FileMaker® Pro 10
Bible

FileMaker® Pro 10 Bible

Ray Cologon, PhD

Wiley Publishing, Inc.

FileMaker® Pro 10 Bible

Published by
Wiley Publishing, Inc.
10475 Crosspoint Boulevard
Indianapolis, IN 46256
www.wiley.com

Copyright © 2009 by Wiley Publishing, Inc., Indianapolis, Indiana

Published simultaneously in Canada

ISBN-13: 978-0-470-42900-6

Manufactured in the United States of America

10 9 8 7 6 5 4 3 2 1

For general information on our other products and services or to obtain technical support, please contact our Customer Care Department within the U.S. at (877) 762-2974, outside the U.S. at (317) 572-3993 or fax (317) 572-4002.

Wiley also publishes its books in a variety of electronic formats. Some content that appears in print may not be available in electronic books.

Library of Congress Control Number: 2009924155

*To my many colleagues in the FileMaker Developer
Community, whose commitment, ingenuity, and passion provide
constant inspiration!*

About the Author

Ray Cologon began using FileMaker in 1990, after having taught and worked with a number of other database tools. He subsequently used FileMaker to compile and analyze data for his doctoral thesis, as well as to design databases for a wide range of other purposes.

Ray has had a diverse career in the creative arts, education, and consulting. Over the past decade, he has developed his own business, NightWing Enterprises, (www.nightwing.com.au/FileMaker) which specializes in the design and development of bespoke FileMaker Pro solutions and provides consulting services to developers and clients in various parts of the world. In 2005, Ray was recipient of the FileMaker Excellence Award for Leadership and Technical Excellence in FileMaker Pro, and he has been a presenter at recent FileMaker Developer Conferences in the United States. He has also been a significant contributor to and moderator of a number of public forums on FileMaker and is a FileMaker Certified Developer.

Ray lives in Melbourne, Australia, where he is known for his sculpture and music, as well as his innovative work with FileMaker Pro.

Credits

Acquisitions Editor
Kyle Looper

Project Editor
Kelly Ewing

Copy Editor
Kelly Ewing

Technical Editors
Corn Walker
Jason DeLooze

Editorial Manager
Jodi Jensen

Vice President & Executive Group Publisher
Richard Swadley

Vice President and Publisher
Andy Cummings

Editorial Director
Mary C. Corder

Project Coordinator
Kristie Rees

Graphics and Production Specialists
Andrea Hornberger
Sarah Philippart

Quality Control Technician
Melissa Cossell

Proofreading and Indexing
Bonnie Mikkelson
Sossity R. Smith
Broccoli Information Mgt.

Contents

Acknowledgments . . . . **xxx**

Introduction . . . . **xxxi**

Part I: The Fundamentals   1

Chapter 1: Databases: The What, Why, and How. 3

The Many Faces of Databases: Lists, Tables and Forms 4
    The limitations of paper-based databases 4
    Entering the digital age...5
    Preparing to get organized...6
The Concept of a Relational Database 6
    Flat-file databases and data redundancy 7
    Opportunities for making connections 7
The Anatomy of a Database Solution...8
    The data: Foundation and substance 8
    The interface: Screens, letters, forms, and reports....................................9
    The hidden helper: Process management 12
How FileMaker Fits In 13
    What FileMaker Pro calls things...13
    Familiar ideas from the real world 17
    Integrating processes and information..18
    Knowledge is power — personal and professional....................................18

Chapter 2: Putting FileMaker Pro in Perspective 21

What Makes FileMaker Pro Different from Other Database Development Tools? 22
    Some common misperceptions...22
    A unique approach to design...25
The FileMaker Product Family..26
    Desktop and server..26
    Scalability and flexibility 27
FileMaker's Hidden Talents...28
    The cross-platform chameleon 28
    Multiple technologies and formats..29
    Plug-ins and extensibility 30
    The FileMaker calculation engine: Simplicity and power............................31
Resources and Exemplars...32
    Examples and brainteasers 32
    Other resources and opportunities 33

Contents

Chapter 3: Getting Acquainted with FileMaker. 35

Getting FileMaker Working for You 35
    Starting and exiting from FileMaker 36
    Creating, saving, and closing files...37
    Handling files and data safely 38
    Earlier file formats and conversion issues 40
Finding Your Way Around...41
    The modes and their uses..43
    Navigating and viewing data 43
    Searching and the FileMaker Find/Omit puzzle.........................45
    Screen elements and what they're for 47
Entering and Editing Data...48
    Creating and duplicating records 48
    Field definitions: Validation and dependencies 49
    The significance of commitment...49
The Ins and Outs 50
    Importing and exporting data...51
    Previewing and printing options 52
    Send/Save as PDF and Excel..53
Getting to Know the Relatives 54
    Ways to view and edit related data...54
    The importance of context 55
    Making complexity simple in practice 55
Optimizing the Application..55
    Preference settings for your workstation...................................56
    File options for the current database 59

Chapter 4: What's New in FileMaker 10 63

Embracing Change...63
Status Area Redesign...64
Live Reports/Sub-summaries 68
Maintain Record Sort Order 70
Saved Find Requests 72
Set Field by Name..76
Script Events Triggers 77
    Layout object triggers 78
    Layout script triggers...81
    Timed interval script triggers..84
    File-based script triggers 85
    Avoiding trigger tangles...85
New Calculation Functions..88
    Get(TriggerKeystroke)..88
    Get(TriggerModifierKeys)...89
    Code(text)...89
    Char(code)..90

GetFieldName(field)..90
Get(DocumentsPathListing) 91
External SQL Data Sources (ESS) Enhancements 92
Additional SQL database support 92
Value lists based on external SQL data 92
Single Sign-On for remote Windows clients..92
Handling of DATETIME values — MS SQL Server 94
Bento Integration 94
File Recovery Improvements...96
Layout Mode Enhancements 98
Inserting an object into the tab order 98
Defining tooltips in Pro 99
Additional font sizes in the format menu...99
Send Mail by SMTP..99
Quick Start Screen Enhancements..100
Import/Export Enhancements 102
Save Target Printer...104
The Manage Scripts Interface 105
Other Useful Enhancements..106
IPv6 Support..106
Format changes for automatically generated log files...106
Updated templates and themes...107
FileMaker Pro Advanced Script Debugger enhancements 107
Relookup Replace and Field Contents no longer commit 107
Only a single sharing error for multiple files..107
Script error codes and control commands 108

Part II: Introduction to Database Design   109

Chapter 5: Creating a Database 111

Before Getting Started 111
Creating a New Database File...112
Adding tables and fields 114
OrderLines 117
Contacts 117
Invoices 117
InvoiceLines 117
Working with the Field Options dialog: Validation and Auto-Entry 118
Setting up simple calculations 124
Capturing simple metadata..127
Creating relationships between tables...129
Adding aggregating calcs 132
Viewing and Interacting with Data 135
Looking at the multiple uses of layouts 136
Creating records and entering data...136

Contents

Editing or deleting data 141

Finding and sorting data you've already entered 141

Using special find symbols 142

Searching with the range and wild card operators 143

Avoiding the Need for Data Duplication 143

Recognizing the visual cues to data relationships 144

Information has a logical flow 144

Anticipating the user 146

Making complex things simple 148

Getting Started with File Security 148

Working with accounts and privilege sets 148

Setting a default account and password 151

Thinking about Usability 152

Moving between records 153

Managing context 153

Moving between tables 154

Using and changing views 154

Using buttons for static and dynamic actions 154

Chapter 6: The Interface: Layout Mode 155

Initial Layouts 155

A map of Layout mode 158

Selection and then Action tools 158

Drag-to-Layout tools 158

Palette and Menu controls 160

Organizing the presentation of information 160

Applying formats to field and text objects 162

Setting up layouts for printing 166

Understanding lists and forms 168

Layout parts and their purposes 170

The Importance of Visual Structure 171

Adding visual pointers and aids 172

Using white space 174

Ergonomics and avoiding visual fatigue 174

Giving information meaning 175

Defining Tooltips 175

Using conditional tooltips 176

Keeping track of tooltips 177

Different Kinds of Layout Objects 177

Static and dynamic objects 178

Inherent object properties 179

Conditional format attributes 179

FileMaker as a Graphical Environment 181

Building graphic objects in FileMaker 181

Default object formats and attributes 183

Controlling stacking and alignment..183
Bringing in graphics from other applications..184
Interacting with Layout Objects 185
Keyboard control of a layout 185
Setting the tab order..186
Assigning names to layout objects 186
Controlling visual spell-checking 187
The Tab Control and Its Uses 188
Defining and creating a tab panel 188
Navigating between tab panels 189
Tab panel limitations...190
Displaying Related Data 191
Working within layout context..191
Setting up a portal...191
The Magic of Buttons 195
Defining buttons 196
Button scope and button commands...198
The button as an object 199
The Web Viewer: Inviting in the World 200
Setting up a Web viewer..200
Controlling a Web viewer..201
Complementary data concepts 202
Reports and Data Output 202
Considerations for printed output 202
Using fonts...202
Page sizes and page setup 203
Paper output versus PDF or Excel output...204
Composite PDFs from multiple layouts 204

Chapter 7: The Structure: The Manage Database Dialog 205
Working with Tables 206
Table concepts: A room with a view..206
Adding, deleting, and renaming tables 206
Moving tables between files...208
Importing tables 209
Specifying Fields..212
Adding, deleting, and renaming fields..213
Understanding field/data types and their significance 214
Auto-Entry options...216
Field validation options 218
Storage and indexing options 221
Summary and Calculation fields..222
Working with global fields 227
Basic Calculations 228
Creating a Calculation field 229
Defining a calculation formula..233

Contents

Entering literal text...234
Referencing fields...235
Understanding calculation functions and their syntax....................................236
    The List( ) function..236
    The Count( ) function...237
    The Date( ) function...237
    The Round( ) function...237
    The Length( ) function...237
Doing some simple calculations...238
    Commission on earnings above a threshold......................................238
    Calculating initials from a person's name...239
    Compound interest at a known rate over a given period....................239
    Current quarter of the calendar year...240
    Changing ampersands to "and" in a block of text.............................240
    Record navigation text (record n of nn)..240
The Relationships Graph...241
Common misconceptions about the Relationships Graph.....................241
Tables versus Table Occurrences..243
Avoiding circular references...244
Named and unnamed data sources..245
Creating references to other FileMaker files.......................................246
Working with External SQL Data Sources..247
Configuring ODBC drivers: Setting up a DSN.....................................247
Integrating SQL tables with FileMaker data.......................................252
Adding supplemental fields...256
The Concept of Data Relationships...257
Why bother with relationships anyway?..257
How relationships work...258
Solving problems by using relationships...258
Deciding what goes where...259
The FileMaker relational model...259

Chapter 8: The Processes: FileMaker Scripting 261

Scripting: What It Is and What It Offers You...261
Building blocks of automation...264
Context is everything...266
Doing things in sequence...267
Addressing objects by name..267
Defining and Editing Scripts...268
Script Editor windows..268
Setting up a basic script..271
How script commands function...273
Changing the order of commands...274
Assigning attributes to a command...276
Using the Scripts Menu..278
Managing the Scripts menu...278
Other ways to trigger a script...279

Using the single-threaded script engine 279
Working with the script stack and paused scripts 280
Controlling Script Execution 280
Using conditional statements..281
Using repetition 282
Pausing for user input 283
Some Notable Script Uses 284
Navigation and view controls 285
Editing information via scripts 286
Printing and managing files 286
Ease of Editing in FileMaker Scripting..287
Selecting and duplicating multiple commands 288
Copying and pasting scripts 288
Copying and pasting script steps..289
Organizing Scripts 289
Creating list separators...289
Script commenting...290
Creating script folders...291
Reordering and grouping scripts 293
Filtering scripts by folder 293
Searching for scripts by name...294
Some Examples to Start With..295
Performing a Find 295
Printing a report 295
Acting on user input..296
Calling Your Scripts 297
The Scripts menu 297
Script hotkeys 297
Scripts assigned to custom menu commands.........................298
Layout buttons 298
Calling scripts from other scripts...298
On Timer Script Triggers..299
File Open and File Close scripts 299
Layout event Script Triggers 299
Object event Script Triggers 300
External script calls 301

Part III: Beyond the Basic   303

Chapter 9: The FileMaker Power User 305

Making Browse Mode Work for You 306
Using multiple windows and views...306
Filtering portals and creating pick lists 306
Jump buttons: Shortcut navigation..313
Controlling one window from another 317

Contents

Performing Complex Search Operations 317
    Compound Find criteria: The AND Find 318
    Stacking Find requests: The OR Find 318
    Constraining and extending the found set 319
    Saving Finds and found sets 319
Sorting Records 323
    Multiple sort keys 324
    Dynamic sort techniques 324
    Creating click-sort columns 327
    Sorting related data 332
Understanding Formatting 333
    The management of formatting: A three-tiered approach 334
    Character-level formatting 334
    Paragraph-level formatting 335
    Layout format filters 335
    Precedence of number, date, and time formats 336
    Controlling formatting programmatically 336
    Creating style buttons 337
Some Notes on Variables 338
    The three kinds of variables 339
    Variables and memory usage 339
    Instantiating and destroying variables 340
    Keeping track of variables 340
Understanding Indexing 341
    Text index types 341
        The word index 341
        The value index 342
    Indexing myths exploded 342
    Differences between numeric and text indexing 343
    Unicode and alternate language indexes 344
    Optimizing field index configurations 345
The Table of Dependencies 346
    Cascading calculation operations 346
    The limits of dependency 346
    Tiers of dependency 347
Caching Join Results 347
    What caching does for you 347
    Solving caching problems 348
    Gaining control of the cache 349
Understanding Global Fields 349
    The behavior of global fields 349
    Uses for global fields 350
    When to avoid global fields 350
    Using global calculation fields 350

Chapter 10: Building Advanced Interfaces **351**

Developing for Mac and Windows Users..352
Selecting fonts...352
Paying attention to differences in screen rendering..353
Considering platform-specific window behavior 354
Using Dynamic Screen Elements...356
Disappearing/reappearing objects..356
The portal invisibility trick 356
Concealed and remotely operated Tab Control..358
Using conditional formatting as a visibility control 360
The hidden power of conditional formatting..360
Multi-state buttons and objects 361
Working with Sub-Summary Parts and Part Controls 362
Building adaptable screens 362
Stacking up multiple Sub-summary parts..363
Using multiple break fields...366
Controlling pagination and page breaks 366
Designing for Print..368
Nonprinting objects 368
Sliding objects and reducing parts...369
Using Merge fields...371
Creating a letter generator 372
Using Multiple Windows and Views 373
Managing window placement and size 373
Windows as pop-ups and drill-downs..374
Simulating modal window behavior 375
Employing Custom Dialogs as an Interface Tool 375
Dialogs as a data-entry device..376
Dynamic dialog attributes..377
Looking at Anchors and Resizable Layout Objects 377
Objects that move according to window size...378
Objects that grow and shrink 379
Managing complex layout resizing 379
Resizing behavior of enclosing objects..382
Centering objects within the viewable area...382
Implementing Shortcut Navigation 382
The power of the Go to Related Record command 383
One interface, many paths...383
Building Back button functionality 384
Building Depth and Dimensionality 385
Using embossing and engraving effects...385
Spatial cues for added meaning...385
Delineation of element groups..386
Color..386
Transparency and translucency 386

Working with Tab Controls 387
    Organizers and space savers 387
    Tab navigation via keyboard..388
    Scripting tab operations 389
Recognizing the Flexibility of Portals 389
    Lists in many guises 389
    Portals as a navigation device 389
    Dynamically sorted portals 390
    Innovative portal implementations 391
Using Advanced Web Viewer Techniques 391
    Access to advanced functionality 391
    Rendering internally calculated content..392
    Scraping data from Web pages 393
Progress Bars and Native Charting Techniques..394
    Creating script progress monitors..395
    Native indicators and graphical displays 396
Using Interface Elements..397
    Splash screens 397
    Main menus 398
    About and version info 398
    Online Help for your users 398
Handling User Preferences 399
    A user-centric development philosophy 399
    Capturing state by user 399
    Example — a multi-lingual solution interface 400

Chapter 11: Data Modeling in FileMaker **405**
Background in Relational Theory..405
    Set Theory in the management of data 406
    Modeling the real world 406
        Think about clarity of organization..407
        Keep the big picture in view 407
    Remembering some guiding principles..408
        Separate entities by type 409
        Delineate fields clearly..409
        Place multiples in a separate table..409
        Store everything once only 410
        Identify the major players 410
        Put it into practice 410
FileMaker Relationships Graph Symbols 410
    Visual cues and clues..410
    The TO as a pointer 412
    Understanding the graph metaphor..412
Relationship Operators 413
    Equi-joins and non-equal joins..414
    Comparative operators (theta joins) 415

Cartesian joins..415
Multi-predicate relationships...415
Alternative Relationship Techniques 416
Multi-Key fields...417
Compound keys...418
One-way relationships..418
Join tables 419
Naturally occurring joins..419
Working with Data Arrays 420
Repeating fields as an array handler 420
Collapsing and expanding arrays..421
Relationship-based techniques for managing data 421
Allowing creation via relationship..421
Using self joins 422
The isolating relationship 423
Graph Techniques — Spiders, Squids, and Anchor-Buoy 423
Constellations and modular centers..424
A satellite-based graph solution...424
Segmentation on functional lines...426
Documenting the Database Structure..427
Graph annotations...427
Naming conventions 428
Field commenting..429
Ancillary notes and documentation..430
The Concept of Layers..431
"Back end" and "front end"...432
The business or procedural layer..432
FileMaker as an integrated environment...433
Separation anxiety...433
File Architecture versus Data Structure 434
Multi-file solutions..434
The modular approach..435
Interface files..436
Approaches to separation of data...438
Costs and benefits of separation 439
Separation and External SQL Sources 439
Understanding the rules...440
Working within constraints...440
Supporting the user...441
Implementing Separation in an Existing Solution..442
Establishing data source(s) 442
Re-pointing Table Occurrences 442
Creating separate graphs 444
Deployment Considerations..445
Your remotest dreams 445
The model of adaptability...445

Contents

Chapter 12: Calculation Wizardry. 447

Compound Calculation Expressions 448
  The language of logic 449
  Functions and schema references 450
    Making context explicit 451
    Avoiding circular references 451
  Structured syntax and nesting 452
  Putting it all together...453
Order of Operations..454
Boolean Operations...456
  Zero, empty, and everything else 456
  Implicit Boolean coding 457
  Explicit Boolean coding...457
Variables — Calculation, Script, and Global 458
  Declaring calculation variables — the Let( ) function 458
  Understanding variables' scope 459
  Benefiting from variables in a calculation 460
Text Processing and Parsing Functions 460
  Substitute, Replace, and Trim..461
  Left, Right, and Middle..462
  Position and PatternCount 463
  The xWords suite 465
  Parsing in practice...466
Text Formatting Operations 467
  Applying text formatting 467
  Removing text formatting..468
  Applying selective formatting 468
  Creating a Format button 469
Dates, Times, and Timestamps...470
  How FileMaker manages dates 470
  Plotting time 470
  The number of seconds in 2009 years..471
  Juggling days, months, and years 472
Summary Data 473
  Using aggregate functions..473
  The ballad of Max and Min 474
  Referencing summary fields...475
Lists and Arrays 476
  Retrieving values as a list 476
  Managing lists — the xValues functions 477
  Extracting one value from a list 478
  Adding or inserting a list value...478
  Removing a value from a list 479

Layers of Abstraction...480
   Building blocks with GetField( )...480
   Completing the circuit with GetFieldName( ).......................................481
   The value of Evaluate( )...482
Unstored Calculations..483
   Why and when calculations are unstored..483
   Understanding the benefits and trade-offs of unstored calculations 484
   Discovering the hidden secrets of unstored calcs................................485
Calculation Fields versus Auto-Enter Calculations 486
   The user over-ride capability...486
   Auto-enter calculations and storage..488
   The Do Not Replace option...488
Global Calculations..489
   The moon follows you everywhere...490
   Managing global dependencies..490
   The freedom and efficiency of global calculations...............................491
Environment and Metadata..492
   The Get( ) functions...492
   Design functions 493
Calculations Using Custom Functions...494
Documenting Your Code 496
   Code formatting...497
   Code commenting...497

Chapter 13: Scripting in Depth 499
Scripting the Control of Objects and Interface 499
   Addressing objects by name..500
   Locking down the interface 501
   Managing user interaction 502
Trapping for Errors...504
   Retrieving error codes appropriately...505
   What the error codes mean 505
   Why bother with error handling?..506
   Handling errors..507
Scripts and Access Privileges 510
   Privilege-based errors 511
   Run script with full access privileges 511
   Determining the substantive privileges 512
Automating the Automation..512
   Defining a script to run on file open..513
   Housekeeping practices for start-up scripts 514
   Scripts that run on file close 515
   Script Triggers...516
Harnessing the Power of Parameters, Results, and Variables......................517
   Getting data into a script 517
   Branching according to state 518

Contents

Declaring variables 519
Passing and retrieving multiple parameters 521
Specifying and retrieving a script result 523
Storing and accumulating data as you go..525
Dynamic and Indirect Controls in Scripts 526
Example — Go to Layout by name or number 526
Dynamic file paths using variables...527
Dynamically building Find criteria 529
Editing field data on the fly (indirection)..530
Using Nonlinear Logic 531
Nested and sequential If/Else conditions 531
Looping constructs..532
Specifying exit conditions..533
Modular Script Code...535
Using sub-scripts..535
Script recursion 536
Scripted Window Management 536
Addressing windows by name (title) 537
Moving and resizing windows..538
Determining window dimensions 539
Creating windows off-screen 540
Freezing and refreshing the screen 541
Scripting Data Import and Export 542
Exporting field contents 542
Exporting table data 543
Selecting fields for export 543
Import options 545
Data matching for import 546
Synchronizing and updating data 546
Other import options 547
Loading and unloading container objects 548
Pivoting Data between Tables...549
Using utility relationships..549
Managing related data (walking through related records) 549
Going over Some Practical Examples..550
Locating unique records...550
Building a multi-part PDF report..551

Part IV: Integrity and Security   553

Chapter 14: In Control with FileMaker Security 555

Concepts of Security 555
Balance and perspective 556
Identifying threats 556
Assessing value 556

Protecting your investment...556
Interface vulnerabilities 557
    Taking things at interface value 557
    More than a semblance of security..558
    File-based security...558
The Privilege Set 558
    Concepts of role-based security..560
    Defining and constraining access..560
    Schema privilege controls...561
Granular Security...562
    Access to value lists and scripts...563
    The two dimensions of layout access..563
    Privileges for table, record, and field access..............................564
    Using and managing extended privileges.....................................566
User Authentication..567
    Creating user accounts 568
    Internal and external authentication...568
Scripted Account Management..570
    Provision for automation of database security..............................570
    Working with multi-file solutions 571
    Safe scripting implementations..572
Creating a Custom Logout Option...573
    The locked-down database..573
    Structuring a solution for logging out...573
    Security logging..575
How Much Security Is Enough?...576
    Ways to evaluate risk 576
    A balanced view of threats...577
    A strategic model for response..577
The Importance of Physical File Security...577
    Layers of protection...578
    Alternative forms of protection..578
    A multi-faceted approach 579
Security in Deployment: FileMaker Server 579
    Filtered display of files 580
    Secure Socket Layer encryption...580
    Server checks and logs 580

Chapter 15: Maintaining Referential Integrity. 581

Pinpointing Common Causes of Referential Integrity Problems.....................581
    The potential impact on your solution 582
    Costs and benefits 582
Using Unique Keys 582
    Key safeguards 583
    Keys and meaning (existence, persistence, uniqueness)...................584

Contents

Generating Keys...584
    Serial numbers 585
    Record IDs 586
    Unique identification (UID) values...587
Exploring Keys and Data Type 588
Retrofitting Keys 590
Deleting Redundant Records...591
    The use of cascading deletion...592
    Configuring relationships for referential integrity 592
    Privilege requirements for cascade delete 593
    Controlled cascading deletes at runtime 594
Considering Other Integrity Issues..595
    Lookups and when to use them 595
    Auto-entry lookups and references..595
    Data design issues 596
Managing Dependencies 597
    Literal text references 597
    Indirect object/element references 597
    Filename references...598
    Structural anomalies...598

Chapter 16: Making FileMaker Systems Fail-Safe 599

Expecting the Unexpected 599
    Successful backup strategies...599
        Backup frequency...600
        An appropriate backup cycle 600
        The integrity of backups..601
        The location of backups 601
        Back up the code, not just the data....................................601
    The hazards of copying open files 601
    Backing up local files..602
    Backing up hosted files...603
A Comprehensive Approach to Error Trapping...............................603
    Dealing with record locking 604
    Techniques to avoid in multi-user or multi-window environments 606
        Replace Field Contents 606
        Record marking and flagging techniques 607
        Uses of global fields 607
Opening Remote Files...607
    Peer-to-peer hosting...608
    File sharing risks 610
    Network spaghetti..610
    Opener files...611

Sending an e-mail link 612
Temporary Edit Interface Techniques 613
The Data Viewer concept 613
The legitimate purpose of record locking 615
Creating double-blind entry systems 615
Field Masking, Filtering, and Error Rejection 616
Applying standard data formations 617
Dealing with trailing spaces and carriage returns 618
Rejecting out-of-scope characters 618
Handling styled source text 619
Built-In Logging Capabilities 619
Making use of auto-enter options 619
Capturing and extending standard metadata 620
Script Logging 621
Infrastructure for script logging 621
Tracking script execution 622
Script-specific context variables 622
Script diagnostics 623
Capturing User Edits in Detail 623
Trapping edits, field-by-field 623
Incorporating ancillary data 624
Logging record deletions 626
Managing the Accumulation of Log Data 626
Archiving options 627
Generating secondary output 627
Implementing Roll-Back Capabilities 627
Chronological roll-back 628
Alternative undo and roll-back capabilities 629
Using logs to roll forward 629
Alternative Logging Approaches 630
Logs as Data 630
Scripted and triggered logging 630

Chapter 17: Maintaining and Restoring Data **633**
Some Notes on File Recovery 633
Debunking common myths and misconceptions 634
The Recover process 635
Salvaging data 637
Understanding file corruption 638
Exporting and Importing Data 639
File format considerations 639
Exporting to and importing from a folder 641
Delimiters and EOL markers 642

Contents

Data Cleansing Operations...643
    Extract, transform, and load...643
    Data format considerations...643
        Data organization..644
        Data presentation..644
        Data domain..645
    Filtering capabilities in FileMaker..................................646
Synchronizing Data Sets..647
    Import matching..648
    Importing selectively..650
Handling Embedded Images and Stored Files................................651
    Assigning and retrieving paths.......................................652
    Scripted field updates...652
Text-Handling Considerations...653
    Export field contents..653
    Designing a custom export process....................................654

Part V: Raising the Bar   655

Chapter 18: FileMaker Pro Advanced Features 657
Script Debugger..657
    Watching code in action..658
    Debugging restricted privilege scripts...............................658
    Getting used to the Debugger controls................................659
Data Viewer..661
    Current and Watch panels...661
        The Current panel..662
        The Watch panel..664
    Using the Viewer with the Debugger...................................665
    The Data Viewer sand box...665
    The Data Viewer and variables..666
Database Design Report...667
    DDR capabilities...668
    Mining the DDR for information.......................................668
    Tools and techniques for interpreting DDR data.......................669
Creating Custom Menus..669
    Defining menus...669
    Editing individual menus...671
        Benefits of the Script Step action..............................672
        Benefits of window widgets......................................672
    Adding menus to sets...673

Assigning menu sets throughout your file 673
   Setting the default menu set for a file... 673
   Determining a menu set for each layout.. 674
   Controlling menu sets via script 675
Custom Functions.. 675
   Defining custom functions 676
   Custom functions as an aid to syntax readability 678
   Maximizing efficiency and ease of use 678
Custom Functions and Recursion 680
   Things that only custom functions can do... 680
   The stack and the limits of recursion... 681
   Tail recursion in practice 681
   Some useful examples 682
      Creating an acronym from a supplied phrase.. 682
      Extracting a character set from a supplied block of text 683
      Removing an unspecified number of leading carriage returns....................... 683
Creating Runtime Applications 684
   Generating a stand-alone solution 684
   Binding for each platform 685
   Hosting runtime files.. 686

Chapter 19: Efficient Code, Efficient Solutions 687
Designing for Scale: Size Considerations 687
   The elephant in the cherry tree.. 688
   Predicting what will scale well... 688
Eliminating Redundancy... 689
   Avoiding duplication of elements 689
   Using portable and reusable code.. 690
      Appropriate use of sub-scripts... 690
      Appropriate use of custom functions 691
Designing for Flexibility and Adaptability 691
   Layouts and adaptable design.. 692
   Concepts of reusability applied to the Relationships Graph 692
Traveling the Shortest Distance Between Two Points.. 693
   Optimal calculation syntax... 693
   Alternative syntax examples 695
      Working with modifier keys... 696
      Working with Boolean values 697
   Avoiding dependency "spaghetti" 698
   Applying simplicity principles.. 701
Transaction Modeling 702
   Live versus batch data 702
   Posting edits and propagating edits to related records 703
   Offline updates and processing 704

Contents

Robots and batch automation..704
Host/server script execution 704
Managing File Size 706
Dealing with data in chunks..706
Modularization strategies..707
Considering segmentation 707
Data archiving..707
Images and Media in Databases..708

Chapter 20: Extending FileMaker's Capabilities 709

External Scripting Calls..709
Using Send Event and VBScript..710
Using VBScript with FileMaker Pro 710
Calling Windows Command-Line scripts 712
Perform AppleScript..713
Cross-platform solutions and external script calls..........715
Third-party helpers and macros 716
Rendering HTML and JavaScript..716
Harnessing HTTP..717
Bringing services to your solution......................................717
Handling hypertext 718
Web Viewer Widgets 719
Charting with Flash..719
Applets and servlets 719
FileMaker Plug-Ins..720
Installing and enabling plug-ins 720
Using external functions..722
Script triggering 723
Robust triggering implementations................................723
Available script triggering plug-ins 725
Dialog capabilities 725
File and media handling..726
E-mail, HTTP, and FTP 727
Charting and other functionality 727
Web Deployment Options 728
Instant Web publishing..728
Custom Web publishing 729
Working with XML and XSLT 729
The FileMaker PHP API 730
FileMaker's PHP Site Assistant......................................730
Finding Third-Party Tools..731
Developer tools 731
Analysis and documentation 732
Shared information 732

Part VI: Appendixes   **733**

Appendix A: Expanding Your Knowledge with Additional Resources. . . 735

Appendix B: About the Web Site 741

Index 743

Acknowledgments

In a project of the size and complexity of this book, many people are involved in the process that delivers the final bound copy into your hands, and 'listing or individually thanking them all isn't feasible. However, I'd like to make a special mention of those at FileMaker, Inc. whose sustained dedication and attention to detail has produced the remarkable application that is FileMaker Pro 10.

Additionally, I'd like to thank my editor, Kelly Ewing, and technical reviewers, Jason DeLooze and Corn Walker, for their attention to detail and their considerable contributions to the success of this project.

Introduction

FileMaker first emerged as a database application in the 1980s and has steadily increased in popularity in the decades since then. FileMaker is a veteran alongside well-established productivity applications, such as Microsoft Excel and Microsoft Word. Moreover, FileMaker Pro has been available as a cross-platform application (Mac and Windows) since 1992.

From its humble beginnings, FileMaker has acquired new features and capabilities with each successive version. Version 10, the most powerful and flexible yet, retains much of the essential core of earlier days, enabling rapid development and providing new users with a moderate initial learning curve. As a longstanding user of FileMaker (I began using FileMaker Pro with Version 2 in 1990), I have seen many of these changes and can unreservedly commend you on your choice. FileMaker Pro has earned its reputation for a combination of ease of use and power — and if you're prepared to take the trouble to look a little more deeply into its capabilities (by reading this book, for example!), you"ll find that it's also extraordinarily versatile and capable.

The *FileMaker Pro 10 Bible* features FileMaker Pro 10 and FileMaker Pro 10 Advanced. As a user wishing to create basic solutions, FileMaker Pro 10 is an ideal place for you to start, and the bulk of the information in this book will be immediately useful to you. For more complex requirements or for serious development work, you'll find that FileMaker Pro 10 Advanced offers numerous advantages, with improved diagnostics and powerful developer-oriented features — and again, you'll find information herein to ensure that you're able to get the most out of your purchase.

In addition, FileMaker, Inc. provides the server-based (Web and local network) deployment products FileMaker Server 10 and FileMaker Server 10 Advanced, providing you with options to host FileMaker solutions for large workgroups. While the Server products aren't the focus of the FileMaker Pro 10 Bible, I nevertheless include some references to design considerations for multi-user deployment.

About This Book

The content of this book leverages the wealth of information and examples in the bestselling FileMaker Pro 9 Bible, re-orienting it to the new features of FileMaker Pro 10 and giving you substantial added value. Radical new features, such as Script Triggers, have been incorporated, and I've reworked the text with these features in mind. This edition and the one immediately preceding it represent a major step forward (the previous book was a total ground-up rewrite) and are a substantial departure from earlier books in the series.

The *FileMaker Pro 10 Bible* brings together practical advice and examples, bringing essential theory together with explanations and techniques covering a wide variety of topics that you won't find covered in other books or in the user guide and Help files that ship with FileMaker Pro. I've designed the book to provide value when read straight-through, as a place to quickly delve into a particular topic or feature, or as a deep reference work when accessing information via the Index.

Although the early chapters (Parts I and II) assume no prior experience with FileMaker, I do assume that you're prepared to refer to the FileMaker Pro User Guide and the application's online Help entries as needed (so I don't repeat the information contained in the documentation that installs by default with the application). In the second half of the book, I cover more advanced aspects of material previously introduced; however, when doing so, I refer you to the relevant introductory passages in case you need to catch up on the basics first. For those occasions when you need to check a fact, find a technique, or solve a problem, the book includes a comprehensive Index and an extensive Table of Contents that help you find topics of interest.

FileMaker Pro 10 is a cross-platform product that operates similarly on Mac and Windows operating systems. In those cases where a feature is specific to one platform, I draw your attention to it and discuss its use (including in cross-platform solutions). When referencing keyboard shortcuts, I include the Mac shortcut and also the Windows shortcut (for example, ⌘+T / Ctrl+T). In those few cases where a dialog is significantly different on Mac or Windows, I provide screenshots of both versions of the dialog the first time it's encountered, but otherwise I show the Mac version in each screenshot.

I've taken care to frame the explanations provided here in standard conventions and terminology wherever possible. For example, I use standard notations, such as 1:n, where applicable and a tilde (~) character to indicate an unspecified object (such as one or many records in a relationship). When terms are used with a special meaning, you can find them in the glossary provided in Appendix A.

Although this is a substantial volume, I nevertheless have a finite number of pages with which to address a vast quantity of information; FileMaker Pro is a very big subject! Rather than reiterating information already covered elsewhere, I have been at pains to employ available space within the book to add value and focus on new material you don't already have at your fingertips. In some cases, this approach means presenting basic information in new ways or elucidating it beyond the common understanding (how FileMaker *really* works, and *why*!). As part of that goal, I present information that isn't documented anywhere else, sharing with you insights gleaned from more than a decade in the trenches with various versions of the FileMaker Pro suite of products.

As part of the *Bible* series, this book is intended to provide self-contained, comprehensive coverage of its subject. With that aim in mind, this edition of *FileMaker Pro Bible* is the most comprehensive ever and does more to help you become productive with FileMaker Pro.

About This Book's Target Audience

If you want to create databases and database solutions using FileMaker Pro 10 or FileMaker Pro 10 Advanced, you're the target audience for this book. Whether you're a serious amateur who's creating a database solution for your family, club, or organization; a professional managing data as part of your wider role; or a developer who's building custom systems or turnkey solutions to sell or license to others, *FileMaker Pro 10 Bible* can help you attain your goals.

I do make a few basic assumptions about you:

- I assume that you know how to use your computer and operating system, whether it's a PC running Windows XP or Windows Vista, or a Mac running Mac OS X.

- I assume that you have, or have access to, FileMaker Pro 10 or FileMaker Pro 10 Advanced. The book is more useful if you have access to FileMaker Pro 10 while you read and work through the examples I present.

- The third assumption is that you want to both understand the database design process and learn how to accomplish a broad range of tasks using FileMaker Pro 10.

How This Book Is Organized

In keeping with *Bible* tradition, *FileMaker Pro 10 Bible* is divided into parts, and each part is divided into chapters. The parts of this book are as follows.

Part I: The Fundamentals

This part covers the basics of database theory and design and provides a high-level overview of the features of FileMaker Pro 10.

Part II: Introduction to Database Design

This part is where you learn more details of database design theory and how to use FileMaker Pro 10 to actually create a database solution.

Part III: Beyond the Basics

In this part, you find out how to use more advanced FileMaker Pro 10 features in such tasks as producing more comprehensive reports, implementing fault-tolerant input forms, designing layouts for cross-platform use, designing target-specific (screen, print, and Web) layouts, and automating data processing.

Part IV: Integrity and Security

This part delves deeply into the concepts and implementation of data integrity, access control, and risk management.

Part V: Raising the Bar

Here, I delve into the additional features and capabilities offered by FileMaker Pro 10 Advanced and explore tools and techniques facilitating professional-level database development processes.

Part VI: Appendixes

The appendixes provide a compendium of other references you might find valuable, such as targeted technical books, related publications, and useful Web sites, and a synopsis of what you can find on this book's companion Web site.

Icons Used in This Book

The book includes a number of icons to call attention to specific passages throughout the book. The icons are as follows:

NOTE Indicates useful, but noncritical, information concerning the material being presented.

TIP Indicates information that makes performing a task easier or describes how a feature can be utilized in a useful, but not obvious, manner.

CAUTION Indicates possible pitfalls or side effects arising from the use of the feature being discussed.

CROSS-REF Indicates where to look for additional (including prerequisite) information about the material being discussed.

NEW FEATURE Indicates a feature introduced in FileMaker Pro 10 or FileMaker Pro 10 Advanced.

ON the WEB Indicates material that you can find on the book's companion Web site at www. wiley.com/go/filemaker10bible.

Where to Go from Here

If you're new to creating databases, you should start with Part I. If you're experienced at database design but new to FileMaker Pro, try skimming Part I to learn the FileMaker Pro interface and feature set. If you're an experienced FileMaker Pro user, you'll probably want to check out Chapter 4 to see what's new in FileMaker Pro 10 and then bounce around the book to those areas of particular interest (so the book's Index should prove immediately useful to you).

All the example files for this book are available for download from the book's companion Web site at www.wiley.com/go/filemaker9bible.

Part I

The Fundamentals

Keeping track of information is a challenge you face in every area of your life, and everything from a grocery list to an inventory of books or music, to a company annual report, is part of that challenge. For your information to be useful, you'll need ways to organize, store, retrieve and present it when needed. I assume that you're reading this book because you recognize that using automated and computer-driven data organizing tools such as FileMaker Pro offers you many advantages — once you've taken the time to gain an understanding of the fundamentals.

In this first part of the FileMaker Pro Bible, I offer you a broad introduction to the terms and concepts that you'll encounter when coming to grips with FileMaker Pro. As well as describing the ways computer database systems can help you to accomplish your goals, I highlight some of the special features and attributes FileMaker Pro offers — those things that set it apart from competing applications, including the support it provides for novice or lay users. Moreover, this part provides a survey of new features in FileMaker Pro 10 that will be of interest to readers who have used previous versions of the application.

IN THIS PART

Chapter 1
Databases: The What, Why, and How

Chapter 2
Putting FileMaker Pro in Perspective

Chapter 3
Getting Acquainted with FileMaker

Chapter 4
What's New in FileMaker 10

Chapter 1

Databases: The What, Why, and How

You'll find no shortage of references to data and databases in books, magazines, TV shows, and Web articles. In fact, referring to databases has become so commonplace that most people take it as shorthand for the use of sophisticated computer techniques to track and analyze information — and indeed computerized databases are everywhere. Despite this, databases have existed much longer than computers, and the basic concept has its origins in much more humble methods of information storage and retrieval.

The term *database* refers to any collection of ordered information, whether a computer is involved or not. So everything from the four-day weather forecast to your grocery list to a pocket dictionary is a database. In fact, this book, with its table of contents and index, is a database too, offering a compendium of useful data and several useful ways to access it. In the same way, computer databases mirror all the other familiar data management techniques that have been used throughout centuries — allowing you to organize information, store it, and access it efficiently.

The first and most important principle of any data organization method is that what you get out is only as good as what went in. In many cases (unless the way the information is organized is carefully conceived and followed), information will always be as easy to find as you would hope. This generalization can apply equally to a handwritten list or a computerized data management tool, depending on the skill and care with which the data has been arranged or entered, and on the suitability of the method for the uses to which you will put the information.

Of course, using a computer to keep track of information offers you many advantages, including speed and reliability, automation of common tasks, and the ability to sort, search, and summarize your information efficiently.

IN THIS CHAPTER

Identifying the elements of a database

Relating data

Solving problems by using a database

Looking at FileMaker's role in streamlining data management

My purpose in this book is to provide you with a comprehensive overview of techniques and strategies for taking control of your information, using the capabilities of one of the best Database Management Systems available — FileMaker Pro 10!

The Many Faces of Databases: Lists, Tables and Forms

The most common form of database is a list — any kind of list. Lists of things to do, shopping lists, lists of names and addresses, and countless others are everyday databases that are so familiar that you scarcely think about them. Lists that hold more than one kind of information are commonly organized into tables with different columns for each kind of fact and a separate row for facts about each item. (For example, a shopping list may have a column naming the items to be purchased and an adjacent column listing the quantity of each item required.) As soon as you have two or more pieces of interrelated information to manage, organizing your data into a tabular form provides a framework that is clear and simple and makes it easy for you to locate the information you need.

A computer database holds one or more tables of information, where your data is held within an organized structure that allows you to easily access it. Instead of columns and rows, however, the elements of a FileMaker database are described by using slightly different language. Here are a few of the basic terms:

- **Field:** In FileMaker, a field holds a discrete piece of information, such as a date, a name, a price, or a ZIP code. Fields correspond to the columns in a conventional table, or to the cells within a row of a spreadsheet.

- **Record:** One of a set of separate instances of a group of fields, containing a set of information about a specific item — for example, a person, a place, or a product. Records are analogous to the rows in a conventional table or spreadsheet.

- **Table:** A collection of records containing information about a number of similar items.

- **Database:** One or more tables containing organized information.

The limitations of paper-based databases

Information is commonly collected by having people fill out forms. Often, the completed forms are filed in cabinets (for example, in alphabetical order), and essential parts of the information may be transcribed into a log or tracked via entries in an index card system.

When information is stored on pieces of paper or on cards, to access it you must delve into the filing system to locate a particular card or form. When you remove it, you must be sure to put it back in the same place. Large number of records take up lots of space, and it can be quite a job to keep them all in order. In addition, this process is pretty inefficient and error prone. Should you need to know general facts (such as the number of single males who have filled out a particular form), you'll have quite a task on your hands working through the entire collection of data and counting up the relevant entries.

After all the effort you might expend getting paper forms sorted and filing them, you'll have them arranged in a single order (for example, by name or date of birth). Should you need the information sorted or grouped differently (such as by ZIP code so that you can claim a price break from the post office when sending mail to all the people who filled out forms), you have a huge manual task ahead. If you're paying someone to assemble the information, such requirements can quickly become too expensive to justify.

Finally, should you need to update any information in the forms stored in such a filing system, someone will have to cross out the old information (such as an out-of-date phone number) and write in different data. After there have been several changes of the same or similar information, the forms (or cards or journal entries and so on) may become jumbled and difficult to read.

Entering the digital age

The impact of computerization has been felt in all corners of the globe. Even folk who don't own and may never aspire to owning computers benefit both directly and indirectly from the many ways computers change the world we live in — from weather forecasting to traffic control to scientific breakthroughs to library loans systems: The digital age is upon us. Databases are at the very center of this world of change, because almost all computerized processes involve storing and manipulating data in some way.

Because you're reading this book, I assume that you're familiar with one or more operating systems. However, it may not have occurred to you that in the process of opening and closing folders and viewing the files they contain, you're navigating a database. Your computer maintains a database that tracks the locations (and names, types, and other characteristics) of all the files on each disk drive. When you double-click a file inside a folder, the operating system looks up its database to find out which application should be used to view or open the file in question. So you've been using databases long before you found your way to a database management application such as FileMaker Pro.

Storing your data digitally offers several compelling advantages:

- The data can easily be edited. (You don't need erasers; you don't make a mess crossing things out; you can automatically track and reverse changes at will. . . .).
- You can use computer programs to search your data and find specific entries much more quickly than you can do manually.
- Computers can repackage your information and present it to you in different formats — or in different sort orders, all at the click of a button or the move of a mouse.

Each of these tasks would be painstakingly laborious to undertake manually by using conventional (paper) records. And the more data you have, the slower a manual process becomes, whereas computers can apply the same processes to 5 records or 5,000, often with barely any perceptible difference in the time they take to complete their task.

Ideally, a computerized database should provide all the advantages of a conventional records system, without any of the disadvantages. As part of that, your computer databases should allow you to transpose information from paper-based forms into screens that have a similar appearance and utility. That is, the information may be arranged in the same configurations, and the screen forms may even resemble the familiar paper forms. When you print a form from a program that has been designed to mirror the appearance of your paper forms, you can move information freely between conventional filing systems and your digital database.

Adding to the advantages a digital database provides for entering, editing, searching, sorting, presenting, and reformatting information, a further benefit is that you can use computers to summarize data (automatically adding up totals or averages and so on), generate new data by using calculations, analyze your data, create graphical representations of your data, or make the data available remotely (such as via a Web page).

Preparing to get organized

Getting started on any significant task requires planning. Databases help you get your information organized, but before you can use them effectively, you may need to spend time organizing the database itself. In turn, to do that, you need to organize your thoughts.

The first thing you must establish in order to approach the task of getting organized is the kinds of information you need the database to store. For example, to keep track of inventory for a retail business, you're likely to need product names, prices, and stock codes. You might also need to know other facts, such as item sizes, availability, sources of supply, or packaging options (boxed or single). In addition, you'll likely need to keep track of how many of each item is on hand so that you'll know when to order more stock from the supplier. When you know what information you need to track, you have a much clearer idea about what you need to put into your database.

Separately, you'll need to determine what information your database should provide as outputs. For example, a products database may be required to produce a catalog or price list, a checklist for stock-take or a summary of items on special, and so on. When you consider what kinds of output will be required, you'll have a clearer idea what information your database will be required to store.

The start of the process of defining and designing your database, therefore, should be to set out the inputs and the outputs and to make sure that what is going in will be sufficient to provide what you require to come out.

The Concept of a Relational Database

When information is arranged in a single table format (such as one you might create with columns and rows on paper or in a spreadsheet program), it's referred to as flat — or as a *flat-file database*. It's flat in the sense that it has only two dimensions — columns and rows. Most simple forms of databases (whether computerized or not) are flat in this way. A flat-file database is a computer database that contains a single table to hold all the fields (or columns or cells) of information together in one place. In that regard, a simple spreadsheet is a prime example of a flat-file database.

Flat-file databases and data redundancy

When working with flat-file databases, you'll frequently encounter situations where the same information must be entered in more than one record (row) of the table. For example, in a database containing information about people, if one of the fields holds the home address and two of the people (John and Mary) live in the same place, the same address must appear twice (once on the record for John and again on the record for Mary). The immediate consequence of this duplication of information is that if you find an error, you're likely to have to correct it in both places — or risk having your data contradicting itself and therefore becoming less dependable and useful.

Another issue you'll encounter when using a flat-file database to deal with large amounts of information is that it's hard to view all the relevant information at once (such as when a table must become very wide to accommodate a lot of fields). To make the process manageable, you may need to work with subsets of the data. If using subsets involves separating the information into two or more tables, you're likely to find that you need to repeat some of the information from one table in the other. For example, if you decide to use separate tables to track people and their addresses and people and their jobs, some of the information (such as people's names) must be in both tables. Again, when this repetition of data occurs, any duplicated information that has to be corrected or updated must be changed in two (or more) places to keep your data accurate and internally consistent.

Almost 40 years ago, an elegant solution to the problem of redundancy in databases was proposed by Edgar F. Codd when he described an idea he called the *relational model* that could be applied to enable Database Management Systems to manage interrelated sets of data more effectively. (You can find a copy of the original article in which Codd described his breakthrough at `http://portal.acm.org/portal.cfm`). The mathematical model Codd proposed applied set theory and predicate logic as the basis of a system that would connect data in different sets (tables). For your purposes, the significant thing is that Codd's work led to the widespread creation of database systems where you can *relate* information in tables based upon a common field.

In fact, long before relational databases became commonplace on computers, a similar concept was in use in various other forms. For example, before teachers began using computers to record attendance, assignment submissions, grades, and so on, many teachers employed special notebooks containing a main page with basic student detail, plus adjacent narrower pages for the teacher to enter columns of details against each student's name (roll call, assignment results, test scores, and so on). When the same basic concept is implemented within a relational database, a table of student information is matched by a unique field value (such as student's name or an ID number) to corresponding information in other tables, where attendance, grades, and the like are recorded.

Opportunities for making connections

You encounter databases just about everywhere you turn. From the telephone book to your bank statements, from game scores to the electoral roll, each time you need to look up some information, you're going to be reaching for a database. While some of these databases reside on computers (for example, Internet search engines are in fact giant databases), even those that are in books or other traditional formats often originate in computers (before being printed and bound into the form in which you access them).

By setting up an appropriate computerized database, you can create a framework within which to work with your data so that you can easily access information you need and see connections between corresponding information (which people live in which houses and so on). FileMaker Pro 10 provides an efficient environment that enables you to create flexible and powerful solutions to store and retrieve your data. As part of the process of configuring your solution, FileMaker Pro lets you set up relationships that link data in one table with corresponding data elsewhere in your solution.

An example of the kind of database solution you might create with FileMaker Pro 10 would be a system to track your music collection, wherein songs, artists, and albums will each appear in separate tables, with links between the tables to associate each song with an artist and with one or more albums on which it appears. In the event you decide to loan some items from your collection to friends, you might add a fourth table to record which items are on loan to whom (and presumably, to mark them off when they're returned).

Similarly, you might choose to create a database to keep track of the names, telephone numbers, and addresses of your friends or business contacts. In this case, you might create a table of people, a table of addresses, and a table of employers (companies or workplaces). In this case, one or more people records may be associated with each address record, one or more people may be associated with each employer, and each employer may be associated with one or more addresses. Note that in this case, because all the addresses would be together in one table, separate joins are required to connect both the people table and the employers table to the addresses table.

While the two examples I mention here are common requirements, there are many other possibilities. From tracking your finances and expenditures to storing trip details and expenses for your vehicle, to organizing your favorite recipes to tracking invitations and responses for as gala banquet, there is no shortage of uses for custom database design skill.

The Anatomy of a Database Solution

You can find a number of basic components in any *database solution,* regardless of its purpose and origins. These elements include tables to hold the organized data, screens or forms to enter and view the data, reports to produce printed (or other) output. All but the simplest solutions can also be expected to include relationships that make the connections between different categories of information (linking people with companies, products with sales, and so on). The combination of the components that make up a database enable you to enter, edit, and extract data in ways that help you to get things done.

The data: Foundation and substance

Nearly everyone has a need to work with information in some area of their life — which is the reason databases are so widely used. The information you need to manage is the whole reason for considering having a database — so your data is the first, most important, and central component of your database. At the simplest level, your *data* and the way they're organized (into tables containing records that in turn are comprised of fields holding individual facts) provide the core of your database.

The way your data is organized provides your database with structure — sometimes called its *data architecture* — which provides the basis for every function and procedure you perform. The decisions you make about data structure are important because they determine what will be possible, and what won't, when you're working with your data.

The model for data relationships developed in the 1970s may seem abstract; however, it provides an effective way of capturing relationships that exist in the real world and replicating them in the information stored in your database. The goal is devising a structure for your data that's a good match for the things that data represents — and the relationships between them.

An ideal database structure is one that captures information about things (people, objects, places, and so on) and also accurately represents the relationships between them. People have relationships with each other — family and work relationships, for example — but they also have relationships of ownership and association with objects and places. Your databases should provide a way to represent information and its interrelations.

The interface: Screens, letters, forms, and reports

When you interact with a computer database, you view and manipulate data onscreen. Different views of data presented onscreen are therefore often called *screens,* irrespective of how they're organized. A screen in this sense combines data, labels, and other control elements, such as menus and command buttons, that enable you to interact with the data and navigate the solution. Frequently, however, the visual elements of a screen are arranged in a way that is analogous to a familiar real-world object, such as a list, form, letter, or report. In many cases, you'll find it helpful to refer to screens as *forms* or *lists,* as these terms are more descriptive.

The most common screen format is the *digital form,* which presents a selection of the fields of a single record, arranged in a logical and useful order. A digital form therefore mirrors familiar real-world paper forms and can be used for the same purposes — to create and update records. Figure 1.1 shows an example of an entry form used in the iTunes music database to interact with information about a song.

If you're familiar with creating lists or using spreadsheets, you've encountered lists or tables containing so much data that they're cumbersome. When a table has too many columns, it becomes unwieldy — making the task of seeing connections and considering the data as a whole very challenging. Database forms provide a way to ameliorate this problem by allowing you to view a subset of the fields (columns) of data, arranged in a way that makes the connections clear. For example, the components of an address — street, city, state, postal code, and so on — can be grouped together and viewed as a whole. Similarly, a person's name, title, and personal details will be grouped together. When viewed in this way — rather than spread out across a row as in a conventional table or spreadsheet — you can much more easily understand what the information means and how it interrelates.

Because you can arrange a selection of fields of data onto a form, you can deal with a situation where there is too much information to fit comfortably on one screen. Just as a real-world paper form may have multiple pages, you can divide a digital form across multiple screens. In this way, the data can be broken into manageable sections, and the user won't be overwhelmed with complexity or clutter. This approach can make data entry simpler and swifter, while reducing the scope for error.

FIGURE 1.1

A form enables you to enter or update information in your database.

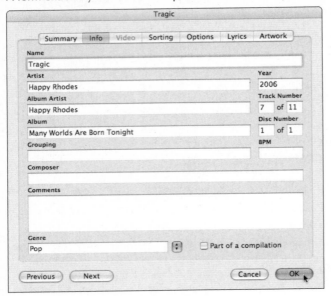

You can also use forms to retrieve your data, but that limits you to viewing one record at a time. Moreover, forms frequently present a subset of a record's data. Although working with forms showing a subset of fields from record data may be advantageous during data entry — allowing you to deal with the data in manageable "chunks" — separate forms may not provide a comprehensive view of the record's data. That may be what you want some of the time, for example, when printing an invoice. However, one of an electronic database's major benefits is that you can quickly and easily get a consolidated report, possibly with summary information, of your data or some defined subset of that data. Figure 1.2 shows such a report — summary data from a music database created with FileMaker Pro.

As the example in Figure 1.2 shows, reports are frequently arranged as a list of data from successive records in rows, along with headings and appropriate summaries or totals. Although the many variations on this concept represent the most common kinds of reports required in a database, there are some exceptions.

When you were in school, you probably received a report card at the end of every quarter or semester that provided an overview of your achievements for the preceding period. Some schools present these reports as a simple list of the classes taken and the grades awarded. However, some school reports are arranged more like a form than a list, with classes and explanatory text arranged in different parts of the page according to the way the curriculum has been structured. Moreover, instead of listing many students, only a single student's results are included. In both respects, this is an example of a report employing the essential elements of a form rather than a list.

Another common use of information is as the basis of correspondence. Letters to colleagues, associates, customers, or clients usually contain information that is relevant and specific to the recipient. These letters can be produced from a database as a kind of report — one in which the elements of data and/or summary information are arranged within appropriate text, in a format that is conventional for correspondence. In this way, using the data that is already in your database, you can efficiently create dozens, or even hundreds, of different letters — each specific to the addressee. This particular type of correspondence, sometimes called a *form letter,* is a common feature of word-processing applications, such as Microsoft Word. In Word, this feature is called Data Merge, and you use it to retrieve data from a separate merge data file (such as an Excel or Access file). FileMaker Pro lets you create such correspondence without involving other applications.

By enabling you to enter your data once and then retrieve it in a variety of configurations and formats (as screens, forms, reports, summaries, lists, or letters), a database turns unwieldy tables of data into a flexible and powerful tool.

FIGURE 1.2

A report shows you multiple records at one time.

The hidden helper: Process management

So far I've talked about putting data into computer databases via forms and getting it back out in reports of various kinds. Between the two ends of the process, however, databases make themselves useful in many other ways. Database solutions can be configured to filter information, confirm its validity, make connections, calculate new data from raw inputs, summarize sets of data, and automate a variety of tasks involving data.

During the process of data entry, you first create a record and then enter information into the fields within the record. Database applications may allow you to specify a default value for some or all fields, so when a new record is created, some of the fields already have data in them. Sometimes the data entered automatically in this way will be *static* (always the same), but on other occasions, it may vary depending on the current situation. Examples of default values that vary are a serial number, which will increment as each new record is created, or a date or time field that takes its value from the computer's internal clock and calendar.

Still more helpful is the ability to define values that will be created automatically, depending on the values you enter. For example, you may enter an item's unit price and the quantity purchased into a database, and the database automatically fills in the sales tax and total price in other fields, saving you time and effort and reducing the potential for mistakes.

Database screens are often set up with lists of values for particular fields, to prompt you to select an appropriate value — and to speed up the process, enabling you to replace the work of many keystrokes with a single click or just one or two keystrokes. Moreover, databases are often configured with rules determining which values are valid and which should be rejected. The user can, thus, be alerted when making an error during data entry, greatly reducing the incidence of data-entry errors.

Because of these capabilities, entering data into a well-designed database solution can be much quicker and easier than typing a table in a word processor or even a spreadsheet, and the results can be more accurate. If you have large amounts of data to manage, or if several different people are involved, using a database has many advantages. These advantages go well beyond data entry because you can automate many other aspects of a database solution.

When you work with data, you'll frequently have to perform repetitive tasks as part of the process of managing information. For example, if you're maintaining a sales and billing system, you may need to go through the purchase invoices, marking and dating those that have been paid and mailing out receipts to the person or company that made each purchase.

If your sales and billing are done within a database, you might instead have the database automatically cross-reference payments with outstanding invoices, update the invoices accordingly, create the corresponding receipts, and send them to the printer in the mailroom. A whole morning's tedious work can be done in the time it takes to pour your first coffee — and without the errors and omissions that are inevitable during manual processing in a busy office with endless interruptions. If implemented well, process automation can free you from much of the drudgery of massaging data, enabling you to do the more important work of dealing with clients, making decisions, and making things happen. Let the computer do what computers are good at so that you're freed to get on with doing the things that *humans* are good at.

How FileMaker Fits In

In contemporary computing, you'll find no shortage of database software — from relatively simple desktop database programs to industrial strength enterprise systems. A few of these products are excellent in the spheres where they operate, but most are not. FileMaker Pro 10, however, stands apart from the rest in several key ways, not least of them being its unusual combination of power, accessibility, and flexibility. However, each Database Management System also has its own terms, techniques, and concepts, as well as its own particular strengths and quirks, with which its users become familiar. To begin your FileMaker journey, I show you a few of the ways to "think" FileMaker.

What FileMaker Pro calls things

In the section "The Many Faces of Databases: Lists, Tables and Forms," earlier in this chapter, I refer to database solutions, using that term's general meaning. However, in the context of FileMaker Pro, a *solution* refers to a database file or a collection of database files that interact with one another to achieve a set of user-defined objectives. Whereas a file containing only a few tables might be referred to as a *database,* the term *solution* is generally reserved for the whole set of (one or more) database files forming a particular database system.

A FileMaker solution is composed of one or more files, which in turn may contain one or more tables in which data can be stored. FileMaker offers a great deal of flexibility regarding the way a solution is configured. You can put many tables into a single file, have many files each holding only a single table — or even have some files that have no tables at all (that is, containing only code or interface). You'll make these choices depending upon the ways you want your solution to work.

The English language is rich with names, and many things have more than one name. In a word-processor table or a spreadsheet, information is entered into cells. In some SQL databases, adhering to the terminology of E. F. Codd (see the section "Flat-file databases and data redundancy," earlier in this chapter), the equivalent place for entering a specific item of data is called an *attribute.* However, in FileMaker, as noted previously, they're called fields. Similarly, what you would refer to as a row in a spreadsheet is called a record in FileMaker.

NOTE Some folk argue that *tuple* is the appropriate term for a record or that *join* is the correct name for a relation. However, in my view, the terms *record* and *relation* have the advantage of being more widely used and understood (including by those who have no background in advanced math). Should you decide to delve into technical papers on the subject of data theory, you'll encounter many such terms employed in discussion of the theory of relational databases. For everyday purposes, including when using FileMaker Pro, the terms in general use are all you'll need.

Most of the terminology used to describe the elements of a FileMaker solution differ little from other database software: FileMaker uses terms such as field, record, table, and relation. However, two notable exceptions are screens and searches. The design surface you use to create forms and reports in FileMaker are called *layouts*. Figure 1.3 shows the appearance of the same solution window in two different modes. At the left, the window is in Layout mode, where the objects on the screen can be edited; at the right, the window appears in Browse mode, and you can see that it is displaying data.

The use of the word *layout* is significant for two reasons. First, FileMaker provides a set of tools for building screens and reports, which are not unlike those you would encounter in a graphic design program — its interface builder is a *layout* builder. Second, layouts are vehicles for creating all different sorts of display and print output and can even create multipurpose screens that can be presented as a form or a list or printed as a report. Instead of providing separate objects and toolsets for building each different kind of display or output (for example, a form builder and a separate report builder), FileMaker provides a single highly flexible object — the layout. With the exception of dialogs, borders, and the Status Area (the gray band at the top), everything you see in a FileMaker window is a layout.

FIGURE 1.3

A layout being edited in Layout mode (left) and displaying data in Browse mode (right).

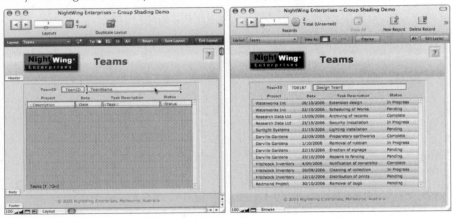

Another way that FileMaker terminology differs from most other database systems is that what others call search or query is referred to in FileMaker as a *find,* and the result of a find is termed the *found set.* To find something in FileMaker, you fill in some information (such as a word or part of a word) into a blank Find screen, shown in Figure 1.4, and FileMaker will subsequently locate any matching records and present them to you. By contrast, to perform a search in many other database environments, you have to create exacting *queries,* usually conforming to a standardized language called SQL (short for *Structured Query Language*). A fairly simple query might be

```
SELECT * FROM Teams WHERE TeamName='Design Team'
```

to locate and return the contents of records in your Teams table where the TeamName field holds "Design Team" as its value. An SQL query also requires that you specify which fields are to be returned. (Otherwise, all fields in the table are returned.) Moreover, if you add further criteria to an SQL query, it soon becomes quite long and complex. By comparison, FileMaker's Find process is quick and intuitive and less vulnerable to user errors. (It involves a lot less typing!)

As you can see in Figure 1.4, other than the tools provided in the panel on the window's left side, there is virtually no visual difference between a new, empty record (as shown in Figure 1.3) and a Find request's layout area.

In FileMaker, to find records that match given criteria, you go into *Find mode*, whereupon the current layout is presented to you with blank fields. You fill in one or more of the blank field boxes with your search criteria (in a layout that has the fields you want retrieved) and when you perform the find (using the Perform Find icon at the top of the window), FileMaker locates the records that match what you've entered. So, for example, when you're viewing a screen that presents data about teams, you can go to Find mode and enter part of a team name, shown in Figure 1.4, to locate records for teams with names beginning with the letters you've entered. After performing the Find, you can browse or print the resulting records.

FileMaker lets you enter find criteria directly, rather than construct complex queries.

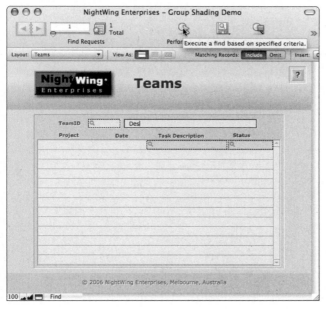

CROSS-REF   I cover Find requests in Chapter 3 and delve more deeply into them in Chapter 5.

Just as searches or queries are made easy via Find requests, retrieving data from related records is made simple. In cases where only a single related record is to be displayed (for example, the name of the school a student is attending), FileMaker allows you to simply place the relevant field from a related table directly onto a layout. The first related value will then be displayed. However, in cases where there is a need to display data other than the first related record or to display a list of related records, FileMaker enables you to achieve this via the use of *portals,* groupings of fields on your layout from tables related to the table on which the layout is based. The name derives from the portal object being a window (or doorway) into related tables — maybe a little trite, but descriptive and easy to remember. The list area appearing in the lower part of the Teams layout featured in Figures 1.3 and 1.4 is an example of a portal that displays a list of projects assigned to the current team.

CROSS-REF   I cover portals in detail in Chapter 6.

In FileMaker, the process by which default values — both static and varying —are assigned to fields is referred to as *Auto-Entry,* and the automatic checking of data input against predefined criteria for completeness and consistency is termed *validation.*

You can generate derived values and dependent variables in FileMaker in several ways, but one of the most common is via the use of special kinds of fields in FileMaker: *calculation fields* and *summary fields.* To support its extensive abilities for logical, textual, and mathematical manipulation, FileMaker provides a sophisticated built-in capability for interpreting and applying your instructions, which is often termed the *calculation engine.* Moreover, in order to keep its calculation results consistent with your data, FileMaker keeps track of which fields depend on the values in other fields. The process of keeping track of calculations so that they can automatically be updated appropriately is done behind the scenes in what is sometimes referred to as FileMaker's *table of dependencies.*

CROSS-REF   Look for additional details about Auto-Entry, validation, and calculation and summary fields in Chapter 7.

In database programs, there is sometimes a need to store a group of values as a cohesive set applying to a single data attribute. Value sets are often known as *arrays.* However, in FileMaker, fields designated to hold data arrays are referred to as *repeating fields* and must be predefined for a specific maximum number of *repetitions.* Both data fields and memory variables in FileMaker can have repetitions.

CROSS-REF   I discuss memory variables in depth in Chapters 9 and 12.

In general, the information held in a field, in a variable, or in a given repetition of a field or variable is referred to as a *value.* However, a text field may hold multiple lines separated by carriage returns — for example, a list — and in such cases, the content of each line is collectively regarded as a value in its own right. In that respect, a single (nonrepeating) FileMaker text field may hold multiple values.

Fields that are used to define *joins* (relationships) between tables are referred to as *Key fields* or *Match fields* in FileMaker, with the default relationship type (an *equi-join*) being one requiring a matching value in the Key fields of both tables being joined. However, if the Key fields are text fields and may be expected to hold multiple values, each value is separately indexed and used to establish a pluralistic relationship. In FileMaker, fields used in relationships in this way are referred to as *Multi-Key fields*.

CROSS-REF   **Relationships and Key fields are explored in detail in Chapters 7 and 11.**

Many computer programs and programming environments provide the ability to create stored procedures or *macros* (collections of instructions, actions, or commands that can be performed automatically or called on at will by the user). In FileMaker Pro, these sets of stored instructions are referred to as *scripts,* and the environment in which they're created is called *ScriptMaker.* Scripts are made up of sequences of *script steps,* sometimes also referred to as *script commands.* When scripts are required to interact with fields, buttons, or other elements on one of the layouts in your solution, the elements they target are referred to as *objects.*

FileMaker provides support for storage of binary objects — movies, images, sounds, and even files — in fields within the database. The type of field that provides this capability is called a *Container field* and is capable of displaying the contents of a range of supported media (images, movies, and sounds in a range of supported formats). Alongside this, FileMaker is able to render HTML and other Web-related technologies within designated layout objects called *Web Viewer objects.*

When multiple database files are designed to operate together and interact as part of a solution, individual files will be programmed to locate and use data or call scripts within other files in the solution. Links and references to other files that allow this interaction to occur are called External Data Sources in FileMaker 10 and can include FileMaker files and also supported SQL databases.

NOTE   **In previous versions of FileMaker Pro, External Data Sources were referred to as *File References* and included only FileMaker database files.**

I've provided you with a quick overview of the central concepts and terms used in FileMaker, with particular emphasis on areas where the terminology or its application differs from that found in other databases. As you read on, you'll encounter many other terms that are either in common use or that I will explain within the text. You'll also find a glossary of terms on the Web site, which will be helpful if you encounter anything unfamiliar while browsing through the chapters.

Familiar ideas from the real world

From its very first versions in the 1980s, FileMaker has provided a rich graphical interface that operates as a metaphor — mimicking familiar objects and ideas from the world around us. One of the clearest illustrations of this is FileMaker's ubiquitous navigation icon, which appears in the Status Area at the top of each window and represents a Rolodex or spiral-bound book. In FileMaker Pro 10, clicking the right page of the spiral-bound book icon moves you forward one record; clicking the left page moves you back one record. The use of the FileMaker Pro navigation icon sets the scene for a program that makes extensive use of visual metaphor and that has powerful graphical capabilities.

FileMaker offers a suite of layout design tools you can employ to create screens and printed output that replicate the appearance of your real-world forms and reports. In addition to a basic suite of drawing and text tools with which you can assemble the layouts that provide screens and printed output, FileMaker supports direct import of image files (including PNG, JPEG, and GIF formats) for display on layouts along with other layout elements. The combination of these elements lends itself to the creation of graphically rich database applications. Moreover, layout elements can be defined to be interactive so that clicking them performs a specific action or gives the user access to a particular record, field, or screen. These capabilities have seen FileMaker used to build a startlingly diverse range of applications, from children's games to boardroom presentation viewers — as well as the many more conventional database exploits.

It would be a mistake, however, to assume that FileMaker's strength lies primarily in its chameleon-like interface capabilities. The real power of any database is in its ability to model information and its relationships in the real world — to find order within complexity. FileMaker responds to this challenge in a very particular way, by providing an extensive palette of tools and capabilities that can be combined in many ways to solve a given problem. In this respect, FileMaker provides an environment in which to model both the problems and the solutions of the real world.

Integrating processes and information

The real value of databases — and FileMaker is no exception — is not in their ability to store and retrieve data, but in their ability to empower you to use your data more effectively. If all you hope to do is store your information, a database is a good way to do so — but most information is part of ongoing processes and is not static.

One of the simplest examples of the power of a database solution is the ability to enter your data in one format (such as a form layout) and then retrieve subsets of it in another format, perhaps in a different sort order and with totals or summary values added. These are everyday feats for a computer database, yet they may be inordinately time consuming to achieve by using traditional record-keeping techniques. This ability alone is empowering.

Even more valuable is the ability to create screens and data views that support a process and follow it through from commencement to completion. This process requires that data be viewed as an essential part of a larger process or project, and that the database be commissioned as a facilitative tool. When viewed in this light, it's clear that the role of the database is significant and can either guide or hinder the progress of a project, depending on its design.

If your aim is to gain a greater command of data and the processes it supports, you have chosen wisely in exploring the capabilities of FileMaker Pro. In the following chapters, I show you how truly flexible and powerful a modern desktop database can be.

Knowledge is power — personal and professional

Without ready access to accurate and well-organized information, you cannot make optimal decisions and that can have immediate and lasting implications for you, your employer, or your business. The old saying *ignorance is bliss* does not apply. (Presumably it was coined by someone who didn't know any better. . . .) Rather, having good data to base your decisions on is the surest way to a profitable day's work and a good night's sleep.

FileMaker Pro provides you with tools to enhance the ways you assemble, interpret, and interrogate your data, enabling you to build and use purpose-built databases that match the way you work, store only the data you need, reduce redundancies and errors, and automate tedious processes. The data in question can be anything from your shopping list, weekly grocery budget, or sporting scores to the sales, inventory, payroll, or research data for your business — any kind of information you need to manage. Using the summary and reporting capabilities FileMaker provides, you're able to analyze your data, quickly viewing totals, averages, trends, or highlights. Alternatively, FileMaker makes it easy to extract relevant data and export it in standard formats so that you can use other applications (such as a spreadsheet program) to perform projections, evaluate scenarios, perform analysis, or render charts from your data.

A further way that FileMaker can assist you is by performing a range of routine checks on your information to ensure that it meets basic error-check criteria. For example, you can define rules that stipulate that a particular field (such as client name) may not be left empty or that a value must fall in a certain range. Similarly, you can save time and reduce the potential for errors by defining default (auto-enter) values that will be generated when a new record is created. A computer program can't do all the work for you, but it certainly can assist you to use your time effectively and focus on the things that matter most (the decisions only you can make)!

Chapter 2

Putting FileMaker Pro in Perspective

FileMaker Pro is a widely used database application and development environment, and it's well established as the best-selling database on Mac OS and among the most prevalent in Windows. However, several things set FileMaker Pro apart from most other Database Management Systems.

The first version of FileMaker made its appearance as a Macintosh-only application in 1985 (as a graphical interface version of an established DOS-based database program called Nutshell, which had been developed and marketed by Nashoba Systems). Early versions of FileMaker were relatively simple by current standards (and were essentially nonrelational), but the program offered a number of innovative features that made a significant impression on the software market of the time.

After establishing a solid user base and undergoing successive enhancements during the latter half of the 1980s, FileMaker was renamed FileMaker Pro in 1990, went cross-platform in 1992, and became relational in 1995. As a cross-platform database, FileMaker Pro shares a common file format between Mac OS and Windows, enabling users to access the same data simultaneously (including over a network). With the advent of relational capabilities, FileMaker Pro became a sophisticated business tool capable of meeting complex requirements efficiently.

FileMaker Pro has continued to evolve with every release, and its flexibility and power has enabled it to retain its position at the forefront of the database market. In 2004, the release of FileMaker Pro 7 provided a radical revision of the power and scope of the application, greatly increasing capacity, flexibility, and power (and allowing multiple tables per file for the first time). FileMaker Pro 10 represents a further leap forward with the introduction of strategically important features such as an interface-based script event trigger architecture and important interface updates along with a host of other improvements.

IN THIS CHAPTER

Understanding what sets FileMaker Pro apart from other database environments

Introducing the FileMaker Pro product family

Identifying surprising capabilities in FileMaker Pro

Finding outside resources and information about FileMaker

Despite the many changes FileMaker has undergone in the 24 years since its debut, it remains elegant and intuitive and is exceptionally easy to use given its power, flexibility, and the sophisticated functionality of which it is capable.

What Makes FileMaker Pro Different from Other Database Development Tools?

Perhaps the most significant difference between FileMaker Pro and the majority of other database environments is that FileMaker provides a seamless environment where the *application* (the components that provide interface and process support) is integrated with the database engine that provides structure and data storage for your solutions.

A further point of contrast is the scalability the FileMaker suite of products offers. While most databases will accommodate a range of requirements, FileMaker is capable of covering an exceptionally broad spectrum. While FileMaker Pro operating alone can accommodate the requirements of single users or small workgroups, FileMaker Pro Advanced provides capabilities for advanced developers and solution providers. When coupled with FileMaker Server or FileMaker Server Advanced, provision can be made for larger-scale networked deployments (up to 250 simultaneous users with FileMaker Server and up to 999 simultaneous users with FileMaker Server Advanced) and online data requirements. However, across this broad spectrum, the user interface, file format, and database engine enjoy a high level of consistency.

NOTE   FileMaker, Inc., also offers Bento, an unrelated single-user database product exclusively for Mac OS X Leopard users. FileMaker 10 supports data imports from Bento; however, live data transfer and multi-user or simultaneous data access isn't possible, and Bento is better suited for personal rather than business or enterprise use. For modest data requirements on Mac OS X 10.5, Bento is an attractive option. Because this text focuses on meeting demanding database requirements, Bento is outside the scope of this book.

Some common misperceptions

Misperceptions abound when it comes to data management and FileMaker Pro:

- **All Database Management Systems are similar.** You may be tempted to consider that all Database Management Systems are similar. However, while database systems may have comparable goals, the approach they take and the skills required to use them effectively to build a solution may differ markedly. In the same way that a speed boat and a dune buggy both provide means of transport yet operate quite differently and within different domains, Database Management Systems serve comparable aims via different means.

- **FileMaker Pro offers a gentle learning curve and therefore must lack power.** The apparent simplicity of use of various features of FileMaker Pro leads some to assume that the program may be inflexible, offer narrow options, or be otherwise limited in scope.

Don't be fooled — the reverse is true! Unlike many applications, FileMaker conceals its complexities, allowing you to make good initial progress without a great deal of technical know-how. However, as you gain confidence, FileMaker exposes deeper layers of functionality and capability that you can use to access a rich resource of complex and advanced features.

To help novice users to be productive, while nevertheless providing power users with advanced features, FileMaker Pro has been designed to simplify complex tasks, revealing complexity only as and when it is needed. In addition, the interface has been designed to work in a consistent way throughout, so that a single skill, when mastered, can be used in a variety of contexts throughout the application. An example of this consistency is the Specify Calculation dialog, shown in Figure 2.1. The Specify Calculation dialog is used throughout the product, wherever you need to determine a result, so instead of presenting separate interfaces for performing math, processing text, defining a script parameter, or composing a URL, the same dialog appears for all these tasks and more.

NOTE In some situations, you can supply a parameter or result without delving into the Specify Calculation dialog. For example, you can enter a static URL for a Web Viewer object or a simple decision for conditional formatting without involving Specify Calculation; however, the dialog is always available for the more complex decisions and computations.

- **Planning your data structure is an optional extra you can postpone until a rainy day.** New users often underestimate the importance of giving thought to the data structure (the tables and relationships between them) for their solution. When you're starting out, lumping everything together into a single table may seem easier. However, doing so leads to complications and closes off opportunities for improved efficiency and clarity as your confidence (and the complexity of your solution) increases.

- **The boxes on the FileMaker Pro Relationships Graph are tables.** FileMaker Pro utilizes a Relationships Graph, shown in Figure 2.2, as the tool for viewing and defining relationships between the tables of your solution. The boxes appearing on the graph aren't the tables themselves but pointers to them, commonly called *Table Occurrences* (TOs). There can be multiple TOs for each table. Each TO in the graph provides a view or connection to a selected table.

- **You can connect anything to anything else on the FileMaker Relationships Graph.** FileMaker Pro doesn't permit circular relationship paths; if you try to add a relationship that would make the path circular, you're prompted to create an additional occurrence of one of the tables so that the circular reference will be avoided. Consequently, there is only ever one path between any two TOs on the Graph. For example, in a company database, you're likely to have a table of employees that includes information about their manager and the staff they supervise. However, the associated records for the manager and subordinate staff will also be located within the employee table. In this situation, FileMaker creates additional occurrences of the employee table for managers and subordinate staff to enable you to implement these relationships without requiring circular relationship paths.

FIGURE 2.1

The Specify Calculation dialog is reused for multiple purposes throughout FileMaker Pro.

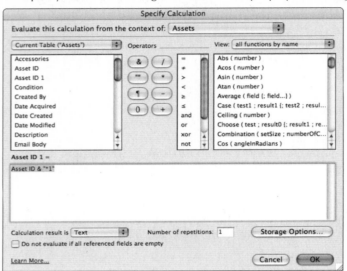

FIGURE 2.2

The Relationships Graph represents relationships between the tables in your solution.

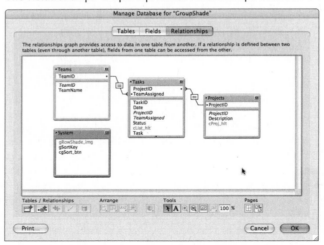

- **The Relationships Graph is like an Entity Relationship Diagram (ERD).** In some respects, the FileMaker Pro Relationships Graph resembles an Entity Relationship Diagram (ERD) commonly used to represent the essential elements of a data model. However, don't assume that you can treat the Relationships Graph as an ERD because of the need to represent tables multiple times on FileMaker's Relationships Graph to avoid circular references (direct or indirect) and to support various navigation and interface requirements — neither of which is required in an Entity Relationship Diagram. Thus, the similarities are mostly superficial and are not generally helpful for understanding how best to use the Relationships Graph in FileMaker.

- **There is one best or correct way of doing anything.** One of the defining characteristics of FileMaker Pro is its flexibility. As part of that, you can frequently approach a problem in more than one way — sometimes many different ways. The first way that occurs to you may not be the best way for your particular situation. The way that is suggested in the manual or Help documentation or in a forum post you locate via a search engine may not be the best for your situation, either, though each method may work. In this book, I encourage you to consider alternatives and to be creative in thinking of some of your own — but I have room only to cover a fraction of the possible techniques in a volume of this size. The fact that you've selected this book and are evidently reading it shows that you're astute, discerning, and resourceful. So I'm assuming that you're also eager to consider all the quirks and possibilities that FileMaker Pro 10 has to offer and to creatively adapt and apply the examples throughout the book to your own situation and your own solutions.

A unique approach to design

FileMaker offers you great breadth of creative scope when designing and implementing your solutions. Everything from the appearance to the structure and the process logic of your solution can be conceived and executed in a wide variety of ways. In that respect, FileMaker provides the tools and the environment, but the ideas and the content are entirely yours. For example, FileMaker's layouts support imported graphics and free-form text, enabling you to produce highly customized screen and report designs. However, you can also use layouts to display help text or instructions on how to use your solution. The demonstration files provided by many solution developers include instructive layouts like the one shown in Figure 2.3. This figure shows the Information layout of the free Calendar View Demo from NightWing Enterprises.

To extend the scope of the design options FileMaker layouts afford, you have a choice of a variety of field formats, allowing you to present users with checkbox, radio button, pop-up menu, or drop-down list interface elements as alternatives to standard text boxes. You can configure field validation requirements to constrain the data users can enter or to require a value in a given field. You can use auto-entry options to prepopulate fields in new records with default values. You can use tab objects to reuse one or more areas of your layouts to present alternative interface options (or to save space and simplify complex layouts), and you can use portals to integrate data from related tables into your layouts. By adding Web Viewers to your layouts, you can incorporate browser capabilities and online content as part of your solution interfaces. In all these ways and many more, FileMaker gives you open-ended creative potential, enabling you to adapt your solution to meet the needs of end-users.

FIGURE 2.3

Including an informational layout (or layouts) is a common practice when providing a solution.

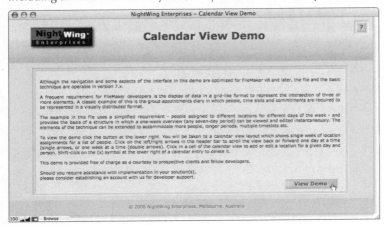

The storage architecture of your solutions is another area where FileMaker provides you with a range of alternatives. While it is possible to have the code, interface, and data tables in a single solution file, you can place the tables in a separate file or distribute them between a number of files. Moreover, you can use FileMaker's External SQL Source (ESS) feature to access one or more data tables in a supported SQL database. Similarly, you can create multiple interfaces to a single solution to serve the needs of different users or to manage version updates.

CROSS-REF For an in-depth discussion of alternative file configurations, including the use of separate files for data and interface, see Chapter 11.

The FileMaker Product Family

Although this book focuses (almost) exclusively on FileMaker Pro 10 and FileMaker Pro 10 Advanced, FileMaker, Inc., offers other related products to fill out its product line. There is considerable integration between the main products in the range, so transitioning from one to another is straightforward.

Desktop and server

FileMaker Pro 10 is a self-contained application that enables you to develop, maintain, and use databases by employing a broad-based set of essential tools for designing, programming, and deploying databases large and small. Included in FileMaker Pro are the layout design tools, relationship and schema editing capabilities, ScriptMaker, and a comprehensive suite of commands and functions. Moreover, FileMaker Pro enables you to share databases from your workstation to up to nine concurrent client connections and access them via a web browser by using built-in Instant Web Publishing for up to five simultaneous sessions.

With FileMaker Pro 10 Advanced, you get an application that includes all the capabilities of FileMaker Pro, plus some key extra powers enabling you to develop more rapidly, access extended capabilities such as custom functions (for example, building a custom calculation function), custom menus (for example, changing the contents and behavior of menus), and other powerful developer features. Moreover, FileMaker Pro 10 Advanced lets you create *runtime solutions* — completely self-contained single-user desktop databases that don't require the user to have a copy of FileMaker Pro. You can configure such solutions to work as kiosk implementations for customers to check on product availability in your store or to sign in or out at the front desk of a business, including the printing of a visitor's badge. Runtime applications can also operate as stand-alone desktop applications serving a wide variety of purposes and needs.

CROSS-REF I provide a more detailed exploration of the additional features and capabilities of FileMaker Po 10 Advanced in Chapter 18.

In addition to the main desktop products — FileMaker Pro 10 and FileMaker Pro 10 Advanced — the FileMaker suite includes two FileMaker Server products that offer enterprise-level distributed database usage, web publishing capabilities, and integration with remote ODBC client applications. FileMaker Server 10 enables you to securely and efficiently make your solutions available to up to 999 simultaneous FileMaker Pro users over a network and to make data available via PHP or XML to an appropriately configured Web site.

When you install FileMaker Server 10 Advanced, you gain access to all the features of FileMaker Server 10, plus two key additional capabilities:

- The ability to make FileMaker data available to remote client applications via ODBC or JDBC protocols
- The ability to publish your databases to as many as 100 simultaneous Web users via Instant Web Publishing (IWP)

Scalability and flexibility

FileMaker's ability to adapt to the task at hand is sometimes surprising. Performing a quick analysis of a few hundred records or sorting the invitations for a party are not too trivial a task for this tool to accomplish. And yet, in some cases, FileMaker has been used to build applications of vast complexity, accommodating millions of records in hundreds of tables. Everything in between these two extremes can be encountered in schools and universities, business, government, and industry the world over.

Despite the breadth of capability and extent of scalability that FileMaker offers, it's nevertheless fair to state that FileMaker is ideally suited to applications accessed by up to several hundred users that typically handle tens of thousands of records. Moreover, the way a solution is designed is a significant determining factor in its capability to scale. Features or designs that are acceptable in single-user or small-scale solutions may be inappropriate for large or complex server-based implementations.

CROSS-REF For a detailed discussion about designing for scale and solution efficiency, refer to Chapter 19.

A key component of FileMaker's strengths is its networkable and multi-user capability. A single FileMaker solution hosted on an appropriate database server can be accessed simultaneously by several hundred users or can be configured to provide the basis of a data-driven Web solution. At its upper limits, FileMaker is capable of integrating with third-party technologies to synchronize multiple servers so as to provide increased security, performance, or extensibility.

As well as providing for both large- and small-scale solutions, FileMaker incorporates a surprisingly diverse feature set, supporting everything from powerful text formatting to workflow automation and document management, to multimedia presentation, playing digital video and sound directly from fields in the database. Moreover, FileMaker provides built-in support for external scripting protocols, such as AppleScript on the Mac and VBScript in Windows, so your solution can interact with other scriptable applications, such as Microsoft Excel or iTunes, to retrieve data or even to control the other application.

FileMaker's Hidden Talents

FileMaker is available in multiple languages and supports multilingual functionality, using Unicode as the technology for managing character sets. Text values can be indexed according to the conventions of more than 26 languages and variants, and techniques are available to create multilingual interfaces within a single solution (see Figure 2.4).

Additionally, the inclusion of ESS to access SQL data, plus ODBC (Open Database Connectivity) support and the ability FileMaker provides to handle several different data formats (text, number, date, time, image, movie, sound, file, and so on) provides a great breadth of scope and functionality, enabling FileMaker to integrate with existing computing applications. FileMaker also provides a plug-in interface that third-party developers can use to provide specialized extended functionality, introducing an extensive array of additional features and further extending the ability to integrate with external systems.

The cross-platform chameleon

Unlike other Database Management Systems, FileMaker Pro provides an almost-seamless cross-platform experience, dealing with most platform differences behind the scenes. The file format is the same on Mac OS and in Windows, and, with very few exceptions, the application controls, menus, dialogs, and features are consistent between platforms. Consequently, you can create a solution on one platform and have it work the same way on the other platform.

CROSS-REF   **For an in-depth discussion of techniques and considerations for cross-platform development, refer to Chapter 10.**

Equally attractive is the capability to have a mix of Mac OS and Windows client computers accessing a single-served solution simultaneously. In mixed-platform work environments, this benefit alone is an outstanding feature.

FIGURE 2.4

The Field Options dialog showing language indexing options for text fields in FileMaker Pro 10.

Multiple technologies and formats

FileMaker has a long history of working alongside a variety of other applications. First and foremost, it includes the capability to import and export data in a variety of formats, including common interchange formats, such as comma-separated values (CSV), tab-delimited files, and Microsoft Excel files, and a number of other common desktop database formats (see Figure 2.5).

Instead of importing, if you simply drag a Microsoft Excel file (or various other supported file formats) onto the FileMaker Pro icon, the file will be converted automatically and presented to you in FileMaker database format. It really is that easy.

Equally significant is FileMaker's ability to import and export eXtensible Markup Language (XML) data, including from online XML data sources, and using parsing via eXtensible Style Language Transformation (XSLT) style sheets. Again, this ability provides broad-based support for data exchange and interoperability.

FIGURE 2.5

The available formats for data import from local files in FileMaker Pro 10.

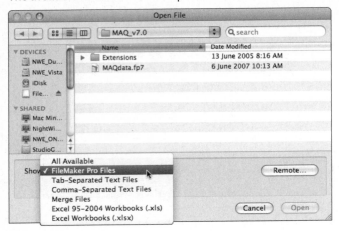

Similarly, FileMaker's ability to read and write seamlessly to data tables in supported versions of MySQL, Oracle, and Microsoft SQL Server gives you extensive options and capabilities from desktop to enterprise systems. Moreover, you can mix and match the formats and technologies, using FileMaker as the conduit. For example, a FileMaker database that uses one or more remote SQL data sources can seamlessly generate reports or data outputs (Excel, PDF, and so on) containing data from any one (or a combination) of the available sources. It's therefore not unrealistic to use FileMaker as the report generator or analysis tool for data that resides in other systems.

Plug-ins and extensibility

FileMaker doesn't restrict you to data entered into a layout via the keyboard or by importing a file from disc. With its plug-in architecture, you can access data from scanners, digital cameras, bar code readers, and other such devices — but FileMaker doesn't stop there.

When the engineers at FileMaker, Inc., first envisioned a plug-in Application/Program Interface (API) for FileMaker, the primary intended purpose was adding the capability to perform complex math and calculation operations outside the core feature set. However, ingenious third-party developers have been devising unexpected uses of the API ever since.

Shortly after the plug-in API was released in 1997, third-party products began to emerge with such diverse features as e-mail client capabilities, drawing and graphics tools, file manipulation tools, charting capabilities, Internet telephony, serial port controllers, custom dialog generators, and encryption tools — the complete list is much too long to include here (and would likely be outdated by the time this book made it to the shelves). Developers found that, via the API, they could pass data from a FileMaker calculation to a compiled application (in the form of a plug-in) and then return a result — and despite some early limitations, this capability has provided the basis of an enormous variety of plug-ins from vendors all over the globe.

Although many plug-ins serve a very specialized purpose — interfacing with specific hardware (such as a TWAIN scanner) or exchanging data with a proprietary application (such as the elegant accounting software suite from Cognito — www.cognito.co.nz) — a number of plug-ins have focused on extending the core feature set of FileMaker itself. As a result, these plug-ins have become widely recognized and used by FileMaker developers the world over. Examples include SecureFM from New Millennium Communications (www.securefm.com), Troi File from Troi Automatisering (www.troi.com), and xmCHART from X2max Software (www.x2max.com/en/products/xmCHART/info.html). These and other plug-in-based products have found a place as part of the mainstream of FileMaker development.

CROSS-REF You can find a more complete discussion of plug-in extensibility in Chapter 20.

The FileMaker calculation engine: Simplicity and power

Starting from promising beginnings in the 1980s, FileMaker's calculation capabilities have been steadily extended to the point where their diversity and scope is considerable. Although FileMaker 10 provides approximately 250 native calculation functions, each designed to accomplish a specific range of objectives, you can combine these functions in compound calculation expressions in myriad ways to solve a wide range of problems.

FileMaker's calculation interface is consistent throughout the application. Additionally, the calculation expression syntax is straightforward and follows consistent rules. Defining simple calculation formulas, therefore, requires no special expertise — it works intuitively and elegantly, so if you enter 2 + 2 into the calculation engine (or quantity * price), you'll get the expected results directly and effortlessly. With a little effort and experience (and with the aid of this book), considerably more challenging tasks are made easy.

CROSS-REF I explore the uses of FileMaker's calculation engine in depth in Chapters 7 and 12.

FileMaker Pro Advanced also provides a developer interface for creating custom functions. Using the building blocks of the calculation engine, you can define new functions within a file, which perform complex operations with a single function call. Significantly, you can define custom functions to use recursive capabilities, further extending their scope and power.

NOTE Even though FileMaker Pro Advanced is required to create custom functions, FileMaker Pro is all that's required to use these functions after they're in the solution.

CROSS-REF I discuss custom functions in greater detail, providing examples of their application, in Chapter 18.

Resources and Exemplars

The first and most important thing to know about FileMaker Pro is that a thriving global developer community exists, made up of consultants and developers with considerable expertise and backgrounds in an extraordinarily diverse range of industries. Although FileMaker Pro is an application that you can use straight out of the box — and I encourage you to do so — be aware that, if you want to extend your reach beyond what you can easily achieve on your own, there is no shortage of professionals available to provide assistance or support.

The FileMaker developer community is vital for a number of other reasons as well. Within this community, new ways to use the application and new insights into its capabilities frequently emerge. An ongoing discourse between active and gifted developers in various parts of the globe often results in new and ingenious approaches to puzzling or elusive problems. Just such a network exists in the FileMaker community, and many have benefited from the resourcefulness and generosity of its many members.

A secondary consequence of the thriving developer community's existence is that the community spawns a plethora of diagnostic tools and development aids, and many such tools and aids exist for FileMaker. Analysis tools Inspector from FMNEXUS (`www.fmnexus.com/products/inspector`), FMDiff from Huslik Verlag GmbH (`www.fmdiff.com`), BaseElements from Goya (`www.goya.com.au/baseelements`), and various other examples provide extensive additional capability and insight to what is already a powerful core product base.

In a further signal of the FileMaker development environment's maturity, recent years have seen the introduction of a worldwide developer certification program by FileMaker, Inc. This certification program increases the visibility and viability of FileMaker as a platform for professional application developers, as well as provides users and business clients with an indication of the skills and credentials of professionals working in the field. Along with annual developer conferences in several countries around the world, certification bodes well for an ongoing wealth of support and expertise in all things FileMaker.

As an important adjunct to its other activities, FileMaker, Inc., offers several support and assistance programs to companies and developers working across the FileMaker product line. Foremost among these programs is FileMaker TechNet (`www.filemaker.com/technet`) — a membership-based network of developers and users who participate on a technical mailing list/forum hosted by FileMaker, Inc. Similarly, FileMaker, Inc., makes FileMaker Business Alliance membership (`www.filemaker.com/fba`) available to businesses that have a substantial interest in or involvement with FileMaker support, sales, or development.

Examples and brainteasers

Flowing directly from the fertile developer community are many thorny questions concerning the best ways to approach particular problems or solve difficult development problems. As part of their participation in this ongoing discourse, a number of developers in various parts of the world publish examples, samples, tips, and tricks that provide insight into novel or elegant solutions to various development challenges.

You can find some of the many free professional-quality examples, tips, demos, and other resources made by participants in the FileMaker developer community at the Web sites of companies in various parts of the world. In addition to the multitude of demos and example files available from NightWing Enterprises (`www.nightwing.com.au/FileMaker`), you can find a wealth of resources and samples at sites such as Database Pros (`www.databasepros.com`), Excelisys (`www.excelisys.com`), SeedCode (`www.seedcode.com`), and numerous others. Moreover, online forums, such as FMForums (`www.fmforums.com`), and resources, such as the inimitable user group network at FMPug (`www.fmpug.com`), provide both depth and breadth of expertise, as well as a host of information and resource directories.

Other resources and opportunities

In addition to the many resources I describe in this chapter, FileMaker, Inc., maintains a network of training partners who are ready and able to provide high-quality support and training to end-users and aspiring developers.

Although I believe that FileMaker is remarkable for its easy learning curve and the way it enables new users to ease into the realm of database design, don't underestimate how much more there is to know. Even after working through the many examples and explanations I provide in this book, you'll find value in exploring the wealth of training and support options available.

Chapter 3

Getting Acquainted with FileMaker

There is no substitute for experience when it comes to using a computer application, so if you haven't already done so, it's time to get in front of a computer and begin to use FileMaker. You can take the book with you, if you wish. (In fact, that's a good way to proceed.)

For the purposes of following the descriptions in *FileMaker Pro 10 Bible*, you'll need a copy of FileMaker Pro 10 or FileMaker Pro 10 Advanced, installed on a supported version of either a Windows or Macintosh operating system. In most respects, the Pro and Pro Advanced applications look identical, although there are a few additional menu commands and features in the Advanced version. Screenshots throughout are generally applicable to both versions and to both Mac and Windows systems, though the appearance of window frames and dialogs differs slightly between platforms.

If this is your very first use of FileMaker, you may need to first run the installer to get the software set up and ready for use. After FileMaker is installed, launch it from the Dock (Mac) or by choosing Start ⇨ All Programs ⇨ FileMaker Pro (Windows).

IN THIS CHAPTER

Starting to use FileMaker

Navigating your database

Entering data in your database

Importing and exporting data

Dealing with related data

Configuring FileMaker

Getting FileMaker Working for You

During installation, FileMaker Pro 10 will prompt you to enter an activation code and register your product. Registering ensures that you will receive update notices and e-mails with information about support, news, and matters of interest to users and developers.

After the launch sequence (during which the opening splash screen is displayed), FileMaker presents the Quick Start screen, providing access to three options, as follows:

- Create Database
- Open Database
- Learn More

Clicking the Create Database icon provides access to 30 starter templates that provide basic pre-programmed functionality for a range of various types of business, education, and home databases. The templates provide a rapid way to get started with a file that has some of the basic elements already created for you; however, as you build your knowledge of FileMaker, you'll want to customize the files to meet your own requirements.

The Open Database icon at the left of the FileMaker Quick Start window provides a convenient list of recently opened files. You may also add favorite files under either the Favorite Files (local) or Favorite Files (remote) subheadings. To add a recently opened file (appearing in the recently opened files list in the Quick Start window) to the relevant favorites menu, select it in the list panel at the right of the window and click the Add to Favorites button appearing below the list. If the selected file is hosted from another computer or server, it will be added to the Favorite Files (remote) group. Otherwise, it will appear in the Favorite Files (local) list.

> **NOTE**   The term *local* refers to FileMaker files that are located on disk drives attached to the computer you are working on, or shared drives accessed from the current computer. *Remote* files are those that are hosted on another computer (that is, opened in FileMaker Pro 10, FileMaker Pro 10 Advanced or FileMaker Server 10) and accessed by using FileMaker's built-in networking.

In addition, the Quick Start screen includes an icon labeled Learn More that provides access to an introductory video, links to the product documentation, and various sites for online information, feedback, and guidance. This gathers together, in one location, a number of resources of interest to you as you become acquainted with the application.

> **TIP**   The Quick Start screen is optional. You can click the Do Not Show Quick Start Again checkbox that appears at the bottom of the panel. If you do this, you can still create new files and open existing files by using commands on the File menu.

Starting and exiting from FileMaker

Your computer operating system provides numerous ways to launch FileMaker Pro. Here are several common methods:

- During installation, an icon for the application is installed (at your option) in the Dock (Mac) or (by default) in the Start ⇨ All Programs menu (Windows). Clicking the program icon in the Dock or choosing it in the Start menu starts FileMaker Pro.

- You may have an alias (in Windows, it's called a shortcut) on your computer's desktop and/or in the Quick Launch toolbar (Windows). Double-clicking an alias/shortcut icon starts FileMaker, as does selecting FileMaker from the Windows Quick Launch toolbar.

- You can locate the application itself and double-click it, or double-click a FileMaker file anywhere on your desktop or within the disk directories on your computer.

NOTE The default path to the FileMaker Pro application on the Mac is Macintosh HD/Applications/FileMaker Pro 10/FileMaker Pro.app. In Windows, it's C:\Program Files\FileMaker\FileMaker Pro 10\FileMaker Pro.exe.

A few seconds after the application launches, you see the Quick Start screen (or if the Quick Start screen has been disabled, a standard Open File dialog appears). You are then ready to create a new database file or to locate and open an existing file.

When you've finished using FileMaker Pro for the moment, you may end the current application session by choosing FileMaker Pro ⇨ Quit FileMaker Pro (Mac) or File ⇨ Exit (Windows). If you have any database files open when you choose to end the application session, the files are automatically saved and closed before FileMaker exits.

Creating, saving, and closing files

The steps in the process of creating a new database file depend on whether FileMaker is already running and whether your computer is configured to use the Quick Start screen.

CROSS-REF Details about how to change the configuration of FileMaker on your computer, including enabling and disabling the Quick Start screen, are included in the "Preference settings for your workstation" section, later in this chapter.

If FileMaker is not yet running, after you launch it you see a dialog with the option to create a new database. If the Quick Start screen is enabled, you can choose whether to create a new empty file or to use one of the starter templates that ship with the application. Otherwise, you're presented with a File dialog. On the Mac, the dialog includes a New button at the lower right; in Windows, you must first enter a filename and then click the Open button, in order to be presented with a dialog confirming that you want to create a new file.

If FileMaker is already running, you can begin creating a new database file by choosing File ⇨ New Database.

NOTE FileMaker database files for all versions from 7 to 10 inclusive use the filename extension .fp7. Using this extension on all your database filenames is important because the operating system uses it to associate the file with the FileMaker Pro application.

When you choose a folder, enter a suitable filename, and confirm the creation of the file, a new database window is displayed. If you selected a template, the new file appears, ready to use or modify. However, if you choose to create a new empty file, a blank layout window appears and the

Manage Database dialog automatically opens. Because a database file cannot hold any data until there are some fields in which to store the data, a default table (with a name corresponding to the file name) is added, and you're prompted to create fields for your new database.

To create one or more fields, enter a name in the Field Name box of the Manage Database dialog, as shown in Figure 3.1, and click the Create button. Then click OK to close the dialog. At this point, FileMaker generates a single default layout containing the fields you've created, plus a single record. The cursor appears in the first field, ready for you to enter some data.

You now have a very simple database file, and you can begin to use it. It doesn't yet have many useful features, but those can follow. For the moment, try entering a few values into the field (or fields) on the layout. If you have several fields you can use the mouse or the Tab key to move between them.

Unlike many other computer applications, FileMaker saves data at two levels. When you change a record or a layout, the change must be saved before you can go on to do anything else. By default, FileMaker handles the saving of records automatically without asking you to confirm — so, when you exit a record, its contents are saved. Similarly, the file must periodically be saved to disk and this, too, is handled automatically. As data is entered and accumulates, FileMaker writes data to disk progressively. You can change the default auto-save behavior for records on a layout-by-layout basis by going to layout mode, choosing a layout, choosing Layouts ➪ Layout Setup, and, in the Layout Setup dialog that appears, deselecting the checkbox labeled Save Record Changes Automatically. Similarly, when you don't want layout changes saved automatically, you can control the auto-save behavior by choosing FileMaker Pro ➪ Preferences (Mac OS) or Edit ➪ Preferences (Windows), and, in the Preferences dialog that appears, navigating to the Layout tab and clicking the checkbox option labeled Save Layout Changes Automatically (Do Not Ask).

FileMaker handles the saving of data behind the scenes, so normally you don't have to worry about it. However, one consequence of this automatic operation is that, when a file is open, it's in a fluid state where, at any point, some parts of the file may not yet have been transferred to disk. Thus, if you duplicate a file while it's open, you can expect the resulting duplicate file to be incomplete because FileMaker Pro has yet to write everything to disk. When the file is closed, any remaining unsaved portions are saved to disk before the file closes.

To close a file, select its window (if you have more than one file or window open in FileMaker) and then choose File ➪ Close (⌘+W or Ctrl+W). You may also close a file by closing all its windows.

TIP A database file cannot be closed while it's still in use. In particular, a file that is a data source for another open file cannot be closed. If you choose File ➪ Close in this situation, the file is hidden rather than closed.

Handling files and data safely

FileMaker reads data from disk into memory when a database file is opened. The contents of the *cache* (data not yet written back to disk) are then maintained as fields and records are updated. Cached data is written back to disk periodically, keeping the cache's size within a defined range.

FIGURE 3.1

Creating the first field in a new database, using the Manage Database dialog.

CROSS-REF You can find instructions for setting the cache size and the frequency with which data is saved to disk in the "Preference settings for your workstation" section, later in this chapter.

While FileMaker has a database open, the current state of the file includes some data that resides on disk and some that is held in cache. Neither the disk nor the cache holds a complete copy of the file. It isn't until the file is closed that FileMaker fully reconciles the data held in cache with the data on disk and thereby ensures that the copy on disk is complete and current. Consequently, in the event that FileMaker quits prematurely — without first closing the files you have open — it is possible that some data held in cache may not have been written to disk.

CAUTION If a FileMaker database file is closed improperly (for example, a forced quit) some recent changes may be lost. It is possible, however, that an untimely end to the application session (for example, a power outage) may occur at a moment when FileMaker is updating the disk and some parts of the record structure — or other file elements — may be only partially written to disk. In such a case, there is a risk that the file may be damaged and may no longer work properly. Fortunately, this is an extremely rare occurrence; however, you should avoid situations where FileMaker is stopped when files have not first been properly closed.

Occasionally, you'll encounter situations where you can't avoid improper closure of files. Hardware failures or power outages do occur, so despite your best efforts, there may be occasional mishaps. In most cases, if a mishap occurs, the file opens again and no data has been lost. If you have difficulty opening a file, refer to Chapter 17, where I discuss the recovery of files.

Unlike other applications, databases manage many different pieces of information, so they require ready access to data from all parts of a file. This is in contrast to an application, such as a word processor, that typically accesses only one or two sections of a file at a time. This, along with the fact that FileMaker holds part of the file in cache, means that it is wise to open files from a reliable hard disk that is directly and permanently connected to your computer, instead of opening files from a network drive. This approach not only improves performance, it also reduces the risk of the network connection to the disk being lost during the session, perhaps compromising the integrity of the file.

TIP   No matter how careful your file handling, or how reliable your computer hardware, I encourage you to make frequent backups of your files. That way, if you run into a problem, you have a recent copy of your database files to go back to and you won't lose much work. The more important your data, and the more intense the rate at which data is added or changed, the more frequently you should make backup copies.

NOTE   Avoid using the Macintosh Finder or Windows Explorer to make a duplicate of a file while it is open. (You won't get the whole file, because some of it is residing in cache when open.) Either close the file first and then copy it, or in FileMaker choose File ➪ Save a Copy As to make a backup copy of your file.

Earlier file formats and conversion issues

FileMaker 10 opens and works directly with files created with versions of FileMaker Pro from version 7 onward. All these files should have been saved with the .fp7 extension as part of their filenames. Because the file format is the same, you can expect all .fp7 files to work in FileMaker 10 in the same way that they worked in the prior version of FileMaker in which they were created.

CAUTION   FileMaker 10 includes some capabilities that aren't supported by previous versions. If you make structural changes to a file in FileMaker 10, be aware that some of the features you add may not work as intended if the file is reopened in an earlier version of FileMaker. For example, Web Viewer objects aren't recognized by FileMaker Pro 7 or 8, but they are recognized by FileMaker Pro 8.5, 9, and 10.

If you want to open a FileMaker file that was created with a version of FileMaker prior to version 7, you first have to convert the file to the .fp7 file format. The first time you attempt to open a file that was created in FileMaker versions 3 through 6, you're prompted to convert the file, and a new file in .fp7 format is created.

NOTE   If you want to convert a file from a version of FileMaker earlier than version 3, for use with FileMaker 10, you must first convert the file to either the .fp3 or .fp5 format by using a copy of FileMaker Pro 3.x, 4.x, 5.x, or 6.x. The resulting .fp3 or .fp5 file can then be converted to the .fp7 format by FileMaker 10. (When you try to open the file with FileMaker 10, you will be prompted to convert it.)

Because versions of FileMaker prior to 7 differed in a number of respects (as well as using a different file format) from more recent editions of FileMaker, some calculations and other functionality may no longer work as intended after conversion. In general, FileMaker does an excellent job of anticipating many of the adjustments that must be made, and it applies them for you during the automated conversion process. Consequently, if the file you're converting is relatively straightforward in function and scope, it may require little or no further adjustment in order to operate to specification in FileMaker 10. Nevertheless, you should test the operation of the file carefully before proceeding.

In the case of complex multi-file solutions that were originally designed to operate in FileMaker version 6 or earlier, some additional preparations for conversion may be warranted. Moreover, a more thorough period of testing and revision to ensure that the solution functions effectively in the .fp7 application environment is advisable. This process may be more or less time consuming, depending on the design and coding approach used in a given solution.

A detailed examination of the intricacies of migrating legacy solutions is outside the scope of this book. However, if you find yourself faced with this challenge, I recommend that you acquaint yourself with resources that are freely available from the downloads area of FileMaker, Inc.'s Web site. These include a comprehensive white paper entitled *Migration Foundations and Methodologies* (www.filemaker.com/products/upgrade/techbriefs.html), which provides extensive information and advice concerning issues that should be addressed to ensure a successful migration of a pre-.fp7 solution.

Finding Your Way Around

When you launch FileMaker Pro 10 and open a file, you immediately encounter two things: a menu bar that includes familiar menus (File, Edit, and so on) and some database-specific menus, and a database window with a title and a few controls at the lower left corner.

The contents of the window depend almost entirely on the particular database file (or collection of files) you have opened. FileMaker windows show the contents of a layout, and their appearance may vary widely. However, you'll likely see a screen containing some mix of data, labels, buttons, and/or images.

Basic FileMaker housekeeping operations (Open, Close, New Database, Print, and so on) are located on the File menu. In Windows, the File menu also includes an Exit command; however, on the Mac, the equivalent command is named Quit and it resides in the FileMaker Pro menu, conforming to the OS X standard. Meanwhile, a list of open windows appears in the Window menu. If you're new to FileMaker, many of the commands in the remaining menus may be unfamiliar to you. The following pages help you to understand how FileMaker works and why, and assist you in locating the commands you seek.

First, you should familiarize yourself with the standard window controls, as shown at Figure 3.2. These appear at the lower left of every FileMaker database window.

The gray area that can be seen spanning the top of the window in Figure 3.2 is the Status Toolbar and includes basic contextual information and navigation controls. At the lower left of the window, are the window zoom controls. The zoom percentage appears at the far left. Clicking the percentage returns it to 100% (normal size) from whatever setting it may have. Clicking the percentage again toggles you back to the last selected zoom ratio. The buttons adorned with close-up and distant horizon icons next to the percentage button are the zoom out and zoom in buttons — their function is to reduce or enlarge the contents of the window.

The Status Toolbar control is beside the zoom controls at the lower left of Figure 3.2. Clicking this button hides or shows the Status Toolbar at the top of the current window. Finally, to the right of the Status Toolbar control is FileMaker's Mini Mode menu, which indicates the current window mode and can be used to change modes. These basic controls are present at the lower left of all FileMaker database windows at all times.

FIGURE 3.2

The standard controls at the lower left of a FileMaker window.

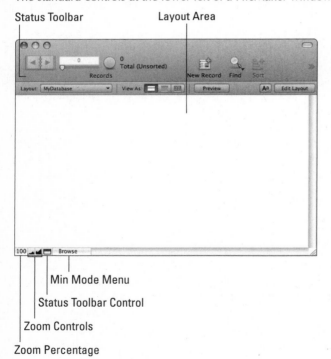

Status Toolbar   Layout Area

Min Mode Menu

Status Toolbar Control

Zoom Controls

Zoom Percentage

The modes and their uses

The first and most important thing to know about FileMaker Pro is that it has several modes of operation. What you can do in each mode is different, and how the application responds to commands is also different. Until you grasp this essential concept, you may find FileMaker a little mystifying; however, the modes actually simplify matters when you understand their functions.

There are four operational modes in FileMaker. They are listed at the top of the View menu as well as in the Mini Mode menu. Buttons and icons provided in the Status Toolbar at the top of the window can also be used to change mode. The four operational modes are

- **Browse:** The mode used for viewing, entering, and editing data in your databases is called the Browse mode. By default, databases open in Browse mode, and much of your day-to-day database work is performed in Browse mode — you can think of it as the normal operational mode. The keyboard command to reinstate Browse mode from any other mode is ⌘+B or Ctrl+B.

- **Find:** So that you can search for records, FileMaker provides a Find mode (⌘+F or Ctrl+F). In Find mode, layouts appear as they did in Browse mode, but the data fields are devoid of data. This enables you to enter criteria for FileMaker to use in a search operation. When the database enters Find mode, the Mini Mode menu changes to read "Find" and the Status Toolbar controls change to provide support for the Find process.

- **Layout:** The third FileMaker mode is called the Layout mode (⌘+L or Ctrl+L) and it is in this mode that FileMaker becomes a screen- and report-building environment. In Layout mode, all the objects within the window take on the behavior of elements in a drawing program, and the Status Toolbar populates with graphical tools you can use to change the size, color, and placement of objects within the layout, and to add and remove objects at will. In Layout mode, rather than changing the data in the database, you're changing the database's interface.

- **Preview:** FileMaker provides a Preview mode (⌘+U or Ctrl+U) to display page images that demonstrate how the current layout, using the current data, looks if printed on the currently selected printer (and with current page size and printer settings).

Navigating and viewing data

Data in your database files can be viewed in Browse mode, using an appropriate layout in a database window. With a new file, or a file relying on FileMaker's built-in interface controls, you can use the Status Toolbar to locate a layout and move around among the records within a table.

At the left of the Status Toolbar, as shown in Figure 3.3, below the navigation slider, you can see a label identifying what you are viewing in the current mode. In Browse mode, you can view and navigate through records, so the label says "Records". (In other modes, it says "Requests", "Pages", or "Layouts".)

FIGURE 3.3

The Status Toolbar controls in Browse mode.

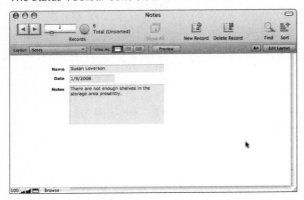

Below the navigation tools and the "Records" label, a menu of viewable layouts is provided. From this menu you're able to select different layouts to provide different views of the data available to the file. The layouts listed may relate to a single table of data, presenting different views or extracts of it, or to a variety of different tables. Layout names ideally should give you some guidance about the contents of each layout.

NOTE The menu of available layouts, as with menus in many dialogs, conform to the User Interface standards of the platform on which you're working. Thus, on a Mac, the menu will be implemented as a pop-up menu; in Windows, the menu will be shown as a drop-down list. Rather than the more cumbersome *pop-up menus/drop-down lists*, I just refer to them as *menus*.

When you select a layout, the controls available in the Status Toolbar change to reflect the state of the records in the table with which the layout is associated. In the example shown in Figure 3.3, the Status Toolbar indicates that you're viewing record 2 of a total of 6 records on a layout called Notes. FileMaker provides a navigation (spiral-bound book) icon and a slider at the left of the Status Toolbar, providing you with the means to navigate through the records in the table being viewed. Clicking the right page of the book icon takes you to the next record; clicking the left page of the book icon takes you back to the previous record. Similarly, the position of the slider control below the Rolodex represents the current location among the available records. Dragging the slider to a new location takes you to the corresponding record in the current table.

NOTE More precisely, dragging the slider takes you to the corresponding record in the currently available records from the current table. Find mode, as I discuss in the next section, can restrict the available records to a subset of the current table's records.

Finally, you can move between records in three other ways:

- If you want to go to a specific record — say record 3 — you can enter the number 3 into the Record field above the slider at the left of the Status Toolbar, and then press the Enter (or Return) key on your keyboard.

- You can choose Records ⇨ Go to Record ⇨ Next, Records ⇨ Go to Record ⇨ Previous, and Records ⇨ Go to Record ⇨ Specify.

- You can move to the next and previous records by pressing Ctrl+up arrow and Ctrl+down arrow.

Searching and the FileMaker Find/Omit puzzle

When you have just a few records in a FileMaker table, scrolling through them and looking for the information you need isn't too difficult. However, when your records accumulate to the point where there are hundreds or even thousands of them in a table, a more efficient method of searching is needed. That's where FileMaker's Find mode comes in.

On entering Find mode, the current layout remains in view, but all the fields that displayed data in Browse mode appear empty, waiting for you to supply search criteria. Depending on the field frames setting of the current layout, unselected searchable fields also show a magnifying glass icon at the upper left when viewed in Find mode. Moreover, the Status Toolbar changes its appearance when you enter Find Mode.

As you can see in Figure 3.4, when you place the database window into Find mode, the layout menu and view buttons remain at the left of the Status Toolbar; however, the text underneath the slider now refers to Find Requests rather than Records. Moreover, Include/Omit buttons and an Insert Operators menu are included, and a Perform Find button appears in the upper toolbar area. While these are the default Status Toolbar options, you can customize the Toolbar — adding, removing, or repositioning icons — by choosing View ⇨ Customize Status Toolbar.

If you want to locate all the records in the current data table referring to a person whose name starts with the letters *Da,* you can simply enter Find mode, type **Da** in the Name field, and click the Status Toolbar's Perform Find button. If any records in the current table contain a name starting with Da, such as Danielle, David, or Damon, those records are found.

FIGURE 3.4

The Status Toolbar controls in Find mode.

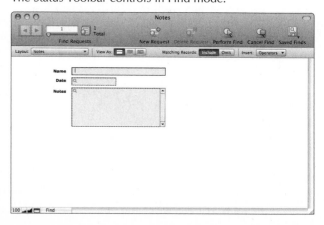

When records are returned as the result of a Find, they are termed the *Found Set* and FileMaker temporarily presents the found records to you in Browse mode — isolated, as though they're the only records available. The rest of the records are not lost at this point; they've simply been omitted (ignored) for the moment.

When a Find has been conducted, the Status Toolbar indicates the number of found records as well as the total number of records in the table. As is shown in Figure 3.5, the six records that were indicated in the Status Toolbar in Figure 3.3 are still present, though only two are presently "found." Just as there is a found set of two records in this situation, there is also an omitted set of four records, bringing the total up to six.

At any point, when the view of a table is split into a found set and (by implication) an omitted set, you can bring the table back into a unified whole by choosing Records ⇨ Show All Records (⌘+J or Ctrl+J) or clicking the Show All icon that appears in the Status Toolbar. (The Show All icon is accessible only when a found set is in place.) Alternatively, you can exchange the found and omitted record sets by choosing Records ⇨ Show Omitted Only. Moreover, choosing Records ⇨ Omit Record (⌘+T or Ctrl+T) and Records ⇨ Omit Multiple (⌘+Shift+T or Ctrl+Shift+T) make it possible to manually fine-tune the found set, isolating a specific group of records of interest.

The found set principle gives you a mechanism to split up the records according to any criteria (or even arbitrarily or manually), isolating any subgroup of records. This is an important feature that provides support for producing extracts, summaries, and analyses of groups and subgroups of your data set.

FIGURE 3.5

Records returned as a result of a Find for *Da* in the Name field.

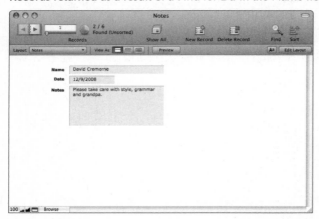

Screen elements and what they're for

So far you've seen the window and Status Toolbar controls for Browse mode and Find mode and you know how they work during navigation and Find procedures. However, much of the action when you're working with a database file takes place within the layouts themselves.

FileMaker database layouts include a variety of elements, some of which are purely visual. For example, text labels, headings, shaded areas, lines, and even images may be included in a layout to provide a frame of reference for the data or to contribute to the appearance of the layout. However, other layout components perform a function in the database and are part of the way users interact with the data. For example, field boxes, such as those in the white layout area in Figure 3.5, dynamically display the data within the current record — and users may click into the field boxes to enter or edit data within them.

The elements that make up layouts, in addition to static text and graphical elements, include fields, buttons, portals, tab controls, and Web Viewers. In addition, layouts may be subdivided into defined horizontal areas such as Header, Body, Footer, and so on, and these are referred to as *parts*.

A *field,* or *field box,* is a rectangular object drawn or placed (pasted) onto a layout in Layout mode that is attached to a data field within a table of the database. Fields may be sized and positioned and given other graphical attributes (color, outlining, embossing, and so on). In addition to their graphical appearance, fields provide direct access to data when the layout is viewed or used in Browse mode. The cursor may be placed into a field and the data inside that field selected, formatted, deleted, or supplemented.

Layout buttons are objects having an action or command assigned to them in Layout mode. When an object has been defined as a button, clicking it in Browse or Find modes causes the assigned action to be performed. FileMaker provides a special type of graphical object (an embossed rectangle with an attached text label) to be used where buttons are required; however, in Layout mode, any object or group of objects (except tab controls and object groups already containing a button) can be designated as a button to perform a corresponding action. Thus images, lines, rectangles, text objects, or even fields themselves can be defined to act as buttons.

Portals are rectangular layout objects that provide a virtual window into the data in another (related) table. So, for example, in a table of kitchen ingredients, you might add a portal to display a list of recipes that use a given ingredient.

Tab Control objects are collections of panels that operate like file index cards with labeled tabs protruding at the top. Clicking the tab of a particular panel brings it to the front. Tab Controls provide an efficient method of organizing layout elements so that groups of related layout objects can be brought forward and accessed as needed. One example might be in an automobile dealership database, where passenger cars and trucks each have their own tabs containing fields specific to that type of automobile (for example, trunk space and number of doors for cars, tow weight and capacity specifications for trucks).

The FileMaker Web viewer is a powerful object capable of retrieving and rendering hypertext and other related Web content, directly on a database layout. This allows your database users to access browser capabilities from within the screens and reports of the database. Moreover, the content of a Web viewer can be controlled directly from the data available within the database.

CROSS-REF I cover Layouts in detail in Chapter 6 and explore interface design in depth in Chapter 10.

The layouts appearing in FileMaker's database windows present you with collections of the various elements mentioned here, organized to provide you with the means to view, interpret, and interact with the data stored within your database files.

Entering and Editing Data

So far I've talked about how you can view records and search for specific data. In many cases, your database usage is not merely as a spectator, but as an active participant, adding data and making changes to data, extending its usefulness or keeping it current.

If you need to make changes to existing data, you first need to locate the data to be changed. First, you should use the layouts menu to go to an appropriate layout — one displaying records from the table in which you want to make changes. Then you should locate the record or records that you want to change — either by navigating through the records or by conducting a Find.

When you've located a record you want to edit, the first step is to place the cursor into a field. You can do this by pressing the Tab key once to enter the first field and then repeatedly to move through the fields, or by clicking directly on the field with the mouse. In either case, the field becomes active and a text cursor appears within it. You can then enter, delete, or modify the data in the field.

If you have changes to make or data to add to several fields in the same record, you can move directly from field to field via the mouse or the Tab key, changing or adding information in each. The changes are not committed (saved) until you exit the record.

NOTE At any time until you commit the data by exiting the record or invoking a script with a Commit command, you can return the record to the state it had upon entry by choosing Records ⇨ Revert Record. In fact, Revert Record will revert *all* record changes made since data was last committed, so a single Revert may simultaneously undo changes in the active record and one or more related records.

Creating and duplicating records

To add a record to the current table, choose Records ⇨ New Record (⌘+N or Ctrl+N) or click on the New Record icon in the Status Toolbar. A new record is added and the cursor is automatically placed into the first field (that is, the first field in the Layout's tab order, which is defined to allow entry in Browse mode), ready for you to enter some data.

In some cases, you may prefer to copy an existing record (for example, a record that has similar data to one you want to create). You can achieve this by choosing Records➪Duplicate Record (⌘+D or Ctrl+D). As with the New Record command, the cursor is automatically placed into the first field, ready for you to begin editing the newly created record.

NOTE When a new record is first created, it initially exists only in memory — it has not yet been stored. If you make a mistake and want to discard the new record, you can do so by choosing Records ➪ Revert Record.

Some layouts show related records (for example, as a list in a portal). An example of such a layout would be an invoice where multiple purchases are shown, one per line — where an invoice table is used to store invoice details, but a separate table stores the details for each line. With a layout designed to include the display of related records, providing the relationship between the tables is appropriately configured, you are able to enter new related records by typing them directly into the portal, dependent upon the relationship specification.

CROSS-REF For additional details concerning relationships and the creation of related records, see Chapter 11.

Field definitions: Validation and dependencies

Databases often include fields designed to hold specific values, or fields that are dependent on the values in other fields. Frequently, such fields are set up to acquire a value automatically when the values they depend upon are entered. In other cases, the database is programmed to confirm that values entered are valid before accepting them and saving the record.

An example of a dependent value is the name of the state, as it can be determined automatically (by linking to a reference table) after the ZIP code for a location or address is entered. Similarly, a total value may be computed for each line of an order, based on the quantity and item price entries.

You can access options for the creation of dependencies between fields, for defining rules for acceptance of valid data, and for setting a variety of default or automatically entered values for each field by choosing File ➪ Manage ➪ Database.

CROSS-REF In Chapter 7, I look in detail at the uses of the Manage Database dialog.

In some cases, default values or values dependent on other inputs can be overwritten if you want. However, fields created by using the explicit calculation field type cannot be overwritten (they always display the result of the calculation with which you have defined them).

The significance of commitment

When you create a new record, duplicate a record, or make changes to the data in a record, the changes are visible only on the current workstation, even if other users are sharing the file. It is not until you finish making changes and exit the record that the new contents are saved as part of the database and may be seen by other users.

The process of exiting a record is called *record commit* — the changes to the data are committed at this point and can no longer be undone or discarded (though of course you can always go back into the record and change it back to how it was).

Because exiting a record commits its contents, there are several different ways to save a record you have been working on. One is to press the Enter key on the numeric keypad. Another is to click in an open area of the layout, outside the field boxes. In some cases a script, button, or menu item (attached to the Commit Records/Requests command) may also be available. When you commit the record, by whatever means, the record is exited (the cursor focus is removed from the fields) and any changes are saved. As noted earlier in this chapter, an optional setting for the Layout (available by choosing Layouts ➪ Layout Setup in Layout mode) lets you specify whether record changes should be saved automatically. When this option is not selected, the user is prompted to save or discard changes when exiting the record in Browse mode.

A record can also be committed in less direct ways: by navigating to a different record, a different table (that is, a layout that is based on another Table Occurrence), or by closing the file. In each case, any changes made to the immediately preceding record are stored and the record becomes available for editing by others (only one user can edit a record at a time).

Prior to the commit point, changes to a record have not been saved and can be reverted. This is done by choosing Records ➪ Revert Record. When a record is reverted, all changes made since the previous time the record was committed are discarded — so if you've changed the value in several fields, all the changes are reversed if you revert the record.

NOTE After a record is committed, the changes made to it are permanent and cannot be undone. At this point, returning the record to its previous state would require that it be edited again to reverse the changes.

When your solution is available to multiple users simultaneously over a network (that is, a multi-user database), the process of committing a record has additional implications. While changes to a record are being made by one user, the record is locked and other users are unable to make changes to it — although they can see it — and can edit *other* records. The commit point releases the lock and the record becomes available for other users to edit. Moreover, it is at the commit point that changes you have made can be seen by other users viewing the record — that is, they see your changes appear when you exit the record.

The Ins and Outs

Manually accessing, entering, and editing information in your solutions is a key part of maintaining your data, but it is labor intensive and can also be error prone. Occasionally, the data you require is already available in computerized form, so you may prefer to avoid entering the data by hand.

Similarly, there are occasions when the best solution to a problem is to take some data from your FileMaker database and view, analyze, or print it in another application. There are a variety of reasons you may choose to do this — to make use of existing chart templates in a spreadsheet application, to submit information for publication in a word-processing format, to examine your data in a statistical analysis tool, and so on.

In any case, FileMaker's powerful data import and export capabilities provide you with options covering a broad range of requirements and support a wide variety of standard formats.

Importing and exporting data

FileMaker Pro makes it extremely easy to get data from text files (comma- or tab-separated data) or Excel spreadsheet files into database files. In its simplest form, you drag and drop such files onto the FileMaker icon and they are automatically converted into databases (you're given the option to use the first row of data in the source text file to provide field names in the resulting database file). In just a few minutes you can start using the powerful searching, sorting, and organizing capabilities of a database to work with your text or spreadsheet tables.

In cases where you already have a database file into which you want to bring data from existing files in other formats, choose File ➪ Import Records ➪ File. When you choose this command, you'll first be prompted to locate the file holding the data you want to import. Then you'll be presented with a dialog prompting you to map the columns or cells in the file you've selected with the fields in the table (Table Occurrence) associated with the current layout of the current database file, as shown in Figure 3.6.

In the Import Field Mapping dialog (see Figure 3.6) the data elements found in the selected file are displayed in a column at the left of the window. Navigation buttons below the column of incoming data allow you to move through the rows of data to ascertain what content the file holds. Meanwhile, the right side of the dialog provides a menu for selecting whether to import data via the Table Occurrence that the current layout is based on, or to create a new table to accommodate the imported data. When you make a selection from the target menu, the right column displays a list of fields in the selected table.

Between the columns of fields in the Import Field Mapping dialog are two rows of symbols — a horizontal arrow and a vertical handle symbol. The arrow can be clicked to enable or disable import into a particular field, while the handle icon can be used to drag Target fields in the column at the right up and down to position them adjacent to appropriate incoming data elements.

NOTE On selecting a field in the right column of the Import Field Mapping dialog, you may press ⌘+up arrow or Ctrl+up arrow and ⌘+down arrow or Ctrl+down arrow to move the field up and down in the list. Similarly, when you select a number of fields in the right column (by pressing Shift+Click or ⌘+Click or Ctrl+Click), clicking an arrow symbol adjacent to any selected field toggles the import state for all selected fields simultaneously.

The lower part of the Import Field Mapping dialog provides additional options relating to the import process — including the capability to add records to the selected table, or to synchronize the data with existing records in the found set. Also included is a key to the meaning of the alternate field mapping symbols. Moreover, if the file chosen as the source of your import is a text file, an additional option is provided, allowing you to choose the character set (text encoding) to use when reading the contents of the file.

In a procedure comparable to the import process, FileMaker enables you to export data into a variety of supported file formats by choosing File ➪ Export Records. After you choose this menu option, you're prompted to choose a file format, provide a filename, and indicate a location for the file to be created.

FIGURE 3.6

The Import Field Mapping dialog — matching incoming data to database fields.

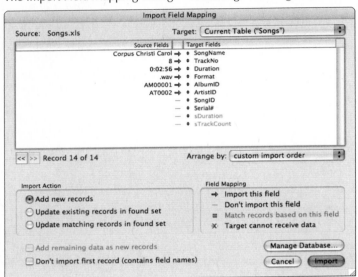

After you click the Save button in the Export Records to File dialog, you're presented with a dialog in which you specify and order the fields to be included in the export (see Figure 3.7). The menu above the list of fields on the left enables you to select the context from which fields are located, and the buttons in the middle of the dialog enable you to add fields to the export.

NOTE The data exported is sourced from the current layout context and includes only the current found set in the frontmost layout. If you add fields from other tables, the values for inclusion depend on their table's relationship to the current layout's table.

If the data in the current found set is sorted, the grouping options at the upper right of the Specify Field Order For Export dialog becomes active. When a group-by-field option is selected, records with matching values in the selected field result in only a single entry in the exported file. This provides a means to export data summaries.

TIP Because exports are based on the found set in the current layout, you can easily perform a Find then Export to create summaries and batch exports of subgroups of records.

Previewing and printing options

One of the most common requirements when it comes to getting data out of your database is the production of printed output. By default, FileMaker layouts operate on the WYSIWYG (what-you-see-is-what-you-get) principle, so, for the most part, if you choose File ➪ Print (⌘+P or Ctrl+P), what comes out of the printer closely resembles what you see onscreen.

FIGURE 3.7

The Specify Field Order for Export dialog is where you determine which fields are to be exported and in what order.

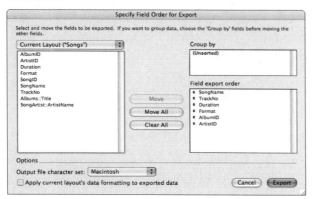

Before printing, however, it's best to check the File ⇨ Page Setup (Mac) or File ⇨ Print Setup (Windows) settings to check the current print driver settings and confirm page size and orientation settings. Before proceeding to print, I also recommend that you pay a visit to the Preview mode (⌘+U or Ctrl+U) to ensure that the way the output is going to be rendered matches your expectations. It's always best to find out there is a problem *before* you've used up the last ream of paper printing the contents of your database.

> **TIP** The available options and the accuracy of the match between the Preview mode display and the actual printed output depend on the installed/selected printer driver, the printer itself, and the match between the two. When constructing the preview image, FileMaker interacts with the printer driver to arrive at a rendering of the instructions the driver prepares to send to the printer. While this is generally accurate, some combinations of drivers and printers produce results that vary slightly from the preview images. If you encounter this, it may signal that an update of the printer driver is required.

Send/Save as PDF and Excel

In addition to its comprehensive printing and data export options, FileMaker Pro 10 provides two special-purpose output options — one to directly generate PDF files from the current found set (using the current layout to format the data) and one to efficiently create an Excel spreadsheet file from the current found set, including fields that appear on the current layout. You can access these options by choosing File ⇨ Save/Send Records As ⇨ PDF and File ⇨ Save/Send Records As ⇨ Excel, respectively.

The Save/Send Records As commands provide an elegant and immediate way to capture the current context in a form that can be archived, viewed, or shared with others (for example, as an e-mail attachment). The two supported file formats can be opened/viewed in a variety of applications on contemporary operating systems — so these options make your data very portable.

> **TIP** The Save/Send as PDF option operates in much the same way as the Print command — it reflects the appearance of the current layout and also the current print driver settings — and it requires database access with printing privileges. By contrast, the Save/Send as Excel option operates along the lines of an export of data and requires database access with exporting privileges.

> **CROSS-REF** The setting of database access privileges, including privileges for printing and exporting, is described in Chapter 14.

Getting to Know the Relatives

In FileMaker solutions containing multiple tables connected via relationships, you require ways to view and edit data from related tables. For example, if you have a customer table and an invoices table, when viewing a customer record, you may want to be able to see details of that customer's invoices — and when viewing an invoice, you need to see the name and address of the customer for whom it was created.

Ways to view and edit related data

You can see a single record from a related table, such as the name of the customer for a particular invoice, by simply placing the Customer::Name field directly onto the invoice layout. FileMaker locates and displays the first matching customer name. Moreover, the data in the corresponding customer record is editable directly from the invoice layout, just as if it were in the invoice table.

In situations where there are multiple related records, viewing just the first is usually inadequate, so FileMaker provides a layout Portal object supporting the display of a list of related records. Thus, in order to display a list of invoices for the current customer (for example, on the Customer layout), you should place a portal based on the Invoice table on the Customer layout. If desired, invoice data can be entered or edited directly in the portal, without visiting the Invoice layout, and any such changes are stored in the Invoice table and displayed on the Invoice layout when you next visit it.

Relationships in FileMaker work in both directions, so a single relationship between the Customer and Invoice tables should be sufficient to enable the relevant invoices to be displayed on the customer layout and the customer details to appear on the invoice layout.

Although the capability to view related data directly on the current layout makes FileMaker's interface powerful and flexible, it's also possible to jump directly to related records in their own table and layout. FileMaker's built-in Go to Related Records functionality (for example, via a button command or a script) can be used to achieve this efficiently.

> **CROSS-REF** I cover advanced interface techniques, using the Go to Related Records command, in Chapter 10.

The importance of context

Everything you do in FileMaker works from the current context. The current mode, the layout displayed in the frontmost database window, and the found set and the current record in that window, determine the context from which data in the solution as a whole are viewed. The effect of any action, therefore, varies depending on context.

When you change records, the values in the match fields for relationships to other tables also change. This means that the sets of related records that are available to view and edit (from the current context) also change. If you navigate to a layout based on a different table — or on a different graph representation (Table Occurrence) of the same table, then the relationship views alter accordingly.

CROSS-REF   For a discussion of the workings of FileMaker's Relationships Graph, see Chapter 7.

Likewise, summary and calculated data may vary according to the found set, so what you see when viewing all records in a table may be different from what you see after performing a Find to isolate a subgroup of records.

Making complexity simple in practice

On your first encounter with a relational data system, you may be tempted to throw up your hands, thinking that it's all too complicated. Surely it would be much easier to keep things in one large table than to divide the data among multiple tables?

It's important to realize that the purpose of setting up appropriate relationships within your data is to simplify matters — to let the computer handle many trivial operations so that you don't have to. So, while it may be true that setting up relationships in your data structure takes a little more thought, planning, and configuration at the outset, the resultant operational simplicity more than justifies the effort.

Optimizing the Application

Many aspects of FileMaker Pro's operation automatically adjust to your working environment. For example, the settings for date, time, and language that are in place on the computer you are using are automatically reflected in the FileMaker interface and in the ways that your solution files operate.

Nevertheless, a number of aspects of the FileMaker feature set are user configurable via two preference settings dialogs. The first of these dialogs sets application preferences applying to all FileMaker work done on the current computer. The second dialog sets preferences specific to the current database file, regardless of the computer it's used on.

Preference settings for your workstation

The Preferences dialog allows you to control the behavior of FileMaker on the current workstation. You can access it by choosing FileMaker Pro ➪ Preferences (Mac) or Edit ➪ Preferences (Windows).

As you can see in Figure 3.8, the Preferences dialog is arranged into five panels, each selectable via a tab at the top of the dialog panel.

The General tab allows several interface options — in the upper section, drag-and-drop text editing functionality, the Quick Start screen, and the recent files submenu are enabled or disabled. Below that, the General tab allows you to assign a custom name to the current workstation. Although this is termed the *User Name*, it refers to the workstation instead of to an individual and isn't to be confused with the login account name. Finally, the General tab allows you to enable or disable automatically checking the FileMaker, Inc., servers for application updates. The Preferences dialog's Layout tab, shown in Figure 3.9, provides access to options affecting the way the application works in Layout mode. The Always Lock Layout Tools setting alters the behavior of the drawing palette in the Status Toolbar in Layout mode so that when a tool (for example, the Line tool or the Text tool) is selected, it remains active until another tool is selected; whereas, by default, a tool only remains active for a single action, unless its icon is double-clicked. Additionally, the Layout tab provides an option to add new fields to the current layout, and to save layout changes automatically.

> **TIP**   If you're doing complex or exacting layout work, you may be well advised to disable the option to add new fields to the current layout (it's on by default) because creation of a new field otherwise results in changes to layouts that you may have spent many hours perfecting. You may also prefer to leave the Save Layout Changes Automatically option disabled so that you have an option to discard changes when leaving a layout (or when leaving Layout mode) after making modifications.

FIGURE 3.8

The General tab of the FileMaker Pro 10 Preferences dialog.

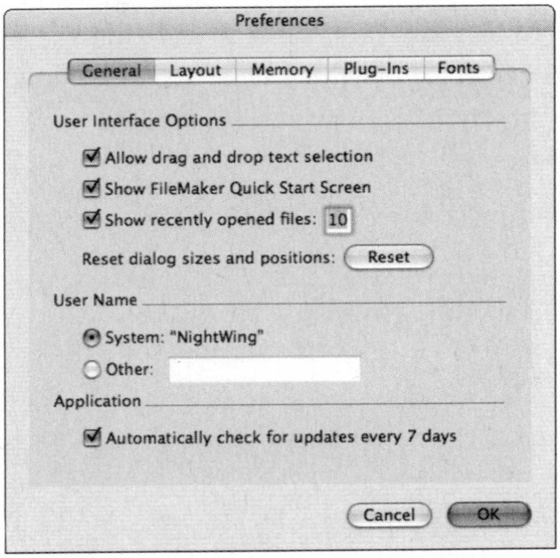

FIGURE 3.9

The Layout tab of the FileMaker Pro 10 Preferences dialog.

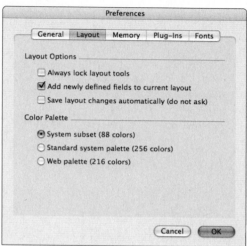

Finally, the Layout tab of the Preferences dialog enables you to constrain or extend the color palette available in Layout mode. The settings you choose here may depend in part on your personal tastes, but should also take account of the color support of the systems (both hardware and software) via which users are to access the interfaces you create in Layout mode.

NOTE The selected color palette gives you the convenience of a ready set of 88, 216, or 256 colors to choose from. However, you have the option to select Other Color from the color palette and adjust the color settings (using Red, Green, Blue values or Hue Saturation and Brightness settings and so on) to create a custom hue for any purpose.

The Preferences dialog's Memory tab, shown in Figure 3.10, provides controls for the cache size and save cycle of the application. When FileMaker is installed, a cache setting adequate for most situations is set. Unless you encounter specific problems that may indicate memory management issues, I recommend that you leave the cache setting at the default value. Similarly, the default save setting During Idle Time is best for the majority of users.

The Plug-Ins tab of the Preferences dialog (see Figure 3.11) allows you to enable/disable and configure third-party plug-ins and the Auto-Update utility (configurable to automatically load plug-in updates from FileMaker Server over a local network).

CROSS-REF In Chapter 20, I provide a more detailed exploration of the use of FileMaker's plug-in architecture.

At the right of the Preferences dialog is the Fonts tab (see Figure 3.12). It provides access to configuration options for default fonts for each supported character system, as well as synchronization and font locking options (controlling the behavior of fields defined for a specific character system when characters from outside that system are entered — for example, Roman characters entered into a field defined to accept Kanji text).

FIGURE 3.10

The Memory tab of the FileMaker Pro 10 Preferences dialog.

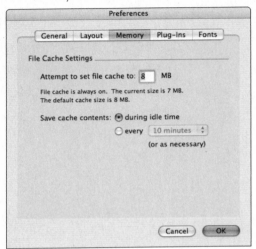

FIGURE 3.11

The Plug-Ins tab of the FileMaker Pro 10 Preferences dialog.

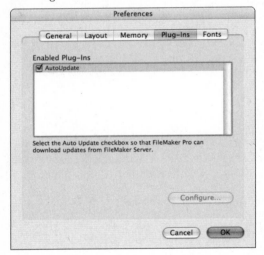

FIGURE 3.12

The Fonts tab of the FileMaker Pro 10 Preferences dialog.

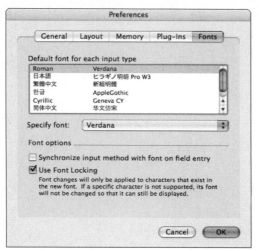

File options for the current database

For each database file, you can access a range of additional configuration options by choosing File ⇨ File Options. Settings defined in this way are saved with the file and affect its behavior whenever, wherever, and however it is opened.

The File Options dialog presents a range of controls grouped within three tab panels in Windows, and with a fourth appearing when the file is open on a Mac (as in the case of the screenshot in Figure 3.13). The first panel, shown in Figure 3.13, provides default settings for the behavior of the file when it's opened, allowing you to specify a default login account, specify a default layout, and specify a script to run automatically when the file is opened. Similarly, an option is provided to have a script run automatically when the file is closed.

The Spelling panel, shown in Figure 3.14, provides access to settings for visual and audible alerts when the spelling of a word during data entry appears questionable (that is, when it is not in the installed FileMaker dictionary).

 **When visual spell checking is enabled, you can override it on a field-by-field basis by choosing Format ⇨ Field Control/Behavior in Layout mode.**

The Text panel of the File Preferences dialog (see Figure 3.15) includes a setting for the use of smart quotes within the file (where straight quotation marks are automatically substituted with curly typesetting quote marks oriented forward or backward, depending on their position with respect to adjacent text). Also included are controls for the specification of line breaking (automatic text line wrapping) for Roman and Asian lettering systems.

FIGURE 3.13

The Open/Close tab of the FileMaker Pro 10 File Options dialog.

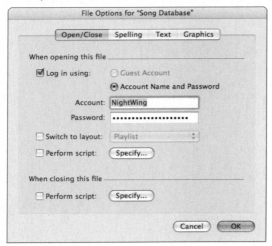

FIGURE 3.14

The Spelling tab of the FileMaker Pro 10 File Options dialog.

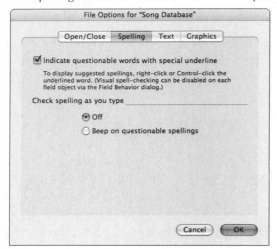

Surprisingly, the Text panel also includes a control to set the behavior of the file with respect to localization settings for number, date, and time (including timestamp) formats. It is perhaps counterintuitive that such a control is located on a tab called "Text," because its effects apply to the storage and display formats of data-entry field types *other than* text and Container fields, but you do enter them as text before FileMaker (re)formats them to match the system-set representations. These controls are important and provide the ability to configure a file to operate consistently on all systems (Always Use File's Saved Settings), to adapt to changing contexts (Always Use Current System Settings), or to require the user to make a choice every time the file is opened on a system with settings that differ from the environment in which the file was created (Ask Whenever Settings Are Different).

NOTE The selection you make in the Data Entry panel of the Text tab in the File Options dialog does not alter the way data is stored internally in your file. However, it does alter the way data will be displayed in the file's interface.

By default, FileMaker Pro 10 applies the Always Use Current System Settings option, which works well in many cases.

TIP I advise against choosing the Ask Whenever Settings Are Different option, because users — unless they programmed the file themselves — are unlikely to appreciate the implications of the choice when it is offered to them. Consequently, in addition to the tedium of being repeatedly presented with a dialog they don't understand, the option frequently forces the user to make an arbitrary rather than informed choice.

Finally, on the Mac, a fourth tab titled Graphics appears at the right of the File Options dialog, as shown in Figure 3.16. The Graphics panel includes a single control that enables/disables the automatic initiation of photo import when a camera is plugged in on the Mac. Because this automation option is not supported in Windows, the option is not displayed when a file is opened in Windows.

FIGURE 3.15

The Text tab of the FileMaker Pro 10 File Options dialog.

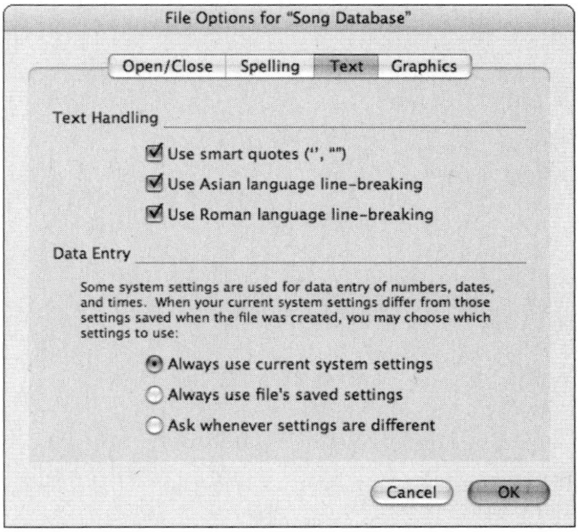

FIGURE 3.16

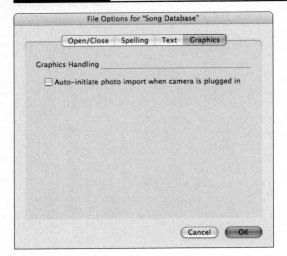

Chapter 4

What's New in FileMaker 10

FileMaker 10 provides a significant enhancement of the application, introducing essential new features to complement and extend its power and versatility, while offering a range of enhancements to previous functionality. The changes in this version provide exciting new options for simplification of processes and automation of your solutions, while also ushering in updates to the look and feel of the interface to lend a more contemporary appearance to your solutions.

This chapter offers an overview of the new features and enhancements in FileMaker 10, along with a discussion of their use and their implications for the ways you design and deploy your solutions.

Embracing Change

If you have created FileMaker solutions in previous versions of FileMaker, you may be pleased to know that FileMaker Pro 10 uses the file format (and the fp7 file extension) that has been current since the release of FileMaker 7 in 2004. Consequently, you can open solutions created in previous editions of FileMaker in FileMaker Pro 10 without conversion, and you can also open solutions created in FileMaker Pro 10 in the preceding versions.

Notwithstanding file format compatibility, you should consider a number of other issues. Before deciding to access a pre-existing solution by using FileMaker Pro 10, to access a FileMaker Pro 10 solution by using an earlier version of FileMaker, or to host a solution to multiple users with mixed versions of FileMaker, consider these important factors:

IN THIS CHAPTER

Introducing the new FileMaker Status Toolbar

Exploring Live Sub-summaries and maintenance of sort order

Using Saved Find Requests

Making use of Set Field by Name

Understanding Script Events Triggers and associated new calculation functions

Taking advantage of ESS Enhancements and Bento integration

Considering File Recovery improvements and changes

Inserting objects in the middle of a layout's object tab order

Importing, Exporting, Quick Start Screen, and printer selection Enhancements

■ Changes to the size and position of the Status Area (now called the Status Toolbar) significantly impact the available/viewable layout area in your database windows, so layout designs that were appropriate for previous versions of FileMaker may not be ideal when the same layouts are viewed in FileMaker 10 (and vice versa). While the file format is the same, the presentation format is not, so your pre-existing solutions may require adjustment to work optimally in FileMaker Pro 10.

■ Several new features of FileMaker 10 (as detailed throughout this chapter) provide opportunities to design solutions that are more responsive to users or that are more efficient in operation. For example, FileMaker Pro 10 Script Trigger capabilities provide some new options for interface design, while the new Set Field By Name command will engender more compact script code in some cases. However, because these and other FileMaker 10 features are not available in earlier versions, solutions that depend on them won't work as intended if accessed in earlier versions. Conversely, solutions that don't make use of these powerful features may not make best use of (or be optimally designed for) FileMaker Pro 10.

NOTE If you intend to make your solution available to users who may be using different versions of FileMaker Pro, consider having your solution check the current version of the application as the file is opened. Your solution can then either make adjustments (such as changing to an appropriate layout) or present a dialog to alert the user to version issues.

To ascertain whether the current FileMaker application is FileMaker Pro 10 (or FileMaker Pro 10 Advanced) or later, you can add an If[ ] / End If script sequence to a script that runs on file open, using a calculation expression such as GetAsNumber(Get(ApplicationVersion)) > 10 as the If[ ] test.

CROSS-REF For additional detail about the process of defining scripts to run on file open in your solutions, refer to Chapter 13.

Status Area Redesign

For anyone who is familiar with previous versions of FileMaker Pro, the significant first impact of opening FileMaker Pro 10 comes from the substantially redesigned interface for standard FileMaker database windows. The Status Area that has been present in successive releases of FileMaker for decades is no longer available at the left of every database window. Gone, too, are the tear-off toolbars that made their appearance below the overhead menus (except in Layout mode, where the Arrange and Align palettes remain available). Instead, FileMaker Pro 10 offers an all-new *Status Toolbar* that appears (when active) across the top of each window, providing ready access to a range of frequently used commands and features, as well as enhanced control and user feedback about the navigation and search options appropriate to the mode of the current window.

The FileMaker 10 Status Toolbar provides you with functionality that is broadly equivalent to the Status Area it replaces. In a few respects, the Status Toolbar offers added functionality, while in others it adds elegance and intuitive touches that new and experienced users alike will appreciate.

Aside from its location and horizontal orientation, the most striking difference between the traditional Status Area and the Status Toolbar is its appearance. The Status Toolbar, shown in Figure 4.1, has a contemporary, graduated and graphically refined appearance, with contrasting elements, intuitive icons, and subtle simplicity.

FIGURE 4.1

The FileMaker Pro 10 Status Toolbar, as it appears in Browse mode.

As with the Status Area, you can invoke or dismiss the Status Toolbar by clicking the (appropriately redesigned) reveal icon at the lower left of a database window. Moreover, you can use the updated View menu, shown in Figure 4.2, to show or hide the Status Toolbar by choosing View➪Status Toolbar (⌘+option+S or Ctrl+Alt+S). The state of the Status Toolbar is specific to the window, so when multiple windows are displayed (whether from the same database or from different database files), each can have an independent (shown or hidden) Status Toolbar state.

NOTE The dimensions of a window designed to accommodate the Status Area in previous versions of FileMaker may no longer be optimal when the same solution is opened in FileMaker 10. It may be appropriate to make adjustments to layouts (to increase their width and reduce their height) in order to achieve equivalent utilization of screen real estate when the Status Toolbar is showing, when your solution is accessed by using FileMaker Pro 10.

FIGURE 4.2

Using the View menu to toggle the display of the Status Toolbar.

The FileMaker Pro 10 Status Toolbar is made up of two parts:

- The main Status Bar containing the record navigation tools at the left (including a pie chart that represents the state of the found set — clicking on the pie swaps the found and omitted record sets

- A row of buttons for a selection of commonly used commands, such as Show All, New Record, Delete Record, Find, and Sort

Immediately below the main Status Bar, shown in Figure 4-1, the Layout Bar appears, providing you with access to controls pertaining to the current window's layout, including the layouts menu, view buttons, a button to invoke Preview mode, a button to toggle the display of the formatting bar, and at the far right, a button to invoke Layout mode.

The Status Toolbar adapts in appearance as you move between modes, presenting you with a range of controls appropriate to the mode of the window. Moreover, the Layout bar becomes darker in Layout mode and lighter in Find mode to help to visually differentiate those modes from Browse and Preview modes. However, the selection of command icons displayed in each mode is not fixed; you can choose a combination of icons to suit your work requirements at will by choosing View ⇨ Customize Status Toolbar. The process for adding or removing commands from the Status Toolbar is a little different on each platform. On Mac OS, you're presented with an editor dialog, as shown in Figure 4.3.

FIGURE 4.3

Using the Mac OS Customize dialog to change the Status Toolbar.

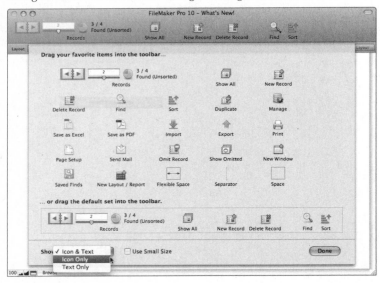

Using the options laid out in the Mac OS Customize dialog, you can drag icons to or from the Status Toolbar. If you have previously made changes, you can restore the default set (for the current mode). Controls are also provided to adjust the display style (Icon & Text, Icon Only, or Text Only) and to adjust the size of the icons displayed.

NOTE The Status Toolbar belongs to the application (and is specific to each application mode), not to the solution or to the individual database window. Each user of your solutions can freely customize the Status Toolbar within his own installation of FileMaker Pro 10, so you can't assume that specific command buttons will be present when your solution is being accessed. Moreover, unlike custom menus, which you can control programmatically, there is no mechanism for you as the developer to automatically configure the user's Status Toolbar appropriately for your solution.

In Microsoft Windows, the process is similar to that described in the preceding paragraph. However, the dialog has a different appearance and is organized into tabs, as shown in Figure 4.4. After choosing View⇨ Customize Status Toolbar, ensure that the Status Toolbar option is selected in the Toolbars tab and then navigate to the Commands tab to access the list of available commands. You can drag commands appearing in the list panel at the right of the Commands tab to the Status Toolbar, as well as rearrange or remove commands on the toolbar.

FIGURE 4.4

Using the Windows OS Customize dialog to change the Status Toolbar.

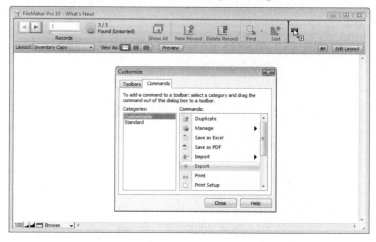

When you finish making changes to the Status Toolbar, dismiss the Customize dialog. The updated toolbar will take effect in the applicable mode (the mode of the currently active window) throughout all windows of the current installation of FileMaker Pro. Customization will remain in effect on the current workstation until you make another change, such as reinstating the default commands.

NOTE Icons appearing on the Status Toolbar, along with their associated label text, are dimmed when the command is unavailable. Toolbar commands will be dimmed and inactive when the corresponding command is not present in the current menu set, so although you can't control which icons will be present on the Status Toolbar within your solution, you can use custom menus to ensure that Status Toolbar icons (if present) will be dimmed and inactive at times when their use would be inappropriate in your solution.

The FileMaker Pro 10 Status Toolbar also provides a control to reveal and hide the new Formatting Bar, replacing the Text Formatting toolbar, as shown in Figure 4.5. The Formatting Bar is available in both Browse and Layout modes.

FIGURE 4.5

Using the Aa button on the Layout Bar to control the display of the Formatting Bar.

CROSS-REF For a detailed guide to the operation of the Status Toolbar in Layout mode, refer to Chapter 6.

Live Reports/Sub-summaries

A significant evolution of the interface of FileMaker Pro 10 focuses on the ability to present sub-summarized data displays in Browse mode. In previous versions of FileMaker, you could preview, print, or export (for example, to a PDF document) grouped and summarized reports, but the reports weren't available while working with your data in Browse mode.

In FileMaker 10, Browse mode presents the data in your List View and Table View layouts in the same grouped and sub-summarized formations as preview and print output, so instead of being static "snapshots" of your data at a particular instant, sub-summarized list and Table Views can be live and editable. This means that you're able to see recalculated Sub-summary values in Browse mode that will update as the data throughout your solution is edited. You can interact with the data in report format and see the changes you make reflected in real time in the report summary data.

Sub-summary parts appear only when the records are sorted by the field on which the part is based (the *break field* for the Sub-summary part). In FileMaker Pro 10, when you sort the found set by a field on which a Sub-summary part is based, the Sub-summary part will appear in Browse mode, as shown in Figure 4.6.

CROSS-REF For additional details about working with Sub-summary parts and part controls, refer to Chapter 10.

FIGURE 4.6

Viewing and editing a Sub-summary report in Browse mode.

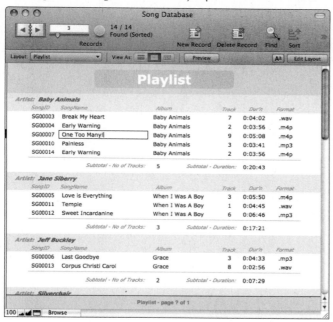

To further consolidate the support for dynamic summary data, FileMaker Pro 10 introduces important enhancements to the way Table View works. In particular, layouts in Table View are no longer restricted to showing the same group of fields that are physically present on the layout. Rather, you can modify the Table View to remove some fields (without deleting them from the layout) and to add others that aren't present on the layout.

To make changes to the Table View configuration of a layout, first view the layout in Browse mode and switch to Table View. Then click the Modify button at the right of the Layout bar. The Modify Table View dialog appears, as shown in Figure 4.7.

By deselecting the checkbox at the left of some of the fields listed in the Modify Table View dialog and by using the + button at the lower left of the dialog to add other fields, you can customize the Table View of a layout without making any changes to the way the layout appears in other views.

Table View in FileMaker Pro 10 also makes provision for the inclusion of Sub-summary parts defined for the layout, according to the sort order of the found records in the current window. FileMaker aligns any summary fields in the Sub-summary part with the column showing the data field being summarized and adds a label according to the type of aggregation the summary field performs (for example, Count or Total, as shown in Figure 4.7).

FIGURE 4.7

Modifying the fields included in the Table View of a layout without changing the layout.

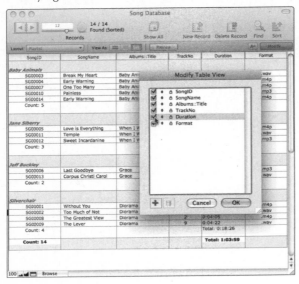

Similarly, leading and trailing Grand Summary parts also now appear when a layout is displayed in Table View. As grand summaries are not dependent on sort order, they will be displayed regardless of the sort state of the found set.

NOTE   Although the Browse mode appearance of layouts in List View and Table View in FileMaker Pro 10 more closely resembles what you see in Preview mode (and in printed output), several significant differences remain. For example, object attributes for sliding, printing, or reducing part size don't take effect in Browse mode, only in preview and print (including PDF output). When you preview or print, what you see may still differ in several respects from what appears in Browse mode.

Maintain Record Sort Order

As soon as the data in a field that is part of the sort order is edited — or a new record is added — the sort sequencing of records that made sense before the change may no longer be appropriate. Previous versions of FileMaker Pro changed the declared state (as shown in the Status Area) of the found set to "Semi-sorted" in such cases. However, FileMaker Pro 10 solves this problem in an entirely different way — by automatically updating the sort order after a data change affecting it is committed. In this way, live Sub-summary data that depends on the sort order of the record set remains current, and, as changes are made to data, the chosen sort order is maintained.

The way FileMaker Pro 10 handles automatic updates of the sort order of the found set is designed to disrupt the user as little as possible. To keep the feature as unobtrusive as possible, refreshes of the sort order will occur during moments of idle time, as the screen refreshes to reflect other changes. Re-sorting will not occur while a user is editing a record (that is, while there are uncommitted changes) nor while a script is in progress, so the sort order will remain predictable during the course of a script that updates records (for example, while looping through a found set of records).

NOTE   **When you create a script to make changes that may affect the current sort order, because re-sorting won't occur while the script is running, if you don't want the records left in a partially sorted state, you should engineer your script to either unsort or re-sort the current table before concluding.**

There are no new controls to adjust to take advantage of the new FileMaker sorting behavior, so there's nothing to turn on or off. You simply apply a sort (for example, by choosing Records ⇨ Sort Records), and FileMaker will keep the records sorted in that order until one of the following events occur:

- The records are unsorted.
- A different sort order is applied.
- The found set changes. (A Find is performed or the Show All Records or Find Omitted commands are selected).

FileMaker Pro 10 maintains the sort order regardless of how the records came to be sorted, whether it's via the Sort Records dialog (accessible from the Records menu and the Contextual menu), by clicking column headers in Table View, by clicking a button that has the Sort Records command attached to it, running a script that includes a Sort Records command, or as a result of calling a Go To Related Records command that acts through a sorted relationship.

When you manually change the value in a field that is defined as part of the current sort order, in the first idle time after commit, the record is moved to a position in the current record set that corresponds to the new value you have entered.

NOTE   **When FileMaker automatically changes the order of records to preserve the current sort order, the active record does not change. However, in List or Table View, the window scroll position is not adjusted when records are automatically re-sorted, so in some cases, the active record in a List or Table View layout will no longer be in view (having been sorted to a new position above or below the bounds of the current window).**

If the current record is no longer in view after being re-sorted automatically, pressing the Tab key (to enter a field on the active record) will cause FileMaker to auto-scroll the window to bring the active record into view.

Every sorted record set (as distinct from sorted portals and sorted relationships) is affected by this new FileMaker Pro sorting behavior. The only notable exception is that FileMaker does not re-sort records after an import operation (one that affects a current sorted found set) so that you'll have an opportunity to view the records in their original order after the import, to decide whether or not you want to re-sort. In this situation, FileMaker Pro 10 declares the records as `"Semi-sorted"` in the Status Toolbar.

An important characteristic of the maintain sort order feature in FileMaker Pro 10 is that the record order is updated to reflect changes made on the current workstation and also on remote workstations when your solution is hosted. When a user elsewhere on the network makes changes that will affect the sort sequence of a record that is part of a list of records you're viewing and then commits the record, your list will be updated (during the first idle time on your workstation) to reflect the change. Moreover, instead of performing a complete re-sort (with the overheads that would entail), FileMaker tracks only the records that have changed and relocates them within the existing sort order so that the process remains efficient.

CAUTION   **Sort order is not always maintained when the sort depends on related fields that are changed indirectly or by other users. Only changes to related data made locally and from the current active record are tracked for the purposes of maintaining sort order.**

Saved Find Requests

A useful new end-user feature introduced in FileMaker Pro 10 is the ability for users to rerun their recent Finds and to save their Finds so that they can run them at will in the future. Using saved Find requests is a great time-saving and convenience feature for individual users, enabling creation of a customized and more efficient work process for Finds within each solution. This feature is of particular benefit where specific users regularly perform complex or multi-request Finds that are laborious to set up, yet they lack the scripting skills (or don't have access privileges that allow scripting) to automate the process for themselves.

Saved and recent Finds using this new feature are particular to each user account, so one user can't see or access Finds performed or saved by any other users of the same solution. Developers wishing to create Finds that multiple users can apply can still do so by providing scripts to apply repetitive complex Finds. However, FileMaker now provides a way for ad hoc Finds performed by individual users to be readily reapplied without being painstakingly re-created each time.

Because the data about saved Finds is stored with the user's account, saved Finds for a given user will be available anywhere on the network they log in and will be maintained from one application or login session to the next. When user accounts are set to log in using external authentication, a separate option becomes available (accessible via the User Data button at the lower left of the Edit Account dialog for any account set to authenticate via an external server) so that when you're administering accounts, you can view the accumulated user data and delete user data associated with defunct user accounts.

CROSS-REF   **If you want to configure your solution so that ad hoc Finds performed by users will be stored and available to be reapplied at will by other users (or groups of users) of your solution, saved Finds will not be suitable and you will need to build your own method of saving Finds so they will be shared among users. You will find an example of one such technique described in detail in Chapter 9.**

The user performing the Finds can reuse his recent Finds without any special effort to save them. Any Find you perform is automatically added to the Recent Finds menu, and you can re-apply it at will by choosing it from the Records ➪ Saved Finds ➪ Recent Finds menu list, as shown in Figure 4.8. The Recent Finds list shows the most recent Finds performed by the current user up to a maximum of ten, with each Find appearing in the form of a summary of the criteria used.

CAUTION **Because the names of Finds stored on the most recent Finds menu don't indicate in which fields the criteria were entered, multiple different Finds may appear with identical names in the Recent Finds menu list. This is a limitation of the recent Finds feature. If you need to reuse Finds that used similar criteria (entered in different fields), you should consider saving the Finds with names that differentiate them.**

A further potential issue is that recent Finds give no indication of the layout or table to which they relate, leaving the user to remember the context for each listed Find. You can address this limitation of the recent Finds feature by creating saved Finds with appropriate detail in their names.

As well as accessing the Saved Finds options from the Records menu, you can also access this new feature from the Status Toolbar, either by clicking and holding on the Find icon (which is part of the default icon set for the Status Toolbar) to access a drop-down menu, shown in Figure 4.9, or, if it has been added via the Customize Status Toolbar option, you can use the Saved Finds Toolbar icon.

FIGURE 4.8

Accessing a recent Find from the Records menu.

CROSS-REF For a description of the process for customizing the Status Area, refer to the "Status Area Redesign" section, earlier in this chapter.

NOTE When you re-use a Find by selecting it from the Saved Finds menu, FileMaker performs the Find afresh against the data currently residing in the table. If you have made changes to data since the Find was previously performed, the results may be different (for instance, some records that previously met the Find criteria may no longer do so).

In addition, FileMaker Pro 10 provides you with the option to save the last Find performed on the current layout, giving it a name so that it will be permanently available (when you are logged into the current file with the current account) in the Records ⇨ Saved Finds ⇨ Saved Finds menu list. To save a Find:

1. Create a Find request and perform the Find in the normal way.

2. Choose Records ⇨ Saved Finds ⇨ Save Current Find. The Specify Option for the Saved Find dialog appears.

3. Enter a descriptive name for the Find you performed in Step 1, as shown in Figure 4.10.

FIGURE 4.9

Accessing a recent Find from the Find icon drop-down menu on the Status Toolbar.

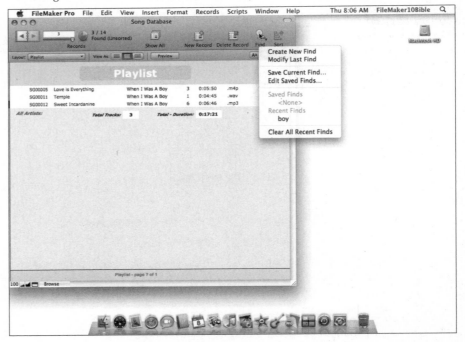

FIGURE 4.10

Entering a Find name into the Specify Options for the Saved Find dialog.

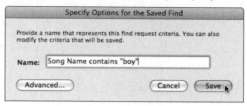

4. If you want to view or edit the criteria for the Find, click the Advanced button at the lower left of the dialog.

5. Click Save to in the Specify Options for the Saved Find dialog to complete the process.

Saved Finds you create by using the preceding procedure are displayed in the Saved Finds menu for the current user account and will be available whenever you log in to the file with the same credentials. To change the order of saved Finds in the menu, to rename a saved Find, to edit the criteria for a saved Find, or to delete a saved Find, choose Records ⇨ Saved Finds ⇨ Edit Saved Finds to invoke the Edit Saved Finds dialog, as shown in Figure 4.11.

FIGURE 4.11

Making changes with the Edit Saved Finds dialog.

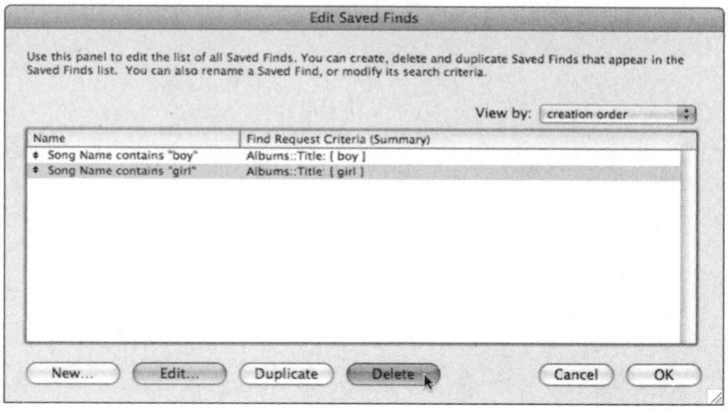

The procedure for editing Find requests in the Edit Saved Finds dialog is comparable to the familiar process used to manage Finds and Find criteria associated with script and button commands, such as Enter Find Mode[ ] and Perform Find[ ].

In all, the saved Find requests feature adds utility and convenience to the user interface of your FileMaker solutions and provides a useful supplement to the functionality that can be provided via the use of FileMaker's scripting capabilities.

Set Field by Name

A favorite of mine among the new features in FileMaker Pro 10 is the ability to set a field programmatically without determining in advance (and specifying in hard code) which field is to be set. The addition of the Set Field by Name [ ] script and button command brings a new level of flexibility and agility to FileMaker programming, enabling developers to supply calculations that will determine which field will be targeted by a Set Field operation.

Users of previous versions will be familiar with the Set Field [ ] command, which remains unchanged in FileMaker Pro 10. Set Field [ ] admits two arguments, the first of which is the target field that must be selected from a list of fields in the Specify Field dialog and the second of which is a calculated result that is to be set into the target field.

The Set Field by Name [ ] command operates in the same way as the Set Field [ ] command with one important exception. The target field is not selected from a list dialog but rather is supplied in the form of a calculation you enter that resolves to provide the name of the target field. Using this new capability, you can set up script sequences with embedded conditions so that different fields will be targeted depending on context. Consider, for example, the following segment of script code that might have been seen in a solution developed in the previous version of FileMaker:

```
If [Get(LayoutTableName) = "Invoices"]
  Set Field [Invoices::Status; "Complete"]
Else If [Get(LayoutTableName) = "Orders"]
  Set Field [Orders::Status; "Complete"]
Else If [Get(LayoutTableName) = "Payment"]
  Set Field [Payment::Status; "Complete"]
Else If [Get(LayoutTableName) = "Requisition"]
  Set Field [Requisition::Status; "Complete"]
Else If [Get(LayoutTableName) = "Diagnosis"]
  Set Field [Diagnosis::Status; "Complete"]
Else If [Get(LayoutTableName) = "WorkBrief"]
  Set Field [WorkBrief::Status; "Complete"]
Else If [Get(LayoutTableName) = "Specification"]
  Set Field [Specification::Status; "Complete"]
End If
```

While the preceding segment of script code extends to 15 lines, seasoned developers will have encountered comparable requirements that extend to many multiples of the length of this example. With the availability of the Set Field by Name [ ] command, the preceding example and many others like it can be reduced to a single line of code, along the lines of

```
Set Field by Name [Get(LayoutTableName) & "::Status"; "Complete"]
```

The example I provide here is one of many possible uses for this new and powerful command. With some ingenuity and a little patience, you can expect to see this command making your solutions more powerful and more agile. Equally important, the ability to make set field operations depend on context lets you create code that is more portable so that you can reuse it in a variety of places in your solution. Re-use of code helps you be more accurate and more efficient in development and makes your code easier to maintain (such as when a change need be made only in one place rather than several).

Of course, like any powerful tool or technique, the ability to calculate the target field to be set carries some risks. If your calculation expression does not anticipate all the conditions that the script will encounter, your command may set the wrong field — or no field at all. Moreover, because the success of the `Set Field by Name [ ]` command depends on the result of the calculation matching the name of a field in your solution, if you change a field name but don't make a corresponding change to the calculation expression, the command will stop working.

To assist in addressing the potential for problems when a field's name is changed, FileMaker Pro 10 provides a new calculation function that enables you to retrieve the name of a field (as a literal string) by referencing it: `GetFieldName ( )`. If you use the calculation function instead of supplying the name of a field as literal text, the correct name of the field will be returned, even if the name of the field has subsequently been changed.

CROSS-REF For additional details about the `GetFieldName ( )` function introduced in FileMaker Pro 10, see the "New Calculation Functions" section, later in this Chapter.

The addition of the `Set Field by Name [ ]` function to the FileMaker Pro script arsenal increases the level of flexibility and power that FileMaker offers to developers, helping them to create and maintain solutions that meet real-world needs.

Script Events Triggers

Speaking of real-world needs, nearly every complex solution developed over the past decade has called for ways to automatically trigger scripts in response to user actions or events or simply on a timer or schedule. Third-party developers have provided a host of plug-ins as a first step toward filling this need, because hitherto FileMaker has provided no native script events framework. However, plug-in script triggering is limiting, being linked to the use of external functions within calculations.

FileMaker Pro 10 introduces interface-driven script triggering that works at two levels: layout objects and layouts. In addition, a third kind of script triggering is provided in the form of timer-based triggers. These new capabilities are in addition to the existing feature that enables you to trigger scripts on file open and/or on file close. Because the new script-triggering capabilities depend on the active layout and/or layout object instead of depending directly on the data residing in your solution, the new features supplement rather than replace the options provided by script-triggering plug-ins. Nevertheless, this new feature significantly extends the power of FileMaker Pro.

Despite its power, I would be remiss if I didn't state upfront that the implementation of triggers in FileMaker Pro 10 is as an interface tool and therefore not a suitable mechanism for enforcing rules or validations in your solutions. That is, triggers can readily be bypassed by the use of an alternative interface or by contriving ways to edit an object while its corresponding interface element is inactive (for example, via drag-and-drop). You should therefore look to script triggers as an aid to the creation of easy interfaces for your users, but not as a means to maintain data integrity or aid security. For those purposes, other mechanisms (including plug-ins that provide calculation-based script triggering) are better suited.

TIP Script triggers are associated with an event that occurs in relation to a specific context. The context is established by the Layout object (for Layout Object triggers) or by the Layout (for Layout triggers and so on, while the event is specific to the type of trigger. For example, an `OnObjectEnter` event can be used to trigger a selected script when a particular layout object is entered. In this example, the event is the user's action (such as pressing the Tab key or clicking the mouse button to enter a field), which causes the object trigger to fire.

Layout object triggers

FileMaker Pro 10 provides five kinds of layout object triggers, each of which can be set to fire when the user (or a script) interacts with a specific layout object. When configured, layout object triggers form part of your solution's interface, responding to specific actions applied to the interface object to which they are attached.

You can configure layout object triggers to operate in Browse mode, Find mode, or both. The layout object script triggers available in FileMaker Pro 10 are as follows:

- `OnObjectEnter`
- `OnObjectKeystroke`
- `OnObjectModify`
- `OnObjectSave`
- `OnObjectExit`

Two of the five layout object triggers, `OnObjectEnter` and `OnObjectModify`, call the associated script after the user performs the corresponding action on the object to which you assign the trigger, in the mode(s) for which you enable the triggers. These two triggers are termed "post" triggers because the user (or script) action occurs and then, immediately afterwards, the associated script runs. For example, if you assign an `OnObjectEnter` trigger to a field in your solution and enable it for Browse mode, when the user presses the Tab key to enter the field in Browse mode (or clicks into the field with the mouse), the field will become active, and then the triggered script will commence. Similarly, when you assign an `OnObjectModify` trigger to a field in your solution, when the field is active (in the mode for which the trigger is enabled) and the user makes a change to the data in the field (such as by pasting or typing), the data in the field will be changed, and then the triggered script will commence.

The remaining three layout object triggers — `OnObjectKeystroke`, `OnObjectSave`, and `OnObjectExit` — call the associated script prior to allowing the user action. These triggers are termed "pre" triggers because the script runs before the corresponding action is processed. Moreover, the action can be allowed or denied depending on the result of the script. For example, when you assign an `OnObjectKeystroke` trigger to a field object and enable it for Browse mode, if the field is active in Browse mode and you press a key on the keyboard, the associated script runs and then, only after the script completes execution and only if the script returns a `True` result (or if the script is not configured to return any result), the keystroke is issued (and affects the field, if it is still active). However, if the script returns an explicitly `False` result (either zero or null), the triggering event — in this case, a keystroke — will be cancelled.

> **NOTE** Script results, which control the fate of pre-event script trigger actions (keystroke, save, and exit) are assigned by supplying an argument to the `Exit Script [ ]` command at the concluding line of the triggered script.

> **CAUTION** If there is no script result defined, either because a triggered script does not conclude with an `Exit Script [ ]` command or because the `Exit Script [ ]` command does not specify a result, the triggering action will proceed as if the script returned a `True` result. Only if an explicit `False` result (either zero or null) is returned will the triggering action be cancelled.
>
> In this case, there is a subtle (but crucial) distinction between a *null* script result and *no* script result; so a concluding script line defined as `Exit Script [ ]` permits the triggering action, whereas a concluding line defined as `Exit Script [Result: "" ]` cancels the triggering action.

You can assign a layout object script trigger to an object by entering Layout mode, selecting the object to which you wish to assign a trigger, and then choosing Format ⇨ Set Script Triggers. The Set Script Triggers dialog appears, as shown in Figure 4.12. On selecting the checkbox adjacent to one of the trigger options in the list box at the top of the dialog, you're prompted to select a script to assign to the trigger and (optionally) enter a script parameter. In the lower panel of the Set Script Triggers dialog, you set associated properties for the selected trigger, including the mode(s) in which the trigger will be enabled.

FIGURE 4.12

Configuring a layout object script trigger in the Set Script Triggers dialog.

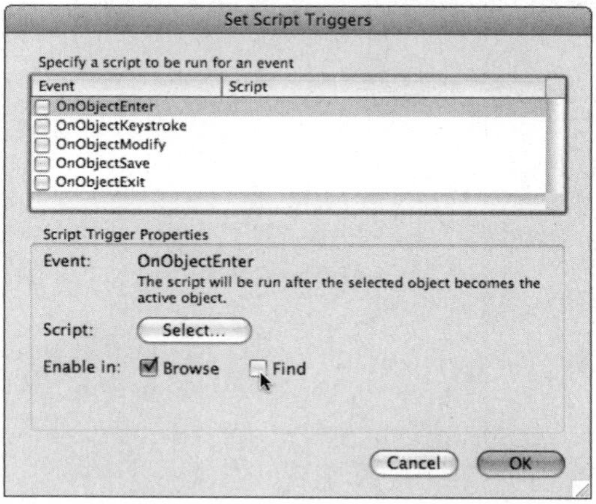

NOTE   You can also access the Set Script Triggers dialog from the object contextual menu in Layout mode.

TIP   When you've defined a script trigger and want to disable it without deleting it, you can do so by deselecting all the mode checkboxes in the settings panel. In this scenario the trigger definition, including the assigned script and associated script parameter, remain in place, but the trigger will not fire in any mode. You can enable the script trigger again at any time by selecting it and enabling one or more modes.

You can assign layout object triggers to field box, button, tab control, portal, and Web Viewer objects in your layouts. You can assign multiple triggers of different types to a single layout object. When you have multiple instances of the same object (for example, field box) on a layout, the trigger configurations are assigned separately for each instance. So whether a script is triggered, and if so, which script, will depend on which instance of the field is active.

When you've assigned one or more script triggers to a layout object, it appears with a red asterisk in the lower right corner of the object in Layout mode, provided that the View ➪ Show ➪ Script Triggers menu option is enabled, as shown in Figure 4.13.

As a part of your solution's interface, assigned script triggers will fire based on interaction with the specific layout objects to which the triggers are assigned — whether the interaction occurs as a result of user input or during the execution of a script. When a script command, such as Go to Field [ ], activates a script trigger assigned to the field that the script has made active, the triggered script will execute before the initiating script proceeds.

FIGURE 4.13

Configuring a layout object script trigger in the Set Script Triggers dialog.

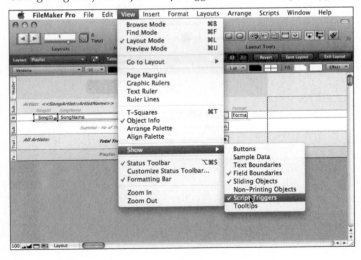

In order for the triggers assigned to a layout object to take effect, the object must be active (have current focus). When you perform an action that changes a field that is not presently the active field, its triggers will not fire. Moreover, if you change the data in a field by any means that does not work directly through the interface object that the script trigger is attached to, the trigger will not fire. For example, if you click a button that uses the Set Field [ ] command to change a value in a field, the field contents will be updated but, because the Set Field [ ] command works behind the scenes, not through the interface, triggers attached to the field object on the layout will not fire. Similarly, when you drag and drop content from one FileMaker field to another, the source field remains active throughout, so triggers attached to the destination field for the drag-and-drop action will not fire. This applies also to content dragged and dropped to a FileMaker field from another application, except in the case where the destination field for the external drag-and-drop is already the active field in FileMaker.

You should also bear in mind that bulk operations (those that may change many records as a result of a single action or command) don't cause object-related script triggers to fire. For the sake of efficiency, as well as for logistical reasons (for example, scripts don't run while modal dialogs are displayed), triggers will be ignored when you perform any of the following operations:

- External scripted operations (such as AppleScript) that work on multiple records
- Find/Replace
- Import
- Refresh Window
- Relookup
- Replace Field Contents
- Spell checking

NOTE Script triggers do not fire as a result of user actions performed via a web interface (either IWP or CWP). However, when a web-compatible script is triggered from a web-user session, triggers activated by script actions will fire in the same way they do if the script is run within the FileMaker Pro client application.

Layout script triggers

FileMaker Pro 10 provides seven kinds of layout triggers, each of which can be set to fire when the user (or a script) interacts with the layout to which you assign one or more triggers. Like object triggers, layout triggers form part of your solution's interface, responding to user and script actions involving the associated layout.

You can configure layout triggers to operate in Browse mode and/or Find mode, and in several cases also in Preview mode. The Layout script triggers available in FileMaker Pro 10 are as follows:

- OnRecordLoad
- OnRecordCommit

- OnRecordRevert
- OnLayoutKeystroke
- OnLayoutLoad
- OnModeEnter
- OnModeExit

As with object triggers, some layout triggers are designed to fire after the associated event has occurred, while some fire before the event. The OnRecordLoad, OnLayoutLoad, and OnModeEnter triggers are "Post" triggers so the assigned script will run after the trigger event has been processed. However the remaining layout triggers, OnRecordCommit, OnRecordRevert, OnLayoutKeystroke and OnModeExit, are implemented as pre-event triggers so the assigned script runs before the trigger event occurs, and the originating event will proceed only if the triggered script returns a True result (or if the triggered script is not defined to return a result). If the script assigned to a pre-event trigger returns a result that is zero or null, the triggering event will be cancelled, and the solution will remain in the state that prevailed before the user action that activated the trigger.

You can assign a layout script trigger by entering Layout mode, choosing Layouts ➪ Layout Setup, and then navigating to the Script Triggers tab of the Layout Setup dialog, as shown in Figure 4.14.

FIGURE 4.14

Configuring a layout script trigger in the Script Triggers tab of the Layout Setup dialog.

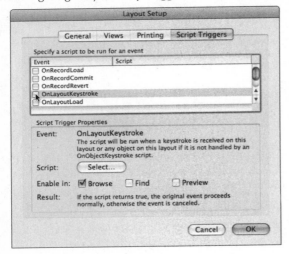

> **TIP** You can also invoke the Layout Setup dialog by Ctrl+clicking/Right-Clicking in the layout background in Layout mode and choosing Layout Setup from the contextual menu.

As with object triggers described in the preceding section, on selecting the checkbox adjacent to one of the trigger options in the list box at the top of the Script Triggers tab, you select a script to assign to the trigger and, if desired, specify a script parameter. In the lower panel of the Layout Setup Script Triggers tab, you can review and/or configure associated properties for the selected trigger, including the mode(s) in which the trigger will be enabled.

You can assign multiple script triggers for each layout, one of each of the available types. Each trigger can be assigned to call a different script and can be configured independently to operate in one or more of the available modes.

TIP   Although you can assign only one of each trigger type to a layout, the script your triggers call can itself call one or more sub-scripts, if desired. By creating a master script that calls several other scripts in sequence and assigning the master script to be triggered by a layout event, you can achieve the effect of assigning multiple scripts to a specific trigger.

NOTE   There is no visual indication that a layout has script triggers assigned. To ascertain the status of script triggers (if any) assigned to a layout, you must navigate to the layout in layout mode, invoke the Layout Setup dialog, and review the settings in the Script Triggers panel.

When you assign multiple script triggers, including layout triggers and object triggers, it is possible for multiple triggers to fire resulting from a single action, in which case FileMaker follows an order of precedence to determine the sequence of the triggered scripts. The following are examples of three typical scenarios:

- When you assign an OnLayoutLoad trigger to a layout and also assign an OnRecordLoad trigger to the same layout and then navigate to the layout, the OnLayoutLoad script will fire first, immediately followed by the OnRecordLoad script for the displayed record.

- When you assign an OnLayoutKeystroke to a layout and an OnObjectKeystroke to a field on the layout, both enabled for Browse mode, and then in Browse mode place the cursor into the field and press an alphanumeric key on the keyboard, the OnObjectKeystroke script fires first. If the OnObjectKeystroke script returns True, the OnLayoutKeystroke script commences. If the OnLayoutKeystroke script also returns True, then the character corresponding to the key you pressed is entered into the active field.

- When you assign an OnRecordCommit trigger and an OnRecordLoad trigger to a layout and an OnObjectEnter trigger to the first field on the layout and then make changes to a record in List View and subsequently click into the first field in another record in the list, the OnCommit trigger fires on the originating record, then subsequently (if the OnCommit trigger script returns True and the commit event succeeds), FileMaker will retry the initiating action of navigating between records, and the OnRecordLoad script commences for the record you clicked into. Then after the OnRecordLoad script completes, the OnObjectEnter script runs. In this example, a single mouse click can result in three scripts being triggered in succession.

TIP When a pre-event script runs and returns an explicit `False` (zero or null) result, the initiating action is not processed. In the preceding example, if the `OnCommit` script returns `false`, the current record is not committed and therefore remains active. Consequently, any follow-on actions including navigation to a different record and entry into a field on that record also fail.

NOTE The `OnLayoutKeystroke` and `OnObjectKeystroke` triggers do not respond to command shortcuts, field changes made via a script or button command, mouse actions (such as selecting a radio button), or a value list entry from a drop-down menu.

CROSS-REF FileMaker Pro 10 introduced new calculation functions to enable you to retrieve and identify keystrokes used to trigger scripts, as described in the next section.

Timed interval script triggers

In addition to layout and object triggers, FileMaker Pro 10 provides the ability to set a timer to trigger a script at a specified recurring interval. This new feature is implemented in the form of an `Install OnTimer Script [ ]` command that can be called either within a script or as a button action. You can find the `Install OnTimer Script [ ]` command in the "Control" group in the list of available commands in the Edit Script and Button Setup dialogs.

The `OnTimer` script trigger is specific to the database window that is active when the trigger is installed. When installed, the `OnTimer` trigger runs the assigned script every time the specified interval (in seconds) has elapsed, provided that the system is idle (no other scripts are running, no modal dialogs are displayed, and so on) and the window is in Browse mode, Find mode, or Preview mode.

NOTE If a script is already running when the interval has passed, the `OnTimer` script will be queued to run at the first idle time.

FileMaker allows you to specify only one timer-based trigger per window at a time. If you install a new trigger in the same window, it supersedes the previous one. An `OnTimer` script trigger continues to trigger the assigned script at the specified interval until

- A different `OnTimer` script trigger is installed in the same window.
- The `OnTimer` script trigger is cancelled.
- The window in which the `OnTimer` script trigger is installed enters Layout mode.
- The window in which the `OnTimer` script trigger is installed is closed.

While the window is in Layout mode, the `OnTimer` script remains in a suspended state and will resume triggering if and when the window is restored to Browse, Find, or Preview mode.

To cancel an `OnTimer` script trigger, you issue a further call to the `Install OnTimer Script [ ]` command, with either a zero or null interval or with no script assigned.

Because you can have multiple windows open simultaneously, you can have multiple `OnTimer` scripts installed, each assigned to a different window.

 OnTimer **scripts can't run from the Web (using either IWP or CWP), nor will they run on FileMaker Server.** OnTimer **scripts are a feature of the FileMaker Pro client application.**

File-based script triggers

As in previous versions of FileMaker, provision is made for scripts to be assigned to run OnFileOpen and OnFileClose. This capability has not changed in FileMaker Pro 10, and the opening and closing scripts are defined by accessing the Open/Close tab of the File Options dialog (choose File ➪ File Options).

Although the dialog options for the file-based script triggers refer to opening and closing the file, in reality, the OnFileOpen script doesn't run until the first window is displayed. Thus, when a file is opened "hidden" (either via script or as a consequence of as an external data source for another open file), the opening script will not be called. Only when and if a window is opened onscreen will the opening script be triggered. Thus, the OnFileOpen script trigger might more properly be considered an "OnFirstWindowDraw" trigger. Similarly, because a file that is referenced by another open file won't close until all the files referencing it also close, but the OnFileClose trigger will fire when the last window associated with the file is closed, the OnFileClose trigger might be better considered an OnLastWindowClose trigger

TIP **When a file has been opened without a window being drawn and is closed again without a window ever having been drawn, neither the** OnFileOpen **script nor the** OnFileClose **script will run.**

Avoiding trigger tangles

Script triggering offers a world of open-ended functionality that is at once inviting and a little awe-inspiring. You may be tempted to run amok attaching triggers to everything in sight, but before you do, take a moment to consider which things triggers can do best and to contemplate some of the potential pitfalls for the unwary developer.

If used sparingly and with careful planning, script triggers can significantly enhance your solution interfaces, providing support to users and navigation finesse. Here are a few of the many things you might consider using script triggering to implement:

- When your users select a value in a field, your solution can automatically navigate them to the corresponding record or layout.

- When your users select a value from a value list, FileMaker can automatically perform a Find to filter the displayed records to include only matching values.

- When your users enter a value that is out of range, FileMaker can post an alert before they even leave the field (avoiding situations such as when the user enters far more text than is permitted in a given field, but does not find out until they have wasted the effort to type the text, leave the field, and only then see the validation error message).

- When your users navigate around your solution, FileMaker can keep a separate log of their movements, allowing you to establish usage patterns as a basis to refine your solution designs.

- When your users type search text into a field, FileMaker can filter an adjacent portal in real time to display a list of possible matching entries.

There are many other examples of uses for script triggering, limited only by your imagination and ingenuity. Notwithstanding the fertile ground that script triggers provide, I encourage you to proceed with caution, keeping in mind the following broad guidelines:

- **Use script triggers sparingly.** Script triggers operate like trip wires in your solution, and you should try to avoid getting your wires crossed or tangled. The actions of a script called from one trigger may cause another trigger to fire. In the event that the actions of the second trigger are such as to cause the first trigger to fire again, your solution will enter a loop, and the user may assume that the application is frozen.

  For example, if the script called from an `OnObjectModify` trigger on field A inserts a value into field B which in turn triggers an `OnObjectModify` script that (among other things) inserts a value into field A, when you edit either field, the two triggered scripts will be called alternately until you abort the running script (such as by pressing ⌘+./esc) or force-quit the application. In either case, the "crossing of the trigger wires" places your solution into an unstable state.

  While the preceding example is a little contrived, you may stumble upon many other configurations with similarly undesirable, unintended, or even spectacular consequences, if you proceed without due caution.

- **Consider all the ways users interact with your solution.** Script triggering is a powerful feature that provides you with scope to radically alter the behavior of FileMaker Pro. However, unless you map out changes to functionality and account for all the ways a user may cause a trigger to run and all the ensuing effects when the trigger script proceeds, you may create situations that are immensely confusing to the user.

  For example, if your solution includes a list-view layout with an `OnCommit` trigger that calls a script that navigates to the next record, users may find the arrangement convenient in some situations. However, when users click another record to navigate to it in List or Table View (or enters a record number into the navigation field in the Status Toolbar), they may be frustrated and mystified to find that they're not on the record they intended. Moreover, in the event a user doesn't notice the sleight of hand your trigger script has caused, they may end up overwriting or deleting the wrong record.

  To minimize the chance of this scenario or others like it, I recommend that you develop a process map for any complex interface procedure involving triggers. In your map, you should plot each of the paths the user might conceivably take that would cause your triggers to fire and ensure that the assigned script will gracefully handle each of the possible process outcomes.

■ **Don't rely solely on script triggers to enforce rules in your solution.** Although script triggers are primarily an interface tool, you may be tempted to use them for a variety of purposes that have more to do with data handling, validation, or security than with supporting the user experience.

For example, if you set an OnObjectExit trigger script to apply validation rules ensuring the integrity or cleanliness of your solution's data or to apply data formats or update other fields to correspond to the data entered, bear in mind that the trigger scripts will run only on those occasions when data is edited by directly interacting with the specific layout object you have applied the trigger to. All bets are off, and your carefully built validation scripts will be bypassed in the following situations:

⬛ Data is modified by a script or a button or via a batch process, such as the Replace Field Contents [ ] or Import [ ] commands.

⬛ The field is present (without the same trigger assigned) on other layouts.

⬛ The solution is accessed via the Web.

⬛ Data is edited via a third-party application or utility, such as AppleScript.

⬛ The user creates a separate file to use as an interface to the data in your solution.

Despite the apparent convenience and flexibility of script triggers, in most occasions, validation constraints applied at the schema level will have greater merit.

While there are few absolutes in solution design and different solution requirements may call for different approaches, I counsel you to view triggers first and foremost as a convenience and a way to make your solutions more efficient and friendly, rather than as part of the core data management functionality your solution depends upon.

From a practical viewpoint, although you can define script triggers freely by using FileMaker Pro 10, the additional capabilities of FileMaker Pro 10 Advanced will prove invaluable when designing and troubleshooting complex operations involving one or more script triggers. In particular, the Script Debugger in FileMaker Pro Advanced enables you to step through a sequence of scripts one line at a time so that you can review the way they affect the data and interface of your solution in different conditions and with different inputs.

It is important to note that when a script performs an action that results in another script being triggered, the triggered script executes before the original script resumes. Moreover, FileMaker treats the triggered script (and any script its actions in turn trigger) as sub-scripts of the substantive script. When using the Script Debugger in FileMaker Pro 10 Advanced, therefore, advancing through a script using the *Step Into* button (F6) will cause the triggered script to be displayed and stepped in the Script Debugger, while pressing the Step Over button (F5) results in execution (outside the Debugger) of the triggered script(s) and allows you to proceed through the original script uninterrupted.

> **TIP** The Script Debugger in FileMaker Pro 10 Advanced has been enhanced so that when a triggered script is running, the area immediately below the control buttons at the top of the Script Debugger window (where the name of the current script is displayed) also states the type of script trigger that fired the script. If the current script did not execute as the result of a trigger, the script name appears as it has in the past.

Because the presence of triggers associated with a script action is not evident when viewing the script in the Script Debugger window, you will gain a more complete picture of the components of a process — including the role of triggered scripts in the outcome — if you use the Step Into button routinely to work through a script sequence in the Debugger, reserving the Step Over button for those occasions when you're aware that the current steps will fire one or more triggers, but want to continue with the underlying script without viewing the step sequence of the triggered scripts.

CROSS-REF For additional discussion about the use of the Script Debugger in FileMaker Pro Advanced, refer to Chapter 18.

New Calculation Functions

FileMaker Pro 10 includes six new calculation functions, four of which provide added support for the use of script triggers based on keystroke events, a further function that is of especial value when you are using the Set Field by Name [ ] command (although it has a range of other uses, too), and a function that will assist with file-handling operations. In all, the new calculation functions are

- Get(TriggerKeystroke)
- Get(TriggerModifierKeys)
- Char(number)
- Code(text)
- GetFieldName(field)
- Get(DocumentsPathListing)

When you use the four functions that provide added support for script triggering, you're able to determine which key was pressed when an OnObjectKeystroke or OnLayoutKeystroke script has been triggered, including when the key pressed was an arrow key or other special key (backspace, tab and so on). This enables you to control the behavior of triggered scripts to ensure that they behave in the ways the user would expect, depending on the keystroke issued.

Get(TriggerKeystroke)

The Get(TriggerKeystroke) function is active while a script that was triggered by an OnObjectKeystroke or OnLayoutKeystroke script trigger (or any subscripts it calls) is in progress. It returns the character associated with the keystroke that triggered the script. For example, when you place the cursor into a field box that has an OnObjectKeystroke assigned and press the **a** key on the keyboard, the assigned script trigger fires. During the course of the script, the Get(TriggerKeystroke) function returns a.

When a script has not been launched by an OnObjectKeystroke or OnLayoutKeystroke, or when there is no script in progress, the Get(TriggerKeystroke) function returns a null result.

The operation of the Get(TriggerKeystroke) function is useful for all cases where you press an alphanumeric key that results in an OnObjectKeystroke or OnLayoutKeystroke trigger firing. However, when the key you press does not return a recognizable character, such as when you press backspace or an arrow key, you need a way to identify which key was pressed. Moreover, if one or more modifier keys (such as Shift, Command, Control, Alt, or CapsLock) were pressed while the keystroke was issued, you may also need a way to ascertain that. FileMaker Pro 10 provides the functions described in the following sections to assist.

Get(TriggerModifierKeys)

Like the function described in the preceding section, the Get(TriggerModifierKeys) function enables you to ascertain the combination of keys that set the script in motion during the course of a script launched by an OnObjectKeystroke or OnLayoutKeystroke trigger. The function returns a result that reflects the modifier keys that were pressed at the time when the trigger was activated, regardless of which keys may be pressed while the triggered script is in process.

The result returned by the Get(TriggerModifierKeys) function is in the form of a number representing the combination of modifier keys (if any) pressed when the keystroke that activated the trigger was received. The format of the result is equivalent to the codified results returned by the existing Get(ActiveModifierKeys) function.

CROSS-REF For detailed information on working with modifier keys, refer to the section by that name in Chapter 19.

Code(text)

The Code( ) function is designed to return the Unicode character number(s) of one or more characters supplied as text. If only one character is in the supplied text, the Unicode code point of that character will be returned. However, if multiple characters are supplied, the code point for the leftmost character in the supplied string will be returned as the low (rightmost) five digits of the returned number; the code point value of the following characters will be in the next (to the left) five digit blocks of the returned value.

TIP Low ASCII characters (7-bit) have the same values in Unicode, so for a range of common purposes, the value returned by the Char( ) function will be equal to the ASCII value of the supplied character.

Therefore, because the Unicode code point for the letter A is 65, for B is 66, for C is 67, and for D is 68, the expression Code("ABCD") returns 68000670006600065.

When you need to identify a keystroke character returned — especially a non-alphanumeric character, such as a backspace, arrow key, or other key such as is returned by the Get(TriggerKeystroke) function, you can do so by using an expression such as Code(Get(TriggerKeystroke)).

Char(code)

FileMaker Pro 10 provides the Char ( ) function to return a character by supplying its index number in the Unicode character set. While this capability may have a range of applications in text processing, cryptography, and so on, it provides a useful partner to the Code ( ) function, enabling you to ascertain the identity of characters passed into code points by the Code ( ) function.

If the number supplied as the parameter to the Char ( ) function contains five or less digits (that is, if it's between 1 and 99,999 inclusive), the result will be a single character from the Unicode standard. However, if the number supplied is comprised of more than five digits, multiple Unicode characters are returned where the rightmost five digits determine the first character, the sixth to the tenth digits from the right determine the second character, and so on.

Therefore, because the letter corresponding to Unicode code point 65 is A, to 66 is B, to 67 is C, and to 68 is D, the expression Code(68000670006600065) returns ABCD.

TIP Because Unicode permits multiple code points as the representation of a composite character (such as an accented letter), number values greater than 99,999 may in some cases be drawn as a single character with inflection.

GetFieldName(field)

There are a variety of situations when it is necessary to pass the name of a field (as a literal text string) as an input parameter for a function or command. That's not too hard to do, because you can just type the field name between quotes and be done — but should you subsequently change the name of the field, the literal text you entered will not match, and the code that depends on it will no longer work.

The GetFieldName ( ) function introduced in FileMaker Pro 10 provides a way to make references to field names in your code more robust by tying them to the field itself. For example, when you use

```
GetFieldName(Invoices::InvoiceDate)
```

rather than

```
"Invoices::InvoiceDate"
```

the fully qualified field name of the referenced field will be retrieved at run time, ensuring that the correct and current name of the field will always be returned. This is very useful as an adjunct to the new Set Field by Name [ ] command, allowing you to ensure that the calculation expressions you use to specify the target field always return a valid field name. However, the ability to calculate the name of a field at run time is also valuable when you're using the GetField ( ) and Evaluate ( ) functions, as well as any of the various design functions that require a field name as an input parameter.

Get(DocumentsPathListing)

If you want to set your scripts to check that a file exists before importing it (or overwriting it), you need a way to check the contents of a directory. Throughout many years, developers have contrived ways to have FileMaker Pro interact with files on the local computer, sometimes using external technologies to supplement the capabilities FileMaker provides in this area. However, FileMaker Pro 10 provides some assistance in the form of the Get(DocumentsPathListing) function.

Using this new function, you can obtain a return-delimited list of files and directories within the user's documents directory on the current workstation. Be aware, however, that the path to the documents folder will vary depending on the platform, operating system version, and configuration of the computer where FileMaker is installed. The path to the documents folder on the current workstation is returned by the Get(DocumentsPath) function in FileMaker Pro. The path may take forms such as those set out in Table 4.1.

TABLE 4.1

Examples of the Documents Path in Different Environments

Platform	Path
On Mac OS X	/Macintosh HD/Users/*yourusername*/Documents/
In Windows XP	/C:/Documents and Settings/*yourusername*/My Documents/
In Windows Vista	/C:/Users/yourusername/Documents/

NOTE The Get(DocumentsPathListing) function operates recursively to build a complete list of the contents of the target (documents) folder, including the files contained within folders that are nested within the documents folder. The function will delve as many layers deep as it needs to, to return the fully specified paths of all the files contained anywhere within the documents folder.

Because the text string returned by the Get(DocumentsPathListing) function is return-delimited, you can use the GetValue( ) function to extract individual lines, or the PatternCount( ) or Position( ) functions to check whether a specific file is present in the user's documents folder.

CAUTION Be aware that users commonly store all their files in the Documents folder (including subfolders within the documents folder), and therefore the documents path contents listing may include many thousands of files. In such cases, the Get(Documents PathListing) function may take some time to evaluate, and the result may be an exceedingly long text string. You should consider providing user feedback about what is happening during this process.

External SQL Data Sources (ESS) Enhancements

When support for External SQL Data Sources (ESS) was first introduced in FileMaker Pro 9, it opened up a wealth of new opportunities and provided solutions for many longstanding problems in integrating data from a variety of sources. FileMaker Pro 10 offers several additions to the capabilities of ESS that increase its usability and extend its reach.

Additional SQL database support

FileMaker Pro 10 adds to the selection of mainstream SQL database management systems that are supported for access via ESS. In addition to the products and versions supported previously, FileMaker Pro 10 adds support for the following:

- Microsoft SQL Server 2008 (10.0.1049)
- Oracle 11g (11.1.0.6)
- MySQL Community Server 5.1

NOTE   When you're working on Mac OS, to configure and use ESS access to the additional database systems supported by FileMaker Pro 10, you will require updated ODBC drivers available from Actual Technologies.

Value lists based on external SQL data

In FileMaker Pro 10, when you're defining a value list, you are now able to choose a field in an ESS shadow table when you select the option to Use Values from a Field.

As shown in Figure 4.15, you can also choose the option to Include Only Related Values, provided you first create an appropriate relationship to the relevant shadow table, in the Relationships Graph of the current FileMaker Pro file.

Single Sign-On for remote Windows clients

When configuring an external data source, it's previously been possible to choose settings to prompt the user to provide authentication details (username and password) or to supply credentials in the data source configuration (either as literal values or via calculation). FileMaker Pro 10 provides a third authentication option, allowing you to use Windows Authentication (Single Sign-on).

To use Single Sign-On for a data source defined to use ODBC, select the third radio button in the Authentication panel of the Edit Data Source dialog. (You can access the Edit Data Source by choosing File ⇨ Manage ⇨ External Data Sources and either selecting a data source and clicking the Edit button, or clicking the New button). After selecting the option to Use Windows Authentication, enter a Service Principal Name (SPN) into the text box provided, as shown in Figure 4.16.

FIGURE 4.15

Configuring a Value List to use values based on an ESS shadow field.

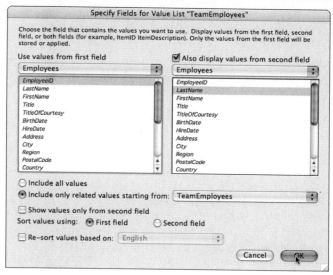

FIGURE 4.16

Configuring an External Sequel Data Source to use Windows Single Sign-On.

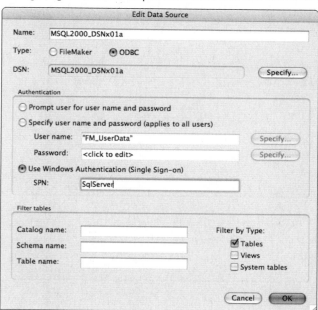

After you select the Windows Authentication option for a SQL data source, provided both the client (FMP) and host (FMS) applications are version 10 (or later), Windows Single Sign-On credentials will be forwarded to the SQL server during ESS connect.

 **If either FileMaker or FileMaker Server is still running version 9, when you connect, you'll be prompted to supply credentials.**

Handling of DATETIME values — MS SQL Server

In Microsoft SQL Server (the 2000, 2005, and 2008 versions), dates, times, and timestamps are all stored as attributes of data type DATETIME or SMALLDATETIME and, when accessed by using ESS in FileMaker Pro, such fields are treated by default as timestamp fields. Previously, this presented some difficulty in cases where the field was intended to be used for a date or a time, because the timestamp format required the user to enter a redundant time value with each date, or a redundant date value accompanying each time.

FileMaker Pro 10 provides you with the flexibility to specify the data type of an ESS shadow field created from a Microsoft SQL Server DATETIME or SMALLDATETIME column. To change a FileMaker shadow field that represents a Microsoft SQL Server column to operate as either a Date or Time field rather than as a Timestamp, choose File ➪ Manage Database, navigate to the Fields tab, and select the shadow table for the SQL table containing the DATETIME or SMALLDATETIME value you want to change. From the Type drop-down menu, select a Date or Time and click the Change button.

When you've specified a Date or Time data type for a DATETIME or SMALLDATETIME field, FileMaker will not prompt for the redundant component (time when the value is to be entered as a date, or date when the value is to be entered as a time), so the user will be able to work with the field as they would if it were a FileMaker field of the appropriate type.

Bento Integration

If you're a Mac user and make use of Bento 2 (or later), the personal database solution available from FileMaker, Inc., you'll be pleased to know that FileMaker Pro 10 includes support for direct import of data from Bento. This provides you with a straightforward way to access your Bento 2 data (including Address Book and iCal data) and integrate it with existing data in your FileMaker solutions.

As shown in Figure 4.17, an additional option has been added to the menu system as File ➪ Import ➪ Bento Data Source, enabling you to load Bento data directly into an existing table in your solution. When you choose Bento as the source of your import, the import field mapping dialog (familiar from previous versions of FileMaker) enables you to align incoming data with fields in a selected table of your FileMaker solution.

In addition to the option to import from Bento 2 into your existing FileMaker Pro 10 solution's tables, an option is provided to create a new database by using the structure and content of a library from your Bento data as a starting point.

To create a new file based on Bento data, invoke the Quick Start screen, select the option to Create a Database From An Existing, and then use the drop-down menu to choose the Bento Source option, as shown in Figure 4.18. After confirming the source data set and field map for import, click OK.

FIGURE 4.17

Selecting Bento as the data source for an import in your FileMaker Pro 10 solution.

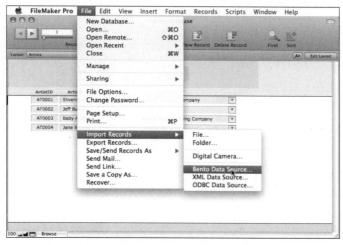

FIGURE 4.18

Creating a new file by using a Bento Source as the starting point.

File Recovery Improvements

There have been significant changes to the way the File Recovery process is implemented in FileMaker Pro 10, making the procedure more flexible and more robust, as well as giving you greater control and additional feedback about what has occurred.

As a part of this change, the Tools ⇨ File Maintenance option has been removed from FileMaker Pro Advanced. In the process of rethinking the approach to salvage and data recovery operations, the file maintenance feature has been superseded by more reliable and more extensive options within the recovery procedure. As part of this change, the Optimize procedure that was previously available from the File Maintenance dialog in FileMaker Pro Advanced is now performed routinely when you select File ⇨ Save a Copy As and choose the Compacted Copy (Smaller) option, using either FileMaker Pro or FileMaker Pro Advanced.

In FileMaker Pro 10, when you choose File ⇨ Recover, you gain access to a new option enabling you to check the consistency of a file. The consistency check is nondestructive; it doesn't change anything in the selected file, but merely reports on its state. Consequently, the consistency check is safe to perform at will as a routine health check on your files. To check the consistency of a file, proceed as follows:

1. Choose File ⇨ Recover. The Select Damaged File dialog appears.
2. Navigate through the folder structure to locate and select the file you want to check.
3. Click the Check Consistency button at the right of the panel appearing below the file list.
4. Review the consistency result dialog that provides results of the consistency check, as shown in Figure 4.19.

FIGURE 4.19

Using the Recover process to perform a consistency check.

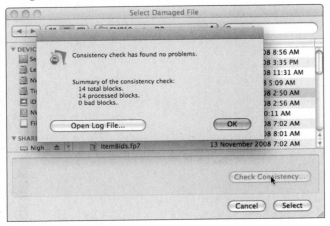

If you conclude that a file is damaged (for example, you're experiencing problems with the file, and it fails the consistency check), select the file in the Select Damaged File dialog and click the Select button at the lower right of the dialog. (The Name New Recovered File dialog appears.) If you click the Save button directly, default recovery options will be used to attempt to rebuild the file. However, if you click the Use Advanced Options checkbox in the panel below the file list, you will see the Advanced Recover Options dialog, shown in Figure 4.20, and you will be able to control the way the Recover process works and which procedures will be applied as FileMaker Pro attempts to rebuild the file.

FIGURE 4.20

Specifying Advanced Recover Options to control the Recover process.

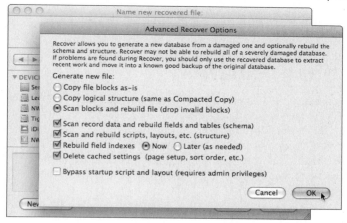

By adjusting the configured options in the Advanced Recover Options dialog, you can perform a wide variety of modifications to the selected file, dealing with specific problem as required. For example, if your file has exhibited anomalies with Finds or relationship matches but appears otherwise intact, you may choose to select only the option to Rebuild Field Indexes. Each of the options provided addresses a specific range of potential issues, resulting in different changes being made in the recovered file.

NOTE   The recovery process does not change the original file. Rather, it creates a newly rebuilt file that contains selected components of the original file. If you try a combination of settings that don't produce the result you desire, you can try again as many times as necessary.

In addition to the control of file rebuild processes, the Advanced Recover Options dialog includes a new option to bypass the startup script. When using this option, you'll be required to authenticate with a [Full Access] account for the file being recovered, whereupon the file options in the resulting (recovered) file will be altered to remove the OnFileOpen script selection. On accessing the

Advanced Recover Options, you also gain access to two options that are new in FileMaker Pro 10, namely the alternate first and second steps allowing you to copy the file as is or copy the logical structure.

NOTE   After each file recovery operation, FileMaker Pro 10 creates a log of the process and stores it in a file called Recover.log located in the same folder as the file being recovered. You can access the log directly by clicking on the button labeled Open Log File in the lower left corner of the dialog reporting the recovery results.

The Recover procedure in FileMaker Pro 10 provides improved feedback and also gives you access to a comprehensive log of the results of each part of the Recover procedure. In this respect, you have considerably improved information about the process and the likely state of the resulting recovered file(s).

CROSS-REF   For additional information about file recovery, refer to Chapter 17.

Layout Mode Enhancements

There have been several changes in FileMaker Pro 10 that affect Layout mode, making it easier to use than in previous versions. One small but useful change is the inclusion of the Manage Layouts command in the Manage submenu of the File menu. This placement means that (among other things) you can now access the Manage Layouts dialog — and from there, the Layout Setup dialog — without first going to Layout mode. In addition, when you are in Layout mode, the menu of layouts on the Layout bar (the lower section of the Status Toolbar) includes the Manage Layouts command at the top of the menu, above the first layout.

Inserting an object into the tab order

Additionally, FileMaker Pro 10 provides you with the ability to insert a layout object into the middle of the tab-through order on a layout. This enhancement addresses a long-standing irritation among many developers, as in the past it was necessary to manually reassign tab sequence numbering to all the layout objects following the inserted object.

To insert an object into the middle of an existing tab order, you simply enter the new object position number for the object in question. If the number you enter conflicts with the sequential number of an existing object in the tab order, the tab order will be automatically resequenced to accommodate the change. For example, if your layout has a tab order that touches a total of 50 objects and you decide to move the 38th object to occupy the 12th position in the tab order, you can do so by simply entering "12" for the 38th object. When you do, the objects previously numbered 12 through 37 are automatically renumbered to positions 13 through 38 in the tab order.

In the same way, you can move an object forward in the tab order, and the subsequent numbers will be moved back to ensure continuity, saving you considerable time and frustration when editing the tab order on layouts that have more than a handful of fields in the tab order.

Defining tooltips in Pro

In the past, mouse-over tooltips were visible in both FileMaker Pro and FileMaker Pro Advanced. However, you could define or edit tooltips only in FileMaker Pro Advanced. However with the advent of FileMaker Pro 10, you can also specify and edit tooltips in FileMaker Pro.

To add or edit tooltips for a layout object in FileMaker Pro, first enter Layout mode, select the object, and then choose Format ⇨ Set Tooltip. The Set Tooltip dialog appears, and you can enter a literal value or a calculation expression to determine the mouse-over tip for the selected object.

Also new in FileMaker Pro 10 is the ability to enable display of Layout mode tooltip icons for objects that have a tooltip attached. When you choose View ⇨ Show ⇨ Tooltips, FileMaker Pro will now add a pale orange note icon at the lower right corner of any layout object that carries a tooltip. (Previously, this view option was available only in FileMaker Pro Advanced.)

Additional font sizes in the format menu

While on the subject of Layout mode (where most of your font formatting likely takes place), I should mention that FileMaker Pro 10 includes 11-point and 13-point sizes in the Format ⇨ Size submenu by default.

This change may not seem like big news until you consider that, previously, developers have had to choose the Format ⇨ Size ⇨ Custom option and enter a custom size into the resulting dialog each and every time an 11-point or 13-point font size was called for. The presence of these commonly used sizes on the menus will save some folk a lot of time.

In addition, FileMaker Pro 10 provides you with menu commands (with associated keyboard shortcuts) to increase and decrease the font size of the currently selected text or active object. The commands are Format ⇨ Size ⇨ Increase Size and Format ⇨ Size ⇨ Decrease Size and the corresponding shortcuts are ⌘+Shift+>/Ctrl+Shift+> and ⌘+Shift+</Ctrl+Shift+< respectively.

Send Mail by SMTP

For many years, it has been possible to have FileMaker pass an outgoing message to the installed (default) e-mail client application. However, exactly how such e-mails are then handled varies between e-mail applications and is outside the scope of the initiating FileMaker action.

In FileMaker Pro 10, you can choose to send an e-mail message either via the e-mail client application or directly via the SMTP server that handles your outgoing mail. When you choose the latter option, FileMaker prompts you to supply sender details, the outgoing SMTP server address, and login credentials, if applicable, as shown in Figure 4.21.

NOTE The setup dialogs and procedure are the same whether the user selects the File ⇨ Send Mail option or whether the Send Mail [ ] script command is used. Moreover, the Send Mail script command can run on the server provided the Via SMTP option is used. In conjunction with scheduled server scripts, the Send Via SMTP option enables you to configure your solutions to handle batch mail operations centrally.

FIGURE 4.21

Providing SMTP server address and credentials to send e-mail directly from FileMaker Pro 10.

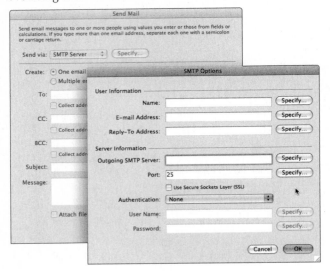

Quick Start Screen Enhancements

The Quick Start screen has had several changes made to it in FileMaker 10. This screen appears when FileMaker Pro is first launched and when you choose File ⇨ New Database command (provided the Show FileMaker Quick Start Screen option has not been disabled in the General tab of the FileMaker Preferences dialog).

As shown in Figure 4.22, the Learn More group of links in the Quick Start screen is arranged into four categories in FileMaker Pro 10. This new arrangement provides ready access to new tutorial materials to provide an introduction to the main features of FileMaker Pro.

FIGURE 4.22

The new organization of the Learn More links on the Quick Start screen FileMaker Pro 10.

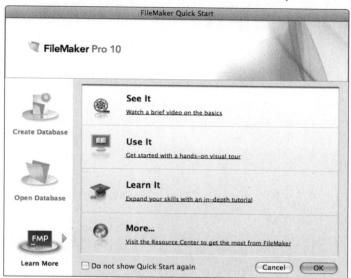

A further change to the Quick Start screen in FileMaker 10 is the inclusion of an additional option in the Create Database tab. As shown in Figure 4.23, a new option to Create a Database from an Existing has been added, with an adjacent pull-down menu providing the following options:

■ Excel 95-2004 workbook (.xls)

■ Excel workbook (.xlsx)

■ Tab Delimited text file

■ Comma Separated Values text file

■ Merge file

■ Bento Source

When you choose the option to create a database file with an existing Excel, Tab delimited, CSV, Merge, or Bento data, FileMaker applies special defaults to create a file with the form (structure) and content of the file you select.

FIGURE 4.23

The additional Quick Start option to create a database from an external file.

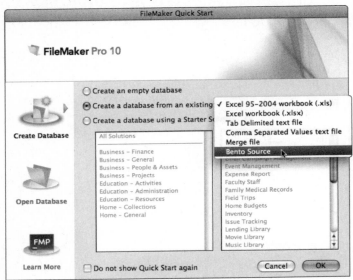

Import/Export Enhancements

The import and export options have undergone a face-lift in FileMaker Pro 10, with arcane and obsolete formats (including VisiCalc, Lotus, Sylk, and dBase DOS) being purged from the menu of supported file options and support for the most recent version of Microsoft Excel being added. In addition to the ability to import from a Bento 2 source (as noted previously) and XML and ODBC imports (also available previously), FileMaker Pro 10 provides you with support for import from the following file types:

- FileMaker Pro Files

- Tab-Separated Text Files

- Comma-Separated Text Files

- Merge Files

- Excel 95 — 2004 Workbooks (`.xls`)

- Excel Workbooks (`.xlsx`)

Similarly, the supported file types for export have been updated and are as follows:

- Tab-Separated Text

- Comma-Separated Text

- Merge
- HTML Table
- FileMaker Pro
- XML
- Excel 95 — 2004 Workbooks (`.xls`)
- Excel Workbooks (`.xlsx`)

You can access these options by choosing File ⇨ Import Records ⇨ File or File ⇨ Export Records commands respectively.

A further significant enhancement of Import and export capabilities in FileMaker Pro 10 is the ability to specify server-side scripts to include the Import Records and Export Records commands. That is, if your solution is hosted on FileMaker Server 10, server-side scripts can perform import and export operations.

TIP In FileMaker Server 10, Server Activated Script Execution (SASE) is able to perform imports and exports.

To underscore the new distinction between commands available for use in different contexts, a new system for filtering available scripting commands has been implemented in the script editing interface. Scripts can be executed now in three environments, and the capabilities of each is different. Hence, FileMaker Pro 10 allows you to select from a Show Compatibility pull-down menu at the lower left of the Edit Script window, as shown in Figure 4.24. When you select the compatibility filters for Server or Web Publishing, script commands that are unavailable in the selected environment appear dimmed in the list of available commands and (where applicable) also in the script definition. Your selection in the Show Compatibility is retained for the duration of your application session in the FileMaker Pro client, but reverts to the default setting (Client) the next time FileMaker Pro is launched.

CAUTION Server compatibility shown in the Edit Script window in FileMaker Pro 10 refers to script commands that are executable in FileMaker Server 10. When you host a FileMaker solution on a different version of FileMaker Server, script compatibility may differ from that shown in FileMaker Pro 10.

NOTE Script steps that can work under SASE in some cases work only with certain configurations of options. For example, the Perform Without Dialog setting is required (because the server can't display a user dialog). When you choose Server from the Show Compatibility pull-down menu and then add a command to your script with settings that are not compatible, it will not appear dimmed in the script definition, but while the unsupported options for the command are in place, FileMaker will append the words NOT COMPATIBLE in parentheses within the arguments for the command.

FIGURE 4.24

Selecting the option to view Server compatible commands in the Edit Script window.

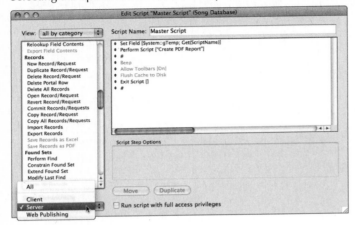

To provide additional support for import and export within SASE, a change to the behavior of the Get(TemporaryPath) function has been made so that it now returns the path to a folder one level deeper than in previous versions. In addition, the temporary path will point to a temporary session folder on the local workstation. The session folder will be automatically created the first time the Get(TemporaryPath) function is evaluated within each FileMaker (client or server) application session. The session folder will be named with a leading S followed by a number assigned by FileMaker to identify the application session.

At the conclusion of the application session (for example, when you quit FileMaker Pro), the temporary files the application has spawned, including the session folder and all its contents, are deleted.

Save Target Printer

When you create a script (or button) that calls the Print[ ] command, you're able to specify print options as one of the arguments for the command, and the resulting configuration dialog allows you to choose (among other things) the target printer for the print operation.

NOTE In previous versions of FileMaker Pro, the identity of the target printer for a scripted print operation was not saved on Mac OS. In Windows, it was saved only if the printer name was 30 characters or less in length.

In FileMaker Pro 10, when you configure the print options for the Print[ ] script or button command, the identity of the target printer is stored with the print settings and reinstated when the command is executed.

In cases where the printer you choose can't be found as the command is (subsequently) executed, or if you don't choose a printer when configuring the Print[ ] command, FileMaker will select the printer that is designated as the default for the current user account on your computer.

The application of the stored printer selection depends on the availability of the selected printer and on the state of the Specify Print Options checkbox for the Print[ ] command. If you have also selected the Perform Without Dialog checkbox, FileMaker will send the print job to the selected printer (or the default printer, if the selected printer is not available). However, if you don't select the Perform Without Dialog checkbox, FileMaker will present the Print dialog with the saved printer pre-selected, if available.

Print options — including the target printer name — are defined separately for each platform. If you define a print command to use a target printer on Mac OS, for example, you'll have to select the print options and choose the printer in Windows as well in order to have the setting work as desired on each platform.

The Manage Scripts Interface

The pull-down menu beside the button labeled New at the lower left of the Manage Scripts window has changed. The option labeled New Script has been replaced by two options, the first being Empty Script and the second being Default Script, as shown in Figure 4.25.

FIGURE 4.25

Accessing the new Default Script option in the Manage Script window.

When you select the Default Script option in FileMaker Pro 10, a new script is created and pre-populated with three script commands for you to use as the basis of your new script. The default steps added to your script are along the lines of the following:

```
Enter Browse Mode [ ]
Go to Layout ["YourCurrentLayout" (CurrentLayoutTable)]
Show All Records
```

Additionally, in Windows, when you open the Manage Scripts window, it opens in a restored state even if the current database window has been maximized — that is, opening Manage Scripts reverts maximized windows to the restored state automatically.

Other Useful Enhancements

By now you've probably concluded that FileMaker Pro 10 is a significant release with a lot of important new features and changes to the behavior of the application. If so, then I am in agreement with you. The inclusion of script triggers alone makes this release a powerhouse of new possibilities. However, while the features I've described in detail earlier in this chapter are what I regard as the highlights of this new version, FileMaker Pro 10 includes a number of other changes that make it more powerful, more flexible, or easier to use. In the closing pages of this chapter, I will take a moment to mention some of the other ways in which this release departs from its predecessors.

IPv6 Support

The Internet is approaching a time when IP addresses conforming to the prevailing standard (IPv4) will be exhausted. In fact, some projections suggest that this is likely to occur within the coming two years. The answer is a move to lengthier IP addresses by using the IPv6 format (which is 128 bits long, as compared to 32 bits for IPv4 addresses).

When FileMaker Pro 10 is running in an IPv6 network, functions such as Get (SystemIPAddress) and Get (HostIPAddress) that return an IP address will return IPv6 addresses. Moreover, it's now possible to enter IPv6 addresses in dialogs (such as Open Remote and Open URL) that require an IP address.

NOTE On Mac OS, the Send Mail command, when configured to use SMTP, is not compatible with IPv6. In Windows, however, IPv6 can be used to specify the address of the SMTP server for outgoing e-mails.

Format changes for automatically generated log files

All log files created automatically by FileMaker (Conversion.log, Import.log, and Recover.log) now use a tab-delimited format. Moreover, the timestamp format used in FileMaker Pro 10 .log files is now the universal time format adopted for logs generated from FileMaker Server 9. That is, the timestamp includes a reference to the UMT adjustment of the time zone where the computer is located.

Updated templates and themes

If you're content with using templates and premade solutions as the basis of your work, you will be pleased to know that the Starter Solution templates (accessible from the Quick Start screen) have undergone a face-lift in FileMaker Pro 10. There are now 30 starter solutions to choose from, and their layout designs have been improved and modernized.

Similarly, the New Layout Wizard in FileMaker Pro 10 will offer you a clutch of new layout themes that will preformat your new layouts with background colors and fonts to save you a little time dealing with the interface design requirements of your solution.

FileMaker Pro Advanced Script Debugger enhancements

In FileMaker Pro 10 Advanced, the Step button in the Script Debugger has been renamed Step Over, and it acts to dismiss paused states invoked by the current script step. Moreover, after you complete a pause by using the Step Over button, the pause step remains the current step until you click the button once again to advance to the next step.

In addition, the Step Over button executes any scripts triggered by the current step's action, without displaying them in the Debugger. If you want to view and step through any scripts triggered by the current script's actions, use the Step Into button instead.

Relookup Replace and Field Contents no longer commit

When you change a value in a field and then, without taking any action that would commit the record, choose Records ⇨ Replace Field Contents or Records ⇨ Relookup Field Contents, FileMaker performs the requested action (including using the new uncommitted data as the basis of the action on the current record) without committing the current record. Thus, even after the Relookup or Replace action has completed its action across the found set, you will still be able to revert the current record.

Only a single sharing error for multiple files

In FileMaker Pro 10, when you open the first file of a multi-file solution, in the event that a file sharing error occurs (for example, you're presented with a dialog that reads along the lines of "FileMaker cannot share files because..."), the error will be displayed only once regardless of the number of files in the solution you have just opened.

This change will be worth the upgrade fee alone if you have a solution that is comprised of 50 or more files.

Script error codes and control commands

In FileMaker Pro 10, the control steps in scripts no longer clear the error code returned by the Get(LastError) function. This makes good sense because control steps can't themselves generate an error — and it makes it easier to handle errors, because you can test for the error and then handle it without losing access to the error result at the point where you test. The script commands that are affected by this change are

- If [ ]
- Else
- Else If [ ]
- End If
- Loop
- Exit Loop If [ ]
- End Loop
- Exit Script [ ]
- Halt Script

With this change, it will no longer be necessary, in most cases, to commit the Get(LastError) result to a variable (or otherwise store it) before testing — making your scripts shorter, quicker, and easier to write, and a little quicker in execution.

Part II

Introduction to Database Design

An essential part of your journey of discovery with FileMaker Pro involves designing and creating a new database from first principles. In this second part of the *FileMaker Pro 10 Bible*, I invite you to roll up your sleeves and work through the creation of an example Inventory System that will allow you to see procedures in context and to acquire many of the basic skills and techniques you'll need as you begin to work with FileMaker.

In the development of the example solution featured here, you'll start with a completely fresh and empty database file, adding structure and features progressively until, after several chapters, you'll have the basis of a simple working solution. Throughout subsequent chapters and parts of the book, I will refer back to the example commenced here, showing how you can use more complex features and advanced techniques to extend and enhance what you have created.

I invite you to follow along with the practical experience of creating the example as described. However, the book's Web site provides copies of the completed example file from each chapter, so you can download and compare (or simply work directly with) the example file I've provided, if you prefer.

IN THIS PART

Chapter 5
Creating a Database

Chapter 6
The Interface: Layout Mode

Chapter 7
The Structure: The Manage Database Dialog

Chapter 8
The Processes: FileMaker Scripting

Chapter 5

Creating a Database

I n Part I, I provide you with broad background information concerning databases, their uses, and FileMaker Pro and its role. I introduce you to many of the terms and concepts that I feature throughout this book. Much of the information thus far has been theoretical rather than practical — but that's about to change, so roll up your sleeves. To jump-start you into the hands-on creation of databases, in this chapter I walk you through the creation of an example database that illustrates many basic techniques and that is developed further in subsequent chapters to explore alternative approaches and more advanced techniques.

IN THIS CHAPTER

Creating an empty database

Working with data

Making sure you avoid duplicating data

Keeping your files secure

Considering usability

Before Getting Started

You need to consider several things before you proceed with the example that follows:

- The completed example file for this chapter is available from the book's companion Web site (see Appendix B) at www.wiley. com/go/filemaker10bible so that you can follow along if you like or download the completed example and review it if you prefer. Either way, the files available on the Web site provide you with a point of reference.

- Although the procedures described in this chapter are lengthy, you can stop and exit FileMaker at any point and then open the files again and resume later. If you're new to FileMaker, you may want to take a break or two along the way.

- The database techniques I describe here are equally applicable to many other kinds of solutions. Although I walk you through a specific example, I assume that you'll be able to transfer what you learn here and apply it within the context of your own solutions.

- The example discussed here isn't offered as a complete solution for any particular need or as an exhaustive representation of techniques for managing inventory. Rather, it's a vehicle to introduce a variety of useful concepts, skills, and methods, and to get you thinking about the ways FileMaker Pro enables you to solve a variety of problems you'll encounter in your own solutions.

As I indicate in Chapter 3, the Quick Start window that appears when you first launch FileMaker, or when you choose File ➪ New Database, includes lists of Starter Solutions. These Starter Solutions provide ready-made files for a range of common purposes. However, the real strength of FileMaker Pro is that it gives you the ability to custom build a solution to meet your own needs. If a ready-made, one-size-fits-all solution were all you needed, then you could probably have found a suitable shareware solution for a few dollars, and you wouldn't be reading this book.

Starter Solutions, then, are what you might use on occasions when you don't want to create a new database file (that is, when you're happy to simply use or adapt a solution that somebody else has created for you). Here, however, I lead you through the process of creating your own database from scratch, working through several stages of development to arrive at a workable and useful solution.

The example I've chosen for this exercise is the creation of a simple system to keep track of inventory. Although this is only one of the many situations where databases are useful, it clearly illustrates many of the challenges you'll encounter when building your own solutions. In fact, an inventory system that tracks products and sales has a lot in common with many other kinds of solutions, such as a school solution that tracks students and courses or a research laboratory database that tracks samples and test results. Consequently, the techniques I cover in this chapter and throughout this book are applicable to many of the challenges you'll encounter when creating your own solutions, even though the names of the things you're tracking may be different.

Creating a New Database File

To get started, follow these steps:

1. Launch FileMaker Pro 10 and wait until the Quick Start screen appears. If FileMaker is already running (and the Quick Start screen isn't on display), choose File ➪ New Database to begin.

2. In the Quick Start screen, confirm that the Create Database icon is selected at the left, select the Create an Empty Database radio button (see Figure 5.1), and click OK.

3. You're prompted to select a location to save the file and to supply a name. I suggest that you name the file `Inventory.fp7` and that you save the file to the Documents folder on a Mac or the My Documents folder in Windows. The database is created, its window appears, and the Manage Database for "Inventory" dialog (shown in Figure 5.2) appears.

TIP The example file developed according to the procedures set out in this chapter (available from the book's companion Web page at the link you'll find in Appendix B) is named `Inventory_Ch05.fp7`.

NOTE All the files you create should be given an `.fp7` suffix because that's the extension used by your computer's operating system to associate files with the FileMaker Pro application.

FIGURE 5.1

Creating an empty database from FileMaker's Quick Start Screen.

When you create a new file in the manner just described in the preceding steps, FileMaker creates a single default table with the same name as the first part of the filename — in this case "Inventory." It then opens the Manage Database dialog to the Fields tab with the default table selected, ready for you to begin adding fields to this new empty database. (A database is not much use without fields in which you can store your data.)

FIGURE 5.2

The new file, showing the Manage Database for "Inventory" dialog, ready to begin.

Adding tables and fields

Your new file is ready and waiting for you to create some fields — and nothing could be easier. To begin, follow these steps:

1. Check that the cursor is in the Field Name box and type the name **Serial#** for the first field.

2. From the Type menu (at the right of the Field Name box), select Number and click the Create button near the lower left of the dialog. A line appears at the top of the list of fields, showing the field that you've just created.

> **TIP** You can use the keyboard to choose the Type for a field: ⌘+T or Ctrl+T for Text, ⌘+N or Ctrl+N for Number, and so on (as you can see when the Type menu is open).

3. Repeat Steps 1 and 2 to create four additional fields, setting each as Text in the Type menu and naming these additional fields: ItemID, Name, Description, and SupplierID.

4. Create two Number fields called Cost and SalePrice, respectively. The dialog should now resemble the one shown in Figure 5.3. Above the list of fields, it shows the name of the table (Inventory) and number of fields (7), and the list of fields displays the name and type of each field in the order in which you entered them.

> **TIP** I recommend that you leave spaces out of field names and, instead, start each new word with a capital letter. This practice is sometimes known as camel case, because of the shape of the word forms it produces, or as intercapping. Alternatively, if you prefer, you can use underscore charactersrather than spaces.
>
> Although FileMaker permits spaces in field names, some other technologies don't (Web and ODBC, for example). So one reason for omitting spaces is that you may need to pass data to another application or environment at some point. Omitting spaces also makes field names slightly shorter, which may be visually convenient in some situations (such as when viewing lists of field names in narrow dialogs).

FIGURE 5.3

Creating fields in the Fields tab of the Manage Database for "Inventory" dialog.

After you enter the first few fields, you've created the basis for a single table in your new file — a place to store some data. However, to make this into a useful solution, you need additional tables to store information about what happens to each of the items listed in the main table. Because this is an inventory solution, its purpose is not simply to list the various kinds of items on hand, but to allow you to record where they come from and when, what they cost, where they go to, and how many of each you have.

Therefore, to provide the basic framework for tracking inventory items, you need to record arrivals of items, departure of items, and their source and destination. At this stage, I propose that you add five more tables to start this example file. To create the additional tables, follow these steps:

1. Navigate to the Tables tab of the Manage Database for "Inventory" dialog by clicking the leftmost tab along the top of the dialog. In the Tables tab, a single table named `Inventory` appears in the list — this is the default table (named according to the name of the file) that FileMaker creates with a new file. The Details column of the Tables list shows that the Inventory table has seven fields (these are the seven fields you just created on the Fields tab) and zero records.

2. Check that the cursor is in the Table Name box (at the lower left of the Tables tab) and type the name `Orders` for the second table.

3. Click the Create button. Two lines are displayed in the list of tables — the original Inventory table, plus the `Orders` table you've just created.

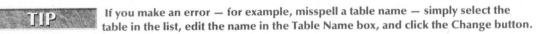

TIP   If you make an error — for example, misspell a table name — simply select the table in the list, edit the name in the Table Name box, and click the Change button.

4. Repeat Steps 2 and 3 to add four more tables to the file, naming them `OrderLines`, `Invoices`, `InvoiceLines`, and `Contacts`, respectively. The dialog now resembles the one shown in Figure 5.4, with the annotation above the tables list reading "6 tables defined in this file."

Now that you have six tables, you're ready to add some appropriate fields to each of them. To accomplish this, you need to select each of the new tables in turn on the Manage Database dialog's Fields tab. Alternatively, from the Tables tab, you can select a table and view the corresponding Fields tab by double-clicking its entry in the list of tables. When you're on the Fields tab, you can move between different tables by selecting them from the Table menu at the upper left of the Fields tab.

Follow these steps:

1. Select the `Orders` table on the Fields tab, using the same procedure you followed when adding fields to the Inventory table (as described earlier in this section).

2. Add a Number field called `Serial#`, a Text field called `OrderID`, a Date field called `OrderDate`, a Text field called `SupplierID`, and a Number field called `Shipping`.

3. Move through the remaining four tables, creating fields with name and field type as outlined in the following tables.

OrderLines

Serial#	Number
OrdLineID	Text
OrderID	Text
Qty	Number
ItemID	Text
Price	Number

Invoices

Serial#	Number
InvoiceID	Text
InvoiceDate	Date
BuyerID	Text
Shipping	Number

InvoiceLines

Serial#	Number
InvLineID	Text
InvoiceID	Text
Qty	Number
ItemID	Text
Price	Number

Contacts

Serial#	Number
ContactID	Text
Title	Text
FirstName	Text
LastName	Text
Organization	Text
AddressLine1	Text
AddressLine2	Text
City	Text
State	Text
PostalCode	Text
ContactType	Text
SupplierID	Text
BuyerID	Text
SupplierID	Text
BuyerID	Text

You've now created a basic set of data fields in each of your tables. These data fields will provide places to enter information that will accumulate, providing you with a history of items. However, there are still several additional steps to complete before your new file's data structure will be truly useful.

> **TIP** If you want to take a break and continue at a later time, simply click OK to dismiss the Manage Database dialog. Then you can close the `Inventory` file and quit FileMaker Pro. When you reopen the file to continue, choose File ⇨ Manage Database to take up where you left off.

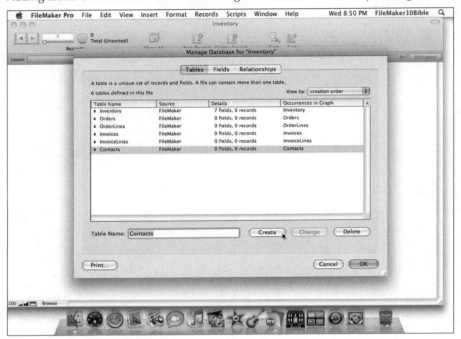

FIGURE 5.4

Adding tables on the Tables tab of the Manage Database for "Inventory" dialog.

Working with the Field Options dialog: Validation and Auto-Entry

Some of the information required in each record in the tables you've created is routine enough that FileMaker can create it for you. The first field in each table is a serial number — a good candidate for automatic data entry. To begin setting up some automation of this kind, use the Table menu near the upper left of the Fields tab in the Manage Database dialog to return to the list of fields for the Inventory table. Then follow these steps:

1. In the `Inventory` table field list, select the first line — the one showing the Serial# field — and then click the Options button. The Options for Field "Serial#" dialog appears.

TIP   You can also invoke the Options for Field dialog by double-clicking a field in the list or by selecting the field and then using the ⌘+O (Ctrl+O) keyboard shortcut.

When the Options for Field dialog appears, it displays the first of four tabs, showing a group of controls under the heading Auto-Enter (see Figure 5.5). The Auto-Enter options available on this panel include the capability to generate data in various ways; however, on this occasion, the option you require is an automatic serial number for each record.

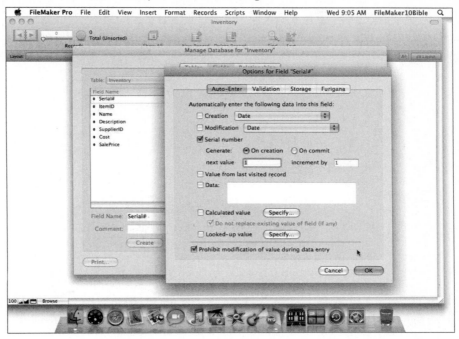

FIGURE 5.5

The Auto-Enter tab of the Options for Field dialog.

2. To set automatic serialization of the Serial# field, follow these steps:

   ■ Select the Serial Number checkbox.

   ■ Leave Generate set to the default On Creation.

   ■ Make sure that Next Value and Increment By are both set to 1.

   ■ Select the Prohibit Modification of Value during Data Entry checkbox.

   When configured, the dialog should resemble the one pictured in Figure 5.5.

3. Click OK to accept the settings and dismiss the dialog. When the Options for Field dialog is closed and you're back in the Manage Database for "Inventory" dialog, the Options/ Comments column of the field list includes the details of the settings you've applied to the Serial# field. If you completed this step correctly, beside the Serial# field it will say Auto Enter Serial, Can't Modify Auto. If it doesn't say this, you've missed a step, and you need to return to the Options for Field dialog to rectify it.

The next field in the Inventory table is named ItemID and has been defined as a text field. At this point, you may be wondering why I've suggested that you create both a serial number field and a separate ID field. This is because for some purposes a numeric serial is useful, while for other purposes a text identifier is preferable. So as a matter of course, it's good practice to create both at the outset for each table. Doing so gives you choices and flexibility later on. Similarly, even in cases where other record identifiers (such as Social Security numbers or license numbers) are available, a separately issued and controlled primary key value is still a good idea because it makes your database more resistant to problems arising from duplicate values, data entry errors, and other mishaps.

CROSS-REF   **For a more detailed discussion of the use of serial and text values as primary record identifiers (keys), refer to the section on alternative relationship techniques in Chapter 11.**

To tie the values of the first two fields together, I recommend that the ID field be based on the Serial number field. That way, you can be confident that the two will never fall out of step — and knowing one, you'll be able to infer the value of the other. Follow these steps:

1. Select the `ItemID` field and click the Options button. The Options for Field "ItemID" dialog appears.

2. Select the Calculated Value checkbox in the Auto-Enter panel. Another dialog appears, prompting you to specify what the calculated value should be. Shortly, I discuss the use of this dialog in more detail. For now, just place the cursor in the main text area in the lower part of the dialog and enter the following formula:

```
SerialIncrement("ITM00000"; Serial#)
```

With the formula in place, the Specify Calculation dialog should look like the one shown in Figure 5.6.

CROSS-REF   **For in-depth explorations of the creation and use of calculations, such as the one shown here, refer to Chapters 7 and 12.**

NOTE   **What this particular calculation does is create IDs consisting of "ITM" followed by the serial number, with the numeric portion of the ID padded, if necessary, by leading zeroes to guarantee ItemIDs of at least eight characters in length.**

3. Click OK to accept the formula and dismiss the Specify Calculation dialog. You're now back at the Options for Field "ItemID" dialog.

4. Enable the Prohibit Modification of Value during Data Entry checkbox and click OK to apply the selected options. In the list of fields showing in the Manage Database dialog, you should now see, in the Options/Comments area adjacent to the `ItemID` field, Auto Enter Calculation, Can't Modify Auto. If you don't see this, retrace your steps to ensure that you've completed the procedure as outlined.

TIP   **If you haven't entered the formula exactly as it is shown in Step 2 of this list, or if your field names don't match the ones I've indicated, an error dialog will prevent you from closing the Specify Calculation dialog. If that occurs, check the formula and make sure that the field names used match the names of the fields as you entered them in the Manage Database dialog.**

FIGURE 5.6

Specifying the Auto-Entry calculation formula for the ItemID field in the Inventory table.

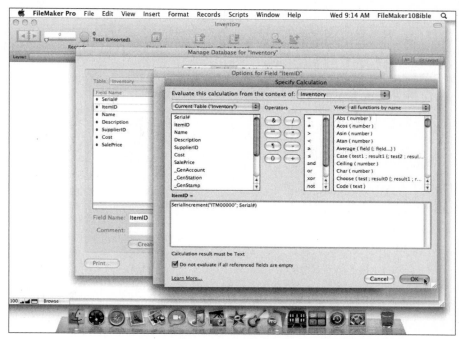

When you successfully complete the preceding set of steps, repeat the process for the first two fields of each table you've created. In each case, however, vary the prefix appearing at the start of the formula for the ID field to provide an appropriate mnemonic for the table in question. I suggest using the following formulas:

Field	Formula
OrderID	SerialIncrement("ORD00000"; Serial#)
OrdLineID	SerialIncrement("OLN0000000"; Serial#)
InvoiceID	SerialIncrement("INV00000"; Serial#)
InvLineID	SerialIncrement("ILN0000000"; Serial#)
ContactID	SerialIncrement("CT00000"; Serial#)

> **NOTE**   Although some of the tables include more than one ID field, only the first ID field in each table — the primary key for the table — should be configured as outlined here.

Now that you've set up the serial and ID fields, the next step is to add validation rules. For example, it makes no sense to add an inventory item without providing a name for it, so it would be appropriate to make the `Inventory::Name` field a required value.

> **NOTE**   The standard convention for referring to a field in FileMaker is to provide the table name, followed by a pair of colons, and then the field name. The table name used for this purpose is the name given to the relevant table reference (usually called a *Table Occurrence* or TO) in FileMaker's Relationships Graph. In a new file, however, the Table Occurrence names default to the same names as the corresponding table (as in case of the `Inventory` TO).

To set up suitable validation for the `Inventory` table's `Name` field, follow these steps:

1. Select the `Inventory` table on the Fields tab of the Manage Database dialog (for example, by selecting Inventory from the Table menu at the upper left of the dialog) and then double-click the Name field. The Options for Field "Name" dialog appears. You want to guarantee that the user enters a name for every item carried in inventory.

2. In the Options for Field "Name" dialog, select the Validation tab and select the Not Empty checkbox.

3. Select the Display Custom Message If Validation Fails checkbox and enter the following message into the text area below it:

   `You are required to enter a name for this item!`

   The dialog should match the one shown in Figure 5.7.

4. When you're satisfied that the configuration is complete, click OK to accept the settings and dismiss the Options for Field dialog. In the Manage Database dialog, you should now see that the Options/Comments column adjacent to the Name field displays the legend Required Value, Allow Override, Message. If you don't see this, retrace your steps to ensure that you haven't omitted anything.

5. Navigate to the field list for the `Contacts` table, select the `ContactType` field, and click the Options button. The Options for Field dialog appears.

6. Click the Validation tab (if it is not already selected) and select the Member of Value List checkbox.

7. Select the Manage Value Lists option from the Member of Value List menu.

8. In the Manage Value Lists for "Inventory" dialog, click the New button. The Edit Value List dialog appears.

9. Enter `ContactType` in the Value List Name box at the top of the dialog.

10. Enter the words `Supplier` and `Buyer` on separate lines within the custom values area at the lower left of the dialog. Figure 5.8 shows how the Edit Value List dialog should now look.

FIGURE 5.7

Specifying validation rules for the Name field in the Inventory table.

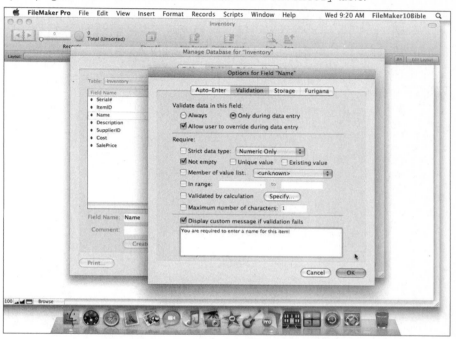

TIP   It is preferable to avoid adding Return/Enter characters after the final entry in your list of values, as trailing returns are hard to see and if you have more than one trailing return, FileMaker will include an extra, empty value in the resulting list.

11. Click OK to accept the settings and dismiss the dialog.

12. Click OK in the Manage Value Lists dialog to accept and dismiss it.

13. Click OK in the Options for Field "Contact Type" dialog to return to the Manage Database dialog.

14. In the field list adjacent to the ContactType field, the text By Value List, Allow Override should now be showing.

You've now established some initial Auto-Entry and validation configurations for the new database. However, some additional settings will depend on creating relationships between the tables, so they can't be added yet. I provide you with instructions for the remaining Auto-Entry options after describing some basic calculation and relationship configurations.

FIGURE 5.8

Creating a value list for validation of the ContactType field.

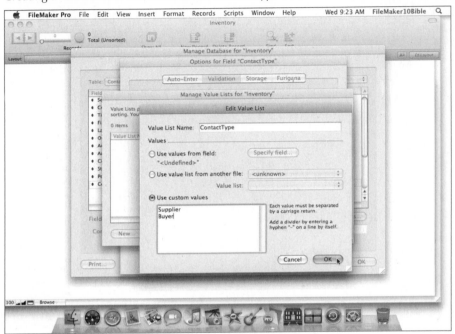

Setting up simple calculations

In addition to automatically entering data into some of the fields, you'll want some data to be calculated from the information you enter. To create such a calculation, follow these steps:

1. Select the `OrderLines` table from the Table menu at the top left of the Manage Database dialog's Fields tab.

2. In the Field Name box, enter `cLineTotal`.

3. From the Type menu select Calculation (⌘+L or Ctrl+L).

4. Click the Create button. The Specify Calculation dialog appears.

> **TIP**   I prepended a lowercase c to the field name so as to be reminded at all times that the field is a calculation field type (that is, it can only acquire information via internal calculation, not by data entry, import, or any other means). Although prepending the lowercase c is not essential, conventions of this sort can prove helpful as your databases become more complex. (In programming terminology, this convention is known as *Hungarian notation* — the use of leading characters in an identifier name to convey data type information.)

CROSS-REF Field naming conventions and other development standards are discussed in greater depth in Chapter 11.

In the Specify Calculation dialog, you see a list of fields at the upper left, a list of functions at the upper right, and, between them, buttons showing mathematical symbols and operators (add, multiply, divide, and so on).

5. Double-click the Qty field in the fields list. It appears in the calculation formula box in the lower part of the dialog.

6. Click the multiplication symbol button (*).

7. Double-click the Price field in the fields list. You should see a complete formula in the calculation area, as follows (see Figure 5.9):

```
Qty * Price
```

8. When you confirm that the formula is correct, click OK to accept and dismiss the Specify Calculation dialog. The Type and Options/Comments columns adjacent to the new cLineTotal field should now show:

```
Calculation        = Qty * Price
```

FIGURE 5.9

Specifying a calculation formula for the cLineTotal field in the OrderLines table.

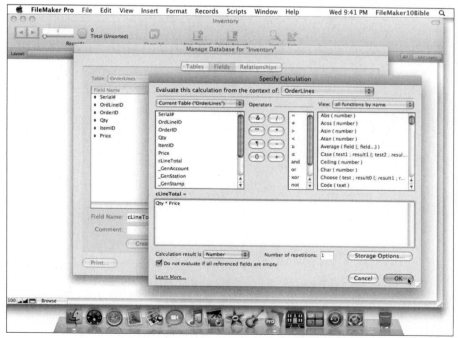

> **NOTE** The calculation you just created is an instruction to multiply the quantity by the price. In other words, the number found in the quantity field will be multiplied by the number found in the price field on each record to return a total for that record. Although you selected the field names from a list, you could have typed them in if you knew what they were.

Although this is a very straightforward computation performing a very simple math operation, the calculation capabilities of FileMaker are extensive, as you discover in later chapters. Many forms of manipulation and formatting of numbers, text, dates, times, and other data types are possible.

9. Now repeat Steps 2 through 8 to create a cLineTotal field along similar lines (same field name and same formula) in the InvoiceLines table.

> **TIP** If you're using FileMaker Pro 10 Advanced, you don't have to repeat the procedure to create a line total calculation in the InvoiceLines table. Instead, you can copy and paste the field from the OrderLines table. Copying and pasting of fields in the Manage Database dialog is not available in FileMaker Pro 10, although nothing is stopping you from copying the formula from the calculation dialog for a field in one table and pasting it into the calculation dialog for a field in a different table.

10. Using a variation on the technique described in steps 3 through 8, go to the Contacts field list, select the SupplierID field, and call up the Options dialog.

11. On the Auto-Entry tab, select the Calculated Value checkbox. The Specify Calculation dialog appears.

12. Enter the following formula and click OK:

    ```
    If(PatternCount(ContactType; "Supplier"); ContactID)
    ```

13. Uncheck the Do Not Replace Existing Value of Field (If Any) checkbox and click OK. This ensures that the Supplier ID value will only exist if the contact is listed as a supplier.

> **NOTE** In FileMaker Pro's calculation syntax, a conditional expression is of the form If (condition; then-clause; else-clause) where the then clause is executed when the condition is true and the optional else clause is executed when the condition is false. Therefore, in the foregoing example, if the character string "Supplier" is present in the ContactType field, the ContactID is placed in the SupplierID field; otherwise, the field's value is left empty.

14. Repeat Steps 10 through 13 for the BuyerID field, this time entering the formula

    ```
    If(PatternCount(ContactType; "Buyer"); ContactID)
    ```

    With both of these formulae in place, a contact can be either a supplier or a buyer, depending on the value entered into the ContactType field.

15. Create a calculation field called cFullName in the Contacts table with the formula

    ```
    FirstName & " " & LastName
    ```

16. Set the calculation result type for the cFullName field to Text by using the Calculation Result Is menu near the lower left of the Specify Calculation dialog and click OK. This calculation brings together the text elements of the name on each record, for convenient display in lists and reports.

Capturing simple metadata

As part of the process of tracking what's happening with your data, it's often helpful to have some additional fields that store reference information. This information can assist you in troubleshooting a problem, if you need to compare two versions of a database file, or if you need to synchronize two copies of your data.

To facilitate such tracking, follow these steps:

1. Return to the field list for the Inventory table (on the Fields tab of the Manage Database dialog) and create a new text field called _GenAccount. This field will be used to track the account associated with the genesis (or generation, if you prefer) of each record. Note that I am suggesting an underscore prefix for your metadata fields to ensure that they're easily separated visually from other fields in your tables.

2. Double-click the _GenAccount field. The Options dialog appears.

3. Select the Creation checkbox, located near the top left of the Auto-Enter tab.

4. Using the menu to the right of the Creation checkbox, choose the Account Name option.

5. Select the Prohibit Modification of Value during Data Entry checkbox, located at the lower left of the dialog. The dialog settings should match those shown in Figure 5.10.

FIGURE 5.10

Configuring a field to automatically capture the creation login account for each record.

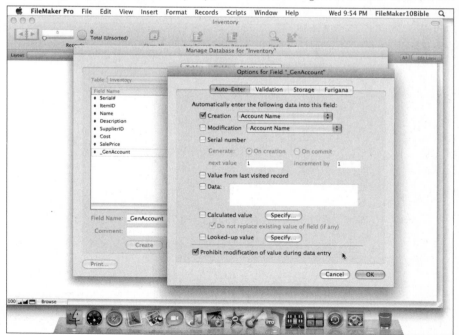

6. Click OK to accept the settings and confirm that the Options/Comments field adjacent to the _GenAccount field says Creation Account Name, Can't Modify Auto.

7. Create two more fields — a text field named _GenStation to capture the name associated with the workstation where each record is created and a timestamp field named _GenStamp to capture the date and time of record creation. Configure options for these two additional fields similarly to the _GenAccount field; however, when selecting from the Creation menu, choose the Name and TimeStamp options, respectively.

> **NOTE** A timestamp is a value generated by FileMaker, combining both date and time in a single value. It is a compact and efficient way to track sequences of events spanning days or even years.

8. Now that you've defined your three _Gen fields in the Inventory table, proceed along similar lines to create three fields capturing the modification account name, workstation, and timestamp. I suggest you name these fields _ModAccount, _ModName, and _ModStamp, respectively. When setting the options for each _Mod field, select the Modification checkbox and choose the associated value from the adjacent menu. When you've completed this process, the field list for the Inventory table should match the one shown in Figure 5.11.

9. Repeat the process outlined in Steps 1 through 8 to add a basic complement of metadata fields to each of the tables in your new database.

FIGURE 5.11

The Inventory table field list, including six metadata fields.

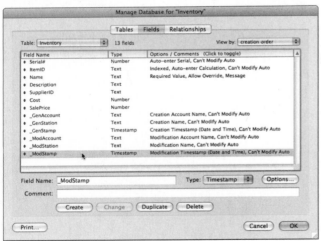

Creating relationships between tables

Although you've added six tables and defined a number of fields in each table, they aren't yet connected in any way. In practice, you'll employ a simple mechanism to associate each record with its related records in other tables. That's where relationships come in — links created in a visual environment referred to as the *Relationships Graph*.

To access the Relationships Graph for your `Inventory` file, click the Manage Database dialog's Relationships tab. You're presented with a series of boxes — one for each table — containing lists of the fields you have defined. These boxes are referred to as Table Occurrences (TOs). The default TO for each table has a header area containing, initially, the name of the table to which it refers. (The default TO names can subsequently be changed if desired.) You can drag the TOs around by their header bars to position them more conveniently.

In order to create relationships between tables, you point the mouse at a field in one TO, click and drag to a corresponding field in another TO, and then release. A line representing the relationship is created.

One of the relationships you'll need is an association between order lines and their corresponding order. To create this relationship, locate the TOs for `OrderLines` and `Orders` (if necessary, reposition them so that they're adjacent to each other) and then drag a line between the `OrderID` field in each, as shown at Figure 5.12.

FIGURE 5.12

Using the mouse to "drag" a relationship between the `Orders` and `OrderLines` TOs.

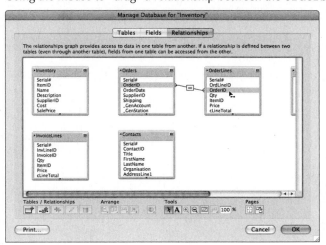

By default, when you create a relationship in this manner, FileMaker sets up the simplest kind of relationship — one where records will be related if the value in the two fields used for the join is the same in both tables. This kind of relationship is called an *equi-join* and is represented by the = sign that appears on the box that bisects the line between the two tables.

CROSS-REF You can find a detailed discussion of different kinds of relationships and their uses in Chapter 11.

The default equi-join relationship is suitable for the join between Orders and OrderLines; however, an additional setting is required. Double-click the box containing the equal sign to bring up the Edit Relationship dialog. As you can see in Figure 5.13, the two tables that the relationship joins are listed on either side of the dialog, with corresponding settings and options listed below. On the side of the dialog where the OrderLines table appears, select the Allow Creation of Records in This Table via This Relationship checkbox.

Similarly, you'll require a relationship between the Invoices and InvoiceLines TOs, so drag a line between the InvoiceID fields in those two TOs and edit the relationship, selecting the checkbox option allowing creation of records in the InvoiceLines table via the relationship.

So far, I've only been working with the default TOs for the six tables in the file. At this point, I need to ensure that the graph reflects the fact that Contacts can be suppliers or buyers — and a way to do this is to represent the Contacts table multiple times on the Relationships Graph. Similarly, I need to monitor orders and invoices to track items purchased and sold. To implement this, proceed as follows:

1. Select the Contacts table's TO and click twice on the third button from the left below the Graph window. (The button bears a double-plus symbol in green.) Two duplicates of the Contacts TO, called Contacts 2 and Contacts 3, respectively, are created.

2. Double-click the Contacts TO. The Specify Table dialog appears.

3. In the Name field, change the name to Suppliers and then click OK.

4. Repeat Step 2, changing the Contacts 2 TO to ItemSupplier and then changing the Contacts 3 TO to **Buyers**.

5. Drag a line from the SupplierID field in the Orders TO to the SupplierID in the Suppliers TO. Similarly, drag a line from the BuyerID field in the Invoices TO to the BuyerID field in the Buyers TO.

NOTE If the fields you're dragging relationship lines between aren't visible in the TOs, you can either scroll the field view in the TO by clicking the arrow at the bottom center of the TO or enlarge the TO by dragging its bottom border downward until the desired fields are visible.

6. Drag a line from the SupplierID field in the Inventory table to the SupplierID field in the ItemSupplier TO.

7. To Select the OrderLines and InvoiceLines TOs and click the double-plus button to duplicate them.

FIGURE 5.13

Configuring the relationship to allow creation of related records in the `OrderLines` table.

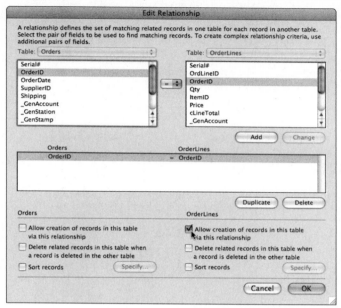

8. Repeat Steps 2 and 3, renaming the `OrderLines` TO duplicate (`OrderLines 2`) to `ItemsPurchased` and the `InvoiceLines` TO (`InvoiceLines 2`) duplicate to `ItemsSold`.

9. Draw lines from the `Inventory` TO's `ItemID` field to the `ItemID` field in the `ItemsPurchased` TO, and from the `Inventory` TO's `ItemID` field to the ItemID field in the `ItemsSold` TO (see Figure 5-14).

TIP When you have created multiple TOs assigned to the same base table, as in Steps 1 and 7 of the preceding instructions, it can be helpful to assign a color to each base table and color each TO according to the base table it points to. You can assign a color to a TO by selecting it and choosing a color from the color palette that appears among the tools along the bottom of the Relationships tab of the Manage Database dialog.

After completing these steps, I enlarged the Manage Database dialog and arranged and colored the TOs so that it's easy to see at a glance what's going on. The result is shown in Figure 5.14. As you can see, three separate groups of related tables are now supporting distinct functions (inventory, ordering, and invoicing).

FIGURE 5.14

Arrangement of the Relationships Graph into three distinct Table Occurrence groups.

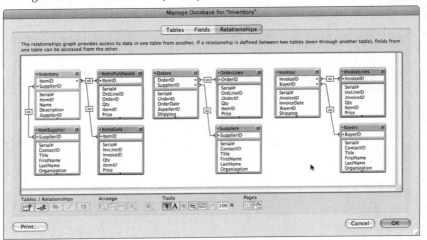

Adding aggregating calcs

When your file has a suitable relationship structure, some additional calculation capabilities become available, enabling you to draw on data from related tables.

To begin setting up aggregating calculations, navigate to the Inventory table on the Manage Database dialog's Fields tab and create a calculation field called cStockLevel, entering the formula

```
0 + Sum(ItemsPurchased::Qty) - Sum(ItemsSold::Qty)
```

Make sure that the Calculation Result Is menu, at the lower left of the Calculation dialog, is set to Number and that the Do Not Evaluate If All Referenced Fields Are Empty checkbox is deselected and then click OK to accept the calculation settings. With this calculation in place, FileMaker subtracts the total number of sales of a given item from the total number of orders for the item to automatically determine how many of each item remain. The Specify Calculation dialog for this procedure is shown in Figure 5.15.

> **NOTE** The leading zero in the calculation provided in the preceding formula may appear redundant, but its inclusion ensures that FileMaker is able to return a value even if no records are in either the ItemsPurchased or ItemsSold tables.

FIGURE 5.15

A calculation using relationships to determine aggregate stock levels.

Next, navigate to the Orders table on the Fields tab of the Manage Database dialog and add a calculation field called cOrderTotal, entering the formula:

```
Sum(OrderLines::cLineTotal) + Shipping
```

Again, confirm that the calculation result menu is set to Number and then click OK to confirm the settings and dismiss the dialog.

Similarly, navigate to the fields list of the Invoices table and add a calculation field called cInvoiceTotal with the formula

```
Sum(InvoiceLines::cLineTotal) + Shipping
```

Check that the result is Number and click OK to accept the dialog.

Next, you instruct FileMaker to retrieve pricing information for the `OrderLines` table from the Inventory table as follows:

1. Choose the fields list for the `OrderLines` table.

2. Double-click the `Price` field. The Options dialog appears.

3. Select the Auto-Enter tab and select the Looked-Up Value checkbox near the bottom of the dialog. The Lookup for Field "Price" dialog appears.

4. From the Starting with Table menu, choose the `ItemsPurchased` TO.

5. From the Lookup from Related Table menu, choose Inventory.

6. Select the `Cost` field from the list at the lower left.

The completed settings for this dialog are shown in Figure 5.16. When the settings are in place, click OK to accept the Lookup dialog and click OK again to confirm the settings for the `OrderLines::Price` field.

FIGURE 5.16

Configuring a lookup to retrieve the cost price of items from the `Inventory` table.

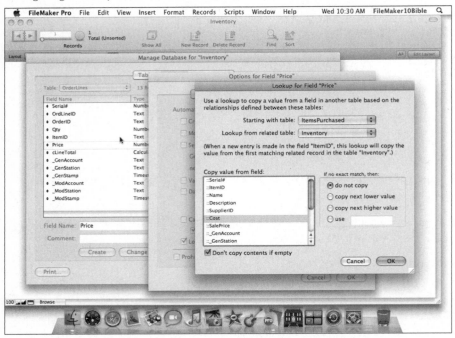

Choose the field list for the InvoiceLines table and repeat Steps 2 through 6 for the InvoiceLines::Price field, configuring the lookup to start from the ItemsSold TO. From the list of fields to copy, select the SalePrice field.

NOTE With these lookups in place, when you select an item for an order or invoice, FileMaker automatically enters the price for you, saving time and increasing the accuracy of your work.

At this point, the initial structure of an inventory system is in place, so click OK to save your work and exit to the new file. When you do, FileMaker creates an initial default layout for each of the tables you created in the file, plus a record in the first (Inventory) table. On first leaving the Manage Database dialog (if you followed my instructions regarding field validations), because the Inventory table has been set to require a name for each item, you'll be prompted to enter an item name before leaving the first record. Enter the name of an item (for example, CD-ROMs) so that you can exit the record and take a look around the file.

NOTE If you took a break and closed the Manage Database dialog before setting up field validations in the Inventory table, you won't see a prompt when you close the dialog at this point.

TIP Instead of entering an item name to satisfy the validation requirement, you can alternatively choose Records ⇨ Revert Record to reverse the creation of the Inventory table record, or you can click the No button on the validation message dialog to override the validation.

Viewing and Interacting with Data

When you first exit the Manage Database dialog, the layouts created by default are very basic — they simply present a list of the fields created, table by table, arranged one above the next in the order in which they occur in the table's list of fields. There is no logical grouping of similar elements (for example, the parts of an address); the layout is unadorned white on white, and the only visual cues are field names positioned to the left of the fields. Nevertheless, you have a sufficient basis to begin entering some initial data and testing the auto-enter fields, validation criteria, and the defined calculations.

Before proceeding, you might find it helpful to take a quick tour of the layouts in the file (selecting each in turn from the Layout menu at the lower left of the Status Toolbar). Note that as you navigate among the layouts, the Status Toolbar indicates that there are presently no records in any of the tables but the first (Inventory).

Looking at the multiple uses of layouts

It's worth pausing again to note that FileMaker layouts are a multipurpose tool. They provide screens for viewing, entering, and editing the data within records, but they also provide options for

List or Table Views and can be configured to provide printed output. Moreover, layouts serve equally well as the query interface when you employ FileMaker's Find mode.

While doing initial tests and familiarizing yourself with the default layouts in the Inventory file, you might find it helpful to consider ways in which the information could be arranged to increase clarity and usability. It won't be long before you begin the process of organizing the information and building the interface for this file.

CROSS-REF   You can find additional details regarding the development of the solution interface in Chapter 6.

Creating records and entering data

In order to test the basic structure that the Inventory file has in place, the first step is to enter some data and observe how the file responds. To complete your preparations for testing, proceed as follows:

1. Navigate to the layout based on the Contacts table (for the moment, it will be called Suppliers — or, if you did not follow earlier directions exactly, it may be called Buyers, or ItemSupplier based on the TO of the same name).

2. Before creating any records, go to the overhead menus and choose View ⇨ Layout Mode and then choose Layouts ⇨ Layout Setup. The Layout Setup dialog appears, providing access to the layout settings.

3. Change the Layout Name to Contacts, shown in Figure 5.17, and click OK to save the change.

TIP   If you exited the Manage Database dialog early in the process of creating tables and TOs (and resumed later to get to this point), a default layout may not have been created based on the Contacts table. In that case, you should now go to Layout Mode and choose Layouts ⇨ New Layout/Report, select Contacts from the Show Records From pull-down menu, enter "Contacts" into the Layout Name field, choose Standard Form as the layout type, and proceed through the layout wizard screens to create a default themed layout with all the fields from the Contacts table on it.

While you are still in Layout mode, double-click the ContactType field. The Field/Control Setup dialog for the ContactType field appears. At the upper left of the dialog, choose Checkbox Set from the Display As menu. Choose ContactType in the Display Values From menu, as shown in Figure 5.18. With the field configured in this way, the user will be presented with a prompt to enter data by selecting from among the values in the value list you defined when setting up the ContactType field's validation rule.

After configuring the control style settings for the ContactType field as indicated, click OK to accept the change and exit the dialog. Then choose View ⇨ Browse mode to see the effects of the changes you've made.

FIGURE 5.17

Editing the layout name in the Layout Setup dialog.

FIGURE 5.18

Attaching the `ContactType` value list to the corresponding field via the Field/Control Setup dialog.

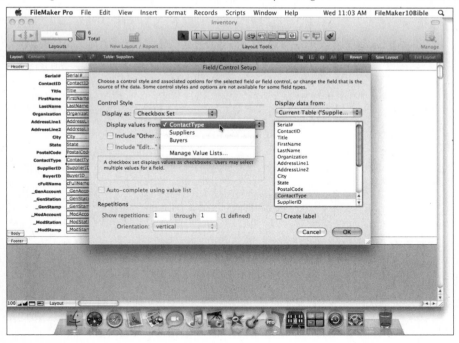

NOTE   When changing mode or navigating to a different layout after making changes to a layout in Layout mode, you may be presented with a dialog prompt to save changes to the layout. If you've selected the option in the Layout tab of FileMaker Preferences dialog to Save Layout Changes Automatically (Do Not Ask), as described in Chapter 3, you won't see the save dialog.

When in Browse mode, choose Records ⇨ New Record and, using the Tab key and/or the mouse to move between fields, enter data into the empty fields. Note that you don't need to use the `AddressLine2` field for most addresses, and that you can't directly fill in the `SupplierID` and `BuyerID` fields — they acquire a value based on the selection in the `ContactType` field.

For testing purposes, the data you enter can be purely fictional — so stretch your imagination and add four or so records to the `Contacts` table, using the `Contacts` layout (by choosing the Records ⇨ New Record command to create each new record in turn and then typing information into the fields). An example `Contacts` record that I entered as described here is shown in Figure 5.19. When entering your test records, add a mix of suppliers and buyers.

FIGURE 5.19

Entering some initial test data into the `Contacts` layout.

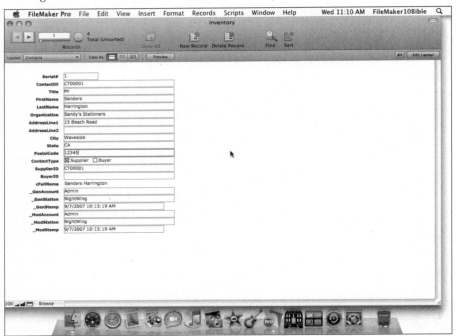

Now that you have some Data in the `Contacts` table, you need to be able to refer to it from elsewhere in the solution. One available option is to create value lists of suppliers and buyers that can be attached to fields on other layouts. To do so, follow these steps:

1. Choose File ➪ Manage ➪ Value Lists to display the Manage Value Lists dialog.

2. Click the New button at the lower left of the dialog. The Edit Value List dialog appears.

3. Type `Suppliers` into the Value List Name box.

4. Select the Use Values from Field radio button. The Specify Fields for Value List "Suppliers" dialog appears, ready for you to configure it, as shown in Figure 5.20.

5. In the Specify Fields for Value List dialog, choose `Suppliers` from the Use Values from First field menu at the upper left. Then locate and select `SupplierID` in the list of fields that appears in the box at the left of the dialog.

6. Select the Also Display Values from Second Field checkbox and locate the Suppliers cFullName field, as shown at Figure 5.20.

FIGURE 5.20

Setting up a value list to display suppliers from the data in the `Contacts` table.

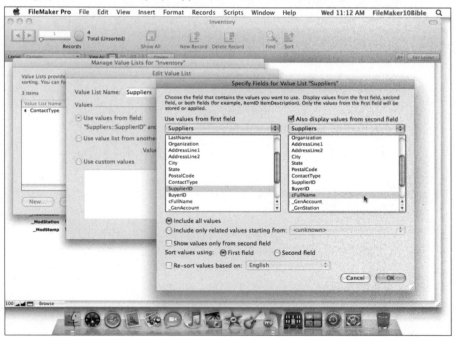

7. When these settings are complete, click OK to exit the Specify Fields for Value List dialog and click OK again to exit the Edit Value Lists dialog.

8. Click the Manage Value Lists dialog's New button again and repeat Steps 3 through 7 to create a Buyers value list, choosing the BuyerID field from the Buyers TO for the first field and the cFullName field (also from the Buyers TO) as the second. When you've created both value lists, click OK to dismiss the Manage Value Lists dialog, saving the changes you made.

9. Navigate to the Inventory layout, choose View➪Layout Mode, and double-click the SupplierID field to invoke the Field/Control Setup dialog.

10. From the Display As menu, select the Drop-Down List option and from the Display Values From menu, select the Suppliers Value List.

11. Click OK to dismiss the Field/Control Setup dialog, and choose View➪Browse Mode.

> **NOTE** FileMaker provides field control options for lists, menus, checkboxes, and radio buttons, giving you alternative methods for selecting field values from a value list. I chose to display the values in a drop-down menu in this instance because a drop-down menu offers maximum user flexibility, works well with lists of differing lengths, and allows you to type a value *or* choose from the list of already existing values.

12. Complete your initial Inventory record by entering values in the Description, SupplierID, Cost, and Sale Price fields. Note that the sale price may include a markup, in line with the practice of buying wholesale and selling at retail prices.

13. After completing the first record, choose Records➪New Record to add several additional Inventory records for testing purposes, completing each with data, either real or fictitious — it doesn't matter for the purposes of the test.

14. Navigate to the Orders layout and create an order record; then go to the OrderLines layout and create a corresponding record, entering the OrderID of the order you have just created, the ItemID for your first inventory item, and a quantity of 20. After you've completed these two records, return to the Orders layout to confirm that the cOrderTotal field is correctly showing the combined price of the 20 items plus shipping.

15. Return to the corresponding Inventory item record in the Inventory layout and confirm that the cStockLevel value is showing 20, which reflects the stock purchase for which you have just entered an order.

16. As a final check, navigate to the Invoices and InvoiceLines layouts and create a record in each, completing them with details for a sale of 5 of the same item for which you have entered an order above.

After completing the InvoiceLines entry, check that the correct total (including shipping) is showing in the Invoices::cInvoiceTotal field, and that the Inventory::cStockLevel field for the first inventory item is now showing 15, reflecting the number of items remaining after you have purchased 20 and sold 5.

During the preceding process, you copied values from layout to layout — not a very efficient way to work — so some additional value lists and interface tools are needed. However, if the various tests have worked, then you've confirmed that the basic structure is operable, and that's enough at this stage. If anything *didn't* work as expected, look back over the process to see what you missed or compare your file to the copy of the file (for this chapter), available from the book's companion Web page at www.wiley.com/go/filemaker10bible, to see what you've done differently.

Editing or deleting data

Now that you have some data accumulating in the Inventory solution, you need to be able to efficiently navigate it and update where necessary, adding, editing, and deleting record and field data. Moreover, you need to know that when you make a change in one part of the solution, it will be reflected elsewhere.

CROSS-REF For an introduction to basic FileMaker navigation techniques, refer to Chapter 3.

Navigate to the test record you entered on the InvoiceLines layout, click in the Quantity field, and change its value from 5 to 3. As you tab or click out of the field, watch to confirm that the InvoiceLines::cLineTotal value updates to reflect the change. Similarly, click in the Shipping field in the Invoices layout, select its value, and make a change — again checking that when you leave the Shipping field, the Invoices::cInvoiceTotal updates to the appropriate new value.

Now that you've changed the number of items sold to 3, the stock level should be 17 rather than 15. Pay a visit to the Inventory layout to confirm that the cStockLevel field is accurately reflecting this change. You might also try switching to the InvoiceLines layout and choosing Records ⇨ Delete Record (you'll be prompted to confirm), and then verify that the stock level appearing on the Inventory layout has returned to 20.

Finding and sorting data you've already entered

In Chapter 3, I describe the workings of the FileMaker Find mechanism. If you haven't already done so, now is a good time to experiment with performing finds on your test data set.

In the Inventory layout, choose View ⇨ Find Mode and enter the first few letters of the name of one of the inventory items in your test data into the Name field. Click the Find button on the Status Toolbar and confirm that FileMaker has located the record matching the Find criteria you entered. If more than one record in your test set included a word in the name field starting with the same characters, confirm that it was also returned as part of the found set after you clicked the Find button.

Because you have a found set in place, try choosing Records ⇨ Show Omitted Only and confirm that the records you're viewing are now the group of items that were *not* found. Choose Records ⇨ Show Omitted Only again, and you'll have swapped back to the original found set. Now choose Records ⇨ Show All Records to cancel the find and bring all the available records back together, noting that as you do so, the text adjacent to the slider on the Status Toolbar updates to reflect the state of the records you're viewing.

When you're viewing multiple records, you may want to sort them so that they display in a predictable order. Unless sorted, records will appear in the order of their creation.

To sort the current found set of records (or all records, if there is no found set at present), choose Records ➪ Sort Records. The Sort Records dialog appears. Select a field in the list of fields at the upper left and click the Move button to add it to the Sort Order list panel at the upper right. If you want to sort by multiple fields, repeat the process to add other fields to the sort order list.

NOTE When sorting by multiple fields, FileMaker sorts the records in the current table by the uppermost value in the sort order. Only if there are multiple records with the same value in the field that is first in the sort order is the next field in the sort order used and then only to determine the presentation order of the records that have the same value in the prior sort field(s).

When sorting by multiple fields, you can alter their precedence in the sort order by dragging them up or down in the list at the upper right. To drag an item, position the mouse pointer over the handle icon appearing to the left of the field name in the sort order list and click and drag it to a new position in the list.

By default, the sequence of values for each field in the sort order will be ascending — for example, from 0 to 99 for numeric values or from A to Z for text values. If you want to modify the presentation order for a particular field in the current sort, select it in the sort order list at the upper right and use the controls in the lower half of the dialog to select an alternative sort method.

When you finish establishing the desired sort order, click the Sort button at the lower right of the dialog to start sorting. When the sorting process is complete, the Status Toolbar will indicate that the records are sorted.

TIP To return the records to their default (creation) order at any time, choose Records ➪ Sort Records or click the Sort icon in the Status Toolbar (the Sort Records dialog appears) and then click the Unsort button at the lower left of the dialog.

Using special find symbols

Searching for a word or number value, as you've just done, is useful but somewhat limited. However, FileMaker presents a range of Find options that extend the scope of searching in various ways.

Choose View ➪ Find Mode and place the cursor in the `Inventory::cStockLevel` field. Now locate the Operators button to access the Symbols menu in the Status Toolbar and click it to bring up FileMaker's menu of built-in Find operators. These symbols alter the way your Find criteria are interpreted. Select the fourth item (less than) from the symbols list and note that a less-than character (<) is placed into the selected field. Now type the numeral 1 into the field after the < symbol. You are requesting that FileMaker locate any inventory items where the stock levels are below 1 (in other words, out of stock).

Click the Find button in the Status Toolbar and confirm that FileMaker locates all test inventory item records for which you have not yet created orders or for which the number of invoices is equal to or greater than the number of orders for the corresponding item.

Searching with the range and wild card operators

Among the special Find operators included in the Find mode's Status Toolbar Operators menu are four worth mentioning of here. The first of these is the Range operator, represented by an ellipsis (...) character.

TIP If you prefer, you can simply type the special Find symbols from the keyboard. In the case of the ellipsis, FileMaker will accept a string of either two or three periods in its place.

Try entering the Find criterion **1...20** into the `Inventory::cStockLevel` field, and note that when you perform the find (for example, by clicking the Perform Find button in the Status Toolbar), FileMaker locates all records that are showing stock levels between 1 and 20, inclusive.

Similarly, FileMaker supports the use of wild card operators in Find mode. Wild cards are special characters that you can use to represent an unknown or unspecified character. The three wild card operators available in FileMaker's Find mode are

- @ One character (either alphabetic or numeric)
- # One digit
- ■ Zero or more characters

As an example, if you enter the criterion `Jo*n` into a text field, FileMaker will locate records that have words such as Joan, John, Jon, or Jordan in that field. If you supply the criterion as `Jo@n`, FileMaker will locate records containing John and Joan, but not Jon or Jordan. I encourage you to experiment with these and other special find operators to become comfortable and practiced with their use.

Avoiding the Need for Data Duplication

If you use paper-based record-keeping systems, or even if you use a spreadsheet or word processor to create and manage invoices, you'll enter the customer details on every invoice — a duplication of effort that is inherently error prone (as well as mind-numbingly tedious and time consuming).

By contrast, the structure of the inventory system under development allows you to store each contact only once in the `Contacts` table and then reference that one record by its ID whenever an item record or a transaction involves that contact. In its present state, however, the database does not show you the related data — you have to take it on faith that when you enter the ID CT00001 on an item record, it creates a link to the corresponding contact record.

Recognizing the visual cues to data relationships

A solution is much more useful if you can see the relationships working and if the data is presented to you in ways that make sense of the connections and data flow. One example of this usefulness is that after you select a `contact` ID for an item record in the `Inventory` layout, you can see brief details of the relevant contact record.

To make the connection between `Inventory` and `Contact` visible, follow these steps:

1. Navigate to the `Inventory` layout and enter Layout mode (click the Edit Layout button at the lower right of the Status Toolbar or choose View ⇨ Layout Mode).

2. Click the `SupplierID` field to select it (it will acquire black selection boxes at each corner) and drag the lower right corner left, reducing the size of the box. It needs to be only about an inch wide to accommodate the ID values it's designed to hold.

3. Click on the Field/Control tool in the Status Toolbar and drag a rectangle on the layout, to the right of the `SupplierID` field. When you release the mouse button, FileMaker draws a new field in the current position and displays the Specify Field dialog.

4. Click the menu near the top of the Specify Field dialog to access a list of available TOs from which to retrieve data for the field you're adding to the layout.

5. Select the `ItemSupplier` TO, as shown in Figure 5.21. With the `ItemSupplier` TO chosen in the Specify Field dialog's menu, the fields from the `Contacts` table appear in the main body of the dialog (each preceded by two colons to indicate that they're located in a different table from the layout's primary table).

6. Click the `cFullName` field to select it, deselect the Create Label checkbox, and click OK to accept the selection.

7. Choose View ⇨ Browse Mode to return to Browse mode.

You've now added the supplier name field from the related record, so selecting a `SupplierID` value immediately displays the corresponding supplier's name. It's important to note that the field you've added simply displays the data located in the corresponding record in the Contacts table. If the Contacts record is edited, the change is automatically reflected on every other record referencing it. Instead of having to manage multiple copies of the same information, keeping them in sync whenever there is a change, the database now manages that for you.

Information has a logical flow

What you've seen so far is that it's possible to create clean demarcations between different types of data, placing each in its own logical group, so that contacts are stored in an ordered way in the Contacts table, items in the Inventory table, and so on. Yet you're able to use the relationships to bring the data together in endless combinations, wherever you need to.

FIGURE 5.21

Selecting a field from a related table to add to the `Inventory` layout.

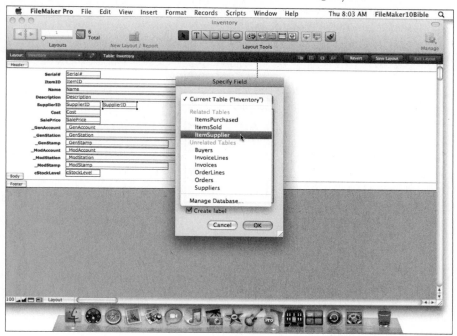

The capability to combine data from different tables without duplicating the data (that is, simply using the relationships to enable you to see the data in its original record) has many advantages and many implications. For example, if a related field is editable, any changes you make when viewing the field from a related table will be stored in the table of origin and will, therefore, be visible everywhere that field appears. If you correct a spelling error in a contact's name, you won't have to find all the items, invoices, or orders referring to that contact and repeat the correction, because the name is stored only once.

The underlying concept driving the approach employed here is one of keeping everything in its proper place. The information about individuals belongs in the `Contacts` table. You refer to it from other places, via relationships, but the information itself stays put in the part of the data structure designed for it.

The key to understanding how you can make the necessary connections is that the relationships you create provide the logic for all information flow in a solution. When setting up relationships, you're defining one or more logical connections between different kinds of "things."

Anticipating the user

When setting up the Inventory file, you defined several Auto-Entry options for fields throughout the structure. In doing so, you are enabling the solution to anticipate the required data in some of the fields. In some cases, the Auto-Entry options are creating information that is not directly useful to the work the user is undertaking — serial numbers, creation timestamp, and so on. However, these items have an essential role in supporting the structure of the database and allowing you to track basic details of the origins of the most recent changes to the data.

The Auto-Entry lookup options you set up for the `OrderLines::Price` and `InvoiceLine::Price` fields don't merely manage solution data; they anticipate the user by looking up and entering the current wholesale or retail price for the item the user has selected. By setting default values and calculated values wherever appropriate, your solution can anticipate users, reducing effort and likelihood of error.

CROSS-REF   **For an in-depth discussion of lookups and when to use them, refer to the section on the subject in Chapter 15.**

Similarly, the data and relationship structure can anticipate the user by grouping information about different kinds of entities and ensuring that each piece of information need be entered only once. This means that you can edit a name or address in the `Contacts` table (or any of the layouts that point to it) and be confident that all references to it are updated. Similarly, it means that you can enter a single value such as `SupplierID`, and all the information on the related `Contact` record becomes available to the current `Item` or `Order` record — no need to enter the address or any other details. They're already there!

To make the relevant contact details visible on the Inventory layout, follow these steps:

1. Return to Layout mode on the `Inventory` layout.

2. Select the `cFullName` field and type ⌘+D or Ctrl+D to duplicate it. The Specify Field list dialog appears.

3. Using the pull-down menu at the top of the dialog, choose the `ItemSupplier` TO and then select the Title field from the list.

4. Repeat the process in Steps 1 through 3 to place copies of the `ItemSupplier::Organization`, `ItemSupplier::AddressLine1`, `ItemSupplier::AddressLine2`, `ItemSupplier::City`, `ItemSupplier::State`, and `ItemSupplier::PostalCode` fields onto the layout.

5. Arrange the fields into an orderly group, as shown in Figure 5.22.

6. Click the Text tool (the one labeled with a capital A) in the Status Toolbar and then click above the group of fields you've just added and type **Preferred Item Supplier Details:**.

7. Click a blank area of the layout (or press the Enter key on the numeric keypad) to conclude text entry.

8. Choose View ➪ Browse Mode to view the results of your work.

TIP If the font face, size, style, or color of fields or text you add to a layout don't match other similar elements already there, a quick way to achieve consistency is to use the FileMaker Pro Format Painter. To use the Format Painter, go to Layout mode, select an item with the appearance you desire, click the format painter icon (the rightmost of the layout tools in the Status Toolbar in Layout mode), and then click the object you wish to transfer the formats to. To reinstate the Format Painter to apply the same format to multiple objects, press the Enter key (on the numeric keypad) and then click another target object to format it.

With the preceding steps complete, you're ready to perform some tests. First, try selecting different values in the `SupplierID` field and confirm that the fields you added update to show the corresponding details from the `Contacts` table. Now, try editing the `AddressLine1` entry for the supplier address, using the field appearing on the Inventory layout, and navigate to the corresponding record on the `Contacts` layout to confirm that the change has been stored there. Finally, edit the same address on the `Contacts` layout and return to the Items layout to confirm that the latest change is visible there, as well.

FIGURE 5.22

An organized group of `ItemSupplier` fields added to the `Inventory` layout.

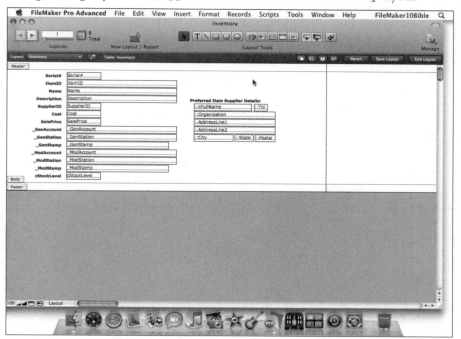

Making complex things simple

If you're new to working with databases, the structure I've proposed for the inventory example may at first have seemed unduly complex. As you can now see, however, its purpose is to introduce both order and simplicity, enabling many data management and organizational tasks to occur automatically or with minimal effort.

A question to ask when considering a data structure — or indeed any aspect of solution design — is "Will this ultimately make things simpler?" It's clearly worth wrestling for a few hours to get a seemingly complex structure in place if it saves you hundreds or even thousands of hours a year by linking up data consistently, fluently, and automatically.

CROSS-REF   For an in-depth discussion of data modeling as a key part of the design of your solutions, refer to Chapter 11.

Getting Started with File Security

Before proceeding further with the development of a solution, it's important to pay some attention to file security. If your work is worth doing and/or your data is worth organizing, then both are worth protecting. Just as you would be unwise to leave your house wide open when going on vacation or leave your car with the keys in the ignition while attending the theater, you'd be unwise to leave your solution or the data it contains unsecured.

Working with accounts and privilege sets

FileMaker enables you to define different levels or kinds of access that can then be assigned to one or more user accounts. These are called *privilege sets,* and they group together a range of settings that define what the user can and cannot do in your solution.

Additionally, FileMaker supports creation of multiple user accounts, each having an Account Name and password and assigned to a privilege set. Both accounts and privilege sets are defined on a file-by-file basis and apply to all elements, layouts, records, value lists, records fields, and so on within the file.

By default, a FileMaker file is created with three privilege sets — [Full Access], [Data Entry Only], and [Read-Only Access] — and one active account named Admin, which has no password and is assigned to the [Full Access] privilege set. Take a moment now to put some more useful and appropriate settings in place, as follows:

1. Choose File ➪ Manage ➪ Accounts & Privileges. The Manage Accounts & Privileges dialog appears.

2. In the Accounts tab of the dialog, double-click the line identified as Admin. The Edit Account dialog appears.

3. In the Password box, enter **BibleExample**. The password will appear as bullets as you type, (to conceal it from others who may have a view of your monitor), as shown in Figure 5.23.

4. In the Description box, enter "Developer access account".

5. Click OK.

 **TIP** FileMaker passwords are case-sensitive (though account names are not).

FIGURE 5.23

Specifying a password for the default Admin account.

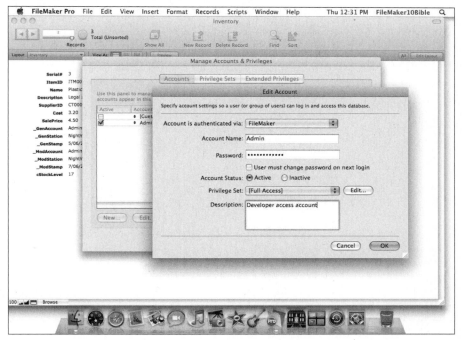

6. Navigate to the Privilege Sets tab of the Manage Accounts & Privileges dialog.

7. Click the New button. The Edit Privilege Set dialog appears.

8. In the Privilege Set Name box, enter **Regular User**.

9. Under the Data Access and Design heading, use the menus to choose the following settings (see Figure 5.24):

   ▪ Records: Create, Edit, and Delete in All Tables

   ▪ Layouts: All View Only

   ▪ Value Lists: All Modifiable

   ▪ Scripts: All Executable Only

FIGURE 5.24

Creating access settings and options for a new privilege set.

10. Under Other Privileges, select the Allow Printing checkbox and the Allow Exporting checkbox.

11. Click OK.

12. Navigate to the Accounts tab of the Manage Accounts & Privileges dialog.

13. Click New.

14. In the Account Name box, enter **User01**; in the Password box, enter **mypassword**; and from the Privilege Set menu select Regular User.

15. Click OK to close the Edit Account dialog and then click OK again to save and close the Manage Accounts & Privileges dialog.

NOTE Before closing the Manage Accounts & Privileges dialog, FileMaker will prompt you to enter a full access account and password. This is to prevent a situation where you have set a full access password inaccurately and could, therefore, permanently lock yourself out of the file.

Setting a default account and password

After you complete the steps outlined in the preceding section, FileMaker prompts you to enter an account name and password every time the file is opened. This provides a way to reserve file access for those you determine should have it — and to protect the structure of the file from inadvertent or inappropriate changes by users whose purpose in using the file is limited to data entry or access to the data (who will, therefore, log in by using an account assigned to the Regular User privilege set).

In some cases, defining a default privilege set is helpful so that the file opens automatically with a particular account (without prompting the user for account name and password). For example, to set the User01 account as the default, choose File ➪ File Options. Then in the upper area of the Open/Close tab of the File Options dialog, ensure that the Log In Using checkbox is selected and enter the account and password into their corresponding boxes.

When you click OK to close the File Options dialog after specifying a default account and password, an alert will appear, as shown at Figure 5.25, confirming that the settings have been accepted (providing you enter valid credentials). If the details you enter don't match the account/password combinations in the file, an error dialog will be displayed.

NOTE As the alert message indicates, after a default account/password has been set, you can still open the file by using a different account by holding down a modifier key as you're opening the file. On the Mac, you use the Option key to perform this function; in Windows, you use the Shift key.

FIGURE 5.25

Specifying a password for the default Admin account.

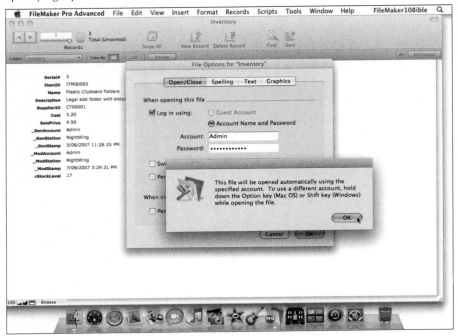

> **TIP**   In most circumstances, except during development, when you choose to set a default account and password for a file, you should select a restricted-access account as the default. In the previous example, the account with Regular User privileges is assigned as the default. If you choose an account with [Full Access] privileges as the default in a deployed file, you're effectively negating all security in the file. (Anyone can then open the file and do anything to it.)

Thinking about Usability

After working through the example described in this chapter, you have a basic file containing data and capable of performing some essential operations. It has passed a few basic tests along the way, but in most respects it isn't yet very useful.

> **ON the WEB**   A copy of the database, as constructed through this chapter, is available on this book's companion Web site. The copy of the file containing the work described in this chapter is named Inventory_Ch05.fp7.

In particular, the file lacks a suitable interface — everything is pretty much wherever it fell, and the only visual or functional aids are those that are provided by default by FileMaker itself. Such a minimal interface is restrictive and inconvenient. In Chapter 6, I examine some of the techniques you can use to build a more suitable interface.

Meanwhile, it is important to begin thinking about how the solution should operate, look, and feel. Most important, this will be determined by the ways you want to use the solution, the order and frequency you'll need to perform different tasks, and the range of processes you need the solution to support.

Moving between records

In this example, you're presently moving between records by using the controls in the Status Toolbar or perhaps the corresponding keyboard or menu commands (as outlined in Chapter 3). However, you can move around your data in many other ways — lists to select from, buttons to automatically take you to particular records, and so on.

As a central part of designing the interaction model for a solution's interface, you need to determine how users will move around the solution and what kinds of support the interface should give them to facilitate this navigation. When considering navigation, think about other computer applications you're familiar with, from music players to photo viewers — all of which provide ways of moving around that may provide models upon which you can draw.

Managing context

When creating the Relationships Graph for the inventory example, you connected TOs into groups. As shown in Figure 5.14, earlier in this chapter, the file presently has three separate "islands" of interconnected graph objects. Sets of TOs of this kind are often termed *Table Occurrence Groups* (TOGs) and operate as separate contextual "environments" — each TO within a group is able to "see" data from the other TOs in its group, according to the rules you set up for the relationships in the group.

When you're using the solution, you navigate to layouts attached to a specific TO and, therefore, present a view of data from the perspective of that TO. This is referred to as *Layout context*. The data you see and interact with depends on the current layout context and on the relationships radiating from the underlying TO.

Because context determines what you see and when, one interface design challenge is ensuring that the users can understand context and know how to interpret what they see on different layouts. You can apply layout headings, colors, and other design cues to make context clear as the user navigates around the solution.

Moving between tables

When you navigate from one layout to another, you may be changing context or not, depending on whether the layouts you're moving between are displaying records from different TOs. If the layouts are displaying records from the same TO, you may be accessing a different view of the same data. Similarly, if the layouts are based on different TOs within the same TOG, you may be accessing alternate views of the same data. Consistent visual themes or elements on layouts based on TOs within a functional group can help the user make these connections when using the solution.

In other situations, navigating to another layout may take you to a vantage point that's underpinned by a TO in a different TOG. For example, moving from the Orders layout to the Inventory layout in the example solution you've been building takes the user to a different TOG context. Both you and other users who may use the solution must be able to determine the operative perspective at all times.

Using and changing views

Instead of changing context or perspective, it's occasionally preferable to view the same data in an alternate presentation format. FileMaker provides options to view a given layout in Form, List, or Table presentations. Frequently, however, it's best to provide separate layouts optimized for a specific view and provide the user with an efficient means to switch between them.

CROSS-REF Details of the commands and processes for selecting alternate views (form list or table) of your layouts are discussed in Chapter 6.

Using buttons for static and dynamic actions

A key to making usable solutions is the addition of control elements that guide and support you. To achieve this, you can add screen devices (that is, layout objects) that perform actions or commands. These provide you with signposts, shortcuts, and other forms of assistance when using your solution.

With all the preceding considerations in mind, Chapter 6 examines a number of key techniques for developing the interface and beginning to build an appropriate user interaction model of your solutions.

Chapter 6

The Interface: Layout Mode

S o far, I've discussed various aspects of Layout mode's role, and you've seen a few of its basic capabilities. However, my primary focus has been elsewhere. In this chapter, you come to grips with the practicalities, working through a hands-on tour of the tools and techniques for building interfaces.

In many respects, a solution is only as good as its interface. Users do not understand information if it's presented in opaque or confusing ways, they don't use features they don't know about, and they avoid working with solutions that are perplexing or tedious to use. By contrast, a thoughtfully designed solution interface makes everything easier and leads the user through the processes that the solution is designed to support. Fortunately, FileMaker Pro provides excellent tools for creating interfaces of the latter kind.

FileMaker's Layout mode exemplifies two of the central concepts of the application — simplicity and common sense. You need to be able to build a variety of screens and reports, so FileMaker gives you a flexible environment and a broad set of tools for your work. Each of the elements and each of the tools are straightforward, and when you understand how they can be pieced together, the power of FileMaker's Layout mode becomes clear.

IN THIS CHAPTER

Setting up Initial layouts

Appreciating visual structure

Working with layout objects

Leveraging the FileMaker graphical environment

Interacting with layout objects

Using Tab Controls

Employing navigation options and techniques

Exploring the magic of buttons

Inviting the world in via the Web viewer

Generating reports and data output

Initial Layouts

As you can see in Chapter 5, when you create a new database file, FileMaker adds default layouts for each of the tables in the file. The default layouts are arranged in a simple form presentation with the fields appearing in a list with their names shown as labels on the left. Both the fields themselves and the labels beside them appear in a default font, with black text and no fill, and the layout's background is white with no other adornments.

Although the initial layouts get you started and enable you to see the fields and (in due course) data in the file, they don't present or group information in meaningful ways, nor do they aid the user in comprehension, navigation, or use of the solution. Before you begin to change and enhance the layouts, however, I recommend a couple of adjustments to FileMaker's preference settings:

1. Choose FileMaker Pro ⇨ Preferences on the Mac or Edit ⇨ Preferences in Windows to display the Preferences dialog.

2. Click the Layout tab.

3. Ensure that the Add Newly Defined Fields to Current Layout checkbox is deselected and the Save Layout Changes Automatically (Do Not Ask) checkbox is selected, as shown in Figure 6.1.

   These recommended settings allow you to work more efficiently when building the interface in a new file. The option to add fields to the current layout is useful in some situations, but when you're designing custom layouts, a change of schema results in undesired changes to the layout if this option is in force. Similarly, when starting a new file, it's generally most convenient to have layout changes save automatically. When the layouts are taking shape and are complex, however, the safety net of a save prompt or the option to revert or reject layout changes can be pretty convenient.

4. In the lower part of the Preferences dialog's Layout panel, select the Standard System Palette (256 Colors) radio button. This ensures that you have a diverse selection of stock colors available in the Formatting bar text, line and fill color palettes, as well as the text color submenu that appears when you choose Format ⇨ Text Color in Browse mode or Layout mode.

FIGURE 6.1

Adjusting settings in the Layout tab of the FileMaker Preferences dialog.

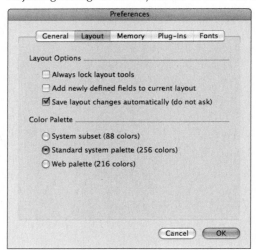

5. Select the Fonts tab.

6. Choose the Roman input type and select a default font from the menu below the list of input types. The dialog should match the settings shown in Figure 6.2.

FIGURE 6.2

Choosing a default font for the input and display of Roman characters.

NOTE I recommend Verdana as the default font — both because it's installed by default on both Mac and Windows operating systems and because it renders well at a number of sizes both onscreen and in printed output.

7. Click OK to save the settings and dismiss the Preferences dialog.

If you haven't already done so, open the copy of the Inventory solution discussed in Chapter 5.

ON the WEB You can download the Chapter 5 Inventory solution from this book's companion Web site to use as your starting point.

CROSS-REF For additional details about setting preferences and file options in FileMaker, refer to Chapter 3.

If you made a change to the font input preference, before proceeding you should go into Layout mode and select all objects on each layout and change their font to the newly selected default font. To accomplish this, follow these steps:

1. Navigate to the Inventory layout, using the Layout menu at the left of the Status Toolbar.

2. Choose View ➪ Layout Mode (⌘+L or Ctrl+L) or click the Edit Layout button at the right of the Status Toolbar.

3. Choose Edit ➪ Select All.

4. Choose Format ➪ Font ➪ Verdana (or whichever alternate font you chose as your default).

5. Now click in an open area of the layout to deselect all the objects and then repeat Step 4. The default font changes, and any new objects you add to the layout subsequently will be in the selected font.

A map of Layout mode

Before you begin serious work in Layout mode, take a moment to acquaint yourself with its various tools and features. When you choose View ➪ Layout Mode, FileMaker's Status Toolbar and Layout Bar populates with a number of controls and tools that, at first glance, may appear daunting. If you have any experience with a drawing or presentation application, some of the tools may seem a little familiar.

As you can see in Figures 6.3 and 6.4, you can access many of the operations you perform in Layout mode via the tools, palettes, and controls located in the Status Toolbar. The Status Toolbar tools work in three distinct ways.

Selection and then Action tools

Using a single click, you can select the tools at the upper right of the Status Toolbar, starting with the Object Selection tool and ending with the Format Painter (excepting the Field tool and Part tool) can be selected with a single click (The tool becomes shaded to indicate that it's active). A subsequent mouse click/drag action in the main layout area selects the enclosed objects (if you chose the Object Selection tool) or creates an object of the corresponding type (all other tools). For example, when you click the Web Viewer tool and then drag across a section of the layout, a Web Viewer object is created in the area where you drag the mouse. Similarly, when you click the line tool and drag between two points in the layout area, a line is created between those points. In all, 12 tools in this group operate in a similar manner.

> **TIP** By default, after each use of any of the 12 select/act tools, the Object Selection tool becomes active. However, if you double-click another tool, the tool is locked as the active tool until you choose a different tool. When a tool is locked, it appears in a darker shade. You can change the behavior to leave tools selected in Layout Preferences (by selecting the Always Lock Layout Tools checkbox; refer to Figure 6.1).

Drag-to-Layout tools

Within the group of layout tools at the upper right of the Status Toolbar are two tools labeled Field and Part, respectively. When the mouse button is depressed with the cursor positioned over either of these tools, it takes the shape of a hand, indicating that you may drag from the tool to the layout area to add the corresponding element (field or part) to the current layout. When you release the mouse button over the layout, a field or part will be added at the location of the mouse coordinates.

FIGURE 6.3

The anatomy of Layout mode.

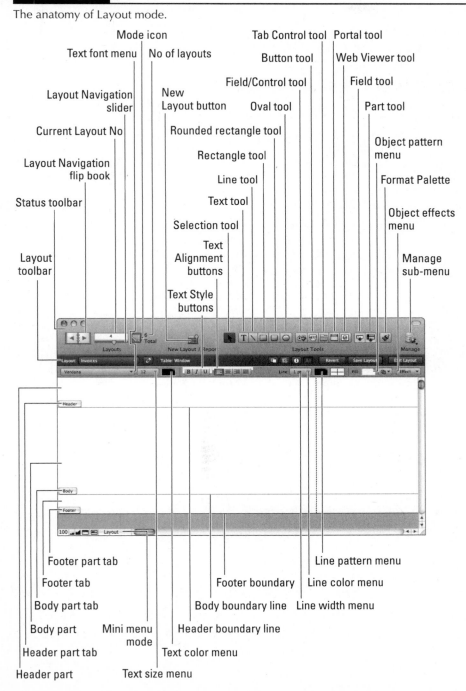

FIGURE 6.4

The controls of the Layout bar.

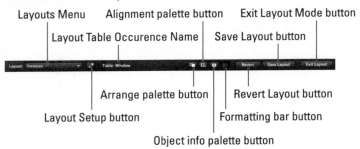

Layouts Menu   Alignment palette button   Exit Layout Mode button

Layout Table Occurence Name   Save Layout button

Arrange palette button   Revert Layout button

Layout Setup button   Formatting bar button

Object info palette button

Palette and Menu controls

When the Formatting bar is displayed (it can be toggled on and off by using the button labeled Aa in the Layout bar — the dark gray area below the main body of the Status Toolbar), you have access to menus of color, pattern, and appearance settings for the line (border) and fill attributes of selected layout objects, and for the color and font attributes of text objects. These controls work like conventional text menus: Click once to reveal the corresponding palette of options and then click a second time on the option (color, pattern, or line/fill attribute) you want to apply to currently selected objects.

TIP   **You can change the arrangement and selection of icons on the Status Toolbar by choosing View ⊏ Customize Status Toolbar and dragging icons (or groups of icons) from the Customize dialog to the Toolbar, dragging icons off the Toolbar, or dragging icons to new positions on the Toolbar. Changes you make to the Status Toolbar remain in effect for all solutions and application sessions on the current workstation, until you make a further change.**

For additional details of the processes for customizing the Status Toolbar, refer to Chapter 4.

Organizing the presentation of information

One of the keys that people use to understand information is its position relative to other information. For example, if the name Martha has the name Samuel immediately to its right, you may conclude that you're seeing the first and last names of an individual. Conversely, if the name Martha has the name Samuel appearing immediately below it, a more likely conclusion is that you're viewing a list of names and that Martha and Samuel are two individuals who belong together in a group of some kind. Simply by positioning information according to conventions of this type, you provide intuitive cues to suggest meaning and relationships. When employing such techniques, labels become a secondary aid, confirming what object placement has already suggested.

As an example of the way information can be grouped to make its meaning clearer, I made some initial changes to the preceding chapter's Inventory layout. You can see the result of these modifications in Figure 6.5.

FIGURE 6.5

Reorganizing the information in the Inventory layout into logical groupings.

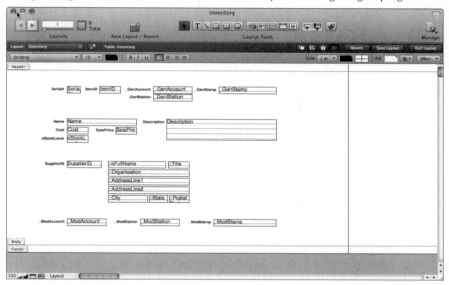

At this stage, the only things that have been altered in the Inventory layout are the relative sizes and placement of the elements. None has been added, removed, or otherwise altered. Yet the layout already makes more sense and is easier to scan.

To make comparable changes in your Inventory layout, follow these steps:

1. Click the Body tab at the lower left of the layout and drag it downward, enlarging the layout area.

2. Click the field and label objects and drag them around the screen to new positions.

> **TIP**
> You can Shift+click objects to make multiple selections and then drag a group of selected objects to reposition them simultaneously. I recommend moving the labels and fields simultaneously.

3. To resize field boxes, click them once to select them — corner handles appear — and then drag the lower right corner handle and release when the box is the desired size.

> **TIP**
> To make fine adjustments to the position of an object or group of objects, first select the objects and then use the arrow keys to move them. They're nudged one pixel at a time in the direction of the arrow key you press.

Applying formats to field and text objects

You can apply a variety of formatting changes to selected layout objects, including text format (font size, style, color, and so on) as well as graphical effects, such as line and fill color, embossing, and drop shadow. You can use combinations of effects to reinforce the groupings and distinctions between elements on your layouts. The following steps walk you through such a process:

1. In Layout mode in the Inventory layout, select the Auto-Entry fields (Serial#, ItemID, _GenAccount, _GetStation, _GenStamp, _ModAccount, _ ModStation, and _ModStamp).

2. Click the Fill Color palette in the Formatting bar of the Status Toolbar and select the lilac fill color, as shown in Figure 6.6.

3. With the Auto-Entry fields still selected, choose the object effects palette (at the right of the row of controls that includes fill color and pattern) and from the resulting menu, select the Engraved option, as shown in Figure 6.7.

NOTE The engraving effect creates an illusion of depth, giving the impression that you're looking into a shallow depression in the layout. This effect imparts the idea of looking into something and is therefore useful for fields or other objects containing information. (That is, one is "looking into" the database to see the contents of a field, so the engraving provides a useful visual analogy.)

4. Choose Format ➪ TextColor and select a medium dark gray from the submenu color palette, as shown in Figure 6.8.

5. Choose Format ➪ Field/Control ➪ Behavior. The Field Behavior dialog appears.

6. Deselect the In Browse mode checkbox in the section labeled Allow Field to be Entered.

7. Select the Do Not Apply Visual Spell-Checking checkbox, as shown in Figure 6.9.

8. Click OK.

9. Select the Name, Description, Cost, SalePrice, and SupplierID fields and apply the lightest gray fill and the Engraved fill effect to them.

10. Select the remaining fields and apply the second gray shade (one shade darker than the lightest gray) fill to them and, again, apply the engraved fill effect.

NOTE The slightly darker fill effect applied to the final group of fields differentiates them from the light gray data entry input fields. The remaining fields acquire their values automatically when the input values are entered.

11. Select the Serial#, ItemID, Cost, SalePrice, cStockLevel, State, and PostalCode fields and choose Format ➪ Align Text ➪ Center.

12. Select the Cost and SalePrice fields.

13. Choose Format ➪ Number. The Number Format for selected objects dialog appears.

FIGURE 6.6

Setting a lilac fill color for selected fields in the Inventory layout.

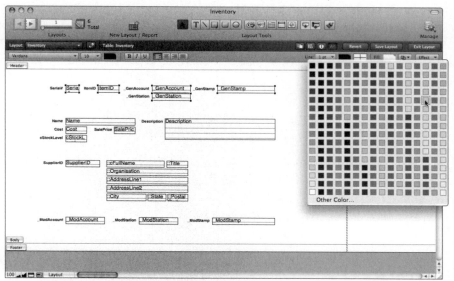

FIGURE 6.7

Applying the Engraved effect to selected fields in the Inventory layout.

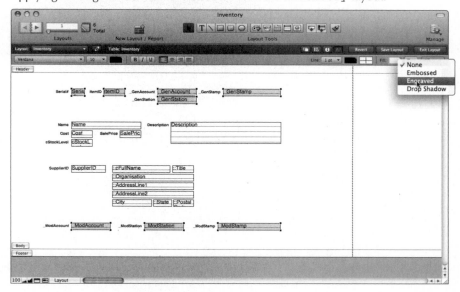

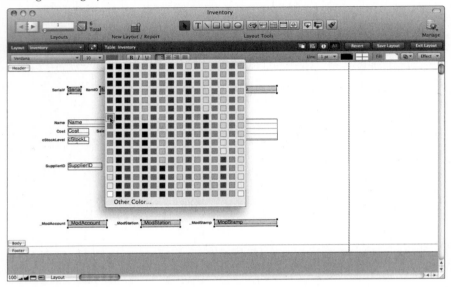

FIGURE 6.8

Setting a dark gray text color for selected fields in the Inventory layout.

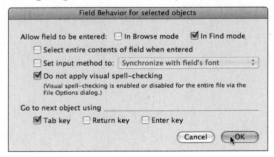

FIGURE 6.9

Configuring field behavior settings for a group of fields.

14. Select the Format as Decimal radio button, the Fixed Number of Decimal Digits checkbox (make sure that the adjacent number is 2), and the Use Notation checkbox (making sure that Currency Leading/Inside is selected in the adjacent drop-down list and that the correct currency symbol appears at the right), as shown in Figure 6.10.

15. Click OK.

16. Choose View ➪ Browse Mode to view the results of your work. Your Inventory layout should now resemble the one shown in Figure 6.11.

FIGURE 6.10

Setting number display options for decimal currency.

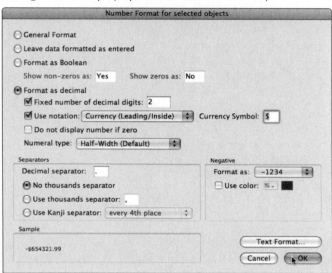

FIGURE 6.11

The Inventory layout in Browse mode with basic field formatting applied.

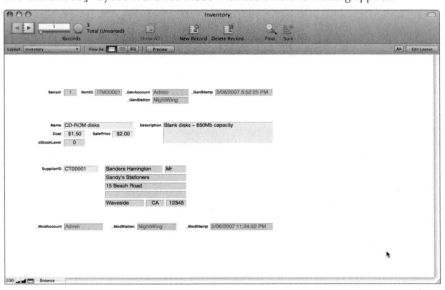

The preceding process is a first step toward providing an interface for the Inventory layout, but already its appearance is transformed — it's now easier to see what different elements are, and the layout is already more usable.

Setting up layouts for printing

What works well onscreen is not always ideal when the document is sent to a printer. One aspect of this is the use of color. Careful and tasteful use of color can make screens more attractive and more readable, but many printers require black and white or grayscale, and even when color is available, ink can bleed, making text against a color background harder to read. Moreover, the orientation and arrangement of elements you want onscreen may not match printed output requirements.

One answer to this dilemma — sometimes the easiest or cleanest solution — is to create separate layouts for printing. It's certainly an option, and for some purposes — such as printing onto irregular or special-purpose paper such as labels or envelopes, or matching pre-existing forms or letter formats — it is necessary. For relatively simple requirements, however, FileMaker provides you with techniques to control the way things print.

Before making adjustments to a layout's printing configuration, choose File ⇨ Page Setup (Mac) or File ⇨ Print Setup (Windows) to choose an appropriate printer and page orientation. Next, go to Layout mode and choose Layout ⇨ Layout Setup and click the Printing tab of the Layout Setup dialog that appears. Here you can set column printing and set fixed margin widths for the current layout.

> **NOTE** Print settings (orientation, scaling, page margins, and so on) also affect the output FileMaker produces when you create PDF documents, such as when you choose File ⇨ Save/Send Records As ⇨ PDF.

On first entering the Layout Setup dialog's Printing tab for a particular layout, the Use Fixed Page Margins option is disabled, and the margin widths are default values based on the current print driver and page setup configuration. As shown in Figure 6.12, after selecting the Use Fixed Page Margins checkbox, you can enter alternative margin widths. Bear in mind when doing so that, if you specify fixed margins less than the minimums for the selected printer, the page is nevertheless cropped. (That is, you can't use margin settings to extend the printable area outside your printer's hardware limits.)

> **NOTE** For exacting printing requirements, you should set fixed page margins to ensure that page dimensions and placement are not dependent on the printer and driver selections. Note, however, that the paper size and orientation settings still impact the layout dimensions.

In Layout mode (refer to Figure 6.3), a vertical dotted line appears to the right side of the main window area. This line identifies the edge of the printable area, based on the current printer, page setup (orientation, scaling, and so on), and the margin settings for the current layout. If you make a change to any of these settings, the line appears in a new position, indicating the new width of the layout that can be printed on the selected paper size.

NOTE You can position objects outside the printable area of the layout. If you do, they nevertheless appear onscreen and behave normally, with the exception that they don't appear (or are cropped, depending on placement) in the printed output.

After setting the Page Setup configuration and specifying margins, choose View ⇨ Preview Mode to view the placement of the current layout within the area of the printed page. With settings in place for U.S. letter and landscape orientation, the preview should resemble Figure 6.13.

TIP You can also choose View ⇨ Page Margins to view the layout in context, with the limits of the selected paper size and margin allowances shown. This technique can be useful for preparing a layout for printing.

FIGURE 6.12

Setting fixed page margins via the Printing tab of the Layout Setup dialog.

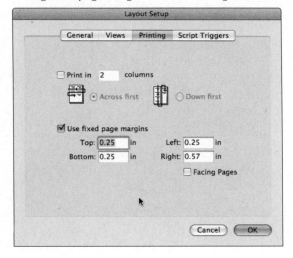

An invaluable feature when setting up pages for printing enables you to exclude particular layout objects from the printed image. (That is, the printed output can optionally present a subset of the layout objects.) In the Inventory layout example shown in Figure 6.13, you may want to print only the data fields and their corresponding text labels, without the ancillary (metadata) fields showing record generation and modification details.

To invoke the Do Not Print option, go to Layout mode and select the metadata fields and their adjacent text labels; then choose Format ⇨ Set Sliding/Printing. In the Set Sliding/Printing dialog that appears (shown in Figure 6.14), select the Do Not Print the Selected Objects checkbox in the lower left and then click OK to dismiss the dialog.

After applying the Do Not Print setting, return to Browse mode and confirm that the fields and their labels still appear and display their data. Now return to Preview mode and note that the metadata fields no longer appear there. If you want, try a test print to confirm that the printed output corresponds to the preview image.

CROSS-REF For a more in-depth discussion of the options for setting up layouts for print, refer to Chapter 10.

FIGURE 6.13

Preview mode shows how the current layout appears on the printed page.

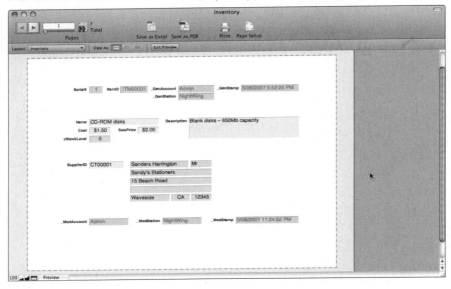

Understanding lists and forms

FileMaker allows you to view a layout in a Form, List, or Table presentation format.

- **Form View** presents the data one record at a time in a manner analogous to paper forms. To view a different record, you must navigate forward or backward (for example, using the Flip book tool in the Status Toolbar).

- **List View,** as the name suggests, presents multiple records (assuming that the current found set has than one record), one below another, allowing you to scroll through the records.

- **Table View** also shows the records as a list but ignores the appearance of the current layout, instead showing records in a display format resembling a spreadsheet.

FIGURE 6.14

Setting selected objects as nonprinting (so that they're not included in printed output).

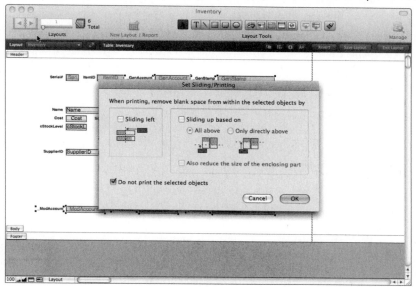

To see the current layout in different views, enter Browse mode, check that you're viewing a found set of two or more records, and then (sequentially) choose the View ⇨ View as Form, View ⇨ View as List, and View ⇨ View as Table commands. As you can see, FileMaker gives you a lot of control over how your layouts are presented.

Commonly, your layouts are designed with a particular presentation format in mind. Form layouts generally take up most of the screen and don't work so well when viewed as List, whereas list layouts are frequently designed to be wide and shallow so that many records fit on the screen. Consequently, you may want to constrain users to view each layout only in the formats for which you have designed them.

To specify the layout views available for selection by the user, navigate to the layout, enter Layout mode, and choose Layouts ⇨ Layout Setup to display the Layout Setup dialog. Select the Views tab, as shown in Figure 6.15. By deselecting one or more checkboxes on the Views tab, you prevent users from choosing to display the current layout in the corresponding presentation format. (The menu commands for the disabled views are dimmed and unavailable when the layout is displayed.)

NOTE When constraining a layout to a single view, you should consider providing an alternate means for users to see data in a variety of appropriate formats. For example, you may want to provide two or more layouts — one or more to show records from a table in a summary list view and another to show more extensive detail of the same records in a form view.

FIGURE 6.15

FIGURE 6.15

Constraining the available (user selectable) views for the current layout.

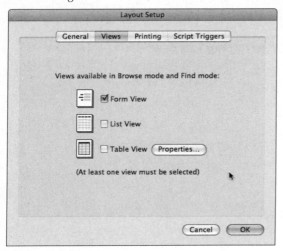

As a general principle, list views are more useful when they include a relatively small number of essential fields, providing a summary of the data in a table, whereas form presentations are better suited to the display of larger numbers (a dozen or more) fields. There is no hard rule about this, but appropriate use of forms and lists reduces clutter and confusion in your solutions.

Layout parts and their purposes

The default layouts generated by FileMaker when you create a new file — or when you choose Layouts ⇨ New Layout/Report (in Layout mode) to generate a new blank layout — are subdivided vertically into three parts identified as Header, Body, and Footer. At the left side of the boundary of each part is a tab bearing its name. Clicking a part tab selects the part, and dragging a part tab up or down changes the corresponding part's size.

The purpose of a layout's Header and Footer parts is to provide a reserved area for layout elements that are to appear only once at the top or bottom of each screen or page (regardless of the number of records displayed). These parts are useful for the display of headings, page numbers, logos, or design elements, and anything else of a general nature (that is, applying to all records).

A layout's Body area is repeated for each record in the layout's table, giving all the detail that is particular to one record. In List View or when printed, multiple instances of the body part (one for each record) may appear between each occurrence of the Header and Footer parts, depending on the size of the body part, the size of the page, the part settings, and the number of records being displayed.

When required, you may include additional layout parts to support summary information. You do this by dragging the Status Toolbar's Part tool to the place in the layout where you want to add a part. In addition to the Header, Body, and Footer, FileMaker supports the following layout part types:

- **Title Header:** Enables you to create a different header to appear on the first page
- **Leading Grand Summary:** Provides a place to include summary information that should appear only once, at the top of a screen or start of a printout or report
- **Sub-Summary When Sorted By:** Enables you to include summary details before and/or after each group of values in a sorted set
- **Trailing Grand Summary:** Provides a place to include summary information that should appear only once, at the bottom of a screen or at the end of a printout or report
- **Title Footer:** Enables you to create a different footer to appear only on the first page

You may create layouts containing many parts. However, with the exception of Sub-summary parts, each part type may only appear once in a layout. You can create up to two Sub-summary parts per field — one leading (that is, preceding the Body part) and/or one trailing.

NOTE A Sub-summary part is displayed in Browse mode, in Preview mode and print (or PDF) output, when the records are sorted according to the corresponding field (the break field associated with the Sub-summary part). You may create multiple Sub-summary parts, each coming into play only if the current found set is sorted by an associated field.

A layout must have at least one part, but that part may be of any kind. Thus, you can define a layout with sub-summaries but no body, for example, to display summary data about groups of records without including details of the records themselves.

CROSS-REF The creation and use of Sub-summary parts is explored in greater detail in Chapter 10.

The Importance of Visual Structure

In the section "Organizing the presentation of information," earlier in this chapter, you moved the fields on the Inventory layout into organized groups to give order and meaning to the data they present. This provided a first step toward an intuitive interface — one leading the eye to the relevant data in an ordered fashion.

To assist in the interpretation of information, you should arrange it in a sequence that users find easiest to comprehend. Frequently, this order entails moving from the general to the specific. (For example, users generally need to know what something is before learning about its history or other attributes, so name and ID fields should generally come before descriptive details.)

Adding visual pointers and aids

In addition to the placement of fields on your layouts, a variety of graphical elements can help to communicate the relationships between the elements and reinforce the visual effect of grouping and placement. These elements may include text, lines, borders, boxes or panels, arrows, logos, or other graphical indicators.

Using the `Inventory` layout as an example, in Layout mode, add a rectangle around the first group of fields. To implement this, proceed as follows:

1. Select the rectangle tool in the Status Toolbar.
2. Draw a rectangle around the first group of fields. (Initially, the rectangle may obscure the fields.)
3. With the rectangle selected, choose Arrange ⇨ Send to Back.
4. Apply a light gray fill by using the Fill tool in the Status Toolbar.
5. Select and apply the Engraved effect from the Object Effects palette in the Status Toolbar.
6. Locate the Line Pattern menu (next to the Line Color tool in the Formatting bar section of the Status Toolbar; see Figure 6.16), and choose the transparent line option at the upper left of the menu of line patterns.

FIGURE 6.16

Selecting the transparent line attribute from the Line Pattern tool in the Status Toolbar in Layout mode.

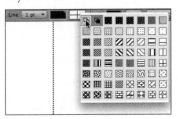

After completing the preceding process, the layout should include an engraved rectangle positioned behind the group of five fields nearest the top of the screen, as shown in Figure 6.17.

Repeat the preceding steps to add boxes behind each of the remaining three groups of fields. Apply the same shade of gray to the box behind the group of fields near the bottom of the layout, but choose a lighter shade for the data fields in the middle two groups. Then proceed as follows:

1. Click the Header part's tab to select it.

2. Select the lightest gray fill color from the Fill Color tool in the Status Toolbar. This changes the Header part's background color to light gray. Select the Footer by clicking its tab and again apply the lightest gray fill to it.

3. Select the Text tool in the Status Toolbar (the one labeled with an A), click near the top left of each rectangle, and type a text label to identify the group of fields.

4. Using the Text tool, click the field labels and (as appropriate) edit their names to conventional English labels for clarity.

5. Using the text tool, click in the Header area and type the word **Inventory**.

6. With the heading text selected, choose Format ➪ Text Color and apply a mid-gray,

7. Choose Format ➪ Size to enlarge the heading and Format ➪ Style to apply a bold type setting.

8. Increase the height of the header area (by dragging the Header tab downward a short distance) and drag the heading label text into a central position above the layout contents.

After completing these steps, return to Browse mode to view the effect of your work. Your Inventory layout should resemble the one shown in Figure 6.18.

FIGURE 6.17

Adding a rectangular box behind the first group of fields on the Inventory layout.

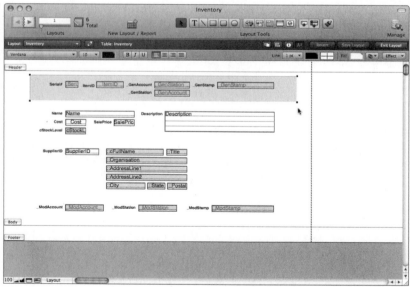

FIGURE 6.18

The Inventory layout, showing added visual cues to improve readability.

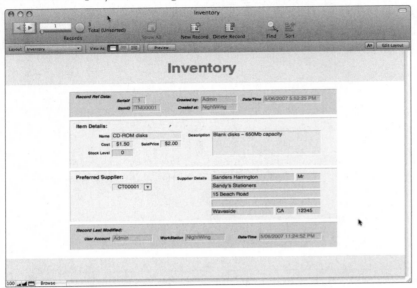

Using white space

The proximity of layout elements is one of the cues indicating relationships between them, so grouping elements is important. To achieve the desired effect, it's equally important to leave space between the groups of elements. In other words, the spaces you leave are as important as the elements you add, when it comes to the user interpreting the screen (or page) content.

It's equally important to avoid clutter. If your table has many fields, consider showing only a manageable number of fields or groups of data on any one screen — use multiple screens or multiple panels of a Tab Control to create separation between groups of fields. Aim to present the user with clear and striking ideas, allowing them to focus on the essential elements that are important at each step.

Ergonomics and avoiding visual fatigue

One of the reasons you should avoid clutter is that it's stressful and fatiguing for the user. As information is processed, mental connections are made and held in memory. It requires much more work and concentration to hold ten connections in mind than four or five. If you're able to present users with no more than a handful of interconnected ideas at any one time, your solutions become much easier to use.

Consider the essential ideas presented by the `Inventory` screen in its present form. In broad terms, the flow of ideas can be expressed as:

- There is an item record created by a certain user at a certain time.
- The item has a name, description, and price.
- I have a certain quantity of the item in stock.
- There is a preferred supplier with an associated address.
- The record was last modified by a certain user at a certain time.

With screen data grouped in this way, your users have a manageable group of ideas to digest at any one time.

Just as a screen's clutter or complexity affects the amount of user effort required, so do various other design aspects. Rich, or bright, colors make a strong impression and grab the user's attention, so if you want to draw attention to important items, you may want to use strong colors. However, if you overuse bright or strongly contrasting colors throughout a layout, the user is torn between many items that are all shouting for attention, which is also fatiguing.

I recommend that you choose subtle and relatively gentle shades for the majority of your layout areas, reserving strong or bright elements for those things that you want your screens to "shout" about.

Giving information meaning

Most of the information you enter into the fields of a database means little on its own. The number 42 may be a profound answer — if your user knows what the question is. A fact such as 17 Priory Lane may solve all problems — if your user knows where it fits or to whom it belongs. The table and record structure of your solution provides a means of storing information in an ordered way, but users rely on the interfaces you design to make the order clear.

While the techniques shown earlier in the chapter help your users understand the immediate connections between fields within a single record, they have to be able to comprehend the wider context. One aspect of the wider context is the overall data set encompassing the data subset displayed on the current layout. Another is the solution process or processes that the current screen supports. To add cues for these larger purposes, some additional techniques are required.

Defining Tooltips

FileMaker Pro 10 includes the ability to define and display *tooltips* (text flags associated with layout objects) in both Browse and Find modes. Tooltips make it easier for users to learn how your interface works, giving ready reminders as users work. Moreover, most users are familiar with tooltips, having experienced them on web browsers and productivity applications.

To define a tooltip for an object in FileMaker Pro, follow these steps:

1. Enter Layout mode and select the object.

2. Choose Format ⇨ Set Tooltip. (You can also access the Set Tooltip command from the contextual menu by Ctrl+clicking/right-clicking with the mouse on the layout object.) The Set Tooltip dialog appears, as shown in Figure 6.19.

3. Type the tooltip text you want to use for a layout object and click OK. The relevant tip rectangle appears when the mouse pointer is stationary above the object (in Find or Browse mode) for a little more than a second, as shown in Figure 6.20.

> **TIP** To efficiently identify objects with tooltips attached when viewing your solution in Layout mode, choose View ⇨ Show ⇨ Tooltips. A small, colored note icon appears at the lower-right corner of objects with a tooltip defined.

FIGURE 6.19

Defining a tooltip for a selected object via the Set Tooltip dialog.

Set Tooltip
Specify the text or calculation to display as a tooltip for the selected object in Browse or Find mode.
Tooltip: "Return to the Main Menu..."   (Specify...)
(Cancel)   (OK)

FIGURE 6.20

A button tooltip displayed in Browse mode.

Using conditional tooltips

In the preceding example, the tooltip was supplied as a literal text value. However, FileMaker Pro supports the use of calculation syntax when defining tooltips, enabling you to define different tooltips to display in different circumstances or to implement a method of turning tooltips on or off according to user preferences.

For example, if you have a script attached to a button that takes users to Find mode (if they're currently in Browse mode) or performs the Find if the solution is already in Find mode, you may want to vary the tooltip text according to the current window's mode. You can achieve mode-dependent tip text with a tooltip definition, using a calculation expression along the lines of

```
Choose(Get(WindowMode); "Go to Find mode..."; "Perform the current Find...")
```

NOTE The `Get(WindowMode)` function returns 0 in Browse mode and 1 in Find mode.

Similarly, if your solution keeps track of user preferences in a Users table, you can set your login script to store the user's tooltip preference (whether or not the user wants tooltips displayed during their sessions) in a global field, such as in a Utility table. With such a mechanism in place, you can determine whether your tooltips appear, based on the user's preference, by using a calculation expression such as

```
If(Utility::gTooltipPref = 1; "Your tooltip text here...")
```

Keeping track of tooltips

If your solution is complex, you'll likely have many tooltips defined, and the same tooltip text may appear in multiple places. For example, when defining a tip such as the one shown in Figure 6.20, you're likely to want the same tip text appearing on all main menu navigation buttons throughout your solution — in other words, on most of the layouts.

When managing the text for a large number of tooltips, you should consider storing the tooltip content in a single location to facilitate managing it and updating it as needed. For example, if your solution has around 25 main menu buttons throughout, a better solution than defining (and subsequently managing) all the tooltip text separately is to create a global field called `gMainMenuButton` in a table called Tooltips in your solution and then specify the tooltip for the main menu buttons as

```
If(Utility::gTooltipPref = 1; Tooltips::gMainMenuButton)
```

With an approach of this kind, you can update the tooltip text for all the main menu buttons at once by editing the default value in the `Tooltips::gMainMenuButton` field.

To enhance the usefulness of a centralized tooltip management approach, I suggest that you store the reference text for each tooltip in your solution in separate records in the Tooltips table, loading the relevant values into the global field(s) referenced by your tooltip calculation expressions, as a sub-routine of your solution's start-up script. That way, when the solution is hosted, the current tooltip text is made available in the global fields in the Tooltips table at the commencement of each client session.

Different Kinds of Layout Objects

In your work so far on the `Inventory` layout, you've dealt with three kinds of layout objects — field boxes, text labels, and graphical rectangles. Of these, the field boxes are the only ones that interact with the user or display different content from mode to mode or record to record. The text labels and graphical rectangles serve their purpose in a more passive fashion.

When using a database, you need a variety of ways to interact with the data and the interface. To this end, FileMaker provides a number of additional object types, as represented by the main group of 11 tools in the Status Toolbar.

Among the tools, the Object Selection tool is used to choose one or more objects in the layout; you can also use it to drag objects (or groups of objects) to new locations in the layout. The remaining two blocks of five tools represent various kinds of layout objects, as follows:

- Text objects
- Graphical line objects
- Rectangular (or square) objects
- Rectangles (or squares) with rounded corners
- Elliptical (or circular) objects
- Field controls (checkboxes, radio buttons, menus, and lists)
- Buttons
- Tab Controls
- Portals
- Web viewers

In addition to the ten layout object types listed here, two more types of objects are supported by FileMaker. You can create the first of these objects, the field box, by using the Field tool immediately to the right of the main groups of tools. The final object type is any supported object (for example, a picture or illustration) created in another application that you can paste into a layout or add by choosing Insert ➪ Picture.

> **NOTE** FileMaker supports more than a dozen common image formats, enabling you to place pictures and graphics from other applications directly onto FileMaker layouts. Supported formats include `.jpg`, `.gif`, `.tif`, `.png`, `.eps`, `.fpx`, and `.pdf` image files.

Static and dynamic objects

Six of the 12 types of layout objects in FileMaker can be described as *static* — they add to the appearance of the layout, but you can't interact directly with them. In that regard, such objects serve their purposes passively. Inherently static layout objects include text objects, lines, squares/rectangles, round-cornered squares/rectangles, circles/ellipses, and inserted graphics/images.

By their nature, the remaining six layout object types support user interaction and can, therefore, be characterized as dynamic objects. In brief, their properties are as follows:

- **Field controls** are dynamic — when you click them, a value in the field they're attached to changes.
- **Portals** display lists of related records that you can (optionally) scroll, select, add, delete, or edit (depending on the portal and relationship configuration).

- **Tab controls** let you click alternate tabs to view different layout content.

- **Web Viewer objects** display content from a remote (or local) Web site; they can be configured to enable you to click hyperlinks and interact directly with the content.

- **Field boxes** enable you to "enter" a record and directly add, edit, or delete data within the fields of the database.

- **Buttons** can be configured to execute any of 127 commands when you click them.

Now that I've told you that some objects are static and others are dynamic, I'm going to risk confusing the issue by telling you that all but one type of object (a Tab Control) can *also* be formatted to act as a button. So you can even give objects that are by nature static (such as lines, circles, imported images, and so on) button properties so that a command is executed when the user selects them (for example, by clicking them).

Inherent object properties

Each of the different kinds of objects has a number of inherent attributes, according to its intended function. For example, you can assign color, style, size, and font attributes to text objects, and line objects can have color, pattern, and thickness attributes. Additionally, you can assign a name to each object you place on a layout, change its size and position, and apply a variety of other formats and properties.

TIP Object names, coordinates, and auto-resize properties are assigned by using the Object Info palette, accessible in Layout mode by choosing View ⇨ Object Info, or by clicking the "i" button in the Layout bar.

According to its different appearance and behavior, each object type accepts a different range of properties and attributes. In the case of dynamic layout objects, each has a configuration dialog, letting you specify its behavior. Double-clicking dynamic objects in Layout mode causes the corresponding configuration dialog to display so that you can edit the object's properties and parameters.

In addition to properties particular to their function, you can assign all objects a variety of appearance attributes, such as line and/or fill color, engraving or embossing effects, and so on. You can apply these attributes efficiently by using the tools and controls in Layout mode's Status Toolbar.

NOTE The effect of applying graphical attributes to different kinds of objects varies according to the nature of the object. For example, fill/line color or transparency does not affect an inserted picture (because the picture's appearance and transparency attributes are set in the application in which it was created), but 3-D object effects can still be applied.

Conditional format attributes

When you create an object, adding it to a layout, you establish its appearance as well as its size and placement on the layout. As you assemble the layout's components, the layout's overall appearance emerges. Moreover, FileMaker 10 provides you with the ability to link the appearance of various kinds of objects to the data within the database.

> **TIP** In the `Inventory` layout, for example, you may want to alert users when the stock level of an item falls below a certain level. One way to do that is to apply conditional formatting so that the text is displayed in a different color when the stock level is low.

To apply conditional formatting, follow these steps:

1. Enter Layout mode with the `Inventory` layout active.

2. Select the `cStockLevel` field.

3. Choose Format ⇨ Conditional. The Conditional Formatting dialog appears.

4. Click the Add button to create a condition.

5. Using the menus in the Condition area of the dialog, enter a value for the condition (for example, "Value is . . . less than . . . 5").

6. In the Format area of the dialog, choose the formatting attributes to be applied when the condition is met. Figure 6.21 shows the settings for a condition that changes the text color of the `cStockLevel` field to red when the stocking level of an item drops to fewer than five.

FIGURE 6.21

Settings to apply conditional text color to the `cStockLevel` field.

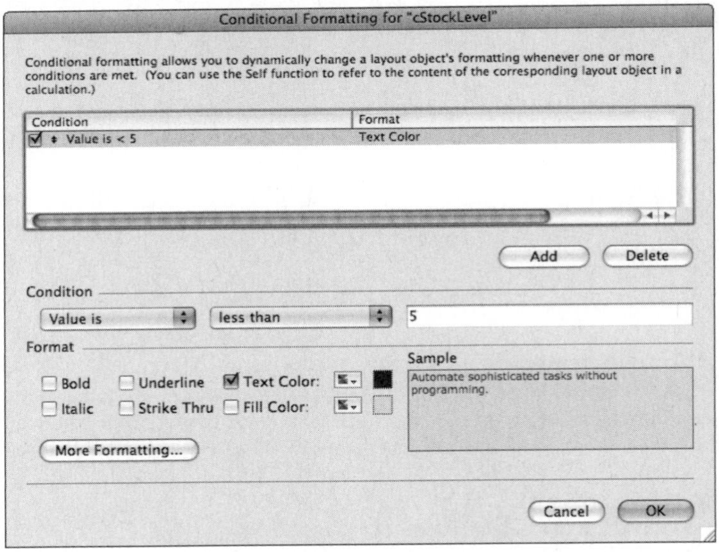

You can apply conditional formatting to textual objects, including fields, buttons, and Web viewers, and use it to control the text style, color, size, font, and background fill of the object. Moreover, you can specify multiple conditions for an object, with conditions being evaluated in the order in which they appear in the list at the top of the dialog.

CROSS-REF For a more detailed discussion of the uses of conditional formatting, see Chapter 10.

FileMaker as a Graphical Environment

FileMaker's Layout mode provides you with a drawing environment, enabling you to create graphical objects and assemble them into layouts. You can create designs, pictures, stationery, forms, slide presentations, and many other visual displays by using Layout mode — with or without displaying data from FileMaker's database tables. The ability to insert images created in other applications further enriches FileMaker's interface-building environment's creative possibilities.

Layout mode's flexibility is such that FileMaker has been used to create everything from boardroom presentations to store window advertising displays, shopping mall kiosks, and children's educational games. FileMaker enables you to arrange some pictures, shapes, and text and make them "do stuff" — the rest is up to your imagination.

Building graphic objects in FileMaker

Using the `Inventory` layout as an example, try creating a graphical logo to appear in the header part, as described in the following steps:

1. Enter Layout mode for the `Inventory` layout.

2. Select the Oval tool and draw an elliptical shape approximately 2 inches wide and 0.75 inch high.

3. Using the fill color control, choose a dark mauve color, apply a dark blue line color and, as shown in Figure 6.22, select the embossed option from the Object Effects palette.

FIGURE 6.22

Applying a 3-D embossed effect from the Object Effects palette.

4. Create a slightly smaller ellipse, giving it a lighter shade (of a similar hue), apply the Engraved effect, and position it centered on top of the first ellipse.

To create a (fictitious) company name for the logo, the process is as follows:

a. Choose the Text tool and type **xyz** as the logo name for this example.

b. Using the Selection tool (arrow), click the text.

c. Choose Format ⇨ Font ⇨ Courier New.

d. Choose Format ⇨ Size ⇨ Custom and, in the resulting dialog, enter a custom size of 32 points. Click OK.

e. Choose Format ⇨ Style ⇨ Italic.

f. Click the text and drag it to the middle of the smaller oval shape.

g. Choose Format ⇨ Text Color and select white from the submenu palette of text colors.

h. Choose Edit ⇨ Duplicate to create a duplicate of the xyz text. The duplicate is positioned one grid space down and to the right. (A grid space defaults to six pixels, but you can set a different value by choosing Layouts ⇨ Set Rulers).

i. Choose Format ⇨ Text Color and select a dark purple color from the submenu palette of text colors.

j. Position the dark purple text object exactly on top of the white text object in the middle of the two oval shapes.

k. With the dark purple text object still selected, press the up arrow key (on the keyboard) to nudge it upward by one pixel and then press the left arrow key to nudge it left by one pixel.

When you've completed these steps, your completed logo should resemble the one shown in Figure 6.23.

FIGURE 6.23

A logo image assembled in FileMaker from four graphical objects.

5. Select all the logo parts at once by dragging a selection rectangle to encompass the entire logo and then choose Arrange ⇨ Group to lock the elements together.

Default object formats and attributes

When you create an object in Layout mode, it appears with default formats including style, font, color and line, although you can subsequently make alterations, if desired. If you're creating a number of similar objects, however, you'll find it advantageous to set default formats before you begin.

To set the default formats, first click with the Selection tool in a blank area of the layout to ensure that no objects are selected. Then choose the formats you want to use as defaults for objects you're about to create (for example, text color, font, style, and size — and, for fields and graphical shapes, fill, effects, and line attributes).

Now, when you select an object tool and create an object, the settings you've stored are used to determine the initial formats and attributes of each object. You can, of course, still select the objects and apply other settings if you want — setting default attributes simply saves you time by allowing you to determine the initial appearance of objects.

> **TIP** If you want to change the formatting on multiple items at once, first select them all (for example, by shift-clicking each in turn). Formatting and other attributes are then applied simultaneously to all selected items.

Controlling stacking and alignment

When creating the xyz logo in the preceding example, each of its parts was created in order so that each new part lay in front of the previous one. In this process, graphical objects are being stacked up in a certain order to achieve the final effect. Each new object added to a layout goes on top of the stack (in front of any other objects already on the layout).

In FileMaker, you have control over the stacking order of objects, so you can change it if necessary to achieve the effect you desire.

To continue the developing visual theme of the Inventory layout, follow these steps:

1. Choose the Rounded Rectangle tool and draw a rectangle approximately 8.5 inches wide and a little less than 1 inch high. (Remember, you can use the Object Info palette — View ⇨ Object Info — to check the size and coordinates of selected layout objects.)

2. With the rectangle selected, use the Object Effects palette to apply the Embossed effect and the Fill Color palette to apply a pale lilac color and then select the transparency option from the Line Pattern palette.

3. Drag the resulting rectangle to a central position in the header. With the rectangle in the header, you can no longer see the header text because the rectangle obscures it. The next step addresses this.

4. Move the mouse to a blank area at one side just below the header area and drag a selection rectangle that encompasses the area where the heading text object is located (but not large enough to fully encompass the new rectangle you've placed in the header). When

you release the mouse after dragging the selection rectangle, four selection boxes should appear to indicate that the text object in the header is selected, even though it is presently out of sight.

5. Choose Arrange ⇨ Bring to Front to alter the stacking order, bringing the selected text object forward so that it appears in front of the colored rectangle.

6. Select the logo object and drag it to a position within the left end of the rectangle in the header. Because the logo was created before the rectangle, it disappears behind the rectangle.

7. Click the rectangle to select it and choose Arrange ⇨ Send to Back (⌘+Option+] or Ctrl+Alt+]) to place it behind the logo.

After you adjust the placement and stacking order of the logo, heading text, and embossed rectangle, the Inventory layout should resemble the one shown in Figure 6.24.

FIGURE 6.24

The Inventory layout with logo and header band stacked and positioned.

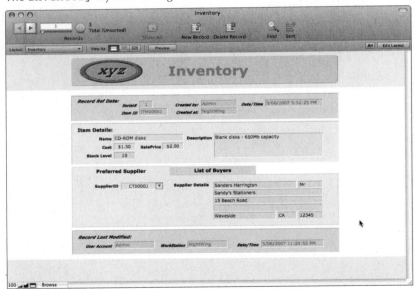

Bringing in graphics from other applications

Instead of building graphics such as logos in FileMaker, you may prefer to create them in another application — or it may be appropriate to use photographs or other images you have on hand. In that case, you can use the images as objects in FileMaker's layouts.

Although you can copy images from other applications and paste them into FileMaker layouts, this method does not always produce optimal results, depending on the attributes of the original image. I recommend that you save the image to disk in a standard format (such as .png, .gif, or .jpg) and then bring the file directly into FileMaker.

To place a picture stored in a supported file format directly onto a FileMaker layout, go to Layout mode, choose Insert ⇨ Picture, locate the file you want to add, and then click OK. The file is inserted and displayed on the layout, and you can move it, resize it, and position it within the stacking order along with other layout objects.

Interacting with Layout Objects

The work you do in Layout mode creates layouts for you to use in other modes, when interacting with your solution via its screens and reports. An important consideration when you build a layout is how efficiently you're able to use the layout in Browse mode and Find mode.

Keyboard control of a layout

Controlling the behavior of layout objects (fields, buttons, Tab Controls, and so on) in Browse mode by clicking them with the mouse isn't always the most efficient way for your users to work. When entering data, many users prefer to perform common actions by using keyboard commands.

With appropriate preparation, you can ensure that your layouts can be navigated and controlled by using the keyboard. Using the Field Behavior dialog (select a field and then choose Format ⇨ Field/ Control ⇨ Behavior), you can specify to go to the next object by using the Tab key, the Return key, and/or the Enter Key. Figure 6.25 shows the Field Behavior dialog, displaying the settings for Go to Next Object Using near the bottom.

FIGURE 6.25

Setting the keystrokes for Go to Next Object Using in the Field Behavior dialog.

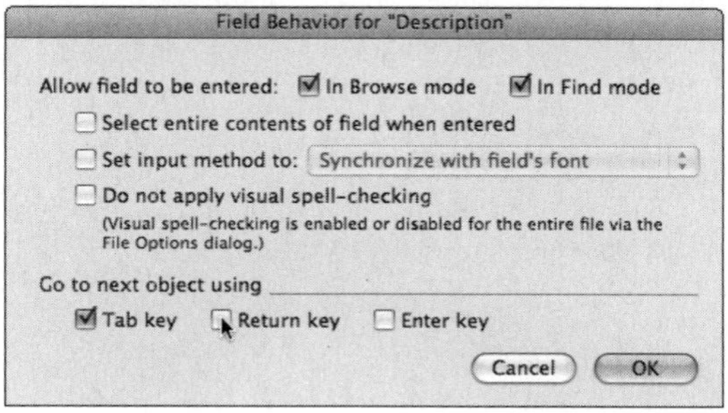

NOTE   The Return key is the carriage return key at the right of the alphabetic section of the computer keyboard (even though on some keyboards, especially those common to Windows systems, it's labeled Enter). In FileMaker, the Enter key refers specifically to the numeric keypad's Enter key.

By default, navigating layout fields follows a sequence that goes from left to right and then top to bottom. By using the keystrokes defined in the Field Behavior dialog, you can move from field to field through the layout in Browse and Find modes. The navigation sequence that enables you to move around the layout in this way is referred to as the *tab order*.

CAUTION   Specifying the Return key as one of the Go to Next Field keystrokes for a field prevents users from typing a carriage return into the field. (However, users are not prevented from pasting carriage returns into the field from the clipboard.)

This technique can, of course, be useful for fields where the inclusion of carriage returns is not desired or may present problems.

Setting the tab order

In many cases, you'll find it beneficial to predetermine the order of navigation through fields in your layouts, perhaps excluding some fields from the tab order. Moreover, you may want to include any Tab Controls, buttons, or Web viewers on your layouts in the tab order so that they can be controlled from the keyboard.

To edit a layout's tab order, go to Layout mode and choose Layouts ⇨ Set Tab Order to display the Set Tab Order dialog. As shown in Figure 6.26, fields (and any other keyboard-controllable objects) are displayed with adjacent arrows. The arrows attached to fields shown in the tab order include numbers indicating the field's position in the tab order sequence. Clicking the Clear All button in the Set Tab Order dialog removes the tab order numbering throughout the layout. Clicking the arrows in sequence enables you to edit the tab order or apply a new tab order.

NOTE   If a Tab Control object is included in the tab order, after you navigate to it by using the keyboard, you can use the left and right arrows to select a specific tab and either the spacebar or the Return key to bring the selected tab to the front. Similarly, if a button object is included in the tab order, after selecting it by using the keyboard, you can execute the button operation by using the spacebar or the Return key.

Assigning names to layout objects

FileMaker 8.5 introduced the ability to name objects on your layouts. Naming objects opens many possibilities — including letting you control or reference an object by its assigned name when you're defining a script or button command.

FIGURE 6.26

Specifying a custom tab order for fields on the `Inventory` layout.

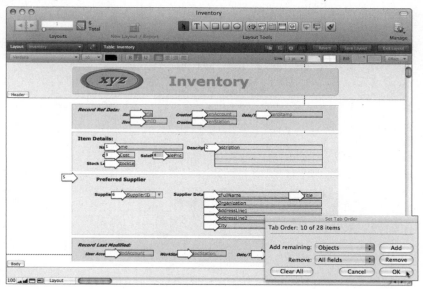

As an example, if you create a button object assigned to the Go to Object command and supply the object name of a field on the same layout, the button, when clicked, places the cursor into the corresponding field. You can use the same procedure to place focus on (or modify the behavior of) portals, Web viewers, Tab Control panels, and so on.

Controlling visual spell-checking

A key usability feature in FileMaker Pro is visual spell-checking — automatic underscoring of questionable words in the active field throughout a FileMaker file. However, it's the nature of databases that some fields are designed to hold values that don't benefit from spell-checking (IDs, codes, names, and so on). In these cases, visual spell-checking is an annoyance and a distraction.

TIP You can disable the visual spell-checking feature for specific field objects on your layouts. Figure 6.27 shows Layout mode's Field Behavior dialog for the `SupplierID` field (Format ➪ Field/Control ➪ Behavior) with the Do Not Apply Visual Spell-Checking option enabled.

FIGURE 6.27

Excluding a field from visual spell-checking via the Field Behavior dialog.

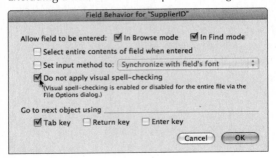

The Tab Control and Its Uses

In complex solutions, layouts can rapidly become cluttered and the clarity of the interface impaired. FileMaker provides a useful organizational tool that lets you put groups of objects away out of sight until you need them: the Tab Control.

One of the best uses of Tab Controls is to provide locations for alternative and low-use views of data. A single click takes you to the data when you need it, but the rest of the time it's not cluttering up your view of the data.

Here is one such example: The Inventory layout shows the preferred supplier for each item, but it may occasionally be useful to be able to view a list of buyers for the item. Because that's a secondary purpose of the layout, it would be better included on a concealed panel until needed.

Defining and creating a tab panel

To add a tab panel to the Inventory layout, perform the following steps:

1. Enter Layout mode for the Inventory layout.

2. Delete the rectangular background behind the Preferred Supplier field.

3. Click the Status Toolbar's Tab Control tool and then drag across the area of the Preferred Supplier fields. The Tab Control Setup dialog appears.

4. Enter **Preferred Supplier** into the Tab Name field and click the Create button.

5. Enter **List of Buyers** into the Tab Name field and click Create again.

6. In the dialog settings at the right, choose Left from the Tab Justification menu and Square from the Appearance menu, set the Tab Width menu to Label Width + Margin of:, enter **55** in the following field, and choose Pixels from the bottom menu, as shown in Figure 6.28.

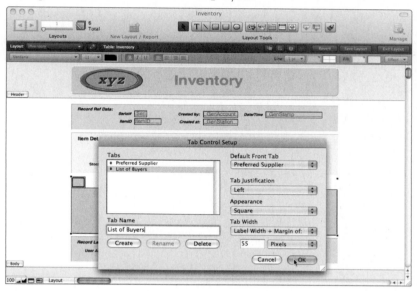

FIGURE 6.28

Adding a Tab Control to the Inventory layout.

7. Click OK to accept the Tab Control settings.

8. Choose Arrange ⇨ Send to Back to place the Tab Control behind the existing supplier fields.

9. With the Tab Control still selected, choose lightest gray fill color and mid-gray line color and select None from the Object Effects menu. If necessary, adjust the sizes and positions of the Tab Control and other elements on the layout to achieve appropriate spacing between objects and check that the font settings are appropriate.

After completing these steps, return to Browse mode to review the effects of your work. If all is well, the modified layout should be similar in appearance to Figure 6.29.

Navigating between tab panels

In Browse mode, the default tab panel (Preferred Supplier) appears at the front, displaying the fields previously enclosed by a static rectangular panel. The tab for the second panel (List of Buyers) appears dimmed.

Click with the mouse on the List of Buyers tab and note that it comes to the foreground, obscuring the Preferred Supplier tab and its contents (the Preferred Supplier tab is now dimmed). Now click the Preferred Supplier tab, and it returns to the front, reinstating your view of the supplier fields.

FIGURE 6.29

The appearance of the `Inventory` Layout tab panel when viewed in Browse mode.

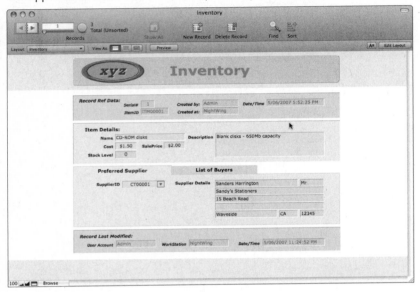

Tab panel limitations

Although Tab Controls are powerful and flexible, an essential feature of their operation is that they provide a view of the data in your database from the same vantage point (TO on the Relationships Graph) as the layout where they're placed. Tab Controls, like everything else on your layouts, are context dependent.

In cases where you need to take the user outside the current layout context, you should consider two options:

■ Place a portal in the Tab Control and build a supporting relationship structure enabling you to display the appropriate data from elsewhere in your solution.

■ Create a separate layout based on an alternative TO that serves in place of the tab. To provide comparable functionality, provide a button on each layout that the users can click to move back and forth seamlessly between the two layouts. (If you set it up with care, the user experience is comparable to the use of a Tab Control.)

CROSS-REF For a more detailed exploration of the uses and advanced options available for Tab Controls, refer to Chapter 10.

Displaying Related Data

The Inventory layout is based on the TO named Inventory and, by default, fields you place on the layout are sourced from the current record in the Inventory table. In some cases, however, you need to show fields from other tables so, as in the case of the Supplier Details group of fields, you choose an alternative (related) TO as the fields' source.

When you're working from a different layout (one based on a different TO), your view of the data in your solution is from a different vantage point. When sourcing data from another table, you must ensure that the TO you use to access fields from the other table is appropriately related to the current table. If in doubt, consult the Relationships Graph.

During the course of this chapter, I've described in detail processes for initial refinement of the Inventory layout. Before proceeding, take a few moments to work through the same processes on the remaining layouts in the file, using the same techniques to bring them into line with the layout and appearance of the Inventory layout.

Working within layout context

When making adjustments to the second layout (Orders) in the file, as well as defining the SupplierID field as a drop-down list (choosing Format ➪ Field/Control ➪ Setup) and setting it to display the Suppliers value list, you need to add relevant fields from the Contacts table.

Whereas on the Inventory layout related suppliers fields were sourced from the ItemSupplier TO (related to Inventory), on the Orders layout, supplier fields must come from a TO that is appropriately related to the Orders TO. If you consult the Relationships Graph (in the Manage Database dialog, accessible by choosing File ➪ Manage ➪ Database), you'll see that the TO named Suppliers is directly related to the Orders TO.

On the Orders layout, when adding related fields to show the supplier details, you should source the fields from the Supplier TO, as shown in Figure 6.30.

The Supplier fields, when placed on the Orders layout, do their job of showing related data. There is one supplier for each order, and the relevant supplier details appear in the related fields (on the Orders layout) when a value is selected in the Orders::SupplierID field.

Setting up a portal

Each order has only one supplier. However, a single order may consist of a number of items. Simply adding fields from the OrderLines TO is not adequate; you need a method to show a list of related records from the OrderLines TO. For this purpose, FileMaker provides the Portal object.

To add a portal to the Orders layout, enter Layout mode, click the Portal tool in the Status Toolbar, and drag the mouse across the area of the layout where you want to add the portal. The Portal Setup dialog appears.

FIGURE 6.30

Using the Specify Field dialog to source fields from the related `Supplier` TO for inclusion on the `Orders` layout.

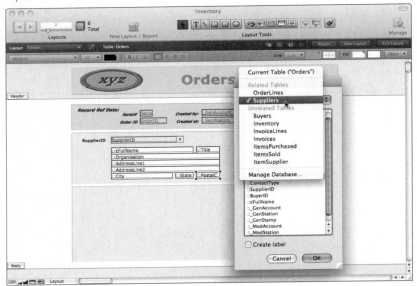

As shown in Figure 6.31, use the Show Related Records From menu near the top of the Portal Setup dialog to choose the `OrderLines` table from the group of related tables appearing in the list. Then select the Allow Deletion of Portal Records checkbox and enter 8 into the Number of Rows field. Also, select the Alternate Background Fill checkbox and choose the second lightest gray from the adjacent color palette. When you're finished, click OK to accept the portal setup.

Immediately upon dismissing the Portal Setup dialog, you see the Add Fields to Portal dialog. In the column at the left, select the `OrderLines::Qty` field and click the button labeled » Move » to include it in the column at the right of the dialog. Repeat this procedure to include the `OrderLines::ItemID` field, the `OrderLines::Price` field, and the `OrderLines::cLineTotal` field (as shown in Figure 6.32). When complete, click the OK button.

You now have a portal on the `Orders` layout, but it needs some further configuration before it's ready for use. To complete the process, proceed as follows:

1. Select the `ItemID` field in your new portal and choose Format ➪ Field/Control ➪ Setup (⌘+Option+F/Ctrl+Alt+F).

2. In the Field/Control Setup dialog, choose Pop-up Menu from the Display As menu at the top left of the dialog.

FIGURE 6.31

Adding a portal object (based on the `OrderLines` TO) to the `Orders` layout.

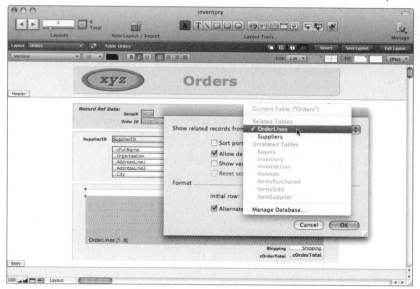

FIGURE 6.32

Adding fields to the `OrderLines` portal.

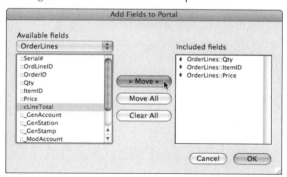

3. Choose Manage Value Lists from the Display values from menu (immediately below the Display As menu).

4. In the Manage Value Lists dialog, click the New button at the lower left.

5. In the resulting Edit Value List dialog, enter `AllItems` into the field labeled Value List Name. Then select the Use Values from Field radio button. The Specify Fields for Value List "AllItems" dialog appears.

6. Choose the `Inventory` TO from the menu above the column at the left of the Specify Fields dialog.

7. In the list in the left column of the Specify Fields dialog, select `ItemID`.

8. Above the column at the right of the Specify Fields dialog, select the Also Use Values from Second Field checkbox and then select the `Name` field in the list in the right column.

9. Near the bottom of the dialog, select the Show Values Only from Second Field checkbox.

10. Click OK to accept and dismiss each of the dialogs in turn.

11. In the portal, select all four fields and apply transparent line and fill attributes.

12. Resize the `OrderLines::Qty` field to approximately 0.5 inch wide and move it to the far left of the portal.

13. Resize both the `OrderLines::Price` and `OrderLines::cLineTotal` fields to approximately 1 inch wide each and move them to the right side of the portal.

14. With the `OrderLines::Price` and `OrderLines::cLineTotal` fields still selected, choose Format ➪ Number and select the options to Format as decimal, fixed number of digits 2, use currency notation, and use thousands separator. Then click OK to accept the number format settings.

15. Choose Format ➪ Align Text ➪ Right.

16. Reposition and resize the portal appropriately, applying a white fill and gray line attributes to it.

17. Immediately above the portal, add text labels for Qty, Item, Price, and Extended Price.

After you complete these steps, return to Browse mode to view the results of your efforts. The `Orders` layout should now resemble Figure 6.33.

Try adding some items to the portal (by entering them into the first blank line). The portal accepts and displays up to eight lines, automatically calculating the price, extended price, and order total values. Of particular note is the way the value list operates in this case, automatically retrieving a list of available items from the `Inventory` table so that you can select them when adding a line to an order. In conjunction with the use of a portal to add `OrderItems` records, the value list in this example provides powerful and flexible support to the user.

Before proceeding, take a little time to look over the other layouts in the file and bring them into line with the changes you've made to the `Orders` layout. In particular, the Invoices layout should be developed to closely resemble the `Orders` layout, including the use of a portal to display invoice lines. The `Contacts` layout is simpler, and its presentation will more closely resemble the `Inventory` layout.

FIGURE 6.33

The `Orders` layout in Browse mode showing the completed `OrderLines` portal.

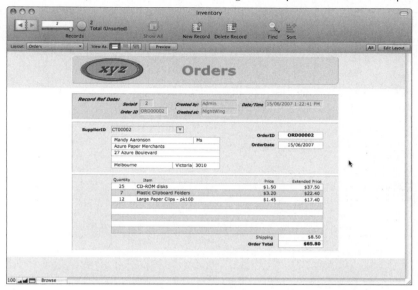

The Magic of Buttons

FileMaker provides a special tool in Layout mode's Status Toolbar for the creation of buttons. Buttons created with the Button tool are embossed rectangular text objects with a command attached.

You should know two things about buttons:

- You can choose Format ⇨ Button Setup to attach a command to any layout object (with the exception of a Tab Control) — not just to objects created with the Button tool. So almost anything can be a button.

- One of the commands you can attach to a button is more important than all the rest combined. It's the Perform Script [ ] command, and it's important because it enables a button to run a script containing many commands, capable of performing complex operations.

CROSS-REF For further discussion about advanced uses of buttons, refer to Chapter 10.

Defining buttons

In the Inventory database, go to Layout mode on the Orders layout. To add a button to the layout, follow these steps:

1. Select the Button tool.

2. Drag a rectangle approximately 2 inches wide into the footer area. When you release the mouse button, the Button Setup dialog immediately appears.

3. Choose the Go to Layout option in the list of commands at the left of the Button Setup dialog, as shown in Figure 6.34.

4. Use the Specify menu in the panel at the upper right to choose the Inventory layout.

5. Click OK to accept the settings and dismiss the dialog.

FIGURE 6.34

Creating a button in the footer area of the Orders layout.

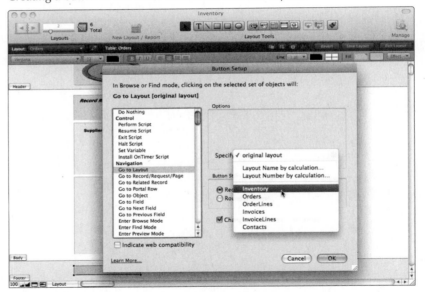

6. After you close the Button Setup dialog, the cursor flashes in the new button you've created, waiting for you to enter a button label — type **Inventory**.

7. Press the Enter key (on the numeric keypad) or click in a blank area of the layout to exit the button.

Now you have a button in the footer area of the layout, and it's assigned to the Go to Layout [ ] command. Further work is required, however, to bring its appearance into line with the design of the layout. To style the button, proceed as follows:

1. With the button selected, choose View ⇨ Object Info. The Object Info command acquires a tick and the Info palette appears.
2. Click the scale values at the right of the palette (the ones that read "in," "cm," or "px") to toggle the scale until it displays measurements in px (pixels).
3. Type **153** as the horizontal dimension and **22** as the vertical dimension.

TIP The horizontal and vertical dimension parameters in the Object Info palette are grouped together and identified by double-ended arrow symbols oriented horizontally and vertically, respectively.

4. Choose Format ⇨ Size ⇨ 12.
5. Choose Format ⇨ Style ⇨ Bold.
6. Choose Format ⇨ Color ⇨ [white].
7. Select a medium gray from the Fill Color palette and the transparent option from the Line Pattern palette.

After you complete these steps, your button has both form and function and is ready for duty as part of the interface of your solution. To create a second button, select the Inventory button and follow these steps:

1. Choose Edit ⇨ Duplicate (or type ⌘+D or Ctrl+D). A second button appears.
2. Position the duplicate button immediately to the right of the original button.
3. Click the text tool in the Status Toolbar and then click the duplicate button and edit the text to **Orders**.
4. Change the text color of the duplicate button to match the background color of the logo and change the fill color to two shades lighter gray.
5. Double-click the Orders button. The Button Setup dialog appears.
6. From the Specify menu in the upper-right area of the dialog, choose the `Orders` layout.

With both buttons complete and functional, the next task is to create corresponding buttons on another layout so that you can navigate back and forth by using the buttons in the footer. To replicate the two buttons you've created so far and to complete the navigation button set, follow these steps:

1. Select both buttons
2. Note the left and top coordinates shown in the Object Info palette.

TIP The left and top coordinates in the Object Info palette are identified by an arrow symbol pointing left and an arrow symbol pointing up, respectively.

3. Choose Edit ➪ Copy.

4. Navigate to the `Inventory` layout.

5. Choose Edit ➪ Paste.

6. Enter the left and top coordinates (as noted before leaving the `Orders` layout) into the Object Info palette and press the Enter key (on the numeric keypad). This step results in the pair of buttons being positioned identically in both layouts.

7. Edit the colors of the text and fill for both buttons on the `Inventory` layout so that the lighter gray fill is on the Inventory button and the mid-gray fill on the Orders button, the text on the Inventory button matches the color of the logo background, and the text on the Orders button is white.

8. Make two duplicates of the Orders button.

9. Change the text on the duplicate buttons to **Invoices** and **Contacts,** respectively.

10. Edit the button setup of the duplicate buttons to go to the layouts corresponding to their names.

11. Position the Invoices and Contacts buttons side by side to the right of the first two buttons on both the `Invoices` and `Orders` layouts.

12. Copy the four buttons and paste them at the same location in the footers of the `Invoices` and `Contacts` layouts.

13. Ensure in each case that the button corresponding to the current layout has lighter gray fill and colored text and that all the other buttons have mid-gray fill and white text.

With these steps complete, return to Browse mode and click your new buttons. You can now navigate to the four main areas of your solution by using simple mouse clicks in the footer, as shown in Figure 6.35.

Button scope and button commands

As you saw in the preceding exercise, creating buttons is not difficult. Moreover, although all four of the buttons you've created so far use the Go to Layout command, you've seen that the Button Setup dialog provides access to a great variety of commands.

FileMaker buttons are an interface tool and have no meaning outside the layouts where they reside; they always act from the context of the layout where you place them. For some button commands — such as the Go to Layout command — context is not critical, and the command can be executed from anywhere in the file. Other commands, however, require access to the data structure of the file and are therefore constrained to operate from the perspective of the layout (and the TO associated with the layout).

FIGURE 6.35

The `Inventory` layout complete with navigation buttons in the footer to provide direct access to the other main screens in the file.

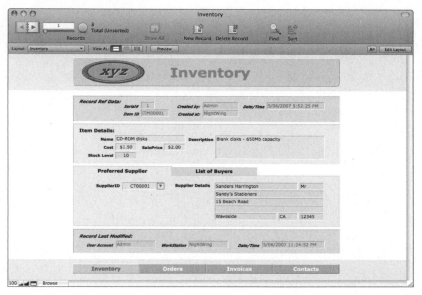

The button as an object

Like other objects, buttons can be assigned an object name. The object name is separate from the label you type onto the button and is only seen in the Object Info palette when the button is selected in Layout mode.

 **Object names for buttons and all other objects are entered and edited via the Object Name field at the top of the Object Info palette.**

When you've assigned a button's object name, scripts or buttons can select it automatically by executing the Go to Object command (supplying the relevant object name as the command parameter).

Similarly, you can include buttons in the layout tab order, along with fields, Tab Controls, and Web viewers. When you add a button to the tab order, you'll be able to select it by using the keyboard command(s) assigned to Go to Next Object for the object preceding the button in the tab order.

When you selecte a button — either via the Go to Object command or via the keyboard — you can execute it by pressing either Return or Space.

The Web Viewer: Inviting in the World

FileMaker's Web Viewer object enables you to incorporate Web browser capabilities within defined areas of the layouts of your solution. In FileMaker 10, you can deploy a Web viewer to retrieve online content from the World Wide Web, render HTML content stored on your computer's drives or on a local network, or display content directly from your database.

Setting up a Web viewer

Implementing a Web viewer on your layout is neither difficult nor time consuming. Simply click the Web Viewer tool in the Status Toolbar in Layout mode and drag across an empty area in your layout. When you release the mouse button, the Web Viewer Setup dialog appears.

The Web Viewer Setup dialog provides automated setup options for a number of useful Web resources. If you know the URL of the location you want to display, however, you can select the Custom Web Address option in the Choose a Website list and enter the desired URL directly into the Web Address field in the lower part of the dialog (see Figure 6.36).

FIGURE 6.36

Specifying an Internet location (URL) in the Web Address field of the Web Viewer Setup dialog.

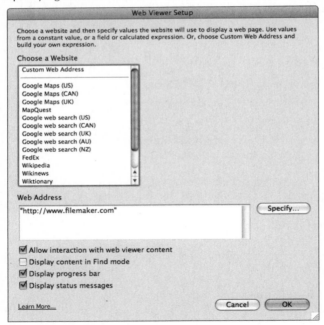

After setting up a Web viewer in this way, you can view the Web page content in your layout in Browse mode. Clicking hyperlinks enables you to navigate to other sites, download files, and so on, just as you do in a browser.

CROSS-REF You can find additional information about alternative configurations and uses for Webviewers in Chapter 10.

Controlling a Web viewer

Although a Web viewer, as outlined in the preceding section, provides the direct Web surfing capability such as you experience in a Web browser, it does not automatically provide the various standard controls for operations such as back, forward, refresh, and so on. If you require additional functions of that kind, you have to build your own controls.

FileMaker provides a button and script command — Set Web Viewer — configurable in various ways to provide either manual or automatic control of a Web viewer. To direct FileMaker to control a specific Web viewer (it's possible to have more than one on the same layout), you must first assign an object name to the Web viewer. You can then enter the Web viewer's name into the Object Name field when configuring the options for the Set Web Viewer command, as shown in Figure 6.37.

FIGURE 6.37

Setting options to control a Web viewer with the Set Web Viewer command.

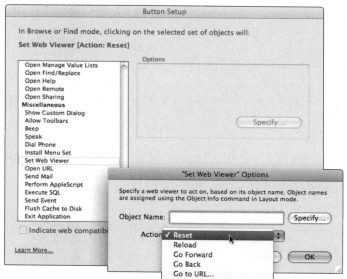

Complementary data concepts

The value of including Web content within your databases is greatest when it directly supports and extends the core functionality of your solutions — such as providing maps to your supplier's dispatch stations or retrieving catalog entries and prices for new products. In other words, data and images from the Web can complement and enrich your solution.

If you have your own organization or business, you're probably publishing key information on a public Web site of your own, keeping your clients, customers, students, patients, or constituents informed. Web viewers provide you with an excellent opportunity to view your organization's public information and your internal data side by side, placing the information you need at your fingertips. For example, you may want to show a picture (from the Web) of each product in your inventory system.

Reports and Data Output

This chapter has focused primarily on ways to make your solution functional and its interface operationally efficient. Consequently, the layouts and examples provided have been directed toward creating screens rather than useful printed output. However, while databases must first enable you to add data, it is equally essential that you retrieve and present data efficiently.

I encourage you to consider making separate screens for printing information from your solution. That way, you don't have to compromise screen designs to accommodate the limitations of paper sizes and printer capabilities — and your letters, lists, and summary reports are not constrained by screen ergonomics.

Considerations for printed output

Most printed matter — from business correspondence to boardroom reports — is printed in black (or dark) ink on white (or at least light) stationery. With a few exceptions, business documents are preferred in portrait orientation, and efficient use of space on the page (packing a lot of information in) is mandated.

In each of these respects, the requirements for printed output are at odds with the things that make good and useable screens. Screens are typically landscape in orientation; judicious use of color is beneficial, and it's preferable to avoid packing the information too densely.

Creation of good reports is frequently an exercise in efficient organization of large amounts of information into compact formats, using clean lines and simple (but elegant!) presentation.

Using fonts

Modern printers are capable of much higher resolutions than computer monitors. So, although many people begin to complain of eye strain when reading screen lettering at sizes of 10 points or less, smaller font sizes are readily accepted in most printed formats. Moreover, the most readable screen fonts are well spaced, rounded, and generally sans serif, whereas compact serif fonts work best for printed output.

I've previously suggested Verdana as a good font for general purpose use, and it's well suited to onscreen data display. For some kinds of reports, Verdana also works well, but substitutions with Trebuchet, Times, or other comparable fonts may be appropriate for more densely packed report formats.

Whatever your choices of font, I offer two essential rules:

- **Be consistent and moderate.** Try to keep to one or two fonts throughout a solution (logos and occasional special headings aside) and make sparing and judicious use of alternate faces and weights (italic, bold, and so on).

- **Ensure that whatever fonts you choose are available on every computer that the solution is to be used on.** If a font is not available, font substitution occurs, and its effects can make an appalling mess of your carefully constructed layouts and reports.

Finally, be aware that fonts (even the same font family) are rendered slightly differently (including different size) on different operating systems and can even vary depending upon the font supplier. Typically, fonts appear slightly larger in Windows than they do on Macintosh, so you may need to allow for this in your screen designs.

 **CROSS-REF** I discuss issues related to developing for cross-platform deployment in greater detail in Chapter 10.

Page sizes and page setup

In most parts of the world, page sizes are standardized — unfortunately, to different standards. In Australia, in Japan, and throughout Europe, the International Standards Organization (ISO) A4 standard is customary, while in the United States, the American National Standards Institute (ANSI) letter format holds sway. With globalization and the increasing use of the Internet, it's no longer safe to assume that all users of a solution have access to the same kinds of stationery. I recommend that you make a margin allowance to ensure that your reports and letters can be accommodated on an alternative page format should the need arise.

Meanwhile, FileMaker Pro is accommodating with regard to the many printers, printer drivers, and stationery formats — it provides you with options to save page specifications and other settings in scripts that automatically generate your reports.

TIP If you frequently switch among different paper sizes or orientations while printing manually, consider making buttons to restore the settings for particular situations (save sets of Page Setup settings in a button command configuration). In this manner, a single mouse-click can (re)set the appropriate configuration for you.

Paper output versus PDF or Excel output

I'm not about to break into song about the dream of the paperless office — but I would neverthe-less like to encourage you to save a few trees by taking advantage of FileMaker's excellent support for generation of data and reports direct to widely used formats such as Excel and PDF.

The capability to index and store documentation in electronic form is not only fast and ecofriendly, it also saves you money, effort, and storage space. You can compress and store an entire filing drawer of text documents on a single DVD. You can store terabytes of information in economical and reliable hard drives. Further, when the inevitable time arrives where you need to update your documentation, even more trees survive.

If you need any more encouragement, we note that FileMaker enables you to create a document and automatically attach it to an e-mail — all as part of a single process. With a little thought and planning, you can design your solutions to take fullest advantage of these capabilities.

> **CROSS-REF**   More detailed coverage of techniques for generating reports and summaries in FileMaker is provided in Chapter 10.

Composite PDFs from multiple layouts

Layouts are the face of your data. When printing or viewing data, you're accessing the underlying tables through a layout. Although layouts are very flexible, they constrain you to a specific perspec-tive or vantage point within the structure of your solution. In some cases, you want a report to combine content from several different vantage points, so you produce reports that combine pages or sections from different layouts.

> **TIP**   FileMaker Pro provides the capability to append pages to an existing PDF file via script — so you can produce compact documents combining elements from any part of your solution.

> **CROSS-REF**   In Chapter 13 you can find a detailed discussion about the process of generating composite PDF reports with FileMaker's scripting engine.

In the last two chapters, you've seen and used most of the basic solution-building techniques, including creating relationships to bring data together from different tables. You've seen some indi-cations of the power at FileMaker's core. Now it's time to delve more deeply into the heart of the database and take a closer look at the workings of the Manage Database dialog, where the structure of your solutions takes shape.

> **ON the WEB**   The example database we've been developing, as it exists at this point, can be found on the companion Web site at www.wiley.com/go/filemaker10bible.

Chapter 7

The Structure: The Manage Database Dialog

FileMaker presents you with different interfaces to perform different tasks — and from the user's perspective, Browse mode, Find mode, and Preview mode cover most requirements. However, when you're in the process of developing or modifying your database, you'll spend much of your time in Layout Mode (discussed in Chapter 6), in the Manage Scripts and Edit Script dialogs (see Chapter 8), and in the various tabs and panels of the Manage Database dialog. The Manage Database dialog is thus one of the three main developer centers within FileMaker and is where the plans and specifications for your database reside, allowing you to build and edit the tables and relationship structures that support your data.

Creating a database is a design process that involves a series of decisions, each of which impacts the subsequent operation of the solution — affecting its efficiency as well as the development time and complexity of the project. A few good decisions early in the development cycle may save you a great deal of stress and frustration later on.

FileMaker Pro is built around principles that take care of much of the tedium of the database design process. FileMaker anticipates your needs in a number of ways — from automatic creation of an initial default Table Occurrence and layout for each table you create, to the automatic update of object names (for example, field and table names) throughout your solution's code whenever you edit them. In these and a variety of other ways, FileMaker can be considered to be a *rapid application development* (RAD). As part of the commitment to RAD principles, a simple change of your solution's field or table definitions in the Manage Database dialog flows on throughout your solution's code and interface, so references to the field in labels on layouts, in scripts, and even in custom function definitions will be automatically updated, saving you what would otherwise be a great deal of painstaking labor.

IN THIS CHAPTER

Organizing data with tables

Creating data structure with fields

Doing basic calculations

Understanding the Relationships Graph

Working with External SQL Data Sources

Looking at data relationships

Notwithstanding the various ways FileMaker anticipates your actions and makes various parts of the process straightforward or even easy, the decisions you make when creating and updating the structure of your database will require thought and skill because they have deep implications for the ways your solution will work (or fail to work). In this chapter, many of the subtleties of the Manage Database dialog are laid bare.

Working with Tables

Database tables are part of the organizing principle for your data. When you have things to organize, you group them together, first into broad (but clear) categories and then into finer categories. All your clothes go into a certain closet, but within that closet, the socks go into a certain drawer, the handkerchiefs into another. Tables provide a receptacle for information about a particular kind or class of things, allowing you to establish hierarchies of order and clarity as a framework for management of the information in your solution.

Table concepts: A room with a view

A good way for you to think about structures for organizing data is to consider how other familiar things around you are organized. For example, houses are comprised of rooms in much the same way as database solutions may incorporate a number of tables. The various rooms in a house have different purposes — the kitchen, the laundry, the bedroom, and so on — and some rooms are connected to others by corridors, doors, serving hatch, and the like.

Just like the rooms of a house, the tables of your solution can be connected to each other so that from the perspective of one table, you have access to related data from another table. FileMaker provides a Relationships Graph where you can manage these data connections to and between the tables you define in your solution. Moreover, FileMaker allows you to place multiple occurrences of each table onto the Relationships Graph — so they operate like multiple doors or windows into a given room, each providing a different path to the data contained there, or, if you will, a different view.

The tabs of the Manage Database dialog are where you create the rooms (tables) for your database and the Relationships Graph is where you add doors and windows to enable you to see from one to another and to navigate between them.

Adding, deleting, and renaming tables

When working with the FileMaker Relationships Graph, you're dealing with TOs that provide views into your tables. Each TO is a specific view (like a window or a doorway) into a particular table. Just as you may require several different points of access to a room in your house (to enable entry from different places or for different purposes), you can add multiple TOs of the same table and position them differently in the logical structure of your database. The Manage Database dialog provides you with a Tables tab to create, modify, or delete tables and a Relationships tab where you create, modify, or delete TOs.

NOTE You can find out how many TOs of each table appear in the Relationships Graph by counting them in the Occurrences in Graph column on the Tables tab of the Manage Database dialog. If you have numerous occurrences, you may need to enlarge the dialog to see them all. Alternatively, you can select one of the Table Occurrences in the Relationships Graph and type ⌘+U or Ctrl+U to select all TOs with the same source table and then count the selected TOs.

The `Inventory` example file developed over the course of the previous two chapters has six tables defined and ten TOs, as you can see in the Tables tab of the Manage Database dialog shown in Figure 7.1. To access a fresh copy of the in-progress `Inventory` example at the end of the preceding chapter (to follow along with the examples here), download the `Inventory_Ch6.fp7` file from the book's companion Web site.

FIGURE 7.1

Create, remove, and rename your tables in the Manage Database dialog's Tables tab.

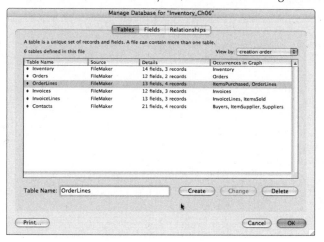

The Tables tab of the Manage Database dialog has relatively few controls, but it provides you with some essential data about the basic structure and content of your solution. Among the information the Tables tab makes available is the list (by name) of each table's occurrences in the Graph that appears in the right-hand column of the list area. This information is not immediately apparent from looking at the Graph itself, nor from viewing layouts or dialogs elsewhere in your solutions. In addition, the Tables tab lists the tables' names, their source (shown as FileMaker if the table is stored in the current file, or as the name of the DSN from which the data is sourced if the table is external), plus summary details regarding the number of fields and records in each table. (If a table is external, its entry will be italicized, and the number of records will appear only if the table has been cached by FileMaker. Otherwise, a question mark will appear in place of the number of records.)

NOTE If you have access to a copy of FileMaker Pro 10 Advanced, you can make use of the Database Design Report (DDR) option to obtain data about the structure and content of your solution. The DDR collects all the information about your solution — tables, fields, relationships, scripts, and so on — into one consolidated report. (See Chapter 18 for additional details.)

In the Manage Database dialog's Tables tab, you can change the width of the columns by dragging the column joins to the left or right. At the upper right, you'll find the View By pop-up menu, from which you can choose the presentation order for tables listed in the main data panel. You can choose to show tables in creation order, alphabetically by table name, or in a custom (user-defined) sequence. To specify a custom order, you can use the handle symbols at the left of the table names to drag the corresponding line to a new position in the list. (Doing so automatically changes the setting in the View By menu to show it's a custom order.)

In Chapter 5, I provide details of the process for creation of a new table: You type a table name into the text box provided below the main list of tables and then click the Create button to the right of the text box. To change the name of a table, first select it (the selected table's name will appear in the Table Name field below the list of tables), modify the name in the Table Name field, and click the Change button. (Note that the Change button is dimmed except when a name edit is waiting to be saved.) Excising a table is equally simple: Just click on it in the list to select it and then click the Delete button at the lower right. (You'll be prompted to also remove occurrences in the Graph of tables you're deleting, which you'll generally want to do unless you intend to assign them to a different table — for example, a table in another file.)

When you make a change to the name of a table, FileMaker Pro updates both direct and indirect references to it throughout the current file. For example, the names of associated TOs (either with the same name as the table or the same name with an appended number) will be updated to reflect the edited table name. Similarly, if you have layouts in the file that are associated with those TOs (and have exactly matching names), they, too, will be renamed automatically. Moreover, if you have references to the TOs that have been renamed (such as in calculations or script code), they, too, will be automatically updated to show the revised naming.

NOTE In some cases, you may not want cascading name changes throughout elements in your solution. If you edit the names of the TOs so that they no longer exactly match the source table name, FileMaker doesn't apply any automatic changes when you change a table name.

Moving tables between files

For a variety of reasons, you may find yourself wanting to move one or more tables between FileMaker files. You may want to do so because you've created a table that would be useful in more than one solution — or because you have a solution that has previously been in multiple files (for example, a solution migrated from an earlier version of FileMaker), and you want to consolidate the tables in a single file (or in a smaller number of files).

Assuming that you have access to a copy of FileMaker Pro 10 Advanced, one option available to you is to open two files simultaneously, choose a source table in the tables tab of one of the files' Manage Database dialog, and then choose Edit ⇨ Copy (⌘+C or Ctrl+C). Then navigating to the Tables tab of the Manage Database dialog for the target file, choose Edit ⇨ Paste (⌘+V or Ctrl+V).

FileMaker Pro Advanced also provides a table import capability in the Tables tab of the Manage Database dialog. This feature adds the table structure (fields and all their calculations validation options and so on) but doesn't import data, relationships, or any other associated elements.

Whether or not you're using FileMaker Pro Advanced, you have the option of importing a table from one solution into another by using the File ⇨ Import Records ⇨ File command, as described in the following section.

Importing tables

Although nowhere near as efficient as copying and pasting, the process of importing a table from another FileMaker file does more than replicate the source table. When you import a table into a different file by choosing the File ⇨ Import Records ⇨ File command, you simultaneously add part or all of the table's field structure and its data contents. As with other kinds of import procedures in FileMaker, if you establish a found set in the frontmost window of an open source file, only the found records will be imported.

> **NOTE** When adding a table to the destination file, FileMaker always creates the entire table. (All fields from the source table are created in the new destination table.) However, you can use the Import mapping process to choose which fields to import data into.

> **CAUTION** Importing a table is an irreversible step; you can't undo it. Before undertaking this procedure, make sure that you have a recent backup copy of your solution.

Following is the procedure for importing a table from the Inventory example file (from the preceding chapter) into a new empty database file:

1. Locate your copy of the Inventory example file named Inventory_Ch06.fp7 (if necessary, download it from the book's companion Web site — you'll find the URL and download details in Appendix B) and make a note of the path to the folder where you've stored it.

2. Choose File ⇨ New Database and then (assuming the QuickStart screen is enabled) select the option to create an empty database.

3. Name the new database **MyItems.fp7** (for the sake of this example). When you click Save, the Manage Database dialog appears. Note that by default, FileMaker has created an empty table with the same name as the file (MyItems).

4. Click OK to dismiss the Manage Database dialog.

5. Choose File ⇨ Import Records ⇨ File. In the Open File dialog that appears, choose the Inventory_Ch06solution you located (or downloaded) in Step 1 and then click Open. The Import Field Mapping dialog (see Figure 7.2) appears.

FIGURE 7.2

Specify what fields to import data from (if any exist in the source file) here.

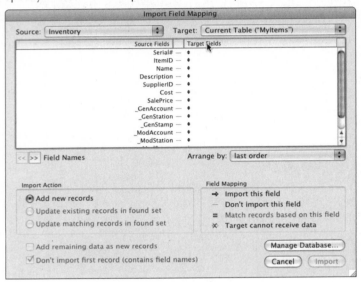

6. Choose New Table ("Inventory") from the Target pop-up menu. The Target Fields column now includes all the fields from `Inventory` table in the Chapter 6 example file, with each source field pointing to its same-named `Target` field in the new table that is to be created.

7. Click Import. The Import Options dialog (see Figure 7.3) appears.

   After you click the Import button in the Import Options dialog, FileMaker creates a new table called `"Inventory"` in the `MyItems.fp7` file, populates it with data from the `Inventory` table in the `Inventory_Ch06.fp7` solution and displays a confirmation dialog, as shown in Figure 7.4.

FIGURE 7.3

You can specify additional import options in the Import Options dialog.

FIGURE 7.4

FileMaker provides a confirmation via the Import Summary dialog.

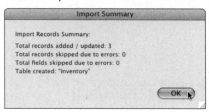

8. Click OK on the Import Summary dialog to complete the import process.

If you were using the procedure described in the preceding steps to commence development of a new solution, the default table added to the file in the third step would presumably be superfluous to your needs. However, it's a simple matter for you to delete the default table and be left only with the newly imported `Inventory` table.

An important part of the process of adding a table to your solution via import is that FileMaker doesn't simply add fields with the same names, but imports all the configurations and specifications for each field, including its data type (number, text, date, time, and so on), its Auto-Entry, validation and storage settings (including indexing settings), and, in the case of calculation fields, formulae. With all these characteristics preserved, plus with the data (if any) from the source table also imported into your file, you have in effect completely transferred the table between files. As shown in Figure 7.5, this procedure results in the `Inventory` table being transferred in its entirety into the `"MyItems"` file.

In cases where an existing calculation field imported references fields in other tables, FileMaker will look for fields with the same TO and field naming in the file to which you're importing. If it finds them, then it will preserve the calculation intact. Where a calculation field references fields (in other tables) that aren't present in the file into which you're importing the table, the calculation formulae will be enclosed within comment braces, and the calculation will not function until you make a manual correction (to remove the comment braces and update the field references to ones that are valid within the table's new location).

CROSS-REF For further details regarding code commenting and the use of comment braces, refer to Chapter 12.

Each element of a FileMaker file — including fields and tables — is assigned its own internal ID within your solution. When a table is being imported (or copied and pasted) between two different files, the internal IDs of fields are preserved after import. So, for example, a field that had an internal ID of 341 in the original file still has the ID 341 in the new file to which the table has been imported. The preservation of field IDs is important because when links are established between files, FileMaker uses the internal IDs to keep track of elements in other files — so if you re-create a table in a new file, the chances are that the IDs will not match (for example, if the fields aren't created in the same order). Because of the way FileMaker handles the assignment of internal IDs during transfer of structure, the ability to import tables enables you to build new files that will work interchangeably within an existing multi-file solution, with field references resolving correctly between files.

The Manage Database dialog showing the fully configured Inventory table after import into the brand new "MyItems" file.

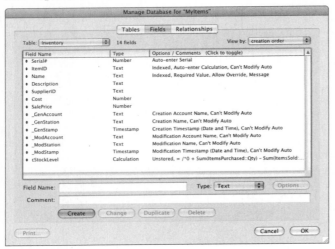

TIP The internal IDs that FileMaker assigns to each field you create are allotted sequentially, just like the Auto-Enter ID fields created in this book's Inventory example. In general, you don't need to worry about Field IDs, because FileMaker manages them behind the scenes. However, when accessing data from outside the current file, FileMaker resolves all references and relationships by using internal IDs.

Specifying Fields

At one time, most database systems required that you allocate a specific number of characters for each field. If field contents were shorter than the allocated length of the field, the difference was made up in spaces — and conversely, if anyone needed to enter a value that was longer than the allocated field length, they were out of luck. Worse still, with such systems, adding a field into the mix after the table was in place was a major headache. Fortunately FileMaker, along with most current database technology, is far more flexible than this, providing for fields of variable size and allowing you to add or remove fields with ease at any time.

Adding, deleting, and renaming fields

Using a technique similar to the one for adding, deleting, or renaming tables in your solution, FileMaker lets you make changes, deletions, and additions to the fields within each FileMaker table. Note, however, that you must have access to the file where a table resides in order to make changes to either the table or the fields it contains. (You can access the table's data from other files, but changes to the table itself must be made from within the file that accommodates it.)

To add a field to an existing table:

1. Navigate to the Fields tab of the Manage Database dialog and choose the table in question from the drop-down menu at the upper left.
2. Enter a name in the Field name box (below the list of fields).
3. Choose a field type from the adjacent drop-down menu and then click the Create button.

To edit an existing field (for example, to change its type or modify its name):

1. Select the field in the field list.
2. Make changes in the type menu and/or name box below the list.
3. Click the Change button.

Similarly, to remove a field permanently from the table, select it in the list and then click the Delete button. (FileMaker will present a confirmation dialog before removing a field from your database.) If you remove a field, any data it previously contained throughout your solution will be lost.

NOTE The fields in an External SQL Data Source are not available for modification (you can't rename or delete them) from within FileMaker — such changes must be made by using utilities provided by the source (SQL) database application. The exception is that you can add summary and calculation fields that exist only in your solution and not in the external file. Moreover, if you delete fields appearing in a SQL table in FileMaker, they're removed from the FileMaker view of the table, but not from the external database. (You can reinstate fields deleted from a shadow table by clicking the Sync button that appears above the shadow table field list in the Manage Database dialog.)

When you rename a field in FileMaker, a lot of useful things happen behind the scenes. FileMaker helps you out by automatically updating all references in the Relationships Graph, scripts, calculations, and any corresponding layout labels to reflect the field's new name. However, in cases where you've modified a field's layout label or moved it to a different part of the layout (so that it's no longer adjacent to the field box to which it relates), FileMaker no longer keeps track of the item, and it won't be updated when you change the corresponding field name.

Field deletion can occur either because you delete a field in the current FileMaker file (using the Delete button on the Fields tab of the Manage Database dialog) or because you delete the table in which a field resides (using the Delete button on the Tables tab of the Manage Database dialog), in which case, all the table's fields also will automatically be deleted.

FileMaker disallows the deletion of any field referenced in a calculation or summary field within the same table or within a calculation determining privileges for the table. In such cases, to delete the field, you must first modify or delete the calculation(s) and/or summary field(s) referencing the field. When the reference is no longer present, you can successfully delete the field. If a field you want to delete is referenced in a script or used as a key field for a relationship, FileMaker posts a warning dialog (citing the first script or relationship depending in the field) but nevertheless allows you to proceed, if you want. If you disregard the warning and delete a field used in one or more scripts or relationships, the relevant script(s) or relationship(s) will not work as intended until you manually repair them. Finally, if a field you delete is referenced in a calculation in another table or file (including within a script in another file), FileMaker will neither prevent deletion nor post a warning, but external references to the field will be rendered inoperable.

When you delete a field that isn't referenced locally (within the same table) or when you delete a table, FileMaker posts a confirmation alert dialog, but doesn't prevent you from proceeding. However, if a field you have deleted on your layouts has references to it or in calculations, scripts, button calculations, tooltips or elsewhere throughout your solution, they will display a placeholder <Field Missing> flag. Moreover, any calculations referencing missing fields will (typically) return null or inaccurate results (the same is true for summaries), while scripts that refer to missing fields may produce undesired and perhaps unpredictable results.

Understanding field/data types and their significance

One of the most significant attributes of FileMaker Pro fields is their data type, which determines the kind of information the field can store, the format for storage, and various other aspects of the field's behavior. Choosing the correct type for a field ensures that FileMaker accepts, presents, indexes, and stores the data appropriately, while also determining what you're able to do with the data. For example, if you designate a phone number field as being numeric, leading zeros may be ignored in some instances (such as sorting), and non-numeric characters common in phone numbers (such as spaces, dashes, or alphabetic sequences) may not be handled or displayed appropriately. Phone numbers are not really numbers!

The data type of a field is determined by the Type pop-up menu below the fields list on the Fields tab of the Manage Database dialog, shown in Figure 7.5. The Type pop-up menu provides eight options, two of which are for derived data (calculation and summary fields), and the remainder of which represent data storage formats. The available field types are as follows:

- **Text** fields can store any kind of alphanumeric data, including anything you can enter directly via the keyboard (up to 1,000,000,000 characters).

- **Number** fields can also store alphabetic characters and may be referenced in some text calculations. However, numeric indexing protocols are applied, so searching for alphanumeric strings will present difficulties. Although number fields can store up to a billion characters, numeric values comprising up to 800 digits on either side of the decimal point (up to 1,600 digits in total) are supported and indexed. Moreover, to be indexed and referenced appropriately, values stored in number fields must be all on one line.

- **Date** fields are stored internally as numeric data and can therefore be employed in calculations to determine the number of days between events. Date fields are restricted to values between 1 January 0001 and 31 December 4000 ce. Values stored in Date fields will sort chronologically, as opposed to dates stored in Text fields, which are subject to alphanumeric sorts. By default, Date fields display according to the date formats determined by the settings on the Text tab of the File Options dialog (that is, in line either with the current system settings or the file defaults established at the time of file creation). Data entry must be in the default date format as specified in File Options. However, you can specify alternative display formats (for example, by choosing Format ⇨ Date in Layout mode).

NOTE If you enter dates in an abbreviated format (that is, with fewer than eight digits and two separators), FileMaker makes certain assumptions about what date you're referring to. The first assumption is that entering only a single number is invalid. However, two numbers separated by a forward slash or period (provided they fall in the 1..12 and 1..31 ranges, respectively — or vice versa in most countries outside the United States) are interpreted as specifying a date in the current year. Similarly, if you enter a two-digit year, FileMaker makes an assumption about which year you're referring to and converts your input into an imputed four-digit year.

- **Time** fields contain a time of day (or a duration) in hours, minutes, and seconds, separated by colons. Times can be stored with a resolution of up to one microsecond. To have a time field display a duration greater than 24 hours, choose Format ⇨ Time in Layout mode for that field and specify either Leave Data Formatted as Entered or 24-Hour Notation. FileMaker stores times internally as numeric data (in seconds since midnight), so they, too, can be used in calculations (for example, to determine the interval between two times).

TIP If you enter a single number, FileMaker treats the entry as an hour value; two colon-separated numbers are treated as hours and minutes. To enter a minute value, the leading 0 for hours (and separating colon) is required. To enter a seconds value, the leading 0s for both hours and minutes are required.

- **Timestamp** fields combine a date and time, separated by a space. You saw examples of Timestamp fields in the Inventory database begun in Chapters 5 and 6. The respective parts of a Timestamp value follow the Date and Time input requirements (except that the time portion must be between 00:00:00 and 23:59:59.999999). FileMaker stores timestamps as a numeric value representing the number of seconds elapsed since 12:00:00 a.m. on 1 January 0001, so you can use these values, too, in computations to determine the duration between two times on given dates.

- **Container** fields are the catchall for a variety of types of nontextual data. You can store graphics, movies/multimedia (QuickTime supported file formats), sounds you record in FileMaker Pro, or an arbitrary disk file. In Windows machines, you can also store Object Linking and Embedding (OLE) objects.

- **Calculation** fields, the first of two derived data field types, consist of a formula specified to returning one of the first six data types (including Container). Calculations are defined in the Specify Calculation dialog. (See the "Basic Calculations" section, later in this chapter.)

■ **Summary** fields bear some similarities to Calculation fields, but instead of acting on values in a single record, they perform their calculation on a group of records (that is, records in the current found set, or the current related set when evaluated from a layout based on another table) in the table where they reside. Summary fields return aggregate results over the current record set (found or related), such as sum, average, count, or standard deviation.

FileMaker supports indexing of text, number, date, time, and timestamp field types. However, the indexing protocols differ according to type. In particular, text fields are indexed and sorted according to conventions that are not applicable to other field types. Number, date, time, and timestamp fields are all numeric in basis, but FileMaker translates date, time, and timestamp values into appropriate formats for display.

CROSS-REF For additional detail regarding field indexing, refer to the section titled "Storage and indexing options," later in this chapter.

Auto-Entry options

As demonstrated in Chapter 5, situations arise where you want some fields to automatically acquire a value when new records are created — serial numbers, account names, and creation/modification dates are examples. In these cases, I chose to invoke the Prohibit Modification of Value during Data Entry option because a user override of such values would compromise the integrity or purpose of the data. Another common example benefiting from Auto-Entry is establishing a default value for a field — for example, initializing the State value in a contact record where most of your customers live in the same state. In this situation, you want users to be able to override the initial value, so the Prohibit Modification option is not appropriate. FileMaker Pro offers you great flexibility when specifying Auto-Entry values through the Field Options dialog's Auto-Enter panel (shown in Figure 7.6). You access the Field Options dialog by selecting a field in the Manage Database dialog's Fields tab and clicking Options (or by double-clicking the field entry).

NOTE I'm happy to report that I love the power and flexibility that FileMaker's Auto-Enter options provide — but to be frank, I also have to admit that I'm not thrilled with the interface. The Auto-Enter panel presents you with seven checkboxes grouped together. In both Mac OS and Windows, a checkbox grouping implies that you can select multiple items, but that's not what's on offer here; the first five checkbox options are mutually exclusive, as are the last two (that is, you can select up to two options — one of the first five and/or one of the last two).

After you get over your puzzlement at the way the Auto-Enter interface works, you can configure FileMaker to auto-enter values representing the record's creation or modification date, time, or timestamp; generate a serial number; populate a field with the value from the last record visited or with a static default value; calculate a default value; or look up a value from a record in another table. Here's how the Auto-Enter options work:

FIGURE 7.6

The Options for Field dialog's Auto-Enter panel.

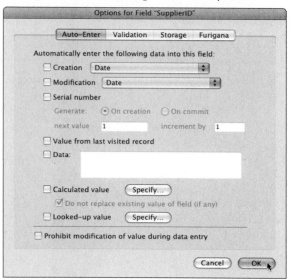

- Select the **Creation** checkbox and choose from the associated pop-up menu to have FileMaker automatically place the date, time, timestamp, *username* (a name assigned to the instance of FileMaker on the current workstation), or *account name* (the user's login credential for the current file) active at the time the user creates the record.

- Select the **Modification** checkbox to have FileMaker enter the date, time, timestamp, username, or account name active when any field in the record is modified.

- Select the **Serial Number** checkbox to have FileMaker generate automatic, incrementing numeric, or alphanumeric serial values. When an alphanumeric serial format (that is, a serial number incorporating both letters and numbers) is specified, only the rightmost numeric portion of the value is incremented.

- Select the **Value from Last Visited Record** checkbox to have FileMaker initialize the field with the previously viewed record's value for the field. For the purposes of this feature, *visited* means entering a record (for example, by placing the cursor into a field — merely scrolling past a record or viewing it does not qualify). Moreover, when a file is closed, the last record visited isn't saved, so if a record is created on first opening a file (before visiting any records), the value from last visited record's Auto-Entry option will return a null result.

- Select the **Data** checkbox to have FileMaker place a default value in the field each time a new record is created— for example, when entering patient data for a local hospital in Dallas, you probably want the State field to default to Texas. Type the default value in the text box next to the Data checkbox.

- Select the **Calculated Value** checkbox to have FileMaker compute a value based upon other field values, system variables (for example, current computer's IP Address), constants, or any mix thereof, as in the `Inventory` example's various ID and line total fields.

NOTE By default, the Do Not Replace Existing Value of Field (If Any) checkbox is selected. When this option is selected, changes the user makes to the auto-entered value persist. If the checkbox is deselected, the field value will be overwritten if values it depends on change.

- Select the **Looked-Up Value** checkbox when you want FileMaker to retrieve and store a value from a field in a related TO.

Field validation options

Your design goal may be to ensure that the data users enter into a field meets specified requirements, such as determining that a Social Security number is comprised of nine digits (with separators after the third and fifth digits); that product attributes, such as color or size, conform to accepted standards (and are spelled correctly); or that product sale quantities do not exceed available stock. There are many such possibilities, depending on the nature of your solution and the rules of the business it serves.

As shown in Figure 7.7, FileMaker provides a broad spectrum of validation capabilities in the Options for Field dialog's Validation panel.

FIGURE 7.7

The Validation panel of the Options for Field dialog.

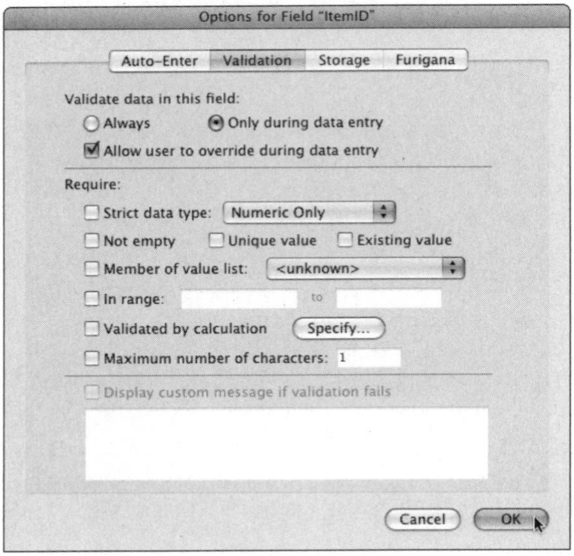

Here is a brief description of the options you'll find on the Validation panel:

- The **Validate Data in This Field** section provides you with two radio buttons and a checkbox that enables you to determine when validation occurs and whether it's to be strictly enforced.

  - The **Only during Data Entry** radio button (the default) enables you to configure FileMaker to validate the data only when the data is entered directly by the user (but not, for example, when data is imported or modified by a script).

  - The **Always** radio button tells FileMaker to also validate imported data and scripted field modifications. When this option is selected, imports will ignore records that don't satisfy validation criteria, and scripts will be prevented from committing records with invalid data (and may fail or otherwise malfunction unless appropriately coded to deal with this condition).

  - The **Allow User to Override during Data Entry** checkbox (selected by default) specifies whether enforcement is absolute (that is, FileMaker will prevent the modified record from being committed unless the criteria are met) or optional (where FileMaker warns the user but permits the user to instruct FileMaker to proceed with the requested change anyway).

CAUTION The validation options fall into two broad groups: those that apply at the field level, such as Strict Data Type or Member of a Value List and so on, and those that apply at the record level (specifically Validated By Calculation and Not Empty). Whereas script or import actions that attempt to make an invalid modification to a field with a validation rule that operates at the field level will fail and other changes to the record will proceed unhampered, modifications that fail record level validation will result in the record either being skipped (during an import process) or being unable to commit (during a script). When Validate Always is selected and a record can't be committed because a record level field validation rule is violated, not even the `Commit Records [Skip validation]` command will permit the record to be committed.

- The **Require** section is where you indicate specific validation rules and requirements.

  - **Strict Data Type** enables you to specify that you want the data to be **Numeric Only** (useful with Number fields), **4-digit Year Date** to only allow entries having a millennium compliant year format, or a **Time of Day** to accept only a valid time value (that is, no durations, or at least none of 24 hours or greater). You can choose one of these three options from the associated pop-up menu.

  - **Not Empty** allows you to require that a value be present in the field. For example, the `Inventory` table's Name field in the book's example `Inventory` solution is an example of a required field.

  - **Unique Value** and **Existing Value** are mutually exclusive, self-explanatory options. Note that both these options use the field's index to determine that the requirement is satisfied during data entry.

■ **Member of a Value List** allows you to constrain the entered values to correspond to values present on a value list you have defined. You can select the option to **Manage Value Lists** from the pop-up menu, if you want to edit the value lists in your solution or create an additional value list.

■ **In Range** enables you to constrain the entered value to fall within a defined domain, by entering minimum and maximum values allowed for a field. The most obvious uses for this option are its application to Number, Date, Time, and Timestamp fields. However, it also works with text values (according to their position in the collating sequence for the field's language — so that you can define a field to accept only names from *Aarom* to *Mulchahey,* for example).

■ **Validated by Calculation** presents you with the Specify calculation dialog, where you can encode validation rules in the form of a formula to determine whether the data is acceptable. For example, you may want to compare the entered value with values in other fields on the record to make sure that the data is internally consistent — such as when users are required to enter a minimum bid amount and a maximum bid amount (where you may want to set up a rule to ensure that the maximum bid amount is greater than the minimum amount entered).

■ **Maximum Number of Characters** provides you with a way to limit the length of the text a user can enter into a field. This option doesn't prevent the user from typing a long entry, but merely prevents the user from leaving the field if the entry is longer than the stipulated maximum.

TIP   If you want to prevent the user from typing more than a specified number of characters into the field (instead of simply preventing the user from committing the record if they have entered more than the specified maximum number of characters), you can do so by assigning an `OnObjectModify` script trigger (and an appropriately configured script) to each instance of the field on your solution's layouts. Additional detail about configuring Script Triggers may be found in Chapter 8.

NOTE   The Not Empty and By Calculation validation criteria are evaluated at record commit. All the other criteria are evaluated when you leave the field. This arises from the distinction between field-level validations and record-level validations and affects the way FileMaker behaves when a validation rule is violated.

■ If you select one or more validation options, you have access to an additional option to **Display Custom Message if Validation Fails.** This feature enables you to enter a message that will be posted on user dialogs to indicate why data entry for the field failed validation (and what to do to address the problem). Note that although multiple validation options may be specified, only one custom message can be defined and must serve for all cases.

In a majority of cases, the built-in validation alert messages are sufficient, although the information they provide is limited, providing only two alternative instructions to the user, depending on the status of the Allow User to Override During Data Entry option. Examples of the two dialog configurations are provided in Figure 7.8.

You don't have control over the size of the native validation alert dialogs or the dialog button labels. Moreover, the Revert button may or may not appear, depending on the state of the record and the validation options in place.

CROSS-REF Details of the options for using scripts to validate field contents and provide more flexibility in communicating with the user are provided in Chapter 16.

FIGURE 7.8

If the current user is permitted to override validation rules, an alert similar to the one on the top appears. Otherwise, FileMaker displays an alert similar to that on the bottom.

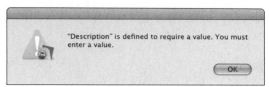

Storage and indexing options

FileMaker has a remarkably no-fuss way of handling indexes — so much so that many basic operations can take place without requiring you to do anything. Indexing is controlled from the Storage panel of the Options for Field dialog and defaults to Automatically Create Indexes as Needed.

Unless you specifically modify the index settings, each field you create will initially be unindexed. Indexes will then be created on demand when any event requiring (or significantly benefiting from) an index for a given field occurs. Examples of events prompting creation of a field index are as follows:

- Performing a Find on the field
- Accessing records from the table where the field resides via a relationship for which the field has been used as a key (that is, a match field)
- Creating a value list defined to use values from the field
- Setting up unique or existing validation for the field
- Displaying the View Index dialog by choosing Insert ⇨ From Index (⌘+I or Ctrl+I)

Additionally, the language option you choose for the indexing of a text field determines the default sorting conventions that FileMaker will apply to it, although the index itself is not directly used for sorting.

NOTE   You can override the default sorting convention for a field in a specific sort by choosing the Override Field's Language for Sort checkbox in the Sort Records dialog, while the field in question is selected in the Sort Order list.

For databases that you access in stand-alone mode, as well as for solutions of moderate size, you generally need not concern yourself with indexing. Let FileMaker handle it. If your solution becomes large and size and network performance are of concern, the details I provide in later chapters about optimizing indexes will be of interest to you.

When indexing numeric data (that is, number, date, time, and timestamp fields), FileMaker creates only a single type of index (a value index) comprising a sorted list of values in the field, referenced to the IDs of the records where each value occurs.

For text fields, FileMaker manages two different types of indexes — a word index that's used to support Finds and a value index that's principally used to support relationships and value lists. However, FileMaker creates either type of index only when needed, so text fields may acquire only one index. The fact that two types of index can exist for a text field is not evident in the Options/Comments area of the Fields tab of the Manage Database dialog (which simply lists the fields as indexed) but is indicated in the Storage panel of the Options for Field dialog, where text fields that have only one type of index are shown with the Minimal indexing setting.

CROSS-REF   For a discussion of indexing in greater depth, including format and optimization options, refer to Chapter 9.

Summary and Calculation fields

While the data users enter into your solution may provide the core of your records, you can configure your database to generate new or additional data by combining or analyzing inputs. A simple example is that when the user enters a number of items on an order, you may require (or desire) that the solution automatically add up the total value of the order and show that in a separate field. FileMaker provides Calculation and Summary fields to enable you to produce derived data that extends the usefulness of the primary (entered) information. Compared to a manual record-keeping process (where totals and other derived values must be separately calculated and entered manually), the ability to automatically calculate and summarize user inputs is one of the great advantages of a well-designed computer database. As well as saving time and effort, the use of calculation and summary fields can improve accuracy (eliminating the human error component).

For each field you create, you select the field type from the Type menu in the lower part of the Manage Database dialog's Fields tab. When you create a calculation field (or change an existing field to calculation type), FileMaker presents the Specify Calculation dialog (as first described in Chapter 2). Like other fields, however, a calculation's result also has a data type, which you must select from the Calculation Result Is pop-up menu immediately below the formula box of the Specify Calculation dialog. The calculation result data type options, shown in Figure 7.9, are Text, Number, Date, Time, Timestamp, and Container.

NOTE Originally, the Specify Calculation dialog was conceived solely as a mechanism for defining calculation fields. However, as FileMaker's functionality has increased, the same interface has been used to allow you to create rules for a wide variety of other purposes throughout the application — including determining record level access privileges, defining conditional formatting, supplying the name of the target field for a `Set Field by Name[ ]` script command, building complex validation rules for a field, assembling the URL for a button that controls a Web viewer, and many more. The Specify Calculation dialog (and FileMaker calculation syntax) appears almost anywhere you require FileMaker to make a runtime decision that's calculated based upon the current status of the user's data or the user's system.

FIGURE 7.9

The Specify Calculation dialog's pop-up menu for choosing the data type of the calculation result.

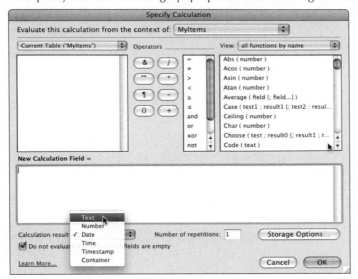

Calculations that reside within a database table and reference other fields within the same table have a predictable point of view (or context). That is, they sit within a record and compute a result from values within that record. However, if you choose to include references to fields in other tables within your calculation, FileMaker must use your solution's relationships to gain access to data located elsewhere. To do that, FileMaker requires both a start point and an end point for the relationship via which it is to source related data. The relationship start point is the current table. However, because you can create more than one TO of the current table (on the Relationships

Graph), FileMaker provides a pop-up menu of context options at the very top of the Specify Calculation dialog (the Evaluate This Calculation from the Context Of pop-up menu). Calculation *context* determines the TO that will be used to establish relationships to fields in other TOs that are referenced in the calculation formula. In cases where a table has only one TO, the pop-up presents only a single (default) option. However, when you have multiple TOs of the current table, the context selection determines which of several possible evaluation paths will be used. For example, the Inventory example's OrderLines table has two occurrences: OrderLines and ItemsPurchased. The OrderLines TO is related to the Orders TO, while the Items Purchased TO is related to the Inventory TO and does not have any relationship path to the Orders TO. If you want to create a calculation within the OrderLines TO that references a field in Inventory, you must choose the ItemsPurchased TO as the context for the calculation (that is, select ItemsPurchased from the Evaluate This Calculation from the Context Of pop-up menu) in order to establish the relationship to be used to resolve the calculation.

When a calculation field's formula references one or more fields within the same record, the calculation result is *dependent* on the values in the referenced fields (so if the value in any of the referenced fields changes, FileMaker re-evaluates the calculation). For example, the Inventory example's OrderLines table includes the cLineTotal Calculation field, defined as = Qty * Price — thus making cLineTotal calculation dependent upon the values in the Qty and Price fields within the same record of the OrderLines table. Through an internal process called the *table of dependencies*, FileMaker keeps track of which calculations (including Auto-Enter calculations) to re-evaluate when a value in another field changes. FileMaker's management of dependencies, however, is limited to the current record of the current context's TO — so references to related fields or global fields are not tracked through the table of dependencies, and calculations will not be automatically re-evaluated when a referenced field outside the current record is modified.

NOTE When a calculation field references global or related fields, FileMaker automatically changes its storage option to Unstored, whereupon the calculation will be re-evaluated whenever it's referenced (such as when the screen is redrawn), because there is no mechanism for managing calculation dependencies outside the current record. Auto-Enter calculations, however, are always stored and are therefore generally unsuitable for tracking the current state of related data.

CROSS-REF If you find you need to store calculated data that references related or global fields (for example, so that the calculation result can be indexed for use in optimized finds, value lists, or as a target key field for a relationship), alternative mechanisms will be required to achieve the desired outcome. Examples of different approaches to problems of this kind are discussed in subsequent chapters, including Chapter 19.

Calculation fields work well with localized computations (using a single set of inputs to derive a result within the context of a single record), and you can use them with aggregating functions (such as Max( ), List( ), Sum( ) and others) to return a result from a related set of records. However, when you need a straightforward way to summarize values spanning a found set, Summary fields provide an attractive alternative. Here are the steps you should follow to create a Summary field:

1. Enter a field name for your new Summary field into the Field Name box on the Fields tab of the Manage Database dialog and then choose Summary (⌘+S or Ctrl+S) in the Type pop-up menu.

2. Click the Create button. The Options for Summary Field dialog appears, as shown in Figure 7.10.

3. Choose a summary function from the radio button options at the left of the dialog.

4. Select the field you want to summarize in the Available Fields list.

NOTE Only Number, Time, Date, and Timestamp fields (or Calculated fields returning one of those data types) are available for summarization. Other field types will be dimmed and cannot be selected in the Available Fields list in the Options for Summary Field dialog.

Where the summary operation you have chosen has additional options available (such as the Running Total and Restart Summary for Each Sorted Group option shown in Figure 7.10), they're presented as checkbox options immediately below the Available Fields list. As appropriate, you can also choose the method by which the values in separate field repetitions (if used) are handled.

FIGURE 7.10

The Options for Summary Field dialog.

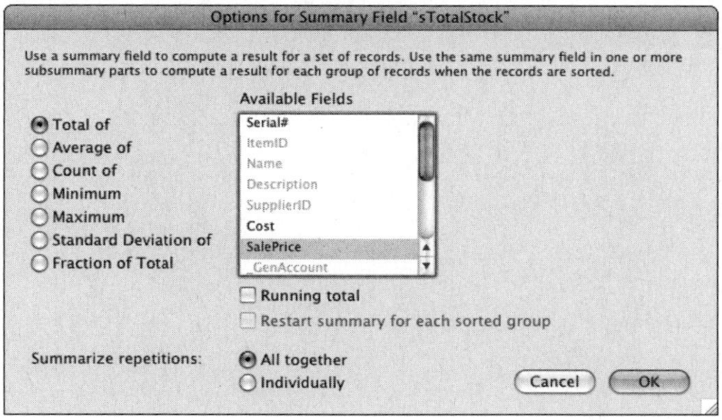

For a detailed overview of the various Summary functions and their options, refer to Table 7.1.

5. Click OK to accept the Summary field definition.

Summary fields produce live statistics reflecting the current state of data in your solution — and this is both their strength and, potentially, their weakness, depending on how you choose to use them. When data sets are relatively small (a few hundred records or less), recalculating complex summaries every time anything changes will be efficient and, in most cases, useful. However, in solutions where the quantity of data is large — or will become large over time — users will tire of delays introduced while summary data is recalculated with every small change.

For extensive data sets, therefore, you may prefer alternative approaches. Because Summary fields are recalculated each time they appear onscreen, one solution is to exclude them from most screens so that they're evaluated and displayed only when the user specifically requires them. Alternatively, you may consider a scripted approach, which computes summary data either progressively (via transactional modeling) or on demand.

TABLE 7.1			

Summary Functions, Descriptions, and Options

Name	Description	Option	Option Description
Total of	Sums the values in the found set (or filtered set when the Summary field is viewed via a relationship)	Running Total Restart Summary for Each Sorted Group	If placed in the Body part, returns the cumulative total for the found set up to and including the current record. The Restart option allows the Running Total to operate separately within sub-summarized data sets.
Average of	Provides a simple arithmetic mean of values in the found or related set	Weighted Average	Returns the average adjusted with respect to (weighted by) another field's value. For example, in a database of maintenance costs, the average cost per repair may be weighted by the frequency of repair for each item, to arrive at a more accurate indication of maintenance costs for a period.
Count of	Returns the number of records where the selected field has a value	Running Count Restart Summary for Each Sorted Group	(See Running Total) The Restart option allows the running count to operate separately within sub-summarized data sets.
Minimum	Returns the numerically lowest (or chronologically earliest) value in the found or related set	N/A	
Maximum	Returns the numerically highest (or chronologically latest) value in the found or related set	N/A	

Name	Description	Option	Option Description
Standard Deviation Of	Returns a statistical measure of dispersion of a group of values (the root-mean-square of the deviation of the values from their mean)	By Population	Uses a probability-based distribution method to estimate the standard deviations of a subset of records against an (imputed) whole population.
Fraction of Total	Indicates the fraction of the total each value in the summarized set represents.	Subtotaled	Returns the fraction of a sub-summarized group of records (rather than all records) represented. For example, the cost of each computer's repair might be expressed as a fraction of the total computer repair costs rather than as a total of all maintenance costs. Expressing the cost as a fraction of the total is done by subtotaling against item type (where computers are one of the item types represented).

Working with global fields

Most database values are specific to each record in a table, but in a few cases, you may find need to store a value that applies to all records in a table. For example, the prevailing currency exchange rate may affect all the records equally. While you could set such a value into a field in each record (and update it throughout the table when the value changes), FileMaker provides global fields as a more effective alternative. To define a global field in FileMaker:

1. Create the field and click the Options button (in the Fields tab of the Manage Database dialog).

2. In the Storage panel of the Options for Field dialog, shown in Figure 7.11, specify that the field should use global storage and then click OK.

When you choose the global storage option for a field, its contents are stored outside the table's record structure, and the field is available with the same value to all records in the table. Global fields values form part of a (hidden) *record zero* of the table, and their values are not lost even if all the records of the table are deleted.

Global fields have some properties in common with variables, as a convenient and efficient place to store temporary values. Unlike variables, however, global fields are persistent as part of the schema of the table where they reside, and, as fields, they can be included on layouts and designated as the input fields for custom dialogs. In single-user solutions, their values persist between application sessions. In both single-user and multi-user solutions, global fields provide an ideal place to store graphics and resources (logos and so on) that will be used throughout the solution's interface. Using global fields to store interface resources has the advantage that any change made (with the solution accessed offline) is propagated to all the instances of the field throughout multiple layouts. Using this technique, your solutions can have an accessible library of images and interface elements that you can manage efficiently.

FIGURE 7.11

The Options for Field dialog's Storage tab lets you set a field to use Global Storage.

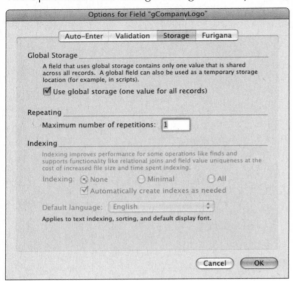

CROSS-REF **Refer to Chapter 9 for coverage of script variables and a more in-depth discussion of the roles, behavior, and uses of global fields.**

Another useful aspect of global fields is that their value is specific to each user when a database is shared over a network. As a result, when a global field is used to store temporary information (for example, while a script is running), two users can use the field simultaneously without "colliding" with the other. However, updates to global field values made by clients of a hosted database are lost when the client session concludes.

Perhaps the most compelling advantage that global fields offer, however, is their accessibility from other tables in your solution without a relationship. You can access global field values from unrelated tables, either for use within calculations or to display (and edit) on your solution's layouts. This easy access allows you to move data around your solution with considerable flexibility and without adding to the complexity of your solution's Relationships Graph.

Basic Calculations

You can use FileMaker calculations for a wide variety of purposes that go well beyond simple arithmetic. While you can use FileMaker calculations to add and multiply numbers with ease by using familiar math syntax, FileMaker extends the power of calculations to address diverse requirements that include logic, text processing, and a broad range of general data-handling operations.

Calculations of all kinds and for all purposes are created in the same way by using the FileMaker Specify Calculation dialog, which, as noted previously, makes its appearance in many places throughout the FileMaker interface — well beyond the confines of the Manage Database dialog.

Most of the terminology you encounter when dealing with calculations in FileMaker is familiar and straightforward, so with only a few pointers, you're able to make the environment work for you. Many of the terms used are common enough that they have entered mainstream conversation. However, there are a few exceptions. Some of the key terms (with special meanings) that you'll encounter are as follows:

- **Result:** The value produced when a calculation is evaluated.
- **Function:** A predefined, named component of a calculation formula that performs a defined computation and returns a single result.
- **Parameter:** An input value to a command or function.
- **Argument:** An input value or expression that forms part of the syntax of a function or parameter.
- **Operator:** A symbol used to denote an arithmetic, textual, or logical operation to be performed, such as + (plus), – (minus), * (times), and & (concatenate).
- **Literal:** A precisely specified (and predetermined) value (42 and "Henry" are literals).
- **Variable:** A placeholder name for a value.
- **Constant:** A placeholder name for a literal value.
- **Syntax:** The order in which FileMaker expects to receive functions, arguments, and operators within a calculation (essentially, grammatical rules).
- **Expression:** A sequence of literals, constants, variables, and operators that, when evaluated, returns a result. For example, `1.075 * (Qty * Price)` is an expression that, when evaluated, returns the amount due for a purchase in a locale with a 7.5 percent sales tax rate. In FileMaker parlance, *expression* is sometimes used a little more loosely to refer to sequences including functions and field references.
- **Formula:** The entire content of a calculation combining elements described in this list to produce a result — sometimes used interchangeably with *expression*.

You'll find it helpful to be familiar with these terms as you're working with calculations because calculation parlance appears frequently in FileMaker.

Creating a Calculation field

Creating a Calculation field is a straightforward operation, and you can see it in action in Chapter 5. The Specify Calculation dialog (see Figure 7.12) provides all the tools and resources you need to create a Calculation expression.

FIGURE 7.12

The Specify Calculation dialog and its many parts.

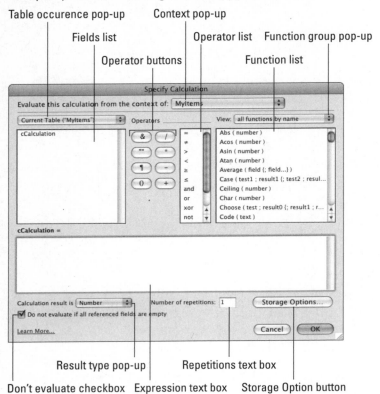

The Specify Calculation dialog's parts are as follows:

- **Context pop-up:** Where you choose a TO from which the calculation is to be evaluated. When the current table in your Relationships Graph has only one TO, the pop-up is disabled.

- **Table pop-up:** Where you choose a TO to source fields you want to reference in the calculation. (The terminology here can be a little confusing — the table pop-up lists *only* TOs, not the base tables they point to.)

- **Fields list:** Lists all the fields of the TO chosen in the Table pop-up.

- **Operator buttons:** Provide a palette of eight of the most commonly used arithmetic and text operators.

- **Operator list:** A scrolling list with an additional 11 operators (logical and comparison) that FileMaker recognizes.

> **NOTE** There is some inconsistency in FileMaker's naming of the Operator list because it includes the caret (which is an exponentiation operator, yet FileMaker documentation refers to the list as logical and comparison operators). The problem is not immediately obvious, however, because the caret hides out of view at the bottom of the list, and you must scroll down to find it.

- **Function View pop-up:** A filtering menu from which you can select a sub-group of FileMaker functions to view them in isolation. The Function View pop-up is shown in Figure 7.13.

- **Function list:** A scrolling list of the available functions, as filtered by your selection in the Function View pop-up.

FIGURE 7.13

The Function View pop-up menu filters your view of the available calculation functions.

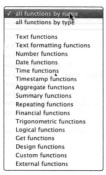

- **Expression text box** (FileMaker Pro's Help calls it the Formula box): The heart of the Specify Calculation dialog. This text box is where your calculation's expression appears as you select functions, operators, fields, and type.

- **Result Type pop-up:** Where you specify what data type your calculation returns as a result.

- **Repetitions text box:** Lets you specify whether your calculation is a repeating field (that is, returns multiple results) and, if so, how many repetitions it comprises.

- **Don't Evaluate checkbox:** Lets you tell FileMaker not to perform the calculation if none of the referenced fields contains a value (such as in a new record). Note that if even one of the referenced fields contains a value, FileMaker will evaluate the calculation.

- **Storage Options button:** Provides you with access to controls that determine how the selected field will be incorporated into the structure of your solution, allowing you to select global storage (one value for all records), control indexing options, specify repetitions, and, in the case of calculation fields, make the field unstored (so that a result is calculated only when needed).

When you become familiar with calculation syntax and the names of all the functions and fields your expression references, you can simply type them directly into the Expression text box (and, I'll admit, that's what I generally prefer to do). When in unfamiliar territory (obscure or lengthy field names or working with infrequently encountered functions), however, employing the following mouse-driven shortcuts the Specify Calculation dialog offers is useful:

- To use a function, double-click the function's name in the Function list. The function appears (along with prompts for the inputs it requires) at the cursor location in the Expression text box and with the argument list preselected. Replace the placeholders in the argument list (called *parameters*) with field names, literals, and/or expressions.

- To reference a field, double-click the field's name in the fields list. The field name appears at the cursor position (replacing a selection, if there was one) in the Expression text box.

- To enter a literal value, type it into the Expression text box. (Remember that numeric literals don't require enclosing quotes, but text literals do.)

- To enter an arithmetic or text operator, click its button.

- To enter a logical or comparison operator, double-click it in the operator list.

> **TIP** If your calculation references fields in related tables and the current table has multiple occurrences in the Relationships Graph, make sure that you select the appropriate context for your calculation, as described in the "Summary and Calculation fields" section, earlier in this chapter. Choosing the appropriate Evaluate From TO enables FileMaker to determine which relationship path to use to source data from related tables.

Specifying an appropriate result type for your calculation is important for several reasons. Perhaps most important, some calculation functions and operations produce different results depending on the data type of the result, as FileMaker determines whether to treat ambiguous elements as text strings or numeric values. Moreover, FileMaker Pro references the result type when performing many operations, such as indexing and sorting. If you specify that a Calculation field (or a regular field) is a text field rather than a number field, 29 appears before 3. Similarly, with dates in a text field, December sorts before November.

> **CROSS-REF** A more detailed discussion of indexing and sorting issues and conventions is included in Chapter 9.

> **TIP** If you occasionally want to present data as a type other than its natural type, you can use Calculation expressions to convert formats through the many type-conversion functions, such as GetAsDate( ), GetAsText( ), and GetAsTimestamp( ).

I urge you to consider the use of descriptive field names, along with the use of Hungarian notation (or some similar, consistent scheme) when naming calculation fields, global fields, and Summary fields to make their nature clear while developing, working with, and maintaining your solution.

Defining a calculation formula

Computers follow rules when interpreting your calculations, so as long as you understand the rules and follow them, the results are consistent and accurate. However, because computers interpret inputs literally, formulas must conform to syntax rules to be parsed correctly. Consequently, calculations take a form that is designed around the need for human comprehension (that is, it resembles human language) but adapted to the requirements of the computer (its format follows clear and unambiguous rules).

An essential principle of calculation syntax is that calculation operations follow a predetermined order of precedence. Among the arithmetic operators, exponentiation has the highest precedence, followed by multiplication and division, and then addition and subtraction. Operators of equal precedence are evaluated from left to right, with expressions in parentheses performed first (from inside out and then left to right). The following examples illustrate the impact of operator precedence:

> 8 + 5 * 4 returns 28, because the multiplication is performed first, followed by the addition
>
> (8 + 5) * 4 returns 52, because the operation in parentheses is performed first
>
> ((8 + 2)^2 * 4) + 1 returns 401
>
> (8 + 2^(2 * 4)) + 1 returns 265 (8 + 256 + 1)
>
> ((8 + 2^2) * 4) + 1 returns 49

To increase the readability (by humans) of the code, it is customary to include white space and line breaks so that the code more closely resembles human language. If you're anything like me, you will find it easier to make sense of

> If(Qty > 10; GetRepetition(gStockIndicator; 1);
>   GetRepetition(gStockIndicator; 2))

than

> If(Qty>10;GetRepetition(gStockIndicator;1);GetRepetition
>   (gStockIndicator;2))

In addition, the need for readability aids becomes increasingly important in longer formulas.

When a function accepts multiple parameters, FileMaker requires that the parameters be separated by semicolons (as demonstrated in the preceding example regarding white space). Many functions follow a fixed format, insofar as they always require the same number of parameters. However, some parameters are optional for several functions.

A classic example of a function with optional parameters is the Case statement. A Case statement includes at least one test and one result. However, Case statements can optionally include additional tests and results and may also include a closing result (to be used by default if none of the tests returns true). For example, if you had a global repeating field containing graphics for "Unavailable" "While Stocks Last" and "In Stock", you could use the following Case statement to display the unavailable graphic when the quantity on hand was zero, to display the While Stocks

Last graphic when only one or two items are left in stock, and the In Stock image when three or more items are available:

```
Case( Qty = 0; gStockStatus[1];
      Qty < 3; gStockStatus[2];
      gStockStatus[3])
```

The successive conditions you can include in a Case statement are evaluated from left to right and top to bottom, with evaluation ceasing with the first test that returns true. Thus, in the preceding example, if zero items are on hand, the second test (Qty < 3) isn't performed.

NOTE The process whereby FileMaker terminates evaluation upon reaching a true test is called *short-circuited evaluation* and has implications. For example, tests can call functions that reference related data requiring calls to a remote server, introducing a brief delay. However, the cumulative impact of a series of such effects is dependent upon how many of the tests are performed. Thus, the order in which tests are performed can influence the time FileMaker takes to determine a result.

Entering literal text

Frequently, your calculations will require known values, which you'll be able to enter directly into the calculation formula. For example, when you need to determine whether the value in a text field contains a specific word (such as "overdue"), you can employ an expression such as If (Pattern Count (Collection::LoanStatus; "Overdue") > 0; "Late") returns the text "Late" when the LoanStatus field contains "Overdue", "Now Overdue", or "More than a Week Overdue". In this calculation, Overdue, and Late are both literals.

FileMaker requires that text literals are enclosed in quotation marks. Consequently, the calculation engine can distinguish between a literal and what may otherwise be interpreted as a function, table, or field reference. Moreover, some functions, such as GetField( ) and Evaluate( ), are designed to process the contents of literal strings and the text results returned from other functions. To ensure that a literal or the text value returned by a function will not be processed, FileMaker provides the Quote( ) function. For example: Evaluate("Pi") returns the value "3.1415926535897932". However, Evaluate(Quote("Pi")) returns the text "Pi".

Keep in mind that when you work with literal strings in a calculation, some FileMaker text-processing functions are case sensitive, while others are not, which can be a significant determinant of the result. For example, Substitute( ) is case-sensitive, but PatternCount( ) is not. Moreover, it pays to keep in mind that some results will be required to be case-specific. (For example, if your calculation is constructing a URL to be sent to a server, it may be required to be in a specific case format because some Internet servers are case-sensitive.)

Within text in calculations, several characters are reserved — they have a special meaning as text operators. Notably, the quote character is used to indicate the start and end of literal text, and the pilcrow (¶) signifies a carriage return. So what can you do if you want to include quotes or pilcrows within your literal text?

To deal with this problem, FileMaker lets you use a prefix character (called an *escape character*) to instruct the calculation engine to read the following character as written. The character used to escape quotes and pilcrows is the backslash. So anywhere you want to insert a quote in literal text, you must use \". For example, the calculation

```
"You're the kind of girl\¶that \"fits in\" with my world."
```

returns

You're the kind of girl¶that "fits in" with my world.

With those two problems (" and ¶) solved, there remains the issue of how to deal with the backslash itself, which now has a special meaning as an escape character for the other reserved characters. Oddly enough, the answer is the same: You can escape the backslash character with itself, if you want FileMaker to interpret it as a backslash rather than an escape character for what follows. In other words:

1.   \" = "
2.   \¶ = ¶
3.   \\ = \

Referencing fields

It's worth noting that when you create a formula referencing fields and tables, FileMaker simply accepts the names you type (or select from lists). But if, after creating a calculation formula, you change the name of one of the fields the calculation references, the next time you open the Specify Calculation dialog, the new field name is already there staring back at you. The first time you see it, it's kind of spooky — although after the thrill wears off, it's just mildly geeky. Either way, it's very cool. Even if you've referenced a field in dozens of places, when you change its name, they're all instantly updated without your having to lifting a finger. The same thing is true of many things that have a name in FileMaker (for example, scripts, tables, layouts, and so on).

FileMaker achieves this feat by storing and tracking everything (behind the scenes) by an ID. When you access a list of tables and fields — for example by opening the Specify Calculation dialog, FileMaker simply looks up and displays the current names for the tables and fields referenced there. The use of internal IDs for objects throughout your solution gives you a lot of freedom to change your mind and modify your solution as you build it.

However, some words and characters are off limits when it comes to field and table names. Function names and various *reserved words* (words that have a special meaning as an argument for a function) don't make good choices for field names. Moreover, field names should not start with a number or include any of the symbols used as operators.

If you do use an inappropriate name for a field or table, FileMaker deals with the problem by enclosing references to the offending field (or `table::field` combination) within prefixed braces as follows: `${ }`. So, for example, if you have a field named `Average`, when you include it in calculations, it will appear as `${Average}` so as not to be confused with FileMaker's `Average()` function.

When you create calculations within a table and reference fields in the same table (from the same TO selected in the table pop-up at the upper left of the Specify Calculation dialog), FileMaker accepts references to the field without a preceding TO name. However, in all other cases, fields must be referenced in the form `TOname::FieldName`.

Finally, FileMaker manages calculation dependencies only within the current record. If a calculation references another field in the record, it will automatically update when the referenced field is edited. However, if you create a calculation referencing a field outside the current record, such as a field from another TO, FileMaker will make the calculation unstored, and it will be evaluated only when a screen it appears on is displayed or refreshed (or when the calculation is otherwise referenced). Similarly, calculation fields referencing global fields (even those defined within the same table) are required to be unstored.

Understanding calculation functions and their syntax

Functions work rather like building blocks, letting you fabricate answers for all sorts of problems. The FileMaker calculation engine includes close to 400 native calculation functions, which you can combine in many interesting and useful ways. You can place one function within another so that its result becomes one of the inputs (arguments) for the function enclosing it.

With so many functions, each able to be used in various ways, I could devote an entire book the size of this one to exploring each in turn. Fortunately, that's not necessary — FileMaker provides the basic syntax for functions in the Function list at the upper right of the Specify Calculation dialog. Moreover, when you get started, you'll discover that the process follows some straightforward predictable patterns. The following sections describe a few examples.

The List( ) function

The `List()` function accepts one or more fields (separated by semicolons) and returns a carriage-return separated list of all values it finds there on the current record (if the supplied fields are in the current table) or on all related records (if the supplied fields are sourced from a related TO).

If the `List()` argument includes only one field, the function will look for multiple instances of the field either in the current record (if it's a local field) or in multiple related records (if it comes from another TO) and will list any values it finds, one per line.

If, in the `Inventory` solution, you wanted to compose an e-mail confirming the contents of an order, you would need a list of the order's item stock numbers to include in the e-mail. From the `Order` record, the expression `List(OrderLines::ItemID)` returns a list of stock numbers on the current order. For example:

- ITM00001
- ITM00003
- ITM00002

The Count( ) function

For the same `Inventory` example and e-mail of order details, the e-mail needs to include a summary line stating how many types of items are being stored. In the same way, as you create a list of items, you can create a count of items: The expression `Count (OrderLines::ItemID)` for the preceding order returns the number 3.

The Date( ) function

To convert a human-readable date into the internal numeric format that FileMaker uses to perform computations with dates, FileMaker provides the `Date ( )` function, which accepts month, day, and year as its arguments. So to supply FileMaker with New Year's Day in a calculation, I can enter **Date(1; 1; 2008).**

Among many other date and time functions, FileMaker provides the function `Get (CurrentDate)` to let you retrieve the current date from the computer's internal clock and calendar. Thus, to determine how long it is to (or since) January 1, you can use the following expression:

```
Date(1; 1; 2008) - Get(CurrentDate)
```

FileMaker returns a result which is the number of days between now and New Year.

The Round( ) function

In cases where fractions or percentages have been multiplied — for example, when you add tax or deduct discounts from a total amount — you need to round the result (because most people don't deal with fractions of a cent) before displaying it in a letter or report. FileMaker's `Round ( )` function accepts two arguments: the amount to be rounded and the number of decimal places to round it to. Thus, the expression `"$" & Round (37.25297; 2)` returns a result of $37.25. In practice, however, the first argument for such a calculation will likely either be a field holding the value to be rounded or a calculation — or perhaps a combination of the two. If the amount is in a field in the `Orders` table, you can achieve the desired result with the following expressions:

```
"$" & Round(32.822 * 1.135; 2)

"$" & Round(Orders::cFinalTotal; 2)

"$" & Round(Orders::cFinalTotal * 1.135; 2)
```

Note that you can supply the arguments (in this case, the first argument) in any form, which will resolve when evaluated to pass the necessary input value to the `Round ( )` function.

The Length( ) function

FileMaker calculations work with all kinds of data (locating a relevant word or phrase, extracting an e-mail address from a paragraph of text, checking that an address will display correctly in an envelope window, and so on. (In fact, many calculations are designed to manipulate text for a wide range of purposes.)

The building blocks that FileMaker provides so that you can work with text in calculations are just as straightforward as the other examples I cite in this list. For example, to determine the number of characters (including all punctuation, spaces, and carriage returns) in a field, you use FileMaker's `Length( )` function. For example,

    Length(OrderItems::Name)

will return a number representing the length of the text in the indicated field.

All the examples listed in this section have several things in common. They start with a function name that is plain English and give a clear and simple indication of the purpose of the function. You could probably guess many of the function names correctly. In parentheses after each function are one or more values (separated by semicolons) to determine what the function will work on and what it will do — for example, what number is to be rounded, to what precision, and so on.

Although initially the building blocks will be unfamiliar, the process is consistent and follows straightforward and largely intuitive principles.

Doing some simple calculations

After you know the basics of how FileMaker calculations are assembled, you're ready to see some concrete examples of formulae that you can use to solve common challenges and problems by the clever use of calculations. The following examples are indicative of the range of tasks you can address by using calculations. They also will give you some ideas to get started with when building your own solutions.

Commission on earnings above a threshold

In any situation where you need to apply a rule to values that exceed a threshold, you will find it a great help to put the logic into a database so that the work will be done for you and your logic will be automatically applied according to the data available. For example, if you need to pay a 50 percent commission to each sales representative in your company on the quarterly company earnings they generate that exceeds an agreed threshold, you can create a field in your table of sales representatives called `QuarterlyEarnings` (where you enter the income generated by each rep) and a field named `Threshold` to store the agreed minimum target each rep must meet to qualify. With these fields in place, you can create an unstored calculation field called `cCommission` with a formula along the lines of the following:

    If(QuarterlyEarnings ≥ Threshold; (QuartlerlyEarnings − Threshold) / 2; 0)

Approaching the problem in this way makes good use of the `If( )` function, a staple of logical expressions, but the formula isn't as compact or as efficient in execution as it could be. If you have a lot of data to process (or if you will in the future), you may want to consider a swifter path to the same result:

    Max(0; (QuarterlyEarnings - Threshold) / 2)

Calculating initials from a person's name

A frequent business practice is to include the initials of persons involved in the preparation of documents in a reference code or document number. This simple mnemonic makes remembering the document's origins or history in a busy organization easier. If your solution includes a table of staff details, you may want to include a field that computes staff initials for inclusion on documents generated by your database. If the staff's names are stored in fields called `FirstName`, `MiddleName`, and `LastName`, it will be a simple matter to create an additional field called `cInitials` in the Staff table, defined with a formula such as

```
Left(Staff::FirstName; 1) & Left(Staff::MiddleName; 1) & Left(Staff::LastName;
    1)
```

This calculation works its way through the values in the three name fields, extracting the first letter from each and concatenating them into a single string of up to three characters. In the event that the middle name field is blank for a given staff member (some people don't have a middle name), the second function will return a null result, and the initials will be two characters long rather than three.

CAUTION While the practice of adding initials to documents as handy mnemonics is reasonable, you should never rely upon it as the definitive method of identifying a document's origins (lest, for example, more than one individual with the same initials enters the company). The separate `StaffID` field should continue to provide the basis of an authoritative link to the related records identifying the subject or originator of the record.

Compound interest at a known rate over a given period

There was once a time when people painstakingly calculated compound interest over lengthy periods as a series of manual computations, the results of which were then summed to arrive at a result. Changing any of the dates or amounts required that the process be repeated — which, no doubt, was enough to try the patience of even the most dutiful clerk. With the advent of programs such as FileMaker — and with the application of a little skill with calculations — the process of computing compound interest becomes effortless and immediate.

Compound interest is calculated by multiplying the principal amount by the interest rate plus one, raised to the power of the number of periods. So, for example, if I were to invest $1,000 at a fixed interest rate of 12 percent per annum (1 percent per month) for a period of 12 months, based on month periods, the compound interest would be calculated as $1000*1.01^{12}$. In FileMaker terms, this formula is not difficult to apply as a calculation. Assuming that you have a table set up with fields for the principal amount, the interest rate, and the number of periods of the investment, you can create a calculation with the following formula:

```
Round(PrincipalAmount * (1 + MonthlyInterestRate) ^ Periods; 2)
```

With this formula in place, when you enter 1000 into `PrincipalAmount`, 0.01 ($1/12$ of the annual interest rate) into `MonthlyInterestRate`, and 12 into `Periods`, you get the result $1,126.83. Change any of the input values, and FileMaker will instantly return the resulting compounded value.

Current quarter of the calendar year

The calendar year is often divided into quarters. Whether for financial reporting, scheduling short courses, product releases, or sporting seasons, you may need to sort dates into the correct quarters so that you can group records appropriately. FileMaker provides no direct method for converting dates into calendar year quarter values, but with a little thought, you can build a calculation to do just that task.

Following the custom where the quarter of the year is identified with the number of the quarter (prefixed with a Q), followed by a slash and the final two digits of the year — for example, Q2/09 for the second quarter of 2009 — you'd require a calculation along the lines of

```
"Q" & Ceiling(Month(EventDate) / 3) & "/" & Right(Year(EventDate); 2)
```

In this expression, the quarter number is produced by applying the `Ceiling()` function to the fraction produced by dividing the month component of the date by the number of months in a quarter (3). Using `Ceiling` raises the resulting fraction to the next highest integer, thus returning the number of the quarter in which the date value in the `EventDate` field falls.

Changing ampersands to "and" in a block of text

FileMaker provides extensive text-processing capabilities, and one of the staple procedures enabling you to manage a variety of text handling requirements is the use of functions such as `Substitute()` and `Replace()`. In this example, you see how you can replace occurrences of the ampersand (&) character in a text field with the word *and*. FileMaker provides two calculations functions that perform text replacement: `Replace()` changes a specified number of characters at an indicated position in the text with a designated replacement string, whereas `Substitute()` changes all occurrences of a search string throughout an indicated text block with the replacement string you supply. In this example, the `Substitute()` function is best suited to the purpose at hand:

```
Substitute(YourTextField ; "&"; "and")
```

> **TIP**   You can use the `Substitute()` function to perform multiple substitutions simultaneously, as exemplified by the following example, which replaces ampersands with *and* and virgules (forward slashes) with *or*.

```
Substitute(TextField; ["&"; "and"]; ["/"; " or "])
```

Record navigation text (record n of nn)

The FileMaker Status Toolbar provides you with controls and information to aid in the navigation of your solution. However, on occasion, you'll not want users to have the complete freedom the Status Toolbar affords. In such cases, you can lock the Status Toolbar out of harm's way and provide users with layout objects (buttons and text) that offer similar functionality.

One of the most useful indicators on the Status Toolbar is the dynamic text area that tells the user where in the table they're presently located. To replicate this functionality within your layouts, you'll require a calculation formula that assembles comparable information about the state of navigation in the current table. With the aid of a couple of built-in FileMaker Get ( ) functions, the task of building an unstored calculation to return custom navigation text is readily achievable as follows:

```
"Record " & Get(RecordNumber) & " of " Get(FoundCount)
```

> **TIP** When you create a calculation that draws upon contextual information, such as the navigation status data referenced in the preceding calculation, you need to set the storage options for the calculation field to "Unstored" to ensure that the calculation will refresh as you navigate from record to record.

In a List (or Table View) layout, a navigation indicator is best displayed in the header or footer. However, on a form layout, you can incorporate navigation buttons and text into the main body of the form, as an integral part of your layout design.

The Relationships Graph

The Relationships Graph in FileMaker Pro is both a visual metaphor to aid your understanding and a tool through which you manipulate your solution's data model. It seeks to provide you with a single, all-encompassing view of your solution's structure. It's an ambitious aim, particularly as a solution becomes complex, yet the Graph is undoubtedly a powerful tool — albeit one peculiarly well suited to visual thinkers.

A number of divergent approaches to working with the Graph have appeared in the years since FileMaker Pro 7 was introduced — one testament to the flexibility of the model it encapsulates. In reality, however, a solution is multi-dimensional and the Graph is two-dimensional, so a certain amount of awkwardness is inevitable. Perhaps the most significant contribution to complexity arises because FileMaker relies on the Graph not only for underlying data frameworks but also for direct support of the interface. TOs that provide data filtering, portal displays, or script support mingle unfettered among core data dependencies defining the data structure fundamentals. Keeping both in an orderly perspective is both the joy and the challenge of the Relationships Graph.

Common misconceptions about the Relationships Graph

Where the Relationships Graph is concerned, various myths and misconceptions abound. Foremost among the misconceptions is the impression that those boxes you see on the Graph *are* tables, rather than merely pointers to tables. The distinction is crucial; grasping it is essential to the ease of understanding of all that flows from FileMaker's context management model. The way the interface is grafted to structure via the layout-TO-table pathway places the Graph at the heart of everything.

Confusion surrounding the distinction between tables and TOs is not helped, perhaps, by the fact that, throughout FileMaker's own interface, the distinction is blurred, with numerous dialogs displaying TO names with labels such as `Current Table`, `Related Tables`, and so on distributed among them. Figure 7.14 shows one such example.

The Specify Field list dialog is one of many that exclusively lists TOs, yet refers to them throughout as "Tables."

The blurring of the distinction between TOs and the tables they point to is unfortunate because it makes grasping the pivotal importance of context more difficult. Further, it makes the necessary existence of multiple TOs for a given base table appear perplexing or even incomprehensible. This misconception leads to a second one about the Relationships Graph — that it is essentially an Entity Relationship Diagram (ERD). In glossing over the distinction between TOs and tables, fundamental differences between the Relationships Graph and a conventional ERD are obscured, and inappropriate patterns of use appear both feasible and viable.

NOTE　**I've yet to see a FileMaker solution of any complexity with a Graph resembling an ERD, although I've seen a few hopelessly mired projects where it seems that the developers tried to envision the Graph in this way.**

Whereas an ERD serves to outline defining structures to tie operations to essentials — the database equivalent of a floor plan — the Relationships Graph exists in curved space around a process better understood as analogous to fission. You solve problems in FileMaker not by referencing back always to a unified core, but by a more organic process of branching and enclosing structures; alternate paths meet only within the substrata (that is, the underlying tables). If you try to work with the Relationships Graph as though it were really an ERD with a different name, you'll encounter the frustration of circular reference errors as a constant frustration — that is simply not how FileMaker works.

Tables versus Table Occurrences

It's a defining strength of FileMaker that the nexus between process and structure is chameleon-like in its flexibility. TOs, as the building blocks of the Graph, operate as tokens — that is, they're analogous to shortcuts or aliases to tables in the underlying database structure and can be multiplied and repurposed at will to perform a variety of major and minor roles spanning the data layer, the process layer, and the interface layer of your solutions.

Although tables are the central structural element in a FileMaker database's data layer, TOs are the conduit between the data and the process and interface layers. The structure of the Relationships Graph is, therefore, dictated as much by process and interface considerations as it is by entity relationships.

Key to the distinction between tables and TOs is that you can have many TOs associated with a single table, each named however you choose. (None of the TO names need to resemble the underlying table name.) For example, a college database may have a table called `People`, which may have spawned TOs named `Students`, `Faculty`, `AdminStaff`, `Alumni`, and `BoardMembers` — each having a distinct and essential role in the solution, each related differently to various other TOs in the Graph.

You can easily tell which table each TO is attached to by moving the mouse pointer over the reveal arrow at the left of the header bar on a TO in the Relationships Graph. As Figure 7.15 shows, an info panel appears indicating the source table, the data source, and (if applicable) the location of the file in which the table is stored. When you have multiple TOs attached to a base table, this feature becomes especially useful.

FIGURE 7.15

_____

Creating multiple TOs pointing to a single table and viewing the info panel that reveals the source of data for a TO.

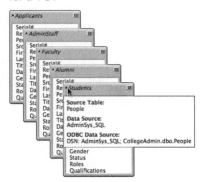

Avoiding circular references

When you create a relationship between two TOs, you can reference related data via the relationship by prefixing the name of a field with the name of the related TO. For this setup to work, you must have only one path (direct or indirect) between any two TOs. Consider a sales force database with a relationship between the customer and sales staff tables and also a relationship between customer and bill-of-sale tables. Figure 7.16 shows what happens when you try to create a relationship between the sale and the cashier who made the sale.

FIGURE 7.16

The Add Relationship dialog prompts you to create an additional TO if a relationship you're creating would result in more than one path between two existing TOs.

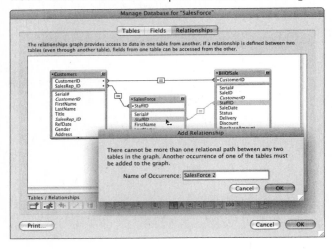

If FileMaker permitted you to add a relationship between the `BillOfSale` and `SalesForce` TOs, a reference to either of the other tables from any of the three would create confusion, because the direct path or the indirect path (via the third table) would be equally valid, yet may produce different results. For example, the cashiers for a customer's purchases may not always have been the sales rep assigned as their contact — so from a Customer layout, the assigned contact would be returned via a direct link to the `SalesForce` TO, but a link that passes via the `BillOfSale` TO may return the name of the cashier who sold the customer an appliance last week.

Instead, FileMaker requires that an additional TO be created, providing an alternate (and distinct) path to the sales staff table, so that confusion is avoided. The result, as Figure 7.17 shows, is an additional TO associated with the `SalesForce` table, supporting the desired logic while avoiding conflict. Instead of being a circular reference, this path formation might be thought of as a spiral form because it returns to the same point, yet a displaced location.

The requirement to avoid circular references and the consequent displacement of points of connection to the underlying table structure are central to grasping the way the Graph works. Unlike a two-dimensional floor plan, it's best thought of as an exercise in multi-dimensional modeling.

A typical spiral formation in the FileMaker Relationships Graph.

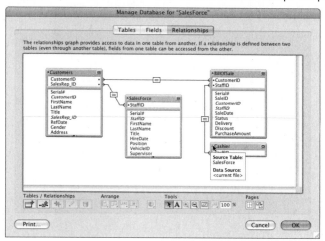

Named and unnamed data sources

FileMaker keeps track of the locations of files you're using. These locations include files containing the tables associated with TOs on the Relationships Graph, files from which you're importing data, and also files your solution will create (files containing exported data, PDF files of database content, and so on).

When storing details about the identity or location of a file that your solution uses, FileMaker differentiates between data sources (files containing one or more of the tables referenced on the Relationships Graph) and all other files. A key aspect of this distinction is that files containing tables referenced on the Relationships Graph are given a name and are stored for reuse. You can view and edit a list of these named data sources by choosing File ➪ Manage ➪ External Data Sources. Named Data Sources can include any mix of FileMaker files (both local and hosted) and SQL databases sourced via ODBC (from hosts running supported versions of SQL Server, MySQL, or Oracle).

Referenced files not containing tables you've associated with TOs on the Relationships Graph include files designated in script or button commands, such as Open File[ ], Import Records[ ], Insert File[ ], Save Records as PDF[ ], and the like. In these cases, the location of the file (its path or server address) is specified and saved as a property of the command to which it relates via the Specify File dialog shown in Figure 7.18.

Whereas you can reuse named data source references, unnamed file specifications are specific to a single command. Even if you've referenced the same file several times in one or more scripts, each instance is specified and stored separately.

FIGURE 7.18

The Specify File dialog that FileMaker provides for entering or editing unnamed file specifications.

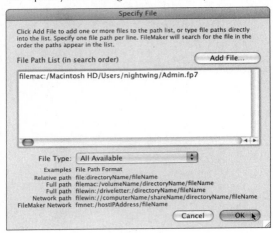

Creating references to other FileMaker files

FileMaker presents the Specify Table dialog showing, by default, a list of the tables in the current file when you add TOs to the Relationships Graph. At the top of the dialog is a pop-up menu of available data sources (see Figure 7.19).

If you want to use a table in another FileMaker file as the basis for a TO in the current file and the file isn't already present in the Data Source list, you can choose to add it to the list by choosing Add FileMaker Data Source (within the group of options at the bottom of the menu). Choosing this option presents the standard Open File dialog, so you can choose a local or remote file. After selecting a file, as long as you have appropriate access privileges to the file, it's added to the menu, and a list of available tables appears in the dialog.

As you add a FileMaker data source (as described in the preceding section), its name and location are stored so that you can later view or edit them (after leaving the **Manage** Database dialog) by choosing File ⇨ Manage ⇨ External Data Sources. When you choose this command, FileMaker displays the Manage External Data Sources dialog, listing each external data source referenced by the current file, its type, and its location.

FIGURE 7.19

Adding a TO to the current file in the Specify Table dialog.

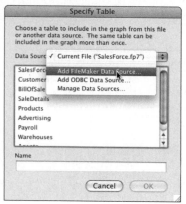

Working with External SQL Data Sources

FileMaker Pro 10 provides you with seamless access to data from a variety of sources — and the ability to combine data from disparate sources. In doing so, it delivers new power and simplicity. When your connections are configured, you can work with remote data from one or more SQL systems in the same ways in which you work with FileMaker data. In many cases, users need not even be aware of the source of the data they're accessing.

Support for External SQL Data Sources (ESS) not only lets you integrate data from FileMaker, MySQL, SQL Server, and Oracle systems — allowing you to search, view, create, edit, and delete records in the remote systems — but also enables you to output data from any mix of these systems to a variety of formats. You won't need to write a single line of SQL to make it all work.

In many cases, systems to which you'll connect by using ESS will be managed by others, and you may have little influence over the form of the data or the nature of access available. Nevertheless, you'll be able to create calculations and summaries by using SQL tables, while working entirely within the familiar environment of FileMaker.

Configuring ODBC drivers: Setting up a DSN

FileMaker Pro 10 lets you work directly with tables stored in supported SQL databases. Prior to doing so, however, you need to configure your computer's connection to the relevant ODBC host. This configuration requires creating a Data Source Name (DSN) that points to the location of the external database.

NOTE ODBC stands for Open Database Connectivity and is a widely supported protocol allowing data exchange between enterprise data systems. FileMaker uses ODBC as the technology that enables its connections to supported SQL database hosts.

If you intend to use the database as a stand-alone solution, you'll need the appropriate ODBC drivers and DSN configuration on your workstation. However, when a FileMaker file is hosted by using FileMaker Server 9 or 10, the ODBC drivers and DSN configuration are required only on the server, not on individual workstations accessing the solution.

To begin, you'll need appropriate ODBC drivers for the versions of SQL you'll be accessing, which, when installed, will be available for selection in the ODBC Data Source Administrator utility on your computer.

TIP If you're working on a Windows computer, you can expect that the required drivers are already installed. (They ship with the operating system.) On the Mac, however, you'll need to purchase and install the required drivers, which are available from Actual Technologies (www.actualtechnologies.com).

To access the ODBC Data Source Administrator in Windows (XP or Vista), go to the Start menu and navigate to Control Panel ⇨ Administrative Tools ⇨ Data Sources (ODBC). After selecting this option, the ODBC Data Source Administrator control panel appears. Choose the System DSN tab (see Figure 7.20).

FIGURE 7.20

The ODBC Data Source Administrator control panel in Windows Vista.

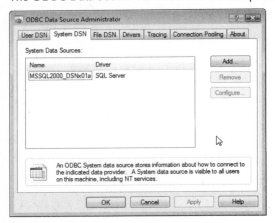

To access the ODBC Administrator on Mac OS, open the Applications folder on your system disk and locate and open the Utilities folder. Inside Applications/Utilities, you'll find an application called ODBC Administrator. Double-click it, and the ODBC Administrator utility window appears. Click the padlock icon at the lower left and authenticate as an administrator for the computer. Choose the System DSN tab to show the panel in Figure 7.21.

After you've accessed the ODBC Administrator on your computer (as described in the preceding paragraphs), click the Add button at the upper right of the window. You'll be prompted to select a driver. Choose the driver appropriate to the source to which you're connecting — MySQL, SQL Server, or Oracle. (If the appropriate driver isn't present in the list, you'll first have to obtain and install it.) Accept the driver selection, and you'll be presented with the driver configuration panel. Although there is some variation between drivers and systems, the process is similar, requiring you to enter a name, a server address, and authentication details.

In the following steps, I show the process for creating a new DSN to connect to SQL Server from Mac OS by using the Actual SQL Server driver:

1. In the first configuration panel (shown in Figure 7.22), enter the name for this connection (I chose to call the connection AdminSys_SQL, but any recognizable name will do) and the connection type (System), along with the address of the server, which may be in the form of an IP address or a domain pointer (for example, `data.yourdomain.com`). The description field, if available, is optional.

FIGURE 7.21

The ODBC Administrator Utility in Mac OS.

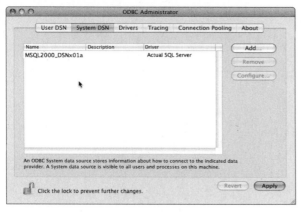

After you accept the settings on the first panel, a second panel asks for authentication details, as shown in Figure 7.23. The login and password you enter here must match a valid account in the host system you're accessing.

2. In this panel, you can click the Client Configuration button to change the network protocol or the connection's port assignment. In my case, the default settings (TCP-IP, port 1433) were appropriate. As long as your login ID and password are valid (and the server address, port, and protocol are correct), the connection is established and you're taken to a third screen (shown in Figure 7.24) that displays settings specific to the server.

FIGURE 7.22

Configuring the DSN, Part 1: Connection name and server address.

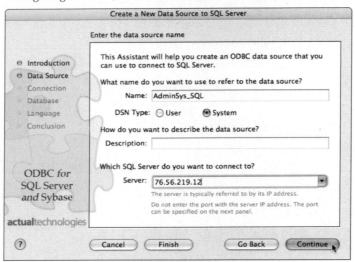

3. If necessary (that is, if your login provides access to more than one database on the selected host), choose a database as the default. Options to change the default language and regional settings and log file locations, plus a confirmation screen, appear.

FIGURE 7.23

Configuring the DSN, Part 2: Authentication.

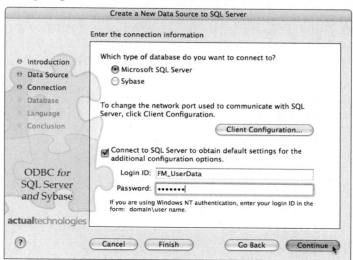

FIGURE 7.24

Configuring the DSN, Part 3: Server-specific settings.

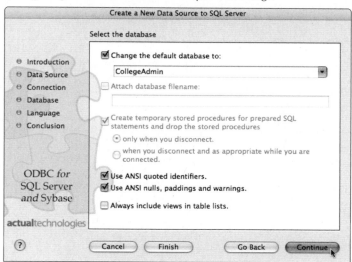

4. I accepted all the default settings. On dismissing the confirmation panel of the driver configuration panel, a new DSN was added to the ODBC Administrator panel, as shown in Figure 7.25.

Although the configuration process described here and the accompanying images are on a Mac using the Actual SQL Server driver, I repeated the process in Windows Vista (using the default SQL Server driver in Windows), and the process was identical.

FIGURE 7.25

The resulting DSN appearing in the ODBC Administrator Utility, after configuration of the ODBC Driver.

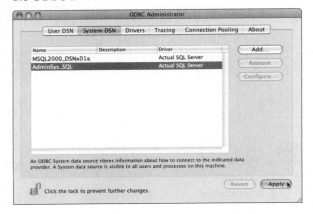

Integrating SQL tables with FileMaker data

After establishing a DSN as described in the preceding section, you can add SQL tables directly onto the Relationships Graph in FileMaker Pro 10. To do so, follow these steps:

1. Choose File ➪ Manage ➪ Database and navigate to the Relationships tab.

2. Click the New TO icon at the far left of the tools along the bottom of the dialog. The Specify Table dialog appears, as shown in Figure 7.26.

3. Select Add ODBC Data Source from the Data Source menu. You're prompted to choose a DSN (from a list of previously configured DSNs).

FIGURE 7.26

Adding an ODBC Data Source via the Specify Table dialog.

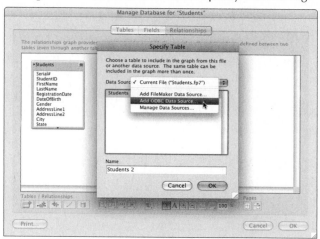

4. Select the appropriate DSN and click Continue. FileMaker displays the Edit Data source dialog, as shown in Figure 7.27.

The only essential settings when configuring your connection to a SQL database are a valid System DSN and a name to identify the external source within FileMaker. (It can be the same as the DSN name if you want.) You will, of course, need a valid username and password to access the SQL host. However, you have the choice of being prompted to authenticate for every connection or to save the authentication details when creating the connection.

CAUTION If you store authentication details for an SQL Host in your FileMaker file, ensure that your solution is appropriately secured with its own account and password authentication (see Chapters 5 and 14).

For most purposes, you can leave the Filter options at the bottom of the Edit Data Source dialog with the default settings, but it may vary depending on the nature and configuration of the SQL database and the settings of the DSN on your computer. If you're unfamiliar with the database to which you're connecting, you may want to confer with the database administrator to ensure that you have an appropriate account and other configuration details.

On accepting the Data Source settings, you're returned to the Specify Table dialog, and a list of tables available in the selected SQL database is displayed, as shown in Figure 7.28.

FIGURE 7.27

The Edit Data Source dialog for configuration of an external SQL connection.

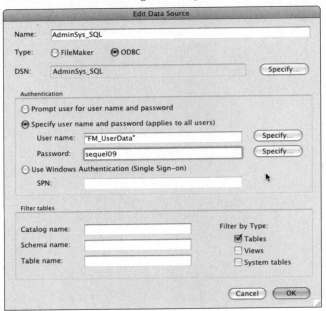

FIGURE 7.28

Selecting from a list of SQL Server tables in the Specify Table dialog.

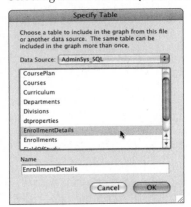

5. For the purposes of this example, I've added three SQL tables to a file alongside a FileMaker table called Students. With SQL tables appearing as TOs on the Relationships Graph, as shown in Figure 7.29, you're able to drag connections between the tables to create relationships, exactly as you do when working with FileMaker tables.

NOTE The names of TOs based on external tables (both FileMaker and SQL) appear in italic in the header band of their boxes on the Relationships Graph.

With relationships in place, you can work with your solution, incorporating SQL data alongside FileMaker data, performing Finds, and creating and editing records (subject to privilege restrictions, if any, of your account to the SQL host).

FIGURE 7.29

Creating relationships to join FileMaker tables and SQL tables.

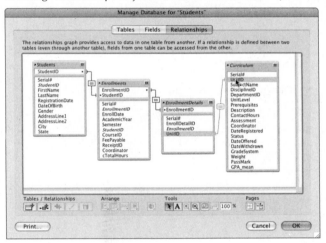

Because some of the tables in your solution are created and hosted elsewhere, you'll be constrained by the available fields and their formats. SQL fields don't always behave in the same ways as FileMaker fields. However, you'll be able to define Auto-Enter options (default values, serial numbers, auto-enter calculations and lookups, and so on) and data validations for the fields in the SQL tables in your solution. To facilitate the application of Auto-Entry options and creation of calculations for ESS tables, FileMaker creates shadow tables representing the content of the SQL tables you've referenced, as shown in Figure 7.30.

FIGURE 7.30

Shadow tables created by FileMaker to support SQL TOs added to the Relationships Graph.

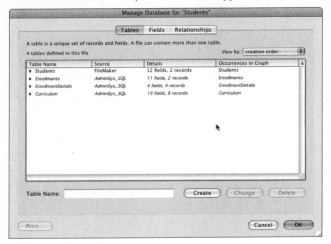

Adding supplemental fields

In addition to specifying Auto-Enter and validation options for fields within shadow tables, FileMaker lets you add summary and calculation fields (for use only within FileMaker).

Using the example shown in Figures 7.29 and 7.30, you can add data to create and update student enrollment records in the remote SQL Server database. As subjects are added to a student's enrollment, the total attendance hours increase. However, the SQL database has no facility to calculate the total. You can resolve an issue of this kind by adding a calculation field to the Enrollment table, exactly as you would if it were a FileMaker table.

Figure 7.31 shows the FileMaker calculation field added to the Enrollments table. Supplemental fields added in this way are re-evaluated as data is displayed in the same way as unstored calculations within native FileMaker tables.

CROSS-REF   For further discussion of the use of SQL data, you may want to consult the discussion on the use of separated data in SQL sources in Chapter 11.

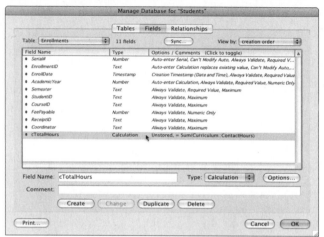

FIGURE 7.31

A FileMaker supplemental field added to the SQL Enrollments table that calculates the sum of course hours by using a FileMaker relationship between two SQL tables.

The Concept of Data Relationships

Previously, I've mentioned the value of investing time and effort in setting up appropriate data relationships in your solutions. Establishing a comfortable and "natural" fit between the information itself and the structures where you store it greatly simplifies effective information management.

As well as mirroring reality, relational data systems make practical sense because they allow you to store each piece of information once and connect it to other relevant information. The reduced duplication not only saves labor but also reduces the scope for error.

Why bother with relationships anyway?

In a solution such as the Inventory example from the previous chapters, each kind of item has a single corresponding record in the Inventory table. Wherever the item is purchased or sold — or included on a list of acquisitions for a customer in the contacts table — the name and description of the item, as stored in its Inventory record, is displayed. If you correct an error in the description of an item, the change instantly propagates to every place in the system referencing the item.

Similarly, each buyer and supplier has a single record in the Contacts table. If a contact's address is updated, the change will be seen throughout the system without further effort on your part.

In coming years, the time and money you invest designing and implementing an appropriate structure (and solution to support it) for your databases will pay off many times over in the improved accuracy and accessibility of your data and the time saved.

How relationships work

Relationships use one or more key fields, which are matched to corresponding values in another table. The values used as keys follow three guidelines:

- They should be unique (duplicates cause instant confusion).
- They should be persistent (not changing periodically).
- They should not be empty.

Using an attribute such as a person's name or initials (or some other data about them) as the key to a record is generally unwise. The information may not be unique (people can have the same name), and it may not be persistent. (People occasionally change their names.) For these and similar reasons, using serial numbers or code values as keys is often safer.

When you've chosen key values, FileMaker builds value indexes for the key fields so that relationship matching can be undertaken efficiently. When your solution retrieves data from another table, it's the other table's index that is used. The value of the key field in the current table is referenced against the index of the related table to instantly locate matching records. For this reason, a relationship will work as long as the "other" table's match field is indexed.

In FileMaker, most fields can be indexed, so most relationships work in both directions (from the perspective of layouts associated with TOs at both ends of the join). However, in cases where a global field or an unstored calculation has been used as the key field on one side of a relationship, the relationship will work in one direction only.

Solving problems by using relationships

A useful feature of FileMaker relationships is that they match field values. In text fields, a value is one line of text. Because text fields can hold multiple lines, however, a text field can hold multiple key values. When you place multiple values (separated by carriage returns) into a text field that you've defined as the key field for a relationship, matches to any of the values will be valid. A key field used in this way is referred to as a *Multi-Key field* (or sometimes just a *Multi-Key*). By employing Multi-Key fields, you increase the possible matches, creating an OR relationship condition. (That is, records will be related to the current record if they match one value *or* the other.) You can use Multi-Key text fields on either side, or both sides, of a relationship. (In the latter case, the join is valid if any of the values on one side matches any of the values on the other.)

FileMaker also lets you narrow the scope of a relationship by specifying additional pairs of key fields, Relationships of this kind are called *multi-predicate relationships*. When more than one pair of key fields has been assigned to a relationship, both criteria are applied, returning an AND condition. (The first pair of keys must match, *and* any subsequent pairs must match in order for the relationship to be valid.)

By far the most common kind of relationship is one in which values on either side of the relationship must exactly match. This kind of relation is called an *equi-join* and is symbolized by the = relationship operator. However, FileMaker provides a number of alternative operators that you can use to control the behavior of relationships.

For example, when you want to relate an invoice record to the record for the customer who you're invoicing, your relationship between the Invoices and Customers TOs will be an equi-join that connects the CustomerID fields in both tables. However, when you want to view a list of previous invoices, your relationship between two TOs based on the invoices table will use the less than operator to match the InvoiceDate fields in both TOs. In this latter example, the invoices with dates earlier than (less than) the date of the current invoice will appear.

 **For additional detail about relationships and relationship operators in FileMaker, refer to Chapter 11.**

Deciding what goes where

A central principle of relational design is that of separating entities and describing their attributes. From a data design perspective, each kind of entity warrants a table, and each attribute of an entity warrants a field in the entity's table.

In practical terms, tables are used to store information about a class of items. Whenever an item has independence from another (with which it is associated), you should consider treating them as separate entities and giving them separate tables.

Persons are entities, and they live at addresses. Because persons are not inseparable from their places of residence, however, storing addresses in a separate table from persons often makes sense. Similarly, employees occupy jobs for periods of time, but they can be viewed as discrete entities, so it makes sense to have separate tables for them and relationships to show who is in which job and when.

CROSS-REF **I provide a more extensive discussion of relational modeling and data design in Chapters 11 and 15.**

The FileMaker relational model

FileMaker offers you a very appealing combination of elements. It provides coverage for a wide range of requirements from stand-alone systems to major server-based installations. It's a stealth weapon, concealing its power behind a demure interface and apparent ease of use.

A defining characteristic of FileMaker has been its integrated approach — wherein data, logic, and interface are combined within a unified format. But in reality, FileMaker's extraordinary flexibility gives you many choices. The ability to work seamlessly with SQL data in FileMaker 10 further extends FileMaker's scope as an all-purpose tool.

However, powerful relational tools and good data modeling aren't the only things that make FileMaker an instant asset. Its capability to automate your work processes adds another dimension. In Chapter 8, I delve into FileMaker's capabilities as a process management tool.

Chapter 8

The Processes: FileMaker Scripting

A key benefit when you choose to embrace technology is that it can make life easier for you. However, getting the most out of technology means not only choosing well, but also using well. It is at the point where you wish to gain maximum benefit from your use of FileMaker Pro that the FileMaker built-in scripting environment comes to the fore.

In the preceding chapters, you've become acquainted with the tools and techniques for building database structures and interfaces. Scripting provides a third essential element that makes everything work together. When you need your solution to take a more active role, you have to provide it with a script. That's where scripting comes in. Scripting enables you to store instructions about tasks to be performed with your data; then a script performs those tasks for you!

Any series of database tasks that you need to do repetitively may benefit from being scripted and performed on demand. Scripting performs this essential automation role, with the potential to take much of the drudgery out of your digital days. The best thing is that you'll find it very easy to get started using scripting — and, when you do, you'll wonder how you ever got by without it!

IN THIS CHAPTER

Getting acquainted with scripting

Creating and modifying FileMaker scripts

Getting acquainted with Script menu

Designing script automation

Identifying some notable script uses

Organizing your scripts

Getting started with some examples

Putting your scripts into action in your solutions

Scripting: What It Is and What It Offers You

At its inception, FileMaker scripting was analogous to a macro environment; its focus was to perform a number of simple tasks in the same ways in which the users would perform the tasks. That was a couple of decades ago, however, and scripting's capabilities have been growing and evolving, version by version, ever since. Nevertheless, scripting retains those original capabilities, making it easy for you to get started.

A FileMaker *script* is essentially a sequence of instructions saved together — a stored procedure. Scripts typically perform a series of actions in the same sequence in which you'd perform those actions if you were stepping through a task manually. When the actions are set out in a script, however, you can perform them as though they were a single action or command. For example, when you create a database to keep track of customer details, you'll find it useful to be able to locate a customer's details and then click a button to see corresponding orders. Similarly, you may want to create an automatic procedure to create banking reconciliations or to delete inactive customer records.

Before beginning a journey into the realm of scripting, it will help you become familiar with some of the terms and concepts you'll encounter as you work with scripts. You can get started creating and organizing your own scripts in the Manage Scripts window in FileMaker by choosing Scripts⇨Manage Scripts or Shift+⌘+S/Ctrl+Shift+S). The instructions within a script are called *commands* and are sometimes also referred to as *steps* or *script steps*. The FileMaker Edit Script windows (you access the Edit Script windows from within the Manage Scripts window) present a list of script commands groups within the following 12 functional categories:

- **Control commands** enable you to manage the flow of your scripts, determining when it will exit, introducing conditions, repeating (looping) particular sequences, detecting errors, and so on.

- **Navigation commands** allow your scripts to move the focus between layouts, fields, layout objects (buttons, tab controls, Web viewers, and so on) and modes within your solution.

- **Editing commands** let your scripts make changes to data in the fields of your database, selecting text, clearing values, inserting data, and cutting, copying, pasting, and replacing data.

- **Fields commands** enable you to programmatically set or update the value in a field or a group of fields or to export the contents of a field.

- **Records commands** allow you to create, delete, save, duplicate, import, or export the records in your database and to generate find requests when scripting search operations.

- **Found Sets commands** enable your scripts to perform and modify Finds, adjust found sets, and sort records.

- **Windows commands** provide your scripts with control over the display, position, and behavior of the database windows of your solution, enabling the creation of new windows, selection of existing windows, closure of windows, and adjustment of window size and position.

- **Files commands** allow your scripts to automatically control database files, creating, opening and closing files; adjusting formats; and selecting printers and printing documents.

- **Accounts commands** give your scripts an interface to file security, allowing them to add and delete user accounts, enable and disable accounts, update passwords, and change the login status of the current file.

- **Spelling commands** provide script options for control of the spell-checking features and dictionary support of FileMaker Pro.

- **Open Menu Item commands** offer your scripts a means to access a range of standard menu actions to display key configuration dialogs, including Online Help, File Options, Preferences, Sharing, Manage Database, and numerous others.

- **Miscellaneous commands** provide additional controls and extended functionality, from toolbars and custom dialogs to Web viewer controls, SMTP e-mail external events, and inter-application scripting.

Scripting in FileMaker is easier than text-based programming (in languages that require you to write code directly) because FileMaker provides Edit Script windows that enable you to build scripts by pointing and clicking. The Manage Scripts dialog and the Edit Script windows provide you with lists of commands to select from, plus buttons, checkboxes, and menus for associated parameters and controls so that you don't have to be so concerned about remembering the syntax or typing things out correctly. Instead, you can select the commands you require from the lists provided and then configure the required parameters in a panel below the main script definition panel. As you can see in Figure 8.1, dialogs such as the "New Window" Options dialog prompt you to enter the necessary details to support each script command. Moreover, many dialogs, like the one in Figure 8.1, include Specify buttons adjacent to many input fields, allowing you direct access to the calculation dialog so that the script command's parameter values can be determined dynamically (that is, calculated as the script runs).

FIGURE 8.1

Specify buttons present calculation dialogs where you can create calculations that will determine command parameters dynamically each time your script is executed.

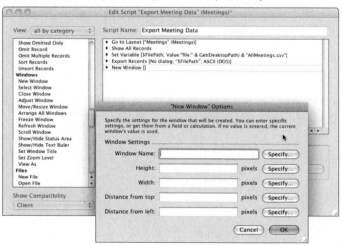

TIP If your solution may be Web hosted or if you're creating a script that you may need to run remotely on FileMaker Server, make sure to visit the Show Compatibility drop-down menu at the lower left corner of the Edit Script dialog. Knowing which steps won't function in a given environment allows you to adjust your approach or disable specific functionality when designing scripts to be run remotely.

Building blocks of automation

The FileMaker Scripting environment offers 15 Control commands, 11 Navigation commands, 8 Editing commands, 16 Fields commands (Mac) or 18 Fields commands (Windows), 14 Records commands, 10 Found Sets commands, 14 Windows commands, 10 Files commands, 6 Accounts commands, 7 Spelling commands, 11 Open Menu Item commands, and 15 Miscellaneous steps (Mac) or 14 Miscellaneous steps (Windows), making a total of 137 script commands on Mac OS and 138 script commands in Windows. However, two of the Miscellaneous commands (Perform AppleScript and Speak) are Mac-only, and three (Insert Object, Update Link, and Send DDE Execute) are Windows-specific, while the Send Event command is present on both platforms but requires different syntax.

I won't provide you with a blow-by-blow account of the operations of each of the 140 commands (both platforms combined) here. If I were to give full details (listing and describing them all) here, you would not get the best value because you already have lists and descriptions in the online Help system that installs with every copy of FileMaker Pro (and the same information is also available on the Web and in downloadable PDF documents from the FileMaker, Inc., Web site)

CROSS-REF Refer to Appendix A for links to free and comprehensive resources detailing the operation of each script command.

The FileMaker Specify Calculation dialog allows (but does not require) you to type your calculation expression. However, the Edit Script dialog requires that you create and edit scripts by selecting items from lists and configuring their predefined options. Some users start out performing these selections and manipulations entirely via the mouse, but you'll quickly find that you can use keyboard commands to control the whole process efficiently. You select script steps (using the mouse, the Tab and arrow keys, or type-ahead selection) in a list box at the left of the Edit Script window. After you've located/selected the step you want, you can add it to the current script (by double-clicking or by pressing Return). By default, new steps appear at the end of the current script, but if you've selected a step in the current script, any new steps will be added immediately after that step.

In the main working area of the Edit Script window, you use the same methods to select a script step to configure, reposition, or delete. You can select options for a selected script step from checkboxes (occasionally with adjoining Specify buttons) in the Script Step Options panel, as shown in the lower portion of the dialog in Figure 8.2.

> **TIP** The Tab key provides a convenient way to shift the focus between the Script Name text box, the Script Step list box, and the Script Definition list box. (Shift+Tab changes focus in the reverse direction.)

When one of the two list boxes in the Edit Script window has focus (a blue border), you can use the keyboard to select items/lines by typing the first letter(s) of the entry. For example, in Figure 8.2, typing **en** selects the End If script command line.

When a line is selected in the list box, press Return (or Enter or the space bar) to add it to the current script. When a line in the script definition window is selected, press Return (or Enter or the space bar) to open a configuration dialog.

FIGURE 8.2

The Edit Script window with a command in the current script selected.

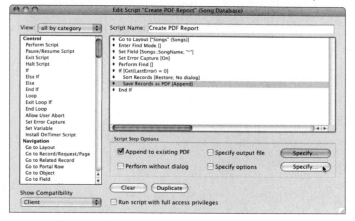

When you select a script command, configuration options are shown in the Script Step Options panel immediately below the script definition panel, as shown in Figure 8.2. Moreover, script command options are summarized in square brackets ([ ]) adjacent to each configurable command in the Script Definition panel. The additional information that command options provide are frequently termed *arguments* or *parameters*. After a brief period working with FileMaker scripting, you'll find that you become familiar with the way commands are presented, and it becomes easier to read a script definition and understand the arguments. Although FileMaker makes it relatively easy, it is nevertheless a programming language that provides complex information in a compact form, ready to be parsed and executed by the FileMaker script engine.

Some script steps are straightforward and have no parameters to be configured. Perhaps the best example is the Halt Script command, which stops the script dead in its tracks. Another example is the New Record/Request step, which requires no parameters and always simply creates a new record (if the database is in Browse mode at the time) or a new Find request (if the database is in Find mode).

Many script commands have multiple options and can perform a variety of different actions, depending on the options you select. A simple example is the Undo/Redo command, which provides a menu of three options: Undo, Redo, or Toggle. In effect, the Undo/Redo command can provide three different behaviors, depending on the parameter you select.

At the opposite extreme, however, are some commands that have many options and can be configured to do a variety of different tasks within a single script step. One such command is `Go to Related Records[ ]`. It can be configured to

- Select records from a related table.
- Choose an appropriate layout to display the selected records.
- Create a new window.
- Give the new window a custom title.
- Size and position the new window.
- Constrain the found set of records in the selected table.

With all these capabilities available simultaneously, this one particular command can do work that would otherwise require a number of steps. In this manner, many of the available script commands may be viewed as "packages" of functionality.

Similarly, when you create a script, you're assembling a number of steps into a particular order (and with particular options selected), such that the script itself becomes a package of functionality in your solution. In other words, you can call your script with one action (for example, from a menu or with an assigned keystroke), and it responds, delivering the full functionality of its sequence of steps, at a single stroke.

Context is everything

FileMaker scripts act as though they're the user — they temporarily take over control of your solution and perform a sequence of actions. In doing so, scripts are constrained to work with the solution's layouts and windows (although they can be programmed to switch layouts or create new windows if desired). Just like the user, a script must be focused on the appropriate screen before it can act on the data that's accessible from that screen.

The way your scripts depend on context is similar to the way you, as a user, depend on context when using your solutions. From a particular layout, you can see data from the associated table and also from related tables (for example, in a portal). Similarly, scripts can act on the current record or on related records, based on the currently active layout and record as each script command executes.

Many script steps require not only that the correct layout be active but that the field or object they're programmed to act on also be present on the layout. For example, when your script includes the command

```
Paste [Select; Contacts::ContactName]
```

The step will fail if you remove the `ContactName` field from the current layout.

> **NOTE** Although scripts act from the context established via the interface, some script commands, such as `Set Field [ ]`, work directly with the data structure available from the current layout context, regardless of the presence of fields on the layout.

To ensure that your scripts work as intended, you should code them to manage context. Doing so entails establishing the correct context before taking context-dependent actions (such as changing data), testing for context where appropriate, and returning the user to a familiar context after completing their operation.

Doing things in sequence

Because scripts control the interface and act on your solution as a user does, they're constrained to perform actions in the same logical sequence that a user would. If you want to create a record in the `Invoice` table, you have to make sure that you're in Browse mode, navigate to an invoice layout and then select the `New Record` command. To script the same procedure, you'd require three commands as follows:

```
Enter Browse Mode [ ]
Go to Layout ["InvoiceList" (Invoices)]
New Record/Request
```

A script is a list of instructions to be performed in the order in which they appear. In this respect, your scripts are a detailed and sequential documentation of a specific process. If you're able to clearly document all the steps required to perform a specific task, then you'll be able to script the task by assembling the commands that represent each user action, in the order in which the actions are to occur.

Addressing objects by name

Many script commands act directly on the solution interface, whether entering data into a field on the layout or setting a URL into a Web viewer. To do this, scripts must move the cursor to the appropriate field or layout, select the appropriate Web viewer, and so on.

Some layout objects types have a special command to place the focus on them. For example, the commands

```
Go to Field [ ]
Go to Portal Row [ ]
```

are specially designed to move the focus to a specific field on the current layout or row of the current portal. However, you can address objects of other types by first assigning an object name (via the Object Info palette) and then using the command:

```
Go to Object [ ]
```

For example, if you have more than one portal on a layout called InvoiceSummary, in order to place the cursor into a particular field in the last row in one of the portals, you could use a script sequence such as:

```
Enter Browse Mode [ ]
Go to Layout ["InvoiceSummary" (Invoices)]
Go to Object ["AvailableItems"]
Go to Portal Row [Last]
Go to Field [Items::QuantityAvailable]
```

By naming the portal in question AvailableItems and then addressing it explicitly by its name in the script, you ensure that the script will locate the desired portal and the correct instance of the Items::QuantityAvailable field.

In any situation where more than one instance of an object may be present on the layout, the Go to Object [ ] command provides a way to ensure that your script will target the desired object. Moreover, you can use the Go to Object [ ] command to place the focus on a variety of different object types including tab panels, buttons, and Web viewers as well as fields and portals.

NOTE   An added advantage of the Go to Object [ ] command is the ability to determine the name of the object it is to target by calculation. This command enables you to program your scripts to behave more intelligently (for example, taking the user to the first empty field, or selecting a field if it has a value in it, but if not, going to a different field).

Defining and Editing Scripts

In the sense that script commands and scripts themselves can be considered packages of functionality, you can view scripting as analogous to an object environment, where larger objects can be assembled from smaller ones and then, in turn, used as components in the assembly of still other objects. Just as you can supply parameters (or *arguments*) to a script command to determine its behavior, you can pass and reference a script parameter within the script to control the behavior of the script.

CROSS-REF   The use of script parameters is explored in detail in Chapter 9.

I encourage you to think about scripts as reusable objects — maps of action and process — and to strive for a mix of simplicity and versatility. As you develop your skills with scripting, you may come to view a script as operating like the roll of a player piano — encapsulating detail while re-creating artistry.

Script Editor windows

When you choose File ➪ Manage ➪ Scripts (⌘+Shift+S or Ctrl+Shift+S), FileMaker displays the Manage Scripts window for the current file.

NOTE   An alternative way to invoke the Manage Scripts window is to choose Scripts ⇨ Manage Scripts. Both commands take you to the same window.

As shown in Figure 8.3, the Manage Scripts window provides a list of scripts in the current file, along with basic search and selection tools at the top of the window and a selection of controls along the bottom.

The Manage Scripts window in FileMaker 10 is nonmodal, so you can leave it open (off to one side of your monitor) while you continue to work with your solution in Browse mode, Layout mode, and so on. Moreover, if you have more than one FileMaker database file open, you can display the Manage Scripts windows for both files simultaneously. This ability is particularly useful for comparing different versions of the same file or copying and pasting scripts between files. The title bars of the Manage Scripts windows show the name of the file to which each belongs.

FIGURE 8.3

The Manage Scripts window and its controls.

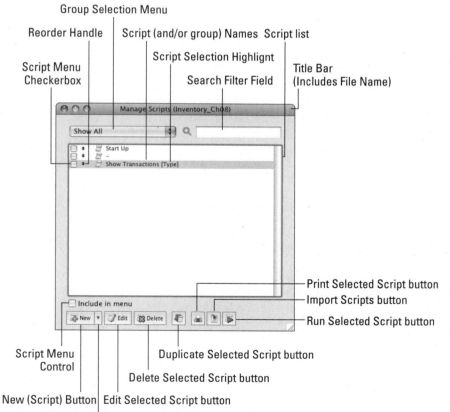

NOTE   The Include in Menu option adds the selected script(s) to the Scripts menu. However, if you have access to FileMaker Pro 10 Advanced, you can create custom menus to add script calls to other menus throughout your solution.

CROSS-REF   For a more detailed discussion of the creation and use of custom menus in FileMaker Pro Advanced, refer to Chapter 18.

Although only three of the controls at the bottom of the Manage Scripts window have text labels, mouse-over tooltips provide reminders about the function of the remaining four icon-only buttons.

To create a script, click the New button at the lower left. To edit an existing script, select it in the list (it appears highlighted, as shown in Figure 8.3) and click the Edit button (or simply double-click the script). In either case, an Edit Script window will be displayed for the script in question, as shown in Figure 8.4.

FIGURE 8.4

The Edit Script window and its controls and parts.

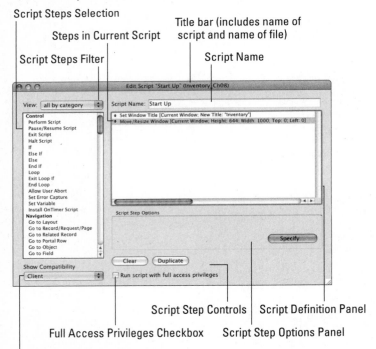

Like the Manage Scripts window, the Edit Script window is nonmodal in FileMaker 10, meaning that you can open the Edit Script window for multiple scripts (from the same or different files)

simultaneously. For comparison and also for copying and pasting commands (or groups of commands) between scripts, this ability is advantageous.

When you open multiple Manage Script or Edit Script windows, each is added to the list of windows appearing at the bottom of the Window menu. Selecting a window from the Window menu will bring it to the front.

To save changes to a script in an Edit Script window, choose Scripts ➪ Save Script. To discard all changes since the script was last saved, choose Scripts ➪ Revert Script.

To close an Edit Script window, or the Manage Scripts window (while either has focus), choose File ➪ Close (⌘+W or Ctrl+W) or click the Close button in the window's title bar. If you've made changes to a script in an Edit Script window and you haven't saved the changes, you'll be prompted to save (or discard) the changes when closing the window.

Setting up a basic script

The process of creating a script to perform a common task requires that you first identify the component actions of the task. After you've done that, creating the script to put the actions into effect is relatively straightforward. For example, to create a script that prints a list of acquired items in the example Inventory database, follow these steps:

1. Choose File ➪ Manage ➪ --Scripts. The Manage Scripts window appears.

2. Click New. A new script is created, and an empty Edit Script window appears.

3. In the Script Name field, replace the default text for the script name with **Acquired Items Report**.

4. In the list of commands at the left (under the heading Navigation), locate the Enter Browse Mode [ ] command, and double-click it. An Enter Browse Mode [ ] step is added to the script definition panel.

5. Choose the Windows option in the View pop-up menu at the upper left of the Edit Script window; then, in the resulting list of commands, double-click the Freeze Window command.

6. Select the Navigation group of commands; then locate the Go to Layout command and double-click it.

7. With the Go to Layout [ ] command selected in the script definition panel, click the Specify menu in the Script Step Options panel and choose the OrderLines layout.

8. Choose Found Sets in the filter menu that sits above the list of commands on the left in the Edit Script window; in the resulting list of commands, double-click the Show All Records command.

9. From the Found Sets group of commands, double-click the Sort Records command.

10. With the Sort Records [ ] command selected in the script definition panel, select the Perform without Dialog checkbox in the Script Step Options panel; then click the Specify Sort Order checkbox. The Sort Records dialog appears.

11. In the Sort Records dialog, locate the `OrderLines` table in the menu at the upper left and double-click the `ItemID` field. It appears in the Sort Order panel at the upper right.

12. Click OK to accept the Sort Records dialog settings.

13. Choose Files in the filter menu at the top of the list of commands at the left of the Edit Script window and, in the resulting list of commands, double-click the `Print Setup` command.

14. With the `Print Setup [ ]` command selected in the script definition panel, select the Perform without Dialog checkbox in the Script Step Options panel and select the Specify Page Setup checkbox. The Page Setup dialog appears.

15. Choose page attributes for portrait orientation and either US Letter or A4 paper size (as appropriate to your region); then click OK.

16. Double-click the `Print` command in the list at the left.

17. With the `Print [ ]` command selected in the script definition panel, select the Perform without Dialog checkbox in the Script Step Options panel and select the Specify Print Options checkbox. The Print Options dialog appears.

18. Choose an appropriate printer, a single copy, and — from the FileMaker Pro section of the dialog options — the Records Being Browsed radio button and click Print (Mac) or OK (Windows).

19. In the Navigation group of commands, locate the `Go to Layout` command and double-click it. The content of the script is now complete, as shown in Figure 8.5.

20. Choose Scripts ⇨ Save Script (⌘+S or Ctrl+S) to save your work.

FIGURE 8.5

The complete Acquired Items Report script definition as it is shown in the Edit Script window.

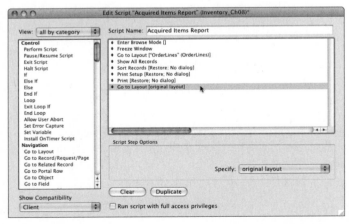

21. Choose File ⇨ Close (⌘+W or Ctrl+W) to close the Script Editor window.

22. In the Manage Scripts window, select the Acquired Items Report and the Include in Menu checkbox.

23. Choose File ⇨ Close (⌘+W or Ctrl+W) to close the Manage Scripts window.

24. Test your new script (by choosing Scripts ⇨ Acquired Items Report) to ensure that it produces a printed data sheet from the `OrderLines` table and returns you to the layout you were in when you chose the script from the Scripts menu.

NOTE For reference purposes, a complete copy of the preceding script, with comments added, is included in the `Inventory` example file for this chapter. For the purpose of viewing the results of the script, I also made some rudimentary changes to the `InvoiceLines` layout in this chapter's copy of the `Inventory` example, so the printout produced presents information in a list format.

CROSS-REF In Chapters 9 and 10, I provide detailed instructions for formatting the `InvoiceLines` and `OrderLines` layouts to achieve more useful output.

After completion of this process, you've created a simple eight-step script that fully automates the process of creating a report from the `OrderLines` layout. You can generate the report by selecting the script from the Scripts menu from wherever you are in the solution. You will be returned to the screen you started from as soon as the report has been created.

How script commands function

Script commands execute an action (or a folder of actions) in real time as the script runs. Some commands, though, are more dependent on the interface than others. For example, commands such as Cut, Copy, Paste, Clear, and Insert work directly with fields in the user interface, placing the cursor into the field and acting on its contents. These commands are not only constrained by the current layout context, but they're also dependent on the relevant field being present on the current layout (if you remove the field from the layout, these script commands will fail). Such commands can be described as *interface dependent*.

A second category of commands replicate the actions of menu commands throughout FileMaker. These commands include script commands, such as New Record/Request, Show All Records, and Save Copy As. There are many commands of this kind, and they provide access to the broad range of activities that are routinely available to the user of a solution.

In addition, scripting provides a number of commands that directly leverage the underlying FileMaker engine. Commands such as `Set Field [ ]`, `Set Next Serial Value [ ]`, `Add Account [ ]`, and `Set Selection [ ]` exemplify this script step category. They allow your scripts to reach around behind the interface, directly manipulating components of the solution.

Finally, a significant number of commands provide control over the script itself, managing the flow of commands and altering their execution. You can find the majority of these commands in the Control group of commands — they include `If [ ]/End If`, `Loop/End Loop`, `Perform Script [ ]`, and numerous others.

A significant aspect of script commands is that they provide controls and options that extend FileMaker's preset capabilities. You can achieve many actions via careful use of scripting that are not available via the standard user interface of FileMaker. A few of the many examples are `Execute SQL [ ]`, `Set Window Title [ ]`, `Dial Phone [ ]` (Windows only) and `OpenURL [ ]`. These commands and others like them extend FileMaker's functional capabilities, enabling you to use scripts to create a rich and varied experience for your solution's users.

Changing the order of commands

When you're editing your scripts, you'll encounter situations where you need to move a command to a position elsewhere within your script. The FileMaker Edit Script dialog offers the capability to move a step by using either the mouse or keyboard. Alternatively, if you prefer, you can achieve a similar result by copying and pasting one or more steps to a new location. (This approach isn't particularly useful for a single line of your script, but it may be worth considering if you need to move a group of commands together.)

NOTE   Unfortunately, no Cut command is available when editing scripts. To simulate the effect of a Cut operation, you need to first copy the command (or group of commands) and then click Clear to delete it. The copied code remains on the clipboard ready to be pasted elsewhere.

When you move the mouse pointer over the column of symbols at the left of the script definition panel, it changes to the familiar FileMaker handle cursor, showing double-headed arrows to signify that you can drag the object up or down. You can click the handle, illustrated in Figure 8.6, and drag the adjacent command to a new position in your script.

FIGURE 8.6

Drag the command handle to move a script step to a new position.

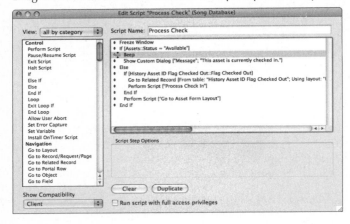

If you prefer, another way to move a script command is to select the step and press ⌘+↑ or Ctrl+↑ to move the selected step upward and ⌘+↓ or Ctrl+↓ to move the step to a position farther down your script.

FileMaker doesn't provide direct support for moving a block of script steps all at once, but two methods are useful when you need to do this task: the copy/clear/paste method and the inline duplication method.

Follow these steps to use the copy/clear/paste method:

1. Select the block of commands you want to move.
2. Choose Edit ⇨ Copy (⌘+C or Ctrl+C).
3. Click the Clear button.
4. Select the script step immediately above the desired new location.
5. Choose Edit ⇨ Paste (⌘+V or Ctrl+V).

Follow these steps to use the inline duplication method:

1. Select the block of commands you want to move.
2. Press ⌘+click or Ctrl+click to select a subsequent command immediately above the desired new location.
3. Click the Duplicate button.
4. Select the final line of the resulting (duplicated) block of commands.
5. Click the Clear button.
6. Reselect the original block of commands.
7. Click the Clear button.

Although inline duplication is less versatile, it has the advantage of working in earlier versions of FileMaker and can be an effective method for some requirements in FileMaker 10. However, inline duplication has the limitation that it's convenient only if you require the duplicate lines below the original lines you're duplicating.

Adding a script command to your script (either by selecting it in the step list and clicking the Move button or by double-clicking it in the step list) places that step immediately below the currently selected line in the script definition window — or, if no line is selected, the command will be added at the end of your script. However, you can easily reposition the step to a different location.

NOTE When you select an item in the list of commands, FileMaker deselects any selected steps in the Script Definition box. Nevertheless, FileMaker remembers which line was selected. However, should you wish to add a command as the first line in your script (after adding other lines), you need to add it first and move it to the top subsequently, because commands are always inserted after, rather than before, the selected (or last) step in the definition panel.

I expand on these and other script-editing techniques in the "Ease of Editing in FileMaker Scripting" section, later in this chapter.

Assigning attributes to a command

Some script commands, such as `Select All` or `Open Record/Request`, are self-contained, requiring no parameters. However, most script commands accept (or require) configuration arguments specifying the scope of (or content for) their action. For example, when your script creates a new window by using the `New Window [ ]` script command, you can (optionally) supply a window name, dimensions, and location for the window that is to be created. In this instance, if you don't supply one or more of the arguments, their values will instead be based on the currently selected window.

The controls that appear in the Script Step Options panel relate to the currently selected script command in the script definition panel, as shown in Figure 8.7. FileMaker assists you and aids clarity by displaying only those controls pertinent to the selected step. The parameters are entered and edited by using a variety of controls, such as checkboxes, pop-up menus, and Specify buttons, which frequently invoke the Specify Calculation dialog (where you can enter a formula to determine the relevant parameter). When you click the relevant controls, FileMaker updates the corresponding command definition in the Script Definition panel.

FIGURE 8.7

Configure your script commands with the controls provided in the Script Step Options panel.

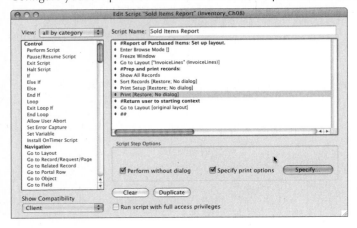

Clicking a Specify button presents a context-appropriate dialog, such as the Specify Field dialog, shown in Figure 8.8, which appears when you select the Specify Target Field checkbox (or its associated Specify button).

FIGURE 8.8

Clicking a Specify button presents a corresponding dialog.

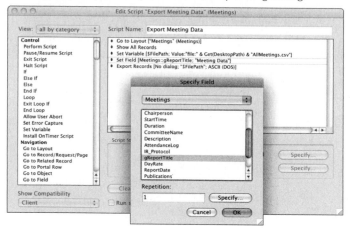

> **NOTE** Double-clicking a command in the Script Definition Panel — or selecting a command and then pressing the Enter key — brings up the default dialog for commands that have one or more parameters configurable by dialog.

You can see examples of the process of setting parameters in the Acquired Items Report script described in the "Setting up a basic script" section, earlier in this chapter, where you selected parameters for the Go to Layout [ ], Sort Records [ ], Print Setup [ ], and Print [ ] script steps.

One of the most frequently used script steps, Set Field [ ], has two Specify options, as shown in Figure 8.8. One of the options determines the field to be set (the target field) via the Specify Field List dialog; the other determines the value to be set in the target field. When the Set Field [ ] command is selected in the Script Definition panel, you can access the Specify Field dialog by any of the following means:

- Clicking the first Specify button
- Pressing the space bar, the Return key, or the Enter key (Mac) or pressing Alt+S (Windows)
- Double-clicking the script step

Similarly, you can access the Specify Calculation dialog by any of the following means:

- Clicking the second Specify button
- Pressing the Ctl+Option+space bar (Mac) or pressing Alt+F (Windows)
- Option+double-clicking or Alt+double-clicking the script step

You can employ the same alternatives to access the Specify dialogs of most script commands that use the Specify Calculation dialog.

You'll encounter many circumstances where you don't know the inputs for a script command in advance. In fact, many script actions will depend on the values in your database at the time the script runs. For example, when your script is designed to add the values in a series of records and place the total into a field, the value it must write depends on the values present when the script is executed. Similarly, you may want the script to act differently depending on the date or day of the week (for example, to send batch reminder e-mails every Friday or as the end of the month approaches).

For these and many other cases, you'll find that you can define script step parameters as a calculation formula (to be resolved when the script runs), rather than a static (literal) value. When you click a Specify button on the Script Step Options panel or within a configuration dialog for a script command, in many cases, FileMaker presents you with the Specify Calculation dialog. This dialog allows you to define a formula that will determine the command parameter when the script is executed. When you have access to the Specify Calculation dialog, you can use any combination of field values from your database and calculation functions, including the many Get ( ) functions FileMaker provides, to return a wide range of environment and status information.

Using the Scripts Menu

FileMaker enables you to display many scripts on the Scripts menu. Because menus provide a widely understood user interface paradigm, this ability is a way of immediately delivering the functionality of your scripts to your users.

If you want to provide a more complex menu interface incorporating your scripts (for example, distributing them among other menus), you can do this via the Custom menus feature of FileMaker Pro 10 Advanced.

CROSS-REF For a more detailed discussion of the creation and use of custom menus in FileMaker Pro 10 Advanced, refer to Chapter 18.

Managing the Scripts menu

The order in which scripts appear in the Scripts menu corresponds to the order of their arrangement in the Manage Scripts window. Thus re-sorting, rearranging, or grouping scripts in the Manage Scripts window directly affects the usability of the Scripts menu.

Only those scripts specifically enabled for menu access (via the checkboxes to the left of each script's name in the Manage Scripts window) appear in the Scripts menu, so the Scripts menu is typically a subset of a file's available scripts. Where a script's functions are specific to only one area of a file (for example, a group of layouts), you may prefer not to include it in the Scripts menu (which is accessible throughout your solution), instead making it available only from those layouts where it's appropriate.

When you add folders to the Manage Scripts window and place scripts within folders, the folders will appear as submenus in the Scripts menu. When you add folders within folders, FileMaker creates corresponding cascading submenus in the Scripts menu.

TIP Don't go overboard with folders within folders. Users find traversing multiple layers of cascading submenus awkward, visually confusing, and frustrating. Although not cast in stone, two levels of submenus is a reasonable limit.

CROSS-REF Additional information is provided in the "Organizing Scripts" section, later in chapter.

Other ways to trigger a script

FileMaker provides a number of alternative ways to call scripts in your solutions:

- Scripts called from the Scripts menu (or submenus of grouped scripts on the Scripts menu)
- Scripts designated to run automatically OnFileOpen and OnFileClose via the File Options dialog (accessed by choosing File ⇨ File Options)
- Scripts launched from Buttons by using the Perform Script [ ] button command
- Scripts called from within other scripts by using the Perform Script [ ] script step
- Scripts called from other menu commands and interface widgets throughout the application, via the use of the FileMaker Pro 10 Advanced Custom Menus capability (see Chapter 18)
- Scripts called by a script trigger assigned to a layout or layout object
- Scripts called by an Install OnTimer Script command on a button or in a script
- Scripts called by plug-ins, using the external function API (see Chapter 20)
- Scripts called by other applications or protocols (for example, AppleScript on the Mac or ActiveX in Windows)

CROSS-REF For a detailed discussion of various methods of triggering a script, refer to the section "Calling Your Scripts," later in this chapter.

Using the single-threaded script engine

Scripts are sequential in nature — they execute one step at a time and one script at a time. Accordingly, script execution in the FileMaker client application is single threaded. Only one script can be active at a time, and when a script is executing, the application is not available to the user.

To manage the execution of scripts, FileMaker keeps track of called scripts on a script stack. The script at the top of the stack is the active script. However, if a script calls another script, the calling script moves down the stack, waiting until the called script (often termed a *sub-script*) completes its run. Then the calling script moves up the stack and continues to execute. In this way, focus may move between a number of scripts during the completion of a single scripted procedure.

Because FileMaker is a multi-user application, each user has the ability to run his own separately executing script thread. Although the client-specific execution of scripts has certain advantages (users aren't delayed while other users run scripts), it does have implications for the way you structure your scripts — you need to consider that multiple instances of a script may be running (on different client workstations) simultaneously. For example, scripts that mark records as part of their process will be apt to conflict if more than one user is running the script because one script may delete marks as the other adds them, or one script may act on records marked by a different script. Similarly, scripts should test for record locking before updating any data because users or scripts may be modifying the current record. (FileMaker locks records while they're being modified.) Without such checks, your scripts may fail intermittently due to conflicts with legitimate activity on other client workstations.

Working with the script stack and paused scripts

When a script is indefinitely paused, it remains active. Meanwhile, the solution interface is made available to the user so that input can be provided or action taken. To facilitate this setup, the solution's functionality while in this state is limited. Because the solution is waiting for input from the user, window switching and file closure are disabled, along with most other options and commands. Such limitations remain until the script resumes and completes execution, or until the user cancels the script. However, if the script includes the Allow User Abort [Off] command prior to the pause, the user won't have access to the Cancel button.

When a script is paused, the user can nevertheless run another script (or another instance of the same script). If you use script pauses frequently in your solution, the user can encounter a situation where a number of scripts are paused and awaiting completion on the script stack. This situation is generally undesirable (because it's hard to predict the effects of part-scripts executing out of sequence) and should, therefore, be managed.

You can limit the likelihood of issues with multiple incomplete (paused) scripts by reducing users' access to scripts during periods when a script is paused or by

- Appropriate use of the Halt Script command to terminate the current script and any other paused scripts.

- Employing the FileMaker controls for script stack management when launching scripts via buttons. An argument accepted by the Perform Script [ ] button command controls the fate of any currently running script when the new script begins, providing you with the option to halt, exit, resume, or pause the current script.

Controlling Script Execution

Manage Scripts provides a meta-command framework — a series of script commands that give you control of the way other commands are executed. Using these process controls enables you to set up scripts to repeat a process (that is, looping and recursion) or to conditionally omit or insert sequences of commands within a process.

Using conditional statements

Occasionally, you need a script to perform the same sequence of actions every time it runs — consistently and uniformly. Sometimes, however, you'll want to set up a script that takes account of different circumstances and responses accordingly. For example, your script that finds all the overdue accounts and sends out reminders should not proceed if no accounts are overdue. Similarly, you may want to have your script post an alert dialog and delete a record only if the user confirms that it should be deleted. These examples and other cases like them require that your code incorporate mechanisms of *conditional execution*. To enable you to implement conditions in the logic of your scripts, the FileMaker Scripting environment provides script commands such as If, Else If, Else, and End If script commands.

> **NOTE** Conditional evaluation occurs in calculations as described in Chapter 7. In addition to the If function, FileMaker provides functions such as Case and Choose. It's important to note that a number of parallels between the logical forms of calculation conditionals and script conditionals, where tests and corresponding results are paired.

One of the most common forms of conditional implementation in scripting is a sequence of commands enclosed between If and End If steps. The If command accepts an argument, and if the argument evaluates as true, the enclosed commands are executed; otherwise, they're skipped. For example, if your invoice table has a PaymentDueDate field, you might include a conditional statement in an invoice-processing script to change the invoice status to "Overdue" if the due date has passed:

```
If [Invoice::PaymentDueDate < Get(CurrentDate)]
    Set Field [Invoice::Status; "Overdue"]
End If
```

> **NOTE** Unlike most other script commands, selecting the If command adds both an If and an End If step to your script, ready to receive your conditional logic. The only other script command that is added with a "partner step" is Loop, which is always accompanied by an End Loop step.

When introducing conditional logic into your scripts, you'll often need to deal with situations where an alternative sequence of steps is required when the If condition fails. For this purpose, FileMaker provides an Else step to delineate sequences of commands associated with true and false results from the If test. For example, if you have a script that navigates to the associated supplier record from the current order, it makes sense to implement a conditional sequence in your script to provide user feedback in the event that there is no supplier record for the current order. One way to achieve that is with the following script code:

```
If [not IsEmpty(Suppliers::ContactID]
    Go to Related Record [From table: "Suppliers"; Using layout: "Contacts"]
Else
    Beep
End If
```

In cases with more than two alternatives, FileMaker provides scripting syntax that allows you to extend the conditional logic, by using the `Else If` command to define successive conditions. For example:

```
If [IsEmpty(Enrollment::Date]
    Set Field [Enrollment::Date; Get(CurrentDate]
Else If [Enrollment::Status = "Draft"]
    Set Field [Enrollment::Status; "In Progress"]
Else If [Enrollment::Status = "Complete"]
    New Record/Request
Else
    Beep
    Show Message [Enrollment is in Progress. Please confirm subject selections.]
End If
```

> **NOTE** A conditional script sequence may contain an extensive number of `Else If` steps, enclosed by a single `If` and `End If` pair. However, you can only use a single `Else` step immediately prior to the `End If` command. (That is, the `Else If`, when used, must precede the final sequence of steps within the `If/End If` construct.)

Using repetition

One of the strongest arguments for using scripting is that it can help you avoid (or at least minimize) repetitive tasks. The more frequently a task is repeated, the more ideal a candidate it is for scripting. In particular, tasks that may need to be repeated many times over in quick succession (such as when you need to update a value on all records in a set) can be very time consuming, and a well-thought-out script makes it possible for you to save a lot of time. For this purpose, FileMaker's `Loop` command and the accompanying `Exit Loop If` and `End Loop` commands provide a convenient mechanism. In addition, several navigation script commands include an Exit After Last option that automatically terminates the loop when no more records remain.

Using looping script sequences allows you to define a series of steps that are repeated until a defined condition is met. For example, to compile a countdown string of values in a text field, you could use the following:

```
Set Variable [$counter; Value:8]
Set Field [Index::Countdown; ""]
Loop
    Exit Loop If [$counter < 0]
    Set Field [Index::Countdown; Trim(Index::Countdown & " " & $counter)]
    Set Variable [$counter; Value:$counter - 1]
End Loop
```

When the script runs, FileMaker will update the `Countdown` field on each pass through the loop, appending a decremented number. The field will acquire a series of numbers (with a space between each) starting from 8 and ending with 0:

```
8 7 6 5 4 3 2 1 0
```

While a countdown of numbers in a field is a simple way to illustrate the action of a looping script, its simplicity is the main thing that makes it useful as an example. However, you can do a great deal more with scripts. Consider for a moment that you can combine both Loop/End Loop and If/ Else/End If syntax to have your script perform a conditional action on each pass of the loop. For example, to have your script work through a set of item records omitting any where the value in a bid field is below the value in a threshold field (on the same record), you can use the following:

```
Go to Record/Request/Page [First]
Loop
        If [Item::Bid < Item::Threshold]
           Omit Record
        Else
           Go to Record/Request/Page [Next; Exit after last]
        End If
End Loop
```

> **TIP** Your loop sequences should always include a valid escape condition — a situation that will arise where the loop will be exited. Otherwise, the loop continues infinitely, and the user will be apt to assume that the computer has stopped responding. (It hasn't, but the user won't know that.) The preceding examples use alternate methods of exiting the loop, the first with the Exit Loop If [ ] command and the second with the Exit after last option on the Go to Record/Request/Page [ ] command. You can use any combination of exit conditions, and the loop will terminate on the first pass when any of the exit conditions is met.

Pausing for user input

Important aspects in controlling your scripts are the ability to pause scripts and determine the timing of their execution. When you want to pause a script to provide the user an opportunity to provide input, you have several options:

- Display a custom dialog allowing the user to make a button selection (in the dialog) or to enter information (into a dialog field).
- Select the Pause argument on a script step, such as a mode change command (for example, Enter Browse Mode [Pause]).
- Add the Pause/Resume Script [Indefinitely] command.

In each case, the script will be placed on hold, and partial control of the solution interface will be returned to the user, enabling the editing or entry of information, navigation in the current table, printing, launching of another script, or resumption of the current script.

FileMaker also provides you with the ability to pause a script for a defined period, placing the database into the same limited state, but automatically resuming the current script at the end of the allotted time. You can achieve this process by configuring the Pause/Resume Script [ ] command, as shown in Figure 8.9.

FIGURE 8.9

The configuration dialog for the Pause/Resume Script [ ] command.

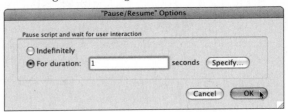

When defining a pause interval, you can enter a finite value in seconds or use the calculation engine to determine a numeric value (also applied as seconds). Timed pauses are useful for creating processes that will run unattended.

NOTE FileMaker will accept sub-second pause durations, and FileMaker 10 will apply them with moderate error tolerances down to periods of around 50 milliseconds (0.05 seconds), below which the margin of error increases. Moreover, error varies between platforms and hardware configurations, so sub-second pauses should be considered indicative. However, FileMaker 10 does provide greater precision than previous versions, which is useful for more accurate control of scripted process and more responsive procedures where pauses need not be defined in whole seconds when shorter durations will suffice.

Some Notable Script Uses

Before you became familiar with the concept of scripting, you may have found it difficult to imagine how you would use it. After you've made a start, though, the possibilities seem limitless. Nevertheless, some processes are better suited to scripting than others, and it's important to identify the best candidates.

Scripting is essentially a process of automation. Any process that is performed in essentially the same way many times over may be a good candidate for automation — especially if it can be constructed to require minimal (or no) human intervention. However, the real test is

- Whether the amount of time saved (over a period of solution use) by scripting a process exceeds the time taken to create the script
- Whether the accuracy of the process will improve significantly if it's scripted (in which case, the reduction in errors may justify the investment of time in automating the process)

In short, spending five hours automating a process doesn't make sense if doing so saves the users five minutes a year. But five hours would certainly be worth spending if the result is a much more substantial saving or if doing so would reduce the scope for operator error.

Navigation and view controls

Although you can provide basic navigation capabilities (such as layout switching and record browsing) by using button commands, scripting such navigation may provide an opportunity to perform other functions, validations, or housekeeping operations, or to provide additional functionality along the way.

In the Inventory example, I had previously configured navigation buttons in the footer area to take the user to other main layouts. However, if these buttons call scripts instead of being attached directly to the Go to Layout [ ] command, you can introduce additional functionality. To demonstrate this concept, I created a script to find incomplete orders or invoices. I structured the script so that

- It finds either orders or invoices, depending on the script parameter it receives.
- It finds all orders or invoices unless the Shift key is depressed.
- If the Shift key is depressed when the script runs, it finds only those orders or invoices not marked as complete (that is, incomplete orders or invoices).

The definition of the script created for this purpose is shown in Figure 8.10. It's called Show Transactions [Type]. The bracketed suffix in the name serves as a reminder that the script requires a parameter to indicate the type of transactions to be shown.

FIGURE 8.10

Definition of the Show Transactions [Type] script in the Inventory example file.

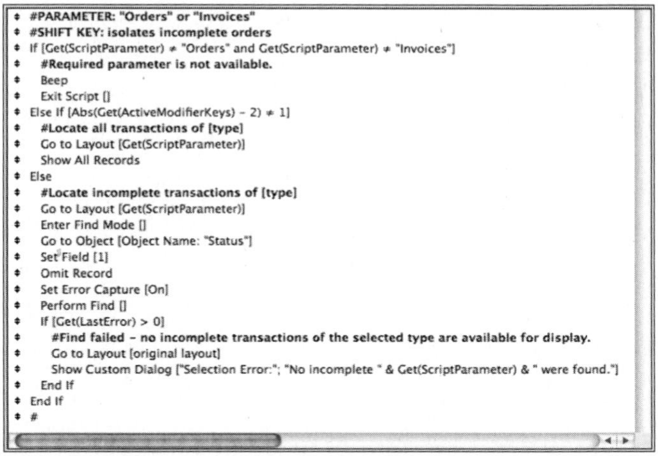

```
#PARAMETER: "Orders" or "Invoices"
#SHIFT KEY: isolates incomplete orders
If [Get(ScriptParameter) ≠ "Orders" and Get(ScriptParameter) ≠ "Invoices"]
    #Required parameter is not available.
    Beep
    Exit Script []
Else If [Abs(Get(ActiveModifierKeys) - 2) ≠ 1]
    #Locate all transactions of [type]
    Go to Layout [Get(ScriptParameter)]
    Show All Records
Else
    #Locate incomplete transactions of [type]
    Go to Layout [Get(ScriptParameter)]
    Enter Find Mode []
    Go to Object [Object Name: "Status"]
    Set Field [1]
    Omit Record
    Set Error Capture [On]
    Perform Find []
    If [Get(LastError) > 0]
        #Find failed – no incomplete transactions of the selected type are available for display.
        Go to Layout [original layout]
        Show Custom Dialog ["Selection Error:"; "No incomplete " & Get(ScriptParameter) & " were found."]
    End If
End If
#
```

After installing the Show Transactions [Type] script and configuring the navigation buttons to call the script (with an accompanying parameter of either Orders or Invoices, depending on the function of the particular button), you can filter the displayed orders or invoices to include only incomplete transactions by holding down the Shift key while clicking the corresponding button.

Editing information via scripts

You can use scripts to provide guidance for data entry or editing and to perform associated checks and validations, providing the user with information and support and improving the quality of the data. You can achieve this goal by

- **Using dialogs and viewer windows for data entry:** Your scripts can present the user with a dialog (or a pop-up window controlled to behave in a way resembling a dialog) with fields for entry of required information. A dialog or pop-up window can be advantageous as a prompt for required information, where the user can't proceed until the relevant input is complete.

- **Scripting for batch processing of data updates:** Where a group of records periodically need to be updated (for example, to reflect the current date or to recalculate with respect to revised budget projections, and so on), a script can gather the necessary inputs and then work its way through a large number of records, applying the required updates to each in turn.

- **Scripting find and data-cleansing routines:** You can use scripts very effectively for locating anomalous records and correcting known or anticipated issues. For example, if data imported into your solution frequently has undesirable characters such as tabs or trailing punctuation in the fields, you can create a script to search for records exhibiting these problems and cycle through them, checking and correcting them.

Printing and managing files

As in the case of the example Acquired Items Report script you created in the section Setting up a basic script," earlier in this chapter, scripts provide an ideal mechanism for generating consistent reports because they can apply the same criteria (find, sort, and so on) each time and produce printed copy by using identical page and print settings. You can set up and refine all the details and settings for a report once (in the script) and then be confident that you'll get the correct output every time you use the script to create the same report.

Similarly, you can use scripts to greatly simplify and improve the repeatability of data import and export procedures, each of which can require painstaking configuration — with an attendant risk of error over repeated occurrences.

Finally, you can create a simple script (employing the Save a Copy as [ ] command) to automate the process of generating backup copies of a solution while it's used in stand-alone mode (or hosted by using FileMaker Pro). An example of such a script is as follows:

```
If [Get(MultiUserState) < 2]
  Set Variable [$path; Value:
                  "file:" & Get(DocumentsPath) & Get(FileName) & "_BU_" &
                  Year(Get(CurrentDate)) &
                  Right("0" & Month(Get(CurrentDate)); 2) &
                  Right("0" & Day(Get(CurrentDate)); 2) & "_" &
                  Right("0" & Hour(Get(CurrentTime)); 2) &
                  Right("0" & Minute(Get(CurrentTime)); 2) & ".fp7"]
  Save a Copy as ["$path"; compacted]
Else
  Beep
  Show Custom Dialog ["Backups must be performed on the host computer."]
End If
```

Whenever the preceding script is called, a fresh backup copy of the current database will be created in the current user's Documents folder with the filename, including the backup's date and time (in a canonical format). An automated backup procedure is a useful way to keep copies of a file as you're developing (enabling you to return to a previous version in case of a mishap).

CROSS-REF For a discussion of the process of setting filenames by calculation, as used in the preceding script, turn to Chapter 13.

ON the WEB I've added the preceding script to the Inventory example file for this chapter so that you can refer to it if you want. Look for the script named Save Local Backup.

NOTE You can perform the preceding backup script only on the computer where the current database is located (that is, being hosted) and is, therefore, not suitable for solutions being accessed via FileMaker Server. FileMaker Server provides its own built-in backup scheduling options.

Ease of Editing in FileMaker Scripting

FileMaker 10 enables you to open multiple Edit Script windows simultaneously, which has the obvious advantage of letting you compare scripts and copy and paste steps or groups of steps between scripts (from the same or different files). A less obvious advantage is that, in a hosted solution, multiple developers can work in Manage Scripts concurrently — while only one user can modify a specific script at a time, users can work on different scripts simultaneously.

TIP When you open a script and make changes to it, an asterisk appears to the right of the script name in the window's title bar, indicating unsaved changes. Whenever the asterisk is present, you can choose Scripts ⇨ Revert Script to discard the changes and go back to the last saved version of the script. Alternatively, you can close the Edit Script window and select the Don't Save option when FileMaker presents a dialog to prompt you to save changes to the script.

Selecting and duplicating multiple commands

To select contiguous blocks of script commands on both Windows and Mac, you can click the first step and then Shift+click the last step of your selection. Similarly, you can select noncontiguous blocks by ⌘+clicking (Mac) or Ctrl+clicking (Windows). You can exclude individual steps from an existing selection by ⌘+clicking or Ctrl+clicking the step(s) you want to deselect.

> **TIP**   **You can use the keyboard to extend a selection downward by pressing Shift+↓ or upward by pressing Shift+↑. After extending a selection, you can reduce it by using the Shift key with the opposite arrow (opposite to the direction in which you extended the selection).**

When you select noncontiguous blocks of script commands by using the methods described here, you can clear, duplicate, or disable all the selected commands at once. When duplicating commands by this method, note that the duplicated commands will be placed together immediately after the last selected command.

An alternative method of duplicating script commands (or groups of commands) is to select them and copy and paste. Note that when you paste, the commands from the clipboard will be inserted after the current selection (or after the last command in the current selection, if multiple commands are selected).

Copying and pasting scripts

In FileMaker Pro 10, you can copy and paste whole scripts in the Manage Scripts window (or between the Manage Scripts windows of different files). You can copy and paste multiple scripts as well as single scripts. The ability to open the Manage Scripts windows for multiple files simultaneously makes copying and pasting scripts easy to use.

In cases where you want to duplicate multiple scripts, copying and pasting them within the same Manage Scripts window is one option.

> **NOTE**   **The naming methodology FileMaker uses when pasting multiple copies of a script is different from the naming technique employed for duplicating scripts. For pasted multiples, FileMaker appends the number 2 (separated from the name by a space), and subsequent copies acquire an incremented number (3, 4, 5, and so on). When using the Duplicate button, the first duplicate has Copy appended to the name (separated from the name by a space) and subsequent duplicates acquire an incrementing number (Copy2, Copy3, and so on).**

Every script in a FileMaker file has a unique internal ID assigned. References to scripts (from buttons and scripts using the `Perform Script [ ]` command) are resolved by using the assigned ID. This ID lets you change the name of a script without affecting references to it.

When you paste a script, FileMaker assigns an internal ID to it. When a script you paste includes references to other scripts, FileMaker will try to resolve those references by name at the point of pasting. If the name doesn't match any existing script (or any script currently being pasted), the reference will be broken and will appear in the script as `<unknown>`. When this situation occurs, you must manually reassign script references to correct the errors.

When copying and pasting scripts that include references to other scripts, you should do one of the following:

- Copy and paste all the scripts (referring to each other) at once.
- Copy and paste the scripts that are referenced first and then copy/paste the scripts that refer to them.

FileMaker resolves references to schema and other elements by name at the point when scripts are pasted into a file in the same way it resolves references to other scripts. If a reference in a script is being pasted to a field called `Invoice::Serial#`, FileMaker will look for an `Invoice::Serial#` field in the file where you paste the script. If there is no exact match, FileMaker won't resolve the reference.

Copying and pasting script steps

FileMaker supports copying and pasting of script steps between scripts — either between scripts in the same file or between scripts in different files. This capability is available in FileMaker Pro 10 as well as in FileMaker Pro 10 Advanced.

Copying and pasting supports multiple (including discontiguous) script steps. The copied step (or steps) will be added immediately after the current selection in the active Script Definition panel.

Organizing Scripts

Scripts are defined within a FileMaker file, and their scope of action is limited to the file where they reside. Each file, therefore, has its own collection of scripts and a separate Manage Scripts window in which to access and organize them.

Scripts accept free-form text names of up to 100 characters on a single line. (Carriage returns aren't permitted.) Within these limits, you can name scripts as you choose, but I recommend avoiding obscure character sets and keeping names brief and explanatory.

Although FileMaker permits duplicate script names, you should take care to avoid duplicates in cases where confusion may result. Moreover, some third-party products (such as plug-ins) reference scripts by name and may produce unintended results if script names are duplicated within a file.

Creating list separators

Using scripts named with a single hyphen as separators in the Manage Scripts window is customary and is supported directly by FileMaker. In fact, the Separator option on the New Item menu (near the lower left of the Manage Scripts window) automatically creates an empty script that uses a hyphen as its name for precisely this purpose.

When you create list separators in the Manage Scripts window and set the Include in Menu option for them, they appear as menu separators in the Scripts menu. The use of a modest number of separators as a grouping or organizational cue can make the Scripts menu easier to use when you have more than a handful of scripts to display there.

You can use scripts, script folders, or a combination of both to introduce order into the presentation of scripts in your solution. (See the section "Creating script folders," later in this chapter.) The ability to organize your scripts into folders serves the dual purpose of improving script manageability during development and maintenance and improving the usability of the Scripts menu.

Script commenting

I counsel you to document your work — I can't say it more directly than that. Unless you have a perfect memory, you'll benefit from a reminder in the future as to what you had in mind about a script's purpose and logic. Should you need to make changes or add new code to your solution, you'll be glad you left some pointers and notes for guidance. Similarly, should other developers have occasion to make changes to your code, they'll be thankful for the pointers that help them understand what you've done and why.

You'll hear different views about the amount of documentation that's desirable. Large organizations, such as government departments, frequently require detailed descriptive and analytical documentation for each component of business applications they use. Frequently, such extensive documentation gets in the road of development and, instead of aiding clarity, simply adds to the bulk and burden of the code — but documentation shouldn't be too burdensome to write, or too tedious to decipher. You should exercise some caution in deciding how much commenting and documentation is enough to be helpful without becoming more hindrance than help.

One general rule that applies in a majority of cases is that the commenting should be less bulky than the code itself — and this is especially true if you're able to create code that is in part self-documenting. That is, the names and structure of the code itself is suggestive of its purpose and its logic. In FileMaker, creating code that is self-documenting is relatively easy, especially if you use human-readable field, table, script, layout, and custom function names. In such cases, relatively simple scripts may need little or no commentary at all. More complex scripts may benefit from the inclusion of comments explaining the presence of particular steps or notes of caution regarding points of ambiguity or possible problems and errors. In lengthy or more complex scripts, it may also be helpful to delineate the main sections of the script so that it's easier to find your way around and to locate blocks of functionality.

As a general rule, you should avoid commenting the obvious. For example, when the New Record/ Request script step appears, it does not require an adjacent comment stating that it creates a new record. Such comments may actually reduce the clarity of the code because they add clutter without amplifying meaning. In such cases, comments may be used to good effect to label groups of steps to indicate their purpose.

Conversely, obscure aspects of the logic of your scripts *should* be elucidated so that they may be readily understood by those who follow. You need to provide pointers not only to the logic of the script itself, but also to its purpose and place in your solution.

FileMaker Scripting's Comment function (appearing in the Miscellaneous category) inserts a comment step represented by a leading hash symbol (#). The comment step provides a Specify button that invokes a simple text entry dialog (see Figure 8.11) into which you can type comments and details about the script.

FIGURE 8.11

Enter your comment's text in the Specify dialog's text box.

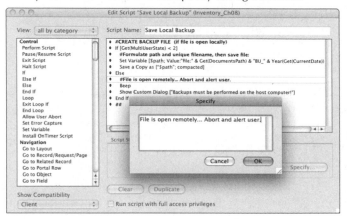

> **NOTE** You may also employ Comment steps with no text as white space, to visually separate blocks of steps. Moreover, an empty comment line at the end of a script may prove useful when debugging sub-scripts in FileMaker Pro Advanced, because the Script Debugger in FileMaker Pro Advanced will stop on the closing comment line if the prenultimate script step has an error and the script is run in the debugger with the Pause on Error option enabled.

Creating script folders

FileMaker lets you create folders, which serve as groups for organizing your scripts in the Manage Scripts window. Folders can contain scripts, separators, and other folders, enabling you to build ordered hierarchies of scripts.

When viewed in the Manage Scripts window, folders appear as a folder icon in the list of scripts, with an adjacent disclosure triangle to display or hide the contents of the folder.

To add a script folder, choose Folder from the New Items drop-down menu at the lower left of the Manage Scripts window. An Edit Folder dialog appears to prompt you to enter a name for the folder. If a script is selected when you create a folder, the folder will be added immediately below the selected item; otherwise, the new folder will appear at the end of the list of items in the Manage Scripts window.

You can move scripts into and out of folders either with the mouse or the keyboard:

1. Open the script folder by clicking its disclosure triangle with the mouse or by selecting the folder (using the keyboard arrow keys) and pressing →/{numeric keypad plus}.

2. Use the mouse or keyboard to position the desired script immediately below the open script folder.

3. With the mouse, grab the desired script by its handle icon (a four-pointed arrow will appear, as shown in Figure 8.12) and drag the handle to the right. (Or press the ⌘+↑ or Ctrl+↑ key combination to add the script to the folder.)

FIGURE 8.12

Using the four-pointed arrow cursor to move the Sold Items Report script into the Reports script folder in the Manage Scripts window of the Inventory example file.

You can move scripts out of folders by dragging them with the mouse or moving them with the keyboard.

After you add scripts to a folder, those set to appear in the Scripts menu will be presented in cascading submenus, as shown in Figure 8.13.

> **NOTE** If items within a folder are set to appear in the Scripts menu but the folder itself is not, the items will appear on the Scripts menu at the previous level (that is, not in a submenu for their enclosing folder). In this way, you can use script folders as an organizational tool in the Manage Scripts window without affecting the arrangement of Scripts menu items.

FIGURE 8.13

The Reports script folder appears as a Reports submenu on the Scripts menu.

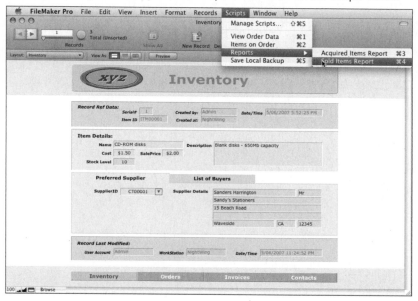

Reordering and grouping scripts

You can drag script folders to new positions by using their handles or by using the keyboard commands, in the same way you can move scripts. Moreover, you can move folders into or out of other folders by using the procedures described in the preceding section. You can also create multiple levels of script folders, although only 20 levels of cascading submenus are supported.

When you move a folder (whether on its own or as part of a larger selection of items) to a new position in the Manage Scripts window, the folder's contents are moved with it to the new location.

Filtering scripts by folder

When you create one or more script folders in the Manage Scripts window, you can filter your view of the Manage Scripts list by folder. To filter, select the desired folder from the folder selection menu at the upper left of the Manage Scripts window, as shown in Figure 8.14.

 If you name a folder with a single hyphen, it will act as a separator in both the folder selection menu and (if enabled for inclusion) the Scripts menu.

CAUTION If you use a script folder as a separator, include it in the Scripts menu, and enclose scripts within it, you won't be able to access the enclosed scripts on the Scripts menu, even if they're enabled to appear there. (The submenu that would otherwise contain them is inaccessible, being presented as a separator.)

FIGURE 8.14

Filtering the Manage Scripts item list to display the contents of a specific folder.

Searching for scripts by name

If you have many scripts in your solution, FileMaker enables you to search for scripts by their names. To do so, enter one or more characters into the search field at the upper right of the Manage Scripts window. All character strings in a script name are targeted by the search.

Script folders containing scripts meeting the search criteria (or partial criteria as the search string is entered) will be pulled open (if they were previously closed) to reveal their contents. Only those scripts matching the entered criteria will be displayed while the search is active.

To disable a script search, delete the search string from the search field. All scripts will again be displayed in the script items list.

NOTE The search status of the Manage Scripts window has no effect on the contents of the Scripts menu.

Some Examples to Start With

Earlier in this chapter, I refer to sample scripts implemented in the Inventory example file to illustrate techniques discussed here. In this section, I describe three straightforward scripts that automate actions common to most solutions.

Performing a Find

If you need to view a list of items ordered but not received, you navigate to the layout listing ordered items (the OrderLines layout) and perform a search for items for which the order status is blank. (Enter Find mode, select the Order Status checkbox, select the Status Area's Omit option, and then click Find.) If any items are found, you may view or print the resulting list and return to where you came from.

If you (or your users) need to perform a find frequently, setting up a script automating the process makes sense. Before creating this script, perform the task manually so that you're clear on the process. Doing so also sets up the Find criteria for the script you're about to create. When you're ready, create a script called Items on Order as follows:

```
Go to Layout ["OrderLines" (OrderLines)]
Set Error Capture [On]
Perform Find [Restore]
If [Get(LastError) ≠ 0]
  Go to Layout [original layout]
  Beep
  Show Custom Dialog ["Error:"; "No items were found."]
End If
```

Printing a report

A frequent requirement in solutions of all kinds is to produce printed output of selected or summarized data in a predetermined fashion. In the "Setting up a basic script" section, earlier in the chapter, I give detailed instructions for the creation of an Acquired Items Report script. Along similar lines, I've created a Sold Items Report script in the Inventory example for this chapter.

The script definition for the Sold Items Report is as follows:

```
Enter Browse Mode [ ]
Freeze Window
Go to Layout ["InvoiceLines" (InvoiceLines)]
Show All Records
Sort Records [Restore; No Dialog]
Print Setup [Restore; No Dialog]
Print [Restore; No Dialog]
Go to Layout [original layout]
```

Acting on user input

You can improve the flexibility and versatility of your scripts by structuring them to receive input from the user. For example, when providing users with a script to display order data, you may want to give them a choice of formats. One way to do so is to display a custom dialog and then use the Get (LastMessageChoice) function to determine which selection the user has made.

For this example script, I configured the custom dialog with three buttons (corresponding to Get (LastMessageChoice) values 1, 2, and 3), as shown in Figure 8.15.

The script definition for the View Order Data script is as follows:

```
Show Custom Dialog ["Note:" Do you wish to view Orders or an Order Items List?"]
If [Get(LastMassageChoice) < 3]
  Go to Layout [If(Get(LastMessageChoice) = 1; "Orders"; "OrderLines")]
  Show All Records
End If
```

 The example file containing the scripts and associated code discussed in this chapter is available among the download materials on the book's Web site.

FIGURE 8.15

Configuration of a custom dialog to prompt for user input.

"Show Custom Dialog" Options

General   **Input Fields**

Specify the title, message and buttons that you wish to display in the dialog. For the title and message, you can enter specific values, or get them from a calculation.

Title
`"Note:"`   (Specify...)

Message
`"Do you wish to view Orders or an Order Items list?"`   (Specify...)

Enter the text to be used as a label for each button that you wish to display. Buttons will only be displayed if they are labeled.

Default Button	Button 2	Button 3
Orders	Items List	Cancel

(Cancel)   (OK)

Calling Your Scripts

When you have created one or more scripts in your solution, you need to determine how and when scripts will be called into action. FileMaker provides you with many options, and you may frequently choose to make the same script available to be triggered in more than one way in your solution interface. pointing the following sections, I provide a brief overview of the script calling options available to you.

The Scripts menu

The most immediate and obvious point of access for your scripts is the Scripts menu. By default, scripts you create are enabled to appear in the Scripts menu. (You have to turn off the checkbox at the left of a script in the Manage Scripts window to remove it from the Scripts menu.)

NOTE If a script is selected in the Manage Scripts window when you create a new script, the new script will be placed immediately below the selected script and will acquire the Include In Menu checkbox status of the selected item, overriding the default behavior noted in the preceding paragraph.

If your solution has only a few scripts, this mechanism may be more than adequate for most users of the solution — and it has the advantage of requiring little action or thought on your part. The chief consideration to bear in mind for scripts that will be accessible from the Scripts menu is that you should choose names for them that will be meaningful to your users (and preferably not too lengthy).

A further consideration when adding items to the Scripts menu is that the scripts on the menu, unlike scripts attached to buttons, will be available from all layouts in your solution. You should therefore take care to ensure that scripts you make accessible from the Scripts menu perform appropriate checks and/or take any necessary steps to ensure that they operate in the intended contexts only.

The Scripts menu is well suited for up to a dozen scripts, or perhaps even a few more. When your solution has more than a moderate number of scripts, however, consider providing alternate ways of launching them because scrolling through a lengthy menu will soon frustrate the users of your solution.

Script hotkeys

The first ten scripts on the Scripts menu are automatically assigned to the keyboard shortcut commands ⌘+1 through ⌘+0 on Mac or Ctrl+1 through Ctrl+0 in Windows. While shortcut keys are convenient, they're limited in several ways:

- The shortcut keys aren't particularly ergonomic.
- The keys aren't easy to remember.

- You're limited to only ten shortcuts.
- The shortcuts are always tied to the position of the scripts in the menu. (If you delete or move a script in the menu, the shortcuts will change, and your users will be apt to be confused.)

Scripts assigned to custom menu commands

A more comprehensive solution to the use of menus and keyboard shortcuts to launch scripts in your solutions is via the creation of Custom Menus. When your solution uses Custom Menus, you can assign scripts to existing or new menu items, and you can edit or add keyboard commands (using the mnemonic of alphanumeric and modifier key combinations to assist users to recollect them).

 **Although you can access Custom Menus, when created, in FileMaker Pro, you need FileMaker Pro Advanced to install and configure them.**

An important advantage of the use of Custom Menus is that you can replace existing features of FileMaker with scripts that provide alternative or supplementary functionality. When you do, the scripts are launched not only when the menu command itself is selected, but also when the user clicks on any associated widget in the Status Toolbar or the database windows of your solution. For example, if you assign a script to the File ⇨ Close menu command, the script will also run when the user clicks the Close box on the title bar of the frontmost database window.

CROSS-REF **An example of the use of Custom Menus to support a Find logging process is provided in Chapter 9.**

Layout buttons

When you add buttons to your layouts, you can assign to them a range of individual commands, including the `Perform Script[ ]` command. Attaching commands enables you to provide a comprehensive and context-appropriate interface for access to scripts associated with specific layouts of your solution.

The use of buttons on your layouts, as exemplified in the `Inventory` example, is an ideal point of access for navigation scripts throughout your solution. If your solution is complex, the ability to locate buttons within the interface will be invaluable as a way to increase your solution's usability.

CROSS-REF **For details of the procedures for defining layout objects as buttons, refer to Chapter 6.**

Calling scripts from other scripts

Just as you can assign a button to the `Perform Script[ ]` command, you can also assign a step within a script to call a script in the current file, or in any other file defined as a data source for the current file. In fact, a script can also call itself via the `Perform Script[ ]` command, giving you an alternative way to achieve a looping or recursive construct.

When a script calls another script, the first script remains in progress awaiting the completion of the second (sub-)script, whereupon the first script resumes, continuing until it concludes. By using a combination of conditional steps and calls to other scripts, you can build a master script that calls any of various other scripts depending on the context, timing, or other factors at the time the script runs.

On Timer Script Triggers

As well as making direct calls to other scripts, FileMaker 10 enables you to configure your scripts to call other scripts (or themselves) indirectly through the use of the Install OnTimer Script[ ] command.

The Install OnTimer Script[ ] command accepts two arguments:

- The script to be called
- The interval (time in seconds) before the script should be called

You can enter the latter parameter as a literal value or calculate it when the script executes. You can queue only one OnTimer script per window at a time, so the script will be called repeatedly at the specified interval (subject to idle time being available on the current workstation) until you cancel it.

To cancel an OnTimer event, you can issue a further call to the Install OnTimer Script[ ] command with either the script or interval left blank, or with an interval specified as zero seconds.

File Open and File Close scripts

FileMaker provides options for you to specify a script to run at file open and a script to run at file close. When you set a script to run at file open, it will be executed the first time a window is drawn after the file is opened. So if a file is opened hidden, as would be the case if it's drawn open by a related file, the OnFileOpen script will not run until/unless the file window is selected for display.

CROSS-REF For details of the procedure for specifying a script to run on file open (and/or on file close) refer to Chapter 13.

Layout event Script Triggers

FileMaker 10 provides seven kinds of event triggers that you can specify for each layout. They include the following: OnRecordLoad, OnRecordCommit, OnRecordRevert, OnLayoutKeystroke, OnLayoutLoad, OnModeEnter, and OnModeExit. You can configure layout Script Triggers by selecting them on the Script Triggers tab of the Layout Setup dialog for the relevant layout, as shown in Figure 8.16.

FIGURE 8.16

Setting up a script to run on record load in the Layout Setup Script Triggers panel.

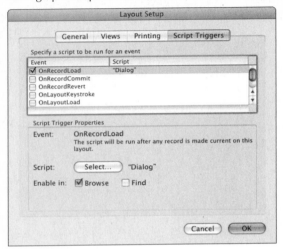

Among the layout triggers provided, `OnRecordCommit`, `OnRecordRevert`, `OnLayout Keystroke`, and `OnModeExit` are designed to execute the selected script prior to the trigger event, and the script when it runs determines whether the trigger event will proceed by passing a script result, using the `Exit Script[ ]` command. That is, a script result of zero will cancel the trigger event.

Object event Script Triggers

In addition, FileMaker 10 provides five more event triggers that you can specify for individual layout objects (such as fields, tab controls, Web viewers, and so on). They include the following: `OnObjectEnter`, `OnObjectKeystroke`, `OnObjectModify`, `OnObjectSave`, and `OnObjectExit`. You can configure object Script Triggers by selecting the relevant object and choosing Format ➪ Set Script Triggers. You then choose from the options presented in the Set Script Triggers dialog, as shown in Figure 8.17.

Among the object triggers provided, OnObjectKeystroke, OnObjectSave, and OnObjectExit are designed to execute the selected script prior to the trigger event, and a script result of zero will cancel the trigger event.

CROSS-REF You can find additional details about Script Triggers in FileMaker Pro 10 in Chapters 4 and 13.

FIGURE 8.17

Setting up a script to run OnObjectEnter in the Set Script Triggers dialog.

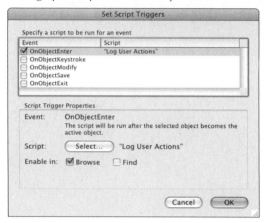

External script calls

While all the script calling methods detailed are native to FileMaker, options also exist for calling a FileMaker script from alternate and external sources. Specifically, FileMaker scripts can be called by AppleScript on Mac OS, by Active X in Windows, and by various third-party script-triggering plug-ins.

CROSS-REF For further discussion of the use of external scripting and third-party plug-ins for FileMaker, refer to Chapter 20.

Part III

Beyond the Basics

FileMaker Pro has something of a reputation for ease of use — and it's certainly true that you can accomplish many things swiftly and without great effort, as you've witnessed in the preceding chapters. Beneath its friendly interface, however, FileMaker conceals considerable power and capability, positioning it as a high-end development environment for desktop and networked solutions. If you're ready for the challenge, there is a great deal more to discover and a wealth of skills and techniques that will help you to gain command of the tools FileMaker provides.

In this part, you begin an exploration of the more advanced options available for creation of sophisticated interfaces, efficient data organization, and enhanced usability and automation in your solutions. It is here that I begin to reveal the flexibility and depth of the development platform provided by FileMaker Pro 10 and FileMaker Pro Advanced 10.

IN THIS PART

Chapter 9
The FileMaker Power User

Chapter 10
Building Advanced Interfaces

Chapter 11
Data Modeling in FileMaker

Chapter 12
Calculation Wizardry

Chapter 13
Scripting in Depth

Chapter 9

The FileMaker Power User

In the preceding chapters, you've employed the fundamental database creation techniques and used FileMaker's scripting, calculation, and interface tools. Along the way, you've glimpsed FileMaker's depth and power.

Because you've come this far, I figure you must be serious — and the fact that you're still reading means you've realized there is much more to learn. You're right — in fact, there is much more to know about FileMaker than I can cover in detail, even in a book of this size. Consequently, I've chosen to encourage you to seek out additional details about the basics, in available resources such as the Users Guide, Help file, and online references. Going forward, I won't cover entire processes in great detail; instead, I'll focus on key insights and development strategies, to make best use of the available pages in this book.

So far, you've acquired the skills to set the core elements of a database in place — techniques that you'll use repeatedly. However, FileMaker is noted for, among other things, providing alternative ways of achieving any given outcome. It is the mark of the experienced user to be aware of the options and to make informed choices.

FileMaker is something of a chameleon insofar as it presents you with a friendly, easy interface for a range of basic tasks, yet possesses the sophistication to deal with more complex requirements when needed. As a result, you'll encounter a steeper learning curve when transitioning to more demanding tasks. This is the transition between FileMaker's legendary ease of use and its hidden power.

In the following chapters, I introduce a range of techniques and capabilities that take you beyond the obvious and into the domain of the FileMaker power user.

IN THIS CHAPTER

Working with Browse mode

Understanding the secrets of search operations

Controlling the sort order of your records

Formatting fields and text

Working with variables

Making sense of indexing

Discovering the table of dependencies

Seeing the benefit of caching

Working with global fields

Making Browse Mode Work for You

When you open a database, a window appears, enabling you to navigate between layouts and records — following the thread of your work processes. Although clear delineations between screens make sense structurally, work is apt to fall outside neat divisions. Interruptions and distractions often require that one task be paused so that another can be performed.

Lucky for you, many more tools are at your disposal in the FileMaker Browse mode. You're not constrained by a single screen and its Status toolbar. Using a combination of advanced techniques, you can greatly increase the power and usability of your solutions.

Using multiple windows and views

When you choose Window ➪ New Window — or use the equivalent button or script command — FileMaker leaves the current window in place and creates a new window in front of it. As you create a new window, FileMaker creates a separate workspace, allowing you to take actions in the new window without affecting the work you were doing in the previous window. This works in a way analogous to having two separate users logged in: Each window can operate separately, but only one can edit a given record at any given time.

One of the immediate advantages of opening a new window is that each window has its own current layout, found set, and selected record. If you're viewing a found set and an interruption requires you to perform a search for a different group of records, you can do so in a new window without disturbing the found set, sort order, or active record in the window you're working in. You can open as many windows as you require, navigating between them by clicking them (if a portion is visible) or selecting them from the list appearing in the Window menu.

You can position windows in a variety of ways so that they overlay each other (the frontmost window obscuring the view of windows behind it), overlapping, or side by side. In the latter cases, users can still view a previous window after opening another, allowing them to see and compare information in different views. Thus, for example, one window may display a summary list of available records while another window shows details of a selected record.

Filtering portals and creating pick lists

Displaying small floating windows configured to operate like dialogs is one way to take advantage of the ability to show multiple windows, inviting the user to make a selection. After a selection is made, the smaller window is closed, and the selection is applied to the original screen in the main (underlying) window. Allowing your users to select items from a list — especially for cases when the number of items on the list may be too long to be conveniently displayed in a radio button field, a list, or a menu — is one common application of this technique.

An example where you can use a selection window is specifying the customer to invoice in the Inventory example discussed in preceding chapters. Currently, the example provides a drop-down menu displaying the contacts identified as buyers. However, as the number of customers increases, the menu becomes unwieldy, and an alternate selection method is desirable.

Implementing a pop-up selection window requires three separate components working in unison:

- A filtering relationship
- A utility portal layout
- A control script

To set up the filtering relationship, open the Inventory file and follow these steps:

1. Choose File ➪ Manage ➪ Database. The Manage Database dialog appears.

2. Select the Tables tab and create a new table named Utility.

3. Double-click the new table's entry in the tables list to select it on the Fields tab.

4. Create a global text field named gFilter_txt.

5. Create a global calculation field named cFilter_key with a result type of text and enter the following formula:

   ```
   If(IsEmpty(gFilter_txt); "0¶z"; gFilter_txt & ¶ & gFilter_txt
       & "zzz")
   ```

6. Create a global text field named gType_key.

7. In the Relationships panel, select the Buyers TO and click the duplicate button at the lower left (third from the left with the double-plus sign icon).

8. Double-click the duplicate TO and rename it ContactFilter.

9. Position the ContactFilter TO next to the Utility TO and drag a join between the Utility::gType_key field and the ContactFilter::ContactType field. Either resize the ContactFilter TO box or scroll its field list until its ContactType field is visible.

10. Drag a second join between the Utility::cFilter_key field and the ContactFilter::LastName field.

11. Double-click the box bisecting the relationship line joining the Utility TO to the ContactFilter TO. The Edit Relationship dialog appears.

12. In the panel in the middle area of the Edit Relationship dialog, select the cFilter_key = LastName join attribute line, choose the ≤ relationship symbol from the menu of operators between the field list boxes at the top of the dialog, and click the Change button.

13. Choose the ≥ relationship symbol from the menu of operators between the field list boxes, and click the Add button to create a third relationship predicate. The Edit relationship dialog now resembles the one shown in Figure 9.1.

TIP   Testing for both ≥ and ≤ against a pair of key field values (as in this case) is a technique to return just those values starting with a sequence of characters. Testing for equality returns only exact matches; however, the ≤ test eliminates any items starting with characters subsequent to those in the second of the pair of search strings, and the ≥ test removes all items starting with characters preceding those in the first of the search string pair.

14. Click OK to close the Edit Relationship dialog and again to close the Manage Database dialog.

FIGURE 9.1

The Edit Relationship dialog showing the completed relationship definition for the join between the `Utility` TO and the `ContactFilter` TO.

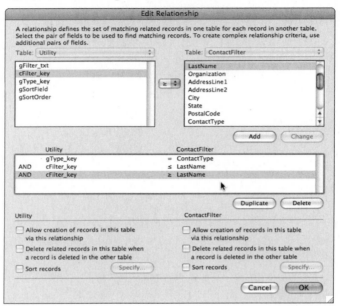

You now have a relationship in place, using `Utility` table global fields to control a relationship with the `Contacts` table. By changing the global field values, the relationship retrieves only a selection of the available Contact records. You can use this mechanism to support selection functionality in a pop-up window.

When you create the `Utility` table as described in the preceding steps, FileMaker creates a default layout named `Utility` based on this table. Select the `Utility` layout and switch to Layout mode to prepare the layout for use as a selection window, by following these steps:

1. Drag the Header tab upward to the top of the layout to delete the Header part.

2. Drag the Footer tab up to the body part boundary to delete the Footer part.

3. Select the Body tab and choose a pale gray/mauve fill color.

4. Delete the `cFilter_key` and `gType_key` fields and their labels.

5. Select the `gFilter_txt` field box, apply the engraved effect, select lightest gray fill, and position it near the upper left of the layout.

6. Edit the text label of the `gFilter_txt` field to read **Filter**:

7. Place a text object (10pt, plain style, centered) near the top of the layout and enter the this instruction: **Enter one or more characters in the filter field to filter the list by last name.**

8. Select the Portal tool and drag across the left area of the layout beneath the `Filter` field to create a portal. Base the portal on the `ContactFilter` TO, specify a sort order by the `LastName` field, enable the vertical scroll bar, enter **12** as the number of rows, and choose an alternate background fill. Figure 9.2 shows the Portal Setup dialog with these settings.

FIGURE 9.2

The Portal Setup dialog for the filtered selection portal on the `Utility` layout.

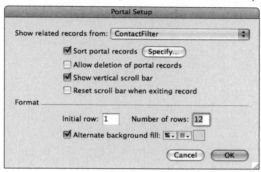

9. Click OK to accept the Portal Setup dialog settings. The Add Fields to Portal dialog appears.

10. Select the `cFullName` field, click the Move button to add it to the portal, and click OK to dismiss the dialog.

11. Create a button, attach it to the Close Window command, label it Cancel, and position it below the portal.

12. Create a button attached to the Go to Next Field command, label it Filter, and position it to the right of the `gFilter_txt` field.

13. Create a button attached to the Set Field command, set the target field as `Utility::gFilter_txt`, specify the calculated result as null (""), label the button Clear, and position it to the right of the Filter button. Your `Utility` layout should resemble the one shown in Figure 9.3.

You now have your selection window's layout ready. The final preparations set a script in place to control the window's behavior. To create the required script, follow these steps:

1. Choose File ➪ Manage ➪ Scripts. The Manage Scripts window appears.

2. Click New to create a new empty script. The Edit Script window appears.

3. In the Script Name field, enter **Select Contact [Type]**.

4. Using the command list at the left of the Edit Script window and, for each command, using the configuration buttons below the script panel, create the following script:

```
If [not IsEmpty(Get(ScriptParameter))]
    #Display Selection Filter Window...
    Set Field [Utility::gFilter_txt; "" ]
    Set Field [Utility::gType_key; Get(ScriptParameter) ]
    New Window [Name: "Select " & Get(ScriptParameter);
    Height: 458;
    Width: 340;
    Top: Get(WindowTop) + (Get(WindowHeight) − 400) / 2;
    Left: Get(WindowLeft) + (Get(WindowWidth) − 340) / 2 ]
    Show/Hide Status Area [Lock; Hide]
    Allow Toolbars [Off]
    Go to Layout ["Utility" (Utility)]
    Enter Browse Mode [ ]
    Go to Field [Utility::gFilter_txt]
Else
    #Select Contact record
    Set Variable [$SelectID; Value:ContactFilter::ContactID]
    Close Window [Current Window ]
    Freeze Window
    Go to Object [Object Name: "ContactID"]
    Set Field [$SelectID ]
    Commit Records/Requests [Skip data entry validation; No
    dialog]
End If
```

5. Save the `Select Contact [Type]` script, close the Edit Script window, and then click the New button in the Manage Scripts window to create another script.

6. In the Script Name field, enter **Refresh Portal**.

7. As in Step 4, create the following script:

```
#Refresh portal by updating key value
Set Variable [$CursorPosn; Value: Get(ActiveSelectionStart)]
Set Field [Utility::gFilter_txt; Utility::gFilter_txt]
Set Selection [Utility::gFilter_txt; Start Position: $CursorPosn;
    End Position: $CursorPosn - 1]
##
```

8. Save the script, close the Edit Script window, and close the Manage Scripts window.

9. Select the `gFilter` field in the `Utility` layout and then choose Format ➪ Set Script Triggers. The Set Script Triggers dialog appears.

10. In the Set Script Triggers dialog, choose the checkbox labeled `OnObjectModify` in the list box. The Specify Script dialog appears.

11. In the Specify Script dialog, choose the `Refresh Portal` script and then click OK to close the dialog. The Set Script Triggers dialog should now be configured, as shown in Figure 9.3.

12. Close the Set Script Triggers dialog and confirm that the left area of the layout is arranged, as shown in Figure 9.3.

13. Select the `cFullName` field in the `ContactFilter` portal of the `Utility` layout.

14. Choose Format ➪ Field/Control ➪ Behavior. The Field Behavior for `"cFullName"` dialog appears.

15. Uncheck the options labeled In Browse mode and In Find mode at the top of the dialog, and then click OK to dismiss the dialog.

16. Choose Format ➪ Button Setup. The Button Setup dialog appears.

17. Choose the Perform Script command in the column at the left.

18. In the Current Script menu at in the panel at the right, choose Exit.

19. Click the Specify button in the panel at the right of the Button Setup dialog. The Specify Script Options dialog appears.

20. Choose the `Select Contact [Type]` script in the list of scripts and click OK to dismiss the dialog.

21. Click OK to close the Button Setup dialog.

FIGURE 9.3

The `Utility` layout configured to include the `ContactFilter` portal and showing the configuration of the Set Script Triggers dialog for the `gFilter` field.

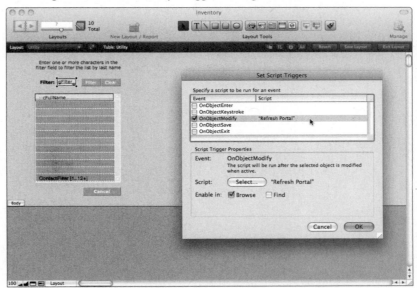

Your preparations are now complete. Now, it's time to add controls to the `Invoices` layout so that users can invoke the new selection window. To make the required adjustments, follow these steps:

1. Navigate to the `Invoices` layout and enter Layout mode.
2. Create a button to the right of the `BuyerID` field and attach the Perform Script command.
3. In the Current Script menu in the panel at the right, choose Exit.
4. Click the Specify button in the panel at the right of the Button Setup dialog. The Specify Script Options dialog appears.
5. Choose the `Select Contact [Type]` script in the list of scripts.
6. In the Optional Script Parameter box, near the bottom of the dialog, enter **Buyer.**
7. Click OK to dismiss the dialog.
8. Label the newly created button **Specify Buyer.**
9. Double-click the `BuyerID` field. The Field/Control Setup dialog appears.
10. In the Display As menu, select Edit Box and click OK to dismiss the dialog.
11. If the Info palette is not currently displayed, choose View ⇨ Object Info.
12. With the `BuyerID` field still selected, enter `ContactID` into the `Object Name` field.

    Your `Invoices` layout should be similar in appearance to the one shown in Figure 9.4.

FIGURE 9.4

The `Invoices` layout with the addition of the Specify Buyer control button.

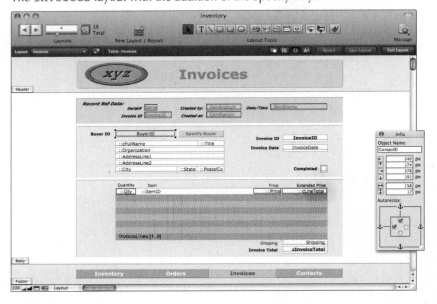

You're ready to test your modifications. To begin, enter Browse mode on the `Invoices` layout and click the Specify Buyer button. The Select Buyer window should appear centered over the Inventory window, as shown in Figure 9.5. The pop-up window displays the portal you created on the `Utility` layout. The portal lists all the `Contacts` who are flagged as buyers in the `Contacts` table. Entering one or more letters into the `Filter` field should automatically reduce the list of names showing in the portal to include only those contacts whose last name begins with the letters you've typed.

Clicking a name in the portal should simultaneously close the window and enter the contact whose name you clicked as the buyer for the current invoice.

Although the number of buyers in the `Contacts` table remains small, the filtering capabilities of the new selection window aren't needed. However, as the number of buyers extends to hundreds or even thousands, the filtered selection list provides users with a very efficient method to locate and select a specific customer for each invoice.

FIGURE 9.5

Testing the Select Buyer pop-up window.

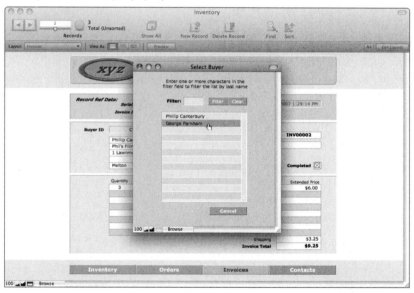

Jump buttons: Shortcut navigation

In Chapter 3, I cover the use of shortcut navigation to enable the user to move efficiently between relevant views of data in your solutions. The `Go to Related Record[ ]` command, which you can use to automatically display associated data in an alternate layout, underpins shortcut navigation.

A useful Go to Related Record[ ] feature is the ability to simultaneously generate a new window to display the results. You can use this feature to show detail or summary data in a convenient pop-up window, without losing the context (found set, sort order, active record) in the window in which you're working.

Using the Inventory example file, if you change the Contacts layout to be based on the ItemSupplier TO, you can add a button to locate and display all the items available from the current supplier.

NOTE   **To change a layout to a different TO, navigate to the layout, go to Layout mode, choose Layouts ⇨ Layout Setup, and then change the setting in the Show Records From menu.**

After you make this change, you also have to reassign any field objects on the layout so that they access the field via the appropriate TO. Double-click each field in turn to access the Field Control Setup dialog and use the menu above the list of fields in the dialog to select the TO identified as the current table.

After you've reassigned the Contacts layout, follow these steps to implement jump navigation to display supplier items in a pop-up window:

1. Navigate to the Inventory layout and choose Layouts ⇨ Duplicate Layout.

2. Choose Layouts ⇨ Layout Setup. The Layout Setup dialog appears.

3. Change the layout name to Inventory List and deselect the option to include it in the Layout menu.

4. Navigate to the Layout Setup dialog's Views panel, deselect the options for Form View and Table View, and click OK to dismiss the dialog.

5. Rearrange the elements on the layout as shown in Figure 9.6, deleting superfluous objects.

6. Navigate to the Contacts layout, create a button at the lower right of the Contact Details panel, and select the Go to Related Record command from the list at the left of the Button Setup dialog.

7. Click the Specify button in the panel at the upper right of the dialog. The Go to Related Record Options dialog appears.

8. Configure the Go to Related Record settings as shown in Figure 9.7.

9. When you select the Show in New Window checkbox, the New Window Options dialog appears. Configure the settings for the new window, as shown in Figure 9.8.

NOTE   **You can either type the formulas in the Window Name, Distance from Top, and Distance from Left text boxes or click the associated Specify buttons and create the formulas in the Specify Calculation dialogs that appear. The latter method reduces the potential for typographic errors.**

FIGURE 9.6

The arrangement of layout objects for the Inventory List layout.

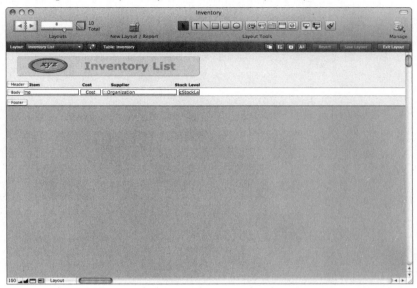

FIGURE 9.7

Settings in the Go to Related Record Options dialog for the Available Items button.

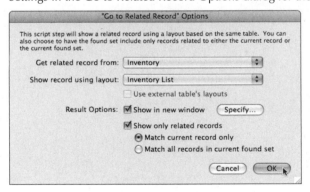

10. Click OK to accept the settings and dismiss each of the dialogs.

11. Label the new button Available Items, size and position it appropriately, and color it to match the Contacts layout's header panel.

FIGURE 9.8

The New Window Options configuration for the Go to Related Record command.

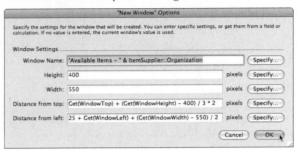

After completing these steps, return to Browse mode and locate a contact record with the Supplier option checked and entered as Preferred Supplier on some inventory items in your `Inventory` file.

Click your new Available Items button to invoke a pop-up window showing a summary list of items for the current supplier, as shown in Figure 9.9.

You can use variations of this technique to provide ease of access to related information and supplementary detail throughout your solutions.

FIGURE 9.9

The pop-up Available Items window listing `Inventory` items supplied by the current contact.

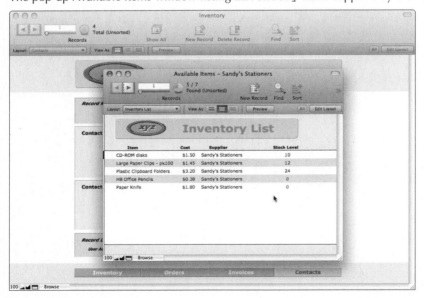

Controlling one window from another

A further example of the flexibility that FileMaker's window management controls afford is the ability to display multiple windows and control their appearance and behavior from a single "main" window. To implement this functionality, you can create buttons and controls attached to scripts by selecting the appropriate window, performing an action on it, and then returning the focus to the controller window.

Careful use of this technique enables you to provide one or more controller palettes that allow the user to navigate or manipulate images, text, or records in one or more windows displayed elsewhere on the screen. For example, you can use such a technique to provide controls for navigating a document preview where the controlling window is in Browse mode, as shown in Figure 9.10.

FIGURE 9.10

Using controls in one window to modify the display in another window.

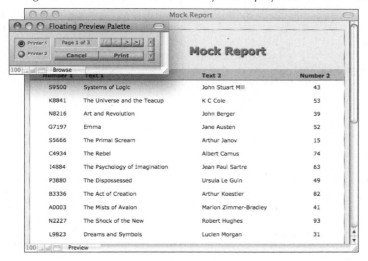

Performing Complex Search Operations

The Find procedures discussed in Chapters 3 and 5 allow you to search for partial word matches or whole word matches. The special Find Symbols you can select from Find mode's Status Toolbar extend the search capability, enabling you to search for ranges or employ wild card operators. But there is much more to searching, as you can see in the following sections.

Compound Find criteria: The AND Find

If your Finds are returning too many results, one option is to make your Find criteria more specific. FileMaker provides you with a straightforward way to approach this problem when constructing your initial Find criteria.

To extend the original Find criteria, you can enter additional detail into the search field (for example, entering **ja** rather than **j** returns Jackson but not Johnson). Alternatively, you can enter criteria into more than one field. For example, entering **j** in the LastName field and **p** in the FirstName field tells FileMaker to return only those records satisfying both criteria (that is, those that have a last name starting with *j* and a first name starting with *p*). You can enter Find criteria into as many fields as necessary to locate the records you're looking for.

Additionally, FileMaker permits the use of multiple sequential Find requests, and you can use the second or subsequent requests to narrow the Find by omitting certain records from the found set. To do so, create a Find request (with appropriate initial criteria) and then, while still in Find mode, choose Requests ⇨ Add New Request. A second find request appears, ready to accept additional criteria. By selecting the Omit checkbox in the Status Toolbar, you can instruct FileMaker to exclude from the found set those records returned by the first request meeting the second request's criteria.

> **NOTE** When you use multiple Find requests, FileMaker processes them in the order in which you create them. When the Find is performed, the first request acts on all records in the current table, and subsequent requests add or omit records from the found set returned by preceding requests.

The processes outlined here provide ways to ensure that more than one criterion is applied in a Find, with additional criteria acting in sequence to make the search more specific.

Stacking Find requests: The OR Find

You can create multiple simultaneous Find requests for Finds that return sets of records meeting any of the request criteria. That is, when multiple requests are created without the Omit option (in the Find mode Status Toolbar) selected, each request is independently evaluated, and its results are added to any preceding requests' results.

In this way, you can instruct FileMaker to search simultaneously according to different criteria, increasing the scope of the search. For example, if you create a Find request and enter **j** in the LastName field and then — before performing the Find — create a second request and enter **p** into the FirstName field, FileMaker returns all records that have an entry in the LastName field starting with j OR an entry in the FirstName field starting with p.

When creating multiple Find requests, you can set specific requests to omit certain records because the Omit option is specific to each request. Thus, you can assemble complex search operations involving multiple Find requests, combining many details to locate records according to very specific requirements.

Constraining and extending the found set

Find criteria assembled in the ways described in the previous sections are applied to all the records in the current table (as determined by the TO associated with the layout in the frontmost window). However, at times, using the results of a previous Find as the starting point for your search is convenient. You can do this in either of two ways:

- **If you want to search only within the records already showing in a found set on the current layout,** go to Find mode, create your Find criteria, and choose Requests ➪ Constrain Found Set. FileMaker locates only records within the current found set that meet the criteria you supply.

- **If you want to preserve the current found set and *add* to it any records meeting your criteria,** go to Find mode, create your Find criteria, and choose Requests ➪ Extend Found Set. When extending the found set, FileMaker applies the supplied criteria to currently omitted records (that is, those not in the current found set), adding the results to the preexisting found set.

In both instances, you're able to refine an existing found set, thereby progressively building the criteria until you've isolated the desired group of records.

Saving Finds and found sets

In any solution where you're frequently performing complex Finds, you'll occasionally want to store Find criteria so that you can efficiently and reliably repeat specific Finds.

FileMaker provides for Find criteria to be stored within the properties of the `Perform Find[ ]` button or script command. When the command is first selected, you have the option to specify Find requests. On selecting this option, the Find properties automatically populate with the criteria of the last Find performed. Thus, one way to store a Find is to first perform it manually and then create a button or script to execute the `Perform Find[ ]` command, reinstating (and storing) the criteria of the Find you just performed. Alternatively, the `Perform Find[ ]` command provides a Specify Find Requests dialog to receive the criteria for one or more Find requests.

Although the creation of scripts or buttons to automate Finds is a great feature, end-users will sometimes perform complex Finds manually and will want to be able to save a record of those Finds. FileMaker Pro 10 provides a partial solution for this problem by allowing users to save their own finds by choosing Records ➪ Saved Finds. This new feature stores finds against the user's login account so that you can reaccess previous finds at a later time. Although this feature is great for cases where each user has his own particular Finds that won't be of interest to other users, it doesn't allow one user to make use of the Finds created by other users of the same database.

If you want users to be able to share complex Finds and see a history of the Finds performed by themselves and others, you need to build a method for capturing and storing find criteria (from finds performed by all users) within the database. Ideally, you want to be able to provide an easy way for users to reinstate saved Finds as well.

When discussing reinstating a Find, it's important to consider that the data may have changed since the Find was performed. Records that matched the criteria at the time of the Find may have been edited so that they no longer match. Records that didn't match may have been edited so that they do, and, of course, records may have been added or deleted. To reinstate a Find, you can either

- **Locate the records that were located previously (if they still exist), whether or not they still match the original Find criteria.** This technique is useful when retrieving historical data.

- **Perform a new Find by using the original Find criteria to locate the records (if any) matching those criteria now.** Use this technique to determine the current status.

Using FileMaker's scripting capabilities, you can configure your solutions to do either of the preceding — depending on the requirements of the solution and its users. In either case, you need a table (in the same file or another file) in which to store each Find and a script to build an array of information and store that information array in a `Finds` table record.

If you decide to store a record of the specific records located in a Find (rather than the criteria), the best way to do so is by gathering the unique key values of records in the found set. Traditionally, developers have used a technique involving the use of the `Copy All Records/Requests[ ]` command on a special layout and then a `Paste` command to store the contents of the clipboard. I don't recommend this approach because it modifies the clipboard and depends on the interface (special layouts with the correct fields present). Instead, I prefer to employ a script looping through the found set, gathering unique key values into a variable, and then to write the variable's contents into a text field in a new record in your `Finds` table.

> **NOTE** If you have access to FileMaker Pro 10 Advanced, another alternative for found sets of moderate size is to create a custom function to recursively retrieve unique keys for the found set via the use of the `GetNthRecord( )` function. See Chapter 18 for a further discussion of custom functions and recursion.

> **CAUTION** If found sets in your solution may be large (for example, tens of thousands of records or more), you should consider carefully whether an approach to gathering and storing unique keys is viable, because doing so involves significant storage and processing overhead.

The second approach to storing Finds entails the capture of the original Find criteria. It requires creating a script to run when a Find is performed, working through the fields on each request to gather the Find criteria into a text array for storage in your `Finds` table.

Because this approach is not as widely known as others, here's an example of the essentials of a script performing this task:

```
If [Get(WindowMode) ≠ 1]
    Beep
Else
```

```
Commit Records/Requests[Skip data entry validation; No dialog]
Go to Record/Request/Page [First]
Go to Next Field
Set Variable [$Layout; Value:Get(LayoutName)]
Set Variable [$FirstField; Value:Get(ActiveFieldName)]
Loop
  Loop
    If [not IsEmpty(Get(ActiveFieldContents))]
      Set Variable [$Criteria; Value:If(not IsEmpty($Criteria);
        $Criteria & ¶) & Get(RecordNumber) & "»" &
        Get(RequestOmitState) & "»" & Get(ActiveFieldName) &
        "»" & Get(ActiveFieldContents)]
    End If
    Go to Next Field
    Exit Loop If [Get(ActiveFieldName) = $FirstField]
  End Loop
  Go to Record/Request/Page [Next; Exit after last]
End Loop
Set Error Capture[On]
Perform Find []
If [Get(LastError) = 0]
  Freeze Window
  Go to Layout ["StoredFinds" (StoredFinds)]
  New Record/Request
  Set Field [StoredFinds::LayoutName; $Layout]
  Set Field [StoredFinds::Criteria_array; $Criteria]
  Go to Layout [$Layout]
Else
  Beep
  Show All Records
  Show Custom Dialog [Message: "No records were found."]
End If
End If
```

The preceding script requires that a StoredFinds table and layout be added to your solution and that it include text fields called LayoutName and Criteria_array. You probably would want to add other fields (such as a serial number, a date and/or time, a field to store the number of records found, the name of the user, and perhaps a brief description of the purpose of the Find). Whenever a Find is performed by using a script such as this one, a record is created containing codified details of the complete criteria used for any and all requests in the Find in the StoredFinds table.

> **TIP** If you have access to FileMaker Pro 10 Advanced, I recommend that you use the custom menus feature to attach the preceding script to the Perform Find command so that it automatically runs whenever a Find is performed.

When you implement a process to store Find criteria sets, your users can browse or search through a complete Find history. You can also provide a simple process for users to automatically reinstate a Find (that is, to rerun the Find against the current data in the relevant table). The essentials of a script to reinstate a Find (stored in the form outlined earlier) are as follows:

```
Set Variable [$Criteria; Value:StoredFinds::Criteria_array]
Go to Layout [StoredFinds::LayoutName]
Freeze Window
Enter Find Mode [ ]
Loop
    Set Variable [$RequestNo; Value:Leftwords($Criteria; 1)]
    Set Variable [$OmitState; Value:Let([
      p1 = Position($Criteria; "»"; 1; 1);
      p2 = Position($Criteria; "»"; 1; 2)];
      Middle($Criteria; p1 + 1; p2 − p1 − 1))]
    If [$OmitState]
      Omit Record
    End If
    Loop
      Set Variable [$FieldName; Value:Let([
        p1 = Position($Criteria; "»"; 1; 2);
        p2 = Position($Criteria; "»"; 1; 3)];
        Middle($Criteria; p1 + 1; p2 − p1 − 1))]
      Go to Next Field
      If [Get(ActiveFieldName) = $FieldName]
        Set Field [Let([
          p1 = Position($Criteria; "»"; 1; 3) + 1;
          p2 = Position($Criteria & ¶; ¶; 1; 1)];
          Middle($Criteria; p1; p2 − p1))]
        Set Variable[$Criteria; Value:RightValues(
          $Criteria; ValueCount($Criteria) - 1)]
      End If
      Exit Loop If[IsEmpty($Criteria) or Left($Criteria;
        Position($Criteria; "»"; 1; 1) − 1) > $RequestNo]
    End Loop
    Exit Loop If [IsEmpty($Criteria)]
    New Record/Request
End Loop
Perform Find [ ]
```

When you attach the preceding script to a button on the `StoredFinds` layout, users are able to click it to automatically view the results of a Find on the layout where the Find was originally performed. A complete history of Finds performed is available in the `StoredFinds` table. Figure 9.11 shows a Find Log, implemented in the updated `Inventory` example file for this chapter.

ON the WEB In case you want to view the preceding scripts in action or review them within the Script Editor in FileMaker, I've added them to the example `Inventory` solution (see the file for this chapter among the Web resources).

FIGURE 9.11

An implementation of the `Stored Find` technique in the `Inventory` example file.

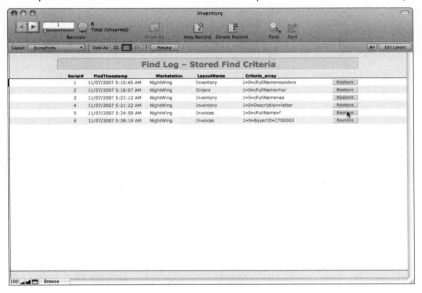

Sorting Records

A common misconception about sorting is that it depends upon (or is made more efficient by) field indexing. However, the truth is that sorting doesn't use field indexes at all. When operating on stored values (as opposed to unstored calculations), your sort operations are processed with the same efficiency irrespective of any field indexing.

Although sorting doesn't use indexes, it does depend on data type and, for text fields, the indexing specification (that is, the selected language). For example, if you select Unicode as the default language for indexing and sorting text on a text field's Options for Field dialog's Storage panel, sorting on the field is case-sensitive (a, b, and c all come *after* X, Y, and Z).

When you choose a numeric data type (including date, time, and timestamp field types), FileMaker applies a different sorting principle. In conventional text sorting, aa comes before b. When this convention is applied to numerals, 11 comes before 2. Hence, a separate methodology is applied when sorting fields having a numeric value.

TIP In cases where you need to store numeric values as text without losing the ability to sort according to numeric sequence, the solution is to pad the values with leading zeros (or spaces) so that they're of consistent length. Whereas a text sort places 11 before 2, 02 sorts before 11 (and 002 sorts before 011, and so on).

Multiple sort keys

Sorting your data by multiple fields is a hierarchical process. FileMaker looks at the first field in the sort order first and applies it across the board. If there are two records with the same value in the first sort field, they're returned in default (creation) order unless there is a second field in the sort order — whereupon they're returned according to the sort order of the second field.

> **TIP** Only with very large or very constrained (that is, containing little variation in values regardless of the number of records) data sets are you likely to need to create sorts depending on more than one or two fields.

For relatively small or simple databases, FileMaker's Sort dialog is easy to use, and end users are able to achieve satisfactory results with it, as long as field names are relatively short and intelligible to the user. However, when sorts must include data from multiple tables and the data model is complex, sorting can present some challenges for end users.

Dynamic sort techniques

To provide a simple and efficient sorting interface for end users, a widely used technique is to store a series of predetermined sorts within a script and provide users with a simplified menu of sort options.

One variant of this technique involves creating a value list of sort options, a global field (where users select a sort option by using a menu of values from the value list), and an adjacent button to run a script configured to apply the appropriate sort. For example, if the desired options are to sort by name, batch, or value, your value list requires values such as the following:

- Unsorted
- Name Order
- Batch Order
- By Value

When the value list is attached to a global text field (for example, called gSortSelecton), you can construct your sort script (attached to the button next to the sort selection field) as follows:

```
If [Utilty:gSortSelection = "Name Order"]
    Sort Records [Restore; No Dialog]
Else If [Utilty:gSortSelection = "Batch Order"]
    Sort Records[Restore; No Dialog]
Else If [Utilty:gSortSelection = "By Value"]
    Sort Records [Restore; No Dialog]
Else
    Unsort Records
End If
```

NOTE In the preceding script, the sort order specified for each of the `Sort Records [ ]` commands must be set to correspond to the selection named in the preceding `If [ ]` or `Else If [ ]` command. For example, the first `Sort Records [ ]` command must be configured to sort by the `Name` field, the second by the `Batch` field, and so on.

Although this technique provides an adequate solution in some cases, occasionally the number of combinations makes it impractical (especially when sorts involving multiple fields are required). For such cases, I offer an alternative technique. To create an open-ended three-tier sorting system, follow these steps:

1. Create a value list of the names of fields you want to be available for sorting.

2. Create a value list called Switch with the value 1.

3. Create three global text fields (`gSortField1`, `gSortField2`, and `gSortField3`), place them on your layout, and configure them as menus, attaching the value list of fields to each of them.

4. Create three global number fields (`gSortOrder1`, `gSortOrder2`, and `gSort Order3`), place them on your layout, configure them as checkbox fields, attach the Switch value list to them, size them to 12px by 12px, and position them beside the three global text fields.

5. Create an unstored text calculation called `cSort1_asc` and enter the following formula:

```
Case(
gSortOrder1 = 1; "";
MiddleWords(FieldType(Get(FileName); gSortField1); 2; 1) = "text";
GetField(gSortField1);
Let([
nF = GetField(gSortField1);
nA = Abs(nF);
nS = nF > 0;
nT = Int(nA);
nM = Mod(nA; 1);
nX = If(nM; nM; ".0")];
Case(
IsEmpty(nF; 0;
nS; "P" & Right("0000000000000000" & nT; 12) & nX;
"N" & (9999999999999999 - nA))
)
)
```

6. Create an unstored text calculation called `cSort1_dsc` and enter the following formula:

```
Case(
gSortOrder1 ≠ 1; "";
MiddleWords(FieldType(Get(FileName); gSortField1); 2; 1) = "text";
GetField(gSortField1);
Let([
```

```
nF = GetField(gSortField1);
nA = Abs(nF);
nS = nF > 0;
nT = Int(nA);
nM = Mod(nA; 1);
nX = If(nM; nM; ".0")];
Case(
IsEmpty(nF; 0;
nS; "P" & Right("0000000000000000" & nT; 12) & nX;
"N" & (9999999999999999 - nA))
)
)
```

NOTE   The calculation formulae presented here are designed to dynamically retrieve the value of the selected sort field. They achieve this via the use of the `GetField( )` function. They then conditionally add leading zeros to ensure that numeric values will sort appropriately although the result is returned as text.

CROSS-REF   The techniques used in these calculations and others like them are explored in greater detail in Chapter 12.

7. Create unstored text calculations called cSort2_asc and cSort2_dsc with the formula along the same lines as those in Step 6, except substitute references to gSortField1 and gSortOrder1 with gSortField2 and gSortOrder2.

8. Create unstored text calculations called cSort3_asc and cSort3_dsc with the formula along the same lines as those in Step 6, except substitute references to gSortField1 and gSortOrder1 with gSortField3 and gSortOrder3.

9. Go to Layout mode, create a button labeled Sort attached to the Sort Records[ ] command, configure the button setup to Perform without Dialog, and Specify the Sort Order configuration depicted in Figure 9.12.

   Take particular note of the assignment of alternate ascending and descending sort order properties to the six calculation fields.

When you complete these steps, return to Browse mode, select one or more field names in the gSortField fields, and click the Sort button to confirm that the sort settings are applied. Selecting the checkboxes in the gSortOrder fields reverses the direction of the sort for the corresponding sort field.

Using this technique, you can create entirely customized sorting control interfaces, providing your users with a clean and simple user experience that doesn't involve scrolling through lengthy lists of field names or negotiating a complex table structure. To illustrate the flexibility of such an arrangement, with lists of ten fields for users to select from, a three-tier sort interface of this kind permits users to select from well over 5,000 possible sort configurations.

Although I've described the process for creating an optional three-tier custom sort interface, you can apply the same principles to the creation of custom interfaces for fewer tiers or for additional tiers, according to the requirements of your solutions.

FIGURE 9.12

The Button Setup sort order settings for your dynamic Sort button.

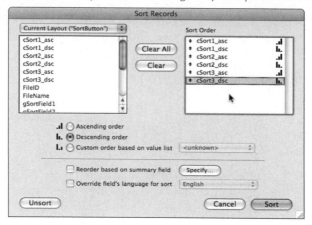

Creating click-sort columns

The dynamic sorting technique described in the preceding section enables you to provide users with a custom sorting interface. You can also adapt the same approach to support a variety of other user interaction models. By way of example, you can configure a three-field sorting mechanism to provide column sorting where the user can click column headings to sort or, if already sorted, reverse the sort order of the corresponding column.

To implement this variant of the technique in the Inventory example file, follow these steps:

1. In the Utility table, create a global text field called gSortField.

2. In the Utility table, create a global number field called gSortOrder.

3. In the OrderLines table, create a calculation field called cSort_asc with result type of text and enter the following formula:

```
Case(
Utility::gSortOrder ≠ 1; "";
MiddleWords(FieldType(Get(FileName); Utility::gSortField); 2; 1) =
    "text";
GetField(Utility::gSortField);
Let([
nF = GetField(Utility::gSortField);
nA = Abs(nF);
nS = nF > 0;
nT = Int(nA);
nM = Mod(nA; 1);
nX = If(nM; nM; ".0")];
```

```
Case(
IsEmpty(nF); 0;
nS; Right("000000000000" & nT; 12) & nX;
"000000000000" & (9999999999999 - nA))
)
)
```

4. In the `OrderLines` table, create a calculation field called `cSort_dsc` with result type of text and enter the formula

```
Case(
Utility::gSortOrder = 1; "";
MiddleWords(FieldType(Get(FileName); Utility::gSortField); 2; 1) =
    "text";
GetField(Utility::gSortField);
Let([
nF = GetField(Utility::gSortField);
nA = Abs(nF);
nS = nF > 0;
nT = Int(nA);
nM = Mod(nA; 1);
nX = If(nM; nM; ".0")];
Case(
IsEmpty(nF); 0;
nS; Right("000000000000" & nT; 12) & nX;
"000000000000" & (9999999999999 - nA))
)
)
```

5. Repeat Steps 3 and 4 to create identical calculation fields in the `InvoiceLines` table.

6. Create a new script called `ColumnSort` and define it as follows:

```
If[Get(ScriptParameter) = Utility::gSortField]
    Set Field[Utility::gSortOrder; Abs(Utility::gSortOrder — 1)]
Else
    Set Field[Utility::gSortField; Get(ScriptParameter)]
    Set Field[Utility::gSortOrder; Abs(Get(ActiveModifierKeys)-2)
  = 1]
End If
Sort Records [Restore; No dialog]
```

Note: When defining the sort order properties for the final step of the script, select the four calculation fields created at Steps 3, 4, and 5, configuring them as shown in Figure 9.13.

7. Go to the `OrderLines` layout and enter Layout mode.

8. Delete the `Serial#`, `_Gen`, and `_Mod` field boxes from the layout and rearrange the remaining fields in a horizontal row at the top of the Body part, with their corresponding labels above them (at the bottom of the Header part).

9. Reduce the height of the Body part so that it's just high enough to accommodate the fields.

10. Choose Layouts ➪ Layout Setup. The Layout Setup dialog appears.

11. Click the Views tab, disable the Form View and Table View checkboxes, and click OK to dismiss the dialog.

12. Click the tabs for the Header and Footer parts in turn, applying the lightest gray fill color to each.

13. Copy the header panel, label, and logo from the `Orders` layout, paste them into the `OrderLines` layout's header, reduce their size, and edit the label to read "Order Lines."

14. Choose File ➪ Manage ➪ Database (Shift+⌘+D or Ctrl+Shift+D), navigate to the Relationships panel, add a TO based on the `Inventory` table called `OrderItems`, and join it to the `OrderLines` TO matching the `ItemID` field in both TOs.

FIGURE 9.13

Sort order properties for the final step of the `ColumnSort` script.

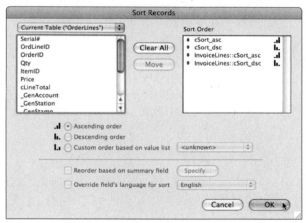

---

15. Repeat Step 14 to add an `InvoiceItems` TO joined to the `InvoiceLines` TO (again, matching the `ItemID` fields in both TOs).

16. Return to Layout mode and add the `OrderItems::Name` field to the `OrderLines` layout, positioning it beside the `ItemID` field.

17. Select the field labels, apply the embossing 3-D effect, and apply gray fill (a shade darker than the background fill of the Header part).

18. Select the `OrdLineID` label and choose Format ➪ Button Setup. The Button Setup dialog appears.

19. Select the Perform Script command in the column at the left, choose Exit from the Current Script pop-up menu in the panel at the upper right, and then click Specify. The Specify Script Options dialog appears.

20. Select the `ColumnSort` script in the list of scripts and then, in the Optional script parameter field near the bottom of the dialog, enter the formula

```
Get(LayoutTableName) & "::OrdLineID"
```

21. Click OK in the Specify Script Options and Button Setup dialogs to return to Layout mode.

22. With the `OrdLineID` label still selected, choose Format ⇨ Conditional. The Conditional Formatting for Selected Objects dialog appears.

23. Click the Add button and, in the field adjacent to the `Formula Is` menu selection, enter

```
Utility::gSortField = Get(LayoutTableName) & "::OrdLineID"
```

24. Select the Fill Color checkbox in the format area near the bottom of the dialog and, from the adjacent color palette, choose a medium-toned highlight color, such as gray-blue).

25. Click the Add button again and in the `Formula Is` field, enter

```
Utility::gSortOrder = 1 and
Utility::gSortField = Get(LayoutTableName) & "::OrdLineID"
```

26. Select the Text Color checkbox in the format area of the dialog and, from the color palette, choose white.

27. Click OK to dismiss the Conditional Formatting dialog.

28. Select each of the remaining text labels in turn, choose Format ⇨ Conditional, and repeat Steps 23 through 27 to configure them, varying the formulas to correspond with the associated field.

29. Adjust the widths of the field labels to correspond to the widths of the fields below them.

30. Select the field boxes, choose Format ⇨ Field/Control ⇨ Borders, and apply light gray side borders. Your `OrderLines` layout should resemble the one shown in Figure 9.14.

31. Repeat the layout formatting process to make comparable changes to the `InvoiceLines` layout.

Now, when you return to Browse mode on either layout, you can click the column headings to apply an ascending sort by the corresponding field. The first click on a heading sorts the column in ascending order, and the column label highlights with a light blue shade, as shown in Figure 9.15. (You can see it in full color by opening the `Inventory` example database from the companion Web site.) A subsequent click on the same column heading toggles the sort order between ascending and descending, and the highlight changes color accordingly. When you hold down the Shift key during your first click on a column label, the initial sort order is reversed.

FIGURE 9.14

The OrderLines layout reformatted as a list with dynamically sorting column headers.

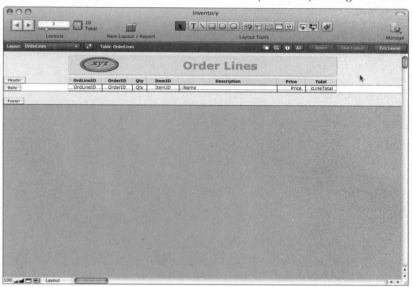

FIGURE 9.15

The InvoiceLines layout sorted by clicking one column heading.

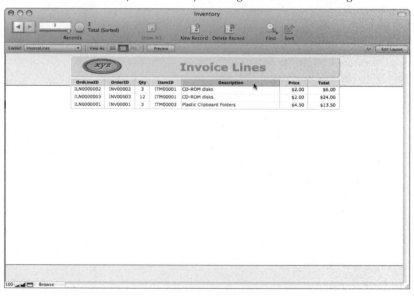

Sorting related data

In the preceding section, you set up a sorting mechanism for a series of fields, including a field outside the table being sorted (for example, the OrderItems::Name field). When a related field is included in the sort order, FileMaker resolves the relationship and sorts the records according to the data it finds (for each record) in the related table.

In addition to letting you sort the current table by related fields, FileMaker provides mechanisms for you to sort the related data so that when multiple records are related to the current record, they're presented in a specified order.

NOTE If related records aren't explicitly sorted, then they're presented by default in the order of their creation.

When defining a relationship between any two TOs, you can specify the sort order for the relationship in either or both directions (that is, you can indicate the order in which records from either table should be presented to the other). You do this by selecting the Sort Records checkbox on the corresponding side of the Edit Relationship dialog, accessible from the Manage Database dialog's Relationships panel. You assign Sort properties by using the same Sort dialog you see when sorting records in Browse mode, as shown in Figure 9.16.

CAUTION Bear in mind that sorting a relationship adds to the work that FileMaker has to do to return records for display in portals and found sets throughout your solution, especially when the number of records in the related table is large. Avoid redundant use or overuse of sorted relationships to avoid unnecessary slowdowns of your solutions.

Regardless of a relationship's sort status, you can independently sort portals. You can set up portal sorting by selecting the Portal Setup dialog's Sort Portal Records checkbox when adding or editing the portal. When alternate sorts of the same data sets may be required in different parts of your solution interface, leaving the relationship(s) unsorted and instead applying sorting to individual portals as required makes sense.

NOTE To provide click-sort column functionality by using portals, you can apply a variant of the dynamic sorting technique to portal data.

CROSS-REF I discuss the use of portals, including interfaces for dynamic portal sorting, in Chapter 10.

FIGURE 9.16

Specifying the sort order for a relationship.

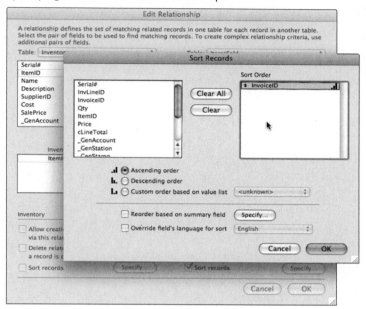

Understanding Formatting

FileMaker provides you with powerful mechanisms for applying and controlling text formatting. However, in order to make full use of these features, you need a thorough understanding of the way the different mechanisms interact. Format options include text style, text size, text font, text color, and a range of paragraph attributes, such as indentation, margins, alignment, tab stops, and line spacing. Moreover, you can apply formatting at several different levels, with attributes at some levels overriding those at other levels.

FileMaker includes support for formatting protocols shared between computer applications, so you can copy formatted content from a word processor, a Web browser, or another application and paste that content into FileMaker with its formatting intact. In fact, if you want to paste text without its original formatting, you need to use FileMaker's Paste Text Only option.

The management of formatting: A three-tiered approach

FileMaker manages formatting at three distinct levels:

- Calculated formatting
- Embedded character and paragraph formatting
- Layout format filtering (including conditional formatting)

Each of these tiers of formatting takes precedence over the next. If calculated formats are in place, they override embedded or layout-based formatting. Embedded character/paragraph formatting overrides attributes applied at the layout level.

Character-level formatting

You can apply formatting to individual characters of text within a FileMaker field. You can select a single word or letter in a field and change its font, size, color, or style. When you do so, the attributes you apply remain in place wherever the text appears, unless overridden explicitly by a calculation within the schema (or via a script). These formats are embedded.

In addition to applying formatting directly to selected text within a database field, you can paste data from other applications, preserving the formatting applied elsewhere. This is part of the same encoded character-level formatting stored with the data and displayed wherever the data appears.

NOTE   **Only formatting options available within FileMaker are preserved. For example, custom kerning or tracking from Adobe Illustrator and double-strikethrough from Microsoft Word aren't preserved.**

To manually apply character-level formatting, click a field box, select one or more characters, and use the commands on the Format menu to change the color, size, font, or style of the selected characters. Any embedded formatting applied is retained by default even if the characters are copied and pasted to another field or combined with other data in a calculation (unless the calculation includes formatting commands to coerce the result into a specific format).

The process for pasting content (copied from other applications or from elsewhere within FileMaker) without including embedded formatting varies between operating systems. On the Mac, you can hold the Option key down while choosing Edit ➪ Paste Text Only or use the keyboard shortcut (Option+⌘+V). In Windows, you can choose Edit ➪ Paste Special and use the resulting dialog to select the option for unformatted text or use the keyboard shortcut (Ctrl+Shift+V).

TIP   **When you paste formatted text into a field in FileMaker Pro 10, FileMaker treats it as performing two operations: pasting the text and then applying the formatting. Thus, choosing Edit ➪ Undo (⌘+Z or Ctrl+Z) removes the formatting, leaving the unformatted text in the field. (A further Undo command is required to remove the pasted text altogether.)**

Paragraph-level formatting

Just as you can apply embedded character formatting to specific text stored within the database, you can also apply embedded paragraph attributes (alignment, line spacing, and orientation) and store them with the data. Paragraph formats apply to the text preceding a carriage return (or text in between two carriage returns, if multiple carriage returns are in a field).

As with embedded font, size, color, and style attributes, you can apply embedded paragraph attributes directly to selected text in a field by using Format menu commands or by interacting with the Text Ruler (accessible from the View menu in Browse mode).

As with character formatting, you can remove paragraph formatting when you paste text, by using the Paste [No style] script step or button command or by choosing Paste Text Only (Mac) or Paste Unformatted Text (Windows).

Unlike character formatting, however, you can't override paragraph formatting by calculation because FileMaker doesn't provide calculation functions to control any paragraph format attributes.

Layout format filters

When you place a field box onto a layout, it includes a full complement of attributes for both character and paragraph formatting. These layout object formats operate as defaults for the single instance they represent, applying only to characters and paragraphs that do not have embedded formatting for a given attribute.

You can regard layout field boxes as passive filters that apply their formats to any unformatted text viewed through them — but allowing formatted text to pass unmodified. The filtering effect applies to all aspects of the displayed text not governed by explicit (embedded) format attributes.

In addition to embedded formats, layout format filtering is also overridden by calculated character formatting.

Conditional formatting dynamically alters the filtering properties of layout objects, also operating as a default applied only to characters that do not carry embedded or calculated format attributes.

A significant feature of the operation of layout object formats is the "apply-if-different" rule. When you're applying formatting to content within the database via a specific field box, formatting instructions are interpreted by FileMaker with reference to the default formats specified for the particular field box. When you select format options matching the formats of the current field box, FileMaker removes embedded formatting. When you select format options different from the field box defaults, they're stored as embedded formats.

For example, if you select the text in a 10pt field box and choose Format ⇨ Size ⇨ 10pt, no embedded character size formats are applied because the selected format matches the field box default. However, if you switch to a different layout and select the same text in a 12pt field box and choose Format ⇨ Size ⇨ 10pt, embedded character size formatting is applied because the selected format differs from the field box default. Immediately, the selected text assumes 10pt size everywhere it appears, regardless of the default sizes specified for the field boxes where it's displayed. Conversely, by applying a format that matches the attributes of the enclosing field box, you remove the attribute instead of applying it. For example, if field text has an embedded size of 12pt and you format it to 9pt in a field box to which 9pt font size has also been applied, not only is the 9pt font size not applied, but the 12pt embedded size attribute is removed.

Precedence of number, date, and time formats

In addition to character and paragraph style and format defaults, layout objects associated with number, date, time, or timestamp fields accept formatting masks to control the way the relevant data is presented (to conform to various date, time, currency, and other numeric conventions). Unlike other layout-level format defaults, data masks take precedence over relevant formatting stored with the data.

In versions up to and including FileMaker 8.5, data masks also suppressed character formatting in some cases. For example, number formatting, including the option to display negative numbers in a different color, took precedence over calculated text color. In FileMaker 10, however, the embedded or calculated formats of the first character are reflected throughout the entirety of a masked field. This applies to merge field text objects to which date, time, or number formats have been applied, as well as to field boxes that carry data presentation formatting.

CAUTION   Although I applaud this behavior change, it may have implications for you if your solution is used in a mixed environment where some users access your files by using earlier versions of FileMaker.

Controlling formatting programmatically

FileMaker provides you with a suite of calculation functions to add and remove text font, size, style, and color settings. You can combine these functions with other functions within calculation expressions, enabling you to fully control the appearance of the text your calculations produce.

To supply a color value to the TextColor( ) function, you can pass individual color values for red, green, and blue to the RGB( ) function. The RGB( ) function computes a composite number by using the formula

```
red * 256² + green * 256 + blue
```

Thus, the entire RGB color spectrum is represented by the sequence of numbers between 0 (black) and 16,777,215 (white). In many cases, when you've determined a specific hue that you want FileMaker to return in certain conditions, it makes sense to calculate the RGB result number once and enter that directly into the calculation, instead of requiring FileMaker to compute it every time it is required. So, for example, you can reduce

```
TextColor("This is purple"; RGB(120; 40; 255))
```

to

```
TextColor("This is purple"; 7874815)
```

TIP Even better is defining a global variable with a suggestive name to hold this constant value (assign it once, when the solution opens). Seven- and eight-digit numeric literals don't tell you all that much when you come back to your solution in a few months to make enhancements or fix a bug.

By combining functions of this kind with logical and match operations, you can provide users with subtle cues to the significance of different elements of the data in your solutions.

NOTE A particularly useful technique is FileMaker's use of auto-enter calculations and their ability to self-reference. You can set up self-referencing by using the `Self` function. By defining an auto-enter calculation to replace itself with colored text, you can set up your database to respond dynamically (and colorfully) to data entry. For example, an auto-enter (replaces existing value) calc applied to a number field with the formula

```
TextColor(Self; If(Self > 10; 11801640; 0))
```

automatically changes the color of any entered values greater than 10 to dark red.

Creating style buttons

Because FileMaker provides fine-grained control over character formatting, you can build interface tools for your users that enable them to perform operations on text like those provided in a range of familiar text-processing environments. You're also able to tailor the functionality to suit your solution's specific requirements.

For example, if you create a button attached to the `Set Field[ ]` command, with the target field left unassigned and the formula entered as

```
Let([
text = Get(ActiveFieldContents);
start = Get(ActiveSelectionStart);
size = Get(ActiveSelectionSize)];
Left(text; start - 1) &
TextStyleAdd(Middle(text; start ; size ); bold) &
Right(text; Length(text) - start - size + 1)
)
```

clicking the button automatically applies bold character formatting to selected text in any field on the current layout.

NOTE A useful aspect of the `Set Field[ ]` command's behavior is that when you do not provide a target field parameter, it acts on the currently selected field (if any).

This example utilizes `Set Field[ ]` with `Get( )` functions to supply selection parameters, the `Left( )`, `Middle( )`, and `Right( )` functions for text parsing, and the `TextStyleAdd( )` function to change the text appearance. When combined appropriately, these functions let you automate the application of selective formatting.

Although this kind of button does its primary task of applying formatting, it has one significant shortcoming: After the formatting is applied, your text is no longer selected (the cursor is moved to the end of the field contents). If this is of concern, you can incorporate the Set Field[ ] functionality into a short script as follows:

```
Set Variable [$size; Value:Get(ActiveSelectionSize)]
If [$size]
    Set Variable [$text; Value:Get(ActiveFieldContents)]
    Set Variable [$start; Value:Get(ActiveSelectionStart)]
    Set Field [Left($text; $start — 1) &
      TextStyleAdd(Middle($text ; $start; $size); Bold) &
      Right($text; Length($text) — $start — $size + 1) ]
    Set Selection [Start Position: $start;
      End Position: $start + $size — 1]
End If
```

You can attach the preceding script to your button by using the Perform Script command so that when you click the button, the selected text acquires bold formatting. However, now the selection is remembered and reinstated, making the process self-contained and seamless.

Style buttons such as the preceding one exploit the behavior of each of these elements (Set Field[ ], TextStyleAdd[ ], Set Selection[ ], and so on) to provide users with useful and context-appropriate interface tools.

Some Notes on Variables

FileMaker enables developers to store and manipulate information in temporary memory locations called *variables*. Variables have several advantages:

■ Variables are very quick because they don't require FileMaker to reference the schema or read/write to disk.

■ Variables aren't tied to the data structure, so you can reference them from a variety of contexts and modes regardless of the availability/accessibility of fields and relationships.

To be fair, variables also have a downside:

■ They're difficult to keep track of in large and complex solutions.

■ They're not particularly secure.

■ They're specific to an individual file session.

Each of these issues simply requires some care and planning on your part as the developer.

Until the release of version 8, FileMaker did not provide native support for variables. Much of the work that you can now do by using variables previously required the use of global fields. However, global fields retain some properties that ensure their continued usefulness, despite the many benefits of memory variables.

The three kinds of variables

FileMaker provides three distinct kinds of variables, each working within a different scope:

■ **Calculation variables:** This kind of variable is defined within the syntax of the Let ( ) function. You can use calculation variables to improve the efficiency and readability of calculations. Any variable you create in a calculation that is not named with a $ or $$ prefix is a calculation variable.

■ **Local variables:** So-called local variables have a lifespan determined by an individual script thread in a single file on the current workstation (that is, they only exist while a given instance of the script they're associated with is running). Local variable names always commence with a single dollar sign ($).

■ **Global variables:** Identified by names commencing with two dollar signs ($$), global variables persist throughout the file where they're defined, while it remains open on the current workstation.

Although these working definitions indicate the way variables are used, the boundaries are somewhat blurred. For example, you can declare local ($) or global ($$) variables within a Let ( ) calculation; then they have scope outside the calculation and can be retrieved by scripts or other calculations.

Similarly, you can declare local variables when no scripts are running — with the result that they're associated with a hypothetical "script zero" and available only when the script stack is empty.

Although variables are sometimes referred to as "script variables," I consider this name something of a misnomer, because you can define and reference all three kinds of variables both inside and outside of scripts. A more apt description is the sometimes used *memory variables,* or simply *variables.*

Variables and memory usage

In FileMaker, variables are created automatically when you assign a value to them; you don't need to specify or name them in advance. You can assign values to variables within any calculation expression (via the use of the Let ( ) function) or via the Set Variable[ ] script and button commands. The value you assign to a variable is held in memory at a fixed location, enabling you to retrieve the value within its scope of availability.

Because variables are stored in memory, they use a portion of the computer memory reserved for FileMaker. If you intend to create a large number of variables or store a large quantity of data in a variable, be aware that the amount of memory available for other operations is reduced, which may impact performance.

FileMaker does not differentiate between an empty (null) variable and a nonexistent variable. Thus, by setting a variable to null (" "), you can release the memory reserved for its contents and take it out of play.

Instantiating and destroying variables

The creation of a variable is sometimes called *instantiation* (that is, creating an instance of the variable). Because you can create and destroy variables at will, a number of instances of the same variable may exist over the course of an application session. A variable is created simply by assigning it a value, so the process of assigning a value to a variable is also frequently referred to as *declaring a variable*.

The most useful and flexible method of declaring variables is via a calculation expression. For example, you can create a variable named `something` by using the calculation expression

```
Let(something = "107%"; "")
```

Because the name of the `something` variable doesn't include any leading $ characters, FileMaker scopes it to the calculation function where it's created (that is, it has meaning only within the enclosing parentheses of the `Let()` function). However, if you add leading $ characters, FileMaker interprets the variable as having local or global scope, and the accessibility and durability of the variable is set accordingly. You can define any mix of differently scoped variables within a single `Let()` expression.

In addition, FileMaker provides button and script commands you can use to directly instantiate a local or global variable. Whether a variable you create by using the `Set Variable[ ]` command is local (confined to the script where it's created) or global is determined solely by whether you prepend a single or a double dollar prefix to the name of the variable. Thus

```
Set Variable [$something; Value:"107%"]
```

creates a local variable that persists only while the current script is at the top of the script stack; it's not accessible by other scripts that the declaring script might invoke via the `Perform Script[]` step.

Deleting the contents of a variable (setting the variable to null) is the only way you can destroy a FileMaker variable. Thus, you destroy variables by using the same functions and commands that you use to create them. For example, you can destroy a global variable by using the command

```
Set Variable [$$name; Value:""]
```

Because calculation variables and local variables have narrowly defined scope and expire after the conclusion of the calculation or script in which they're defined, explicitly destroying them is rarely necessary. However, global variables persist throughout the current file session unless you destroy them — so when a global variable is no longer needed, I suggest you destroy it so that FileMaker can reclaim the memory it has occupied.

Keeping track of variables

When you configure a script or calculation to declare or reference a variable, you choose a name for the variable. FileMaker has no mechanism to determine whether the name is correct (for example, that it won't overwrite an existing variable that is still needed). An ever-present danger when working with variables is that you lose sight of them, writing or referencing them with mismatched names or inadvertently overwriting them.

When you work with calculation variables and local variables, because their scope is constrained, the task of managing them and ensuring that you know what they're for and how they're named is finite. Global variables, however, present you with a significant challenge. For this reason, some developers prefer to avoid the use of global variables. Although I'm not about to tell you not to use them, I recommend that you do so sparingly and with caution.

When you do use variables —global variables in particular — you need a reliable way of keeping track of them. One way is to keep a register of variables in each solution, updating it each time you create or reference a variable. This method is almost certainly preferable to tracking variables retroactively — after you've forgotten where they originated and what exactly they were for.

Understanding Indexing

FileMaker does a great job keeping the complexities hidden from the user and even the developer. Sometimes it does this a little too well so that few people know how the program actually works or how best to use it. Field indexes in FileMaker have been the subject of myths of various kinds — in part because the interface obscures their status and role.

Indexes have two primary roles and a number of secondary roles. The two primary roles are to

- Establish relationships
- Facilitate Finds

Both of these roles are important. However, although an index is essential for a relationship (it won't work without one), Finds can proceed (albeit more slowly) on unindexed fields.

Text index types

Many FileMaker users are aware that indexes support both relationships and Finds, but fewer users understand that, for text fields, there are, in fact, two distinct types of index — one providing primary support for Finds and the other providing support for relationships.

The word index

The index that FileMaker uses to support Finds on text fields is an index of words stored in a field. FileMaker treats most characters other than letters and numbers as word separators. So in addition to spaces, characters (such as &, ?, +, $, ~, and so on) are also used to delimit words.

NOTE The list characters used as word separators may vary on a field-by-field basis depending on the default language setting on the Options for Field dialog's Storage panel. For example, if Unicode is chosen as the default for a field, most characters other than a space, including those mentioned in the preceding paragraph, are indexed as part of words rather than treated as word separators.

The word index is created for a field the first time you perform a Find on the contents of the field, unless the default Automatically Create Indexes as Needed option has been disabled in the Storage panel for the field.

If indexing is enabled for a field, you can view its word index by placing the cursor in the field, choosing Insert ⇨ From Index, and, in the resulting dialog, selecting the Show Individual Words checkbox. As shown in Figure 9.17, FileMaker shows you each word as a separate entry in the index list.

CAUTION If a word index has not been created for a field, displaying the View Index dialog as described here causes FileMaker to create one, as long as the Automatically Create Indexes as Needed option is enabled for the selected field.

The value index

FileMaker uses a value index to support relationship matching, value lists, some special Find operations — for example, a duplicate values search — and uniqueness validation. Value indexing is applied to numeric fields as well as text fields.

When FileMaker creates a value index for a text field, each line of text is treated as a single separate index entry. When a field contains no carriage returns, its contents are treated as a single value. However, when carriage returns are present, they serve as value separators.

NOTE Although FileMaker indexes very long values, only approximately 110 characters are used when determining uniqueness or matching values (the precise number varies depending on the bit length of the characters involved). In other words, if the first 110 characters of two values are the same, FileMaker treats the values as a match regardless of what follows.

FileMaker creates value indexes when the Automatically Create Indexes as Needed option is enabled for a field, and a relationship or value list depending on the field index is used, or any other user action is taken (for example, insert from index) requiring the value index.

Indexing myths exploded

Because I'm talking about myths, I start off by reminding you that indexes aren't used for sorting, even though the default language selection in the indexing area of the Options for Field dialog does affect sort order. However, a field without an index sorts in exactly the same amount of time as a field with an index.

Another area of frequent confusion centers on the relationship between storage and indexing. Stored fields aren't necessarily indexed. However, unstored calculations can't be indexed. The fact that a field is unstored means that it can't be indexed. However, the fact that it's stored doesn't signify that it *has* an index.

Finally, you'll encounter a common belief that the index settings None, Minimal, and All in the storage tab of the Options for Field dialog equate to none, value index, and both value and word index. However, the Minimal option refers to any case where only one of the indexes for a text field has been created. If you create a value list by using values from an unindexed field with the Automatically Create Indexes as Needed option enabled, the Minimal setting appears selected. However, if you perform a Find on an unindexed field with the Automatically Create Indexes Needed option enabled, the Minimal setting also appears selected. Thus, the minimal setting, as shown in Figure 9.18, indicates that only one index is present, but it doesn't indicate which one.

FIGURE 9.17

Viewing the contents of the word index for a text field.

If you encounter a solution (perhaps developed by someone else) with the Minimal index indicator showing and the Automatically Create Indexes as Needed option disabled, how can you tell what kind of index the field has? One answer would be to try to use the field as the basis of a value list — if the field's index is a word index, an error dialog is displayed. Perhaps the simplest method is to choose Insert ⇨ From Index to expose the View Index dialog. The Show Individual Words setting is inaccessible but nevertheless appears enabled (checked) if the field has a word index or disabled (unchecked) if the field has a value index.

Differences between numeric and text indexing

The most significant difference between the indexing of text and numeric fields is that text fields provide the option for two indexes that operate independently, as noted earlier. However, the sequence and behavior of a numeric index differs from a text index. As shown in Figure 9.19, if you view the index of a number field, the index entries appear as you'd expect, arranged in ascending order according to their numeric value.

If a text field containing the same data as the field that produced the numeric index shown as Figure 9.19 is indexed, the presentation order follows a different convention.

The convention for sorting text data follows different rules, so numeric data stored in a text field is presented in a different format, as shown in Figure 9.20. In this circumstance, when you follow the rules for alphabetic sorting, an ascending order places 12 before 2 and 207 before 21.

TIP When you create relationships, make sure that the data types of the match fields are the same so that the indexing rules produce predictable results for all cases. Similarly, because the sorting conventions that FileMaker applies are adjusted to correspond to the data type, you should use numeric fields in cases where you expect to see data sorted according to ordinal values.

FIGURE 9.18

The Minimal Indexing indicator in the Options for Field dialog.

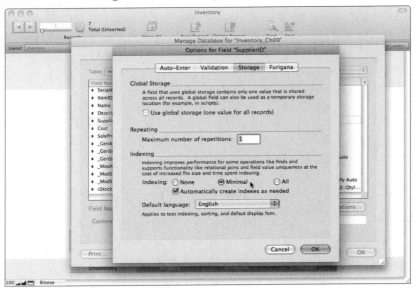

FIGURE 9.19

Index entries for a numeric field.

Unicode and alternate language indexes

The way FileMaker treats a text field's character set is contingent on the Default language for indexing and the sorting text setting in the Storage tab of the Options for Field dialog. For most purposes, you'll achieve the desired results by using a language selection that corresponds to the language of the operating system in the region where your solution is used. However, there are some notable exceptions:

- If you specify Unicode as the language for indexing and sorting for a field, uppercase and lowercase characters are indexed, sorted, and searched separately, enabling you to set up case-sensitive relationship matching.

- If you choose the Default option for the Indexing and Sorting Language setting, then sorting, searching, and matching aren't case-sensitive, but nevertheless, accented characters are differentiated from unaccented equivalents (for example, *é* does not match to *e*).

FIGURE 9.20

The index of a text field containing numeric data.

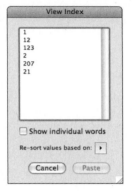

Optimizing field index configurations

To support your solution design, some field indexes are essential. Relationships and field-based value lists, in particular, require that the field they address be indexed. In most other cases, indexes are optional.

When a field is used in a Find (especially if the record count is large), FileMaker can use the field index to significantly improve the Find's execution speed. This benefit comes at a cost because FileMaker must do additional work to maintain the index as values in the database are added, deleted, and changed, and the file's size increases to accommodate the indexes (impacting server and network performance in some cases).

It's a trade-off between faster Finds and slower overall performance, or faster overall performance, with some lengthy Finds on unindexed fields. In most cases, the best answer is to allow indexes to remain on frequently searched fields (as well as value indexes on fields used for relationships and value lists) and disable indexing on other fields. That may sound like a great theory, but it only works well if you have reliable information about the fields where users frequently perform Finds. In large solutions with many users, this information may not be readily available.

In the "Saving Finds and found sets" section, earlier in this chapter, I describe a technique for capturing and storing a complete history of Find criteria. One useful side benefit of implementing such a system is that it provides a comprehensive and reliable source of data about the frequency of Finds on each field in the solution. With a little ingenuity and a small amount of additional code, you'll be able to capture other useful information about Finds performed by the users of your solutions — such as the execution times of Finds and the number of records found.

The Table of Dependencies

The FileMaker Pro calculation engine is a thing of joy, with its combination of power and simplicity. A significant part of the reason you can "set and forget" with FileMaker calculations is because FileMaker does an excellent job of keeping track of things behind the scenes. In particular, calculations in FileMaker are supported by an internal table of dependencies. There is no direct user interface to the table of dependencies; it works almost entirely behind the scenes, keeping track of fields that reference other fields within a FileMaker table.

Cascading calculation operations

As noted in Chapter 7, when you define a calculation referring to values in other fields in the record, you're creating a *dependency* — thus, creating a flow-on effect of the initial change. The plot thickens when you create calculations referencing other calculations. Then FileMaker keeps track of dependencies extending through multiple stages (for example, when an input value changes, a calculation referencing it is targeted for re-evaluation). However, it isn't until FileMaker has computed and returned a new result for this first calculation that other calculations depending on that result can begin re-evaluation. Thus, complex dependencies can result in a cascade of operations.

CAUTION Inexperienced developers sometimes create extensive chains of dependent calculations where every calculation is dependent on several others, which are dependent on still others, and so on. In this situation, FileMaker is given a great deal of work to do when a single input value is changed. Moreover, it must work sequentially through the chain of logical dependencies until it has resolved them all. This type of poor solution design leads to performance issues in large or complex solutions.

The limits of dependency

FileMaker manages calculation dependencies within the record structure of each table. In that sense, a record in a table is a discrete entity that's internally managed and resolved by the application. However, FileMaker doesn't track dependencies outside of the individual record.

You may be aware of several apparent exceptions to this rule. Lookups, for example, draw data from a field in another table, but their dependency is on the relationship key field residing in the same table, not on the related field. Similarly, unstored calculations may reference values in other tables, but they're re-evaluated when the screen is refreshed and not as a consequence of a change in any field outside the table where they reside.

The constraints on FileMaker's internal management of dependencies establish a discipline with which you must become familiar in order to anticipate the behavior of the application. Doing so helps you design solutions harnessing and exploiting FileMaker's strengths.

Tiers of dependency

When calculations reference other calculations, FileMaker uses its table of dependencies to determine an appropriate order of evaluation. In this respect, *tiers* of dependency are created where directly dependent fields are re-evaluated before indirectly dependent fields. In many cases, you don't need to worry about this — it just happens!

In some cases, however, calculation logic does not resolve in a simple linear way. If Field C depends on Field B, which in turn depends on Field A, FileMaker can establish a clear chain of dependency, enabling it to perform evaluation A, then B, and then C. However, in a more complex arrangement — for example, where C depends on both A and B, but B depends on both A and C — the logic does not resolve into a clear evaluation order. In this type of case, fields B and C are evaluated in the order in which the fields were created.

Caching Join Results

One of the challenges of relational data management is the way compound data accumulates. Via a one-to-many relationship, a single record may reference several. Each of these several related records may in turn reference several others. If the average number of related records is 10, as you reference data from more remote tables, 10 becomes 100, and 100 becomes 1,000 — an exponential burden, potentially requiring retrieval of large numbers of records to calculate and display a single screen of data.

What caching does for you

FileMaker tackles the potentially exponential challenge of delivering related data by storing related data sets in a cache, thus reducing the number of disk reads and network calls required as you work. The object of caching is transparency — holding data until needed, yet refreshing data automatically as changes occur. FileMaker monitors the user to achieve this transparency, responding to actions impacting cached data and anticipating requirements for fresh data from the host.

In most cases, caching increases the responsiveness of the application without perceptible compromises. However, FileMaker can't anticipate every possible combination of elements, so occasionally situations arise when an update of cached data needs prompting. This occurs most commonly when an action occurring outside the frame of reference of the current window (for example, via a script) has implications for data on display.

Solving caching problems

FileMaker provides a direct and disarmingly simple remedy to cache control issues arising as a consequence of scripted actions. The `Refresh Window[ ]` command includes options to flush cached join results and/or flush cached SQL data. By including an appropriately configured `Refresh` command at strategic positions in your scripts, you can correct most script-related caching issues.

In FileMaker Pro 10, a `Refresh` command is also available on the Records menu (Shift+⌘+R or Ctrl+Shift+R), shown in Figure 9.21, as well as via a button command — so manual control of the cache is possible.

If you're confronted by a refresh issue not solved via these options, a further alternative that may be useful in some cases is to make use of dependencies in the current table (that is, the table the current layout is associated with). Any calculation dependency between a relationship key field and a modified field in the local table prompts a refresh of related data.

FIGURE 9.21

The Records ⇨ Refresh Window command.

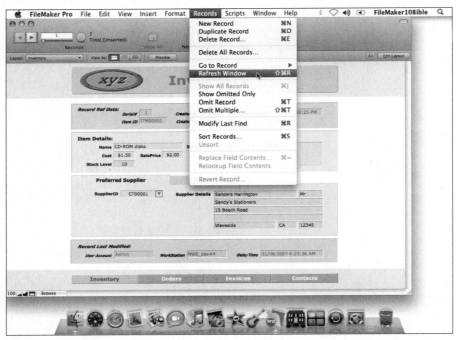

Gaining control of the cache

Although I've suggested several ways you can ameliorate cache refresh problems should they arise, prevention is better than cure. If you approach your solution design with a view to minimizing complex dependencies on related data, issues are less likely to arise.

You can adopt several strategies to reduce the potential for refresh issues:

- By breaking down data views into focused groups of fewer elements and providing a modular series of screen displays, you reduce the reliance on caching and gain greater control over the data presentation sequence. Tab controls provide a useful interface mechanism supporting data modularization.

- Another technique that assists you to avoid potential caching issues is the use of a scripted solution interface. This approach is one where buttons and custom menu commands are provided for all the basic operations the user undertakes. Because you can script all interface actions, you can determine how and when displayed data is refreshed.

Understanding Global Fields

It's all a matter of perspective, but I've been known to remark that global fields are not as global as their name suggests. One of the notable characteristics of global fields is that in a multi-user solution, each user sees his own separate set of values. When viewed in this way, the behavior of global fields seems decidedly parochial. So why are they called global?

A global field holds one value for all records within the table where it is defined. It's global specifically with respect to the table. However, another useful (and more recently acquired) characteristic of global fields is the fact that they're accessible from anywhere in a file without a relationship. That's a rather different sense in which they might be considered global.

From their inception well over a decade ago, global fields have provided repositories for constants, variables, and interface elements, as well as scratch fields and temporary storage. Several of these uses have diminished with the advent of memory variables, but other uses have arisen to make global fields indispensable.

The behavior of global fields

You have to understand several aspects of global field behavior before you can use them to best advantage:

- They hold a single value (although that value might be a repetition) for all records and can be accessed without a relationship.
- They can be read and written even when no records are in their table.

- Their value is saved only on the host computer (or when the file is edited in stand-alone mode). Each user sees the saved values from the host when the file first opens, but any changes the user makes are specific to that user's workstation.
- They're persistent in Find mode.

Uses for global fields

Global fields provide input fields for custom dialogs, key fields for utility relationships, filter and option fields for interface controls, scriptable summary data fields for reports, portable accommodation for interface elements and corporate logos, and flexible containers for layout text, instructions, or labels.

In short, resourceful developers have thought of many ingenious global field uses, and they have become an essential ingredient in FileMaker's interface tool box.

When to avoid global fields

The use of global fields isn't desirable in several situations. Some of the most notable of these are

- When the persistency of values (between sessions) matters
- When data is to be shared among users in a multi-user solution
- When more expedient options are available

For many purposes, variables offer a good alternative to global fields — and they have certain advantages:

- Variables don't have to be defined within the schema — they can be created and destroyed as needed.
- Reading and writing to variables is more efficient than reading and writing to fields.

Using global calculation fields

In the Storage Options dialog accessed from the Specify Calculation dialog, you can choose to define a calculation as globally stored. When you do so, the calculation takes on several of the key properties of all global fields, most notably one value for all records in the table, accessibility without a relationship, and persistence in Find mode.

You can use global calculations to compute a result from values stored in global fields. However, global calculation fields also have some useful attributes when used to reference standard data fields. When used to reference standard data fields, they're re-evaluated with respect to the record where the referenced fields have been most recently edited on the current client workstation.

CROSS-REF For a more detailed discussion of the use of global fields, including an overview of the rules for re-evaluation of global calculations, refer to Chapter 12.

Chapter 10

Building Advanced Interfaces

Computer software may be powerful and innovative, but, with few exceptions, software is only as useful as its interface allows. The user's ability to understand what his computer is telling him and effectively interact with it is an essential measure of a solution's effectiveness. Thus, your solutions' success is determined as much by your command of interface technique and design as any other single factor.

In Chapter 6, I introduced many of the essential concepts supporting FileMaker's interface building environment — Layout mode — showing you how to use essential interface building tools. I also introduced a number of design concepts, helping you make interface design choices that will enhance the ergonomics and intuitiveness of your solutions.

The goals of good interface design are clarity and consistency, as well as ease and efficiency of use. However, you also have to consider aesthetics. If you expect users to spend lots of time working with your solution, you have to keep in mind that your interface design choices will have a significant impact on user fatigue. Don't underestimate the solutions' cumulative impact on the user's mood and morale.

In the following pages, I delve into a series of deeper challenges, providing specific techniques and recommendations and enabling you to address a variety of challenges, remedy shortcomings, and lend increased professionalism to your solution interfaces.

IN THIS CHAPTER

Developing for the cross-platform world

Changing layouts dynamically

Summarizing, reporting, and printing

Working with windows and views

Dealing with custom dialogs

Building enhanced layouts

Making use of Tab Controls and portals

Exploring advanced Web viewer techniques

Delivering native charts and progress bars

Customizing the user experience

Developing for Mac and Windows Users

One of several key benefits that FileMaker brings to the world of desktop databases is its cross-platform capability. Users have every expectation that they'll be able to choose freely among available operating systems and hardware platforms, without forgoing access to critical business applications. FileMaker's ability to run the same solutions on both Macintosh and Windows operating systems is a powerful plus.

Many businesses accommodate a mix of computer operating systems. And many of those that don't *currently* accommodate a mix of operating systems have done so at some time in the past. Staff members change, policies adapt, companies that resolutely embraced one technology for years sooner or later find themselves confronted with the unexpected need to support another.

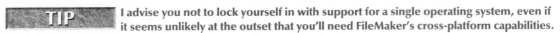 **I advise you not to lock yourself in with support for a single operating system, even if it seems unlikely at the outset that you'll need FileMaker's cross-platform capabilities.**

In the following sections, I examine the key issues you must address to deliver solutions that work well and look good on both Mac and Windows computers.

Selecting fonts

When you choose a display font for text in your solution, you may be surprised and disappointed to see the result when the solution is opened on another computer (even if the operating system is the same) where the chosen font is not installed. When the specified font is not available, operating systems use a process of font substitution to find an alternative. However, the sizing, spacing, and general appearance of characters may vary. On occasion, text is clipped or cropped, and lines wrap in unattractive ways — sometimes to the point where legibility is compromised. Even if it isn't that bad, your efforts in creating a polished appearance for your screens will be lost if the screens aren't rendered as intended.

For solution portability, carefully select fonts installed as standard with the operating system. That way, you have a high probability that, wherever the solution is viewed, the necessary fonts will be available. Ideally, the fonts you choose should also offer a high level of readability and intelligibility, consistency between operating systems, and a crisp and open appearance.

TIP **For best results, I recommend Verdana, Times New Roman, Trebuchet MS, Georgia, and Tahoma. For occasional touches, Impact, Arial Black, Comic Sans MS, Symbol, and Webdings are other alternatives. All these fonts are part of the standard installation on current and recent versions of both Mac OS and Windows.**

Even with the most careful selection of fonts, differing font imaging technologies will result in the same fonts rendering in different sizes on different platforms, with variations according to the sizes and weights used. Frequently, plain styles render with slightly greater width in Windows, while italic styles generally render with a shallower slant on the Mac. Both of these effects are most evident at smaller font sizes (that is, below 12 points).

When working with small font sizes, leave an allowance to accommodate different rendering characteristics.

TIP When designing layouts on the Mac, I recommend adding 2- to 3-pixel additional height (per line) on field boxes and text objects and approximately 10 percent extra length. This approach prevents overlapping and truncation of text when viewed in a Windows workstation.

Paying attention to differences in screen rendering

To illustrate differences in font rendering between platforms, I created some text at three common sizes on a Mac. I took screenshots of the text (still on a Mac) and pasted them above the text objects. On opening the file in Windows, the text objects as rendered by the Windows operating system could be directly compared to the adjacent images of the appearance of the text on the Mac. I enlarged the results and show them in Figure 10.1.

As Figure 10.1 shows, differences in rendering of screen fonts at moderate sizes occur on the Mac and Windows, for one commonplace cross-platform font in plain face. Comparable differences also exist for other fonts. If you don't allow for these differences when designing your layouts, they won't transition well between computers.

FIGURE 10.1

Enlargement of screen renderings of Verdana at three difference sizes on Mac OS and Windows showing differences in appearance and spacing.

9 pt Verdana on MacOS

9 pt Verdana on Windows

10 pt Verdana on MacOS

10 pt Verdana on Windows

11 pt Verdana on MacOS

11 pt Verdana on Windows

In addition to font rendering issues, several other factors affect the appearance of solutions on alternate platforms:

- **Color differences:** FileMaker uses the same color palette on both Windows and Macintosh. However, minor differences in operating system and hardware configurations (such as a different white point — 1.8 on Macs and 2.2 in Windows) generally result in perceptible differences in color rendering and overall color temperatures. Differences of this type may also be observed between computers of the same operating system, particularly where different color bit depths have been set in System Preferences (Mac) or the Control Panel (Windows). You'll also often notice differences when using different monitors, particularly when comparing LCD with CRT implementations.

- **Screen layering:** FileMaker renders layouts progressively, building them in layers according to the layout objects' stacking order (working from back to front). This often results in some flickering or flashing, which is generally more noticeable in the Windows platform due to different graphics handling.

TIP You can reduce or eliminate screen display artifacts such as flashing by avoiding the use of large and unoptimized images on layouts (these images load more slowly, generating flicker) and by applying opaque fill to as many layout objects (including graphics) as possible. You can further refine the appearance of screens as they're rendered by altering the stacking order of elements on the layout — particularly avoiding clusters of large graphical objects loading early (that is, at the back of the stacking order), thus delaying the load of other layout elements. Placing larger objects near the front of the stacking order generally results in a more pleasing rendering sequence.

- **Button click-shade highlighting:** Another notable difference between the appearance of your FileMaker solutions on Macintosh and Windows is the way buttons change appearance when you click them with the mouse. In Windows, the button changes to a color negative (inverted) image while the mouse button is depressed, whereas on Mac the button is shadowed (rendered several shades darker). This difference in visual effect is dramatic, especially when the buttons are large and/or rendered in bold tones. Check the appearance of the click-shade effect on both platforms before finalizing your button designs.

TIP Very dark buttons lose most of the impact of the click-shading effect on the Mac. (They can't get much darker.) Conversely, mid-gray buttons show little click-shading in Windows. (Their inverse is also mid-gray.) Because extremely light or dark buttons in Windows show such a marked Click Shade effect, they may be unappealing. Mid-toned and colored buttons give the most pleasing overall effect when viewed on either platform.

Considering platform-specific window behavior

The most notable difference between the appearance and behavior of FileMaker on Macintosh and Windows is that in Windows, all database windows are contained within a single larger application window with the application's menu bar across the top of the application window. By contrast, database windows on the Mac appear separately, not enclosed by an application window, while the application's menus are fixed across the top of the screen.

The application window in Windows (see Figure 10.2) has its own discrete borders, title bar, and controls, including the Application menus incorporated into the band immediately below the application window title bar.

NEW FEATURE A notable feature of the application window in previous versions of FileMaker Pro in the Windows operating system is that, by default, a gray band called the status bar (not to be confused with the Status Toolbar, which is the control strip at the top of each database window) appeared along the bottom of the application window. The status bar is no longer present in FileMaker 10. It didn't do very much (and was mainly an annoyance), so its loss is unlikely to cause any grief.

TIP You can turn the status bar on the application window off or on by choosing View ⇨ Status Bar.

A less obvious — but no less important — consideration regarding the way FileMaker works on Macintosh and Windows is the way dialogs work. In Windows, the general convention places the Cancel dialog button at the lower right of dialogs and other buttons (for example, the OK button — usually the default) to the left. However, FileMaker custom dialogs use the rightmost button as the default, and only this button will result in data entered or edited into Custom Dialog Input Fields being stored in the database. Unless you choose dialog and button text with care, Windows users may find this inconsistency confusing.

FIGURE 10.2

The application window contains all FileMaker database windows in the Microsoft Windows operating system.

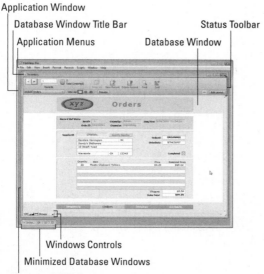

Application Window
Database Window Title Bar · · · · · · · · · · · · · Status Toolbar
Application Menus · · · · · · · · · · · Database Window

Windows Controls
Minimized Database Windows
"Restored" Window

Using Dynamic Screen Elements

Computer users are accustomed to seeing interfaces change to reflect the currently available options or program state. Buttons light up when ready to be clicked or dim when not applicable. This is one way in which applications communicate their state to users. Even on the Web (commonly considered stateless), many sites devise ways to provide visual cues regarding state.

Because your solution's user experience is dependent on how well the interface communicates to the user, you need to provide visual cues about what's going on. How well you deliver an intuitive and appealing user experience depends on your command of dynamic interface techniques — ways of changing what users see to help them understand what's required or expected.

Disappearing/reappearing objects

One key way to make your interfaces dynamic is to add or remove elements according to the current situation or context. For example, if your database requires users to enter only an e-mail address for contact records where the preferred communication method is e-mail, you may want to have the `E-Mail` field remain hidden except when `E-Mail` is selected in a `MethodOfContact` field.

There are a number of ways you can use FileMaker's interface tools to make things appear or disappear conditionally. In the following sections, I provide three examples.

The portal invisibility trick

This technique has been around in a variety of forms for many years. It relies on the fact that, when a relationship is invalid (for example, if the key field on which it depends is empty), the contents of a portal depending on the relationship will not be displayed. If you apply transparent line and fill characteristics to the portal, neither it nor its contents will be visible until the relationship is established.

Using the example file from the previous chapter's `Inventory` layout, I provide an example of the portal invisibility trick, displaying the Preferred Supplier tab's supplier details only when the user selects a valid value in the `SupplierID` field. To accomplish this, add a portal based on the `ItemSupplier` table, as shown in Figure 10.3.

Configure the portal to show a single row (`Initial row: 1, Number of rows: 1`). On the Preferred Supplier tab, size the portal just large enough to enclose the `Supplier Details` fields and label, position it behind the fields, and apply transparent line and fill.

When you return to Browse mode, you'll see that if you delete the value from the `SupplierID` field, the `Supplier Details` fields no longer appear empty. Instead, the fields and their label disappear completely, as shown in Figure 10.4.

The portal trick described in the preceding paragraphs has the advantage of being driven by the data — no separate action (by the user or by a script) is required to determine and apply the visibility state. Because it's possible to create a calculation field to use as the key field for a portal relationship to determine visibility, you can define calculation rules to determine the visibility of different layout objects.

FIGURE 10.3

Setting up a single-row portal on the `Inventory` layout.

FIGURE 10.4

Portal invisibility in action — hiding the `Supplier Details` fields until a `SupplierID` is entered.

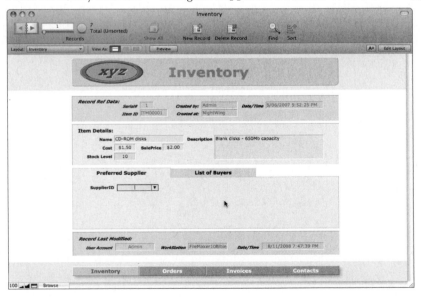

CAUTION   Although the portal invisibility trick can be useful for occasional requirements, overuse can lead to undesirable clutter of additional calculation fields and relationships. The example described here has the advantage of leveraging an existing relationship and, therefore, has minimal impact on the solution.

Concealed and remotely operated Tab Control

Another way you can control what appears when on your layouts is to provide a Tab Control that is remotely operated by scripts or buttons so that it changes to show (or hide) layout elements at will. In FileMaker 10, you can assign a script that changes the state of a Tab Control to the Tab Control itself (as an OnObjectModify script trigger) so that user actions that change the state of the Tab Control will invoke a script that conditionally reverses the change or performs other actions. Similarly, you can assign a script that selects an appropriate tab (according to the current user's access privileges, for example) as an OnLayoutLoad script trigger.

NOTE   To assign an ObjectModify script trigger to a Tab Control, go to Layout mode, select the Tab Control, and choose Format ⇨ Set Script Triggers. The Set Script Triggers dialog appears. Choose the checkbox event labeled OnObjectModify and select a script to be performed. To assign an OnLayoutLoad or OnRecordLoad script trigger, navigate to the relevant layout, choose Layouts ⇨ Layout Setup, and then navigate to the Script Triggers tab of the Layout Setup dialog, where you can choose the relevant script event and select a script to be performed. When assigning a script trigger, you can also choose whether it is to be active in Browse and/or Find modes by using checkboxes provided in the lower part of the ScriptTriggers dialogs.

NOTE   The visibility state created by using a Tab Control object will persist only for the duration of the display of the current layout. When the user leaves the layout and returns, the layout will be presented in its default state, unless an OnLayoutLoad script trigger has been assigned to select a different tab or restore a previous tab selection when you return to the layout. Moreover, the state of the Tab Control is not dependent on which record is displayed. If you require the state to change when the user navigates to a different record, a script will be required. To manage tab changes on record navigation, you should assign a script to the OnRecordLoad script trigger.

To implement this technique, follow these steps:

1. Add a Tab Control to your layout with two (or more) tab panels. Give the tabs brief names (such as numbers) to differentiate them and then click OK.

2. Select each of the tabs in turn and, via the Object Info palette (View ⇨ Object Info), specify a unique object name. For example, if you're creating only two tabs, name them "invisible" and "visible," respectively.

3. Leave the first tab blank, but add the objects that you want to conditionally appear or disappear on the subsequent tab(s).

4. Apply a fill color to the tabs matching the layout background's fill color.

5. Select both tab panels, choose Format ⇨ Size ⇨ Custom, and enter a size of 1 point.

6. With the Tab Control selected, choose Format ⇨ Tab Control Setup. The Tab Contol Setup dialog appears.

7. From the Tab Width pop-up menu at the lower right of the dialog, choose Fixed Width Of. In the field that appears below it, enter **0**, and select Pixels from the adjacent measurement pop-up.

8. Still in the Tab Control Setup dialog, choose a default front tab from the pop-up menu at the upper right of the dialog, as shown in Figure 10.5. Select the tab you've assigned the "invisible" object name to if you want the tab contents to be invisible by default. Otherwise, select the other (another) tab as the default.

FIGURE 10.5

Setting up the Tab Control for tab width and default tab.

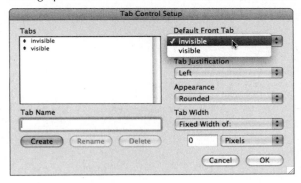

9. Click OK to accept the dialog settings.

10. Finalize the size and position of the Tab Control and its contents on the layout.

11. With the Tab Control selected, apply transparent line attributes and set the 3-D effects to None. After you make these changes, the tab will blend into the background.

12. Create a script or button using the following command:

```
Go to Object [ "visible" ]
```

This displays the contents of the visible panel of the Tab Control.

13. Create a script or button using the command:

```
Go to Object [ "invisible" ]
```

This renders the contents of the tab panel invisible.

When these changes are complete, the scripts (and/or buttons) in your solution have control over the state of the Tab Control and will, therefore, display or hide its contents when appropriate.

One advantage this technique has over the portal-based technique is that, by using additional tabs, a number of alternate options can be invoked in the same area of the screen. Conversely, its chief disadvantage is that it requires scripted control to activate changes in the state of the Tab Control.

If you want to combine the flexibility of the Tab Control visibility approach with the comparatively automatic operation of the portal visibility technique, you may want to set up a script trigger to ensure that the relevant script will be called whenever a user changes tab panels.

CROSS-REF For additional details about configuring Script Triggers in your solutions, refer to Chapters 4 and 8.

Using conditional formatting as a visibility control

In addition to the many possible variations of portal and Tab Control techniques for controlling object visibility, FileMaker 10 includes options that, in some circumstances, provide an attractive alternative to the preceding techniques.

In the following section, I take a closer look at some of the ways you can use conditional formatting to achieve dynamic interface effects, including control of visibility.

The hidden power of conditional formatting

FileMaker's conditional formatting options enable you to set up rules for applying formatting to text objects, including fields, buttons, and layout text. Using these options, you can configure FileMaker to make objects visible under specific conditions.

If you apply transparent line and fill characteristics to a text object, everything except the text it contains will be see-through. Similarly, if you set an object's font size to 1 point and choose a font color that matches the background, the object will disappear from view. When you subsequently apply conditional formatting to set the font color, font size, and/or fill color under specific conditions (determined via calculation), the object becomes visible according to the rules you've defined.

As an example of this technique, you may want to adapt the widely used Web form prompt of an asterisk next to required fields. Ideally, the asterisk should no longer appear after the field in question has a value. To achieve that, using conditional formatting for the `Inventory` solution's `SupplierID` field, navigate to the `Inventory` layout and follow these steps:

1. Add a text object to the layout to the right of the `SupplierID` field and enter an asterisk (*).
2. Select the asterisk and choose Format ⇨ Size ⇨ 18 Point.
3. Choose Format ⇨ Conditional. The Conditional Formatting dialog appears.
4. Click the Add button and, in the `Formula Is` field, enter

   `IsEmpty(Inventory::SupplierID)`
5. Select the Text Color checkbox and, from the adjacent color menu, choose a dark red, as shown in Figure 10.6.

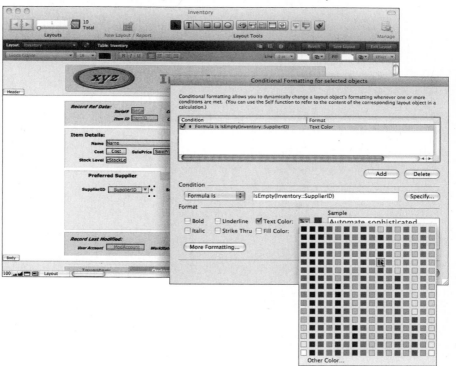

FIGURE 10.6

Applying conditional formatting attributes to an asterisk text object.

6. Click the OK button to dismiss the Conditional Formatting dialog.

7. With the asterisk text object still selected, choose Format ➪ Text Color and select a light gray to match the color of the tab panel behind the asterisk.

When these changes are complete, return to Browse mode and note that the asterisk appears when the SupplierID field is empty, disappearing when a value is entered or selected.

Using variations of this technique, you can configure your solution's interface to direct the user's gaze to areas or elements on the screen requiring attention, post flags or messages, and/or highlight point(s) where the next data entry should occur. When you employ a thoughtful combination of measures of this kind, you achieve an interactive and adaptable visual interface, increasing the intuitive quality of the user experience.

Multi-state buttons and objects

You can use variations of the technique outlined in the preceding section to create state-aware button objects that light up when the function they perform is available (and that otherwise dim). For example, a button that performs the Show All Records command after a Find has been performed will be of use only when a found set is in place. To have such a button light up when the user is viewing a found set and dim when all records are displayed, set default text and fill colors in pale gray with low contrast (for the dimmed state) and then specify conditional formatting to apply fill color and strong contrast (between text color and fill color), using the following formula:

```
Get(FoundCount) < Get(TotalRecordCount)
```

With this condition in place, the button automatically lights up when one or more records are omitted, dimming again as soon as all records are returned to the display.

> **NOTE**   **For an example of dynamically configured Show All buttons using the technique described here, refer to the lower right corners of the OrderLines and InvoiceLines layouts in the copy of the Inventory example file for this chapter.**

Similarly, you can use conditional formatting to change the appearance of background panels and dividers according to the current context. For example, a layout text object can readily be repurposed to provide a colored background panel in Find mode. This useful visual cue reduces the likelihood that users will inadvertently attempt data entry in Find mode (and lose their work on returning to Browse mode).

A transparent text object placed at the back of the layout and formatted to apply colored fill with the conditional formatting formula creates a sharp visual delineation between Find and Browse modes:

```
Get(WindowMode) = 1
```

If, before applying transparent fill to the text object, you first apply a 3-D effect (such as engraving), the effect also becomes active when the fill color changes, further enhancing the drama of the effect.

Working with Sub-Summary Parts and Part Controls

To enable you to group data and introduce summaries of the grouped data, FileMaker provides a special type of layout part called the Sub-summary part. Sub-summary parts only appear in Browse mode and Preview mode, when the previewed data is sorted according to a particular field.

Using Sub-summary parts, you can instruct FileMaker to dice up a data set, presenting it grouped according to predetermined criteria — or even to dice your data multiple ways simultaneously (for example, to summarize by groups within groups in a hierarchical arrangement).

Building adaptable screens

Clearly, not having to create a new layout for every version of a screen or report is preferable — and in many cases, you don't have to. Two factors work in your favor, enabling you to create layouts that serve as both screen displays and versatile reports.

One of the keys to FileMaker's adaptability is its support for nonprinting objects. Select any layout object (or group of objects), choose Format ➪ Set Sliding/Printing, and, in the resulting dialog, enable the Do Not Print the Selected Objects checkbox, and you can determine what prints. This enables you to build a layout in layers, with the frontmost elements providing the screen view, yet disappearing in preview and print output to reveal the layer of items behind them.

This technique lets you provide graphically rich screens employing color and subtlety, yet produce clean and elegant grayscale printed output from the same layouts. Moreover, because Sub-summary parts operate dynamically to introduce summary data into the layout according to the prevailing sort order, they add a further dimension of flexibility.

Sub-summary parts are associated with values in a sort sequence. When adding a Sub-summary part to your layout, you're prompted to select a When Sorted By field, as shown in Figure 10.7. A *leading Sub-summary part* (one that's placed above the Body part) produces a heading above a group of records within the sort sequence with which it's associated, whereas a *trailing Sub-summary part* appears below each sorted group. You can have both a leading and trailing Sub-summary part associated with the same sort field. In FileMaker 10, Sub-summary parts appear in both Browse and Preview modes, whenever the database is sorted by the designated field.

Stacking up multiple Sub-summary parts

FileMaker permits you to add multiple Sub-summary parts above and below the body part on your layouts. You may have two (one above and one below) for a given sort field, but you may add many additional Sub-summary parts associated with other sort fields. When the layout is viewed as a list, each Sub-summary part remains dormant until the field with which it's associated is included in the sort order. Thus, by stacking up multiple Sub-summary parts, you can configure a single layout to provide a variety of alternate presentation formats dependent upon the current sort order.

FIGURE 10.7

Specifying the When Sorted By field for a Sub-summary part.

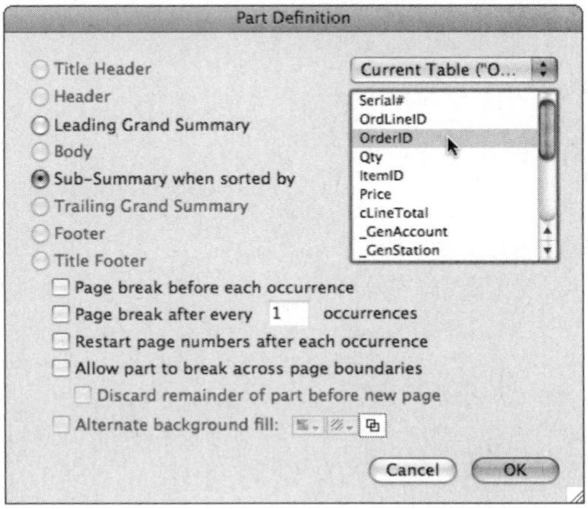

As an example, the Inventory database for this chapter has Sub-summary parts added to the OrderLines layout for both ItemID and OrderID sorts, as shown in Figure 10.8. In addition, the OrderLines layout has been reconfigured, as described under the preceding heading, to print only some of the layout items, thus producing a clean and simple appearance when the layout is previewed or printed.

With the OrderItems layout so configured, the browse, preview, or print output can be broken out and summarized by either Orders or Items, simply by changing the sort order. You can see examples of layouts showing the alternate options in Figures 10.9 and 10.10. As well as illustrating the differently summarized content of the report, Figures 10.9 and 10.10 also show the different appearance of the Browse mode and Preview mode views of the layout. (See the section on "Designing for Print," later in this chapter, for additional details).

In the OrderLines layout, I chose to configure the appearance of the Sub-summary parts for the two different sort configurations differently, so the content of the reports shown in Figure 10.9 and Figure 10.10 are distinct in appearance. However, you can choose to make the appearance of the Sub-summary parts identical if it suits the purposes of your solution.

FIGURE 10.8

Configuration of multiple Sub-summary parts on the OrderItems layout.

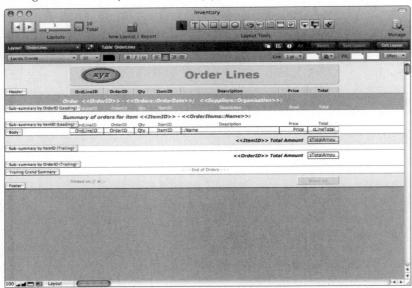

FIGURE 10.9

A Browse mode view of the `OrderItems` layout sorted by `ItemID`.

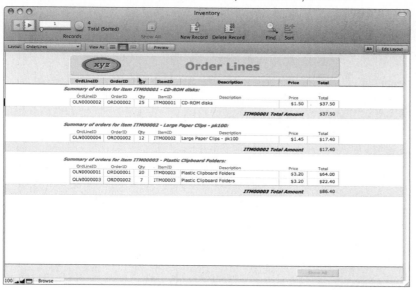

FIGURE 10.10

A Preview mode view of the `OrderItems` layout sorted by `OrderID`.

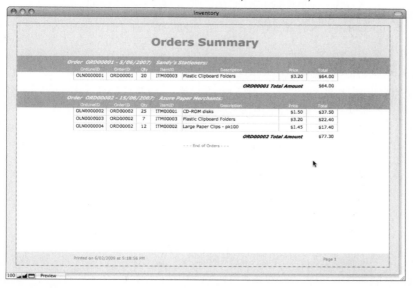

Using multiple break fields

Sub-summary parts are included (in Browse mode, Preview mode, and print output) whenever the field with which they're associated is included in the sort order. When you create Sub-summary parts for multiple sort fields and then sort by multiple fields, FileMaker presents a hierarchical breakout with group summaries nested within enclosing groups according to the order of precedence of the sort order.

> **NOTE** In FileMaker 10, sort order is preserved in Browse mode, so when you add records or edit data (in a field that is specified as part of the sort order), records will automatically be repositioned to reflect the appropriate sort sequence. This means that Sub-summary displays in Browse mode are "live" and will remain up-to-date as data changes.

If, for example, you sort the `OrderLines` entries by `ItemID` and then `OrderID`, the result will be order summaries within each item summary. Conversely, by reversing the order of the sort fields, you can generate a tiered report that summarizes items separately within each order. Figure 10.11 shows the appearance of the `OrderLines` layout when sorted simultaneously by `OrderID` and `ItemID` (in that sequence).

As it happens, the dual-sort report in Figure 10.11 is not particularly useful — other than to illustrate a possibility. Rarely does an order have more than one line for the same item, so summarizing the items per order doesn't tell you anything. However, in many other cases, it may be highly advantageous to produce a groups-within-groups summary report. For example, when a class of students has completed a series of assessment tasks each term, you'll want to be able to summarize each term's task results by student — and you may also want to summarize each student's task results by term.

Applying the logic of the preceding example, after creating Sub-summary parts for term and student, the required reports would be achieved by sorting the data in the task results table by `Term` and then `Student` (for the first report) and by `StudentID` and then `Term` for the second.

Controlling pagination and page breaks

Using Sub-summary parts in your layouts, in addition to controlling your reports' content and summary characteristics, also affords you a number of controls over where and how page breaks occur when your layout is prepared for preview and printing.

As shown in Figure 10.7, the part controls for pagination include

- Page break before each occurrence
- Page break after every *n* occurrences
- Restart page numbers after each occurrence
- Allow part to break across page boundaries
- Discard remainder of part before new page

FIGURE 10.11

A preview of the `OrderItems` layout sorted by `OrderID` and `ItemID`.

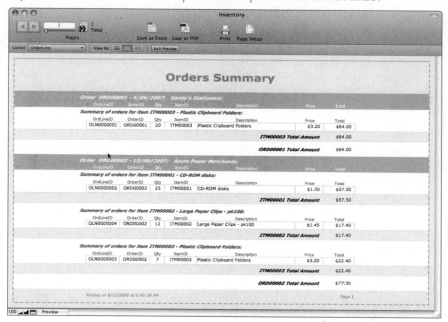

The descriptions of these pagination controls are for the most part self-explanatory. However, keep in mind that these controls all relate to the position of page breaks with respect to parts — they don't give you control over the position of breaks relative to objects within parts. You need to make separate provisions to ensure that page breaks don't occur in the middle of a field or line of text.

When you specify a given report's or printout's paper size and orientation, adjust the size of the margin allocation and/or header and footer parts so that the amount remaining for the body part (or other parts) is an exact multiple of the line height of the text you'll include on the layout. It may help to set the line height to a specific fixed value to ensure consistent behavior.

TIP To specify line height, select the relevant objects in Layout mode and choose Format ➪ Line Spacing ➪ Custom. The Paragraph dialog will appear, and, at its upper right, you'll find controls for line height. You can specify line height in lines, pixels, inches, or centimeters. When the height of all objects on the layout sums to a multiple of the line height you've determined, and the layout itself is also a multiple of the line height, you can be confident that page breaks will fall between lines.

NOTE The importance of designing complex print layouts to a height in multiples of the set line height forms a general rule for achieving clean/unbroken lines of text at page breaks. This *rule of multiples* becomes still more important when using sliding and reducing features, as described in the "Sliding objects and reducing parts" section, later in this chapter.

Designing for Print

When preparing layouts for printing, consider the printed page as a cohesive whole, arranging elements on the page to direct the reader's eyes to the salient information. The factors making a printed report easy to read and understand are its simplicity, clean lines, use of white space separating distinct items, and the alignment and proximity of associated or related elements. FileMaker provides you with a number of techniques to assist you in creating clean and intelligible printed output, including the ability to determine which objects print (or are visible only onscreen), to control the size and placement of objects with sliding and reducing settings and techniques for merging data with static text.

Nonprinting objects

You can use FileMaker's setting for nonprinting objects, a setting located in the Set Sliding/Printing dialog (Format ⇨ Set Sliding/Printing), shown in Figure 10.12, as part of the process of making adaptable layouts. For example, your screens may include various button objects for navigation or script control — objects that will serve only as a distraction on a printed report, so they should be set as nonprinting.

FIGURE 10.12

Setting an object (or group of selected objects) as nonprinting.

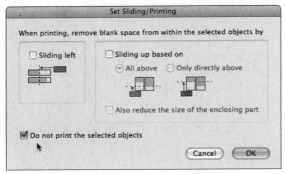

A further use of FileMaker's option for nonprinting objects is to create alternate backgrounds for screen and print. Your screen designs will benefit from subdued, colored, or dark-toned backgrounds and may include graphical elements. By contrast, printed output generally serves best with light or white backgrounds and clear, open arrangement of elements.

TIP   To help you see at a glance which layout objects are set to print and which are not, choose View ⇨ Show ⇨ Non-Printing Objects. Objects set as nonprinting will then be displayed with a screen border around them.

By creating layout objects to serve as screen backgrounds (for example, graphical rectangles) and setting them as nonprinting, you can ensure that your layouts show one background when viewed on screen but another when printed. Foreground objects set as nonprinting are stripped away to reveal background elements more appropriate for print (especially monochrome print).

The header area of the layout pictured in Figures 10.9 and 10.10 is an example of this technique. The various items appearing in the header of the layout in the Browse mode display shown in Figure 10.9 are eliminated from the Preview mode and print output to leave a clear and simple heading at the top of the page, as shown in Figure 10.10.

Sliding objects and reducing parts

When setting out fields for screen display, it's customary to size them so that they're large enough to show the largest amount of content likely to be entered. For example, if you'll be entering descriptions of up to four lines, you make the description fields four lines high so that they show all the text. Although that works well for screen display, fields with fewer lines of text will leave the appearance of unwanted gaps when printed.

FileMaker enables you to configure fields to collapse and the fields beneath (or to the right) to slide up (or across) to close unwanted gaps when the layout is previewed or printed. These settings are applied by selecting the relevant objects in Layout mode and choosing Format ⇨ Set Sliding/Printing. The resulting dialog (refer to Figure 10.12) includes separate controls for horizontal and vertical sliding.

> **TIP** As a reminder of which layout objects are set to collapse and slide, choose View ⇨ Show ⇨ Sliding Objects. Objects set to slide and remove white space will be identified with small black arrows. Text objects appear with arrows on their right and/or bottom sides (according to the directions in which they're set to collapse and slide), while other objects will display corresponding arrows on the top and left sides.

When objects are set to collapse and/or slide upward, an additional control labeled Also Reduce the Size of the Enclosing Part becomes available. Activating this option prevents blank pages from appearing at the end of a printout (or a section of a printout) where collapsing or sliding fields have been accommodated on a preceding page.

> **TIP** In order for a field or text object to collapse to the left, its contents must be left-aligned. Similarly, in order to collapse upward, an object's contents must be top-aligned. This applies to container fields as well as text objects.

As an example, when printing a layout including names composed of a title, first name, and last name, you don't want the printed copy to include large gaps after each part of a name. Figure 10.13 shows a Browse mode view of fields arranged in columns with generous spacing — perfect for data entry, but less than ideal for a printed list (or an address on a letter and so on).

FIGURE 10.13

Name fields in Browse mode — with ample room for long names.

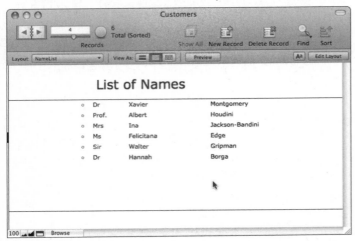

By selecting each of the fields in layout mode, choosing Format ➪ Set Sliding/Printing, and setting the option to slide left, as shown in Figure 10.14, the fields can be configured to print their contents as a continuous line of text without gaps. Figure 10.15 shows the Preview mode appearance of the same layout, where you can see the effect of the sliding attributes.

FIGURE 10.14

Name fields set to slide left to remove blank space.

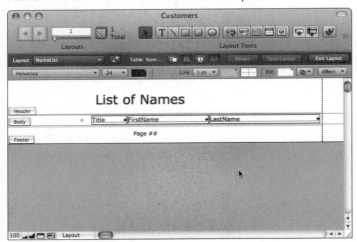

The result: Name fields sliding left to remove blank space.

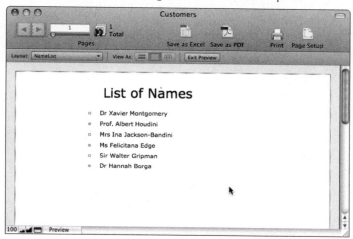

The careful application of sliding and reducing attributes helps you control field arrangement in printed output such as reports, labels, letters, invitation cards, and so on. However, although sliding deals with whole fields, it doesn't have the flexibility to combine blocks of text from multiple fields or text objects in a seamless way (for example, so that line wrapping will flow naturally throughout). For that, you require Merge fields.

NOTE When objects on your layouts are set to slide upward, the white space between them is maintained. Even in cases where an object collapses entirely (for example, a text field that is empty), the white space between it and the next object on the layout will remain.

Using Merge fields

Merge fields enable you to create layout text objects that include references to fields in the current record within the static text. Using this capability, standard text constructions can include dynamic elements, such as names, amounts, addresses, dates, and so on.

To use Merge fields, first create a text object in layout mode and then choose Insert ➪ Merge Field (⌘+Option+M or Ctrl+M). The Specify Field dialog appears, prompting you to choose a field to insert into the current text object. After you select a field, it will be added at the cursor as a tagged reference enclosed in double angle brackets. The syntax for a Merge field reference is

```
<<TableOccurrenceName::FieldName>>
```

NOTE The delimiters for a Merge field are two successive left angle brackets, paired with two successive right angle brackets. Do not use the « and » single character quote marks — they aren't an acceptable substitute.

If the field you select is sourced from the table the current layout is based on, the field name is used for the Merge field placeholder. For all other cases, the table occurrence name and the field name are required. Moreover, if you know the name of the table occurrence (if required) and the field, you can type the Merge field placeholder directly from the keyboard; you don't have to use the menu command for this purpose.

> **TIP** A Merge field placeholder will be formatted according to the text formats (size, color, style, and so on) applied to the leading chevron bracket enclosing it (except where character formatting has been applied to the field contents of the referenced field — in which case the character formatting will take precedence).

In addition, FileMaker supports a number of generic text placeholders for system and contextual information:

//   Resolves to the current date when the layout is displayed or printed

::   Resolves to the current time when the layout is displayed or printed

|| Resolves to the workstation username when the layout is displayed or printed

Resolves to the current page number when the layout is previewed or printed

@@ Resolves to the current record number (according to its current position in the found set or in the current portal display) when the layout is displayed or printed

> **TIP** When a text object includes generic placeholders or Merge fields including dates, times, timestamps, or numbers, you can control the format of the data when displayed by selecting the text object and choosing Format ➪ Number, Format ➪ Date, and/or Format ➪ Time.

Merge fields and placeholders have a variety of uses. However, they have the limitation that you can't use them to edit field data in Browse mode. Thus, they're suitable for displaying and printing data, but not as an editing interface. Consequently, Merge fields are most frequently used on special-purpose layouts, such as form letters, certificates, or various formal documents. In some situations, the non-editable nature of Merge fields is a strength, so you may choose to use Merge fields to display field contents in cases where you don't want the user to be able to copy or edit the data.

Creating a letter generator

Although Merge fields provide a flexible way to create free-form letters using your database's data, they require a familiarity with Layout mode and high-level access privileges. As a developer or advanced user, you should have no hesitation creating or editing documents using layout text and Merge fields. However, there are a few limitations:

- Solution users may not have the skills to make professional-looking letters in layout mode.

- If the data architecture of the solution is complex, users may have difficulty locating the appropriate fields and table occurrences to base Merge fields on.

- Giving a large number of users access to creating or modifying your solution's layouts may be risky.

- If a lot of slightly different letters are required, over time the number of layouts required to accommodate them all may grow to unacceptable — or at least, unwieldy — levels.

- Layouts are not tied to specific records (only to a table occurrence), so they provide no indication which records were used to create which letters/documents or when.

If any of these issues are of concern, you require a different alternative — one that enables users to create letters dynamically without creating or editing layouts, meanwhile maintaining a record of the recipients of each letter. One way to achieve this aim is to set up a single letter layout where the text of the letter is supplied by a calculation field. You can then provide users with a letters table in which they can compose letters, using merge placeholders where they want to reference fields in your solution. Your calculation field (the one producing the letter text) can then perform a substitution to replace the merge placeholders with the appropriate field values for each record as the letters are printed.

When you structure your solution in this way, each letter will be stored in its own record in a letters table. Therefore, it's a simple matter to record in a separate table, such as a join table, which contacts were sent which letters and on which date(s).

If your letters are stored in a field called `MergeLetterText` in a table named `Letters` — and if the text in `MergeLetterText` includes properly formatted field references in double angle brackets — you can use a calculation formula along the lines of the following to resolve the embedded placeholder tags, constructing the appropriate letter text for the current record in your `Contacts` table:

```
Evaluate("\"" & Substitute(Letters::MergeLetterText ; ["<<"; "\" & "]; [">>"; " &
    \""]) & "\"")
```

Using Multiple Windows and Views

FileMaker enables you to display multiple windows showing the same or different views of a file's contents. Windows can be spawned manually by choosing Window ➪ New Window or via button or script. In the latter case, your script can control the location and size of the displayed window, as well as selecting which layout to present to the user.

Given that you have a high degree of programmatic control over the scripted display of database windows, you can use them to perform the roles of pop-up information panels, graphs, auxiliary and drill-down displays of data, selection windows, detail windows, image viewers, and countless other related interface roles.

Managing window placement and size

When you use the `New Window[ ]` script or button command to create a window, the options are available to set the window name, its height and width (in pixels), and its location. The location is also set in pixels, supplied as coordinates relative to the monitor's upper left corner of the desktop area (Mac) or the Application window (Windows). You can enter each of these window parameters either as a literal value or as a calculation to be evaluated at runtime.

For example, if you specify the Distance from Top parameter using the following formula, the new window will be positioned 50 pixels farther from the top of the screen than the current active window:

```
Get(WindowTop) + 50
```

Similarly, if you have specified the height and width of a window (for example, as 500 pixels wide by 300 pixels high) and want to locate the window in the center of the viewable desktop area of the user's monitor, you can do so by using formulas for the Distance from Top and Distance from Left attributes as follows:

- Distance from top: `(Get(WindowDesktopHeight) - 300) / 2`
- Distance from left: `(Get(WindowDesktopWidth) - 500) / 2`

When these formulas are evaluated, they return the correct coordinates to center the 500 x 300 window on the user's monitor.

CAUTION When naming a window, bear in mind that window names are not required to be unique. However, if a window does not have a unique name, script commands won't be able to reliably select the window by name.

In addition to creating new windows at desired locations, you can move and resize existing windows, addressing them by their window names. This is achieved by using the `Move/Resize[ ]` script or button command, using similar parameter options to those described for the `New Window[ ]` command. Similarly, the `Select Window[ ]` command brings a specified window (or the current window, if none is specified) to the front, making it active.

NOTE Parameters for size and location in both the `New Window[ ]` and `Move/Resize Window[ ]` commands are optional. If you don't specify a parameter, FileMaker makes no change to it. In the case of the `New Window[ ]` command, the result is that the window takes on attributes for size and/or location from the currently active window. However, where no window name is specified, the window name will be generated based on the active window name, but with a hyphen and incrementing number appended.

Windows as pop-ups and drill-downs

FileMaker packs a lot of power and flexibility into the `Go To Related Record[ ]` command (GTRR), enabling you to locate related records, determine the found set, independently select a suitable layout, spawn a new window (or target the current window), and, if creating a new window, set the name, position, and size of the new window and select it, all in one step. That's a lot of functionality in a tiny package.

Using the `Go To Related Record[ ]` command, you can create simple layout buttons to move around your solution, including to spawn pop-up windows showing details or related data for content of a current screen, or drilling down into additional detail (showing the source data for an aggregate calculation and so on).

As a further example of the use of windows as pop-up "reveal" interaction elements, if you're storing images of products or people in your solution, it may be appropriate to display a thumbnail-sized image on the data-entry screen, configured so that clicking the thumbnail brings up a full-sized image in a window in the foreground of the user's monitor.

Simulating modal window behavior

A common feature of computer interfaces is the *modal window* — a window or dialog that remains in front until the user takes an action to dismiss it. Most dialogs are modal, requiring you to click OK or Cancel before you can resume other activities. In some cases, you may want to have your database windows mimic modal behavior.

One of the ways developers achieve an effect similar to a modal window is by creating a new window in a script and terminating the script within a loop so that the window will be held frontmost by the action of the script until the user cancels or takes some other action. The following script demonstrates the technique:

```
New Window [Name: "Select Item"; Height: 400; Width: 340; Top: 200; Left: 350]
Go to Layout ["Select Item" (Items)]
Show/Hide Status Area [Lock; Hide]
Loop
   Select Window [Name: "Select Item"; Current File]
   Pause/Resume Script [Indefinitely]
End Loop
```

With this script sequence in place, the new Select Item window is displayed and locked as the frontmost window until the user takes an action halting the script. You must, therefore, ensure that the displayed layout provides access to one or more buttons that will halt the looping script and restore control of the interface to the user.

CAUTION   Although simulation of modal window behavior may provide a useful mechanism to guide the user, it should not be relied upon to enforce security. You can use various techniques (including the use of the Mac OS's Exposé feature) to partially or fully circumvent a loop-locked window.

Employing Custom Dialogs as an Interface Tool

Although harnessing database windows for a variety of dynamic interaction modeling techniques provides power and flexibility, simpler requirements can frequently be met by employing FileMaker's native custom dialogs. Custom dialogs can include a heading label, up to four lines of text, up to three buttons, and up to three input fields.

Providing standard and familiar interface techniques has a number of advantages, and users are familiar with the interaction models associated with dialogs. All computer users understand dialogs as alerts and as information entry prompts.

Dialogs as a data-entry device

Using custom dialogs to accept input from the user requires using the Input Fields option. You configure these via the "Show Custom Dialog" Options dialog's Input Fields tab, as shown in Figure 10.16.

Custom dialog field input is always received as text, regardless of the data type of the fields selected to store the data. Moreover, standard data type error alerts won't be displayed when data is entered into fields via a custom dialog. When using dialogs, you must, therefore, perform your own checks for data type consistency.

Using global text fields to accept dialog input and then perform data checks and conversions (if necessary) before writing the content into the appropriate fields in the current record has some value. A single global text field with three repetitions (for example, located in a utility table in your solution) suffices for this purpose.

When using a script to present a dialog containing input fields, placing the dialog call within a loop with an exit loop condition based on a check for the presence of the required input is a common technique to confirm that data has been entered. A simple example of a script sequence achieving this is as follows:

FIGURE 10.16

Configuring input fields via the "Show Custom Dialog" Options dialog.

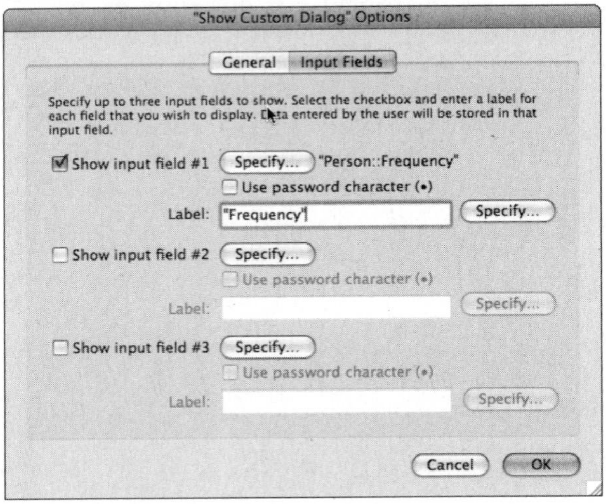

```
If [IsEmpty(Person::Frequency)]
  Loop
    Show Custom Dialog ["Enter the contact frequency." Person::Frequency]
    Exit Loop If [not IsEmpty(Person::Frequency) or Get(LastMessageChoice) = 2]
  End Loop
End If
```

Note that the `Exit Loop If [ ]` condition includes the `Get(LastMessageChoice)` test to determine if the user has clicked Cancel.

CAUTION Data entered into a custom dialog's input field is discarded unless the user clicks the first button (the button appearing at the far right of the dialog) when accepting/dismissing the dialog.

Dynamic dialog attributes

FileMaker's custom dialog's heading and message attributes can be determined by calculation. Thus, you can set them to reference fields in your solution or to incorporate system variables such as time, account name, operating system, and so on.

To take advantage of the ability to set dialog attributes dynamically, click the Specify buttons in the General and Input Fields panels of the "Show Custom Dialog" Options dialog. A Specify Calculation dialog appears, and you can enter a formula to determine the text for use on the relevant dialog caption.

NOTE Although heading, message, and field labels can be calculated, the fields themselves, plus the button text, must be specified in advance.

Looking at Anchors and Resizable Layout Objects

Over the course of the past decade, computer users' experience with Web browsers and Internet content has increasingly influenced their expectations. Browsers are designed to reposition the content — and sometimes also resize it — according to the size of the browser window. The arrival of ever-larger-format monitors increases appreciation of this capability.

In some cases, resizing components of a database window makes sense (so a field accepting free-form text can be enlarged when there is a lot of text to read or enter/edit). Even when you think that there's no merit to resizing layout elements, you should consider setting window contents to maintain their position with respect to the center of the window.

Objects that move according to window size

FileMaker provides a deceptively simple control mechanism for positioning and resizing layout objects, in the form of a set of four anchor checkboxes. These controls appear on the lower section of the Object Info palette (View ⇨ Object Info). When you select an object in Layout mode (with the Info palette in display), its anchor settings are shown and can be modified.

By default, all layout objects are anchored to the top left. That means when you select an object and view its settings in the object Info palette, the default state is top and left anchors on, right and bottom anchors off, as shown in Figure 10.17.

When you disable one or both of the default anchors, the selected object is free to move away from the edge of the layout to which it was anchored. This means that if the window is enlarged above the original layout size, the object moves in order to maintain an equal distance from the center (horizontal) or middle (vertical) of the layout area.

NOTE   The original size of the layout (used as the reference size to determine object moving and scaling) is based vertically on the combined height of the layout parts and, horizontally, on the distance from the left side of the layout to the right border of the rightmost layout object.

A layout's moving and resizing behavior in Browse and Find modes depends on the view format of the layout. When you set a layout to List View (View ⇨ View as List), vertical resizing is disabled (enlarging the window exposes additional records rather than increasing the vertical size of records). When you set a layout to Table View (View ⇨ View as Table), both vertical and horizontal resizing are disabled. Only in Form View (View ⇨ View as Form) are both vertical and horizontal resizing (and repositioning) attributes activated.

NOTE   Vertical repositioning and resizing is applied to objects in all layout parts. However, if a layout part contains no objects set to reposition or resize vertically, that part will not resize. Layout parts containing objects set to reposition or resize are scaled proportionally in Browse and Find modes when the vertical height of the window is enlarged to a size greater than the combined height of all layout parts.

FIGURE 10.17

The default anchor state for all layout objects — anchored to the top and left.

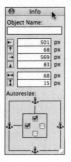

It's common to leave some "breathing room" at the left and right sides of your layouts. In other words, fields or labels are not positioned flush against the edges of the layout. When using repositioning and resizing (as when using the `Adjust Window [Resize to Fit]` command), you need a way to ensure that FileMaker respects the surrounding space at the right side of your layouts. One way to achieve this is to include an invisible object (for example, a graphical rectangle) at the right edge of the layout area you're using. This establishes a boundary that FileMaker respects when resizing windows and the objects they contain.

> **TIP** I suggest that you use an empty text object to establish the right boundary. You can then format it to acquire the same fill color as the background except when in Layout mode (the conditional formatting formula to achieve this is `Get (WindowMode) ≠ 4`). This means that the boundary object will always be visible in Layout mode (so that you can keep track of it) but not in other modes or in printed output.

Objects that grow and shrink

When an object is simultaneously anchored to opposing edges of the layout (both top and bottom, or both left and right), it will increase in size as the size of the window exceeds the size required to accommodate the contents of the layout.

If your layout is area is configured to be 500 pixels wide (that is, the right edge of the rightmost object is 500 pixels from the left edge of the layout), the width of a window sized to exactly accommodate the layout will be 515 pixels on the Mac and 528 pixels (in a restored database window) in Windows. The difference of 13 pixels is due to the added size of the scroll bars and window borders in Windows.

When an object is anchored to both the left and right of the layout, its size will be increased in Browse and Find modes when the window width exceeds the minimum width required to accommodate the layout. Given a layout width of 500 pixels, if the window size on the Mac is set to 600 pixels, an object anchored at both left and right will be increased in width by 16 pixels (600 − 584 = 16).

> **CAUTION** Because the size increase of resizing objects is equal (rather than proportional) to the size increase of the window, adjacent objects anchored to opposing sides will overlap as the window size increases.

Managing complex layout resizing

Multiple objects set to resize in the same direction, within the same area of the screen, will collide and overlap as the window size is increased. This may be ugly or disconcerting, but regardless, it compromises usability in most cases. It's incumbent on you to ensure that this sort of unintended side effect is avoided when resizing.

I recommend a "zoning" approach to the management of resizing — zones being arbitrary horizontal or vertical segments of your layout parts. Identify only one object to resize vertically within a given vertical zone and horizontally within a horizontal zone. (You can choose to work with multiple notional zones if you want.) To illustrate this approach, Figure 10.18 shows a layout comprising nine fields, in which, by using the zoning method, you should identify one column for horizontal resizing and one row to resize vertically.

FIGURE 10.18

An example layout of nine fields, at the minimum (default) layout size.

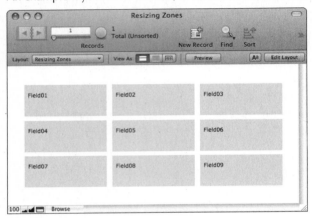

When determining how to gracefully apply resizing properties to the fields in the example layout shown here, I first visualized the layout as comprising three horizontal zones and determined that one field within each zone would expand horizontally. I chose to set `Field02`, `Field04`, and `Field09` as the horizontally expanding fields. In addition, I visualized the layout as comprised of three vertical zones and chose to apply vertical resizing to `Field07`, `Field08`, and `Field09`.

NOTE   When you've anchored an object to both left and right, all objects to the right of it should be anchored to the right and not anchored at the left. Likewise, all objects to the left of it should be anchored to the left and not the right. This ensures that as the dual-anchored object increases in size, objects to the right of it will move across to accommodate it. Similarly, when an object is anchored at both the top and bottom, other objects below it in the same layout part should be anchored at the bottom and not at the top. Likewise, all objects above it should be anchored to the top and not the bottom.

With the appropriate anchor properties applied, the fields resize as the window is enlarged, without colliding with one another, as shown in Figure 10.19.

Although the zoning method allows you to design layouts that work within the resizing limits of FileMaker Pro 10, sometimes you may want to be able to resize all fields proportionally. Proportional horizontal resizing is not supported in FileMaker 10.

There is, however, a technique you can use for proportionally resizing fields vertically in a Form View screen layout. Because Sub-summary parts are displayed in form view, different "zones" can be assigned to Sub-summary parts. A modified version of the file used as the example for this section is pictured in Figure 10.20, showing the application of this technique to provide proportional vertical resizing to all nine fields.

CAUTION The proportional vertical resizing technique described here is best suited for layouts that will not be used for printing, because further work would be required to ensure that layout parts used to control resizing appear in printed output (and in a desired sequence).

FIGURE 10.19

Resizing according to the zone method to avoid overlapping objects.

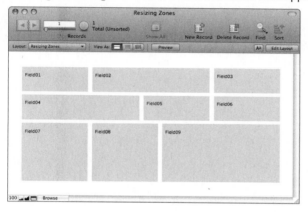

FIGURE 10.20

A workaround to achieve proportional vertical resizing for a screen-only layout.

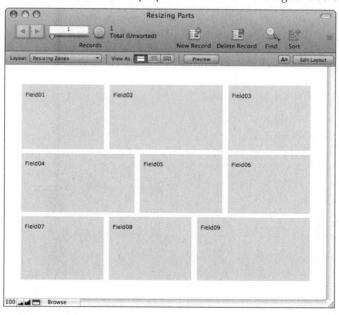

Resizing behavior of enclosing objects

Unlike other layout objects, Tab Controls and portals influence the behavior of the objects they enclose. The first thing to note is that when an object is placed within a portal or a Tab Control object, its anchor settings no longer refer to the edges of the layout. The object is, instead, anchored to the boundaries of the enclosing object. Thus, objects within an enclosing object inherit (or are limited by) the anchor properties of the enclosing object.

Additionally, portals exhibit different vertical resizing behavior depending on the anchor properties of the objects within them. If all the objects within a portal are anchored to the top (but not to the bottom) and the portal is anchored to top and bottom, when the portal height increases, it will display additional rows. However, if any items within the portal are anchored to the bottom and/or not anchored to the top (that is, set to move or resize vertically), the portal rows will increase in height rather than number: The number of rows will remain constant, and their sizes will increase proportionally as the portal is enlarged.

Centering objects within the viewable area

By disabling the anchors on opposing sides, an object is treated by FileMaker as being anchored to the center of the viewable area of the layout (or, vertically, to the layout part). For example, this setting allows you to ensure that a heading remains in the center of the header part when increasing the window size.

Similarly, if an object in the body part has all its anchors disabled, it will float free and remain equidistant from the center (both vertically and horizontally) of the body part as the window is enlarged above the size required to accommodate the layout.

Although this technique does not increase the usability of individual layout objects in the way that resizing may, it can contribute to the sense of balance, aesthetic appeal, and/or dynamism of your solutions. This is clearly evident if you open an old solution designed for a small-format (for example, 800 x 600) monitor and set to maximize on start-up. On a modern, large-format monitor, the blank area at the right and bottom of the layout dwarfs the small usable area at the upper left. Centering objects in the usable area of the window allows your solutions to transition between screens of different sizes more gracefully.

NOTE For examples of object centering, repositioning, and resizing, see the layout header and footer objects in the `Inventory` example for this chapter. If your monitor is not large enough to increase the window above the layout size, you'll be able to view the effect by zooming the layout to 75 percent or 50 percent.

Implementing Shortcut Navigation

A well-configured relational database manages the connections between all the components of your data. Items having relationships to other items are intrinsically connected to them via the solution's structures.

Why not exploit the structure of the relationships in your solution to provide navigational pathways from one place to other related places? Instead of requiring the user to laboriously exit from an invoicing screen and then navigate into the products module and search for a product to view its record, why not allow the user to jump directly to any product that appears on any invoice? If you set up your solutions appropriately, the schema can serve as a network of "rabbit holes" for the user to jump through.

The power of the Go to Related Record command

In Chapter 9, I describe in detail the implementation of jump buttons for shortcut navigation using the Go to Related Record [ ] command (GTRR), and earlier in this chapter (in the "Windows as pop-ups and drill-downs" section), I looked at some other applications of the same command.

Instead of providing isolated and idiosyncratic navigation options, well-thought-out use of the GTRR command can provide a central and essential framework for navigation of your solution. Each instance of a GTRR saves users multiple steps versus conventional navigation methods.

An important option that GTRR provides is its ability to isolate a group of records within a found set on a layout associated with the related table (that is, the table where the related records are stored). The resulting found set can be presented to the user in the current window, in a new window, or in another file (if the related table is stored elsewhere). This effectively enables you to "find" a group of records without using Find mode.

Equally important is the ability of the GTRR command to transfer found sets between layouts based on the same underlying table (but on different table occurrences). If you've performed a find to locate a subset of records on the current layout, you can use any other layout associated with a TO that (in turn) is associated with the same base table, to view the found set, by using GTRR to navigate to the desired layout.

One interface, many paths

Sophisticated computer users are aware that you can access many computer features in multiple ways. Menus, buttons, keyboard shortcuts, and so on all provide access to the same commands. Similarly, in your solutions, alternative mechanisms should be available to move from one point to another. In the interest of both utility and ergonomics, you should provide your solutions' users with alternatives suitable to different work processes and styles.

When your solution navigation is designed ergonomically and paths through layouts and records are intuitive and follow work processes and business rules, users will rely less upon FileMaker's Status Toolbar tools and will use Find mode less frequently.

CROSS-REF For further discussion of the design and implementation of navigation and menu structures for your solutions, refer to the "Using Interface Elements" section, later in this chapter.

Building Back button functionality

Something all users of the Internet rapidly learn is the value of being able to go back. Providing similar functionality in FileMaker, however, may require that your solution keep a log of where the user has been in relation to both layouts and records.

One relatively straightforward way to achieve an automatically updating log of where the user has been is to set up an unstored calculation to capture the current context and append it to a global variable. This can be done with a calculation along the following lines (where `CurrentTable::Serial#` is a reference to the primary key in the current table):

```
Let([
Sn = CurrentTable::Serial#;
Bn = ValueCount($$trace);
Vc = GetValue($$trace; Bn);
Sc = RightWords(Vc; 1);
Lc = LeftWords(Vc; WordCount(Vc) - 1);
La = Get(LayoutName);
$$trace = $$trace & If(Sn ≠ Sc or La ≠ Lc; Left(¶; Bn) & La & " " & Sn)];
"")
```

Such a calculation would be required in every table on which a user-accessible layout is based — and although empty, the field would be required to be present on each layout (it may, however be both invisible and inaccessible). This method is seamless in operation, automatically capturing a history of navigation steps between both records and layouts, regardless of the method(s) the user uses to move around your solution.

> **TIP**   If your solution includes fields that calculate values for display (for example, navigation text or the current user/account name, and so on), you can readily combine the `$$trace` calculation with an existing calculation.

When a mechanism is in place to capture user navigation, you can use a single script, structured as follows, to return through the list of previous locations in your solution:

```
If [ValueCount($$trace) < 2]
 Beep
Else
 Set Variable [$PrevCtxt; Value:GetValue($$trace; ValueCount($$trace) - 1)]
 Set Variable [$LastLayout; Value:LeftWords($PrevCtxt; WordCount($PrevCtxt)-1)]
 Set Field [Utility::gTrace_key; RightWords($PrevCtxt; 1)]
 Freeze Window
Go to Layout ["-" (Utility)]
 If [$LastLayout = "Inventory"]
  Go to Related Record [From Table:"Inventory_trace"; Using layout:$LastLayout]
 Else If [$LastLayout = "Orders"]
  Go to Related Record [... ]
  # etc
 End If
 Set Variable [$$trace; Value:Let(Nt = LeftValues($$trace; ValueCount($$trace) - 1);
  Left(Nt; Length(Nt) - 1))]
End If
```

The technique as presented here requires a utility relationship for each base table in the solution and a single corresponding GTRR command in the script to invoke the relevant relationship.

 **A working example of Back button functionality has been implemented in the accompanying Inventory example file for this chapter.**

Building Depth and Dimensionality

A long time ago, humans discovered that the world is not flat. But even before that discovery, people's minds were wired for three dimensions. Humans are geared for spatial concepts and understand the world in terms of three-dimensional space.

When you use a computer, your understanding and experience aid the interpretation of what the monitor presents to you. Thus, the best computer interfaces are those you perceive as metaphors for tangible objects and mechanisms you've encountered in the world around you.

Using embossing and engraving effects

The embossing effect (available in an elementary form on FileMaker's 3-D effects pop-up menu in Layout mode) provides a simple but effective illusion of depth, creating the appearance of a foreground and background, introducing the semblance of spatial and even tactile qualities to the screen image. As embossing raises, engraving recesses — and stacked (nested) 3-D objects increase the perceived layers of depth.

Although the effect is a simple visual illusion, things that appear raised (with embossing) have the illusion of inviting you to press on them — like buttons — or intruding upon you like neon signs or placards. Conversely, engraved objects carry the illusion of depth, inviting you to enter or suggesting interior or enclosed spaces. Moreover, engraved objects enclosed inside other engraved objects appear to take you additional layers inward, suggestive of hierarchical structures.

For added impact, you may also want to create an embossed or engraved effect for key text elements in your interfaces. Although FileMaker does not directly support embossing and engraving effects for text objects, you can produce such effects using native layout text objects by duplicating the object, stacking the duplicate atop the original, shifting it 1 pixel left and 1 pixel up, and changing its hue (darker for engraving, lighter for embossing). Alternatively, you can add text effects in a third-party program and import the results.

CAUTION **I recommend that imported graphics be optimized and used sparingly, to avoid unduly enlarging file sizes or impacting solution performance. This is a significant consideration for solutions that will be remotely hosted.**

Spatial cues for added meaning

The illusion of depth enhances your perception of a screen layout in several ways. The simplest of these is the way in which it tricks the eye — the illusion helps reduce the fatigue associated with long periods viewing flat objects at close range. Equally important, it taps into spatial associations, assisting you to visualize the relationships between groups of objects — it invokes spatial metaphors and, thus, makes screen arrangements easier to view and easier to interpret.

Careful and consistent use of protruding objects and receding or enclosing spaces creates a much stronger sense of separation and spatial relationships than any flat lines and borders could. This can aid the comprehension of information being presented. Understanding how these tools work is the first step to using them effectively when designing interfaces for your solutions.

Delineation of element groups

Engraved areas of the screen create catchments within which you naturally understand elements to be grouped in a relationship. An additional level, or tier, of engraving can enhance this effect. However, employing more than two levels begins to lose impact and risks complicating rather than simplifying the visual order being imparted.

Similarly, one or (at most) two levels of embossing can enhance the perceived order and separation of elements in a layout. Moreover, embossed elements, seeming closer to the user, take on a more present, urgent, or immediate quality.

Color

Bright colors grab attention and impress themselves vividly upon your eyes. Thus bright colors are best reserved for those screen elements the user should see first, the ones that are most urgent or important.

Overuse of strong or bright colors creates an impression of conflict and competition and is visually fatiguing. An overly bright (or overly strong-colored) screen may seem loud and/or angry. Conversely, softer tones are less fatiguing but also leave a fainter impression. Ideally, a screen should contain a few splashes of color (used to draw the user's eye to key elements) among ordered and more subdued elements.

The use of clean subtle lines throughout your interface provides maximum scope for emphasis of key elements and alerts, while serving to gently guide the user. After you have the user's attention, you don't need to keep shouting (and it's better if you don't). I recommend the use of coordinated themes of subtle tones and backgrounds, with one or two brighter colors for emphasis and contrast.

Transparency and translucency

Although FileMaker's native graphic elements are basic, imported graphics are supported in a range of formats. These include support for translucent and transparent effects in formats such as PNG (Portable Network Graphics, an Internet graphic standard). Judicious use of graphics and visual effects created in third-party graphics environments can significantly extend and enhance the visual appeal of your FileMaker interfaces.

> **TIP** To preserve the integrity of translucent and transparent images in supported formats, choose Insert ➪ Picture in Layout mode. Images pasted from the clipboard will not retain these properties.

Including graphical elements can also increase the tactile and dimensional quality of your screens, introducing subtle shadows and light effects. This sort of subtle touch lends a strengthened illusion of depth and space, reinforcing the spatial metaphors throughout your interface.

However, avoid excessive use of graphical elements in the interest of maintaining performance, particularly overly busy network connections. For best performance, optimize your graphics for smallest size, and after inserting once, duplicate the graphic within FileMaker, pasting copies to other locations. FileMaker stores a single library copy of the graphic and references it elsewhere, thus reducing the resources required to download and display interface images.

> **NOTE** The example `Inventory` database for this chapter includes several imported graphical elements (in PNG format) to add shadow, light, and enhanced depth and dimensionality to the screens.

Working with Tab Controls

In addition to designing your screens to form data into logical groups and present the user with a natural sequence of information, it's important to avoid presenting too much information at once. Clutter is problematic because the user's focus becomes lost.

One solution to the problem of clutter is to spread information out over a larger number of screens. However, this introduces a different problem — fragmentation. An alternative solution that avoids either problem is to nest data within a single screen, keeping data out of sight until it's needed. Tab controls provide an elegant way to achieve that aim.

Organizers and space savers

FileMaker's Tab Controls can be as large as the layout or as small as a postage stamp. They can work side by side in multiple arrays. Tab control panels can contain any combination of other objects including fields, Web viewers, portals, or other Tab Controls. If you place Tab Controls inside other Tab Controls, your layouts will be capable of holding large amounts of data in an ordered hierarchy, while presenting the user with a clean and simple interface design.

The hierarchical principle introduced by Tab Controls is a familiar way of creating order, and your users will instinctively understand. Just as buildings have levels that contain apartments that contain rooms that contain cupboards that contain drawers, your solutions can organize information into multiple levels of order. As long as the allocation of data to each place in a hierarchy makes simple and logical sense, your users will have no difficulty grasping the principle and locating the data they need.

Tab navigation via keyboard

By default, Tab Controls are mouse-driven. However, you can include a Tab Control into the layout tab order so that users can select it by using the keyboard Tab key, just as they can move between fields on your layouts (see Figure 10.21).

When a tab control has been added to the layout tab order:

■ The first (or default) tab becomes selected when the user tabs to the Tab Control.

■ The right arrow and left arrow keys will select alternate tabs across the top of the selected Tab Control.

■ The Return key or the space bar will bring the currently selected tab to the front.

By default, a Tab Control isn't included in the layout's tab order. However in FileMaker Pro 10, you can insert a Tab Control object — or any other object (such as a field or button) that can receive keyboard focus — into an existing tab order by selecting the arrow next to the object, typing the number corresponding to the desired position in the tab order, and then clicking another arrow or OK on the Set Tab Order dialog. After inserting a number that falls within the sequence of an existing tab order, the object that previously held the same number (the number you entered) is incremented, and all objects that follow it in the preexisting tab order are resequenced to preserve (and increment) their positions within the new tab order.

FIGURE 10.21

Assigning a Tab Control to the layout tab order so it can be selected via the keyboard.

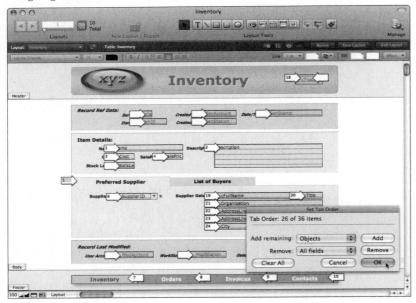

Scripting tab operations

Alternatively, you can provide scripted navigation to take users directly to a specific tab on a given layout. To do this, you must first select the tab panel in layout mode (the tab area of the panel will become outlined in black when it's selected) and assign an object name via the Object Info palette. After you've named the panel, you'll be able to script the selection of a specific tab with a sequence such as

```
Go to Layout ["YourLayout"]
Go to Object ["YourTabPanel"]
```

Similarly, you can build custom menus including menu commands (using FileMaker Pro Advanced) to take the user to specific tabs. To achieve this, a script such as the preceding one should be assigned to a menu selection.

 **For additional information about the use of FileMaker Pro Advanced features, such as custom menus, refer to Chapter 18.**

Recognizing the Flexibility of Portals

FileMaker's portal object is a powerful tool — providing you with the ability to create windows into alternate spaces in your solutions, using them to combine data from multiple tables within a single layout. Portals are also adaptable, enabling you to implement them in a variety of different ways according to the needs of your solution.

Lists in many guises

By default, FileMaker portals present a range of records from a related table, appearing in a continuous list. However, you can specify a commencing row for a portal (other than the first related record), thus creating portal editions and displaying noncontiguous record sets.

Portals can include a scroll bar, configurable to snap back to the first related record (or first record for the current portal) when the record is exited or to remain at the scrolled position. When the scroll bar option is disabled, a portal presents a fixed list of a predetermined number of related records.

By using multiple portals in conjunction with a tab panel, portal displays can be paginated. For example, the first 20 records can be shown on one tab, records 21 to 49 on a second tab, and so on. This can provide a more convenient interface for addressing related records in defined ranges, in situations where the maximum number of records you'll need to display can be predicted.

Portals as a navigation device

A portal row can contain a button so that clicking the row (either a button contained within and sized to occupy the entire row, or a button located at the edge of the row) executes a GTRR command, navigating to the relevant record on another layout. This navigation technique is useful for moving the user between related locations in your solution. By providing a portal based on the current table (for example, via a self-join relationship), a portal can provide an efficient navigation tool for the current table.

When displaying records from the current table in a portal, you should consider how to treat the portal display of the current record. One option is to configure the portal to display all records except the current record. Another option is to display all records and highlight the current record in the portal.

To omit the current record from a self-join portal, you should structure the relationship as a *Cartesian product* (one where all records in the first table are matched with all records in the second table, regardless of the value in the match fields), with an added predicate for a nonequal join (also known as an anti-join), matching the primary key to itself. This compound join criterion will be expressed in the relationship definition as the following (where `TableID` is the primary key for the current table):

```
            TableID        ×        TableID
    AND     TableID        ≠        TableID
```

Alternatively, to highlight the current record in a self-join portal, you first need a method to capture and declare the ID of the current (displayed) record. One such method is to include an expression declaring a global variable (setting it to the primary key of the current record) and including the expression within an object set to evaluate as the layout (displaying the current record) is drawn onscreen. The calculation can be included in an unstored calculation field displayed on the layout, in a Web viewer, or in a conditional formatting argument. The form of the expression declaring the variable will be

```
    Let($$ActiveRecord = YourTable::TableID; "")
```

After the mechanism for capturing the ID of the active record is in place, you can set a conditional formatted object to highlight the portal row with the following formula:

```
    $$ActiveRecord = PortalTO::TableID
```

> **NOTE** The layout object being used to capture the ID of the current record should be set at the back of the layout's stacking order so that it's drawn first, ensuring that its calculation expression is evaluated (and the `ActiveRecord` variable instantiated) prior to evaluating the conditionally formatted object highlighting the portal row.

Dynamically sorted portals

A variety of methods are available for setting up dynamic portal sorting. One of the easiest to configure involves the use of a Tab Control and a series of portals, each configured with a different sorting criterion.

By setting the Tab Control's tabs to match the columns and column widths of the portal, the tabs can serve as portal heading labels. Multiple copies of the portal can then be positioned within each panel of the Tab Control and adjusted to present the related records in the appropriate order. The result is an efficient portal sorting mechanism that's implemented in a matter of minutes.

Innovative portal implementations

Occasionally, a conventional list of related records is a less-than-ideal way to view or interact with related data. For example, calendars are customarily viewed in grids with one week occupying each block in sequential rows of data.

Displays of data requiring grids or matrices call for a little extra ingenuity (and some additional work) in implementing portals on your layouts. To create the effect or a horizontal portal or grid, you can add a series of single-row portals each starting with a different related row. Thus, each separate portal shows one row — a different row — of the data in the related table. These separate "cells" of related data can then be arranged in whatever configuration you choose — according to the seating plan of a theater, according to a calendar of the lunar cycles, according to the grid positions of a football team. . . . All these things and more are possible.

Using Advanced Web Viewer Techniques

In Chapter 6, I introduce the concept of using Web viewers as a way to extend your solution's scope, providing a window into related online information from a company's own Web site or from other online resources. The Web viewer has a number of other potential uses.

Because FileMaker's Web viewer taps directly into the same operating system resources as Web browsers, it provides access to the range of Web-compliant technologies including HTML, JavaScript, CSS, Flash, and others. If you have skills in these or other related areas, the Web viewer allows you to exploit them, and even if you don't, the Web viewer still lets you tap into the vast collections of Internet resources made available by others. I don't propose to go into these fathomless possibilities in great detail — that's not the focus of this book (and there are boundless resources available if you need to explore Web technologies). However, I would like to outline the scope of this FileMaker feature.

Access to advanced functionality

The FileMaker Web viewer can load and display Web-compliant code objects and widgets created with Flash, JavaScript, or other technologies, without needing to load them from a remote site — they can be stored locally. The most obvious way to achieve this is to reference objects as resources stored on a local hard disk. Moreover, FileMaker 10 enables you to store resources as data and output them at start-up to the Temp directory on the current computer. To script this process, you can use the following code (where gSWFresource is a global container field holding a resource file — in this case, a Flash file — that you want to export with the filename, Resource.swf, into the Temp directory):

```
Set Variable [$path; Value:"file:" & Get(TemporaryPath) & "Resource.swf"]
Export Field Contents [Utility::gSWFresource; "$path" ]
```

You can use this technique to make a variety of resources available, including images, to be referenced via Web viewers in your solutions.

After you've created the required resources locally, they can be referenced directly (for example, in a Web viewer) by dynamically inserting path references as URLs, using a calculation construction such as

```
"file:/" & Get(TemporaryPath) & "FileName.xtn"
```

Using these supporting techniques, you can configure a Web viewer to address local resources as well as remote URLs. The ability to so configure a Web viewer becomes much more useful and powerful when you embed references to local or remote resources into source content that your solution generates on demand.

Rendering internally calculated content

When you load a URL into a FileMaker Web viewer, the content of the file at the specified location is retrieved, interpreted, and rendered in the Web viewer. However, FileMaker 10 makes it possible for you to generate content within FileMaker and pass it directly to the Web viewer. For example, you could store the text content of a page of HTML in a text field and have the Web viewer display it.

To pass content directly to the Web viewer (rather than a URL pointing to the location of some content), you need to employ the data URL protocol. Assuming that you've placed the text of a fully formed HTML page in a field called Content in a table in your solution called ViewerData, you're able to load the page into a Web viewer by specifying a Web viewer address as follows:

```
"data:text/html," & ViewerData::Content
```

Because you're calling upon FileMaker's calculation engine to form the syntax of the content to be displayed, however, you can manipulate the HTML source via calculation, or combine elements from a number of fields for the definition of the page to be displayed. For example, to produce a fully formed HTML report based on a tagged report template stored in a global field in your solution, you can use a calculation such as the following:

```
"data:text/html," &
Substitute(SystemData::gReportTemplate;
["«Heading»"; SystemData::CompanyName & " Report"];
["«ReportYear»"; Year(Get(CurrentDate))];
["«Preamble»"; ReportData::Notes]
["«QuarterSum»"; ReportData::QuarterlyRevenue]
["«YTD»"; Sum(Income::AmountReceived)]
["«Projected»"; Sum(Budget::Income)]
)
```

This approach takes a basic, premade page layout (complete with hypertext formatting, links, images, and other content), inserts relevant data from your solution, and passes the result to be displayed in your Web viewer. Moreover, the content of the Web viewer is then linked live to your data via the calculation engine — so in the preceding example, if a staff member on the next floor processes an additional payment, you'll see the Year to Date amount on your dynamic report change to include the additional amount.

Although this example is relatively simple, you can apply the same principles to dynamically modify almost every aspect of the content of a page to be displayed in a Web viewer. You can use variations on this approach to create and display live graphs of your data, dynamic summaries, diaries, calendars — essentially any formatted representation of information in your solution.

Scraping data from Web pages

In addition to enabling you to create displays and render data by sending information directly to the Web viewer, FileMaker provides tools you can use to retrieve data from the Web viewer and store it in fields in your solution. This is the process commonly known as *Web scraping*.

Before attempting to retrieve data from a Web page on a remote Web site, you must first provide the URL of the page you want to "scrape" and ensure that it has fully loaded into a Web viewer in your solution. To start the process, begin a script with a command to load the required Web address, such as the following:

```
Set Web Viewer [Object Name: "YourViewer"; URL: "http://www.RemoteSite.com"]
```

If you attempt to retrieve the content of the Web viewer before the page has fully loaded, you may either get nothing or get only part of the page source. To ensure that the page has fully loaded, pause and check for the presence of the closing body tag (</body>) before proceeding. In case the Internet connection fails or the remote site is not available, you'll require a timeout. Here's an example of a script sequence implementing the required pause and check:

```
Set Variable [$start; Value:Get(CurrentTimeStamp)]
Loop
  Pause/Resume Script [Duration (seconds): .1]
  Set Variable [$html; Value:GetLayoutObjectAttribute("YourViewer"; "content")]
  Set Variable [$elapsed; Value:Get(CurrentTimeStamp) - $start]
  Exit Loop If [PatternCount($html; "</body>") or $elapsed > 9)]
End Loop
If [PatternCount($html; "</body>") < 1]
  Show Custom Dialog ["Timeout Error: Remote site not responding."]
Else
  # $html has been retrieved for processing:
  # etc...
End If
```

When this process runs, as long as the remote site responds within the allotted timeout (in this case, approximately ten seconds), the source of the targeted page will be returned as text via the variable named $html. It can then be parsed for use in your solution.

CAUTION If a process such as this — which may entail a processing delay — will run while users are accessing your solution, it's important to provide ongoing feedback to ensure that they're aware the process is under way. This reduces frustration and avoids situations where users force-quit under the impression that the solution has stopped responding. (In the "Progress Bars and Native Charting Techniques" section, later in this chapter, I suggest some of the ways you might address this requirement.)

To successfully complete the process of retrieving data from a remote site, you need to extract the relevant information from the HTML source returned by the previous script sequence. To do that successfully, first examine the HTML content to locate elements that identify the location of the information you require.

If, for example, your script is automatically retrieving a list of movies shown at a local chapter clubhouse, as posted on its Web site, it's likely that the information you require will routinely follow the segment of text `Now Showing:<big><b>` and will always immediately be followed by `</b></big><br>`. In that case, the required calculation expression to retrieve the name of the currently showing movie will be

```
Let([
p1 = Position($html; "Now Showing:<big><b>"; 1; 1) + 20;
p2 = Position($html; "</b></big><br>"; p1; 1)];
Middle($html; p1; p2 - p1)
)
```

By adding a `Set Field [ ]` command configured to write the result of the preceding calculation into a field in your solution, you'll complete the process so that each time the script runs, the name of the current movie feature will be retrieved and stored in your solution.

While the example used here involves a single piece of information (which you can look up and copy/paste into your solution without a great deal more time or trouble), you can use the same procedure to automate complex processes where hundreds of items are retrieved at intervals throughout the day or night, saving a great deal of labor and bringing significant benefits to your users. Alternatively, you could be extracting image source (`IMG SRC`) hyperlink references to retrieve a graphic associated with the data, such as a book cover thumbnail from Amazon or a product image from an online catalog.

Progress Bars and Native Charting Techniques

User feedback is always a good idea, but when your solution runs a process that takes more than a few seconds, it's essential. Without it, the user is left hanging, wondering what's going on and worrying that the solution is nonresponsive. At best, users will become frustrated; at worst, they'll force-quit or restart, interrupting the process partway and risking damage to the solution files.

You can provide user feedback in many ways, some of which are very simple to implement. For example, you can post a dialog before a lengthy process begins, saying, "This may take a while — please come back after your coffee break." However, contriving a form of feedback that stays in place while the process is ongoing, providing a clear indication that the process is active, and that gives some indication of the state of the process and how much longer it has to run, is even better.

Creating script progress monitors

One of the simplest ways to display a dynamic progress indicator is to show a window, such as the one in Figure 10.22, with a percentage-complete updating as the task progresses.

A simple numeric progress indicator in a floating FileMaker window.

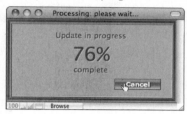

To update a percentage-complete progress indicator, first you need to estimate the size of the task being undertaken and then update the display at intervals to indicate how much has been completed. Many intensive and time-consuming scripting tasks involve repetitive processing (for example, when looping through a series of records). The following is an example of a looping script used to control a progress display while summing the values in the found set:

```
Set Variable [$task; Value:Get(FoundCount)]
Set Field [System::gProgressPercent; 0]
New Window [Name: "Processing: please wait..."; Height: 200; Width: 370; Top:
   Get(WindowTop) + 120; Left: Get(WindowLeft) + 350]
Go to Layout ["ProgressIndicator" (Meetings)]
Set Zoom Level [Lock; 100%]
Show/Hide Status Area [Lock; Hide]
Adjust Window [Resize to Fit]
Freeze Window
Loop
  Set Variable [$summary; Value:$summary + Meetings::Attendees -
  Count(Apologies::Serial#)]
  Set Variable [$completed; Value:Int(Get(RecordNumber) / $task * 100)]
  If [$completed > System::gProgressPercent]
    Set Field [System::gProgressPercent; $completed]
    Refresh Window
  End If
  Go to Record/Request/Page [Next; Exit after last]
End Loop
Set Field [Person::Frequency; $summary]
Close Window [Name: "Processing: please wait..."; Current file]
```

With a few added steps, the preceding script maintains a record of its progress in a global number field (`System::gProgressPercent`), with the result displayed onscreen as an incrementing percentage complete. Although this technique is not difficult to implement, with very little additional effort, a variety of other attractive progress indicators are possible.

For solutions that will be deployed in a mixed environment, a graphical progress indicator can be created relatively simply. For example, to create a text-based progress bar, you can create a global calculation field with a formula such as

```
Substitute(10^System::gProgressPercent - 1; "9"; "|")
```

The preceding formula will return a row of pipe characters (|) representing the percentage completion of the process task (as per the incrementing number in the `System::gProgressPercent` field). By stacking several copies of the field (offset by 1 pixel), applying transparent fill, and using bold condensed text format, the appearance of a solid bar can be produced, as shown in Figure 10.23.

FIGURE 10.23

A text-based progress bar in a floating FileMaker window.

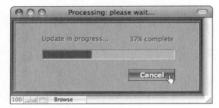

If your solution will be accessed only by using FileMaker 9 or FileMaker 10, several additional possibilities are available for the creation of graphical progress indicators, using either conditional formatting or a Web viewer.

Native indicators and graphical displays

The FileMaker 10 Web viewer alternative for creating progress indicators provides an excellent example of the ease with which data can be displayed visually using Web technologies. The progress indicator shown in Figure 10.24 uses a small rectangular Web viewer in place of the text field used in the previous example.

To create the progressive movement of the indicator, the relative widths of two cells in an HTML table are varied according to the value in the `System::gProgressPercent` global field. The table cells can have graphic backgrounds (using standard HTML tags), including animated GIFs if desired. The result is aesthetically pleasing, while having a very light footprint. The essence of the calculation code used to implement this (enclosed within a standard HTML table with a single row) is:

```
"<td height=\"17\" width=\"" & System::gProgressPercent * 2 & "\"> </td>
<td height=\"17\" width=\"" & 200 - System::gProgressPercent * 2 & "\"> </td>"
```

FIGURE 10.24

A Web viewer progress bar in a floating FileMaker window.

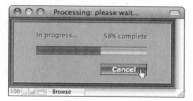

A further advantage of the Web viewer progress-bar technique is that the same viewer can be used to display other kinds of indicators — such as a barber's pole indicator for processes of indeterminate duration, or a variety of other animations, using Web-based image manipulations.

A wide variety of other graphical renderings of FileMaker data can easily be created using variations and alternate applications of this technique. As discussed in the section "Rendering internally calculated content," earlier in this chapter, graphs and live data visualizations can be achieved by making use of the data URL capabilities of the Web Viewer object.

Using Interface Elements

Being different and challenging prevailing wisdom is fashionable, but it isn't always wise. Computer users have become accustomed to a number of ways of interacting with computer applications, and collectively, these familiar patterns form a language. You, as a solution developer, use this language to communicate with your users, and they communicate (impart information) in response. Users do not want or need to learn a new interface vocabulary for every new computer application.

A number of widely understood user interface elements are common to most modern applications. Because they're familiar in function and (often) in operation, standard interface techniques can provide guideposts, focusing the users' attention on the tasks they're supposed to perform.

Splash screens

The splash screen provides a first point of reference, often appearing as an application is first launched. The splash screen performs a welcoming and orienting function — letting the user know he is entering your solution and providing the context for what is to follow. As a first impression, the splash screen sets the standard for your solution.

It is of most help to the user if your splash screen is distinctive in appearance and contains brief essentials about version, authorship, and support of your application. Including ownership, copyright, and/or brief acknowledgments on the splash screen is customary. However, avoid clutter and stick to essentials.

Users should be able to return to the splash screen at any time if they want to check the information set out there (for example, the solution version). After doing so, users should be returned to the place (screen or menu) they left.

Main menus

All but the simplest of solutions have too many functions for users to remember all at once. Ideally, users should be presented with no more than five or six choices at any one time. Any more than that and users have to work much harder to keep track of what the options do.

You can make it easier for users to find their way around your solution by grouping controls into broad logical categories. When you've done that, you'll have the essence of a main menu. How you present that to users is a matter of style; users will rapidly adapt to your style provided it has clear logical underpinnings and you're consistent in its usage.

I recommend that all your decisions about the grouping of functions and controls in your interfaces be based on the way users do their work. The system should follow the natural workflow, minimizing the frequency with which users must switch between sections/modules during a work session. You may find it helpful to consider your interface as a series of interconnected role-based modules.

As a general principle, users should always be able to return to familiar territory with a single click of the mouse, and they should always be able to tell where they are.

About and version info

Although I've mentioned that splash screens often incorporate vendor, copyright, and version information, providing this information separately can make sense. A simple menu command can be invoked (for example, returning a custom dialog) to set out authorship, version, and support information. Doing so leaves the splash screen less cluttered and creates a more positive impression. If you want, a link or button on the splash screen can invoke the version information.

Online Help for your users

I encourage you to consider providing built-in documentation for your solutions. In many cases, the extent of documentation required to get users started and answer basic questions is not great, and, if the system design conforms to intuitive principles, users may only infrequently have to call to check the documentation. Providing answers to the top 10 or 20 questions that a user may ask goes a long way toward building confidence in your solution and your work.

Ideally, because FileMaker is so good at managing data, your support documentation should be made available as a searchable database within your solution. This has the advantage that it can be readily updated and can provide a facility for users to make notes and additions or ask questions. However, the documentation should also be available in a printed format or PDF and, preferably, generated fresh from your solution's Help database on request.

A further option to consider is providing Help content via a Web viewer, where the source documentation is hosted remotely. This approach can have a number of advantages, allowing the developer to update and extend the documentation as questions are asked, problems are solved, or changes are made to the solution.

Handling User Preferences

The best solutions are those that directly respond to the needs of the user, providing a tool to accelerate productivity. However, unless you create solutions for only one user, you have the dilemma of reconciling competing users' needs and preferences.

The ideal answer to many competing requests and concerns is to accommodate a variety of system behaviors by enabling users to control how some features work. When you do this, be sure to structure your solution so that it keeps track of the selections made by each user, reinstating them automatically when the user returns.

A user-centric development philosophy

One of the essential purposes of most solutions (including, but not limited to, FileMaker solutions) is to free users from a variety of mundane and repetitive actions or tasks. Many solutions, however, bring with them a host of new mundane and repetitive tasks, specifically because the developer does not understand how the users want to get from point A to point B.

One answer is to have the developer watch users to determine repetitive sequences of tasks and build the solution around the emerging patterns. Another approach is to build flexibility into the interface and permit users to select how the solution will operate.

Capturing state by user

To capture information about users' preferences and their use of your solution, I recommend you include a users table, with a record automatically created for each login account. The users table provides a place to store preference settings for each user so that when the user logs in again (whether from the same or a different workstation), your login script can locate the user record, retrieve the user's preference settings, and configure the solution accordingly.

A convenient way to manage this process is to

1. Load the user's account name (after login credentials have been accepted) into a global key field.
2. Use a GTRR to isolate the corresponding record in the user table.
3. Load the preference settings into global fields. Because global fields can be accessed without a relationship, the user preferences will be available for read and write from anywhere in your solution throughout the user's login session.

4. Restore the state (selected layout and record) where the user last left the solution. In most solutions, this step should be optional — the user should be able to select whether he wants his logout state restored on next login — and this should be stored as one of the user preference settings.

At the conclusion of the user's session (either logout or file close) your scripts should capture the current state and return to the user table to write the current contents of the preference and state global fields back to the appropriate record in the user table.

Example — a multi-lingual solution interface

One of the most profound kinds of user preferences is language. Many solutions are used by people who speak different languages and who require (or desire) an interface that speaks their language. Although I've seen a number of methods used to create multi-lingual interfaces, most of them require many additional relationships; some stop working when the user enters Find mode and may make working in Layout mode a chore. Here is a method that avoids these problems.

The technique I recommend entails some extra work during development, but after it's in place, providing support for additional languages requires only an additional record in the language resource table. The technique adds two tables to your solution, but they don't have to be related to anything else (just to each other), and no other relationships are required. Moreover, field labels remain reasonably compact and intelligible in Layout mode.

To implement a multilingual interface, follow these steps:

1. Gather a list of the fields, headings, labels, tooltips, dialog messages, window titles, and other text elements required throughout your solution.

2. Create a table called LanguageResources with a primary key (LanguageID), a LanguageName field, and a flag field (container type), plus one text field for every entry in your list from Step 1. Name each field with the logical name (in your own native language) of the element to which it corresponds.

3. Create two or more records in the LanguageResources table, entering the appropriate translations of the element names and text into their respective fields.

4. Create a table named **I**. The uppercase I stands for Interface but is abbreviated for compactness.

5. In the I table, create a global field called gLanguageID, of the same data type as the LanguageID field in the LanguageResources table.

6. Create a relationship from I::gLanguageID to LanguageResources:: LanguageID.

7. For every field in the `LanguageResources` table, create a corresponding field in the I table, making the I field a global calculation field with the following formula (where the field in question is `I::FirstName`):

   `Evaluate("LanguageResources::FirstName"; gLanguageID)`

8. Create a value list called `InterfaceLanguages` and define it to use values from a field. Configure the value list to draw values from the `LanguageResources::LanguageID` and `LanguageResources::LanguageName` fields and to show values only from the second field, as illustrated in Figure 10.25.

9. On your user preference screens (and elsewhere as appropriate), place the `I::g LanguageID` field and attach the `InterfaceLanguages` value list.

10. Adjacent to the `I::LanguageID` field, place the `I::LanguageFlag` field so that the selected language will be identified with a corresponding national flag (for the benefit of those not familiar with the language names).

11. Configure the layouts throughout your solution with labels next to them in the form `<<I::FirstName>>` where the field in question is called `FirstName` (as shown in Figure 10.26).

12. For all window titles and dialog messages, reference the relevant field in the I table.

13. Create a field in your user table for preferred language.

FIGURE 10.25

Configuration for the `InterfaceLanguages` value list.

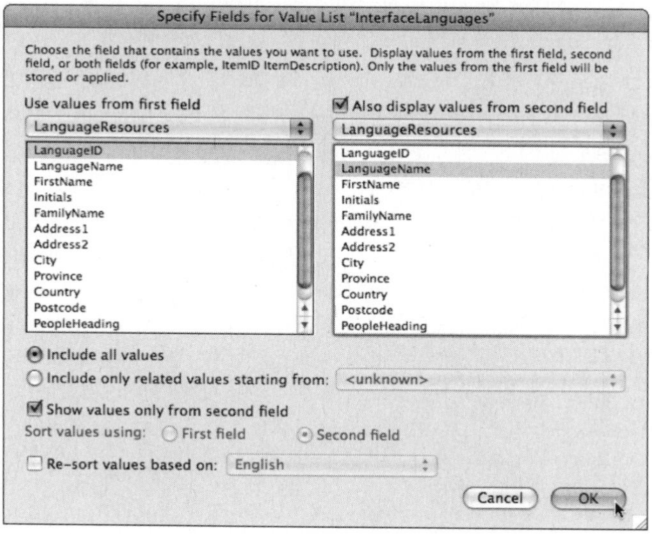

FIGURE 10.26

The format for field labels and headings in Layout mode.

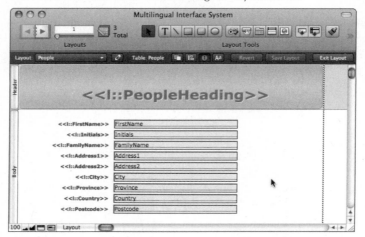

14. Script a prompt for preferred language the first time each user logs in.

15. Set your login script to write the ID of the user's preferred language into the `I::gLanguageID` field.

16. Set your logout and file close scripts to write the current value of the `I::gLanguageID` field into the `LanguagePreference` field of the current user's table. If the user changes interface language preference during the session, the change will be remembered.

Whenever the user makes a new selection in the `I::gLanguageID` field, all the text on the layouts throughout your solution's interface of your solution's layouts changes to the new language selection.

TIP If you require the window title to change when a new language selection is made, you have to script the language change procedure and reset the window title according to the user's new language selection.

The field labels, headings, and so on will be present in both Find and Browse modes. In Layout mode, however, you can readily read and work with the labels, and adding more languages only requires an additional record in the LanguageResources table.

NOTE Although the language selection will control layout and custom dialog text, FileMaker's native dialogs will continue to display text in the language chosen at the operating system level. For a full language makeover, system preferences must be updated as well.

CAUTION FileMaker doesn't provide an option to programmatically specify the button text for custom dialogs, so if your solution will require language specific dialog button labels, you'll require a workaround. One option is to create separately specified dialogs for each language (where the button text is required to be language-sensitive) and use conditional statements within your scripts to select the dialog that corresponds to the current language choice. Another way you can address this is to invoke dialogs via external script calls (using AppleScript on Mac OS, VBScript in Windows) or by using a third-party dialog plug-in.

CROSS-REF For additional discussion of the use of external scripting and third-party plug-ins, refer to Chapter 20.

For international vertical market, runtime, or shrink-wrapped solutions, consider verifying the current operating system language using Get (SystemLanguage) during your solution's on-open script, and making a corresponding language selection as the commencing (default) language for your solution.

Chapter 11

Data Modeling in FileMaker

FileMaker is as much a problem-solving tool as it is a development platform. As such, it provides you with the means to achieve a wide variety of ends (and in the process, solve many problems). How you use the tools FileMaker makes available is less important than the functionality your solutions are able to deliver. Nevertheless, considering the underpinnings of a well-formed relational data model is helpful — not so much so that you will be bound to adhere rigidly to it, but so that you'll be able to make informed choices about how and when to depart from it.

Regardless how you choose to work in FileMaker, you need a clear plan for the storage of data, including the main connections and interactions between different data types. This over-arching plan is your data model. It doesn't matter where it exists — it could be in your solution itself, on a whiteboard in your office, on a diagram in your diary, or a vision in your imagination. However, without such a plan, little will work well, and your solutions will quickly become mired in confusion and complexity.

A data model's purpose is to establish clarity and simplicity, enabling you to see — from any vantage point — what belongs where, and how to bring together the available elements to achieve required outcomes.

Background in Relational Theory

Modern database applications — including FileMaker — take a set of ideas based on the theoretical work of Edgar F. Codd (first made public in 1970, while Codd was working at IBM) as a starting point for implementation of a relational data management model. Databases implementing Codd's central ideas are commonly referred to as *Relational Database Management Systems* (RDMS). Although relational principles are now widely used, no commercially available RDBMS fully implements the detailed model articulated by Codd and his colleagues.

IN THIS CHAPTER

Understanding relational theory

Recognizing the FileMaker Relationships Graph symbols

Using relationship operators

Exploring different relationship techniques

Working with data sets and arrays

Managing your Relationships Graphs

Documenting the structure of your database

Working with layers in your solution

Understanding the differences between file architecture and data structure

Using separation and external SQL sources

Implementing separation retroactively

Considering deployment

An essential tenet of data theories (including relational theory) is that data form part of a model of the universe. Each datum describes (accurately or otherwise) something in the universe. Thus, an organized data collection represents a model of the universe (and this is true, whether or not the organizers of the data recognize it).

The shortcomings, such as they are, of computer implementations of relational data management concepts are due in part to pragmatism. In other words, rather than exhaustively modeling all the intricacies of the universe, real-world system designers introduce compromises for various reasons. Some of the reasons for compromise (economy, expediency, and business imperatives) are more admirable than others (ignorance or carelessness).

Despite Codd's efforts — publishing dozens of papers on the relational model between 1968 and 1988 — myths and misconceptions about its central tenets abound.

Set Theory in the management of data

When you collect and manage data (by whatever means), you're collecting many facts to describe the properties of an entity or class of entities. In the simplest analysis, you have sets of facts about sets of things, which gives rise to the forms of tables where rows and columns organize things and the facts about them, respectively.

An essential problem when the information you require pertains to more than one kind of thing is that you then have multiple sets of data comprising part of a whole. For example, you can consider an organized group of facts about people and an organized group of facts about houses a unified fact set when it becomes clear that people live in houses. At this point, 19th-century posits regarding Set Theory (first proposed by Georg Cantor) provide a way to resolve seeming conflicts in the organization of complex data.

By using an organizing principle where facts about things (attributes of entities) are organized into tables (one table per entity) and the relationships between those entities are expressed or managed mathematically (which people live in which houses), you can model relationships in the real world. This insight is at the heart of Codd's genius.

Giving form to this concept are the applications of ratio principles to describe relations as one-to-one (1:1), one-to-many (1:n), many to one (n:1), or many to many (m:n), and the concept of join types such as the equi-join (=) and others describing the kinds of relationships between entities within different tables (sets and subsets). These abstract concepts rapidly acquire concrete meaning and usefulness within applications, such as FileMaker, where they enable you to solve problems organizing your data.

Modeling the real world

To model the world (or, at any rate, a part of it) using relational principles, you first need to be clear about the entities each group of facts pertains to. Using the example of people and houses, you may have a number of facts about each person, such as an address. In this simple scenario, you have two entities (each requiring a table) and a relationship between them (based on people's residency). Because more than one person may live at a house, the relationship from houses to people may be one-to-many. By breaking information down into entities and defining relationships between them, you establish a relational model of the real-world "things" your database describes.

A relational solution's data organization centers around using tables to hold information about each class of item (object, thing, or entity). Each row in the table holds all the information about a particular instance of the kind of item, and each column holds a particular fact about the thing. For example, if you have a people table, each person has a single row in the table, and each column holds a different kind of fact, such as eye color, date of birth, sex, and so on. A separate table about vehicle models may have columns for engine capacity, number of seats, manufacturer, paint color, and so on.

Think about clarity of organization

When applying the concept of relational modeling to your data, the first step is to separate different kinds of entities and to group fundamentally similar entities. The purpose of this exercise is to gain clarity about what belongs where — confusion at this first stage leads to conflicts in the data model. An *entity* is a "thing in the modeled universe," so people, vehicles, houses, and jobs are all entities of different kinds.

CAUTION **Don't describe different kinds of entities within the same table. Vehicles don't belong in a people table, for example. Similarly, you should avoid describing different attributes in the same column within a table — for example, in a people table, eye color doesn't belong in the date of birth column, and vice versa. In addition, don't separate fundamentally similar entities into different tables. You don't need to put sports cars in one table and sedans in another — rather, they're all vehicles, and chassis type is one of their attributes, so it's properly represented as a column in the vehicle table. Similarly, you don't require a separate table for people with brown eyes, as eye color is clearly one of the attributes of a person and should be represented as data in a column of a people table.**

Keep the big picture in view

Although in simple examples the choices may appear obvious, other times the decision isn't so clear or easy. For example, if you're designing a college database, you may think it's reasonable to have separate tables for staff and students — and many such implementations are in existence. However, all of them produce anomalies when a staff member enrolls in a class or a student is offered employment at the college. (The "solution" then involves creating a duplicate record for that person and then manually keeping the two records in sync by entering everything twice.) This situation is one example of how a departure from one of the central principles of relational design can lead to confusion and burden you with extra work.

In the college database example, an alternative data model, in keeping with relational principles, is to create three tables, not two. Instead of having two marginally different people tables for staff and students, you could create tables for people, enrollments, and job roles, which then allows you to have a single table for all people, with associated records in either or both of the related tables. By the time a college expands its data requirements to keep track of donors, alumni, governors, and visiting fellows (at which point some individuals may require six separate entries if each type of person is in a separate table), it becomes clear that storing each of these associated characteristics as an attribute of a single record in the `People` table — with an associated table for accompanying details or donations, visits, enrollments, and so on — is preferable.

Data structures are a way of describing reality. If, in reality, one person may be associated with several different kinds of roles, a data model in which a single person's record is associated with role records in a number of related tables more accurately reflects reality.

NOTE   Any discussion of relational data modeling principles can rapidly descend into a minefield of purist ideologies, conflicting interpretations, debates about "normal forms," and deeper esoterica. However, my interest here is to provide guiding insights and practical advice. A wealth of specialist resources exists for those who want to explore the intricacies of relational theory.

Remembering some guiding principles

You need to be clear about the reasons for modeling data in a particular way. The central purposes of relational modeling are clarity, simplicity, accuracy, and efficiency in managing the data (and, incidentally, in representing the reality the data seeks to describe).

One essential way a good relational model achieves these aims is by storing each piece of information only once (while providing access to it as needed, via data relationships). If your solution has multiple people tables, then almost inevitably, you'll end up having multiple records for some people. As soon as this event happens, the following occur:

- **Efficiency** is compromised because data must be updated in two different places every time a change occurs.

- **Accuracy** suffers because of the risk that data will be updated in some places but not others. In other words, the potential for data integrity problems is increased.

- **Clarity** is reduced because it's no longer obvious where to go to locate a particular piece of information — and because when the information in alternate parts of the system differs, it's not clear which is correct.

- **Simplicity** is eroded as increasing numbers of duplicate records move the data farther away from a representation of reality, and system users are burdened with additional work, such as the need to search in multiple tables to find data about a person, collate multiple reports to summarize all information about one person, or aggregate information about all persons. In such cases, working with the system involves negotiating burgeoning lists of exceptions.

There are good reasons for investing your time and effort in clarifying data relationships early in the solution design process. Of course, one solution isn't necessarily right for all cases, and you must make your own judgments about how and when to apply the principles I outline in the following sections. You should note, however, that the principles I am about to outline apply to the data model rather than to specific fields and tables as you define them within FileMaker Pro — I address details of schema design principles subsequently.

Separate entities by type

Relational principles are best served by creating separate tables for each basic kind of entity, with fields (columns) only for the attributes reasonably expected to apply to all the table's entities. Similarly, you should consolidate information about essentially similar entities in one table.

CAUTION Although you may be tempted to view the methodology described here as absolute, form your decisions with due consideration of the importance and purpose of each kind of entity in relation to the business at hand.

For example, in a sales system, you may want to treat everything being sold as the same kind of entity, storing it in the Products table. In a social club database, however, cars may belong in a Vehicles table, whereas trampolines belong in a Facilities table. In yet another kind of solution, both cars and trampolines may belong in an Assets table. You should consider an entity's basic nature, as well as its purpose, in context.

Delineate fields clearly

Each field in a table should hold a specific kind of fact, such as a date, color, or measurement, about the entity described in the table. Try to minimize fields with general names like Appearance or Facts, which are so nonspecific that they could hold all sorts of different kinds of information. Try to minimize reliance on Notes, Comments or Other fields in each table.

TIP Your users may insist on including a Notes or Comments field, and if so, I encourage you to consider doing so. If you have modeled the users' data requirements effectively, however, such ancillary fields will prove superfluous. (Take it as a measure of your success when such fields are largely or entirely unused.)

Place multiples in a separate table

Frequently, multiple instances of an attribute for a particular entity are an indication that the attribute should instead be classed as an associated entity and should be in a table of its own (with a relationship to the current table). For example, where students may enroll in a variety of classes, it's clear that enrollments aren't a student attribute; instead, they belong in a separate table.

As part of separating multiples, storing abstract objects, such as ownership or association, in separate tables is often desirable. For example, if you have a table of people and a table of car models, you may find that one person can own multiple vehicles (at once, or over time), in which case you may want to create a separate table where the multiple cars for each individual are recorded (one record for each). This kind of table is sometimes referred to as a *join table* or an *association table*. An enrollment table is a good example because it joins a student with courses or classes.

CROSS-REF I discuss techniques for implementing join tables — along with other methods of managing multiple related values — in the section "Alternative Relationship Techniques," later in this chapter.

Store everything once only

An objective of successful relational data modeling is that it allows you to store each piece of information only once, yet refer to it from multiple locations within the solution. One benefit of achieving this goal is that when information is updated via one part of your solution interface, the modified information then appears everywhere else the information is referenced.

A successful data model, therefore, is one where you can store each piece of information only once, where it's clear where the information should reside, and where the single instance of each piece of information can nevertheless be accessed wherever required throughout your solution.

Identify the major players

In addition to the practical steps outlined in the preceding sections, I encourage you to discover the centers around which your solution's processes or workflow revolve. Most solutions have several centers, while a few have only one. While it's likely you'll identify a number of entities requiring tables in your solution, knowing which tables are the main focus points for the activities your solution supports greatly aids the clarity of your model.

Put it into practice

A key to successful data design — in FileMaker or any other application — is establishing a clear understanding about the nature of the information to be stored and accessed and the relationships between its elements. By applying the broad guidelines outlined in the preceding sections, you arrive at a map of the data your solution must support. The exercise I propose here is designed to help you to get clear about the data model for your solution, prior to commencing implementation in FileMaker Pro. Hence, at this preliminary stage, your outline is necessarily somewhat abstract. In the ensuing sections, you give concrete form to a data framework supporting your data model, using the relational toolset provided by FileMaker.

FileMaker Relationships Graph Symbols

The FileMaker Relationships Graph — as a spatial and visual metaphor for the data structure — provides you with an environment where you can give form to your solution's data architecture. Nevertheless, given the practical and procedural implications for your solution's operation, the Relationships Graph is more an implementation tool than a visual model. Moreover, as your solution becomes more complex, essentials of the data model are obscured (on the Graph) as it becomes increasingly crowded with components serving functional, rather than structural, purposes.

To make best use of the Graph and the tools it provides for creating and managing data relationships, you need a deep understanding of the way each of its components fit together.

Visual cues and clues

The Graph presents a collection of miniaturized table icons commonly called *Table Occurrences* (TOs) that are aliases or pointers to tables, not the actual tables. This is an essential distinction. Several TOs can point to the same base table, and TO names need not relate in any way to the names you've assigned to the underlying tables.

> **TIP** Because TOs aren't tables, as such, the Tables panel in the Manage Database dialog provides more direct insight into the data structure. However, bear in mind that in a multi-file solution, some or all of the tables may be defined in other files.

The lines connecting TOs on the Graph represent relationships and are drawn between the operative key fields in the tables represented by the TOs they join. However, FileMaker displays different line endings according to the status of the field at each end of the relationship.

Figure 11.1 shows four relationships between a Main table and a Related table, where a different Main field is used as the key field for each relation. Note that the lines all end in the "crows foot" terminator where they connect to the Related~ TOs. This terminator signifies that the connection to Related is valid and capable of supporting a ~to-many (1:n or m:n) join to records in the Related table. The two determinants of this status are

1. The match field in Related ("Key") is indexed (or indexable), thus supporting the retrieval of record data from the Related table via this relationship.

2. There is no constraint or mechanism for uniqueness of the match field's values.

In the Main TO, however, the line terminators show as

- A straight line connecting to the Serial# field, because the field is set to auto-generate unique numbers

- A terminal line connecting to cUnstored because the field is an unstored calculation and therefore can't be indexed (so retrieval of record data from Main via this connection isn't supported)

- A terminal line connecting to gGlobal because, as a global field, it also can't be indexed and doesn't support retrieval of record data from Main

- A crows-foot line connecting to Main::Indexed because it's an indexable and (potentially) non-unique data field supporting retrieval of record data from Main

These line terminators provide visual clues to the operative abilities of each of the relationships, according to the definitions of the fields they connect. The crows-foot symbol doesn't signify that a relationship *is* used to support a ~to-many join, but merely that it *may* be.

Bisecting each relationship line on the Graph is a small, white box displaying a join symbol describing the kind of relationship. By default, the join symbol is an equal sign (=), as shown in Figure 11.1.

FIGURE 11.1

Alternative relationship line representations.

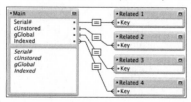

 The relationship operators and their uses are explained in the upcoming section "Relationship Operators."

The TO as a pointer

Because TOs aren't actually tables but pointers to tables, you can refer to the same table in multiple ways or in multiple places on the graph. By using separate TOs for multiple references to a table, you avoid circular references so that there is never more than one relationship path between any two TOs on the Graph, thus avoiding referential ambiguity.

Because you can have multiple instances of the same table on the Graph, you can establish multiple views of the content of the same table. For example, by setting up a relationship based on a field holding the current date, you can display all of today's transactions in a portal. At the same time, a relationship to the `Transactions` table on status will give you a portal display of outstanding payments. Meanwhile, in the `Customer` table, you may require a filtered view of transactions for each customer. By creating three separate TOs, each a pointer to the `Customer` table, you're able to connect in different ways (and from different places on your graph) to the same underlying table.

Similarly, the ability to add multiple occurrences of a table enables you to connect a table to itself. For example, you may want to show fellow team members in a portal on a staff member's record. Joining two TOs of the relevant table (for example, matching `TeamID` in both TOs) achieves this goal.

Understanding the graph metaphor

The FileMaker Relationships Graph may contain elements of your data model, but it must also contain a variety of functional and procedural elements supporting interface requirements and process logic in and around those parts supporting the data model. If you try to use the Graph as the locus of your data design, you risk becoming mired in a mass of extraneous information.

 A more extensive discussion of alternative graph modeling techniques appears in the section "Graph Techniques — Spiders, Squids, and Anchor Buoy," later in this chapter.

Two alternative ways to consider the Relationships Graph are

- As a map of data flows and data controls
- As a context diagram linking interface to data structure

In either case, choose a TO as the current TO, and the Graph becomes instructional for data availability, access to records and tables, and related options possibilities and constraints from the current layout's vantage point.

Relationship Operators

FileMaker creates relationships displaying an = symbol by default. The symbol is referred to as the relationship operator and indicates the type of join. The = symbol signifies a type of join referred to as an *equi-join,* where the relationship is based on matching values on opposing sides of the join. Only records with the same value in the fields in both tables used for the relationship will be related.

> **NOTE** The fields used in relationships are commonly referred to as *match fields* or *key fields.* The unique ID field used to identify the records in a table is often referred to as the *Primary Key* in that table. A Primary Key from another table may be referred to as a *foreign key.*

The equi-join is one of seven relationship operators supported in FileMaker. To change the default "=" operator to one of the other alternatives, you must edit the relationship. For an existing relationship, double-click the symbol box bisecting the relationship line to view the Edit Relationship dialog. As shown in Figure 11.2, a drop-down list in the upper center of the dialog (between the two field lists for the connected TOs) gives you access to the alternative operators.

FIGURE 11.2

Accessing alternative relationship operators in the Edit Relationship dialog.

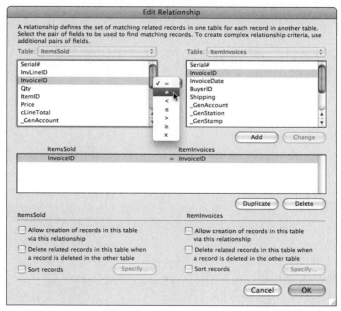

Each relationship operator engenders different relationship behavior, giving you the capability to filter and connect data to serve a variety of purposes, as detailed in the following sections.

Equi-joins and non-equal joins

Most relationships are based on exactly matching values in the connected fields in both tables and therefore use the equi-join (=) operator. FileMaker looks up the value in the current record of the current table in the index of values for the matching field in the related table and returns records having a matching index entry.

Because the matching process uses the field index of the related table, the indexing method chosen for the field(s) used in the relationship affects the way matching occurs. Thus, the data type, such as whether it's text or number, is significant, because numbers and text are indexed differently. To achieve expected results, the key fields on both sides of a relationship should be of the same data type.

If you're using text fields for a relationship, alternative indexing protocols are available (via the Options for Field dialog's Storage tab). For example, if you choose English language indexing, relationship matches aren't case sensitive (although punctuation and spaces are still observed when matching), whereas if you choose Unicode as the indexing protocol, full-case sensitivity is observed in relationship matching. Conversely, if you choose Default text indexing, accented characters are differentiated from unaccented equivalents, but matching is not case sensitive.

TIP The text index protocol for the key field in the related table determines the method of matching.

For many purposes, you'll require relationships matching key values (for example, to link invoice items to an invoice or courses to a study program). In most cases, text matches based on the native language of your solution (for example, English) will suffice. However, note that indexing in external SQL tables is generally case-sensitive by default.

CROSS-REF For an in-depth discussion of indexing and its implications, refer to Chapter 9.

FileMaker also provides an inverse of the equi-join, in the form of the not-equal join operator (≠), also known as the anti-join. This operator makes a join for all records in the related table key field values (including an empty value) that *don't* match the key field value in the current record. On the other hand, an empty key field value in the current record will not match any related records, even though the empty value in the current record does not match non-empty values in the related key field.

Note regarding theta joins in relational algebra

In relational algebra, the category of joins known as *theta joins* also includes the equi-join and anti-join. In common parlance, however, the term is frequently reserved for those members of the join set other than equi- and anti-joins.

Comparative operators (theta joins)

FileMaker provides four comparative operators (commonly referred to as *theta joins*), represented by the less-than (<), greater-than (>), less-or-equal (≤), and greater-or-equal (≥) symbols, enabling you to establish relationships based on a range of values.

Using the available comparative operators, you can make use of range-based joins with text, number, date, time, and timestamp data types, creating relationships for uses such as the following:

- Identifying records with a due date prior to the current date (in other words, overdue)
- Listing records with a family name in the range m to z
- Displaying records of customers with more than $200 outstanding

Cartesian joins

The last of the seven relationship operators is the Cartesian product operator (×), which provides a join where all records in one table are matched to all records in the other, regardless of the values (or lack of values) in the match fields. For this type of relationship, the selection of key fields is immaterial, as their contents are ignored. In fact, if the fields chosen for the relationship are subsequently deleted, the relationship will nonetheless continue to function.

Cartesian product relationships (also referred to as a cross-join) are useful for relationships used to aggregate whole-of-table data (for example, returning the Max( ) and Min( ) values for a related table), for portal navigation where users will select from all available records, and a variety of purposes, such as reference tables, preference tables, or logs, where access to a continuous data display is desired.

Multi-predicate relationships

FileMaker supports *multi-predicate* (sometimes also called *multi-criteria*) relationships where you select more than one pair of key fields to define the join. The effect of multiple predicates is cumulative — all the matches must be satisfied for the join to be valid, meaning that only AND predicate operators are permitted.

Multi-predicate relationships are created in the Edit Relationship dialog by selecting additional pairs of match fields (and an associated operator) and clicking the Add button, as shown in Figure 11.3.

The relationship definition shown in Figure 11.3 is the one used for filtering a portal of contacts by name and contact type in the Inventory example file, as discussed in Chapter 9. However, multi-predicate relationships have many other uses. For example, you can use a relationship definition to locate records with dates falling between two dates:

```
          ItemDate      >   StartDate
    AND   ItemDate      <   EndDate
```

Multi-predicate relationships employing a mix of different operators are represented in the Relationships Graph by the generic dyadic operator, as shown in Figure 11.4.

FIGURE 11.3

Defining a multi-predicate relationship in the Edit Relationship dialog.

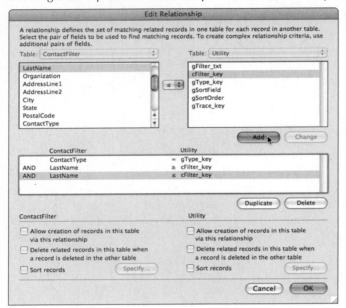

FIGURE 11.4

The dyadic operator representing a mixed-operator, multi-predicate join.

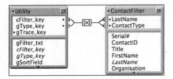

Alternative Relationship Techniques

Frequently, FileMaker offers you a variety of methods to achieve similar outcomes. That's certainly the case when working with relationships, where you can use other means to produce many of the effects you can achieve with different relationship operators and multi-predicate joins.

In the interests of an expanded toolkit of relationship management techniques, here is a brief survey of alternative techniques.

Multi-Key fields

When you enter more than one line of text into a text field (separated by earriage returns), FileMaker treats each line as a separate value. Related records that match either value (in accordance with the relationship operator) are deemed valid. Key fields holding more than one value are termed *Multi-Key fields*.

Because any value in a list of values (in a relationship key field) will provide a match, Multi-Key fields provide one mechanism to support one-to-many or many-to-many joins. Moreover, because multiple value matches occur simultaneously, Multi-Key techniques enable you to relax relationship constraints, introducing OR logic into relationship definitions (whereas multi-predicate relationships permit only AND logic).

Among the many uses of the Multi-Key techniques in FileMaker is the calculation of exploded keys to support partial match filtering. For example, if the target key in the related table is a calculation rendering the value of a field in the related table as an exploded array in the form

```
e
ex
exp
expl
explo
explod
explode
exploded
```

then incomplete matches from a related table (via an equi-join relationship) become possible. As a result, users can start typing part of a word or name and then select from a portal list of possible matches. While this technique is useful in some situations, it imposes a penalty of increased storage and indexing requirements in the related table.

An alternative application of a Multi-Key technique achieving similar functionality in some circumstances is the use of a calculation in the parent table, generating two values to represent the lower and upper limits of a text range. For example, set up a field for user-entered data (say, a global text field called gSearch) and an unstored calculation called cSearch (of result type text) in the same table defined as

```
gSearch & ¶ & gSearch & "zzz"
```

Set up a relationship based on the calculation field defined along the following lines:

```
        cSearch        ≤ RelatedKey
AND     cSearch        ≥ RelatedKey
```

With the preceding calculation and relationship in place, when the user enters **ex** into the gSearch field, the cSearch field will produce a Multi-Key value array containing two values:

```
ex
exzzz
```

Because Multi-Key matches are evaluated simultaneously on all values (as an OR sequence), values in `RelatedKey` that are both greater than and less than the two values in `cSearch` are those falling between ex and exzzz in alphabetical sequence. This method is suitable for a variety of range matching, filtering, and partial completion relationships.

CROSS-REF See Chapter 9 for implementation notes for a filter relationship using the essentials of this technique.

Compound keys

Compound keys (usually calculation fields) concatenate the several values into a single value (or group of values) for matching purposes. You frequently encounter keys of this type in solutions migrated from earlier versions of FileMaker (for example, solutions created in FileMaker 6 or earlier) because multi-predicate relationships were not directly supported prior to Version 7.

An example of the former use of concatenated keys is a relationship based on a concatenation of last name and date of birth in both tables. When compound keys are matched in this way, only records with the same value in both last name and date of birth will match — so the relationship is functionally equivalent to a multi-predicate relationship referencing both fields. For this reason, most uses of compound keys in current solutions serve other purposes.

A useful contemporary technique using compound keys is the creation of *multi-purpose relationships* (relationships you can switch between different purposes at will). For example, if you have three key fields in `Table1` (keyA, keyB, and keyC) and three corresponding key fields in `Table2` and you need at various times to relate `Table1` and `Table2` according to different pairs of keys, you can achieve this with a single relationship by creating a compound key in `Table2` (as a stored text calc named `cMasterKey`) defined as:

```
"keyA" & Table2::keyA & "¶keyB" & Table2::keyB & "¶keyC" & Table2::keyC
```

In `Table1`, create a global text field called `gKeySelection` and an unstored calculation field called `cDynamicKey` with the formula

```
gKeySelection & GetField(gKeySelection)
```

With the preceding fields in place, define a single relationship between `Table1` and `Table2` as

```
Table1::cDynamicKey              = Table2::cMasterKey
```

With such a relationship in place, you can modify the relationship between `Table1` and `Table2` to match any pair of the three original (`Table2`) key fields by putting the name of the desired key field for the relationship into `Table1::gKeySelection`.

One-way relationships

In most cases, FileMaker relationships work in both directions. So, for example, an `InvoiceLines` layout can display data from the Invoices table sourced via the same relationship you use to display `InvoiceLines` data on the Invoices layouts.

Relationships that are dependent on an unstored calculation work in one direction only, however, because the matching of records utilizes the index of the key field(s) in the related table — and unstored fields can't be indexed. Although you can use such relationships to retrieve data from other tables, data won't flow in the other direction.

Similarly, global fields cannot be indexed, so relationships where the destination key field is a global field do not return matching records. Instead, they act as Cartesian joins (when retrieving records from the table where the global key field is located), returning all records, regardless of the value (or lack of value) in the global field.

NOTE The behavior of relationships that terminate with a global field is consistent regardless of the data type of the global field because no index matching occurs. However, if the relationship is used in the opposite direction (assuming that opposing match field is not a global field), the data types of the fields should match.

Despite their limitations, one-way relationships prove useful in a variety of situations because they have other helpful behaviors. In many cases, a utility relationship from a global field to a related table is useful for addressing individual records in the related table. Similarly, relationships where one of the keys is an unstored calculation field exhibit more dynamic behavior than their stored-key counterparts.

Join tables

While you can use Multi-Key fields to support various forms of one-to-many and many-to-many relationships, in many cases storing associations between entities in an intermediary table is preferable. Tables used in this way are commonly known as *join tables*.

The use of join tables is particularly advantageous in any situation where

- You need to store or process data connected with each join event.
- You need to track the joins and report on join activity.

For example, when associating people with clubs, you can create a Memberships table to manage the connections. Each person would then have a record in the Memberships table for each club they were a member of. In such a case, you need to store data connected with the join (such as the person's membership expiration date, their status, and perhaps the fee paid). You also need to be able to track memberships — for example, producing membership pattern reports by year for each club — which is much easier to do when you can search, sort, and summarize the records in the memberships table.

Naturally occurring joins

Like the preceding memberships example, many types of data that are a familiar part of life that, in database terms, are a join table. For example, a college `Enrollments` table is, in fact, a join table connecting `People` and `Courses`. An `Employees` table is a join tables between `People` and `Companies`. The `Tickets` register in an airlines database is a join table between `Passengers` and `Flights`.

The preceding examples are so familiar that you're likely to think of them as entities in their own right. However, in each case (and there are many other examples), the joins have no independent existence — they're not tangible entities in the way that, say, people and companies are.

For the efficient management of data relationships involving ~to-many joins, facilitation of organizational clarity and ease of reporting/summarizing available information often warrants creating one or more join tables.

Working with Data Arrays

In any work you do with structured data, arrays make an appearance (whether you're aware of it nor not). An *array* is a group of data elements you can access via an index (value number). It can be as simple as a numbered list or as complex as a compilation of keys and associated values from a set of related records.

Any time you store a list of record IDs in a field, you have, in effect, an array — you can reference the record IDs by their position in the list, using functions such as `GetValue ( )`. Similarly, value lists, delimited text, and name/value pairs may all be considered array types.

Repeating fields as an array handler

FileMaker provides a built-in method of storing multiple discrete values in a single field and referencing them according to a value's index (position) within the set of values assigned to the field. FileMaker calls this feature a Repeating Field. Moreover, FileMaker also supports repeating variables, so arrays can be stored and accessed efficiently in memory (and therefore outside your solutions' data structures).

Most programmers know that arrays can be really useful, yet repeating fields gets a bad rap among old hands in the FileMaker developer community for two reasons:

- Historically (prior to the release of FileMaker Pro v3 in 1995), FileMaker provided only rudimentary relationship support, so repeating fields provided a surrogate (albeit an inadequate one). When relational structures became available, this type of use of repeating fields was deprecated.

- Inexperienced users without grounding in relational theory have been known to tie themselves in knots trying to use repeating fields for purposes far better served by related tables.

Although these concerns have a legitimate basis, a variety of valid and appropriate uses of repeating fields as array-handling mechanisms exist. In particular, using global repeating fields as index references or repositories for system resources, such as text and graphics for use in your solution interface, aids efficiency and clarity.

Collapsing and expanding arrays

FileMaker provides a number of alternative forms for lists and arrays. On occasion, you may consider using arrays to extend your data structure — for example, storage of anything from test measurement sets in research databases to binomial indices in quantum plotters to rolling transaction logs in audit systems.

In some cases, such as when a *static array* (one fixed in size) is appropriate to your needs, repeating fields may be adequate. However, in many cases, you may not know in advance how many elements you need to accommodate. In those cases, you should consider using text arrays (managed using FileMaker's ~Values ( ) functions) for stored arrays or variables for temporary arrays. In both cases, you can achieve dynamic array functionality, where the array size may be extended at will, within the limits of available memory or FileMaker's text field size limit of 1 billion characters.

TIP Arrays are a great way to pass more than one parameter to a script — or returning more than one result. Name/Value pair syntax is one of the formats many developers find ideal for this purpose.

Relationship-based techniques for managing data

One of the choices you make as soon as you start building a solution is what values to use as the keys for relationship match fields. For each table in a relational database, it's a good idea to have a unique ID field to use as the primary key (and for all other purposes, to identify the record).

CROSS-REF For a discussion of the selection requirements for key field values (especially primary keys), refer to Chapter 7.

When you have relationships in place, a variety of useful options become available to you. For example, you can use relationships in place of Finds to locate groups of records instantly (by using the Go to Related Record [ ] command), and it becomes possible to automatically generate *dynamic* (data-driven) value lists filtered via relationships.

From a single vantage point (layout or base table) within your solutions, your users (and the scripts you provide them) can access related data and create, update, or delete related records. A brief overview of techniques available for these purposes appears in the following sections.

Allowing creation via relationship

When you define a relationship, you can choose for either (or both) TOs of the relationship to Allow Creation of Related Records in This Table via This Relationship. You make this specification via a pair of settings in the lower panel of the Edit Relationship dialog, shown in Figure 11.5.

NOTE The Allow Creation of Related Records option requires that key fields in either or both tables be writable so that FileMaker can automatically synchronize key field values when establishing the relationship to a new record. Moreover, the relationship definition may only include the =, ≥, and ≤ operators. (Otherwise, FileMaker is unable to determine an appropriate corresponding key value to establish a relationship match.)

FIGURE 11.5

Setting the Allow Creation option to enable creation of new records in the `OrderLines` TO from layouts based on the `Orders` TO.

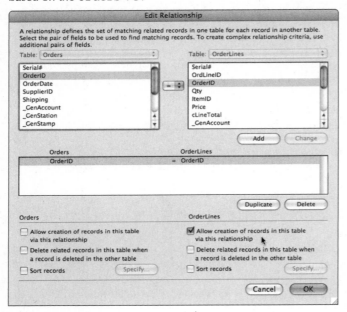

When this setting is enabled, portals based on the TO in question acquire an empty last line into which you can enter data to automatically create a new record. Thus, with a portal based on such a relationship present on the current layout, a script sequence along the following lines will generate a new related record:

```
Go to Portal Row [Last]
Set Field [RelatedTable::AnyWritableField; AnyValue]
```

NOTE In the absence of a portal, you can still create related records via a relationship set up as noted. However, a new related record is created only when no related records exist for the current match key value(s). Nevertheless, you can use a utility relationship to generate new related records (see "The isolating relationship" section, later in this chapter).

Using self joins

The self-join relationship is an important technique in creating sophisticated solutions. Self-joins require two TOs of the same base table for the purpose of connecting them. The primary purpose of self-join relationships is to permit records to read from and/or write to other records in the same table.

Self-join relationships serve a variety of different needs, including joins on the primary key to isolate the current record (by using a GTRR to present it alone in a found set), joins on foreign keys, or other attributes grouping or summarizing records on common characteristics (to see other person records listing the same profession, other employee records in the same work group, other invoices for the same customer, and so on). Self-joins are also frequently used for navigation, filtering, selection summarization, and new record creation.

The isolating relationship

You can employ utility relationships to create a temporary one-to-one relationship to any record in a table so that its data can be retrieved or updated. Such relationships generally match a global field in the current table to the primary key field in a TO based on the same or a different table. By writing the ID (of any related record) into the global field, you can establish a temporary relationship isolating the related record, without changing layouts or modifying the found set.

By this means, you can create a script to work its way through a group of related records (without using a portal), updating each in turn. Alternatively, with a relationship configured to allow creation of related records, you can clear the global field and generate a corresponding related record by writing a value into a field in the related table via the relationship. FileMaker will generate a new auto-entered ID in the related table and will automatically add it to the global field to complete the relationship.

> **TIP** After creating one or more related records via an Allow Create relationship, provided that you don't commit records during the process, the whole operation can be committed or reverted as a batch and therefore operates as a single transaction.

> **CROSS-REF** For a detailed description of scripted processes using an isolating relationship to address groups of related records, refer to Chapter 13.

Graph Techniques — Spiders, Squids, and Anchor-Buoy

When FileMaker first introduced the Relationships Graph (FileMaker Pro 7), many users assumed it was primarily a data modeling tool and tried to build ERD-like structures. However, the required supporting relationships for interface and process added complexity, and the original concept was almost invariably lost. With a certain amount of irony, some developers have described the Relationships Graphs from their early efforts as *spider graphs,* meaning that the clusters of TOs amid myriad relationship lines resembled spiders in webs.

Over time, developers confronted with the need to manage the relationship structures of complex solutions came up with alternative strategies for organizing the Graph's elements and increasing its manageability. One of the first — and perhaps least useful — methods to emerge (though it can be argued that it has helped some developers make the transition to the .fp7 format) is an approach that in its variants is sometimes referred to as either *squid* or *anchor-buoy.* These Graph management models introduce an orthodoxy in which a specific TO of each table is reserved for layouts, and each reserved TO becomes the anchor (or squid-head) for a discrete group of TOs built entirely and independently to support the needs of layouts based on the anchor TO. These methods make no use of two-way relationships, introduce high levels of redundancy, and trap the developer in a confined (though predictable) paradigm of relationship management closely analogous to the constraints operating in FileMaker 6 and earlier.

Meanwhile, among developers dissatisfied with the limits of these approaches, several other useful Graph management models have emerged. Although I don't propose to exhaustively explore the possible techniques in the following sections, I'd nevertheless like to indicate some directions for you to consider.

Constellations and modular centers

A useful emerging technique for managing the Relationships Graph in complex solutions is to group Graph activity into modules around several functional centers that form a natural focus of activity in the solution. Many solutions support several overlapping areas of activity and readily lend themselves to being conceptualized in this way.

This *modular-centric approach* enables you to begin by building several independent ERD-like Graph structures from the foundation tables of each modular center. These structures remain separate, while you extend them by adding supporting TOs (drawn in some cases from base tables represented in the cores of other modular centers) to serve the range of process, interface, and reporting requirements within each module.

While the Relationships Graph example shown in Figure 11.6 supports a solution of moderate complexity, where five interactive functionality centers are used as the basis of organizing the supporting relationship structures, it's clear that each of the TO groupings is of manageable size and complexity. In this solution, the ratio of TOs to tables is approximately 4:1, so there is moderate redundancy, and the solution is efficient in operation and relatively straightforward to maintain. I compare this solution to one of equivalent size and functionality developed using an *anchor-buoy approach,* requiring over 500 TOs (ratio approx 15:1) and presenting a significant challenge to development.

Some solutions lend themselves more readily to a modular Graph management approach than others. This implementation style works best when each center has relatively few supporting tables (in the case of my example, an average of seven tables per operational group) and where not all tables from other groups are required to be accessed throughout the solution.

A satellite-based graph solution

When modularization of the Graph begins to reach burdensome levels of redundancy, you have other alternatives. For example, you can draw together the essential elements of the data model into a simplified cluster at the heart of your Graph design. For all operational requirements not catered to within the simplified central group of TOs, you can add separate utility structures that control specific functions, reports, and processes.

FIGURE 11.6

An implementation of Graph modeling based on the modular-centric approach, in a 35-table solution.

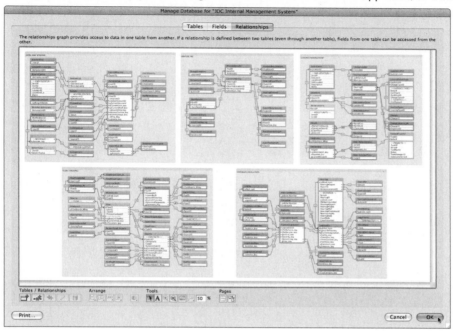

The Relationships Graph displayed in Figure 11.7 represents the final result of a process commencing with solution design around an anchor-buoy graph model requiring more than 350 TOs. When the original developer sought a more streamlined design, a modular approach was first considered. However, due to the nature of the solution, a modularized Graph would still have required around 180 TOs.

By stripping the Graph model back to bare essentials and defining a limited number of two-directional reusable satellite structures, you can deliver the same functionality using only 73 TOs, as shown in Figure 11.7.

Although alternative approaches to Graph modeling, as illustrated by the preceding examples, can result in more manageable and efficient data designs and Graph structures, the more radical reductions, such as the satellite-based approach, have implications for the solution's logic. To use such a model, the solution is heavily dependent on scripted processes transferring the action to appropriate layouts to access Graph element utility clusters. So the solution is more tightly scripted than would be required for some other data designs — and requires a significant number of ancillary layouts to support the scripted processes.

FIGURE 11.7

A Graph implementation based on a cluster and satellite approach in a 23-table solution.

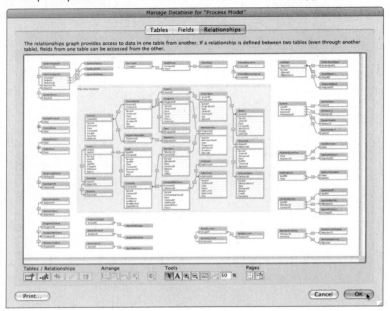

The use of a satellite Graph model, therefore, becomes a trade-off between competing concerns. A reduction of complexity in one area of your solution may be counterbalanced by constraints or complications elsewhere. When determining an appropriate Graph model, consider the balance of requirements for your particular solution to identify a harmonious mix of elements.

Segmentation on functional lines

The foregoing examples of Relationships Graph models are best suited for solutions of moderate size and complexity. To varying degrees, they take a task focus rather than an entity relationship model as their alternative organizing principle. While these techniques are scalable within reason, if you use this type of structure, you'll encounter problems supporting solutions with hundreds of base tables.

You need to think about the overhead any complex Relationships Graph imposes on FileMaker's cache management processes. To support a data-on-demand usage model, FileMaker maintains an internal map of joins with respect to the layout (and its associated TO) of each window. When the user (or a script) takes action impacting the joins, FileMaker must work its way through each affected join, discarding outdated cache and (subsequently, when required) rebuilding it. A layout that reaches out through hundreds of relationship joins therefore imposes a greater burden than one with a more moderate Graph overhead.

To ease concerns about interactions between large numbers of tables, you could consider separating the Graph between two or more files. Even though all the base tables may reside in a single file, placing some components of the Graph functionality into alternate files (to support various script and interface requirements) can yield noticeable benefits in both manageability and solution performance.

One of the candidates for segmentation is reporting. A large solution can benefit from separating and modularizing reporting requirements, enabling them to be served by separate graph structures that come into play only when the reporting functionality is required. Thus, data entry and business process support can proceed without the added cache management associated with reporting relationship structures. Conversely, reporting can operate unencumbered in a Graph environment of its own when required.

> **NOTE** A deeper exploration of the separation of solutions into elements — including the separation of data and interface — is provided in the section "Implementing Separation in an Existing Solution," later in this chapter.

Documenting the Database Structure

In every area of every solution, the value of documentation increases as the mix of elements and structure becomes more complex, as time passes and memory fades, or as the number of people working on a system increases or changes.

In a solution of less than a hundred lines of code, even if you've never seen it, you can probably comprehend its entire scope and purpose in the space of an afternoon. A solution of a thousand (or 10,000) lines of code, however, is a different proposition. At this point, some well-placed sign posts may be the only thing preventing you from becoming hopelessly lost.

A problem, however, arises when you put off documenting your solutions — at first because they're small (everything starts small, after all), and then because you're onto the next thing (and, besides, you can remember where you've been). But soon, a solution grows to the point where retrospectively documenting it is a major undertaking. When it comes to documentation, "Don't wait, or it will be too late" is an excellent motto.

Graph annotations

The FileMaker Relationships Graph provides a text tool for adding notes to the Graph. Conveniently, the notes always sit behind TOs and relationship lines, so the essentials aren't obscured. You can add text notes as sticky labels, headings, explanatory notes, or frames and bounding boxes for groups of TOs. Figure 11.8 shows a selection of styles and uses of Graph notes objects created with the Text tool.

The upper right corner of the Graph text object (see Figure 11.8) provides a disclosure button. Clicking the button collapses the note into a heading; subsequent clicks toggle the display of the body area of the note. You can use this feature to add information and then tuck it out of sight until it's needed.

You can create a variety of text notes to provide supporting information on the Relationships Graph.

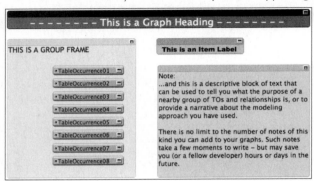

You can also apply color to notes, note text, and TOs on the Graph. By using color systematically to identify TOs (either by the base table they point to or according to their function), you can make the Graph considerably more comprehensible.

Naming conventions

A significant aspect of the trail you leave behind for yourself or others to follow is the way you name the components of your solutions. Nowhere is naming more important than for tables, Table Occurrences, and fields.

NOTE   **FileMaker accepts free-form text names for most elements in the schema — you can use spaces, alphanumeric characters, plus a variety of other characters or punctuation marks. However, integration with other systems and technologies can be problematic if your naming is nonstandard. For compatibility, use only alphanumeric characters, underscore, and hash characters**

I'm not about to instruct you to follow standards. The problem with standards is that they're all different. Numerous public documents recommend various possible approaches to naming in FileMaker. Most recently, in November 2005, FileMaker, Inc. published a Development Conventions paper documenting the practices and recommendations of a number of developers. Although it contained some useful advice, along with a broad range of suggestions, it has gained no more widespread acceptance than various other proposed standards that preceded it.

While I don't insist on a specific standard, I strongly recommend that you take care to be consistent — and to strive for simplicity, logic, and readability. I recommend the use of Hungarian notation (in other words, a prefixed c or g) to identify calculation fields and global fields, along with the use of CamelCase (often called *intercapping*) to delineate words in a compact way without spaces.

While some developers recommend suffixes such as _pk for primary keys and _fk for foreign keys, I think the inclusion of ID in the name of a key field is sufficient for clarity in most cases. It's already obvious that an `InvoiceID` field is the unique identifier and serves as the primary key in an Invoices table — and it's equally obvious when it appears in another table that it is a foreign key. In both cases, suffixes would clutter without clarifying.

As a part of a common-sense and minimalist approach to naming, I do recommend care in ensuring that your names are clear and descriptive. Try to avoid similarly named fields with different purposes — and differently named fields with similar purposes. Aim for clarity.

Field commenting

In complex solutions, the importance of brevity in field names limits the amount of meaning or explanation you can reasonably hope to pack into field and TO names. While FileMaker permits names of up to 100 characters, long names are problematic and counterproductive. For example, the long field name shown in Figure 11.9 is only 48 characters long — but only the first 27 characters show in the default column width in the Fields panel of the Manage Database dialog. Moreover, other dialogs, such as the Sort dialog, show even fewer characters of the field name and can't be enlarged.

In fact, if you choose the same starting characters for several fields, differentiating them only by the characters at the end of the name, such as

```
Companies_Selection_update_ALL

Companies_Selection_update_CURRENT

Companies_Selection_update_NEXT_c

Companies_Selection_update_NEXT_g
```

FIGURE 11.9

Long field names are truncated in many dialogs, including the Field Name list on the Fields tab of the Manage Database dialog.

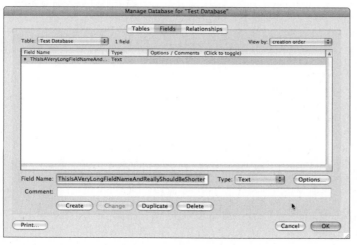

you'll encounter a usability issue when the field names are truncated in dialogs throughout the application. Figure 11.10 displays fields that are indistinguishable from others because they all start with the same characters.

FIGURE 11.10

Long field truncated in the Sort Records dialog — presenting a usability issue for both developer and end users.

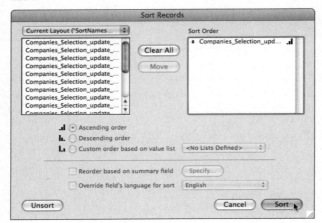

> **NOTE** You can resize some FileMaker dialogs to enlarge the viewing area, but it doesn't solve the problem in cases where only the right-hand column is resizable.

I recommend field names of 25 characters or less. If you want to include more information than fits comfortably within these constraints, use the field commenting facility to add an explanatory note. As shown in Figure 11.11, you can enter field comments directly below the field name and, if desired, view these in the main field list in the Manage Database dialog by clicking the column heading labeled Options/Comments.

> **CROSS-REF** In addition to field comments and Graph notes, FileMaker supports the use of C and C++ style commenting within calculation expressions. Refer to Chapter 12 for additional details about the use of commenting in calculation expressions.

Ancillary notes and documentation

You can also leave additional notes within the database itself. For example, you might consider adding a table called DeveloperNotes where you can store design concepts and annotations regarding aspects of the structure and code so that you can have ready access to your notes about things you need to remember.

Adding and viewing field comments via the Manage Database dialog.

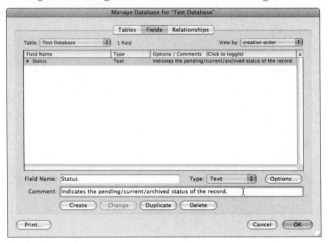

In addition, accumulating programming notes during the course of solution development can provide various forms of input information as you begin to assemble user documentation and help text for your solution. Users generally need slightly different information — and may need it expressed in different terms. However, both kinds of documentation should often cover many of the same broad issues.

The Concept of Layers

Database systems are frequently comprised of a collection of elements working together to provide data storage, logical processing, and user interaction. Thus, it can be helpful to think about solution design in terms of the data layer, the logic layer, and the interface layer. FileMaker's unified file structure incorporates some elements of all three layers in every file — and permits you to deliver your entire solution in one file, if you want.

FileMaker is nothing if not flexible, however. If you choose to do so, you can divide your solution to some degree, delineating the purpose of different files according to layers of functionality — or other criteria as dictated by the needs of your solution and its users.

Some developers believe that a benefit of considering the layers of your solution independently (whether or not you choose to use a single file or multiple files) is that it gives you an opportunity to think through the data structure and get it right before worrying about the logic or interface aspects. I'm not persuaded by this viewpoint because in FileMaker the requirements of logic and interface are substantially imposed on the Graph model (and vice versa); thinking about any one layer in isolation may lead to decisions that are ultimately detrimental.

"Back end" and "front end"

Another concept familiar to many database developers is the back end or data end of a solution. Although FileMaker has layouts in the same files as tables, you enter a different environment (the Manage Database dialog) to create or change the data structure, so it's not difficult to recognize that the data end requires somewhat different skills and has its own rules.

Because FileMaker enables you to set up references to external data — in other FileMaker files or in SQL data sources — you have the option to create some degree of distinction between the data storage function and the logic and interface functions in your solutions. For example, you can choose to use a specific file primarily to store data and little else (giving it only the most rudimentary interface and few scripts) and then create one or more files to use the data in the first file as the basis of layouts and scripts to make a presentation layer for your solution. Arrangements of this kind form the basis of what has become known as the *separation model* of FileMaker development.

The separation model is important to understand — not merely because it provides you with additional architectural options for your solutions, but also because understanding it is essential to grasping the elements of the structural model FileMaker provides.

FileMaker ties code to data to the extent that a back-end file must always have more than just data in it. For example, calculations or lookups require some supporting relationships in the file where they're defined. Moreover, FileMaker's security model is file-based; to protect the data, you need to build appropriate security in the data file. With this security in place, some scripts will be necessary to let users log in appropriately in the data file so that they can access the information it contains. In all these respects and others, it becomes clear that a purist approach to the separation of data from the remaining frameworks of a solution is neither feasible nor desirable when working with FileMaker. Nevertheless, you may choose to create one or more files primarily as data files and others primarily as interface files.

Just as a FileMaker data file will never be purely or exclusively data, a FileMaker interface file will necessarily include the logic (security and scripting) and probably also at least some data (if only user preferences, global filter attributes, and the like).

The business or procedural layer

In some database development environments, the process or logic layer of a solution subsists in a collection of stored procedures. FileMaker, on the other hand, distributes your solutions' logic layers throughout a number of places.

The first and perhaps most important logical and procedural control FileMaker affords you is its calculation capabilities. When you define a calculation, you're in effect setting up a process that automatically responds to certain inputs and follows the rules you specify to produce corresponding outputs. This is true of calculations residing in the tables of your solution, but it's also true of calculations in scripts, on buttons, in conditional formatting, or anywhere else in your solution. Calculations are one expression of rules governing how your solution should work and what should happen when the user acts in a certain way.

FileMaker's scripting capability is the second focus of logic and process in your solutions. In many respects, scripts more closely resemble the procedure methods available in other environments and their implementation provides self-contained process logic.

CROSS-REF For a more detailed discussion of the FileMaker scripting engine's logical capabilities, refer to Chapter 13.

FileMaker as an integrated environment

One reason to consider a solution structure separating data and interface is the ability to modify one part without affecting the other. Because FileMaker is designed as an integrated database tool, you can view using it to create solutions comprising separate data and logic interface components either as perverse or ingenious — your choice. You may not choose to adopt such an approach for all cases, but it's important to be aware that separation is available for occasions when it may be desirable or even necessary.

When a solution created in a version of FileMaker prior to Version 7 is migrated to the current file format (identified by the file suffix .fp7), it acquires a structure that reflects the constraints of the legacy environment. Prior to the release of FileMaker 7, solutions were constrained to a single table per file, so all relationships were between files. (Even self-join relationships were defined as a link from a file to itself.) Migrated solutions, therefore, typically start out with tables distributed across multiple files and with the interface elements related to a particular table residing in the same table as the file.

Other reasons to depart from the obvious (single-file) architecture for your FileMaker solution include

- **Network performance considerations:** You can keep your dependence on a slow network connection to a minimum if you separate a solution into two components and place the shared data component on a remote server and the static reference data, archival data, and graphics-intensive interface files on the user's local workstation.

- **Divergent user requirements:** If your solution serves different groups of users with different preferences or different needs (but common data requirements), you can provide access to a single data source via multiple interfaces representing the different groups' requirements.

FileMaker has the power to leverage a range of different structural models to deliver a variety of user experiences — all underpinned by a seamless application delivering a holistic database environment.

Separation anxiety

No matter how you're considering separating your solution on data and interface lines, on modular lines, or in some other way, you need to be aware of several issues and weigh the potential benefits against possible concerns:

- When you choose a multiple-file structure, you need to duplicate some components of code, content, and/or structure. For example, if you create a two-file solution, some scripts may be required in both files (and some processes may require that a script in one file call a script in the other and vice versa). Moreover, you need to configure appropriate security settings in each file. These requirements add complexity and, therefore, may increase development time.

- When you deploy a multi-file solution, you need to decide what goes where and (when you have a choice) what combination or distribution of elements best serves the needs of the users and the requirements of the solution. For example, you don't want to have users perform some actions, such as logging in, twice just because you have two files.

- You also need to be aware of what works where, such as how environment variables are evaluated when a calculation is being performed in a different file. You must also understand the scope of action of all the elements in play (variables, security, scripts, and so on).

File Architecture versus Data Structure

There is a long history of confusion between file architecture and data architecture. Since the inception of the .fp7 file format, FileMaker has supported multiple tables per file up to 1 million, according to the technical specifications published by FileMaker, Inc. (I'll leave it to you to test that assertion!)

A database system's file architecture, however, doesn't determine the relational structure — FileMaker Pro has supported relational data architectures since the release of Version 3. Prior to the release of Version 7, each file was constrained to contain only a single table, so a multi-table relational solution required multiple files. Solutions converted to the .fp7 format from earlier versions retain their multi-file architecture initially — and, in fact, you can create new solutions in FileMaker 10 that work this way, if you choose.

Remember that although the file structure has implications for how you work and how your solution appears to users, it's entirely independent of the data structure. You get to choose where to store and access each data table your solution uses.

Multi-file solutions

In a few situations, it's advantageous to have every table in a single file, but it's frequently useful (or necessary) to build a solution around data residing in more than one file. Occasionally, a multi-file solution architecture is required so that you can incorporate or reference data in a pre-existing system (either a separate FileMaker solution or an external SQL database). Even when there is no imperative to use multiple files for your solution, you may choose to do so for a variety of reasons:

- To improve network performance by storing static data or interface components on users' local workstation

- To make installing an update of the interface or process components of a solution easier (without the need to import current data into each new version)
- To give different users different views of the data or different functionality according to their needs or preferences
- To reduce the complexity and overhead associated with each "module" in a complex system where, for example, a single Relationships Graph supporting the entire solution would be unduly complex

Your objectives dictate whether you seek to gather all data into a single file while providing one or more other files to access it, present your interface in a single file with data being sourced from multiple locations, or some combination of both. In other words, you may choose to create

- A single file comprising both data and interface
- A single data file and a single (separate) interface file
- Multiple data files supporting one interface file
- Multiple interface files accessing a single data file
- Multiple interface files sourcing data from multiple files
- A mixed-model solution incorporating multiple files, which may have both interface and data elements within them

The modular approach

If you can readily divide your solution's functionality into discrete (though perhaps overlapping) areas of functionality, a mixed model or multiple interface approach may provide several benefits. For example, you may choose to provide separate modules to support sales, inventory, and accounts, even though the data for all three subsystems is stored in a single file.

With a modular approach, each department in an organization can have immediate access to the results of the work being done elsewhere (using other system "modules"), yet each works within a system specifically designed to support the needs, preferences, and business processes at hand. For example, the screens, scripts, reports, and menus seen by Accounts personnel need bear no resemblance to those used in the warehouse or on the shop floor, even though the supporting tables and relational structure of the back-end data file are common to all.

Other uses of a modular approach may involve separation of functionality along process lines. For example, you can create a single file or pair of files (interface and data) to support data entry and general solution functionality but provide a separate file for reporting. One advantage is that end users may be given considerably broader access to make changes in the reporting file, while the scripts and interface of the main files remain tightly secured.

While a modular approach can serve a number of needs, the advantages must be counterbalanced against the additional file infrastructure requirements, version control, and complexity introduced. There is, nevertheless, often a payoff from using a modular approach to solution architecture.

Interface files

Whenever you have a FileMaker file containing data and interface, you can create an interface file by establishing an External Data Source reference from a new file to the existing file. For example, in a new file, if you choose File ➪ Manage ➪ External Data Sources and then click the New button in the lower left of the Manage Data Sources dialog (to expose the Edit Data Source dialog), you can create a link to a copy of the Inventory example file, as illustrated in Figure 11.12.

When you're working on the Relationships Graph (in the Manage Database dialog), you can also access the Manage External Data Sources dialog from the Data Sources menu in the Specify Table dialog.

With a named reference to an external database in place, you can then begin to add TOs to the interface file's Graph (by clicking the + tool button in the lower left of the dialog, as described in Chapter 5) referring to tables located in the external file, as shown in Figure 11.13. Once TOs are in place, you're able to work with the interface, developing scripts and layouts in the same ways as if the tables were defined and stored within the file. However, all changes to the definitions of tables and fields — and associated access privileges — must still be made directly in the file housing the tables.

FIGURE 11.12

Creating a link between two files.

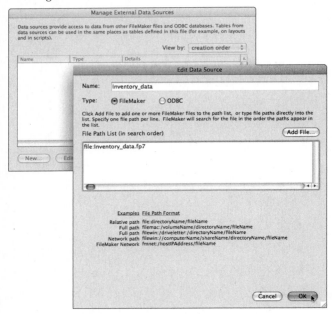

436

FIGURE 11.13

Choosing an external file when adding a TO to the Relationships Graph in an interface file.

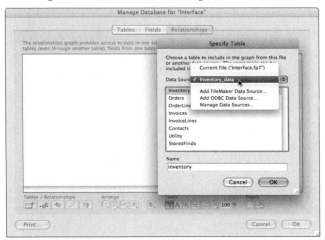

The most significant difference when you develop in a separated solution where the interface is in one file and the data in another is the need to maintain an awareness of the location of different elements and the scope of each component of the solution. For example:

- The Run Script with Full Access Privileges setting only influences the access privileges in the file where the script resides — so a script in your interface file won't gain full access to data in the external data file when this option is selected. To achieve full access to the data, you must either call a script (with appropriate privilege settings) in the data file, run a re-login process to temporarily change the level of privileges in the data file, or otherwise modify settings affecting the privilege status of the data file.

- Variables are scoped to the file where they're declared — so calculations in the data file won't be able to "see" variables declared in the interface file and vice versa. To pass values between files, your solutions will have to write the values to a field (for example, a global field) or pass them as a script parameter or script result so that they can be accessed externally.

- You should be mindful that environment data returned by Get ( ) functions in the interface file won't always be applicable in the data file and vice versa. For example, if a script in the data file evaluates the function Get (ActiveSelectionStart), it returns a result with respect to whatever is (or is not) selected in the data file. Even if the user's cursor is in a data-file field in the current active window of the interface file, the function being evaluated in the data file will not recognize it. To achieve the desired result, you need to structure the scripted sequence to pass the relevant value(s) from the interface to the data file via a script parameter or script result.

These concerns, and other examples like them, introduce some constraints and stringencies to multi-file development. However, taken as a whole, FileMaker's support for external data sources is broad and effective, with most features operating the same way regardless of the file architecture.

One of the most challenging issues in a multi-file solution is the management of security, because you need to script processes — such as login, logout, account creation, and password change — to occur simultaneously in all files. That way, the user is not prompted for credentials multiple times, and the appropriate access privileges are in place in all files throughout a work session.

Approaches to separation of data

Some developers take the view that to achieve separation of data and interface, the data file should ideally contain nothing but data, and that one should aim to get as close to this ideal as possible. Doing so, however, presents some challenges when working with FileMaker, preventing you from using some of FileMaker's features to the best advantage. For example, FileMaker's calculation fields and the schema to support them can be viewed as part of the logic of the solution rather than strictly part of the data and therefore a strict separation would exclude their use.

Such an approach may enhance the ability to perform updates to a solution without a need to import data to a new file by reducing the likelihood that updates will require modifications to the data file. In extreme cases, however, this convenience is achieved at a considerable cost in foregone functionality and produces inconvenience in other areas. I take the view that the more extreme approaches to separation cost more than they gain in a majority of cases, and you should carefully weigh the trade-offs before going to lengths to achieve "pure" separation.

A more conservative approach to separation, however — where schema, scripts, and calculations are present in the data file, but kept to moderate levels and the majority of code and configuration resides in the interface file — is highly tenable and provides a viable option for many solutions.

In this latter method, some redundancy occurs because the data file requires the essentials of a data model for the solution, much of which may also be required in the interface file. Moreover, in addition to login and security management scripts, some supporting sub-scripts (able to be called from scripts in the interface file) may also be present in the data file, especially where actions beyond the user's access privileges are required.

Although the essential calculation requirements of a solution may be performed in the original data file in a separation model solution, if you want to minimize changes to the data files after deployment, you can structure your solution to script the calculation and storage of derived values for all calculation requirements not covered in the original implementation. Similarly, the addition of reserved (unused) fields in tables in the data file can enable you to anticipate changes and make adjustments to the implementation without modifying the data file.

CAUTION Although the practice of adding unused fields to tables in a data file may help you reduce the need to modify the data file in the event changes are needed in the future, the practice is disadvantageous in some respects, because the unused fields can't be meaningfully dealt with in the scripting or security model for your solution, nor adequately detailed in the solution documentation.

Costs and benefits of separation

Data separation introduces a well-understood architecture common to many other data systems with clarity regarding the independence of the interface and logic layers from the data layer of your solution. This clarity is poised in counterbalance against the minor penalties and added complexities noted in the preceding sections, making the decision to opt for a separated solution difficult to justify in the absence of other considerations.

One of the most frequently repeated arguments in favor of the separation of data and interface is the added ease and efficiency of updates after deployment. In some cases, this contention is more valid than others. For example, when a solution is in use around the clock and holds millions of records, you want to avoid the inconvenience of taking the system offline to transfer records to an updated database file, if possible. In such cases, if you're able to construct the solution so as to minimize the impact of updates, it makes sense to do so.

Conversely, if your solution is of moderate size or doesn't need 24/7 availability, offline updates involving migration of the data to a new master copy of the updated file are feasible and often desirable because they

- Allow updates to the data structure, including calculations, additional fields, and data relationship definitions to support changed or extended functionality.
- Enable you to refresh the file at each update with a pristine master copy of the development file, thus minimizing the risk of corruption or data loss.

In the latter case, I recommend creating a migration utility to automate the transfer of data between versions of the file. This utility increases the efficiency of an offline update so that it can be performed routinely as required. You can view the creation and maintenance of an update utility as a cost or trade-off associated with your decision to work with an integrated (single file) solution. You can avoid the additional burden of creating and maintaining an update utility if you opt instead to separate the data and interface between two or more files.

In addition to the considerations regarding updates, potential benefits for network optimization and added deployment flexibility make various forms of separation and multi-file solution architectures attractive in a number of cases.

Separation and External SQL Sources

As part of the repertoire of options for accessing external data, FileMaker 10 provides support for live access to data in supported external SQL databases. Because SQL systems can't contain any FileMaker script or calculation code, an instance of the use of live SQL data requires you to adopt strategies for dealing with separation of data and interface, as outlined in the preceding section ("File Architecture versus Data Structure"). In such a solution, you can rely entirely on one or more SQL data sources for the data content of a solution, while using FileMaker to provide the interface and business process logic.

The use of SQL data with FileMaker has several potential advantages, chiefly being the capability to integrate seamlessly with other systems supporting SQL standards and the relative ease with which supported SQL databases can accommodate very large data sets, making them available simultaneously to thousands of users.

Understanding the rules

You may be tempted to consider FileMaker a candidate for duties as a front end for SQL databases. However, bear in mind that FileMaker doesn't provide some capabilities normally found in SQL front ends, including the ability to modify schema in the SQL back end and the ability to incorporate SQL syntax in its normal interactions with the data source.

NOTE   FileMaker includes an Execute SQL command you can use for scripted queries against an ODBC data source. However, normal Find operations on SQL tables in FileMaker use the native FileMaker Find interface, which is translated internally into SQL syntax for transmission to the host database.

You should also be aware that FileMaker's ability to deal with very large data sets (such as when performing finds, sorts, or other data-management tasks) is constrained by its internal architecture and may not be optimal when dealing with extremely large numbers of records. The performance limits you encounter when working with data stored in a SQL database will not necessarily be significantly different from those you deal with in native FileMaker deployments.

Also consider the absence of stored calculation capabilities in SQL databases. If you're used to defining calculations for a variety of purposes in FileMaker tables, you'll have to adopt alternate strategies when working with SQL data, which reduces some of the data modeling flexibility characteristic of an all-FileMaker implementation.

Working within constraints

To work efficiently with SQL data sources, consider adopting some different solution design approaches to compensate for the reduced data model flexibility. For example, one option is to provide an editing interface where the data is presented in holding fields (for example, global fields in the FileMaker interface file) and written back to the SQL database via script at the conclusion of user editing. Such a model where all changes to the remote data are made via script allows you to add calculations and perform operations on the data prior to storage.

If you're working with SQL databases holding very large sets of data, consider defining your links to the SQL data via views rather than direct to the SQL tables, as views can present more manageable subsets of the data in large tables. Figure 11.14 shows the configuration at the lower right corner of the Edit Data Source dialog where you can specify the form of SQL data to be presented to FileMaker.

NOTE   The extent of flexibility you have to set up links to an SQL database that use views in an optimal way will depend on the way the SQL database is configured. If you don't have access to make changes to the configuration of the SQL system, you should communicate with the administrator for the SQL database to ascertain the most appropriate options for making connections to the SQL data.

> **NOTE** SQL data views don't necessarily have predefined primary key values. If you choose to access such a view in FileMaker, you're required to identify a suitable key value for use as a unique key.

FIGURE 11.14

Configuring the settings for an external ODBC data source to present views instead of tables.

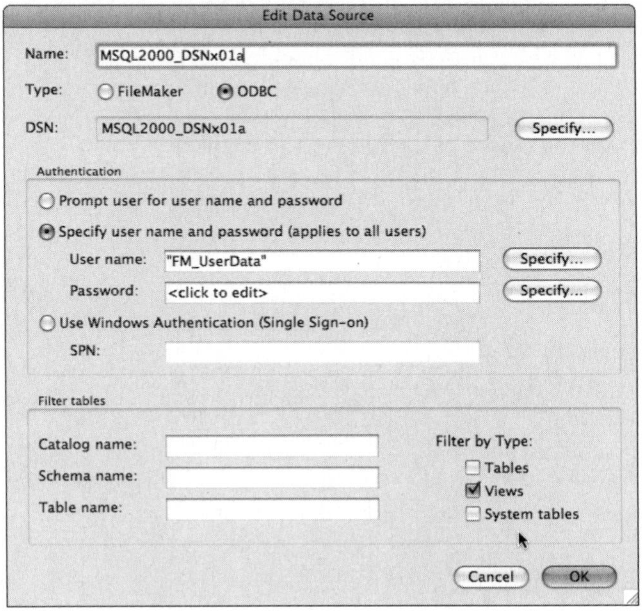

Supporting the user

Delivering solutions combining data from a variety of environments — even connecting simultaneously to multiple remote host systems — is challenging as well as exciting. The effort required to resolve differences in the way different technologies are implemented is worthwhile because it gives you the ability to provide enhanced support to the users of your solutions.

With user requirements in play, it's important to set aside theoretical models and examine the practical realities. The functional requirements and the best interests of the solution's owners and users dictate the decision to build a separated solution, an integrated solution, or a part FileMaker and part SQL solution.

The starting point for any solution modeling exercise should be a user requirements audit. When developers listen, it's been my experience that users are more than ready to talk.

Implementing Separation in an Existing Solution

When you create a single-file solution in FileMaker Pro 10, all the elements of the file — tables, layouts, scripts, accounts and privileges, and so on — connect directly within FileMaker's integrated file format. Even after a solution is in an advanced stage of development, however, you can redeploy with an alternative solution architecture, introducing layers of separation.

The simplest method for adding multi-file functionality to an existing solution is to create an additional file with links to the tables in the main file and configure the new file to provide specific additional functions (for example, a search interface, an Instant Web Publishing interface, a reporting interface, and so on). However, converting the file into a completely separate data/interface architecture is a more challenging task.

Establishing data source(s)

To begin the process of converting a solution from a single-file architecture to a separated architecture, you should first store a backup copy of the file in a secure place and then create a duplicate of the file, naming it appropriately for the data file of the solution. You now have two copies of the file, both containing the existing interface and the existing data. Here's how you convert a solution:

1. Add the data file as an external data source in the interface file.
2. Reassign the TOs in the interface file to point to the corresponding tables in the data file.
3. Remove data tables (and their contents) from the interface file.
4. Test to restore any functionality affected by the change.
5. Remove or disable interface elements in the data file.
6. Add scripts to manage security (login and logout) as required across the two files.

Figure 11.12 shows the method of adding a data file as an external data source by choosing File ➪ Manage ➪ External Data Sources. After adding the path to the data source to the interface file, it appears as an available option on the Data Sources menu when selecting or assigning a TO to a data table in the Manage Database dialog.

Re-pointing Table Occurrences

The second step in implementing separation is to select each of the TOs in the Relationships Graph and reassign it to the corresponding table in the external data file, as shown in Figure 11.15. Here's how to do so, making sure that you keep the same TO names:

1. Note the table the TO is attached to.
2. Copy the TO name.
3. Select the external data source.

4. Reattach it to the corresponding table in the external file.

5. Paste the original TO name into the name field.

6. Repeat Steps 1–5 for each TO.

After you've changed each TO, its name in the header band appears in italics to indicate that the table it references is in an external file. After completing this process, visit the Manage Database dialog's Tables panel in the interface file. As shown in Figure 11.16, you now see nothing in the Occurrences In graph column of the tables list. (If you do see some, then you missed one and should go back to the Relationships tab to reassign it to the external data file.)

After you've confirmed that all the tables in the interface file are unreferenced, you can delete them from the file. The solution now uses data exclusively from the data file.

As an important part of the redeployment procedure, you should conduct tests to confirm that the solution's functionality is intact, making any required modifications to restore the intended behavior. In the case of the example `Inventory` solution, my testing revealed that the Back button functionality required modifications because it depended on a `$$trace` variable declared within the `cTrace` calculations in schema. The value of a variable declared in the data file where the schema now resides is no longer available to the Go Back script in the interface file. This example is typical of the kind of issue that arises when you change to a separation architecture, as noted in the section "File Architecture versus Data Structure," earlier in this chapter.

FIGURE 11.15

Reconnecting a TO to the corresponding table in an external data source.

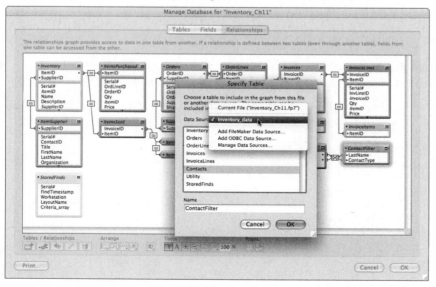

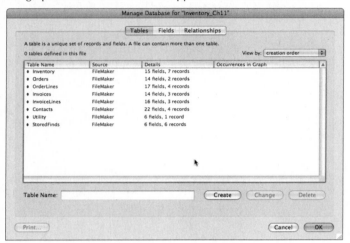

FIGURE 11.16

No graph occurrences of tables appear in the Interface file.

I addressed this issue in the example files for this chapter by placing a variant of the cTrace calculation expression into the conditional formatting calculation of replacement Back buttons in the interface file. After this change, I deleted the cTrace fields from the tables in the data file.

Additionally, I made minor changes to the Go Back script to address a refresh issue arising from cached external data in the Utility relationship used by the script. With these changes, I restored the example solution to its former functionality, yet in a separated architecture.

Creating separate graphs

Once data sources for all TOs have been reassigned according to plan, rationalization of the two identical Relationships Graphs can begin.

The first step toward tailoring each file for its new role is removing extraneous process and interface support elements from the data file's Relationships Graph. In the example Inventory solution, I identified that 12 of the 24 TOs on the original Graph were required for script or interface support, but they were nonessential to the schema in the data file. Consequently, I was able to halve the number of TOs in the data file. Similarly, I removed scripts and layouts from the data file.

When making changes to both files at this stage in redeployment, multiple test cycles are a good precautionary measure. Extra testing ensures that adjusting Graph and/or other elements in either of the files allows preservation (or restoration, if necessary) of required functionality.

After making the preceding changes, the Inventory example reached the desired redeployment aim: a more flexible architecture without sacrificing features or usability. The programming style adjustments required to accommodate the structural change are minimal, and I could efficiently make the required modifications at this stage of development.

The more complex a solution is at the time a change of deployment strategy is indicated, the greater the risks involved and the greater the work and testing required to ensure that the solution will not be adversely affected by the change. However, while determining an appropriate architecture for your solutions at the outset is desirable, change can be achieved.

Deployment Considerations

The option to separate elements of a solution makes a number of innovative deployment models viable, including modularization, separation of data, and interface and integration of external SQL data. However, I encourage you to carefully weigh the options to determine a mix that best serves your solution.

The conventional deployment mode — where one or more FileMaker database files (comprising both data and interface) reside on a network server and are accessed over a high-speed internal network — is giving way to other innovative solution topographies.

Your remotest dreams

Employing solution separation architectures enables some elements of your solutions to reside on network hosts (including multiple or remote/WAN hosts) while others are stored and accessed locally from the end user's workstation. Deployment models of this type permit new levels of flexibility and performance for distributed systems.

Systems drawing agency data for supporting databases in branch offices at considerable distances can now achieve satisfactory performance with appropriate optimizations — and a single server can be used as the conduit for data from any mix of FileMaker and supported SQL data systems.

The model of adaptability

The introduction of FileMaker's .fp7 file format in 2004 signaled a shift in focus only fully realized with the release of the FileMaker 10 suite of products. FileMaker has evolved and, with the introduction of support for external SQL data sources, the evolutionary leap is evident.

With FileMaker 10 as your tool of choice, a robust and ambitious feature set is available to you. FileMaker delivers its own flexible relational database management system — and puts it, along with a plethora of alternative (and even competing) technologies, into your hands. Access to these capabilities enables you to combine technologies in new ways and to solve new problems by doing so. It is up to you to devise data models and solution architectures to take advantage of FileMaker's new horizons.

Chapter 12

Calculation Wizardry

I n Chapter 7, I introduce you to the Specify Calculation dialog and demonstrate a few aspects of its utility and capability. However, if you have the impression that calculation is mainly about numbers, I have some surprises in store for you. Calculating in FileMaker is about getting the computer to work things out, but not necessarily just with numbers. In fact, calculations are great for people who aren't all that impressed with numbers. A bit of clear thinking will go a very long way, and the computer can do the rest!

Like scripting, calculations are integral to structuring and automating your solution. You can use calculations to determine access, control displays, and implement a variety of other features in your solution, as demonstrated in this chapter.

With FileMaker, a little work upfront can save you a lot of work later on. Calculations are one of the most extreme examples of this principle. Set one up, and it will keep chugging away producing results for thousands or even millions of records — enough to wear the buttons off a whole storeroom full of portable calculators.

You can employ the 249 built-in calculation functions FileMaker Pro 10 offers, each of which is designed to do something very particular. However, what calculation functions can do on their own isn't the subject of this chapter, but how you can combine them together to achieve everything from clever tricks to downright astonishing feats is.

> **NOTE** An alphabetical list of the calculation functions in FileMaker Pro 10, including links to descriptions and basic examples, is available at www.filemaker.com/help/html/help_func_alpha.html. Moreover, you can find a complete FileMaker 10 Functions Reference in a PDF document at www.filemaker.com/downloads/pdf/fmp10_functions_ref.pdf.

IN THIS CHAPTER

Building compound calculation expressions

Understanding order of operations and Boolean constructs

Using variables in different contexts

Processing, parsing, and formatting text

Calculating with dates and times

Working with summaries and arrays

Dealing with Layers of Abstraction

Working with different kinds of calculations

Employing global calculations

Making use of environment and meta-data

Extending your code with Custom Functions

Keeping track of what you've done

Because these materials are so readily available, I don't repeat their content in this book, reserving the space instead for usage recommendations and examples. I recommend that you download the PDF reference and refer to it as a supplement to this book.

Compound Calculation Expressions

A *formula* is the statement of your calculation, and an *expression* is something that can be evaluated. Thus, a formula is an expression, but not all expressions are necessarily formulas. Therefore, when I say formula, I mean the entirety of what appears in the Specify Calculation dialog's formula box, and that formula will consist of one or more expressions.

A *function* is a named expression that, when provided with zero or more arguments (frequently called *parameters*), returns a value. FileMaker Pro 10 provides a collection of precisely 249 calculation functions for you to employ in your formulae; however, they are *black boxes* in that you don't get to see the code that implements them.

Symbols such as +, -, *, /, ^, and also and, or, xor, and not are termed operators and instruct FileMaker how to treat adjacent parts of your calculation expressions. The adjacent parts acted upon by operators are often termed *operands*. In the calculation 2 + 3, for example, the 2 and the 3 are operands and the + is the operator.

CROSS-REF   You can supplement FileMaker's built-in functions by creating your own custom functions using FileMaker Pro 10 Advanced, as described in Chapter 18.

In the simplest of formulas, a function receives appropriate input parameters and returns a result. For example, the expression `Rightwords("The Jean Genie"; 1)` returns `Genie`, extracting one word from the right of the supplied phrase. However, each parameter you supply to a function such as `RightWords()` can be a literal value (as in the preceding example), a field (in which case the function acts on the field's value for the current record), or an expression combining one or more functions, constants, and/or operands.

Because one function's result can be passed as the input to another function, you can assemble complex structures according to simple rules, using functions and expressions like the words and phrases of a magical language that does the things it says.

If you begin with a simple function such as `Get(CurrentDate)` (which returns the current date as per the current computer's system clock) and enclose it within the `Month()` function as in `Month(Get(CurrentDate))`, FileMaker returns the number of the current month (for example, 3 for March, 7 for July, and so on). Similarly, enclosing `Get(CurrentDate)` within the `Year()` function returns the number of the current year (for example, 2009).

All these numbers are moderately useful in themselves, but they're more useful if you use them in turn to supply arguments to the `Date` function:

```
Date( Month(Get(CurrentDate)) + 1; 1; Year(Get(CurrentDate)) )
```

In this formula, 1 is added to the month number, and it's passed as the month parameter to the `Date()` function. The day is specified as the constant value 1, and the current year is provided as the year parameter. Thus, the entire expression returns the date of the first day of the following month.

An important thing to understand about the foregoing Date trick is that it will still work even when the current month number is 12. FileMaker is smart enough to accept the resulting month parameter of 13, convert the month to 1 (January), and increment the year so that a valid date is returned for all cases. This sleight of hand is typical of the FileMaker box of tricks.

NOTE The `Date()` function also resolves zero and negative parameter values. So, for example, if zero (0) is passed as the second parameter (day number) in the preceding example, the result will be the last day of the current month, regardless of how many days are in the current month.

The language of logic

In the example

```
Date( Month(Get(CurrentDate)) + 1; 1; Year(Get(CurrentDate)) )
```

you're instructing FileMaker to tell you the date where the month is the current month plus 1, the day is the first of the month, and the year is the current year. The form — also called *syntax* — that FileMaker requires you to use when asking it for a date is

```
Date(Month, Day, Year)
```

This form imposes a structure like any other language. First, you must say what you want to do and then (in parentheses afterward) you must say how, when, or where (as the case may be). FileMaker's calc syntax is based on the English language, presented in a simplified and codified form. After you get used to the structured language, it becomes easier to scan, write, and understand.

The calculation language's rules are consistent and straightforward, and the vocabulary (function names, operators, constants and some reserved words, plus the table and field names in your solution) isn't too challenging. Most of the rules simplify things; prepositions and conjunctions are omitted, and parentheses, semicolons, or operators are used in their place, as appropriate.

FileMaker's native function set defines not only the core of the vocabulary of calculations, but also the form and syntax. Each function in the vocabulary has simple rules for the inputs it requires and the outputs it returns, all of which are defined in the FileMaker 10 Function Reference. (To access this reference, go to `www.filemaker.com/downloads/pdf/fmp10_functions_ref.pdf`.)

Almost all native FileMaker calculation functions require parameters. The only five exceptions are

- `DatabaseNames`
- `Pi`
- `Random`
- `Self`
- `WindowNames`

Each of the first four functions stands alone, returning its appropriate value without qualification, whenever you use it. The last, `WindowNames`, can stand alone or can accept an optional parameter specifying the name of the file for which it is to return the names of current windows. All other functions, however, require one or more parameters, either to control the way they work or to provide input.

When parameters are required, they're always enclosed in parentheses immediately after the name of the function they're associated with. Multiple parameters are separated by semicolons. A few functions (22 in total, including `WindowNames`) include optional parameters. Whereas `WindowNames` has only one parameter, all other functions with optional parameters have one or more required parameters. An example of a function with an optional parameter is the `If( )` function:

```
If(test; resultIfTrue {; resultIfFalse})
```

The `If( )` function can accept either two or three parameters — the first two are required, and the third is optional. The first parameter is the test to determine the result the function returns. The second parameter supplies the result if the test succeeds (is evaluated as true). The final, optional parameter supplies a result to be returned if the test fails (proves false). A simple expression using `If( )` can therefore be written as

```
If(
Month(DateOfBirth) = Month(Get(CurrentDate)) and
Day(DateOfBirth) = Day(Get(CurrentDate));
"Happy Birthday, " & FirstName
)
```

This formula returns a message such as "Happy Birthday, Jan" when the value in the `FirstName` field is "Jan" and the month and day of the value in the `DateOfBirth` field is the same as the current date on your computer's system clock. However, if you want the function to return a result on days other than Jan's birthday, you can use the optional third parameter:

```
If(Month(DateOfBirth) = Month(Get(CurrentDate)) and
Day(DateOfBirth) = Day(Get(CurrentDate));
"Happy Birthday, "; "Welcome, ") & FirstName
```

In this example, whenever it is not the anniversary of Jan's birthday, the optional second result is returned, so the text will simply read "Welcome, Jan". One day per year, the text returned will be Happy Birthday, Jan".

Functions and schema references

You can supply parameters to your functions in one of three ways:

- **As text or numbers entered directly into the calculation:** Parameters supplied in this way are usually referred to as a *constant* or a *literal* value. Commonly, constant refers to numeric values and literal to text values, but the names are applied somewhat interchangeably.

- **As a reference (by name) to a field or a variable in your solution:** In this case, FileMaker retrieves the current value of the field or variable at the time it evaluates the calculation, using it as input to the function.

- **As an expression:** This expression can be made up of one or more functions, operators, and other elements combined in such a way as to produce a result that will provide the required parameter.

When you enter text literals into a calculation, they must be enclosed within quotes (" "). Numeric literal values don't require quotes. When you enter more than one item, an operator is required in between them (and which operator you choose controls how they're interpreted). For example, the + operator tells FileMaker to add the numeric values of the supplied values, whereas the & operator tells FileMaker to append them as text. So the expression 23 + 4 will return 27, whereas the expression 23 & 4 will return 234.

CROSS-REF For a detailed discussion of the mechanics of defining calculations in the Specify Calculation dialog, refer to Chapter 7.

Making context explicit

When you want FileMaker to retrieve the value from a field in your database, you must generally supply the name of the field, preceded by the name of the relevant TO, in the form

```
TableOccurrenceName::FieldName
```

The only exception is when you define the calculation within the schema, and the field is returned from the current record — in which case the TO name is optional.

Adding the TO name enables FileMaker to determine the relationship path to use when retrieving a value from the field. Resolving the path requires both a start point and an end point. The TO name you supply with the referenced field name defines the end point. The start point is set via the Evaluate This Calculation From The Context Of menu at the top of the Specify Calculation dialog, as shown in Figure 12.1.

Avoiding circular references

Because FileMaker requires that only one relationship path be between any two TOs on the Relationships Graph (thus avoiding circular references on the Graph), supplying the starting and ending TOs for a field reference is sufficient to indicate exactly from which instance of the field to retrieve a value.

NOTE When a relationship you use to reference a field in the current record points to multiple related records, FileMaker returns the first related record (according to the sort order for the relationship, if specified, or otherwise according to the creation order of records in the related table). To reference a field in a record (other than the first related record), enclose the field reference within the GetNthRecord( ) function, supplying (as the second parameter) the number of the record you want to reference.

FIGURE 12.1

Setting the context for evaluation of a calculation via the Specify Calculation dialog.

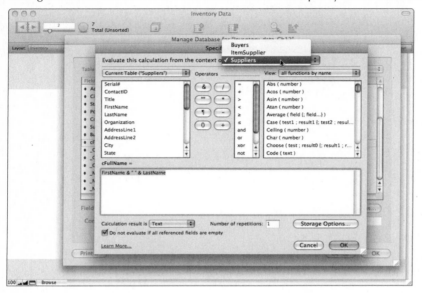

Structured syntax and nesting

Although I recommend that you obtain a copy of the FileMaker 10 Functions Reference and use it as a supplementary resource, you don't need to refer to it to remember the syntax required for each calculation function. FileMaker lists all its available functions in the panel at the upper right of the Specify Calculation dialog, along with a key to the syntax requirements of each function. The listed functions may be filtered by category (in 16 predefined categories) to make it easier to find what you're looking for.

Two of the 16 categories of functions — Get functions and External functions — are included only as a single reference each in the list of all functions by name. To see the available options in each of these groups, you must choose the respective function category.

NOTE Functions in the Specify Calculation dialog list are categorized by data type according to the kind of input value they're expected to receive, rather than the kind of output they generate. For example, GetAsTimestamp ( ) is listed as a text function because it receives a text input, even though it returns its result as a timestamp value.

Similarly, the Length ( ) function is listed among text functions because it treats the input value as a text string, even though the result it returns will be a number (representing the length of the supplied string).

When you select a function from the Specify Calculation dialog functions list, it's inserted into the calculation panel at the current cursor position, along with the prompt for its syntax, such as parentheses, semicolons, and names of the required parameters. For example, if you select the Upper ( ) function, it is inserted into your calculation as Upper (text) with the parameter name (text) selected, ready for you to overwrite it with an appropriate value. You can supply the parameter as a literal value (within quote marks):

```
Upper("Strawberry Fields Forever")
```

or as a reference to a field or variable:

```
Upper(Songs::SongName)

Upper($$CurrentSongName)
```

or as an expression, incorporating any combination of literal values, field or variable references, and/or functions:

```
Upper("Song Title: " & Songs::SongName)
```

In each case, FileMaker first resolves any expressions within the enclosing parentheses and then converts the result to uppercase text.

Putting it all together

To connect components of a calculation together, FileMaker provides six basic types of operators:

- **Arithmetic operators:** +, -, /, *, ( ), and ^ .
- **Comparison operators:** <, >, ≥, ≤, =, and ≠.
- **Logical operators:** and, or, not, and xor.
- **Text operators:** &, " ", \, and ¶.
- **Comment operators:** /* */ and //.
- **Reserved Name operator:** ${ }.

NOTE If you prefer, you can use the combinations <> in place of ≠, >= in place of ≥, and <= in place of ≤.

Frequently, your calculations will involve a decision, taking action or applying logic accordingly. For this purpose, the comparative and logical operators are indispensable. When two or more values are compared, FileMaker returns a true or false (Boolean) result that you can use to determine the outcome of the calculation. For example, if you're inviting interested parties to a house inspection on a different date depending on where in the alphabet their name falls (for example, A to M on date 1 and N to Z on date 2), you might use a simple logic calculation along the following lines:

```
If(Visitors::LastName < "N"; VisitDates::Day1; VisitDates::Day2)
```

In this example, the logic hinges on the test `Visitors::LastName < "N"` returning either of the two possible dates from the `VisitDates` table contingent on the test outcome. However, if you also want to ensure that anyone who has made telephone contact is also invited on the first available date, you need a more complex logic. Your calculation now appears as

```
If(Visitors::LastName < "N" or Visitors::PhoneContact = "Yes"; VisitDates::Day1;
    VisitDates::Day2)
```

Again, the formula includes an expression and two alternative results; however, this time the test brings together two comparisons (using the comparative operators < and = respectively) with the logical operator or to accommodate the additional requirement. Note that the meaning of the calculation is clear, and it reads almost like a narrative.

Order of Operations

When you place parentheses around part of a calculation, FileMaker resolves that part first. Therefore, adding parentheses makes the order of evaluation explicit. Consider the classic example of a simple arithmetic calculation:

```
24 - 2 * 3
```

The rules of math require that multiplication and division take place before addition and subtraction, so the correct answer is 18 (24 minus 6). However, if parentheses are used to re-order the calculation as in

```
(24 - 2) * 3
```

the parentheses change the normal order of computation so that the subtraction must be performed first — making the correct answer now 66 (22 times 3). Similarly, all FileMaker's operators have a natural or default order of operations for all cases except where you specify the order by including one or more sets of parentheses. In fact, parentheses themselves are an operator acting on the calculation to determine the outcome.

Although some operators take precedence over others, some are of equal weight (for example, addition and subtraction). When these equal operators are combined in a calculation, the evaluation proceeds from left to right (again, unless parentheses are included).

Each kind of operator serves a different purpose and produces a different kind of result. Arithmetic operators perform sums and produce numeric results, whereas comparative operators perform tests and return a Boolean result. Logical operators combine multiple tests to determine a composite test result, and so on. Each has a clear role and operates according to basic (and largely intuitive) principles.

Filemaker Pro 10 applies the following default order of operations:

1. Comment operators take precedence over all else.
2. Reserved name operators and quotation marks are evaluated second, with whichever occurs first or outside the other taking precedence.

3. Expressions in parentheses are evaluated next.

4. The not operator is evaluated before all remaining operators.

5. ^ is evaluated before any other arithmetic operator; * and / are evaluated before + and −.

6. With the exception of quotation marks (see Step 2 on this list), arithmetic operators are evaluated before text operators.

7. Arithmetic and text operators are evaluated before comparison operators.

8. With the exception of the not operator, comparison operators evaluate before logical operators.

9. The and operator is evaluated before or or xor.

This order of operations determines how your expressions are evaluated, except where you use parentheses to determine the order of evaluation. Where no parentheses are included and operators are at the same level in the preceding hierarchy, evaluation takes place from left to right.

Although the order of operations I provide here may appear daunting at first glance, in most cases the order supports natural flow and readability in your calculation expressions. In many cases, beyond the rules of simple arithmetic, you don't need to pay any special attention to evaluation order because the default order determined by FileMaker is the correct order for a significant number of cases.

Take, for example, the test in the If ( ) function cited in the preceding section:

```
Visitors::LastName < "N" or Visitors::PhoneContact = "Yes"
```

Because comparative operators take precedence over logical operators, both comparisons take place first and are then joined by the evaluation of the or operator and no parentheses are required to deliver the expected and desired outcome. In many such cases, FileMaker makes the same sense of your code as you would make reading it, making your task simple.

You can combine elements to produce a desired result in many ways, and you can achieve many calculations using alternative approaches. Some methods may be easier to read, while other methods may be more compact. Still others may be more efficient in operation. You get to decide which is best for your purposes.

Because the parameters for a function can be supplied by a combination of calculation elements (including functions), you can nest calculation functions within themselves. For example, you can use the Replace ( ) function with a size parameter of zero, to insert a phrase into a block of text:

```
Replace("The fox jumps over the dog."; 5; 0; "quick ")
```

This syntax returns "The quick fox jumps over the dog." However by passing the preceding expression as the input parameter to a further Replace ( ) function, you can insert a text string at a second point in a single operation:

```
Replace(Replace("The fox jumps over the dog."; 5; 0; "quick "); 30; 0; "lazy ")
```

This expression returns "The quick fox jumps over the lazy dog." Although the preceding expression is a conventional example of nesting, extending the scope of the original operation, you can also place one function within another to perform complementary operations. For example, you can make sure that a number never goes below 1 with the following expression:

```
Max(1; YourNumber)
```

The `Max( )` function returns the highest number from those supplied to it as parameters, so if the value in the field called `YourNumber` is greater than 1, it will be returned, but if it is lower, 1 will be returned instead. Similarly, the `Min( )` function can be used to determine an upper limit:

```
Min(10; YourNumber)
```

Here, the result will never exceed 10 because FileMaker will return the lesser of the two values supplied. You can nest one expression within the other to ensure that `YourNumber` always falls within the range from 1 to 10:

```
Max(1; Min(10; YourNumber))
```

With this expression in place (using a technique such as an *auto-enter calculation/replaces existing value*, on the `YourNumber` field), you have set both upper and lower bounds for `YourNumber`, using a single formula.

Boolean Operations

Many tasks you perform in a database implement decisions. If a student has achieved a certain score, he may be admitted to the next grade. If the full amount of an invoice has been paid, its status may be changed to Closed. These decisions are simple logical determinations you can build into your database via calculations.

When you write a formula to compare values and determine a result, you use comparison operators. Comparison operators return a true/false result in numeric format where 1 is true and 0 is false. This true/false result is called a *Boolean result* — meaning that the result is always either true or false, and no other possibilities exist.

Zero, empty, and everything else

FileMaker interprets numbers (in fields, variables, and literal values) as Boolean according to the rule that zero and empty values are false and other numbers (whether positive or negative, integer or decimal fraction) are true. Text strings (containing no numerals), because they have no numeric value, are treated as empty for the purposes of a Boolean test. However, text values that contain a number (such as "Julie has 3 socks") are interpreted as having a true Boolean value.

Date, time, and timestamp fields, because they also stored numeric values, are interpreted as true when they hold a non-empty, nonzero value. Otherwise, they're interpreted as false. Container fields do not hold numeric data, but FileMaker interprets them as true if they're not empty and false if empty.

If invalid data is imported into date, time, or timestamp fields, they can return false when evaluated as a Boolean due to the presence of invalid data (that is, data that doesn't conform to the requirements of the field's data type).

If you set up a number field to display a value list with only a single value of 1, checking or unchecking the checkbox will change the value of the field from null (empty) to 1 and back. Because FileMaker interprets null values as false and other values (such as 1) as true, such a field can be used as a logical switch to control other calculations.

Implicit Boolean coding

Alternately, if you reference the AmountPaid field within an operation calling for a Boolean result, FileMaker registers it as true if it contains an amount or false if it contains zero or is empty. This coding is an implicit conversion of the field value to a true/false status. You might use this, for example, to set a Paid flag on the invoice.

Although FileMaker handles this conversion for you, it is generally preferable to code your solution explicitly rather than relying on FileMaker to interpret it for you. (That way, when you or another developer looks at your code, you'll have no doubt as to what you intended.)

Explicit Boolean coding

You can make Boolean behavior explicit in several ways. Perhaps the clearest and simplest is to enclose the reference within FileMaker's GetAsBoolean() function. So, for example,

```
GetAsBoolean(Invoice::AmountPaid)
```

always returns either zero (false) or one (true). Not only is this simple and direct, but it plainly states the purpose of the expression.

Another way to make a reference to a field explicitly Boolean is to use it in a comparative operation:

```
Invoice::AmountPaid > 0
```

Because comparative operations always return a Boolean result, this expression is an acceptable alternative way to make a field reference in your solution explicitly Boolean. However, in the case of this example, you may want to avoid situations where a part-payment will set the payment flag, so comparing the AmountPaid value to the TotalPayable value for the invoice is preferable, rather than merely confirming that it is a nonzero amount. So the formula for your paid flag field may best be

```
If(Invoice::AmountPaid ≥ Invoice::TotalPayable; "PAID IN FULL")
```

When written in this way, your Boolean code is clear and unequivocal, leaving you in no doubt as to its intent — and leaving FileMaker no room for alternative interpretations of your code.

FileMaker's interpretation of null values is also affected by the setting labeled Do Not Evaluate When All Referenced Fields Are Empty. If this checkbox is enabled in the Specify Calculation dialog, the calculation will return no result if the referenced fields are null.

Variables — Calculation, Script, and Global

Memory variables — values such as calculation results or data held temporarily in application memory — are both convenient and efficient (much faster than referencing a field, for example) as ways to pass information between calculations or between expressions within a calculation.

FileMaker supports three essential kinds of memory variables for use in your solution:

- **Calculation variables:** Calculation scoped variables are those that have names that don't begin with a $ character.
- **Local variables:** This category includes all variables that have names commencing with single $ character.
- **Global variables:** Global variables have names commencing with a pair of dollar sign characters ($$).

The variable types differ in their scope and/or persistence and are therefore useful in different ways. However, their usages aren't immediately obvious from the names appearing in official documentation and common use. In particular, the use of the term *script variables* is misleading.

Significantly, all three kinds of variables can be defined in a calculation anywhere in your solution, via the use of the Let ( ) function. Moreover, although calculation variables can't be defined or referenced outside a calculation, the calculation in which they're defined can occur within a script or anywhere else in your code — for example, in schema, in a calculation defined as part of a button command, in a formula evaluated as part of conditional formatting, and so on.

Declaring calculation variables — the Let( ) function

Calculation variables exist only within the confines of a Let ( ) statement within a single calculation expression. Such variables are defined singly or in a list at the beginning of the Let ( ) function and persist only through to the closing parenthesis of the function they're defined in (unless explicitly cleared or redefined earlier in the function syntax). For example, the expression

```
Let(x = 10; 70 / x)
```

returns 7 because for the duration of the expression (between the enclosing parentheses of the Let ( ) function), the variable x has been declared as having a value of 10. When the expression 70 / x is evaluated, x resolves to its declared value, and the formula is treated as 70 / 10. Similarly,

```
Let([x = 10; y = 70]; y / x)
```

also returns 7 because both the operative values x and y have been declared with their respective values in the list expression (between the square brackets). Moreover, once a variable has been declared, you can use it as part of the argument in the declaration of subsequent variables:

```
Let([x = 10; y = x * 7]; y / x)
```

In this way, each named variable acquires a declared value for the purposes of the enclosed expression. If a variable name is reused in the list of variables in a single Let ( ) statement, the later declared values supercede earlier ones. If Let ( ) statements are nested, the value of variables declared in the enclosing statement can be accessed within enclosed statements, but not vice versa. In other words, enclosed statement variables aren't accessible outside the specific instance of the Let ( ) function where they're declared.

Understanding variables' scope

Variables with names not starting with dollar symbols are operable only within the confines of the function where you define them. Thus, their scope is tightly constrained, they expire instantly, and they can't be referenced, even while evaluation is in process, anywhere else in the solution.

When a Let ( ) statement variable's name commences with a single dollar sign (for example, $x), you can access the variable outside the calculation where you define it, but only while the current instance of the currently running script is *active* (in other words, at the top of the script stack).

CROSS-REF For a detailed discussion of FileMaker's script-threading and the operation of the Script Stack, refer to Chapter 8.

Such variables are termed *local* because, though accessible throughout the current file, they persist only for the duration of the current script. They may also be considered *script variables* because in addition to being declared in a Let ( ) statement within a calculation expression, they can be created independently by the use of the Set Variable[ ] script step or button command.

TIP When no scripts are running, FileMaker deems a hypothetical Script Zero to be at the top of the script stack. Therefore, if a local variable is declared while no scripts are active (that is, in a calculation expression), it retains its value throughout the file whenever the script stack is empty, for the remainder of the current file session.

When you declare a variable with a name commencing with two (or more) dollar signs, FileMaker makes its value available throughout the current file regardless of the status of the script stack. Variables of this type are called *global* variables because of their wider scope; however, they're not persistent — in other words, they're constrained to the current file session. If you want a value to persist between FileMaker sessions, you should store it in a standard (nonglobal) field and then set your solution's start-up script to retrieve and reinstate the value in a subsequent file session. Global fields, like global variables, are session specific in a hosted solution.

NOTE A file session is the period between when a file is opened and subsequently closed on a particular workstation. If a file is closed and reopened, a new file session begins, and any $$ variable values associated with the previous file session are lost.

Within their respective scope, each type of variable persists until explicitly destroyed. A variable is destroyed in FileMaker by setting its value to null (" "), at which point the memory it has occupied is released.

Benefiting from variables in a calculation

The use of the Let ( ) function to declare variables in calculation syntax has several potential advantages, especially in compound or complex expressions. Foremost among these advantages are

- The capability to calculate a component value once and use it multiple places in the calc expression, thus reducing redundancy and minimizing the processor cycles required to evaluate the expression

- The capability to break logic of a compound statement down into its elements and improve readability, simplicity, and clarity

As an example of the elimination of redundancy, consider the following simple expression:

```
Item::Qty * Item::Price +
If(Item::Qty * Item::Price < 100; Item::Shipping)
```

The logic of this expression is straightforward: Customers aren't charged shipping on orders over $100. To resolve the logic, however, FileMaker must retrieve the Item::Qty and Item::Price values from their respective fields twice and perform the multiplication twice, consuming slightly more resources (processor cycles, memory, network bandwidth, and so on) in the process and taking slightly longer.

Instead, the components of the preceding calculation can be reworked as

```
Let(
Amt = Item::Qty * Item::Price;
Amt + If(Amt < 100; Item::Shipping)
)
```

In this reworking, you calculate the product of quantity and price only once, significantly reducing the work involved in evaluating such a calculation — it's almost halved. In more complex functions where the time taken to calculate a component of the expression is significant, and especially where one or more components may recur multiple times, the reduction in evaluation time is greater and may make a significant difference to your solution usability.

CROSS-REF For a further discussion of elimination of redundancy and efficient coding practices in your solutions, refer to Chapter 19.

Text Processing and Parsing Functions

One useful capability in FileMaker's calculation repertoire is the ability to modify text in your databases in a wide variety of ways, including correcting errors; updating entries; organizing; sorting; merging; separating words, lines, and sentences; and more.

When your database contains e-mail addresses such as `mary@greatgizmos.com`, you'll likely need to convert them into a corresponding URL, such as one for the GreatGizmos Web site. Or perhaps you need to extract all the part numbers from a file full of correspondence with a major client. These tasks and many others are trivial when you're familiar with the use of FileMaker's text processing functions.

Substitute, Replace, and Trim

One of FileMaker's most versatile functions is `Substitute( )`. You can use this function to swap all occurrences of any character or sequence of characters in a field or text string for text you specify. For example, if you have a list of values (one on each line) that you'd prefer were presented with a comma and space between each, you can achieve that elegantly with a calculation expression, such as

```
Substitute(YourList; ¶; ", ")
```

If the items on your list are preceded by bullet characters that have no place in your new comma separated presentation, you can remove them as part of the same function call by using the list syntax:

```
Substitute(YourList; [¶; ", "]; ["• "; ""])
```

> **TIP** Wherever parameter lists are supported in FileMaker calculations, each list item, as in the preceding example, is enclosed within square brackets, and successive items are separated by a semicolon.

The ability to perform multiple substitutions in a single function call makes your calculations both powerful and efficient. Because the `Substitute( )` function is case sensitive, if you need to replace a word or phrase regardless of case, you may need to list all likely permutations. For example, to ensure that the name of your database software is correctly capitalized wherever it occurs in a text field, you could use

```
Substitute(YourTO::YourTextField;

["filemaker; "FileMaker"];

["Filemaker; "FileMaker"];

["FILEMAKER; "FileMaker"];

["FIleMaker; "FileMaker"];

)
```

When you need to replace a specific sequence of characters without regard to what they are, you'll be better served by the `Replace( )` function. Unlike `Substitute( )`, `Replace( )` enables you to specify the text to be modified by its position in the target string, rather than by matching it to a string you supply.

Suppose that the value in a field always begins with a letter of the alphabet, followed by a punctuation mark (but not always the same punctuation mark), a space or tab, and then some subsequent text, and your objective is to make all of the second and third characters consistent. In such a situation, Substitute() is less useful — not only because the combination of characters to be replaced may be different each time, but also because you don't want to change other punctuation later in the field. (You're concerned only with the second and third characters in each field.) You can achieve an update with surgical precision using a formula such as

```
Replace(YourTO::YourTextField; 2; 2; ". ")
```

which tells FileMaker to start at the second character and replace two characters with the string you're providing (a period followed by a space).

> **TIP**   If you supply a zero as the third parameter for the Replace() function, it doesn't remove any text. Instead, it inserts text at the point determined by the second parameter. For example, you can use this feature to add a space between the third and fourth characters of a telephone number.

Before long, when editing or cleaning up text in your solutions, you face the challenge of superfluous spaces at the start or (particularly) the end of a field value or text string. Spaces at the end of a field can go unnoticed until you compare text or combine text together, such as when you're adding names to the top of a letter. As soon as you do, the extra spaces can create problems and produce unwanted results.

FileMaker provides the Trim() function to enable you to efficiently discard leading and trailing spaces without disturbing the spaces between words). So

```
Trim("     The Hendersons will all be there…    ")
```

returns "The Hendersons will all be there…" without all the extra space before and after. Similarly,:

```
TrimAll("  For     the    benefit    of  Mr     Kite…   "; 1; 1)
```

returns "For the benefit of Mr Kite…" with just a single space between each word, as well as the superfluous leading and trailing spaces removed.

> **NOTE**   The TrimAll() function also has uses controlling full- and half-width spaces when working with non-Roman characters and words. Consult the online help entry on this function for full details of all its configuration options.

Left, Right, and Middle

When you get down to working with text, you frequently need to extract part of the text from a larger block. For example, if names have been imported into your solution in a single field, but you require them to be separated into Title, FirstName, and LastName fields, you're facing a minor challenge known as *parsing*.

The Left( ), Middle( ), and Right( ) functions provide you with the means to extract a specific number of characters from either end, or anywhere within a string of text. For example, if your ClientDetails field contains the name Mr Fandangle Pranderghast, the following three expressions return the three separate text strings Mr, Fandangle, and Pranderghast, respectively:

```
Left(Contacts::ClientDetails; 2)

Middle(Contacts::ClientDetails; 3; 9)

Right(Contacts::ClientDetails; 12)
```

These functions are powerful and precise — provided that you're able to accurately supply them with the correct coordinates (more on that in the following section, "Position and PatternCount").

Another example of using these great functions is the elimination of unwanted characters at the start or end of a text string. For example, if you want to remove the punctuation from the end of a sentence in a field, you can use

```
Left(YourSolution::YourTextField; Length(YourSolution::YourTextField) - 1)
```

Whatever is in the text field when this expression is evaluated will be returned with one character removed from the right.

Similarly, when you have fields containing To Do list items in the form

A: *Don't forget your lunch!*

and you want to discard the first three characters and the trailing punctuation mark, you can accomplish that in a single stroke with the expression

```
Middle(ThingsToDo::Reminder; 4; Length(ThingsToDo::Reminder) - 4)
```

By starting at character 4, it leaves off the first three characters, and by running for the length of the string minus 4, it stops short of the last character, giving as its result "Don't forget your lunch".

Position and PatternCount

The text processing operations' capability increases greatly when you can instruct FileMaker to look for particular characters or text strings and return their position or the number of them encountered. FileMaker provides the Position( ) and PatternCount( ) functions for this purpose, and they add flexibility and precision to the text-handling arsenal.

For example, in the following example, FileMaker is extracting text from the middle of a string commencing at the fourth character:

```
Middle(ThingsToDo::Reminder; 4; Length(ThingsToDo::Reminder) - 4)
```

However, this syntax produces the desired result only if all the strings you apply the procedure to are structured the same. If any of them has an additional (leading) character or missing initial character, the fixed start parameter results in an inappropriate result. In other words, the first character of the required text may sometimes be 5 or 3 rather than 4.

Because `Position( )` returns the exact location of a specified character or starting location of a string, it can be incorporated to lend greater accuracy to the text extraction:

```
Position(ThingsToDo::Reminder; ": "; 1; 1)
```

This expression returns the location (in characters starting from the left) of the first occurrence of a colon and space. By using the result of the `Position( )` expression as a reference point (adding two to it to determine the start of the extract string), you can make your `Middle( )` operation responsive to changes in the format of the Reminder text.

In the form shown in the preceding example, the `Position( )` function is set (via its last two parameters) to locate the first occurrence of the search string (": ") starting from the first character of the content of the `ThingsToDo::Reminder` field. However, you can structure the function to operate differently by supplying different values for these parameters:

```
Position(ThingsToDo::Reminder; ": "; Length(ThingsToDo::Reminder); -1)
```

The preceding syntax instructs FileMaker to begin its search at the end of the field (`Length (ThingsToDo::Reminder)`) content and to search backwards(`-1`). Thus, with this variant of the expression, the last occurrence of the search string's location is returned, rather than the first.

> **NOTE**   If the search string is not present in the supplied text (or field value), the Position( ) function returns a zero.

In some cases, however, you'll want to confirm the presence or frequency of occurrence of the search string before proceeding to act on it. For example, when you need to locate the middle occurrence of an item in a continuous text sequence (where each item is prefaced by a label and colon, as in the previous example), you can determine the number of items using the following syntax:

```
PatternCount(ThingsToDo::Reminder; ": ")
```

Thus, to calculate the middle occurrence, you should divide by two and enclose the result in the `Ceiling( )` function:

```
Ceiling(PatternCount(ThingsToDo::Reminder; ": ") / 2)
```

To ascertain the location of the middle occurrence of the search string, you can use a compound formula, where the preceding expression is supplied as the *occurrence* parameter for the `Position( )` function:

```
Position(ThingsToDo::Reminder; ": "; 1; Ceiling(PatternCount(ThingsToDo::Reminde
  r; ": ") / 2))
```

This result, in turn can supply the *start* parameter to the `Middle( )` function, when you are seeking to extract text from the middle To Do list item in a text block. By using a comparable technique to determine the location of the end of the middle item (and subtracting the end from the start to determine the size of the middle item), you're able to neatly extract (parse) the middle item from a block of text containing multiple items. For example, when the text in the `ThingsToDo::Reminder` field is as follows,

> *A: Don't forget your lunch! B: Deliver term papers to office. C: Collect bus pass! D: Pay electricity bill. E: Photocopy timetable.*

you can use a compound construction along the following lines to extract the middle item (Collect bus pass!) from the field:

```
Let([
    ItemNo   = Ceiling(PatternCount(ThingsToDo::Reminder; ": ") / 2);
    StartPos = Position(ThingsToDo::Reminder; ": "; 1; ItemNo) + 2;
    EndPos   = Position(ThingsToDo::Reminder; ": "; StartPos; 1) - 2];
Middle(ThingsToDo::Reminder; StartPos; EndPos - StartPos)
)
```

NOTE In the preceding example, I employed the `Let( )` function to separately calculate the expression's components, declaring each as variables, and then combined those variables in the final line. Determining parameters dynamically increases the clarity and efficiency of a compound expression used to parse elements dynamically from a text string.

While combinations of `Position( )` and `PatternCount( )`, along with the `Left( )`, `Middle( )`, `Right( )` functions, are sufficient to isolate and extract a word or phrase from a longer text string, doing so can be challenging. FileMaker makes it easier by giving you a variety of other options, including the ability to extract text in whole words rather than individual characters.

The xWords suite

The `LeftWords( )`, `MiddleWords( )`, `RightWords( )`, and `WordCount( )` functions streamline many text operations, giving you a direct and simplified method of performing many language and narrative related manipulations and analyses. Working in whole words takes much of the drudgery out of parsing and assembling text.

When parsing text by whole words, FileMaker uses separator characters to recognize the start and end of each word. The most obvious example of a word separator is the space, but FileMaker also treats many common punctuation marks and glyphs as word separators. For example, in addition to spaces, the following characters are treated as word separators:

- `< > ? / ; " { } [ ] | \ ~ ` ! @ # $ % ^ & ¶ • * ( ) _ + =`

Additionally:

- A period is treated as a word separator if the characters on either side of it are a letter and numeral, but not if both characters are of the same type, such as two letters or two numerals.

- A forward slash, colon, comma, and hyphen are treated as word separators except when the characters on both sides of them are numerals (useful for selecting dates, times, and numbers as single words).

- An apostrophe is treated as a word separator except when the characters on both sides of it are letters.

- Both a tab character and a carriage return, as well as a literal pilcrow (¶) character, are treated as word separators for all cases.

By applying these rules, FileMaker offers a relatively automatic method of text manipulation. Using this capability, text in the form

A: *Don't forget your lunch!*

can be more easily reduced to "Don't forget your lunch" with the expression:

```
RightWords(ThingsToDo::Reminder; 4)
```

Because an artifact of the xWords functions is that they omit leading and trailing word separator characters from the returned (or counted) string, they're often exploited as a way to strip unwanted characters, including spaces, carriage returns, and punctuation, from the ends of a text string. For example, the expression

```
LeftWords(" •  Endless rain into a paper cup??!  ¶ "; 9999)
```

returns "Endless rain into a paper cup", cleanly excising the bullet, tab, punctuation, carriage return, and associated spaces from both ends of the text string — rather like a Trim( ) function on steroids!

Parsing in practice

The logic of parsing operations (location and extraction of text within a field or other string or value) conforms to a common set of principles whether you're using functions such as Left( ), Middle( ), and Right( ), or the powerful yet simple xWords functions. Either way, you must locate a start point and an end point and then pass these parameters to the appropriate function to grab everything in between.

Sometimes, however, what you leave out, not what you include, makes the difference. Consider a situation where you want to omit a particular text string that occurs in several thousand records. For example, in a tournament database, each match will be entered in the following form:

Peter Van Elking - challenging - Jerry Glover

Janice Thorn - rematch - Jenny-Lee Shackles

Gemma P. Harding - face-off - Susan Marchent

However, you may be asked to produce a program where the names are listed with a simple comma between the opponents' names instead. One way to do this is to use the `Position( )` function to locate the "–" characters and use that to reassemble the strings as follows:

```
Left(Game::Set; Position(Game::Set; " - "; 1; 1) - 1) & ", " &
Right(Game::Set; Length(Game::Set) - Position(Game::Set; " - "; 1; 2) - 2)
```

When this expression is applied to each line (that is, each `Game::Set` field value) in turn, the names are returned with a comma in place of the intermediary dashes and words.

In this expression, the location of each of the en dashes is determined by the `Position( )` functions and passed respectively to the `Left( )` and `Right( )` functions to extract the name from either end of each string, despite the fact that the length of the intervening text is not consistent. The two names are then joined in a new string using the concatenation operator (`&`), along with a separating comma and space supplied as a text literal (and therefore enclosed within quote marks).

Text Formatting Operations

FileMaker's suite of text formatting calculation functions enables you to control character level (embedded) formats applied to text within fields in your database, including applying and removing custom text style, color, size, and font attributes.

You can display text you've formatted via calculation in calculation fields, set it into conventional data fields via script, or apply (or remove) formatting using auto-enter calculations, depending on the content of the field (or other fields in the record).

Applying text formatting

You can use any combination of the `TextFont( )`, `TextColor( )`, `TextSize( )`, and `TextStyleAdd( )` functions to apply formatting. Formatting you apply with any one of these commands is added to the specified text's existing character formatting (if any).

To apply more than one style at once, you can list multiple style parameters within a single instance of the `TextStyleAdd( )` function:

```
TextStyleAdd("Mad World"; bold + italic + underline)
```

The preceding expression results in the text ***Mad World***.

Similarly, you can apply multiple formats simultaneously by nesting two or more format functions. For example, to simultaneously change the font of a text string to Verdana and the size to 11 point, you can use

```
TextSize(TextFont("I Saw Her Standing There"; "Verdana"); 11)
```

Formatting applied in this way overrides field formats applied to the field object on a layout (and also conditional formats applied to the layout field object).

 For a detailed discussion of formatting and the different ways it's applied and managed in FileMaker Pro, refer to Chapter 9.

Removing text formatting

You can remove text formatting either selectively or indiscriminately. To remove all fonts, styles, font size, and font color attributes from a text string, use the formula

```
TextFormatRemove(YourTable::YourTextString)
```

This calculation returns the text in the `YourTable::YourTextString` field as plain text that is stripped of all character styles and paragraph formatting

However, if you prefer to remove some aspects of the custom formatting while retaining others, you can do so with precision by using the `TextFontRemove( )`, `TextColorRemove( )`, `TextSizeRemove( )`, and `TextStyleRemove( )` functions. You can remove a single format with each of these functions by supplying an associated format parameter. Or you can remove all formats of the relevant type by supplying a text string and no format (size, color, style, or font) parameter. For example, to remove bold character styling while leaving other styles (italic, underline, and so on) in place, use an expression such as:

```
TextStyleRemove(YourTable::YourTextString; Bold)
```

As when adding formatting, you can nest multiple functions (if desired) to remove a number of specific format attributes simultaneously (while leaving others in place).

Applying selective formatting

You can combine logic and formatting functions to apply to text (or parts of the text, such as individual words) according to the data in your solution. For example, to display part of a sentence in italics depending on the data available, you can use the following formula:

```
"This issue is " &
TextStyleAdd(Issues::Status; If(Issues::Status = "Urgent"; Italic; Plain))
```

Alternatively, to spotlight all occurrences of a search term in a block of text using bold formatting, you can use

```
Substitute(Issues::Description; Issues::gSearchTerm; TextStyleAdd(Issues::gSearch
    Term; Bold))
```

This formula locates all occurrences of the value in the `gSearchTerm` field within the content of the `Description` field, changing each to bold formatted text. Because formatting functions can be nested, the preceding example can be extended to apply color as well as style attributes, by enclosing the final part of the expression within an additional function:

```
Substitute(Issues::Description; Issues::gSearchTerm; TextColor(TextStyleAdd(Issu
    es::gSearchTerm; Bold); RGB(0; 0; 255)))
```

> **TIP**
> The `TextColor( )` function accepts, as its second parameter, a color number in the range from 0 (black) to 16777215 (white), where the 8-bit color value of red, green, and blue (each in the range from 0 to 255) is combined using the following formula:
>
> ```
> Red * 256^2 + Green * 256 + Blue
> ```
>
> For convenience, FileMaker provides the `RGB( )` function for computing this value from the individual values for red, green, and blue. However, if you know or can precalculate the number for a desired color, you can enter the number directly into the `TextColor( )` function.

Creating a Format button

If you routinely need to mark words or passages in a text field, you can easily create a button that applies the marking to the selected text. For example, to underline text, follow these steps:

1. Attach the `Insert Calculated Result[ ]` button command to your button.

2. Disable the Select Entire Contents checkbox.

3. Leave the Go To Target Field checkbox unchecked and specify the calculation as
   ```
   Insert Calculated Result[
   TextStyleAdd(Middle(Get(ActiveFieldContents);
       Get(ActiveSelectionStart); Get(ActiveSelectionSize));
       Underline)
   ]
   ```

4. Close the Button Setup dialog and name the button (for example, with the U symbol).

You can then click the button to apply character formatting to selected text in any accessible field.

> **NOTE**
> Because the button described here works on the basis of insertion (overwriting the current selection with a formatted copy of itself), the selection will be lost, and the cursor will appear at the end of the selected text after the formatting is applied. If you don't want this to happen, consider attaching a script to the button and configure the script so that it captures and stores the selection (in a local variable), inserts the formatted text, and reinstates the selection of the formatted text.
>
> You can use the `Get(ActiveSelectionStart)` and `Get(ActiveSelectionSize)` functions to capture the current selection (or cursor position) and the `Set Selection[ ]` script command to reinstate the selection subsequently.

In this case, the button applies but doesn't remove the formatting. If you need to also simplify the process of removing formatting, you can provide a second button using the essentials of the same procedure while employing the `TextStyleRemove( )` function. Alternatively, you can use a more complex calculation to determine whether the selected text is underlined and either remove or apply underlining accordingly. This enables a single button to toggle the underline formatting.

To determine within a calculation whether text is underlined, you can retrieve the selected text as CSS using FileMaker's `GetAsCSS( )` function, search it for the presence of the `text-decoration:underline;` tag, and modify the result accordingly. You can incorporate such an expression into a scripted process to provide buttons that add or remove formats dynamically.

CROSS-REF The appendixes include references to online resources where you will find examples of techniques for creating scripted style buttons for Filemaker Pro 10.

Dates, Times, and Timestamps

As part of almost every solution I've seen, storing and tracking dates or times is needed, whether to record the creation date of records, the acquisition date of assets, the start time of a recording session, the expiration date of perishable goods, or myriad other temporal factors. In many cases, you can significantly increase a solution's utility by performing checks and calculations using date and time values.

FileMaker uses a robust method of storing and manipulating date, time, and timestamp values, and when you comprehend the basics, many operations become simple to understand and execute.

How FileMaker manages dates

FileMaker stores all dates internally as a numeric value representing the number of days since 1/1/0001 inclusive. For example, 2 January 0001 is stored as 2, whereas 1/1/2010 is stored internally as the number 733773. You don't normally see this value because FileMaker receives and displays accepted date formats (according to the current file or system regional settings) — but you don't need to take my word for it. Enter this calculation:

```
GetAsNumber(Date(1; 1; 2010))
```

FileMaker returns the number 733773.

What is great about this storage format is that you can add and subtract using dates, and FileMaker will resolve the calculation appropriately. For example, the expression

```
GetAsNumber(Date(3; 1; 2008)) - GetAsNumber(Date(2; 1; 2008))
```

returns 29, because there are 29 days between February 1 and March 1, 2008 (it was a leap year).

Although the examples here cite explicit dates for the sake of clarity, the calculations work the same way when the values involved are references to date fields, variables containing date values, or functions or expressions returning dates, such as Get(CurrentDate).

Plotting time

FileMaker stores all times internally as a numeric value representing the number of seconds since midnight. For example, when you enter 9:25 a.m. into a time field, it's stored internally as the number 33900 but displayed as 9:25:00. Enter the following calculation expression:

```
GetAsNumber(Time(9; 25; 00))
```

It returns the number 33900.

Storing values in this form enables you to perform calculations comparing times (to get the difference between them in seconds). So, for example, the following expression returns 180 — the number of seconds in three minutes:

```
GetAsNumber(Time(9; 28; 00) - Time(9; 25; 00))
```

However, if you remove the enclosing `GetAsNumber( )` function, FileMaker returns the difference as a time value in the form 0:03:00.

Using these temporal arithmetic capabilities in your solutions could not be easier. For example, when you have a start and stop time for any activity, you can determine the duration of the activity with an expression such as:

```
Meeting::ConcludeTime - Meeting::StartTime
```

Similarly, you can calculate the appropriate end time of a scheduled 90-minute meeting that starts at, say, 10:42:16 a.m., by entering the start time into a time field in FileMaker and using the following calculation expression:

```
Meeting::StartTime + 90 * 60
```

Such calculations enable you to deal with time calculations falling within a given day with ease. However, when you encounter the need to calculate time periods spanning several days, the Timestamp data format is better suited to the task.

The number of seconds in 2009 years

FileMaker stores timestamps internally as a numeric value representing the number of seconds since midnight preceding 1/1/0001. In this way, a timestamp value combines both date and time into a single reference value. Thus, the timestamp value for 9:25 a.m. on 1/1/2010 is stored internally as 63397934700— a fact that you can readily demonstrate by having FileMaker resolve the expression:

```
GetAsNumber(Timestamp(Date(1; 1; 2010); Time(9; 25; 00)))
```

Working with timestamp data, you combine the benefits of both date and time calculations, enabling you to compare times many days apart to easily determine the amount of time elapsed between them. For example, the expression

```
Timestamp(Date(1; 1; 2010); Time(9; 25; 00)) -
Timestamp(Date(1; 1; 2009); Time(9; 25; 00))
```

returns 8760:00:00, which is the number of hours in 365 days (365 × 24 = 8760).

Even if you've chosen to store date and time values in their own respective formats, you can still take advantage of timestamp capabilities when resolving calculations spanning days or weeks. For example,

```
Timestamp(Trip::EndDate; Trip::EndTime) -
Timestamp(Trip::StartDate; Trip::StartTime)
```

is one of the more straightforward ways to calculate a trip of several days' duration's total length.

Juggling days, months, and years

When you're working with either date or timestamp values, being able to perform simple math operations on the component values can prove invaluable. For example, just as subtracting one date from another works to give a duration, you can also add or subtract numbers from date values. For example:

```
Get(CurrentDate) + 7
```

returns the date of the corresponding day of the following week. Similarly,

```
Timestamp(Get(CurrentDate) + 7; Time(9; 0; 0))
```

returns 9:00am on the corresponding day of the following week.

By combining other options from among FileMaker's date and time functions, you can calculate many other useful intervals and dates. For example:

```
Get(CurrentDate) - DayOfWeek(Get(CurrentDate)) + 6
```

always returns the date of the current week's Friday.

> **NOTE** FileMaker assigns day numbering based on a week starting on Sunday (day 1) and concluding on Saturday (day 7). If you want to work with weeks that start on a different day (such as Monday), you'll have to adjust your calculations for this.

Moreover, using the same principle, but with a little additional sleight of hand, you can use an expression such as

```
DateValue + Choose(Mod(DayofWeek(DateValue), 7), -1, 1)
```

to return the date of the nearest week day. In other words, if the date falls on a Saturday, the date returned is the preceding Friday; if the date falls on a Sunday, the date returned is the following Monday; but if the date is a week day, it is returned without change.

By extending these techniques, you can calculate the date of the corresponding day of the next month with the expression

```
Date(Month(Get(CurrentDate)) + 1; Day(Get(CurrentDate)); Year(Get(CurrentDate)))
```

> **NOTE** If no corresponding day is in the following month (such as when it is the end of the month and the next month is shorter than the current month), FileMaker will return an equivalent date value counting forward in days from the start of the next month. For example, if the current date is 31 January 2009, the calculation provided will return 3 March 2009.

or the date of the last day of the preceding month (even when the current month is January) using

```
Date(Month(Get(CurrentDate)); 0; Year(Get(CurrentDate)))
```

or the date of someone's birthday in the current year, using

```
Date(Month(Person::DateOfBirth); Day(Person::DateOfBirth);
    Year(Get(CurrentDate)))
```

Moreover, you can combine the preceding elements to accurately calculate a person's current age in whole years using a relatively simple expression such as

```
Year(Get(CurrentDate)) - Year(Person::DateOfBirth) -
GetAsBoolean((Month(Get(CurrentDate)) + Day(Get(CurrentDate)) / 100) <
(Month(Person::DateOfBirth) + Day(Person::DateOfBirth) / 100))
```

Many other examples are possible, using different combinations of FileMaker Pro 10's available date and time functions. With a little logic and ingenuity, you have all the resources you need to gain mastery over a wide range of date and time calculation requirements.

Summary Data

FileMaker's summary field options (Total, Average, Count, Minimum, Maximum, Standard Deviation, and Fraction of Total) accommodate a variety of basic requirements for analyzing and reporting on your data. However, you can greatly extend these capabilities' scope by bringing FileMaker's calculation capabilities into play.

To complement summary fields, FileMaker provides you with a comparable range of calculation functions to aggregate data in various ways, producing calculated summary data.

Using aggregate functions

You can use aggregate functions in three essentially different ways:

- To summarize values in a supplied array or in multiple designated fields on the current record
- To summarize values in nonempty instances of a repeating field
- To summarize values in a field across all related records

FileMaker does not support combinations of the first two methods. If you supply a list of fields to an aggregate function such as Sum ( ), the returned result ignores values in the second or subsequent repetitions of those fields. (In other words, only values in the first repetition of each referenced field are summed.) Only where a single field is referenced do the aggregating functions address values in field repetitions.

Similarly, you can't combine the first and last methods. If you include a reference to a related field in an array of fields being passed to a summary function, FileMaker ignores values in the second or subsequent related records, summarizing the values on the current record along with the first related record only.

You can, however, combine the last two methods. When you reference a related repeating field in an aggregate function, FileMaker summarizes the values in all repetitions of all related records.

When you reference fields in the current TO within an aggregating calculation as in

```
Average(Score1; Score2; Score3)
```

FileMaker determines an average with respect to values in the Score1, Score2, and Score3 fields in the current record only, without regard to other records in the found set. Similarly, if you reference a repeating field, such as

```
Average(Score)
```

in a record where the Score field has three repetitions, FileMaker determines an average of the nonblank repetition values in the current record only. Meanwhile, if you reference a related field within an aggregating function, such as

```
Average(Games::Score)
```

where Games is a related TO, FileMaker returns the average of values in nonempty instances of the Score field on all Games records related to the current record.

When supplying an array of values to an aggregate function, you can include any mix of constant values, field references, variables, and expressions. For example, if you enter the following expression into a calculation in an InvoiceLines table:

```
Min(100; InvoiceLines::Value; InvoiceLines::Qty * InvoiceLines::Price; $$var)
```

FileMaker returns a result representing the lowest of the four values:

- 100
- value (if any) in the InvoiceLines::Value field
- product of Qty * Price on the current InvoiceLines record
- numeric value (if any) of the $$var variable at the time the calculation is evaluated

 Should any of the supplied references or expressions in an array of values passed to an aggregate function evaluate to null, they're excluded from the calculation.

The ballad of Max and Min

Among the aggregating functions, Max( ) and Min( ) are particularly useful for the ways they work together when you define limits or ranges.

In the example in the preceding section, given that the number 100 appeared as one of the values in the array being passed to the Min( ) function, the number returned by the expression will never be higher than 100. Thus, the Min( ) function is being used to set a maximum value for the field to which it is applied. At first glance, this setup may seem counterintuitive, but its logic is sound (so much for intuition!).

Similarly, by applying `Max(N; YourValue)` to a value in your solution, you can establish a minimum — the resulting value will never be lower than N. You can combine the two functions into a single expression to set both an upper and lower limit, containing a value within a fixed or variable domain.

> **CROSS-REF** For additional details on the use of the `Max( )` and `Min( )` functions, refer to the example of their use with `Evaluate( )` in the section titled "The value of Evaluate( )", later in this chapter.

Referencing summary fields

An essential difference between the ways summary fields and aggregate calculations behave lies in the fact that summary fields always calculate with respect to the found set, whereas aggregate functions act on the current record or the related record set, without regard to the found set. Moreover, summary fields depend upon the sort order to tabulate and break the data into Sub-summaries when viewed in Browse mode, Preview mode, or in printed output.

You can, however, combine calculation capabilities with the behavior of summary fields in various ways, by including references to summary fields within calculations. For example, in a table containing scheduled examinations for a college semester, summary fields defined to return the Minimum of the `ExamDate` field and the Maximum of the `ExamDate` field will dynamically return the start and end of the exam period for the semester. Additionally, when a Find is done to locate the exams for a particular course or a particular student, the summary fields update to show the start and end of the exam period for that course or individual.

In this example, when you need to determine the length of the exam period — either overall or for a particular found set of exams — you can do so by defining a calculation field referencing the summary fields:

```
1 + sLastExam - sFirstExam
```

Here, `sLastExam` and `sFirstExam` are the summary fields providing the maximum and minimum of `ExamDate`, respectively. This example produces a valid result across the found set in the exams table as a whole, but will not produce separate Sub-summary results for each student or course when the data in the examinations table are included in a report. To have the calculation return separate Sub-summary results for each group of records when the found set is sorted, you should enclose the references to the summary fields within the `GetSummary( )` function, as follows:

```
1 + GetSummary(sLastExam; cSortBy) - GetSummary(sFirstExam; cSortBy)
```

In this example, `cSortBy` is the field used to sort the examination table records by course or student according to the report required. The calculation result returned now correctly reflects the Sub-summary values of the `sLastExam` and `sFirstExam` summary fields for grouped data.

> **CROSS-REF** For a further discussion of techniques for calculating a multiple-use sort field for retrieval of summary data according to two or more break fields (as per the `cSortBy` field in the preceding example) refer to the section "Layers of Abstraction," later in this chapter.

Lists and Arrays

In solutions of all kinds, you frequently require ways to retrieve and manage sets of values — often as lists or arrays. The essential techniques are much the same whether you're retrieving a list of the most common symptoms of an illness, a list of the top three students in each class, a list of low-stock items to be reordered, or a list of tasks to be performed before next Monday's meeting.

A *list* is any sequence of data elements (generally of the same or similar type), and an *array* is the mechanism use to store or handle such data. The simplest structure for an array is a delimited list, where each list item is separated from the next by a known (reserved) character or sequence of characters — and the most ubiquitous form of such arrays is the carriage-return (CR) delimited list where each list value is on a separate line. In this context, the character used as a delimiter is reserved arbitrarily by the user or developer rather than by FileMaker (though FileMaker does provide support for external file formats using a variety of common delimiter characters, such as tabs and commas).

Retrieving values as a list

FileMaker provides several powerful features for the retrieval of lists of values, each applicable to different requirements and operating according to its own rules.

The first and longest-standing method is the creation of value lists (either custom lists, or lists dependent on field indices), and the retrieval of their contents via the `ValueListItems ( )` function. This method requires the separate configuration of the list (via the Manage ⇨ Value Lists command and associated dialogs) and a reference to it by name from within the preceding calculation function. Values are returned as a CR-separated list in an order determined by the value list referenced — in other words, where values are sourced from a database field, listed values are sorted in ascending order according to the data type assigned to the referenced field.

A second method of retrieval of CR-separated values is via the `List ( )` function. As an aggregating function, you can use `List ( )` to return a list from an array of supplied elements including any combination of constant values, referenced fields, expressions, and variables:

```
List(100; InvoiceLines::Value; InvoiceLines::Qty * InvoiceLines::Price; $$var)
```

As is the case for other aggregating functions, null values are ignored (and do not appear as empty lines in the resulting list of values).

Similarly, you can use `List ( )` to return all nonblank values from a repeating field on the current record, or from a related field (in which case values from all related records will be returned).

In addition, you can use the `GetNthRecord ( )` function, alone, in a compound expression, or in a custom function to assemble a custom list of values, either from field values among records in the found set, or from field values among related records.

CROSS-REF   **For additional information regarding custom functions and their uses, refer to Chapter 18.**

Similarly, if you're working with repeating fields or repeating variables, you can use standard array notation, such as `YourField[7]` or `$YourVariable[8]`, to build a custom CR-separated list of values for further manipulation. In the case of repeating fields, you can also use the `GetRepetition( )` function to reference the values in specific repetitions (cells).

Managing lists — the xValues functions

Extending the parsing functions detailed in the section titled "Text Processing and Parsing Functions" earlier in this chapter, FileMaker provides you with a suite of functions purpose-built for managing values in lists: `LeftValues( )`, `RightValues( )`, `MiddleValues( )` and `ValueCount( )`. In combination, these functions enable you to combine lists, separate lists, and add and remove list values.

CAUTION Although the `LeftValues( )`, `RightValues( )`, and `MiddleValues( )` functions are in many respects equivalent in operation to the `Left( )`, `Right( )`, and `Middle( )` functions, dealing with whole lines of text rather than individual characters, an important difference is that the **xValues** functions always include a trailing carriage return on the result, even in cases where no trailing carriage return was present in the original string being interrogated. For example:

```
LeftValues("Line One."; 1)
```

returns "Line one.¶" In other words, it adds a trailing carriage return not present in the original string.

NOTE Carriage return characters are always represented in calculation code by the pilcrow (¶) character.

The `PatternCount( )` function lets you measure a text string's contents. This useful test helps you confirm that a string contains what you're looking for, before your calculation proceeds to extract it, and also helps to determine the contents of a string without examining it exhaustively. Why not let FileMaker do the work for you?

One of the many invaluable uses of `PatternCount( )` is determining the number of times an entry appears in a list. For example, if you have a list of late returns to your school Library, you may want to check how many times the name of a certain student appears on the list. Although `PatternCount( )` can do this search for you, there is a trick to making it work reliably.

If you simply have FileMaker search the list for a name — say, "Mary" — you risk also inadvertently counting entries for **Mary**anne or perhaps Rose**mary**, or some other name of which Mary is a substring. (Note: `PatternCount( )` is not case-sensitive.) To address this problem, I recommend that you enclose the search item within word or list delimiter characters. For example, with a carriage-return delimited list, place a carriage return at either end of the search string to ensure that only complete-value matches are counted. For this search to work, you must also ensure that the list and each item within it is enclosed within leading and trailing carriage returns; otherwise, the first and last list values, and any adjacent values, will not qualify to be counted because they won't match to a search value having a carriage return on either side. The resulting expression is

```
PatternCount(¶ & Substitute(Library::LateReturnsList; ¶; "¶¶") & ¶; "¶Mary¶")
```

The preceding expression returns 3 if Mary's name appears three times in the `LateReturnsList` field.

Extracting one value from a list

As is often the case, FileMaker provides multiple ways to solve a given problem. And the extraction of a specific value from a list is no different. One of several ways to extract, say, the third value from a list is to use the `MiddleValues()` function, with a "start" parameter of 3 and "size" parameter of 1:

```
MiddleValues(Library::LateReturnsList; 3; 1)
```

While the preceding method works and is straightforward to implement, it returns the text of the third list entry with a trailing carriage return. If the purpose of your calculation is assembly of a new list and you're adding the extracted item to it, the trailing carriage return is of benefit because you won't have to add a carriage return before appending a subsequent item. However, for most other purposes, the trailing carriage return is either redundant or problematic.

For cases where you want to extract a single list value without a trailing carriage return, FileMaker provides the `GetValue()` function. Thus, the expression

```
GetValue(Library::LateReturnsList; 3)
```

performs the task with simplicity and efficiency, returning the referenced value (in this case, the third) without a trailing return.

Adding or inserting a list value

Adding an item to the end of a list is straightforward if you know whether the list already has a trailing carriage return. If it does, and assuming that the list is in a field called `Roster` in a table called `Library` and the new value to be added is in a global field called `gNewValue` in a `Utility` table, you can use

```
Library::Roster & Utility::gNewValue
```

If the same list doesn't have a trailing return, you should use

```
Library::Roster & ¶ & Utility::gNewValue
```

The preceding example appends the required return as well as the new value. However, both these approaches are fragile and may produce undesired results if the field is not in the state you expect. A far more robust approach is to have your calculation check for the presence of a trailing carriage return, adding one only if necessary:

```
Library::Roster & If(Right(Library::Roster; 1) ≠ ¶; ¶) & Utility::gNewValue
```

The preceding technique is a robust way of adding a value to the end of your list, but if you want to insert the new value into the midst of the list, you require a different approach. For example, if you want to insert a value after the fourth value in a lengthy list, you could split and recombine the list (inserting the new value between the parts) using an expression such as

```
LeftValues(Library::Roster; 4) &
Utility::gNewValue & ¶ &
RightValues(Library::Roster; ValueCount(Library::Roster) - 4)
```

By altering the number in the first and last lines of the formula, you can vary the position in the list where the new value will be inserted. In the example, the new item becomes the fifth item in the list. However, when you change both 4s to 7s, the new item is inserted as the eighth list item.

Although you can insert a value in other ways, such as by using the `Replace()` function, the preceding method has the advantage that it gracefully handles a situation where the list contains fewer items than the position specified in the formula. For example, if the list in the `Library::Roster` field contains only two items, the preceding expression simply appends the contents of `Utility::gNewValue` to the end of the list.

Removing a value from a list

You can approach the task of removing a value from a list in different ways, depending on the nature of the list and the information you have about the item to be removed. For example, if you are confident that the items on the list are unique, you can remove the value by substitution, using an expression such as

```
Middle(
Substitute(¶ & Library::Roster & ¶; ¶ & Utility::gValueToRemove & ¶; ¶)
; 2; Length(Library::Roster) - 1 - Length(Utility::gValueToRemove))
```

Note that both the list and the value to be removed are first enclosed in carriage returns to ensure that partial matches do not occur, and the `Substitute()` function is enclosed within a `Middle()` expression (with a starting parameter of 2) to remove the leading and trailing carriage returns that would otherwise be appended.

This method is unsuitable if the list may include duplicate values, because multiple non-adjacent occurrences of the target value will be removed. However, by first identifying the list position of the value to be removed, you can cleanly excise it using a variation of the split list technique. For example, to remove the fourth item from the list, you could use the following expression:

```
LeftValues(Library::Roster; 3) &
RightValues(Library::Roster; ValueCount(Library::Roster) - 4)
```

This technique is clean and simple, but requires that you know — or can first determine — the list position of the item to be removed. Assuming that you know the item but not its list position, you can calculate the list position of the item's first occurrence by using an expression such as

```
ValueCount(Left(Library::Roster;
Position(¶ & Library::Roster & ¶; ¶ & Utility::gValueToRemove & ¶; 1; 1)))
```

By incorporating the logic of this process into a composite expression with the preceding calculation, you can remove an item's first occurrence in your list as follows:

```
Let ([
p1 = Position(¶ & Library::Roster & ¶; ¶ & Utility::gValueToRemove & ¶; 1; 1);
n1 = ValueCount(Left(Library::Roster; p1));
v1 = LeftValues(Library::Roster; n1 - 1);
v2 = RightValues(Library::Roster; ValueCount(Library::Roster) - n1)];
v1 & Left(v2; Length(v2) - 1)
)
```

 For simplicity and brevity, I have used algebraic naming for the variables in the Let ( ) function. However, you're at liberty to employ more descriptive names if you prefer.

Layers of Abstraction

The previous calculation formula introduces a form of abstraction in that you don't have to know which list item is to be removed; the calculation determines where the item is in the list and then uses that information to complete the process of item removal. Although this is a simple and relatively minor form of abstraction, FileMaker's calculation engine supports a number of more profoundly abstract techniques, letting you structure your solution so that different outcomes occur depending on the state of the data your calculations encounter.

The essential principle of code abstraction is the use of FileMaker to calculate what should be calculated. A simple and direct example of this is the GetField( ) function.

Building blocks with GetField( )

The GetField( ) function returns the value in the field named in its parameter, enabling you to calculate the name of the field from which a value is to be retrieved, at the time the calculation is evaluated.

At the conclusion of the "Summary Data" section earlier in this chapter, I proposed employing a calculation field named cSortBy as the GetSummary( ) function's break field parameter in a case where it might be used to return exam period data either by course or by student. To achieve this task, you can create a reference field (a global field in a Utility table) and store a value there determining which field (CourseID or StudentID) the cSortBy calculation should reference. A simple logical expression to achieve this would be

```
Case(
Utility::gSortField = "StudentID"; StudentID;
Utility::gSortField = "CourseID"; CourseID
)
```

Although this approach is adequate when you have only two options that can be defined in advance, an alternative and more flexible way to achieve the same result is with the expression

```
GetField(Utility::gSortField)
```

This expression returns the contents of whichever field (if any) is named in the `Utility::g SortField` field. It has the advantage of simplicity and directness, but more importantly, it is open-ended and can accommodate a variety of other sort fields of the same data type (requiring only that they be named in the `Utility::gSortField` global field).

The `GetField( )` function's various uses enable you to build calculation code that can source input values from different fields in your solution according to need or context, enabling you to build a single calculation with multiple uses.

Completing the circuit with GetFieldName( )

Supplying the name of a Table Occurrence and field — for example, as a literal text parameter for the `GetField( )` function — is a risky proposition. There is a risk that at some later time, the Table Occurrence name or field name will be edited, and the text literal will no longer be accurate. If you have many references to a field located in calculations within calculations, scripts, conditional formatting, custom dialog messages and so on, any number of things will break when someone changes the field name.

FileMaker 10 provides a way to set up your code so that parameters requiring that fields be named will not break if the field or Table Occurrence names change. The `GetFieldName( )` function in FileMaker 10 returns the fully qualified field name from a supplied field reference. With `GetFieldName( )`, you can pass a text literal, while preserving FileMaker's ability to automatically propagate field (and Table Occurrence) name updates throughout your solution. For example, rather than supplying a literal text reference to a field in your solution in a form such as

```
GetField("SalesItems::cSaleTotal")
```

you can instead achieve the desired result in a more durable fashion with

```
GetField( GetFieldName(SalesItems::cSaleTotal) )
```

Apart from the opportunity to avoid typographical errors when defining your code, the clear advantage here is that the field name will always be retrieved afresh when the calculation is evaluated — so in the event the name is subsequently edited, the latter expression will still be valid.

CAUTION As with `Get( )` functions and **Design** functions, the `GetFieldName( )` function won't prompt re-evaluation of an expression where it has been used, if the name of the field it references changes. When you use the `GetFieldName( )` function in conventional calculation field formulas, you'll generally need to make the calculation unstored to ensure that it updates appropriately.

The GetFieldName ( ) function has application wherever a literal reference to a field may be required. In addition to calculation functions such as Evaluate ( ) and GetField ( ), it is well suited to use in expressions supplying the target field to the Set Field By Name [ ] script and button command.

The value of Evaluate( )

While your solutions can operate more flexibly with judicious use of the GetField ( ) function, a range of considerably more powerful options is provided by the Evaluate ( ) function, enabling you to determine part or all of the syntax of a calculation expression within the calculation itself.

As usual, FileMaker's online help gives a number of basic examples. Using the Evaluate ( ) function, however, opens a range of new possibilities and provides alternate ways to solve problems. Consider for a moment that you can use the Max ( ) function to ascertain the highest value in a related field, but there is no obvious way to use a calculation to determine the second-highest value, should you need to.

One way to solve such a problem is to

1. Retrieve all the related values using the List ( ) function.

2. Determine the maximum related value using the Max ( ) function.

3. Use the list management techniques described in the section titled "Lists and Arrays" earlier in this chapter, to remove the first occurrence of the maximum related value from the list of related values.

4. Present the list of remaining values as an array formatted appropriately for the syntax required by FileMaker's aggregate functions.

5. Pass the resulting string, enclosed within Max ( ) function syntax, to the Evaluate ( ) function.

In this way, you use text and list manipulation functions to modify the inputs to the calculation, eliminating the highest related value. Rather than acting on the raw related data, Evaluate ( ) is used to apply the Max ( ) function to the modified text string.

The following composite calculation expression uses Evaluate ( ) to determine the second-highest related value in the Entries : : Points field:

```
Let([
Lv = List(Entries::Points);
Lc = ValueCount(Lv);
Mv = Max(Entries::Points);
p1 = Position(¶ & Lv & ¶; ¶ & Mv & ¶; 1; 1);
v1 = ValueCount(Left(Lv; p1));
Lr = LeftValues(Lv; v1 - 1) & RightValues(Lv; Lc - v1);
Mf = "Max(" & LeftWords(Substitute(Lr; ¶; "; "); Lc - 1) & ")"];
Evaluate(Mf)
)
```

When seven related records contain values in the points field of 77, 65, 83, 22, 91, 58, and 63, the function retrieves all the values as a list (Lv), identifies the maximum of 91 (Mv), eliminates 91 from the list (Lr), and then substitutes semicolon characters for carriage returns in the resulting list, placing it in the text format of the `Max()` function (Mf). The value of the Mf variable is therefore resolved to the following text string:

```
"Max(77; 65; 83; 22; 58; 63)"
```

When the text string Mf is passed to the `Evaluate()` function on the final line of the calculation, the calculation is resolved, and the second-highest related value — 83 — is returned. By using a calculation to determine what is to be calculated, this procedure is able to produce a result outside the primary scope of native FileMaker calculation functions (there is no native function to return the second-highest related value).

Although this example is somewhat arbitrary (albeit a useful technique in solutions where you need to calculate penalties or handicaps or plot top scores), I offer it as an indication of the extended scope of calculation capabilities made possible by creative uses of calculation abstraction.

Unstored Calculations

FileMaker manages dependencies within each record of each table so that if a field is updated, other fields (stored within the same record) referencing it are re-evaluated. However, FileMaker provides an option for calculation fields to be unstored, in which case they're evaluated whenever referenced or displayed (as well as when referenced fields in the same record are modified, if they're currently referenced or displayed when the modification occurs). Moreover, calculations directly referencing fields outside the current record (global fields or related fields) are required to be unstored. (FileMaker converts them to unstored data automatically when accepting the formula.)

> **NOTE** Unstored fields are commonly confused with unindexed fields, but they're not the same thing. There is a connection between storage and indexing insofar as a field must be stored to be indexed. However, although all unstored fields are always necessarily unindexed, stored fields my also be unindexed.

Unstored fields have both advantages and disadvantages. They have some capabilities and useful properties that other fields don't, but they also have several notable limitations.

Why and when calculations are unstored

An unstored calculation comes into being for one of several possible reasons:

- The calculation directly references one or more global fields, and FileMaker has automatically converted it to unstored storage.

- The calculation directly references one or more related fields, and FileMaker has automatically converted it to unstored storage.

- The calculation directly references one or more unstored fields, and FileMaker has automatically converted it to unstored storage.

- The unstored option has been manually enabled in the Storage Options dialog for the field.

The first three reasons are required by FileMaker, because they introduce dependencies outside the record and not tracked by FileMaker's internal dependencies table. The fourth is optional; you may decide to make a field unstored to save on storage space, to improve the performance of certain tasks, or to enable the field to update to reflect the current state of system variables such as those returned by FileMaker's Get ( ) functions. For example, a calculation defined with the expression

```
Get(CurrentTimestamp)
```

has no dependencies on fields or objects in your solution — it derives its value from your computer's system clock. If the calculation is stored, it records the date and time at its evaluation (when you leave the Manage Database dialog after defining the calculation). If your intent is to simply display the current date and time (when a layout is displayed) you should make the calculation unstored. Note, however, that unstored calculations are re-evaluated only when the screen is re-drawn, so the value shown on screen will not always be current.

Similarly, calculations created to display navigation details, such as the number of the current record in the found set, login details, or a variety of other system or environment variables, will only refresh if you define them as unstored.

Understanding the benefits and trade-offs of unstored calculations

Unstored calculations have several benefits. When a calculation is unstored, the file size is reduced because the results of the calculation are not written to disk. Some operations, such as the update of dependent field values or import of records, may proceed with greater efficiency given that they don't require re-evaluating the calculation. Moreover, changing data in unstored calculations is refreshed frequently; for example, every time a layout containing an unstored calc is refreshed, the calculation is re-evaluated.

Conversely, unstored calculations use many processor cycles over time because they're evaluated whenever needed and, therefore, may be evaluated many times in the course of a work session rather than being evaluated once and stored. The re-evaluation of unstored calculations can lead to a processing burden that affects your solution's speed of operation if the number of unstored calculations is large, and particularly if unstored calculations are implicated in actions repeated across large record sets. If you're sorting records by an unstored calculation field, for example, the sort duration may be noticeably slower if the record set's size is larger than a few thousand — especially on older, slower hardware.

CAUTION In cases where unstored calculations reference other unstored calculations, FileMaker must resolve each in turn before a result can be displayed. If you create multiple cascading dependencies of this kind, serious performance degradation often results because you're requiring FileMaker to resolve an extensive chain of dependencies at every turn.

Design flaws of this kind can result in an unresponsive and inefficient solution and should be avoided.

Discovering the hidden secrets of unstored calcs

Because an unstored calculation placed on a layout is re-evaluated each time it is referenced, you can use it to track user activity, increment values in your solution, or, with the aid of a third-party plug-in, perform other operations (for example, sending e-mail, updating a log file or polling a server) automatically as users interact with your solution. These capabilities provide a useful supplement to the automation options that script triggers make available to you.

For example, when you define an unstored calculation to increment or update a local or global variable, the variable is re-created each time a user performs an action resulting in screen re-draw. A practical example of one of the many uses of this capability is in Chapter 10 with the example of adding "back-button" functionality to the `Inventory` sample file.

Similarly, you can use a calculation defined to declare the current record ID to a variable each time the user navigates to a new record or layout as the basis of a conditional row-highlight in a portal. In other words, where the portal displays the results of a self-join relationship, you can highlight the current record's row in the portal. Here's how:

1. Create a stored calculation field called `RecordID` in the current table defined with the formula

   `Get(RecordID)`

2. Define (or modify) an unstored calculation displaying on the current layout to commence with the expression

   `Let($$CurrentRecord = Get(RecordID); ...`

3. Add a text object containing only a space to the layout to provide the portal row's background and apply conditional formatting to invoke a custom fill color with the formula

   `$$CurrentRecord = PortalTO::RecordID`

   where `PortalTO` is the name of the Table Occurrence your portal is based on.

4. Apply transparent fill to the text object, size it to fit in the portal row, and set it behind other objects in the portal.

5. Adjust the stacking order on the layout so that the unstored calculation field in Step 2 is further back in the object order than the portal. To do so, select the portal and all its contents and then choose Arrange ➪ Bring To Front.

On records where the portal display includes the current record, after you complete these steps the portal row showing the current record is highlighted with the fill color you selected in Step 3.

Because other kinds of calculations, such as tooltip calculations, conditional formatting calculations, Web Viewer calculations, and so on, are also evaluated when the screen refreshes or when users interact with your solution, you can exploit several alternatives to invoke functionality depending on evaluation of calculations embedded in layout objects.

Calculation Fields versus Auto-Enter Calculations

A FileMaker calculation field acquires a value according to the formula specified for it, updating when local fields it references are edited. The same is true of an auto-enter calculation, when the option labeled Do Not Replace Existing Value Of Field (If Any) is disabled, as shown in Figure 12.2. Consequently, some commentators have suggested that the calculation field is redundant, and auto-enter capabilities suffice.

FIGURE 12.2

De-selecting the Do Not Replace Existing Value of Field (If Any) option for an auto-enter calculation.

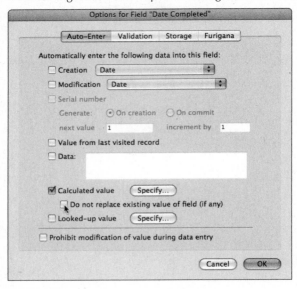

The functionality of conventional FileMaker calculation fields and auto-enter calculation fields overlap. However, both kinds of calculations are useful in their own right, making them both highly desirable in different circumstances.

The user over-ride capability

FileMaker calculation fields do not accept user input under any circumstances; their result is always determined by the calculation expression defining them. Users can enter a calculation field if you make it accessible on a layout, but although they can select and copy the contents, they can't overwrite them. Any attempt immediately results in the error dialog shown in Figure 12.3.

FIGURE 12.3

Users can't modify conventional calculation fields.

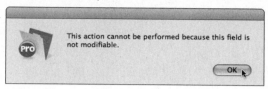

Auto-enter calculation fields can partially mimic the behavior of conventional calculations when you select the Prohibit Modification of Value During Data Entry option in the Options for Field dialog. However, you can override this option using a variety of methods, including disabling the Perform Auto-Enter Options While Importing option or by using a `Set Field[ ]` command on either a button or a script.

In most cases, however, the user can freely overwrite auto-enter calculations. This feature is valuable for occasions when your users need to manually over-ride a value, such as to mark down the price of a damaged stock item or waive a fee for a needy student. Whenever business rules call for the exercise of discretionary powers, mechanisms to depart from calculated norms are called for.

Just as auto-enter calculations offer the user the capability to over-ride the calculation result, so, too, can they be configured to respond to data input, overwriting the data entered by the user with the result of the calculation expression. This feature is useful for automatically applying or removing formatting or cleaning up sloppy data entry. For example, an auto-enter calculation with the formula

```
TextFormatRemove(Trim(Self))
```

accepts user input but immediately and automatically (as the user leaves the field) removes leading and trailing spaces and formatting. Similarly, a phone number field (defined as a text field, with an auto-enter/replaces existing value calculation) automatically updates to apply a standard telephone number presentation format (mask), regardless of the way the data is entered, thanks to the following formula:

```
Replace(Replace(Filter(PhoneNo; "0123456789"); 4; 0; "-"); 8; 0; "-")
```

With this formula and configuration, entering any of the following

0123456789

012.345.6789

012 345 6789

results in the field displaying and storing the value 012-345-6789.

NOTE The phone format formula is a simple and single example that indicates a way to solve this genre of problem. You may need to vary this formula to match the requirements of phone numbers in your area or to support multiple formats if your solution will contain contact details from different provinces or countries.

Auto-enter calculations and storage

Auto-enter calculation options apply only to stored fields, so they don't share the capability of conventional calculations to be unstored and therefore to refresh "spontaneously" on screen re-draw. The capability to define unstored calculations has a number of specific uses and benefits. (See the section "Understanding the benefits and trade-offs of unstored calcs," earlier in this chapter.) These advantages are therefore unattainable with auto-enter calculations.

Conversely, in some cases, you can use auto-enter calculations to address shortcomings of unstored calculations. Because an auto-enter calc can never be unstored, even if it references global fields or related fields, the result of its calculation will be stored in the current record. In cases where the related data will not change — or where changes will not be relevant to the current record, such as where the data are part of a historical transaction record — incorporating related data into a stored auto-enter calc result has the advantage that the field can then be indexed and used for optimized searches, relational filtering and matching, and/or as a source of data for field-based value lists.

CAUTION Because calculation dependencies do not extend beyond the current record, an auto-enter calculation field referencing related data will not automatically update when the related fields it references are changed. Therefore, you should reference the data in place in the related table (that is, place the calculation in the same table as the fields it references) or use an unstored calculation, whenever current data is required.

The Do Not Replace option

Figure 12.2 shows the Options for Field dialog, containing the Do Not Replace Existing Value of Field (If Any) setting. The way this option is named is perverse insofar as it results in a double negative when you deselect it — by turning it off, you are instructing FileMaker to "*Do Not Do Not Replace…*" — all very sensible if you're the kind of person who drives to work in reverse; for the rest of us, it can be downright confusing.

Notwithstanding the convolutions of its naming, this option is a powerful and essential feature in its own right, enabling you to configure auto-enter calculations to dynamically determine a default value for a field and then remain in the background allowing free-form data entry thereafter.

When the Do Not Replace checkbox is selected, auto-enter calculations support the user unobtrusively, leaving the user entirely in control of the data and the process of updating/maintaining it. When the option is turned off, the auto-enter calculations more closely mimic the behavior of conventional calculations, overwriting their current contents whenever local fields they reference are edited.

Global Calculations

A rather underrated (and perhaps, poorly understood) feature of FileMaker is the global calculation field.

To define a calculation field as global, go to the Storage Options dialog by clicking Storage Options in the lower right of the Specify Calculation dialog and, as shown in Figure 12.4, select the checkbox labeled Use Global Storage (One Value for All Records).

A calculation field defined to use global storage acquires the same essential (and valuable) characteristics as other types of global fields, to wit:

- As indicated in the Storage options dialog, it returns a single value for all records in the current table.

- It is accessible throughout your solution without requiring a relationship between the current context and the TO where it is defined.

- Its value (if changed during a user session in a multi-user solution) is specific to the current user and session.

- Its value does not depend on any records being present (or being present in the found set) of the table where it resides.

- Its value is persistent in Find mode.

These advantages are surely powerful, providing reason enough to make use of global calculations. However, global calculations exhibit some additional characteristics, making them especially useful for a range of requirements.

FIGURE 12.4

Defining global storage for a conventional calculation field.

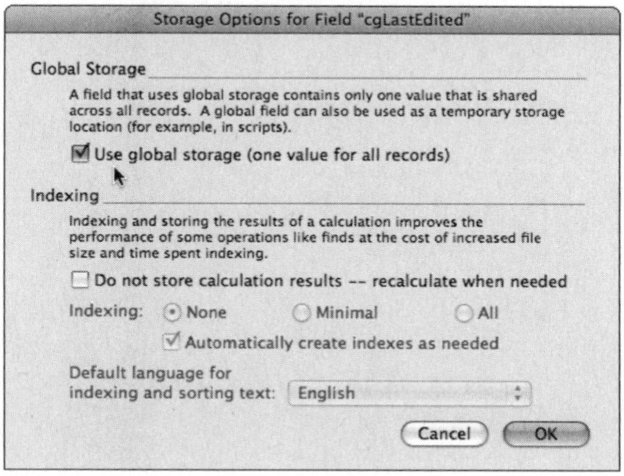

The moon follows you everywhere

Like a full moon in the late afternoon sky, global calculations shadow your movements, recalculating always with respect to the current user's current context. Like all other calculation fields, their dependencies are restricted to fields in the current table. However, they update according to changes in the current record — whichever record that may be from the context of the current user.

Global calculations also have a unique role in relation to other kinds of global fields. Normally, a calculation based on a global field value must be unstored. However, if the calculation is global, it will respond to global fields as a regular calculation field responds to data fields within the record — updating according to internally managed dependencies.

These two important behavioral attributes of global calculations give them considerable power. Unfortunately, their unique combination of behavioral attributes has resulted in some confusion about how they interact with other field types and when they will and won't update. To assist you in coming to grips with the behavior of global calculations and to understand and predict their behavior, I've assembled a brief description of their characteristics.

Managing global dependencies

If you're uncertain about the way global calculations behave with respect to changes in fields they reference, the following 12 observations provide you with guidance. These characteristics of global calculations apply to all versions of FileMaker supporting the .fp7 file format:

- A global calculation updates automatically if it references a global field that is located in the same table and that field is edited by the current user.

- A global calculation updates automatically if it references a regular field that is located in the same table (and referenced directly) when that field is edited on any record by the current user. In this instance, the value of the global calculation depends on the value of the referenced field in the record in which that field has most recently been edited.

- When a global calculation references multiple regular fields, its value depends on the values in the instances of all those fields located on the particular record where the most recently edited (by the current user) of any of those fields resides.

- A global calculation does *not* update if it references a global field that is located in another table, if that field is edited by the current user.

- A global calculation does *not* update if it references a global field (in the same table and referenced directly, or in another table) that is edited by different user. (Users see their own separate global values.)

- A global calculation does *not* update automatically if it references a regular field that is located in the same table (and referenced directly) when that field is edited on any record by another user.

- A global calculation does *not* update automatically if it references a regular field that is located in a related table (even if a self-relation) if that field is edited on any record by the current user or by another user.

- If a global calculation references one or more related fields and *also* directly references a local field, either global or regular, the value of the global calc depends on the related values that are current (for the current user) at the time when the local (to the table in which the global calc resides) value(s) are edited.

- The value of a global calculation when a solution is opened remotely is the value that it had on the host when last closed. (Sound familiar?)

- The values of global calculations in a hosted solution can be prompted to update at login by changing a local field which they reference. For example, if you have several dozen global calculations with formulas constructed along the lines of

```
If(not IsEmpty(GlobalsTable::RegularTriggerField);
    RelatedTable::DataField)
```

they all update to reflect the current (related) values at start-up when the start-up script includes the command

```
Set Field [GlobalsTable::RegularTriggerField; "1"]
```

- Changes made to referenced regular fields on another workstation do not appear in global calculation results until a refresh event has occurred on the current workstation — such as the next time the start-up script runs. If no triggering mechanism occurs, then remote changes do not appear at all until the solution is taken offline, updated in a client session, closed, and reopened on the server, as is the case with noncalculating globals.

- When a global calculation field references regular fields located in the same table, it retrieves values from the record in that table that is the current record at the time the calculation is evaluated. If no current record exists at the time of such an update (for example, the active layout is not based on the table containing the global calculation field and there is no relationship from the current layout's TO to the TO containing the field), the current record is imputed to be "record zero" and the values of regular fields will be read as null.

Within these constraints and guidelines, the behavior of global calculations is entirely consistent and predictable. After you're familiar with their behavior, they're an invaluable addition to your technical repertoire.

The freedom and efficiency of global calculations

In addition to their useful characteristics as global fields — they're session specific, accessible without a relationship, and so on — global calculation fields also share several key behaviors common to regular calculations:

- They're automatically triggered by dependencies according to specific rules as set out in the preceding section titled "Managing global dependencies."

- Their values are determined and cannot be overwritten, deliberately or inadvertently, as a result of either user error or script error.

Taken as a whole, these attributes make global calculation fields indispensable for a variety of purposes related to handling of user, state, and reference data, as well as process support and interface elements in your solutions.

CROSS-REF As an illustration of the use of global calculation fields to support extended solution functionality, refer to the multilingual solution interface example in Chapter 10.

Environment and Metadata

Enabling your solutions to interact sensitively and dynamically with the environments where they operate, FileMaker includes a significant number of functions allowing you to retrieve information about the solution and the state of the hardware and operating system.

The Get( ) functions

An essential part of the calculation process, FileMaker provides Get ( ) functions to return information about process, context, and environment. Filemaker Pro 10 has 92 Get ( ) functions, and I urge you to familiarize yourself with each of them. The online Help files are a great place to start for brief descriptions of each function.

As a simple illustrative example, the Get (ApplicationVersion) function returns a text string identifying both the kind of access the current user has to the solution and the specific version and revision number if applicable. Obtaining the application version number can be useful in several ways. For example, the expression

```
GetAsNumber(Get(ApplicationVersion))
```

returns 10.01 when the solution is currently being accessed by FileMaker Pro 10.0v1, FileMaker Pro Advanced 10.0v1, or a runtime created using FileMaker Pro Advanced 10.0v1. If your solution has been created using features introduced in Filemaker Pro 10, such as script triggers, Set Field By Name, or SMTP-direct email, it won't work as intended if opened using an earlier version of FileMaker. You should consider including a test, like the following, in the On Open script of your solution, configured to alert the user to the required version and close the file if it evaluates as false:

```
GetAsNumber(Get(ApplicationVersion)) ≥ GetAsNumber( "10.01")
```

Alternatively, when your solution is accessible by a variety of means, you will find it useful to calculate script branching (or otherwise tailor the functionality of your solution) using the following expressions:

```
If(PatternCount(Get(ApplicationVersion); "Web"); ...
```

and

```
If(PatternCount(Get(ApplicationVersion); "Pro"); ...
```

These calculation expressions enable you to determine whether the current user is accessing your solution via Instant Web Publishing or one of the FileMaker client application versions (Pro or ProAdvanced). With the information the calculations provide, you can set up calculation or script functionality to branch according to version.

Similarly, when your solution may be accessed on a variety of computers, you should routinely test for the computer platform and operating system version using `Get(SystemPlatform)`, `Get(SystemVersion)`, and/or `Get(SystemLanguage)`, enabling your solution to respond differently according to the requirements of different computing environments.

The many available `Get( )` functions in FileMaker Pro 10 offer you a rich source of information about many aspects of your solution, its use, and the environment in which it is operating, each offering enhanced control over the results your calculations return and the ways your solution operates.

> **CROSS-REF** Refer to the appendixes for references and additional resources regarding the abundant collection of `Get( )` functions in FileMaker Pro 10.

Design functions

Like the `Get( )` functions, design functions in FileMaker are principally concerned with the retrieval of metadata and environmental information. Functions such as `DatabaseNames`, which returns a list of the filenames of FileMaker databases open on the current workstation, or `FieldType( )`, which indicates the data storage type (number text, date, etc.) of a named field, enable you to code your solution to adapt to present conditions.

Design functions also serve many more central purposes in your solution design. For example, if you build code in your solution to refer to a specific layout by its layout number, the code may cease working correctly if the layouts are reordered. However, if you refer to the layout by name instead, you risk the code failing if the layout is renamed in the future. Instead, you can use design functions to refer to a layout by its layout ID, which can never change. For example, to determine the internal ID of a specific layout, you can first use a calculation expression such as

```
Let([
Ln = LayoutNames(Get(FileName));
ID = LayoutIDs(Get(FileName));
p1 = Position(¶ & Ln & ¶; ¶ & "Name of Layout" & ¶; 1; 1);
n1 = Left(Ln; p1);
p2 = ValueCount(n1)];
If(p1; GetValue( ID; p2 ))
)
```

Having ascertained FileMaker's internal ID number for a specific layout, you can then code your solution to determine the current name of the layout at any time, based on its ID, by passing the ID to a calculation reversing the process:

```
Let([
ID = LayoutIDs(Get(FileName));
Ln = LayoutNames(Get(FileName));
```

```
p1 = Position(¶ & ID & ¶; ¶ & "ID of Layout" & ¶; 1; 1);
n1 = Left(ID; p1);
p2 = ValueCount(n1)];
If(p1; GetValue( Ln; p2 ))
)
```

NOTE   You can adapt these techniques to enable you to refer to a variety of other solution elements by ID, including fields, Table Occurrences, scripts, and value lists.

Although this example shows you one way you can use design functions to improve the robustness and adaptability of your solutions, you have many other options. FileMaker Pro 10 offers 21 design functions to provide dynamic information about the essentials of your solutions.

Calculations Using Custom Functions

FileMaker Pro includes a category of functions available in calculation dialogs for custom functions. You can see the functions listed in the menu of function types appearing at the top right of the Specify Calculation dialog, as shown in Figure 12.5.

In a new database file created in FileMaker Pro 10, the Custom Functions category is empty. You must create and install custom functions into a file using FileMaker Pro 10 Advanced. However, this capability alone is well worth the cost difference between FileMaker Pro 10 and FileMaker Pro 10 Advanced, and I encourage you to consider the benefits of designing additional calculation functions to serve the needs of your solutions.

FIGURE 12.5

Selecting the Custom Functions category from the menu of function types in the Specify Calculation dialog.

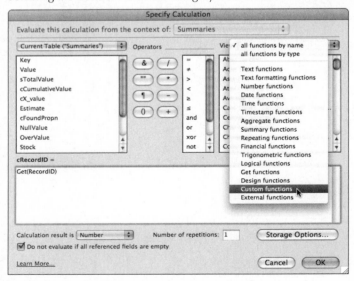

Once a custom function has been created and installed, you can select and use custom functions in calculations in the same way that you use other kinds of functions, assuming that your account does not have restricted access.

Here are three chief reasons why custom functions can significantly enhance the calculation code of your solutions:

- You can use custom functions to simplify calculation syntax and improve legibility and convenience in calculation code.

    For example, when your solution contains a custom function called Platform Is MacOS defined as:

    ```
    Abs(Get(SystemPlatform)) = 1
    ```

    you can check which platform your solution is presently running on with plain English readable code, such as

    ```
    If [Platform Is MacOS]
    ```

    This and many other examples like it can streamline development and add clarity to your code.

- Custom functions can encapsulate complex, but frequently used, code in a compact and convenient form, enabling you to reference the code with a single function call. Incorporating complex code within a custom function is not merely a simplifying move; it also enables you to maintain the block of code in one place (the custom function definition) knowing that any change to the stored function definition will propagate everywhere the function is called throughout your solution.

NOTE When you change a Custom function definition, previously stored values created using the function will not automatically change, but any new values will be calculated using the revised function definition. If you want to update previous values, you'll have to prompt reevaluation of stored calculations using the Custom function.

For example, in the preceding section, I provide a sample function to retrieve the current name of a layout based on its ID number. If you plan to use such a function frequently, it may be preferable to place the code within a custom function with the syntax

```
GetLayoutName ( LayoutID )
```

where the function definition is

```
Let([
ID = LayoutIDs(Get(FileName));
Ln = LayoutNames(Get(FileName));
p1 = Position(¶ & ID & ¶; ¶ & LayoutID & ¶; 1; 1);
n1 = Left(ID; p1);
p2 = ValueCount(n1)];
If(p1; GetValue( Ln; p2 ))
)
```

With a `GetLayoutName ( )` custom function installed in your file, you can incorporate it in your code whenever you want instead of repeating the more unwieldy expression it represents.

■ You can configure custom functions to perform feats not available to ordinary calculations. In particular, you can design custom functions to use *recursion,* a process where a function repeatedly calls itself until predetermined conditions are met.

As an arbitrary example of a recursive process, consider the elementary example of a custom function defined with the syntax `ShuffleString(text)` and with the definition

```
Let([
a = Length(text);
b = Int(Random * a) + 1];
If(a; Middle(text; b; 1) &
ShuffleString(Left(text; b - 1) & Right(text; a - b)))
)
```

This simple recursive function is designed to receive a text string and return the supplied characters in random order. The following example expression returns a result such as BLFVWNAQUMOIRTGPYCSDJKHXEZ:

```
ShuffleString("ABCDEFGHIJKLMNOPQRSTUVWXYZ")
```

Because the recursive process repeats its work until complete, the function can process input strings of variable length. In doing so, it achieves a result that cannot readily be matched using a conventional calculation expression. There are many kinds of problems — both common and obscure — that you can solve elegantly using an appropriately constructed recursive function.

A comprehensive tutorial on the creation and use of custom functions is beyond this chapter's scope. Nevertheless, the calculation capabilities in FileMaker are powerful and extensible, well beyond the limits of the 249 built-in calculation functions in FileMaker Pro 10.

 **For further discussion about the creation and use of custom functions using FileMaker Pro Advanced, refer to Chapter 18.**

Documenting Your Code

As you work with the calculation expressions in FileMaker, their syntax becomes increasingly familiar, and you find them intelligible. To a degree, therefore, calculation code in FileMaker is self-documenting. With only the most basic familiarity with the calculation engine, the following expression can be accurately interpreted:

```
If(IsEmpty(Invoices::TimeField); Get(CurrentTime))
```

So much so that including an explanation along the lines of "if the invoice time field is empty, get the current time" adds bulk without aiding clarity.

The use of descriptive field, table, and variable names aids the readability of your calculations. When combined with the intelligibility of much of the FileMaker calculation syntax, the use of relatively transparent naming makes it much easier to read and understand your calculations. In addition, keeping field and table names relatively short contributes to ease of comprehension of calculation expressions.

In some cases, however, your calculation code's meaning or purpose is difficult to discern without additional information — particularly when calculation expressions are long or complex, or where they form a small part of the logic distributed between a number of solution components. In such cases, the judicious use of code formatting and code commenting can improve intelligibility.

Code formatting

A variety of styles for the formatting of code are available, including use of line breaks and indenting to delineate enclosing elements and map out the logic of compound expressions.

Although simple one-line expressions rarely require formatting, longer expressions do benefit from some attention to the arrangement of elements for readability. For example, the definition of the GetLayoutName ( ) custom function in the previous section titled "Calculations Using Custom Functions" would have been considerably more difficult to interpret if presented as follows:

```
Let([ID=LayoutIDs(Get(FileName));Ln=LayoutNames(Get(FileName));p1=Position(¶&ID&
    ¶;¶&LayoutID&¶;1;1);n1=Left(ID; p1);p2=ValueCount(n1)];If(p1;GetValue(Ln;
    p2)))
```

As the expression is of moderate complexity, I chose to include line breaks to delineate the components of the code. For more convoluted expressions, indenting may also help to clarify meaning. For example, a fully formatted rendering of the same function definition is

```
Let(
    [
        ID = LayoutIDs( Get( FileName ) );
        Ln = LayoutNames( Get( FileName ) );
        p1 = Position( ¶ & ID & ¶; ¶ & LayoutID & ¶; 1; 1 );
        n1 = Left( ID; p1 );
        p2 = ValueCount( n1 )
    ];
    If( p1; GetValue( Ln; p2 ) )
)
```

Here, like elements and enclosing braces are aligned to give the syntax maximum form and structure.

Code commenting

Another aid to comprehending complex code is the judicious use of commenting. FileMaker supports the inclusion of either C or C++ style commenting (or any mix thereof) within calculation expressions. In general, C++ comment syntax is best suited to labeling and brief annotations, whereas if you need to include extensive explanatory notes, C syntax will be preferable.

To add comments in C++ syntax, precede each comment with a pair of slashes and terminate it with a line break:

```
//this is a C++ comment
//you can include multiple lines
//but each line must commence with a new pair of slashes.
```

Alternatively, you can provide more discursive multi-line comments by adopting the C syntax, where a comment is preceded by a slash and asterisk (/*) and terminated with an asterisk and slash (*/):

```
/* This is a C style comment, running across multiple lines
and enclosed at either end with the appropriate terminators.*/
```

As a general rule, commenting should highlight important or obscure points, providing signposts and pointers to aid understanding. However, it should remain unobtrusive, contributing as little as possible to code bloating.

Chapter 13

Scripting in Depth

hapter 8 describes what FileMaker scripting does and how to use it —
I provide various practical examples of scripts automating a number of
frequently performed database tasks. The examples I show you in
Chapter 8, however, barely exercise the FileMaker scripting engine's power. In
this chapter, I provide you with deeper insight into a number of central scripting concepts in FileMaker.

The FileMaker Pro 10 scripting engine evolved through previous versions
and has grown into a powerful coding environment. Originally, FileMaker
scripting offered a way to automate repetitive or tedious user actions.
Consequently, many scripts and script commands work with and through
the solution interface, performing actions and accomplishing work in the
same ways the user does. However, scripts can go far beyond mimicking the
user and provide an environment of power and extended functionality.

Scripts in FileMaker Pro 10 have the ability to act directly on data and file
elements and interact with other applications and services. Nevertheless, the
scripting framework retains some of its original focus on the interface as the
primary way of interacting with a solution. In this chapter, I explore a number of essential techniques to increase the depth of your command of
FileMaker scripting.

Scripting the Control of Objects and Interface

Consider for a moment the ways your FileMaker solutions interact with
users. A FileMaker solution's user interface is comprised of a series of layouts
containing a variety of objects, some of which are static, but many of which
have embedded attributes linking them to the solution's data and code.

IN THIS CHAPTER

Controlling interface objects via script

Handling errors gracefully

Scripting around access privilege issues

Applying principles of automation

Using parameters, results, and variables in your scripts

Utilizing dynamic and indirect controls in scripts

Applying nonlinear logic

Working with modular script code

Managing database windows via script

Automating import and export of data

Moving data efficiently between tables

The variety of FileMaker layout objects include static objects (text labels, graphical lines and shapes, plus inserted images) augmenting the visual appearance of your solution but without an active or interactive role. Other layout object types are designed as controls or devices with which the user can access and interact with the solution's code and data. These include

- Field boxes
- Buttons
- Portals
- Tab controls
- Web viewers

In FileMaker Pro 10, you can assign names to both layouts and layout objects. The object names that you assign provide a basis for scripts to target and interact with specific objects. In fact, you can explicitly name each of these kinds of objects and then have scripts specify an object by name when the script needs to interact with the object.

> **TIP** You can assign or edit layout names while in Layout mode by choosing Layouts ➪ Layout Setup and entering a name in the name field in the upper part of the Layout Setup dialog.

> Object names are assigned when you enter them into the Object Name field in the Info palette after selecting the object in Layout mode. Choose View ➪ Object Info command to display the Info palette.

Addressing objects by name

After you create an object and place it on a layout in Layout mode (and after you save the changes to the layout), it immediately becomes visible and available to users viewing the layout in Browse or Find modes. Additionally, the object becomes accessible to scripts running in either of those modes. When you assign a name to an object, scripts are able to select the object using its name. Selected objects (by the user or via script) are said to be *active* or to *have focus*. Similarly, only one layout — the layout showing in the frontmost window — is active at a time.

When interacting with objects, your scripts are constrained to those objects present on the current (active) layout. Moreover, FileMaker's current mode determines the possible forms of interaction with each kind of object. Consequently, to ensure that your script can perform the intended action, you should commence your script code with a command explicitly establishing the required mode and then add commands navigating to the appropriate layout and (if appropriate) the desired record.

For example, to have your script place the focus on the FirstName data field (with an object name of "Contact first name") on the Contact Details layout in Browse mode in the most recently added record of the Contacts table, commence it with the following six script steps:

```
Enter Browse Mode [ ]
Go to Layout ["Contact Details"]
Show All Records
```

```
Unsort Records
Go to Record/Request/Page [Last]
Go to Object [Object Name: "Contact first name"]
```

The preceding sequence of commands sets the focus where you want it — on the FirstName field. However, it only succeeds if a number of conditions are satisfied. In this case, the script requires that the "Contact Details" layout exists, that there are (one or more) records in the Contacts table, and that an instance of the FirstName field on the Contact Details layout has been assigned the object name Contact first name. If any of these conditions aren't met, the script fails.

> **TIP** Each object type mentioned at the start of this section can have focus. Consequently, you can use the Go to Object [ ] script command in a sequence such as the one shown here, to direct the focus toward named objects of any of the kinds listed.

The names you assign to objects must be unique within a given layout. FileMaker won't accept an object name if it's already used on the current layout. Therefore, you can employ a single instance of the Go to Object [ ] command to address an object even if it's enclosed inside other objects on the layout. For example, suppose that a named field object is located inside a named portal that, in turn, is located inside a named tab control panel. You can place the focus on the field and both its enclosing objects simply by addressing the named object's unique name. This is sufficient for the relevant tab and portal to also automatically acquire focus. You can use this behavior to address a layout's objects in a straightforward manner.

You should bear in mind that while object names must be unique within a layout, objects with the same names may appear on other layouts. The process of directing focus to a named object with the Go to Object [ ] command is valid only when the correct layout is active. Avoid using the Go to Object [ ] command unless your script has previously established or confirmed the layout context. In this and many other respects, context is crucial.

In fact, the concept of context, as outlined in Part I, governs every action that your scripts take. The methods outlined in this section provide a key part of the strategy you can use to ensure that your scripts manage context throughout their execution by placing the focus where required for each scripted action.

> **TIP** I suggest that you first ascertain and store the user's current context (mode and record or request) so that the script can reinstate context at its conclusion and return control of the database to the user in the same state as when it started.

Locking down the interface

When you configure your script to establish focus on a specific field, your purpose may be to have the script prompt the user to enter a name for the most recent client contact record. If so, to achieve its aim, your script relies on the user to provide necessary input.

To ensure that such a scripted procedure is completed successfully, you must ensure that the user is unable to leave the selected layout until the required information is entered. In this case — and other similar situations — it makes sense to prevent the normal use of navigation controls until the matter at hand has been addressed. In this manner, you can configure your scripts to guide and constrain users. Doing so establishes and enforces procedures and business rules in keeping with the solution's objectives.

Frequently, hiding and locking (disabling) the FileMaker Status Toolbar suffices to constrain navigation. However, you may also want to set the layout size and magnification (zoom) level to ensure that the field is in view and to ensure that the layout is being viewed as a form rather than a list or table (so that the user cannot scroll to other records). You can implement these restrictions by configuring the following four additional script commands:

```
Show/Hide Status Area [Lock; Hide]
Set Zoom Level [100%]
View As [View As Form]
Adjust Window [Resize to Fit]
```

Although a sequence of commands such as this one adds to the length of my script, it enhances the script's ability to meet its objectives, so its inclusion is justified.

> **TIP**   When the Status Toolbar is hidden and locked, not only are the navigation controls (the layout menu, rolodex, slider, and so on) inaccessible to the user, the scroll wheel, standard keyboard navigation shortcuts, and menu commands for navigating between layouts and records are also disabled.

Managing user interaction

In the previous sections, I describe a script that takes the user to a particular layout and record, locks the interface, adjusts the window, and places focus on the FirstName field. However, you can't be certain that the user will know what to do next. Users are apt to have minds of their own. Moreover, no process has been implemented for returning the users to their starting point after they complete the required task.

In addition to setting the conditions for the task at hand — and doing all the heavy lifting — your scripts should inform users what is required of them. One method is to post a dialog prompting the user to enter a name in the name field. You can find the Show Custom Dialog[ ] script command in the Miscellaneous group of commands near the bottom of the Edit Script window's script step list, as shown in Figure 13.1.

After adding and configuring the dialog command (to display a prompt along the lines of "Enter the contact's first name, then press enter"), you need a way to maintain scripted control of the process. One way to do so is by having the script pause for user input and then return the user to his previous location or context.

If using the pause-for-input approach, you should add a pause command after the Show Custom Dialog[ ] command, followed by a further pair of commands that return the user to their previous layout and reinstate the Status Toolbar. The whole script now looks like

```
Enter Browse Mode [ ]
Go to Layout ["Contact Details" (ItemSupplier)]
Show All Records
```

```
Unsort Records
Show/Hide Status Area [Lock; Hide]
Set Zoom Level [100%]
View As [View As Form]
Adjust Window [Resize to Fit]
Go to Record/Request/Page [Last]
Show Custom Dialog ["Enter the customer's name, then press Enter."]
Go to Object [Object Name: "Contact first name"]
Pause/Resume Script [Indefinitely]
Go to Layout [original layout]
Show/Hide Status Area [Show]
```

With the script paused, as indicated at the third-last line of the script as set out here, pressing the Enter key causes the script to resume from its paused state, at which point the subsequent command takes the user back to whichever layout was active when the script was triggered. However, if the user presses Enter without first typing a name in the FirstName field, the script will proceed without the requested input.

So far, so good — the sequence of steps now appears workable. However, the process is more heavy-handed than necessary, in part because it's modeled on the series of actions a user would take to perform the same task manually. While it's not a bad starting place, you can use other options to achieve similar results in a more streamlined fashion.

In this case, rather than taking the user on a whirlwind tour to the customer table and back, an alternative is to use the custom dialog to collect the required information in one step (before even changing layouts) and then perform the remaining action(s) efficiently behind the scenes without the user's knowledge or intervention. This process makes use of the custom dialog's ability to include input fields.

FIGURE 13.1

You can select Show Custom Dialog from the Miscellaneous group of commands in the Edit Script window.

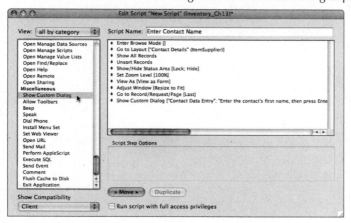

To achieve more graceful execution, try using alternative sequencing of essentially the same script, such as the following:

```
Show Custom Dialog ["Enter the customer's name, then press Enter.";
    Contacts::gTempText]
Freeze Window
Enter Browse Mode [ ]
Go to Layout ["Contact Details"]
Show All Records
Unsort Records
Go to Record/Request/Page [Last]
Set Field [Contacts::FirstName; Contacts::gTempText]
Go to Layout [original layout]
```

This modification improves the script in several respects. The script accomplishes the same task with fewer steps but, more importantly, it accomplishes its work with less interruption and visual discontinuity for the user. The dialog appears and, after it's closed, the window is frozen momentarily while the rest of the work is done unseen.

> **NOTE** To collect the user input up front using a dialog requires a temporary place to store the data until it can be used. A global text field is suitable for this purpose.

Trapping for Errors

A clean and simple user experience is certainly an improvement, but truly graceful execution also requires that your script detect problems and handle them efficiently.

The script in the preceding section is vulnerable to a number of possible problems that you can anticipate. Think about the following:

- The user might dismiss the dialog without entering anything into it.
- The Contact Details layout may have been deleted.
- While the user was entering a name in the dialog, another user on the network may have deleted all the records in the contacts table.
- Another user may have added a new record to the Customer table, so that the last record is no longer the one that the current user's value should be entered against.
- Another user may presently be editing the last record in the Customer table, so it may be temporarily locked, and the script is consequently unable to apply the change.

These and other similar conditions can cause one or more of the script commands to fail, in which case the script may not complete or may complete with unintended results. At worst, the script may write its data into the wrong record, perhaps overwriting data already stored there. Such occurrences threaten a solution's data integrity and are more common than many people suppose.

You can achieve a more robust script in two ways:

- Introduce additional code into the script to detect errors and respond appropriately.
- Further modify the design of the script so that it's less vulnerable to error.

Both of these techniques are possible. For example, FileMaker Pro 10 provides error management capabilities within scripts. As a script is executed, step by step, it returns a succession of error codes (each of which refers to a specific error class or condition). The calculation function Get (LastError) provides a means to determine whether an error was encountered and, if so, of what type.

Retrieving error codes appropriately

At any point in time, only one error code is available — the code relating to the most recently executed script command. If another command executes (aside from the exceptions noted in this section), its error code replaces the previously stored result. In other words, FileMaker does not maintain a history or log of errors. It is up to you to retrieve the error codes and then act on them or store them as you see fit when designing and implementing a script.

 **In all cases, when no error has occurred (including when no script steps have yet been executed), the Get (LastError) function returns zero.**

Not all script commands return an error code. Most notably, #comment script lines are not evaluated or executed in FileMaker Pro 10, so they return no code. Similarly, the Halt Script and Exit Script [ ] commands are ignored by the error handler (the error result from the preceding command will continue to be available). Additionally, various commands — including those in the Control group, such as Allow User Abort [ ], Beep, Pause/Resume Script [ ], among others — are not vulnerable to failure and routinely return a zero error result.

NEW FEATURE A change in the behavior of scripts in FileMaker Pro 10 has been made so that the most recent error code (the value returned by the Get (LastError) function) is not cleared by the controls steps If, Else, Else If, End If, Loop, Exit Loop If, End Loop, Exit Script, and Halt Script. This change makes it easier to test for an error from a preceding step and then act on it in the following step.

The error code relating to the most recent script's last action remains available even after the script has concluded, so you may evaluate the Get (LastError) function at any time to discover the error result of the most recent script's last command. Moreover, error result codes are specific to the FileMaker application session but not to the file, so even if the most recently run script was in Solution A, its closing error result will remain available even after switching to Solution B — until another script is executed (in either solution) or until you quit from FileMaker.

What the error codes mean

FileMaker Pro 10 provides a total 137 script commands. However, more than 200 error codes are available, each relating to a particular problem (or category of problem) preventing a command or process from executing successfully. You can find a complete list of the codes, with a brief explanation of each, in FileMaker Pro 10 online help under the heading FileMaker Pro error codes.

In some circumstances, an error code is returned even though the script command may be regarded as having succeeded. For example, a Go To Related Records[ ] command with the Match All Records in Found Set option enabled will return error code 101 (Record is missing) if the current record had no related records, even though other records in the found set had related records that have been located and displayed. If there were no related records for any of the records in the found set, FileMaker returns error code 401 (No records match the request), and the command fails.

Not all the error conditions represented in the list of error codes are relevant to any one script command. For example, error code 400 is defined as "Find Criteria are empty." This error code is clearly applicable only to those few script commands that you can use to execute a find and that may therefore fail if no Find criteria have been provided. Similarly, error code 209 is defined as New password must be different from existing one, which is applicable only to the Change Password[ ] script command.

However, other results (such as error code 1, User canceled action or error code 9, Insufficient privileges) can arise in a variety of situations and may be associated with many of the available script commands. Although you may be able to anticipate specific error conditions when using particular script steps, accounting for the possibility that other errors may also arise is prudent.

Why bother with error handling?

In most cases, when an error is returned, something is amiss, and there are likely to be consequences. FileMaker, as an application, is relatively tolerant of errors (that is, it rarely crashes or hangs), but if a sequence of commands fail, the following scenarios may result:

- The user will be confused.
- Data will be inappropriately written or overwritten.
- Data that should be written won't be.
- The wrong records will be deleted or duplicated.
- The user will be left stranded on the wrong layout.
- Any of a range of other unexpected events will occur.

The purpose of a script is generally to improve the efficiency, accuracy, and usability of your solution. It is somewhat self-defeating if the script itself becomes the cause of errors or usability problems.

Scripts are executed sequentially from the first step to the last, so when a command partway through a script can't be performed, it may be problematic if the script proceeds. Conversely, if the script stops partway through its run, the procedure it was intended to implement may be left in an incomplete or otherwise unacceptable state (for example, an address that is partially updated may be rendered meaningless).

In general, users are likely to embrace your solution if it supports their work, increases their efficiency, or makes life easier, but not if it produces unpredictable results and leaves them confused. To address this concern, you should selectively add code to trap errors as they occur during the execution of your scripts.

Handling errors

FileMaker Pro 10 applies default error handling to many processes, which is what you see when an error occurs while you're operating the database manually. For example, if you go to Find mode and then try to execute the Find without having entered any criteria, FileMaker posts a standard alert dialog, as shown in Figure 13.2.

When a comparable error is encountered as a result of a script's execution, FileMaker (by default) posts an essentially similar dialog, with the addition of a button allowing the user to continue the script regardless. In this case, the Cancel button not only cancels the current action but also terminates the script. Figure 13.3 shows the variation of the dialog that appears by default when the same error is encountered as a result of a failed `Perform Find [ ]` script command.

When comparing the dialogs shown in Figures 13.2 and 13.3, notice that apart from the addition of a Continue button, the dialogs are identical. However, while the default dialog in Figure 13.2 is generally adequate for a situation when the user initiates a Find without first providing criteria, the dialog appearing when a script throws the same error is less helpful — especially because the user, not being closely acquainted with your script code, may be unable to discern the cause or consequences of the error.

FIGURE 13.2

The native FileMaker error dialog for the empty Find criteria condition.

FIGURE 13.3

The default script error dialog for the empty Find criteria condition.

> **NOTE** When a scripted Find procedure is preceded by the `Allow User Abort [Off]` command, a variant of the dialog shown in Figure 13.3 appears, with the Cancel button omitted.

The default error dialog is unable to tell the user what role the failed command had within the script or why it has failed on this occasion. Similarly, it does not explain the consequences of canceling or continuing, or what criteria it would be appropriate to enter if choosing the Modify Find option. The user is placed into a position of uncertainty, if not confusion, and the choices he makes to resolve this dilemma may only compound the problem. This is an inherent limitation with reliance on default error handling within the context of a scripted procedure.

The first thing to do when implementing appropriate error handling within a script is to turn off the default error messages within the script. You do this by adding the script command `Set Error Capture [On]`.

> **NOTE** After error capture is turned on, all default error handling is disabled until the script concludes or error capture is explicitly turned off. Notable exceptions are errors arising from failed file handling procedures (such as import or export) and errors generated by the operating system arising from a script action (for example, out of memory or permissions errors).
>
> A script's error capture state is also "inherited" by any and all sub-scripts that the script may call. Changes to the error capture state occurring within sub-scripts will subsequently be inherited by the calling script (when it resumes execution).

When you include the `Set Error Capture [On]` command at the start of a script, it is important to ensure that you provide adequate error handling within the ensuing script sequence, because no default error messages will be displayed. Otherwise, when the script encounters an error while error capture is on, it will continue regardless.

> **TIP** You can use the `Set Error Capture [ ]` command to turn error capture on and off at will during the course of a script (or script thread involving calls to sub-scripts).

If you determine that native error trapping will be adequate for some portion of a script, you may want to turn on error trapping for only those passages that require custom error handling.

Whenever you enable error capture, you should add an error-check sequence after each command that you might reasonably expect to fail under some conditions. I recommend that you trap for less likely errors as well as highly probable ones.

Here is a practical example of a simple two-step script to which error trapping might be added:

```
Go to Layout ["Invoices" (Invoices)]
Perform Find [Specified Find Requests: Find Records;

Criteria: Invoices::Status: "Open"]
```

The preceding script is designed to locate and display open invoices, if there are any. Of course, if no open invoices are in the `Invoices` table at the time of script execution, the second line produces an error, and the user is left stranded. Here's a revised copy of the same script, including error handling:

```
Set Error Capture [On]
Go to Layout ["Invoices" (Invoices)]
If [Get(LastError) ≠ 0]
   Beep
   Show Custom Dialog [Title: "Find Open Invoices: Error Alert";
      Message: "The Invoice Layout required for this process could not
      be accessed.¶¶Please report this problem to the developer.";
      Buttons: "OK"]
   Exit Script [ ]
End If
Perform Find [Restore; Specified Find Requests: Find Records;
   Criteria: Invoices::Status: "Open"]
Set Variable [$LastError; Value:Get(LastError)]
If [$LastError ≠ 0]
   Beep
   Show Custom Dialog [Title: "Find Open Invoices: Error Alert";
      Message: Case(
      $LastError = 401; "There are no open invoices at present.";
      $LastError = 9; "Your privileges do not permit this action.";
      "An unexpected error occurred [ref#" & $LastError & "].¶¶Please
      report this problem to the developer."
      ); Buttons: "OK"]
   Go to Layout[original layout]
End If
```

The original two-step script is now expanded to 14 steps, with the inclusion of the Set Error Capture [ ] command and an If[ ]/End If sequence after each of the substantive steps.

NOTE The example shown here illustrates two different approaches to error trapping. The first (which follows the Go to Layout [ ] command) is generic and responds without regard to the cause of the error, while the second approach stores the error code so as to be able to respond in a way that is specific to the nature of the error.

At first glance, the implementation of error handling may seem unduly onerous. Consider the following before you throw your arms up in despair:

■ In practice, you can greatly reduce the work required by placing the repetitive error trapping code into a sub-script. (An example of this technique is described in detail in the "Using sub-scripts" section, later in this chapter.)

■ When the script is executed, if no errors are detected, the steps within the enclosing If/ End If commands will be bypassed, so the revised script does not take significantly longer to run.

■ Adding error handling is a significant enhancement that greatly improves the user experience. In many cases, the quality of the data and reliability of the solution also improves substantially.

Scripts and Access Privileges

FileMaker scripts assume control of your solution for the duration of the tasks they perform, working with your solution's code and interface like a powerful (and extremely efficient) user. By default, therefore, your scripts inherit the current user's login account access privileges and constraints.

CROSS-REF For a detailed discussion of security configuration and user accounts and privileges, see Chapter 14.

You can take three approaches when dealing with access privileges within your scripts. You can

- Design your scripts to work within the limits of the current user's account privileges, working on the basis that if, for example, the user does not have record creation privileges, then scripts running while the user is logged in should be similarly limited.

- Designate your scripts as super-users, granting them access to everything in the file regardless of the privileges of the current user.

- Configure your scripts to re-login under an account of their own, changing the applicable access restrictions one or more times during the course of execution (perhaps requiring the user to re-authenticate at their conclusion).

Needless to say, you may mix and match — take one approach for some scripts and another for others. Whichever approach you take, however, must be reflected in the way your script tests for and handles privilege-related error conditions.

When you take the first approach indicated, your scripts will encounter different permissions depending on the current user's login account. Moreover, user access privileges may change over the solution's life, so you should assume that access restrictions may arise subsequently, even if they're not a consideration when your script is first created.

To take the second listed approach, you should enable the checkbox option at the lower edge of the Script Editor window labeled Run Script with Full Access Privileges, as shown in Figure 13.4.

When your script is set to run with full privileges, access restrictions of the privilege set assigned to the current user's account are overridden for the duration of the script.

CAUTION If a script set to run with full access privileges script calls other scripts via the Perform Script [ ] command, the called scripts do not inherit the full privileges setting (unless they're also set to run with full access privileges; they're constrained by the privilege set assigned to the current user's account).

If you decide to have your script log in with a different account to perform certain operations, be aware that the user's login session will be terminated. If you intend that users continue to use the database by using their own login accounts after the script completes its task, you need to request (or otherwise supply) the user's password to re-login with the user's account.

FIGURE 13.4

Select the full access privileges option for a specific script by using the checkbox at the bottom center of the Script Editor window.

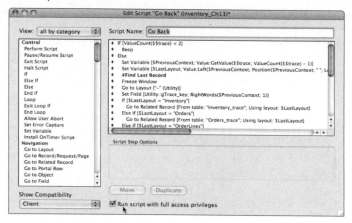

Privilege-based errors

When a script action fails due to privilege restrictions, the error code returned is not necessarily directly related to privileges. For example, if the `Contacts::FirstName` field is configured as "no access" for the Privilege Set assigned to the current user's login account, the following script command will return `error 102, Field is missing`:

```
Go to Field [Contacts::FirstName ]
```

FileMaker returns this same error code if the field targeted by the `Go to Field[ ]` script command is not present on the current layout. In this example, and others like it, the error returned may arise from a number of causes, of which privilege restrictions are only one.

In light of this, I recommend that you trap for a variety of errors in addition to the `Insufficient privileges` error, when dealing with processes subject to access restrictions.

Run script with full access privileges

As indicated in Figure 13.4, you can set individual scripts to run with full access privileges. When this option is enabled, your script behaves in all respects as though the current user is logged in with an account assigned to the file's default [Full Access] privilege set. As part of this, the `Get(PrivilegeSetName)` function will return `"[Full Access]"` if evaluated while the script is active. However, the `Get(AccountName)` function will continue to return the name of the current user's account.

Be aware that the Run with Full Access Privileges option affects access only within the file where the script is defined. If your users are accessing data, scripts, or other elements stored in other files (either FileMaker files or external SQL data sources), privilege restrictions in those files remain unchanged. When working with data or other content distributed between multiple files, the options for overriding privilege restrictions within your scripts are consequently limited.

 **If your script needs to act on an external FileMaker file's content and may encounter privilege restrictions in the source file, one possible solution is to create a script within the external file to perform the required operations, set that external script to run with full access privileges, and use the `Perform Script[ ]` command in your original script to call the external script.**

Determining the substantive privileges

If you've created a script to perform actions outside the privilege restrictions of the current user (and have enabled the Run Script with Full Access Privileges option for the script), you may want to set the script up to function differently according to the user's assigned privileges. To do so, your script will require access to the name of the current (substantive) user's privilege set. However, the Get(PrivilegeSetName) function does not return the substantive privilege set during the execution of such a script. Here are two alternative options allowing your script to nevertheless ascertain the current user's assigned privilege set:

■ **Ensure the script is always called via a method that supports script parameters** (for example, a button or a custom menu command) and specify the script parameter using the Get(PrivilegeSetName) function. Because the parameter expression is evaluated prior to the script's commencement, it's not affected by the Run Script with Full Access Privileges setting, and your script can retrieve the name of the substantive privilege set by using the Get(ScriptParameter) function.

■ **Create a single step script** (without the Run Script with Full Access Privileges option enabled) containing the following command:

```
Exit Script [Result: Get(PrivilegeSetName)]
```

Then call the script from within your original script, afterwards retrieving the name of the user's substantive privilege set by using the Get(ScriptResult) function. Note that the same one-step script can serve this purpose for all the scripts in a solution file set to run with full access privileges.

CROSS-REF **For additional details about defining custom menus using FileMaker Pro 10 Advanced, see Chapter 18.**

Automating the Automation

Every solution has processes that can benefit from automation, so the question is not whether to make use of Scripting's ample capabilities, but which tasks to automate first and how to design the automation so that it requires as little user input or intervention as possible.

Most scripts — even the most self-contained and robust — require user initiative to launch them. In Chapter 8, I detail seven methods of calling scripts, most of which depend on an explicit action from the user (a button click or a menu selection). However, several script-triggering methods offer less direct ways to set scripted procedures in motion.

I encourage you to consider all options for setting your scripts in motion at the appropriate times — both in the interests of saving work for your users and also to improve the reliability and integrity of the processes your scripts encapsulate. The most elegantly conceived script is only useful if it's used!

Defining a script to run on file open

Among the *indirect* methods of launching a script are the "when opening" and "when closing" perform script options accessible in the Open/Close tab panel of the File Options dialog (File ⇨ File Options), as shown in Figure 13.5.

When you specify a script to run on file open, it's automatically triggered every time the file is opened, the first time a window from the file is displayed. When a file is opened in a hidden state — such as when FileMaker opens it via a relationship or script call — the start-up script is not invoked. However, if the file is selected for display, the start-up script will then be activated. When you open a file directly, either by double-clicking its icon or by choosing File ⇨ Open or File ⇨ Open Recent, the start-up script will run. However, if the file is opened indirectly as a result of a relationship or a script call, it will open hidden, and the start-up script will be delayed to run if and when a window from the file is first displayed.

Specifying a script to run when opening your solution files is as simple as selecting a checkbox and choosing the script from a list of scripts defined in your file. However, determining what to include in your opening script is a challenge of a different order.

FIGURE 13.5

Setting the options to perform a script when opening or closing a file, via the File Options dialog.

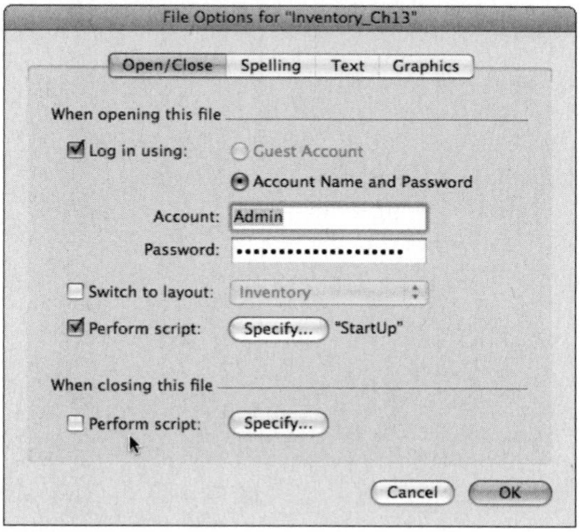

Housekeeping practices for start-up scripts

The processes you include in your start-up scripts vary according to the needs of your solution, but a range of operations common to many solutions' start-up scripts are worth considering.

You should also keep in mind that a start-up script is considerably more useful if you can be confident it has launched and completed its run on every occasion your solution is accessed. One part of ensuring this is to include the command.

```
Allow User Abort [Off]
```

Placing this command at or near the commencement of the script reduces the likelihood that the user will (intentionally or inadvertently) interrupt your script before it executes fully (for example, by pressing the Escape key).

CAUTION Don't assume that the Allow User Abort option is an absolute guarantee of uninterrupted passage for your start-up script — or any other script, for that matter. A knowledgeable user can contrive a number of ways to halt a running script. However, this option is a reasonable first-line safeguard.

CROSS-REF For a further discussion of start-up scripts and security considerations, refer to Chapter 14.

Consider including the following when configuring your start-up scripts:

- **Application verification:** When your solution has been developed to take advantage of the features of a recent version of FileMaker, it may be prudent to have your start-up script confirm that it's being opened with the required version (or later).

- **Security and login procedures:** Unless your solution is configured to prompt the user for credentials prior to opening, your start-up script is an opportunity to present a scripted login procedure.

- **Window placement and management:** Positioning and sizing of the window (or windows) required for your solution's optimal use should not be the first task for your solution's users.

- **Setting user preferences:** When you've configured your solution to store a range of settings, preferences, state variables, or other user-specific or computer-specific usage information, the start-up script is a convenient place to restore the appropriate configuration for the current user or workstation. The configurations sequence in your start-up scripts may also include loading custom menu sets and ensuring your solution and/or its interface options conform to the current computer's language and regional settings.

- **Usage logging:** For diagnostic and planning purposes, have your solution maintain a record of the history of its use, including opening and closing on different computers. This, too, may be a job for the start-up script.

- **Initialization of third-party plug-ins:** If your solution's functionality depends on plug-ins, start-up is a good time to verify the availability of compatible versions of plug-ins and to pass any registration or enabling codes to them for the current session.

- **Refreshing any external resources required by your solution:** For example, if you've configured Web viewers to display Flash files, images, and so on, the start-up script provides an opportunity to install or update the required resources on the current workstation.

- **Uploading or updating online content:** When your solution depends on current information from remote servers or Web sites, the start-up script can check the current online information, downloading fresh data when necessary.

- **Restoring global values and declaring variables:** The start-up script is a good place to establish the default state of any values and variables on which your solution depends. Moreover, the practice of establishing solution-wide reference values in the start-up script is a good discipline (and a point of reference for the existence and operational state of any/all such values required by your solution).

- **Providing the user with solution version confirmation, basic usage statistics (last used, last back-up, file size, number of records, and so on), and/or support resources and contact information:** A splash layout displayed for the duration of the starting script may be a good way to achieve this task.

You might also consider assigning a variety of other tasks to a start-up script in your solutions. The previous list includes only some of the more common usages. However, as you can see, there is no shortage of work in store for you as you prepare your solution for an encounter with its users.

Scripts that run on file close

Just as a start-up script can perform a wide variety of useful operations, a script set to run on file closure can take care of numerous important checks, updates, and other housekeeping. Because the user can choose to terminate the application (or file) session at any time, a first concern to be addressed by the closing script is whether the data is in a valid state (for example, your closing script might prompt the user to provide data to finalize a partially complete record, or to either correct an invalid entry or discard the record containing it).

Like the start-up script, your closing script should restore the solution to its default state by

- Capturing and storing any preference or state data for the current user (for example, so that the user's session can be restored on next login)
- Updating any solution logs to indicate closure of the client session
- Ensuring any ancillary or supporting files are gracefully closed
- Presenting the user with any relevant statistics or exit system messages or data

You should also consider that in the event of a system or hardware failure (power outage or force-quit, for example), your closing script may not run or execute completely. You may need to include an additional subroutine in the start-up script that verifies that the previous session was terminated appropriately and, if not, undertakes whatever checks and other remedial steps are appropriate (updating logs, for example). To detect whether your closing script has run correctly, have it set a value into a utility field when it runs and then have the start-up script reset the value to indicate the file is open. If the start-up script finds the utility field with a value indicating an open session, you've established that the shut down sequence did not execute completely.

Script Triggers

While your database is in use, a variety of circumstances will necessitate the execution of a script. For this purpose, FileMaker 10 provides script trigger events that allow you to attach a script to a layout or layout object.

You can assign a script trigger to a layout by choosing Layouts ⇨ Layout Setup and navigating to the Script Triggers tab. FileMaker 10 provides support for seven kinds of layout based script trigger events:

- OnRecordLoad: Runs a script after a record becomes active on the layout to which the trigger has been assigned.

- OnRecordCommit: Runs a script prior to committing a record on the layout. The script can forestall the commit action by returning a script result of zero.

- OnRecordRevert: Runs a script prior to reverting a record on the layout. The script can forestall the revert action by returning a script result of zero.

- OnLayoutKeystroke: The assigned script will run when an (noncommand) input keystroke is issued while on the layout, provided the keystroke isn't intercepted by an OnObjectKeystroke trigger. The script runs before the keystroke takes effect and can be forestalled by returning a script result of zero.

- OnLayoutLoad: Runs a script each time the layout becomes active.

- OnModeEnter: Runs a script after entering a new mode on the layout.

- OnModeExit: Runs a script prior to exiting the current mode on the layout. The assigned script can forestall the mode change by returning a script result of zero.

Similarly, FileMaker 10 provides a further five script trigger events that can be assigned to individual layout objects, as follows:

- OnObjectEnter: Runs a script after the selected object becomes active.

- OnObjectKeystroke: The assigned script will run when an (noncommand) input keystroke is issued while the selected object is active. The triggered script runs before the keystroke takes effect and can be forestalled by returning a script result of zero.

- OnObjectModify: Runs a script after the selected object is modified. Modification can include an edit action in a field box, a tab change in a tab control, and so on.

- OnObjectSave: Runs a script before a change to the object's contents is validated and saved. The assigned script can forestall the save event by returning a script result of zero.

- OnObjectExit: Runs a script before the selected object loses focus (is no longer the active object). The assigned script can forestall the exit event by returning a script result of zero.

You can assign Layout object triggers, as well as the OnRecordLoad, OnRecordCommit, and OnRecordRevert triggers, to run in Browse mode, Find mode, or both. You can assign the OnLayoutKeystroke, OnLayoutLoad, OnModeEnter, and OnModeExit triggers to run in Browse, Find, and/or Preview modes.

You should exercise caution when assigning script triggers because they're a powerful feature that can take control of your solution. Used sparingly and wisely, triggers can provide seamless automation and invaluable assistance to your solution's users. Take care, however, to avoid overuse of triggers and test to ensure that one trigger event does not set off others resulting in a loop sequence or creating other unintended or undesirable effects.

Harnessing the Power of Parameters, Results, and Variables

In Chapter 8, I mention that a script parameter can be passed to a script and referenced within the script as a way of controlling the script's behavior. However, the concept isn't pursued in depth in the examples I provide. In the example provided in the "Scripts and Access Privileges" section, earlier in this chapter, I suggest that you use a single line script to declare the name of the substantive privilege set as a script result, for retrieval by a *parent* script, where the Run Script with Full Access Privileges option is enabled. There are, however, many other benefits to the ability to pass data directly to and retrieve data from your scripts.

Getting data into a script

FileMaker provides you the option to specify a script parameter — data to be passed as input to the script — either literal text or the result of a calculation expression evaluated as the script is queued when a script is triggered by the following methods:

- Using the `Perform Script[ ]` button command
- Being called as a sub-script from the current script
- Selecting an item in a Custom menu
- Using an external function (using FileMaker's plug-in API with an appropriate third-party plug-in installed)

For example, when configuring the `Perform Script[ ]` button command, the Specify Script Options dialog, shown in Figure 13.6, includes a field for an optional script parameter below the list of available scripts.

In Figure 13.6, the script parameter has been specified as literal text (enclosed in quotes). However, the Edit button to the right of the parameter field provides access to the Specify Calculation dialog in which you can define a calculation to determine the content of the parameter based on the state of your solution at runtime (for example, when the button is clicked).

NOTE An expression determining the parameter to be passed to a script is evaluated before the script commences — which determines the state of local variables in play, the scope of any local variables declared in the expression itself, the status of privileges with respect to the "Run with Full Access Privileges" setting, and the value returned by the `Get(ScriptName)` function. In all these respects, the context of evaluation of the script parameter expression reflects the state of play immediately before commencement of the script.

FIGURE 13.6

Specifying a script parameter when defining a button on the Specify Script Options dialog.

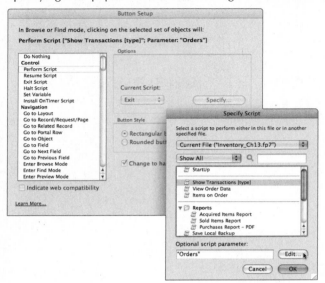

Branching according to state

Your solution's state when a script is triggered is largely beyond your control. By restricting the means of triggering your script to a specific layout button (or to a set of custom menus assigned to particular layouts), you can constrain users' options a little — for example, you can be confident that they are on an appropriate layout when launching the script. However, you can't predict what mode the user will be in, what record (or request) will be active, what the found set will be, what other windows will be open, or what processes are running.

By capturing data about your solution's state either at the commencement of the script or by passing the data as a script parameter (evaluated immediately prior to the script's commencement), you can ensure that your script has crucial information about the environment it is to act upon. Additionally, you have the option to call the same script from different buttons, passing a different parameter from each to determine alternate script behavior. For example, you may choose to use the same script for two buttons, requiring different behavior for Browse and Find modes, thereby producing four alternate script sequences.

One way to implement a branching of process and functionality within your script is to create a control structure for your script by using FileMaker script control commands (those grouped in the Control category of commands in the Edit Script window). For example:

```
If [Get(WindowMode) = 0]
   #Solution is in Browse mode
   If [Get(ScriptParameter) = "Button 1"]
```

```
      >>> {insert script sequence 1 here}
    Else If [Get(ScriptParameter) = "Button 2"]
      >>> {insert script sequence 2 here}
    End If
  Else If [Get(WindowMode) = 1]
    #Solution is in Find mode
    If [Get(ScriptParameter) = "Button 1"]
      >>> {insert script sequence 3 here}
    Else If [Get(ScriptParameter) = "Button 2"]
      >>> {insert script sequence 4 here}
    End If
  End If
```

A simple control framework such as the one shown in this example lets you apply process differentiation to part or all of your script, contingent on mode and the trigger button selected. However, although simple to design and implement, such a structure may lead to redundancy or repetition in your scripting model.

CROSS-REF For alternative approaches to branching and alternate script functionality according to state or context, refer to the discussion of dynamic and indirect controls later in this chapter.

By first mapping out an appropriate control structure for your scripts, you can accommodate varying (though related) functional requirements within a single script, enabling one script to serve for diverse situations and contexts.

Two concerns you must address when structuring scripts for dynamic execution are the frequent need to pass more than a single datum to the script as parameter and the desirability of establishing a consistent framework of context indicators for the duration of the script. For example, the simple control framework described earlier in this section directly tests for window mode during its execution. However, in a more complex script where branching may occur at intervals throughout its execution, the mode may change during the course of the script. Thus, it's necessary to capture and store context at the commencement of the script to provide a consistent point of reference throughout.

Declaring variables

I recommend that you declare relevant information in local ($var) variables during the commencing steps of your script so that you can capture context at the start of a script (or at key points throughout its execution) and maintain the data for reference during the script. For example, you can restructure the control framework discussed in the previous section as follows:

```
#Declare state variables:
Set Variable [$Mode; Value:Choose(Get(WindowMode); "Browse"; "Find")]
Set Variable [$Button; Value:GetAsNumber(Get(ScriptParameter))]
#Process control:
If [$Mode = "Browse"]
  If [$Button = 1]
    >>> {insert script sequence 1 here}
  Else If [$Button = 2]
```

```
       >>> {insert script sequence 2 here}
     End If
  Else If [$Mode = "Find"]
    If [$Button = 1]
       >>> {insert script sequence 3 here}
    Else If [$Button = 2]
       >>> {insert script sequence 4 here}
    End If
  End If
```

In this rudimentary example, with only two state variables in play and a basic branching structure, you can notice an improvement in readability because intelligible variable names replace function calls and potentially convoluted expressions throughout the script's body. The work of retrieving parameter and environment data is performed once at the script's commencement, and the variables are then available throughout the course of the script. Overall, structuring your scripts in this way offers potential improvements in

- **Efficiency:** Functions and calculations determining state need be evaluated only once and thereafter variables are available to be referenced. Variables are held in memory; referencing uses minimal resources.

- **Reliability:** Given values are determined once and remain in memory throughout, so if a script action changes the state of your solution, the execution of the script's logic is not impacted.

- **Readability:** Variable names and values can be chosen to aid clarity and transparency of the ensuing logic throughout the main body of the script.

- **Maintainability:** An adjustment to the calculation used to retrieve and declare a mode variable requires a change in only one place. (Otherwise the change would be required to be repeated throughout logical expressions distributed through the script.)

Although a series of Set Variable[ ] commands at the top of your script is moderately compact, yet accessible and readable, an alternative approach is to use a single command containing a Let ( ) calculation declaring multiple variables within its syntax. Some developers prefer this approach because it increases compactness of the code, tucking the variable definitions out of the way until needed. I regard this decision as largely a matter of style or personal preference, and I acknowledge that the desirability of having all the variables laid out may vary according to the solution's nature and complexity. If you prefer to use the hidden-until-needed approach, the first three lines of the example cited previously would become

```
Set Variable [$All State Variables; Value:Let([

$Mode = Choose(Get(WindowMode); "Browse"; "Find");

$Button = GetAsNumber(Get(ScriptParameter))]; "")]
```

Because the bulk of the code in this construction is contained within the parameter of a single Set Variable[ ] command, only one line of the script is used, and it stays out of sight until you select and open the step for viewing.

Either of the methods outlined in this section provides the means to pass data efficiently into appropriately named local variables to serve the needs of your script. The usefulness of these techniques remains limited, however, until you find a way to pass more than a single parameter value to your scripts.

Passing and retrieving multiple parameters

Although FileMaker accommodates a single text parameter when calling a script, you need not regard it as a limitation. You can contrive to pass multiple parameter values several ways.

One of the most straightforward techniques for passing multiple parameter values is to place each value on a separate line in a predetermined order and then write your script to retrieve each line of the parameter separately, such as by using the GetValue() function to selectively appropriate the individual values from the composite string passed as the original parameter. For example, when you have a script designed to write a new value into a given field for a specific contact record, you require the ability to pass three values to the script: ContactID, FieldName, and NewValue.

When a script you define requires parameters, I recommend that you append their names to the name you give the script (preferably listed at the end in square brackets), as in

```
Update Contact Record [ContactID, FieldName, NewValue]
```

Having determined the order that you will pass the parameter values, you can then specify the script parameter using an expression such as

```
Contacts::ContactID & "¶AddressLine1¶" & Utility::gUpdateValue
```

This expression passes to the script a carriage-return separated list of values such as

CT00004

AddressLine1

17 Coventry Road

Within the opening lines of your script, you can then efficiently retrieve the separate elements of the parameter, declaring them as separate named variables, with the following commencing steps:

```
Set Variable [$ContactID; Value:GetValue(Get(ScriptParameter); 1)]
Set Variable [$FieldName ; Value:GetValue(Get(ScriptParameter); 2)]
Set Variable [$NewValue; Value:GetValue(Get(ScriptParameter); 3)]
```

This procedure is easy to implement for small numbers of values and, provided that the values will not contain carriage returns, gives satisfactory results. However, such a procedure is vulnerable to error if you're not careful about the order you provide the variables. The risk of error and intelligibility of the parameter and code rapidly diminish if you have more than two or three values to pass to your script.

To address these shortcomings — and especially to serve more demanding requirements — I recommend an approach where each component value is passed together with its name. The resulting array format is what is commonly termed *name/value pairs*. The most frequently encountered format for name/value pairs is the FileMaker internal display of command parameters (in the script definition panel of the Edit Script window, for example). The value name is supplied, followed by a colon, and then the value followed by a semicolon. For example, the three parameters in my preceding example could be represented as name/value pairs as follows:

```
ContactID: "CT00004"; FieldName: "AddressLine1"; NewValue: "17 Coventry Road"
```

A set of parameter values passed in this format has several advantages. It is extensible; you can include additional values at will. Each value is clearly identifiable regardless of how many there are. The order of the values is immaterial, because each value will be located according to its name.

The downside is that retrieving the values requires a more complex calculation. For example, to retrieve the individual values from the preceding parameter string, you could use a parsing expression (such as those in Chapter 12), such as

```
Let([
Vn = "FieldName";
Ln = Length(Vn);
Sp = Get(ScriptParameter);
p1 = Position(Sp; Vn & ": \""; 1; 1) + Ln + 2;
p2 = Position(Sp & "; "; "\"; "; p1; 1)];
Middle(Sp; p1; p2 - p1)
)
```

This expression returns `AddressLine1`, but if you change the value of the `Vn` calculation variable to `"ContactID"`, it returns `CT00004`, and if you change `Vn` to `"NewValue"`, it returns 17 Coventry Road.

In this technique, you have the rudiments of an extensible system, but in the form described here, the unwieldy calculation is a drawback. Either creating a sub-script to perform the task or defining a custom function (using FileMaker Pro 10 Advanced) to encapsulate the required code obviates needing to repeat an exacting expression to parse individual parameter values.

In fact, if you have access to FileMaker Pro 10 Advanced, I recommend taking this process a step further using the capabilities of custom functions. You can design a self-contained custom function to parse an unlimited number of name/value pairs and declare them as local variables in a single call. With such a function in place, a parameter string, whether containing one or several dozen name/value pairs, can be declared as local variables in a single opening script command.

Here's one custom function definition example:

```
//Custom Function Syntax:  DeclareVariables ( ParameterString )
Case(
  not IsEmpty( ParameterString );
  Let(
```

```
        [
          p1 = Position( ParameterString; ": "; 1; 1 ) + 2;
          q1 = Middle( ParameterString; p1; 1 );
          s1 = (q1 = "\"");
          t2 = Choose(s1; "; "; "\"; ");
          q2 = Left("\""; 1 - s1);
          p2 = Position(ParameterString & t2; t2; 1; 1);
          n1 = Left(ParameterString; p1 - 3);
          c1 = Middle(ParameterString; p1; p2 - p1 + s1);
          v1 = Evaluate("Let( $ " & n1 & " = " & q2 & c1 & q2 & "; \"\")" );
          r1 = Right(ParameterString; Length( ParameterString ) - p2 - 1 - s1)
        ];
        DeclareVariables( Trim( r1 ) )
      )
    )
```

NOTE   Custom functions must be defined in your file using FileMaker Pro Advanced, but once installed, you can use and deploy them in FileMaker Pro.

CROSS-REF   For more information about the creation and use of custom functions, see Chapter 18.

The preceding custom function is structured so that the enclosing quotation marks on the values in your name/value pairs are optional, being required only when semicolons are present in a particular value. With this custom function in place, you can convert this script parameter,

> date: 8/12/2005; address: 33 Drury Lane; city: Gemmaville; state: Louisiana; amount: $343.00; process: recursive; title: FileMaker Pro 10 Bible; url: http://www.wiley.com/

which includes eight name/value pairs, to eight separate local variables (with names corresponding to those supplied in the parameter string) by using the following single line of script code:

```
Set Variable [$x; Value: DeclareVariables ( Get(ScriptParameter) )]
```

NOTE   The `Inventory` example file for this chapter includes the `DeclareVariables( )` custom function and employs the function to declare name/value pairs in the supplied parameter for the Show Transactions [type; filter] script.

Specifying and retrieving a script result

Script results are specific to the situation where you program one script to call another using the `Perform Script[ ]` command. In such situations, the calling script (sometimes called the parent script) may need to receive a confirmation or error message back from the sub-script, after the sub-script concludes and the parent resumes.

When one script calls another, a parameter can be passed to the sub-script. A script result can be viewed as the inverse functionality, allowing the sub-script to pass a value back to the calling script. Like a script parameter, the script result value is available only to the specific script to which the sub-script passes it. To declare a script result, the sub-script must conclude with the `Exit Script[ ]` command, with the result value declared as its parameter. For example, a sub-script that creates a record in a related table can be structured as follows:

```
#Create child record:
Set Variable [$layout; Value:GetValue(Get(ScriptParameter); 1)]
Set Variable [$parentID; Value:GetValue(Get(ScriptParameter); 2)]
Freeze Window
Go to Layout [$layout]
Set Variable [$ErrorLog; Value:Get(LastError)]
If [GetAsBoolean($ErrorLog)]
  Exit Script ["ResultLog: " & $ErrorLog]
End If
New Record/Request
Set Variable [$ErrorLog; Value:$ErrorLog & ¶ & Get(LastError)]
If [GetAsBoolean($ErrorLog)]
  Go to Layout [original layout]
  Exit Script ["ResultLog: " & $ErrorLog]
Else
  Set Variable [$NewID; GetField(Get(LayoutTableName) & "::ID")]
End If
Go to Object[Object Name: "ParentID"]
Set Variable [$ErrorLog; Value:$ErrorLog & ¶ & Get(LastError)]
If [not GetAsBoolean($ErrorLog)]
  Set Field [$parentID]
  Set Variable [$ResultLog; Value:$ErrorLog & ¶ & Get(LastError)]
End If
Go to Layout [original layout]
Exit Script ["ResultLog: " & $ErrorLog & "; NewID: " & $NewID]
```

This example sub-script has several important features. It does the following:

- Receives direction as to the layout of the child table and the ID of the intended parent record

- Traps (cumulatively) for errors throughout, storing them in a local variable

- Declares a script result at each point of exit, including a complete log of error values returned by the four error-sensitive commands in the sequence

- Returns (if successful) the ID of the newly created child record

The example provided here is structured so that it can be reused (subject to layout, field, and object naming) to create related records in any table in a solution, returning a result in name/value pair format to the calling script.

 **You can use whatever method you use for passing and parsing multiple parameters to declare and retrieve multiple values through the FileMaker script result mechanism.**

With a utility script in place in your solution and assuming that your solution has implemented the `DeclareVariables( )` custom function described in the previous section, a controlling script can create a child record for the current record using a sequence along the lines of

```
#Create child record in Invoices table:
Perform Script ["Create child record"; Parameter: "Invoices¶" & Products:ID]
Set Variable [$x; Value: DeclareVariables ( Get(ScriptResult) )]
If[GetAsBoolean($ResultLog)]
  Beep
  Set Field [SystemLog::Errors; $ResultLog]
  Show Custom Dialog ["An error occurred - child record not created!"]
  Exit Script
End If
Set Field [Products::gNewInvoice; $NewID]
#New child record successfully created...
```

> **NOTE** The preceding code is a fragment of a larger script. For brevity and clarity, I have shown here only the segment of the parent script calling the sub-script and receiving/handling the result.

The foregoing process provides you with a framework for handling errors progressively throughout a multi-script sequence, enabling two-way communication between your scripts.

Storing and accumulating data as you go

A significant feature in the `Create child record` sub-script's error-trapping process is the use of a local variable ($ErrorLog) to store a cumulative log of error codes returned by key steps in the process. Because variables are passed directly to and from memory, they're stored and retrieved with little or no overhead (delay or processor cycles). This method is far more efficient than writing to or referencing fields in your solution's database schema.

You can use variations of the logging technique exemplified in the previous example to perform a range of tasks requiring the accumulation of data. For example, if you need an on-the-spot summary to show you the proportion of radio airtime devoted to local talent in the current days' broadcast program, you could set up a script as follows:

```
#Local talent airtime:
Go to Layout ["Air Schedule" (Prog)]
Enter Find Mode [ ]
Set Field [Program::AiredDate; Get(CurrentDate)]
Perform Find [ ]
If [Get(LastError) = 0]
  Go to Record/Request/Page [First]
  Loop
    Set Variable [$all; Value:$all + Prog::Duration]
    Set Variable [$local; Value:$local + If(Prog::Local = 1; Prog::Duration)]
    Go to Record/Request/Page [Next; Exit after last]
  End Loop
  Show Custom Dialog ["Local talent: " & Round($local / $all * 100; 1) & "%"]
Else
  Beep
  Show Custom Dialog ["Sorry - nothing has been scheduled for today yet!"]
End If
Go to Layout [original layout]
```

This is another of many examples of scripted data accumulation using variables. Although this example is by no means the only way (nor necessarily the best way) to calculate quick summary data, it may be an ideal method in cases where

■ You don't want to (or can't afford to) clutter schema with additional fields (such as summary fields) for the purposes of performing such a check.

■ The summary or calculation you require isn't readily supported by the FileMaker built-in summary and aggregation operations.

■ You need to spot-check a host of different things at different times (in which case your script can be repurposed — for example, via script parameters — to perform a variety of calculations at will).

■ The information to be extracted is solely as input to a subsequent script operation.

If one or more of these conditions applies, scripted data aggregation should be among the options you consider. There are many instances when the aggregation of information available during the course of a script is both opportune and practical — with variables providing the ideal mechanism for all such operations.

Dynamic and Indirect Controls in Scripts

You can configure many FileMaker scripting commands to explicitly target a specific layout, field, or object in your solution. When you do, your scripts are clear, direct, and simple but not very flexible.

For example, when you create a script with the Go to Layout [ ] command and you assign a specific layout as the command's target, your script is easy to read and interpret, but it can be used only for operations to be performed on that one layout.

Example — Go to Layout by name or number

In the case of the Go to Layout [ ] command — as with many other script and button commands — FileMaker provides options for the destination object (in this case, layout) to be determined by calculation. This has two profound implications:

■ The target layout will be determined as the command is evaluated, based on the result of the calculation (and, therefore, on the inputs available at the time).

■ The script or button can be configured to serve different purposes in different circumstances, making the code more flexible and dynamic and allowing it to be repurposed.

As shown in Figure 13.7, the Go to Layout [ ] command offers two By Calculation options. It can be configured to select a target layout by either its name or its number. When choosing either option, make sure that the calculation expression you supply will return a valid result in all cases.

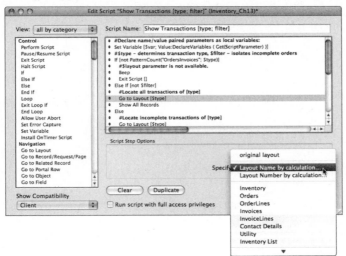

NOTE In the context of the Go to Layout [ ] command, "by number" means according to the numeric position of the layout in the layout order of the file (including any layouts used as separators or not set to appear in the layouts menu).

CAUTION If you choose to target a layout by name and the layout names are subsequently edited, or to target a layout by number and the layouts are subsequently reordered, the command may either fail or select the incorrect layout.

If you're concerned about the possibility of changes in the future impacting the accuracy or applicability of calculated results used to control commands dynamically, you can devise a more robust method by using FileMaker design functions to determine an object's name or number from its internal ID.

CROSS-REF A method for calculating a layout's internal ID from its name (and vice versa) to enable you to increase the robustness of references to objects in your code is provided in Chapter 12.

FIGURE 13.7

Configuring the Go to Layout command to determine the target layout at runtime using a calculation.

Dynamic file paths using variables

In most cases, the option to determine a target object by calculation appears in the FileMaker script and button command interface — at least when you know where to look, as in the case illustrated in Figure 13.7. However, one of the less obvious examples is the ability to provide the filename and/or file path for import and export of files (including the creation of PDF and Excel files using the Save Records as PDF [ ] and Save Records as Excel [ ] commands).

FileMaker accepts a variable as the specification (path and filename) of a file in the Specify File dialog you use to set the target file for all import and output file operations. Figure 13.8 shows a variable named $ReportPath being entered into the Specify Output File dialog in this chapter's Inventory example file's Acquired Items Report script (in the Save Records as PDF[ ] command).

For a file operation to complete successfully when the file has been specified using a variable, the variable must have a value resolving to a valid file path and filename for the current computer when the command is executed. Therefore, a preceding step in your script must declare the variable, giving it a value in the appropriate format (the accepted syntax for paths and files of various types is indicated in the lower portion of the Specify File dialogs for each operation).

To assist in the creation of appropriate paths for the configuration of the current computer, you have recourse to a number of useful functions, including

```
Get(DesktopPath)
Get(DocumentsPath)
Get(FilemakerPath)
Get(FilePath)
Get(PreferencesPath)
Get(TemporaryPath)
```

Moreover, the Get(SystemPlatform) function will enable you to ensure that your calculation expression returns a path and filename in keeping with the requirements of the current computer's operating system.

FIGURE 13.8

Supplying a predefined variable to provide the path and filename to create a file on the current workstation.

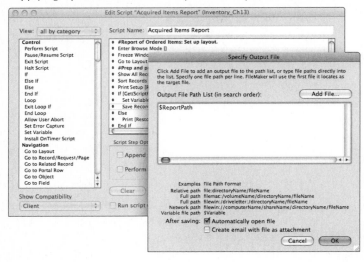

Dynamically building Find criteria

Although many script and button commands provide for indirect or dynamic targeting, several are lacking in this capability. For example, although you can configure the `Perform Find[ ]` command to apply specific search criteria, there is no provision for the criteria themselves to be determined by calculation. You can, nevertheless, achieve dynamic search capability in a reasonably straightforward way.

If you followed Chapter 8 closely, you already encountered a simple example of a dynamically scripted Find procedure in the `Show Transactions [Type]` script section. The script is designed to find incomplete records in either of two tables and therefore places criteria into a different field in each case (though the criteria placed into the field is always "1"). The technique for scripting a dynamic Find is, essentially, to build the find step-by-step using a series of discrete script steps, rather than using the "Restore" option to pre-populate Find criteria within the `Perform Find[ ]` step.

> **NOTE** Because performing a dynamic Find requires multiple commands in sequence, it can't be performed directly by a single button command — it requires a script. (However, your button can call the script to achieve the desired effect.)

The essence of a dynamic Find is a script sequence in which you enter Find mode, specify criteria, and then perform the Find — thus, at a minimum, three lines of script code are required. For example, when you need a script to locate all agenda submissions entered within the past 28 days, you can set it up as follows:

```
Enter Find Mode [ ]
Set Field [Submissions::Date; "≥" & (Get(CurrentDate) - 28)]
Perform Find [ ]
```

In this case, a single Find request is used (FileMaker creates a request automatically when entering Find mode), with a single criterion entered into the `Submissions::Date` field. However, the criterion is calculated with respect to the current day's date, as a calculation using the `Set Field[ ]` command.

By extension, you can use the same technique to build more complex Finds. For example, when scripting a Find similar to the one described, to locate all `"topic"` submissions since the start of the current month but excluding those marked as `"deferred"`, you can build a two-request dynamic Find script as follows:

```
Enter Find Mode [ ]
Set Variable [$now; Value:Get(CurrentDate)]
Set Field [Submissions::Date; "≥" & Date(Month($now); 1; Year($now))]
Set Field [Submissions::Type; "Topic"]
New Record/Request
Set Field [Submissions::Status; "Deferred"]
Omit Record
Perform Find [ ]
```

When used in Find mode, the `Omit Record` command toggles the state of the Omit checkbox option appearing in Find Mode's Status Toolbar.

In this more complex example, two Find requests are created:

- The first with compound criteria in the Date and Type fields
- The second configured to omit records matching a criterion in the Status field

Because the parameter of the `Enter Find Mode[ ]` command is empty, the sequence is executed without pausing. As the parameter of the `Perform Find [ ]` command is empty, the extant criteria, such as that created by the preceding steps, are used for the Find.

CAUTION For the sake of clarity and compactness, I have omitted additional error trapping commands from the foregoing script code. This may be acceptable where a script concludes with the `Perform Find[ ]` command, but in most cases, as discussed in the section "Trapping for Errors," earlier in the chapter, error trapping steps would be appropriate in addition to those shown here.

Editing field data on the fly (indirection)

A further area of frequently desired (and often required) dynamic functionality is the ability to determine at runtime the field to be set (for example, by the `Set Field[ ]` command) or selected (for example, by the `Go to Field[ ]` command). In either case, the functionality is only indirectly achievable in FileMaker Pro 10.

One of the more elegant methods for having your script target a field without predetermining which field (determining which field via runtime calculation) is employing the `Go to Object[ ]` command to select a named field on the current layout. This technique requires that

- An instance of each of the fields to be targeted be present on the current layout when the `Go to Object[ ]` command executes.
- Each field to be targeted is assigned an object name on the current layout.
- Your calculation for the `Go to Object[ ]` command returns the appropriate field's object name, rather than its logical (schema) name.

Thus, to reliably replicate the behavior of the `Go to Field[ ]` command with or without its Select/Perform parameter enabled, but with the target field being determined by calculation, you require (in addition to the earlier conditions set out) two lines of script code. To choose the field and select its contents:

```
Go to Object [If(Submissions::Status = "Pending"; "Reason"; "Action")]
Select All
```

To place the cursor at the end of the selected field's current content:

```
Go to Object [If(Submissions::Status = "Pending"; "Reason"; "Action")]
Set Selection [Start Position: Length(Get(ActiveFieldContents)) + 1]
```

NOTE   These field selection methods are applicable to field types other than containers. The Select All command does not prompt the commencement of multimedia program content in a container field.

In cases where you need to dynamically target a field for the purposes of having your script update its value, the Go to Object[ ] command can also be pressed into service for the first part of the task. Rather than using a subsequent selection command, however, you can use a Set Field[ ] command with no target field specified. (When the cursor is in a field and a Set Field[ ] command with no target is executed, the result of the Set Field[ ] calculation replaces the contents of the current field.)

Thus, to set a field without specifying which field in advance, you can use a two-step sequence such as

```
Go to Object [If(Submissions::Status = "Pending"; "Reason"; "Action")]
Set Field ["Prep for next meeting"]
```

You can apply a similar approach to achieve the effect of indirection using other editing and inserting commands, such as Cut, Copy, Paste, Clear, Insert, and so on.

In addition, FileMaker Pro 10 includes an additional Set Field By Name[ ] command that allows you to determine the field to be set using a calculation that supplies the fully qualified name of the field (that is, the TO name and the field name separated by double colons). The use of this new command enables you to select a field as the target of a set field operation dynamically based on context or other variables that may not be known until runtime. For example, if your solution has fields named tp correspond to the days of the week, you can place the value 9 into a field corresponding to current day as follows:

```
Set Field By Name [Get(LayoutTableName) & "::" & DayName(Get(CurrentDate)); 9]
```

Using Nonlinear Logic

Although the basic structure of FileMaker scripting processes is linear, several of the control options let you construct script sequences that execute in a nonlinear way. These can result in repeated sequences, alternate or parallel logical paths, and a variety of conditional code options.

Throughout the execution of all script processes, however convoluted, FileMaker nevertheless remains single-threaded: Only one command is executed at any point in time, and the process remains sequential in nature. (Each command completes its task before the next begins.)

Nested and sequential If/Else conditions

A mainstay of scripting control is provided by the logical controls If[ ], Else If[ ], Else, and End If sequence of commands. You can use them to introduce dynamic elements to your code to satisfy a wide range of requirements. They're not as compact or dynamic as the indirection methods discussed in the previous section, but they're nonetheless invaluable for their breadth of application and their explicit control of any sequence of steps in your scripts.

In some cases, you can use a sequence of If[ ] and Else If[ ] conditions where indirection capabilities are not provided by FileMaker. For example, to call a different sub-script according to which TO the current layout is based on, you might define the following sequence:

```
If [Get(LayoutTableName) = "Contacts"]
  Perform Script ["Add Contact Address Record"; Parameter: Contacts::ContactID]
Else If [Get(LayoutTableName) = "Invoices"]
  Perform Script ["Create InvoiceLines Record"; Parameter: Invoices::InvoiceID]
Else If [Get(LayoutTableName) = "Orders"]
  Perform Script ["Create OrderLines Record"; Parameter: Orders::OrderID]
Else If [Get(LayoutTableName) = "Products"]
  Perform Script ["Create ProductPrice Record"; Parameter: Products::ProductID]
End If
```

Although this code is entirely explicit regarding what should happen and when, it is nonetheless extensible. And although I include provision for only four conditions, much longer conditional statements are possible.

When FileMaker evaluates a conditional sequence such as the one shown here, it works down from the top evaluating the If[ ] and Else If[ ] expressions until it finds one that returns true (a non-empty and non-zero value). It then performs the enclosed commands and jumps to the following End If command.

For logical purposes, therefore, the order of the conditions is significant. For example, if more than one condition could evaluate as true, the one coming first will gain focus, and the subsequent one(s) will be bypassed. However, if the conditions you supply are mutually exclusive, it's preferable to order the conditions from the most probable (or frequently occurring) to the least probable, because doing so reduces the number of evaluations performed (and therefore execution time) for a majority of cases.

CROSS-REF For further discussion of techniques for optimizing your script and calculation code, see Chapter 19.

Looping constructs

FileMaker includes control commands you can use to create recursive script sequences. Direct support for this functionality is provided in the form of the Loop, Exit Loop If[ ], and End Loop group of script steps (refer to Chapter 8).

In Chapter 9, I present a method of saving and restoring Finds using a pair of loops. However, I do not discuss in detail the mechanism used to support this. The relevant steps from the first example script I do include (the script appears in the Inventory example as "...Perform/Store Find") are as follows:

```
Go to Record/Request/Page [First]
Go to Next Field
Set Variable [$FirstField; Value:Get(ActiveFieldName)]
```

```
Loop
  Loop
    If [not IsEmpty(Get(ActiveFieldContents))]
      Set Variable [$Criteria; Value:If(not IsEmpty($Criteria);
        $Criteria & ¶) & Get(RecordNumber) & "»" &
        Get(RequestOmitState) & "»" & Get(ActiveFieldName) &
        "»" & Get(ActiveFieldContents)]
    End If
    Go to Next Field
    Exit Loop If [Get(ActiveFieldName) = $FirstField]
  End Loop
  Go to Record/Request/Page [Next; Exit after last]
End Loop
```

As you can see from the two adjacent Loop steps, the construction of this sequence sets up a loop within a loop. The outer loop contains only two elements: the inner loop, plus the Go to Record/Request/Page[Next; Exit after last] command. Therefore, the outer loop serves to *walk* the current requests starting from the first and exiting after the last.

While the first (outer) loop is working its way through the current set of Find requests, the inner loop executes multiple times on each record, working its way through all the fields in the current layout and assembling details of the Find criteria (if any) in each field.

The number of times each loop executes depends on the circumstances when the script is executed. In the case under discussion, when there are three Find requests, the outer loop will execute three times — and when there are 12 fields on the current layout, the inner loop will execute 12 times on each pass of the outer loop for a total of 36 passes.

Specifying exit conditions

Whether you use an incrementing or decrementing counter, as I describe in Chapter 8, or an exit condition such as those employed in the loops in the preceding example, the essentials of the technique are the same — the loop iterates through the enclosed steps until the exit condition is satisfied.

In some cases, the use of a loop with an enclosed pause (set for a specific time interval) can be used to confirm completion of a task before proceeding. For example, when your script issues the Set Web Viewer[ ] command to load a page from a remote site, you can use a loop and pause technique to wait until the page has completely loaded before proceeding. One way of doing this is to check the html source of the loading Web viewer to confirm that the closing body tag has been received. For example:

```
Set Variable[$counter; Value: 0]
Loop
  Set Variable[$counter; Value: $counter + 1]
  Set Variable [$source; Value:GetLayoutObjectAttribute("Viewer"; "content")]
  Exit Loop If [PatternCount($source; "</body>") or $counter > 100]
```

```
       Pause/Resume Script [Duration (seconds): .1]
  End Loop
  If [not PatternCount($source; "</body>")]
     Show Custom Dialog ["Web Connection time-out"]
     Exit Script [ ]
  End If
```

In this code example, note that I've included a counter in addition to the check for the presence of the closing body tag so that in the event the network is unavailable, the script will not be indefinitely locked within its loop.

NOTE FileMaker provides support for pauses of durations less than a second, but the accuracy of pause timing in FileMaker Pro 10 for very short pauses (less than one tenth of a second) is low. However, you can specify pauses as short as 0.1 of a second, and FileMaker will pause for a corresponding interval (approximately 100 milliseconds).

One occasion when your loop will not require an exit condition is when the loop's purpose is to force a pause (for example, holding the active window in frontmost position) until the user clicks a button. In this case, the button the user clicks may be defined to halt or exit the current script — as shown in Figure 13.9.

NOTE The Current Script option is available only on buttons you attach to the `Perform Script[ ]` command, though you can separately define a button to halt or exit the current script (by attaching the separate `Halt Script` or `Exit Script` commands).

FIGURE 13.9

Defining a button to halt or exit the current running script to terminate a paused looping sequence.

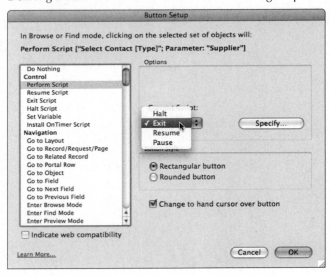

TIP By default, when you define a button to execute the `Perform Script [ ]` command, the Current Script control is set to the Pause option. However, this choice is rarely the most appropriate, so it is a good practice to consider the circumstances where a button will be used and select accordingly.

In most cases, looping conditions aside, it's been my experience that the most appropriate Current Script setting for a `Perform Script [ ]` button is either Exit or Resume, with Pause or Halt rarely giving the most acceptable or desirable behavior.

Modular Script Code

When your scripts are long and complex, you may want to consider breaking them up into self-contained smaller blocks of code that can be called in sequence to complete longer tasks. However, I counsel against doing this for its own sake. A lengthy scripted procedure does not necessarily become more manageable when its contents are split between several scripts, and, in fact, the reverse can be true. Keeping track of a scripted sequence when it ducks and weaves between multiple scripts can be a considerable challenge.

So when should you divide a scripted process into multiple scripts? Here are some things to consider:

- Is a section of your script code repeated at intervals during the process (in which case a single sub-script might be called at each of those points)?

- Could part of the process of your script be shared with one or more other scripted processes in your solution? (Again, if there is common code, separating it into a self-contained module may have benefits.)

- Does part of your script require a different level of access than the rest (for example, should one part run with the Run Script with Fill Access Privileges option enabled, while the remainder does not)?

- Is it desirable or necessary that part of your scripted process reside in one file while another part resides in another of your solution's files?

Unless you answered a resounding "yes" to one or more of the preceding questions, you're unlikely to benefit from introducing component logic into your script. In fact, it's likely that the added complexity and overhead (more scripts to manage, more convolutions, and dependencies to keep in view) will outweigh any advantages.

Using sub-scripts

When you design a script so that it can serve a particular kind of need in a number of contexts in your solution, ideally it becomes a self-contained parcel of code available to you whenever you need it when creating other scripts. In the section "Using Nonlinear Logic," earlier in this chapter, I cited the example of a script designed to create child records from various locations in your solution.

Another example would be a script designed to display a progress bar while other processes are under way. The code to manage either of these processes might best be located in one place for your whole solution — so that when you need to update it, you know exactly where to find it and a single change will be reflected throughout the solution (for example, wherever the sub-script is used).

A further area that is frequently a good candidate for separation into a sub-script is error trapping. Many steps in many scripts require similar checks and error-handling mechanisms. If you centralize all your error handlers into one script designed to receive the error code as a parameter, you can then provide error handling throughout all your other scripts by adding the following line of code:

```
Perform Script ["Error Handler"; Parameter: Get(LastError)]
```

You can add it after each script step where an error condition is possible. Such a script should, as its opening line, exit if the parameter is equal to zero (no error) so that the parent script can continue.

An advantage of using a sub-script for error trapping is that it enables you to apply much more exhaustive interpretation and response to various error types (and logging of errors) than would be feasible if you are required to repeat the error-handling code in every script throughout your solution. When you've created an appropriate error-handling script, it becomes a simple matter to reuse it wherever there is potential for error.

Script recursion

Intentionally or otherwise, the use of sub-scripts creates the possibility of circular logic and, therefore, infinite loops. This is one of many ways FileMaker gives you enough rope to hang yourself. Whenever you create a call from one script to another script, it is wise to confirm that the script you are calling does not itself call the current script. If it does — and you haven't added an intercept or exit condition — calling either script will bring your workstation to its knees.

While you should be mindful of the risks, the possibility of script recursion may be useful in some situations. Provided that you enclose a script's call to itself (or its call to another script that, in turn, calls it) within an If [ ]/End If condition with an appropriate expression to terminate the cycle when the desired aim is achieved, such a code model is viable.

In general, I recommend the use of Loop/End Loop structures in situations where recursive functionality is required within your scripts. It is clear and readable, while providing support for a variety of code architectures. Moreover, loop structures avoid the relative inconvenience and added overhead of repeated script calls that are a necessary part of recursively calling scripts.

Scripted Window Management

Among the 14 script commands appearing under the Windows group of commands in the list at the left of the Edit Script window, you can use 7 commands to control the appearance of the content display in the current window. Seven — highlighted in Figure 13.10 — act on the window itself.

FIGURE 13.10

Seven of the available Windows script commands act on windows themselves rather than the current window's contents.

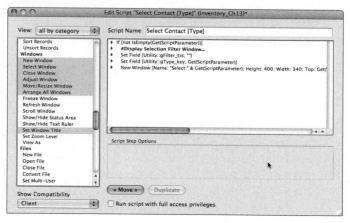

Addressing windows by name (title)

I'd love to have been able to provide a less equivocal subheading here, but the fact is that the text appearing across the top of windows is referred to as the window name in some places in FileMaker Pro 10, while in others it's called the window title. But rest assured that they're both referring to the same thing — for example, when you execute the command Set Window Title ["xyz"] and then subsequently evaluate the Get(WindowName) command, it returns "xyz".

Nowhere is this quirk more evident than in the "Set Window Title" Options dialog (shown in Figure 13.11) where the dialog itself is labeled "Title" but the fields within the dialog prompt you for "Window Name."

FIGURE 13.11

Filling in the Window Name fields in the "Set Window Title" Options dialog.

When you first open a solution file, FileMaker sets the window name to the file's name. When you create a new window using the `New Window[ ]` script or button command, FileMaker allows you the option of specifying the new window's name. If you don't provide a window name at this point, however, FileMaker uses a default naming convention where the new window is assigned a name based on the current window name (with a trailing hyphen and number appended — such as "Inventory – 2"). If you create a window manually by choosing Window ➪ New Window, FileMaker applies the same default naming procedure to determine the name (or should that be title?) of the new window.

Whatever it's called and however it got there, the label across the top of the window is useful for a variety of purposes:

- It gives you a way to let your users know which window is which and what each window is for.

- It lets you differentiate between windows in calculations throughout your solutions (for example, by using the `WindowNames( )` and `Get(WindowName)` functions to apply window-specific highlighting or other attributes in your solution).

- It provides scripts with a mechanism to control the behavior of one window from a script running elsewhere (even from a script in another file).

For all these reasons, I encourage you to supply unique and descriptive names to the windows in your solutions and keep window naming in mind when managing windows through your scripts. As part of this, you can issue custom (calculated) names to all new windows created by using the `New Window[ ]` command, as shown in Figure 13.12.

When you name a window, its name remains in place until it is closed unless your scripts or button commands explicitly change it. Thus, care in window naming provides you with a way to be explicit when subsequently selecting, moving, resizing, hiding, or closing a window.

NOTE   If you configure your solution to explicitly name windows, then the names will be those you assign. Otherwise, FileMaker will assign window names that incorporate the file name, which may include the name of the host where the file is located and/or a sequential number appended to differentiate similarly named windows.

Moving and resizing windows

When you script the creation of a window, the New Window Options dialog, shown in Figure 13.12, provides the option to specify the size (height and width in pixels) and location coordinates (distance from top and left of the main monitor in pixels).

TIP   On Mac OS, the window position is measured (in pixel coordinates) with respect to the top left corner of the screen display area immediately below the menu bar, while on Windows, the coordinates are referenced to the top left of the display area of the Multiple Document Interface (MDI) Application window that frames all database windows on Windows.

FIGURE 13.12

Specifying a name by calculation when scripting the creation of a new window.

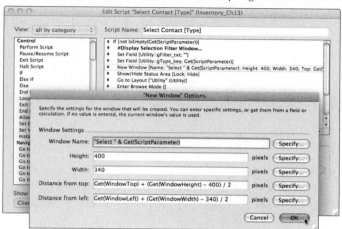

Whether or not you've chosen to make use of the options to set a window's initial dimensions and location when creating a new window by script, you can subsequently modify the window's position or proportions by using the Move/Resize Window[ ] command. Like the New Window Options dialog, the Move/Resize Window Options dialog accepts values for height and width in pixels, and for top and left in pixels from the upper left corner of the main monitor.

Determining window dimensions

Because the values for all four Move/Resize values can be determined by calculation, you can size and position the window with respect to other windows on the screen. For example, if you're setting your window to a width of 340 pixels and your monitor size is 1024 × 768 pixels, the unused horizontal space on either size of your window will be 768 – 340 = 684 pixels. Thus to position a window with a width of 340 pixels in the center of a 1024 pixel monitor, the "Distance from left" coordinate should be supplied as 342 (half of 648).

NOTE When you're calculating the available are for your solution's windows, you should take account of the allowance required for window "chrome" — the borders, scroll bar, controls, and other adornments that are included on your database windows be default. The sizes of these window components differ between operating system and operating system versions and are also affected by appearance settings, themes, and task bar preferences in Windows and the location and size of the Dock on Mac OS.

In cases when your solution may be opened on a number of monitors of different sizes, you can set your window placement calculations to determine the correct placement of your window by using the appropriate Get() functions. For example, to center a 340-pixel window horizontally on a monitor of any size, you can specify the distance from left coordinate as

```
(Get(ScreenWidth) - 340) / 2
```

Similarly the vertical location (for a 400-pixel-high window) can be set to find the middle of the monitor according to its height with

```
(Get(ScreenHeight) - 400) / 2
```

NOTE When determining sizes and locations of windows on the Windows operating system, remember that they will be contained within the Application window frame. It is preferable to calculate your window coordinates with respect to the application window dimensions rather than the screen size. You can do so by using the Get(WindowDesktopHeight) and Get(WindowDesktopWidth) functions. On Mac OS, Get(WindowDesktopHeight) returns the main monitor height minus the height of the menu bar.

Alternatively, if you prefer to center a new (say, 400 × 340) window with respect to an existing window (for example, the foremost window), it is easiest to use the Get(WindowHeight) and Get(WindowWidth) functions to pass the current window's coordinates to the expressions specifying the new window's location when creating the new window. As shown in Figure 13.12, you can do so with the following expressions:

```
Distance from top:  Get(WindowTop) + (Get(WindowHeight) - 400) / 2
Distance from left: Get(WindowLeft) + (Get(WindowWidth) - 340) / 2
```

Creating windows off-screen

Extending the ability to control the placement and size of windows, you can create windows off-screen and therefore (potentially) invisible to the user. This documented feature of FileMaker Pro 10 is useful for cases where you require a scripted procedure to undertake actions in another window so as to leave the user's environment undisturbed, while avoiding the visual discontinuity of a new window appearing and disappearing onscreen during the process.

NOTE FileMaker keeps track of found sets and relationship caching — along with other environment and state characteristics such as current layout, active record, commit state, and so on — separately for each window. Therefore, if your script changes some of these attributes (especially the found sets, which may be onerous to reinstate), creating a separate window to give your script its own separate contextual environment in which to operate (and closing the window upon script completion) is advantageous.

Using this technique, you might, for example, activate a message in the user's current window (or a floating window positioned above it) saying "processing — please wait…" perhaps accompanied by a progress indicator (especially if your script procedure may take more than a few seconds). Bear in mind that the visual effects of this technique vary between platforms, and window placement requires restored window states on the Windows operating system.

CROSS-REF For a detailed discussion of various approaches to the implementation of progress indicators, refer to Chapter 10.

After user feedback is in place, your script can create a window out of view and undertake its processing in a discreet contextual environment without impacting the user's selections and environment. From its point of focus in the off-screen window, your script can update a global variable value controlling the progress indicator onscreen, to provide up-to-date user feedback throughout the process.

> **CAUTION** If the user's computer is equipped with multiple monitors, a window created a short distance off-screen may simply appear on a different monitor (this applies particularly to Mac OS where the visibility of windows is not constrained by the limits of an Application Window). I recommend using negative coordinates and/or coordinates above 10,000 pixels to place your script's window well out of the user's visual range (values up to 32,766 in all directions are supported on all platforms — higher values are supported in some cases, but I don't recommend their use for reasons of cross-platform compatibility).

Freezing and refreshing the screen

In some circumstances creating off-screen windows will not suit your requirements — for example, if your approach is maximizing your solution's windows on the Windows platform, creation of windows of specified dimensions and placement causes FileMaker to revert to the restored window state. Moreover, creation of off-screen windows on Windows OS causes the application window to acquire scroll bars indicating the presence of objects outside the user's field of view.

For these and other reasons, in certain circumstances, you may prefer to maintain the focus on the current window while your script is in progress, yet don't want to expose a screen display of the script's actions. In such cases, issuing the Freeze Window script command prior to script steps that would otherwise change the display in the current window is an alternative. The Freeze Window command frees your script to proceed without updating the screen.

A common misconception is that when your script freezes the window, it should subsequently refresh the window using the Refresh Window[ ] command; however, this is not the case. The Freeze Window command carries an implicit window refresh after the freeze is released (such as when the script pauses or concludes). Therefore, adding a Refresh Window[ ] command is not only superfluous but may cause screen flicker as the screen is refreshed twice in quick succession.

I recommend that you only use the Refresh Window[ ] command at the conclusion of a script sequence if either

- You have not used the Freeze Window command throughout the course of the script.
- You need to explicitly flush cached join results or cached SQL data (both of which are options of the Refresh Window[ ] command).

> **CAUTION** Overuse of the Freeze and Refresh commands may add to rather than ameliorate screen flickering. I recommend that you use them sparingly and only when needed. However, lengthy scripts — such as those looping through the found set — generally benefit from including a Freeze command before commencing the loop.

TIP In addition to off-screen windows and scripted `Freeze/Refresh` sequences, a further option for performing processes out of the user's field of view is the use of a utility file with a window that has been explicitly hidden using the `Adjust Window [Hide]` command. You can call a script in a utility file as a way of ensuring that the action is separated from the interface being viewed by the user.

Scripting Data Import and Export

One of many strengths of FileMaker is its ability to import data from and export data to a wide variety of formats. This ability makes it a good player in medium to large organizational environments where a number of tools and technologies are in use. These capabilities become considerably more powerful when you're able to control them within your solution's scripts.

CROSS-REF My description of the technique for specifying dynamic file paths using variables (in the section "Dynamic file paths using variables," earlier in this chapter) is pertinent to the following examples. You can use a calculation to determine the filename and file path for any of the file creation and import operations discussed here.

Exporting field contents

With very few exceptions, you can export anything that is stored in a FileMaker field to a file on your computer, and the process can be scripted. The exceptions are limited to container images not in a supported external graphical format (such as layout vector objects pasted directly into container fields). All other data — including text, movies, sounds, images, and files — can be used as the basis of creation of a file or files on the current computer or any volume (such as network file server) accessible to it.

The `Export Field Contents[ ]` command requires only that you select a target field and specify an output file. For example, if your solution includes a text field called `Description` in a `Library TO`, you can use the following two lines of script code:

```
Set Variable [$FilePath; Value "File:Description.txt"]
Export Field Contents [Library::Description; "$FilePath"]
```

Doing so results in the creation of a text file called `Description.txt`, containing the text in the targeted field.

TIP The suffix of the filename you specify for an output file must be one your computer's operating system recognizes as valid for the kind of data you are exporting. If the suffix does not conform to system requirements the export may return an error. Or, if the file is successfully created, it may be associated with an inappropriate application (and therefore not recognized when a user attempts to open it).

Exporting table data

When you choose to export structured data from your solution, by default FileMaker exports from the table associated with the current layout and includes only the records in the current found set. The same applies when your export is scripted — the export is conducted from the current context at the time the `Export Records [ ]` command executes.

To script a successful export, you must therefore structure your script to first

- Select an appropriate layout (providing table context, including relationships to other tables if you're including data from related fields in the exported data set, including calculations in your primary TO referencing related table data).
- Establish an appropriate found set for the records you want to export.
- (Optionally) Set a path and filename for the file to be created.

In addition to the preceding preparatory steps, you must configure the `Export Records [ ]` step to include the selection of fields to be exported (and the order they're to appear in the export file), the output file path and the file format for the export (csv, tab separated text, XML, Excel, and so on), as shown in Figure 13.13.

The rudiments of a script exporting the contents of all Meetings table records in your solution in ASCII text in a CSV (comma separated values) format, into a file called `"AllMeetings.csv"` on the desktop of the current computer, are as follows:

```
Go to Layout ["Meetings" (Meetings)]
Show All Records
Set Variable [$FilePath; Value "file:" & Get(DesktopPath) & "AllMeetings.csv"]
Export Records [No Dialog; "$FilePath"; ASCII(DOS)]
Go to Layout [original layout]
```

This script (with the addition of appropriate error handling) executes efficiently, creating a file ready for transfer into another system or for a variety of other purposes.

> **TIP** If your objective is to move records from one table to another in your solution or to move them to another FileMaker file, rather than exporting, you can perform a direct import into the other table or file.

Selecting fields for export

When setting up an export, the settings you create in the Specify Field Order for Export dialog, shown in Figure 13.14, determine the fields to be included in the export, as well as their order.

Using the Field Order dialog, you can choose the source table for each field from the pop-up menu at the upper left and then select fields from the list at the left and use the buttons in the center to move them to the Field Export Order or Group by list boxes at the right.

FIGURE 13.13

Specifying the file type in the Specify Output File dialog for the `Export Records[ ]` command.

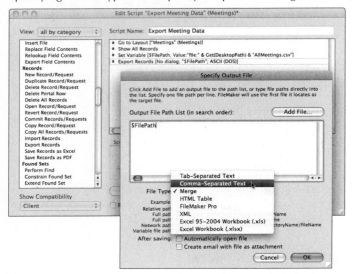

FIGURE 13.14

Specifying the fields and field order for export from the Meetings table.

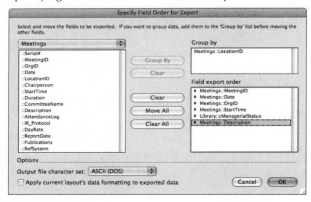

NOTE The checkbox option at the lower left of the Specify Field Order for Export dialog refers to the data format (such as number, date, and time presentation formats) rather than to character styles and formats applied to text.

Most export file options are suited for plain text only, so you can't include container field data, and any embedded text styles (including colors, fonts, and font sizes) will be lost. An exception is when you're exporting to a FileMaker file — both container data and embedded character styles are retained.

After you've added fields to the Field Export Order list, you can change their order by selecting them and then using ⌘+↑ or Ctrl+↑ and ⌘+↓ or Ctrl+↓ to move them up and down, or by dragging them with the handle icon to the left of each field, as shown in Figure 13.14.

Import options

When scripting a data import process into your solution, several steps of the process mirror the export procedure described in the preceding section. In particular, specifying a source file from which the data is to be imported and choosing an appropriate file type are achieved in the same way using a variant of the Specify File dialog, as shown in Figure 13.15.

FIGURE 13.15

Specifying the file path and type for import of data into your solution.

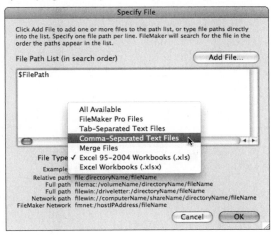

The choice of file type you make when specifying the file for import determines how FileMaker interprets the data and parses the values in the file you select (for example, FileMaker breaks fields using the appropriate delimiter for the chosen file format).

To configure the settings for an import, you must select a specific file as the source of the import. If you intend to supply a dynamic file path using a variable, you should first configure the import with a file path selected and then overwrite the file path with the name of the variable that will supply the path for the import.

Data matching for import

The configuration of options to match fields from the incoming data (or database) file to the field structure of a table in your solution requires that you select a destination table in your solution and then designate fields or values in the external file to align with some or all of the fields in the selected table, as shown in Figure 13.16.

Individual fields in the Target Fields column at the right of the Import Field Mapping dialog can be moved up and down to correspond to incoming data by selecting them and using the ⌘+↑ or Ctrl+↑ and ⌘+↓ or Ctrl+↓ to move them up and down, or by dragging them with the handle icon to the left of each field. Moreover, you can click the arrow in the center column adjacent to any field to enable or disable import into a specific field.

Synchronizing and updating data

You can import data into only one table at a time. However, you can choose a variety of import, matching, and synchronization options, enabling you to add new data, update existing data (to match the corresponding records in the external file or table), or a mix of both. The controls for these options are found at the lower left of the Import Field Mapping dialog, as shown in Figure 13.16.

FIGURE 13.16

Aligning incoming data to fields in your solution by using the Import Field Mapping dialog.

> **TIP** If you Shift+click or ⌘+click or Ctrl+click to select multiple contiguous or discontiguous fields in the Import Field Mapping dialog, as shown in Figure 13.16, you can enable or disable them all as a group by clicking the symbol in the center column.

Additionally, you can choose from the Arrange By pop-up menu (below the field list at the right), one of six field presentation orders for the fields in your solution, as follows:

- Matching names
- Last order
- Creation order
- Field names
- Field types
- Custom import order

> **CAUTION** If new fields are created in the destination table (in your solution) after you've defined a scripted import, they will be automatically added to the end of the import order. If you do not want new fields included in subsequent imports (or you want them in a different place in the import map), you should revise all script import maps targeting the table after adding fields.

Other import options

In addition to the import of raw data as described previously, FileMaker provides options to import from a Bento data source, enabling you to access the content of address book, calendar, and other related data from your computer, via the Bento desktop database. To import Bento data, choose File ⇨ Import Records ⇨ Bento Data Source. This option requires that you have Bento 2 (or later) installed on your computer.

Another import option allows you to import from an XML source. If the source data is formatted using the FMPXMLRESULT encoding format, you can import it directly. Otherwise, you need an appropriately formed XSLT style sheet to enable FileMaker to interpret and transform the XML data. Many data sources are available for which style sheets already exist or can readily be adapted.

After you've specified an XML source and (if necessary) an XSLT document to interpret it, FileMaker lets you configure an import field map to import the XML data as described in the previous section.

Additionally, FileMaker supports import from Open Database Connectivity (ODBC) data sources. To take advantage of this option, you first need to install an appropriate ODBC driver and employ it to define a Data Source Name (DSN).

> **CROSS-REF** For full details of the process of installing and configuring an ODBC driver and defining a DSN, refer to Chapter 7.

When your driver and DSN are configured, you're prompted to authenticate for the remote data source and then passed to the SQL Query Builder for the remote data source, letting you select fields from the ODBC data to be included in the import mapping process in FileMaker.

Loading and unloading container objects

Although container data aren't supported in import and export formats, you can batch import text or multimedia (picture or movie) files by using the Folder Import option. This option has a number of advantages, including the ability to simultaneously import (into different fields in your table) the Text Content, File Name, and File Path (for text file folder imports) or the Image, File Name, File Path, and Image Thumbnail (for image or movie imports).

Alternatively, you can readily script a process by using FileMaker's scripting commands to Insert Picture[ ], Insert QuickTime[ ], Insert File[ ], and/or Export Field Contents[ ] to loop through a group of records inserting or exporting container field contents to or from a predetermined directory (using filenames calculated and passed to the relevant commands via the attendant Specify File dialog, as noted earlier in this section). So, for example, to export student photos from the Students table to a pix folder in the current solution directory on your computer, using the StudentID as the filename, you could use a script structured in essentials along these lines:

```
Enter Browse Mode [ ]
Freeze Window
Go to Layout ["Students" (Students)]
Show All Records
Go to Record/Request/Page [First]
Loop
  Set Variable [$ImagePath; Value "file:pix/" & Students::StudentID & ".jpg"]
  Export Field Contents [Students::StudentPhoto; "$ImagePath"]
  Go to Record/Request/Page [Next; Exit after last]
End Loop
Go to Layout [original layout]
```

By using a similarly structured script with the Go to Field[ ] and Insert Picture[ ] commands in place of the Export Field Contents[ ] command, the reverse procedure can be accomplished, and appropriately named files can be uploaded from the pix directory. The variant of the script to achieve this is as follows:

```
Enter Browse Mode [ ]
Freeze Window
Go to Layout ["Students" (Students)]
Show All Records
Go to Record/Request/Page [First]
Loop
  Set Variable [$ImagePath; Value "image:pix/" & Students::StudentID & ".jpg"]
  Go to Field [Students::StudentPhoto]
  Insert Picture ["$ImagePath"]
  Go to Record/Request/Page [Next; Exit after last]
End Loop
Go to Layout [original layout]
```

CAUTION Both scripts described in this section require the addition of error handling as discussed in the section "Trapping for Errors," earlier in this chapter, particularly to deal with the situation where, in the second script, no image is available to match a given record in the Students table.

Pivoting Data between Tables

While import and export provide a number of essential methods for moving your data around in a number of circumstances, you will require more control over the process — for example, when modifying or massaging data into the appropriate form and structure for the table it is to occupy.

When you're working with data stored according to a different data model (such as FirstName and LastName in the same field — something you're most unlikely to have done in your own solutions, having read Chapters 7 and 11 of this book!), you'll require what is sometimes referred to as an Extraction, Transformation, and Loading (ETL) process between your data and the destination data structure.

Using utility relationships

One of the most powerful methods of data transfer and transformation in FileMaker is via a scripted update using a utility relationship. Such a relationship is based on a global field in the table from which the data is to be sourced, and relates either to the primary key of the destination table, or to an intermediary table you will use for final data vetting before export or before importing to the destination table.

The relationship between the tables should be set to Allow Creation of Related Records, as described in Chapter 11. By populating the global key field in your source table with each of the primary keys for the remote table in turn, you are able to write to or create corresponding records using the data in your primary source table and any tables related to it, within the structure of your solution.

Managing related data (walking through related records)

Using your utility relationship to isolate individual records to be created or updated in the target table, you can build a transformation script in your solution along the following lines:

```
Enter Browse Mode [ ]
Freeze Window
Go to Layout ["SourceData" (Source)]
#Locate records to be loaded to external system via ETL
Perform Find [Restore]
Go to Record/Request/Page [First]
Loop
   #Load external system key to activate utility relationship
   Set Field [gETL_key; Source::LegacySystemID]
```

```
      Set Variable [$ETL; $ETL + 1]
      #perform required transformations for each external data field
     .Set Field [External::Name; Source::FirstName & " " & Source::LastName]
      Set Field [External::Chk; Choose(Source::Status; "pending"; "complete")]
      Set Field [External::Date; Day(Billed::Date) & "." & Month(Billed::Date)]
      Set Field [External::NetCost; Billed::Amount - Source::Discount]
      #etc - to complete full set of required data transformations
      Go to Record/Request/Page [Next; Exit after last]
   End Loop
   Go to Layout [original layout]
   Show Custom Dialog ["Extract/Transform/Load of " & $ETL & " records completed"]
```

This process outlined in its essential form pivots data through the utility relationship from the
Source TO to the External TO, drawing on data from the Source and Billing TOs (and
others as required) to modify and transform the data into the appropriate form and content for
upload to the external system.

> **TIP**   An ETL process along the lines set out in the previous script can be used effectively
> to pass data between external data sources and FileMaker data tables to facilitate
> reporting on ESS data, archiving or warehousing of FileMaker data, or the interchange of data
> between complementary systems.

Going over Some Practical Examples

Throughout this chapter, I've delved into a selection of the essentials of scripting, providing you
with guidance, tips, and examples designed to help you solve problems and elevate your solution's
scripts to new levels of power and efficiency. To add to the wealth of examples included in this
chapter, here are two useful techniques to round out your repertoire.

Locating unique records

A common problem encountered in all database systems is identifying unique examples of an
entity or attribute when duplicates exist. For example, if your parking register has a field for the
car model of each client and you need to produce a list of car models (including each only once),
you can use the following script:

```
   Enter Browse Mode
   Show All Records
   Sort Records [Restore; No dialog {by Clients::CarModel}]
   Go to Record/Request/Page [First]
   Freeze Window
   View As [View as Form]
   Loop
     Set Variable [$prevNo; Value: Get(RecordNumber) - 1]
     Set Variable [$prevValue; Value: GetNthRecord(Clients::CarModel; $prevNo)]
     If [$prevValue = Clients::CarModel]
       Omit Record
```

```
      Else
        Go to Record/Request/Page [Next; Exit after last]
      End If
    End Loop
    Unsort Records
    View As [View as List]
    Go to Record/Request/Page [First]
```

In this disarmingly simple procedure, your script sorts the records in the Clients table (by the field where you want to isolate unique values) and then walks the records, comparing each with the preceding record to selectively omit those already represented in the found set.

Building a multi-part PDF report

FileMaker Pro 10 includes the ability to combine several reports or report components into a single, composite PDF document. For example, you can generate a polished presentation document with a cover page, data pages, and a concluding summary page within a single document.

Generating a composite report of this kind first requires three layouts: one providing the summary page, one formatted as a list layout providing the report document's body, and one containing header, footer, and sub-summary parts only to generate an overview of grouped data. With the required report layouts in place, you can then set in place a script along the following lines:

```
    Set Variable [$ReportPath; Value:"file:PurchasesReport.pdf"]
    Go to Layout ["ReportCover" (InvoiceLines)]
    Save Records as PDF [Restore; No Dialog; "$ReportPath"; Current record]
    Go to Layout [ "PurchaseReport" (InvoiceLines) ]
    Show All Records
    Sort Records [Restore; No dialog ]
    Save Records as PDF [Restore; Append; No Dialog; "$ReportPath"; Records being
        browsed]
    Go to Layout ["BuyerSummary" (InvoiceLines)]
    Sort Records [Restore; No dialog ]
    Save Records as PDF [Restore; Append; No Dialog; "$ReportPath"; Automatically
        open; Records being browsed]
    Go to Layout [original layout]
```

With this script in place, a multi-page PDF report will be created representing current data and then opened on your computer.

 This script is implemented in the Inventory example file for this chapter and is available among the download materials on the book's Web site.

Part IV

Integrity and Security

Making your solutions operate efficiently and respond to the needs of users is an excellent start, but it's important that your solutions also be robust, reliable, and secure. A focus on preventative measures in the design, configuration, and deployment of your solutions will be of great benefit in ensuring that your solutions continue to deliver what is required.

When you encounter situations where different users require different levels of access to data and functionality in your solutions, it's time to make use of FileMaker security to set in place granular controls on user access privileges.

In this part, you'll find insider tips, explanations, and techniques to help you understand how best to design and deploy solutions that will survive real-world use and abuse. The chapters included here include detailed coverage of user account management, robust relational design techniques, error trapping, backup strategies, and more, to equip you with the best practices for developing dependable solutions.

IN THIS PART

Chapter 14
In Control with FileMaker Security

Chapter 15
Maintaining Referential Integrity

Chapter 16
Making FileMaker Systems Fail-Safe

Chapter 17
Maintaining and Restoring Data

Chapter 14

In Control with FileMaker Security

I f data doesn't matter to you, you're unlikely to store it at all, much less build a database solution to accommodate it — so the fact that you've done so is as good an indication as any that the data matters. Because it matters, it should be protected — from unauthorized access or sabotage or simply from mishap or loss. Security takes a number of forms and helps protect your data in a variety of ways.

FileMaker provides a robust database environment with a multi-faceted security architecture that you can configure to meet various needs — from a simple single-user database to a diverse multi-user system with dozens or even hundreds of users. FileMaker conforms to industry standards in its security framework implementation and supports a range of best practices for secure handling of sensitive data.

Technology, however, is effective only when used skillfully and appropriately, and an arsenal of security capabilities is of no use whatsoever if it remains unused. Security should form part of your solution's design from the outset and should be built into the fabric of your code. Too often security is added as an afterthought.

Concepts of Security

In the broadest sense, security represents a collection of safeguards against potential risks, threats, and problems. An important first step toward creating an appropriate security strategy is planning, which involves assessing the possible risks, understanding their impact, and considering the probability of the various risks.

IN THIS CHAPTER

Exploring security concepts

Understanding privilege sets

Working with granular security

Dealing with user authentication

Managing accounts via script

Creating a custom logout option

Deciding how much security you need

Recognizing the importance of physical file security

Implementing secure deployments with FileMaker server

There is no one way to address all aspects of security, so I encourage you to think and act broadly and to implement a mix of strategies addressing your solution's needs. Security can't be considered in isolation; it's an essential and core part of every aspect of your solutions' creation and use.

Balance and perspective

Among life's copious ironies are a collection of sad stories about misplaced effort, including backup files that can't be opened, passwords on sticky notes along the tops of computer monitors, and heavily secured buildings with open access Wi-Fi networks. It's a long and sorry tale.

Keeping things in perspective is important when considering solution security. It's too easy to focus your attention on one area of concern while largely overlooking others. For example, a beautifully implemented login system won't protect your data from the hazards of disk failure or human error — each presenting a real risk of potentially equal magnitude. You need different kinds of security to address different risks.

Identifying threats

Taking time to identify the various risks, threats, and contingencies impacting your solutions makes sense. These risks include the possibility of malicious acts, unauthorized access to your data or your solution's code, and careless modification or deletion of data, not to mention hardware failure or errors within your solution's code.

I suggest a measured approach to security. Address the various hazards and potential issues by responding to them in proportion to their relevance (the probability of each type of issue arising in your particular situation) and make sure that the level of security you implement is in line with your solution's value.

Assessing value

Your solution has value in several ways, the most readily identifiable being the expenditure (of both time and money) to develop, implement, and maintain it. In many cases, however, the value of your solution is best measured by the amount of work it does for you, your business, or your employer — and the costs that would be incurred or the amount of income foregone if your system failed or were unavailable.

Against this background, even the simplest of solutions has a value sufficient to warrant some thought, time, and resources devoted to identifying its vulnerabilities and setting strategies in place to manage those vulnerabilities.

Protecting your investment

Before deciding on a security strategy for your solutions, take a moment to consider what's at stake. Security is a way of protecting your investment, and the level of your investment may be greater than you first think. You invest in your database solutions in several ways:

■ The solution is almost certainly an investment in time and ingenuity. It may well be worth more than the software or computers it runs on.

■ Your solutions, by nature, contain the essentials of many of your business rules, operating procedures, and work preferences. (A solution is in fact a way of codifying your way of working.) A solution may also incorporate your "mental map" of ways to solve a host of problems.

■ The accumulation of work collecting, processing, refining, and organizing information in your solution has a value. Whether you enter information yourself, pay others to do so, or acquire information in a variety of other ways, it nevertheless has a value.

■ When information is sensitive or privileged, it must be protected — as required by law as well as common sense. Whether the reasons are positive (competitive advantage) or negative (breach of privacy), they amount to a compelling need for controlling the flow of information.

Each way your solution has value presents a range of different issues and security concerns. Maintaining data confidentiality is of little use if the data itself has become subject to corruption or is generously peppered with user errors. Conversely, protecting your solution from a malicious attack won't help if your scripts malfunction and delete the wrong records.

Although in some cases risks are low or security isn't a paramount concern, nonetheless, you need to consider the investment, both in the data and in the solution itself. Even for solutions operating in a secure environment or including no private or sensitive data, the levels of risk are needlessly high if security is left to chance.

Interface vulnerabilities

Your solution interface can challenge or threaten security in several ways. The simplest of these are the impact of clutter and confusion. Confusion leads to errors, misplaced data, incomplete processes, and the diminishing returns arising from user frustration and incomprehension.

Taking things at interface value

Care and attention to interface design can lend clarity and simplicity to your solutions, resulting in great improvements in data integrity and worker productivity. Rather than bolting your interface down, adding layers of code to prevent users from doing the wrong things, and using still more layers to detect and correct errors after they're made, with some changes to the interface, many problems evaporate.

Along with your solution's interface layer, you should also consider the interaction model. If your solution has a natural flow to it and users find that it mirrors their work processes, they'll be engaged and energetic in maintaining the solution, because they understand and appreciate its value. Conversely, when you introduce onerous login processes and complex or convoluted requirements, the easy flow turns to a struggle, with users working in opposition to the system.

More than a semblance of security

An entirely different way your solution's interface can get you into trouble is by providing the appearance of security in place of real security. You may be tempted to consider fields not in view as being inaccessible or to suppose that users will be constrained to follow the processes laid out in your scripts.

Don't allow your interface and script designs to lull you into a false sense of security. They are the front door to your solution, and it's certainly important that they guide the user and present only the appropriate information in layouts and reports. Be aware, however, that many alternate ways exist for a solution to be accessed by a resourceful or mischievous user — so the fact that a field doesn't appear on any layouts doesn't mean that it's secure. Similarly, having your scripts impose a certain sequence of events doesn't guarantee that users can't contrive other passages through your solution.

FileMaker supports links to external files, so you can structure solutions to include data from other files. Unless you've given careful thought to security, a user can create a file with a reference to your solution and use it to view and edit data in every corner of your solution, regardless of the interface you've set in place.

CAUTION Unless you have set safeguards in place — in the form of robust security measures assigning appropriate privileges to each user — every field can be accessed and edited by anyone with a mind to do so.

File-based security

To provide you with the tools to control access to key components of your solution (including layouts, scripts, and value lists as well as field data), FileMaker provides a security architecture centered on assigned user privileges in each file. Therefore, if a user is accessing the contents of your file from another file, the constraints and privileges in place will be those (if any) you have defined in your file, not those they define in the external file being used to gain access.

The file-centered security model has numerous advantages — allowing you to offset a variety of security concerns — but also presents some challenges, especially when your solution is comprised of multiple files. In such cases, it's incumbent on you to build appropriate security into each file, while ensuring that the solution files can nevertheless interact and provide a seamless user experience.

CROSS-REF The implications of file-based security for aspects of the design and use of your solutions are explored in Chapters 11 and 13.

The Privilege Set

At the heart of the FileMaker security model is the concept of the *privilege set,* a named collection of specifications for access levels and restrictions throughout the file where it's defined.

By default, all FileMaker files contain the following three privilege sets:

- [Full Access]
- [Data Entry Only]
- [Read-Only Access]

NOTE The enclosing square brackets around FileMaker's default privilege set names enable you to easily differentiate them from other privilege sets in your solution files. When creating your own privilege sets, you can choose to enclose their names in square brackets. However, I recommend against doing so, to preserve and underscore the distinction between default privilege sets and those created specifically for the solution.

The default [Full Access] account provides the level of access required for solution development and is an essential component of any file under development or maintenance.

By choosing File ⇨ Manage Accounts & Privileges and navigating to the Privilege Sets panel, as shown in Figure 14.1, you can view the current privilege sets in each solution file, as well as create and configure new ones.

FIGURE 14.1

Default privilege sets showing in the Manage Accounts & Privileges dialog.

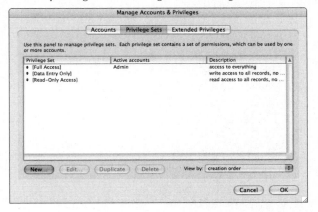

Before your solution's initial deployment and preferably early in its development, you should begin building appropriate privilege structures to support and enhance your solution's operations and to define the scope and limits of use. In fact, establishing the security model will help you achieve clarity about what the purpose and scope of the components of your solution are, and is therefore an important component of the design process.

Concepts of role-based security

A privilege set comprises a comprehensive definition of field, layout, value list, and script access permissions, as well as a number of broad functional capability permissions (such as printing and exporting). Collectively, these permissions are assembled to meet the requirements of a particular user or (better still) a group of users.

When you define a privilege set to meet the needs of a group of users, you tailor the permissions according to the role or roles to be performed by the users. If a different group of users performs different roles, you create another privilege set. Thus, a collection of privilege sets is modeled on the various roles performed by users of the solution. Organizing privileges in this way provides a framework of clarity that helps you determine appropriate access for each group and enables efficient management of privileges. For example, a single change to the privileges assigned to a particular privilege set affects a change for all users assigned to that set.

Each user logs in with personal credentials (account name and password), but each account is assigned to a privilege set that determines the access levels the account enjoys. By assigning multiple accounts (requiring similar access privileges, according to the users' roles) to each privilege set, you simplify the setup and management of access for multiple users. The grouping of accounts with similar requirements against appropriate privilege sets is the essential principle of role-based security management.

Defining and constraining access

To create and configure privilege sets for your solution's users, click the New button (lower left of the Privilege Sets panel of the Manage Accounts & Privileges dialog) to open the Edit Privilege Set dialog and then enter a name for the privilege set in the field at the top left. You can also enter an optional description in the adjacent field as a reminder of the privilege set's purpose. By default, a new privilege set provides no access to any part of your solution, so you must add privileges before the privilege set will allow users to view any data or perform any actions.

The Edit Privilege Set dialog is divided into three sections, as shown in Figure 14.2. The Data Access and Design section lets you specify access controls for records and fields in the file's data structure (data stored in tables within the file, for example), as well as access levels to layouts, value lists, and scripts.

NOTE   While unstored calculation fields don't represent stored data as such, access to the results they return can be controlled using access privileges in the same way as other types of fields.

The Extended Privileges section lets you enable or disable each of a list of access modes or options. By default, FileMaker includes seven extended privilege options associated with different modes of access to your data. You can add to or modify the list. Each extended privilege optionally associates a keyword with the privilege set. You can see the keywords listed in parentheses to the right of each entry in the Extended Privileges list box at the lower left of the dialog, as shown in Figure 14.2.

FIGURE 14.2

Configuring a privilege set in the Edit Privilege Set dialog.

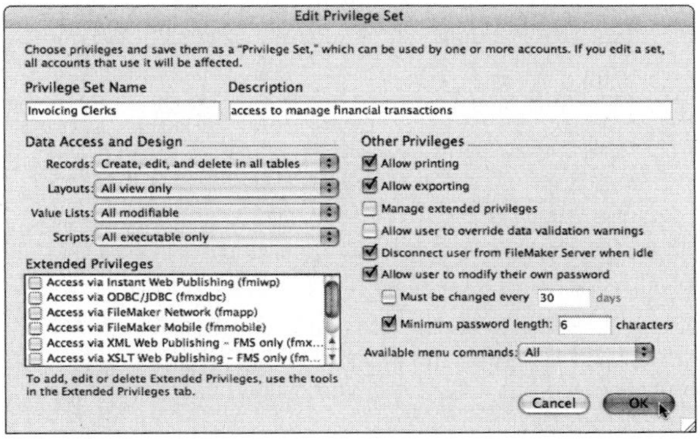

NOTE Extended privileges allow you to specify keywords that are associated with a privilege set to allow you to set up extensible control of access and application behavior according to your own requirements. When viewed or retrieved in the application (for example, using the `Get(ExtendedPrivileges)` function), the names of the assigned extended privileges for the current user's privilege set are returned as words, without the brackets that appear in the dialogs where they're defined.

Finally, the Other Privileges section (on the right) gives you access to a series of general controls over the current solution file's behavior for users whose logins are associated with the privilege set. Among the most significant of the privilege settings in the Other Privileges section are the controls for ability to print or export data and the ability to override data validation warnings.

CAUTION Be aware that disallowing printing or exporting of data will not stop determined users from taking screen captures, copying and pasting data from your solution into other applications on their workstation, or using other methods of access to circumvent your file-based security measures. These controls determine only the range of functionality available within the file where they are defined.

Schema privilege controls

At the center of the FileMaker security model is the ability to control users' access to the elements of schema — the fields and tables throughout your solution's data structure — as part of Data

Access and Design privilege controls. In the Edit Privilege Set dialog's Data Access and Design section, the pop-up menus provide several categories of access, each offering several predetermined access levels including

- All Modifiable
- All View Only
- All No Access

The first pop-up menu is labeled Records and differs from the others in that in place of the All Modifiable option are two more explicitly defined options, as shown in Figure 14.3, supporting editing capabilities either with or without the ability to delete records. As the wording in these options indicates, the selection you make at this level applies equally to all tables within the file.

The generic access options presented in the Data Access and Design settings will be adequate for your requirements in many cases. If you need more fine-grained control, however, you can choose a Custom Privileges option to modify the scope of action permitted (per privilege set) in each area of the file. These options appear below a separator at the bottom of each pop-up menu.

FIGURE 14.3

Access options in the Data Access and Design privileges pop-up menus.

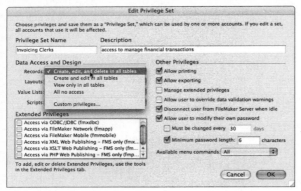

Granular Security

On each of the pop-up menus, the Custom Privileges options give you access to dialogs listing the corresponding elements in the current file (records, value lists, scripts, and layouts), letting you specify a range of access attributes separately against each component of the solution file.

The range of access controls operates at a number of levels from the broadest categories (for example, granting or denying access to a whole table) down to the most finely granular (controlling access for the individual record or field). In this section, I describe the processes for configuring granular access appropriate for the needs of your solution.

Access to value lists and scripts

The Custom Privileges options open list dialogs that allow you to select items and choose the desired access levels. For example, the Custom Script Privileges dialog, shown in Figure 14.4, offers radio button settings for Modifiable, Executable Only, or No Access on a script-by-script basis.

As you can see near the top left of the dialog shown in Figure 14.4, a checkbox is provided to control the user's ability to create new scripts. A similar control is provided in the Custom Layout privileges dialog to regulate users' ability to create new layouts. Furthermore, the Custom Script Privileges layout includes a Notes column at the right to display indicators generated by FileMaker that are relevant to the access status of the script. For example, scripts set to Run with Full Access are annotated as such in the Notes column. The Custom Value List Privileges dialog is also similar to the dialog shown in Figure 14.4, offering options for Modifiable, View Only, or No Access for each value list in the current file.

FIGURE 14.4

Specifying access levels for individual scripts.

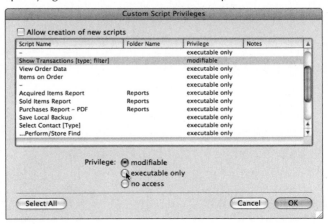

The two dimensions of layout access

The Custom Layout Privileges dialog provides dual controls for each layout — one relating to the layout itself (to allow or deny layout design changes or layout viewing, for example) and another to control access to records when viewed using the layout.

Figure 14.5 shows that you can independently select the options provided by the dual controls when configuring layout privileges.

FIGURE 14.5

Setting access for both layouts and records via layouts in the Custom Layout Privileges dialog.

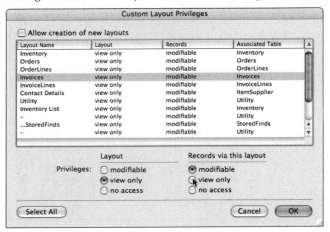

Privileges for table, record, and field access

The Custom Record Privileges dialog differs from the three custom privileges dialogs described in the previous section. This dialog provides multiple access controls for records in each table and governs View, Edit, Create, Delete, and Field Access permissions, as shown in Figure 14.6. The pop-up menus for View, Edit, and Delete include an option labeled Limited. Selecting this option opens a Specify Calculation dialog where you can define an expression that determines on a record-by-record basis the level of access to individual records users assigned to the current privilege set enjoy. For example, in the Inventory example file for this chapter, if you select the Orders table, choose Limited from the Edit pop-up menu and then enter this expression:

```
Status ≠ 1
```

Users logging in against the privilege set so defined are prevented from editing records flagged as complete in the `Orders::Status` field (that is, only incomplete records may be edited). In this example, it would be appropriate to apply a similar control to the Delete option so that only incomplete orders can be deleted.

Using the Field Access menu option (lower right of the Custom Record Privileges dialog), you gain access to a further layer of granular control over users' access to individual fields in the selected table. As shown in Figure 14.7, you can independently designate each field in the table as No Access, View Only, or Modifiable for the current privilege set.

FIGURE 14.6

Specifying record level access permissions by table in the Custom Record Privileges dialog.

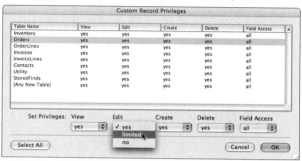

Using these controls as described, you can configure explicit and dynamic access privileges for individual elements throughout the current file, ensuring access at all levels as appropriate to users assigned to the selected privilege set.

Additionally, each Custom Privileges dialog includes an option to set the default access level applicable to new elements added to the file. For example, in Figure 14.6, the last line specifies access for [Any New Table]. Similarly, the Custom Privileges dialogs for Layouts, Value Lists, and Scripts include a checkbox option at the top left allowing users to create new items — for example, at the upper left of Figure 14.5 the Allow Creation of New Layouts option is shown.

FIGURE 14.7

Specifying field-level access privileges for the selected table.

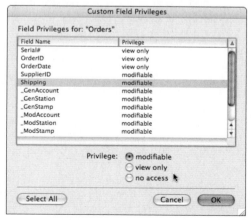

NOTE   At the bottom of each custom privileges list is a line that allows you to set default access privileges for new (subsequently created) entities. For example, Figure 14.6 shows the entry for [Any New Table] at the bottom of the Custom Record Privileges list.

In the case of the Custom Layout Privileges dialog shown in Figure 14.5, there is an interplay between the Allow Creation of New Layouts option and the default [Any New Layout] privilege setting. When you grant users the privilege to create new layouts using the checkbox setting, you can also determine the level of access they'll have to those new layouts using the [Any New Layout] privilege setting.

Using and managing extended privileges

FileMaker Pro and FileMaker Server use the seven default extended privileges keywords to control a range of network and remote access capabilities. You can enable or disable each of these keywords independently for each privilege set, giving you precise control over the means of interaction with the solution available to each role-based group of users.

FileMaker provides a number of default extended privileges in each new file, including the fmapp extended privilege to control access to the file when hosted (for example, using FileMaker Server). The default extended privileges also provide various forms of web access, mobile access, and external connectivity (ODBC/JDBC) access.

You can also create keywords of your own and associate each with one or more privilege sets, as a means of establishing granular and customized access control over your solution's elements (such as calculations and scripts). For example, when you have a script — say, a reports script — that should include monthly totals for some groups of users (but not others), you can create an extended privilege keyword to manage this for monthly reports. To do so, follow these steps:

1. Navigate to the Extended Privileges panel of the Manage Accounts and Privileges dialog.
2. Click the New button at the lower left. The Edit Extended Privileges dialog appears.
3. Enter a brief keyword (such as MthRep) and a description of the purpose of the privilege, as shown in Figure 14.8.
4. Select one or more privilege sets for access to the extended privilege you've created.

After an extended privilege, as outlined, is in place, you can code your calculations and scripts to refer to it. In this example, you can set up a script to include the additional (month report summary) functionality, conditional on the current user's login having the MthRep privilege assigned, by adding script code, such as:

```
If [PatternCount(¶ & Get(ExtendedPrivileges) & ¶; "¶MthRep¶")]
    Go to Layout ["Month Summary Report" (Orders)]
    Sort Records [Restore; No dialog]
End If
```

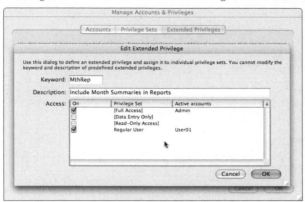

FIGURE 14.8

Entering details for a new Extended Privilege in the Edit Extended Privilege dialog.

With this additional code in your report script, users whose login account is assigned the MthRep extended privilege will see an alternate report based on the Month Summary layout, whereas other users will not.

NOTE You can assign the Manage Extended Privileges option to one or more privilege sets, enabling some users (managers and team leaders, for example) to edit and reassign extended privileges to existing privilege sets. Extended privileges, like all privilege set characteristics, are available only to scripts and calculations in the file where you define them. For a multiple file solution, you may need to define extended privileges in more than one file.

User Authentication

You can create privilege sets for groups of users according to their role within the solution and create multiple accounts in each solution file. You can assign each account to an existing privilege set in the file to facilitate assigning appropriate privileges without having to individually specify and manage each user account's permissions.

Each user of your solution should therefore be assigned an account, giving them personal credentials (account name and password) to log in to your solution — and users should be made aware of measures to keep their credentials private and secure.

NOTE An essential principle underpinning security and solution access management is that accounts and credentials are never shared. Each user has his own login account name and a password he should be expected to keep secret. Moreover, each user should be encouraged to avoid leaving his computer unattended (or handing control to another person) while logged in with his credentials.

Creating user accounts

User accounts provide you with a basis to control the access of individual users to a solution file. You should therefore add a separate account for every person who will access the solution (and to each file within the solution). To add accounts in your solution files, follow these steps:

1. Choose File ⇨ Manage Accounts & Privileges. The Manage Accounts & Privileges dialog appears with the Accounts panel selected as the default.

2. In the Accounts panel of the Manage Accounts & Privileges dialog, click the New button at the lower left. The Edit Account dialog appears, as shown in Figure 14.9.

FIGURE 14.9

Creating a new account using the Edit Account dialog.

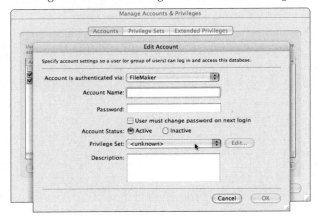

3. Click OK to accept the settings and close the Edit Account dialog.

TIP I recommend that you assign intelligible and recognizable account names so that when data about the current user is returned (by the Get (AccountName) function, for example), the user's identity will be evident. Straightforward naming conventions, such as first name and last initial (JulietteB, GeoffreyR, and so on) or first initial and last name (RFiennes, CBlanchett, for example), are compact, yet readily recognizable.

Internal and external authentication

By default, FileMaker accounts are set to authenticate with a password you supply (that is, a password stored internally in your FileMaker file), as shown in Figure 14.9. However, when you choose the external authentication option from the pop-up menu near the top of the Edit Account dialog (Figure 14.10), user credentials are retrieved from the domain server when the file is hosted using FileMaker Server, within a network managed by an Open Directory (Mac OS) or Active Directory (Windows) domain controller.

FIGURE 14.10

Choosing external authentication for an account, in the Edit Account dialog.

When creating user accounts, rather than supplying an account name and password, when you choose external authentication, you need supply only the name of a group corresponding to a group assigned to users in the domain authentication server.

NOTE The authenticating computer for an external authentication configuration may be the same computer where FileMaker Server is installed — though in most cases, a separate domain controller will already be performing this function.

When a user logs in at the domain level and then accesses a FileMaker file, FileMaker compares the groups associated with the user's network login with groups assigned to externally authenticated accounts in the file. The file is opened with the first externally authenticated account with a name matching one of the group names for the current user's network login (working downwards from the top of the accounts in FileMaker, when viewed in authentication order). A Windows-based domain configuring external authentication as described here provides users with single sign-on functionality.

On Mac OS, the user is still presented with the familiar login dialog to access the file (or server, if so configured). However, a similar level of functionality is available via the use of the Mac Keychain to manage credentials for the user, enabling the user to bypass the FileMaker authentication dialog and providing a convenience proximate to single sign-on.

TIP You can change the authentication order of accounts in the Manage Accounts & Privileges dialog by dragging the accounts up or down in the list on the Accounts pane. You can display the authentication order by selecting Authentication Order in the View By drop-down menu.

When you create accounts configured for external authentication, the FileMaker external server account operates as a connection between existing network credentials and a defined privilege set within your FileMaker files. All the work of verifying the user's credentials takes place outside of FileMaker. (This step happens at the designated authentication server, as configured in FileMaker Server settings.)

One significant benefit of using external authentication is that the accounts and passwords are managed centrally for multiple FileMaker files. So, for example, when users change their password, you don't need to provide a mechanism to apply the change separately to each FileMaker file — the credentials for such accounts are not stored within your solution.

CAUTION   I advise against assigning any externally authenticated accounts to the [Full Access] privilege set, as this presents a potential vulnerability if users can gain access to the physical files.

Scripted Account Management

For the purpose of setting up the initial security configuration for the database files in your solution, you must use the controls in the Manage Accounts & Passwords dialog's panels, as I describe in the previous sections — no alternative exists. After your solution's security infrastructure is in place, FileMaker lets you automate a number of the key maintenance and usage operations associated with logging in and manipulating accounts. You can use scripts to manage these and other tasks.

Provision for automation of database security

As shown in Figure 14.11, ScriptMaker provides you with six essential commands for controlling security in your files, including adding and deleting accounts, resetting or changing passwords, and activating or deactivating accounts, as well as account login and re-login.

NOTE   Contrary to expectation, the Enable Account command is not used to enable an account. Instead, its function is either to activate or deactivate a designated account. (In fact the latter option seems directly contrary to the function suggested by its name.) Despite this oddity, the function efficiently performs its activation and deactivation tasks.

FileMaker also provides three calculation functions you can use to determine the current security status of the solution:

```
Get(AccountName)
Get(ExtendedPrivileges)
Get(PrivilegeSetName)
```

CROSS-REF   As noted in Chapter 13, the Get(PrivilegeSetName) returns [Full Access] when evaluated during the course of a script set to Run with Full Access Privileges. A method of determining the name of the user's substantive privilege set in this situation is detailed in Chapter 13.

FIGURE 14.11

FileMaker's suite of Account and Security Management Script commands.

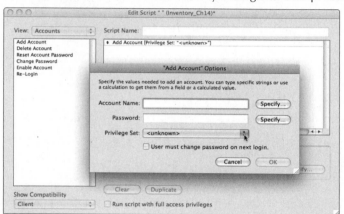

Moreover, although you can't directly change the privilege set to which an account is assigned, you can delete an account and recreate it. And when you recreate an account, it can be assigned to any privilege set in the file.

CAUTION   Avoid having your scripts deactivate or delete the account of the current login session (lest the script and the current user be orphaned without access to the file). Instead, if you need to modify the current user's account, have your script log in to a different account first, modify the user's account, and then log back in to the modified account.

Working with multi-file solutions

If your solution contains more than one file, having a synchronized security configuration is helpful. In particular, you should ensure that the same accounts are present in each file (and with comparable privileges).

If you're using external authentication, you should ensure that accounts exist in the same authentication order for all the same groups in all files in your solution, so when a user's credentials are accepted, their access is simultaneously granted to all required components of your solution.

If you're using the FileMaker internal password authentication and if the account names and passwords in each file match, opening one solution file (where the user is prompted to login before the file opens) will generally pass the user's credentials to other files. However, if your solution provides an option for users to re-login during a file session, it will fall to your scripts to coordinate synchronous re-logins in all the required files, to keep the security status in alignment across all the solution files.

Similarly, if users are allowed to change passwords in your solution, in order to ensure the passwords remain in sync across multiple solution files, I recommend that you provide a scripted password change procedure. The procedure should prompt the user for old and new passwords, authenticate them, and then apply the change automatically in each file. For this purpose, the initial script can collect the required password (or passwords) from the user and then transmit them (for example, as script parameters) to scripts in the other solution file (or files) configured to apply the same authentication update (login, password change, and so on) in those files.

Safe scripting implementations

A potential security risk arises when you have your script collect a password from the user and then transmit it as data. The concern is that while the password is being held and transmitted as data, it might be intercepted or otherwise revealed to an unauthorized party. Configuring your scripts to avoid these types of risks is very important. To achieve this, I recommend that your controlling script is implemented as follows:

1. Turns off the `Allow User Abort [ ]` capability, presents the user with a layout devoid of any buttons that could halt the script, and then hides and locks the Status Toolbar.

2. Displays a custom dialog requesting the user's password (and new password, in the case of a password change procedure).

3. Retrieves the password(s) supplied by the user immediately (storing them as variables) and deletes them from the global fields used for the custom dialog, before proceeding.

> **NOTE**   For all processes involving user password entry, you should configure the custom dialogs your scripts display to use the bullet character to conceal the actual password entry. This option is available in the Input Fields panel of the Show Custom Dialog Options dialog.

When your scripts follow these steps, the period of time when the password is held as data is constrained to the time from when the user accepts the dialog until the global fields are cleared immediately afterwards. The vulnerability is limited to the user's computer, because global field values are specific to the client workstation — and the client workstation is in use with its interface and abort options locked during the millisecond or so while the password is held as data. This setup minimizes any risk of a password being intercepted as data.

After your scripts retrieve passwords the user enters (clearing the global fields used for this purpose), the passwords exist in memory but not in data. With unauthorized access to the workstation at this juncture, a third party might contrive to pause the script and retrieve the contents of variables. However, because the process follows immediately from the user dismissing the dialog, such an intervention is unlikely in practice. However, if you're concerned about this potential threat, then you might consider encoding or encrypting passwords when declaring them as variables and/or transmitting them as parameters to other files.

> **TIP**   You can use text-processing functions or custom functions (created using FileMaker Pro Advanced) to modify the format of passwords for added security — provided you create calculations in the scripts in the receiving files to reverse the process and extract the original password text.

Creating a Custom Logout Option

The way the FileMaker security system works, you log into a file when first opening it and remain logged in until you either close the file or use a script or button command to re-login (using the Re-login[ ] command). As long as a file is open, a user (or at least, an account) is logged in. For best security, however, it can be advantageous for users to be able to secure your solution while they're away from their desk, without the tedium of closing the solution files and reopening them on their return.

In such cases, you can create a process analogous to a logout where your solution remains open but is in a secured state — requiring that the user enter their account name and password to regain operational access and resume working with the solution. Because responding to a password prompt may be considerably quicker and less onerous than reopening the solution files from the host, users appreciate this convenience and are likely to use it.

The locked-down database

A first step toward securing your solution's files to provide the effect of a logged out state is to create a layout with limited options, attached to a utility table. Typically, such a layout should include your solution's name, version, support or admin contact information, a button to exit the solution (close all solution files), and a button to login (to run a login script requesting the user's credentials).

The second step completes the securing of your solution, giving you a lockdown state. The three additional features of a secured solution required for this step are as follows:

- The Status Toolbar is hidden and locked (using the Show/Hide Status Area[ ] command). This has the effect of also disabling the menu commands for Go to Layout and Go to Record (and also the corresponding keyboard commands, including the mouse scroll wheel) to restrict users' navigation options.

- The menus are restricted so that the user cannot use them to perform any significant actions or to navigate away from the current record or layout. This can be achieved using the custom menus capability of FileMaker Pro Advanced (if available), or by using a restricted Privilege Set as described in the following topic.

- The access privileges are constrained by logging in to the solution with an account assigned to a special privilege set having minimal capabilities. (Essentially, only the ability to run the login script or close the solution – along with read-only access to the logged-out layout and any utility fields displayed there.)

CROSS-REF For additional information about using FileMaker Pro Advanced to create and deploy custom menus, turn to Chapter 18.

Structuring a solution for logging out

Strange though it may sound, the third step in securing your solution, as I discuss in the previous section, involves logging in with a "logged out" account.

The procedure required to complete custom log-out functionality is for you to create a special restricted lockdown privilege set where the user has no record creation, deletion, or editing capabilities, where the only accessible layout is your login layout, and the only executable scripts are the start-up script, your exit script (if any), and a login script attached to the corresponding button on your "logged out" layout.

> **TIP**   **If your login script will use a custom dialog to have the user enter an account name and password, you must provide fields in your solution to temporarily accommodate the values entered into the dialog (global fields in a utility table will suffice). These fields must be accessible while the login script is running, either because they're assigned as writable fields under the lockdown privilege set or because you have set the login script to run with full access privileges.**

As Figure 14.12 shows, your lockdown privilege set should constrain the user, including applying the Minimum setting for the Available Menu Commands option.

FIGURE 14.12

Setting up a lockdown privilege set with constrained access and minimum available menu commands.

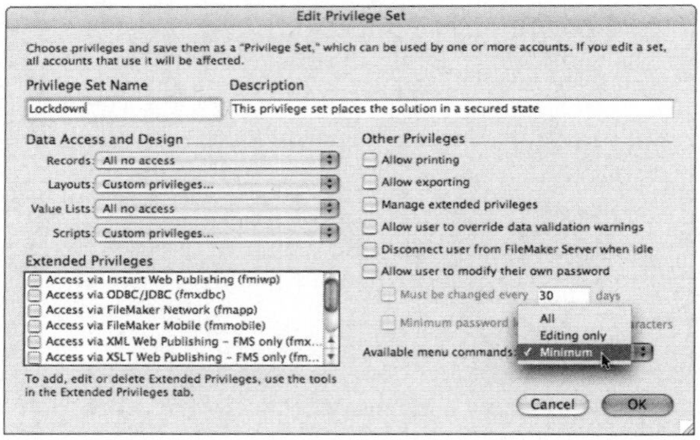

With the lockdown privilege set, you can create a lockdown account assigned to this privilege set, for use as the default account for your solution files and for occasions when users want to temporarily log out of the solution without closing it.

> **TIP**   **When your solution has multiple files, you should create a lockdown privilege set and associated lockdown account in each file so that your logout script can call a sub-script in each file, placing it into a secured state as part of a single-user action.**

To complete the securing of your solution, I recommend that you specify your lockdown account as the default account for each solution file, as shown in Figure 14.13.

Additionally, you should configure your solution's start-up script (or scripts) to take the user to the login layout and hide and lock the Status Toolbar, ensuring that the user must provide valid credentials before proceeding.

FIGURE 14.13

Defining the lockdown account as the default account for when each solution file is opened.

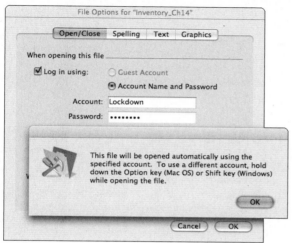

As an added security measure, you can set your login scripts to automatically activate the requested account prior to login and deactivate it again on logout. This step can reduce the solution's vulnerability in the event the solution files fall into the wrong hands.

CROSS-REF Security can be further strengthened by using the Developer Utilities in FileMaker Pro Advanced to remove full access accounts from all production copies (or published copies) of your solution files, as outlined in Chapter 18.

I've updated this chapter's Inventory solution example file to include a basic security architecture along the lines described here, including a dual-file custom logout system and a master script to manage the login and logout procedures. Passwords for the two accounts in the file are provided via a button labeled "get passwords" appearing at the lower right of the main panel on the login screen.

ON the WEB The Inventory example files may be downloaded from the book's Web site, as detailed in Appendix B.

Security logging

As a further aid to security, I recommend you include a script process that tracks user activity. The tracking process should capture login and logout times and associated workstation and network locations. To do so, you need to add a user sessions table to your solution, plus a few extra steps in your login/logout script(s) to create and update a record for each user login session.

A security log serves a number of purposes, including enabling users to see an up-to-date register of who is logged in and from which workstations, at any time during their use of the system. Moreover, a security log can provide important diagnostic information in the event of data anomalies or malfunctions of any kind. (You can match record creation and modification times to the details in the sessions table.)

In addition, a security log is a useful monitor of access and login attempts, providing you with an overview of system activity and alerting you to potential flaws, vulnerabilities, or irregularities in the solution's security or related to its usage patterns.

How Much Security Is Enough?

Realistically, all security measures (in FileMaker or anywhere else) can be defeated, given unlimited time and resources. However, potential thieves or saboteurs do not have infinite time or money to devote to the task of getting around your security — so your job is to ensure that your solution's security exceeds any reasonable expectation of threat. Additionally, some security threats, such as spyware (keystroke loggers, for example), are system-wide and are therefore beyond the purview of an application or solution developer.

Ways to evaluate risk

When evaluating risk, begin by determining the incentives for a range of possible attacks on your system. For example, perverse human actions may be motivated by greed or spite, but whatever the motive, you can reasonably assess the value their perpetrators may place on success. If your solution supports a business with an annual turnover of $10 million in a highly competitive market, an unscrupulous competitor may be prepared to spend millions mounting corporate espionage or sabotage. The value you and others may place on (or derive from) the solution or the data it contains is the first and best indication of the extent of security warranted.

When considering possible threats, think about positive and negative value as well as indirect value. For example, the privacy of client records may not be a salable commodity as such, but nevertheless is highly valued by the clients to whom it belongs. A breach of client or customer privacy may expose you to legal challenges, but its indirect implications may be still more serious. The flow-on effects of a compromise of privacy may result in indirect consequences, such as a loss of confidence in the business or the business practices your solution supports. Although you may not regard client details as saleable, identity thieves and Internet marketers may take a different view.

In all these respects, the nature of your solution, the data it contains, and the investment it represents form the basis of your assessment of its value. In simple terms, your job is to ensure the cost and inconvenience of any effort to circumvent your solution's security exceeds any perceived gain.

A balanced view of threats

When you deadbolt your front door, the adjacent open window becomes the most likely area of vulnerability for your home's security. When the window is also bolted and shuttered, the point of least resistance moves elsewhere. To achieve reasonable levels of security, you must pay adequate attention to all potential vulnerabilities, raising each potential vulnerability above the threshold of incentive for those who might pose a threat.

When considering the range of potential risks, in addition to threats from deliberate attack, you should also be mindful of the many ways your solution may be compromised by actions or events that don't involve any malicious intent. User error, hardware failure, or a variety of other mishaps may present as great a risk as any other and should be kept in view when considering how to safeguard your solution.

Additionally, make sure that the ways you address potential risks don't create new risks. For example, if your password security implementation is cumbersome for users, they'll be reluctant to use it and may ultimately (actively or inadvertently) undermine it. A classic example of this is the organization so concerned about security that they implement multiple levels of password screening for various different functions or procedures — with the direct consequence being that users who cannot remember all their many passwords end up writing them on notes stuck up and down the sides of their computer monitors. The net effect of this ill-conceived strategy is a diminution rather than an enhancement of security.

A strategic model for response

After pondering the range of possible vulnerabilities for your solution and the data it accommodates, considering the relative impact of potential mishaps of different kinds, and assessing the value of your solution and its contents to various contenders, you have the model for strategic risk management.

Using your appraisal of the potential threats, I encourage you to map out priorities for solution safeguard measures, paying heed to each identified risk in accordance not only with the perceived likelihood of mishap, but also with the consequences (direct and indirect) should a mishap occur. By doing so, you achieve a balanced strategy providing a reasoned response to a broad view of hazards and susceptibilities. Error correction, audit systems, data backup, and login security can all work together to address risks and provide recovery options when a problem is encountered.

The Importance of Physical File Security

In any situation in which third parties can gain direct physical access to copies of your solution files, a number of avenues of attack are open, and your files are vulnerable. Would-be hackers can attempt to use software other than FileMaker to try to read, interpret, or even change the content of your files — or they may use other tools to try to break past your login security systems.

Whenever external authentication is used, the importance of the physical security of your solution's files is further increased. Someone obtaining copies of the database files may seek unauthorized access by configuring a bogus domain (with groups named according to the group names in the legitimate server environment). Bear in mind that backup copies of the solution represent as much of a risk as the deployed copy and should therefore be safeguarded with similar measures.

Layers of protection

As I mention in the last section, you want to consider ways to maximize the physical security of your solution. If the only (or primary) means of access to your solution will be through a network (if your solution resides on a server), the location and accessibility of the server is an important consideration. If possible, the server should be located in a secure environment (such as a locked room) where unauthorized persons can't access or remove it.

Similarly, restricting access to the network where your solution operates and to the workstations commonly used to access your solution helps ensure your security's integrity. Be aware that keystroke logging software (spyware) and other malware finding its way onto client computers may compromise the security of your data, despite your best efforts in other areas.

NOTE FileMaker files do not store user passwords internally. Instead, a *hash* (a complex checksum) is computed and stored — in a form that can't be used to reconstruct the original password. This makes some forms of attack more difficult, but it does not stop third-party tools from overwriting the relevant sections of the file with bogus password hashes to break your file's security, replacing the legitimate passwords with impostors. This is one of several ways someone who has physical access to your files may wreak havoc, potentially compromising the integrity and security of the files and their contents.

Alternative forms of protection

In cases where you can't safeguard the physical security of your files — for example, when your solution is to be distributed to end users to run on their own computers, rather than being accessed from a server — I recommend that you use the FileMaker Pro Advanced capability to permanently remove [Full Access] accounts from all copies of your solution files distributed to others or used in production.

The removal of [Full Access] accounts provides good protection against direct access to your solution's code (file structure, calculations, scripts, and so on) within your database files. Additionally, it provides some protection against various methods that might be used to gain indirect access to the code. However, the removal of [Full Access] accounts may not prevent a skilled user from using third-party tools to tamper with the remaining accounts or to directly read or modify your solution's files.

CROSS-REF For additional details regarding the removal of [Full Access] accounts using FileMaker Pro Advanced, see Chapter 18.

A multi-faceted approach

Using a variety of methods to guard against potential hazards and threats is the best approach to take for your solution's security. If your solution's start-up script and File Options configuration place the files into a secured state and direct the user to use your login scripts to present credentials and gain authorized access to your solution, it's important to ensure that your scripts will be used — and that other avenues to the use of your solution will not be viable.

One way to constrain users to operate within the limits of your scripts is to have the start-up script and login script generate dynamic token values and place them in fields in your solution (such as global fields created for the purpose). You can then configure other key scripts and calculations throughout your solution to check for the presence of valid tokens before proceeding (or calculating). By doing this, you can effectively disable your solution unless the current user has logged in using the scripts you have provided.

Another part of your approach — to guard against tampering with your solution's security structure — is to build in a second lockdown account and then have your start-up script perform a re-login (into the second lockdown account) by using a fixed password. If the password verification data stored in the file have been tampered with, the scripted re-login will fail, and your start-up script (detecting the failure of this procedure via the Get(LastError) function) can lock and close the solution.

In addition to these approaches, consider using various third-party products including

- Data encryption systems (either native or plug-in based)
- External dongles, hardware keys, and locking devices
- Identification card readers and biometric scanner systems
- Online authorization and activation services

Using the range of available techniques and tools, your solution can be configured to provide efficient and convenient, yet effective measures to guard against a broad range of potential problems and hazards.

 **For additional information about plug-ins and third-party resources, see Chapter 20, and for details of some sources of information and tools, see Appendix A.**

Security in Deployment: FileMaker Server

In several respects, the deployment of your solutions through the use of FileMaker Server software running on an appropriately configured and secured machine is advantageous from a security perspective (as well as in various other respects). One of the advantages, as noted in the "User Authentication" section, earlier in this chapter, is the support for external authentication enabling your FileMaker Server deployments to conform to domain or external credential checks, providing, in effect, single sign-on capabilities for one or more solutions on a local network.

FileMaker Server provides several additional options that are worth taking a few moments to consider (and to configure).

Filtered display of files

FileMaker Server gives you an option to filter the display of files to users accessing the list of available databases (by using File ⇨ Open Remote in the FileMaker Pro client application) based on a user's account name and password.

By enabling this option, you can prevent unauthorized individuals from seeing or presenting credentials to any database files other than those they are approved to access.

Secure Socket Layer encryption

FileMaker Server 10 provides an option to encrypt data in transit between the server and client workstations using industry standard SSL (Secure Socket Layer) encryption.

You can activate network encryption simply by selecting it as an option in configuring your server deployment (and then restarting the server). I have seen no performance penalty resulting from the use of SSL encryption for data transfers with FileMaker Server — and I recommend its use as a further means of protection for your hosted solutions.

Server checks and logs

As a standard part of its operation, FileMaker Server 10 provides automatic logging and optional e-mail notifications for a variety of events and potential problems. This includes commencement and conclusion of client sessions (remote connections, not user account logins), automated backups, and consistency checks.

The availability of server event and error logs is an important additional step toward ensuring the health and security of your solution, giving you insight into its use as well as alerting you to problems and issues arising as your solution is accessed. E-mail notifications provide a way to extend your monitoring of the health of your database server installation.

In addition to its performance capabilities, the added safeguards and security of FileMaker Server represent a significant benefit over peer-to-peer hosting options (for example, hosting files with FileMaker Pro). Of course, the increased expense of a dedicated server and the FileMaker Pro Server license is an element in your security cost-benefit analysis. However, only in a few cases do the benefits of this deployment model not outweigh the costs.

> **NOTE** Bear in mind that when you consider costs and benefits, the costs of deploying an appropriately configured server include those associated with providing for an adequately experienced and trusted user or IT professional's time to administer the server and software. Logs and e-mail notifications are of little value if there is no one to read and respond to them.

Chapter 15

Maintaining Referential Integrity

Referential integrity, an essential concept, lies at the very heart of relational database development. Ideally, the end users of your solutions take referential integrity for granted — and you, as developer, place it before many other considerations. I think it's important enough to devote an entire chapter to the topic because I know that without referential integrity, all your beautifully built solutions will crumble and amount to nothing.

Pinpointing Common Causes of Referential Integrity Problems

Referential integrity has many dimensions, the problem of orphaned records foremost among them. Consider, for a moment, an invoicing system where you have an invoice table and a line items table storing the items for each invoice. However, an invoice has been deleted without the corresponding line item records being deleted. Now, when you perform a search, you get a different result when you search in the `Invoices` table than when you search in the `Line Items` table. The difference arises because the deleted invoice's items remain in the `Line Items` table, so they appear there, but no related record exists in the `Invoices` table, so they don't appear when you search there.

When you get different results searching in different places, you no longer know what is correct, and you have a lot of work to do to determine the discrepancy's cause. This example is one of several common problems affecting referential integrity. Three of the most common causes of referential integrity problems are

IN THIS CHAPTER

Surveying threats to referential integrity

Understanding the importance of relational keys

Working with keys and data types

Bringing data into line with optimal relational design

Automating the removal of redundant data

Considering data integrity in wider contexts

Managing a solution's data dependencies

- Deleting records without deleting related or dependent records or values
- Modifying key field values without modifying the corresponding foreign key values in related tables, so corresponding field values no longer match
- Non-unique (duplicate) primary key values

The potential impact on your solution

On rare occasions, these problems may go undetected, and the consequences may be minimal. However, even a single instance of one of these problems means that your data is no longer in sync — the data in one table no longer agrees and fully conforms with data elsewhere in your solution. Such issues can rapidly erode confidence in a solution and may have profoundly negative consequences when business decisions are based on compromised data.

If your data ever falls out of sync, you'll understand why I say that prevention is better than cure. Vetting and correcting anomalies in a large data set can be a thankless and enormously time-consuming task.

Costs and benefits

You have a great deal to gain from using relational data structures in your solutions. Key information is stored once and is instantly available elsewhere — wherever it is needed. An update in one part of the system is propagated instantly throughout the solution. These significant benefits depend on taking the time to understand and implement robust and reliable links throughout your solution, to support its relational data architecture.

In Chapters 7 and 11, I address many of the concepts that underpin the design and implementation of relational structures in FileMaker Pro. Although I comment on some relational integrity issues in those chapters, I don't spell out exactly why it matters or how best to avoid the potential pitfalls when working with complex data interdependencies. Several strategies are essential to successful management of complex related data sets, as outlined in the following sections.

Using Unique Keys

Should the keys for a relationship in your solution be edited, deleted, or duplicated, relationships depending on them will break. Re-establishing relationship connections after such a mishap is, at best, an unenviable task. A first checkpoint when assessing the relational integrity of your solution is, therefore, the appropriateness of selected keys and methods of handling them.

Consider using ways to generate key values automatically (for example, using auto-enter serial numbers, calculations, or scripts) to ensure their integrity. On occasions when keys aren't generated automatically, you need to implement some safeguards to ensure the key values are appropriate.

Key safeguards

The validation options in FileMaker let you require that a field has a value ("Not empty") and that it is unique, as shown in Figure 15.1. If your solution requires user entry of primary key values, such as when records originate within another system, using both these validation checks can help minimize errors.

In cases where users import data into your solution, validation rules will be applied during import if the Validate Data In This Field: Always option is selected (rather than the Only During Data Entry option). With the Always option selected, records in the import source data with field values that do not satisfy the validation rules you specify will be skipped (that is, they will not be imported), and this will be mentioned in the Import Summary dialog. In the case of a scripted import procedure, if records were skipped due to validation errors, error code 729 will be returned for the Import Records command.

> **CAUTION** Any situation where users directly enter or edit key values is risky, even if you have existence and uniqueness validations in place, because any unique value will be accepted and then used for relationship matching (and the creation of related records). Any errors the user subsequently corrects will post a risk for relational joins involving the record in question.

FIGURE 15.1

Setting Unique, Not Empty validation for a `PrimaryID` field.

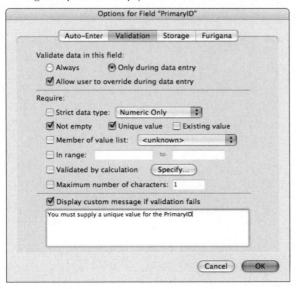

Few values originating outside your solution can be relied upon to be unique — or to exist for all cases. Even purportedly unique values, such as a Social Security Number (SSN), have been known to be duplicated on occasion — and you can't assume that they will always be available. Input data types that can be relied upon as suitable for use as a key value in all cases are the exception rather than the rule.

Keys and meaning (existence, persistence, uniqueness)

Relational keys should be unique, persistent, and non-empty, and these requirements are frequently best met by assigning special values for the purpose. There is no absolute rule about this. Classical relational theory proposes that key values be derived from data, if suitable. However, if you do so, you introduce risks and should proceed carefully. In general, I counsel against using keys based on or derived from data, as data is subject to data-entry errors, the correction of which may compromise the persistence of key values. Instead, I recommend that your key values be generated automatically (via auto-entry options) and protected by selecting the Prohibit Modification of Value During Data Entry option in the Auto-Enter tab of the Options for Field dialog.

One case where key values are frequently legitimately derived from data is within the context of an association table (also known as a join table), where the primary key is commonly formed from the conjoining of two or more foreign keys. This is an example of a situation where the data provides a suitable basis for relational keys.

In situations where an ID value, such as an SSN, bank account number, or vehicle registration number, is required to be entered, you can also generate a separate unique value to use as the record's primary key. When you do so, even if the entered value changes (or is entered inaccurately and subsequently corrected), referential integrity is maintained.

NOTE For most purposes, you don't need to display key values to the user; in fact, doing so may complicate matters needlessly. However, where you can't rely on any of the data values to be unique, a serial number or other unique value can be useful to users.

In a student database, for example, where several students are named Peter John Smith, a student ID may be a convenient way for users to identify to which Peter Smith a given piece of information refers.

Generating Keys

A majority of database solutions are designed to operate as single or separate instances — in other words, only one copy of the solution is deployed at a time. Or, if there are multiples, data from them will never be combined. In most cases, an efficient way to generate suitable key values is to produce record serial numbers in each table. The auto-entry serial option is an ideal way to address this need. Even so, it has several possible variations, described in the following sections.

Serial numbers

The option to auto-enter serial numbers is the cleanest and simplest way to generate key values for single-instance solutions. Although the concept and name suggest that values created via this mechanism will be numeric, you can store the values in either text or number fields. If the values are stored as text, they may include alphabetic prefixes. For example, as shown in Figure 15.2, you can configure serial values to include leading zeros or other characters.

CROSS-REF For a detailed discussion of the use and limitations of the available data types, refer to Chapter 7.

FileMaker also provides you with the option to have serial values assigned either on creation of a new record or when the record is first committed. You can use the radio buttons shown in Figure 15.2 to specify which option you want. In situations where consecutive serial numbers are desired, using the On Commit option avoids serial number incrementation in a case where users change their mind and revert the new record. In this situation, however, be aware that relationships or other operations depending on the presence of the serial value will not be available until after the record is committed.

To assist you in managing serial numbers, FileMaker provides the `GetNextSerialValue( )` and `SerialIncrement( )` calculation functions and the `Set Next Serial Value[ ]` script command. Thus, in a script designed to import records into your solution, you can sort the records and reset the serial number for the table so that serial numbers assigned to subsequently created records will not overlap those among the imported data. For example, you can structure the relevant portion of such a script along the following lines:

```
Import Records [No dialog; "OldFile.fp7"; Add; Windows ANSI]
#Re-set next serial value:
Show All Records
Sort Records [Restore; No dialog]
Go to Record/Request/Page [Last]
Set Next Serial Value [Data::Serial#; SerialIncrement(Data::Serial#; 1)]
Unsort Records
```

NOTE This script sequence's correct operation requires that the `Sort Records[ ]` command be configured to sort the records in ascending order by the `Data::Serial#` field and on the data type and content of the `Data::Serial#` field. Note, however, that the correct operation of the script (including the correct sort sequence) depends on the `Data::Serial#` field being defined as a number field (since in a text field 10 will sort before 9 and so on).

Additionally, FileMaker can reassign serial numbers to a field, at the same time resetting the auto-entry options to follow sequentially from the last assigned number, using the Records ⇨ Replace Field Contents menu command or the corresponding script or button commands. As shown in Figure 15.3, if the selected field is defined to auto-enter a serial number, the procedure can simultaneously update the serial number (the next value) in Entry Options.

FIGURE 15.2

Defining an alphanumeric serial value with an alphabetic prefix.

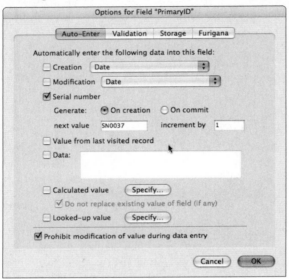

> **CAUTION**   **Using the Replace Field Contents command to modify a key field's contents will compromise any relationships already depending on existing key field values. You can't revert or undo changes made using this command.**

> **NOTE**   **You should avoid using a Replace Field Contents procedure while your solution is hosted because locked records, if any, are skipped. In the case of serialization, skipping locked records can lead to duplications, where the skipped records may hold the same value as some of the values assigned elsewhere during the process.**

If the Prohibit Modification of Value During Data Entry option is in force for the selected field, the Replace Field Contents menu command isn't available. However, scripts or buttons calling the corresponding command can still succeed. Therefore, you should consider the implications for relational integrity and the potential for error (especially if the solution is hosted) before using this procedure on a primary key field.

Record IDs

In addition to auto-enter serial numbering, FileMaker automatically assigns an internal sequential record ID to each record in every instance of a file. Record IDs are a numeric value starting from 1 in each table. You can retrieve this internal value for the current record by using the Get(RecordID) calculation function. Although the record ID value is useful in some circumstances, it isn't well suited as a key value's sole basis because:

- The record ID sequence is particular to a specific copy of the file. If records are imported into another copy of the file, they will be assigned new record IDs in the receiving file.

- All record IDs are reset (and therefore commence again from 1) within a copy saved as a clone of your file.

For these reasons, if you use record IDs as keys you can't prevent the assignment of duplicate values in all situations. However, it has the advantage of not being vulnerable to being reset inappropriately (for example, via the Replace Field Contents command) or not being reset when it should, such as when records are imported. It can, however, be used as a component of a key field value in cases where records will be combined from multiple files into a single set (and where it is desirable to avoid key field duplications in the combined record set).

Unique identification (UID) values

The concept of a universally unique ID value, commonly known as a UUID, is known and used in a variety of computing contexts. However, FileMaker does not support it directly. This kind of value is called for in distributed solutions where multiple sets of new records will be created separately and later combined (and where it is essential to avoid duplication of ID values when the record sets are merged or synchronized).

One way to meet this requirement is by allocating reserved serial ranges, where each instance of the solution files assigns IDs within its own separate range. Whereas the allocation of reserved ranges is feasible in limited cases, it requires careful management, and its success depends on accurately configuring every instance for an appropriate range. As a result, the scope for error becomes greater if more than a few instances of the solution are in operation.

FIGURE 15.3

Generating a new serial number sequence and resetting the next serial value in auto-entry options via the Replace Field Contents dialog.

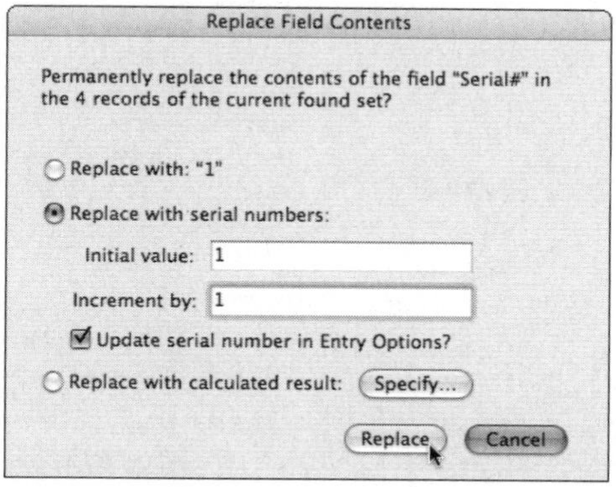

In cases where you can't reliably predict the number of copies of the database that will be in use, or where managing the assignment of serial ranges is difficult, one solution is to assemble a unique identifier. You do this by combining the identity of the current computer, the assigned ID of the current record, and the timestamp of the second when the record is created. FileMaker provides the means to assemble a UID in several ways:

- You can determine the identity of the computer by retrieving its unique network address — the ID of the hardware Network Interface Card (NIC) installed in the computer — using the `Get(SystemNICAddress)` function. Because a computer may be equipped with more than one network interface device, you can obtain a sufficient identifying value by retrieving the address of the first available device, using the calculation expression

  `GetValue(Get(SystemNICAddress); 1)`

- You can access the sequential number of the current record within the current copy of the file via the `Get(RecordID)` function.

- You can generate the current time (in the form of a number representing the seconds elapsed since midnight on 1st January 0001) using the calculation expression

  `GetAsNumber(Get(CurrentHostTimestamp))`

By concatenating the three values — NIC address, record ID, and timestamp — you can produce a key value that will be unique regardless of the circumstances of its creation. The chief drawback of this approach is that the resulting string will be lengthy. I recommend ameliorating this concern by converting the values first to base 10 (the NIC address is supplied as a hexadecimal value) and then to base 36 for compactness. Using this approach, a record created with the record ID 123,456,789 on a computer with an NIC address of 00:14:51:65:4d:6a and generated at 5:47:37 pm on October 21st 2007 is allocated the UID NI1PM Z3J50 JG9ZH 6HI2H.

The base conversions required to transmute the source data into the compact base36 format require some mathematical manipulation of the original values that is best performed via a custom function.

 **An example of a custom function you can use to create UIDs along these lines is included among the materials referenced in Appendix B.**

Exploring Keys and Data Type

Because serial numbers and record IDs may be numeric, defining ID fields as number fields is tempting. However, you'll frequently have occasion to use multi-key relationship capabilities (for example, to filter a portal or to use the `Go to Related Record[ ]` command to isolate a group of records in a found set). In a multi-key relationship, multiple values in a key field are simultaneously matched to values in the related table. If you have used number fields as the key fields in either table, however, matching won't work as desired because number fields aren't designed to hold multiple values. You must use text fields to take advantage of multi-keyed relations. For maximum flexibility, I recommend using text fields as keys.

Using text fields as keys presents a different kind of problem. If you have conventional numeric sequences stored as text, they will not be sorted appropriately — for example, 3 will be sorted after 12. You can address this problem in two ways:

- Pad the numbers with leading zeros so that they're all the same length. They then will sort correctly in a text field.

- Use a number field to generate the serial values (and for sorting) but use a text calculation referencing the number field as the key field.

For maximum flexibility, I suggest that you consider using both these strategies simultaneously. You then have both a numeric and text field you can use for relationships, for sorting, and for other purposes, as appropriate.

An added benefit of using text values as relational keys is that you can prefix them with one or more letters identifying their table of origin. For example, INV0001 is recognizable as an invoice number and ORD0001 as an order number. Although this classification may be of little consequence in the table of origin, when data containing a primary key and several foreign key values is exported or imported, the prefixes greatly reduce the likelihood that the keys will be imported into the wrong fields (or, if they are, the problem will be considerably easier to detect and correct).

Consider, for example, an import procedure where the import mapping dialog presents you with the following:

Source Fields		Target Fields
21 Jan 2008	→	TransactionDate
1217	→	ReceiptID
1921	→	ClientID
921	→	AccountID
3119	→	InvoiceID
2174	→	StaffID
3550	→	Amount

In this example, importing a data set from a delimited file is error prone, because the source values other than the transaction date are not differentiated. If, however, text key values are used with the appropriate prefixes, you can more readily see that the correct import order in this case is as follows:

Source Fields		Target Fields
21 Jan 2008	→	TransactionDate
1217	→	Amount
R00001921	→	ReceiptID
CL00921	→	ClientID
AC03119	→	AccountID
ST02174	→	StaffID
INV003550	→	InvoiceID

Whereas the use of redundant (text and numeric) serials and padded keys adds slightly to the amount of data your solution must store, the improved flexibility, reliability, and diagnostic transparency offered usually outweighs the penalty.

NOTE **The ID fields throughout the `inventory` example file created in previous chapters of this book provide an example of a structure incorporating a numeric serial and a prefixed text ID value, along the lines I recommend.**

Retrofitting Keys

When you encounter a situation where the key fields in use are unsuitable and their format is presenting a threat to referential integrity, you may need to retroactively add key fields to existing tables. For example, suppose that you have inherited a solution where the client table's `LastName` field has been used as a key field to associate invoices with clients, but it's come to your attention that two more families named Johnson have moved into the neighborhood and will soon be added to the clients table along with the Johnson client you already have.

Rather than loading the new clients as `Johnson2` and `Johnson3` — a kludge at best — you can correct the structure by adding appropriate key fields to the solution and reconstructing the relationship between `Clients` and `Invoices` tables to use them. To retrofit appropriate keys to the solution in this example, proceed as follows:

1. Take the database offline if it is hosted. You can't make a change such as this one reliably while other users are accessing the solution.

2. Create a text field called `ClientID` in the `Clients` table. In field options, configure the `ClientID` field to auto-enter a serial number.

3. Place the `Clients::ClientID` field on a layout based on the `Clients` TO.

4. In Browse mode, choose Records ⇨ Show All Records.

5. Place the cursor into the `ClientID` field and choose Records ⇨ Replace Field Contents. The Replace Field Contents dialog appears.

6. Select the Replace with Serial Numbers option, enter **CL0000001** in the Initial Value field and **1** in the Increment By field, check the option to Update Serial Number in Entry Options and then click the Replace button.

7. Choose File ⇨ Manage ⇨ Database, navigate to the Clients table on the Fields tab, and double-click the `ClientID` field. In the Auto-Enter tab of the Options for Field dialog, select the Prohibit Modification of Value During Data Entry option and click OK to accept the change.

8. Select the Invoices table on the Fields tab of the Manage Database dialog and create a text field called `ClientID`. Click OK to close the Manage Database dialog.

9. Navigate to a layout based on the `Invoices` TO and add the `Invoices::ClientID` field to the layout.

10. In Browse mode, still on the `Invoices` layout, choose Records ⇨ Show All Records.

11. Place the cursor in the `Invoices::ClientID` field and choose Records ➪ Replace Field Contents. The Replace Field Contents dialog appears.

12. Select the Replace with Calculated Result option; in the resulting Specify Calculation dialog, enter `Clients::ClientID`.

13. Choose File ➪ Manage ➪ Database, navigate to the Relationships tab, and double-click the box bisecting the relationship line connecting the `Clients` and `Invoices` TOs. The Edit Relationship dialog appears.

14. Select the `ClientID` field in the `Clients` TO's field list, select the `ClientID` field in the `Invoices` TO's field list, and click the button labeled Change in the middle right of the dialog.

15. Click OK to dismiss the Edit Relationship dialog and again to dismiss the Manage Database dialog.

16. Choose File ➪ Manage ➪ Value Lists. If an existing value list of clients was used to select a related client for each invoice, select it and click Edit; otherwise, click New.

17. Configure the value list to use values from a field, choosing the `Clients::ClientID` field as the first field. Select the Also Display Values from the Second Field option and then choose the `Clients::LastName` field in the second field list. Click the OK button to save the value list and then dismiss the Manage Value List dialog.

18. In Layout mode on the Invoices layout, configure the `Invoices::ClientID` field to use the Clients value list (the one edited or created in Step 17) and position the field in place of the `ClientName` field previously used as the key field.

After completing these steps, your solution is updated to use the new `ClientID` field as the basis of the relationship between `Clients` and `Invoices`. After testing the solution to confirm that the update has been successful (and assuming that no relationships, calculations, or scripts depend on it), you can delete the `Invoices::Client` field and instead use a related field (`Clients::LastName`) to display the name of the client on the invoice.

If other relationships depend on the `Clients::LastName` field, you should repeat the process from Step 8 onward to update each of the related tables to include `ClientID` as a foreign key field. Once the change is complete, the relationship architecture of the solution is significantly improved.

Deleting Redundant Records

The usefulness of your data is proportional to its accuracy. The harvest from a garden of weeds is not sustaining. As well as taking the trouble to add the data you need, you must take the time to excise erroneous, obsolete, irrelevant, or duplicated data. If you don't, you can't rely on the results of any find, calculation, or report as encompassing only current or accurate content.

In a relational database, data is distributed among tables according to its type. Data about cars is in the Vehicles table, and data about their owners is in the People table. To ensure that your database does not become a repository for accumulations of redundant and obsolete information — not merely a dead weight but a compromise of data integrity — you should configure your solution to manage group deletion of related records, wherever appropriate.

The use of cascading deletion

To assist you in maintaining referential integrity, FileMaker provides an option to automatically delete related records when deleting a record in any table in your solution. You can enable this option by accessing the Edit Relationship dialog for the join between the two Table Occurrences in question and selecting the checkbox option labeled Delete Related Records in This Table When a Record Is Deleted in the Other Table. This capability is commonly known as *cascading deletion* because it can be configured for a series of relationships such that deletion of a record in one table can result in follow-on deletion of records in a number of related tables.

Figure 15.4 shows the Edit Relationship dialog for the join between the Orders and OrderLines TOs in the current chapter's Inventory example. As you can see, the Delete Related Records option is enabled on the OrderLines side of the relationship; if an Order is deleted, the associated item records will automatically also be deleted.

The cascading deletion option imposes an essential referential integrity constraint ensuring that the dependency between associated entities is preserved. Without it, the integrity of your data will be compromised.

Configuring relationships for referential integrity

When setting up your data model, take care to enable cascading deletion only where an entity's existence is fully contingent on the associated "parent" entity. Moreover, consider the flow-on effects of cascading deletion, lest their scope exceed your intent. To avoid unintentional consequences of the use of integrity constraints, I recommend

- No more than one TO for each base table be configured with the Delete Related Records option

- The TO targeted by the Delete Related Records option be named to match the underlying table

- The Delete Related Records option be enabled only in the file where the corresponding base table is defined

In addition (and especially should you have occasion to depart from any of these recommendations), you may want to consider making a separate record or annotation regarding the cascading deletion configuration in each file. A text note on the Relationships tab of the Manage Database dialog in the data file is often appropriate.

CAUTION   **Although FileMaker permits you to activate the Delete Related Records option on both sides of a relationship, it's generally not appropriate to do so. In fact, activating this option, depending on the nature of the relationships and data, may set up a ricochet effect as deletion calls pass back and forth between the two tables, with the result that deleting a single record in one table may decimate the contents of both tables.**

FIGURE 15.4

Enabling cascading deletion for the Orders-to-OrderLines relationship.

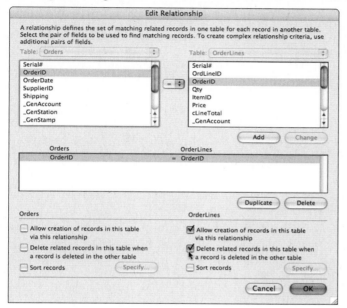

Privilege requirements for cascade delete

Users must have sufficient privileges to delete all the dependent records in order to be able to delete a record in the current table when referential integrity constraints (via cascading deletion) are configured. For example, if the user is viewing a record from table A and a constraint has been applied that requires that records in table B be deleted if a record is deleted in table A, the user will be able to delete the current record in table A only if

- The Privilege Set assigned to the user's login account permits deletion of records in both table A and table B.
- No records in table B relate to the current record in table A (and the user's privileges allow deletion of records in table A).

In the event that there are records in table B and the user's account doesn't include privileges to delete records in the related table, deletion of the current record in table A will fail, and FileMaker will post an error dialog, as shown in Figure 15.5.

If the deletion command is issued via script with error capture enabled, no error dialog will appear, but the deletion will nevertheless fail, and FileMaker will return error code 200 (defined as Record Access Is Denied).

FIGURE 15.5

FileMaker posts an error if the user doesn't have sufficient privileges for cascading deletion to occur, even if the user's privileges permit deletion of records in the current table.

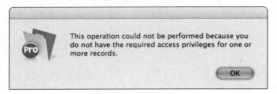

TIP If record deletion is undertaken by script and you enable the Run Script with Full Access Privileges option, the deletion will succeed regardless of the privileges assigned to the current user's account, and all cascading deletions will succeed.

Controlled cascading deletes at runtime

Configuring your files to delete records automatically can save your users a lot of work and/or a lot of headaches when configured appropriately. However, in some situations, cascading deletes may result in problems. For example, if your solution requires that data in one of the tables be refreshed from an external source, such as via selective deletion and re-import of updated records from a reference file, the presence of cascading deletes may interfere with the desired process, requiring that related record sets also be refreshed/imported (because they'll be deleted as a result of referential integrity constraints, when the parent records are deleted).

You can respond to such a requirement so that cascading deletion does not prevent you from delivering the required functionality in several ways:

- Avoid the necessity to delete and re-import parent records by restructuring the process around synchronization or conditional update of the existing records. In some cases, you can do so by using the Update Existing import option. In others, it may warrant importing the reference data into a holding area, such as a utility table, and providing a scripted reconciliation process.

- Script the process to delete the values from the primary key fields in the parent table (the key field used for the relationship defined to delete related records) before deleting the parent records. Alternatively, if this step introduces an unacceptable delay to the procedure, set up the cascading delete to operate via a secondary (utility) relationship where the parent key is an unstored calculation depending on a global field. For example, use a calculation formula for the key field along the lines of:

  `If(ParentTable::gRI_Switch = 1; ParentTable::PrimaryID)`

  Clearing the `gRI_Switch` global field can disable the relationships depending on the unstored calculation throughout the table at a single stroke; you can re-enable them by setting a 1 into the global field. With this mechanism in place, your scripts can turn cascading delete functionality on and off by controlling the value in the `gRI_Switch` field.

- Build a separate file containing a reference to your solution data file(s) and build a graph in the separate file containing your referential integrity constraints, such as all Delete Related Records options. Then script your solution to open the file (as in open hidden) when you require the constraints and close it when you want to switch off the constraints.

  I recommend this last technique for cases in which cascading deletion will not be part of normal operation but is to be invoked for specific procedures.

By using these techniques (and other variations and permutations), you can control your solution's functionality, ensuring that cascading deletion serves its intended purpose, yet avoiding circumstances where it interferes with the required functionality.

Considering Other Integrity Issues

One essential of efficient data management is a solution designed to store each piece of information only once — displaying it whenever and wherever it's needed. The fact that you can update the data once and expect the change to flow throughout your solution is an efficiency advantage. However, the integrity advantages are greater still.

When you store the same information twice, you risk that one instance will be edited so that it no longer agrees with others, and then you no longer know which instance is the correct one. Any time you duplicate data, you're compromising solution integrity as well as solution efficiency.

Lookups and when to use them

FileMaker supports auto-entry lookups where a field is set to automatically copy the contents of a related field. The `OrderLines::Price` field in the `Inventory` example demonstrates the use of this functionality, as shown in Figure 15.6.

When is it appropriate to use a lookup, and when is it preferable to reference the data in place in its source table? The straightforward answer is that `Data` should be referenced in place if its meaning is undifferentiated.

Auto-entry lookups and references

In the case of the price field discussed in the preceding example, the `Inventory` table's cost field represents the current purchase price of the item. When the item is ordered, the price against the individual order line takes on a different meaning because it represents the price at the date of the order. If a price change occurs in the future, the price in the `Inventory::Cost` field may change, but the change won't apply automatically to the history of previous orders. Only subsequent orders will be affected. Moreover, a discount or bulk order price may be negotiated for a specific purchase, but it will not be reflected in the list price for the item. Thus, the ongoing reference price is a different piece of information from the specific price for any one instance of a purchase of the item, so it makes sense to store each instance independently. They may, in fact, all be different.

By contrast, you can't expect other details about an item to change or differ from one transaction to another. The name of an item and its description are immutable facts about the item. If you were to set lookups to create copies of each of these item attributes for every order, referential integrity and solution efficiency would be compromised by data duplication.

Data design issues

The principle of making data storage decisions according to differentiation of meaning is broadly applicable to a range of design decisions you make when determining your solution's data model. In addition to lookups, it applies to auto-entry calculations, relationships, and even regular calculations. Unless an element has a distinct role and meaning, it's redundant and should not be included in your solution's data model.

Throughout your solution, avoid duplicating data, structure, and code. This general maxim is part of a larger framework considered part of the DRY (Don't Repeat Yourself) programming principle.

CROSS-REF Issues relating to the elimination of redundancy and the application of the DRY principle are discussed in depth in Chapter 19.

FIGURE 15.6

The use of a data lookup for the `OrderLines::Price` field.

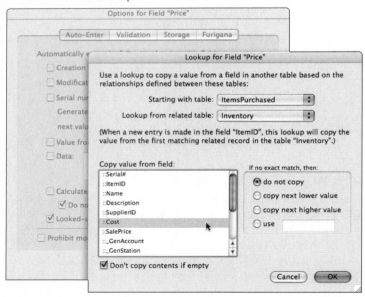

Managing Dependencies

The handling of data about the design elements of your solution (fields, tables, scripts, layouts, and so on) in FileMaker operates in a framework where, when you change an element's name, the new name is reflected in all references to the element throughout your solution. For example, if you rename a field referenced in scripts and calculations, the next time you open the calculation to review its definition or open the script in the Edit Script window, you see the updated name.

FileMaker uses internal IDs to track references to solution elements, looking up their current names as required. The process is analogous to your use of relational data structures to store your data only once (yet make it available throughout multiple contexts).

Literal text references

A notable exception to automatic handling and updating references to solution elements in FileMaker arises when you incorporate references to elements as literal text within your calculations. For example, if you supply a layout name by calculation when defining a Go to Layout[ ] script or button command, FileMaker does not change the literal text values (the text within the quotes) if the names of your layouts are subsequently changed:

```
Go to Layout [If(User::Preference = "Tips"; "Instructions"; "Report Listing")]
```

Where you've used literal references to layouts, files, fields, scripts, layout objects, or any other elements of your solution, you must keep track of them and update them manually if you change the name of the object to which they refer.

Indirect object/element references

Given that FileMaker doesn't automatically update literal text references to elements and objects for you, you may prefer to minimize your use of them. However, including literal references in your code is occasionally advantageous because doing so enables you to construct dynamic code referring to different elements according to the current context. Thus, you have a trade-off between richer and more flexible code and maintenance convenience.

Ironically, you can produce compact and reusable code by incorporating calculated references to solution elements and objects. Literal references to objects by name, like those used in the Go to Layout example shown in the preceding section, are easier to troubleshoot and maintain in most other respects (in particular, because the technique allows you to greatly reduce repetition and duplication in your code). You must strike a balance.

Filename references

One area in which the use of literal references can compromise referential integrity is in the use of the FileMaker Design functions, many of which require you to supply the name of the file containing the required information. For example, you can retrieve the contents of a value list using the following function syntax:

```
ValueListItems ( FileName; ValueListName )
```

You can supply both parameters required by the `ValueListItems ( )` function as text literals, so the resulting expression may be incorporated into your solution along the lines of

```
ValueListItems ( "Inventory.fp7"; "Suppliers" )
```

Declaring calculation arguments as text literals, as in this example, is high maintenance because if the filename or value list name ever changes, you will have to manually edit the names in quotation marks to restore the intended functionality. You can solve this problem in several ways. In relation to the filename:

- When the reference is to the current file, you can structure your syntax to retrieve the name of the file using the `Get (FileName)` function. This function continues to work without any adjustment in the event the file is renamed.

- In a multi-file solution, including a reference table containing details such as the names of the solution files may be advantageous. If all functions referring to a particular file reference its name in the relevant data field (rather than as a text literal), you only have to update the file's name in the reference table if it changes, rather than separately locating and updating each function referring to it.

CROSS-REF A method of making references to field, layout, value list, script, and Table Occurrence names impervious to name changes (referring to them by their internal ID rather than by their current name) is detailed in Chapter 12.

Structural anomalies

On occasions when you have included literal text references to an object or element (or where others may have done so) and you need to change that object's (or element's) name, you'll need a reliable way of locating the literal references so that you can update them.

One option is to select all tables (in the Manage Database dialog's Tables tab) and all scripts (in the Manage Scripts window) and print them, sending the output not to a printer but to a PDF or text file. Then you can search the file for the text string to locate all occurrences of text references to the object or element you are renaming.

CROSS-REF Third-party diagnostic tools, such as BaseElements from Goya or Inspector from FM::Nexus, in conjunction with FileMaker Pro Advanced can also provide invaluable help when tracing dependencies. For additional details about the uses of FileMaker Pro Advanced with these and other third-party diagnostic tools, refer to Chapters 18 and 19.

Chapter 16

Making FileMaker Systems Fail-Safe

Database solutions serve many purposes, including supporting essential, even critical, processes. Whether the consequences of data errors or problems are dire — or merely inconvenient — designing your solutions to be as robust as possible is beneficial. In many cases, additional cost or effort to make your solution resistant to failure and improve the ability to recover from a variety of errors is more than justified.

Fortunately, you can take many steps to safeguard your solution's data, improve user accountability, avert mishap, and recover from calamity. In this chapter, I gather together a number of techniques and options you can use to strengthen your solution's defenses against a variety of potential hazards.

Expecting the Unexpected

Systems fail for any number of reasons — usually, they're the reasons you didn't consider, because otherwise you'd have taken preventive measures. The circumstances that cause your system most harm, therefore, will be the problems you didn't anticipate.

Although you can't anticipate every possible error or mishap, you can be confident that sooner or later something will crop up. Luckily, you can take steps to ensure that when a difficulty arises, you have some options available to minimize its impact and recover with a minimum of fuss.

Successful backup strategies

Foremost among survival strategies for any computer system — and especially any database solution — is a backup regime. A reliable backup routine can get you out of trouble almost regardless of the cause. Accidentally deleted records,

IN THIS CHAPTER

Being prepared for problems

Taking care of error trapping

Opening databases remotely

Working with temporary edit interfaces

Screening errors with masks and filters

Building audit trails and script logs

Offering undo and roll-back functionality

Considering logging alternatives

power failure, disk corruption, bugs in your code — you can alleviate all these things if you have previous copies of your database to which you can revert.

Several questions arise when you're considering your approach to solution backup, and the way you resolve them determines your backup strategy's viability. The key questions are

- How often should you back up?
- How long should you retain each backup?
- How will you be sure that your backup copies are sound?
- How and where should your backups be stored?
- Which components of your solution should you back up?

Backup frequency

Backing up too infrequently reduces protection against mishap and leaves you exposed to the possibility of greater loss of data. In the event of a catastrophic system failure, you may lose all the data entered or edited since the last backup. If you backed up less than an hour ago, you're in a much better position than if your last backup was a week or a month ago.

Frequent backups, however, consume time and resources. If your solution is large, they may begin to impact the solution's performance. Often, the ideal backup regimen is one that sets the frequency of backups just below the level where their impact on performance would begin to affect productivity. The level that adversely affects productivity varies depending on the size of your system, the deployment configuration, and the number of users. However, you should aim to avoid any significant slowing or interruption or work due to backup cycles. (If sufficiently frequent backups present a performance problem, consider upgrading server hardware.)

You also need to consider the relative costs of data loss. If the labor costs of repeating a day's work are significant, then you should consider running backups more frequently than once a day. Determine how much time and data you (and your solution's owners and users) can afford to lose.

An appropriate backup cycle

If you overwrite each backup with the next one, at any point you have only one backup copy. This situation is risky for several reasons, including the possibility that an error or problem may not be immediately detected. If several hundred records were erroneously deleted some time in the last week, but you're only keeping backups from the last day or hour, backups won't enable you to recover the lost data.

If storage capacity is limited, I recommend that you keep backups for two weeks. However, in any situation in which the preservation of data is critical, consider archiving backups to cheap long-term storage media, such as a DVD-ROM.

As part of your short-term backup strategy, I recommend setting up an external process. For example, you might consider deploying a third-party backup application or operating system script (AppleScript or VBScript or Shell script) to transfer the backup files to a remote volume (for example, a network share or ftp directory) after the creation of each backup file set is completed.

The integrity of backups

All too frequently, it's not until *after* a system failure — when they attempt to restore from a backup — that people discover that all their backups are empty, corrupt, or otherwise useless. Backup failure can occur for a variety of reasons, including simple hardware failures (such as write errors) on the media where the backups are being stored.

To be certain, therefore, you need a procedure in place that confirms the integrity of the backup files. If your solution is hosted using FileMaker Server 9 or 10, you can configure it to perform both the scheduled backups and their verification automatically. Otherwise, you'll need a manual process to regularly verify that backup copies of your files are accessible and usable. In fact, even where Server verification is enabled, periodic manual checks are good practice, helping to place focus on the restore process, which is where backup strategies most frequently fail.

The location of backups

It may seem obvious, but if your backups are stored on the same disk drive (and on the same workstation) that the solution itself resides on, failure of that drive will cause your backups to be lost — along with the deployed copy of your solution.

Ideally, your backups should be stored not just on a different system, but at a different location. In the event of a fire, flood, earthquake, or other physical calamity, multiple computers in the same room, building or wider area may be affected simultaneously. Ideally, you should store frequent copies of backups at a secure remote location, such as on an ftp server accessed over the Internet.

Back up the code, not just the data

Keep in mind that the investment in your solution's structure, logic, and interface may be at least as valuable as the data it contains. Thus, you should back up not only while your solution is deployed, but also while it's under development. Keep a pristine (never deployed, never improperly closed) reference copy of your solution from each stage of its development. In the event your file's code or structure is compromised, the existence of a reference master will prove invaluable.

The hazards of copying open files

Some ways to create backup files are right — and some are wrong. One of the riskiest actions you can take is to use external applications (third-party backup utilities or your computer's operating system) to make copies of your solution files while they're in use.

> **CAUTION** Copying database files while they're being accessed by users can result in corruption, not only of the copies but also of the original files. Avoid copying open database files under any circumstance.

Copying database files while they're open is a bad idea for two reasons:

- FileMaker and FileMaker Server read substantial amounts of an open file into cache, maintaining the data there, writing parts of it back to disk only when necessary or during idle time. Therefore, the valid structure and content of the file is an amalgam of what is on disk and what is in memory — with neither, alone, representing a valid or complete file. If you attempt to copy the file while it's in this state, you are at best copying only the disk component of the file, which will be neither current nor complete.

■ FileMaker and FileMaker Server require exclusive access to a file they're hosting so that data can be read and written with maximum efficiency and integrity. External applications copying files frequently place successive locks on sectors of the disk while reading data from them. If FileMaker needs to flush data from its cache while part of the current file is locked by a third-party application, the consequences can include data loss and/or file corruption.

Of similar concern are ancillary programs, such as indexing and anti-virus applications, which may interfere with the connection between FileMaker Server and the files it is hosting. Any external process that accesses database files while they're being hosted presents a threat to file integrity.

TIP   **Always use FileMaker or FileMaker Server to create a separate backup copy of open files. Only use the operating system or third-party procedures to subsequently copy the backup files, not the deployed files. This way you can securely transfer copies of the backup files to remote storage locations.**

Backing up local files

If you're hosting a solution using FileMaker Pro or FileMaker Pro Advanced (rather than FileMaker Server), you must create backups by using the File ➪ Save a Copy As command or by closing the solution files and then using your computer's operating system (or a third-party application) to make copies.

You can, however, simplify the process of making solution backups in a stand-alone solution (or a solution hosted using FileMaker Pro) by creating a script along the following lines:

```
If [Get(MultiUserState) < 2]
  #Set Backup reference time
  Set Variable [$time; Value: Year(Get(CurrentHostTimeStamp)) &
        Right("00" & Month(Get(CurrentHostTimeStamp)); 2) &
        Right("00" & Day(Get(CurrentHostTimeStamp)); 2) & "_" &
        Right("00" & Hour(Get(CurrentHostTimeStamp)); 2) &
        Right("00" & Minute(Get(CurrentHostTimeStamp)); 2)
  #Set Backup path
  Set Variable [$path; Value: "file:" & Get(FileName) & "_BU" & $time & ".fp7"]
  #Create backup of current file:
  Save a Copy as ["$path"; compacted;
Else
  Beep
  Show Custom Dialog ["Backups can only be run on the host computer"]
End If
```

Where your solution has multiple files, an efficient way to configure it is to create a backup script in each file and then, from the main file (the interface file), add steps to the backup script to call the backup scripts in each of the other files.

 Example backup scripts similar to the one provided here have been added to the `Inventory` example files for Chapter 16 on this book's Web page.

Such a script is useful only if you remember to run it on the host computer at regular intervals. Relying on someone remembering to run backups at regular intervals may be adequate for a small or single-user solution. For all other cases, I recommend the use of FileMaker Server, where automatic backup scheduling is built in.

Backing up hosted files

If your solution files are hosted (multi-user), backup copies can be generated only on the computer on which the files reside. The script shown under the previous topic includes a check to confirm that the file is hosted on the current computer before it creates a backup copy. If your solution is hosted using FileMaker Pro, you need to ensure that the backup procedure is completed at regular intervals.

If you're using FileMaker Server to host your solution, you can use the option (recommended) to create automatic backup schedules. FileMaker Server 9 and 10 also provide the means to automatically verify the integrity of each backup file after it's created and to generate an e-mail notification confirming task completion.

Regardless of the way your solution is hosted, a separate procedure to transfer the backup files to an appropriate secure location is required. FileMaker Server includes the ability to schedule OS-level scripts. If you create an appropriate script on the host computer to archive and/or transfer backups to a secure location, you'll be able to schedule it to run after each backup has been created.

CAUTION When scheduling a file transfer procedure to copy backup files to a remote storage location, ensure that the copy procedure does not commence before FileMaker Server has had time to complete the creation of the backup files.

CROSS-REF See the resources listed in Appendix A for sources of information about the creation of external scripts for archiving backup files.

A Comprehensive Approach to Error Trapping

While anticipating problems and setting in place appropriate backup procedures is an essential first step toward protecting your solution, prevention is undoubtedly better than a cure. Adopting a broad-based approach to error handling when designing your solution's code can help you avoid a significant class of possible problems before damage occurs.

FileMaker, Inc. provides documentation listing more than 200 error codes FileMaker may return, so trapping independently for all of them at every step would be an onerous task. Fortunately, you don't need to because many errors are particular to specific circumstances. For example, error 508 (Invalid value entered in Find mode) is specific to actions in which field contents are updated while the database is in Find mode — so unless both these conditions apply, you won't see an error 508. Similarly, error 100 (File is missing) is specific to an action involving a reference to an external file (and that file is unavailable).

CROSS-REF Full details of all FileMaker Pro error codes and their definitions appear in the online help and are listed in resources referenced in Appendix A of this book.

Bearing in mind the context of a given script and script action, you can narrow the range of possible errors and associated error codes considerably and then test explicitly for those errors you deem most likely to occur in context. When you do, I suggest that you ensure the final lines of your error-handling code test for any other errors and handle them generically.

NOTE Not all error codes indicate that the preceding command has failed (or failed inappropriately). For example, error 1 is defined as User cancelled action. This error can occur only in a situation where the user has been presented with an option (for example, in an application dialog) that includes a Cancel button and has clicked it. Because Cancel is a valid option for the user in such a situation, your scripts should handle it, but it need not be considered an error.

Similarly, a `Go to Related Record[ ]` command with the Match All Records in Current = Found Set option enabled will return error 101 (Record is missing) if the current record had no related records, even though other records in the found set did and they have been successfully displayed.

In such cases, the error code FileMaker returns provides information about the result of the previous action but need not be considered an indication of an error as such.

In all cases, when implementing error trapping, I recommend that you also maintain a log of errors within your solution. Have your scripts create an entry in an error table indicating what error was encountered, at what point in what script, on what record in which layout, which user was logged in, and so on. Creating a log greatly aids system maintenance and problem diagnosis if errors should occur.

Dealing with record locking

When your solution is hosted on a busy network, one of the most frequent errors your scripts may encounter is 301 (Record is in use by another user). However, this error can be produced even if your database is not hosted, when the record currently being edited is already being edited in another window on the current user's workstation. In this situation, FileMaker produces the error dialog shown in Figure 16.1 (if error capture is not enabled).

With multiple users working simultaneously on a hosted solution, error 301 is apt to occur more whenever users or scripts simultaneously attempt to open or edit the same record.

NOTE You can view records while another user is editing them and place the cursor into a field without seeing an error message. FileMaker returns an error only when an attempt is made to change the contents of a field while the record is being edited by another user.

FIGURE 16.1

The error dialog associated with an attempt to edit a record already being modified (in a different window) on the current user's computer.

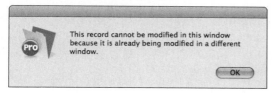

When someone else on the network causes the record lock, FileMaker displays an error dialog (if error capture is off) that indicates the identity (workstation "user name" and login account name) of the user currently modifying the record and provides an option to display a message to the user encountering the error, as shown in Figure 16.2.

FIGURE 16.2

The error dialog associated with an attempt to edit a record already being modified by another user on the network.

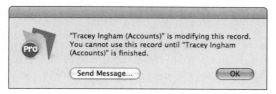

Although the error dialogs FileMaker displays when encountering these two distinct error conditions are different (see Figures 16.1 and 16.2), the error code returned in both cases is the same (301), so you need to construct your error handling to deal appropriately with both issues.

I recommend that you build window management procedures into your scripts to handle situations where the user may have several windows open, closing those not required and ensuring that the state of those remaining open do not impede subsequent scripted edits. If you build appropriate context management (including window management) procedures into your scripts as a matter of course, you can minimize or eliminate situations where error 301 results from the current record being edited in another window.

Regarding occurrences of error 301 resulting from the activities of other users, your error handling code should do the following:

1. Pause and try again several times. If the other workstation edit is brief, such as when it results from another user's computer performing a scripted update, you can expect the record to be released quickly, and your script can then continue.

2. Time out after several attempts and store the unique ID of the record where the error occurred.

3. If the script has significant processing to do on other records, consider structuring it so that it returns to records skipped because of error 301 and tries again after concluding its work on other records. Frequently, the locked records will have been released in the interim.

4. Notwithstanding Step 3, if the record(s) remain locked through timeout and after the conclusion of the script, have your script either report the error to the user (with the IDs of records not updated) and/or log the errors (including the IDs of the records where errors occurred and the details of the update that failed on those records) to an error log for later attention.

5. Consider having your script's error-handling sequence automatically generate and send an e-mail to the solution administrator with details of the error.

Although this mix of steps may vary according to the nature of the update your script is applying, following such a process provides the best protection against data anomalies arising when records in a set being updated are unavailable due to record locking in a hosted solution. The way of dealing with record locking described here addresses one of the most common causes of data integrity issues arising from inadequate code and error handling.

Techniques to avoid in multi-user or multi-window environments

Several development techniques you can effectively employ in single-user solutions present risks or have adverse consequences when used in a multi-user solution — either because they cause errors or because error-handling procedures can't adequately protect their use. Several techniques deserve special mention here.

Replace Field Contents

Although the scripted update of a batch of records (such as via a script looping through the found set and updating each record in turn) is vulnerable to record locking in a multi-user solution, appropriate error handling, as described in the previous section, can mitigate the associated risks. However, if your solution (or its users) use the Replace Field Contents [ ] script step in a button, script, or menu command, error data regarding locked records (if any) will not be available during or after the update. In other words, if records were locked, they're skipped. While a generic error code (201, defined as Field Cannot Be Modified) is returned, the identities of the locked records remain unknown.

For this reason, you should avoid using the Replace Field Contents [ ] command in a multi-user solution. Because it doesn't lend itself to error handling, it poses an unacceptable risk when used in a hosted database.

> **TIP** If you have access to a copy of FileMaker Pro Advanced, you may want to create a custom menu set for your hosted files, with the Records ⇨ Replace Field Contents command disabled or removed.

CROSS-REF   You can find additional detail about the creation of custom menus using FileMaker Pro Advanced in Chapter 18.

Record marking and flagging techniques

Inexperienced developers sometimes build procedures depending on setting flag values on or marking certain records so that they can be summarized, found again, or included in a process being performed by the current user. If the number of records involved is moderate, these techniques can provide an acceptable method in a single-user solution. However, as soon as the solution is made available to multiple simultaneous users, problems arise because the marks applied or removed by one user's workstation are overridden by another's.

I've encountered solutions in which one user's order items routinely ended up on another user's invoices or where records marked by one user for archiving are instead duplicated by another user's script. These errors, and others like them, arise from the use of flagging and marking techniques that are inappropriate for multi-use deployments.

NOTE   The use of flags to indicate the status of a record with the purpose of enabling other users to see the record's status is multi-user friendly and falls outside the caution mentioned here.

An example of the legitimate use of a flagging technique to manage custom record locking is discussed in the "Temporary Edit Interface Techniques" section, later in this chapter.

Uses of global fields

One further technique you should avoid when developing solutions that may at some point form part of a hosted data system is the use of global fields to store persistent data.

When a solution is accessed in stand-alone mode, the contents of global fields are saved when the solution files are closed and are therefore available again when the file is subsequently reopened. In this situation, global field values persist between sessions. However, in a multi-user database, changes made to global field values during each client session are seen only on the workstation where they're made (every user "sees" their own set of global field values) and are discarded at the conclusion of the client session.

Once understood, global field behavior in a hosted solution is valuable and even essential. However, procedures predicated on the behavior of global fields in stand-alone mode fail spectacularly — and without returning any error codes — when hosted.

Opening Remote Files

The method you use to access database files has a bearing on their performance and their vulnerability to corruption.

Database applications, especially for hosted databases, are I/O (input/output) intensive. A lot of data is read and written to disk, sometimes in short periods of time, so FileMaker (or FileMaker Server) performs a lot of two-way communication with the disk on which your database files are stored. The speed and reliability of the connection between the CPU where the host application is running and the volume where the files are stored are therefore critical determining factors in the response times and reliability of the application.

> **TIP** **Always open and/or host database files from the computer where they're stored. Opening files from a remote (network) volume is both risky and suboptimal. I acknowledge that technology advances rapidly and new storage protocols are emerging, including new mass storage opportunities in high bandwidth networked environments. While each case must be considered on its merits, I presently consider local hardware connected storage to be the safest and (in most cases) best performing option.**
>
> **For additional information about the reasons for this caution, refer to the sections "File sharing risks" and "Network spaghetti," later in this chapter.**

Peer-to-peer hosting

You can use FileMaker Pro 10 to host a solution for up to ten concurrent users (nine client connections, plus the host itself), so you can start sharing files straight away over a local network, directly from your desktop computer. To do so, you should follow these steps:

1. Make sure that your computer is connected to a TCP/IP network and that other computers on the network have copies of FileMaker Pro 10 (or FileMaker Pro 10 Advanced) installed.

2. Open the solution you want to install (including all solution files, if your solution comprises more than one file) from a disk drive directly connected to the current computer (either an internal hard drive or an external drive attached through high-speed USB, FireWire, SCSI, or SATA connections).

3. Choose File ➪ Sharing ➪ FileMaker Network. The FileMaker Network Settings dialog, shown in Figure 16.3, appears.

4. Select the Network Sharing On radio button in the upper section of the dialog.

5. Select each of your solution's database files in the Currently open files lists (lower left of the dialog) and enable network access to the file in the panel at the lower right — either for all users or users by privilege set.

6. If the computer where the files are open has a firewall enabled, confirm that port 5003 is open in the firewall settings, to permit traffic between the FileMaker host and client workstations.

> **TIP** **If your solution has a main file and one or more ancillary files, consider enabling the checkbox labeled Don't Display in Open Remote File Dialog for the ancillary file(s) so that remote users will be guided to open your main file first.**

7. Click OK to accept the settings and close the FileMaker Network Settings dialog.

FIGURE 16.3

Enabling Network File Sharing from the FileMaker Pro client application.

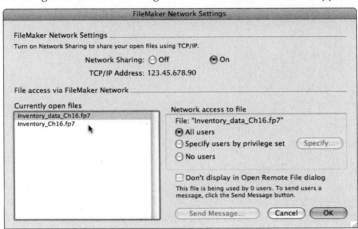

After following the preceding preparatory steps, other workstations elsewhere on your network running FileMaker Pro are now able to open the solution files remotely. To confirm that your solution is shared over the network, go to another computer on the network, launch FileMaker Pro, and choose File ➪ Open Remote. The Open Remote File dialog appears, as shown in Figure 16.4.

FIGURE 16.4

Select a file to open in the Open Remote File dialog.

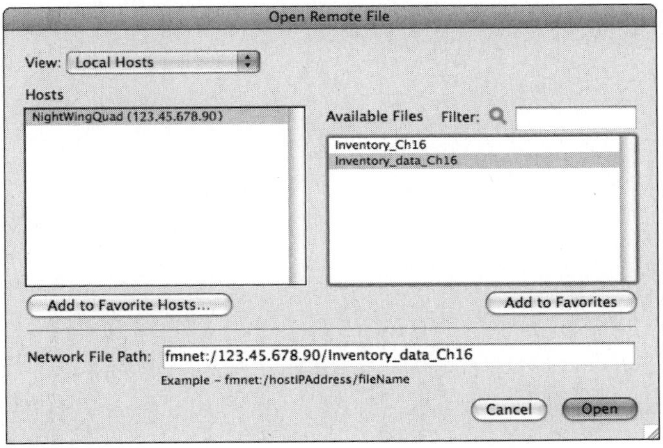

The list of available hosts in the Open Remote File dialog, when Local Hosts is selected in the View pop-up menu at the top left, shows computers on the local network configured for FileMaker sharing. When you select the workstation where your solution is hosted, the files enabled for network sharing appear in the Available Files list at the right of the dialog. When you select your solution's main file and click OK, the solution opens remotely on the current workstation.

File sharing risks

FileMaker network sharing provides you with a built-in data sharing protocol available with minimal setup, right within FileMaker Pro on your computer. There is an important distinction between this capability and conventional file sharing, where users open a file directly from a disk on another computer. The key difference is that with FileMaker Network sharing, multiple users can open the solution simultaneously, whereas file sharing permits only one user at a time to have write access to a file.

When you enable your solution for FileMaker Network Sharing, avoid having the same computer available for conventional file sharing on the network for several reasons. Foremost among them is that doing so provides two alternative ways users can open the solution — one via FileMaker Network sharing and the other by opening the files directly with file sharing. Should users open your files directly (as host) via file sharing rather than through FileMaker's Open Remote dialog, your files are placed at risk (for example, if a network drop-out occurs), and performance is severely compromised.

Another significant risk presenting itself whenever database files are stored on a volume enabled for file sharing is that multiple copies of the files will be available, and users may make their own copies. If they do, users are highly likely to inadvertently open the "wrong" copy of the database for a given work session. Then, when they next log in (to the correct copy of your solution), all the work from their previous work session is absent. Even if users realize immediately what has occurred and where all their work from the previous day is located, reconciling the data between the two copies of your solution may present significant challenges (particularly if some users have been updating one version while others were updating another).

You can avoid all these problems and potential pitfalls by ensuring that file sharing is never enabled for volumes where copies of your database files are stored and, particularly, for the computer (or computers) you're using to host databases via FileMaker Network Sharing.

Network spaghetti

Risks of file corruption, data loss, and general confusion aside, additional issues arise when database files are accessed via file sharing. Every element of data to be displayed, edited, or entered when a database is opened via file sharing must be passed to and fro between the computer accessing or hosting the databases and the network volume where they're stored. Moreover, the computer's access to the storage media is impeded not only by network traffic and inherent network latency but by other tasks being serviced simultaneously by the file share.

When users connect remotely to a database file open on a computer, if that computer has in turn opened the files via file sharing from elsewhere on the network, all remote calls for data must travel to the host computer, then to the file sharing computer, then back to the host — and then on to the client workstation. Data entered or edited must negotiate the same obstacle course in reverse. By the time you have several client workstations connected, network traffic becomes convoluted, and multiple bottlenecks can arise.

In a busy office or production environment, the last thing you need is an overburdened and slug-gish network configuration — notwithstanding the risks to file integrity should the connection between host and file server/file share ever be interrupted.

Opener files

One way of simplifying the remote connection procedure for users of your solution is to provide a file to be stored on the user's desktop as a gateway to your solution. Such files are commonly termed *opener* files.

The basic principle of an opener file is a simple one. It opens the solution file(s) from a remote net-work address (the computer configured as host) and then closes itself. In the process, it gives the user an icon on the desktop that simultaneously launches FileMaker Pro and opens the remote database, saving the user a number of intermediary steps. For users who access your database infrequently — and who may be relatively unfamiliar with FileMaker Pro — an opener file pro-vides a direct and easily remembered way to access your solution.

Within your opener file, you create a link to your solution as an external data source so that the opener can find your solution on the network. Enter the syntax for the data source in the following form:

```
fmnet:/hostIPAddress/FileName
```

If your solution may be hosted in one of several alternate locations, you can list them, each on a sepa-rate line. (FileMaker opens the solution from the first location where it finds it, working down from the top of the list.) You can set up the start-up script in your opener file along the following lines:

```
Set Error Capture [On]
Open File ["Inventory_Ch16"]
Set Variable [$result; Value: Get(LastError)]
#Create opener log entry
New Record/Request
Set Field [OpenerLog::CurrentIP; Get(SystemIPAddress)]
Set Field [OpenerLog::DateTime; Get(CurrentTimestamp)]
Set Field [OpenerLog::ConnectionStatus; $result]
If[Result ≠ 0]
  Show Custom Dialog ["The solution is not currently available"]
End If
Close File [CurrentFile]
```

You can define a script such as this one to run automatically on file open (via the Open/Close tab panel of the File Options dialog). When you configure it in this way, the opener file automatically launches your solution remotely, logs the event, and then closes. If an error is encountered (if the solution isn't available on the network, for example), the opener file posts a dialog stating this before closing.

NOTE   I have included several lines in the suggested opener script to log the result of its use in a table within the opener file itself. This means that if a user is reporting problems or as part of routine maintenance, you can verify the exact times and details of any failed connections, including the specific error code FileMaker returned on each occasion.

Sending an e-mail link

New in FileMaker 10 is the ability to send an e-mail link to a hosted database. This capability is a useful alternative to an opener file in cases where those accessing your solution may change frequently or be spread far and wide. An e-mail link doesn't require that any files be added to the user's desktop, and you can distribute the e-mail bearing the link to large numbers of users speedily and efficiently.

To create an e-mail containing an embedded link (URL), users can click to access a hosted solution and then choose File ⇨ Send Link, as shown in Figure 16.5.

The Send Link command creates an unaddressed e-mail containing a URL for the current host and solution file, in the form

```
fmp7://123.45.678.90/Inventory_Ch16.fp7
```

The IP address of the host computer on the network in this example is 123.45.678.90, and Inventory_Ch16.fp7 is the name of the hosted file. The text of the automatically generated e-mail also includes a summary of the conditions that are required when clicking the link.

In order to connect to the database using this link:

- The client must have FileMaker installed on their computer.
- The database file must be open on the host machine.
- Any firewalls between the client and server must allow FileMaker sharing.
- The client must have a valid account and password.
- The client and the host must be on the same local area network.

E-mail links may be sent from FileMaker 10 databases hosted either peer-to-peer or by using FileMaker Server 9.

TIP   Users receiving an e-mail link may save the e-mail or add the link to bookmarks in their Web browser. The link works whenever the solution file is open on the host computer indicated in the URL.

FIGURE 16.5

You can send an e-mail link for the current (hosted) FileMaker database file to a prospective user.

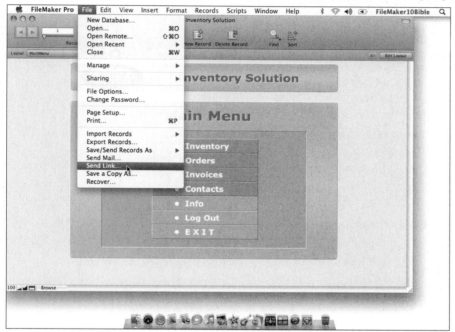

Temporary Edit Interface Techniques

When you exit a field or record (click in an inactive area of the layout outside of FileMaker's fields, buttons, and so on), the record is automatically committed, validation rules are evaluated, and the data (if validation succeeds) is written to the record. After a record is committed, the Records⇨Revert Record and Edit⇨Undo commands are no longer available, and the changes become permanent.

In cases where the accuracy of data entry and editing is of paramount importance, you're likely to require greater control over what goes into the database and how it gets there. You can create a holding area where data entry can occur and be subject to more rigorous checks or screening before being stored in your solution's main data tables.

The Data Viewer concept

You can create a separate Data Viewer interface so that users can edit in an offline area where you control how and when the data is saved to the database. You can create a FileMaker Data Viewer interface by following these steps:

1. Set user access privileges to View Only for the table(s) in question.

2. Create global fields (for example, in a utility or temporary data table) corresponding to each of the user-editable fields in your table.

3. Make a copy of the main form layout for the data to be edited via a viewer screen and re-point the fields on the copy to the temporary global fields created in Step 2.

4. Create an Edit script that

   a. Opens the current record (if necessary looping until it is available).

   b. Checks a lock flag on the current record and, if it isn't set, sets it (but if it is set, exits the record and posts an error alert telling the user the record is locked).

   c. Writes the values from each field in the current record to the corresponding global field (as per Step 2).

   d. Switches to the layout showing the global fields

   e. Locks down the interface (so that the user can't navigate using menus or the Status Toolbar).

5. Attach the Edit script to a button on the original layout.

6. Create a Save script that

   a. Checks all the values in the global fields and performs all required validations (alerting the user and exiting whenever a problem is found).

   b. On successful completion of all checks, opens the current record (if necessary, looping until it's available).

   c. Writes the values from the global fields back to the current record.

   d. Clears the lock flag on the current record.

7. Attach the Save script to a button on the copy of the layout with the global fields.

 **TIP** **Because the user's privilege set doesn't have write access to the main data table, both the Edit and Save scripts must be set to run with full access privileges.**

With this configuration in place, you have a custom record editing procedure, one in which changes to the record can't be committed until the Save button is clicked — and then only in accordance with requirements built into your Save script. No data can be entered or updated in the live solution table until (and unless) all your validation requirements are met.

One advantage of this approach is that it enables you to perform multiple validation tests on each field, returning a custom error message for each, indicating the exact nature of the problem encountered and what to do to resolve it. (The FileMaker built-in validation system provides only a single custom message regardless of the validation rule breached.)

The legitimate purpose of record locking

You may have encountered cases where a Data Viewer concept somewhat like the one described under the preceding topic has been proposed (or even implemented) as a palliative for issues arising from record locking. Such an approach resembles the one described in the preceding section but omits the custom record locking (the lock flag) procedure. I strongly caution against disabling record locking without providing a viable alternative.

Record locking serves an essential purpose in a multi-user database. It prevents one user's changes from being overwritten by another's and, perhaps more importantly, prevents data integrity from being threatened by the merging together of data of different origins. For example, without a record lock procedure, two users can select the same record for editing more or less simultaneously. If one user replaces a contact address while another user corrects the spelling of the suburb of the existing address, there is a risk that when both users confirm their changes, the result will be the new address but with the old suburb — an address that doesn't exist and therefore corrupts data. Each user independently did the right thing, but a flawed solution design crunched their data together inappropriately.

To preserve data integrity, you should either use record locking (either FileMaker's native record locking, or a custom alternative as described in the preceding topic) or

- Ensure that all fields are overwritten with new data when the edited record is saved (so that data from two separate user edits can never be blindly combined).

- Store the modification time when a record is opened for editing and check that it hasn't changed before writing changes back to the record.

- If the record has been modified since the user began editing, post an error dialog and either discard the changes or require that the user review changes made by the other user to decide which value to keep for each field (and subject the combined result to a further round of validations).

With these additional measures, your edit interface provides a viable alternative method of dealing with potential editing conflicts. Permitting multiple edits and then warning if a problem arises resembles the "optimistic" locking model FileMaker itself uses when dealing with data in *ESS* (External SQL Source) tables.

Creating double-blind entry systems

You can extend temporary edit interface techniques to provide support for *double-blind data entry* — where each record or edit must be processed independently and identically by two operators before being accepted into your solution's data. Double-blind entry is a requirement in some data processing environments and is considered desirable in others to safeguard against error and fraud.

Implementing a double-blind entry system requires all the essentials of the Data Viewer outlined in the preceding pages, with the addition of a holding table. Moreover, data to be entered requires a unique ID number prior to entry (for example, from serialized stationery). The Save script then performs an additional procedure as follows:

1. After completing data validations on the entered/edited data (refer to Step 6 in the procedure to create a Data Viewer earlier in this chapter), the script checks for the presence of a corresponding record (by unique form ID) in the holding table. Then one of the following happens:

   - If no corresponding record is found in the holding table, the data is transferred to a new record in the holding table.

   - If one (or more) corresponding record is found in the holding table, the values in each field of the entered or edited data are compared with the values in the holding record.

   - If there is an exact match between the entered/edited data and any holding record, the corresponding holding record (or records) is deleted, and the entered edited data is saved to the main table.

   - If the entered or edited data does not match any of the holding records, the data is transferred to a new record in the holding table.

2. Returns the user to the main viewing layout.

With this additional procedure in place, data can't become part of the main system unless entered identically by at least two operators. In such an implementation, it's normal practice to record the user IDs of both operators (those creating each of the matching entries) either with the updated record or in a separate log table. When an entry or edit is transferred to the main table, some businesses require that records from the holding table be transferred to an archive rather than deleted. Doing so provides a comprehensive audit trail of additions and modifications to the data. The presence of errors is greatly reduced, while user accountability is enhanced.

Because double-blind entry systems require a more complex solution design — and twice as much staff time for data entry — their use is restricted to solutions where the accuracy of data (and accountability of staff) is of critical importance. Nevertheless, the double-blind technique provides an added option in the design of a fail-safe system.

CROSS-REF   Methods of creating audit trails without requiring double-blind entry or separate edit interfaces are discussed in detail in the later sections of this chapter.

Field Masking, Filtering, and Error Rejection

When your data is required in a standard format and you want to avoid variations or rogue characters accumulating amidst your data, validations are only one of the options — and not necessarily the best option — for achieving your objective.

An alternative approach is to intercept data at the point of entry and modify it to conform to your requirements. In FileMaker Pro, you can intercept and modify data via the use of Auto-Entry calculations that reference the current field (and with the Do Not Replace Existing Value of Field option disabled). A field with Auto-Entry options configured by using this option automatically replaces the contents of an entry into it with the result of the calculation expression.

 Data modification at entry is generally best suited for use with text fields because they're designed to accept data in a variety of presentation styles and configurations.

Applying standard data formations

A frequent requirement when setting up database fields is to store telephone numbers according to a common convention — for example, the 123-456-7890 format is common in some parts of the world.

If you require all values entered into your `Contacts::PhoneNo` field converted onto a standardized 3-3-4 format, you'll require an auto-enter (replaces existing) calculation to remove characters other than numerals and to insert hyphens at the appropriate places. The following is an example of a calculation formula that achieves this:

```
Let(
Dgts = Filter(Contacts::PhoneNo; "0123456789");
If(not IsEmpty(Dgts);
Left(Dgts ; 3) & "-" & Middle(Dgts; 4; 3) & "-" & Middle(Dgts; 7; 4)
)
)
```

When this calculation expression is entered as an auto-enter calculation definition and the Do Not Replace option is disabled, entries such as the following are automatically converted:

(12) 345 678 90

1-2345-678 #9

123 456 7890

1234567890

Each of these input values is converted and stored as

123-456-7890

CAUTION **Before enabling strict filter formatting, consider the possibility that users may need to enter international or out-of-state numbers according to a different convention. If so, an override option (using a modifier or a global field checkbox, for example) may be appropriate.**

The following is an example of a variation of the formula configured to provide an override (accepting data in whatever fashion it is presented) if the Shift key is depressed while leaving the field after entering or editing a value:

```
Let(
Dgts = Filter(Contacts::PhoneNo; "0123456789");
```

```
Case(
Abs(Get(ActiveModifierKeys) - 2) = 1; Contacts::PhoneNo;
not IsEmpty(Dgts); Left(Dgts ; 3) & "-" & Middle(Dgts; 4; 3) & "-" &
   Middle(Dgts; 7; 4)
)
)
```

Dealing with trailing spaces and carriage returns

Using variations of the masking technique discussed in the preceding topic, you can configure a field to reject trailing spaces or carriage returns automatically as the user leaves the field. For example, to remove leading and trailing spaces from entered values in the Contacts::Address field, select the Auto-Entry by calculation option, deselect the Do Not Replace checkbox, and enter the formula

```
Trim(Contacts::Address)
```

Alternatively, to remove trailing carriage returns from values entered into the same field, specify the auto-enter calculation expression as

```
Let([
Rchar = Right(Substitute(Contacts::Address; ¶; ""); 1);
Pchar = Position(Contacts::Address; Rchar; Length(Contacts::Address); -1)];
Left(Contacts::Address; Pchar)
)
```

> **NOTE** The previous formula removes carriage returns only if they occur at the end of the text string entered into the field. Carriage returns included elsewhere in the entered string are left in place.

Building on the previous two examples, if you want to simultaneously remove trailing carriage returns and leading and trailing spaces, you can do so using a calculation expression such as the following:

```
Let([
Rchar = Right(Substitute(Contacts::Address; [¶; ""]; [" "; ""]); 1);
Pchar = Position(Contacts::Address; Rchar; Length(Contacts::Address); -1)];
Trim(Left(Contacts::Address; Pchar))
)
```

> **TIP** You can combine the logic of these expressions with other filtering requirements by nesting additional code within the example expressions.

Rejecting out-of-scope characters

FileMaker's Auto-Entry calculation technique, in combination with the Filter( ) function, lets you cleanly eliminate inappropriate characters, defining the character set to be retained and stored in a field.

For example, to ensure that the `Contacts::Address` field contains only letters, numbers, and spaces, you can use a formula such as the following:

```
Let (
Charset = "ABCDEFGHIJKLMNOPQRSTUVWXYZabcdefghijklmnopqrstuvwxyz 0123456789";
Filter(Contacts::Address; Charset)
)
```

With this expression applied as an Auto-Entry (replaces existing) calculation, all punctuation, carriage returns, and other extraneous characters are stripped from the text string entered by the user.

Handling styled source text

If users paste data into fields in your solution (after copying text from a word processor or Web browser, for example), the text may include embedded character formatting — text colors, text styles, fonts, or nonstandard font size attributes. These styles can wreak havoc on the data legibility in your solution's screens and printed output. You can strip these styles out at data-entry time cleanly and simply with an auto-enter (replaces existing) calculation employing a formula such as

```
TextFormatRemove(Contacts::Address)
```

With this auto-enter calculation configured, users can paste styled text into the field, but as soon as they leave the field, all styles and character format attributes are removed.

 **If desired, you can also use the techniques described in this section to conditionally apply text styles and character formats to data at the point of entry.**

Built-In Logging Capabilities

Your data's safety depends on your solution being able to detect errors and, when errors are detected, acting to correct them and prevent their recurrence. To achieve that goal, you need information about the data and the sources of errors. FileMaker provides several ways to capture additional information that can be of assistance in tracing and troubleshooting errors.

Making use of auto-enter options

As a first line of defense, you should add a standard set of metadata fields to each table users will edit directly.

In Chapter 5, I describe adding fields to capture creation account, creation workstation, creation timestamp, modification account, modification workstation, and modification timestamp for every record in each table. I recommend this practice to you as a standard procedure for data entry tables. Although standard metadata fields provide a first port of call when checking the origins of your data, you can explore a number of more useful options.

Capturing and extending standard metadata

In addition to the basic set of metadata fields provided among FileMaker's standard Auto-Entry options, you can capture a number of additional pieces of information regarding the circumstances of each record's creation and modification, including

- The user's IP Address and/or network hardware address — such as their computer's MAC address (Media Access Control, not an Apple computer)
- The version of FileMaker being used to make the change
- The operating system version and platform of the user's workstation
- The layout the user is using the make the edit
- The name of the script (if any) running when the record is committed
- The name of the account the user uses to login to their computer (not the database)

You can capture each of these items (except the last) with a text field that is set to auto-enter based on a reference to the record modification time field and then use one of FileMaker's native Get ( ) functions. For example, an auto-enter text calculation field can capture the IP address (or addresses if there is more than one network interface available) of the computer used to make the most recent modification to the current record, with the following calculation expression:

```
If(_ModStamp; Get(SystemIPAddress))
```

To obtain the name of the user's login account on the current computer, you can extract it from the result returned by FileMaker's Get (DesktopPath) function using the following calculation expression:

```
Let([
Dp = Get(DesktopPath);
Ln = Length(Dp);
p1 = Position(Dp; "/"; Ln; -3) + 1;
p2 = Position(Dp; "/"; Ln; -2)];
Middle(Dp; p1; p2 - p1)
)
```

> **TIP** If you require extensive data about this information, rather than adding a large number of fields to every table, I recommend that you create a session table and have your login script add a record to it each time a user logs in or out. With all the required information stored in the session table, you'll be able to reference it as required based on the user's account name and the creation or modification timestamp value.

A significant limitation of the metadata capture process is that it contains information only about the most recent modification. If the record has been modified multiple times, information about the previous modifications is overwritten. However, you can readily build a variation that captures the account names and dates/times of all changes or recent changes to each record. For example, if you want to capture a rolling log of the date, time, and associated login account of the last six modifications of the current record, you can do so by defining an auto-enter text calculation (replaces existing) called _ModHistory, with the following calculation expression:

```
LeftValues(
If(_ModStamp; GetAsText(Get(CurrentHostTimeStamp)) & " - " & Get(AccountName)) &
¶ & _ModHistory
; 6)
```

NOTE As an example, I've added a _ModHistory field using this formula to this chapter's Inventory example's Inventory table. I used FileMaker Pro Advanced to add a tooltip displaying the recent modification history, as captured by the _ModHist field to the Record Last Modified panel near the bottom of the Inventory layout.

CROSS-REF For additional information about defining tooltips using FileMaker Pro Advanced, see Chapter 18.

Script Logging

An important part of the reference information about the access, performance, and data history of your solutions is the timing, context, and results of script execution. If things go awry, in either a small or a significant way, your ability to determine what has been occurring and why depends on the quality of information available — including information about what happens when each of your scripts executes.

For any solution where performance, reliability, and data integrity are crucial, I recommend that you consider incorporating a script logging procedure to capture details about script activity as your solution is used.

Infrastructure for script logging

To keep track of script activity in your solution, create a ScriptLog table with a single table occurrence, no relationships, and one layout. (The layout may remain blank because only the script accesses the table.) In your StartUp script, create a window called ScriptLog, either off-screen or hidden.

In the ScriptLog table, create the fields as set out in Table 16.1

TABLE 16.1

Name	Type	Options
ScriptLog#	Number	Auto-Entry serial number, Can't Modify Auto
Script	Text	Auto-Entry Calc with formula Get(ScriptName)
Parameter	Timestamp	Auto-Entry Calc with formula Get(ScriptParameter)
Start	Timestamp	Auto-ENTRY Calc with formula Get(CurrentHostTimestamp)
Account	Text	Auto-entry Calc with formula Get(AccountName)
Workstation	Text	Auto-Entry Calc with formula Get(UserName)

(continued)

TABLE 16.1	*(continued)*	
Name	**Type**	**Options**
Layout	Text	Auto-Entry Calc with formula `$layout`
Mode	Number	Auto-Entry Calc with formula `$mode`
RecordNo	Number	Auto-Entry Calc with formula `$record`
Window	Text	Auto-Entry Calc with formula `$window`
Conclude	Timestamp	
ResultArray	Text	

Tracking script execution

With the script log table in place, commence each significant script with a sequence along the lines of the following:

```
#Capture Context and Log Script Start
Set Variable [$x; Value:Let([
                   $window = Get(WindowName);
                   $record = Get(RecordID);
                   $mode = Get(WindowMode);
                   $layout = Get(LayoutName)]; "")]
Select Window [Name: "ScriptLog"; Current file]
If(Get(LastError))
   New Window [Name: "ScriptLog"; Top: -5000; Left: -5000]
   Go to Layout ["ScriptLOG" (SCRIPTLOG)]
End If
New Record/Request
Select Window [Name: $window; Current file]
```

After each significant or error-vulnerable step, include the step:

```
Set Variable [$result; Value: $result & "|" & Get(LastError)]
```

At the conclusion of the script, include the following:

```
Select Window [Name: "ScriptLog"; Current file]
Set Field [ScriptLog::Conclude; Get(CurrentHostTimestamp)]
Set Field [ScriptLog::ResultArray; $result]
Select Window [Name: $window; Current file]
```

NOTE When using the error logging method to build an array in the `$result` local variable, the expression `RightWords($result; 1)` retrieves the error code of the most recently logged script command (as the script progresses).

Script-specific context variables

As part of the opening lines of the script described in the preceding topic, the starting context of the script (window, record ID, layout, and mode) are captured, and these values are subsequently logged, along with several others.

An added benefit of this procedure is that where appropriate, you're able to use the same values at the conclusion of the script to return the user to the context as it was when the script began. Exceptions depend on the nature and purpose of the script.

Script diagnostics

With a script logging procedure in place, you'll be able to export the accumulating history of solution use into a separate developer database in which you can analyze script usage patterns, identify performance bottlenecks, and locate errors indicating where revisions of your solution's code are appropriate.

In some solutions, you may conclude that only a few of the scripts warrant logging; in complex solutions, it may be appropriate to include logging on all scripts. When you include script logging in your solution from the outset, you'll discover its value immediately during the build and beta testing phases of development.

Capturing User Edits in Detail

In the earlier section "Built-In Logging Capabilities," I provide you with techniques for capturing data about who has modified each record and when. To provide a true audit trail, however, you need to know which fields were edited and what their values were before and after the change.

A number of methods enable you to build an audit trail capability into your solutions. If you're using a temporary edit interface technique, your Save script can store a record of the changes. However, if your users edit data directly in layouts attached to the main solution tables, you need to create a calculation field to automatically capture field changes.

> **NOTE** When your scripts change data in your solution, it's a simple matter to have them also record the change to a record of edits — so scripts can be self-logging. However, capturing edits made by users presents a challenge of a different order. The following techniques focus on methods of capturing a reliable history of user-initiated changes.

Trapping edits, field-by-field

If you want to capture a history of values in a single field, you can efficiently achieve that goal via a slight extension to the Auto-Entry method I describe in the section "Capturing and extending standard metadata," earlier in this chapter. For example, to add a field audit log to capture the history of values in the `Contacts::Organization` field in the `Inventory` example database, proceed as follows:

1. In the `Inventory Data` file, choose File ➪ Manage ➪ Database. The Manage Database dialog appears.

2. Navigate to the Fields tab panel and select the `Contacts` table from the pop-up menu at the upper left of the dialog.

3. Create a text field called _DataLog.

4. In Field Options for the _DataLog field, navigate to the Auto-Enter tab panel and select the checkbox labeled Calculated value. The Specify Calculation dialog appears.

5. Enter the following calculation formula:

```
Let([
p1 = Position(_DataLog; "-»"; 1; 1) + 3;
p2 = Position(_DataLog; ¶; 1; 1);
Prv = If(p1 < 4; "[---]"; Middle(_DataLog; p1; p2 - p1));
Crt = If(IsEmpty(Organization); "[null]"; Substitute(Organization;
   ¶; "‡"))];
Get(AccountName) & " " &
GetAsText(Get(CurrentHostTimeStamp)) & "   " &
Prv & "        -» " & Crt & ¶ & _DataLog
)
```

6. Click OK to accept the Specify Calculation dialog.

7. Disable the checkbox option labeled Do Not Replace Existing Value of Field (If Any).

8. Select the checkbox option labeled Prohibit Modification of Value During Data Entry.

9. Click OK to close the Options for Field dialog and again to close the Manage Database dialog.

With this method in place, the _DataLog field accumulates a history of edits for the Organizations field, as shown in Figure 16.6. The history includes the account name of the person performing the edit, the data and time the edit occurred, the previous value (if any) of the field, and the value it was changed to.

NOTE I have made these modifications (shown in Figure 16.6) in the copy of the Inventory example files for this chapter. You can view the field modification history for the current record by holding the mouse over the Organization field on the Contacts screen to display its tooltip. (See Chapter 18 for additional information about tooltips.)

Incorporating ancillary data

You can use the method I describe in the previous section to log any text or number field. And with minor adjustments, it can also log date, time, and timestamp values. However, if you're using this approach, you need an additional field in each table for every field you need to audit. Instead, you can use a more complex formula to log user edits of multiple data-entry fields within a single (log) text field.

The following example is a formula to capture edits from multiple fields (including any mix of text, number, date, time, or timestamp fields, and including repeating fields) within a single text field.

```
Let([
Trg = Field1 & Field1[2] & Field2 & Field3 & Field4;
Lval = Length(AuditTrail);
Scpt = Get(ScriptName);
```

```
Rpt = Get(ActiveRepetitionNumber);
Rflg = If(Rpt > 1; "[" & Rpt & "]") ;
Fnm = Get(ActiveFieldName) & Rflg;
Pref = Position(AuditTrail; "          " & Fnm & "        "; 1; 1);
Pst = Position(AuditTrail; "          -»          "; Pref; 1) + 4;
Pnd = Position(AuditTrail & ¶; ¶; Pref; 1);
Pval = If(Pref; Middle(AuditTrail; Pst; Pnd - Pst); "[---]");
Tval = Get(CurrentHostTimeStamp);
Fval = GetField(Fnm);
Sval = Substitute(Fval; ¶; "‡");
Nval = If(Length(Fval); Sval; "[null]")];
If(Length(Fnm) and Length(Scpt) = 0;
GetAsDate(Tval) & "          " &
GetAsTime(Tval) & "          " &
Get(AccountName) & "          " &
Fnm & "          " & Pval & "          -»          " &
Nval & Left(¶; Lval) & AuditTrail; AuditTrail)
)
```

In this formula, the fields listed on the second line (`Field1 & Field1[2] & Field2 & Field3 & Field4`) are the fields to be logged, and the name of the log field itself appearing throughout the formula is AuditTrail.

FIGURE 16.6

A tooltip in the `Contacts` layout of the `Inventory` example for this chapter shows the history of edits of the `Contacts::Organization` field on the current record.

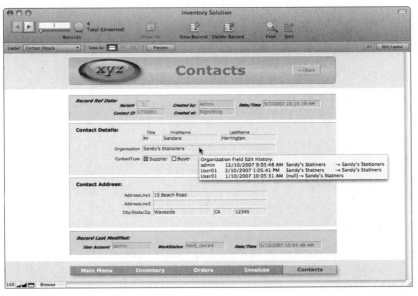

Because this formula is unwieldy, I recommend that you use a custom function to incorporate its logic. Doing so allows you to use it with a single function call and two parameters. A custom function that provides logging capabilities along the lines of this example was the basis of the FileMaker SuperLog demo (a free online download example file) published by NightWing Enterprises in 2006.

The calculation expression shown previously (and the `SuperLog( )` custom function, on which it is based) produces a composite (multi-field) audit trail for the current record, in the form shown in Figure 16.7.

FIGURE 16.7

The audit trail text for a record, as shown in the `SuperLog` example file.

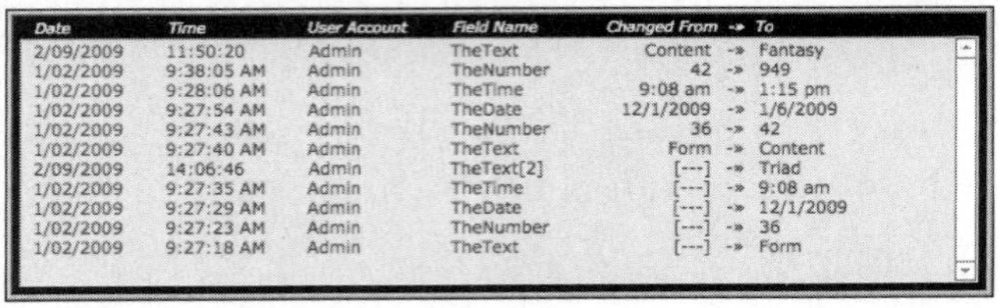

Date	Time	User Account	Field Name	Changed From → To	
2/09/2009	11:50:20	Admin	TheText	Content → Fantasy	
1/02/2009	9:38:05 AM	Admin	TheNumber	42 → 949	
1/02/2009	9:28:06 AM	Admin	TheTime	9:08 am → 1:15 pm	
1/02/2009	9:27:54 AM	Admin	TheDate	12/1/2009 → 1/6/2009	
1/02/2009	9:27:43 AM	Admin	TheNumber	36 → 42	
1/02/2009	9:27:40 AM	Admin	TheText	Form → Content	
2/09/2009	14:06:46	Admin	TheText[2]	[---] → Triad	
1/02/2009	9:27:35 AM	Admin	TheTime	[---] → 9:08 am	
1/02/2009	9:27:29 AM	Admin	TheDate	[---] → 12/1/2009	
1/02/2009	9:27:23 AM	Admin	TheNumber	[---] → 36	
1/02/2009	9:27:18 AM	Admin	TheText	[---] → Form	

CROSS-REF You can find a link to the NightWing Enterprises `SuperLog` example file among the resources included in Appendix A.

Implementing an audit trail mechanism throughout your solution by using a technique such as the preceding one requires an `AuditTrail` field in each table, alongside other metadata fields. Field modification data is then captured automatically as users work.

Logging record deletions

Although the processes described in the preceding sections provide mechanisms for tracking user edits, the method is such that if a record is deleted, its recent log entries are deleted with it.

One way to address this shortcoming is to provide (and require the use of) a script for deletion of records and to have the script first transfer details of the record being deleted (including all its data) to a log table. This way, you can keep track of which records have been deleted by whom as well as have the basis to restore lost information, if necessary.

Managing the Accumulation of Log Data

A potential disadvantage when you set up a field in each table to capture user edits is that in solutions where data changes frequently, the history of edits and previous field values can accumulate, adding significantly to the size of the file and thereby impacting performance. In fact, the volume of data associated with logging each record's history is necessarily larger than the current data in the solution. In addition, while audit data is stored in a single text block within each record, you can't readily search or sort it.

You can mitigate both these shortcomings by periodically archiving audit data to a separate table and/or file for reference.

Archiving options

Audit log data is more useful when you store it in a separate data table, where a separate record holds the details of each field edit in your main solution tables. When stored separately in this way, you can search and analyze log data, as well as access and update it independently of the main database. Separate data storage provides a more convenient format for audit log data when it is archived. When you allocate a separate record per field edit, each column of data from the originating log field array can be stored in a separate field in your log table. A script that loops through the lines of each record's audit log and parses each to the fields of a separate record in an audit utility table provides the first step toward consolidating audit data in a convenient indexed and searchable format.

CROSS-REF For details of techniques for looping through data and parsing elements from data arrays, refer to Chapters 12 and 13.

With your audit data stored in its own table, you can search for all changes made by a specific user or containing a particular value. Your ability to pinpoint errors and to discern patterns in the evolution of your solution's data is increased exponentially.

Generating secondary output

Depending on the volume of data edits taking place in your solution, you may consider running a maintenance script that transfers log data to an audit table nightly (after close of business), weekly (over the weekend), or on some other convenient cycle. If you need to review up-to-date audit summaries, you may want more frequent consolidations.

Your secondary repository of audit data is generally most useful if it spans a recent period (for example, ranging from a quarter to a year), rather than being an accumulation of edits for all time. In most cases, periodically transferring aged transaction logs to external storage (either an archive database or delimited text files) is appropriate. Once exported, you can delete these data from secondary storage.

Implementing Roll-Back Capabilities

A key benefit of implementing logging procedures — both for user edits and for record deletions — is the opportunity it affords to detect errors and reverse them. At its simplest, it means going back through the logs to locate an entry made in error and manually re-entering (or copying and pasting) the original value back into the relevant field and record.

A much more useful and powerful feature is the automated roll-back of log entries. In effect, this feature provides multiple undo capabilities at the record level.

Chronological roll-back

By using a record-based text field log as described in the preceding pages, you can create a relatively straightforward script to reverse the most recent edit on the current record. By running such a script multiple times, you can step a record back through its previous states in reverse chronological order.

As an example, the following script applies record-specific roll-back, one edit at a time, based on a log field in the format shown in Figure 16.7.

```
Set Variable [$LogEntry; Value:LeftValues(Data::AuditTrail; 1)]
Set Variable [$field; Value:Let([
                p1 = Position($LogEntry; " "; 1; 3) + 1;
                p2 = Position($LogEntry; " "; 1; 4) - p1;
                f1 = Middle($LogEntry; p1; p2);
                Ln = Position(f1 & "["; "["; 1; 1) - 1];
                Left(f1; Ln)
                )]
Set Variable [$repetition; Value:Let([
                p1 = Position($LogEntry; " "; 1; 3) + 1;
                p2 = Position($LogEntry; " "; 1; 4) - p1;
                f1 = Middle($LogEntry; p1; p2)];
                If(PatternCount(f1; "[") = 0; 1; RightWords(f1; 1))
                )]
Set Variable [$value; Value:Let([
                p1 = Position($LogEntry; " "; 1; 4) + 1;
                p2 = Position($LogEntry; " "; 1; 5) - p1];
                Middle($LogEntry; p1; p2)
                )]
If [$value = "[--]" ]
    Beep
Else
    Go to Object [Object Name: $field; Repetition: $repetition ]
    Set Field [If($value ≠ "[null]"; $value) ]
    Set Field [Data::AuditTrail; RightValues(Data::AuditTrail;
                ValueCount(Data::AuditTrail) - 1)]
    Commit Records/Requests [Skip data entry validation; No dialog]
End If
```

NOTE   The preceding script requires that the fields being logged have object names matching their field names assigned on the current layout so that the Go to Object [ ] command can locate each field by its name.

Although the previous script implements a roll-back procedure that is chronological with respect to a specific record in isolation, it allows you to roll back one record without affecting others edited during the same time period. A possible shortcoming of this roll-back procedure is that because it deals with a single record in isolation, associated changes to child records (if any) aren't automatically rolled back as part of the same action, potentially leaving related data sets in an erroneous state unless comparable roll-back procedures are performed in each related record.

Alternative undo and roll-back capabilities

By using the principle that provides the basis for the chronological roll-back discussed in the previous section, you can implement a roll-back option for audit log records in a consolidated log table.

Because you can search and sort records in a consolidated log table in various ways, selective roll-back is possible. You can adjust the scope of selective roll-back to include all references to a particular event, all edits made by a particular user, all edits made to a particular field — or any other criterion you choose to apply to the edit history.

To implement selective roll-back capabilities, first create a script that reverses a single edit by following these steps:

1. Have your script transfer the name of the edited field, the before-edit value, the location, and the ID of the edited record into variables.

2. Your script should then navigate to the appropriate record and place the before-edit value into the edited field.

3. Your script should return to the log table and update the status of the current log record to indicate it has been reverted.

With this script in place, selective rollback of a group of edits can be achieved by performing a find in the log table to locate the edits that are to be reverted and then calling a master script that loops through the found set applying the revert script to each.

CAUTION **If you roll back edits to a particular field and record out of chronological sequence (for example, reinstating a value other than the second-last value of the field), the remaining log records may not have continuity.**

I recommend that if you're rolling back log table entries, rather than deleting the entries you have reversed, you mark them as rolled back. Using a log status field to indicate which log records have been reverted has the added advantage that you can provide a counterpart procedure to roll forward.

Using logs to roll forward

If you've implemented comprehensive audit logging capabilities in your solution, a further option providing additional fail-safe security is a generic roll-forward script. Again, such a script operates on the same principle as the roll-back example provided in this chapter.

Rolling forward enables you to do the following:

■ Reverse a roll-back. If you have rolled back too far or where you wanted to roll the database back to the state it was in on a previous date to run a report or summary of the data as at that date, then roll the database forward to the present.

■ In the event of file corruption, providing your consolidated logs are intact, roll-forward enables you to apply the logged edits to a backup copy of the database, bringing the backup forward to the state the solution was in at the most recent consolidation.

If you provide a mechanism for the reversal of roll-back, I recommend inclusion of a status check to ensure that each log entry to be rolled forward has previously been rolled back. (Log entries not marked as rolled back should be skipped.) This requirement should be waived when applying a roll-forward through consolidated edit logs to a backup copy of your solution.

Alternative Logging Approaches

Although I've explored several facets of audit logging in the closing pages of this chapter, a variety of other approaches are possible. With a little research, you can find examples of other methods suited to a number of different requirements.

In particular, logging methods depending on third-party tools can provide additional flexibility and improved protection against unforeseen events. You must weight these potential benefits against the additional costs and deployment considerations for such products.

CROSS-REF Additional information about extending FileMaker capabilities with third-party tools is provided in Chapter 19.

Logs as Data

The accumulation of audit logs and journals as additional data in your solution has advantages for searching, sorting, summarizing, and reporting based on log data. However, it also presents a risk. If your solution encounters a problem that can be rectified by referring to the logs, the logs may possibly be affected by the same event.

If, for example, your server crashes, you might be able to rebuild the current state of the data if your logs are intact. For this reason, I suggest recording your log data on a server in a different location and outputting your logs to a different format. (For example, a text file format on a remote file server.) According to the needs of your solution, you must balance convenience and flexibility of data logs against the additional safeguards of remote or external log formats.

Scripted and triggered logging

When your audit trail of user edits is captured within the record by using the FileMaker calculation engine, compiling consolidated logs is necessarily a two-step process, with log data being stored first in the calculation used to capture it and subsequently transferred to a separate table or file.

Using the Script Event Triggers capabilities of FileMaker Pro 10, you're able to set up layout script triggers to perform an action every time a record is committed on a layout. You may choose to harness this capability to trigger the transfer of logged data to a consolidated log table. Be aware, however, that this approach is inherently fragile because the available triggers are all associated with the interface rather than with the schema — so logging will only occur if a data change is committed on a layout where the appropriate trigger has been defined. In fact, it would be relatively easy for a user to circumvent logging if it were based on native event triggers. For this reason, script triggers as implemented natively in FileMaker Pro 10 are more ideally suited to roles as interface tools and navigation aids than for audit, data validation, enforcement of business rules, or other mission critical purposes within your solutions.

By using a fully scripted approach to audit logging, you can avoid the necessity for a two-step approach, instead writing details of each change directly to a consolidated log table. This approach requires either of the following:

- The use of a scripted edit interface where changes are always committed and written to the main data tables via a script. In this situation, you can include log maintenance procedures within the Save scripts when you use this approach to editing your solution data.

- The use of a third-party tool to trigger a script or external event when an edit occurs (or when the record is committed). You can use a variety of products, such as plug-ins, in conjunction with FileMaker Pro 10 to support script-driven or event-driven logging functionality. Because script trigger calls provided via plug-ins can be embedded within the schema, processes that depend on them will occur whenever the schema is affected. Third-party triggering methods therefore continue to be better suited to logging and related requirements requiring robust and fail-safe implementation.

Chapter 17

Maintaining and Restoring Data

IN THIS CHAPTER

Understanding file recovery

Working with data export and import

Cleansing your data

Setting up data synchronization

Managing stored files and embedded images

Transforming text and text formats

When handled appropriately, FileMaker Pro solutions give years of faithful and trouble-free service — and, in fact, they've been known to survive a variety of forms of abuse. Nevertheless, problems can and do arise, and you need to know what to do — and what not to do — when responding to them.

As is frequently the case in many areas of computing, fiction and misinformation abound. In this chapter, I set out the facts for you so that you're able to address any potential problems with confidence and dependable strategies.

For more techniques to increase your solutions' fault tolerance and robustness, see the previous chapter. Here, I provide you with techniques to manage your solution's data.

Some Notes on File Recovery

The Recover command (File ➪ Recover) is arguably one of the most universally misunderstood features in FileMaker Pro. Despite many theories about what it does and how and when you should use it, much of the original confusion persists.

The uncertainty surrounding the Recover command stems in part from the fact that its name is misleading. *Recover* simultaneously suggests regaining full health and regaining something lost or misappropriated. Neither sense aptly conveys what the Recover command in FileMaker Pro actually does: a task that may be better characterized as a "partial salvage" in a brutal jaws-of-life kind of fashion.

Debunking common myths and misconceptions

The first and most egregious misconception you'll encounter regarding the Recover procedure is that running a full recovery on your files is a reasonable measure as a maintenance health check, and it's okay or even advisable to do it routinely — whether your files have exhibited problems or not. If you're the kind of person to clean your new Porsche with a belt sander, then go right ahead — but otherwise, please think again.

As an alternative to running a recover procedure, FileMaker 10 provides a Check Consistency option that you can access from the Select Damaged File window. This procedure is nondestructive, so you can perform it on healthy files without risk. To run a consistency check, choose File ➪ Recover. In the Select Damaged File dialog that appears, locate the file you want to check and click the Check Consistency button at the lower right of the dialog. FileMaker performs a basic analysis of the structure of the selected file and then posts a dialog, as shown in Figure 17.1, indicating whether any anomalies were found in the block structure of the file.

FIGURE 17.1

The result of the Check Consistency procedure shown in a summary dialog.

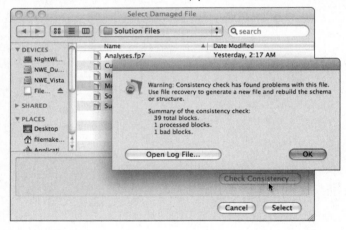

Although the Check Consistency procedure does not alter the file (and can therefore be run at will), it doesn't exhaustively analyze the file, so the Check Consistency process may not detect all problems.

A second widely circulated fallacy is that a database file, if it survives the Recovery procedure, is whole, intact, clean, and safe to use or develop further. You may be able to drive your car — after a fashion — following a nasty crash and an encounter with hydraulic salvage machinery. The stereo may even work. However, the safety of such an undertaking is in serious doubt. FileMaker Pro 10 provides some additional control over the procedures performed during a Recover cycle, as well as additional detail about what has transpired after recovery is complete, to provide a basis for making a judgment about the extent of the changes that occurred during recovery. However, it's important to bear in mind that the procedure is essentially a salvage operation.

A further myth, arising all too frequently, is that the Recover procedure *not* being a reliable repair utility — a dependable machine for restoring files to pristine condition — is itself a myth and that no one has ever experienced severe problems with recovered files. This myth seems to be a curious extension of "It will never happen to me" thinking.

The Recover process

Before deciding when and how to use file recovery in FileMaker Pro, you should know that this feature's mandate is to do whatever it takes to get a file in a state such that its *data* can be extracted. While the precise steps included in the recovery procedure may vary depending on the selections made in the Advanced Records Options dialog (see Figure 17-2), consider, for a moment, the broad basis of the process Recover follows:

1. The Recover command produces a copy of your original file.

2. As the copy of the original file is created, each piece of the original file is examined by using an algorithm designed to swiftly identify possible corruption.

3. When a component of the original file's code or structure is identified (accurately or otherwise) as potentially problematic, a pessimistic approach is taken, and the element containing the suspect code is omitted from the recovered version of the file. Recovery, therefore, is an aggressive process placing priority on getting your data out of a severely compromised file — and it will sacrifice code, interface, or the essential logic of your solution in service of this aim.

4. On completion of the Recovery operation, a dialog appears with a report providing edited highlights of its journey of recovery, as shown in Figure 17.3.

While a default set of Recover steps applies, a significant innovation in FileMaker 10 is the ability to configure a number of options that determine the steps Recover will apply, as shown in Figure 17.2. Using the options in the Advanced Recover Options dialog, you can choose to apply recovery procedures only to specific areas of the file and to choose the method used to deal with inconsistencies in the block structure as well. The generate new file options allow you to configure the Recover process to perform the equivalent of a Save a Copy or Save a Copy Compacted commands as the basis of creating the recovered file, rather than rebuilding the file as part of the recovery process.

In cases where you experience problems associated with a specific area of functionality in your file, such as indexing, you can use the advanced recovery options in FileMaker 10 to target Recover procedures on the problem area, leaving other parts of the file unmodified. To achieve a minimal procedure, you should choose the Copy Blocks As-Is option in the Advanced Recover Options dialog and then enable only the checkbox (or checkboxes) associated with areas of the file where you've been experiencing problems.

Although recovery passes through 16 multi-part stages, working through file structure, data blocks, layouts, tables, indexes, relationships, scripts, dependencies, and more, the confirmation dialog, as shown in Figure 17.3, mentions only five of these steps and provides only brief summary details about what occurred. In other words, the confirmation dialog doesn't mention a great deal of what occurs (including most of the checks resulting in file components being included or skipped) during recovery. The dialog's focus is primarily on your data (Records, fields, field definitions, and indexes).

FIGURE 17.2

The default selection of options in the Advanced Recover Options dialog.

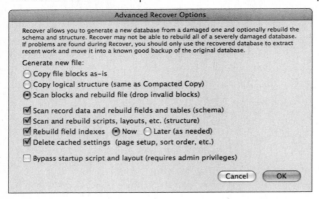

FIGURE 17.3

The overview dialog appearing on completion of a Recovery cycle.

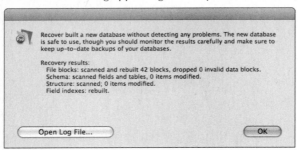

Although the result summary as shown in Figure 17.3 may state that The New Database Is Safe to Use, that message doesn't signify that the file is complete or intact, but rather that the Recover tests seem to indicate that the file is restored to a stable point. (In other words, you can expect to open the file without causing an application or system crash on your computer.)

Conversely, should the Recovery confirmation dialog indicate that the resulting file is *not* safe to use, that message doesn't necessarily indicate that the file won't open or that the contents of the file will not appear normal. Rather, it signifies that the Recover procedure produced a file in a state that *may* still render the file unstable. Thus, while a file that is Safe to Use is not necessarily complete or fully functional, a file that is described as Not Safe to Use may appear to be complete and operable.

Based on considerable experience, both good and bad, with this feature (including previous and current versions of FileMaker), I can confirm that the Recover process:

- Typically (but not invariably) omits items preventing a file from opening
- May omit items (scripts, layout objects, and so on) not among the elements mentioned in the concluding dialog summary
- May remove logical components of a file (layout, layout element, script step, and so on) suspected to be corrupt, even though they were causing no apparent problems
- May skip damaged or corrupt content, leaving it in the recovered file if the presence of that content doesn't prevent the file from opening

Damaged files usually open after recovery and may even appear to operate normally. However, don't assume (regardless of what the confirmation dialog stated or omitted to state) that your recovered file is complete and contains all the code and logic of the original — nor that it will work as intended in all respects.

WARNING In rare cases, recovered files have been known to contain duplicates of some records or to reinstate deleted records. My observation has been that the Recover procedure uses as its guiding principle "When in doubt, exclude it" regarding file structure and code content, while using "When in doubt, include it" with respect to your data.

Occasionally, damaged files may continue to exhibit problems after recovery. Furthermore, I have seen cases where otherwise normal and fully operational files are missing essential components and therefore malfunction after recovery.

Salvaging data

File recovery provides you with a fallback option if you encounter difficulties resulting from a system crash, hardware failure, and so on. However, the process is imperfect and is not exhaustive (see preceding section), so don't assume that your file is complete or will function as you intended after recovery.

Rather than take the risk of running the Recover process, the preferable options, in priority order, are

1. Revert to a recent backup of your file — one predating any problems leading to your file becoming inaccessible — and then re-enter data or otherwise modify the backup to bring it up to date. If you've been making frequent backups, this path may be the least onerous or inconvenient to take, particularly if you've employed transaction logging as described in Chapter 16.

2. Locate a clean and uncompromised (never crashed or improperly closed) copy of your solution file(s), make a clone, and then import data from a recovered copy of your solution into the clean clone(s).

Because the data in a recovered file may not exactly match the data in the original file (damaged records may have been omitted, deleted records reinstated, or duplicates included), if you opt for making a clone, you should expect to comprehensively check the resulting data set's completeness and accuracy. Unless your most recent backup is well out of date, the combined effort to recover, re-import, and verify your data will likely be greater than the work of re-entering information to bring a backup up to date.

Consider deploying a recovered file only if neither of the preceding options is available. (For example, your file has crashed, and you have no suitable backups or clean clones of the current file structure.) Before doing so, be prepared to undertake a thorough check of both the data and the code (including all layouts, layout objects, scripts and script steps, and calculation definitions) to confirm the solution is in a deployable state. If your solution is of any size and complexity, an adequate check of the deployment-worthiness of a recovered file is likely to be more onerous than preferred options 1 and 2 combined.

Understanding file corruption

You can define *file corruption* in several ways, with the broadest definition perhaps being "anything that is not as you intended." FileMaker, however, can't know what you intended and must therefore use a considerably less ambitious definition. For this purpose, FileMaker looks for block integrity throughout a file by applying the rules of well-formed data, seeking to restore lost pointers when file architecture contiguity is compromised.

FileMaker manages its own (internal) file structure, independent of the block structure of the storage device and, in doing so, depends on internal pointers to establish the status and order of each segment. When the integrity of the pointers is compromised or FileMaker is unable to resolve and interpret the contents of one or more segments of your file, FileMaker determines the file to be corrupt and posts an alert dialog, such as the one shown in Figure 17.4.

FIGURE 17.4

The warning FileMaker provides when file integrity problems have arisen.

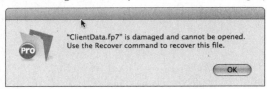

"ClientData.fp7" is damaged and cannot be opened.
Use the Recover command to recover this file.

OK

The most common problems affecting FileMaker files arise from improper closure, and FileMaker is able to correct these anomalies in most instances, with nothing more onerous than a consistency check when the file is next opened. More serious problems can result if data was partially written to disk at the time of a crash, power outage, or hardware failure — in which case one or more segments of your file's data may be incomplete and/or damaged. File corruption may result from a variety of other causes, such as power spikes, faulty device drivers, operating system errors, malicious software, or plain-old bugs, process conflicts with background utilities, and user errors, such as copying a file at the Operating System level while it's still open in FileMaker or FileMaker Server. Fortunately, file damage from these various causes is relatively rare.

The kind of damage your files may sustain when impacted by one of the events I mention may vary, from a single overwritten bit to whole sections of the file missing. For the most part, damage is random and therefore unpredictable. Occasionally, damaged data resembles valid data, and occasionally it is valid data (written into the wrong place), whereas on other occasions damaged bits are simply unintelligible. Faced with almost infinite possibilities in the forms corruption may take, the Recover procedure in FileMaker balances efficiency and efficacy by checking for the most commonly encountered and problematic issues.

Exporting and Importing Data

An important consideration when deploying any database is your ability to get data into and out of it in bulk, in formats appropriate for a variety of requirements. FileMaker Pro helps you out by supporting a broad range of data formats for both import and export.

In addition to general utility and exchange of data with other applications (for example, drawing in data from legacy systems, sharing data with others, and using information from your solution for word processing or publishing tasks), data exchange enables you to take advantage of the summarizing, reporting, or data analysis capabilities of other desktop applications or to share data with external accounts or financial management suites.

Several of the further purposes of data export and import include archiving data from your system, moving data between versions of your solution or processing, filtering, or validating your data externally as part of maintenance and/or restoration procedures in the event of solution integrity problems.

CROSS-REF Refer also to details about importing and exporting procedures and automating data transfers provided in Chapters 3 and 13.

File format considerations

One of the essential issues when you're considering moving data between formats is supported functionality. While your data remains in FileMaker, you benefit from a variety of automatic calculation, summary, and data presentation options. Because other applications don't support many of these options, you may face compromises when preparing to export to an alternative format. As a result, you may want to perform calculation, filtering, sorting, or summarizing in FileMaker prior to export.

When transferring data, it's usually preferable to deal with each table separately. However, where data relationships are central to your solution but can't be replicated in the destination application, you can accumulate data from multiple tables into a single (flat) file export. Figure 17.5 shows a simple example where the cFullName field from the Suppliers Table Occurrence is included in an export of data from the Orders table.

Along with relational and data presentation limitations in many of the available export file formats, most formats don't support inclusion of container data, such as files, images, sounds, or movies. Unless you choose FileMaker Pro as the export file format, FileMaker posts an alert dialog and prevents you from adding container fields to the field export order, as shown in Figure 17.6.

Even though you can't include container data in most data exports, you can output container fields' contents into a folder, from which you can later import them (if desired).

FIGURE 17.5

Inclusion of related fields in the Field Export order.

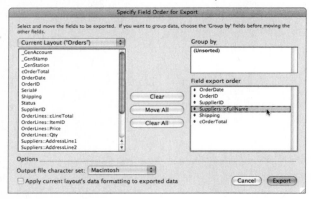

FIGURE 17.6

FileMaker displays an error alert if you choose a container field for export.

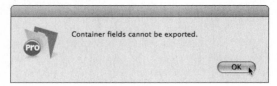

Exporting to and importing from a folder

In most cases, you can export container field contents individually (one field and one record at a time) by choosing Edit ➪ Export Field Contents command. In situations where you need to export a batch of container field contents — for example, from a found set of records or a whole table — you should create a script to automate the process, including assigning an appropriate (and unique) filename to each exported file.

> **NOTE** In one particular case, you can't export container contents directly to a file using the Export Field Contents command: when container data has been pasted from the clipboard and is not in a supported file format.
>
> In this case, you can copy and paste the contents into a graphics application where you are able to select a suitable file format to save it, or, if you prefer, you can use a third-party plug-in in conjunction with FileMaker to automate the process.

Chapter 13 describes methods for scripting export or selective import of container field data, including details of scripts for accomplishing each of these tasks and also briefly covers the ability to import an entire folder of files. To commence this process, choose File ➪ Import ➪ Folder. You select the options for folder import, including text files, pictures, or movie files, from the Folder of Files Import Options dialog shown in Figure 17.7.

FIGURE 17.7

Selection options for a folder import.

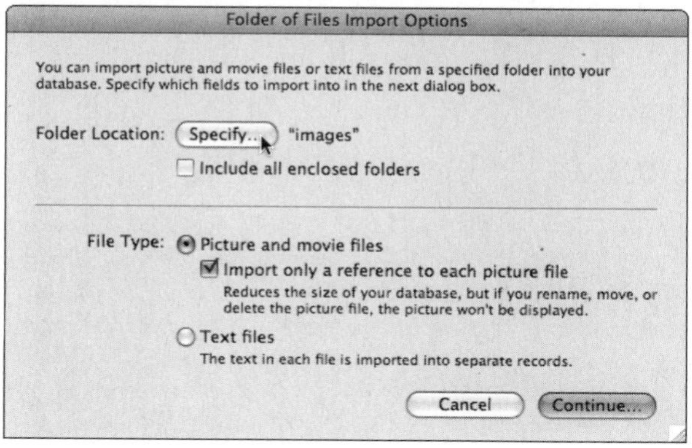

After you select an appropriate folder (one that contains files of the selected type), you're then prompted to select up to four values for import. As shown in Figure 17.8, you can simultaneously import the file (into a container field), the filename and file path (into a text field), and a thumbnail image (also into a container). When importing text files, only the first three of these options are available.

When your data includes both text and files, you may require separate processes to bring both types of data into FileMaker from other data formats. However, you can script both processes, if desired, even managing them sequentially within a single script.

Setting the import field map to upload a folder of picture files into FileMaker.

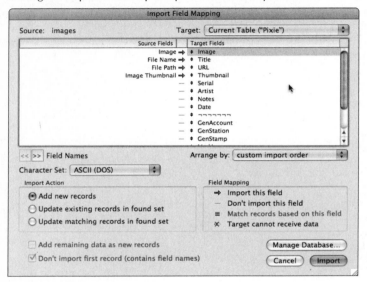

Delimiters and EOL markers

Most data formats represent each record as a separate line or paragraph of text, containing one or multiple field values. The field values within each line are separated by a character or sequence of characters, referred to as *delimiters*. For example, a tab delimited file has tab characters separating field values within each record and carriage returns marking each end-of-line (EOL), which separates each record from the next.

So what happens when carriage returns or tab characters appear in a field in your FileMaker data? FileMaker solves this dilemma for you:

- Carriage returns within fields are converted to vertical tab characters (ASCII character number 11) in the exported data. This conversion takes place automatically when you use the Export Records command in FileMaker.

- Tab characters within fields are converted to standard spaces (ASCII character number 32) when you choose the tab-delimited text export format. When you choose other formats where tabs are not treated as delimiters, such as in comma-separated values (CSV), the tab characters are preserved in your export output.

You should consider your data content when choosing your export formats. In other words, if your data includes tab characters, the tab-separated export format is less suitable than others because your tab characters are translated to spaces during the import. Fortunately, FileMaker Pro 10 provides eight different export file formats, letting you find a suitable way of preserving your data in most cases.

CROSS-REF Import and export options and procedures are addressed in detail in Chapters 3 and 13.

Data Cleansing Operations

Exporting and importing data is a relatively straightforward task if the data is clean and well formed, and you're either transferring data between two systems using identical data structures or have control over both the applications (so that you can make changes to facilitate data transfer).

In situations where the data has integrity issues or isn't compatible with the required format or structure, you face an additional challenge: You have to transform the data as part of the data transfer procedure.

Extract, transform, and load

The process of modifying data to correct formation and structural issues or mismatches is called an *Extract, Transform, and Load* (ETL) cycle and is especially important when migrating data between different kinds of systems. For example, when you need to load data into a data-warehousing or external-reporting tool, you invariably require a modified organizational format and possibly require individual values in a data format specific to the destination system. Similarly, migrating data between a legacy database system and a new solution environment necessitates converting data to the structure and format required by the new system.

You may also require an ETL cycle if your data has been subject to abuse or system malfunction and must be retrieved from a damaged solution file (such as a recovered file). After extraction from a damaged file, you should perform checks and cleansing procedures on the data prior to loading it into a clean reference copy (clone) of your solution.

Depending on the nature of transformation and/or data cleansing required, you may want to build a rapid FileMaker transformation tool. To do so, first drag the extracted file onto the FileMaker application icon to create a temporary database file containing the migratory data. Within the temporary file, you can then build scripts and calculations to correct issues with the data, combine groups of data together, separate concatenated values, remove unwanted characters, and eliminate unneeded duplicates. Your FileMaker calculation and scripting skills will get a thorough workout!

Data format considerations

Data organization, data presentation, and data domain are three aspects of data formation you should consider separately during the transformation process — each requiring a different set of skills and strategies to successfully update your data.

Data organization

First and foremost, your data must be aligned with the receiving application's data model. This alignment includes an appropriate delineation of data elements to conform to the entity/table definitions and the data model used in your data's new home. Moreover, within grouped records, you may require a different distribution of attributes. For example, when migrating data from a legacy database, you may find the extracted data has a single field for address, whereas the destination data model may require street address, city, state, and postal code each in a separate field. The legacy system's address data must be parsed during the transformation stage — using appropriate calculation techniques — to separate the original single address value into the required four (or more) values to match the requirements of the receiving system.

Other aspects of the data organization challenge may include

- Eliminating redundant or duplicated data
- Allocating appropriate unique key values
- Establishing metadata or summary data if required
- Setting a suitable sort order for the records in each data subset

As part of the data organization procedure, you should also prepare a basic inventory of available data so that you can confirm the transfer's success. This inventory may be as simple as the number of data subsets (tables), the number of fields in each subset, and the record count of each subset. If the data will include null values, a count of nulls per subset (including null rows, null columns, and individual null values per table) is also a useful check.

Data presentation

The foremost data presentation issue relates to the receiving system's data type requirements. If your data currently includes alphabetic characters in attribute data required to be numeric, you need to either eliminate or substitute values to meet the presentation requirements. Similarly, you should pay attention to the strings used to express date and/or time values. For example, if your legacy system has produced date columns in dd/mm/yy presentation format and the destination solution is configured to receive mm/dd/yyyy dates, your transformation stage must modify all the dates to conform to the latter requirement. You can make such a change in a FileMaker transformation tool by running a `Replace Field Contents [ ]` on the data as text, using a formula such as

```
Let([
txt = Substitute(TransformationTool::LegacyDate_ddmmyy; "/"; " ");
mm = MiddleWords(txt; 2; 1);
dd = LeftWords(txt; 1);
yy = RightWords(txt; 1);
yyyy = (19 + (GetAsNumber(yy) <= 50)) & yy];
mm & "/" & dd & "/" & yyyy
)
```

CAUTION This calculation deals with conversion of the two-digit years to four-digit years by placing all years less than 50 (00 through 50) into the 21st century and dates with year values above 50 into the 20th century. This conversion is likely to be appropriate for transaction dates or budget projection dates, but may be inappropriate for dates of birth or other historical data (which may include dates prior to 1951, but will not include dates in the future).

An alternative form of the date text transformation calculation suitable for dates including only past values (such as date-of-birth data) is

```
Let([
txt = Substitute(TransformationTool::LegacyDate_ddmmyy; "/"; " ");
mm = MiddleWords(txt; 2; 1);
dd = LeftWords(txt; 1);
yy = RightWords(txt; 1);
yyyy = (19 + ((2000 + yy) <= Year(Get(CurrentDate)))) & yy];
mm & "/" & dd & "/" & yyyy
)
```

By varying your approach according to the needs of each data element, you can automate the transformation of large sets of data to efficiently address each data presentation issue.

A further dimension of data presentation relates to the data format itself — the delimiter and end-of-line characters determined by the export and import formats. In cases where you need to prepare data for upload into a system not supporting any of the standard export formats provided by FileMaker, you may need to use text calculation operations to generate data using different delimiters, such as pipe characters or square brackets. Again, you can accomplish this task with relative ease by using text calculations in a temporary transformation tool.

Data domain

Data transformation considerations also encompass confirming that your data falls within acceptable ranges, both with respect to the characters occurring within the data, and the range of values occurring across all instances of fields, cells, or attributes within each data set or subset. This transformation involves addressing several specific requirements:

- Establishing that the range of values in each field is within the range of values supported for the field in the destination solution — for example, within the permissible numeric or date range, or for text, within the character limit (if any) of the destination field

- Ensuring that the data is appropriately current — in other words, if the data includes records due for archiving due to a long period of inactivity, they should be segregated during transformation

- Eliminating redundant or inappropriate characters from data, including leading or trailing spaces or carriage returns, superfluous punctuation, or characters outside the required or approved character set (such as low or high ASCII characters not forming part of the language of the data)

> **TIP** Although you can perform a variety of transformation operations within FileMaker, if you have extensive requirements, consider using a special-purpose external data cleansing application.

The transformation stages do have some overlap, and some data problems may relate to more than one stage. For example, extraneous characters included in a date or number field are a data presentation problem, because the affected field values do not conform to data type requirements of the destination system. However, these cases should also be regarded as data domain problems, as the characters are also out of range and redundant.

You ensure that key data integrity, structure, and content issues are not overlooked by considering and addressing each of the transformation stages.

Filtering capabilities in FileMaker

FileMaker is very forgiving regarding what is stored in the fields of your database. Field validation and data type constraints aside, you can store any string of characters from the vast compendium of the Unicode character set. However, in practice, you'll likely require a considerably narrower scope, and in many solutions, you can define the permissible character set to include no more than a few hundred characters.

The presence of out-of-range characters may present several problems for your solution. Most fundamentally, it compromises your data's meaning and may lead to calculations producing unexpected results. In particular, low-range characters (generally referred to as *control characters* — those in the range from 0 to 31) are frequently invisible, and their presence leads to confusion at the very least. For example, take a calculation including the following expression:

```
If(Deliveries::DestinationState = "Utah"; Amount * TaxRate; Amount)
```

Your users will be concerned if they can see "Utah" in the `DestinationState` field, but the state tax has not been included. However, the presence of an invisible control character (an ASCII #011, a.k.a. DC1) on one end of the value in the field prevents it from matching the literal comparison value in the calculation expression.

The concept of invisible characters seems contradictory. Although you may not be familiar with all the control characters supported in the ASCII and Unicode character sets, you have probably encountered programs, such as word processors, that include the ability to *show invisible characters*. Invisible characters include tabs, carriage returns, line feeds, and numerous other characters serving as instructions or placemarkers. While tabs and carriage returns are standard fare, most control characters have no place in your solution's data, yet the fact that they're invisible can make them difficult to detect and remove.

> **TIP** Rarely are invisible characters entered from the keyboard, but users may paste them in inadvertently, having copied text from another application or (more commonly) from a Web site. You can also import out-of-range characters into your solution if data has not undergone appropriate cleansing transformations prior to import.

Provided you can determine an "approved" character set for use in your solution, the most straightforward way to reject undesired characters is via the use of the `Filter( )` function. For example, to constrain a field to contain only characters suitable for numeric values (integers and decimal fractions), you can use a calculation with the expression

```
Filter(YourTable::YourField; "0123456789,.")
```

 If the values you're filtering may include negative numbers or numbers in scientific notation, you should include both the characters e and – within your filter string.

NOTE This filter only removes invalid characters from the field and does nothing to validate that the resulting string is a valid numeric representation. For example, it doesn't verify that only one decimal point is present or that the comma separators are appropriately placed.

If you apply such a formula as an Auto-Entry calculation (replaces existing), the field automatically rejects out-of-range characters. Similarly, to constrain a text field to include only alphanumeric characters, spaces, and hyphens, you can use the calculation formula

```
Filter(YourTable::YourTextField;
    "0123456789ABCDEFGHIJKLMNOPQRSTUVWXYZabcdefghijklmnopqrstuvwxyz -")
```

When you use calculation expressions such as the preceding ones as an argument within the `Replace Field Contents [ ]` command, you can efficiently constrain the character set across significant numbers of records. The use of filters (along with selective substitution in cases where the permitted character set is too large to be readily defined or included in a Filter calculation) forms an essential part of data cleansing and transformation processes.

NOTE Alphanumeric value filtering using the 64 characters shown in the preceding example is suitable only for limited cases. In many circumstances, you'll want to include a considerably larger range of characters (including punctuation, accented characters, glyphs, and so on).

Synchronizing Data Sets

As part of the process of managing data in your solutions, you may have call to synchronize disparate data sets in separate copies of the same solution (or in comparable solutions). For example, when your main database resides on the server at your office, and you go on offline field visits, taking a copy on your laptop (modifying records and adding new records as you go), a problem of synchronization of the two record sets (the server database and the laptop database) arises. On your return, you need to load the added and edited work from your laptop into the main solution file, but without deleting new records added by your colleagues while you were gone.

An important feature of the import and export functionality in FileMaker is that it acts on the found set of records in the frontmost window showing a layout based on the Table Occurrence from which you're importing. To import only the new records you added while on your field trip:

1. Copy the file from your laptop onto a client machine logged in to the main copy of your solution.

2. Open the field copy and perform a Find to locate the records you added while on your trip. One way to locate the added records is to perform your search on the record creation timestamp field in your table.

3. With the found set of new records still showing in the window of the field copy, switch to the main solution.

4. Perform an import in the main copy of the solution, importing records from the field copy.

5. Only the new records (those in the current found set in the field copy of the file) are added to the main solution.

> **CAUTION** When consolidating records from different copies of a solution file, take care to ensure that you're not introducing duplicate primary key values (for example, serial numbers).

> To avoid duplication of key values, consider allocating separate ranges of serial numbers to each copy of the file or try generating unique IDs using a combination of timestamp, NIC address, and recordID values.

> **CROSS-REF** Chapter 15 covers methods of generating robust unique IDs (UIDs).

If your work while traveling offline with your laptop also involved editing some of the pre-existing records originating in the main solution, you'll need to use a different process to upload modified records as well as new additions. Import matching allows you to merge records from the original and secondary copies of the file into a single data set.

> **NOTE** When merging data sets as described here, the incoming data is given preference, overwriting corresponding data (if any) in the receiving file. If you require a more finely tuned synchronization process (such as one that retains the most recently modified version of each record), you need to build an intermediary transformation process to compare the data in both sets and selectively update either or both files.

Import matching

To match records while importing, select the file for import via the normal import process (choose File ➪ Import Records ➪ File) and proceed to the Import Field Mapping dialog. As well as ensuring that the fields shown in the current table at the upper right align appropriately with the data in the column at the upper left area, select the Update Matching Records in Found Set option in the panel at the lower left, as shown in Figure 17.9.

> **NOTE** Assuming that the source and destination are both FileMaker files and the source and destination table structures are the same, you should select the Matching Names option from the Arrange By pop-up list in the Import Field Mapping dialog.

For synchronization during import, FileMaker provides you with two options, as represented by the Update Existing Records in Found Set and Update Matching Records in Found Set options appearing in the lower left area of the dialog, as shown in Figure 17.9.

When you choose the Update Existing Records in Found Set option, the selected fields in records in the found set are overwritten with values from corresponding (according to sort order) records in the source table. Alternatively, when you select the Update Matching Records in Found Set option, you can identify one or more match fields to synchronize existing records in the current table with corresponding records in the source. With this option selected, you choose the match ("=") symbol adjacent to the relevant fields in the import order list, as shown beside the ItemID field (the selected field) in Figure 17.9.

CAUTION When determining match fields for an Update Matching Records in Found Set import, take care to ensure that the field (or combination of fields) you choose will be unique. If more than one match is found, the subsequent matches will overwrite data imported from previous matches, resulting in the last match in the source file determining the final value for a record in the current file.

FIGURE 17.9

Setting the import field map to update modified records.

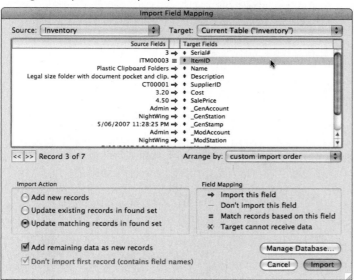

When performing an update import process, you can select the checkbox option to add remaining data as new records. Note, however, that if you're updating the values in a subset of fields in the current table (as determined by your configuration of the import field map), only the selected values (and match values, if any) are imported into the resulting new records.

> **NOTE**   If you require additional fields uploaded for the records added in an Update import, you should isolate the new records in a reduced found set after the import completes and then run a second import using the Update Matching Records in Found Set option to populate the remaining fields in the new records.

Importing selectively

To import selectively, one option is to open both the source and target files and perform a find in either or both files and then run an Update Records in Found Set import. Providing the file containing the source table is open and is showing the required found set in its frontmost window, only the found records are included in the import. (Otherwise, all records in the source table are imported.)

In cases where data synchronization requires the application of more complex criteria than you can address by performing a find in either or both files prior to import, such as when you need to compare the values in corresponding records in both data sets to determine whether to import values from a given record, you'll require a custom synchronization process. Custom synchronization requires one of the following:

- One file is defined as an external data source for the other so that a relationship between the source and target tables can be established (and a script can then loop through records comparing them and selectively transferring values in either direction).

- A utility table is created in one of the files as a temporary holding place for data from the source file. Selected records can then be imported into the utility table, and a post-processing script can perform the required comparisons and selective transfers prior to deleting the records from the utility table.

- An external control file is created with the source and target files defined as external data sources and containing the logic for comparison and selective transfer of data between one or more tables in the two original files.

The use of a control process, as described in the first and last options, is powerful and flexible, giving you the option to

- Selectively transfer data in both directions, achieving two-way synchronization of data between tables in two files

- Efficiently synchronize data between systems with different data structures, where some data transformation and/or cleansing is required as part of the procedure

- Selectively transfer records from tables in other supported database environments, such as external SQL data sources

The utility table method described in the second option introduces additional processing time, because external data must first be imported and then separately reconciled. However, the absence of calculations, Auto-Entry actions, or validations (and minimization of the use of indexes) in the utility table enables the initial import to proceed efficiently. Moreover, this method's added flexibility lets you build synchronization procedures for data extracted or exported from a wide variety of sources, including unsupported mobile databases, spreadsheets, online sources, and third-party data systems.

Handling Embedded Images and Stored Files

The container fields in FileMaker Pro can store a wide variety of files containing text, images, or other media content. A significant number of files of this kind, however, will add to the bulk of your solution file(s), impacting performance, making backups and other procedures slower, and complicating some data transfer procedures. (Keep in mind that container fields can't be exported directly, as noted in the "Exporting and Importing Data" section, earlier in this chapter.)

One option to consider if your solution is carrying a significant quantity of container data is to place container fields into tables in separate files, defining those files as external data sources and creating 1:1 relationships from your existing tables to the tables housing container data. This approach enables you to back up your data more efficiently by setting a different backup schedule for the file(s) containing large quantities of container content.

Another option FileMaker provides is external storage of container objects, where you instruct FileMaker to store only a reference to the file (for example, the path to the file's location on your computer or an accessible volume such as a file server). For example, when inserting a picture into a container field in Browse Mode by choosing Insert ⇨ Picture, the resulting dialog, shown at the lower left of the dialog in Figure 17.10, includes a checkbox option to Store Only a Reference to the File. This option is also available when using script or button commands to insert a file into a container.

Storing a reference to a file, rather than storing the file itself, has both advantages and disadvantages. Among the advantages:

- You can access or update the files independently of FileMaker.
- The references don't cause your database files to bloat with their extra content.
- You can back up the files separately from your database backups.

Among the disadvantages:

- The path to the files must be the same from all client workstations if the files are to be accessible by multiple users when your solution is hosted.
- Your solution may break (or its content may no longer make sense or be complete) if the files are moved, renamed, or deleted.

You are, however, able to choose the most convenient method of storage depending on your priorities and the deployment considerations for your solution. Among other things, the ability to choose the storage mode can lead to

- Some containers being stored in the database and others stored only as a reference
- Changes of circumstance wherein you need container contents stored via the alternate method

FIGURE 17.10

The Insert Picture dialog, showing the Store Only a Reference to the file setting.

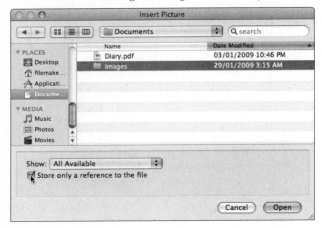

Fortunately, the decisions you make aren't final; the means are available to convert container fields (individually, or as a batch) between the two modes of storage.

Assigning and retrieving paths

When a file has been stored (embedded) in a container field using the Insert menu commands (or an equivalent script or button command), you can ascertain the file's name by passing the container field's name to the GetAsText ( ) function. Similarly, if a file is stored as a reference in a container field, you can retrieve the path to the file (along with other information about the file, if available) by the same method.

When you script the insertion of a file into a container field, you can use a variable to supply the path, as described in Chapter 13. Additionally, when you set a valid path to a file (as text) into a container field, FileMaker stores the reference and displays the file (or its icon) in the container.

By exploiting the capabilities of the GetAsText ( ) function and the Set Variable[ ] command, you can build scripts to control the storage state of container fields.

Scripted field updates

A script along the following lines toggles the storage state of a container field used to store image files between embedded images and store-as-reference images:

```
If [IsEmpty(Products::Image)]
  Beep
Else If [PatternCount(GetAsText(Products::Image); "image:")]
  #Container is stored as path. Embed image:
```

```
Set Variable [$Path; Value:Let([
                      pf = GetAsText(Products::Image);
                      p1 = Position(pf; "image:"; 1; 1);
                      p2 = Position(pf & ¶; ¶; p1; 1) — p1];
                      Middle(pf; p1; p2)
                      )]
    Go to Field [Products::ProductImage]
    Insert Picture ["$Path"]
Else
    #Image is embedded: Store as path
    Set Variable [$Path; Value:"file:images/" & GetAsText(Products::Image)]
    Export Field Contents [Products::Image; "$Path"]
    Set Field [Products::Image; "image" & Right($Path; Length($Path) — 4) ]
End If
```

> **TIP** You can readily adapt the scripting techniques used in the preceding script to pro-
> duce a script that loops through the found set — or all records in the current table —
> converting the contents of a container field between embedded and stored-as-reference storage
> modes.

Text-Handling Considerations

In this chapter, I provide you with strategies and techniques for dealing with a broad range of data migration, transformation, and synchronization challenges. However, another issue deserves special mention. When presenting data in a range of export formats, FileMaker uses the standard convention of including a carriage-return character (ASCII character 13) as the delimiter between successive records in the exported data. Consequently, carriage returns appearing within fields in your data are substituted with alternate characters (ASCII character 11) in the exported data. This substitution presents a challenge when situations arise requiring that exported data include the original carriage-return characters.

Export field contents

One way to solve the problem of ensuring carriage returns will be preserved in text output from your database is to gather content for export, such as data from multiple records, into a single text field, including carriage returns as required. You can then output the text field's complete contents — with carriage returns in place — using the Export Field Contents[ ] script command.

You can employ this technique to script a custom export process to build a text report document containing lines of text and carriage returns in configurations outside the normal constraints of the FileMaker export formats. For example, if you're required to export the contents of a series of Description fields in a Products table as continuous text, including any carriage returns residing within the text in the field, you do so by creating a global text field (for example, Products::gExportText) and a script along the following lines:

```
Set Error Capture [On]
Perform Find [Restore]
If [Get(LastError) ≠ 0]
  Beep
  Exit Script []
End If
Go to Record/Request/Page [First]
Set Field [Products::gExportText; ""]
Loop
  Set Field [Products::gExportText; Products::gExportText & If(not
          IsEmpty(Products::Description); ¶ & Products::Description)]
  Go to Record/Request/Page [Next; Exit after last]
End Loop
If [not IsEmpty(Products::gExportText)]
  Set Variable [$path; Value:"Products_" & Year(Get(CurrentDate)) & Right("0" &
          Month(Get(CurrentDate)); 2) & Right("0" & Day(Get(CurrentDate)); 2)
          & ".txt"]
  Export Field Contents [Products::gExportText; "$path"; Automatically open]
  Set Field [Products::gExportText; ""]
End If
```

After running this script, you have a text file containing the description field entries with their carriage returns preserved, providing there are records meeting the criteria you specified for the Perform Find [Restore] command, and the Products::Description has text in it on one or more of the found records.

Designing a custom export process

The process of passing data first into a global text field and exporting from there provides you with, in effect, a customized export where you gain increased control over the resulting file's form and content. By extension, you can use this process to build export files employing custom delimiters and to perform a variety of other procedures on the data — substitutions, character filtering, and so on — before exporting to the external file.

If you need still greater control over the export process, I recommend that you create a transformation utility within your solution. To create this utility, create a Transformations table where your scripts can create records (for example, via a relationship from the source table for the export, set to Allow Creation of Related Records). In this way, you can create Transformations table records for export in whatever form is required, applying calculations to the content to combine or separate data, or to address data presentation or domain requirements.

Once the transformation process is complete, your script can either export the transformed data directly from the Transformations table or perform further processing by compiling output content in a global field as described in the "Export field contents" section, earlier in this chapter. By combining these techniques, you can attain a high degree of control over the resulting data export, generating data in whatever form circumstances may require.

Part V

Raising the Bar

As a mature application development environment, FileMaker provides open ended scope for the creation of commercial and professional solutions to serve the needs of a wide variety of industry, business, and organizational requirements. To provide the necessary flexibility, FileMaker provides open ended capabilities for integration with third-party applications and utilities, as well as a number of built-in options for extending and refining the operation of your solutions.

In this fifth part of the book, I give you a tour of the additional capabilities that FileMaker Pro 10 Advanced provides, with its custom menus, custom functions, design reporting, runtime applications, and more. I also offer insight into the art of designing your solutions for elegance and streamlined simplicity, and I survey available options for extending your solutions' reach with external scripting, third-party plug-ins, and available Web-deployment options. In addition, this part includes pointers to some of the available third-party tools that will assist you to diagnose problems and maintain the health of your solutions.

IN THIS PART

Chapter 18
FileMaker Pro Advanced Features

Chapter 19
Efficient Code, Efficient Solutions

Chapter 20
Extending FileMaker's Capabilities

Chapter 18

FileMaker Pro Advanced Features

I f you're reading this chapter, I figure the fact that you're here means you're serious, right? When the going gets tough, FileMaker developers' reach for FileMaker Pro Advanced, an extended version that does everything FileMaker Pro can do, with a host of powerful additions.

FileMaker Pro Advanced makes things easier, giving you professional tools to debug and document your code. By itself, this benefit may be reason enough to pawn your second computer and buy a copy, but FileMaker Pro Advanced offers you several other powerful features.

In this chapter, I walk you through what I consider the key features of this leading-edge FileMaker Pro version, giving you insights into where your development can take you when you become an Advanced developer.

Script Debugger

Scripts run at blinding speed, doing their thing. When they work, it's a bit magical, but when your scripts don't do what you expect them to do, figuring out the cause can be quite a challenge. To help, FileMaker Advanced provides a Script Debugger that lets you step through your script one line at a time, watching what happens, and checking for errors.

Choosing Tools ➪ Script Debugger prior to running a script activates the Script Debugger. While the Script Debugger is active, its window "floats" over your solution's windows. When you run a script, the text of the script appears in the Debugger window, as shown in Figure 18.1.

IN THIS CHAPTER

Employing the Script Debugger

Making use of the Data Viewer

Documenting solutions with the Database Design Report

Building and controlling custom menus

Working with custom functions

Understanding custom functions and recursion

Distributing solutions as runtime applications

FIGURE 18.1

Viewing the Show Transaction script (from the `Inventory` example file) in the Script Debugger.

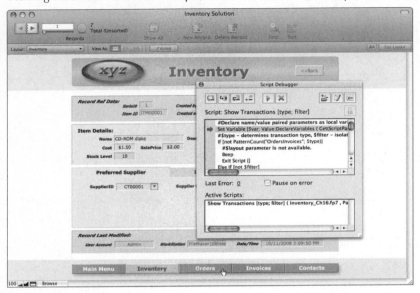

Watching code in action

Along the top of the Script Debugger window are ten buttons and immediately below them the definition of the current script appears, with the current step highlighted. Below the script pane, the Last Error code is displayed. Most of the time when using the Debugger, you'll be stepping through a script using one of the two buttons nearest the left along the top of the Script Debugger window (Step Over and Step Into), while checking the effect on your solution and noting the error code at each step.

Even if your script isn't malfunctioning, stepping through it with the Script Debugger activated enables you to better understand how FileMaker scripting works and how to improve your script's code and make it more fault tolerant.

When your script calls other scripts (via the `Perform Script [ ]` command), the Script Debugger displays the stack of active scripts in the pane at the bottom, allowing you to select and review any script in the stack.

 You can double-click any script listed in the Active Scripts pane to open it for editing in a corresponding Edit Script window.

Debugging restricted privilege scripts

An important feature of the FileMaker Pro 10 Advanced Script Debugger and Data Viewer is the ability to separately authenticate the Debugger so that you can view and debug a script while logged in with a privilege set that doesn't have edit access to the script.

To authenticate the Data Viewer for debugging while in restricted privilege access accounts, click the button with the padlock symbol at the upper right of the Current tab. In the authentication dialog that appears, enter a [Full Access] account and password. When you do, the access account and privileges for your current database session are unchanged, but the Data Viewer and Script Debugger nevertheless admit you "behind the scenes" to see what is going on.

After authenticating with [Full Access] credentials, the padlock icon shows in its unlocked state, and the Script Debugger and the Current tab of the Data Viewer both provide an unfettered view of the workings of your solution. Clicking the padlock icon again, however, concludes the authentication session, requiring you to re-authenticate to view scripts and data values in the Debugger and the Data Viewer's current tab.

> **NOTE** Authentication applies to the Data Viewer (see next topic) as well as the Script Debugger. If you authenticate in one, the authentication provides coverage of the other as well, and if you de-authenticate in one, the de-authentication also applies to both.

Getting used to the Debugger controls

The buttons along the top of the Script Debugger (see Figure 18.2) take a little getting used to, mainly because they're adorned by rather obscure icons and aren't labeled. They do, however, have tooltips you can view by holding the mouse over them for a few seconds so that you aren't totally in the dark.

The buttons along the top of the Script Debugger window operate as follows:

- **Step Over:** Advances through the current script one line at a time, without stepping into (debugging) any sub-scripts.

- **Step Into:** Advances through the current script sequence line-by-line, stepping into and debugging any sub-scripts encountered as it goes.

- **Step Out:** Ceases debugging the current script or sub-script, allowing it to run normally until its conclusion. (If you're debugging a sub-script, you'll be returned to the parent script at the line after the `Perform Script [ ]` command calling the sub-script.) However, if the current script includes breakpoints, the Step Out button causes it to run until the next breakpoint is reached.

- **Set Next Step:** Allows you to designate a selected step as the next step to execute. Using this control lets you modify the execution sequence while debugging, either skipping over steps or repeating steps.

- **Run/Pause:** Sets the script running until the next break point (if any) or until its conclusion.

- **Halt Script:** Cancels all active scripts, regardless of state at the current step, and exits the Script Debugger.

- **Set/Clear Breakpoint:** Adds or removes a marker (appearing as a red tag at the left) on the currently selected script step. When a breakpoint has been set, you can use the Run/Pause button to run the script through to the next breakpoint. (It will pause automatically when it reaches the tagged step.) You can also add or modify breakpoints in the Edit Script window by clicking in the gray band to the left of the script pane or at the left of the Script Debugger window in FileMaker Pro Advanced.

FIGURE 18.2

The main controls of the Script Debugger.

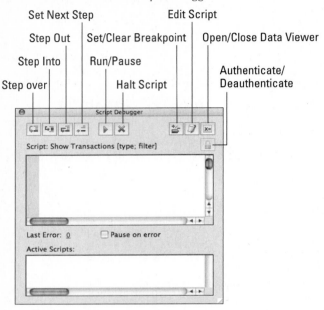

- **Edit Script:** Opens the current script for editing or viewing in its Edit Script window. The current step of the script will be automatically pre-selected in the script when it opens for editing. When you are logged in with a restricted access account and have authenticated with [Full Access] privileges, the Edit Script button allows you to use the higher privilege status to directly access a running script in its Edit Script window and make changes to it.

- **Open/Close Data Viewer:** Displays or hides the Data Viewer window, allowing you to see the values of fields, variables, or calculations as the script progresses.

 Closing the Script Debugger does not halt execution of the active scripts. Instead, it sets them in motion for the remainder of their run without the Debugger.

In addition, below the main script pane, the Script Debugger in FileMaker Pro 10 Advanced includes a checkbox option for Pause on Error. With this option enabled, running the script, either by clicking the Run/Pause button or closing the Script Debugger, results in the script pausing when an error code other than zero is encountered. If the Script Debugger has been closed, it reopens when an error is encountered. When the Script Debugger reopens following an error, it does so with the step following the one that produced the error selected as the current step (even if the next step is in a different script from the one that produced the error — which can occur if the error occurred on the final step of a sub-script). However, if an error occurs on the final step of a script sequence, the Script Debugger will not reopen.

Data Viewer

The FileMaker Pro 10 Advanced Data Viewer lets you see your calculation results without having to add them to your solution or place them on a layout. You can test ideas — and get the calculation syntax right — by trying them out in the Data Viewer before adding them to your scripts or field definitions. Moreover, you can keep an eye on the values of variables and an assortment of application or system parameters, by adding calculations using selected Get ( ) functions to the Data Viewer.

You can access the Data Viewer — whether a script is running or not — by choosing Tools ➪ Data Viewer. As with the Script Debugger, the Data Viewer window permanently floats above other windows (with the exception the Script Debugger window), as shown in Figure 18.3.

FIGURE 18.3

Viewing the Data Viewer window floating over a solution window.

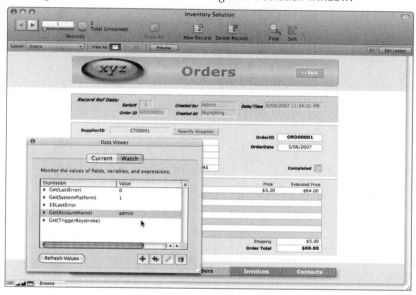

You can close and reopen the Data Viewer window at any time (except when viewing a modal dialog), and it will retain the calculations or values you manually added to it.

Current and Watch panels

The Data Viewer in FileMaker Pro 10 Advanced includes two tab panels, one automatically displaying variables in use and values referenced in the active script and the other enabling you to create calculations and monitor their results regardless of the current script context.

You can switch between the Current and Watch panels whenever the Data Viewer is open, providing you with access to two complementary modes of operation.

The Current panel

Values tracked on the Data Viewer's Current panel update automatically to include current global variables (if no script is running) and current local and global variables (if a script is active). Moreover, when a script is in progress, fields referenced by the script are automatically added to the Current panel. As a script commences its run in the Script Debugger, the Data Viewer's Current panel performs a "pre-flight load" of all fields (including fields referred to by calculations) referenced by the script.

The Current panel is always available when you're logged in with an account that's assigned [Full Access] privileges. At other times, you're required to authenticate within the Data Viewer, as shown in Figure 18.4, to access the Current panel's display.

FIGURE 18.4

The Current panel requires authentication when you're logged in with a restricted access account.

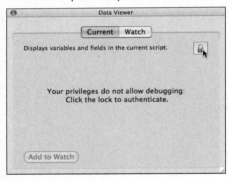

Authenticating with a [Full Access] account in the Data Viewer applies only to the Data Viewer and the Script Debugger in the current file; it has no effect on the login account for the rest of the file. If you have multiple files open with accounts assigned to restricted access privilege sets, you'll need to authenticate the Data Viewer separately in each file in order to see script values in the Current panel in all the open files.

When you hold the mouse pointer over a selected line in the Current panel, a tooltip appears showing the result in its entirety. This tooltip is useful when the result is too long to appear fully in the limited space of the Value column — and especially if the value has multiple lines, as shown in Figure 18.5.

In addition, you can view a line's values — and in the case of variables, directly edit them — by double-clicking the line in the Current panel. FileMaker displays the value in its entirety in a scrollable list in the Current Value dialog, as shown in Figure 18.6.

The Current Value dialog is resizable, so you can use it to display long values without truncation. Moreover, you can select values in the Current Value dialog and copy them to the clipboard. However, you can use the other enabled Edit menu commands (Paste Cut and Clear) only to perform actions on variable values.

Where referenced fields have repetitions, the repetitions containing a value are loaded into the Data Viewer's Current panel. Repetitions (for either fields or variables) are shown in the Data Viewer using array notation, such as YourField[3] for the third repetition of YourField.

FIGURE 18.5

The Current panel hover technique reveals long or multi-line viewer values.

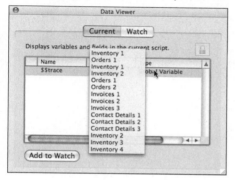

FIGURE 18.6

Viewing or editing a variable value in the Current Value dialog.

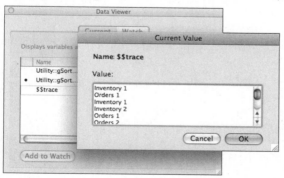

> **NOTE** You can copy fields or variables appearing in the Data Viewer's Current panel to the Watch panel by selecting them and clicking the Add to Watch button at the lower left of the Current panel.

The Watch panel

The Data Viewer's Watch panel lets you specify calculation expressions and tracks their evaluation in the Value column, as shown in Figure 18.7.

The controls at the lower right of the Watch panel of the Data Viewer are as follows:

- **Add Expression:** Brings up an Edit Expression dialog (a variant of the Specify Calculation dialog) where you can enter a field, variable, or calculation formula to be monitored in the Watch panel.

- **Duplicate Expression:** Creates a copy of the selected expression (or expressions) in the list area of the Watch panel.

- **Edit Expression:** Opens the Edit Expression dialog for the currently selected expression in the Watch panel, allowing you to view a long calculation expression or copy or revise it. Double-clicking an expression is an alternative way to open the Edit Expression dialog.

- **Remove Expression:** Deletes the currently selected line (or lines) from the Watch panel.

FIGURE 18.7

The controls of the Data Viewer's Watch panel.

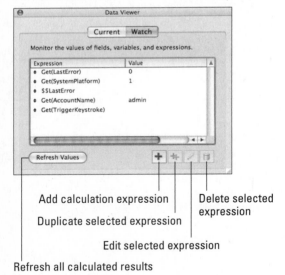

The values you enter into the Watch panel are retained until you delete them. They're not specific to the current file or files set, but apply to all files opened in the current copy of FileMaker Pro Advanced. However, expressions in the Watch panel are evaluated in the current context — so if they refer to fields in your solution, they only produce valid/meaningful results while those fields remain accessible.

 **You can sort either of the columns of the Data Viewer (in the Current panel as well as the Watch panel) by clicking the corresponding column heading.**

Using the Viewer with the Debugger

You can use the Data Viewer as a stand-alone feature by choosing it from the Tools ⇨ Data Viewer. However, the Data Viewer is an invaluable adjunct to the Script Debugger, enhancing your ability to observe the results of scripts as you advance through them one step at a time. You can invoke or dismiss the Data Viewer from within the Script Debugger window by clicking the Open/Close Data Viewer button (bearing the "X=" symbol) in the upper right corner of the Script Debugger window.

In particular, the Current panel automatically monitors the values of all the current variables and all fields referenced by the current script. Each value is updated with every line of the script as you step through it in the Debugger window.

 **Global variables are listed in the Current panel while you're debugging a script, whether or not the current script references them.**

The Data Viewer sand box

While the Data Viewer is a powerful adjunct to the Script Debugger, it has a variety of other uses in its own right. It is a very useful environment for building calculation expressions for use in your solution — either in scripts or field definitions — because it allows you to test the expression and view its result as you're writing it. In this way, the Data Viewer enables you to debug your calculation code in a safe sand-pit environment, copying the final expression and pasting it into your solution when you're satisfied with the result.

The Data Viewer's Edit Expression dialog, shown in Figure 18.8, includes a Result box below the Expression box, where the current expression's result appears when you click the Evaluate Now button.

NOTE When you enter references to your solution's field and table occurrence structures into the Data Viewer via the Edit Expression dialog, FileMaker evaluates the references from the context of the current record and layout showing in the frontmost window of the active file.

FIGURE 18.8

The Edit Expression dialog accessible from the Watch panel of the Data Viewer.

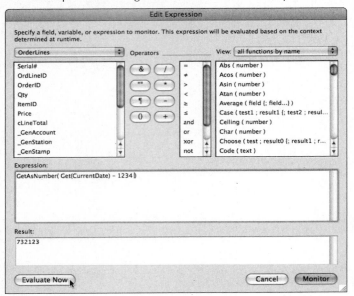

The Data Viewer and variables

The Data Viewer is a convenient way to view the values assigned to variables in your solution, enabling you to keep track of their changing values as you test your scripts and calculations. Additionally, you can use the Data Viewer to modify a variable's value, either by editing it directly in the Current panel or by including it in a Let ( ) expression in the Edit Expression dialog.

Bear in mind that anyone with a copy of FileMaker Pro Advanced can access the Data Viewer's Watch panel, even without a [Full Access] login, and can therefore modify the values assigned to variables in your solution. Keep in mind the following caveats regarding variables:

- Global variables are unsuitable for holding or handling sensitive or confidential information, including passwords, because a user who guesses the name of the variable can access its value using the Data Viewer (if they open your solution using a copy of FileMaker Pro Advanced).

- Variables aren't suitable for the storage of essential values your solution (and particularly your solution's security) depends upon because they can be edited directly by users who have access to the Data Viewer.

Concerns about the security of variable values with respect to the Data Viewer apply primarily to global variables because local variables are extant only while the script where they were declared is active (during which time a user without the ability to authenticate with a [Full Access] account is not able to use the Data Viewer). An exception to the normal expiration rules exists with respect to local variables associated with script zero.

 **For a detailed discussion of variables, including variables associated with script zero, refer to Chapter 9.**

Database Design Report

Documenting your work is an important part of the professional development process. You can do some limited documentation in FileMaker Pro by printing scripts, tables, and layouts. However, FileMaker Pro Advanced substantially extends your ability to document the finer details of your solutions by including the Database Design Report (DDR).

To create a Database Design Report, follow these steps:

1. Open the file or file set you want to document.
2. Choose Tools ⇨ Database Design Report. The Database Design Report dialog appears, as shown in Figure 18.9, enabling you to specify the files, tables, and kinds of detail to be included in the report, as well as the report's output format.

FIGURE 18.9

Selecting report options in the Database Design Report dialog.

Database Design Report
Create an XML or HTML report on the structure of your database(s). The file can be viewed in a web browser. Only files open with full access privileges can be included. A file is marked with a "*" when a subset of its tables are selected.

Available files:
- ☑ Inventory_Ch18.fp7
- ☑ Inventory_data_Ch16.fp7

Include fields from tables in selected file:

Include in report:
- ☑ Accounts
- ☑ Custom Menu Sets
- ☑ Custom Menus
- ☑ Data Sources
- ☑ Extended Privileges
- ☑ Functions
- ☑ Layouts

Report Format:
- ○ HTML
- ◉ XML

File Handling: ☑ Automatically open report when done

Cancel   Create

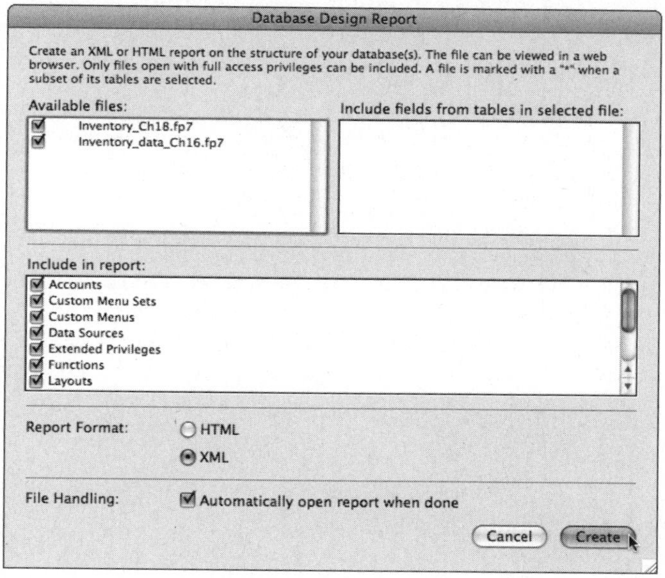

3. Select your desired options in the Database Design Report dialog.

4. Click the Create button and then choose a location to save the report files.

5. Click the Save button to accept the settings and commence creation of your Database Design Report.

> **NOTE** If your solution is large and/or you choose to include most or all of the report detail options, be aware the report may take some time to compile. A coffee break may be in order while FileMaker prepares your report.

DDR capabilities

A full DDR captures, in detail, almost every aspect of your solution's design, from scripts and script steps to tables, relationships, and calculation code. Data concerning all these elements and more are compiled into a structured and searchable document that defines and captures the current state of your solution files.

You can open the DDR in a Web browser — or any other HTML or XML compatible application — to peruse, search, or manipulate its contents or to extract details for inclusion in other documents, archives, and so on. You can also use information in the DDR as a reference for further development or to build or repair parts of your solutions. For example, you can copy and paste the syntax of complex calculations, custom functions, and other code available in your DDRs into new field and function definitions in your solutions.

> **TIP** Running a new DDR at intervals during your development work is one way of keeping track of your work, enabling you to refer to the details of earlier versions of your data structure and code.

Mining the DDR for information

At the most basic level, the DDR provides an index of organized data about your solution's structure and code, enabling you to browse and locate information in broad categories and giving you a useful overview of each file's contents. However, you can also call the DDR into service to solve problems.

The DDR provides a direct resource for locating specific references to elements in your solutions. For example, if you need to locate all the places where a particular field is referenced, you can generate a complete DDR and then search it for the name of the field in question. Similarly, to locate unresolved references such as missing fields (for example, a field has been referenced but subsequently deleted), you can search the HTML version of the DDR for the text string "Missing Field."

By performing HTML searches or by opening the DDR files in a text editor or other tool, you can perform various kinds of basic analysis of your solution content. If you want access to additional capabilities, use the optional XML output option and consider investing in one of the available tools for detailed analysis of your DDR's contents.

Tools and techniques for interpreting DDR data

When you create DDR output in XML format, FileMaker generates a series of files containing the complete contents of the DDR, in a form you can readily convert into a variety of other formats (or upload into a database) for analysis.

You can create your own tools, such as a custom-built FileMaker database, to import DDR's XML version for analysis or to develop reports of your own using the data contained in one or more of your solution's DDRs. You can find more details about the XML Output Grammar used in the Database Design Report at the FileMaker, Inc., Web site to assist you in working with the XML content.

Additionally, a number of developers have created and published tools ready-made to perform a variety of analyses of DDR data. The best of these provide instant access to a wealth of information that can save you time and help you to produce better solutions.

 For additional details regarding the use of third-party tools, including tools for analysis of Database Design Report output, refer to Chapter 20.

Creating Custom Menus

The FileMaker Pro menu system provides users with access to all the basic application features and functions, but it does so in a generic way without reference to the particular needs, habits, preferences, or vocabulary of your users.

You can improve your solutions' usability by modifying the menus to remove commands not required by your users, to rename commands so that their meaning is specific to your solution (for example, "New Contact" instead of "New Record"), and/or to change the way commands operate, according to the needs of your users.

Defining menus

The Custom Menu functionality in FileMaker enables you to define menu sets and then choose which menu set will be the default for each layout in your file, as well as change the current menu set using the `Install Menu Set [ ]` script or button command.

 The standard menus in FileMaker are always available as one of the options for you to assign to a layout or invoke via the `Install Menu Set [ ]` command.

To create a menu set for use in your solution, choose File ➪ Manage ➪ Custom Menus. The Manage Custom Menus dialog appears, as shown in Figure 18.10.

Creating a custom menu set requires you to configure elements at three levels:

- Setting the attributes — name and action to be performed — for the commands on each menu

- Naming and configuring each individual menu (groups of commands)

- Gathering a number of menus into a named set

To perform the first two tasks, select a menu in the Manage Custom Menus dialog's Custom Menus panel and click the Edit button at the bottom of the panel, causing the Edit Custom Menu dialog to appear.

FIGURE 18.10

Selecting a menu for editing in the Custom Menus tab of the Manage Custom Menus dialog.

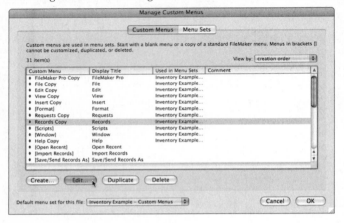

> **TIP** When defining menus and menu items, you can supply a calculation expression that will determine the name of the menu item. When you do so, however, the calculation will be evaluated when the menu is installed, and the menu and menu item names will then remain static until the menu set changes and the same or another menu set is installed. A change of menu set can occur when navigating to a new layout that has a different menu set assigned, or when a script of button calls the `Install Menu Set[ ]` command.

When building a custom menu, you can choose to modify an existing menu, make a copy of a menu and modify the copy, or start from scratch and build a whole new menu. These options correspond to the Create, Edit, and Duplicate buttons along the bottom of the Custom Menus panel shown in Figure 18.10.

You can't copy *default menus* (those with names enclosed in square brackets). However, copies of most menus are ready for editing or duplication when a file is first created. Because the menu copies originate at the point when you create a file, the menu configuration they reflect matches the configuration of the version of FileMaker used to create the file (so menu commands added in later versions aren't included). For example, the Edit Copy custom menu available by default in a file created with a previous version of FileMaker includes a single Edit ⇨ Undo command, whereas the Edit Copy custom menu in a file created with FileMaker Pro 10 includes Edit ⇨ Undo and Edit ⇨ Redo.

CROSS-REF For a detailed discussion of the process for determining which version of FileMaker is opening your solution so that you can prevent earlier versions from accessing the solution (or warn them about restricted functionality) refer to Chapter 12.

TIP When you create a menu, you can use it in multiple menu sets throughout your solutions — each menu set is made up of a collection of menus defined in the file — including FileMaker's default menus.

Editing individual menus

The Edit Custom Menu dialog, shown in Figure 18.11, allows you to specify overall settings for the menu in the upper part of the dialog. These settings include the name of the menu, both as it appears in the Custom Menus dialogs and its *display title* (the name users will see when accessing it in your solution). You can also specify the platform(s) and mode(s) where the menu is to appear.

NOTE FileMaker's standard menu sets always appear in Layout mode.

FIGURE 18.11

Assigning a script to a menu command in the Edit Custom Menu dialog.

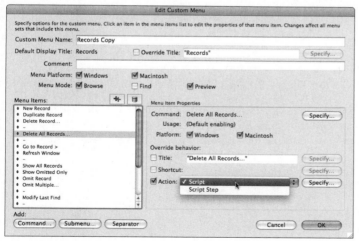

In the lower part of the Edit Custom Menu dialog, you edit the commands on the menu, configuring each to perform a default or custom (Script or Script Step) action, as well as setting the command's name, the platform(s) it's to be available on, and an associated keyboard shortcut. You can make each setting in the Menu Item Properties panel in the Edit Custom Menu dialog, after selecting the item in the Menu Items list.

Benefits of the Script Step action

Assigning custom menu commands to the Script Step action rather than the Script action does have some benefit, even when your goal is to have the command you're configuring run a script. Using the Script Step option, you can select the Perform Script[ ] command to launch a script, with the advantage that you can then also configure the controls to manage any running scripts (selecting whether running scripts should Halt, Exit, Resume, or Pause when the script you attach to the command is triggered).

When configuring menus using the Edit Custom Menu dialog, you can add or remove items, submenus, and separators using the buttons immediately above and below the Menu Items list.

> **TIP** When adding a menu item, you can base it on an existing FileMaker menu command or create it with No Command Assigned. The significance of the decision whether or not to repurpose an existing FileMaker command is that the command's availability is determined by the availability context of the command on which it is based.
>
> For example, commands such as Duplicate Record and Delete Record aren't available (and therefore appear dimmed) when no records are in the current found set. If you want to create a command that is dimmed and unavailable when there are no records in the found set, you could choose to base it on one of these commands. (Its availability will be determined accordingly, even though you assign it a different name and a different action.)

Benefits of window widgets

An important aspect of custom menu operation is that when you modify the actions associated with a standard menu command, window buttons and widgets performing the same task also acquire the new behavior. For example, if you reassign the Close Window command to run a script, clicking the Close button in the title bar of a database window also runs the assigned script.

When configuring the custom find log in the Inventory example in Chapter 9, I used custom menus to reassign the Perform Find command to run the Perform/Store Find script instead — so when users perform a Find (whether by using the menu command, clicking the Find button in the Status Toolbar, or by pressing the Enter key), the script runs and the Find is logged.

In any situation where a command is associated with a window widget, you can employ custom menus to change the behavior of the widget by modifying the attributes of the associated command. The same is true regarding contextual menus and toolbar actions — like window widgets, their behavior is changed when the corresponding menu action is reassigned using custom menus.

Adding menus to sets

Once you've created required menus and configured them with the menu commands you need, the next step is to assemble them into sets. You do so by navigating to the Menu Sets panel of the Manage Custom Menus dialog and using either the Edit (to modify an existing set) or Create (to assemble a new set) button to access the Edit Menu Set dialog, as shown in Figure 18.12.

In addition to adding or removing menus from the selected menu set, you can use the Edit Menu Set dialog to determine the order menus will appear (from left to right in the menu bar). To do so, drag the menus up and down by their handle icon in the Edit Menu Set dialog's Menus in <...> list.

FIGURE 18.12

Assigning a menu to a Menu Set via the Edit Menu Set dialog.

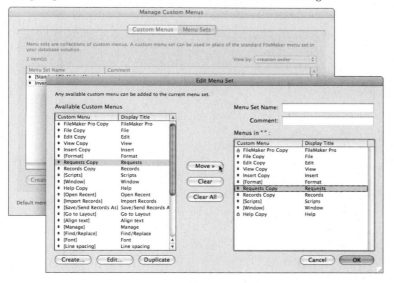

Assigning menu sets throughout your file

Once you've created one or more custom menu sets, you have several options available to you to specify when and where your users will have access to your custom menus.

Setting the default menu set for a file

The simplest option for deploying your custom menu set is to assign it as the default menu set for the file where it is defined. You can do so via the pop-up menu setting on the bottom of the Manage Custom Menus dialog (see Figure 18.10). When you define a menu set, it appears in the pop-up list and can be selected as the file default.

Determining a menu set for each layout

You can also associate a default menu set with each layout in your file. To assign a default menu for a layout, proceed as follows:

1. Navigate to the layout in question.

2. Enter Layout mode

3. Choose Layouts⇨Layout Setup. The Layout Setup dialog appears, as shown in Figure 18.13.

4. Choose the desired menu set for the layout from the Menu Set pop-up menu near the bottom of the Layout Setup dialog's General panel.

5. Click OK to save the selection and dismiss the Layout Setup dialog.

FileMaker uses the term [File Default] to refer to a menu set assigned to the file via the pop-up menu setting at the bottom of the Manage Custom Menus dialog. The menu set specified as the file default applies everywhere in the file, except where you've chosen an alternative menu for a particular layout, or where your scripts have used the Install Menu Set[ ] command to change the current menu set.

FIGURE 18.13

Setting the default menu set for the current layout via the General tab of the Layout Setup dialog.

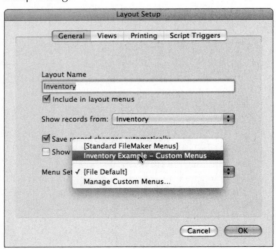

Conversely, the term [Standard FileMaker Menus] refers to the menu set that FileMaker uses when no custom menus have been created or selected. When a file is first created (and before you've made any custom menu configuration changes), [Standard FileMaker Menus] is set as the [File Default] menu set.

TIP To quickly see which menu sets have been assigned as the defaults for each layout, choose File ⇨ Manage ⇨ Layouts....

The resulting dialog lists all the layouts in the file, showing in the right column the default menu set assigned to each layout.

Double-clicking a layout line in the Manage Layouts dialog invokes the Layout Setup dialog for that layout, allowing you to edit the layout's properties, including its assigned menu set.

Controlling menu sets via script

Once you have set the default menu sets for the current file and/or for each layout in the file, you have established a basic operational environment for your users. You also have the option to further customize the user experience by providing access to alternative menus via script and button actions using the Install Menu Set [ ] command to vary the menus available on the current layout.

NOTE A menu set invoked by a button or script normally remains in place only until the user switches to a different layout (when the default menu set for the new layout takes priority). If the user returns to the previous layout, the original menu set is reinstated until changed again by a script or button.

An exception is when you select the option on the Install Menu Set [ ] command to Use As File Default, in which case the selected menu set remains in place for all layouts configured to use the [File Default] menu set until the conclusion of the current file session. However, since this setting doesn't alter the default menu set in the Manage Custom Menus dialog, the file reverts to the pre-existing default menu set after it's closed and re-opened.

Custom Functions

FileMaker Pro 10 provides you with a total of 243 calculation functions. However, you can extend that number in FileMaker Pro Advanced by defining your own functions using combinations of the original 249 functions as building blocks to assemble powerful new calculation functions of your own.

Custom functions are a great idea and should be part of your standard development toolkit for three compelling reasons:

- You can use custom functions to simplify the language of calculations, making your solution's code more readable and giving you shortcuts to commonly used code snippets.

- By encapsulating frequently repeated code (especially long or complex blocks of code) within a custom function, you can maintain the code in one place. When you change the custom function definition, calculations employing it throughout your solution automatically use the new function definition the next time they're evaluated.

- You can structure custom functions to produce *recursion* (repetition of a task until a condition is met), enabling them to tackle complex tasks beyond the scope of ordinary calculations.

CROSS-REF See Chapter 12 for a more complete discussion of the three advantages of custom functions.

Defining custom functions

Custom functions are available only in the file where they're defined. If you want to have access to a particular custom function in multiple files, you will have to define it separately in each file.

Once defined, however, custom functions appear in the list of available functions in calculation dialogs throughout the field definitions, scripts, button commands, and everywhere else calculation formulae are accepted. Although custom functions can only be defined with FileMaker Pro Advanced, once defined you can use them in calculations created using FileMaker Pro.

To create a custom function:

1. Choose File ➪ Manage ➪ Custom Functions. The Manage Custom Functions dialog appears, as shown in Figure 18.14.

FIGURE 18.14

Creating or editing a custom function via the Manage Custom Functions dialog.

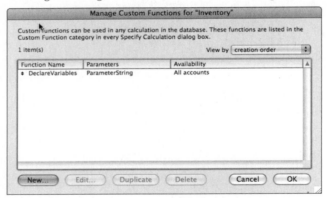

2. Click the New button. The Edit Custom Function dialog appears.
3. In the Function Name field, enter the custom function's name, as shown in Figure 18.15.
4. (Optional) After naming your custom function, add parameters in the Function Parameters field. *Parameters* enable you to pass values to your function when you reference it in calculations throughout your solution. Parameters are used as placeholders in the definition of your custom function, but are substituted with the values passed by your calculations when the custom function is evaluated.

FIGURE 18.15

Specifying a Custom Function definition in the Edit Custom Function dialog.

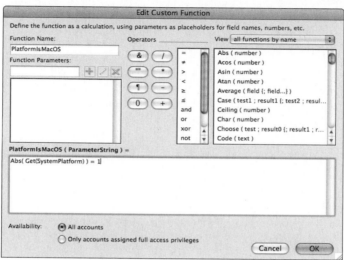

5. Specify a calculation expression in the main text box occupying the lower area of the Edit Custom Function dialog. The function definition is created according to the same calculation syntax as used elsewhere in FileMaker, except that you can also refer to the parameters defined for the function, and to custom functions defined in the current file (including the current custom function).

6. Use the radio button options at the bottom of the Edit Custom Function dialog to determine whether the custom function you're creating will be available in calculations specified by users whose login account is not assigned to the Full Access privilege set. If you choose to limit the function's use to Full Access accounts as described here, calculations referencing the function will still work for all users, but will not be able to be defined or modified by users with restricted privileges. For example, if you've granted some users the ability to create or modify their own scripts, they won't be able to build calculations in their scripts using your custom function unless you've selected the All Accounts availability option for the function.

7. Click OK.

NOTE Custom functions operate and are available for use by users (including users accessing the solution using FileMaker Pro) providing the users have sufficient privileges. That is, if a function is defined to be available only to users with full access privileges, it will be unavailable to users with restricted accounts, whether they log in with FileMaker Pro or FileMaker Pro Advanced.

Custom functions as an aid to syntax readability

Custom functions offer an opportunity to simplify calculation syntax in your solutions. A simple but elegant example is provided by the custom function definition shown in Figure 18.15:

```
Abs(Get(SystemPlatform)) = 1
```

This somewhat arcane syntax is specified as the definition of a custom function named `PlatformIsMacOS`, making it possible to use more easily scannable code in your solution. For example, with the preceding function installed in your file, a script requiring a different window width for each platform (to account for the difference in window borders between Macintosh and Windows) may use the expression

```
If(PlatformIsMacOS; 865; 878)
```

instead of

```
If(Abs(Get(SystemPlatform)) = 1; 865; 878)
```

You can simplify many other commonly used expressions in your solutions — from tests for modifier keys to paths to shared directories to error results — making the resulting calculation code shorter and easier to read.

Maximizing efficiency and ease of use

When you place long or complex calculation expressions into a custom function, you can use a single custom function name in your calculations in place of a much more convoluted expression. For an expression used only once in your solution, there may be little value in replacing it with a custom function because the complexity of the code is simply moved from the calculation definition to the custom function definition. However, if your solution references the expression in multiple places, defining its logic as a custom function provides a number of benefits.

The first and most obvious benefit of placing a complex calculation into a custom function is that it makes coding easier throughout the various occurrences of the logic in your solution. An added benefit is that if you need to update the logic of the calculation, a single update (to the custom function definition) propagates throughout your solution.

> **CAUTION** Previously calculated (and stored) values do not automatically update if the definition of a custom function used to calculate them changes. To apply a changed definition to stored values, you must separately prompt their recalculation — such as by updating the value of a referenced field.

For example, if your solution requires that a progressive (tiered) tax rate be applied in three salary bands to calculate net income, you can achieve the required result using a formula such as

```
Let([Cap1 = 7500; Cap2 = 45000; Rate1 = 0; Rate2 = .33; Rate3 = .5];
Income::Gross -
(Min(Income::Gross; Cap1) * Rate1) -
If(Income::Gross > Cap1;
(Min(Income::Gross; Cap2) - Cap1) * Rate2) -
If(Income::Gross > Cap2;
(Income::Gross - Cap2) * Rate3)
)
```

An alternative technique, however, is to define the logic of the preceding calculation as a custom function where the rates and salary cap values are passed in as parameters, as shown in Figure 18.16.

With the `NetIncome( )` custom function installed in your file, the previous calculation can be performed throughout your solution (in scripts and other calculations) with the new simplified syntax

```
NetIncome(Income::Gross; 7500; 45000; 0; .33; .5)
```

Moreover, should the rules for the application of progressive tax rates change in the future, a modification of the definition of the `NetIncome( )` custom function implements the revised logic going forward.

FIGURE 18.16

Defining a NetIncome custom function to apply a three-tiered tax structure.

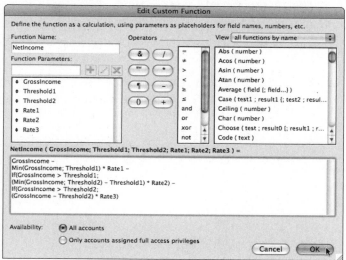

Custom Functions and Recursion

Custom functions can do several tasks that regular FileMaker calculations cannot, because custom functions are capable of recursion. *Recursion* is when a process explicitly and repetitively invokes itself until its work is accomplished. Recursion is analogous to a looping construction, excepting that a loop is explicitly iterative, whereas recursion achieves an equivalent logical outcome implicitly. Examples of recursion and iteration exist elsewhere in FileMaker Pro, such as when you define a script to loop until an exit condition is satisfied. Looping constructs (as well as requiring a script to implement them) tend to be longer and less efficient in operation, though they may sometimes be easier to read and interpret.

Elsewhere in FileMaker Pro, calculation expressions are evaluated only once; however you can define custom functions to call themselves, creating a looping effect. To successfully implement recursion in a custom function, you need to observe two simple rules:

- The function must call itself within its own syntax (supplying the appropriate parameter values).
- The function syntax must include an escape condition so that it will stop calling itself when the intended goal has been achieved.

Following these two basic rules, you can set up custom functions to perform a wide variety of tasks — including many not otherwise readily (or efficiently) accomplished within calculations.

Things that only custom functions can do

Using the power of recursion, your calculation can perform operations in an extensible way, repeating a process until the required result is reached (according to the exit condition you build into its syntax).

Consider a very simple example, where you need to generate a series of numbers — say, for houses in a street, starting at one number and ending at another, where some streets may have many thousands of houses and the start and end numbers can be almost anything. This task is quite difficult, if not impossible, to do reliably for all cases using a conventional calculation, but achieved quite simply with the following function, which uses the power of recursion:

```
    //  SYNTAX:  NumRange ( From ; To )
If(From < To;
From & ", " & NumRange(From + 1; To);
From
)
```

When you define a custom function in this way and then employ it in a calculation expression, supplying the From parameter as, say, 52972 and the To parameter as, say, 53007:

```
NumRange ( 52972 ; 53007 )
```

FileMaker returns the result:

> 52972, 52973, 52974, 52975, 52976, 52977, 52978, 52979, 52980, 52981, 52982,
> 52983, 52984, 52985, 52986, 52987, 52988, 52989, 52990, 52991, 52992, 52993,
> 52994, 52995, 52996, 52997, 52998, 52999, 53000, 53001, 53002, 53003, 53004,
> 53005, 53006, 53007

Using this same function, you can generate number ranges starting anywhere and running for hundreds or even thousands of numbers, if need be. While this example is simple, you can perform much more complex tasks using the same essential principle, thanks to the power and flexibility recursion offers. In this case, the `If ( )` function test provides an escape condition, while the work of the function is performed on the second line of the `If ( )` expression:

```
From & ", " & NumRange(From + 1; To);
```

Here, on its first call, the function returns the `From` value, appends a comma and space, and then calls itself again with the `From` value incremented for the next iteration — so the expression continues to call itself until the `If ( )` test fails (that is, until `From` is no longer less than `To`), at which point the accumulated sequence of `From` values is returned, spanning all the way from the original `From` value to the `To` value.

The stack and the limits of recursion

To execute a procedure such as the one described in the previous section, FileMaker must hold the result of each call to the `NumRange ( )` function in memory until the process completes, and it can return the combined result of all the iterations. To do so, FileMaker uses an internal memory stack, where it stacks up each result in turn, in memory, until the task is complete, and then it retrieves each value in turn from the memory stack.

A potential risk when using a memory stack is that the process will continue until available memory is exhausted, resulting in an out-of-memory error that causes a problem for the application. To avoid this risk, FileMaker places an arbitrary limit on the depth of the stack at 10,000. If the process hasn't completed by the time the memory stack is 10,000 values deep, the process is aborted, and an error value ("?") is returned. This limit protects FileMaker from the possibility of an out-of-memory condition, but imposes an upper limit on recursive processes that make use of the memory stack.

In cases where 10,000 iterations is insufficient, you need a different approach. If you plan to use recursion, the conventional "stack-based" approach won't do, and you need to use an alternative calculation syntax known as *tail-end recursion*, or simply tail recursion.

Tail recursion in practice

A custom function using tail recursion is designed to complete all its work at each call so that nothing need be held in memory while subsequent calls are evaluated. To do so, the function must be structured to pass its result to the next call (via the defined parameters or via a variable) rather than holding it on the stack.

For example, you can restructure the `NumRange ( )` function from the preceding discussion to no longer require use of the memory stack by changing its definition to

```
      //  SYNTAX:  NumRange ( From ; To )
Let(
pN = GetAsNumber(RightWords(From; 1));
If(pN < To; NumRange(From & ", " & (pN + 1); To); From)
)
```

Here, rather than each successive value being held in memory until the complete sequence has been compiled, the string of numbers is built within the From parameter and passed whole from each iteration to the next. Because nothing is left to be held in memory, the stack depth limit is not relevant, and this version of the function can return number ranges spanning more than 10,000 integers.

Tail recursion syntax enables functions to continue until FileMaker's limit of 50,000 total function calls for a single calculation operation is reached, so the revised (tail recursive) version of the `NumRange ( )` function can produce ranges containing up to 49,999 numbers before it, too, will fail.

NOTE The 50,000 upper limit for sequential calls within a single calculation evaluation prevents you from locking your solution in an infinite loop, such as when you code your function with an invalid escape argument. Moreover, even with a powerful CPU, your computer will take a while to crunch through 50,000 nontrivial computations, so the limit is a good compromise between functionality and usability.

Some useful examples

The example I provide in the preceding discussion is designed to help you comprehend the fundamentals of recursion, but in itself is of limited use. However, many other uses of recursive functions can become central and even essential components of your solution functionality, taking over where the built-in capabilities of the FileMaker calculation engine leave off.

While I'd love to provide many more examples (and I have enough of them to fill a book), the constraints of space are such that I limit ourselves to the ones described in the following sections.

Creating an acronym from a supplied phrase

Producing an acronym by calculation is straightforward if you know in advance the maximum number of words occurring in the supplied text. You need not be concerned about that, however, if you use a recursion, as in this example:

```
      // SYNTAX: Acronym ( Phrase )
Case(
WordCount(Phrase) > 1;
Upper(Left( Phrase; 1)) &
Acronym(RightWords( Phrase; WordCount( Phrase ) - 1));
Upper(Left( Phrase; 1))
)
```

This function accepts an input parameter such as "Your mileage may vary" and returns the acronym YMMV. It uses conventional (iterative) recursion. It is useful for generating initials from names, company acronyms from company names, and so on. Because it can also create very long acronyms, you can use it for generating an "imprint" of a longer block of text for quick identification. For example, using it, I've created the following imprint of this paragraph:

TFAAIPSAYMMVARTAYIUCIRIIUFGIFNCAFCNESICACVLAICBUFGAIOALBOTFQIFEUIWCTFIOTP

Extracting a character set from a supplied block of text

To establish the character domain of a text value (or a series of values), you need to be able to produce a list of all the characters used in the text — in other words, a character set. The following recursive function makes the task easy:

```
// SYNTAX: CharacterSet ( text )
Case(
Length ( text );
Let([
K1 = Left(Text; 1);
Kn = Substitute(text; K1; "")];
K1 & If(Length(Kn); CharacterSet(Kn))
)
)
```

The `CharacterSet ( )` function returns one of each character occurring in the text string you supply as input. Using it, you can develop appropriate collections of characters occurring in sample text, for use in filtering applications (where you need to constrain the character set to eliminate rogue or garbage content).

Removing an unspecified number of leading carriage returns

Removing undesired characters from a text string is another task that's straightforward if you know how many characters to remove. If you use a recursive function, with an appropriately formed escape clause, the problem is solved, as in the following example:

```
// SYNTAX: TrimLeadingReturns ( text )
If(
Left(text; 1) = ¶;
TrimLeadingReturns(Right(text; Length(text) - 1));
text
)
```

The task of eliminating leading carriage returns is humble, yet practical and useful. I have selected this function as my third example because it provides another delightfully simple example of tail recursion — completing its task without invoking the memory stack.

CROSS-REF   **For links to resources containing a broad selection of documentation and examples of custom functions, refer to Appendix A.**

Creating Runtime Applications

Complementing its wealth of customization options and developer tools, FileMaker Pro Advanced offers you the ability to generate royalty-free, stand-alone, runtime applications from your solutions. This ability means you can distribute stand-alone copies of your database solutions to users who don't own FileMaker Pro, and they'll be able to install them and use them as discrete applications.

Before generating a runtime application from your solution, it pays to give some thought to making your solution interface self-contained, adding appropriate branding and building in help and support information and contact details.

> **NOTE** Apart from being good practice and basic professionalism, providing an "About" layout that includes your name and contact details for technical support is one condition of FileMaker, Inc.,'s license agreement, permitting you to create and distribute runtime copies of your solution. Refer to the FileMaker Pro Advanced product documentation for full details.

Generating a stand-alone solution

To create a self-contained application from your completed solution, open FileMaker Pro Advanced (leaving your solution files closed) and proceed as follows:

1. Choose Tools ⇨ Developer Utilities. The Developer Utilities dialog appears.

2. Click the Add button and select all the database files required by your solution. These files will be added to the Solution Files list in the Developer Utilities dialog.

3. Ensure that the red arrow indicator at the left of the file list is pointing to your solution's primary file.

4. Choose a project folder by clicking the corresponding Specify button and making a selection.

5. Click the Specify button for Solution Options in the lower part of the Developer Utilities dialog. The Specify Solution Options dialog appears, as shown in Figure 18.17.

6. Select from the five available options in the Specify Solution Options dialog (you can select more than one) and, with the Create Runtime Solution application(s) option highlighted, enter an application name and unique extension. (*Note:* Runtime applications can't use the fp7 extension.)

7. If desired, select a closing splash screen image and enter the preferred closing splash delay.

8. Enter a bindkey of your own choosing or make note of the bindkey value generated by FileMaker. You may need this value in the future.

9. Click OK to accept the Solution Options and dismiss the Solution Options dialog.

10. In the Developer Utilities dialog, click Create.

FIGURE 18.17

Specifying runtime solution options using Developer Utilities.

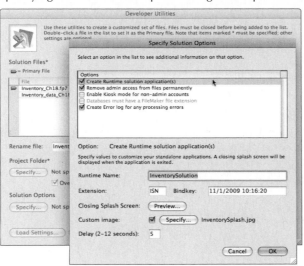

NOTE You can select the five options available in Developer Utilities in any combination — so you can use the procedure to permanently remove admin access accounts or enable kiosk mode, without choosing the option to create a runtime application.

Kiosk mode enables you to configure your files to run in a blacked-out screen with no menu bars or desktop visible or accessible. This mode is useful for computers that are available to the public for information purposes or for front-desk applications to log visitors and print name tags. However, the kiosk mode is less useful for general desktop productivity applications.

TIP When you apply kiosk mode to your solution files using Developer Utilities, your solution opens into kiosk mode whenever it's opened with a restricted access account, either in FileMaker Pro or with a runtime application engine.

Binding for each platform

As part of the process of creating a runtime application, a simplified version of FileMaker Pro (without database design capabilities) is created and specifically bound to your solution files (so that it can only operate with the bound files). Because this version is an application in its own right, it is specific to the platform you create it on.

If you want a runtime to operate on Windows, you have to bind your files to the Windows runtime on the Windows operating system. If you require a runtime for the Mac OS PowerPC platform, you need to bind on PowerPC. A separate runtime is required to run natively on an Intel Macintosh computer.

When you need to produce multiple versions of your solution, to work on different operating systems, you need to bind the same files, using the same bindkey value, on each destination platform. The executable file from each bind procedure is required to run the solution on that platform.

Hosting runtime files

Runtime applications are strictly single user. However, if you need to provide multi-user access to a runtime solution, you can configure FileMaker Server to open and host your runtime database files.

When runtime solution files are hosted by FileMaker Server, users will require full licensed copies of FileMaker Pro (or FileMaker Pro Advanced) to log in and use the solution. It can't be accessed over a network using the runtime application engine.

Chapter 19

Efficient Code, Efficient Solutions

FileMaker's reputation as a user-friendly database is legend — and, for the most part, well deserved. Users with no background in programming (but with self-motivation, good logical thinking, and some design sense) can make great progress from a standing start with FileMaker.

In fact, FileMaker draws you in with what it can do, leading the new user to try more complex and even daring feats only a short time after becoming familiar with the application. But FileMaker has a great deal more to it than you can see from the outset. FileMaker is a program with deep roots and hidden power, and it takes time and dedication to fully tap its potential.

A proportion of enthusiastic beginners, having had a ball making their first attempts at building a database, get serious and start looking for robust, fault tolerant, and efficient ways to code their solutions. They are the ones who make the transition to achieve professionalism as FileMaker developers (whatever their job title). If you fall into this group, this chapter is especially for you.

IN THIS CHAPTER

Designing your solutions for scalability

Finding ways to avoid redundancy

Seeking the most efficient ways to produce the desired outcomes

Building solutions around transactional principles

Keeping file sizes within limits

Working with images and media

Designing for Scale: Size Considerations

One of the greatest problems you face — whether working with FileMaker or any other database application — is designing solutions that continue to work well as they grow. Some designs succeed when modeled using only a small number of records and survive beta testing (also with moderate-sized record sets), but then founder in deployment, when encumbered with the accumulation of serious quantities of business data.

When a solution develops problems operating under load, many developers are tempted to blame the tool, but frequently such problems are a reflection of the design. What works well in small single-user databases does not necessarily translate well to situations calling for tens or hundreds of thousands of records in multi-user networked systems.

The elephant in the cherry tree

Well, it's an old joke — and if you don't know it, you're not missing much — that an elephant can't really hide in a cherry tree by painting his toenails red. However, elephants notwithstanding, while you can accommodate surprisingly large data sets in your FileMaker Pro solutions by paying heed to good design and avoiding bottlenecks and performance impediments, the qualities needed for scalability are fundamental, not cosmetic.

In itself, FileMaker is one of the most scalable development environments available, working with ease and elegance in the smallest of desktop solutions, yet capable of producing server-based solutions delivering large and complex functionality to hundreds of users simultaneously. Across this range, however, are a variety of approaches you can use to produce viable solutions in high-volume, high-output deployments.

CAUTION **Solutions need room to grow over time. Bear in mind that FileMaker Server supports up to a maximum of 250 client connections, so if a new solution's requirements already approach this number, it will have little scope for expansion.**

Enterprise-wide solutions delivering data to thousands of users may still have a place for FileMaker as part of a larger mix of strategies, but not as a whole solution.

Predicting what will scale well

Scale takes three main forms:

- Number of users
- Functional or logical complexity
- Volume of data

Each form of scale brings its own issues and may be considered in isolation, though it is the combination of scale in multiple dimensions that presents the greatest challenge.

Some techniques are strictly single user — they break or cause problems when a solution is hosted. Notably, the use of global fields to store data across multiple sessions is a strictly single-user-only technique. Procedures depending on flag fields and record marking, or involving the use of the `Replace Field Contents [ ]` command, are also problematic in multi-user solutions. Finally, a lack of adequate error handling for record locking (and for a range of other conditions) becomes a serious impediment to functionality and data integrity when your solution is hosted.

When requirements are relatively simple, a variety of techniques can achieve the desired ends without unduly impacting performance. For example, a heavy dependence on unstored calculations to provide the solution interface, gather data across multiple tables, or pass data through an ungainly data structure is scarcely problematic while requirements remain relatively simple. However, such techniques become unsustainable, and their impact on performance increases exponentially as additional requirements are introduced and complexity increases.

In solutions with modest volumes of data (up to about a thousand records in each table), FileMaker is very forgiving:

- Finds performed on unindexed fields scarcely cause users to blink.

- Summary data calculated live in real time does not introduce unacceptable delays.

- Scripts looping through found sets do not take hours to complete.

Techniques depending upon real-time data summarization become problematic, though, when the volume of data is expected to become large. Similarly, many actions involving updating indexes and using unstored calculations (especially those aggregating data) and multi-predicate relationships encounter performance issues.

Conversely, solutions that are clean, simple, and concisely coded, with almost all values stored, indexing optimized, and with an efficient and unencumbered data model, scale well and can support tables with hundreds of thousands or even millions of records in FileMaker.

Eliminating Redundancy

A first step toward the optimization of your solutions is avoidance or elimination of redundancy. The DRY (Don't Repeat Yourself) development principle should be at the forefront of your thinking. While eliminating redundancy makes sense from the point of view of speed and efficiency of development, its impacts are greatest in the fluency and responsiveness of the resulting solutions.

By consolidating similar elements and functions and repurposing solution components to serve multiple purposes, you can reduce bloated and ungainly solutions to a fraction of their size, with comparable performance benefits. You can recast awkward and suboptimal scripts that take hours to complete simple processes so that they complete in minutes or seconds.

Combining the techniques I suggest in this section and the following section throughout your solutions, you achieve a considerable reduction in file sizes and corresponding improvements in solution performance. Your solutions will be lean and powerful.

Avoiding duplication of elements

Whenever two processes are similar in essentials, consider using a single script to serve both requirements (with a script parameter determining context-appropriate behavior, and internal branching to deal with variations). Before you begin, reflect on whether you really need 45 report scripts, or whether a single report controller script, with some additional lines and internal branching — plus a handful of small supporting sub-scripts for various special cases — will serve the same requirements. If so, when reporting requirements change, what would otherwise have been a week's work updating each report and its associated script may be a task that you can complete in a couple of hours. In such a case, the reduction in size and complexity of your file has benefits that flow right through your solution, making your design tight, efficient, and powerful. Now, consider applying the same essential approach to layouts. I have seen files with several hundred layouts that, after some rethinking and repurposing, could achieve the same functionality with only a few dozen layouts — again, reducing complexity and overhead in every direction.

Your Relationships Graph is another area where duplication and redundancy produces a sub-optimal result. A solution design requiring more than the minimum number of table occurrences to achieve the desired functionality incurs performance penalties and complicates development and maintenance, because FileMaker must manage join results and concomitant cache updates across the Graph.

As in many aspects of development, you need to make a judgment call when deciding the optimal path to take. In some cases, a graph that includes redundant elements may support work practices that are more comfortable — and in a solution of moderate size, the trade-off in performance may be small enough to be considered acceptable. There is no single "correct" answer, and you must weigh the competing imperatives and decide what works best for each case.

Using portable and reusable code

While scripts are a key area where the reusability of code gives you many opportunities to increase efficiency and do more with less, relationship specifications and your calculation code's design provide scope for streamlining and introducing reusability.

Appropriate use of sub-scripts

When you have a number of scripts where similar sequences of steps occur, even though those scripts may be substantially different in intent, consider placing those sequences into a sub-script and calling it from each of the main scripts. For example, error handling procedures for various conditions are apt to be repeated throughout many scripts. While I don't necessarily recommend having only a single, all-encompassing error handler script in your solutions, it certainly does make sense to consolidate the trapping and handling of certain errors or groups of errors. A single script to deal with record locking errors and another to deal with Perform Find [ ] errors (and so on) is a reasonable compromise between efficiency and manageability.

While sub-scripts enable you to consolidate code into a procedural model, reducing fragmentation and redundancy in your solution, the inappropriate use of sub-scripts can have the opposite effect. I recommend that you avoid breaking logically unified processes into multiple scripts without a compelling reason to do so.

A good general rule is that unless a sub-script is called from multiple parent scripts in your solution, you should include its content in the body of the main script instead of making it a sub-script. I've been called in to troubleshoot lengthy processes where the logic is distributed across a dozen or more scripts, to no benefit. In fact, splitting a process into sub-scripts may introduce redundancy because each script must separately instantiate and manage its own (local) parameters, variables, and so on. Exceptions to this rule are when

- One or more parts of an action are required to be performed with [Full Access] privileges, while the remainder of the process should be constrained by the privileges of the current user's account. In this situation, placing the part (or parts) of process requiring the Run Script with Full Access Privileges option enabled in a separate script makes good sense.

- Components of a process need to be performed in different files of a multi-file solution. This approach may be required so that a script can act on variables (all variables are scoped within the file where they are defined), logins, or access privileges (also specific to the file where they're defined).

You should limit your use of sub-scripts to occasions where they're necessary or where doing so significantly increases the efficiency of your code. In other cases, sub-scripts add needless clutter and complexity.

Appropriate use of custom functions

One benefit of using custom functions in your solutions is the ability to avoid repetition of complex logic in your calculation code. By placing the essentials of calculation logic common to multiple scripts, schema calculations, or various other solution pieces (tooltips, button parameters, conditional formatting expressions, and so on) where calculations are used into a custom function, you can greatly simplify and streamline your solution's code.

As with script code, I counsel against separating calculation into custom functions unless you have a clear rationale for doing so. However, the benefits of using custom functions are several:

- A custom function's calculation logic is reusable and can be more efficiently managed in one place than if it were repeated throughout your solution's structures.

- Custom functions using recursion give access to functionality not available with calculation code elsewhere in FileMaker.

- Using custom functions enables you to make functionality available to end users without revealing proprietary or sensitive logic contained within the function definition.

Remember that custom functions are specific to the file where they're defined, so managing a large number of custom functions across all the files in a multi-file solution can itself become burdensome. Nevertheless, many situations arise where the benefits of custom functions more than compensate for the time required to create and manage them.

CROSS-REF For detailed information about the design and use of custom functions, refer to Chapters 12 and 18.

Designing for Flexibility and Adaptability

FileMaker, as a development environment, is notable for its flexibility, lending itself to innumerable ingenious and sometimes unexpected problem resolutions. One consequence of this flexibility is that you can approach almost any problem in several ways. If you can see only one path forward, chances are you aren't looking hard enough.

As a developer, your task is to choose the most effective method to address each requirement and provide each function point. However, some choices will lock you in, constraining subsequent design choices, while others leave your options relatively unencumbered. In most cases, choosing the paths offering greatest versatility is the wisest choice, even if doing so requires additional work.

In the preceding section, I suggest techniques for creating flexible and adaptable script and calculation code. However, other areas of your solution designs, including schema and interface, also benefit significantly from adopting design practices aimed at maximizing reusability and portability.

Layouts and adaptable design

You can design layouts for flexibility and reusability using a variety of available techniques, several of which have been covered in preceding chapters.

Defining screen elements as nonprinting objects and positioning print-ready content behind them supports combining print and screen versions of some layouts. Moreover, the ability to include multiple Sub-summary parts, invoking only those needed for a given report, according to the selected sort order lets you generate a variety of alternate reports from a single layout in your solution. Chapter 10 discusses examples of these techniques.

In addition, the FileMaker tab control layout object is well suited to circumstances where some screen or report elements should remain constant while others vary. Because you can control tabs either manually or via script, they also provide rich possibilities for condensing alternate interface and print content into single reusable layouts.

Combining tab control techniques with sliding objects, conditional formatting, and calculated interface elements, your interfaces can be dynamic and varied, while remaining compact and versatile.

Concepts of reusability applied to the Relationships Graph

Another area where it pays you to minimize redundancy is FileMaker's Relationships Graph, because FileMaker must manage and update its cache of join results for every dependency affected by actions ranging from editing a key field (or a value upon which a key field depends) to creating or deleting a record. Any such change requires FileMaker to revisit all cached join results where dependencies may require that current cache contents be discarded. Consequently, when your Graph contains a large number of redundant connections, your solution is unnecessarily encumbered and its responsiveness degraded.

Relationship joins, where key fields on both sides of the join are indexed, are operable in both directions. I recommend that you avoid creating two or more essentially similar relationships where a single relationship may be repurposed (used in both directions) to provide the same functionality.

Utility relationships — such as those where a global field is used to establish temporary joins to related tables — should be designed to be reusable for various purposes where possible. To facilitate this goal, consider using a prefixed composite key (in other words, a calculation field combining multiple key values) in the targeted table so that you can reassign the global key used to filter the utility relationship by adding or alternating its prefix value.

Traveling the Shortest Distance Between Two Points

A direct relationship exists between the ways you choose to structure your calculation code and the time it takes to execute. Lengthy and convoluted calculations tie up your workstation for many CPU cycles, unraveling their twisted logic. Calculations addressing related record sets require the retrieval of data from the host and carry a cost in network time, as well as processor cycles, on both server and client.

The unpleasant truth is that a single severely sub-optimal calculation can bring your solution to its knees, slowing users to a crawl and needlessly using vast computing resources. While this case is rare, a more common but equally problematic scenario is the solution where a number of calculations are sub-optimal and, while the effect of each is marginal, the combination is enough to severely impact performance. In either case, a few well-placed adjustments can yield significant and immediate gains.

Optimal calculation syntax

The DRY principle, as it applies to calculations, mandates that you should structure expressions to calculate each value or logical unit of a computation only once. (For more on the DRY principal, see the section "Eliminating Redundancy," earlier in this chapter.)

Consider the seemingly inoffensive little calculation in the Customer table of an invoicing solution:

```
If(Sum(Invoices::BalancePayable) < 5; 0; Sum(Invoices::BalancePayable))
```

As a single line of code, it may hardly seem worthy of close attention. However, whenever the balance of amounts payable on related invoices equals or exceeds $5, the calculation must determine the balance twice over — first to evaluate the If ( ) test and again to deliver the result. When you consider that the number of related invoices involved in the computation may be large and, if the Invoices::BalancePayable is itself also an unstored calculation retrieving and reconciling related LineItems and Payments values for each Invoice record, several thousand values may be computed producing the result. The preceding line of code, requiring as it does that the task of summing balance payable amounts be done twice, carries a potentially heavy performance burden.

You can recast the calculation as follows:

```
Let(Bal = Sum(Invoices::BalancePayable); If(Bal < 5; 0; Bal))
```

The work required to evaluate the expression will be halved in many cases, because the values in the Invoices::BalancePayable field are summed only once for each record in the found set. If screen draws of list layouts including the original calculation were sluggish, this one small change increases its speed (up to doubling it, depending on the number of balances of $5 or more in the rows being listed).

NOTE The If ( ), Case ( ), and Choose ( ) functions use short-circuit evaluation, so only those arguments required to be evaluated to return a valid result are processed. Consequently, in the original version of the preceding example, the second Sum ( ) function is not evaluated when the result of the first is less than 5.

In the preceding example, the `Let ( )` function is used to avoid repetition of calculation syntax, while preserving the logical form of the original expression. The relatively minor adjustment has a marked effect on performance. Now consider a more profoundly sub-optimal calculation:

```
Case(
Sum(Invoices::BalancePayable) > 0 and Sum(Invoices::BalancePayable) < 50;
Sum(Invoices::BalancePayable) - Sum(Invoices::BalancePayable) * .05;
Sum(Invoices::BalancePayable) ≥ 50 and Sum(Invoices::BalancePayable) < 100;
Sum(Invoices::BalancePayable) - Sum(Invoices::BalancePayable) * .1;
Sum(Invoices::BalancePayable) ≥ 100 and Sum(Invoices::BalancePayable) < 150;
Sum(Invoices::BalancePayable) - Sum(Invoices::BalancePayable) * .15;
Sum(Invoices::BalancePayable) ≥ 150 and Sum(Invoices::BalancePayable) < 200;
Sum(Invoices::BalancePayable) - Sum(Invoices::BalancePayable) * .2)
Sum(Invoices::BalancePayable) ≥ 200;
Sum(Invoices::BalancePayable) - Sum(Invoices::BalancePayable) * .25)
)
```

This calculation is so poorly formed that you could be forgiven for thinking I made it up to illustrate a point. Not so; I copied both the examples in this section directly from a real (albeit poorly designed) solution. As you can see, the latter example requires evaluation of the `Sum(Invoices::BalancePayable)` expression a minimum of 4 times and up to a maximum of 11 times, depending on the cumulative amount owing for a given customer record.

In this instance, I recast the expression as

```
Let([
Bal = Sum(Invoices::BalancePayable);
Rate = .95 - Min(4; Int(Bal / 50)) * .05];
Bal * Rate
)
```

Here, I eliminate redundancy, I no longer repeat the sum expression, and, after a single expression is used to calculate the discount rate, I apply it with the compact closing argument (`Bal * Rate`). The changes are twofold: The use of `Let ( )` function's variables to avoid needless repetition, plus the reworking of the logic of the calculation to achieve a more straightforward formula. Not surprisingly, with this change, the client reported approximately 900 percent performance gains in the processes (screen draws and reports) where the calculation was used, after this one change was implemented.

Throughout your calculation code, considering alternative ways to structure each expression and also choosing syntax requiring fewer steps (and therefore fewer CPU cycles and/or disk or network calls) during evaluation confer many benefits. While optimizing a single calculation formula may yield tangible benefits — as in the preceding example — the cumulative effect of optimizations throughout your solutions will be considerably greater.

Alternative syntax examples

The examples discussed in the preceding section are calculations designed to act on related data sets. However, when you choose calculation syntax with care, your solution benefits in a number of ways. More compact and efficient calculations are frequently easier to read and understand (and therefore easier to maintain) and also provide improved performance.

When looking for opportunities to optimize calculation syntax, established methods such as eliminating repetition and eliminating redundant steps are a first step. However, a more radical rethinking of your approach will frequently take you further. For example, consider a situation where data imported into an Income table includes a delimited array of monthly balance amounts for the year, in the form:

1171|554|2034|943|1623|878|1340|2552|2154|3515|2091|3027|

Extracting the August income balance amount (the eighth value in the array) may lead you to first consider parsing the string using the pipe delimiter characters to break out the eighth value with an expression such as

```
Middle(
Income::MonthBalances;
Position(Income::MonthBalances; "|"; 1; 7) + 1;
Position(Income::MonthBalances; "|"; 1; 8) —
Position(Income::MonthBalances; "|"; 1; 7) — 1
)
```

A quick glance over this formula shows it is sub-optimal because the expression Position(Income::MonthBalances; "|"; 1; 7) occurs twice. A conventional approach to optimization, therefore, produces a slight improvement, as follows:

```
Let([
p1 = Position(Income::MonthBalances; "|"; 1; 7) + 1;
p2 = Position(Income::MonthBalances; "|"; 1; 8];
Middle(Income::MonthBalances; p1; p2 — p1)
)
```

While the revised form of the calculation is a little more compact, a little quicker to evaluate, and perhaps a little more readable, the change is scarcely revolutionary. However, because I can be confident that the income amounts will all be numeric values, with some lateral thinking, I can adopt a quite different approach, arriving at the expression:

```
GetValue(Substitute(Income::MonthBalances; "|"; ¶); 8)
```

Each formulae in the preceding example produces the same result (2552), given the input string indicated. However, the last does so using considerably fewer steps.

> **NOTE** The method depending on the **GetValue( )** function works reliably in cases where the values in the delimited string being parsed will never include carriage returns, as in the case with an array of numeric values.

Elsewhere in the same solution, you may need to convert a text value representing the month into its corresponding numeric value (for example, a month number). I've seen various solutions set up to accomplish this conversion using expressions like the following:

```
Let(
MonthName = Left(Income::IncomeMonthName; 3);
Case(
    MonthName = "Jan"; 1;
MonthName = "Feb"; 2;
MonthName = "Mar"; 3;
MonthName = "Apr"; 4;
MonthName = "May"; 5;
MonthName = "Jun"; 6;
MonthName = "Jul"; 7;
MonthName = "Aug"; 8;
MonthName = "Sep"; 9;
MonthName = "Oct"; 10;
MonthName = "Nov"; 11;
MonthName = "Dec"; 12
)
)
```

Consider, however, the fact that you can return the same result using a strikingly different — and rather more compact approach — by employing FileMaker's Position() function:

```
Position("xxJanFebMarAprMayJunJulAugSepOctNovDec";
Left(Income::IncomeMonthName; 3); 1; 1) / 3
```

These examples are selected somewhat arbitrarily to illustrate that you can bring a variety of techniques to bear to solve a given problem — and rarely is there only one viable approach. My purpose here is to present you with the concepts so that you can apply them yourself to myriad calculation requirements, rather than to limit you to the specific approaches of the examples I am able to include here. Nevertheless, in the following sections, I include several additional examples to illustrate the ways alternate coding approaches may be beneficial.

Working with modifier keys

A frequent calculation challenge — often associated with scripted procedures where different functionality is made available depending on whether the user holds down a keyboard modifier (such as Shift, Control, Option/Alt) while running the script — is to determine by calculation whether a particular modifier key is depressed.

When you hold down a modifier key, the FileMaker Get(ActiveModifierKeys) function returns a number representing the combination of modifier keys currently engaged. An issue arising when testing for a specific modifier, such as Shift, is the possibility that the Caps Lock key will be engaged, adding 2 to the value the function returns. So rather than testing for the Shift Key alone

```
Get(ActiveModifierKeys) = 1
```

it's desirable to test for the Shift key both with and without the Caps Lock engaged, as in

```
Get(ActiveModifierKeys) = 1 or GetActivceModifierKeys) = 3
```

You can create an equivalent expression, however, evaluating as true when the `Get(ActiveModifierKeys)` function returns either 3 or 1, using the Abs( ) function:

```
Abs(Get(ActiveModifierKeys) - 2) = 1
```

To detect the presence of the Control key (on either Mac OS or Windows) regardless of the state of the Caps Lock, you can use

```
Abs(Get(ActiveModifierKeys) - 5) = 1
```

In these examples, the expressions evaluate as true only if the Shift key or Control key (respectively) is the only modifier key (aside from Caps Lock) engaged. However, if you need to determine whether the Shift key is pressed regardless of the state of any of the remaining modifier keys, rather than using longhand and the pedestrian approach of testing against all 16 possible combinations (across both Mac and Windows), consider using

```
Mod(Get(ActiveModifierKeys); 2)
```

To test whether the Control key is pressed regardless of the state of any of the other modifier keys, consider using either of the two following expressions:

```
Mod(Get(ActiveModifierKeys); 8) > 3
```

or

```
Mod(Div(Get(ActiveModifierKeys); 4); 2)
```

These more succinct methods arise from taking a step back and looking at the values returned by the `Get(ActiveModifierKeys)` function. Each of the five possible modifier keys (Shift, Caps Lock, Control, Option/Alt, ⌘) toggles a separate bit of a five-bit binary value. By isolating the relevant bit — by combined use of `Mod( )` and `Int( )` — you can efficiently read the state of a single key.

Working with Boolean values

The implementation of Boolean logic in FileMaker operates on the principle that nonzero numeric values are true, and zero and empty values are false. A basic understanding of this principle leads novice users to construct Boolean tests, such as the argument for the `If [ ]` step in a script, resembling the following:

```
If(IsEmpty(Receipts::AmountPaid) or Receipts::AmountPaid = 0; 0; 1)
```

Conversely, to toggle the state of a Boolean checkbox field, the novice may use

```
If(IsEmpty(Receipts::ReceiptStatus) or Receipts::ReceiptStatus = 0; 1; 0)
```

While these methods achieve their intent, they don't represent the shortest distance between points. In the case of the first example, the If ( ) function is redundant, because the required Boolean result (0 or 1) is returned by the expression

```
Receipts::AmountPaid = 0 or IsEmpty(Receipts::AmountPaid)
```

However, a still more elegant (yet equally robust) way to meet the requirement is by using FileMaker's purpose-built (but remarkably under-utilized) function:

```
GetAsBoolean(Receipts::AmountPaid)
```

Similarly, the expression frequently used to set a Boolean checkbox to its alternate state is unnecessarily verbose and may instead be replaced by

```
not GetAsBoolean(Receipts::ReceiptStatus)
```

Or, depending on your mood,

```
Abs(Receipts::ReceiptStatus − 1)
```

Either of these alternatives is both more compact and more efficient in execution than the earlier method using the If ( ) function. The first may be regarded as slightly more robust, as it still works even if the value in the Receipts::ReceiptStatus field is out of bounds (that is, neither empty, 0. nor 1), but both methods are viable alternatives.

Avoiding dependency "spaghetti"

When you define a calculation field with an expression referencing a field of the same table in your solution, you're creating a *dependency*; when the referenced field is updated, FileMaker automatically re-evaluates the calculation. FileMaker manages these dependencies internally, so you don't have to set or manage them. However, it pays to be aware of them when designing your solutions' code architecture.

One consequence of dependencies is a predetermined sequence of calculation "events" when you update a value. For example, take the following steps:

1. Create a number field.
2. Create a calculation field adding 1 to the value in the number field.
3. Create an equi-join relationship using the calculation field (as defined in Step 2) as the match field.
4. Create a text field defined as an auto-enter lookup to copy a value from the related table via the relationship established at Step 3.
5. Create a calculation field performing a substitution on the looked-up value in the text field defined at Step 4.
6. Apply a conditional formatting formula to the field defined at Step 5, changing its color if it matches the value of another field in the current record.

Each field created in Steps 2, 4, and 5 depends on the resolution of the preceding steps, so you've set up an implicit chain of dependencies for FileMaker to manage. When you change the value in the number field created in Step 1, FileMaker must work its way down the dependency tree triggering consequent actions at every level. When updating the calculated key field (Step 2), FileMaker must dump the cached join results for the relationship at Step 3, re-establishing it (replacing the cached values), and then perform the lookup for the field created at Step 4. Only after the fresh looked-up value is written to the text field at Step 4 can FileMaker begin to re-evaluate the calculation field defined at Step 5 — and only when the calculation has returned a result can FileMaker commence resolving the conditional formatting expression. Figure 19.1 illustrates this process.

FIGURE 19.1

The sequence of events required to resolve a chain of dependencies.

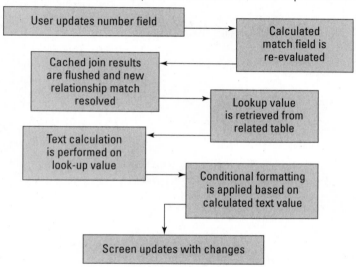

What's significant about this dependency scenario is that it's entirely sequential. Each step commences after the preceding step has completed. No amount of parallel processing efficiency will improve the speed of execution of such a process; its inefficiency is inherent.

NOTE Sequential dependencies are most problematic when they involve unstored calculations (as they are re-evaluated each time they're displayed or referenced, using up large numbers of processor cycles as users work and hampering the responsiveness of your solution) and especially where unstored calculations are included in list views (requiring computation of the whole dependency chain multiple times over to draw a single screen).

It's likely when you define a series of dependent actions in the preceding steps that editing the value in the number field imposes a slight but perceptible pause before the conditional formatting at Step 6 is displayed. On a high-performance workstation running on a fast network, the delay may be minimal. You should, however, be aware of the performance implications when creating long chains of dependency. I've seen solutions where sluggish calculations followed dependency chains from table to table all over the solution and back (and therefore using unstored calculations at each step), sometimes 15 or more steps deep. Small wonder that the users experienced long pauses and mounting frustration!

You can do three things to avoid creating "logical spaghetti" throughout your solutions:

- Keep dependencies in view. Be aware of the implications of each dependency as you create it. If necessary, plot your dependency tree as part of your code design, updating it as you work.

- Aim to keep sequential dependencies at four levels or less in all cases, with most dependencies being either direct or dependent on only one other dependency. With most modern computer hardware, FileMaker can resolve two calculations concurrently more quickly than it can process two calculations in succession.

- When a sequential dependency chain arises, look for opportunities to break it or branch it to achieve the desired result with fewer tiers (successive stages) of dependency.

In the case of the preceding example, to reduce the length of the chain of sequential dependencies, consider two steps:

- Create a stored calculation field in the related table defined to subtract 1 from the value being used as the key for the equi-join and then use it as the match field for a relationship (Step 3) matching direct to the number field (Step 1). By doing so, you eliminate the need for the calculation field (Step 2), reducing the chain of dependencies from five to four.

- Create a stored calculation field in the related table defined to apply the required substitution (as at Step 5) to the text value looked up in Step 4 and then re-point the lookup to the field holding the calculated value. By doing so, you eliminate the dependent calculation in Step 5 from the dependency chain, further reducing the length of sequential dependencies.

With these changes in place, when you change the value in the original number field, FileMaker has to perform only the re-lookup and then apply conditional formatting to the result. Yet the outcome is functionally the same.

In this scenario, each calculation is still performed. However, the calculations in Steps 2 and 5 are performed separately when the values they reference in the related table are updated. When reevaluation of the calculations occurs, because they're directly dependent on fields in the related table, they introduce no perceptible delay. Yet the lengthy chain of dependencies has been significantly reduced.

Whether the specific techniques discussed in this example are appropriate for a given situation depends on what else you have in place in your solution. A variety of other strategies are possible. What matters is that you're aware of the dependency overhead as you work, taking opportunities to structure your solution design to minimize daisy-chain logic.

Applying simplicity principles

The process of simplifying your code isn't as simple as it seems. That may be a great one-line jest, but it's nonetheless true.

A single line of code capable of replacing (and performing the same function as) half a page of code is obviously more powerful. In addition, the resulting solution is cleaner, simpler, easier to maintain and easier to use. Once you've taken the trouble to comprehend how and why the single line of code works, the solution containing it becomes easier to read and understand than the solution containing more verbose code. I doubt that the argument that longer code is preferable because it's "more explicit" or "easier to understand" is ever more than a rationalization.

One way you can view the concept of simplicity is in terms of elements. The elements are powerful. When you reduce your solution to its elemental properties, you remove extraneous and verbose material and invest a great deal in the remaining essentials. Mature computer applications such as FileMaker are inherently complex, permitting myriad paths toward any goal you identify. Your challenge is to find or create simplicity and harmony among the burgeoning complexity. If you succeed, your code and the solutions it supports will be powerful and elegant — as well as robust and scalable.

The following general principles govern the achievement of simplicity in solution development:

■ **Simplicity doesn't simply happen.** In fact, if you have anything more than a shopping list to design, simplicity is frequently harder to achieve than complexity. Moreover, arriving at a set of simple principles requires a more profound understanding of both the solution requirements and the development environment.

When you sketch out the design for a relational model, a challenging calculation, or a crucial screen design, you're probably approaching it from the wrong direction if it seems impressively complex. Take that complexity as a sign and look for an alternative way to conceptualize the problem.

■ **The ideal solution is usually the simplest.** When you can achieve more with less, everybody wins. That's true whether you're talking about increased data accuracy with fewer error alerts, better system performance with more compact code, or more flexibility with less confusion.

If your solution has 20 tables and you can build a fully functioning solution requiring only 50 table occurrences on the Relationships Graph, your achievement is superior — and evidence and experience indicate that it will perform better (all other things being equal) than a comparable solution where there are 100 table occurrences on the Graph.

- **The deepest organizational model frequently is the simplest in operation.** Collapsing too many things together (when their fit is poor) leads to conflict and confusion, whether they're ideas, operational procedures, or entities and attributes in your relational model.

  By working from first principles and breaking the components down into their essential units, you establish clean lines of separation and workable models of the real world.

- **Simple for the user matters more than simple for the developer.** Avoid the temptation to rationalize with "If simple is good, then my job should be easy" — it just isn't so. Development is in part a process of creating order out of chaos, offering smooth and streamlined paths in place of clutter and obstacles. The greater your thought and comprehension, the more likely it is that your users will find the result simple to use and easy to like.

- **There is always room for improvement.** Perfection is unattainable, but improvement is not. However powerful and elegant a piece of code may be, remain open to the possibility of other ways and other ideas. Continually revisit design principles, removing the unnecessary, refining, condensing, and simplifying.

  Excellence arises from a continuous process of questioning and a sustained commitment to improvement.

A number of the principles in this list (along with others, perhaps) may aid you in a variety of pursuits, beyond the bounds of FileMaker development. However, if you're able to keep these five principles in mind throughout the development of your solutions, I'm confident you (and your solution's users) will see direct benefits as a result.

Transaction Modeling

Many database systems, especially those supporting large data sets and enterprise-wide network demands (perhaps serving up data to thousands of users concurrently), provide no equivalent for FileMaker's calculation and summary field types. All data, whether input data or derived data, is calculated on the spot (for example, using a stored procedure), verified, and then stored.

FileMaker's calculation and summary field capabilities are a convenience I would not have you forego, but they carry a price. As the size and complexity of your solutions grows, reliance on calculations and summaries becomes less desirable. In large and heavily loaded systems, data integrity and solution responsiveness is best served by adopting a transaction-based approach to use-case definition — that is, design and define the user experience and the solution's response to user inputs in terms of transactions.

Live versus batch data

When your solution uses calculation and summary fields throughout, every action a user takes has flow-on consequences. Change the value of the quantity field in an invoice, and the change instantly propagates to the calculated totals and summaries showing on the user's screen. The automatic and immediate update of dependent values is the essence of live data interaction — as illustrated in Figure 19.2 — and many of the processes in FileMaker are built around this principle.

FIGURE 19.2

A dynamic interaction model where each user action produces a result.

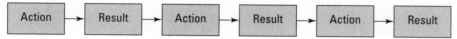

An alternative way to conceptualize a data management process is to separate input actions from consequential actions. In such a process, you enter all the required information and then press a key or click a button, and all the resulting computations (along with validations and integrity checks) are performed. If the process is complete and all validation requirements are satisfied, the data is written to the database (committed) as a single transaction, as shown in Figure 19.3.

FIGURE 19.3

A transactional interaction model — the final user action precipitates a result (reflecting all the preceding actions).

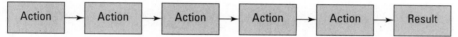

Posting edits and propagating edits to related records

When you implement a transaction-based interaction model, a complete set of changes is committed as a whole, in a single action. At the time of that action, all interdependencies are resolved, validation checks performed, derived values are generated and stored, and data summaries are updated in a single closing procedure.

In FileMaker, the closing procedure for a transaction is best managed by a script, where the script commits the record and all related records updated as part of the transaction at the close of its process. Because a script manages the user's interaction with the stored data, you can use the script to generate and store derived (calculated) values and update summaries at the point where each change is committed.

With this type of interaction model in place, summary values are computed and stored at the conclusion of each transaction rather than being recalculated across vast record sets in real time (consuming CPU resources constantly as the user navigates the database and works with the data). Each time the user commits a record, such as by clicking a custom Save Changes button on each layout, a short delay occurs while FileMaker adjusts the summary data. However, summary recomputation, even at this point, is not required. The script can simply increment or decrement each stored summary value to reflect the current transaction's contribution. Because all calculations and summaries are stored, navigation, screen refresh, and reporting are instantaneous regardless of the size of your solution.

Offline updates and processing

Another dimension of transactional systems is the potential for periodic data refresh using separate system processes not dependent on direct interaction between each client workstation and the host.

Overnight generation of updated summary data and reports is one implementation model for periodic processing. If you choose this approach, you schedule an extensive operation to occur during off-peak hours (overnight, for example) to generate queued reports, re-compute and store updated summary data (stock levels and so on), and perform various other batch processing tasks.

The strategic use of periodic updates (performed elsewhere — not on the client workstation) can relieve performance bottlenecks for a variety of non-time-critical requirements, freeing live computation or transactional updates to deal exclusively with immediate data requirements. For example, in a transaction process where the user records a customer payment and issues a receipt, the calculations generating the balance of account for the receipt and updating the customer balance record are required immediately, so you include them as part of the transaction work cycle. However, updates to the company profit and loss statements and general ledger aren't required instantly and can occur in an overnight batch run gathering all receipts and payments in the preceding 24-hour period. In this way, you free user transactions of much of the burden of consequential processing, enabling the system to be deft and responsive for end users, yet all the required data is available according to appropriate timelines.

Robots and batch automation

When you want to implement batch processing in a multi-user solution, several options are available. One of the most powerful and versatile options is deployment of a workstation dedicated to batch processing. Such a workstation is commonly termed a *robot,* as it self-regulates and performs a variety of preprogrammed tasks as an unattended client on the network.

A database robot has its own user account and remains logged in to the host database, as shown in Figure 19.4. Because its tasks are scheduled to occur without user intervention, you need to choose a late model or well-specified machine — if it meets the requirements to run FileMaker Pro 10 and is robust enough to run 24/7, it will suffice. Its job is to work quietly in the background, relieving the client workstations of non-urgent process work and ensuring lengthy and process-intensive tasks are routinely completed.

You don't need to limit robot deployments to overnight processing of lengthy batch jobs. You can use them as fax or database print managers, monitoring queues as users commit jobs for processing, generating the required documents throughout the daily work cycle, and then resuming routine batch processing outside scheduled work hours.

Host/server script execution

FileMaker Server permits you to schedule database scripts to run on the server at predetermined times. This approach provides you with a viable alternative to employing a robot workstation for some kinds of process work.

FIGURE 19.4

Overview of a server-based system incorporating a robot-processing station.

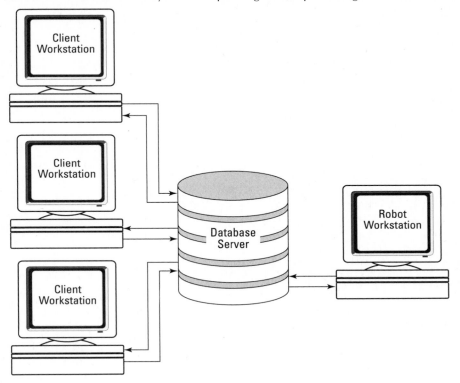

When you define a script to be executed on FileMaker Server, you're constrained to use Server-compatible script step subset. You can view the available commands by choosing Server from the pop-up menu labeled Show Compatibility in the lower left of the Edit Script window. Incompatible Script steps appear dimmed in the list of script commands at the left of the Edit Script window, as shown in Figure 19.5.

Despite the limited selection of commands available for use in scripts you want to schedule to run on FileMaker Server, you can address various operations using this mechanism. In general, I recommend that you schedule scripts to run during low-use times on FileMaker Server to minimize server load.

CAUTION Scripts scheduled to run on FileMaker Server fail if they include unsupported script steps (in other words, commands not indicated as Server compatible). A script containing incompatible steps either halts when the first such step is encountered (leaving the process incomplete and possibly leaving the solution of the data in an inappropriate state) or, if the `Allow User Abort[ ]` setting is off, continues, while skipping the incompatible step or steps.

FIGURE 19.5

Viewing the Server-compatible script command subset available for use in scripts executed on FileMaker Server 10.

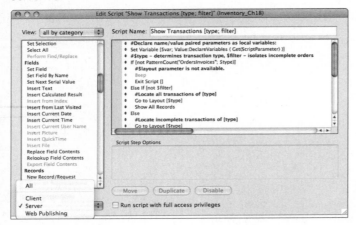

Managing File Size

A factor affecting both the manageability of your solution and its performance under load is the size of your database files. Large files are less efficient for several reasons.

One issue with very large files is that data segments are necessarily stored further apart on disk media, so more head movement is required to return nonsequential data sets, such as the results of a Find or records for display in a portal. FileMaker manages data caching to minimize performance impacts from this cause, but the performance you observe in a 200K file will outstrip your experience with a file approaching 5GB.

When files sizes become very large, a more profound impact arises because the backup process for the file takes considerably longer, which introduces periodic delays if your backups are frequent (and I recommend that they are)!

NOTE   The storage of text and numeric data — especially where a majority of fields are not indexed — is very efficient and is not generally the primary cause of large file sizes. Images and files stored as data are the most frequent cause of large file sizes.

Dealing with data in chunks

One way to mitigate the performance impact arising from large database files is to separate your data between two or more files. As part of this strategy, you can set separate backup schedules for each file. Because the files are smaller, performance impact when their backups occur will be less noticeable. Moreover, you don't need to back up less used files, such as reference data that rarely changes, as frequently.

Modularization strategies

If you need to address issues arising from file size, making modularization of your solution necessary, consider the following three approaches:

- Create separate database files to store container data — images, files, and multimedia content — using 1:1 relationships between records storing container data and the corresponding data records in your existing solution files.

- Build files to store any large reference data sets and/or low-use data tables, because you don't need to back them up as frequently as other files. This strategy is of greatest use where you have very large reference sets of historical or geographic data that rarely changes.

- Define functional centers based on the operational requirements of different groups of users of your solution, separating the main data sets for each functional center into a different file. For example, accounts payable may be in a separate file from product inventory.

One or more of these strategies may enable you to adapt your solution's deployment strategy to improve performance and minimize storage and backup issues.

Considering segmentation

An alternative approach to the management of large data sets is *segmentation,* where you subdivide data into ranges or subcategories, storing alternate blocks of data in separate "edition" files. For example, if your solution stores the content of newspaper articles spanning a century or so, you can consider segmenting data by decade, giving you ten files of manageable size, rather than one vast and unmanageable file.

Supporting segmentation requires an index file containing enough information, including keywords and titles, to let users search and summarize data across multiple segments. However, viewing a record's content in its entirety requires the user to navigate to the appropriate segment file. You can automate the navigation process, making the user's task a relatively straightforward one.

 Data segmentation is most useful for historical data sets where most segments are not expected to change or grow significantly.

Data archiving

At some point in any solution's life, the question of archival storage of old or low-use data arises. If you're concerned about the impact of file size on your solution's performance, archiving aged data may present a viable option.

The simplest method of archiving is to create a copy of your solution structure and import records older than a given date into the copy. However, I recommend that you make significant changes to the interface and scripts to ensure the following:

- **Users can't mistake an archive file for the current file.** You don't want users mistakenly entering new data into the wrong file or searching in vain for current data in a file of ancient records.

■ **Scripts, buttons, and screens associated with new record creation and other processes relevant only to current data are removed or disabled.** As part of this change, you should consider modifying all privilege sets assigned to user accounts to read-only in the archive file.

With an archive file established, build a scripted process in your solution to automate the process of locating candidate records for archiving and their transfer to the archive solution file.

CROSS-REF For details of the processes of transferring data sets between files or alternate systems, refer to Chapter 17.

NOTE When your solution includes an archive, all future changes of data structure should be replicated in the archive to a sufficient extent that the archive is always able to accommodate data from the current solution structure without transformation.

Images and Media in Databases

A significant cause of overly large database files is the storage of images and media content files, such as PDF or QuickTime, as part of your solution data. Be aware, however, of the range of options available to you for handling these content types.

If file size is the primary cause of performance issues, and that in turn is due to the storage of files and/or media content, one option you should consider is storing files separately, such as on a file server, and referencing them in your solution.

CROSS-REF For techniques and procedures for handling images and stored files, refer to the details in the closing pages of Chapter 17.

By defining a media file as an external FileMaker data source for your solution, and selecting the Allow Creation of Related Records in This Table via This Relationship option, the location of the container content in a different file will not be evident to users.

When considering options for efficiently storing and handling container data, you should consider the capabilities of Web viewers as a means to present image and media content stored remotely.

To incorporate Web storage and viewer access and display of media data as a primary content strategy in your solution, you need to employ external scripting and/or third-party tools to aid in the transfer of files to and from online server locations. Even so, the merits of online content management, including the options for integrating database operations with Web support, make this option worthy of further consideration.

CROSS-REF For additional details about external tools and products to assist in management of content via remote servers, see Chapter 20.

Chapter 20

Extending FileMaker's Capabilities

There is a great deal to know about FileMaker — so much that doing justice to its native capabilities, without providing coverage of the many related environments, technologies, products, and deployment options, in a book of this size is no small challenge. In this chapter, however, I provide you with a brief survey of products, tools, and techniques available to extend the reach of your solutions.

Many of the technologies I refer to here are the subject of a rich variety of books and other resources in their own right. I encourage you to consider the range of technologies available and choose appropriate resources for further exploration.

Because FileMaker's capabilities are extensive and provide support for wide-ranging functional requirements, you can create many solutions with FileMaker Pro without recourse to external tools or applications. When you reach the limits of the program's native capabilities, however, many options enable you to employ other technologies and push past those limits.

IN THIS CHAPTER

Making use of external scripting calls

Rendering Web source code in FileMaker

Using Web viewer widgets

Getting acquainted with FileMaker plug-ins

Exploring Web deployment options

Reviewing available third-party tools

External Scripting Calls

Among FileMaker's 137 (Mac) or 138 (Windows) scripting commands are two commands allowing you access to the repertoire of external capabilities made available via your computer's operating system and the scripting languages installed by default on your computer:

```
Perform AppleScript [ ]
```

and

```
Send Event [ ]
```

These commands enable you to configure your FileMaker scripts to execute AppleScript code on Mac OS and VBScript code on Windows. These scripting languages, in turn, let your solution execute command-line (OS Shell) calls and control other applications running on the current workstation. Moreover, the Send Event [ ] command can pass messages (open application/document, print document) to other applications on Windows.

> **NOTE** Send Event [] also passes messages (called *AppleEvents*) on the Mac. However, the syntax of the messages differs between the platforms, and events that succeed on one platform may fail on the other. I strongly recommend that you ensure that you are on the correct platform for the event your solution is going to send. The Get (CurrentPlatform) function is extremely useful in this determination.

Despite the wealth of possibilities you can access via these commands, be aware of the following issues:

- Whereas FileMaker solutions are cross-platform, AppleScript, VBScript, and command-line syntax are specific to each platform. While the capabilities of these technologies overlap, they work differently.

- When part of your script process occurs outside FileMaker scripting via calls to external script languages, conventional FileMaker error handling is not available. Therefore, your solution cannot as readily determine if the external script process has completed or succeeded.

- Some variations exist in script capabilities and syntax between operating system versions, so what works in your test environment may not work (or may produce different results) on an end user's computer. Moreover, dependencies on the end user's computer configuration may make some scripts vulnerable.

For these reasons, I recommend that you use FileMaker's native script capabilities as much as possible, invoking alternative script capabilities only for requirements falling outside the scope of FileMaker's scripting vocabulary.

Using Send Event and VBScript

On Microsoft Windows, you can execute either VBScript or command-line instructions from within your FileMaker scripts. Several methods are available for accessing external scripting capabilities. (I provide examples in the next two sections.) The process is relatively straightforward, giving you access to an immense vocabulary of instructions on the current workstation.

Using VBScript with FileMaker Pro

The Microsoft Visual Basic Scripting engine (VBScript) installs by default on current versions of the Windows Operating System (including the versions FileMaker Pro 10 requires to operate), making it a freely available resource for you to tap when your FileMaker solutions are deployed on Windows.

If you have a VBScript file already created and saved on your computer, you can run it using the Send Event [ ] script command. If desired, you can store a ready-made file containing VBScript code in a container field in your solution so that your script can export it and then run it as needed. For maximum flexibility, you can use FileMaker's calculation and scripting capabilities to create and run VBScript code dynamically.

In FileMaker 10, you can create a file containing a VBScript definition on a local disk drive and then have the Windows Script Engine run the file. You can efficiently accomplish this task by having your FileMaker script write the VBScript instructions into a global text field, then export them to a *.vbs file and open the file. The process requires a script sequence such as

```
Set Variable [$vbs; Value:"file:" & Get(TemporaryPath) & "FMPmessage.vbs"]
Set Field [Utility::gVBS; "MsgBox \"You've run VBScript from FileMaker Pro.\""]
Export Field Contents [Utility::gVBS; "$vbs"; Automatically open]
```

To create the VBScript file and open it in a single step, select the Automatically Open File checkbox option in the Specify Output File dialog for the Export Field Contents [ ] command, as shown in Figure 20.1.

FIGURE 20.1

Setting the Exported .vbs file to open automatically.

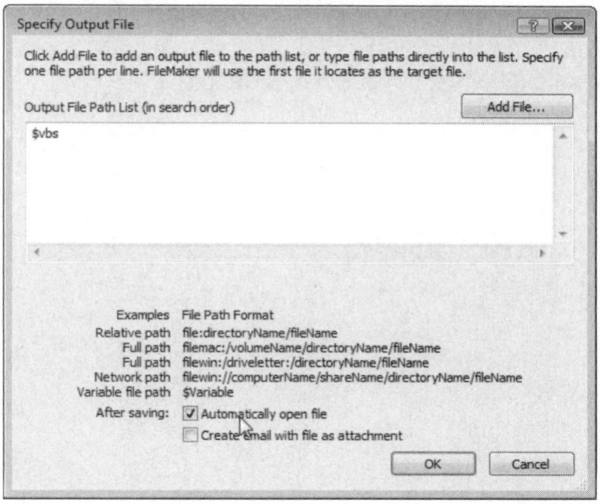

The example script shown here uses a single line of code containing the VBScript MsgBox command to invoke a dialog onscreen, as shown in Figure 20.2.

While the one-line VBScript that produces the dialog in Figure 20.2 is a useful, albeit basic, demonstration of the technique, you can use VBScript's extensive capabilities to automate a great variety of processes.

FIGURE 20.2

A VBScript dialog invoked from a FileMaker Pro script.

CROSS-REF You can find links to resources containing thousands of ready-to-use VBScript examples in Appendix A.

Calling Windows Command-Line scripts

You can also issue instructions to the Windows Command Line Interpreter using the FileMaker `Send Event [ ]` script command. For example, Figure 20.3 shows the Options dialog for the `Send Event [ ]` script command configured with appropriate syntax to create a folder at an explicit path.

FIGURE 20.3

Using `Send Event [ ]` to call a command script creating a folder on the current workstation.

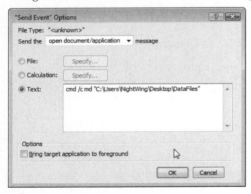

The example shown in Figure 20.3 provides a fixed text command-line instruction to create a new folder called DataFiles on the desktop of a user named NightWing on drive C:\ of the current workstation. The syntax of the code used in this example is formed as follows:

1. The instruction opens with `cmd` to invoke the Windows command-line interpreter (the cmd.exe application on the current computer).

2. The `/c` suffix is a command-line switch instructing the interpreter to exit after completion of the instruction.

3. The program call, md, is the command-line instruction for "make directory."

4. The closing argument `"C:\Documents and Settings\NightWing\Desktop\DataFiles"` provides the path (including the folder name) of the folder to create. The enclosing quotes are required only if the path contains spaces (as in this case).

NOTE When you use `Send Event [ ]`, a scripted pause may be required before any subsequent step that depends on the outcome. In this case, for example, if your script's next action is to place a file in the newly created folder, a short pause of 1 to 2 seconds is required to give the command-line interpreter time to create the folder and exit.

While this example illustrates the technique, in practice, you'll frequently find it more useful to determine paths dynamically. You can achieve the dynamic determination of paths using the option to employ a calculation specifying the `Send Event [ ]` command. For example, to build the path for creation of a folder named DataFiles, you can specify a calculation using as its basis the value returned by the built-in `Get(DesktopPath)` function, with an expression along the following lines:

```
Let([
UserDesk = Substitute(Get(DesktopPath); "/"; "\\");
MD_path = Right(UserDesk; Length(UserDesk) - 1)];
"Cmd /c md \"" & MD_path & "DataFiles\""
)
```

When you use a calculation to determine command-line syntax dynamically, as shown here, the procedure is more robust because it accurately reflects the extant environment on the user's computer.

CROSS-REF The command-line instruction used in the preceding examples (md) is one of a large number of available Windows commands. For additional information about available commands and their uses, refer to the resources listed in Appendix A.

The Windows `Send DDE Execute []` script step (DDE stands for Dynamic Data Exchange) provides added Windows-specific capabilities. In particular, it allows you to send service requests to other applications (such as a request to Internet Explorer to open a particular URL). The services available depend upon the application with which you're trying to communicate, so you need to examine that application's documentation for what it supports and the request syntax. While FileMaker Pro can send DDE requests, it isn't configured to respond to any DDE requests.

Perform AppleScript

On the Macintosh Operating System, your FileMaker scripts can make use of the built-in AppleScript scripting language, providing extensive control over the operating system and many applications. Moreover, through AppleScript, you can gain access to Shell Scripts (UNIX command-line instructions).

Executing AppleScript code from within your FileMaker scripts is as simple as configuring the `Perform AppleScript [ ]` command with an appropriate AppleScript instruction. For example, to have AppleScript display a dialog similar to the one in the preceding section's example, you can configure the Perform AppleScript options to run a line of Native AppleScript, as shown in Figure 20.4. When the script containing the Perform AppleScript instruction shown in Figure 20.4 executes, Mac OS presents a dialog displaying the specified message text, shown in Figure 20.5.

Needless to say, the one-line AppleScript shown here does not do justice to AppleScript's expansive capabilities. However, it serves to illustrate the basic technique for integrating external script calls into your FileMaker scripts.

FIGURE 20.4

Running a line of Native AppleScript code with the `Perform AppleScript` command.

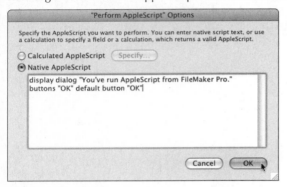

FIGURE 20.5

An AppleScript dialog invoked from a FileMaker Pro script.

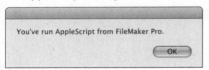

CROSS-REF   **You can find links to resources containing detailed AppleScript syntax and a broad collection of useful examples in Appendix A.**

In addition to its native powers, AppleScript gives you access to the operating system's command-line capabilities.

For example, rather than using AppleScript instructions to create a folder (which is certainly possible), you can use it to execute a Shell script. The example in Figure 20.6 shows an AppleScript call configured to run an OS script, hard-coded to create a new folder called DataFiles on the desktop of a user named nightwing on a volume named Macintosh HD on the current workstation.

FIGURE 20.6

Using AppleScript to call a Shell command creating a folder on the current workstation.

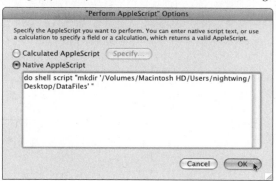

In practice, dynamically determining paths is frequently far more useful. You can, for example, use the shell syntax `"~/Desktop/DataFiles"` to determine the path to the DataFiles directory on the current user's desktop. Alternatively, you can employ the Calculated AppleScript option to specify the command syntax. For example, you can specify a calculation to build the required shell script instruction with an expression such as

```
"do shell script \"mkdir '/Volumes" & Get(DesktopPath) & "DataFiles' \""
```

Because you can create both AppleScript and OS Shell commands via calculation and execute them using the `Perform AppleScript[ ]` command, you have a great deal of scope and flexibility.

CROSS-REF For information and examples of Shell commands and their associated arguments, refer to the resources listed in Appendix A.

Cross-platform solutions and external script calls

While the external script options differ between MacOS and Windows, the command-line and script engine capabilities have significant overlap, so you can accomplish many external scripting tasks on both platforms with the appropriate syntax.

To make best use of external script calls in your solutions, consider including a platform test and execute the external scripts according to the result. For example, to create a folder named DataFiles at the root directory of the boot drive, regardless of platform, you can use the following script code:

```
If [Abs(Get(CurrentPlatform)) = 1
   # Current Platform is MacOS-execute AppleScript/Shell Script:
   Perform AppleScript ["do shell script "mkdir 'DataFiles' ""]
Else
   # Current Platform is Windows — call Command-Line instruction:
   Send Event ["aevt"; "odoc"; "cmd /c md C:\DataFiles"]
End If
```

With strategic branching according to platform, your solution's scripts can respond appropriately wherever the files are opened. Using this technique, you can successfully incorporate a significant number of external script actions into your cross-platform solutions.

> **TIP** Because the `Perform AppleScript [ ]` command is not available on Windows, the third line of the preceding script must be tested with the file open on MacOS. Although the `Send Event [ ]` step is available on both platforms, I recommend that you create and test the external script calls for each platform on the appropriate operating system.

On Mac OS, the `Send Event [ ]` command provides you with the capability of directly sending AppleEvents to other applications (or even to your currently running copy of FileMaker Pro). When you install FileMaker Pro 10 (or FileMaker Pro 10 Advanced) on a Mac, a FileMaker Pro database of AppleEvents is installed in the English Extras folder within the FileMaker folder within Applications.

On Windows, you can use the `Send Event [ ]` command to pass open or print events to designated applications, pass single lines of script, or invoke the command-line interpreter. A FileMaker database of script commands and code operable on Windows is available as a free download from the ConnectingData Web site (`www.connectingdata.com`).

Third-party helpers and macros

Beyond FileMaker scripting, you can use a variety of external tools to automate common procedures, including repetitive FileMaker tasks.

Depending on the platform, you can use AppleScript or VBScript to initiate processes, opening files and setting scripts in motion (script calls require the use of ActiveX on Windows) and controlling your solution's interface.

Other third-party automation and scheduling tools are also worthy candidates for the automation of both developer and end-user processes involving your solution (or your solution's interaction with other applications). For example, QuicKeys (available for both Mac OS and Windows) is a versatile macro environment providing user-configurable automation options for most sequences of keyboard and mouse input.

Other useful tools for enhancing productivity include TextExpander (Mac OS), As-U-Type (Windows), and AIM Keys (Windows) — each offering aids to the efficiency and accuracy of a wide variety of data-entry and computer management tasks — within and beyond your database solutions.

Rendering HTML and JavaScript

FileMaker's `Open URL [ ]` script step and the Web viewer layout object give you direct access to content from a wide variety of sources, including Web services and output from a variety of applications capable of generating hypertext or Web-compliant content.

With the advent of FileMaker 10 and its increased support for Data URLs, FileMaker itself is now one of the applications you can use to generate Web viewer content. You can render calculations and stored data directly in FileMaker Web viewers using the following syntax:

```
"data:text/html,"  & YourTO::YourHTMLcontent
```

In this example, the trailing field reference (or a calculation expression in its place) produces HTML and/or browser-compatible content (Flash, Javascript, and so on).

Harnessing HTTP

When you produce Web content using any third-party tool, such as Dreamweaver, Netbeans IDE, or Eclipse, you can substitute placeholder flags for content or page rendering values (colors, sizes, coordinates). When you store the resulting content in FileMaker in a text field, your calculations can substitute values from the current record's fields (and its related data) for the embedded place-holder values.

This process's output is a dynamic rendering of your solution content. You can pass the result directly to a Web viewer for screen viewing or printing (or output to pdf, e-mail, and so on) or save the result to an external file, such as on a Web server for public access.

Using variations on the techniques described here, your solutions can incorporate the full depth of interface, data display, and dynamic visualization available using current Web and browser technologies.

Bringing services to your solution

With a Web viewer pointed to any URL on the Internet, your solution can retrieve the page source using the following simple FileMaker calculation expression:

```
GetLayoutObjectAttribute ( "ViewerObjectName" ; "content" )
```

To reliably retrieve the source code from a designated Internet address, you must account for load times, pausing until the full content of the destination page has been recovered. You can do so with a scripted loop procedure.

CROSS-REF For a detailed description of script technique for scraping data from Web pages, refer to Chapter 10.

Using Web viewers in your solution lets you choose to render the content for screen or print output or to store the content as data in your solution. By combining the techniques discussed here with those described in previous sections, you can recover the source from a remote Internet address and then use it as a template or *wrapper*, interleaving or embedding data from your solution and rendering or printing the result.

Alternatively, these techniques allow you to draw source content from multiple sites, combining them and presenting them in a format of your choosing.

CAUTION Always ensure that your use of content not originating within your solution is in accordance with the terms of use and copyright provisions of its owners, authors, and publishers.

Handling hypertext

Moving content between conventional data storage, such as text and number fields, and hypertext presents some challenges regarding formatting. By using FileMaker's native `GetAsCSS( )` function, you can convert embedded text character formatting, including styles, sizes, fonts, and colors, to a tagged form appropriate for display in a Web viewer or browser environment.

For example, to display formatted text content from your database in a Web viewer, configure the Web viewer (in Layout mode, via the Web Viewer Setup dialog) to enclose the data URL content within the `GetAsCSS( )` function, as shown in Figure 20.7.

FIGURE 20.7

Configuring a Web viewer to render embedded character formatting from content originating in data fields.

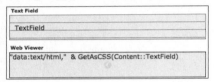

Using this technique, any character formatting applied to the text in the TextField field will be replicated in the CSS-tagged content the Web viewer renders. You can see the rendering of styled field text in a Web viewer in the Browse mode image of the same layout reproduced in Figure 20.8.

FIGURE 20.8

Web viewer in Browse mode, displaying data formatting.

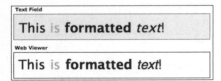

NOTE A Web viewer renders unformatted text (that is, text without embedded character formatting) according to the default Web style — not necessarily matching the field box's display formatting. The application of default formatting applies separately to each aspect of formatting (font, size, style, and color).

Web Viewer Widgets

Web viewers bring additional functionality to FileMaker. There is a world of innovation on the Web, much of it leaking into FileMaker layouts through Web viewers large and small.

With the gathering momentum of Web 2.0, dynamic and interactive content forms are appearing and evolving at an alarming rate — so I'm resigned to anything I write here being old news almost before the words hit the page. You can assume that what I say here applies equally to a variety of technologies — including some not yet revealed.

Charting with Flash

Data visualization tools are far more abundant with every passing year. Many of these tools cropping up in recent years are compact Shockwave Flash (.swf) files capable of receiving and rendering arrays of user data. The variety and quantity of this class of tools is steadily increasing, and a number of the tools are available free (and others are licensed for modest shareware fees).

The significance of this burgeoning technology for FileMaker lies in the opportunities you have to incorporate Flash charting into your solution. You can perform this feat by

1. Storing the required Flash resource file in a container field.

2. Exporting the file to a known path on the user's workstation (for example, to the `temp` directory).

3. Setting a calculation to append arrays of solution data to the path to the Flash resource file.

4. Loading the resulting string into a Web viewer on your solution's layout.

Moreover, while this process requires a script to render your data in graphical form on your layout, by placing the required resources during your solution's start-up script and setting the path calculation as the default path for your Web viewer, you can make the process fully dynamic. Your solution's data will be charted "live" as users navigate records and edit field contents.

Applets and servlets

The process outlined in the preceding section isn't limited to data visualization. In addition to graphical and rendering widgets, a generation of calculation, communication, and analysis utilities is emerging in the form of miniature Web-capable, self-contained code snippets. Some of these emerging tools — commonly called *servlets* — are designed to operate in a fixed environment on a remote server, yet are accessible to anyone with a Web connection. Others are entirely portable, compatible with the models of use I've described for charting utilities, and are referred to as *applets*.

FileMaker is positioned to make full use of emerging technologies of this kind — and their continuing availability appears assured. Whatever the future of computing may hold, component technologies are set to be a significant part of it.

FileMaker Plug-Ins

No survey of FileMaker's options for extensibility would be complete without mention of the plug-in API (Application-Program Interface) and the extraordinary variety of plug-in utilities (some so sophisticated they might be better thought of as ancillary applications) developers have made available as FileMaker plug-ins.

Although the plug-in interface was first envisaged (with the introduction of FileMaker 4) as an adjunct to the calculation engine — a way for developers to provide support for obscure computation functions — it rapidly became the base of wide-ranging innovation, with plug-ins emerging to serve such diverse purposes as script scheduling, systems integration, e-mail handling, and image manipulation.

As with almost every technology available for extending the program's scope, I could fill a book in its own right with detailed coverage of FileMaker plug-ins, their capabilities, and their use. I can't hope to do justice to even a fraction of the available tools here. However, I can provide you with an overview of the main techniques used to control plug-ins and some guidelines for their use.

Installing and enabling plug-ins

To install and fully enable a plug-in on your client workstation installations of FileMaker Pro or FileMaker Pro Advanced, follow these steps:

1. Obtain the correct version of the plug-in for your computer's operating system and place it in the `Extensions` folder inside the folder containing your copy of FileMaker Pro 10 (or FileMaker Pro 10 Advanced). Plug-ins on Mac OS have the file extension `.fmplugin`, whereas Windows plug-ins use the `.fmx` extension.

2. Launch FileMaker Pro 10 (if it's already running, quit and relaunch it to load the new plug-in) and choose FileMaker Pro ➪ Preferences (MacOS) or Edit ➪ Preferences (Windows). The Preferences dialog appears.

3. Navigate to the Plug-Ins tab, confirm the new plug-in appears in the list, and (if it's not already selected) select the checkbox next to its name, as shown in Figure 20.9.

   In your solution, configure the start-up script to call the plug-in's version function confirming its availability (and verifying the required version of the plug-in — or later — is installed). If the required plug-in version isn't available, try the following:

   - If your solution is hosted and you're using AutoUpdate to retrieve required plug-ins from the Server, have your script call the `FMSAUC_FindPlugIn( )` external function to search for the plug-in on the server and, if found, subsequently call the `FMSAUC_UpdatePlugIn( )` external function to retrieve and install the plug-in.

   - If the plug-in isn't available and your solution's functionality depends on it, post a dialog alerting the user to the problem and close your solution.

NOTE Commercial and shareware plug-ins must be licensed and generally require that a valid license code be supplied by your solution before first use of the plug-in in each application session.

Passing a required license code to a plug-in is usually achieved by calling an external "register" function provided by the plug-in. Consult the documentation supplied by your plug-in vendor for details of the appropriate syntax for plug-in registration.

FIGURE 20.9

Enabling a plug-in via the Preferences Plug-ins tab.

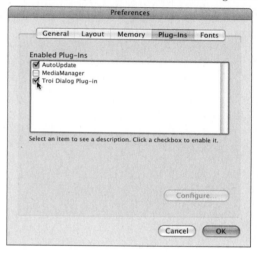

FileMaker Pro installs by default with a plug-in named AutoUpdate enabled. AutoUpdate enables you to configure your solutions to retrieve current versions of required plug-ins when they're stored in the designated plug-ins folder on the current FileMaker Server host computer.

To take advantage of plug-in auto-update capabilities, you must configure the following in accordance with the operational requirements of the AutoUpdate process:

- FileMaker Server
- FileMaker Pro
- Your solution's start-up script

When each of these components are configured appropriately, the required plug-in versions are checked and, if necessary, are downloaded from FileMaker Server and enabled on the user's workstation, as your solution starts up.

A notable change in the operation of the auto-update feature with FileMaker 10 is that plug-ins are automatically downloaded to new locations on the user's workstation. The target locations, depending on the user's operating system and platform, are

- On **Mac OS X:**

  Mac OS X: Macintosh HD/Users/User Name/Library/Application Support

- On **Windows XP:**

  C:\Document Settings\User Name\Local Settings\ApplicationData\ FileMaker\Extensions

- On **Windows Vista**;

  C:\Users\User Name\AppData\Local\FileMaker\Extensions

The same plug-in folder locations are accessed by both FileMaker Pro 10 and FileMaker Pro 10 Advanced.

> **TIP** The user can choose to place plug-ins in the local folders manually if desired, rather than placing them into the FileMaker Pro application folder. This method may be preferable in cases when the user doesn't have privileges allowing them to modify the Applications folder (on Mac OS) or Program Files folder (Windows).

> **NOTE** For additional information about the configuration requirements for automatic update of solution plug-ins, refer to the document named FileMaker Server 10 — Guide to Updating Plug-ins provided with the FileMaker Server 10 manuals and documentation. (It's also available from the Downloads section of the FileMaker, Inc., Web site.)

Using external functions

Invoking plug-in capabilities requires you to call an external calculation function provided by the plug-in, supplying appropriate arguments to control the behavior of the plug-in, and pass it required data or parameters. The purpose of each external function — and its required syntax — is specific to the individual plug-in and should be detailed in documentation available from the plug-in vendor.

> **TIP** Simply including an external function in a calculation is not sufficient. FileMaker's calculation engine must evaluate the function. For example, if you have the MediaManager plug-in installed and you call the external function Media_RecordSoundStop in the following calculation expression:

```
If(DayOfWeek(Get(CurrentDate)) = 5; Media_RecordSoundStop)
```

the sound recording function of the MediaManager plug-in will be stopped on Fridays.

You can take advantage of this behavior by using calculation code to determine how and when external functions are evaluated.

Most plug-ins are designed to be called via calculations occurring in your solution's scripts (by including external functions in the formula for a `Set Field [ ]` or `Set Variable [ ]` command, for instance). However, you can include plug-in functions wherever calculations are supported so that you can add plug-in calls in schema calculations, access privileges calculations, conditional formatting expressions — wherever is appropriate for the plug-in functionality you require.

> **NOTE** Ideal techniques for including external function calls in your solutions may vary according to a given plug-in's nature and functionality. Most plug-in vendors provide example databases showing a range of recommended techniques for calling the external functions provided by their plug-in. Such examples are indicative of the range of viable and supported triggering methods for the plug-in.

Script triggering

One of the most ubiquitous plug-in capabilities is *script triggering,* which offers you the ability to trigger a script from a calculation in your solution. Script triggering capabilities can substantially extend and enhance your solution's capabilities. However, it can also lead to problems if not implemented expertly. For example:

- If your solution triggers a script from a schema calculation, and the script modifies the current record resulting in re-evaluation of the same calculation, your solution may become trapped in an infinite loop. The risk is no greater than pertains to the use of the FileMaker `Loop`/`End Loop` script commands (where failure to include a valid exit condition also results in an infinite loop) or the `Perform Script [ ]` command (where an inattentive developer can set a script to call itself). Nevertheless, you should be aware of the need to plan your implementation of script triggering with care.

- Calculations are evaluated when leaving a field or record, and you can use them to trigger a script (by inclusion of an external function call within the calculation expression). However, when you intend to have the script act upon the current record and the user exits the field by navigating to a different record, by the time your script commences, the current record is not the one where the trigger calculation was evaluated. Therefore, you must allow for this possibility and design your scripts accordingly, avoiding unintended outcomes from such uses of script triggering.

You can address both these issues by designing an appropriate framework for your script triggering plug-in calls, mindful of the potential issues, as I discuss in the next two sections.

Robust triggering implementations

To ensure that your script triggers aren't activated by the actions of the script they call, becoming loop-locked, enclose schema (and schema-dependent) trigger calls within a condition preventing the evaluation of the external function if the script is already running. For example, to use the popular zippScript plug-in to call a script named `"Check"` in the current file (without the optional parameter or control settings), you can use the external function syntax:

```
zippScript_PerformScript(Get(FileName); "Check")
```

However, to ensure that the external function will not be evaluated if the Check script is already active, enclose the function in a conditional expression, as follows:

```
If(Get(ScriptName) ≠ "Check"; zippScript_PerformScript(Get(FileName); "Check"))
```

If the Check script calls other scripts that may in turn modify the field (or fields) used to trigger the external function call, you may need to guard against indirect recursion as well. To do so, extend the If( ) test in the preceding expression to forestall the trigger action while any of the implicated scripts are active.

By controlling the evaluation context of script triggering function calls as outlined in the preceding example, you can manage the external calls, determining the context when triggering occurs (also including other criteria if desired). This approach is appropriate in cases where the called script may have consequences leading to re-evaluation of the external function activating the trigger, including schema calculations, privilege (Record Level Access) expressions, and layout calculations, such as Web viewer and conditional formatting expressions.

In cases where a triggered script is required to act on the record where the external function is evaluated, such as for data-entry validation, data updates, and other record-specific script processes, you need to capture the context where triggering originates. You can do so by using the external function call to pass a parameter to the called script, including the ID of the calling record in the parameter. In the following example, the zippScript function passes the primary ID of the current customer record to the Check script:

```
zippScript_PerformScript(Get(FileName); "Check"; CustomerID)
```

You should then structure your check script so that when run, it first confirms that the calling record is current and, if not, accesses it — for example, you can use one of the following methods:

- Structure your script to
  - Capture the current context (mode, layout, record, and window)
  - Freeze the screen, navigate to a utility layout, and enter Browse mode
  - Enter the script parameter value into a global field you've configured to establish a relationship to the relevant customer record

  The script can then proceed to perform its check procedure while accessing the appropriate record via the utility relationship, subsequently returning the user to the script's commencing context.

- Have your script create a new temporary database window out of the user's field of view (for example, off-screen), navigate to the customers layout and perform a Find to locate the relevant customer record, perform the required check, and then close the temporary window.

In either case, your script ensures that its actions are applied to the appropriate record, yet faithfully reinstates the context (active window, layout, found set, and current record) invoked by the user on leaving the field at the point the external function call triggers the Check script. With this implementation, the user can leave the current record by changing layouts, navigating to a different record, entering a different mode, or closing the current window, without compromising the script's ability to perform its intended function.

One further condition you should account for to ensure that your script triggering implementation is robust is the case where a user leaves the current record by closing the file or exiting the application. Because it's likely that your script trigger will not succeed in such a case, if it's essential that the script runs when data is edited, I recommend that you set the script trigger in an auto-enter calculation set to return a session ID value (for example, user login account and workstation ID) when triggered and have your script clear the value when it runs.

With this configuration, your file's closing script should check for the presence of the current session ID in the current table and, if found, call the check script before completing its run.

When you set in place a thoughtfully designed (and thoroughly tested) implementation along the lines set out in this example, you can be confident that your scripts will always run when triggered, will never lock your solution in a loop, and will always act on the appropriate record.

Available script triggering plug-ins

A number of excellent script triggering plug-ins are available, and many provide triggering in addition to a variety of other features. Worthy offerings include MenuMagic from New Millennium Communications (http://newmillennium.com), ScriptMaster from 360Works (www.360works.com), and Troi Activator from Troi Automatisering (http://troi.com). Each of these plug-ins provides additional functionality (and, in the case of MenuMagic, an extensive suite of security and menu customization options).

NOTE An FMExample plug-in supplied on the FileMaker Pro Advanced installation CD includes script-triggering capabilities. However, I advise against its use for most script-triggering purposes because it does not include the ability to pass a parameter to the called script. Consequently, the FMExample plug-in is unsuitable as a trigger for any script where context is relevant to the actions the script performs.

Dialog capabilities

The FileMaker Show Custom Dialog [ ] script step offers a core set of capabilities enabling you to perform two or three of the tasks commonly handled using dialogs in modern computer systems. Several leading third-party vendors — perhaps the best known being 24U Simple Dialog from 24U Software (www.24usoftware.com) and Troi Dialog Plug-in from Troi Automatisering (www.troi.com) — offer plug-ins with dialog capabilities.

Dialog plug-in capabilities include adding custom icons or graphics to your dialogs and altering the dialog's size or placement, including pop-up lists, checkbox options, radio buttons, fields of various sizes, and dynamically labeled buttons. Figure 20.10 shows an example of a dialog produced by calling an external function.

FIGURE 20.10

A customized text display dialog produced using the Troi Dialog Plug-in.

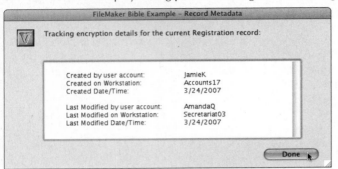

The customized dialog example shown in Figure 20.10 was created by calling three of Troi Dialog's external functions in succession, to specify the custom icon, the dialog title, and the parameters for the dialog to be displayed respectively. The syntax for the relevant script code is as follows:

```
Set Variable [$x; Value: Dial_IconControl("-SetCustomIcon"; I::gDialogIcon)]
Set Variable [$x; Value: Dial_SetDialogTitle( "" ; "FileMaker Bible Example -
                         Record Metadata" )]
Set Variable [$x; Value: Dial_BigInputDialog( "-Width=600 -Height=280
                         -CustomIcon -DefaultButton1 -StopOnESC" ; "Tracking
                         encryption details for the current Registration
                         record:" ; "Done" ; "" ; "" ; "" ; Registrations::cRec
                         ordMetadata)]
```

NOTE **Many other dialog formats and options are available. Full details of the syntax options for each external function — with examples of their use — are available from the vendors' sites.**

While the example provided here gives you an indication of what is involved — and what results you can expect — from using a dialog plug-in, I have barely scratched the surface in an effort to point you in the right direction. I recommend that you download trial copies of plug-ins to determine the most appropriate options for your solution.

File and media handling

One of several other areas of plug-in functionality worth highlighting is the broad range of file and media capabilities brought to FileMaker by a number of premier third-party providers — plug-ins such as CNS Image from CNS (www.cnsplug-ins.com), File Manipulator from Productive Computing (www.productivecomputing.com), MediaManager from New Millennium (www. newmillennium.com), and Troi File from Troi Automatisering (www.troi.com).

These plug-ins and others like them simplify the process of managing external content and extend your reach beyond what can readily be achieved with the combination of FileMaker Pro's native file management capabilities, and those available to you via the use of external scripting, as outlined in the "External Scripting Calls" section earlier in this chapter.

Also noteworthy with respect to content management tools is the SuperContainer plug-in from 360Works (www.360works.com), designed to provide coordinated access to remote server storage of files and media content using a Java servlet in conjunction with a Web viewer in your solution.

E-mail, HTTP, and FTP

An ever-expanding selection of plug-ins providing support for online connectivity continues to emerge from established and new third-party vendors. Long-standing contenders such as mail.it (http://dacons.net), SMTPit, POP3it, FTPit (http://cnsplug-ins.com), and Troi URL Plug-in (http://troi.com) have been joined by the 360Works Email Plugin (http://360works.com) and the TCPdirect and SendMail offerings from Fusion (http://fusionplugins.com).

Recently, however, vendors are providing connectivity tools that combine broad-based and mixed capabilities in a single powerful plug-in. One of the difficulties these products face is their breadth and the potential to overlook them when targeting specific (and more traditional) niches. The release in recent years of Smart Pill from Scodigo (www.scodigo.com), the MBS FileMaker Plugin from Monkeybread Software (www.monkeybreadsoftware.de), and Fusion Reactor from Digital Fusion Ltd. (www.fusionplugins.com) — each exciting and ground-breaking in their own right — are equally hard to categorize in light of their versatility and breadth of applicability.

Charting and other functionality

Another area of plug-in functionality with an established user base is charting and data visualization. Here the plug-in contenders include xmCHART from X2max Software (www.x2max.com), 24U SimpleChart Plugin from 24U Software (www.24usoftware.com), and the Charts Plugin from 360Works (www.360works.com). The breadth and depth of functionality varies between vendors, but continues to provide many users a viable alternative to more recent Web viewer–based charting options.

Also notable for the variety of options available are interapplication communication and data transformation plug-ins. Some of the many available options provide data conduits between FileMaker and established accounts, CRM, e-mail, address book, and organizer applications.

NOTE If you're interested in writing your own plug-ins, you can find an example plug-in project on the installation disk for FileMaker Pro Advanced. Moreover a plug-in development template and tutorial is available from 24U (www.24Usoftware.com).

Suffice it to say, innovative plug-in developers around the globe cover an extraordinarily large number of bases, extending the uses of the API in every direction conceivable. A great deal more is on offer than I have been able to touch on here. If you have a problem, the chances are somebody has already solved it with FileMaker plug-in.

CROSS-REF For additional details regarding the broad range of third-party plug-ins, refer to the online resources listed in Appendix A.

Web Deployment Options

In addition to its power and versatility as a desktop and client-server database system, FileMaker provides options for Web deployment, enabling you to use your FileMaker data as the basis of Web site content. If your data includes schedules, catalogs, collections, facts, or figures, the chances are someone would like to look it up on the Web.

If you don't require users to enter data into your database (and if your data changes only infrequently), one option is to export your data as an HTML table (one of FileMaker's built-in data export formats) and incorporate it into an appropriate HTML framework by adding HTML frames, headers, and/or style sheets. But if your data requires two-way interaction or needs more than periodic updates, a live Web connection direct to your solution is preferable.

Instant Web publishing

If the fmiwp extended privilege is enabled for one or more privilege sets in your solution, you can make your database available to up to five concurrent Web users in a matter of minutes by choosing File ➪ Sharing ➪ Instant Web Publishing and configuring the open databases for access, as shown in Figure 20.11.

Once Instant Web Publishing (IWP) is enabled, users will be able to open your solution using a supported web browser, by entering the IP address of your computer (preceded by http://) in their browser's address bar. Your solution's layouts are rendered in the user's browser and navigation, data entry, and limited scripts (those containing only Web-compatible script commands) are available.

Because of the nature of web browsers — an inherently stateless user experience — FileMaker layouts are not as dynamic and responsive in IWP. The user experience is less suited to the FileMaker interface model than the FileMaker client application, and some layout objects exhibit different behavior when accessed via a web browser. Nevertheless, IWP is a remarkable technology and serves a range of purposes well.

NOTE To access your solutions via Instant Web Publishing, the user's browser is required to provide full support for Cascading Style Sheets (CSS). That limits users to Internet Explorer 6.*x* (or later) or Firefox 1.*x* (or later) on Windows and Safari 1.2.*x*, Safari 2.0.*x*, Safari 3.*x* or Firefox 1.*x* (or later) on Mac OS.

FIGURE 20.11

Configuring your database for web browser access via the Instant Web Publishing dialog.

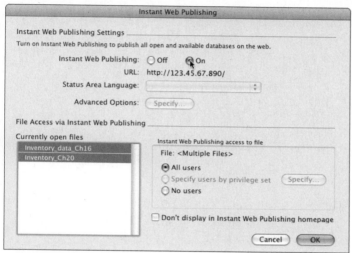

If you can work within the IWP format's functional constraints, but require more than five simultaneous users, you should consider hosting your solution on FileMaker Server Advanced to make your solution available to up to 100 simultaneous Instant Web Publishing users.

> **TIP** When using IWP, you can use the Web folder in your FileMaker Pro folder to store external files, such as images and referenced container files, to share via Instant Web Publishing. You can also include a customized entry page of HTML using the `filename iwp_home.html`, plus other pages of static HTML if required.

Custom Web publishing

If you require more than 100 simultaneous Web-based users, support for a larger selection of Web browsers, or greater flexibility and control over the Web-browsing experience than is achievable within the constraints of Instant Web Publishing, FileMaker Server provides support for other forms of Web access to your solutions.

Custom Web Publishing enables you to build an alternative Web-specific interface to your solution, reading and writing directly to your solution's data structure in real time. Support is available for Web-publishing strategies based on XML/XSLT or PHP.

Working with XML and XSLT

When your solution is hosted using FileMaker Server, you can make data access (for both read and write) available via XML (Extensible Markup Language) and XSLT (Extensible Stylesheet Language

Transformation). By using XSLT, you can extract and transform your data into appropriate presentation formats for a variety of applications, such as Web forms, news feeds, or special-purpose downloads from your Web site.

Similarly, using XML with XSLT can also dynamically generate the source and content for your Web pages, including data from FileMaker and, if desired, from other sources as well. To generate Web content using XML, you require an appropriate XSLT style sheet as the intermediary between FileMaker Server and its Web-publishing engine.

The FileMaker PHP API

If you host your solution using FileMaker Server, you can make use of its built-in PHP support, making content from your solution available directly to external Web sites, receiving input from Web users. The support for PHP's open source standards for the Web enables you to rapidly assemble Web-based applications to access your FileMaker data via live, real-time connections with FileMaker Server.

With your installation of FileMaker Server, you receive a standard install of the PHP engine, the FileMaker API for PHP and sample code, and documentation. Once the server is operational, you have everything you need to begin publishing your FileMaker data via PHP.

 To prepare your solution for use with the PHP API, first activate the fmphp extended privilege for privilege sets in your solution files, as shown in Figure 20.12.

FIGURE 20.12

Activating the fmphp extended privilege in your solution files.

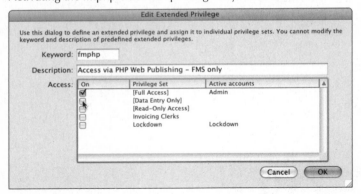

FileMaker's PHP Site Assistant

FileMaker Pro 10 includes a PHP Site Assistant to walk you through the processes required to produce PHP-based Web pages, replicating a range of common Web design elements and formats such as data collection forms, list searching, and database record editing. You can take the resulting pages and place them directly on your Web server or open them in the Web-design environment of your choice (such as Dreamweaver, RapidWeaver, or GoLive) to edit and further refine the HTML.

By using the PHP Site Assistant, along with FileMaker's PHP API, you achieve an efficient method of creating direct links between your FileMaker solution and a new Web application forming the basis of your Web site. If you're an experienced PHP developer, you can bypass the Site Assistant and work directly with the FileMaker API for PHP. By doing so, you gain direct access to the broad range of capabilities PHP provides in conjunction with the functionality of your existing FileMaker solution.

CROSS-REF Refer to the documentation provided with your installation of FileMaker Server for additional detail and instructions about the use of the PHP Site Assistant and the FileMaker PHP API.

Finding Third-Party Tools

The catalog of third-party tools you can find a use for in your FileMaker development is well beyond the scope of the advice I can offer here. It's an ongoing adventure for us, as it will be for you. However, several FileMaker-specific third-party tools are so useful or particularly suited to use with FileMaker that they deserve a mention here.

Developer tools

When you're confronted with a challenging development task involving extensive manual updating of complex FileMaker solution files, you'll be relieved to know that powerful third-party automation tools can reduce the labor and increase the accuracy of your work. FMRobot from New Millennium (www.newmillennium.com) re-creates field definitions, custom functions, value lists, and privilege sets in a new FileMaker Pro 10 file, based on the structure and content of a source file, which can be in any version from FileMaker 6 onward.

Also from New Millennium is Security Administrator, which enables you to manage passwords and privileges centrally across a multi-file FileMaker solution. This tool lets you automate multi-file account management in FileMaker 10.

As an alternative or adjunct technology for generating PHP Web pages and developing and customizing Web applications that integrate closely with FileMaker data, FMStudio and FXForge from FMWebschool (www.fxforge.net) cover a lot of ground and help you leverage multiple technologies to meet complex Web requirements.

For pure convenience and peace of mind when your solution is running on FileMaker Server, AdminAnywhere from 360Works (www.360works.com) lets you access Server administration features, monitor backups, and manage users remotely from a variety of devices via a browser interface you can run on a handheld device, such as iPhone or Palm Treo.

Analysis and documentation

Beyond the capabilities of the DDR generated by FileMaker Pro Advanced, several third-party tools give you direct access to an abundance of detailed information about your solution files.

Foremost among the new breed of FileMaker analysis tools is FMDiff from Huslik Verlag GmbH (www.fmdiff.com), a deceptively simple tool capable of directly examining alternate versions of your FileMaker Pro files and detecting the differences between them. FMDiff also has a range of other useful capabilities, such as detecting and reporting possible structural anomalies and revealing embedded metadata, such as the version of FileMaker used to create your solution files, the versions used to open the file, and the number of times (if any) the file has been recovered.

Operating on different principles, yet no less impressive, is BaseElements from Goya (www.goya.com.au). When you generate a DDR from your solution, BaseElements can import, organize, and analyze the content, enabling you to rapidly detect errors, locate references to specific database objects, and identify unreferenced objects at all levels in your solution. Built in FileMaker, BaseElements massively extends the scope and value of the DDR, giving you the ability to comprehensively analyze and document your solution and to compare different versions of your solution.

At the time of writing, other well-known and useful tools include MetaDataMagic from New Millennium (www.newmillennium.com) and Inspector from FMNexus (www.fmnexus.com). MetaDataMagic presently supports files in the .fp5 format and is an invaluable tool for use prior to and during the conversion of solutions from the .fp5 format. Inspector supports the .fp7 format and is a versatile and impressive analysis tool. Both tools remain invaluable for analysis of files created in previous versions, and I look forward to their support for FileMaker Pro 10 in the future.

Shared information

Undoubtedly the most powerful tool of all is the information shared generously among members of the international developer community. Developers at all levels of expertise from countries on all continents willingly solve problems and exchange knowledge and expertise. Rather than jealously guard trade secrets and nurse competitive advantage, FileMaker developers have a long history of collegiality, where problems are shared and solutions debated in open forums.

I encourage you to build your skills and share them with others that you in turn may benefit from the collective expertise of FileMaker developers across the globe.

CROSS-REF A variety of resources, including Web links to community-sponsored forums and online archives of FileMaker-related information, are available in Appendix A.

Part VI

Appendixes

Despite the size of this volume and the scope of its coverage of FileMaker techniques and functionality, there is a great deal more to learn and to discover. I have given you examples and pointers that should make the journey easier and more enjoyable, but it doesn't end here. To continue to develop your skills as a FileMaker developer, you'll need access to a variety of supplementary resources.

This part contains an overview of additional sources, references, and resources that you'll find useful for further exploration and details about the book's companion Web site, which contains links to download the example solution discussed throughout Chapters 5 through 16.

IN THIS PART

Appendix A
Expanding Your Knowledge with Additional Resources

Appendix B
About the Web Site

Index

Appendix A

Expanding Your Knowledge with Additional Resources

This book and the documentation accompanying your FileMaker Pro 10 software provide a solid foundation for using FileMaker Pro 10 and leveraging its power. However, a worldwide community of FileMaker users and developers exists, and many of them share useful information, tips, and examples of both general and specific nature.

In this appendix, I describe and enumerate many of these other useful FileMaker information sources. These sources include consulting and development services, FileMaker technical support, online and published periodicals, and references to online discussion groups and mailing lists. You can find links to this appendix's references on the book's companion Web site for those sources with an Internet presence (see Appendix B).

From the Horse's Mouth

The FileMaker, Inc., Web site (www.filemaker.com) is your contact point for online product support. But, more than just providing a technical and customer support contact point, the site is a repository of information, including links to tutorials, sample files, a directory of consultants, and a compendium of various FileMaker add-ons, plug-ins, and developer tools (some freeware, some shareware, and some commercial).

In addition to these general categories, the FileMaker Web site includes viewable *Webinars* (recorded Web seminars); access to a broad online Knowledge Base of product issues; solutions and answers to specific questions; PDF copies of the various product manuals; and links to purchasing books (including this one) and magazines devoted to FileMaker. You can find a treasure trove of these and a wealth of other downloadable resources at www.filemaker.com/support/downloads/index.html.

IN THIS APPENDIX

Finding accurate and current information

Locating professional support and services

Sourcing examples and technique demos

Discussing FileMaker online

Using FileMaker printed and periodical resources

NOTE While FileMaker's Web site provides online support access, talking to a person is sometimes beneficial. The Product Technical Support number of 800-325-2747 or 408-727-8227 (if outside North America) fills that bill. Be aware that, unless you purchase an extended support option (FileMaker calls it *Priority Support*), this phone support is limited to one call related to installing the software and one call related to usage problems. Priority Support offers single-case, five-case, and annual options.

Beyond the resources available from the FileMaker, Inc., Web site, resources and mailing lists are available via the membership-based programs (TechNet and the FileMaker Business Alliance) offered to developers and businesses working with FileMaker. Through these resources, users and developers around the globe stay abreast of news, changes, updates, and new releases of the software, and exchange notes with each other and the Developer Relations contacts at FileMaker, Inc. Other resources, such as white papers and technical briefs, are available exclusively to members of FileMaker developer organizations.

NOTE Membership in TechNet and the FileMaker Business Alliance includes significant benefits in addition to providing access to a communication network dedicated to improving the state of the FileMaker development art. Ancillary software, access to prerelease versions, and even copies of FileMaker applications are included, based upon the membership chosen. See the FileMaker Web site for further details.

As an annual event, the FileMaker Developers Conference provides four days of intense information, resources, and exchange between attendees from many parts of the globe. At the time of publication, the next such event is scheduled to take place in San Francisco in August 2009 and will attract speakers and delegates from all major continents. In addition, regional conferences and special-purpose events (colloquia, briefings, meetings, and the like) are conducted in other cities with either sponsorship or involvement of FileMaker, Inc.

Professional Consulting and Development Services

A global network of professional FileMaker developers exists, many of whom provide and support complex applications for clients in a vast range of industries and in many countries of the world. FileMaker provides a certification program through a network of external test centers worldwide as a step toward the assurance of the knowledge and skill of professionals working in the field. Because FileMaker has been in use since 1985, professionals with extensive experience are available.

For those located in Canada and the United States, FileMaker, Inc., publishes a *FileMaker Resource Guide* listing individuals and companies providing FileMaker-based solutions and consultancy services. The current edition is available online from the FileMaker Web site at `www.filemaker.com/downloads/pdf/resource_guide.pdf`.

Regrettably, the community is heavily shortchanged by the Resource Guide's predominant focus on businesses located in the Americas, as it excludes much of the worldwide network of developers and numerous other world-class FileMaker resource providers. With the ready availability of the Internet, you need not be limited to one region or country when looking for the best support or solutions.

To access information about developers the world over, visit the FileMaker, Inc., regional Web sites listing consultants and developers in many other countries. These sites are available separately and managed by their respective regional offices of FileMaker, Inc. For example, FileMaker in France is represented at `www.filemaker.fr`, FileMaker in the Asia Pacific region is represented at `www.filemaker.com.au`, in the United Kingdom FileMaker's Web site is `www.filemaker.co.uk` in Japan FileMaker's Web address is `www.filemaker.co.jp` and so on. You can find a full list of international Web locations at `www.filemaker.com/company/intl/index.html`.

You can find alternative sources of information about professionals working with FileMaker on public resource Web sites, such as FMPug.com and FMPro.org, FileMaker forums, or via the ubiquitous Internet search engines. For example, a search for "FileMaker Pro developers" on Google.com presently produces more than 1.2 million hits.

NOTE   **Due to the dynamic nature of the Internet and technology companies, I don't include a comprehensive list of URLs because they frequently become out of date. Instead, I encourage you to use the directories and resources outlined in this section to locate the help you need. In the following sections, I do, however, provide URLs for a few sites of particular interest.**

Online Design and Development Tips and Tricks

While I provide you with a broad base of design principles and techniques, as well as more than a modicum of examples and tips for developing your solutions, a book this small (yes, I said "small") can't begin to cover the breadth and depth of specific approaches you can employ, problems and solutions you may encounter, nor all the specific challenges you will face.

Fortunately, in addition to the professional FileMaker consultants referenced in this appendix and the publications listed in the upcoming section "Books and Periodicals," other resources also provide high-quality examples, tips and tricks, and developer techniques. Foremost among these are the collections of example files freely available from Database Pros in California (`www.databasepros.com`); NightWing Enterprises in Australia (`www.nightwing.com.au/FileMaker`); and from commercial providers, such as ISO FileMaker Magazine (`www.filemakermagazine.com`) and FMWebschool (`www.fmwebschool.com`). Specialist FileMaker Custom Function resources are available from Cleveland Consulting (`www.clevelandconsulting.com`) and BrianDunning.com (`www.briandunning.com`). Information, tips, and techniques are also plentifully available among innumerable blogs including those from The FileMaker Collective (`www.fmcollective.`

com), Six Fried Rice in Arizona (`www.sixfriedrice.com`); Tokerud's FileMaker Fever (`http://tokerud.typepad.com/FileMaker`), and FileMaker Addict (`http://file makeraddict.blogspot.com`). Also, topics of interest are regularly placed under the microscope (or at any rate, in front of the microphone) on the periodic Adatasol FileMaker Podcasts (`http://podcast.adatasol.com`).

An international network of FileMaker Pro user groups operates and is coordinated from the FMPug.com Web site (`www.fmpug.com`). FMPug provides a vast collection of other useful resources, including a desktop compendium of code and other resources called "The Everything Reference for FileMaker Developers"; online directories of trainers, developers, and consultants from the world over; a database of feature and enhancement requests; and reviews of books and third-party products for FileMaker Pro users and developers.

In addition, innumerable professional development companies offer tips and examples of their work, sometimes giving generally applicable insights or approaches to problems encountered in a variety of contexts. Many of these resources are available free of charge, for the trouble of seeking them out!

 **A search for "FileMaker demos" produces more than a million hits each on both Yahoo! and Google's search engines.**

Online Forums and Mailing Lists

The Internet is teeming with mailing lists and online forums, many of which are free, publicly accessible, and full of rich and varied content about many facets of FileMaker Pro programming and use. A selection of the more targeted FileMaker-specific mailing lists and forums are provided at `www.filemaker.com/support/mailinglists.html` and `www.filemaker.com/support/forums.html`. If you have Usenet access, a newsgroup, `comp.databases.file maker`, is an active discussion group covering FileMaker topics.

 **You can also use the Google Groups (`http://groups.google.com`) interface to access Usenet groups.**

Foremost among online forums for all things FileMaker is FMForums.com, boasting more than 40,000 members and approaching a decade online. The largest single online community of FileMaker users and developers, FMForums attracts a diverse group of participants representing all levels from the merest of beginners to the most accomplished professionals.

Also worthy of mention is the RealTech list operated for members of FMPug and dealing with a broad range of technical issues and challenges relating to FileMaker and FileMaker-related products and solutions. In addition, a number of the user groups listed on the FMPug site sponsor their own mailing lists, wiki Web sites, or online resource pages.

Books and Periodicals

Numerous books are available about FileMaker Pro and related technologies, some repeating material available among the resources mentioned in the preceding sections, or offering little that is not amply covered in this book. I would, however, like to recommend several volumes that provide explorations or detail on matters that go beyond the scope of this book:

- *The Everything Reference for FileMaker Developers* by Andy Gaunt and Stephen Dolenski (FMPug.com)

- *FileMaker 9 Developer Reference* by Bob Bowers, Steve Lane, and Scott Love (Que Publishing)

- *FileMaker Security: The Book* by Steven H. Blackwell (New Millennium)

- *Web Publishing with PHP and FileMaker 9* by Jonathan Stark (Sams Publishing)

Each of these publications offers a wealth of additional information that will prove useful to the professional developer and serious amateur alike. I recommend these titles for the accuracy, quality, and depth of information they provide.

Additionally, while you can occasionally find articles about FileMaker Pro usage in general computer print magazines, such as *Macworld* or *PCWorld,* the following publications contain more concentrated coverage:

- *FileMaker Pro Advisor* is dedicated to FileMaker and related subjects. ADVISOR MEDIA, Inc.; PO Box 429002; San Diego, CA 92142. Web site: `http://my.advisor.com/pub/filemakerAdvisor`.

- *Databased Advisor* covers database issues and includes FileMaker among the database management systems covered (although Access, xBase, and other platforms consume the bulk of the ink). ADVISOR MEDIA, Inc.; PO Box 429002; San Diego, CA 92142. Web site: `http://my.advisor.com/pub/DataBasedAdvisor`.

- *MacTech Magazine* covers popular Macintosh technologies from the perspective of the "serious" user (and FileMaker is one of the many technologies covered). MacTech Magazine; PO Box 5200; Westlake Village, CA 91359-5200; 877-622-8324 805-494-9797 outside US/Canada); `http://www.mactech.com`.

Appendix B

About the Web Site

This appendix describes what you can find on this book's companion Web site at www.wiley.com/go/filemaker10bible. While you can use any relatively current Web browser and operating system to peruse the site's pages, using much of the available content will impose additional requirements. For example, using the sample files will necessitate running FileMaker Pro 10 or FileMaker Pro 10 Advanced, with their consequent Mac OS and Windows requirements.

IN THIS APPENDIX

Locating resources accompanying the book

Taking steps to solve any problems that arise

> **TIP** You can download a free 30-day trial copy of FileMaker Pro 10 from www.filemakertrial.com.

In addition to the preceding requirements, you need an Internet connection and appropriate computer hardware to access the Web site and run the required operating systems and other software.

What's on the Web Site

The following list provides an overview of what the book's Web site contains:

- **Author-created materials:** I include copies of all the referenced example files used in this book, in the corresponding chapter link, in the Author section. In particular, I have made each iteration of the Inventory example solution available so that you can look at it in various stages of evolution, comparing it to experiments you may have created while working through the book's examples. Additionally, I offer a few referenced special examples. I also include a glossary

- **Application and documentation links:** Exhaustive coverage of FileMaker's capabilities would require a book far larger than this one, and the ancillary information grows daily. Consequently, I avoid including reference data that is readily available elsewhere. For example, comprehensive lists of calculation functions and script commands for FileMaker Pro 10 are available as PDF downloads from the FileMaker Web site. Rather than include this extensive material as part of the text of this book, I use the space otherwise and encourage you to download the companion documents from the links I provide on the companion Web site.

In this section of the Web site, I include links to the trial version of FileMaker Pro 10 provided as a free download by FileMaker, Inc., as well as links to a variety of documents FileMaker, Inc., makes available that I believe to be particularly useful as an adjunct to the information I have collected in this volume.

I also provide links to useful utilities, including plug-ins, from a variety of third-party vendors such as 360Works, New Millenium, 24U Software, Troi Automatisering, Digital Fusion, and others, and utilities from companies such as FM::Nexus, FXForge FMDiff, and Goya. Finally, I include links to groups and periodicals devoted to the FileMaker development community, including FMPug user group resource, FileMaker TechNet, FileMaker Forums, the ISO FileMaker Magazine, FileMaker Advisor, and significant providers of demo and example files such as Database Pros and my own company, NightWing Enterprises.

Troubleshooting

If you have difficulty accessing the Web site or downloading any of the provided materials (not including items downloaded from other sites to which I provide links), please contact the Wiley Technical Product Support Center at 800-762-2974 (outside the United States, call 1-317-572-3993) or online at www.wiley.com/techsupport.

Additionally, if you have trouble installing or using software from any of the linked sites:

- Check to ensure that you have the requisite system software version, disk space, and memory required for that software.
- Ensure that the files or applications have been extracted from archives (.dmg or .zip and so on) in which they are provided for download.
- Disable any virus-protection software during the installation. Many viruses mimic the actions necessary for an installer to function, and the virus-protection software is prone to confuse the two. (Remember to re-enable your virus-protection software after completing the installation.)
- Quit other programs you have running. In addition to freeing up memory for the installation to proceed, the absence of other running programs removes any conflict as to files the installer may need to access, update, or replace.

Should you experience ongoing problems after following each of these steps, contact the site from which you obtained the software to seek advice or assistance. Note that some sites may require a purchase or fee to provide you with personal support.

Index

Numerics and Symbols

#comment script, 505
$ character, 340
$$trace variable, 384, 443
$$var variable, 474
$ReportPath variable, 528
$result local variable, 622
$YourVariable[8] array notation, 477
& (ampersands), 240
*.vbs file, 711
... (Range operator), 143
\ (backslash character), 235
| (pipe character), 396
< (less-than) symbol, 415
</body> tag, 393
= (equi-join) operator, 414
= symbol, 411, 413
> (greater-than) symbol, 415
× (Cartesian product operator), 415
≤ (less-or-equal) symbol, 415
≤ relationship symbol, 307
≠ (not-equal join operator), 414
≥ (greater-or-equal) symbol, 415
≥ relationship symbol, 307
360Works AdminAnywhere, 731
360Works Charts Plugin, 727
360Works Email Plugin, 727

A

about information, 398
Abs( ) function, 697
abstraction
    Evaluate( ), 482–483
    GetField( ), 480–481
    GetFieldName( ), 481–482
access privileges. *See also* granular security
    defining and constraining access, 560–561
    full, running script with, 511–512
    overview, 510–511, 558–559
    privilege-based errors, 511
    role-based security, 560
    schema privilege controls, 561–562
    setting default, 150–152
    substantive, determining, 512
Account Management Script command, 571
accounts, user
    creating, 568
    internal and external authentication, 568–570
    overview, 148–150, 567
    scripted management of, 570–572
    setting default, 150–152
accounts commands, 262
Accounts tab, Manage Accounts & Privileges dialog, 149
Acquired Items Report script, 272, 528
Active Directory, 568
active object, 500
active script, 459
ActiveRecord variable, 390
Actual SQL Server driver, 249–252
adaptable design, 692
adaptable screens, 362–363
Adatasol FileMaker Podcasts, 738
Add Expression control, Watch panel, Data Viewer, 664
Add Fields to Portal dialog, 192–193, 309
Add Newly Defined Fields to Current Layout checkbox,
        Layout tab, Preferences dialog, 156
Add Relationship dialog, 244
addressing windows by name, 537–538
Adjust Window [Hide] command, 542
Adjust Window [Resize to Fit] command, 379
AdminAnywhere, 731
Advanced Records Options dialog, 635
Advanced Recover Options dialog, 97–98, 635–636
aggregate functions, 473–474, 476
aggregating calculations, 132–135
aggregation, scripted data, 526
AIM Keys, 716
alert dialogs, 151, 214, 220–221
alias icon, 37

alignment of graphic objects, 183–184

Allow Creation of New Layouts option, Custom Layout Privileges dialog, 565–566

Allow Creation of Related Records in This Table via This Relationship option, 421–423, 708

Allow User Abort[ ] command, 280, 508, 514, 572, 705

Allow User to Override during Data Entry checkbox, Validation tab, Options for Field dialog, 219

alphabetic prefix, 585–586

alphanumeric serial value, 586

Also Reduce the Size of the Enclosing Part option, 369

alternate language indexes, 344–345

Always Lock Layout Tools setting, Layout tab, Preferences dialog, 56

Always radio button, Validation tab, Options for Field dialog, 219

AmountPaid field, 457

ampersands (&), 240

analysis tools, 732

anchor-buoy graph, 423–425

anchoring objects
    centering, 382
    complex layout resizing, 379–381
    enclosing, 382
    moving according to window size, 378–379
    overview, 377
    that grow and shrink, 379

ancillary data, incorporating in user edits, 624–626

ancillary notes, 430–431

AND Find, 318

and operator, 455

AND predicate operator, 415

annotations, Relationship Graph, 427–428

anticipating users, 146–147

anti-join, 390, 414–415

[Any New Layout] privilege setting, 566

API (Application/Program Interface) plug-in, 30–31

appending PDF pages, 204

AppleEvents, 710

AppleScript, 713–715

applets, 719

application links, 741–742

Application menu, 355

application verification, 514

Application/Program Interface (API) plug-in, 30–31

archiving
    backup files, 603
    data, 707–708

arguments, 229, 265, 268

arithmetic operators, 453–455

Arrange By pop-up menu, 547

array notation, 477

arrays
    collapsing, 421
    defined, 16
    expanding, 421
    overview, 420
    relationship-based techniques for managing data, 421–423
    repeating fields, 420

arrow keys, 161, 186

assistance programs, 32

association table, 409

As-U-Type, 716

audit log, 627, 630

AuditTrail field, 626

authentication, user
    creating user account, 568
    internal and external, 568–570
    overview, 567

Authentication panel, Edit Data Source dialog, 92–94

author-created material, 741

auto-enter calculations
    data modification at entry, 617
    Do Not Replace option, 488
    handling styled source text, 619
    order of operations, 456
    overview, 486
    storage, 488
    trailing spaces and carriage returns, 618
    user over-ride capability, 486–488

Auto-Enter tab, Options for Field dialog, 118–124, 216–218, 584, 590

Auto-Entry
    anticipating user, 146
    ESS tables, 255
    lookups, 595–596
    Manage Database dialog, 216–218
    serial, 584–586

Automatically Create Indexes as Needed option, 341–343

Automatically Open File checkbox option, 711

automation
    of database security, 570–571
    process, 12

auto-save behavior, 38

AutoUpdate utility, 56, 721–722

Available Items button, 315–316
Available Menu Commands option, 574
Average of summary function, 226

B

Back button functionality, 384–385
backslash character (\), 235
backups
    appropriate cycle, 600
    automating, 286–287
    code, 601
    copying open files, 601–602
    frequency of, 600
    hosted files, 603
    importance of, 40
    integrity of, 601
    local files, 602–603
    location, 601
    overview, 599–600
BaseElements, 732
batch automation, 704
batch data, 702–703
Batch field, 325
batch processing, 286, 704
Bento personal database solution, 22, 94–95, 547
black boxes, 448
Body, layout, 170, 308
body tag, 393
Boolean operations, 456–457, 697–698
break fields, 68, 366
bright colors, 386
Browse mode
    controlling one window from another, 317
    data formatting, 718
    defined, 43
    filtering portals, 306–313
    overview, 14
    pick lists, creating, 306–313
    shortcut navigation, 313–316
    Sub-summaries, 68–70
    using multiple windows and views, 306
business layer, 432–433
button click-shade highlighting, 354
Button Setup dialog, 196–197, 311, 314, 329–330, 469
Button Setup option, Format menu, 195
Button tool, Status Toolbar, 195–196

buttons
    calling scripts via, 298
    commands, 198–199
    defining, 196–198
    launching script via, 280
    for moving between layouts, 190
    multi-state, 361–362
    as objects, 199
    overview, 47, 195
    for paper configurations, 203
    scope, 198–199
    for static and dynamic actions, 154
    tooltips, 176
BuyerID field, 312
Buyers TO, 307
By Calculation option, 526

C

cache setting, Memory tab, Preferences dialog, 56
cache update, 690
cached data, 38–39
caching join results
    advantages of, 347
    gaining control of cache, 349
    solving problems with, 348
Calculated AppleScript option, 715
Calculated Value checkbox, Auto-Enter tab, Field Options dialog, 218
calculation fields
    versus auto-enter calculations, 486–488
    creating, 229–232
    defined, 16, 215
    global, 489
    letter generators, 373
    overview, 222–227
    unstored, 483
calculation functions
    Char(code), 90
    Code(text), 89
    Count( ), 237
    Date( ), 237
    Get(DocumentsPathListing), 91
    GetFieldName(field), 90
    Get(LastError), 505
    Get(TriggerKeystroke), 88–89
    Get(TriggerModifierKeys), 89
    Length( ), 237–238

calculation functions *(continued)*
    List( ), 236
    overview, 447–448
    Round( ), 237
    schema references, 450–452
    structured syntax and nesting, 452–453
    syntax, 449–450
calculation variables, 339–340, 458–459
calculations
    abstraction, 480–483
    aggregating, 132–135
    auto-enter, 486–488
    Boolean operations, 456–457
    calculation fields, creating, 229–232
    capabilities of FileMaker, 31
    compound calculation expressions, 448–453
    custom functions, 494–496, 691
    documenting code, 496–498
    environment and metadata, 492–494
    formulas, defining, 233–234
    global, 489–492
    lists, 476–480
    literal text, entering, 234–235
    order of operations, 454–456
    overview, 228–229, 447–448
    referencing fields, 235–236
    setting up, 124–126
    simple, 238–241
    standard data formations, applying, 617
    summary data, 473–475
    syntax, 449–450
    text formatting operations, 467–470
    text parsing, 462–463, 466–467
    text processing, 460–466
    time, 470–473
    unstored, 483–485
calendar year calculations, 240
calling scripts
    buttons, 298
    Custom Menus, 298
    external script calls
        AppleScript, 713–715
        cross-platform solutions, 715–716
        macros, 716
        overview, 301, 403, 709–710
        Send Event [ ] command, 710–713
        third-party helpers, 716
        VBScript, 710–713

file open and file close scripts, 299
    hotkeys, 297–298
    layout event Script Triggers, 299–300
    object event Script Triggers, 300–301
    from other scripts, 298–299
    overview, 279
    Scripts menu, 297
    on timer script triggers, 299
camel case, 115, 428
Cancel dialog button, 355
capital letters, 115
Caps Lock key, 696–697
carriage returns
    dealing with, 618
    delimited lists, 476
    delimiters, 642
    text-handling, 653
Cartesian joins, 415, 419
Cartesian product, 390
Cartesian product operator (×), 415
cascading calculation operations, 346
cascading deletion, 592–595
cascading name changes, 208
Cascading Style Sheets (CSS), 728
Case statement, 233–234
case-sensitivity, 234
cDynamicKey unstored calculation field, 418
Ceiling( ) function, 240, 464
centering objects, 382
certification program, 32
cFilter_key =LastName join attribute, 307
cFilter_key field, 308
cFullName field, 309, 640
Change Password[ ] script command, 506
character-level formatting, 334
CharacterSet( ) function, 683
Char(code) function, 90
charting plug-ins, 727–728
Charts Plugin, 727
Check Consistency option, 634
Choose( ) function, 693
chronological roll-back, 628–629
circular references, 244–245, 451–452
cleansing, data
    ETL cycle, 643
    filtering capabilities, 646–647
    format considerations, 643–646
    overview, 643

Clear All button, Set Tab Order dialog, 186
Cleveland Consulting, 737
click-shading effect, 354
click-sort columns, 327–331
ClientDetails field, 463
ClientID field, 590–591
Clients table, 551, 590
Clients::ClientID field, 590–591
Clients::LastName field, 591
Close Window command, 309
closing files, 38
closing scripts, 515
cMasterKey text calc, 418
cmd command, 712
CNS Image, 726
Codd, Edgar F., 7, 405–406
code backups, 601. *See also* efficient code
code objects, 391–392
Code(text) function, 89
collapsing arrays, 421
color
    depth and dimensionality, 386
    differences in screen rendering, 354
    effect on user, 175
    formatting for printing, 166
    in printed reports, 202
    of text, 162–163
    TOs, 131
color palette
    Layout tab, Preferences dialog, 56
    Relationships tab, Manage Database dialog, 131
ColumnSort script, 328, 330
command-line interpreter, 712
commands. *See also* specific commands by name
    button, 198–199
    control, 262, 273
    Custom Menus, 298
    editing, 262
    fields, 262
    files, 262
    found sets, 262
    interface dependent, 273
    keyboard shortcut, 297–298
    navigation, 262
    records, 262
    script
        assigning attributes to, 276–278
        branching according to state, 518–519

changing order of, 274–276
    groups, 262–265
    overview, 273–274
    window management, 536–537
spelling, 263
Status Toolbar, 68
windows, 262
comma-separated values (CSV), 543, 642
comment braces, 211
Comment function, 291
comment operators, 453
commenting, script, 290–291
Comments field, 409
commission on earnings above threshold, 238
committing records, 49–50, 107
community-sponsored forum, 732
comparative operators, 414–415, 453–455, 457
compatibility filters, 103
compound calculation expressions
    functions, 450–452
    logic, 449–450
    nesting, 452–453
    overview, 448–449
    schema references, 450–452
    structured syntax, 452–453
compound Find criteria, 318
compound interest, 239
compound keys, 418
concatenation operator, 467
conditional execution, 281
conditional expressions, 126
conditional formatting, 179–181, 360–362
Conditional Formatting dialog, 180, 330, 360–361
Conditional Formatting for Selected Objects dialog, 330
conditional statements, 281–282
conditional tooltips, 176–177
configuration dialogs, 179
consistency check, 96
constants, 229, 450
constellations, 424
contact databases, 8
contact details, 146
Contact Details layout, 500, 504
ContactFilter table occurrence, 307–308
ContactFilter::ContactType field, 307
ContactFilter::LastName field, 307
ContactID value, 312, 521
Contacts table, 146, 308, 313–314, 501, 625

Contacts::Address field, 618, 619
Contacts::FirstName field, 511
Contacts::Organization field, 625
Contacts::PhoneNo field, 617
container fields, 17, 215
container objects, 548–549
Content field, 392
context
    layout, 152
    managing, 153
    relationships, 55
    scripting, 266–267
Context pop-up, Specify Calculation dialog, 230
control characters, 646
control commands, 262, 273
controller palettes, 317
conversion, file, 40–41
Copy All Records/Requests[ ] command, 320
Copy Blocks As-Is option, 635
copy/clear/paste method, 275
copying
    commands, 274
    open files, 601–602
    and pasting, 126, 288–289
correspondence, 11
Count ( ) function, 237
Count of summary function, 226
Create child record sub-script, 525
Create Database tab, Quick Start screen, 36, 101–102
Create Runtime Solution application(s) option, 684
Creation checkbox, Auto-Enter tab, Options for Field dialog, 127, 217
Criteria_array field, 321
cross-platform development, 28–29
"crows foot" terminator, 411
cSearch field, 417–418
cSort1_asc text calculation, 325
cSort1_dsc text calculation, 325
cSort2_asc text calculation, 326
cSort2_dsc text calculation, 326
cSortBy field, 475, 480
CSS (Cascading Style Sheets), 728
CSV (comma-separated values), 543, 642
cTrace field, 443–444
cUnstored field, 411
Current panel, Data Viewer, 661–664
current quarter calculations, 240
Current Script menu, 311–312, 330

Current Script option, 534
Current tab, Data Viewer, 659
Current Value dialog, 663
custom delimiter, 654
custom dialogs
    attributes, 377
    as data-entry device, 376–377
    overview, 355, 375–376
custom functions, 494–496, 523, 572, 676–677
Custom Layout Privileges dialog, 563–564, 566
Custom Menus, 278, 298, 669–671
Custom Privileges dialog, 565
Custom Privileges options, 562
Custom Record Privileges dialog, 564–565
Custom Script Privileges dialog, 563
custom synchronization, 650
Custom Value List Privileges dialog, 563
Custom Web Publishing
    FileMaker PHP API, 730
    FileMaker PHP Site Assistant, 730–731
    overview, 729
    XML and XSLT, 729–730
Customer table, 412, 504
Customize dialog, 66–67

D

damaged files, 39
Data Access and Design section, Edit Privilege Set dialog, 149, 560–562
data architecture. *See* data structure
data archiving, 707–708
data arrays, 16
Data checkbox, Auto-Enter tab, Field Options dialog, 217
data cleansing operations
    ETL cycle, 643
    filtering capabilities, 646–647
    format considerations, 643–646
    overview, 643
data domain, 645–646
data entry. *See* entering data
data files, 435
data maintenance. *See* maintaining data
data modeling
    alternative relationship techniques, 416–420
    arrays, 420–423
    deployment considerations, 445
    documenting database structure, 427–431

external SQL sources, 439–441
file architecture versus data structure, 434–439
implementing separation in existing solution, 442–445
layers, 431–434
overview, 405
relational theory, 405–410
relationship operators, 413–416
Relationships Graph symbols, 410–412
Relationships Graph techniques, 423–427
data modularization, 349
data organization, 644
data presentation, 644–645
data redundancy, 7
data relationships, 408
data separation
approaches to, 438
costs and benefits, 439
external SQL sources, 439–442
implementing in existing solution, 442–445
data sets, synchronizing
import matching, 648–650
importing selectively, 650
overview, 647–648
Data Source Name (DSN), 247–252, 547
Data Sources menu, 442
data structure
interface files, 436–438
modular approach, 435
multi-file solutions, 434–435
overview, 9, 434
separation of data, 438–439
data types, 214–216
data updates, 286
Data Viewer
Current panel, 661–664
debugging restricted privilege scripts, 658–659
sand box, 665–666
temporary edit interfaces, 613–614
using with Script Debugger, 665
variables, 666–667
Watch panel, 661, 664–665
Database Design Report (DDR)
capabilities, 668
interpreting data, 669
mining for information, 668
overview, 208, 667–668
Database Design Report dialog, 667
Database Management Systems, 22

Database Pros, 737
database robots, 704
database solutions
data, 8–9
FileMaker Pro 10, 13–19
interface, 9–11
overview, 8
process management, 12
Databased Advisor, 739
DatabaseNames function, 449–450, 493
databases
calculations, 124–126, 132–135
digital age, 5–6
documenting structure, 427–431
duplicating data, 143–148
Field Options dialog, 118–124
fields, adding, 114–118
file security, 148–152
forms, 4–6
lists, 4–6
metadata, capturing, 127–128
overview, 3–4, 112–114
paper-based, 4–5
planning, 6
preparing for, 111–112
relational, 6–8
relationships, creating, 129–132
security, automation of, 570–571
tables, 4–6, 114–118
usability, 152–154
viewing data, 135–143
[Data Entry Only] privilege set, 559
DataFiles folder, 712–713
_DataLog field, 624
data-on-demand usage model, 426
Data::Serial# field, 585
Date( ) function, 237, 448–449
date fields, 215
date formats, 336
DateOfBirth field, 450
dates
juggling days, months, and years, 472–473
managing, 470
DATETIME values, 94
DDE (Dynamic Data Exchange), 713
DDR (Database Design Report)
capabilities, 668
interpreting data, 669

DDR (Database Design Report) *(continued)*
  mining for information, 668
  overview, 208, 667–668
Debugger window, 657
decimal currency, 164–165
DeclareVariables( ) custom function, 523–524
declaring variables, 340
default error dialog, 508
default menus, 670
default script error dialog, 507
Default Script option, 105–106
Delete Related Records option, 592, 595
deleting
  data, 141
  fields, 213–214
  redundant records, 591–595
  tables, 206–208
delimiters, 642–643
delineation of element groups, 386
dependencies
  cascading calculation operations, 346
  filename references, 598
  indirect object/element references, 597
  limits of, 346–347
  literal text references, 597
  overview, 49
  simplicity, 698–701
  structural anomalies, 598
  table of, 224
  tiers of, 347
deployment, 445
depth, computer interface, 385–387
Description field, 468, 542
Description.txt text file, 542
design. *See also* interface design
  adaptable, 692
  custom export process, 654
  layout, 18, 25–26
  online development and, 737–738
  screen, for users, 174–175
design functions, 493–494
desktop products, 26–27
DestinationState field, 646
developer certification program, 32
Developer Utilities dialog, 684
DeveloperNotes table, 430
Development Conventions paper, 428

dialog command, 502
dialogs. *See also* specific dialogs by name
  custom, 375–377
  plug-ins, 725–726
  user, 286
digital forms, 9–10
dimensionality, interface
  color, 386
  delineation of element groups, 386
  embossing effect, 385
  engraving effect, 385
  spatial cues, 385–386
  translucency, 386–387
  transparency, 386–387
disappearing objects
  concealed and remotely operated Tab Control, 358–360
  conditional formatting, 360
  overview, 356
  portal invisibility, 356–358
Display Custom Message if Validation Fails option, Validation tab, Options for Field dialog, 220
display titles, 671
displaying related data
  within layout context, 191
  overview, 191
  portals, setting up, 191–195
Distance from Left attribute, 374
Distance from Top attribute, 374
Do Not Apply Visual Spell-Checking option, 187–188
Do Not Evaluate When All Referenced Fields Are Empty checkbox, 457
Do Not Print option, 167, 169
Do Not Print the Selected Objects checkbox, 363
Do Not Replace checkbox, 488, 618
Do Not Replace Existing Value of Field (If Any) setting, 488
Do Not Replace Existing Value of Field option, 486, 617, 624
Do Not Replace option, 488, 617
documentation, 290–291, 398–399
documentation links, 741–742
documenting
  code
    commenting, 497–498
    formatting, 497
    overview, 496–497
  database structure
    ancillary notes, 430–431
    field commenting, 429–430

graph annotations, 427–428
naming conventions, 428–429
overview, 427
documents path, 91
Don't Evaluate checkbox, Specify Calculation dialog, 231
Don't Repeat Yourself (DRY) programming
principle, 596, 689, 693
double-blind entry systems, 615–616
drag-to-layout tools, 158–160
drill-downs, windows as, 374–375
DRY (Don't Repeat Yourself) programming
principle, 596, 689, 693
DSN (Data Source Name), 247–252, 547
Duplicate Expression control, 664
duplicates
button, 197
file, 40
script name, 289
duplicating
data, 143–148
multiple commands, 288
records, 49
dyadic operator, 415–416
dynamic actions, using buttons for, 154
dynamic arrays, 421
Dynamic Data Exchange (DDE), 713
dynamic execution, 519
dynamic interface technique, 356
dynamic objects, 178–179
dynamic rendering, 717
dynamic screen elements
conditional formatting, 360–361
disappearing/reappearing objects
concealed and remotely operated Tab
Control, 358–360
conditional formatting, 360
overview, 356
portal invisibility, 356–358
multi-state buttons and objects, 361–362
dynamic sorting technique, 327–330
dynamic value lists, 421

E

Edit Account dialog, 149, 568
Edit Copy custom menu, 671
Edit Custom Function dialog, 676–677
Edit Custom Menu dialog, 670–672

Edit Data Source dialog, 92–94, 253–254, 436, 440
Edit Expression control, 664
Edit Expression dialog, 664–666
Edit Extended Privileges dialog, 566
Edit Folder dialog, 292
Edit menu command, 663
Edit Menu Set dialog, 673
Edit Privilege Set dialog, 149, 560–562
Edit Relationship dialog, 130–131, 307–308, 332, 413,
415–416, 421, 591–592
Edit Saved Finds dialog, 74–75
Edit Script button, Script Debugger window, 660
Edit Script windows
changing order of commands in, 274
controlling selection window, 310
overview, 270–272
script commands groups, 262–265
Script Step Options panel, 276
Show Compatibility pull-down menu, 103–104
simultaneous editing in, 287
Edit Value List dialog, 138
editing
data, 49–50, 141
information via scripts, 286
menus
overview, 671–672
Script Step action, 672
window widgets, 672
related data, 54
scripts, 287–289
editing commands, 262
efficient code
adaptability, 691–692
file size, 706–708
flexibility, 691–692
images and media in databases, 708
redundancy, eliminating, 689–691
simplicity
applying, 701–702
dependencies, 698–701
examples, 695–698
optimal calculation syntax, 693–694
overview, 22–23
size considerations, 687–689
transaction modeling
batch automation, 704
host/server script execution, 704–706
live versus batch data, 702–703

efficient code (*continued*)
  offline updates and processing, 704
  posting and propagating edits, 703
  robots, 704
`Else` command, 281–282
`Else If` command, 282, 325, 532
e-mail
  containing embedded link, 612
  disappearing/reappearing objects, 356
  plug-ins, 727
  sending by SMTP, 99–100
  sending links, 612–613
embedded images
  assigning and retrieving paths, 652
  overview, 651–652
  scripted field updates, 652–653
embedded links, 612
embedded paragraph attributes, 335
embedded placeholder tags, 373
embossed effect, 181, 183, 385
`Employees` table, 419
empty key field value, 414
empty variable, 339
Enable Account command, 570
enclosing objects, 382
encryption, 580
`End If` command, 281–282, 532
`End Loop` command, 282–283, 532
end-of-line (EOL) markers, 642–643
engraved effect, 162–163, 182, 385
`Enrollments` table, 419
`Enter Find Mode[ ]` command, 530
Enter key, 186
entering data
  committing records, 49–50
  creating records, 48, 136–141
  duplicating records, 49
  field definitions, 49
  literal text, 234–235
  overview, 48
entities, 407
Entity Relationship Diagram (ERD), 25, 242
`Entries::Points` field, 482
environment calculations, 492–494
EOL (end-of-line) markers, 642–643
equi-join (=) operator, 414
equi-joins, 130, 259, 413–415
ERD (Entity Relationship Diagram), 25, 242

ergonomics, 174–175
error capture, 508
error codes, 505–506, 603–604
error handling, 506–509, 536, 605–606
error trapping
  error codes, 505–506
  error handling, 506–509
  global fields, 607
  overview, 504–505, 603–604
  record locking, 604–606
  record marking and flagging techniques, 607
  replacing field contents, 606–607
  sub-scripts, 536
error-check criteria, 19
escape characters, 235
escape conditions, 283
ESS (External SQL Data Sources)
  adding supplemental fields, 256–257
  `DATETIME` values, 94
  integrating SQL tables, 252–256
  modifying fields, 213
  ODBC drivers, configuring, 247–252
  overview, 26
  separation, 439–441
  SQL database support, 92
  value lists based on, 92
  Windows Authentication, 92–94
ETL (Extract, Transform, and Load) cycle, 643
`Evaluate( )` function, 234, 475, 482–483
Evaluate This Calculation From The Context Of menu, 451
evaluation, short-circuited, 234
event-driven logging, 631
Everything Reference for FileMaker Developers, The, 739
`ExamDate` field, 475
Excel files
  exporting as, 53–54
  versus printed output, 204
Execute SQL command, 440
execution, script. *See* scripts
Existing Value option, 219
exit conditions, 283, 533–535
`Exit Loop If [ ]` command, 282–283, 377, 532
`Exit Script[ ]` command, 79, 505, 524
exiting FileMaker Pro 10, 36–37
exploded keys, 417
`Export Field Contents[ ]` command, 542, 548, 641, 653–654, 711
Export Records to File dialog, 52

Export Records[ ] command, 543–544
exporting data
    capabilities, 29–30
    container objects, 548–549
    delimiters, 642–643
    end-of-line markers, 642–643
    enhancements to, 102–104
    as Excel files, 53–54
    field contents, 542
    file formats, 639–640
    from folders, 641–642
    overview, 50–52
    as PDF files, 53–54
    selecting fields for export, 543–545
    table data, 543
Expression text box, Specify Calculation dialog, 231
expressions, 229, 448, 451
extended privileges, 566–567
Extended Privileges panel, Manage Accounts and Privileges
    dialog, 566
Extended Privileges section, Edit Privilege Set dialog,
    560–561
extensibility
    analysis and documentation tools, 732
    developer tools, 731
    external scripting calls, 709–716
    HTML, 716–718
    JavaScript, 716–718
    overview, 30–31
    plug-ins, 720–728
    shared information, 732
    Web deployment options, 728–731
    Web viewer widgets, 719
Extensible Markup Language (XML), 29, 669, 729–730
Extensible Stylesheet Language Transformation (XSLT),
    729–730
Extensions folder, 720
external authentication, 569–571, 579
external backup strategy, 600
External Data Sources, 17, 436, 442
external files, 437
external function calls, 723–724
External functions, 452
external resources, 515
external scripting calls
    AppleScript, 713–715
    cross-platform solutions, 715–716
    macros, 716

    overview, 301, 403, 709–710
    Send Event [ ] command, 710–713
    third-party helpers, 716
    VBScript, 710–713
external server account, 570
External SQL Data Sources (ESS)
    adding supplemental fields, 256–257
    DATETIME values, 94
    integrating SQL tables, 252–256
    modifying fields, 213
    ODBC drivers, configuring, 247–252
    overview, 26
    separation, 439–441
    SQL database support, 92
    value lists based on, 92
    Windows Authentication, 92–94
External table occurrence, 550
Extract, Transform, and Load (ETL) cycle, 643

F

fail-safe systems. *See also* logging
    backups, 599–603
    capturing user edits, 623–626
    intercepting data, 616–619
    modifying data, 616–619
    opening remote files, 607–613
    roll-back capabilities, 627–630
    temporary edit interface techniques, 613–616
    trapping errors, 603–607
favorite files, 36
Field Access menu option, 564
field audit log, 623–624
Field Behavior dialog, 162, 164, 185–188
field boxes, 179, 353
Field Control Setup dialog, 314
Field Export Order list, 545, 640
Field Options dialog. *See* Options for Field dialog
Field Order dialog, 543
Field tool, Status Toolbar, 178
Field/Control Setup dialog, 136, 138–139, 192–193, 312
FieldName value, 521
fields. *See also* calculation fields; global fields
    access to, 564–566
    activating, 48
    adding, 114–118, 213–214
    applying formats to, 162–166
    Auto-Entry options, 216–218
    automatically entered information, 12

fields *(continued)*
  commenting, 429–430
  controls, 178
  copying and pasting, 126
  creating, 38
  data types, 214–216
  deleting, 213–214
  dependencies, 49
  editing, 48
  formats, 25
  in imported tables, 211–212
  indexing, 221–222
  names, 115
  other terms for, 13
  overview, 4, 47, 212
  referencing, 235–236
  renaming, 213–214
  resizing, 161
  Summary, 222–227
  supplemental, 256–257
  for tracking, 127
  validation, 49, 218–221
  values in, 16–17
fields commands, 262
Fields list, Specify Calculation dialog, 230
Fields tab, Manage Database dialog
  adding fields, 113–117
  adding fields to tables, 213–214
  data tracking, 127–128
  filtering portals, 307
  retrofitting keys, 590
  trapping edits, 623–624
FieldType( ) function, 493
file architecture
  approaches to separation of data, 438
  costs and benefits of separation, 439
  interface files, 436–438
  modular approach, 435
  multi-file solutions, 434–435
file close scripts, 299
File dialog, 37
file handling plug-ins, 726–727
File Manipulator, 726
File menu, 41, 100
file open scripts, 299
File Options dialog, 59–62, 85, 151, 513, 579, 612
file recovery
  file corruption, 638–639
  improvements to, 96–98

myths, 634–635
  overview, 633
  Recover process, 635–637
  salvaging data, 637–638
file size
  data archiving, 707–708
  modularization strategies, 707
  overview, 706
  segmentation, 707
File Transfer Protocol (FTP) plug-ins, 727
file-based script triggers, 85
[File Default] menu, 674–675
FileMaker 9 Developer Reference, 739
FileMaker Addict, 738
FileMaker Collective, 737
FileMaker Custom Function resources, 737
FileMaker Developers Conference, 736
FileMaker Fever, 738
FileMaker Network Settings dialog, 608
FileMaker Network Sharing dialog, 610
FileMaker PHP API, 730
FileMaker PHP Site Assistant, 730–731
FileMaker Pro 10
  advantages of, 18–19
  compared to other database development tools, 22–26
  examples, 32–33
  exiting, 36–37
  features of, 28–31
  interface, 17–18
  navigating, 41–48
  optimizing, 55–62
  overview, 21–22, 35–36
  process and information integration, 18
  product family, 26–28
  starting, 37
  terminology, 13–17
  Web site, 735–736, 741–742
FileMaker Pro 10 Advanced, 87, 107
FileMaker Pro Advisor, 739
FileMaker Resource Guide, 736
FileMaker Security: The Book, 739
FileMaker Server, 22, 603, 729
FileMaker Server Advanced, 22
FileMaker Server 10, 27
FileMaker Server 10 Advanced, 27
filename extensions, 37, 40
filename iwp_home.html file, 729
filename references, 598

files. *See also* file architecture; file recovery; file size
  accounts, 148–152
  closing, 38
  conversion, 40–41
  corruption of, 638–639
  creating, 37–38
  filtered display of, 580
  formats, 40–41, 63
  handling safely, 38–40
  links between two, creating, 436
  managing via scripts, 286–287
  passwords, 150–152
  physical security, 577–579
  printing via scripts, 286–287
  privilege sets, 148–152
  saving, 38
  sharing, 107, 608–611
files commands, 262
filing systems, 4–5
Fill Color checkbox, 330
fill effects, 162–163
Filter( ) function, 618, 647
Filter field, Select Buyer window, 313
filtering
  data cleansing operations, 646–647
  layout format, 335–336
  portals, 306–313
  scripts by folder, 293–294
Find icon drop-down menu, Status Toolbar, 73–74
Find mode
  constraining and extending found set, 319
  dynamically building criteria, 529–530
  AND Find, 318
  finding data already entered, 141–142
  OR Find, 318
  overview, 14–15, 43
  saving Finds and found sets, 319–323
  saving requests, 72–75
  special find symbols, 142–143
  Status Toolbar controls in, 45–46
Finds table, 320
FirstName data field, 318, 401, 500–501, 503
fixed margins, 166
_fk (foreign key), 413, 428, 589
flag field, 400
flagging technique, 607
Flash, 719
flat-file databases, 6–7

flexibility, 25, 27–28, 691–692
floating window, 306
FMDiff analysis tool, 732
FMForums, 738
fmphp extended privilege, 730
.fmplugin file extension, 720
FMPug, 738
FMPXMLRESULT encoding format, 547
FMRobot, 731
FMSAUC_UpdatePlugIn( ) external function, 720
FMSAUC_FindPlugIn( ) external function, 720
FMStudio, 731
FMWebschool, 737
.fmx extension, 720
Folder of Files Import Options dialog, 641
folders
  filtering scripts by, 293–294
  importing/exporting data to and from, 641–642
  script, creating, 291–293
  submenus, 279
fonts
  initial layout, 157–158
  printing, 202–203
  selecting for Mac and Windows users, 352–353
  size of, 99
Fonts tab, Preferences dialog, 58–59, 157
Footer, layout, 170, 173, 308
foreign key (_fk), 413, 428, 589
form letters, 11
Form View, 168, 329, 378
Format button, creating, 469–470
Format menu, 99, 335
Format Painter, 147
formats. *See also* formatting
  applying to field and text objects, 162–166
  for automatically generated log files, 106
  converting from earlier, 40–41
  data cleansing operations, 643–646
  default graphic object, 183
  image, 178
formatting
  character-level, 334
  code, 497
  conditional, 179–181, 360–362
  controlling programmatically, 336–337
  embedded, 334
  instructions, 335
  layout format filters, 335–336

formatting (*continued*)
  overview, 333
  paragraph-level, 335
  precedence of number, date, and time formats, 336
  style buttons, creating, 337–338
  text, 467–470
  three-tiered approach, 334
Formatting Bar, Status Toolbar, 68, 160
forms, 4–6, 9–10, 168–170
Formula box, Specify Calculation dialog, 231
`Formula Is` field, 330
formulas
  defining, 233–234
  overview, 229, 448
found sets
  constraining, 319
  defined, 14, 46
  extending, 319
  saving, 319–323
found sets commands, 262
`.fp3` file format, 40
`.fp5` file format, 40
`.fp7` file format, 37, 40–41, 434, 445
Fraction of Total summary function, 227
free-form text name, 428
`Freeze Window` script command, 541
`Freeze/Refresh` sequence, 542
freezing screen, 541–542
From parameter, 680–681
FTP (File Transfer Protocol) plug-ins, 727
[Full Access] privilege set
  authenticating, 662
  as default, 152
  overview, 559
  running script with, 511–512
Function list, Specify Calculation dialog, 231
Function Parameters field, 676
Function View pop-up, Specify Calculation dialog, 231
functions
  as aid to syntax readability, 678
  defined, 229, 448
  defining, 676–677
  efficiency and ease of use, 678–679
  eliminating redundancy, 691
  optional parameters, 233
  overview, 675–679
  recursion, 680–683
  structured syntax and nesting, 452–453

Fusion Reactor, 727
FXForge, 731

G

General Fields panel, "Show Custom Dialog" Options
    dialog, 377
General tab
  Layout Setup dialog, 674
  Preferences dialog, 56–57
Get( ) functions. *See also* specific functions by name
  capturing metadata, 620
  creating style buttons, 337
  Data Viewer, 661
  environment data, 437
  overview, 452, 492–493
  recording navigation text, 241
  unstored calculations, 484
  window dimensions, 539–540
`Get(AccountName)` function, 511
`Get(ActiveModifierKeys)` function, 696–697
`Get(ActiveSelectionSize)` function, 469
`Get(ActiveSelectionStart)` function, 437, 469
`Get(ApplicationVersion)` function, 492
`GetAsBoolean( )` function, 457
`GetAsCSS( )` function, 469, 718
`GetAsNumber( )` function, 471
`GetAsText( )` function, 652
`Get(CurrentDate)` function, 448
`Get(CurrentPlatform)` function, 710
`Get(DesktopPath)` function, 620, 713
`Get(DocumentsPathListing)` function, 91
`Get(ExtendedPrivileges)` function, 561
`GetField( )` function, 234, 326, 480–482
`GetFieldName( )` function, 77, 90, 481–482
`Get(FileName)` function, 598
`Get(LastError)` function, 108, 505, 579
`GetLayoutName( )` custom function, 495, 497
`GetNextSerialValue( )` calculation function, 585
`GetNthRecord( )` function, 320, 451, 476
`Get(PrivilegeSetName)` function, 511–512, 570
`Get(RecordID)` function, 586, 588
`GetRepetition( )` function, 477
`Get(ScriptName)` function, 517
`Get(ScriptParameter)` function, 512
`Get(ScriptResult)` function, 512
`GetSummary( )` function, 475, 480
`Get(SystemLanguage)` function, 403, 493
`Get(SystemNICAddress)` function, 587

Get(SystemPlatform) function, 493, 528

Get(SystemVersion) function, 493

Get(TemporaryPath) function, 104

Get(TriggerKeystroke) function, 88–89

Get(TriggerModifierKeys) function, 89

GetValue( ) function, 91, 420, 478, 521, 695

Get(WindowDesktopHeight) function, 540

Get(WindowDesktopWidth) function, 540

Get(WindowHeight) function, 540

Get(WindowName) function, 537–538

Get(WindowWidth) function, 540

gFilter field, 310–311

gFilter_txt field, 308–309

gGlobal field, 411

gKeySelection global text field, 418

gLanguageID field, 400

global calculations
    creating field, 307
    freedom and efficiency of, 491–492
    managing, 490–491
    overview, 489
    shadowing movements, 490

global container field, 391

global fields
    behavior of, 349–350
    capturing state by user, 399
    characteristics of, 489
    dynamic sort techniques, 324
    one-way relationships, 419
    trapping errors, 607
    uses for, 350
    using, 350
    when to avoid, 350
    working with, 227–228

global key, 692

global number field, 325, 396

global storage, 489

global text field, 307, 324–325, 376, 504

global values, restoring, 515

global variables, 337, 339, 458–459, 665

gNewValue global field, 478

Go Back script, 443–444

Go to Field[ ] command, 511, 530, 548

Go to Layout[ ] command, 197–198, 526–527, 597

Go to Next Field command, 309

Go to Next Object Using section, Field Behavior
    dialog, 185–186

Go to Object[ ] command, 199, 267–268, 501,
    530–531, 628

Go to Record/Request/Page[Next; Exit after
    last] command, 533

Go to Related Record[ ] command (GTRR)
    error codes, 506, 604
    overview, 383
    relationship-based techniques, 421
    shortcut navigation, 313–316
    uses of, 266
    windows as pop-ups and drill-downs, 374–375

Go To Target Field checkbox, 469

Google Group, 738

Goya BaseElements, 732

granular security
    extended privileges, 566–567
    field access, 564–566
    layout access, 563–564
    overview, 562–563
    record access, 564–566
    script access, 563
    table access, 564–566
    value list access, 563

graphic objects
    alignment, 183–184
    building, 181–182
    default formats and attributes, 183
    importing from other applications, 184–185
    stacking, 183–184

graphical attributes of objects, 179

graphical displays, 396–397

graphical element, 387

graphical interface, 17–18

Graphics panel, File Options dialog, 61–62

graphs. *See* Relationships Graph

greater-or-equal (≥) symbol, 415

greater-than (>) symbol, 415

GreatGizmos Web site, 461

gRI_Switch global field, 594

grouping options, Specify Field Order For Export dialog, 52

grouping scripts, 293

gSearch field, 417

gSearchTerm field, 468

gSortField field, 326–327

gSortField1 global text field, 325–326

gSortField2 global text field, 325–326

gSortField3 global text field, 325–326

gSortOrder field, 326–327
gSortOrder1 global number field, 325–326
gSortOrder2 global number field, 325–326
gSortOrder3 global number field, 325–326
gSWFresource global container field, 391
GTRR (Go to Related Record[ ] command)
   error codes, 506, 604
   overview, 383
   relationship-based techniques, 421
   shortcut navigation, 313–316
   uses of, 266
   windows as pop-ups and drill-downs, 374–375
gType_key field, 308

H

Halt Script button, Script Debugger window, 659
Halt Script command, 265, 280, 505
handle icon, script, 292
hash, 578
Header, layout, 170, 172–173, 308
horizontal portal, 391
horizontal resizing, 378
horizontal zone, 379
hosted files, backing up, 603
hotkeys, calling scripts via, 297–298
Hungarian notation, 124
Hypertext Transfer Protocol (HTTP), 717, 727
hyphens, 289, 294

I

ID fields, 119–120
If command
   Boolean values, 697–698
   commission on earning above threshold, 238
   custom functions, 681
   optimal calculation syntax, 693
   optional parameters, 450
   robust triggering implementations, 724
   sequential, 532
   use of, 281–282
If[ ]/End If sequence, 509, 536
If/Else conditions, 531–532
I::gLanguageID field, 401–402
I::LanguageFlag field, 401
I::LanguageID field, 401
image formats, 178

image source hyperlink, 394
images
   in databases, 708
   embedded, 651–653
Import Field Mapping dialog, 51–52, 209–210,
    546–547, 648
import matching, 648–650
Import Options dialog, 210
Import Records command, 583
Import Summary dialog, 211, 583
importing
   Bento integration, 94–96
   container objects, 548–549
   data matching for, 546–548
   delimiters, 642–643
   end-of-line markers, 642–643
   enhancements to, 102–104
   file formats, 639–640
   to folders, 641–642
   graphic objects from other applications, 184–185
   options for, 545
   overview, 29–30, 50–51, 589
   selectively, 650
   synchronizing data sets, 647–648
   tables, 209–212
In Browse mode, 311
In Find mode, 311
In Range fields, Validation tab, Options for Field dialog, 220
Include In Menu checkbox, Manage Scripts window, 297
Income table, 695
indexing
   alternate language indexes, 344–345
   equi-joins and non-equal joins, 414
   myths, 342–343
   numeric, 343–344
   optimizing configurations, 345–346
   options for, 221–222
   overview, 341
   rules, 343
   text, 341–342
   Unicode, 344–345
Indexing and Sorting Language setting, 345
indirect object/element references, 597
indirection, 530–531
inherent object properties, 179
Initial Value field, 590
initials, calculating, 239
inline duplication method, 275

input, database, 6
input field, 350, 503
Input Fields panel, Show Custom Dialog Options dialog, 376–377, 572
input/output (I/O) database, 607
Insert Calculated Result[ ] button command, 469
Insert File[ ] command, 548
Insert Picture dialog, 651–652
Insert Picture[ ] command, 548
Insert QuickTime[ ] command, 548
inserting
    objects into tab order, 98
    pictures, 185, 651–652
Install Menu Set[ ] command, 669–670, 674–675
Install OnTimer Script[ ] command, 84, 299
installing plug-ins, 720–722
Instant Web Publishing (IWP), 728–729
Insufficient privileges error, 511
Int( ) function, 697
integrity of backups, 601. *See also* referential integrity
interaction model, 557, 703
intercapping, 428
interface, FileMaker, 17–18
interface dependent commands, 273
interface design
    custom dialogs
        attributes, 377
        as data-entry device, 376–377
        overview, 375–376
    dimensionality
        color, 386
        delineation of element groups, 386
        embossing effect, 385
        engraving effect, 385
        spatial cues, 385–386
        translucency, 386–387
        transparency, 386–387
    dynamic screen elements
        conditional formatting, 360–361
        disappearing/reappearing objects, 356–360
        multi-state buttons and objects, 361–362
    interface elements
        about and version info, 398
        main menus, 398
        online help, 398–399
        splash screens, 397–398

    for Mac and Windows users
        fonts, selecting, 352–353
        platform-specific window behavior, 354–355
        screen rendering differences, 353–354
    multiple windows and views
        placement, 373–374
        as pop-ups and drill-downs, 374–375
        simulating modal window behavior, 375
        size, 373–374
    overview, 351
    portals
        dynamically sorted, 390
        innovative implementations, 391
        lists, 389
        as navigation device, 389–390
    for print
        letter generator, 372–373
        Merge fields, 371–372
        nonprinting objects, 368–369
        reducing parts, 369–371
        sliding objects, 369–371
    progress bars
        graphical displays, 396–397
        overview, 394
        script progress monitors, 395–396
    resizable layout objects
        centering within viewable area, 382
        complex layout resizing, 379–381
        objects that grow and shrink, 379
        objects that move according to window size, 378–379
        overview, 377
        resizing behavior of enclosing objects, 382
    shortcut navigation
        Back button functionality, 384–385
        Go to Related Record [ ] command, 383
        multiple paths, 383
        overview, 382–383
    Sub-summary parts
        adaptable screens, 362–363
        multiple break fields, 366
        page breaks, 366–367
        pagination, 366–367
        stacking up multiple, 363–365
    Tab Controls
        navigation via keyboard, 388
        organizers, 387
        scripting tab operations, 389
        space savers, 387

interface design *(continued)*
   user preferences
      capturing state by user, 399–400
      multi-lingual solution interface, 400–403
      user-centric development philosophy, 399
   Web viewers
      advanced functionality, 391–392
      rendering internally calculated content, 392–393
      scraping data from Web pages, 393–394
interface files, 432, 435–438, 443
interface vulnerabilities, 557–558
`InterfaceLanguages` value list, 401
internal IDs, 211–212, 235, 288
Internet Protocol version 6 (IPv6) support, 106
`Inventory` file, 307, 316, 356–357, 360
Inventory List layout, 315
`Inventory::Cost` field, 595
invisible characters, 646
`InvoiceID` field, 428
`InvoiceItems` TO, 329
`InvoiceLines` TO, 328–331, 362, 418
Invoices table, 312, 508, 581, 590
`Invoices::BalancePayable` field, 693
`Invoices::Client` field, 591
`Invoices::ClientID` field, 590–591
I/O (input/output) database, 607
IPv6 (Internet Protocol version 6) support, 106
ISO FileMaker Magazine, 737
`ItemID` field, 649
`Item::Price` value, 460
`Item::Qty` value, 460
ItemSupplier TO, 144–146, 314
IWP (Instant Web Publishing), 728–729

J

join results, caching
   advantages of, 347
   gaining control of cache, 349
   solving problems with, 348
join tables, 373, 409, 419
joins
   Cartesian, 415, 419
   equi-joins, 130, 259, 413–415
   naturally occurring, 419–420
   non-equal, 390, 414–415
   overview, 17
   relationship, 692

self, 422–423
theta, 414–415, 455, 457
jump navigation, 313–316

K

key fields, 17, 413
keyboard control of layouts, 185–186
keyboard shortcut commands, 297–298
keyboards, tab navigation via, 388
keys
   exploring, 588–590
   generating
      overview, 584
      record IDs, 586–587
      serial numbers, 585–586
      unique identification values, 587–588
   retrofitting, 590–591
   unique
      meaning of, 584
      overview, 582
      safeguards, 583–584
keystroke logging software, 578
kiosk mode, 685

L

`LanguageID` field, 400
`LanguagePreference` field, 402
`LanguageResources` table, 400–401
`LanguageResources::LanguageID` field, 401
`LanguageResources::LanguageName` field, 401
languages, 28
`LastName` field, 309, 318, 590
`LateReturnsList` field, 478
launching FileMaker Pro, 36
layers
   business, 432–433
   integrated environment, 433
   issues with, 433–434
   overview, 431
   separation model, 432
Layout Bar, 66, 160
layout context, 152
layout event script triggers, 299–300
Layout mode. *See also* layout objects
   buttons
      defining, 196–198
      as objects, 199

overview, 195
    scope and button commands, 198–199
displaying related data, 191–195
drag-to-layout tools, 158–160
enhancements to
    defining tooltips, 99
    font sizes, 99
    inserting objects into tab order, 98
graphic objects
    alignment, 183–184
    building, 181–182
    default formats and attributes, 183
    importing from other applications, 184–185
    stacking, 183–184
initial layouts
    applying formats, 162–166
    forms, 168–170
    lists, 168–170
    organizing presentation of information, 160–161
    overview, 155–158
    parts of, 170–171
    setting up for printing, 166–168
interface, 159
menu controls, 160
multilingual interfaces, 400–402
output, versus Excel, 204
overview, 43
palette controls, 160
preparing layout for use as selection window, 308–309
printed output
    composite PDFs, 204
    fonts, 202–203
    overview, 202
    page setup, 203
    page sizes, 203
    versus PDF, 204
select/act tools, 158
tab panels
    creating, 188–189
    limitations of, 190
    navigating between, 189–190
tooltips
    conditional, 176–177
    icons, 99
    keeping track of, 177
    overview, 175–176
visual structure
    ergonomics, 174–175
    giving information meaning, 175

overview, 171
    visual fatigue, avoiding, 174–175
    visual pointers and aids, 172–174
    white space, 174
Web viewers
    complementary data concepts, 202
    controlling, 201
    setting up, 200–201
layout objects
    format filters, 335–336
    interacting with
        assigning names, 186–187
        keyboard control, 185–186
        tab order, setting, 186
        visual spell-checking, 187–188
    object names, 500
    overview, 500
    resizable
        centering, 382
        complex layout resizing, 379–381
        enclosing, 382
        moving according to window size, 378–379
        overview, 377
        that grow and shrink, 379
    script triggers, 516
    triggers, 78–81
    types of
        conditional format attributes, 179–181
        dynamic objects, 178–179
        inherent object properties, 179
        overview, 177–178
        static objects, 178–179
layout script triggers, 81–84
Layout Setup dialog
    accessing, 98
    click-sort columns, 329
    determining menu set for layout, 674–675
    General tab, 136–137
    jump navigation, 314
    Printing tab, 166–167
    Script Triggers tab, 82–83, 299–300
    scripting, 500
    Views tab, 169–170
Layout tab, Preferences dialog, 56–57, 156
LayoutName field, 321
layouts. See also Layout mode; layout objects
    access to, 563–564
    design, 18, 25–26
    elements in, 47–48

layouts (*continued*)
    format filters, 335–336
    menu of viewable, 44
    multiple uses of, 136
    overview, 13–14
    related records in, 49
    script triggers, 516
    tab order, 388
    viewing related records, 54
Leading Grand Summary layout part, 171
leading Sub-summary part, 363
Learn More icon, Quick Start screen, 36, 100–101
Left( ) function, 337, 462–463, 467, 477
LeftValues( ) function, 477
LeftWords( ) function, 465–466
Length( ) function, 237–238, 452
less-or-equal (≤) symbol, 415
less-than (<) symbol, 415
Let( ) function, 458–459, 465, 480, 520, 666, 694
letter generator, creating, 372–373
Library field, 478
Library table occurrence, 542
Library::Roster field, 479
line breaking, 59
line height, 367
Line Items table, 581
Line Pattern tool, Status Toolbar, 172
LineItems value, 693
List( ) function, 236, 476, 482
List View, 168, 378
lists
    managing, 477–478
    overview, 4–6, 168–170
    separators, 289–290
    Substitute( ) function, 461
    values
        adding, 478–479
        extracting one from, 478
        inserting, 478–479
        removing, 479–480
        retrieving as, 476–477
literal text
    entering, 234–235
    references, 597
literal values, 229, 450
live data, 702–703
local files
    backing up, 602–603
    overview, 36

local networks, 608–609
local variable, 339–340, 458–459, 519, 525
lock flag, 615
lockdown account, 574–575, 579
lockdown privilege set, 574
locking, record, 280
locking down interface, 501–502
log data, 627
log files, format changes for automatically generated, 106
logging
    alternative approaches, 630–631
    built-in capabilities
        auto-enter options, 619
        capturing and extending standard metadata, 620–621
    managing accumulation of data, 626–627
    record deletions, 626
    script
        infrastructure for, 621–622
        tracking script execution, 622–623
    using logs to roll forward, 629–630
logic calculation, 453–454
logic function, 468
logic interface, 433
logic layer, 432
logical operator, 453, 454
login procedure, 514
login script, 574
logo image, 181–182
logout option
    locked-down database, 573
    security logging, 575–576
    structuring solution for, 573–575
Looked-Up Value checkbox, Auto-Enter tab, Field Options dialog, 218
lookups, 133, 135, 146, 595–596
Loop command, 282–283, 532
Loop/End Loop script command, 536, 723
looping script, 282–283, 395
loop-locked window, 375
loops, 532–535, 680

M

macros, 716
Macs
    Customize dialog, 66–67
    documents path in, 91
    ESS, 92
    fonts, 203

interface design for users of
fonts, selecting, 352–353
platform-specific window behavior, 354–355
screen rendering differences, 353–354
IPv6 format, 106
ODBC drivers, 248
setting up DSN, 249–252
MacTech Magazine, 739
main menus, 398
Main table, 411
maintaining data
data cleansing operations
ETL cycle, 643
filtering capabilities, 646–647
formats, 643–646
embedded images
assigning and retrieving paths, 652
overview, 651–652
scripted field updates, 652–653
file recovery
file corruption, 638–639
myths, 634–635
overview, 633
Recover process, 635–637
salvaging data, 637–638
importing/exporting data
delimiters, 642–643
end-of-line markers, 642–643
file formats, 639–640
from folders, 641–642
stored files
assigning and retrieving paths, 652
overview, 651–652
scripted field updates, 652–653
synchronizing data sets
import matching, 648–650
importing selectively, 650
overview, 647–648
text
designing custom export process, 654
Export Field Contents[ ]
command, 653–654
malware, 578
Manage Accounts & Passwords dialog, 570
Manage Accounts & Privileges dialog, 149–150, 559,
566, 568–569
Manage Custom Functions dialog, 676
Manage Custom Menus dialog, 669–670, 673–675

Manage Data Sources dialog, 436
Manage Database dialog
calculations
Calculation fields, creating, 229–232
defining formulas, 233–234
entering literal text, 234–235
functions, 236–238
overview, 228–229
referencing fields, 235–236
simple, 238–241
creating files, 38–39
establishing data sources, 442
External SQL Data Sources
adding supplemental fields, 256–257
integrating SQL tables, 252–256
ODBC drivers, configuring, 247–252
field commenting, 429–431
fields
adding, 213–214
Auto-Entry options, 216–218
Calculation, 222–227
data types, 214–216
deleting, 213–214
global, 227–228
indexing, 221–222
overview, 212
renaming, 213–214
Summary, 222–227
validation, 218–221
Fields tab, 113–117, 127–128, 132–133
filtering portals, 307–308
interface files, 436
overview, 205–206
relationships
functioning of, 258
locations, 259
overview, 257–258
relational model, 259–260
solving problems using, 258–259
Relationships Graph
avoiding circular references, 244–245
misconceptions, 241–242
named and unnamed data sources, 245–246
references to other files, 246–247
tables versus table occurrences, 243
Relationships tab, 129, 131, 255, 592
retrofitting keys, 590

Manage Database dialog *(continued)*
  tables
    adding, 206–208
    concepts, 206
    deleting, 206–208
    importing, 209–212
    moving between files, 208–209
    renaming, 206–208
  Tables tab, 116, 118
  trapping edits, 623
Manage Extended Privileges option, 567
Manage External Data Sources dialog, 246, 436
Manage Layouts dialog, 98, 675
Manage Scripts window
  controlling selection window, 310
  enhancements to, 105–106
  filtering scripts by folders, 293–294
  folders in, 291–293
  Include In Menu checkbox, 297
  list separators, 289
  overview, 262–263, 268–271
  script searches, 294
  Scripts menu, 278
Manage Value Lists dialog, 138
maps, process, 86
margin settings, 166
master script, 629
Match All Records in Current = Found Set option, 604
match fields, 17, 413
Max( ) function, 456, 474–475, 482–483
Maximum Number of Characters field, Validation tab,
    Options for Field dialog, 220
Maximum summary function, 226
MBS FileMaker Plugin, 727
md command, 713
MDI (Multiple Document Interface) Application
    window, 538
media, in databases, 708
media handling plug-ins, 726–727
Media_RecordSoundStop function, 722
MediaManager, 726
Member of a Value List menu, Validation tab, Options for
    Field dialog, 220
Memberships table, 419
Memory tab, Preferences dialog, 56, 58
memory variable, 338–339, 458
menu controls, 160
Menu Item Properties panel, Edit Custom Menu dialog, 672

Menu Set pop-up menu, Layout Setup dialog, 674
menu sets
  controlling via script, 675
  determining for each layout, 674–675
  setting default, 673
Menu Sets panel, Manage Custom Menus dialog, 673
MenuMagic, 725
menus
  defining, 669–671
  editing individual
    overview, 671–672
    Script Step action, 672
    window widgets, 672
  layout, 44
  menu sets
    controlling via script, 675
    determining for each layout, 674–675
    setting default, 673
Merge fields, 371–372
MergeLetterText field, 373
metadata
  calculations, 492–494
  capturing, 127–128
MetaDataMagic, 732
MethodOfContact field, 356
Mf variable, 483
Microsoft Visual Basic Scripting engine, 710
Microsoft Windows
  command line interpreter, 712
  Customize dialog, 66–67
  documents paths in, 91
  external scripting calls, 710
  fonts in, 203
  interface design for users of
    fonts, selecting, 352–353
    platform-specific window behavior, 354–355
    screen rendering differences, 353–354
  and IPv6 format, 106
  ODBC drivers, 248
Microsoft Word, 11
Middle( ) function, 337, 462–465, 477, 479
MiddleValues( ) function, 477–478
MiddleWords( ) function, 465–466
migration, 41, 439
Min( ) function, 456, 474–475
Mini Mode menu, 42
Minimal Indexing indicator, 344
Minimum summary function, 226

mixed-operator, multi-predicate join, 416

mnemonics, 239

Mod( ) function, 697

modal windows, 375

modeling

    data

        alternative relationship techniques, 416–420

        arrays, 420–423

        deployment considerations, 445

        documenting database structure, 427–431

        external SQL sources, 439–441

        file architecture versus data structure, 434–439

        implementing separation in existing solution,
          442–445

        layers, 431–434

        overview, 405

        relational theory, 405–410

        relationship operators, 413–416

        Relationships Graph symbols, 410–412

        Relationships Graph techniques, 423–427

    transaction

        batch automation, 704

        host/server script execution, 704–706

        live versus batch data, 702–703

        offline updates and processing, 704

        posting and propagating edits, 703

        robots, 704

modes, 43

_ModHist field, 621

_ModHistory field, 620–621

Modification checkbox, Auto-Enter tab, Field Options dialog,
    217

modifier keys, 696–697

Modify Table View dialog, 69–70

modular approach, file architecture, 435

modular script code

    script recursion, 536

    using sub-scripts, 535–536

modular-centric approach, Relationship Graph, 424–425

modularization, 349, 445, 707

Month( ) function, 448

Month Summary layout, 567

Move/Resize Window[ ] command, 374, 539

Move/Resize[ ] script, 374

multi-criteria relationship, 415

multi-file solutions, 434–435, 571–572

multi-key fields, 17, 258, 417–419

multi-key relationships, 588

multilingual functionality, 28

multi-lingual solution interface, 400–403

multiple break fields, 366

Multiple Document Interface (MDI) Application window,
    538

multiple-file structure, 434

multi-predicate relationships, 259, 415–416

multi-state buttons and objects, 361–362

multi-user capability, 28

music collection database, 8

N

named data sources, 245–246

names

    calculation field, 232

    field, 235

    layout object, 186–187

    methodology for, pasted script, 288

    script, 289, 297

    table, 208

    window, 538

name/value pair array format, 522

Name/Value pair syntax, 421

naming conventions, 428–429

Native AppleScript, 714

native function, 449

naturally occurring joins, 419–420

navigating. *See also* shortcut navigation

    FileMaker Pro 10

        modes, 43

        overview, 41–42

        screen elements, 47–48

        searching, 45–46

        viewing data, 43–45

    between tab panels, 189–190

    via keyboard, 388

navigation commands, 262

navigation controls, 285–286

navigation icon, 17, 44

navigational pathways, 383

negative parameter value, 449

nested If/Else conditions, 531–532

nesting calculation functions, 452–453

NetIncome( ) custom function, 679

network encryption, 580

Network Interface Card (NIC), 588

network latency, 610

networkable capability, 28

New Layout Wizard, 107
New Millennium Communications, 725
New Record icon, 48
New Record/Request step, 265
New Window Options dialog, 314, 316, 538, 539
New Window[ ] command, 373–374, 538
NewValue value, 521
NIC (Network Interface Card), 588
NightWing Enterprises, 737
non-equal joins, 390, 414–415
nonlinear logic
    looping constructs, 532–533
    nested and sequential If/Else conditions, 531–532
    specifying exit conditions, 533–535
nonprinting objects, 368–369
Not Empty checkbox, Validation tab, Options for Field
        dialog, 219–220
not operator, 455
not-equal join operator (≠), 414
Notes field, 409
Now Showing:<big><b> tag, 394
number fields, 214
Number Format for selected objects dialog, 162, 164–165
number format, precedence of, 336
numeric indexing, 343–344
NumRange( ) function, 681–682

O

Object Effects palette, 181, 183
object event script triggers, 300–301
Object Info palette, 179, 197–199, 358, 378, 389
Object Name field, 312, 500
Object Selection tool, Status Toolbar, 158, 178
objects. *See also* layout objects
    anchored, 380
    defined, 17
occurrence parameter, 464
ODBC (Open Database Connectivity), 247–252, 440–441,
        547
ODBC Administrator utility window, 249, 252
ODBC Data Source Administrator control panel, 248
offline updates, 704
Omit checkbox option, 530
Omit option, 318
Omit Record command, 530
omitting record sets, 45–46
On Commit option, 585

one-to-one relationships, 423
one-way relationships, 418–419
OnFileClose script triggers, 85
OnFileOpen script triggers, 85
OnLayoutKeystroke trigger, 82–84, 516
OnLayoutLoad trigger, 82–83, 358, 516
online content, uploading or updating, 515
online help, 398–399
online support, 735–736
Only During Data Entry option, 583
Only during Data Entry radio button, Validation tab, Options
        for Field dialog, 219
OnModeEnter trigger, 82, 516
OnModeExit trigger, 82, 516
OnObjectEnter trigger, 78, 83, 516
OnObjectExit trigger, 78, 516
OnObjectKeystroke trigger, 78, 83–84, 516
OnObjectModify trigger, 78, 220, 358, 516
OnObjectSave trigger, 78, 516
OnRecordCommit trigger, 82–83, 516
OnRecordLoad trigger, 82–83, 516
OnRecordRevert trigger, 82, 516
OnTimer script triggers, 84–85
Open Database Connectivity (ODBC), 247–252,
        440–441, 547
open database files, copying, 601–602
Open Database icon, Quick Start screen, 36
Open Directory domain controller, 568
Open Menu Item commands, 263
Open Remote File Dialog, 608–610
Open URL [ ] script, 716
Open/Close Data Viewer button, Script Debugger
        window, 660, 665
Open/Close panel, File Options dialog, 59–60, 85, 151, 513
open-ended three-tier sorting system, 325–326
opener files, 611–612
opening remote files, 607–613
operands, 448
operations, default order of, 454–455
Operator buttons, Specify Calculation dialog, 230
Operator list, Specify Calculation dialog, 230
operators
    and, 455
    AND predicate, 415
    arithmetic, 453–455
    in calculations, 451
    comment, 453
    comparative, 414–415, 453–455, 457

concatenation, 467
defined, 229
dyadic, 415–416
logical, 453–454
not, 455
precedence, 233
Range, 143
relationship
    Cartesian joins, 415
    comparative operators, 414–415
    equi-joins, 414
    multi-predicate relationships, 415–416
    non-equal joins, 414
    overview, 413–414
Reserved Name, 453–454
text, 453, 455
wildcard, 143
optimization, FileMaker Pro 10
File Options dialog, 59–62
overview, 55
Preferences dialog, 56–59
Optional Script Parameter box, Specify Script Options
    dialog, 312, 330
Options dialog, 712
Options for Field dialog
Auto-Enter tab, 216–218
Auto-Entry, 118–124
Creation checkbox, 127
indexing, 342, 344
language indexing options, 29
Prohibit Modification of Value during Data Entry
    checkbox,, 127
retrofitting keys, 590
Storage tab, 221–222, 227–228
trapping edits, 624
user over-ride capability, 487–488
validation, 118–124
Validation tab, 122–123, 218–219
Options for Summary Field dialog, 225
OR Finds, 318
OR logic, 417
order of operations, 454–456
OrderItems layout, 364, 367
OrderLines layout, 330, 362, 364, 366
OrderLines table, 327–328
OrderLines table occurrence, 422
OrderLines::Price field, 595
Orders table, 640

Orders::Status field, 564
OrdLineID label, 329
Organizations field, 624
Other Privileges section, Edit Privilege Set dialog, 561
out-of-scope characters, rejecting, 618–619
output. *See also* printed output
    database, 6
    Layout mode, 204
Oval tool, 181

P

page breaks, 366–367
page layout, 392
Page Margins option, View menu, 167
page setup, 203
page sizes, 203
pagination, 366–367
Palette (256 Colors) radio button, Layout tab, Preferences
    dialog, 156
palette controls, 160
paper-based databases, 4–5
paragraph attribute, 333
Paragraph dialog, 367
paragraph-level formatting, 335
parameters
    assigning, 276
    branching according to state, 518–519
    custom function, 676
    defined, 448
    getting data into script, 517–518
    logic, 449–450
    optional, 233
    overview, 229, 265
    passing multiple, 521–523
    retrieving multiple, 521–523
    for size and location, 374
parent script, 517
parsing, 462
Part tool, Status Toolbar, 171
parts, layout, 47
passive filter, 335
passwords
    account, 149–152
    encoding or encrypting, 572
Paste [No style] script, 335
Paste command, 320
Paste Text Only option, 333

pasting, 126, 288–289
PatternCount( ) function, 91, 463–465, 477
paused scripts, 280
Pause/Resume Script [ ] command, 283–284
pausing for user input, 283–284
Payments value, 693
PDF (Portable Document Format) files
    composite, 204
    exporting as, 53–54
    versus printed output, 204
peer-to-peer hosting, 608–610
People table, 408
Perform AppleScript [ ] command, 713–716
Perform Auto-Enter Options While Importing option, 487
Perform Find [ ] command, 319, 321, 507,
        529–530, 672, 690
Perform Find [Restore] command, 654
Perform Script [ ] command
    click-sort columns, 330
    Current Script option, 534–535
    external scripts, 512
    getting data into script, 517
    instantiating variables, 340
    overview, 195, 298
    reducing user access to scripts, 280
    Script Step action, 672
    selection windows, 311–312
permissions, 560
PHP Site Assistant, 731
physical file security
    alternative forms of protection, 578
    layers of protection, 578
    multi-faceted approach, 579
    overview, 577–578
Pi function, 449–450
pick lists, 306–313
pilcrow, 234–235
pipe character (|), 396
pipe delimiter character, 695
pivoting data between tables
    managing related data, 549–550
    using utility relationships, 549
pixel, 379
_pk (primary key), 413, 428, 589
placeholder, 372
PlatformIsMacOS custom function, 678
platform-specific window behavior, 354–355

plug-ins
    Application/Program Interface, 30–31
    AutoUpdate, 721
    charting, 727–728
    dialog capabilities, 725–726
    e-mail, 727
    enabling, 720–722
    extensibility, 30–31
    external functions, 722–723
    file handling, 726–727
    FTP, 727
    HTTP, 727
    installing, 720–722
    interface for, 28
    media handling, 726–727
    script triggering, 77, 723–725
Plug-Ins tab, Preferences dialog, 56, 58, 720–721
PNG (Portable Network Graphics), 386
pop-up windows, 286, 307, 374–375
Portable Document Format (PDF) files
    composite, 204
    exporting as, 53–54
    versus printed output, 204
Portable Network Graphics (PNG), 386
Portal Setup dialog, 191–192, 309, 332
Portal tool, 191, 309
portals
    behavior of enclosed objects, 382
    dynamically sorted, 390
    filtering, 306–313
    innovative implementations, 391
    interaction with, 178
    invisibility, 356–358
    lists, 389
    as navigation device, 389–390
    overview, 16, 47
    setting up, 191–195
    in Tab Control, 190
    viewing related data, 54
    visibility technique, 360
PortalTO stored calculation field, 485
Position( ) function, 91, 463–465, 467, 696
post-event triggers, 78, 82
potential vulnerability, 577
precedence, calculation operations, 233
pre-event triggers, 78, 82, 84
Preferences dialog, 56–59, 156–157, 720–721

prefix character, 235

presentation formats, 168–170

Preview mode, 43, 53, 167–168, 362, 365, 369, 475

previewing data, 52–53

primary key (_pk), 413, 428, 589

PrimaryID field, 583

Print Options dialog, 272

Print[ ] command, 104–105

printed output

    composite PDFs, 204

    versus Excel, 204

    fonts, 202–203

    overview, 202

    page setup, 203

    page sizes, 203

    versus PDF, 204

printers, target, 104–105

printing

    data, 52–53

    files via scripts, 286–287

    interface design for

        letter generator, 372–373

        Merge fields, 371–372

        nonprinting objects, 368–369

        reducing parts, 369–371

        sliding objects, 369–371

    reports, 295

    setting up layouts for, 166–168

Printing tab, Layout Setup dialog, 166–167

Priority Support, 736

privilege set

    defining and constraining access, 560–561

    overview, 148–150, 558–559

    role-based security, 560

    schema privilege controls, 561–562

    setting default, 150–152

Privilege Sets tab, Manage Accounts & Privileges dialog, 149, 559

privilege-based errors, 511

privileges, extended, 566–567

procedural layer, 432–433

procedures, 501–502

process automation, 12

process layer, 432

process maps, 86

Product Technical Support, 736

Products::Description field, 654

progress bars

    graphical displays, 396–397

    overview, 394

    script progress monitors, 395–396

Prohibit Modification of Value During Data Entry option, Auto-Enter tab, Options for Field dialog, 127, 487, 584, 586, 590

Q

queries, 14–15

Quick Start screen, 36, 100–102, 112–113

QuicKeys, 716

quote character, 234–235

R

RAD (rapid application development), 205

radio buttons, 306, 585

Random function, 449–450

Range operator (...), 143

rapid application development (RAD), 205

RDMS (Relational Database Management Systems), 405–406

[Read-Only Access] privilege set, 559

RealTech, 738

real-time data summarization, 689

reappearing objects

    concealed and remotely operated Tab Control, 358–360

    conditional formatting, 360

    overview, 356

    portal invisibility, 356–358

Receipts::ReceiptStatus field, 698

Recent Finds menu, 73

RecordID stored calculation field, 485

recording navigation text, 240–241

records

    access to, 564–566

    committing, 49–50, 107

    creating, 48

    deleting redundant

        cascading deletion, 592–595

        configuring relationships for referential integrity, 592–593

        overview, 591

    duplicating, 49

    flagging, 607

    locking, 280, 604–606, 615

    maintaining sort order, 70–72

records *(continued)*
  marking, 607
  moving between, 44, 153
  overview, 4, 13
  record IDs, 586–587
  related, 16
  sorting
    click-sort columns, creating, 327–331
    dynamic sort techniques, 324–327
    multiple sort keys, 324
    overview, 323
    related data, 332–333
records commands, 262
Records menu, 73–75
Recover command
  file corruption, 638–639
  overview, 96–98, 633–635
  recovery process, 635–637
  salvaging data, 637–638
Recover.log file, 98
rectangle tool, Status Toolbar, 172–173
recursion
  defined, 496, 675
  examples, 682–683
  limits of, 681
  overview, 680–681
  tail, 681–682
reducing parts, 369–371
redundancy
  avoiding duplication of elements, 689–690
  data, 7
  data design issues, 596
  portable and reusable code, 690–691
redundant records, deleting, 591–595
referencing fields, 235–236
referential integrity
  auto-entry lookups, 595–596
  data design issues, 596
  deleting redundant records
    cascading deletion, 592–595
    configuring relationships for referential
      integrity, 592–593
    overview, 591
  dependencies
    filename references, 598
    indirect object/element references, 597
    literal text references, 597
    structural anomalies, 598

keys
  exploring, 588–590
  generating, 584–588
  retrofitting, 590–591
  unique, 582–584
lookups, 595
pinpointing causes of problems, 581–582
`Refresh` command, 348
`Refresh Portal` script, 311
`Refresh Window[ ]` command, 348, 541
refreshing screen, 541–542
registration, 35
Regular User privileges, 152
related data
  displaying, 191–195
  pivoting data between tables, 549–550
  sorting, 332–333
related records, 16, 49
`Related` table, 411
`RelatedKey` field, 418
relational data
  modeling principle, 408
  structure, 582
Relational Database Management Systems (RDMS), 405–406
relational databases
  connections between corresponding information, 7–8
  data redundancy, 7
  flat-file, 7
  overview, 6
relational filtering, 488
relational key, 589
relational matching, 488
relational theory. *See also* data modeling
  guiding principles, 408–410
  modeling real world, 406–408
  overview, 405–406
  set theory, 406
relations, 13
relationship joins, 692
relationship operators
  Cartesian joins, 415
  comparative operators, 414–415
  equi-joins, 414
  multi-predicate relationships, 415–416
  non-equal joins, 414
  overview, 413–414
relationships
  alternative techniques, 416–420
  configuring for referential integrity, 592–593

context, 55
creating, 129–132
editing related data, 54
functioning of, 258
locations, 259
overview, 257–258
relational model, 259–260
simplicity, 55
solving problems using, 258–259
viewing related data, 54
visual cues to, 144
Relationships Graph
circular references, avoiding, 244–245
constellations, 424
data sources, named and unnamed, 245–246
duplication in, 690
establishing relationships, 129–132
misconceptions about, 241–242
modular centers, 424
overview, 206, 423–424
references to other files, creating, 246–247
reusability concepts, 692
satellite-based graph solution, 424–426
segmentation on functional lines, 426–427
shadow tables, 255–256
symbols, 410–412
Table Occurrences, 23–25, 191, 243
tables, 243
Relationships tab, Manage Database dialog, 129, 131, 255, 307, 592
Re-login[ ] command, 573
Relookup Field Contents option, 107
remote files
defined, 36
file sharing risks, 610–611
opener files, 611–612
overview, 607–608
peer-to-peer hosting, 608–610
sending e-mail links, 612–613
Remove Expression control, Watch panel, Data Viewer, 664
renaming
fields, 213–214
tables, 206–208
reordering scripts, 293
repeating fields, 16, 420
repetition, controlling script execution using, 282–283
Repetitions text box, Specify Calculation dialog, 231
repetitive tasks, 399
Replace( ) function, 240, 455, 461–462, 479

Replace Field Contents [ ] command, 585–587, 606, 644, 647, 688
Replace Field Contents dialog, 587, 590
Replace Field Contents option, 107
Replace with Serial Numbers option, 590
reporting, 427
reports
composite PDFs, 204
versus Excel, 204
fonts, 202–203
page setup, 203
page sizes, 203
versus PDF, 204
printed, 202
printing, 295
Require section, Validation tab, Options for Field dialog, 219
Reserved Name operators, 453–454
reserved words, 235
resizable layout objects
centering, 382
complex layout resizing, 379–381
enclosing, 382
moving according to window size, 378–379
overview, 377
that grow and shrink, 379
resizing windows, 538–540
re-sorting, 71–72
resources
books, 739
mailing lists, 738
online design and development, 737–738
online forums, 738
overview, 32–33
periodicals, 739
professional consulting and development services, 736–737
Web site, 735–736
restoring data. *See* maintaining data
restricted-access accounts, 152
Result Type pop-up, Specify Calculation dialog, 231
results
defined, 229
retrieving, 523–525
specifying, 523–525
retrofitting keys, 590–591
Return key, 186
Return/Enter characters, 123
Revert Record option, 48, 50, 134
Revert Script option, 287

RGB( ) function, 336, 469
Right( ) function, 337, 462–463, 467, 477
RightValues( ) function, 477
RightWords( ) function, 465–466
robots, 704–705
role-based security, 560
roll-back
    alternative undo, 629
    chronological, 628–629
    overview, 627–628
    using logs to roll forward, 629–630
roll-forward, 629–630
Roster field, 478
Round( ) function, 237
Rounded Rectangle tool, 183
rule of multiples, 367
Run Script with Full Access Privileges option, 437, 510, 512, 517, 535, 594, 691
Run/Pause button, Script Debugger window, 659
runtime applications
    binding, 685–686
    hosting runtime files, 686
    overview, 27
    stand-alone solution, 684–685
runtime files, hosting, 686

S

safeguards, key, 583–584
SASE (Server Activated Script Execution), 103–104
satellite-based graph solution, 424–426
Save a Copy as [ ] command, 286–287, 602
Save a Copy command, 635
Save a Copy Compacted command, 635
Save Changes button, 703
Save dialog, 137
Save Layout Changes Automatically (Do Not Ask) checkbox, Layout tab, Preferences dialog, 156
Save Records as Excel[ ] command, 527
Save Records as PDF[ ] command, 527
Saved Finds sub-menu, Records menu, 73–75
Save/Send Records As commands, 53–54
saving
    files, 38
    Find requests, 72–75
    found sets, 319–323
    records, 50
    target printer, 104–105
scalability, 27–28

schema privilege controls, 561–562
schema references, 450–452
scope
    button, 198–199
    variable, 459
Score field, 474
screen elements
    conditional formatting, 360–361
    disappearing/reappearing objects, 356–360
    multi-state buttons and objects, 361–362
    overview, 47–48
screens
    adaptable, 362–363
    font, 353
    illusion of depth, 385–386
    layering, 354
    lists of values for fields, 12
    rendering differences for Mac and Windows, 353–354
    separating for printing information, 202
script commands
    assigning attributes to, 276–278
    branching according to state, 518–519
    changing order of, 274–276
    groups, 262–265
    overview, 273–274
    window management, 536–537
Script Debugger
    controls, 659–660
    debugging restricted privilege scripts, 658–659
    empty comment lines, 291
    enhancements to, 107
    issues with triggers, 87–88
    overview, 657–658
    using Data Viewer with, 665
Script Definition panel, Edit Script window, 276–277
Script Editor windows, 268–271, 510–511
script error codes, 108
script logging
    infrastructure for, 621–622
    overview, 630–631
    tracking script execution, 622–623
Script Name field, 310
script parameters, 512, 517–518, 523
script progress monitors, 395–396
script recursion, 536
script results, 523–524
script stacks, 279–280
Script Step action, 672
Script Step Options panel, Edit Script window, 265, 276

script steps, 262–263
script triggering
file-based, 85
layout object triggers, 78–81
layout script triggers, 81–84
logging, 630–631
overview, 77–78, 516–517
pitfalls of, 85–88
plug-ins, 723–725
Tab Controls, 358–359
timed interval, 84–85
Script Triggers tab, Layout Setup dialog, 82–83, 299–300, 516
script variables, 458–459
Script[ ] command, 510
scripted data aggregation, 526
scripted queries, 440
scripting
access privileges
full access, 511–512
overview, 510–511
privilege-based errors, 511
substantive, 512
account management
automation of database security, 570–571
multi-file solutions, 571–572
safe scripting implementations, 572
addressing objects by name, 267–268
automation
housekeeping practices, 514–515
overview, 512–513
running on file close, 515
running on file open, 513
script triggers, 516–517
blocks of automation, 264–266
context, 266–267
dynamic and indirect controls
building Find criteria, 529–530
example, 526–527
file paths using variables, 527–528
indirection, 530–531
examples
building multi-part PDF reports, 551
locating unique records, 550–551
exporting data
container objects, 548–549
field contents, 542
selecting fields for export, 543–545
table data, 543

importing data
container objects, 548–549
data matching for, 546–548
options for, 545
interface object control via
addressing objects by name, 500–501
locking down interface, 501–502
managing user interaction, 502–504
overview, 499–500
modular script code
script recursion, 536
using sub-scripts, 535–536
nonlinear logic
looping constructs, 532–533
nested and sequential If/Else conditions, 531–532
specifying exit conditions, 533–535
overview, 261–264
parameters
branching according to state, 518–519
getting data into script, 517–518
passing and retrieving multiple, 521–523
performing actions in sequence, 267
pivoting data between tables
managing related data, 549–550
using utility relationships, 549
results, specifying and retrieving, 523–525
tab operations, 389
trapping errors
error codes, 505–506
error handling, 506–509
overview, 504–505
variables
declaring, 519–521
storing and accumulating data, 525–526
windows
addressing by name, 537–538
creating off-screen, 540–541
freezing and refreshing screen, 541–542
moving, 538–540
overview, 536
resizing, 538–540
ScriptLog table, 621–622
scripts. *See also* calling scripts; script commands; scripting
access to, 563
controlling execution
overview, 280
pausing for user input, 283–284
using conditional statements, 281–282
using repetition, 282–283

scripts *(continued)*
   creating, 310
   duplicate names, 289
   editing
      copying and pasting, 288–289
      overview, 287
      selecting and duplicating multiple commands, 288
   error handling, 506
   examples
      acting on user input, 296
      performing finds, 295
      printing reports, 295
   organizing
      filtering scripts by folder, 293–294
      grouping scripts, 293
      list separators, creating, 289–290
      reordering scripts, 293
      script commenting, 290–291
      script folders, creating, 291–293
      searching for scripts by name, 294
   overview, 17
   Script Editor windows, 268–271
   Scripts menu
      managing, 278–279
      paused scripts, 280
      script stacks, 280
      single-threaded script engine, 279–280
   self-logging, 623
   setting up, 271–273
   uses for
      editing information via, 286
      managing files, 286–287
      navigation controls, 285–286
      overview, 284
      printing files, 286–287
      view controls, 285–286
Scripts menu
   calling scripts via, 297
   list separators, 290
   managing, 278–279
   paused scripts, 280
   Reports submenu, 292–293
   script stacks, 280
   single-threaded script engine, 279–280
script-threading, 459
scroll bar, 389
searches
   constraining and extending found sets, 319
   databases, 143

AND Finds, 318
OR Finds, 318
overview, 45–46, 317
saving Finds and found sets, 319–323
for scripts by name, 294
Secure Socket Layer (SSL) encryption, 580
security
   accounts, 148–152
   amount of
      balanced view of threats, 577
      strategic model for response, 577
      ways to evaluate risk, 576
   concepts of
      interface vulnerabilities, 557–558
      overview, 555–556
      perspective, 556
      protecting investment, 556–557
   deployment
      filtered display of files, 580
      overview, 579–580
      Secure Socket Layer encryption, 580
      server checks and logs, 580
   file-based, 432
   granular
      extended privileges, 566–567
      field access, 564–566
      layout access, 563–564
      overview, 562–563
      record access, 564–566
      script access, 563
      table access, 564–566
      value list access, 563
   logout option
      locked-down database, 573
      security logging, 575–576
      structuring solution for, 573–575
   management of, 438
   passwords, 150–152
   physical file
      alternative forms of protection, 578
      layers of protection, 578
      multi-faceted approach, 579
      overview, 577–578
   privilege sets
      defining and constraining access, 560–561
      overview, 148–152, 558–559
      role-based security, 560
      schema privilege controls, 561–562
   risks, 577

scripted account management
    automation of database security, 570–571
    multi-file solutions, 571–572
    safe scripting implementations, 572
  start-up scripts, 514
  user authentication
    internal and external, 568–570
    overview, 567
    user accounts, creating, 568
Security Administrator, 731
security logs, 576
Security Management Script command, 571
segmentation, 427, 707
Select Buyer pop-up window, 313
Select Contact [Type] script, 310–312
Select Damaged File dialog, 96–97, 634
Select Entire Contents checkbox, 469
Select Item window, 375
Select Window[ ] command, 374
select/act tools, 158
Self function, 337, 449–450
self joins, 422–423
self-contained applications, 684
self-join portal, 390
self-join relationship, 485
self-logging script, 623
Send DDE Execute [ ] script, 713
Send Event [ ] command, 710–713, 716
Send Link command, 612
Send Mail option, File menu, 100
Send Mail[ ] script command, 100
sending e-mail links, 612–613
SendMail, 727
separation, data
    approaches to, 438
    costs and benefits, 439
    external SQL sources, 439–442
    implementing in existing solution, 442–445
separation model, 432
separators, 294, 465–466
sequential dependency, 700
sequential If/Else conditions, 531–532
Serial Number checkbox, Auto-Enter tab, Field Options
        dialog, 217
serial numbers, 119–120, 585–586
Serial# field, 411
SerialIncrement ( ) calculation function, 585
Server Activated Script Execution (SASE), 103–104
server products, 27

Server-compatible script command, 706
servlets, 719
Set Error Capture [ ] command, 508–509
Set Error Capture [On] command, 508
Set Field [ ] command, 76, 267, 277, 309, 337–338,
        394, 487, 531, 723
Set Field by Name [ ] command, 76–77, 90,
        482, 531
Set Next Serial Value[ ] script command, 585
Set Next Step button, Script Debugger window, 659
Set Script Triggers dialog, 79–80, 300–301, 310–311
Set Selection[ ] script command, 469
Set Sliding/Printing dialog, 167, 169, 368, 370
Set Tab Order dialog, 186–187, 388
Set Theory, 406
Set Tooltip dialog, 99, 176
Set Variable[ ] command, 339–340, 459, 520,
        652, 723
Set Web Viewer[ ] command, 201, 533
Set Window Title ["xyz"] command, 537
Set/Clear Breakpoint button, Script Debugger window, 659
sFirstExam summary field, 475
shadow tables, 255–256
Shell Scripts, 713–715
Shift key, 288
Shockwave Flash, 719
short-circuit evaluation, 234, 693
shortcut icon, 37
shortcut keys, 297–298
shortcut navigation
    Back button functionality, 384–385
    Go to Related Record [ ] command, 383
    multiple paths, 383
    overview, 313–316, 382–383
shortcuts, Specify Calculation dialog, 232
Show All icon, 46
Show All Records command, 362
Show Compatibility menu, Edit Script
        window, 103–104, 705
Show Custom Dialog Options dialog, 376, 572
Show Custom Dialog[ ] script command, 502–503,
        725
Show in New Window checkbox, 314
Show Individual Words checkbox, 342–343
Show Omitted Only option, Records menu, 141
Show Transactions [Type] script, 529
Show/Hide Status Area[ ] command, 573
ShuffleString (text) syntax, 496

simplicity
    applying, 701–702
    dependencies, 698–701
    examples, 695–698
    optimal calculation syntax, 693–694
    overview, 22–23
single character quote mark, 371
Single Sign-on (Windows Authentication), 92–94
single-file architecture, 442
single-threaded script engine, 279–280
Six Fried Rice, 738
sLastExam summary field, 475
sliding objects, 369–371
SMALLDATETIME fields, 94
Smart Pill, 727
smart quotes, 59
SMTP server, e-mailing via, 99–100
solutions
    overview, 13
    simplicity in development of, 701
    steps to add accounts, 568
    using script triggers to enforce rules in, 87
something variable, 340
Sort dialog, 324
sort order, 222
Sort Portal Records checkbox, Portal Setup dialog, 332
Sort Records dialog, 142, 271–272, 430
Sort Records[ ] command, 325–326, 585
sorting data, 141–143
sorting records
    click-sort columns, creating, 327–331
    dynamic sort techniques, 324–327
    multiple sort keys, 324
    overview, 323
    related data, 332–333
Source table occurrence, 550
spatial cues, 385–386
Specify buttons, 263
Specify Buyer button, 313
Specify Calculation dialog
    accessing, 277–278
    aggregating calcs, 132–134
    custom functions, 494
    field names in, 120–121
    formula box, 448
    global calculations, 489
    making content explicit, 451–452
    mouse-driven shortcuts, 232
    overview, 23–24, 222–224

parts of, 229–231
    privileges for table, record, and field access, 564
    setting up calculations in, 124–126
    structured syntax and nesting, 452–453
    trapping edits, 624
Specify Field dialog
    accessing, 276–277
    ItemSupplier TO, 144–146
    Merge fields, 371
    in portal creation process, 194
    sourcing fields in, 191–192
Specify Field Order For Export dialog, 52–53, 543–544
Specify Fields for Value List dialog, 138, 140
Specify File dialog, 245–247, 528, 545, 548
Specify Find Requests dialog, 319
Specify Options for the Saved Find dialog, 74–75
Specify Output File dialog, 544, 711
Specify Script dialog, 311
Specify Script Options dialog, 330, 518
Specify Solution Options dialog, 684
Specify Table dialog, 252–254, 436
spell-checking, 59, 187–188
spelling commands, 263
Spelling panel, File Options dialog, 59–60
spider graph, 423
spiral formation, Relationships Graph, 244–245
splash screens, 397–398
spreadsheets, 6, 51
spyware, 578
SQL Query Builder, 548
SQL tables, integrating, 252–256
squid graph, 423
SSL (Secure Socket Layer) encryption, 580
stacking Find requests, 318
Standard Deviation Of summary function, 227
[Standard FileMaker Menus] menu set, 674
start parameter, 465
Starter Solutions, 107, 112
starting FileMaker Pro 10, 37
start-up scripts, 512–515, 621, 719
state
    branching according to, 518–519
    capturing by user, 399–400
static actions, 154
static array, 421
static data, 434
static objects, 178–179, 500
stationery formats, 203
Status Area, 64–68

status bar, 355
Status Bar, Status Toolbar, 66
Status Toolbar
    Button tool, 195–196
    controls, 42–46
    Field tool, 178
    Find icon drop-down menu, 73, *74f*
    Find mode, 306, 317, 502
    icons, 160
    Line Pattern tool, 172
    Object Selection tool, 158, 178
    overview, 42, 64–68
    Part tool, 171
    Portal tool, 191
    rectangle tool, 172–173
    Text tool, 173
    tools, 158
Step Into button, Script Debugger window, 659
Step Out button, Script Debugger window, 659
Step Over button, Script Debugger, 107, 659
steps, 262–263
storage
    auto-enter calculations, 488
    data, 627
    protocols, 608
Storage Options button, Specify Calculation dialog, 231
Storage Options dialog, 350, 489
Storage tab, Options for Field dialog, 221–222, 227–228
Store Only a Reference to the File option, 651
stored calculation field, 485, 700
stored files
    assigning and retrieving paths, 652
    overview, 651–652
    scripted field updates, 652–653
`Stored Find` technique, 323
stored-as-reference storage mode, 653
`StoredFinds` layout, 321–322
Strict Data Type menu, Validation tab, Options for Field
        dialog, 219
structure
    data
        interface files, 436–438
        modular approach, 435
        multi-file solutions, 434–435
        overview, 9, 434
        separation of data, 438–439
    database, 9, 23
    documenting database
        ancillary notes, 430–431
        field commenting, 429–430

graph annotations, 427–428
    naming conventions, 428–429
    overview, 427
multiple-file, 434
relational data, 582
visual
    ergonomics, 174–175
    giving information meaning, 175
    overview, 171
    visual fatigue, avoiding, 174–175
    visual pointers and aids, 172–174
    white space, 174
style buttons, creating, 337–338
styled source text, 619
submenus, Script menu, 279, 292–293
`Submissions::Date` field, 529
sub-scripts
    defined, 279
    eliminating redundancy, 690–691
    script results, 524
    use of, 535–536
sub-second pause durations, 284
subsets, data, 7, 9
`Substitute( )` function, 240, 461–462, 479
Sub-summary parts
    adaptable screens, 362–363
    multiple break fields, 366
    overview, 68–70, 171
    page breaks, 366–367
    pagination, 366–367
    stacking up multiple, 363–365
    zones, 380
`Sum( )` function, 473, 693
`Sum(Invoices::BalancePayable)` expression, 694
summaries, data, 52
summary data
    aggregate functions, 473–474
    `Max( )`, 474–475
    `Min( )`, 474–475
    referencing summary fields, 475
summary fields, 16, 216, 222–227, 473, 475, 702
SuperContainer, 727
`SuperLog( )` custom function, 626
`Supplier Details` field, 356–357
`SupplierID` field, 356, 360–361
Suppliers Table Occurrence, 640
support programs, 32
`.swf` file format, 719
synchronized security configuration, 571

synchronizing
    data, 546–547
    data sets
        import matching, 648–650
        importing selectively, 650
        overview, 647–648
syntax, 229, 449
System DSN tab
    ODBC Administrator utility window, 249
    ODBC Data Source Administrator control panel, 248
system failure, 601
System Preferences color palette, 354
System::gProgressPercent field, 396

T

Tab Control Setup dialog, 188–189, 359
Tab Controls
    adaptable design, 692
    concealed and remotely operated, 358–360
    defined, 47
    as dynamic objects, 179
    hierarchical principle, 387
    navigation via keyboard, 388
    organizers, 387
    resizing behavior of enclosing objects, 382
    scripting tab operations, 389
    space savers, 387
    uses of, 188–190
Tab key, 265
tab order, setting, 186
tab panels
    creating, 188–189
    limitations of, 190
    navigating between, 189–190
    scripting tab operations, 389
Tab Width pop-up menu, 359
tab-delimited format, 106
Table Occurrence Groups (TOGs), 152–153
Table Occurrences (TOs)
    displaying related data with, 191
    GetFieldName( ) function, 481
    interface files, 436–437
    modifying in Manage Database dialog, 206–207
    names in edited tables, 208
    overview, 23, 410–412
    as pointer, 412
    relationships, 422
    re-pointing, 442–443

Specify Calculation dialog menu, 224
table names, 122
    versus tables, 242–243
    using in Relationships Graph, 129–131
table of dependencies, 224
Table pop-up, Specify Calculation dialog, 230
Table View, 69–70, 168, 329, 378
tables
    access to, 564–566
    adding, 114–118, 206–208
    concepts, 206
    deleting, 206–208
    files, moving between, 208–209
    importing, 209–212
    moving between, 154
    overview, 4–6
    pivoting data between
        managing related data, 549–550
        using utility relationships, 549
    relationships, creating between, 129–132
    renaming, 206–208
    SQL, integrating, 252–256
    versus table occurrences, 243
Tables tab, Manage Database dialog, 116, 118, 206–209, 307, 443, 598
tail recursion, 681–682
Target Fields column, Import Field Mapping dialog, 546
TCPdirect, 727
TechNet, 736
Temp directory, 391
templates
    Create Database, 36
    updated, 107
    using techniques as, 717
temporary edit interface techniques
    Data Viewer concept, 613–614
    double-blind entry systems, 615–616
    record locking, 615
temporary files, 104
terminal line, 411
testing, graph, 444
text
    color of, 162–163
    font sizes, 99
    formatting operations
        applying, 467–468
        creating Format button, 469–470
        removing, 468
        selective, 468–469

handling
  designing custom export process, 654
  `Export Field Contents[ ]` command, 653–654
parsing, 462–463, 466–467
processing functions
  `Left( )`, 462–463
  `LeftWords( )`, 465–466
  `Middle( )`, 462–463
  `MiddleWords( )`, 465–466
  overview, 460–461
  `PatternCount( )`, 463–465
  `Position( )`, 463–465
  `Replace( )`, 461–462
  `Right( )`, 462–463
  `RightWords( )`, 465–466
  `Substitute( )`, 461
  `Trim( )`, 462
  `WordCount( )`, 465–466
underlining, 469–470
Text Color checkbox, 330, 360
text fields, 16, 214, 222, 463
text indexing
  versus numeric, 343–344
  value indexes, 342
  word indexes, 341–342
text objects, 162–166, 353
text operators, 453, 455
Text panel, File Options dialog, 59–61
text placeholder, 372
Text Ruler, 335
text string, 455–456, 466–467
Text tool, Status Toolbar, 173
text value, 589, 683
`TextColor( )` function, 336, 467, 469
`TextColorRemove( )` function, 468
`textdecoration:underline;` tag, 469
TextExpander, 716
TextField field, 718
`TextFont( )` function, 467
`TextFontRemove( )` function, 468
text-processing function, 572
`TextSize( )` function, 467
`TextSizeRemove( )` function, 468
`TextStyleAdd( )` function, 337, 467
`TextStyleRemove( )` function, 468–469
themes, updated, 107
theta joins, 414–415, 455, 457
`ThingsToDo::Reminder` field, 464–465

third-party analysis and documentation tools, 732
third-party automation, 716
third-party backup utilities, 601
third-party developer tools, 731
third-party diagnostic tool, 598
third-party plug-ins, 403, 514
third-party scheduling, 716
third-party shared information tools, 732
360Works AdminAnywhere, 731
360Works Charts Plugin, 727
360Works Email Plugin, 727
time calculations
  juggling days, months, and years, 472–473
  managing, 470
  number of seconds, 471
  plotting time, 470–471
time fields, 215
time format, precedence of, 336
timed interval script triggers, 84–85
timed pauses, 283–284
timer script triggers, 77, 299
timestamps, 106, 128, 215, 471
Title Footer layout part, 171
Title Header layout part, 171
TOGs (Table Occurrence Groups), 152–153
tooltips
  conditional, 176–177
  defining, 99
  keeping track of, 177
  overview, 175–176
TOs (Table Occurrences)
  displaying related data with, 191
  `GetFieldName( )` function, 481
  interface files, 436–437
  modifying in Manage Database dialog, 206–207
  names in edited tables, 208
  overview, 23, 410–412
  as pointer, 412
  relationships, 422
  re-pointing, 442–443
  Specify Calculation dialog menu, 224
  table names, 122
  versus tables, 242–243
  using in Relationships Graph, 129–131
Total of summary function, 226
`TotalPayable` value, 457
trailing carriage return, 477
Trailing Grand Summary layout part, 171
trailing returns, 123

trailing spaces, 618
trailing Sub-summary part, 363
transaction modeling
    batch automation, 704
    host/server script execution, 704–706
    live versus batch data, 702–703
    offline updates and processing, 704
    posting and propagating edits, 703
    robots, 704
`Transactions` table, 412
transformation tools, FileMaker, 643
Transformations table, 654
translucency, 386–387
transparency, 347, 386–387
trapping errors
    error codes, 505–506
    error handling, 506–509
    global fields, 607
    overview, 504–505, 603–604
    record locking, 604–606
    record marking and flagging, 607
    replacing field contents, 606–607
    sub-scripts, 536
trial copy, 741
triggered logging, 630–631. *See also* script triggering
`Trim( )` function, 462, 466
`TrimAll( )` function, 462
Troi Activator, 725
Troi Automatisering, 725
Troi dialog plug-in, 725–726
Troi File, 726
Troi URL Plug-in, 727
tuples, 13
Type pop-up menu, Fields tab, Manage Database dialog, 214

U

UID (unique identification) values, 587–588
Undo/Redo command, 266
Unicode, 89–90, 344–345, 414, 646
unique identification (UID) values, 587–588
Unique Value option, Validation tab, Options for Field
    dialog, 219
unnamed data sources, 245–246
unstored calculation field, 419, 483–484
unstored calculations
    advantages and disadvantages of, 484–485
    hidden secrets of, 485
    reasons for, 483–484

Update Existing import option, 594
Update Existing Records in Found Set option, 649
Update Matching Records in Found Set option, 648–649
Update Records in Found Set import, 650
updating data, 286, 546–547
`Upper( )` function, 453
usability, database
    buttons, using, 154
    context, managing, 153
    overview, 152–153
    records, moving between, 153
    tables, moving between, 154
    views, using and changing, 154
usage logging, 514
Use Fixed Page Margins checkbox, Printing tab, Layout Setup
    dialog, 166
Use Global Storage option, 489
Usenet group, 738
user accounts
    creating, 568
    internal and external authentication, 568–570
    overview, 567
    scripted management of, 570–572
    setting default, 150–152
user names, 56
user over-ride capability, 486–488
user requirements audit, 441
users. *See also* user accounts
    acting on input, 296
    anticipating, 145–147
    capturing edits
        field-by-field, 623–624
        incorporating ancillary data, 624–626
        logging record deletions, 626
    complications with triggers, 86
    dialogs for, 286
    interaction, managing, 502–504
    pausing for input, 283–284
    pop-up window, 286
    preferences of
        capturing state by user, 399–400
        multi-lingual solution interface, 400–403
        setting, 514
        user-centric development philosophy, 399
    screen design for, 174–175
    tooltip preferences, 177
utility relationships
    pivoting data between tables using, 549
    Relationships Graph, 692

Utility table, 307–311, 327, 478
Utility::cFilter_key field, 307
Utility::gFilter_txt field, 309
Utility::gNewValue field, 479
Utility::gSortField field, 481
Utility::gType_key field, 307

V

Validate Data In This Field: Always option, 583
Validate Data in This Field section, Validation tab, Options
    for Field dialog, 219
Validated by Calculation checkbox, Validation tab, Options
    for Field dialog, 220
validation, 49, 118–124, 218–221, 583, 614
Validation tab, Options for Field dialog, 122–123, 218–219
Value from Last Visited Record checkbox, Auto-Enter tab,
    Field Options dialog, 217
value indexes, 342
value lists
    access to, 563
    based on external SQL data, 92
    dynamic sort techniques, 324
ValueCount( ) function, 477
ValueListItems( ) function, 476, 598
variables
    benefiting from, 460
    calculation, 458–459
    Data Viewer, 666–667
    declaring, 340, 515, 519–521
    defined, 229
    destroying, 340
    dynamic file paths using, 527–528
    instantiating, 340
    interface files, 437
    keeping track of, 340–341
    kinds of, 339
    memory usage, 339
    overview, 338
    scope, 459
    storing and accumulating data, 525–526
VBScript, 710–713
Verdana font, 157, 203, 353
version information, 398
vertical resizing, 378, 381
vertical zone, 379
View By menu, Tables tab, Manage Database dialog, 208
view controls, scripting, 285–286
View Index dialog, 342–343

View menu, 43, 65
ViewerData table, 392
viewing data
    editing, 141
    entering data, 136–141
    Find operators, 142–143
    finding, 141–143
    layouts, 136
    overview, 43–45, 135
    Range operator (...), 143
    records, creating, 136–141
    related, 54
views
    changing, 154
    multiple
        placement, 373–374
        as pop-ups and drill-downs, 374–375
        simulating modal window behavior, 375
        size, 373–374
        use of, 306
Views tab, Layout Setup dialog, 169–170
visual fatigue, 174–175
visual pointers and aids, 172–174
visual spell-checking, 187–188
visual structure
    ergonomics, 174–175
    giving information meaning, 175
    overview, 171
    visual fatigue, avoiding, 174–175
    visual pointers and aids, 172–174
    white space, 174
Vn calculation variable, 522

W

Watch panel, Data Viewer, 661, 664–665
Web Address field, Web Viewer Setup dialog, 200
Web deployment
    Custom Web Publishing
        FileMaker PHP API, 730
        FileMaker PHP Site Assistant, 730–731
        working with XML and XSLT, 729–730
    Instant Web Publishing, 728–729
Web Publishing with PHP and FileMaker 9, 739
Web scraping, 393
Web site
    contents of, 741–742
    overview, 735–736
    troubleshooting, 742

Web Viewer Setup dialog, 200, 718
Web viewers
    advanced functionality, 391–392
    complementary data concepts, 202
    controlling, 201
    defined, 17, 179
    overview, 48, 158
    rendering internally calculated content, 392–393
    scraping data from Web pages, 393–394
    setting up, 200–201
web-compatible script, 81
Webinars, 735
When Sorted By field, 363
white space, 174
widgets, 391
wildcard operators, 143
Wiley Technical Product Support Center, 742
Window menu, 306
window widgets, 672
WindowNames ( ) function, 449–450, 538
windows
    addressing by name, 537–538
    controlling one from another, 317
    creating off-screen, 540–541
    freezing screen, 541–542
    management, 514, 605
    moving, 538–540
    multiple
        placement, 373–374
        as pop-ups and drill-downs, 374–375
        simulating modal window behavior, 375
        size, 373–374
        use of, 306
    overview, 41–42, 536
    placement, 514
    refreshing screen, 541–542
    resizing, 538–540
Windows Authentication (Single Sign-on), 92–94
windows commands, 262
Windows operating system
    command line interpreter, 712
    Customize dialog, 66–67

documents paths in, 91
external scripting calls, 710
fonts in, 203
interface design for users of
    fonts, selecting, 352–353
    platform-specific window behavior, 354–355
    screen rendering differences, 353–354
and IPv6 format, 106
ODBC drivers, 248
word indexes, 341–343
Word program, 11
word separators, 465–466
WordCount ( ) function, 465–466
wrappers, 717

X

xmCHART, 727
XML (Extensible Markup Language), 29, 669, 729–730
XSLT (Extensible Stylesheet Language Transformation), 729–730
xValues function, 477
xWords function, 466
xyz logo, 181–182

Y

Year ( ) function, 448
YourField[7] array notation, 477
YourNumber field, 456
YourTable::YourTextString field, 468

Z

zero error, 505
zero parameter value, 449
zippScript function, 724
zones, resizing, 379–380
zoom controls, 42

THOMSON

JRSE TECHNOLOGY ™

ssional ▪ Trade ▪ Reference

GAME PROGRAMMING ALL IN ONE

2ND EDITION

JONATHAN S. HARBOUR

INCLUDES CD-ROM

Premier
Press

GAME PROGRAMMING
ALL IN ONE,
2ND EDITION

JONATHAN S. HARBOUR

THOMSON

─────── TM

COURSE TECHNOLOGY

Professional ■ Trade ■ Reference

ISBN: 1-59200-383-4

Library of Congress Catalog Card Number: 2004091915
Printed in the United States of America

04 05 06 07 08 BH 10 9 8 7 6 5 4 3 2

THOMSON

COURSE TECHNOLOGY

Professional ■ Trade ■ Reference

Course PTR, a division of Course Technology
25 Thomson Place
Boston, MA 02210
http://www.courseptr.com

SVP, Thomson Course Technology PTR:
Andy Shafran

Publisher:
Stacy L. Hiquet

Senior Marketing Manager:
Sarah O'Donnell

Marketing Manager:
Heather Hurley

Manager of Editorial Services:
Heather Talbot

Acquisitions Editor:
Mitzi Koontz

Senior Editor:
Mark Garvey

Associate Marketing Managers:
Kristin Eisenzopf and Sarah Dubois

Project Editor/Copy Editor:
Cathleen D. Snyder

Technical Reviewer:
Joshua Smith

Thomson Course Technology PTR Market Coordinator:
Amanda Weaver

Interior Layout Tech:
Shawn Morningstar

Cover Designer:
Steve Deschene

CD-ROM Producer:
Brandon Penticuff

Indexer:
Kelly Talbot

Proofreader:
Sean Medlock

For Jeremiah

ACKNOWLEDGMENTS

A book of this size involves a lot of work even after the writing is done. It takes a while just to read through a programming book once, so you can imagine how difficult it is to read through it several times, making changes and notes along the way, refining, correcting, and preparing the book for print. I am indebted to the hard work of the editors, artists, and layout specialists at Premier Press who do such a fine job. Thank you Mitzi Koontz, Emi Smith, and Stacy Hiquet for your encouragement and support.

I owe many thanks to Cathleen Snyder, one of the most amazing editors in the business, who both managed the project and copy edited the manuscript, and to Joshua R. Smith, who offered his technical expertise and long experience in the game industry to point out my mistakes and to offer advice. I believe you will find this a true gem of a game programming book due to their efforts.

I thank my wife, Jennifer, for her love and support.

I would also like to thank Bruno Miguel Teixeira de Sousa for writing the first edition of this book. Some of his original work may still be found in this new edition, in Chapters 6, 18, 19, and 20.

ABOUT THE AUTHOR

JONATHAN S. HARBOUR has been an avid gamer and programmer for 17 years, having started with a TI-99, a Commodore PET, and a Tandy 1000. In 1994, he earned a bachelor of science degree in computer information systems. He has since earned the position of senior programmer with seven years of professional programming experience. Jonathan is a member of the *Starflight III* team, working with the original designers and other volunteers on a sequel to the first two *Starflight* games (using Allegro), originally published by Electronic Arts in 1985 and 1989, respectively. Jonathan has released two retail Pocket PC games, *Pocket Trivia* and *Perfect Match*, and has authored or coauthored five other books on the subject of game programming, including *Pocket PC Game Programming, Visual Basic Game Programming with DirectX, Visual Basic .NET Programming for the Absolute Beginner, Beginner's Guide to DarkBASIC Game Programming,* and *Beginning Game Boy Advance Programming.* He maintains a Web site dedicated to game programming and other topics at http://www.jharbour.com. Jonathan lives in Arizona with his wife, Jennifer, and children, Jeremiah and Kayleigh.

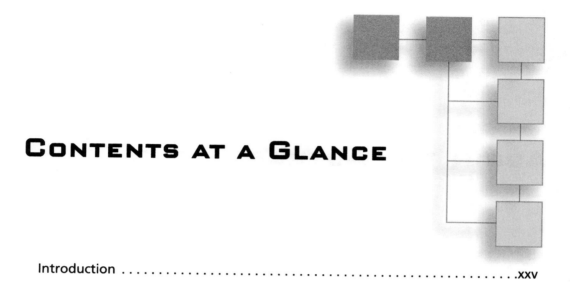

CONTENTS AT A GLANCE

Introduction xxv

PART I: INTRODUCTION TO CROSS-PLATFORM GAME PROGRAMMING   1

CHAPTER 1   Demystifying Game Development 3

CHAPTER 2   Getting Started with Dev-C++ and Allegro 33

CHAPTER 3   Basic 2D Graphics Programming with Allegro 71

CHAPTER 4   Writing Your First Allegro Game 119

CHAPTER 5   Programming the Keyboard, Mouse, and Joystick 145

PART II: 2D GAME THEORY, DESIGN, AND PROGRAMMING   185

CHAPTER 6   Introduction to Game Design 187

CHAPTER 7   Basic Bitmap Handling and Blitting 215

CHAPTER 8   Basic Sprite Programming: Drawing Scaled, Flipped, Rotated, Pivoted, and Translucent Sprites 237

CHAPTER 9   Advanced Sprite Programming: Animation, Compiled Sprites, and Collision Detection 279

CHAPTER 10 Programming Tile-Based Backgrounds with Scrolling 339

CHAPTER 11 Timers, Interrupt Handlers, and Multi-Threading 381

CHAPTER 12 Creating a Game World: Editing Tiles and Levels 429

CHAPTER 13 Vertical Scrolling Arcade Games 455

CHAPTER 14 Horizontal Scrolling Platform Games 489

PART III: TAKING IT TO THE NEXT LEVEL   **509**

CHAPTER 15 Mastering the Audible Realm: Allegro's Sound Support 511

CHAPTER 16 Using Datafiles to Store Game Resources 539

CHAPTER 17 Playing FLIC Movies 551

CHAPTER 18 Introduction to Artificial Intelligence 563

CHAPTER 19 The Mathematical Side of Games 585

CHAPTER 20 Publishing Your Game 611

PART IV: APPENDIXES   **631**

APPENDIX A Chapter Quiz Answers 633

APPENDIX B Useful Tables 651

APPENDIX C Numbering Systems: Binary and Hexadecimal 657

APPENDIX D Recommended Books and Web Sites 663

APPENDIX E Configuring Allegro for Microsoft Visual C++
and Other Compilers 671

APPENDIX F Compiling the Allegro Source Code 685

APPENDIX G Using the CD-ROM 691

Index 693

Contents

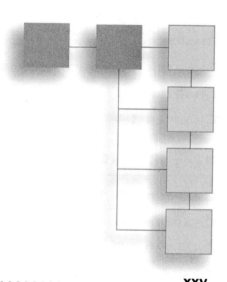

Introduction xxv

Part I: Introduction to Cross-Platform Game Programming   1

Chapter 1   **Demystifying Game Development** .3
     Introduction 4
         Practical Game Programming 5
         Goals Revisited 6
     The High-Level View of Game Development 6
     Recognizing Your Personal Motivations 9
         Decision Point: College versus Job 10
         Every Situation Is Unique 10
         A Note about Specialization 12
         Game Industry Speculation 13
         Emphasizing 2D 14
         Finding Your Niche 15
     Getting into the Spirit of Gaming 18
         Starship Battles: An Inspired Fan Game 18
         Axis & Allies: Hobby Wargaming 22
         Setting Realistic Expectations for Yourself 24
     An Introduction to Dev-C++ and Allegro 25
         DirectX Is Just Another Game Library 25

Introducing the Allegro Game Library 26
Supporting Multiple C/C++ Compilers 29
Summary 30
Chapter Quiz 31

Chapter 2   Getting Started with Dev-C++ and Allegro 33
Introduction 34
Installing and Configuring Dev-C++ and Allegro 35
Installing Dev-C++ 36
Updating Dev-C++ 37
Installing Allegro 41
Taking Dev-C++ and Allegro for a Spin 43
Testing Dev-C++: The Greetings Program 44
Testing Allegro: The GetInfo Program 53
Gaining More Experience with Allegro 63
The Hello World Demo 63
Allegro Sample Programs 65
Summary 68
Chapter Quiz 68

Chapter 3   Basic 2D Graphics Programming with Allegro 71
Introduction 72
Graphics Fundamentals 74
The InitGraphics Program 75
The DrawBitmap Program 79
Drawing Graphics Primitives 82
Drawing Pixels 82
Drawing Lines and Rectangles 84
Drawing Circles and Ellipses 95
Drawing Splines, Triangles, and Polygons 103
Filling in Regions 109
Printing Text on the Screen 112
Constant Text Output 112
Variable Text Output 113
Testing Text Output 114
Summary 115
Chapter Quiz 116

Chapter 4   **Writing Your First Allegro Game** **119**
Tank War 119
   Creating the Tanks. 120
   Firing Weapons 122
   Tank Movement. 125
   Collision Detection 126
   The Complete Tank War Source Code 126
Summary 141
Chapter Quiz 142

Chapter 5   **Programming the Keyboard, Mouse, and Joystick** **145**
Handling Keyboard Input 146
   The Keyboard Handler 146
   Detecting Key Presses 147
   The Stargate Program. 148
   Buffered Keyboard Input 152
   Simulating Key Presses 153
   The KeyTest Program. 154
Handling Mouse Input 155
   The Mouse Handler 156
   Reading the Mouse Position. 156
   Detecting Mouse Buttons 157
   Showing and Hiding the Mouse Pointer 157
   The Strategic Defense Game 158
   Setting the Mouse Position. 165
   Limiting Mouse Movement and Speed 167
   Relative Mouse Motion. 167
   Using a Mouse Wheel 167
Handling Joystick Input 170
   The Joystick Handler 170
   Detecting Controller Stick Movement 171
   Detecting Controller Buttons 174
   Testing the Joystick Routines 175
Summary 182
Chapter Quiz 182

PART II: 2D GAME THEORY, DESIGN, AND PROGRAMMING   **185**

Chapter 6   **Introduction to Game Design** .187

Game Design Basics 188
    Inspiration 188
    Game Feasibility. 188
    Feature Glut. 189
    Back Up Your Work 189
    Game Genres 190
Game Development Phases 195
    Initial Design 196
    Game Engine 196
    Alpha Prototype 196
    Game Development. 197
    Quality Control 197
    Beta Testing 198
Post-Production 198
    Official Release 199
    Out the Door or Out the Window? 199
    Managing the Game 199
    A Note about Quality 200
    Empowering the Engine 200
    Quality versus Trends. 201
    Innovation versus Inspiration 202
    The Infamous Game Patch 202
    Expanding the Game. 203
Future-Proof Design 203
    Game Libraries. 204
    Game Engines and SDKs 204
What Is Game Design? 204
The Dreaded Design Document 205
The Importance of Good Game Design 206
The Two Types of Designs 206
    Mini Design 206
    Complete Design 207
A Sample Design Document Template 207
    General Overview 208
    Target System and Requirements. 208

Story 208

Theme: Graphics and Sound. 208

Menus. 208

Playing a Game 208

Characters and NPCs Description 208

Artificial Intelligence Overview 208

Conclusion 209

A Sample Game Design: Space Invaders 209

General Overview 209

Target System and Requirements. 209

Story 209

Theme: Graphics and Sound. 210

Menus. 210

Playing a Game 210

Character and NPC Description 211

Artificial Intelligence Overview 211

Conclusion 211

Game Design Mini-FAQ 212

Summary 212

Chapter Quiz 212

Chapter 7   **Basic Bitmap Handling and Blitting** **215**

Introduction 215

Dealing with Bitmaps 217

Creating Bitmaps. 219

Cleaning House 221

Bitmap Information. 221

Acquiring and Releasing Bitmaps. 223

Bitmap Clipping. 224

Loading Bitmaps from Disk. 224

Blitting Functions 227

Standard Blitting 227

Scaled Blitting 228

Masked Blitting 229

Masked Scaled Blitting 229

Enhancing Tank War—From Graphics Primitives to Bitmaps 229

Summary 234

Chapter Quiz 234

Chapter 8   **Basic Sprite Programming: Drawing Scaled,**
Flipped, Rotated, Pivoted, and Translucent Sprites . . .237

Basic Sprite Handling 238
   Drawing Regular Sprites 238
   Drawing Scaled Sprites 242
   Drawing Flipped Sprites 244
   Drawing Rotated Sprites 245
   Drawing Pivoted Sprites 252
   Drawing Translucent Sprites 256
Enhancing Tank War 259
   What's New? 260
   Modifying the Source Code 262
Summary 276
Chapter Quiz 276

Chapter 9   **Advanced Sprite Programming: Animation,**
Compiled Sprites, and Collision Detection 279

Animated Sprites 280
   Drawing an Animated Sprite 280
   Creating a Sprite Handler 283
   The SpriteHandler Program 286
   Grabbing Sprite Frames from an Image 291
   The SpriteGrabber Program 293
   The Next Step: Multiple Animated Sprites 298
   The MultipleSprites Program 300
Run-Length Encoded Sprites 306
   Creating and Destroying RLE Sprites 307
   Drawing RLE Sprites 307
   The RLESprites Program 307
Compiled Sprites 313
   Using Compiled Sprites 314
   Testing Compiled Sprites 315
Collision Detection 317
The CollisionTest Program 319
Enhancing Tank War 324
Summary 336
Chapter Quiz 337

Chapter 10   **Programming Tile-Based Backgrounds with Scrolling 339**

Introduction to Scrolling 340

A Limited View of the World 341

Introduction to Tile-Based Backgrounds 345

Backgrounds and Scenery. 346

Creating Backgrounds from Tiles 347

Tile-Based Scrolling 347

Creating a Tile Map. 351

Enhancing Tank War 355

Exploring the All-New Tank War 356

The New Tank War Source Code 359

Summary 378

Chapter Quiz 378

Chapter 11   **Timers, Interrupt Handlers, and Multi-Threading 381**

Timers 381

Installing and Removing the Timer 381

Slowing Down the Program 382

The TimerTest Program 383

Interrupt Handlers 392

Creating an Interrupt Handler 392

Removing an Interrupt Handler 393

The InterruptTest Program 393

Using Timed Game Loops 395

Slowing Down the Gameplay...Not the Game 395

The TimedLoop Program. 396

Multi-Threading 397

Abstracting the Parallel Processing Problem. 398

The Pthreads-Win32 Library 399

Programming with Posix Threads. 400

The MultiThread Program. 403

Enhancing Tank War 413

Description of New Improvements. 414

Modifying the Tank War Project 415

Future Changes to Tank War 426

Summary 426

Chapter Quiz 426

Chapter 12   Creating a Game World: Editing Tiles and Levels 429
Creating the Game World 429
    Installing Mappy 430
    Creating a New Map. 430
    Importing the Source Tiles 432
    Saving the Map File as FMP 433
    Saving the Map File as Text 435
Loading and Drawing Mappy Level Files 436
    Using a Text Array Map. 437
    Using a Mappy Level File 442
Enhancing Tank War 445
    Proposed Changes to Tank War 446
    Modifying Tank War 447
Summary 453
Chapter Quiz 453

Chapter 13   Vertical Scrolling Arcade Games 455
Building a Vertical Scroller Engine 455
    Creating Levels Using Mappy 457
    Filling in the Tiles. 459
    Let's Scroll It. 460
Writing a Vertical Scrolling Shooter 464
    Describing the Game. 464
    The Game's Artwork 466
    Writing the Source Code. 468
Summary 487
Chapter Quiz 487

Chapter 14   Horizontal Scrolling Platform Games 489
Understanding Horizontal Scrolling Games 490
Developing a Platform Scroller 490
Creating Horizontal Platform Levels with Mappy 491
    Separating the Foreground Tiles 495
    Performing a Range Block Edit. 497
Developing a Scrolling Platform Game 498
    Describing the Game. 498
    The Game Artwork 499
    Using the Platform Scroller. 500
    Writing the Source Code. 501

Summary 506
Chapter Quiz 507

PART III: TAKING IT TO THE NEXT LEVEL   509

Chapter 15   Mastering the Audible Realm: Allegro's Sound Support .511

The PlayWave Program 512
Sound Initialization Routines 514
    Detecting the Digital Sound Driver 515
    Reserving Voices 515
    Setting an Individual Voice Volume 515
    Initializing the Sound Driver. 516
    Removing the Sound Driver 516
    Changing the Volume 516
Standard Sample Playback Routines 517
    Loading a Sample File 517
    Loading a WAV File 517
    Loading a VOC File 517
    Playing a Sample 517
    Altering a Sample's Properties 518
    Stopping a Sample. 518
    Creating a New Sample. 518
    Destroying a Sample 518
Low-Level Sample Playback Routines 518
    Allocating a Voice 519
    Removing a Voice 519
    Reallocating a Voice 519
    Releasing a Voice. 519
    Activating a Voice 519
    Stopping a Voice 519
    Setting Voice Priority. 520
    Checking the Status of a Voice. 520
    Returning the Position of a Voice 520
    Setting the Position of a Voice. 520
    Altering the Playback Mode of a Voice. 520
    Returning the Volume of a Voice. 521
    Setting the Volume of a Voice 521
    Ramping the Volume of a Voice. 521
    Stopping a Volume Ramp 521

Returning the Pitch of a Voice 521
Setting the Pitch of a Voice 521
Performing a Frequency Sweep of a Voice 521
Stopping a Frequency Sweep 522
Returning the Pan Value of a Voice. 522
Setting the Pan Value of a Voice 522
Performing a Sweeping Pan on a Voice. 522
Stopping a Sweeping Pan 522
The SampleMixer Program 522
Enhancing Tank War 525
Modifying the Game. 525
Final Comments about Tank War. 536
Summary 537
Chapter Quiz 537

Chapter 16   **Using Datafiles to Store Game Resources** **539**
Understanding Allegro Datafiles 540
Creating Allegro Datafiles 541
Using Allegro Datafiles 544
Loading a Datafile. 544
Unloading a Datafile. 545
Loading a Datafile Object. 545
Unloading a Datafile Object. 545
Finding a Datafile Object 545
Testing Allegro Datafiles 545
Summary 547
Chapter Quiz 548

Chapter 17   **Playing FLIC Movies** **551**
Playing FLI Animation Files 551
The FLI Callback Function 552
The PlayFlick Program. 552
Playing an FLI from a Memory Block 554
Loading FLIs into Memory 554
Opening and Closing FLI Files. 555
Processing Each Frame of the Animation 555
The LoadFlick Program 556
The ResizeFlick Program 558
Summary 561
Chapter Quiz 561

Chapter 18   **Introduction to Artificial Intelligence** **563**
The Fields of Artificial Intelligence 564
  Expert Systems 564
  Fuzzy Logic 565
  Genetic Algorithms 567
  Neural Networks 569
Deterministic Algorithms 570
  Random Motion 571
  Tracking 572
  Patterns 573
Finite State Machines 575
Fuzzy Logic 577
  Fuzzy Logic Basics 577
  Fuzzy Matrices 579
A Simple Method for Memory 580
Artificial Intelligence and Games 581
Summary 581
Chapter Quiz 582

Chapter 19   **The Mathematical Side of Games** **585**
Trigonometry 586
  Visual Representation and Laws 586
  Angle Relations 589
Vectors 590
  Addition and Subtraction 591
  Scalar Multiplication and Division 593
  Length 594
  Normalization 594
  Perpendicular Operation 595
  Dot Product 596
  Perp-Dot Product 597
Matrices 598
  Addition and Subtraction 598
  Scalars with Multiplication and Division 598
  Special Matrices 599
  Transposed Matrices 600
  Matrix Concatenation 601
  Vector Transformation 602

Probability 603
  Sets 603
  Union 603
  Intersection 604
Functions 605
  Integration 606
  Differentiation 607
Summary 608
Chapter Quiz 608

Chapter 20   Publishing Your Game .611
Is Your Game Worth Publishing? .611
Whose Door to Knock On 612
  Learn to Knock Correctly 613
  No Publisher, So Now What? 613
Contracts 614
  Non-Disclosure Agreement 614
  The Actual Publishing Contract 614
Milestones 615
  Bug Report 615
  Release Day 615
Interviews 616
  Paul Urbanus: Urbonix, Inc. 616
  Niels Bauer: Niels Bauer Software Design 622
  André LaMothe: Xtreme Games LLC 624
Summary 625
References 626
Chapter Quiz 626

Epilogue 629

PART IV: APPENDIXES   631

Appendix A   Chapter Quiz Answers 633
Chapter 1 633
Chapter 2 634
Chapter 3 635
Chapter 4 635

Chapter 5 636
Chapter 6 637
Chapter 7 638
Chapter 8 639
Chapter 9 639
Chapter 10 640
Chapter 11 641
Chapter 12 642
Chapter 13 643
Chapter 14 643
Chapter 15 644
Chapter 16 645
Chapter 17 646
Chapter 18 647
Chapter 19 648
Chapter 20 648

Appendix B   Useful Tables 651
Integral Equations Table 651
Derivative Equations Table 652
Inertia Equations Table 652
ASCII Table 653

Appendix C   Numbering Systems: Binary and Hexadecimal 657
Binary 657
Decimal 659
Hexadecimal 659

Appendix D   Recommended Books and Web Sites 663
All in One Support on the Web 663
Game Development Web Sites 663
Publishing, Game Reviews, and Download Sites 664
Engines 664
Independent Game Developers 664
Industry 665
Computer Humor 665
Recommended Books 665

**Appendix E   Configuring Allegro for Microsoft Visual C++
and Other Compilers** **671**
Microsoft Visual C++ 672
Dev-C++ 673
KDevelop for Linux 679
Final Comments 683

Appendix F   Compiling the Allegro Source Code **685**
Microsoft Visual C++ 685
Borland C++/C++Builder 687
Dev-C++ 688
KDevelop for Linux 689

Appendix G   Using the CD-ROM **691**

Index **693**

INTRODUCTION

Greetings! This book is the second edition to the best-selling *Game Programming All in One* by Bruno Miguel Teixeira de Sousa, to whom I am indebted for the original work. This new second edition is a complete rewrite of *Game Programming All in One*, with a completely new direction, new goals, new assumptions, and new development tools. *All in One 2E*, as I have come to call it, has done away with the C++ tutorials, Windows programming tutorials, and DirectX tutorials. In fact, this book does not cover Windows or DirectX at all. Instead, this book focuses on the subject of game programming using a cross-platform game library called Allegro. This library is extremely powerful and versatile. Allegro opens up a world of possibilities that are ignored when you focus specifically on Windows and DirectX. A full quarter of the first edition was devoted to a C++ language primer, while another fourth of the book focused on Windows and DirectX basics. I decided that for this second edition, we did not need to cover those subjects again; thus, this book uses the standard C language, and the sample programs will compile on multiple platforms.

The Windows version of Allegro uses DirectX, as a matter of fact, but it is completely abstracted and transparent, hidden inside the internals of the Allegro game library. Instead, you are provided with a basic C program that includes the Allegro library and is capable of running in full-screen DirectDraw mode using any supported resolution and color depth. Additionally, Allegro provides a uniform interface for sound effects, music, and device input, which are implemented on the Windows platform with DirectSound, DirectMusic, and DirectInput. Specifically, Allegro supports DirectX 8. Imagine writing a high-speed arcade game using DirectX, and then being able to recompile that program (without changing a single line of code) under Linux, Mac OS X, Solaris, FreeBSD, IRIX, and other operating systems! Allegro is a cross-platform game library that will double or triple the user base for the games you develop with the help of this book, and at no loss in performance.

Cross-Platform Game Programming

This book will teach you to write complete games that will run on almost any operating system. Specifically, I focus on three compilers—Visual C++, Dev-C++, and KDevelop— and the sample programs will be written using both Windows and Linux, with screenshots taken from both operating systems. In all likelihood, you will have the opportunity to use your favorite development tool because Allegro supports several C compilers, including Borland C++, Borland C++Builder, Apple Development Tools 2002, and several other compilers on various platforms, including the ubiquitous GNU C++ (GCC).

The target audience for this book is beginning to intermediate programmers who already have some experience with C or C++. Also, those who want to learn to write games using C or C++ can use this book as an entry-level guide. The material is not for someone new to programming—just someone new to *game programming*. I must assume you have already learned C or C++ because there is too much to cover in the game libraries, interfaces, and so on to focus on the basic syntax of the actual language. It was difficult enough to support three different compilers and integrated development environments without also explaining every line of code. Intermediate-level programming experience is assumed, while extreme beginners (newbies) will definitely struggle.

In Appendix D, "Recommended Books and Web Sites," I recommend introductory books for those readers. I encourage you to keep a C primer handy while reading through *All in One 2E* because this book moves along at a rapid pace. My goal was not to cover a *lot* of information, but to quickly get into the *important* information you'll need to write good games. This book is not extremely advanced—the source code is straightforward, with no difficult libraries to learn per se, but I do not explain every detail. I do cover most of the function library in Allegro, since that is the focus of this book, but I do not explain any standard C functions. The goal is to get up and running as quickly as possible with some game code! In fact, you will be writing your first graphics programs in Chapter 3 and your first game in Chapter 4. You will, however, quickly ramp up to advanced topics, such as creating game levels and scrolling the game world on the screen, with sample code, such as the *PlatformScroller* program (see Chapter 14).

Yes, it is true, this book focuses entirely and exclusively on 2D games. This is a huge genre that includes many real-time and turn-based strategy games, such as *Civilization III*, the *Age of Empires* series, *Diablo*, *Starcraft*, and so on. If you scoff at 2D games, then I encourage you to pick up *3D Game Programming All in One* (Premier Press, 2004) instead of (or in addition to) this volume. I make no apologies for ignoring 3D because these two books were designed to complement each other in the *Game Development* series.

Someone who has done some programming in Visual C++, CodeWarrior, Watcom C, Borland C++, GNU C++, or even Java or C# will understand the programs in this book.

Those with little or no coding experience will benefit from a C primer before delving into these chapters. I recommend many good C primers and C programming books in Appendix D. The emphasis of this book is on a cross-platform, open-source compiler, integrated development environment, and game library. You will not need to learn Windows or DirectX programming, and these subjects are not covered. The primary IDE is an open-source (freeware) program called Dev-C++, released by Bloodshed Software (http://www.bloodshed.net), and it is included on the CD-ROM. The game library is called Allegro; it is also freeware, open-source, and included on CD-ROM that accompanies this book. You have all the free tools you need to run the programs in the book, and then some! Using these tools, you can write standard Windows and DirectX programs with or without Allegro, and without the cost of an expensive compiler, such as Visual C++. This book is highly accessible to all C programmers, regardless of their platform of choice.

Use Your Favorite Compiler

Dev-C++ is a capable compiler package that includes an editor with source code highlighting. It uses the infamous GNU C++ compiler (GCC) to convert your chicken-scratch code into real programs with targets for Win32 or console programs and full support for DirectX 9. In other words, you might find Dev-C++ a useful companion for writing games with or without Allegro, and many of the sample programs in other Premier Press game development books will compile with Dev-C++ as well. It is a worthy, free, and easy-to-use alternative to a commercial compiler.

This book's source code and sample programs will run without modification on all of the following systems: Windows 9x/2000/Me/XP/2003, Mac OS X, Linux (any version), BeOS, QNX, and many other UNIX systems (IRIX, Solaris, Darwin, FreeBSD, to name a few) with X Windows. Believe it or not, these programs will also run under MS-DOS (DJGPP, Watcom C). That is almost every computer system out there. It's a sure bet if someone wants to use an old but mainstream C compiler, it will probably run the code in this book (with perhaps some limitations on compiling the Allegro library itself, which uses a modern makefile). I tell you this, not believing that you will need to write a game for MS-DOS, but just to demonstrate the versatility of Allegro.

Yet, at the same time, the Windows version of Allegro supports DirectX. The programs in this book will run in full-screen or windowed mode with support for just about any video card out there. Allegro is not an advanced, next-generation 3D engine; it is a cross-platform game library with a long history that dates back to the original Atari ST version. You might not care about cross-platform programming at this point, but imagine the possibilities if you were able to double the number of people who would play your game, just by compiling your game for other operating systems—and all without modifying any of your source code. When is the last time you saw an online multiplayer game with Mac, Linux, and Windows players? Although I do not cover online multiplayer games in this book, they are a very real possibility using Allegro and standard TCP/IP socket libraries. As an example, I cover multi-threading in this book using a Windows port of the Posix Thread library, and the sample program I wrote to demonstrate multi-threading compiles under Windows and Linux without modification! The same is true for other libraries that conform to a standard, such as Berkeley Sockets for TCP/IP network programming.

This book is not *entirely* about cross-platform programming, though. I do discuss the subject in the first two chapters, but from that point forward, I simply focus on Allegro and specific game concepts, such as scrolling and animation. The overall theme and focus of this book are on writing games. To that end, you will develop a complete game and add to it in each chapter of the book, starting in Chapter 4.

Is This Book for You?

If you have any experience with the C language, then you will be able to make your way through this book. If you are new to the C language, I recommend against reading this book as your first experience with C because it will be confusing due to the extensive use of Allegro. (Very few standard C functions are used.) The example programs use a simple C syntax with no complicated interfaces or lists of include files. In fact, most of the programs will have a simple format like this:

```
#include "allegro.h"
int main(void)
{
    allegro_init();
    allegro_message("Welcome To Allegro!");
    return 0;
}
END_OF_MAIN();
```

This is a very simple program that is used as a test program for Appendix E, "Configuring Allegro for Microsoft Visual C++ and Other Compilers," just as an example. This program simply verifies that the Allegro library has been linked with the main program and is working as expected. This particular program outputs to the console and does not run in graphical mode. Allegro provides comprehensive support for all of the video modes supported on your PC, including full-screen and windowed DirectX modes used by most commercial games. On the UNIX side, Allegro supports the X Window system, SVGAlib, and other libraries (as appropriate to the platform), providing a similar output no matter which system it is running on. For instance, the allegro_message function is displayed in a pop-up message box in Windows, but prints a message to a terminal window in Linux.

If you are a Windows user and you don't care about Linux, that won't be a problem. The screenshots presented in this book look exactly the same no matter what operating system you are using, and my choice of Windows or Linux in each particular case is simply for variety. Likewise, if you are a Linux user and you care not for Windows, you will not be limited in any way because every program in this book is tested on both Windows and Linux. The CD-ROM that accompanies this book includes the complete source code for the sample programs in this book, with project files for Visual C++ (Windows), Dev-C++ (Windows), and KDevelop (Linux). The tools on the CD-ROM include both Windows and Linux versions in most cases. If you are using an operating system other than these two, you should have no problem adapting the source code to your compiler of choice.

Do you like games, and would you like to learn how to create your own professional-quality games using some of the same tools used by professional game developers? This book will help you get started in the right direction toward that goal, and you'll have a lot of fun learning along the way! This is a very practical programming book, not rife with theory, so you will find many, many sample programs herein to reinforce each new subject.

System Requirements

The programs in this book will run on many different operating systems, including Windows, Linux, Mac OS X, and almost any UNIX variant that supports the X Window system. All that is really required is a decent PC with a video card and sound card.

Here are the recommended minimum hardware requirements:

- Pentium II 300 MHz
- 128 MB memory
- 200 MB free hard disk space
- 8 MB video card
- Sound card

Book Summary

This book is divided into four parts:

- **Part I: Introduction to Cross-Platform Game Programming.** This first section provides all the introduction you will need to get started writing cross-platform games with Allegro and Dev-C++, with screenshots from both Windows and Linux. By the time you have completed this first set of chapters, you will have a solid grasp of compiling Allegro programs. This section concludes with a sample game called *Tank War* that you will enhance throughout the book.

- **Part II: 2D Game Theory, Design, and Programming.** This section is the meat and potatoes of the book, providing solid tutorials on the most important functions in the Allegro game library, including functions for loading images, manipulating sprites, scrolling the background, double-buffering, and other core features of any game. This section also provides the groundwork for the primary game developed in this book.
- **Part III: Taking It to the Next Level.** This section is comprised of more theoretical chapters covering basic artificial intelligence, a chapter on basic game physics, and a chapter about publishing your game.
- **Part IV: Appendixes.** This final section of the book provides answers to the chapter quizzes, a tutorial on numbering systems, a set of useful mathematical tables, tutorials on installing and using Allegro, a list of recommended resources, and an overview of the CD-ROM.

PART I

INTRODUCTION TO CROSS-PLATFORM GAME PROGRAMMING

CHAPTER 1

Demystifying Game Development 3

CHAPTER 2

Getting Started with Dev-C++ and Allegro 33

CHAPTER 3

Basic 2D Graphics Programming with Allegro 71

CHAPTER 4

Writing Your First Allegro Game 119

CHAPTER 5

Programming the Keyboard, Mouse, and Joystick 145

W elcome to Part I of *Game Programming All in One, 2nd Edition*. Part I includes five chapters that introduce you to the basic concepts of game development with Allegro. Starting with an overview of game development roots and covering the subject of motivation, this part goes into detail about how to use the free Dev-C++ compiler/IDE and the Allegro game programming library. Also, this part shows how to write, compile, and run several Allegro programs.

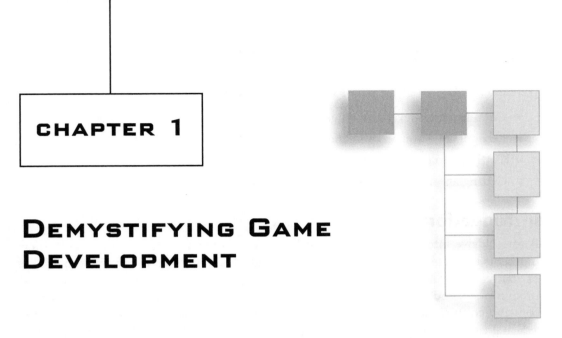

CHAPTER 1

DEMYSTIFYING GAME DEVELOPMENT

This chapter provides an overview of the game industry, the complexities of game development, and the personal motivations that drive members of this field to produce the games we love to play. Herein you will find discussions of game design and how your world view and upbringing, as well as individual quirks and talents, have a huge impact on not only whether you have what it takes to make it big, but also whether it is a good idea to work on games at all. There is more to writing games than motivation. While some programmers see game development purely as a monthly salary, some perceive games at a higher level and are able to tap into that mysterious realm of the unknown to create a stunning masterpiece. In this chapter, I discuss that vague and intangible (but all too important) difference.

I also give you a general overview of what it is like to work as a programmer. If you are interested in game programming purely for fun or as a hobby, I encourage you to absorb this chapter because it will help you relate to those on the inside and judge your own creations. When you consider that it takes a team to develop a retail game—and you are an individual—it is not unreasonable to believe that your own games are high in quality and worthy of note. What you must consider are total invested project hours and the size of the team. How does your solo project compare to a team game development project? You see, your solo (or rather, "indie") game may be comparable to a retail game, all things being equal. One goal of this chapter is to help you realize this fact, to encourage you to continue learning, and to create games from your imagination. Whether you are planning a career in the game industry or simply partaking in the joy of writing games to entertain others, this chapter has something beneficial for you. After all, there are employed game programmers who only make their mark after going solo, and some solo game programmers who only make their mark after joining a team. Taking games seriously from the start is one way to attract attention and encourage others to take your work seriously.

Here is a breakdown of the major topics in this chapter:

- Gaining a high-level view of game development
- Recognizing your personal motivations
- Getting into the spirit of gaming
- Getting an introduction to Dev-C++ and Allegro

Introduction

Before I delve into the complexities of learning to write a game, I want to take a few moments to discuss the big picture that surrounds this subject. I'd like to think that some of you reading this book very likely will enter the game industry as junior or entry-level programmers and make a career of it. I am thrilled by that possibility—that I may have contributed in some small way to fulfilling a dream. I will speak frequently to both the aspiring career game programmer and the casual hobbyist because both have the same goals—first, to learn the tricks and techniques used by professional game programmers, and then to learn enough so it is no longer difficult and it becomes fun. Programming is difficult already; *game* programming is exponentially more difficult. But by breaking down the daunting task of writing a modern game, you can learn to divide and conquer, and finish a great game! Thus, my goal in this chapter is to provide some commentary along those lines while introducing you to the technologies used in this book—namely, the C language and the Allegro game library.

First, a disclaimer—something that I will repeat several times to nail the point home: DirectX is *not* game programming. DirectX is one library that is indisputably the most popular for Windows PCs. However, consoles such as the Sony PlayStation 2, Nintendo GameCube, Nintendo Game Boy Advance, and the many other handheld devices do not use DirectX or anything like it (although Xbox does use DirectX). There are dozens of DirectX reference books disguised as game programming books, but they often do little other than expose the interfaces—DirectDraw, Direct3D, DirectInput, DirectSound, DirectMusic, and DirectPlay. Talk about getting bogged down in the details! In my opinion, DirectX is the means to an end, not the goal itself. Learning DirectX is optional if your dream is to write console games (although I recommend learning as much as possible about every subject).

For the newcomer to game development, this misconception about the nature of some so-called game programming books can be a source of consternation. Beginners can be impatient (as I have been myself, and will discuss later in this chapter). Let me summarize the situation: You want to get something going quickly and easily, and *then* you want to go back and learn all the deep and complicated details, right? I mean, who wants to read an 800-page programming book before they actually get to write a game?

Practical Game Programming

This book focuses on the oft-misused phrase "game programming" and has no prerequisites. I don't discuss Windows or DirectX programming at all in this book. For some excellent reference books on those subjects (which I like to call *logistical* subjects), please refer to Appendix D, "Recommended Books and Web Sites." If I may nail the point home, allow me to present a simple analogy—one that I will use as a common theme in this and other chapters. Writing a game is very similar to writing a book. There are basic tools required to write a game (such as a compiler, a text editor, and a graphic editor), just as there are tools required to write a book (such as a word processor, a dictionary, and a thesaurus). When you are planning a new project, such as a game, do you worry about electricity? As such, when you are planning a new book, would you worry about the alphabet? These things are base assumptions that we take for granted.

I take the operating system completely for granted now, and I try to abstract my computing experience as much as possible. It is a liberating experience when I am able to get the same work done regardless of the electronics or operating system on my computer. Therefore, I take those things for granted, whether I am using Windows Explorer or GNOME, Internet Explorer or Mozilla, Visual C++ or Dev-C++. This is an important concept that I encourage you to consider because the game industry is in a constant state of flux that conducts the vibrations of the entire computer industry.

The concept of a "new computer" is important to the general public, but to a computer industry professional, "new" is a very relative term that only lasts a few weeks or months at most. Everyone has his or her own way of dealing with constant change, and it is part of the experience of working with computers. (Those who can't handle it never last long in this industry.) Rather than seeing change as a tidal wave and trying to keep ahead of it, I often let the wave crash over my head, so to speak, and wait for the next wave. It's an intriguing experience, allowing high technology to pass you up and zoom ahead. But do you know why there is some wisdom in skipping a trend now and then? Because technology is not only in a constant state of change, but it is also in a constant state of experimentation. Not every new "improvement" is good or accepted. Remember videodiscs? Probably not! The movie industry had to rethink videodisc technology in part because the discs resembled vinyl records, which the public perceived as old technology.

For example, the computer hardware industry markets heavily for the need to constantly upgrade computers. It is logical that these companies would do so because the general public really believes that everything is obsolete year by year. In fact, it is the gross inefficiency of the software that makes this so. Rather than grasping at the latest everything with a must-have belief system, why not continue to use known, stable systems and stand up to the frequent tidal waves of technology? What one calls progress, another calls marketing. Games have single-handedly pushed the personal computer industry to extraordinary new heights in the past decade due for the most part to advances in graphics technology. But that cutting edge leaves a lot of well-meaning and talented folks out in the cold when they might otherwise be developing well-loved games.

So we come back to the point again: What is the cutting edge of game development, and what must I do to write great games? For the first part, the cutting edge is gameplay, not the latest 3D buzzword. Second, to write a great game, you must be passionate and talented. Studying the subject at hand (game programming) is another factor—although it is the focus of this book! For my own inspiration, I look at games such as *Sid Meier's Civilization III* and *Age of Wonders: Shadow Magic*, among other recent 2D titles. You can find your inspiration in whatever subject interests you, and it need not always be a video game.

Goals Revisited

One of the aspects of this book that I want to emphasize early on is that my goal is to reach a majority of hobbyists and programmers who are either aspiring to enter the game industry as career programmers or who are simply writing games for the fun of it. As I explained in the Introduction, this book won't hold your hand because there is so much information to cover. At the same time, it's my job to make a difficult subject easy to comprehend; if you have some fun along the way, that's even better. I don't want to simply present and discuss how to write 2D graphics code; my goal is for you to master it.

By the time you're finished with this book, you'll have the skills to duplicate any game released up to the late 1990s (before 3D hardware acceleration came along for PCs). That includes a huge number of games most often not regarded by the "twitch generation"—that is, those gamers who would describe "strategy" as which direction to circle strafe an enemy in a first-person shooter, the best kind of car to "jack" to make the most money, or how to escape via a side alley where the cops never follow you. We can poke fun at the twitch generation because they wouldn't know what to do with a keyboard, let alone how to write game code; therefore, they are not likely to read this book. But if there are any twitch gamers now reading, I congratulate you!

The High-Level View of Game Development

Game development is far more important to society than most people realize. Strictly from an economic point of view, the design, funding, development, packaging, delivery, and sale of video games (both hardware and software) employs millions of workers around the world. There are electronics engineers building the circuit boards and microprocessors. Programmers write the operating systems, software development kits, and games. Factory workers mass-produce the packaging, instructions, discs, controllers, and other peripherals. Technical support workers help customers over the phone. There are a large number of investors, business owners, managers, lawyers, accountants, human resource workers, network and PC technical support personnel, and other ancillary job positions that support the game industry in one way or another. What it all amounts to is an extraordinarily complex system of interrelated industries and jobs, and millions of people who are employed solely to fill the shelves of your local video game store. The whole point of this is simply to entertain you. Because we're talking about high-quality interactive entertainment, we have a tendency to spend a lot of money for it, which increases demand, which drives everyone involved to work very hard to produce the next bestseller.

Although this narrative might remind you of the book publishing industry, where there are many people working very hard to get high-quality books onto store shelves, I submit that games might be more similar to motion pictures than to books. All three of these subjects are closely related forms of entertainment, with music included. Books are turned into movies, movies into video games, and both movies and video games into books. All the while, music soundtracks are available for movies and video games alike. Much of this has to do with marketing—getting the most income from a particular brand name. One excellent side effect of this is that many young people grow up surrounded by themes of popular culture that spawn their imaginations, thus producing a new generation of creative people every few years to work in these industries.

Consider the effect that science fiction novels and movies have had on visionaries of popular culture, such as Gene Roddenberry and George Lucas, who each pushed the envelope of entertainment after being inspired by fantastic stories of their time, such as *The Day the Earth Stood Still* and *The Twilight Zone*, to name just two. Before these types of programs were produced, Hollywood was enamored with westerns—stories about the old West. What was the next great frontier, at least for an American audience? Having spread across the continent of North America, and after fighting in two great and terrible world wars, popular culture turned outward—not to Earth's oceans, but to the great interstellar seas of space. What these early stories did was spurn the imaginations of the young up-and-coming visionaries who created *Star Trek*, *Lost in Space*, *Star Wars*, and action/adventure themes such as *Indiana Jones*, set in a past era (where *time* is often associated with *space*). These are identifiable cultural icons.

The game industry is really the next generation of entertainment, following in the footsteps of the great creative powerhouses of the past few decades. Games have been growing in depth and complexity for many years, and they have come to be so entertaining that they have eclipsed the motion picture industry as the leading form of entertainment. But just as movies did not replace books, neither will games replace movies as a dominant player. Although one might eclipse the others in revenue and profit, all of these industries are interrelated and interdependent.

Thinking hypothetically, what do you suppose will be the next stage of cutting-edge entertainment, the likes of which will supercede games as the dominant player? In my opinion, we have not seen it yet and we might never see it. I believe that books, music, movies, and video games will continue unheeded to inspire, challenge, and entertain for decades to come. But I do hold an opinion that is contrary to my last statement. I believe that western society will embrace entertainment less and adopt more productive uses for games in the decades to come. Why do I feel this way, you might ask? Momentum and progress. Games are already being used for more than just entertainment. They are being used by governments to train soldiers in the strategy and tactics of a modern battlefield, one in which military commanders no longer have the luxury of experiencing for real. Without real long-term engagements like those during World War II (battles since that time have been skirmishes in comparison), modern militaries must rely on alternative means of training to give troops a feel for real battle. What better solution than to play games that are visceral, utterly realistic, shocking in unpredictability, and awe-inspiring to behold? Who needs a real battlefield when a game looks and feels almost like the real thing?

I have now explored several areas of our society that benefit from the game industry. What about gamers themselves—you, me, and other video game fanatics? We love to play games because it is exhilarating to conquer, pillage, destroy, and defeat an opponent (especially if he or she is a close friend or relative). But there is the converse to this point of view, regarding those games that allow you to create, imagine, build, enchant, and express yourself. Some games are so artistic that it feels as if you are interacting with an oil painting or a symphonic orchestra. To conclude this game brings forth the same set of emotions you feel upon finishing a good book, an exceptional movie, or an orchestral performance—exhilaration, joy, pride, fascination, appreciation, and yet a tinge of disappointment. However, it is that last emotion that draws you back to that book, movie, game, painting, or symphony again, where it brings you some happiness in life. This experience transcends mere entertainment; it is a joy felt by your soul, not simply a sensual experience in your mind and through your eyes and ears.

Interactivity has much to do with some of the new lingo used to describe the game industry. Although insiders won't mince words, those who are concerned with public consumption and opinion prefer to call the game industry a form of interactive or electronic entertainment. Game programming has become game development. Outlining the plot of a game has become game design. Very lengthy scripts are now written for games, and some designers will even storyboard a game. Do you begin to see similarities to the movie industry?

Storyboarding is a process in which concept artists are hired to illustrate the entire game scene by scene. This is a very expensive and time-intensive process, but it is necessary for complicated productions. Some films (or games, for that matter) are rather simple in plot: Aliens have invaded Earth, so someone must stop them! Although a storyboard might help a hack-and-slash type of game, it is often not necessary, particularly when the designer and developers are intimately familiar with the subject matter. For instance, think about a game adaptation of a novel, such as Michael Crichton's *Jurassic Park*. The developers of a game based on a novel do not always have the benefit of a feature film, as was the case with *Jurassic Park* and other movies based on Michael Crichton novels. Simply reading the book and watching the movie is probably enough to come up with a basic idea for what should happen in the game; you probably don't need to storyboard.

Why do I feel that this discussion is important? It is absolutely relevant to game development! In fact, "game programming" has become such a common phrase in video game magazines, on Web sites, and in books that it is often taken for granted. What I'm focusing on is the importance of perspective. There is a lot more to consider than just what to name a program variable or what video resolution to use for your next game. You need to understand the big picture, to step away from the tree to see the entire forest.

Recognizing Your Personal Motivations

Why do you want to learn game programming? I want you to think hard about that question for a moment, because the time investment is great and the rewards are not always up to par in terms of compensation. *You must love it.* If you don't love absolutely everything about video games—if you don't love to argue about them, review them online, and play them obsessively—then I have some good but somewhat hard advice. Just treat video games as an enjoyable hobby, and don't worry too much about "breaking in" to the game industry or getting your game published. Really. Because that is a serious source of stress, and your goal is supposed to be to have fun with games, not get frustrated with them.

note

For a fascinating insider narration of the video game industry's early years, I highly recommend the book *Hackers* by Steven Levy, which puts the early years of the game industry into perspective. For a historic ride down memory lane, be sure to read *High Score! The Illustrated History of Electronic Games* by Rusel DeMaria and Johnny Wilson (former editor of *Computer Gaming World*), a full-color book with hundreds of fascinating photos. Browsing the local bulletin board systems in the late 1980s and early 1990s to download shareware games was also a fun pastime. For an intriguing look into this era, I recommend *Masters of Doom: How Two Guys Created an Empire and Transformed Pop Culture* by David Kushner.

I was inspired by games such as *King's Quest IV: The Perils of Rosella, Space Quest III: The Pirates of Pestulon, Police Quest, Hero's Quest: So You Want To Be A Hero?*, and other extraordinarily cool adventure games produced by Sierra. There were other companies, too, such as Atari, Electronic Arts, Activision, and Origin Systems. I spent many hours playing *Starflight*, one of the first games that Electronic Arts published in 1985 (and one of the greatest games made at the time) and the sequel, *Starflight II: Trade Routes of the Cloud Nebula*, which came out in 1989.

Decision Point: College versus Job

In the modern era of gaming, a college education is invaluable. What if you grow tired of the game industry after a few years? Don't cringe; this is a very real possibility. A lot of hardcore gamers have moved on to casual gaming or given it up entirely while pursuing other careers.

Focus every effort on writing complete and polished games, however big or small, and consider every game as a potential entry on your résumé. If you want to work on games for a living, go for it full tilt and don't halfheartedly fool around about it. Be serious! Go get a job with *any* game studio and work your way up. On the other hand, if you want to get involved in high-caliber games, then go to college and focus heavily on your studies. Let the game industry pass you by for a short time, and when you graduate, you will be ready and equipped to get a great job. There are some really great high-tech colleges that are offering game programming degree programs. University of Advancing Technology in Tempe, Arizona, for instance, has associate's, bachelor's, and master's degree programs in game development! Take a look at http://www.uat.edu.

Once you have made the decision to go for it, it's time to build your level of experience with real games that you will create on your own. Don't assume that one of your hobby games isn't good enough for an employer to see. Most game development managers will appreciate brimming enthusiasm if you have the technical skills to do the job. Showing off your previous work and recalling the joy of working on those early games is always enjoyable for you and the interviewer. They want to see your *personality*, your *love* of games, and how you spent *hundreds* of hours working on a particular game, fueled by an uncontrollable drive to see it completed. Your emphasis should be on completed games. Most important, always be genuine.

I would go so far as to say that having a dozen shareware games (of good quality) on your résumé is better than having worked on a small part of a commercial game. Yes, suppose you did work on a retail game. That doesn't guarantee choice employment with another company. What sort of work did you do on that game—level editors, unit editors, level design, play testing? These are common tasks for entry-level programmers on a professional team where the "cool" positions (such as 3D engine and network programming) are occupied by the highly skilled programmers with proven track records who always get the job done quickly.

The best hobbies will often pay for themselves and might even earn a profit. If you have a full-time job that is otherwise fine, then you might turn the hobby of game programming into a money-making adventure. Who knows—you might release the next great indie game.

Every Situation Is Unique

There are many factors to consider in your own determination, and there is no best direction to take in life. We all just try to do the best that we can do, day by day and year by year. I recommend that you pursue a career that will bring you the most enjoyment while still earning the highest possible salary. You might not care about salary at this point in your life; indeed, you might feel as if you would pay someone to hire you as a game programmer. I know that feeling all too well! I thought it was a strange feeling, getting paid to work on a retail game. When that game came out in stores and I saw it on the shelf, then it was an exhilarating feeling.

However, most of the world does not feel the same way that you do about video games. Very few people bother to read the credits. The feeling of exhilaration is really an internal one, not widely shared. You might already feel that this is true, given your own experience with relatives and friends who don't understand why you love games so much and why you wig out over the strangest things.

I remember the first time I discovered Will Wright's *Sim City*; it was in the late 1980s. It was quite an educational game, but extremely fun, too. Traveling with my parents, I would point out along the road, "Residential zone. Commercial zone. Ah ha! There's an industrial zone. Sure to be a source of pollution." I would note traffic jams and point out where a light rail alongside the road would ease the traffic problems. The fact is, the way you feel about video games has a strong bearing on whether you will succeed when the going gets rough, when the hours are piled on and you find yourself with no free time to actually play games anymore. All you have time to do is write code, and not even the most interesting code at that. But that spark in your eye remains, knowing that you are helping to complete this game, and it will go on your résumé as an accomplishment in life, maybe as a stepping stone in your career as a programmer.

Another argument that you might consider is the very real possibility that you could always go to college later and focus on your career now, especially if you have a lead for a job at a game company. That trend seems to be dwindling because games are now exceedingly complex projects that require highly trained and educated teams to complete them. Any self-taught programmer might have found corporate employment in the 1970s and 1980s, but the same is no longer the case with game companies. Now it has become an exceedingly competitive market. As you already know, competition causes quality to rise and costs to go down. A programmer with no college degree and little or no experience will have a very difficult time finding employment with a recognizable game company. Perhaps he can find work with one of the few hundred independent studios, but even private developers are in need of highly skilled programmers.

You might find more success by taking the indirect route to a career in game development. Many developers have gone professional after working on games in their spare time, by selling games as shareware or publishing them online. And there are as many success stories for high school graduates as there are for college graduates. As I said, every situation is unique. During this period of time, you can hone your skills, build your résumé of games (which is absolutely critical when you are applying for a job in the game industry), develop your own game engines, and so on. Even if you are interested in game programming (which is a safe bet if you are reading this book!) just as a hobby, there is always the possibility that you will come up with something innovative, and you might be surprised to receive an unexpected job offer.

A Note about Specialization

As far as specialization goes, there is very little difference between programming a game for console or PC—all are based on the C or C++ language. These are two distinct languages, by the way. It is out of ignorance that many refer to C and C++ interchangeably, when in fact they are very different. C is a structured language invented in the 1970s, while C++ is an object-oriented language invented in the 1980s. It is a given that you must know both of these languages (not just one or the other) because that is the assumption in this industry —you simply must know them both, without exception, and you should not need a programmer's reference for most of the standard C or C++ libraries (although there are some weird functions that are seldom used). If you are a capable programmer (from a Windows, Linux, Mac, or other background), you know C and C++, and you have some experience with a game engine or library (such as Allegro), then you should be able to make your way when working on a console, such as the PlayStation 2, Xbox, or GameCube.

The software development kits for consoles typically include libraries that you must link into your program when the program is compiled and linked to an executable file. Many game companies now produce games for all of the console systems and the PC, as well as some handheld systems (such as the Game Boy Advance). Once all of the artwork, sound effects, textures, levels, and so on, have been created for a game, it is economically prudent to reuse all of those game resources for as many platforms as possible. That is why many games are released simultaneously for multiple consoles. The cost of porting a game is just a fraction of the original development cost because all of the hard coding work has been done. The game's design is already completed. Everything has been done for one platform already, so the porting team must simply adapt the existing game for a different computer system (which is essentially what a video game system is). Since all of the code is already in C or C++ (or both), the porting team must simply replace platform-specific function calls with those for the new platform.

For instance, suppose a game for the PC is being ported to Xbox—something that is done all the time. The Xbox is very similar to a Windows PC, with a Windows 2000 core and a custom version of DirectX. There is no keyboard or mouse, just a controller. Porting a PC game requires some forethought because there is a lot of input code that must be converted so the game is operated from a controller. As an example, one of the most popular online PC games of all time, *Counter-Strike*, was ported to Xbox and features online play via the Xbox Live! network.

The usual setup for a PC game includes the use of keyboard in tandem with mouse—usually the ASDW configuration (A = left, D = right, W = forward, D = backward) while using the mouse to aim and shoot a weapon. Also, you use the CTRL key to crouch and the space-bar to jump. If your mouse has a mouse-wheel, you can use that to scroll through your available weapons (although the usual way is with the < and > keys).

I have always found this to be a terribly geeky way to play a game. Yes, it is faster than a controller. But it's like we have been forced to use a data entry device for so long just to play games that we not only accept it, but we defend it. I've heard many elite *Counter-Strike* players proclaim, "I'll never switch to a controller!" The fact of the matter is, when you get used to controlling your character using dual analog sticks and dual triggers on a modern console controller (such as the Xbox Controller S, shown in Figure 1.1), it is easy to give up the old keyboard/mouse combo.

Figure 1.1 Xbox Controller S

Counter-Strike was originally a Half-Life *mod* (or rather, expansion). To play the original *Counter-Strike*, you had to already own *Half-Life*, after which *Counter-Strike* was a free (but very large) download. Porting the game to Xbox must have been a major undertaking if it was truly rewritten just for the Xbox. Based on the similarity to the now-aged PC game, I would suspect that it is the same source code, but very highly modified. There are no Xbox enhancements that I can see after having played the game for several years on the PC. It is interesting to see how the developers dealt with the loss of the keyboard/mouse input system and adapted the game to work with a controller. The in-game menus use a convenient, intelligent menu system in which you use the eight-way directional pad to purchase gear at the start of each game round.

Regardless of the differences in input control and hardware, the source code for a console or a PC game is very similar, and all of it is written in C or C++. (The biggest difference are the development environment and game libraries, or SDKs.) One common practice at a game studio is to fabricate a development system in which the SDK of each console is abstracted behind *wrapper code*, which is a term used to describe the process of wrapping an existing library of functions with your own function calls. This not only saves time, but it also makes it easier to add features and fix bugs.

Game Industry Speculation

According to Jupiter Research (http://www.jupiterresearch.com), the game industry will continue to grow, having reached an estimated $12 billion revenue during 2003. Although console sales amount to more than PC game sales, there are many more PC gamers than console gamers, and the gap will continue to widen.

I have a theory about this apparent trend. I have seen the growth of consoles over the last five years, and I am convinced that console games will be more popular than PC games in a few years. It is just a simple matter of economics. A $200 console is as capable and as powerful as a $1,500 PC. Not too long ago I was a frenetic upgrader; I always found an excuse to spend another $500 on my PC every few months.

When I stopped to look at this situation objectively, I was shocked to learn that I had been spending thousands annually—on games, essentially. Not just retail games, but the hardware needed to run those games. It seemed to be a conspiracy! The hardware manufacturers and software game companies were in league to make money. Every six months or so, new games would be released that required PC upgrades just to run. One benefit that the consoles have brought to this industry is some platform stability, which makes it far easier to develop games. Not only can you (as a game programmer) count on a stable platform, but you can push the boundaries of that platform without worrying about leaving anyone with an aging computer behind. No newly released PC game will run on a computer that is five years old (in general), but that is a common practice for the average five-year lifespan of a game console.

Given this speculation and the trends and sales figures that seem to back it up, it is very likely that the PC and console game industries—which were once mostly independent of each other—will continue to grow closer every year. That is why it is important to develop a cross-platform mindset and not limit yourself to a single platform, such as Windows. Mastery of C and C++ are the most important things, while your specific platform of choice comes second. Regardless of your proficiency with Windows and DirectX, I encourage you to learn another system. The easiest way to gain experience with console development is to learn how to program the Nintendo Game Boy Advance (GBA) because open-source tools are available for it.

Emphasizing 2D

There is a misunderstanding among many game players as well as programmers (all of whom I will simply refer to as "gamers" from this point forward) that 2D games are dead, gone, obsolete, forever replaced by 3D. I disagree with that opinion. There is still a good case for working entirely in 2D, and many popular *just-released* games run entirely under a 2D game engine that does not require a 3D accelerator at all. Also, numerous games that can only be described as cult classics have been released in recent years and will continue to be played for years to come. Want some examples?

- Sid Meier's *Civilization III* with *Play the World* and *Conquests* expansions
- *StarCraft* and the *Brood War* expansion
- *Diablo II* and the *Lord of Destruction* expansion
- *Command & Conquer: Tiberian Sun* and the *Firestorm* expansion

- *Command & Conquer: Red Alert 2* and *Yuri's Revenge*
- *Age of Empires* and the *Rise of Rome* expansion
- *Age of Empires II* and *The Conquerors*
- *Age of Mythology* and *The Titans* expansion
- *The Sims* and a dozen or so expansions and sequels
- *Real War* and the *Rogue States* expansion

What do all of these games have in common? First of all, they are all bestsellers. As you might have noticed, they all have one or more expansion packs available (which is a good sign that the game is doing well). Second, these are all 2D games. This implies that these games feature a scrolling game world with a fixed point of view and various fixed and moving objects on the screen. Fixed objects might be rocks, trees, and mountains (in an outdoor setting) or doors, walls, and furniture (in an indoor setting). With a few exceptions, these are all PC games. There are several-hundred console and handheld games that all feature 2D graphics to great effect that I could have listed. For instance, here are just a handful of exceptional games available for the Game Boy Advance:

- *Advance Wars*
- *Advance Wars 2: Black Hole Rising*
- *Super Mario World: Super Mario Advance 2*
- *Yoshi's Island: Super Mario Advance 3*
- *The Legend of Zelda: A Link to the Past*
- *Sword of Mana*
- *Final Fantasy Tactics Advance*
- *Golden Sun: The Lost Age*

What makes these games so compelling, so hot on the sales charts, and so popular among the fans? It is certainly not due to fancy 3D graphics with multi-layer textures and dynamic lighting, representative of the latest first-person shooters. What sets these 2D games apart are the fantastic gameplay and realistic graphics for the characters and objects in the game.

Finding Your Niche

What are your hobbies, interests, and sources of entertainment (aside from your PC)? Have you considered that what interests you is also of interest to thousands or millions of other people? Why not capitalize on the fan base for a particular subject and turn that into a game? Nothing beats experience. When it comes to designing a game, there is no better source on a particular subject than a diehard fan! If you are a fan of a particular sci-fi show or movie, perhaps, then turn it into your vision of a game. Not only will you have a lot of fun, but you will create something that others will enjoy as well. I have found that when I work on a game that *I* enjoy playing and I create this game for my own enjoyment, there are people who are willing to pay for it.

Pocket Trivia Takes a Bow

Entirely for my own enjoyment and for nostalgia, I wrote a trivia game about one of my favorite sci-fi shows (*Star Trek*). The game featured 1,600 questions, 400 photos, theme-based sound effects, and a very simple multiple-choice interface (see Figure 1.2).

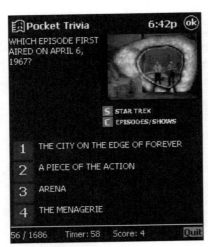

Figure 1.2 *Pocket Trivia* features multiple-choice trivia questions.

I decided to put the game up on my Web site and on a few game sites as a free download. Then I started to think about that decision for a moment. I had spent about two years working on that trivia game off and on during my free time, without setting any deadlines for myself. (Don't let the simplistic graphics and user interface fool you; it is very difficult to so fully cover a subject like this.) So I set a very low price on the game, just $12.00. The game sold 10 copies in the first week. That's $120.00 that I didn't have a week before, and for doing…well, nothing really, because I hadn't written that game for sale, just for fun. One month and 30 sales later, I decided to port the game to the Pocket PC platform, running Windows CE. This was about the time when my book, *Pocket PC Game Programming: Using the Windows CE Game API*, came out. (For more information about this book, see Appendix D.) I was fully immersed in Pocket PC programming, so it was not a difficult job. Oddly, I wrote the original PC game using Visual Basic 6.0, so the Pocket PC version had to be written from scratch using eMbedded Visual C++ 3.0.

Long story short, over the next year I made enough money from this little trivia game to buy myself a new laptop. That is not enough to live on, but it occurred to me that having 10 to 15 similar games in the "trialware" (try before you buy, synonymous with shareware) market, one could make a good living from game sales. The key is to continue cranking out new games every month while existing games provide your income. To do this, you need to hire out the artwork. (A professional artist will not only do far better work than the typical programmer, but he or she will do so very quickly.) I consider artwork to be at least as important as programming. Do you see how you could make a living as a game programmer by filling in niche products? You work for yourself and report to no one. If you can produce enough games to make a living, then you will be on the heels of many giants in the business.

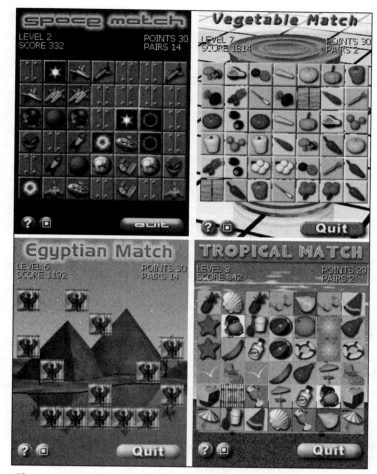

Figure 1.3 *Perfect Match* is a tile matching game with high-quality rendered graphics (four screens shown).

Perfect Match for the Fun of It

Another interesting game that I wrote is called *Perfect Match* (see Figure 1.3). It is a good example of the significant improvements you will see in the quality of your games when you collaborate with a professional artist. This game was written in about a month (again, during my spare time), and it features seven levels of play. The artwork in this game was completely modeled and rendered in 3D, and each level is a specific theme. This is another game that I personally enjoy playing, especially with such high-quality graphics (courtesy of Edgar Ibarra).

In addition to selling trialware, you can also approach a "budget" game publisher such as Xtreme Games LLC (http://www.xgames3d.com), operated by André LaMothe. Some publishers of this kind produce game compilations on CD-ROM, which have a good market at superstores, such as Wal-Mart. But the trend is heading more toward online sale and download. This is a very good way to make money by selling games that aren't "big enough" for the large retail game publishers, such as Electronic Arts. Companies such as Xtreme Games LLC make it possible for individual ("indie") developers to publish their games with little or no startup or publishing costs. Simply work on the games in your spare time and send them in when they're complete. Thereafter, you can expect to receive royalties on your games every month. Again, the amount of income depends on the quality and demand for each game.

Getting into the Spirit of Gaming

In this section I want to show you a hobby project I worked on when I was just getting started. This game is meager and the graphics are terrible, but it was a labor of love that became a learning tool when I was first learning to write code. This is an unusual approach, I realize, so I hope you will bear with me. My goal is to show you that you can turn any subject or hobby into a computer game of your own design, and no matter how good or bad it turns out to be, you will have grown significantly as a programmer from the experience.

I remember my first two-player game, which took a year to complete because there were no decent game programming books available in the late 1980s (only a handful that focused on the BASIC language), and I was literally teaching myself while working on this game. I called the game *Starship Battles*, and it was an accurate simulation of FASA's now-defunct *Tactical Starship Combat* game, right down to the individual starship specifications. This was a very popular pen-and-paper role-playing game in the 1980s, and at the time I had a collection of pewter miniature starships that I hand-painted for the game. Apparently, Paramount Pictures Corporation reined in many popular licensed products in the late 1980s, which is why this game is no longer available.

Starship Battles: An Inspired Fan Game

I wrote *Starship Battles* with Turbo Pascal 6.0 using 16-color EGA graphics mode 640×350. It featured double-buffered graphics, support for dual joysticks, and Sound Blaster effects. Figure 1.4 shows the game in action.

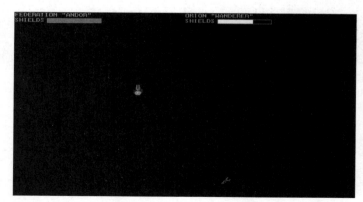

Figure 1.4 *Starship Battles* was a game of one-on-one starship combat set in the *Star Trek* universe.

Figure 1.5 shows the player selection screen in *Starship Battles*. This was a simplistic front-end for the game.

Overview of the Game

This simple-looking game took me a year to develop because I had to teach myself everything, from loading and drawing sprites to moving the computer-controlled ship to providing dual joystick support. This game also made use of the Sound Blaster Developer Kit (shown in Figure 1.6), which was very exciting at the time. I was able to produce my own sound effects (in VOC format) using the included tools and play real digital sound effects in the game. For the joystick support, I had a joystick "Y" adapter and two gamepads, requiring some assembly language programming on my part.

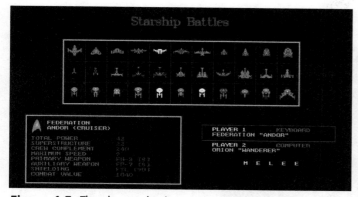

Figure 1.5 The player selection screen in *Starship Battles*

The game included a starship editor (shown in Figure 1.7) and my own artwork (as you probably already guessed). The original hex-based pen-and-paper game with cardboard pieces was the space battle module of FASA's larger *Star Trek: The Role Playing Game*. There were episodic add-on booklets available for this role-playing game, as well as ship recognition manuals and die-cast starship miniatures. The editor included fields for beam weapon and missile weapon types, which the game used to determine how fast a ship was able to shoot in the game, as well as how many shots could be fired at a time.

Figure 1.6 The Sound Blaster Developer Kit by Creative Labs included the libraries and drivers for multiple programming languages.

The Andor-class starship was one of my favorites because it was classified as a missile ship, able to fire eight missiles (or rather, photon torpedoes) before reloading. Some ships featured more powerful beam weapons (such as phasers or disruptor beams), which dealt great damage to the enemy ship. Figure 1.8 shows the specification sheet for the Andor, from FASA's *Federation Ship Recognition Manual* (shown in Figure 1.9). It is always interesting to see the inspiration for a particular game, even if that game is not worthy of note.

My goal is to help you to find inspiration in your own hobbies and interests.

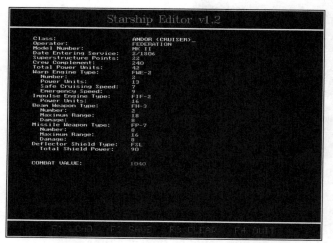

Figure 1.7 The starship editor program made it possible to change the capabilities of each ship.

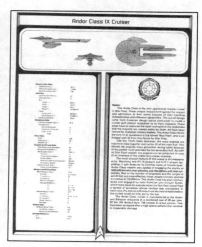

Figure 1.8 The specification sheet for the Andor-class starship

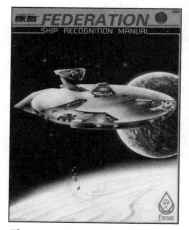

Figure 1.9 FASA's *Federation Ship Recognition Manual* provided the data entered into the starship editor, and thus affected how the game played.

Creating Game Graphics: The Hard Way

I spent a lot of time on this game and learned a lot from the experience, all of which had to be learned the hard way—through trial and error. First of all, I had no idea how to load a graphic file, such as the then-popular PCX format, so I started by writing my own graphic editor. I called this program *Sprites*; over time I wrote a 16-color version and a 256-color version. The 16-color version (shown in Figure 1.10) included limited animation support for four frames and rudimentary pixel-editing features, and was able to store multiple sprites in a data file (shown in Figure 1.11). Most importantly, I learned to program the mouse with assembly language. This sprite editor was very popular on bulletin board systems in the late 1980s.

tip

For the curious fan, the best modern implementation of FASA's tactical starship combat game is Activision's *Starfleet Command* series, excellent Windows PC games that have kept this sub-genre alive.

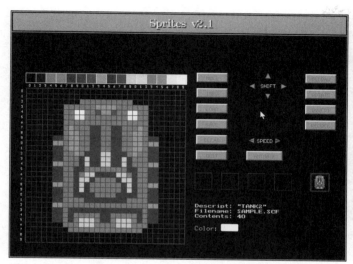

Figure 1.10 *Sprites v2.1* was a pixel-based graphic editor that I wrote in the late 1980s while working on *Starship Battles*.

Figure 1.11 The *Sprites* graphic editor could load and save multiple sprites in a single SPR file.

After completing *Starship Battles*, my plan was to convert the game to 256-color VGA mode 13h, which featured a resolution of 320×200 and support for double-buffering the screen inside the video buffer (which was very fast) for ultra-smooth, flicker-free animation. I came up with *Sprites 3.1* (shown in Figure 1.12) with an entirely new menu-driven user interface.

Rather than finish the sprite editor (which was not compatible with the previous version and lacked support for multiple sprites) and rather than focus on a new version of the game, I stopped using the program. About that time I became frustrated with limitations in Turbo Pascal and I decided to switch to Turbo C. At the same time, I switched to using Deluxe Paint instead of my sprite editor, storing game artwork in a PCX file rather than inside a custom sprite file. This being such a huge step, I never did get around to improving *Starship Battles*, which suffered from its EGA (*Enhanced Graphics Adapter*) roots. Making the transition from Pascal to C was not the most difficult part; the hardest part was rethinking my entire self-taught concept of building a game. During the development of *Starship Battles*, I had no access to a good graphic editor, such as Deluxe Paint, so I had no idea how to rotate the sprites. Instead, I wrote small utility programs to convert a single sprite into a rotated one with 16 frames.

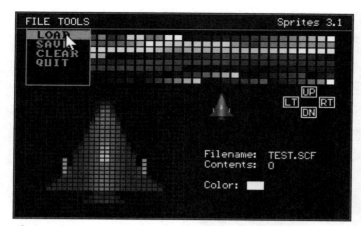

Figure 1.12 *Sprites 3.1* was a 256-color VGA mode 13h graphic editor.

Talk about doing things the hard way! I actually found some matrix math functions in a calculus book and used that knowledge to write a sprite rotation program that generated all of the rotated frames for each starship in the game.

Had I known about Deluxe Paint and Deluxe Animation, with features for drawing and animating sprites onscreen, I might have cried. At any rate, with new technology comes new power, so I gave up this game and moved on to another one of my hobbies—war games.

Axis & Allies: Hobby Wargaming

I have been a fan of Milton Bradley's *Axis & Allies* board game for 20 years, recently getting into the expanded editions, *Axis & Allies: Europe* and *Axis & Allies: Pacific*. This game is still huge, as evidenced by Web sites such as http://www.axisandallies.org. After completing *Starship Battles*, I decided to tackle the subject of *Axis & Allies* using the "proper" tools that I had discovered (namely, the C language and PCX files). The result of the effort is shown in Figure 1.13. What was truly awesome about this game was not the gameplay, per se, but the time spent with friends. (This is another factor in my belief that console games will continue to gain popularity—for all the effort, the greatest appeal of console games is taking on a friend.)

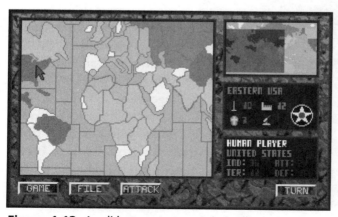

Figure 1.13 A solid attempt at an *Axis & Allies* computer game

What some would consider fond memories, I look back on as additional inspiration.

What made *Axis & Allies* so much fun? Winning the game? Hardly! I rarely beat my archrival, Randy Smith (as a matter of fact, I beat him two times out of perhaps sixty games!). When you design your next game, come to terms with the fact that winning is not always the most important thing. Having fun should be the primary focus of your games. And when your game is irresistibly fun, people will continue to play it. This is so contrary to modern game designs that focus on discrete goals; I feel that this trend coincides with the mechanical feel of the modern 3D game. Only after several years of refinement have gameplay and enjoyment started to enter the equation again. Gamers don't want a whiz-bang 3D technical demo, suitable for the crowds at GDC or E3; they want to have fun.

Overview of the Game

This single screen is packed with information that I believed would be helpful to a fan of the game. For instance, simply moving the mouse over a territory on the world map displayed the territory name, country flag, production value, attack strength, defense strength, and anti-aircraft capability. In addition, the bottom-right displayed global information about the current player, including total industrial capacity, number of territories owned, and global attack and defensive capabilities. Clicking on a territory (such as Eastern USA) would bring up a unit selection dialog, in which the player could select units to move or attack (see Figure 1.14).

Figure 1.14 The unit selection dialog was used to move units from one territory to another.

After moving units onto an enemy territory, the player would then engage in battle for that territory against the defending units. Figure 1.15 shows the battle screen.

Each round of a battle allowed attacker and defender a chance to fire with simulated rolls of the dice (one die for each unit, according to the board game's rules). Figure 1.16 shows the defender's counterattack.

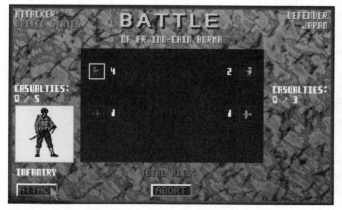

Figure 1.15 The battle screen automatically calculated all attack and defense rolls.

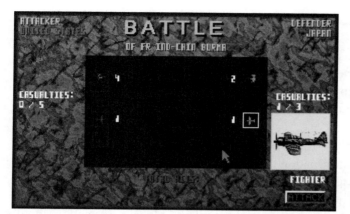

Figure 1.16 The defender makes a counterattack using remaining units.

Concluding the Game

This was the largest game I had attempted at that point, and it was difficult with the constant desire to return to Turbo Pascal, the language most familiar to me. Making strides in a new direction is difficult when it is easier to stay where you are, even if the technology is inferior. I constantly struggled with thoughts like, "It would be so much easier to use my sprite editor." But persistence paid off and I had a working game inside of a year, along with the experience of learning C and VGA mode 13h (the then-current game industry standard). This game really pushed me to learn new things and forced me to think in new ways. After much grumbling, I accepted the new technology and never looked back, although that was a difficult step. When I look back at the enormous amount of time I spent writing the most ridiculously simple (and cheesy) games, it really helps me put things into perspective today—there are wonderful software tools (many of them free) available today for writing games.

Setting Realistic Expectations for Yourself

My goal over the last few pages was not just to traverse memory lane, but to provide some personal experiences that might help explain how important motivation can be. Had I not been such a big fan of these subjects, I might have never completed the games that I have shown you here. Who cares? Touché. Whatever your opinion of reason and motivation, game development is a personal journey, not simply a skill learned solely to earn money. I will admit that these games are poor examples. They were labors of love, as I mentioned, and they suffered from my lack of programming experience. I worked with themes that I enjoyed and subjects that were my hobbies, and I can't stress enough how important that is! However, I will also point out that these game examples got me a job as a game programmer back in the day.

tip

Don't be ashamed of your work, whatever your opinion of it, because you are your own worst critic, and your work is probably better than you think. Be humble and ask the opinion of others before either praising or derailing your work.

My own personal motivations are to have fun, to delve deeper into a subject that I enjoy, to recreate an event or activity, and to learn as I go. With this motivation, I will share with you my own opinion of what makes a great game and, in later chapters, explain exactly how a game is made.

An Introduction to Dev-C++ and Allegro

I want to try to find the best balance of pushing as far into advanced topics as possible in this book while still covering the basics. It is a difficult balance that doesn't always please everyone because while some programmers need help at every step along the way, others become impatient with handholding and prefer to jump right into it and start. One of the problems with game development for the hobbyist today is the sheer volume of information on this subject, in both printed and online formats. It is very difficult to get started learning how to write games, even if your goal is just to have some fun or maybe write a game for your friends (or your own kids, if you have any). I find myself lost in the sheer magnitude of information on the overall subject of game development. It truly is staggering just looking into personal compilers, libraries, and tools, let alone the commercial stuff. If you have ever been to the Game Developers Conference in San Jose, California, then you'll know what I mean. This is a huge industry, and it is very intimidating! Getting started can be difficult. But not only that, even if you have been a programmer for many years (whether you have worked on games or not), just the level and amount of information can be overwhelming.

DirectX Is Just Another Game Library

One subject that is rather universal is DirectX. I have found that the more I talk about DirectX, the less I enjoy the subject because it is basically a building block and a tool, not an end in and of itself. Unfortunately, DirectX has been misunderstood, and many talk about DirectX as if *it* is game programming. If you learn the DirectX API, then you are a game programmer. Why doesn't that make sense to me? If I can drive a car, then am I suddenly qualified to be a NASCAR driver? DirectX is just a tool; it is not the end-all and be-all of game development.

In fact, there are a lot of folks who don't even like DirectX and prefer to stick with cross-platform or open-source tools, in which development is not dictated by a company with a stake in the game industry (as is the case with Microsoft and the Xbox console, in addition to Microsoft Game Studios). The professionals use a lot of their own custom libraries, game engines, and tools, but an equal number use off-the-shelf game development tools such as RenderWare Studio (http://www.renderware.com). This is a very powerful system for game development teams working on multi-platform games. What this means is that a single set of source code is written and then compiled for PC, Xbox, PS2, and GameCube (with support for any new consoles that come out in the future through add-on libraries).

Have you seen any games come out recently for multiple platforms at the same time? (One example is LucasArts' *Secret Weapons Over Normandy.*) It is a sure bet that such games were developed with RenderWare or a similar cross-platform tool. RenderWare includes source code management and logistical control in addition to powerful game libraries that handle advanced 3D graphics, artificial intelligence, a powerful physics system, and other features. And this is but one of the professional tools available!

I have found that there are so many books on DirectX now that the subject really doesn't need to be tackled in every new game development book. My reasoning is logical, I think. I figure that no single volume should try to be the sole source of information on any subject, no matter how specific it is. Should every game development book also teach the underlying programming language to the reader? We must make some assumptions at some point, or else we'll end up back at square one, talking about ones and zeroes!

You should consider another very important factor while we're on the subject of content. Windows is not the only operating system in the world. It is the most common and the most dominant in the industry, but it is not the only choice or even necessarily the best choice for every person (or every computer). Why am I making a big deal about this? I use Windows most of the time, but I realize that millions of people use other operating systems, such as Linux, UNIX, BeOS, FreeBSD, Mac OS, and so on—whatever suits their needs. Why limit my discussion of game development only to Windows users and leave out all of those eager programmers who have chosen another system?

The computer industry as we know it today was founded on powerful operating systems such as UNIX, which is still a thriving and viable operating system. UNIX, Linux, and the others are not more difficult to use, necessarily; they are just different, so they require a learning curve. The vast majority of consumers use Windows, and thus most programmers got started on Windows.

Introducing the Allegro Game Library

I want to support systems other than Windows. Therefore, this book focuses on the C language and the Allegro multi-platform game development library (which does use DirectX on the Windows platform, while supporting many others). Allegro was originally developed by Shawn Hargreaves for the Atari ST; as a result of open-source contributions, it has evolved over time to its present state as a powerful game library with many advanced 2D and 3D features also included. The primary support Web site for Allegro is at http://www.talula.demon.co.uk/allegro. I highly recommend that you visit the site to get involved in the online Allegro community because Allegro is the focus of this book.

Rather than targeting Xbox, PS2, and GameCube (which would be folly anyway because the console manufacturers will not grant licenses to unofficial developers), Allegro targets multiple operating systems for just about any computer system, including those in Table 1.1.

Table 1.1 Allegro and Operating Systems

Operating System	Compiler/Tools
Mac OS X	Apple Developer Tools 2002
Windows	Microsoft Visual C++ 4.0 (or later)
Windows	Borland C++ 5.5, C++Builder 1.0 (or later)
Windows	MinGW32/Cygwin
MS-DOS	DJGPP 2.01 with GCC 2.91 (or later)
MS-DOS	Watcom C++ 10.6 (or later)
IRIX	GCC 2.91 (or later)
Linux	GCC 2.91 (or later)
Darwin	GCC 2.91 (or later)
FreeBSD	GCC 2.91 (or later)
BeOS	Be Development Tools
QNX	QNX Development Tools

Table 1.1 presents an impressive and diverse list of operating systems, wouldn't you agree? Allegro abstracts the operating system from the source code to your game so the source code will compile on any of the supported platforms. This is very similar to the way in which OpenGL works. (OpenGL is another open-source game development library that focuses primarily on 3D.)

Allegro itself is not a compiler or language; rather, it is a game library that must be linked to your main C or C++ program. Not only is this practice common, it is smart. Any time you can reuse some existing source code, do so! It is foolish to reinvent the wheel when it comes to software, and yet that is exactly what many programmers do. I suspect many programmers prefer to rewrite everything out of a sense of pride or arrogance—as in, "I can do better." Let me tell you, game development is so extraordinarily complicated that if you try to write all the code yourself without the benefit of a game library or some help from the outside world, you will quite literally never get anywhere and your hard work will never be appreciated!

Allegro's 2D and 3D Graphics Features

Allegro features a comprehensive set of 2D and 3D graphics features.

Raster operations	Pixels, lines, rectangles, circles, Bezier splines
Filling	Pattern and flood fill
2D sprites	Masks, run-length encoding, compiled sprites, translucency, lighting

Bitmaps	Blitting, rotation, scaling, clipping
3D polygons	Wireframe, flat-shaded, gouraud-shaded, texture-mapped, z-buffered
Scrolling	Double- or triple-buffers, hardware scrolling (if available)
Animation	FLI/FLC playback
Windows drivers	DirectX windowed and full-screen, GDI device contexts
DOS drivers	VGA, Mode-X, SVGA, VBE/AF, FreeBE/AF
UNIX drivers	X, DGA, fbcon, SVGAlib, VBE/AF, Mode-X, VGA
BeOS drivers	BWindowScreen (full-screen), BDirectWindow (windowed)
Mac OS X	CGDirectDisplay (full-screen), QuickDraw/Cocoa (windowed)

Allegro's Sound Support Features

Allegro features some excellent support for music playback and sound effects.

Wavetable MIDI	Note on, note off, volume, pan, pitch, bend, drum mappings
Digital sound	64 channels, forward, reverse, volume, pan, pitch
Windows drivers	WaveOut, DirectSound, Windows Sound System
DOS drivers	Adlib, SB, SB Pro, SB16, AWE32, MPU-401, ESS AudioDrive, Ensoniq
UNIX drivers	OSS, ESD, ALSA
BeOS drivers	BSoundPlayer, BMidiSynth
Mac OS X drivers	CoreAudio, Carbon Sound Manager, QuickTime Note Allocator

Additional Allegro Features

Allegro also supports the following hardware and miscellaneous features.

Device input	Mouse, keyboard, joystick
Timers	High-resolution timers, interrupts, vertical retrace
Compression	Read/write LZSS compressed files
Data files	Multi-object data files for storing all game resources
Math functions	Fixed-point arithmetic, trigonometric lookup tables
3D functions	Vector, matrix, quaternion manipulation
Text output	Proportional fonts, UTF-8, UTF-16, Unicode

Supporting Multiple C/C++ Compilers

Not only is this book focusing on a free open-source game library in the form of Allegro, I will also use an open-source C/C++ compiler and IDE (*Integrated Development Environment*) called Dev-C++, which is shown in Figure 1.17.

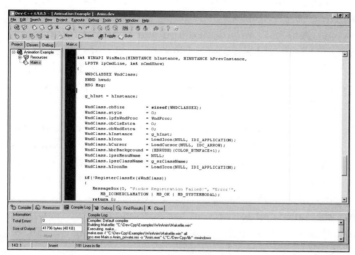

Dev-C++ includes an open-source C++ compiler called GCC (*GNU Compiler Collection*) that is the most widely used C++ compiler in the world. I used this compiler to develop the sample programs for my Game Boy Advance book, too! GCC is an excellent and efficient compiler for multiple platforms. In fact, many of the world's operating systems are compiled with GCC, including Linux. It is a sure bet that satellites in orbit around Earth have programs running on their

Figure 1.17 Dev-C++ is the open-source C/C++ compiler and IDE used in this book.

small computers that were compiled with GCC. This is not some small niche compiler—it is a global phenomenon, so you are not limiting yourself in any way by using GCC. Most of the console games that you enjoy are compiled with GCC. In contrast, the most common Windows compilers, such as Microsoft Visual C++ and Borland C++Builder, aren't used as widely but are more popular with consumers and businesses.

This brings up yet another important point. The source code in this book will compile on almost any C/C++ compiler, including Visual C++, C++Builder, Borland C++, Watcom C++, GCC, CodeWarrior, and so on. Regardless of your compiler and IDE of choice, the code in this book should work fine, although you might have to create your own project files for your favorite compiler. I am formally supporting Dev-C++, Visual C++, and KDevelop (under Linux), so you will find the source code for these compilers on the CD-ROM. All that means is that I have created the project files for you. The source code is all the same! Incidentally, Dev-C++ is also included on the CD-ROM. Due to its very small size (around 12 MB for the installer), you might find it easier to use than Visual C++ or C++Builder, which have very large installations. Dev-C++ is capable of compiling native Windows programs and supports a diverse collection of DevPaks—open-source libraries packaged in an easy-to-use file that Dev-C++ knows how to install.

Allegro is one such example of an existing code library, and it's just plain smart to use it rather than starting from scratch (as in learning to program Windows and DirectX). But what if you are really looking for a DirectX reference? Well, I can suggest several dozen good books on the subject that provide excellent DirectX references (see Appendix D, "Recommended Books and Web Sites"). The focus of this book is on practical game programming, not on providing a primer for Windows or DirectX programming (which is quite platform-specific in any event). As I have mentioned and will continue to do, I am a big fan of Windows and DirectX. However, I am also a big fan of console video game systems, and programming a console will open your eyes to what's possible. This is especially true if you have limited yourself to writing Windows programs and you have not experienced the development possibilities on any other system.

Dev-C++ is just one of the IDE/compiler tools you can use to compile the code in this book. Feel free to use any of the compilers listed back in Table 1.1. It might be possible to use older compilers (such as Turbo C++ or an early version of Microsoft C++) for MS-DOS, but I wouldn't recommend it. Who is still using MS-DOS today? I only mention it because Allegro does support MS-DOS and the DJGPP compiler. While GCC is guaranteed to work with Allegro, the same cannot be said for obsolete compilers, which very likely do not support modern library file structures. If you insist on using MS-DOS, then by all means make use of DJGPP because it is based on GCC.

Summary

This chapter presented an overview of game development and explained the reasoning behind the use of open-source tools such as Dev-C++ and Allegro (the primary benefit being that these tools are free, although that does not imply that they are inferior in any way). I explained how Windows and DirectX are the focus of so much that has already been written, and that this book will delve right into game programming rather than spending time on logistical things (such as tools). I hope you will embrace the way of thinking highlighted in this chapter and broaden your horizons by recognizing the potential for programming systems other than Windows. By reading this book and learning to write platform-independent code, you will be a far more flexible and versatile programmer. If you don't fully understand these concepts quite yet, the next chapter should help because you will have an opportunity to see the capabilities of Dev-C++ and Allegro by writing several complete programs.

Chapter Quiz

You can find the answers to this chapter quiz in Appendix A, "Chapter Quiz Answers."

1. What programming language is used in this book?
   A. C
   B. Pascal
   C. C++
   D. Assembly

2. What is the name of the free multi-platform game library used in this book?
   A. Treble
   B. Staccato
   C. Allegro
   D. FreeBSD

3. What compiler can you use to compile the programs in this book?
   A. Dev-C++
   B. Borland C++Builder
   C. Microsoft Visual C++
   D. All of the above

4. Which operating system does Allegro support?
   A. Windows
   B. Linux
   C. Mac OS X
   D. All of the above

5. Which of the following is a popular strategy game for the PC?
   A. *Counter-Strike*
   B. *Splinter Cell*
   C. *Real War*
   D. *Advance Wars*

6. What is the most important factor to consider when working on a game?
   A. Graphics
   B. Sound effects
   C. Gameplay
   D. Level design

7. What is the name of the free open-source IDE/compiler included on the CD-ROM?
   A. Visual C++
   B. Dev-C++
   C. Watcom C++
   D. C++Builder

8. What is the name of the most popular game development library in the world?
   A. OpenGL
   B. DJGPP
   C. DirectX
   D. Allegro

9. Which of the following books discusses the gaming culture of the late 1980s and early 1990s with strong emphasis on the exploits of id Software?
   A. *Masters of Doom*
   B. *The Age of Spiritual Machines*
   C. *The Inmates Are Running the Asylum*
   D. *Silicon Snake Oil*

10. According to the author, which of the following is one of the best games made in the 1980s?
   A. *Civilization III*
   B. *Counter-Strike*
   C. *King's Quest IV: The Perils of Rosella*
   D. *Starflight*

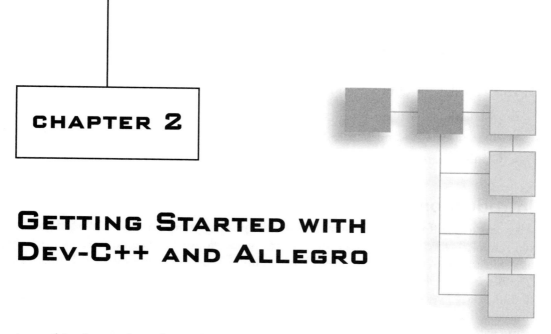

CHAPTER 2

GETTING STARTED WITH
DEV-C++ AND ALLEGRO

This chapter introduces the Dev-C++ integrated development environment, the GNU C++ compiler, and associated tools. You will learn how to install and configure Dev-C++ for game development with the Allegro game library. Because these programs are all available on the book's CD-ROM, everything you need to start writing cutting-edge games was included in the price of this book! However, if you prefer to use a different compiler, such as Microsoft Visual C++ (any version from 4.0 on will work), please refer to Appendix E, "Configuring Allegro for Microsoft Visual C++ and Other Compilers."

There was a time when installing Allegro involved more than just running a setup utility; you had to compile Allegro before using it. The extremely talented contributors to Dev-C++ and Allegro have made things so much easier with the latest versions of these tools. Dev-C++ now includes an update tool that will install the latest version of Allegro automatically, right off the Web! Although this chapter focuses on setting up Dev-C++ and Allegro for Windows, I have added an appendix that will explain how to compile Allegro for systems that might not support the update tool. Please refer to Appendix F, "Compiling the Allegro Source Code" for details.

Everything you need to know to get up and running with Dev-C++ and Allegro is fully explained in the following pages. Unlike some programming books that try to offer stand-alone chapters as a series of independent tutorials, the chapters in this book should be read sequentially because each chapter builds on the one before it. This chapter in particular is critical in that respect because it explains how to set up the development tools used in the rest of the book.

Here is a breakdown of the major topics in this chapter:

- Installing and configuring Dev-C++ and Allegro
- Taking Dev-C++ and Allegro for a spin
- Gaining more experience with Allegro

Introduction

Allow me to go off topic for a moment. I love role-playing games. I am especially fond of the old-school 2D RPGs that focus on strong character development, exploration, and questing as a solo adventurer. I am still amazed at the attention to detail in games such as *Ultima VII: The Black Gate*, which is now more than 10 years old. This game was absolutely amazing, and its legacy lives on today in the form of *Ultima Online*. The music in this game was so ominous that it actually affected most players on an emotional level, drawing them into the game with a desire to help the Avatar save Britannia. The open storyline and freedom to explore the world made it so engaging and engrossing that it completely suspended my sense of disbelief—that is, while playing, I tended to forget it was merely a game.

Contrast that experience with modern games that are more focused on eye candy than exploring the imagination! It reminds me of the difference between a movie and a book; each has a certain appeal, but a book delights at a more personal level, opening the mind to new possibilities. I am drawn into a good game, such as *Ultima VII*, just as I am with a good book; on the other hand, even an all-time favorite movie usually fails to draw me into the story at a personal level. I am experiencing the imagination and vision of another person, and those impressions are completely different than my own. Teasing the imagination is what separates brilliance from idle entertainment, and it is the difference between a long remembered and beloved memory (found in a good book or a deeply engaging game) and a quickly forgotten one (such as in a typical movie).

It is a rare game that is able to enchant one's imagination while also providing eye candy. One such game is *Baldur's Gate: Dark Alliance* (a console implementation of the best-selling PC game). This game is intelligent, challenging, imaginative, enjoyable, engaging, and still manages to impress visually as well as audibly. The layout of this game is an overhead view, although it is rendered in 3D, giving it a 2D feel that resembled the orientation of *Ultima VII* and *Diablo II*. That someone is still building fantastic RPGs like this is a testament to the power of a good story and the joy of character development and leveling up. The pizzazz of highly detailed 3D graphics simply satisfies the picky gamers.

As you delve further into this chapter, try to keep in mind what your ideal game would be. What is your all-time favorite game? What genre does it represent? How would you improve upon the game, given the opportunity? I will continually encourage you to keep your ideal game design in mind while working through this book. I hope you will start to develop that game as you progress through each chapter. To that end and to form a basis for building your own game, I will walk you through the creation of a complete game—not just a sample or demonstration program, but a complete, full-featured game with all the bells and whistles! Although I would really enjoy building an RPG, that is far too ambitious for the goals of this book. RPGs are so enormous that even the simplest of RPGs is a huge undertaking, and there are so many prerequisites just to get started. For instance, will the hero be able to wield different weapons? Animating a single character can require more than 100 animation frames for a single sprite—and that is just with one weapon, one set of armor. What if you want your character to be equipped with different kinds of weapons and armor in the game (in my opinion, one of the best aspects of an RPG)? You could design the game with a fixed character image, but you are still looking at a huge investment in artwork.

My second choice is a strategy game, so that is the approach I have taken in this book. Strategy games are enormously entertaining while requiring a meager initial investment in artwork. In fact, in the spirit of the open-source tools used in this book, I will also be using a public domain sprite library called SpriteLib. This library was produced by Ari Feldman, a talented artist who was kind enough to allow me to use his fantastic high-quality artwork in this book. As you will see in the next two chapters, each great game idea starts with a basic prototype, so you will develop the first prototype version of this strategy game in Chapter 4, "Writing Your First Allegro Game." Following that, each major chapter will include a short section on enhancing the game with the new information presented in each chapter. For instance, the first version of the strategy game will have a fixed background, but when I cover scrolling backgrounds I'll show you how to enhance the game to use that new feature. The same goes for animated sprites, sound effects, music, special effects, and so on.

Installing and Configuring Dev-C++ and Allegro

I know you are looking forward to jumping into some great source code and working on some real games. I feel the same way! But before you can do that, I have to explain how to configure the development tools used in this book. Regardless of whether you are a newcomer to programming or a seasoned expert looking for an entertaining diversion, you will find the information in this chapter valuable because it is important to get set up properly before you delve into the advanced programming chapters to come! I think you will come to enjoy using Dev-C++ regardless of your experience level. However, if you don't like the editor and IDE for any reason, you can configure your favorite IDE to use Allegro; see Appendix E. This appendix covers several compilers, such as Visual C++, Borland C++, and KDevelop.

Dev-C++ is an open-source integrated development environment (IDE) for the infamous GCC (*GNU Compiler Collection*), a multi-platform C/C++ compiler. Dev-C++ and GCC are both distributed under the GNU General Public License, which means they are freely redistributable as long as the source code is provided for the tools themselves and any derivative works. In case you were wondering, GNU stands for "GNU is Not Unix." This is something of an inside joke in the open-source community, in that the name is recursive.

note

The GNU General Public License is printed in the back of the book.

Dev-C++ was developed by Bloodshed Software (http://www.bloodshed.net), and the primary Web site for Dev-C++ is located at http://www.bloodshed.net/devcpp.html. The version of Dev-C++ included on the book's CD-ROM includes an updating tool that will download updates to the compiler or tools, although I still recommend visiting Bloodshed Software's site to get up-to-date news and information.

Although I am not going to cover it in this book, Bloodshed Software also has a very interesting product called Dev-Pascal that uses the same IDE as Dev-C++ but features syntax highlighting for the Pascal language (including support for Delphi) and makes use of the GNU Pascal compiler. I sure would have enjoyed this product back in the day, when I was a Turbo Pascal fan!

Installing Dev-C++

The installation process for Dev-C++ is so simple that I'm not even going to go over it here. If you have any problems installing it, refer to the Bloodshed Software Web site. Simply run the executable file containing the Dev-C++ files; the version included on the CD-ROM is called devcpp4980.exe. I do want to make a recommendation on the install location: I recommend installing Dev-C++ on the same hard drive as Allegro (and your game projects). It just makes things easier when everything is readily available, especially when you consider that browsing for files on multiple drives can be a nuisance. I have several drives in my PC and I choose to install game development software on one of the partitions that I have set aside exclusively for that purpose. I also recommend installing things on the root (such as C:\Dev-Cpp). The installer for Dev-C++ is provided on the CD-ROM in the \dev-cpp folder; it is called devcpp4980.exe. Feel free to use your favorite IDE and compiler as long as it's capable of compiling standard C/C++ code for Windows, Linux, Mac OS X, or one of the other supported systems. If you are living in Antarctica and are stuck with an old PC running MS-DOS, then you can use DJGPP or Watcom.

When is the last time you came across a retail game box in a store that listed MS-DOS, Windows, Linux, and Mac OS X support? Yep, Allegro (the library that makes this possible) is awesome.

Updating Dev-C++

The easiest way to update Dev-C++ is to use the built-in update tool. I have also provided the latest update (at the time of this writing) of 4.9.8.5; it is located in \dev-cpp and it is called devcpp4985.zip. You can simply unzip this file inside your C:\Dev-Cpp folder to perform a manual update. I highly recommend this simple manual update because it supercedes the process involving the old update tool, providing you with WebUpdate right from the start. If you prefer to use the update tool, I'll explain how it works. Once you have installed Dev-C++, open the Tools menu and select Check for Updates/Packages (see Figure 2.1). This will open the update program for Dev-C++.

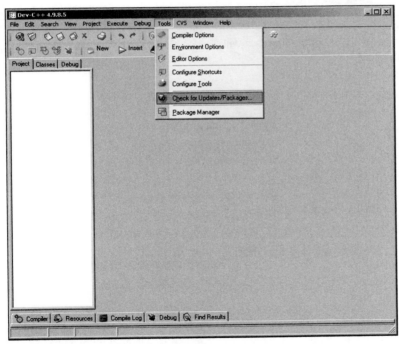

Figure 2.1 The Tools menu in Dev-C++

Dev-C++ includes an update tool to automatically download and install updates. The update program connects to an online server to download packages for Dev-C++, and it is wonderfully easy to use. (In contrast, how often have you ever updated Visual C++ or

Borland C++Builder over the Net? The typical Microsoft service pack is hundreds of megabytes in size.) The update program is shown in Figure 2.2. This default updater has been replaced with a more useful WebUpdate program, but first you must get an update to Dev-C++ to take advantage of this great new updater. Referring to Figure 2.2 again, you will see four buttons on the right. Click on the top button (the one with the purple check-mark on it). This will bring up a dialog box asking you to shut down Dev-C++, which you should do; then click on the Retry button to continue.

The list of updates might change by the time you read this, but at this time there are two updates available (see Figure 2.3). Check both files and click on the Start button to proceed with the download.

Figure 2.2 Dev-C++ comes with an update tool that will download updates and packages.

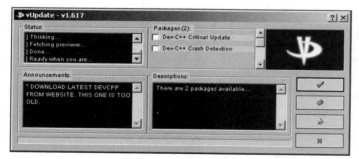

Figure 2.3 The update program displays the available downloads for updating Dev-C++.

tip

It is very likely that Dev-C++ will be updated at regular intervals, at which point the screenshots and tutorials in this section might not apply. If you are using at least version 4.9.8.5 of Dev-C++, that is all you really need while working through this book. The advantage of updating is that you receive bug fixes and new features. For instance, the 8.5 revision includes the newer WebUpdate tool.

After you have completed this initial update process and installed the new version of Dev-C++ (which is done automatically by the update program), your copy of Dev-C++ will be ready to use the more advanced WebUpdate feature. If the Package Manager opens at this point, you can just close it. Once again, start Dev-C++, and you will notice that the version displayed in the caption bar is Dev-C++ 4.9.8.5. Open the Tools menu and select Check for Updates/Packages again. Now you should see the WebUpdate tool, as shown in Figure 2.4.

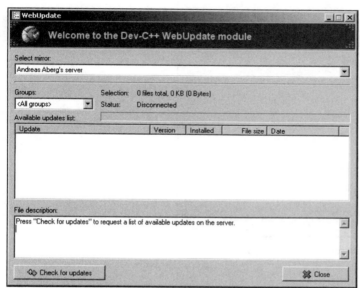

At the bottom-left corner is a button called Check for Updates. Click on this button to retrieve a list of updates for Dev-C++ (see Figures 2.4 and 2.5).

Figure 2.4 Dev-C++ is now equipped with the WebUpdate tool, making it very easy to install new DevPaks.

note

Several Dev-C++ DevPaks have been included on the CD-ROM that accompanies this book so you can install the critical packages you need to compile the source code in this book. The most important DevPak is Allegro! To install a DevPak from Dev-C++, go to Tools, Package Manager and click on the Install icon to browse for a DevPak file (such as Allegro.Devpak). I recommend compiling and installing Allegro yourself; see Appendixes E and F.

I recommend that you not download all of the DevPaks right away, although the temptation is great. Although you can browse the installed DevPaks using the Package Manager, it makes more sense to download only what you need. This not only saves bandwidth for others trying to download files from the update site, but it also gives you time to learn about the packages one at a time. And there are many—just take a look at the list! You will find everything from a MySQL database library to a CD audio extraction library to a DirectX 9 package for Dev-C++. In addition, you will see a Windows API reference, a GNU C library reference, and many more.

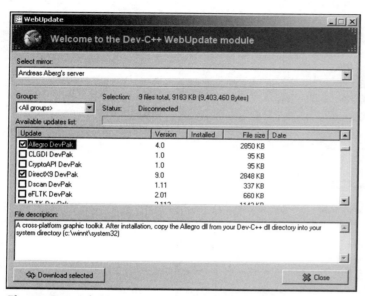

Figure 2.5 Selecting some of the available packages to be installed by WebUpdate

Definitely grab all of the Dev-C++ update packages (the first five or six files), such as Dev-C++ Update, PackMan, and so on. You also must get the Allegro package to run the programs in this book. While you are at it, also select whatever DirectX library is available. (The current package as of this writing is DirectX 9, but you really only need DirectX 8.) Most importantly, I recommend installing the packages one at a time! The Package Manager opens every time an update is installed, so it is much easier to get the updates one at a time.

tip

The DevPaks available on the update site for Dev-C++ are not always up to date because they are maintained by volunteer contributions. If you want to install only the minimum tools needed for this book, they are all provided on the CD-ROM. In particular, the Dev-C++ packages are located in the \DevPaks folder. It might be a good idea to ensure consistency by simply installing everything off the book's CD-ROM rather than relying on WebUpdate.

Installing Allegro

If you followed the steps in the previous section, you should now have Allegro installed from the WebUpdate tool in Dev-C++. If you do not have online access, you can install the Allegro.Devpak off the CD-ROM that accompanies this book (look in \DevPaks). You do not need any of the other DevPaks to compile the code in this book, but you absolutely must have Allegro installed. As was the case with Dev-C++, the version of Allegro provided by default is out of date and must be updated. It is entirely possible to install Allegro manually (see Appendix F). But one benefit that comes with the Allegro package is the convenience of the project templates added to Dev-C++. So what you should do is install the Allegro.DevPak and then copy the Allegro update files.

I have already compiled Allegro 4.0.3 (using the processes covered in Appendix F) and placed the updated library files on the CD-ROM in \allegro. If you are lost at this point, don't worry—I'm just providing an overview of what will be explained in more detail over the next few pages. Installing Allegro is just as easy as installing Dev-C++, but there is an added level of complexity because this software is never set in stone. As is the case with almost every open-source program, Dev-C++ and Allegro both undergo changes frequently to improve functionality and correct bugs. Understanding this and the fact that no single corporation is responsible for the software is a big step toward understanding how open-source works. Indeed, the major difference between commercial and open-source software is the matter of support. The high cost of commercial software pays for not just the development costs, but also the support costs (for those users who need to call the technical support line for assistance). Open-source software basically has no formal support at all, although there are hundreds of other users on the Web who are willing to help.

Figure 2.6 Allegro is an open-source, multi-platform game programming library.

Just as an aside, there are several logos available for Allegro, including the one shown in Figure 2.6. Is it ironic that even the logos for this software were donated?

The Package Manager comes up to install each DevPak after download. Make sure that you have correctly downloaded and installed Allegro by looking at the packages listed in the Package Manager (see Figure 2.7).

tip

If you want to double-check the installation of a particular library (such as Allegro), you can browse to the Dev-Cpp folder and look inside lib. The Allegro library's main file is called liballeg.a; this is specified in the linker options with -lalleg (note the "lib" and ".a" parts of the filename are assumed).

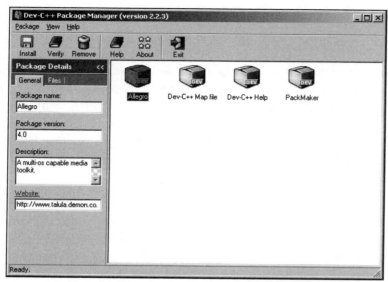

I encourage you to read Appendix F to learn how to compile Allegro for yourself.

Figure 2.7 The Package Manager displays the packages that have been installed for Dev-C++.

The Allegro DevPak and Source Code

There are two versions of Allegro that you can use—the prepackaged version or the source code version. The prepackaged version (Allegro.DevPak) for Windows includes a DLL that you must distribute with any program you compile. This isn't a big deal because you can simply install this DLL with any game or other program that you produce and distribute. The DLL is also useful if you have a Windows compiler that has a hard time compiling the Allegro library and is otherwise not compatible with the Allegro LIB files produced by GCC. Most Windows compilers produce code that is compatible with a standard DLL (not the ActiveX/COM variety, just a standard library). On most systems other than Windows, you will want to use the static library. However, the DevPak also includes a static library that you can have linked right into your programs, nullifying the need for the DLL. I will primarily use the dynamic version of Allegro for the sample projects in the book, but I will lean more toward the static library in later chapters. It's a little more difficult to configure a static project; it is extremely simple to create a new Allegro project using the dynamic library.

The second option is to compile the Allegro source code yourself, creating both the dynamic and static libraries. Rather than get sidetracked setting up GCC to compile the Allegro source code at this point, I refer you to Appendix F for detailed instructions on how to compile the Allegro source code with GCC. This would also be advisable if you are running an operating system other than Windows because the appendix explains how to compile Allegro under both Windows and Linux (which should be enough to get you going with any other OS). To make things simple while you're just getting started, I will use the Allegro (DLL) version and the projects provided by the DevPak.

note

Are you confused yet? I realize this is a lot of information to absorb all at once, but it is basically how I present information. I prefer to provide an overview of any process (or program, for that matter) to give a bird's-eye view, and then go over that subject in detail. I believe it helps to understand the big picture when you are learning something new.

Allegro's Versatility

Allegro is useful for more than just games. It is a full-featured multimedia library as well, and it can be used to create any type of graphical program. I can imagine dozens of uses for Allegro outside the realm of games (such as graphing mathematical functions). You could also use Dev-C++ and Allegro to port classic games (for which the source code is available) to other computer systems. I have had a lot of fun porting old graphics programs and games to Allegro because it is so easy to use and yet so powerful at run time.

For instance, Relic Entertainment released the source code to *Homeworld* in September, 2003, to great acclaim in the game development community. You can download the *Homeworld* source code by going to http://www.relic.com/rdn. You will need to sign up for an account with the Relic Developer's Network (which is free) to download the source code, an 18-MB zip file. Although *Homeworld* was written for DirectX and OpenGL, it could be adapted to Allegro with a little effort—if you are interested in a challenge, that is! The source code for many other commercial games has been released in the last few years, such as the code for *Quake III*. John Carmack from id Software seems to have started this trend by originally releasing the *Doom* source code a few years after the game's release, and following that with the code for most of id's games through the years. Why? Because he shares the opinion of many in the game industry that software should not be patented, that education and lifelong learning should be encouraged. Carmack is also a cross-platform developer.

Taking Dev-C++ and Allegro for a Spin

It's time to start writing some actual programs with Dev-C++ and Allegro. In this section I will walk you through several short programs. In the process, you will learn how to create a new C project and write the initialization code for Allegro before calling on the Allegro-specific functions. First you need to make sure that Allegro was installed properly, so you'll start by writing a short program to verify that Allegro is available for use. Then I'll go over some more interesting programs with you.

Testing Dev-C++: The Greetings Program

The first step in testing the installation is to write a short program in Dev-C++ to verify that GCC is working as expected because Dev-C++ is just the IDE/editor, and it calls gcc.exe to compile programs. Start Dev-C++. In Windows, it is located in the Start menu under Programs, Bloodshed Dev-C++. Because this is a small, tight IDE, it comes up immediately and presents you with a blank project workspace, as shown in Figure 2.8.

note

For the sake of brevity, I will often refer to both the compiler and IDE collectively as "the compiler." This applies to Dev-C++, Visual C++, or any other compiler system where the IDE actually runs the command-line compiler and presents the programmer with the results returned by the compiler (such as error messages).

Figure 2.8 The Dev-C++ IDE works with GCC to compile programs.

Becoming Familiar with the Compiler

I understand that working with an open-source compiler can be a little unsettling. Not only is it very different than the compiler you might be used to, but it can be a little surprising to learn that the ultra-expensive commercial compiler that you (or your employer) purchased works exactly the same way that the free compiler does. Even more surprising is the fact that GCC is an optimizing compiler capable of compiling code with every bit as much efficiency and speed as Visual C++ or Borland C++Builder. I think there is a false impression (furthered by marketing forces) that open-source software is inferior to commercial software and that proponents have simply gotten used to it. Although there is a small margin of truth in that, the fact remains that Dev-C++ works just as well as Visual C++ for constructing Windows programs. What you will not find is a dialog editor, a resource editor, a toll-free customer support number, or case-sensitive help (depending on the IDE).

Case-sensitive help is a very convenient feature if you are used to a commercial compiler package, such as Visual C++. Being able to hit F1 with the cursor over a key word to bring up syntax help is a difficult feature to do without. As an alternative, I like to keep a C reference book handy (such as *C Programming Language* (Prentice Hall PTR, 1988) by Brian Kernighan and Dennis Ritchie or *C: A Reference Manual* (Prentice Hall, 2002) by Samuel Harbison and Guy Steele) as well as an online Web site, such as http://www-ccs.ucsd.edu/c. I also keep the Allegro reference Web site open; the site is located at http://www.talula. demon.co.uk/allegro/onlinedocs/en. After you have programmed for a while without an online help feature, your coding skill will improve dramatically. It is amazing how very little some programmers really know about their choice programming language because they rely so heavily upon case-sensitive help! I don't suggest that you memorize the standard C and C++ libraries (although that wouldn't hurt). This might sound ridiculous at first, but it makes sense: When you have to make a little extra effort to look up some information, you are more likely to remember it and not need to look it up again.

In addition, open-source tools, such as Dev-C++, are not suited for .NET development—which, I might add, is not relevant because .NET is a framework for building business applications, not games, and it is not well suited for games. (In all fairness, Visual Basic .NET and Visual C# .NET are very good languages that do work well with DirectX, but they are not the ideal choice for game development.) You can treat my opinion on this matter as unbiased and objective because I use these tools on a daily basis, both commercial and open-source, and I appreciate the benefits that each tool brings with it. In general, commercial software is just more convenient. To an expert programmer, items of convenience usually only get in the way.

note

You might be using Visual C++ 7.0 in conjunction with this book. That is perfectly fine! Visual C++ is capable of compiling standard C/C++ code (this is called *unmanaged code* by Microsoft) as well as code that is reliant upon the .NET Framework (this is called *managed code*). Many commercial PC games are developed with Visual C++ 7.0 and DirectX, and this version will work with Allegro.

Creating the Greetings Project

Now then, back to Dev-C++. Open the File menu and select New, Project, as shown in Figure 2.9. This will bring up the New Project dialog box showing the types of projects that are available (see Figure 2.10). If you look at the tabs at the top of the dialog box, you will see Basic, Introduction, MultiMedia. These are the three different categories of project templates built into Dev-C++. Click on the Introduction tab to see a Hello World project (see Figure 2.11). The MultiMedia tab (shown in Figure 2.12) includes a sample project template for an OpenGL program. Note that if you have already installed Allegro.DevPak, you should see two Allegro project templates in the MultiMedia section.

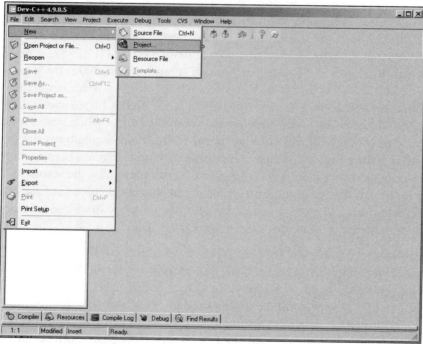

Figure 2.9 Creating a new project in Dev-C++

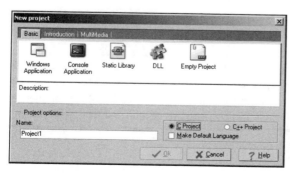

Figure 2.10 The New Project dialog box in Dev-C++ includes numerous project templates.

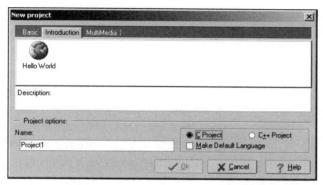

Figure 2.11 The Introduction tab includes a Hello World project template.

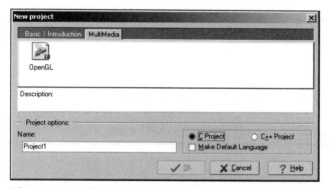

Figure 2.12 The MultiMedia tab includes an OpenGL project template.

Feel free to create a new project using any of these project templates and run it to see what the program looks like. After you are finished experimenting (which I highly recommend you do to become more familiar with Dev-C++), bring up the New Project dialog box again and select the Basic tab. At this point, allow me to provide you with a disclaimer, or rather, a look ahead. Allegro abstracts the operating system from your source code. Therefore, you need not create a Windows Application project (one of the options in the New Project dialog box). Allegro includes the code needed to handle Windows messages through WndProc, WinMain, and so on, just as the versions of Allegro for Linux, Mac OS X, and so on include the specific functions needed for those operating systems.

tip

For more information about the specifics of Windows programming, please refer to Charles Petzold's book *Programming Windows* (listed in Appendix D). Any edition will do, including the fifth edition or some of his newer books. I like the fifth edition because it covers Visual C++ 6.0, which is very similar to Dev-C++ and is easily configurable.

Referring to Figure 2.13, you want to select the Empty Project icon, and for the language choose C Project. For the project name, type Greetings, and then click on OK.

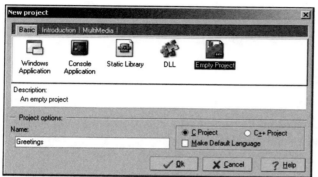

The Project Save dialog box will then appear, allowing you to select a folder for the project. The default folder is inside the main Dev-Cpp folder. I recommend creating a folder off the root of your drive for storing projects.

Figure 2.13 Choosing Empty Project from the New Project dialog box

tip

For future reference, the sample programs in this book are being developed simultaneously under Windows 2000 and Mandrake Linux, and the screenshots reflect this. If you are using another OS, such as Mac OS X or FreeBSD, your user interface will obviously look different.

After you save the new project, Dev-C++ will show the new empty project (see Figure 2.14). Note that Dev-C++ didn't even bother to create a default source file for you to use. That is because you selected Empty Project. Had you chosen Windows Application or another type of project, then a populated source code file would have been added for you. To keep things simple and to fully explain what's going on, I want to go over each step.

Now you need to add a new source code file to the project. Open the File menu and select New, Source File, as shown in Figure 2.15. Alternatively (and this is my preference) you can right-click on the project name to bring up a pop-up menu from which you can select New File (see Figure 2.16). Either method will add a new empty file called Untitled1 to your project.

Now right-click on the new file and select Rename File, and then type in **main.c** for the filename. After you do that, your project should look like the one shown in Figure 2.17.

note

If you are an experienced developer with Visual C++, Borland C++, Dev-C++, or another tool, these steps will be all too familiar to you. I am covering as much introductory information as possible now so it is not necessary to do so in later chapters.

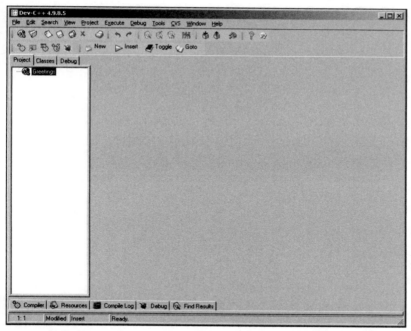

Figure 2.14 The new Greetings project has been created and is now ready to go.

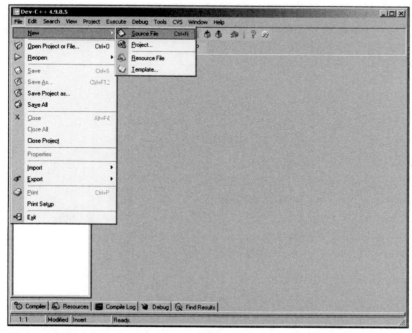

Figure 2.15 Adding a new source code file to the project using the File menu.

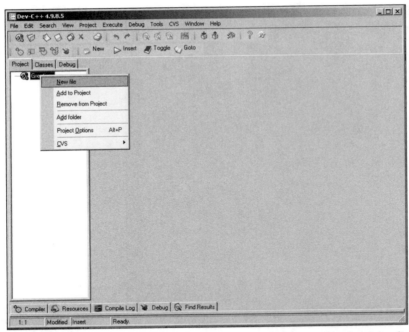

Figure 2.16 Adding a new source code file to the project using the right-click menu.

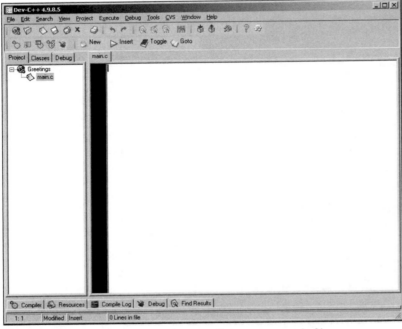

Figure 2.17 The Greetings project now has a source code file.

The Greetings Source Code

Now that you have a source code file, type in some source code to make sure Dev-C++ is configured properly. Here is a short program that you can type in:

```c
#include <conio.h>
#include <stdio.h>
int main()
{
    printf("Greetings Earthlings.\n");
    printf("All your base are belong to us!\n");
    getch();
}
```

You can compile and run the program using several methods. Note that this program doesn't require Allegro to run at this point. (I'll stick to basic C right now.) The easiest way to compile and run the program is by pressing F9. You can also click on the Compile & Run (F9) icon on the toolbar or you can open the Execute menu and select Compile & Run. While you are browsing the toolbar and menus, note some of the other options available, such as Compile, Run, and Rebuild All. These options are occasionally helpful, although the compiler is so fast that I typically just hit F9. Because this is not an introductory book on C programming and I assume you have some experience writing C programs, I won't get into the basics of debugging and correcting syntax errors.

However, there is one thing that might prevent this program from running. If you look at the code listing, you'll notice that it doesn't include any header files and it is about as simple as things can get for a C program. This program assumes that it will be run on a console (such as a DOS prompt or shell prompt). Therefore, the project must be configured as a console project. The terminology will differ based on your OS, but for Windows the two most common project types are Windows Application and Console Application. Open the Project menu and select Project Options. The Project Options dialog box will appear, as shown in Figure 2.18.

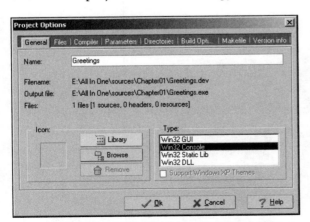

Figure 2.18 The Project Options dialog box is where you can change the project settings.

Pay special attention to the list of project types and make sure that Win32 Console is selected. (This should have been the default when you created a new blank project; however, future versions of Dev-C++ may change the default option or any other feature deemed necessary to improve the IDE.) If Win32 Console is selected, then you are ready to run the program. Close the dialog box, and then press F9 to compile and run the program.

note

Feel free to open multiple instances of Dev-C++ if you are working on several C or C++ projects at the same time or if you would like to copy code from one source listing to another. Dev-C++ has a small footprint of only around 12 MB of memory, and multiple instances of it run off the first memory instance.

Running the Greetings Program

If all goes well you should see the program run as in Figure 2.19, which shows the console window superimposed over Dev-C++. As the source code indicates (note the getch() function), press a key to end the program.

If the compile process failed, first check to make sure there are no typos in the source code you entered. If the code looks good, you might want to refer back to the "Installing and Configuring Dev-C++ and Allegro" section to see whether you might have missed a step

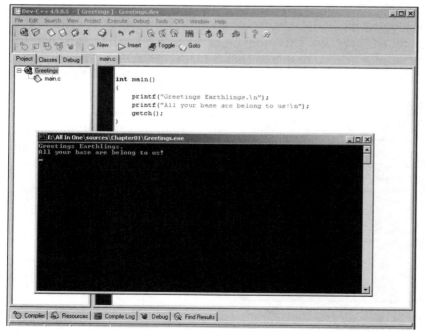

Figure 2.19 The *Greetings* program is running in a console window.

that is preventing the compiler from running as it should. The install process is fairly simple and straightforward (ignoring the update process, at any rate), so if you continue to have problems, you might seek help at the Dev-C++ Web site at http://www.bloodshed.net/devcpp.html. A program this simple should compile and run without any problem, so any error at this point is an installation problem if anything.

Testing Allegro: The GetInfo Program

Now you should give Allegro a spin and make sure it was compiled and installed correctly. The next program you'll write will be similar to the last one because it will be a console program. The difference is that this program will include the Allegro library. Go ahead and open a new instance of Dev-C++ (or close the current project). Open the File menu and select New, Project as before. This time, however, instead of creating an empty project, select Console Application (see Figure 2.20). For the project name, type **GetInfo**.

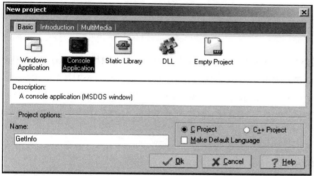

When the new project is created, Dev-C++ will add a main.c file for you and fill it with some basic code. Delete the template code because you'll be typing in your own code.

Figure 2.20 Creating a new console application in Dev-C++

Introducing Some of Allegro's Features

The first function that you need to know is allegro_init, which has this syntax:

```
int allegro_init();
```

This function is required because it initializes the Allegro library. If you do not call this function, the program will probably crash (at worst) or simply not work (at best). In addition to initializing the library, allegro_init also fills a number of global string and number variables that you can use to display information about Allegro. One such variable is a string called allegro_id; it is declared like this:

```
extern char allegro_id[];
```

You can use allegro_id to display the version number for the Allegro library you have installed. That is a good way to check whether Allegro has been installed correctly, so you should write some code to display allegro_id. Referring to the *GetInfo* project you just created, type in the following code:

```
#include <conio.h>
#include <stdlib.h>
#include "allegro.h"

int main()
{
        allegro_init();
        printf("Allegro version = %s\n", allegro_id);
        printf("\nPress any key...\n");
        getch();
        return 0;
}
END_OF_MAIN();
```

You are probably wondering what the heck that END_OF_MAIN function at the bottom of the source listing is. This is actually a macro that is used by Allegro and helps with the multiplatform nature of the library. This is odd, but the macro simply must follow the main function in every program that uses Allegro. You'll get used to it (and quickly begin to ignore it after a while).

Including the Allegro Library File

One more thing. Before you can run the program, you must add the Allegro library file to the *GetInfo* project. The library file is called liballeg.a and can be found in the \allegro\lib folder. (Depending on where you installed it, that might be C:\allegro\lib.) To add the library file, open the Project menu and select Project Options. There are a number of tabs in the Project Options dialog box. Locate the Parameters tab, which is shown in Figure 2.21.

You now want to add an entry into the third column (labeled Linker) so the Allegro library file will be linked into the executable program. You can type in the path and filename directly or you can click on the Add Library or Object button to search for the file. Navigate to your root Allegro folder and look inside a folder called lib.

If you installed Allegro using the Dev-C++ WebUpdate or by installing the DevPak off the CD-ROM, then Allegro will be installed to C:\Dev-Cpp\Allegro by default. If you are at all confused about this issue, then I recommend you visit Appendix F to get a better feel for how Allegro and Dev-C++ work together.

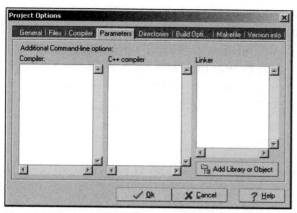

Figure 2.21 The Parameters tab in the Project
Options dialog box

You should see eight compiler-specific folders inside lib:

- bcc32
- beos
- djgpp
- mingw32
- msvc
- qnx
- unix
- watcom

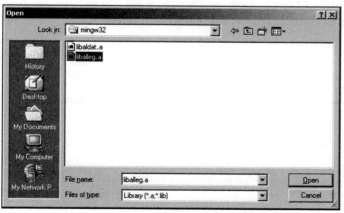

As you might recall from the "Installing and Configuring Dev-C++ and Allegro" section, the version you want to use for Windows is mingw32, so go ahead and open that folder. If you have compiled Allegro for mingw32 you should see two files inside— libaldat.a and liballeg.a (see Figure 2.22).

Figure 2.22 Locating the liballeg.a library file for Allegro

Select the liballeg.a file and click on Open to load the path name for the file into the Linker list. If you look at the path name that was inserted, you'll notice that it includes a lot of folder redirection (../../../../allegro/lib/mingw32/liballeg.a). This will probably look different on your system due to where you saved the project file. (Mine is stored several folders deep in the source code folder.) For future reference, note that you only need to refer to the absolute path name for liballeg.a (or any other library file). Therefore, you can edit the Linker text so it looks like this:

```
/allegro/lib/mingw32/liballeg.a
```

The result should look like Figure 2.23.

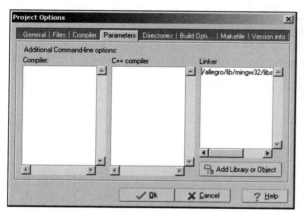

Figure 2.23 You can also type the path name to a library file directly into the Linker list.

Before you get too comfortable with this plan, let me give you a heads up on an even easier way to include the Allegro library! Regardless of whether you installed Allegro.DevPak or compiled the Allegro source code, the liballeg.a file will be installed at \Dev-Cpp\lib. So you really don't need to reference the file in \allegro\lib directly. Referring back to Figure 2.23, you can substitute the path to liballeg.a with a simple linker command (-lalleg) and that will suffice! I will remind you how to set up the projects as we go along, using both methods. This chapter is really thorough in these explanations because future chapters will skim over these details. If you ever have trouble configuring a new project for Allegro, this is the chapter you will want to refer back to as a reference.

tip

If you are using Visual C++, you will want to reference alleg.lib (and no other library files) in the linker options field. See Appendix E for details.

Running the GetInfo Program

If you haven't already, press F9 to compile and run the program. If all goes well, you should be rewarded with a console window that looks like the one in Figure 2.24. If you have problems running the program, aside from syntax errors due to typos you might want to double-check that you have the correct path to the liballeg.a library file.

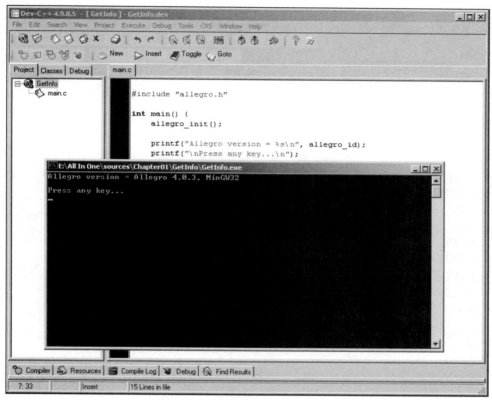

Figure 2.24 The *GetInfo* program displays information about the Allegro library.

Adding to the GetInfo Program

Now you can add some more functionality to the *GetInfo* program to explore more of the functions available with Allegro. First, let me introduce you to a variable called os_type, which has this declaration:

```
extern int os_type;
```

This variable returns a value for the operating system that Allegro detected, and may be one of the values listed in Table 2.1.

To display the operating system name, you'll need to use the switch statement to determine which OS it is. This would be easier using a string array, but unfortunately the list might not be in consecutive order within Allegro, so it is safer to use a switch. Add the following function above the int main() line:

Table 2.1 Operating Systems Recognized by Allegro

Identifier	Description
OSTYPE_UNKNOWN	Unknown (may be MS-DOS)
OSTYPE_WIN3	Windows 3.1 or earlier
OSTYPE_WIN95	Windows 95
OSTYPE_WIN98	Windows 98
OSTYPE_WINME	Windows Me
OSTYPE_WINNT	Windows NT
OSTYPE_WIN2000	Windows 2000
OSTYPE_WINXP	Windows XP
OSTYPE_OS2	OS/2
OSTYPE_WARP	OS/2 Warp 3
OSTYPE_DOSEMU	Linux DOSEMU
OSTYPE_OPENDOS	Caldera OpenDOS
OSTYPE_LINUX	Linux
OSTYPE_FREEBSD	FreeBSD
OSTYPE_QNX	QNX
OSTYPE_UNIX	UNIX variant
OSTYPE_BEOS	BeOS
OSTYPE_MACOS	Mac OS

```
char *OSName(int number)
{
    switch (number)
    {
        case OSTYPE_UNKNOWN: return "Unknown or MS-DOS";
        case OSTYPE_WIN3:    return "Windows";
        case OSTYPE_WIN95:   return "Windows 95";
        case OSTYPE_WIN98:   return "Windows 98";
        case OSTYPE_WINME:   return "Windows ME";
        case OSTYPE_WINNT:   return "Windows NT";
        case OSTYPE_WIN2000: return "Windows 2000";
        case OSTYPE_WINXP:   return "Windows XP";
        case OSTYPE_OS2:     return "OS/2";
        case OSTYPE_WARP:    return "OS/2 Warp 3";
        case OSTYPE_DOSEMU:  return "Linux DOSEMU";
        case OSTYPE_OPENDOS: return "Caldera OpenDOS";
        case OSTYPE_LINUX:   return "Linux";
        case OSTYPE_FREEBSD: return "FreeBSD";
```

```
         case OSTYPE_QNX:      return "QNX";
         case OSTYPE_UNIX:     return "Unix variant";
         case OSTYPE_BEOS:     return "BeOS";
         case OSTYPE_MACOS:    return "MacOS";
    }
}
```

Now you can modify the main routine to display the name of the operating system. Add the following line of code following the first printf line:

```
printf("Operating system = %s\n", OSName(os_type));
```

When you run the program (F9), you should see a console window with output that looks like the following lines. (Note that your operating system should be displayed if you are not running Windows 2000.)

```
Allegro version  = Allegro 4.0.3, MinGW32
Operating system = Windows 2000

Press any key...
```

Now you can use a few more of Allegro's very useful global variables to retrieve the operating system version, desktop resolution, multitasking flag, color depth, and some details about the processor. Since you are already raring to go, I'll just list the definitions for these functions and variables, and then you can add them to the *GetInfo* program. (Remember that none of these variables and functions will work unless you have called allegro_init() first.)

```
extern int os_version;
extern int os_revision;
extern int os_multitasking;
int desktop_color_depth();
int get_desktop_resolution(int *width, int *height);
extern char cpu_vendor[];
extern int cpu_family;
extern int cpu_model;
extern int cpu_capabilities;
```

The first three variables provide information about the operating system version, revision, and whether it is multitasking. The following lines of code will display those values:

```
printf("OS version       = %i.%i\n", os_version, os_revision);
printf("Multitasking     = %s\n", YesNo(os_multitasking));
```

I wrote a short function called YesNo() to display the appropriate word (yes = 1, no = 0); this function should be typed in above int main():

```
char *YesNo(int number)
{
    if (number==0)
        return "No";
    else
        return "Yes";
}
```

Next are the desktop resolution and color depth values, which you can add to the program with the following lines:

```
int width, height;
get_desktop_resolution(&width, &height);
printf("Desktop resolution = %i x %i\n", width, height);
printf("Color depth        = %i bits\n", desktop_color_depth());
```

Notice how you must pass the width and height variables to get_desktop_resolution()? The variables are passed by reference to this function so you can then use the variables to display the desktop resolution. Color depth is a direct function call.

Next come the functions associated with the processor. I don't know about you, but I personally find this information very interesting. You could use these values to directly affect how a game runs by enabling or disabling certain features based on system specifications. When it comes to a multi-platform library, this can be essential because there are many older PCs running Linux and other OSs that perform well on older hardware (whereas Windows typically puts a high demand on resources). Here are the processor-specific variables and functions:

```
extern char cpu_vendor[];
extern int cpu_family;
extern int cpu_model;
extern int cpu_capabilities;
```

The first three variables are easy enough to read, although they are manufacturer-specific values. For instance, a cpu_family value of 6 indicates a Pentium Pro for the Intel platform, while it refers to an Athlon for the AMD platform. The cpu_capabilities variable is a little more complicated because it contains packed values specifying the special features of the processor. Table 2.2 presents a rundown of those capabilities.

I have always enjoyed system decoding programs like this one, so it is great that this is built into Allegro. To decode the cpu_capabilities variable, you can AND one of the identifiers with cpu_capabilities to see whether it is available. If the AND operation equals the identifier value, then you know that identifier has been bit-packed into cpu_capabilities. Here is the code to display these capabilities. (Note that spacing is not critical—I just wanted all of the equal signs to line up.)

Table 2.2 Processor Features Identified by Allegro

Identifier	Description
CPU_ID	cpuid is available.
CPU_FPU	x87 FPU is available.
CPU_MMX	MMX is available.
CPU_MMXPLUS	MMX+ is available.
CPU_SSE	SSE is available.
CPU_SSE2	SSE2 is available.
CPU_3DNOW	3DNow! is available.
CPU_ENH3DNOW	Enhanced 3DNow! is available.

```
int caps = cpu_capabilities;
printf("Processor ID             = %s\n",
    YesNo((caps & CPU_ID)==CPU_ID));
printf("x87 FPU                  = %s\n",
    YesNo((caps & CPU_FPU)==CPU_FPU));
printf("MMX                      = %s\n",
    YesNo((caps & CPU_MMX)==CPU_MMX));
printf("MMX+                     = %s\n",
    YesNo((caps & CPU_MMXPLUS)==CPU_MMXPLUS));
printf("SSE                      = %s\n",
    YesNo((caps & CPU_SSE)==CPU_SSE));
printf("SSE2                     = %s\n",
    YesNo((caps & CPU_SSE2)==CPU_SSE2));
printf("3DNOW                    = %s\n",
    YesNo((caps & CPU_3DNOW)==CPU_3DNOW));
printf("Enhanced 3DNOW           = %s\n",
    YesNo((caps & CPU_ENH3DNOW)==CPU_ENH3DNOW));
```

For reference, here is the complete listing for the main function of *GetInfo*, with some additional comments to clarify what each section of code is doing.

```
int main() {
    //initialize Allegro
    allegro_init();

    //display version info
    printf("Allegro version   = %s\n", allegro_id);
    printf("Operating system  = %s\n", OSName(os_type));
```

```
        printf("OS version          = %i.%i\n", os_version, os_revision);
        printf("Multitasking        = %s\n", YesNo(os_multitasking));

        //display system info
        int width, height;
        get_desktop_resolution(&width, &height);
        printf("Desktop resolution = %i x %i\n", width, height);
        printf("Color depth        = %i bits\n", desktop_color_depth());
        printf("Processor vendor   = %s\n", cpu_vendor);
        printf("Processor family   = %i\n", cpu_family);
        printf("Processor model    = %i\n", cpu_model);

        //display processor capabilities
        int caps = cpu_capabilities;
        printf("Processor ID       = %s\n",
            YesNo((caps & CPU_ID)==CPU_ID));
        printf("x87 FPU            = %s\n",
            YesNo((caps & CPU_FPU)==CPU_FPU));
        printf("MMX                = %s\n",
            YesNo((caps & CPU_MMX)==CPU_MMX));
        printf("MMX+               = %s\n",
            YesNo((caps & CPU_MMXPLUS)==CPU_MMXPLUS));
        printf("SSE                = %s\n",
            YesNo((caps & CPU_SSE)==CPU_SSE));
        printf("SSE2               = %s\n",
            YesNo((caps & CPU_SSE2)==CPU_SSE2));
        printf("3DNOW              = %s\n",
            YesNo((caps & CPU_3DNOW)==CPU_3DNOW));
        printf("Enhanced 3DNOW     = %s\n",
            YesNo((caps & CPU_ENH3DNOW)==CPU_ENH3DNOW));

        printf("\nPress any key...\n");
        getch();
        return 0;
}
```

Running the program now produces the following results. (Note that it will reflect the hardware in your own system.)

```
Allegro version    = Allegro 4.0.3, MinGW32
Operating system   = Windows 2000
OS version         = 5.0
```

```
Multitasking          = Yes
Desktop resolution    = 1280 x 1024
Color depth           = 32 bits
Processor vendor      = AuthenticAMD
Processor family      = 6
Processor model       = 4
Processor ID          = Yes
x87 FPU               = Yes
MMX                   = Yes
MMX+                  = Yes
SSE                   = No
SSE2                  = No
3DNOW                 = Yes
Enhanced 3DNOW        = Yes

Press any key...
```

Gaining More Experience with Allegro

Now that you have learned how to set up the compiler to use Allegro by manually adding the library file to the project, I will show you the easy way to do it! I believe it's always best to know how to set up a project first, but the Allegro.DevPak includes two project templates you can use, so it's a cinch to create a new Allegro project and get started writing code without having to go into the Project Options at all.

I mention this after the fact because a default installation of Dev-C++ and Allegro does not include these Allegro project templates. Only after you install Allegro via WebUpdate will you find these templates installed (which is one good reason for using the WebUpdate tool).

The only drawback to using these Allegro project templates is that they are specifically limited to C++ code, not C (which is mainly what this book focuses on). That is not a limitation really, because you can still write straight C code and it won't make any difference (due to the way C++ headers are handled in the project template). However, you can feel free to write C or C++ code as you wish, so this might be a better solution than limiting the project to C by default.

The Hello World Demo

Now let's see how easy it is to create a new Allegro project. Fire up Dev-C++ and open the File menu. Select New, Project and click on the MultiMedia tab, and you should see three project types—Allegro (DLL), Allegro (Static), and OpenGL—as shown in Figure 2.25.

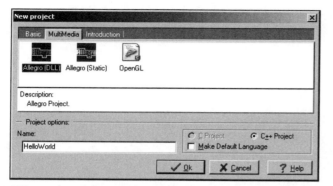

Select the Allegro (DLL) project template, type a new name for the project, and click on OK. A new project will be created in Dev-C++, and you will be asked to choose a location for the project file. After the project has been created, you should see the sample source code shown in Figure 2.26.

Figure 2.25 Creating a new Allegro (DLL) project in Dev-C++

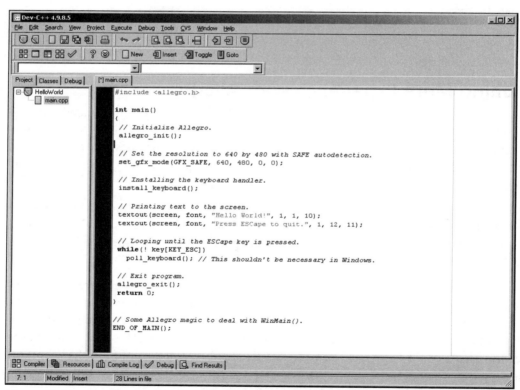

Figure 2.26 The new Allegro (DLL) project has been created from the template.

If you run the program by pressing F9, you should see the program run full-screen with the message "Hello World" displayed (see Figure 2.27).

Hello World!
Press ESCape to quit.

Figure 2.27 The *HelloWorld* program runs in full-screen 640×480 mode.

This is a fully-functional Allegro program that didn't require any configuration. If you are using a Windows system, Allegro automatically supports DirectX and takes advantage of hardware acceleration with DirectDraw. On other platforms (such as Linux), Allegro will use whatever library has been compiled with it to make the most out of that platform (in other words, the DirectX equivalent on each system).

If for any reason you are not able to run the program as shown, go back to the "Installing Allegro" section to make sure it is installed correctly.

Allegro Sample Programs

Allegro comes with a large number of sample programs that demonstrate all of the various features of the library. If you installed Allegro as described in this chapter using the DevPak, you will find these sample programs in the main Dev-Cpp folder on your hard drive. Assuming you have installed it at C:\Dev-Cpp, the example programs are located in C:\Dev-Cpp\Examples\Allegro.

Before you can run an individual C source program in Dev-C++, you need to copy it into an existing project that has been configured with the Allegro library. Otherwise, the compiler will complain that one or more Allegro functions could not be found. The easiest way to do this is to create a new Allegro (DLL) project, as you did with *HelloWorld* a few minutes ago. Then you can open one of the sample programs in Dev-C++ and paste the new code into main.c to run it. That way the project template is configured for Allegro and you can repeatedly paste sample code into main.c to see the sample programs run. The alternative is to create a separate project for each program or compile them all using a make file or by running GCC from the command line (which is probably easier than using Dev-C++, but not as convenient).

note

The Allegro sample programs are contributions from many Allegro developers and fans. They are not all guaranteed to work, especially considering that new versions of Allegro are released frequently and the examples are not always kept up to date.

For an example, take a look at the ex3buf.c example program. You can load this program from \Dev-Cpp\Examples\Allegro (assuming you have installed Dev-C++ to this folder), as shown in Figure 2.28. This program is a triple-buffer demonstration written by Shawn Hargreaves. Although it was primarily written for MS-DOS (as evidenced by the 320×200 video resolution), you can still run the program in Windows or any other system in full-screen mode.

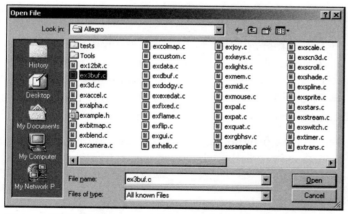

Figure 2.28 Opening one of the sample programs installed with Allegro

This is actually a very interesting program because it uses an early polygon rendering routine that was written before the 3D features were added to Allegro. You could adapt this code to produce a shaded 3D game, but that would be hard work—better to wait until I cover the 3D functionality built into Allegro first! Figure 2.29 shows the program running.

Another interesting program is called exblend.c; it is also found in \Dev-Cpp\ Examples\Allegro. This was also written by Shawn Hargreaves, and it shows an interesting alpha-blend effect that I will cover in the next chapter (see Figure 2.30).

There are many more sample programs just like these in \Dev-Cpp\Examples\Allegro that I encourage you to load and run to see some of the things that Allegro is capable of doing.

Figure 2.29 The ex3buf.c program (written by Shawn Hargreaves) is one of the many sample programs included with Allegro.

Figure 2.30 The exblend.c program shows how two bitmaps can be displayed with translucency.

These aren't full programs or games per se, but they do a good job of demonstrating simple concepts.

Summary

That sums up the introduction to Dev-C++ and Allegro. I hope that by this time you are at least familiar with the IDE and have a good understanding of how the compiler works, as well as what Allegro is capable of (with a little effort on your part). This chapter has given you few tools for building a game as of yet, but it was necessary along that path. Installing and configuring the dev tools is always a daunting task for those who are new to programming, and even experienced programmers get lost when trying to get up and running with a new IDE, compiler, and game library. Not only did you learn to configure a new IDE and open-source compiler, you also got started writing programs using an open-source game library. But now that the logistics are out of the way, you can focus on learning Allegro and writing a few sample programs in the following chapters.

Chapter Quiz

You can find the answers to this chapter quiz in Appendix A, "Chapter Quiz Answers."

1. What game features an Avatar and takes place in the land of Brittania?
    A. *Baldur's Gate: Dark Alliance*
    B. *Ultima VII: The Black Gate*
    C. *The Elder Scrolls III: Morrowind*
    D. *Wizardry 8*

2. GNU is an acronym for which of the following phrases?
    A. GNU is Not UNIX
    B. Great Northern University
    C. Central Processing Unit
    D. None of the above

3. What is the primary Web site for Dev-C++?
    A. http://www.microsoft.com
    B. http://www.bloodshed.net
    C. http://www.borland.com
    D. http://www.fsf.org

4. What is the name of the compiler used by Dev-Pascal?
    A. GNU Pascal
    B. Turbo Pascal
    C. Object Pascal
    D. Microsoft Pascal

5. What is the name of the powerful automated update utility for Dev-C++?

   A.   DevUpdate

   B.   AutoUpdate

   C.   Windows Update

   D.   WebUpdate

6. What are the Dev-C++ update packages called?

   A.   DevPacks

   B.   DevPaks

   C.   DevPackages

   D.   DevSpanks

7. What distinctive feature of Dev-C++ sets it apart from commercial development tools?

   A.   Dev-C++ is open-source

   B.   Dev-C++ is free

   C.   Dev-C++ is multi-platform

   D.   All of the above

8. What is the name of the game programming library featured in this chapter?

   A.   DirectX

   B.   Gnome

   C.   GTK+

   D.   Allegro

9. What function must be called before you use the Allegro library?

   A.   `main()`

   B.   `byte_me()`

   C.   `allegro_init()`

   D.   `lets_get_started()`

10. What statement must be included at the end of `main()` in an Allegro program?

   A.   `END_OF_THE_WORLD()`

   B.   `END_OF_MAIN()`

   C.   `END_OF_FREEDOM()`

   D.   `AH_DONUTS()`

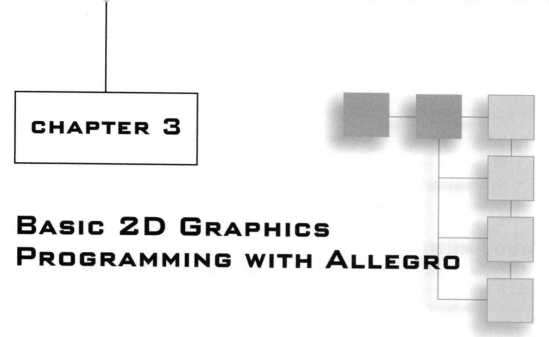

CHAPTER 3

BASIC 2D GRAPHICS
PROGRAMMING WITH ALLEGRO

This hands-on chapter introduces you to the powerful graphics features built into Allegro. In the early years of personal computers, at a time when 3D accelerators with 256 MB of DDR memory were inconceivable, vector graphics provided a solid solution to the underpowered PC. For most games, a scrolling background was not even remotely possible due to the painfully slow performance of the early IBM PC. While competing systems from Atari, Amiga, Commodore, Apple, and others provided some of the best gaming available at the time with performance that would not be matched in consoles for many years, these PCs fell to the wayside as the IBM PC (and its many clone manufacturers) gained market dominance—not without the help of Microsoft and Intel. It is a shame that Apple is really the only contender that survived the personal computer revolution of the 1980s and 1990s, but it was mainly that crucible that launched gaming forward with such force.

This chapter is somewhat a lesson in progressive programming, starting with basic concepts that grow in complexity over time. Because we are pushing the 2D envelope to the limit throughout this book, it is fitting that we should start at the beginning and cover vector graphics. The term *vector* describes the CRT (*Cathode Ray Tube)* monitors of the past and the vector graphics hardware built into the computers that used this early technology.

A more descriptive term for the subject of this chapter would be "programming graphics primitives." A *graphics primitive* is a function that draws a simple geometric shape, such as a point, line, rectangle, or circle. This chapter covers the graphics primitives built into Allegro with complete sample programs for each function so you will have a solid understanding of how these functions work. I should point out also that these graphics primitives form the basis of all 3D graphics, past and present; after all, the mantra of the 3D card is the holy polygon. But above all, I want you to have some fun with this chapter.

Whether you are a skilled programmer or a beginner, try to have some fun in everything you do. I believe even an old hand will find something of interest in this chapter.

Here is a breakdown of the major topics in this chapter:

- Understanding graphics fundamentals
- Drawing graphics primitives
- Printing text on the screen

Introduction

I don't know about you, but I was drawn to graphics programming before I became interested in actually writing games. The subject of computer graphics is absolutely fascinating and is at the forefront of computer technology. The high-end graphics accelerator cards featuring graphics processors with high-speed video memory, such as the NVIDIA GeForce FX and ATI Radeon 9800, are built specifically to render graphics insanely fast. The silicon is not designed merely to satisfy a marketing initiative or to best the competition (although that would seem to be the case). The graphics chips are designed to render graphics with great efficiency using hardware-accelerated functions that were once calculated in software. I emphasize the word "graphics" because we often take it for granted after hearing it used so often. Figure 3.1 shows a typical monitor.

The fact of the matter is that video cards are not designed to render games; they are designed to render geometric primitives with special effects. As far as the video card is concerned, there is only one triangle on the screen. It is the programmer who tells the video card to move from one triangle to the next. The video card does this so quickly (on the order of 100 million or more polygons per second) that it fools the viewer into believing that the video card is rendering an entire scene on its own. The triangles are hidden away in the matrix of the scene (so to speak), and it is becoming more and more difficult to discern reality from virtual reality due to the advanced features built into the latest graphics chips (see Figure 3.2).

Figure 3.1 A typical monitor displays whatever it is sent by the video card.

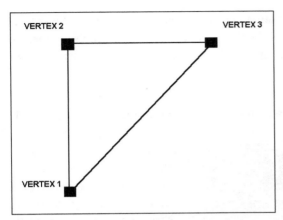

Figure 3.2 A typical 3D accelerator card sees only one triangle at a time.

Taken a step closer, one would notice that each triangle is made up of three points, or *vertices*, which is really all the graphics chip cares about. Filling pixels between the three points and applying varying effects (such as lighting) are tasks that the graphics chip has been designed to do quickly and efficiently.

Years ago, when a new video card was produced, the manufacturer would hire a programmer to write the device driver software for the new hardware, usually for Windows and Linux. That device driver was required to provide a specific set of common functions to the operating system for the new video card to work correctly. The early graphics chips were very immature (so to speak); they were only willing to switch video modes and provide access to the video memory (or frame buffer), usually in banks—another issue of immaturity. As graphics chips improved, silicon designers began to incorporate some of the software's functionality right into the silicon, resulting in huge speed increases (orders of greater magnitude) over functions that had previously existed only in software.

The earliest *Windows accelerators*, as they were known, produced for Windows 3.1 and Windows 95 provided hardware blitting. *Blit* is a term that means bit-block transfer, a method of transferring a chunk of memory from one place to another. In the case of a graphical blit, the process involves copying a chunk of data from system memory through the bus to the memory present on the video card. In the early years of the PC, video cards were lucky to have 1 MB of memory. My first VGA card had 256 KB (see Figure 3.3)!

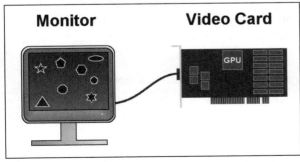

Figure 3.3 The modern video card has taken over the duties of the software driver.

Contrast this with the latest 3D cards that have 256 MB of DDR (*Double Data Rate*) memory and are enhanced with direct access to the AGP bus! The latest DDR memory at the time of this writing is PC-4000, also called DDR-500. This type of memory comes on a 184-pin socket with a throughput of 4 gigabytes per second. Although the latest video cards don't use this type of high-speed memory yet, they are close, using DDR-333. The point is, this is insanely fast memory! It simply must be as fast as possible to keep feeding the ravenous graphics chip, which eats textures in video memory and spews them out into the frame buffer, which is sent directly to the screen (see Figure 3.4).

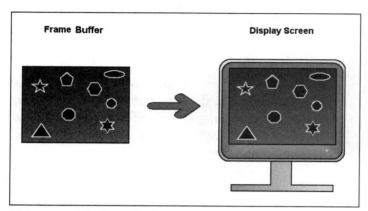

Figure 3.4 The frame buffer, located in video memory, is transferred directly to the screen.

In a very real sense, the graphics card is a small computer on its own. When you consider that the typical high-end PC also has a high-performance sound processing card (such as the Sound Blaster Audigy 2 by Creative Labs) capable of Dolby DTS and Dolby Digital 5.1 surround sound, what we are really talking about here is a multiprocessor system. If your first impression is to scoff at the idea or shrug it off like an old joke, think about it again. The typical $200 graphics card or sound card has more processing power than a Cray supercomputer had in the mid-1980s. Considering that a gaming rig has these two major subsystems in addition to an insanely fast central processor, is it unfounded to say that such a PC is a three-processor system? All three chips are sharing the bus and main memory and are running in parallel. The difference between this setup and a symmetric multiprocessing system (SMP) is that an SMP divides a single task between two or more processors, while the CPU, graphics chip, and sound chip work on different sets of data. The case made in this respect is valid, I think. If you want to put forth the argument that the motherboard chipset and memory controller are also processors, I would point out that these are logistical chips with a single task of providing low-level system communication. But consider a high-speed 3D game featuring multiplayer networking, advanced 3D rendering, and surround sound. This is a piece of software that uses multiple processors unlike any business application or Web browser.

This short overview of computer graphics was interesting, but how does the information translate to writing a game? Read on....

Graphics Fundamentals

The basis of this entire chapter can be summarized in a single word: pixel. The word *pixel* is short for "picture element," sort of the atomic element of the screen. The pixel is the smallest unit of measurement in a video system. But like the atom you know from physics, even the smallest building block is comprised of yet smaller things. In the case of a pixel, those quantum elements of the pixel are red, green, and blue electron streams that give each pixel a specific color. This is not mere theory or analogy; each pixel is comprised of three small streams of electrons of varying shades of red, green, and blue (see Figure 3.5).

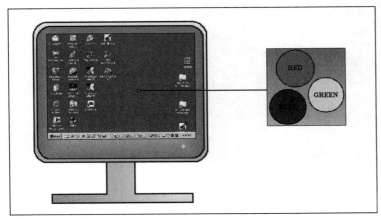

Figure 3.5 The pixel is the smallest unit of measurement in a video system.

Starting with this most basic building block, you can construct an entire game one pixel at a time (something you will do in the next chapter). Allegro creates a global screen pointer when you call allegro_init. This simple pointer is called screen, and you can pass it to all of the drawing functions in this chapter. A technique called *double-buffering* (which uses offscreen rendering for speed) works like this: Drawing routines must draw out to a memory bitmap, which is then blitted to the screen in a single function call. Until you start using a double-buffer, you'll just work with the global screen object.

The InitGraphics Program

As you saw in the last chapter, Allegro is useful even in a text-based console, such as the command prompt in Windows (or a shell in Linux). But there is only so much you can do with a character-based video mode. You could fire up one of the two dozen or so text adventure games from the 1970s and 1980s. (*Zork* comes to mind.) But let's get started on the really useful stuff and stop fooling around with text mode, shall we? I have written a program called *InitGraphics* that simply shows how to initialize a full-screen video mode or window of a particular resolution. Figure 3.6 shows the program running.

The first function you'll learn about in this chapter is set_gfx_mode, which sets the graphics mode (or what I prefer to call "video mode"). This function is really loaded, although you would not know that just from calling it. What I mean is that set_gfx_mode does a lot of work when called—detecting the graphics card, identifying and initializing the graphics

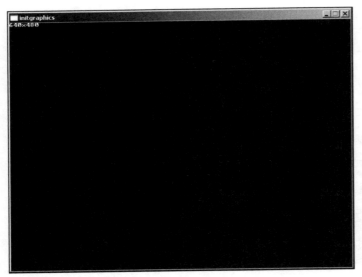

Figure 3.6 The *InitGraphics* program

system, verifying or setting the color depth, entering full-screen or windowed mode, and setting the resolution. As you can see, it does a lot of work for you! A comparable DirectX initialization is 20 to 30 lines of code. This function has the following declaration:

```
int set_gfx_mode(int card, int w, int h, int v_w, int v_h);
```

If an error occurs setting a particular video mode, set_gfx_mode will return a non-zero value (where a return value of zero means success) and store an error message in allegro_error, which you can then print out. For an example, try using an invalid resolution for a full-screen display, like this:

```
ret = set_gfx_mode(GFX_AUTODETECT_FULLSCREEN, 645, 485, 0, 0);
```

However, if you specify GFX_AUTODETECT and send an invalid width and height to set_gfx_mode, it will actually run in a window with the resolution you wanted! Running in windowed mode is a good idea when you are testing a game and you don't want it to jump into and out of full-screen mode every time you run the program.

The first parameter, int card, specifies the display mode (or the video card in a dual-card configuration) and will usually be GFX_AUTODETECT. If you want a full-screen display, you can use GFX_AUTODETECT_FULLSCREEN, while you can invoke a windowed display using GFX_AUTODETECT _WINDOWED. Both modes work equally well, but I find it easier to use windowed mode for demonstration purposes. A window is easier to handle when you are editing code, and some video cards really don't handle mode changes well. Depending on the quality of a video card, it can take several seconds to switch from full-screen back to the Windows desktop, but a windowed program does not have this problem.

The next two parameters, int w and int h, specify the desired resolution, such as 640×480, 800×600, or 1024×768. To maintain compatibility with as many systems as possible, I am using 640×480 for most of the sample programs in this book (with a few exceptions where demonstration is needed).

The final two parameters, int v_w and int v_h, specify the virtual resolution and are used to create a large virtual screen for hardware scrolling or page flipping.

After you have called set_gfx_mode to change the video mode, Allegro populates the variables SCREEN_W, SCREEN_H, VIRTUAL_W, and VIRTUAL_H with the appropriate values, which come in handy when you prefer not to hard-code the screen resolution in your programs.

The *InitGraphics* program source code listing follows. Several new functions in this program are included for convenience; I will go over them shortly.

```c
#include <conio.h>
#include <stdlib.h>
#include "allegro.h"

void main(void)
{
    //initialize Allegro
    allegro_init();

    //initialize the keyboard
    install_keyboard();

    //initialize video mode to 640x480
    int ret = set_gfx_mode(GFX_AUTODETECT_WINDOWED, 640, 480, 0, 0);
    if (ret != 0) {
        allegro_message(allegro_error);
        return;
    }

    //display screen resolution
    textprintf(screen, font, 0, 0, makecol(255, 255, 255),
        "%dx%d", SCREEN_W, SCREEN_H);

    //wait for keypress
    while(!key[KEY_ESC]);

    //end program
    allegro_exit();
}

END_OF_MAIN();
```

In addition to the set_gfx_mode function, there are several more Allegro functions in this program that you probably noticed. Although they are self-explanatory, I will give you a brief overview of them.

The allegro_message function is handy when you want to display an error message in a pop-up dialog box (also called a *message box*). Usually you will not want to use this function in production code, although it is helpful when you are debugging (when you will want to run your program in windowed mode rather than full-screen mode). Note that some operating systems will simply output an allegro_message response to the console. It is fairly common to get stuck debugging a part of any game, especially when it has grown to a fair size and the source code has gotten rather long, so this function might prove handy.

You might also have noticed a variable called allegro_error in this program. This is one of the global variables created by Allegro when allegro_init is called, and it is populated with a string whenever an error occurs within Allegro. As a case in point for *not* using pop-ups, Allegro will not display any error messages. It's your job to deal with errors the way you see fit.

Another interesting function is textprintf, which, as you might have guessed, displays a message in any video mode. I will be going over all of the text output functions later in this chapter, but for now it is helpful to note how this one is called. Because this is one of the more complex functions, here is the declaration:

```
void textprintf(BITMAP *bmp, const FONT *f, int x, y, color,
        const char *fmt, ...);
```

The first parameter specifies the destination, which can be the physical display screen or a memory bitmap. The next parameter specifies the font to be used for output. The x and y parameters specify where the text should be drawn on the screen, while color denotes the color used for the text. The last parameter is a string containing the text to display along with formatting information that is comparable to the formatting in the standard printf function (for instance, %s for string, %i for integer, and so on).

You might have noticed a function called makecol within the textprintf code line. This function creates an RGB color using the component colors passed to it. However, Allegro also specifies 16 default colors you can use, which is a real convenience for simple text output needs. If you want to define custom colors beyond these mere 16 default colors, you can create your own colors like this:

```
#define COLOR_BROWN makecol(174,123,0)
```

This is but one out of 16 million possible colors in a 32-bit graphics system. Table 3.1 displays the colors pre-defined for your use.

The last function that you should be aware of is `allegro_exit`, which shuts down the graphics system and destroys the memory used by Allegro. In theory, the destructors will take care of removing everything from memory, but it's a good idea to call this function explicitly. One very important reason why is for the benefit of restoring the video display. (Failure to call `allegro_exit` might leave the desktop in an altered resolution or color depth depending on the graphics card being used.)

All of the functions and variables presented in this program will become familiar to you in time because they are frequently used in the example programs in this book.

Table 3.1 Standard Colors for Allegro Graphics (8-Bit Only)

Color #	Color Name
0	Black
1	Dark Blue
2	Dark Green
3	Dark Cyan
4	Dark Red
5	Dark Magenta
6	Orange
7	Gray
8	Dark Gray
9	Blue
10	Green
11	Cyan
12	Red
13	Magenta
14	Yellow
15	White

The DrawBitmap Program

Now that you have an idea of how to initialize one of the graphics modes available in Allegro, you have the ability to draw on the screen (or in the main window of your program). But before I delve into some of the graphics primitives built into Allegro, I want to show you a simple program that loads a bitmap file (the supported formats are BMP, PCX, TGA, and LBM) and draws it to the screen using a method called *bit-block transfer* (or *blit*, for short). This program will be a helpful introduction to the functions for initializing the graphics system—setting the video mode, color depth, and so on.

While I'm holding off on bitmap and sprite programming for the next two chapters, I believe you will appreciate the simplicity of this program, shown in Figure 3.7. It is always a significant first step to writing a game when you are able to load and display a bitmap image on the screen because that is the basis for sprite-based games. First, create a new project so you can get started on the first of many exciting projects in the graphical realm.

Fire up Dev-C++, open the File menu, and select New, Project. Click on the MultiMedia tab. If you have installed the Allegro DevPak as described in Chapter 2, you should see two Allegro project templates—Allegro (DLL) and Allegro (Static). Hold off on the static projects for now; you'll have plenty of time to delve into that later. For now, stick to the simple

DLL-type projects. Name this project DrawBitmap (see Figure 3.8). If you prefer, you can load the project from \sources\chapter03\DrawBitmap on the CD-ROM. After you have created the new project, you'll have a sample code listing in main.c. Delete most of that code and enter the following code in its place.

Figure 3.7 The *DrawBitmap* program

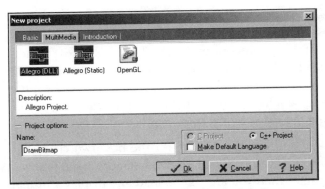

Figure 3.8 The New Project dialog box in Dev-C++

```c
#include "allegro.h"

void main(void)
{
```

```
    char *filename = "allegro.pcx";
    int colordepth = 32;
    BITMAP *image;
    int ret;

    allegro_init();
    install_keyboard();

    set_color_depth(colordepth);
    ret = set_gfx_mode(GFX_AUTODETECT_WINDOWED, 640, 480, 0, 0);
    if (ret != 0) {
        allegro_message(allegro_error);
        return;
    }

    //load the image file
    image = load_bitmap(filename, NULL);
    if (!image) {
        allegro_message("Error loading %s", filename);
        return;
    }

    //display the image
    blit(image, screen, 0, 0, 0, 0, SCREEN_W, SCREEN_H);

    //done drawing--delete bitmap from memory
    destroy_bitmap(image);

    //draw font with transparency
    text_mode(-1);

    //display video mode information
    textprintf(screen, font, 0, 0, makecol(255, 255, 255),
        "%dx%d %ibpp", SCREEN_W, SCREEN_H, colordepth);

    //wait for keypress
    while (!key[KEY_ESC]);

    //exit program
    allegro_exit();
}

END_OF_MAIN();
```

As you can see from the source code for *DrawBitmap*, the program loads a file called allegro.pcx. Obviously you'll need a PCX file to run this program. However, you can just as easily use a BMP, PNG, GIF, or JPG for the graphics file if you want because Allegro supports all of these formats! That alone is reason enough to use a game library like Allegro! Do you know what a pain it is to write loaders for these file formats yourself? Even if you find code on the Web somewhere, it is never quite satisfactory. Not only does Allegro support these file formats, it allows you to use them for storing sprites—and you can load different file formats all in the same program because Allegro does all the work for you. Feel free to substitute allegro.pcx with a file of your choosing; just be sure it has a resolution of 640×480! Allegro determines the file type from the extension and header information within the file. (Yeah, it's a pretty smart library.)

Drawing Graphics Primitives

While the first two programs in this chapter might have only whetted your appetite for graphics, this section will satisfy your hunger for more! Vector graphics are always fun, in my opinion, because you are able to see every pixel or line in a vector-based program. The term "vector" goes back to the early days of computer graphics, when primitive monitors were only able to display lines of varying sizes (where a vector represents a line segment from one point to another).

All of the graphics in a vector system are comprised of lines (including circles, rectangles, and arcs, which are made up of small lines). Vector displays are contrasted with bitmapped displays, in which the screen is a bitmap array (the video buffer). On the contrary, a vector system does not have a linear video buffer.

At any rate, that is what a vector system is as a useful comparison, but you have far more capabilities with Allegro. I always prefer to start at the beginning and work my way up into a subject of interest, and Allegro is definitely interesting. So I'm going to start with the vector-based graphics primitives built into Allegro and work up from there into bitmap- and sprite-based games in the next few chapters.

Drawing Pixels

The simplest graphics primitive is obviously the pixel-drawing function, and Allegro provides one:

```
void putpixel(BITMAP *bmp, int x, int y, int color);
```

Figure 3.9 shows the output of the *Pixels* program, which draws random pixels on the screen using whatever video mode and resolution you prefer.

```
#include <conio.h>
#include <stdlib.h>
```

Figure 3.9 The *Pixels* program fills the screen with dots. (The Linux version is shown.)

```
#include "allegro.h"

void main(void)
{
    int x,y,x1,y1,x2,y2;
    int red, green, blue, color;

    //initialize Allegro
    allegro_init();

    //initialize the keyboard
    install_keyboard();

    //initialize the random number seed
    srand(time(NULL));

    //initialize video mode to 640x480
    int ret = set_gfx_mode(GFX_AUTODETECT_WINDOWED, 640, 480, 0, 0);
    if (ret != 0) {
        allegro_message(allegro_error);
        return;
```

```
    }

    //display screen resolution
    textprintf(screen, font, 0, 0, 15,
        "Pixels Program - %dx%d - Press ESC to quit",
        SCREEN_W, SCREEN_H);

    //wait for keypress
    while(!key[KEY_ESC])
    {
        //set a random location
        x = 10 + rand() % (SCREEN_W-20);
        y = 10 + rand() % (SCREEN_H-20);

        //set a random color
        red = rand() % 255;
        green = rand() % 255;
        blue = rand() % 255;
        color = makecol(red,green,blue);

        //draw the pixel
        putpixel(screen, x, y, color);
    }

    //end program
    allegro_exit();
}
END_OF_MAIN();
```

This program should be clear to you, although it uses a C function called srand to initialize the random-number seed. This program performs a while loop continually until the ESC key is pressed, during which time a pixel of random color and location is drawn using the putpixel function.

Drawing Lines and Rectangles

The next step up from the lowly pixel is the line, and Allegro provides several line-drawing functions. To keep things as efficient as possible, Allegro divides line drawing among three functions—one for horizontal lines, one for vertical lines, and a third for every other type of line. Drawing horizontal and vertical lines can be an extremely optimized process using a simple high-speed memory copy, but non-aligned lines must be drawn using an algorithm to fill in the pixels between two points specified for the line (see Figure 3.10).

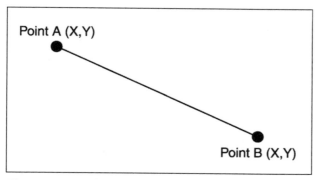

Figure 3.10 A line is comprised of pixels filled in between point A and point B.

Horizontal Lines

The horizontal line-drawing function is called `hline`:

```
void hline(BITMAP *bmp, int x1, int y, int x2, int color);
```

Because this is your first function for drawing lines, allow me to elaborate. The first parameter, `BITMAP *bmp`, is the destination bitmap for the line, which can be `screen` if you want to draw directly to the screen. The next three paramters, `int x1`, `int y`, and `int x2`, specify the two points on the single horizontal Y-axis where the line should be drawn. The *HLines* program (shown in Figure 3.11) demonstrates how to use this function.

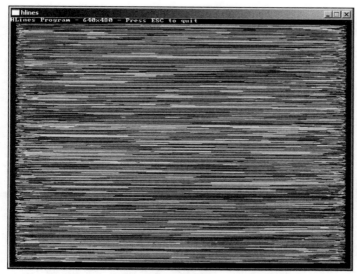

Figure 3.11 The *HLines* program draws horizontal lines.

```
#include <conio.h>
#include <stdlib.h>
#include "allegro.h"

void main(void)
{
    int x,y,x1,y1,x2,y2;
    int red,green,blue,color;

    //initialize Allegro
    allegro_init();

    //initialize the keyboard
    install_keyboard();

    //initialize random seed
    srand(time(NULL));

    //initialize video mode to 640x480
    int ret = set_gfx_mode(GFX_AUTODETECT_WINDOWED, 640, 480, 0, 0);
    if (ret != 0) {
        allegro_message(allegro_error);
        return;
    }

    //display screen resolution
    textprintf(screen, font, 0, 0, 15,
        "HLines Program - %dx%d - Press ESC to quit",
        SCREEN_W, SCREEN_H);

    //wait for keypress
    while(!key[KEY_ESC])
    {
        //set a random location
        x1 = 10 + rand() % (SCREEN_W-20);
        y = 10 + rand() % (SCREEN_H-20);
        x2 = 10 + rand() % (SCREEN_W-20);

        //set a random color
        red = rand() % 255;
        green = rand() % 255;
        blue = rand() % 255;
```

```
        color = makecol(red,green,blue);

        //draw the horizontal line
        hline(screen, x1,y,x2,color);
    }

    //end program
    allegro_exit();
}


END_OF_MAIN();
```

You have probably noticed that the *HLines* program is very similar to the *Pixels* program, with only a few lines that differ inside the while loop. I'll just show the differences from this point forward, rather than listing the entire source code for each program, because in most cases you simply need to replace a few lines inside main. It is pretty obvious that just a few lines inside the while loop need to be changed. The programs are available on the CD-ROM in complete form, but I will provide only partial listings where such changes are needed to demonstrate each of these graphics primitives.

Vertical Lines

Vertical lines are drawn with the vline function:

```
void vline(BITMAP *bmp, int x, int y1, int y2, int color);
```

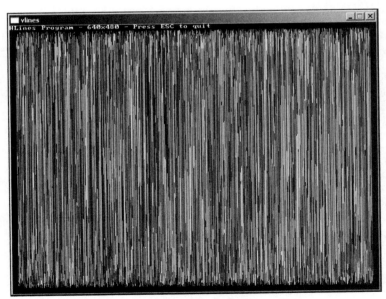

Figure 3.12 The *VLines* program draws vertical lines.

The *VLines* program (see Figure 3.12) is the same as the *HLines* program except for a single function call inside the `while` loop. Also note that this program uses a single X variable and two Y variables, `y1` and `y2`. Here is the listing:

```
//display screen resolution
textprintf(screen, font, 0, 0, 15,
    "VLines Program - %dx%d - Press ESC to quit",
    SCREEN_W, SCREEN_H);

//wait for keypress
while(!key[KEY_ESC])
{
    //set a random location
    x = 10 + rand() % (SCREEN_W-20);
    y1 = 10 + rand() % (SCREEN_H-20);
    y2 = 10 + rand() % (SCREEN_H-20);

    //set a random color
    red = rand() % 255;
    green = rand() % 255;
    blue = rand() % 255;
    color = makecol(red,green,blue);

    //draw the vertical line
    vline(screen,x,y1,y2,color);
}
```

Regular Lines

The special-case lines functions for drawing horizontal and vertical lines are not used often. The following `line` function will simply call `hline` or `vline` if the slope of the line is perfectly horizontal or vertical:

```
void line(BITMAP *bmp, int x1, int y1, int x2, int y2, int color);
```

The *Lines* program uses two complete sets of points—(x1,y1) and (x2,y2)—to draw an arbitrary line on the screen (see Figure 3.13).

```
//display screen resolution
textprintf(screen, font, 0, 0, 15,
    "Lines Program - %dx%d - Press ESC to quit",
    SCREEN_W, SCREEN_H);

//wait for keypress
while(!key[KEY_ESC])
```

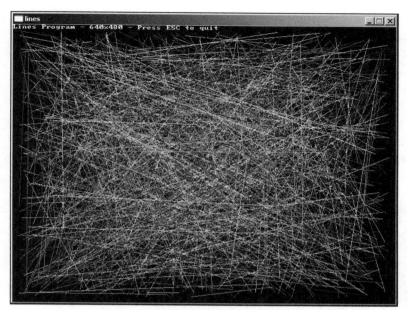

Figure 3.13 The *Lines* program draws random lines on the screen.

```
{
    //set a random location
    x1 = 10 + rand() % (SCREEN_W-20);
    y1 = 10 + rand() % (SCREEN_H-20);
    x2 = 10 + rand() % (SCREEN_W-20);
    y2 = 10 + rand() % (SCREEN_H-20);

    //set a random color
    red = rand() % 255;
    green = rand() % 255;
    blue = rand() % 255;
    color = makecol(red,green,blue);

    //draw the line
    line(screen, x1,y1,x2,y2,color);
}
```

Rectangles

Yet again there is another logical step forward in geometry that is mimicked by a primitive graphics function. While a single pixel might be thought of as a geometric point with no mass, a line is a one-dimensional object that theoretically goes off in two directions toward infinity. Fortunately for us, computer graphics engineers are not as abstract as mathematicians. The next logical step is a two-dimensional object containing points in both the X-axis and the Y-axis. Although a triangle would be the next best thing, I believe the rectangle is easier to deal with at this stage because triangles carry with them the connotation of the mighty polygon, and we aren't quite there yet. Here is the rect function:

```
void rect(BITMAP *bmp, int x1, int y1, int x2, int y2, int color);
```

As you might have guessed, a rectangle is comprised strictly of two horizontal and two vertical lines; therefore, the rect function simply calls hline and vline to render its shape (see Figure 3.14).

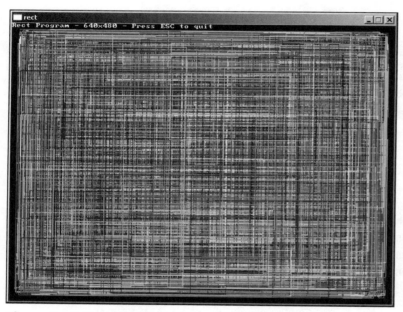

Figure 3.14 The *Rect* program draws random rectangles.

```
//display screen resolution
textprintf(screen, font, 0, 0, 15,
    "Rect Program - %dx%d - Press ESC to quit",
    SCREEN_W, SCREEN_H);

//wait for keypress
while(!key[KEY_ESC])
{
    //set a random location
    x1 = 10 + rand() % (SCREEN_W-20);
    y1 = 10 + rand() % (SCREEN_H-20);
```

```
x2 = 10 + rand() % (SCREEN_W-20);
y2 = 10 + rand() % (SCREEN_H-20);

//set a random color
red = rand() % 255;
green = rand() % 255;
blue = rand() % 255;
color = makecol(red,green,blue);

//draw the rectangle
rect(screen,x1,y1,x2,y2,color);
}
```

Filled Rectangles

Outlined rectangles are boring, if you ask me. They are almost too thin to be noticed when drawn. On the other hand, a true rectangle is filled in with a specific color! That is where the rectfill function comes in handy:

```
void rectfill(BITMAP *bmp, int x1, int y1, int x2, int y2, int color);
```

This function draws a filled rectangle, but one that otherwise has the exact same parameters as rect. Figure 3.15 shows the output from the *RectFill* program.

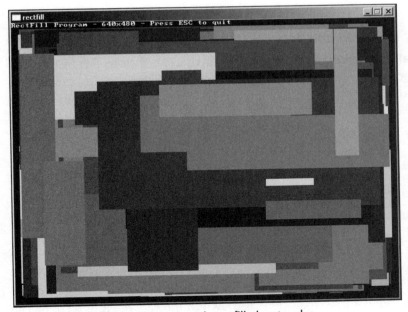

Figure 3.15 The *RectFill* program draws filled rectangles.

```
//display screen resolution
textprintf(screen, font, 0, 0, 15,
    "Rect Program - %dx%d - Press ESC to quit",
    SCREEN_W, SCREEN_H);

//wait for keypress
while(!key[KEY_ESC])
{
    //set a random location
    x1 = 10 + rand() % (SCREEN_W-20);
    y1 = 10 + rand() % (SCREEN_H-20);
    x2 = 10 + rand() % (SCREEN_W-20);
    y2 = 10 + rand() % (SCREEN_H-20);

    //set a random color
    red = rand() % 255;
    green = rand() % 255;
    blue = rand() % 255;
    color = makecol(red,green,blue);

    //draw the filled rectangle
    rectfill(screen,x1,y1,x2,y2,color);
}
```

The Line-Drawing Callback Function

Allegro provides a really fascinating feature in that it will draw an abstract line by firing off a call to a callback function of your making (in which, presumably, you would want to draw a pixel at the specified (x,y) location, although it's up to you to do what you will with the coordinate). To use the callback, you must call the do_line function, which looks like this:

```
void do_line(BITMAP *bmp, int x1, y1, x2, y2, int d, void (*proc))
```

The callback function has this format:

```
void doline_callback(BITMAP *bmp, int x, int y, int d)
```

To use the callback, you want to call the do_line function as you would call the normal line function, with the addition of the callback pointer as the last parameter. To fully demonstrate how useful this can be, I wrote a short program that draws random lines on the screen. But before drawing each pixel of the line, a check is performed on the new position to determine whether a pixel is already present. This indicates an intersection or collision. When this occurs, the line is ended and a small circle is drawn to indicate the intersection. The result is shown in Figure 3.16.

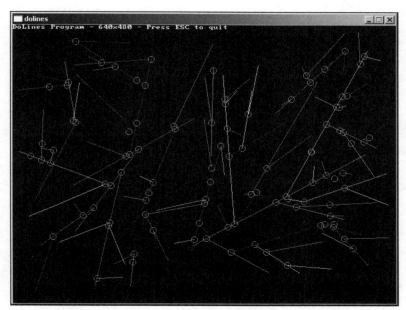

Figure 3.16 The *DoLines* program shows how to use the line-drawing callback function.

```
#include <conio.h>
#include <stdlib.h>
#include "allegro.h"

int stop = 0;

//doline is the callback function for do_line
void doline(BITMAP *bmp, int x, int y, int color)
{
    if (!stop)
    {
        if (getpixel(bmp,x,y) == 0)
        {
            putpixel(bmp, x, y, color);
            rest(5);
        }
        else
        {
            stop = 1;
            circle(bmp, x, y, 5, 7);
```

```
            }
        }
}

void main(void)
{
    int x1,y1,x2,y2;
    int red,green,blue,color;
    long n;

    //initialize Allegro
    allegro_init();

    install_timer();
    srand(time(NULL));

    //initialize the keyboard
    install_keyboard();

    //initialize video mode to 640x480
    int ret = set_gfx_mode(GFX_AUTODETECT_WINDOWED, 640, 480, 0, 0);
    if (ret != 0) {
        allegro_message(allegro_error);
        return;
    }

    //display screen resolution
    textprintf(screen, font, 0, 0, 15,
        "DoLines Program - %dx%d - Press ESC to quit",
        SCREEN_W, SCREEN_H);

    //wait for keypress
    while(!key[KEY_ESC])
    {
        //set a random location
        x1 = 10 + rand() % (SCREEN_W-20);
        y1 = 10 + rand() % (SCREEN_H-20);
        x2 = 10 + rand() % (SCREEN_W-20);
        y2 = 10 + rand() % (SCREEN_H-20);

        //set a random color
        red = rand() % 255;
```

```
        green = rand() % 255;
        blue = rand() % 255;
        color = makecol(red,green,blue);

        //draw the line using the callback function
        stop = 0;
        do_line(screen,x1,y1,x2,y2,color,*doline);

        rest(200);
    }

    //end program
    allegro_exit();
}
END_OF_MAIN();
```

Drawing Circles and Ellipses

Allegro also provides functions for drawing circles and ellipses, as you will see. The circle-drawing function is called circle, surprisingly enough. This function takes a set of parameters very similar to those you have seen already—the destination bitmap, x, y, the radius, and the color.

Circles

The circle function has this declaration:

```
void circle(BITMAP *bmp, int x, int y, int radius, int color);
```

To demonstrate, the *Circles* program draws random circles on the screen, as shown in Figure 3.17.

```
#include <conio.h>
#include <stdlib.h>
#include "allegro.h"

void main(void)
{
    int x,y,radius;
    int red,green,blue,color;

    //initialize some stuff
    allegro_init();
    install_keyboard();
```

```
    install_timer();
    srand(time(NULL));

    //initialize video mode to 640x480
    int ret = set_gfx_mode(GFX_AUTODETECT_WINDOWED, 640, 480, 0, 0);
    if (ret != 0) {
        allegro_message(allegro_error);
        return;
    }

    //display screen resolution
    textprintf(screen, font, 0, 0, 15,
        "Circles Program - %dx%d - Press ESC to quit",
        SCREEN_W, SCREEN_H);

    //wait for keypress
    while(!key[KEY_ESC])
    {
        //set a random location
        x = 30 + rand() % (SCREEN_W-60);
        y = 30 + rand() % (SCREEN_H-60);
        radius = rand() % 30;

        //set a random color
        red = rand() % 255;
        green = rand() % 255;
        blue = rand() % 255;
        color = makecol(red,green,blue);

        //draw the pixel
        circle(screen, x, y, radius, color);

        rest(25);
    }

    //end program
    allegro_exit();
}
END_OF_MAIN();
```

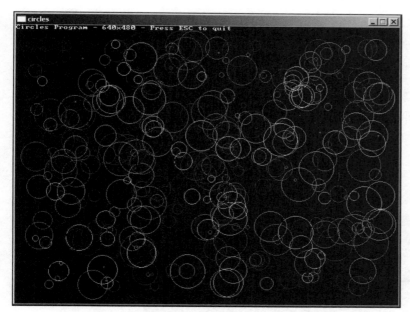

Figure 3.17 The *Circles* program draws random circles on the screen.

Filled Circles

The hollow circle function is interesting, but really seeing the full effect of circles requires the `circlefill` function:

```
void circlefill(BITMAP *bmp, int x, int y, int radius, int color);
```

The following program (shown in Figure 3.18) demonstrates the solid-filled circle function.

```
//display screen resolution
textprintf(screen, font, 0, 0, 15,
    "CircleFill Program - %dx%d - Press ESC to quit",
    SCREEN_W, SCREEN_H);

//wait for keypress
while(!key[KEY_ESC])
{
    //set a random location
    x = 30 + rand() % (SCREEN_W-60);
    y = 30 + rand() % (SCREEN_H-60);
    radius = rand() % 30;
```

```
//set a random color
red = rand() % 255;
green = rand() % 255;
blue = rand() % 255;
color = makecol(red,green,blue);

//draw the filled circle
circlefill(screen, x, y, radius, color);

rest(25);
}
```

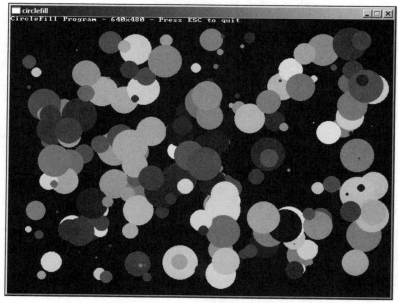

Figure 3.18 The *CircleFill* program draws filled circles.

Ellipses

The ellipse function is similar to the circle function, although the radius is divided into two parameters—one for the horizontal and another for the vertical—as indicated:

```
void ellipse(BITMAP *bmp, int x, int y, int rx, int ry, int color);
```

The *Ellipses* program draws random ellipses on the screen using two parameters—radiusx and radiusy.

```c
#include <conio.h>
#include <stdlib.h>
#include "allegro.h"

void main(void)
{
    int x,y,radiusx,radiusy;
    int red,green,blue,color;

    //initialize everything
    allegro_init();
    install_keyboard();
    install_timer();
    srand(time(NULL));

    //initialize video mode to 640x480
    int ret = set_gfx_mode(GFX_AUTODETECT_WINDOWED, 640, 480, 0, 0);
    if (ret != 0) {
        allegro_message(allegro_error);
        return;
    }

    //display screen resolution
    textprintf(screen, font, 0, 0, 15,
        "Ellipses Program - %dx%d - Press ESC to quit",
        SCREEN_W, SCREEN_H);

    //wait for keypress
    while(!key[KEY_ESC])
    {
        //set a random location
        x = 30 + rand() % (SCREEN_W-60);
        y = 30 + rand() % (SCREEN_H-60);
        radiusx = rand() % 30;
        radiusy = rand() % 30;

        //set a random color
        red = rand() % 255;
        green = rand() % 255;
        blue = rand() % 255;
        color = makecol(red,green,blue);
```

```
        //draw the ellipse
        ellipse(screen, x, y, radiusx, radiusy, color);

        rest(25);
    }

    //end program
    allegro_exit();
}
END_OF_MAIN();
```

Filled Ellipses

You can draw filled ellipses using the ellipsefill function, which takes the same parameters as the ellipse function but simply renders each ellipse with a solid fill color:

```
void ellipsefill(BITMAP *bmp, int x, int y, int rx, int ry, int color);
```

Figure 3.19 shows the output from the *EllipseFill* program.

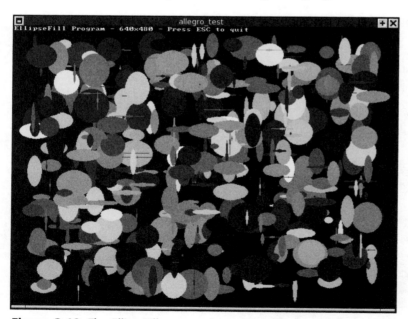

Figure 3.19 The *EllipseFill* program draws filled ellipses. (The Linux version is shown.)

```
        //display screen resolution
        textprintf(screen, font, 0, 0, 15,
            "EllipseFill Program - %dx%d - Press ESC to quit",
            SCREEN_W, SCREEN_H);
```

```
    //wait for keypress
    while(!key[KEY_ESC])
    {
        //set a random location
        x = 30 + rand() % (SCREEN_W-60);
        y = 30 + rand() % (SCREEN_H-60);
        radiusx = rand() % 30;
        radiusy = rand() % 30;

        //set a random color
        red = rand() % 255;
        green = rand() % 255;
        blue = rand() % 255;
        color = makecol(red,green,blue);

        //draw the ellipse
        ellipsefill(screen, x, y, radiusx, radiusy, color);

        sleep(25);
    }
```

Circle Drawing Callback Function

Surprisingly enough, Allegro provides a circle-drawing callback function just as it did with the line callback function. The only difference is, this one uses the do_circle function:

```
void do_circle(BITMAP *bmp, int x, int y, int radius, int d);
```

To use do_circle, you must declare a callback function with the format void docircle(BITMAP *bmp, int x, int y, int d) and pass a pointer to this function to do_circle, as the following sample program demonstrates.

```
#include <conio.h>
#include <stdlib.h>
#include "allegro.h"

void docircle(BITMAP *bmp, int x, int y, int color)
{
    putpixel(bmp, x, y, color);
    putpixel(bmp, x+1, y+1, color);
    rest(1);
}

void main(void)
{
```

```
    int x,y,radius;
    int red,green,blue,color;

    //initialize Allegro
    allegro_init();

    //initialize the keyboard
    install_keyboard();
    install_timer();

    //initialize video mode to 640x480
    int ret = set_gfx_mode(GFX_AUTODETECT_WINDOWED, 640, 480, 0, 0);
    if (ret != 0) {
        allegro_message(allegro_error);
        return;
    }

    //display screen resolution
    textprintf(screen, font, 0, 0, 15,
        "DoCircles Program - %dx%d - Press ESC to quit",
        SCREEN_W, SCREEN_H);

    //wait for keypress
    while(!key[KEY_ESC])
    {
        //set a random location
        x = 40 + rand() % (SCREEN_W-80);
        y = 40 + rand() % (SCREEN_H-80);
        radius = rand() % 40;

        //set a random color
        red = rand() % 255;
        green = rand() % 255;
        blue = rand() % 255;
        color = makecol(red,green,blue);

        //draw the circle
        do_circle(screen, x, y, radius, color, *docircle);
    }

    //end program
    allegro_exit();
}
END_OF_MAIN();
```

Drawing Splines, Triangles, and Polygons

I have now covered all of the basic graphics primitives built into Allegro except for three, which might be thought of as the most important ones, at least where a game is involved. The `spline` function is valuable for creating dynamic trajectories for objects in a game that needs various curving paths. Triangles and other types of polygons are the basis for 3D graphics, so I will show you how to draw them.

Splines

The `spline` function draws a set of curves based on a set of four input points stored in an array. The function calculates a smooth curve from the first set of points, through the second and third, toward the fourth point:

```
void spline(BITMAP *bmp, const int points[8], int color);
```

The *Splines* program draws an animated spline based on shifting points, as shown in Figure 3.20.

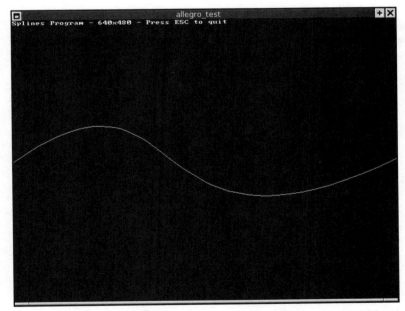

Figure 3.20 The *Splines* program draws an animated spline curve. (The Linux version is shown.)

```
#include <conio.h>
#include <stdlib.h>
#include "allegro.h"
```

```
void main(void)
{
    int red,green,blue,color;

    //initialize Allegro
    allegro_init();
    install_keyboard();
    install_timer();

    //initialize video mode to 640x480
    int ret = set_gfx_mode(GFX_AUTODETECT_WINDOWED, 640, 480, 0, 0);
    if (ret != 0) {
        allegro_message(allegro_error);
        return;
    }

    //display screen resolution
    textprintf(screen, font, 0, 0, 15,
        "Splines Program - %dx%d - Press ESC to quit",
        SCREEN_W, SCREEN_H);

    int points[8] = {0,240,300,0,200,0,639,240};
    int y1 = 0;
    int y2 = SCREEN_H;
    int dir1 = 10;
    int dir2 = -10;

    //wait for keypress
    while(!key[KEY_ESC])
    {
        //modify the first spline point
        y1 += dir1;
        if (y1 > SCREEN_H)
        {
            dir1 = -10;
        }
        if (y1 < 0)
            dir1 = 10;
        points[3] = y1;
```

```
        //modify the second spline point
        y2 += dir2;
        if (y2++ > SCREEN_H)
        {
            dir2 = -10;
        }
        if (y2 < 0)
            dir2 = 10;
        points[5] = y2;

        //draw the spline, pause, then erase it
        spline(screen, points, 15);
        rest(30);
        spline(screen, points, 0);


    }

    //end program
    allegro_exit();
}
END_OF_MAIN();
```

Triangles

You can draw triangles using the triangle function, which takes three (x,y) points and a color parameter:

```
void triangle(BITMAP *bmp, int x1, y1, x2, y2, x3, y3, int color);
```

The *Triangles* program (shown in Figure 3.21) draws random triangles on the screen.

```
#include "allegro.h"

void main(void)
{
    int x1,y1,x2,y2,x3,y3;
    int red,green,blue,color;

    //initialize Allegro
    allegro_init();

    //initialize the keyboard
    install_keyboard();
    install_timer();
```

```
//initialize video mode to 640x480
int ret = set_gfx_mode(GFX_AUTODETECT_WINDOWED, 640, 480, 0, 0);
if (ret != 0) {
    allegro_message(allegro_error);
    return;
}

//display screen resolution
textprintf(screen, font, 0, 0, 15,
    "Triangles Program - %dx%d - Press ESC to quit",
    SCREEN_W, SCREEN_H);

//wait for keypress
while(!key[KEY_ESC])
{
    //set a random location
    x1 = 10 + rand() % (SCREEN_W-20);
    y1 = 10 + rand() % (SCREEN_H-20);
    x2 = 10 + rand() % (SCREEN_W-20);
    y2 = 10 + rand() % (SCREEN_H-20);
    x3 = 10 + rand() % (SCREEN_W-20);
    y3 = 10 + rand() % (SCREEN_H-20);

    //set a random color
    red = rand() % 255;
    green = rand() % 255;
    blue = rand() % 255;
    color = makecol(red,green,blue);

    //draw the triangle
    triangle(screen,x1,y1,x2,y2,x3,y3,color);

    rest(100);
}

//end program
allegro_exit();
}

END_OF_MAIN();
```

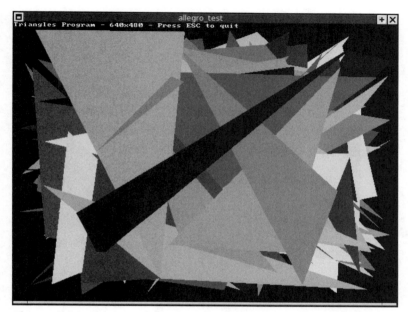

Figure 3.21 The *Triangles* program draws random triangles on the screen. (The Linux version is shown.)

Polygons

You have already seen polygons in action with the *Triangles* program, because any geometric shape with three or more points comprises a polygon. To draw polygons in Allegro, you use the polygon function with a pointer to an array of points:

```
void polygon(BITMAP *bmp, int vertices, const int *points, int color);
```

In most cases you will want to simply use the triangle function, but in unusual cases when you need to draw polygons with more than three points, this function can be helpful (although it is more difficult to set up because the points array must be set up prior to calling the polygon function). The best way to demonstrate this function is with a sample program that sets up the points array and calls the polygon function (see Figure 3.22).

There is more to the subject of polygon rendering than I have time for in this chapter. Rest assured, you will have several more opportunities in later chapters to exercise the polygon functions built into Allegro.

```
#include <conio.h>
#include <stdlib.h>
#include "allegro.h"
```

```
void main(void)
{
    int vertices[8];
    int red,green,blue,color;

    //initialize everything
    allegro_init();
    install_keyboard();
    install_timer();
    srand(time(NULL));

    //initialize video mode to 640x480
    int ret = set_gfx_mode(GFX_AUTODETECT_WINDOWED, 640, 480, 0, 0);
    if (ret != 0) {
        allegro_message(allegro_error);
        return;
    }

    //display screen resolution
    textprintf(screen, font, 0, 0, 15,
        "Polygons Program - %dx%d - Press ESC to quit",
        SCREEN_W, SCREEN_H);

    //wait for keypress
    while(!key[KEY_ESC])
    {
        //set a random location
        vertices[0] = 10 + rand() % (SCREEN_W-20);
        vertices[1] = 10 + rand() % (SCREEN_H-20);
        vertices[2] = vertices[0] + (rand() % 30)+50;
        vertices[3] = vertices[1] + (rand() % 30)+50;
        vertices[4] = vertices[2] + (rand() % 30)-100;
        vertices[5] = vertices[3] + (rand() % 30)+50;
        vertices[6] = vertices[4] + (rand() % 30);
        vertices[7] = vertices[5] + (rand() % 30)-100;

        //set a random color
        red = rand() % 255;
        green = rand() % 255;
        blue = rand() % 255;
        color = makecol(red,green,blue);
```

```
        //draw the polygon
        polygon(screen,4,vertices,color);

        rest(50);
    }
    //end program
    allegro_exit();
}
END_OF_MAIN();
```

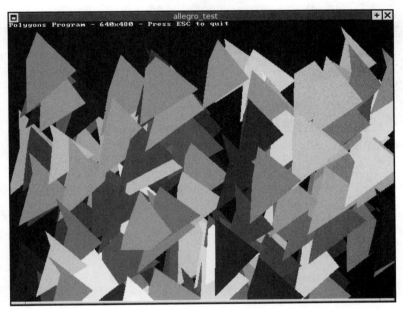

Figure 3.22 The *Polygons* program draws random polygons on the screen.
(The Linux version is shown.)

Filling in Regions

The last function I want to introduce to you in this chapter is floodfill, which fills in a
region on the destination bitmap (which can be the screen) with the color of your choice:

```
void floodfill(BITMAP *bmp, int x, int y, int color);
```

To demonstrate, the *FloodFill* program draws a circle on the screen and fills it in using the
floodfill function while the "ball" is moving around on the screen. I will be the first to
admit that this program could have simply called the circlefill function (which is very
likely faster, too), but the object of this program is to demonstrate floodfill with a basic
circle shape that has historically been difficult to fill efficiently (see Figure 3.23).

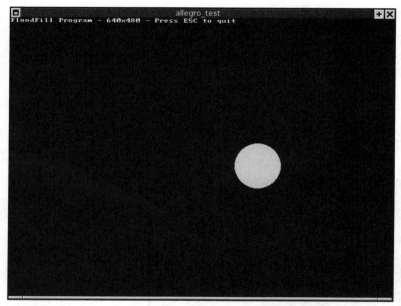

Figure 3.23 The *FloodFill* program moves a filled circle around on the screen. (The Linux version is shown.)

```
#include <conio.h>
#include <stdlib.h>
#include "allegro.h"

void main(void)
{
    int x = 100, y = 100;
    int xdir = 10, ydir = 10;
    int red,green,blue,color;
    int radius = 50;

    //initialize some things
    allegro_init();
    install_keyboard();
    install_timer();

    //initialize video mode to 640x480
    int ret = set_gfx_mode(GFX_AUTODETECT_WINDOWED, 640, 480, 0, 0);
    if (ret != 0) {
        allegro_message(allegro_error);
        return;
```

```
}

//display screen resolution
textprintf(screen, font, 0, 0, 15,
    "FloodFill Program - %dx%d - Press ESC to quit",
    SCREEN_W, SCREEN_H);

//wait for keypress
while(!key[KEY_ESC])
{
    //update the x position, keep within screen
    x += xdir;
    if (x > SCREEN_W-radius)
    {
        xdir = -10;
        radius = 10 + rand() % 40;
        x = SCREEN_W-radius;
    }
    if (x < radius)
    {
        xdir = 10;
        radius = 10 + rand() % 40;
        x = radius;
    }

    //update the y position, keep within screen
    y += ydir;
    if (y > SCREEN_H-radius)
    {
        ydir = -10;
        radius = 10 + rand() % 40;
        y = SCREEN_H-radius;
    }
    if (y < radius+20)
    {
        ydir = 10;
        radius = 10 + rand() % 40;
        y = radius+20;
    }

    //set a random color
    red = rand() % 255;
```

```
        green = rand() % 255;
        blue = rand() % 255;
        color = makecol(red,green,blue);

        //draw the circle, pause, then erase it
        circle(screen, x, y, radius, color);
        floodfill(screen, x, y, color);
        rest(20);
        rectfill(screen, x-radius, y-radius, x+radius, y+radius, 0);
    }

    //end program
    allegro_exit();
}
END_OF_MAIN();
```

Printing Text on the Screen

Allegro provides numerous useful text output functions for drawing on a console or graphical display. Allegro's text functions support plug-in fonts that you can create with a utility bundled with Allegro, but I'll reserve that discussion for later. For now I just want to give you a heads-up on the basic text output functions included with Allegro (some of which you have already used).

Constant Text Output

There are four primary text output functions in Allegro. The text_mode function sets text output to draw with an opaque or transparent background. Passing a value of −1 will set the background to transparent, while passing any other value will set the background to a specific color. Here is what the function looks like:

```
int text_mode(int mode);
```

The textout function is the basic text output function for Allegro. It has the syntax:

```
void textout(BITMAP *bmp, const FONT *f, const char *s, int x, y, int color);
```

The BITMAP *bmp parameter specifies the destination bitmap. (You can use screen to output directly to the screen.) FONT *f specifies the font, which is just font if you are using the default font. const char *s is the text to display, int x, y is the position on the screen, and int color specifies the color of the font to use. (Passing −1 will use the colors built into any custom font.) Here is an example usage for textout:

```
textout(screen, font, "Hello World!", 1, 1, 10);
```

This line draws directly on the screen using the default font at the position (1,1), using the color 10 (which can also be a custom color with makecol).

The other three text output functions are based on textout but provide justification. The textout_centre function has the same parameter list as textout, but the position is based on the center of the text rather than at the left.

```
void textout_centre(BITMAP *bmp, const FONT *f, const char *s,
        int x, y, color);
```

The textout_right function is also similar to textout, but the text position (x,y) specifies the right edge of the text rather than the left or center.

```
void textout_right(BITMAP *bmp, const FONT *f, const char *s,
        int x, y, color);
```

A slightly different take on the matter of text output is textout_justify, which includes two X coordinates—one for the left edge of the text and one for the right edge—along with the Y position. In effect, this function tries to draw the text between the two points. You want to set the diff parameter to a fairly high value for justification to work; otherwise, it is automatically left-justified. This really is more useful when you are using custom fonts.

```
void textout_justify(BITMAP *bmp, const FONT *f, const char *s,
        int x1, int x2, int y, int diff, int color);
```

Variable Text Output

Allegro provides several very useful text output functions that mimic the standard C printf function, providing the capability of formatting the text and displaying variables. The base function is textprintf, and it looks like this:

```
void textprintf(BITMAP *bmp, const FONT *f, int x, y, color,
        const char *fmt, ...);
```

The syntax for textprintf is slightly different than the syntax for the textout functions. As you can see, textprintf has the character string passed as the last parameter, with support for numerous additional parameters. If you are familiar with printf (and you certainly should be if you call yourself a C programmer!), then you should feel right at home with textprintf because it supports the usual %i (integer), %f (float), %s (string), and other formatting elements. Here is an example:

```
float ver = 4.9;
textprintf(screen, font, 0, 100, 12, "Version %.2f", ver);
```

This code displays:

```
Version 4.90
```

There are three additional functions that share functionality with `textprintf`. The `textprintf_centre` produces the same output as `textprintf`, but the (x,y) position is based on the center of the text output (comparable to `textout_centre`). Here is the syntax:

```
void textprintf_centre(BITMAP *bmp, const FONT *f, int x, y, color,
        const char *fmt, ...);
```

As you might have guessed, there is also a `textprintf_right`, which looks like this:

```
void textprintf_right(BITMAP *bmp, const FONT *f, int x, y, color,
        const char *fmt, ...);
```

Likewise, `textprintf_justify` mimics the functionality of `textout_justify` but adds the formatting capabilities. Here is the function:

```
void textprintf_justify(BITMAP *bmp, const FONT *f, int x1, int x2,
        int y, int diff, int color, const char *fmt, ...);
```

Testing Text Output

To put these functions to use, let's write a short demonstration program (see Figure 3.24). Open your favorite IDE (I am using Dev-C++ in Windows and KDevelop in Linux) and create a new project called TextOutput. In Dev-C++, you can click on the MultiMedia tab in the New Project dialog box and choose Allegro (DLL) to configure the project automatically. In KDevelop and other IDEs, you'll want to add a reference "-lalleg" to the linker options to incorporate the Allegro library file.

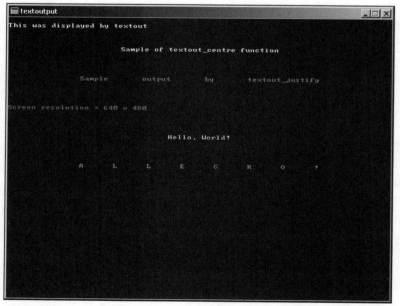

Figure 3.24 The *TextOutput* program demonstrates the text output functions of Allegro.

```
#include <allegro.h>

int main()
{
    //initialize Allegro
    allegro_init();
    set_gfx_mode(GFX_AUTODETECT_WINDOWED, 640, 480, 0, 0);
    install_keyboard();
    text_mode(-1);

    //test the text output functions
    textout(screen, font, "This was displayed by textout", 0, 10, 15);

    textout_centre(screen, font, "Sample of textout_centre function",
        SCREEN_W/2, 50, 14);

    textout_justify(screen, font, "Sample output by textout_justify",
        SCREEN_W/2 - 200, SCREEN_W/2 + 200, 100, 200, 13);

    textprintf(screen, font, 0, 150, 12, "Screen resolution = %i x %i",
        SCREEN_W, SCREEN_H);

    textprintf_centre(screen, font, SCREEN_W/2, 200, 10,
        "%s, %s!", "Hello", "World");

    textprintf_justify(screen, font, SCREEN_W/2 - 200,
        SCREEN_W/2 + 200, 250, 400, 7, "A L L E G R O !");


    //main loop
    while(! key[KEY_ESC]) { }

    allegro_exit();
    return 0;
}
END_OF_MAIN();
```

Summary

This chapter has been a romp through the basic graphics functions built into Allegro. You learned to draw pixels, lines, circles, ellipses, and other geometric shapes in various colors, with wireframe and solid filled color. I also covered text output in Allegro, and you learned about the different text functions and how to use them. This chapter included many sample programs to demonstrate all of the new functionality presented.

Chapter Quiz

You can find the answers to this chapter quiz in Appendix A, "Chapter Quiz Answers."

1. What is the term used to describe line-based graphics?
    A. Vector
    B. Bitmap
    C. Polygon
    D. Pixel

2. What does CRT stand for?
    A. Captain Ron Teague
    B. Corporate Resource Training
    C. Cathode Ray Tube
    D. Common Relativistic Torch

3. What describes a function that draws a simple geometric shape, such as a point, line, rectangle, or circle?
    A. `putpixel`
    B. `Graphics Primitive`
    C. `triangle`
    D. `polygon`

4. How many polygons does the typical 3D accelerator chip process at a time?
    A. 16
    B. 8
    C. 1
    D. 256

5. What is comprised of three small streams of electrons of varying shades of red, green, and blue?
    A. Superstring
    B. Quantum particle
    C. Electron gun
    D. Pixel

6. What function is used to create a custom 24- or 32-bit color?

A.   makecol

B.   rgb

C.   color

D.   truecolor

7. What function is used to draw filled rectangles?

A.   fill_rect

B.   fillrect

C.   filledrectangle

D.   rectfill

8. Which of the following is the correct definition of the circle function?

A.   void circle(BITMAP *bmp, int x, int y, int radius, int color);

B.   void draw_circle(BITMAP *bmp, int x, int y, int radius);

C.   int circle(BITMAP *bmp, int y, int x, int radius, int color);

D.   bool circle(BITMAP *bmp, int x, int y, int color);

9. What function draws a set of curves based on a set of four input points stored in an array?

A.   jagged

B.   draw_curves

C.   spline

D.   polygon

10. Which text output function draws a formatted string with justification?

A.   textout_justify

B.   textprintf_right

C.   textout_centre

D.   textprintf_justify

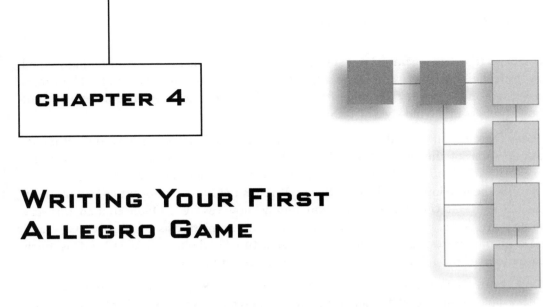

CHAPTER 4

WRITING YOUR FIRST ALLEGRO GAME

This chapter forges ahead with a lot of things I haven't discussed yet, such as collision detection and keyboard input, but the *Tank War* game that is created in this chapter will help you absorb all the information presented thus far. You'll see how you can use the graphics primitives you learned in Chapter 3 to create a complete game with support for two players. You will learn how to draw and move a tank around on the screen using nothing but simple pixel and rectangle drawing functions. You will learn how to look at the video screen to determine when a projectile strikes a tank or another object, how to read the keyboard, and how to process a game loop. The goal of this chapter is to show you that you can create an entire game using the meager resources provided thus far (in the form of the Allegro functions you have already learned) and to introduce some new functionality that will be covered in more detail in later chapters.

Here is a breakdown of the major topics in this chapter:

- Creating the tanks
- Firing weapons
- Moving the tanks
- Detecting collisions
- Understanding the complete source code

Tank War

If this is your first foray into game programming, then *Tank War* is likely your very first game! There is always a lot of joy involved in seeing your first game running on the screen. In the mid-1980s I subscribed to several of the popular computer magazines, such as *Family Computing* and *Compute!*, which provided small program listings in the BASIC language, most often games. I can still remember some of the games I painstakingly typed in from the magazine using Microsoft GW-BASIC on my old Tandy 1000. The games never ran on the first try! I would often miss entire lines of code, even with the benefit of line numbers in the old style of BASIC.

Today there are fantastic development tools that quite often cost nothing and yet incorporate some of the most advanced compiler technology available. The Free Software Foundation (http://www.fsf.org) has done the world a wonderful service by inspiring and funding the development of free software. Perhaps the most significant contribution by the FSF is the GNU Compiler Collection, fondly known as GCC. Oddly enough, this very same compiler is used on both Windows and Linux platforms by the Dev-C++ and KDevelop tools, respectively. The format of structured and object-oriented code is much easier to read and follow than in the numbered lines of the past.

Tank War is a two-player game that is played on a single screen using a shared keyboard. The first player uses the W, A, S, and D keys to move his tank, and the Spacebar to fire the main cannon on the tank. The second player uses the arrow keys for movement and the Enter key to fire. The game is shown in Figure 4.1.

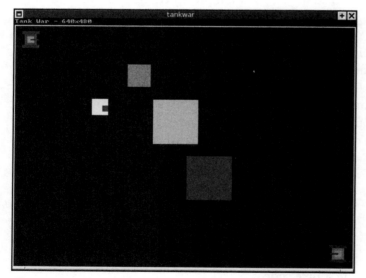

Figure 4.1 *Tank War* is a two-player game in the classic style.

Creating the Tanks

The graphics in *Tank War* are created entirely with the drawing functions included in Allegro. Figure 4.2 shows the four angles of the tank that are drawn based on the tank's direction of travel.

Figure 4.2 The tanks are rendered on the screen using a series of filled rectangles.

The drawtank function is called from the main loop to draw each tank according to its current direction. The drawtank function looks like this:

```
void drawtank(int num)
{
    int x = tanks[num].x;
    int y = tanks[num].y;
    int dir = tanks[num].dir;

    //draw tank body and turret
    rectfill(screen, x-11, y-11, x+11, y+11, tanks[num].color);
    rectfill(screen, x-6, y-6, x+6, y+6, 7);

    //draw the treads based on orientation
    if (dir == 0 || dir == 2)
    {
        rectfill(screen, x-16, y-16, x-11, y+16, 8);
        rectfill(screen, x+11, y-16, x+16, y+16, 8);
    }
    else
    if (dir == 1 || dir == 3)
    {
        rectfill(screen, x-16, y-16, x+16, y-11, 8);
        rectfill(screen, x-16, y+16, x+16, y+11, 8);
    }

    //draw the turret based on direction
    switch (dir)
    {
        case 0:
            rectfill(screen, x-1, y, x+1, y-16, 8);
            break;
        case 1:
            rectfill(screen, x, y-1, x+16, y+1, 8);
```

```
                    break;
                case 2:
                    rectfill(screen, x-1, y, x+1, y+16, 8);
                    break;
                case 3:
                    rectfill(screen, x, y-1, x-16, y+1, 8);
                    break;
            }
    }
```

Did you notice how the entire tank is constructed with rectfill statements? This is one example of improvisation where better technology is not available. For instance, bitmaps and sprites are not yet available because I haven't covered that subject yet, so this game actually draws the tank sprite used in the game. Don't underestimate the usefulness of rendered graphics to enhance a sprite-based game or to create a game entirely. To erase the tank, you simply call the erasetank function, which looks like this:

```
void erasetank(int num)
{
    //calculate box to encompass the tank
    int left = tanks[num].x - 17;
    int top = tanks[num].y - 17;
    int right = tanks[num].x + 17;
    int bottom = tanks[num].y + 17;

    //erase the tank
    rectfill(screen, left, top, right, bottom, 0);
}
```

The erasetank function is calculated based on the center of the tank (which is how the tank is drawn as well, from the center). Because the tank is 32×32 pixels in size, the erasetank function draws a black filled rectangle a distance of 17 pixels in each direction from the center (for a total of 34×34 pixels, to include a small border around the tank, which helps to keep the tank from getting stuck in obstacles).

Firing Weapons

The projectiles fired from each tank are drawn as small rectangles (four pixels total) that move in the current direction the tank is facing until they strike the other tank, an object, or the edge of the screen. You can increase the size of the projectile by increasing the size in the updatebullet function (coming up next). To determine whether a hit has occurred, you use the getpixel function to "look" at the pixel on the screen right in front of the bullet. If that pixel is black (color 0 or RGB 0,0,0), then the bullet is moved another space.

If that color is anything other than black, then it is a sure hit! The fireweapon function gets the bullet started in the right direction.

```c
void fireweapon(int num)
{
    int x = tanks[num].x;
    int y = tanks[num].y;

    //ready to fire again?
    if (!bullets[num].alive)
    {
        bullets[num].alive = 1;

        //fire bullet in direction tank is facing
        switch (tanks[num].dir)
        {
            //north
            case 0:
                bullets[num].x = x;
                bullets[num].y = y-22;
                bullets[num].xspd = 0;
                bullets[num].yspd = -BULLETSPEED;
                break;
            //east
            case 1:
                bullets[num].x = x+22;
                bullets[num].y = y;
                bullets[num].xspd = BULLETSPEED;
                bullets[num].yspd = 0;
                break;
            //south
            case 2:
                bullets[num].x = x;
                bullets[num].y = y+22;
                bullets[num].xspd = 0;
                bullets[num].yspd = BULLETSPEED;
                break;
            //west
            case 3:
                bullets[num].x = x-22;
                bullets[num].y = y;
                bullets[num].xspd = -BULLETSPEED;
                bullets[num].yspd = 0;
```

```
        }
    }
}
```

The fireweapon function looks at the direction of the current tank to set the X and Y movement values for the bullet. Once it is set up, the bullet will move in that direction until it strikes something or reaches the edge of the screen. The important variable here is alive, which determines whether the bullet is moved accordingly using this updatebullet function:

```
void updatebullet(int num)
{
    int x = bullets[num].x;
    int y = bullets[num].y;

    if (bullets[num].alive)
    {
        //erase bullet
        rect(screen, x-1, y-1, x+1, y+1, 0);

        //move bullet
        bullets[num].x += bullets[num].xspd;
        bullets[num].y += bullets[num].yspd;
        x = bullets[num].x;
        y = bullets[num].y;

        //stay within the screen
        if (x < 5 || x > SCREEN_W-5 || y < 20 || y > SCREEN_H-5)
        {
            bullets[num].alive = 0;
            return;
        }

        //draw bullet
        x = bullets[num].x;
        y = bullets[num].y;
        rect(screen, x-1, y-1, x+1, y+1, 14);

        //look for a hit
        if (getpixel(screen, bullets[num].x, bullets[num].y))
        {
            bullets[num].alive = 0;
            explode(num, x, y);
        }
    }
```

```
        //print the bullet's position
        textprintf(screen, font, SCREEN_W/2-50, 1, 2,
            "B1 %-3dx%-3d   B2 %-3dx%-3d",
            bullets[0].x, bullets[0].y,
            bullets[1].x, bullets[1].y);
    }
}
```

Tank Movement

To move the tank, each player uses the appropriate keys to move forward, backward, left, right, and to fire the weapon. The first player uses W, A, S, and D to move and the Spacebar to fire, while player two uses the arrow keys to move and Enter to fire. The main loop looks for a key press and calls on the getinput function to see which key has been pressed. I will discuss keyboard input in a later chapter; for now all you need to be aware of is an array called key that stores the values of each key press.

```
void getinput()
{
    //hit ESC to quit
    if (key[KEY_ESC])
        gameover = 1;

    //WASD / SPACE keys control tank 1
    if (key[KEY_W])
        forward(0);
    if (key[KEY_D])
        turnright(0);
    if (key[KEY_A])
        turnleft(0);
    if (key[KEY_S])
        backward(0);
    if (key[KEY_SPACE])
        fireweapon(0);

    //arrow / ENTER keys control tank 2
    if (key[KEY_UP])
        forward(1);
    if (key[KEY_RIGHT])
        turnright(1);
    if (key[KEY_DOWN])
        backward(1);
    if (key[KEY_LEFT])
```

```
        turnleft(1);
    if (key[KEY_ENTER])
        fireweapon(1);

    //short delay after keypress
    rest(10);
}
```

Collision Detection

I have already explained how the bullets use `getpixel` to determine when a collision has occurred (when the bullet hits a tank or obstacle). But what about collision detection when you are moving the tanks themselves? There are several obstacles on the battlefield to add a little strategy to the game; they offer a place to hide or maneuver around (or straight through if you blow up the obstacles). The `clearpath` function is used to determine whether the ship can move. The function checks the screen boundaries and obstacles on the screen to clear a path for the tank or prevent it from moving any further in that direction. The function also takes into account reverse motion because the tanks can move forward or backward. `clearpath` is a bit lengthy, so I'll leave it for the main code listing later in the chapter. The `clearpath` function calls the `checkpath` function to actually see whether the tank's pathway is clear for movement. (`checkpath` is called multiple times for each tank.)

```
int checkpath(int x1,int y1,int x2,int y2,int x3,int y3)
{
    if (getpixel(screen, x1, y1) ||
        getpixel(screen, x2, y2) ||
        getpixel(screen, x3, y3))
        return 1;
    else
        return 0;
}
```

All that remains of the program are the logistical functions for setting up the screen, modifying the speed and direction of each tank, displaying the score, placing the random debris, and so on.

The Complete Tank War Source Code

The code listing for *Tank War* is included here in its entirety. Despite having already shown you many of the functions in this program, I think it's important at this point to show you the entire listing in one fell swoop so there is no confusion. Of course, you can open the *Tank War* project that is located on the CD-ROM that accompanies this book; look inside a folder called chapter04 for the complete project for Visual C++, Dev-C++, or KDevelop. If you are using some other operating system, you can still compile this code for your favorite compiler by typing it into your text editor and including the Allegro library. (If you need some pointers, refer to Appendix E, "Configuring Allegro for Microsoft Visual C++ and Other Compilers.")

The Tank War Header File

The first code listing is for the header file, which includes the variables, structures, constants, and function prototypes for the game. You will want to add a new file to the project called tankwar.h. The main source code file (main.c) will try to include the header file by this filename. If you need help configuring your compiler to link to the Allegro game library, refer to Appendix E. If you have not yet installed Allegro, you might want to go back and read Chapter 2 and refer to Appendix F, "Compiling the Allegro Source Code."

```c
///////////////////////////////////////////////////////////////////
// Game Programming All In One, Second Edition
// Source Code Copyright (C)2004 by Jonathan S. Harbour
// Chapter 4 - Tank War Game
///////////////////////////////////////////////////////////////////

#ifndef _TANKWAR_H
#define _TANKWAR_H

#include "allegro.h"

//define some game constants
#define MODE GFX_AUTODETECT_WINDOWED
#define WIDTH 640
#define HEIGHT 480
#define BLOCKS 5
#define BLOCKSIZE 100
#define MAXSPEED 2
#define BULLETSPEED 10
#define TAN makecol(255,242,169)
#define CAMO makecol(64,142,66)
#define BURST makecol(255,189,73)

//define tank structure
struct tagTank
{
    int x,y;
    int dir,speed;
    int color;
    int score;
```

```
} tanks[2];

//define bullet structure
struct tagBullet
{
    int x,y;
    int alive;
    int xspd,yspd;

} bullets[2];

int gameover = 0;

//function prototypes
void drawtank(int num);
void erasetank(int num);
void movetank(int num);
void explode(int num, int x, int y);
void updatebullet(int num);
int checkpath(int x1,int y1,int x2,int y2,int x3,int y3);
void clearpath(int num);
void fireweapon(int num);
void forward(int num);
void backward(int num);
void turnleft(int num);
void turnright(int num);
void getinput();
void setuptanks();
void score(int);
void print(const char *s, int c);
void setupdebris();
void setupscreen();

#endif
```

The Tank War Source File

The primary source code file for *Tank War* includes the tankwar.h header file (which in turn includes allegro.h). Included in this code listing are all of the functions needed by the game in addition to the main function (containing the game loop). You can type this code in as-is for whatever OS and IDE you are using; if you have included the Allegro library, it will run without issue. This game is wonderfully easy to get to work because it requires no bitmap files, uses no backgrounds, and simply draws directly to the primary screen buffer (which can be full-screen or windowed).

```
///////////////////////////////////////////////////////////////////
// Game Programming All In One, Second Edition
// Source Code Copyright (C)2004 by Jonathan S. Harbour
// Chapter 4 - Tank War Game
///////////////////////////////////////////////////////////////////

#include "tankwar.h"

///////////////////////////////////////////////////////////////////
// drawtank function
// construct the tank using drawing functions
///////////////////////////////////////////////////////////////////
void drawtank(int num)
{
    int x = tanks[num].x;
    int y = tanks[num].y;
    int dir = tanks[num].dir;

    //draw tank body and turret
    rectfill(screen, x-11, y-11, x+11, y+11, tanks[num].color);
    rectfill(screen, x-6, y-6, x+6, y+6, 7);

    //draw the treads based on orientation
    if (dir == 0 || dir == 2)
    {
        rectfill(screen, x-16, y-16, x-11, y+16, 8);
        rectfill(screen, x+11, y-16, x+16, y+16, 8);
    }
    else
    if (dir == 1 || dir == 3)
    {
        rectfill(screen, x-16, y-16, x+16, y-11, 8);
        rectfill(screen, x-16, y+16, x+16, y+11, 8);
    }

    //draw the turret based on direction
    switch (dir)
    {
        case 0:
            rectfill(screen, x-1, y, x+1, y-16, 8);
            break;
        case 1:
            rectfill(screen, x, y-1, x+16, y+1, 8);
```

```
                break;
            case 2:
                rectfill(screen, x-1, y, x+1, y+16, 8);
                break;
            case 3:
                rectfill(screen, x, y-1, x-16, y+1, 8);
                break;
        }
}


////////////////////////////////////////////////////////////////////
// erasetank function
// erase the tank using rectfill
////////////////////////////////////////////////////////////////////
void erasetank(int num)
{
    //calculate box to encompass the tank
    int left = tanks[num].x - 17;
    int top = tanks[num].y - 17;
    int right = tanks[num].x + 17;
    int bottom = tanks[num].y + 17;

    //erase the tank
    rectfill(screen, left, top, right, bottom, 0);
}


////////////////////////////////////////////////////////////////////
// movetank function
// move the tank in the current direction
////////////////////////////////////////////////////////////////////
void movetank(int num)
{
    int dir = tanks[num].dir;
    int speed = tanks[num].speed;

    //update tank position based on direction
    switch(dir)
    {
        case 0:
            tanks[num].y -= speed;
            break;
        case 1:
            tanks[num].x += speed;
```

```
                break;
        case 2:
                tanks[num].y += speed;
                break;
        case 3:
                tanks[num].x -= speed;
    }

    //keep tank inside the screen
    if (tanks[num].x > SCREEN_W-22)
    {
        tanks[num].x = SCREEN_W-22;
        tanks[num].speed = 0;
    }
    if (tanks[num].x < 22)
    {
        tanks[num].x = 22;
        tanks[num].speed = 0;
    }
    if (tanks[num].y > SCREEN_H-22)
    {
        tanks[num].y = SCREEN_H-22;
        tanks[num].speed = 0;
    }
    if (tanks[num].y < 22)
    {
        tanks[num].y = 22;
        tanks[num].speed = 0;
    }
}


///////////////////////////////////////////////////////////////////////
// explode function
// display random boxes to simulate an explosion
///////////////////////////////////////////////////////////////////////
void explode(int num, int x, int y)
{

    int n;

    //retrieve location of enemy tank
    int tx = tanks[!num].x;
    int ty = tanks[!num].y;
```

```
        //is bullet inside the boundary of the enemy tank?
        if (x > tx-16 && x < tx+16 && y > ty-16 && y < ty+16)
            score(num);

        //draw some random circles for the "explosion"
        for (n = 0; n < 10; n++)
        {
            rectfill(screen, x-16, y-16, x+16, y+16, rand() % 16);
            rest(1);
        }

        //clear the area of debris
        rectfill(screen, x-16, y-16, x+16, y+16, 0);

}

////////////////////////////////////////////////////////////////////
// updatebullet function
// update the position of a bullet
////////////////////////////////////////////////////////////////////
void updatebullet(int num)
{
    int x = bullets[num].x;
    int y = bullets[num].y;

    if (bullets[num].alive)
    {
        //erase bullet
        rect(screen, x-1, y-1, x+1, y+1, 0);

        //move bullet
        bullets[num].x += bullets[num].xspd;
        bullets[num].y += bullets[num].yspd;
        x = bullets[num].x;
        y = bullets[num].y;

        //stay within the screen
        if (x < 5 || x > SCREEN_W-5 || y < 20 || y > SCREEN_H-5)
        {
            bullets[num].alive = 0;
            return;
        }
```

```
        //draw bullet
        x = bullets[num].x;
        y = bullets[num].y;
        rect(screen, x-1, y-1, x+1, y+1, 14);

        //look for a hit
        if (getpixel(screen, bullets[num].x, bullets[num].y))
        {
            bullets[num].alive = 0;
            explode(num, x, y);
        }

        //print the bullet's position
        textprintf(screen, font, SCREEN_W/2-50, 1, 2,
            "B1 %-3dx%-3d   B2 %-3dx%-3d",
            bullets[0].x, bullets[0].y,
            bullets[1].x, bullets[1].y);

    }
}

///////////////////////////////////////////////////////////////////////
// checkpath function
// check to see if a point on the screen is black
///////////////////////////////////////////////////////////////////////
int checkpath(int x1,int y1,int x2,int y2,int x3,int y3)
{
    if (getpixel(screen, x1, y1) ||
        getpixel(screen, x2, y2) ||
        getpixel(screen, x3, y3))
        return 1;
    else
        return 0;
}

///////////////////////////////////////////////////////////////////////
// clearpath function
// verify that the tank can move in the current direction
///////////////////////////////////////////////////////////////////////
void clearpath(int num)
{
    //shortcut vars
    int dir = tanks[num].dir;
```

```
int speed = tanks[num].speed;
int x = tanks[num].x;
int y = tanks[num].y;

switch(dir)
{
    //check pixels north
    case 0:
        if (speed > 0)
        {
            if (checkpath(x-16, y-20, x, y-20, x+16, y-20))
                tanks[num].speed = 0;
        }
        else
            //if reverse dir, check south
            if (checkpath(x-16, y+20, x, y+20, x+16, y+20))
                tanks[num].speed = 0;
        break;

    //check pixels east
    case 1:
        if (speed > 0)
        {
            if (checkpath(x+20, y-16, x+20, y, x+20, y+16))
                tanks[num].speed = 0;
        }
        else
            //if reverse dir, check west
            if (checkpath(x-20, y-16, x-20, y, x-20, y+16))
                tanks[num].speed = 0;
        break;

    //check pixels south
    case 2:
        if (speed > 0)
        {
            if (checkpath(x-16, y+20, x, y+20, x+16, y+20 ))
                tanks[num].speed = 0;
        }
        else
            //if reverse dir, check north
            if (checkpath(x-16, y-20, x, y-20, x+16, y-20))
                tanks[num].speed = 0;
```

```
            break;

        //check pixels west
        case 3:
            if (speed > 0)
            {
                if (checkpath(x-20, y-16, x-20, y, x-20, y+16))
                    tanks[num].speed = 0;
            }
            else
                //if reverse dir, check east
                if (checkpath(x+20, y-16, x+20, y, x+20, y+16))
                    tanks[num].speed = 0;
            break;
    }
}


///////////////////////////////////////////////////////////////////
// fireweapon function
// configure a bullet's direction and speed and activate it
///////////////////////////////////////////////////////////////////
void fireweapon(int num)
{
    int x = tanks[num].x;
    int y = tanks[num].y;

    //ready to fire again?
    if (!bullets[num].alive)
    {
        bullets[num].alive = 1;

        //fire bullet in direction tank is facing
        switch (tanks[num].dir)
        {
            //north
            case 0:
                bullets[num].x = x;
                bullets[num].y = y-22;
                bullets[num].xspd = 0;
                bullets[num].yspd = -BULLETSPEED;
                break;
            //east
            case 1:
```

```
                        bullets[num].x = x+22;
                        bullets[num].y = y;
                        bullets[num].xspd = BULLETSPEED;
                        bullets[num].yspd = 0;
                        break;
                //south
                case 2:
                        bullets[num].x = x;
                        bullets[num].y = y+22;
                        bullets[num].xspd = 0;
                        bullets[num].yspd = BULLETSPEED;
                        break;
                //west
                case 3:
                        bullets[num].x = x-22;
                        bullets[num].y = y;
                        bullets[num].xspd = -BULLETSPEED;
                        bullets[num].yspd = 0;
            }
        }
}


////////////////////////////////////////////////////////////////////////
// forward function
// increase the tank's speed
////////////////////////////////////////////////////////////////////////
void forward(int num)
{
    tanks[num].speed++;
    if (tanks[num].speed > MAXSPEED)
        tanks[num].speed = MAXSPEED;
}


////////////////////////////////////////////////////////////////////////
// backward function
// decrease the tank's speed
////////////////////////////////////////////////////////////////////////
void backward(int num)
{
    tanks[num].speed--;
    if (tanks[num].speed < -MAXSPEED)
        tanks[num].speed = -MAXSPEED;
}
```

```
///////////////////////////////////////////////////////////////////////
// turnleft function
// rotate the tank counter-clockwise
///////////////////////////////////////////////////////////////////////
void turnleft(int num)
{
    tanks[num].dir--;
    if (tanks[num].dir < 0)
        tanks[num].dir = 3;
}


///////////////////////////////////////////////////////////////////////
// turnright function
// rotate the tank clockwise
///////////////////////////////////////////////////////////////////////
void turnright(int num)
{
    tanks[num].dir++;
    if (tanks[num].dir > 3)
        tanks[num].dir = 0;
}


///////////////////////////////////////////////////////////////////////
// getinput function
// check for player input keys (2 player support)
///////////////////////////////////////////////////////////////////////
void getinput()
{
    //hit ESC to quit
    if (key[KEY_ESC])
        gameover = 1;

    //WASD / SPACE keys control tank 1
    if (key[KEY_W])
        forward(0);
    if (key[KEY_D])
        turnright(0);
    if (key[KEY_A])
        turnleft(0);
    if (key[KEY_S])
        backward(0);
    if (key[KEY_SPACE])
        fireweapon(0);
```

```
        //arrow / ENTER keys control tank 2
        if (key[KEY_UP])
            forward(1);
        if (key[KEY_RIGHT])
            turnright(1);
        if (key[KEY_DOWN])
            backward(1);
        if (key[KEY_LEFT])
            turnleft(1);
        if (key[KEY_ENTER])
            fireweapon(1);

        //short delay after keypress
        rest(10);
    }


//////////////////////////////////////////////////////////////////////
// score function
// add a point to the specified player's score
//////////////////////////////////////////////////////////////////////
void score(int player)
{
    //update score
    int points = ++tanks[player].score;

    //display score
    textprintf(screen, font, SCREEN_W-70*(player+1), 1, BURST,
        "P%d: %d", player+1, points);
}


//////////////////////////////////////////////////////////////////////
// setuptanks function
// set up the starting condition of each tank
//////////////////////////////////////////////////////////////////////
void setuptanks()
{
    //player 1
    tanks[0].x = 30;
    tanks[0].y = 40;
    tanks[0].dir = 1;
    tanks[0].speed = 0;
    tanks[0].color = 9;
    tanks[0].score = 0;
```

```
    //player 2
    tanks[1].x = SCREEN_W-30;
    tanks[1].y = SCREEN_H-30;
    tanks[1].dir = 3;
    tanks[1].speed = 0;
    tanks[1].color = 12;
    tanks[1].score = 0;
}


////////////////////////////////////////////////////////////////////////
// setupdebris function
// set up the debris on the battlefield
////////////////////////////////////////////////////////////////////////
void setupdebris()
{
    int n,x,y,size,color;

    //fill the battlefield with random debris
    for (n = 0; n < BLOCKS; n++)
    {
        x = BLOCKSIZE + rand() % (SCREEN_W-BLOCKSIZE*2);
        y = BLOCKSIZE + rand() % (SCREEN_H-BLOCKSIZE*2);
        size = (10 + rand() % BLOCKSIZE)/2;
        color = makecol(rand()%255, rand()%255, rand()%255);
        rectfill(screen, x-size, y-size, x+size, y+size, color);
    }


}


////////////////////////////////////////////////////////////////////////
// setupscreen function
// set up the graphics mode and game screen
////////////////////////////////////////////////////////////////////////
void setupscreen()
{
    //set video mode
    int ret = set_gfx_mode(MODE, WIDTH, HEIGHT, 0, 0);
    if (ret != 0) {
        allegro_message(allegro_error);
        return;
    }
```

```
        //print title
        textprintf(screen, font, 1, 1, BURST,
            "Tank War - %dx%d", SCREEN_W, SCREEN_H);

        //draw screen border
        rect(screen, 0, 12, SCREEN_W-1, SCREEN_H-1, TAN);
        rect(screen, 1, 13, SCREEN_W-2, SCREEN_H-2, TAN);


}


////////////////////////////////////////////////////////////////////
// main function
// start point of the program
////////////////////////////////////////////////////////////////////
void main(void)
{
    //initialize everything
    allegro_init();
    install_keyboard();
    install_timer();
    srand(time(NULL));
    setupscreen();
    setupdebris();
    setuptanks();

    //game loop
    while(!gameover)
    {
        //erase the tanks
        erasetank(0);
        erasetank(1);

        //check for collisions
        clearpath(0);
        clearpath(1);

        //move the tanks
        movetank(0);
        movetank(1);

        //draw the tanks
        drawtank(0);
        drawtank(1);
```

```
        //update the bullets
        updatebullet(0);
        updatebullet(1);

        //check for keypresses
        if (keypressed())
            getinput();

        //slow the game down (adjust as necessary)
        rest(30);
    }

    //end program
    allegro_exit();
}
END_OF_MAIN();
```

Summary

Congratulations on completing your first game with Allegro! It has been a short journey thus far—we're only in the fourth chapter of the book. Contrast this with the enormous amount of information that would have been required in advance to compile even a simple game, such as *Tank War*, using standard graphics libraries, such as DirectX or SVGAlib! It would have taken this amount of source code just to set up the screen and prepare the program for the actual game. That is where Allegro truly shines—by abstracting the logistical issues into a common set of library functions that work regardless of the underlying operating system.

This also concludes Part I of the book and sends you venturing into Part II, which covers the core functionality of Allegro in much more detail. You will learn how to use animated sprites and create scrolling backgrounds, and we'll discuss the next upgrade to *Tank War*. That's right, this isn't the end of *Tank War*! From this point forward, we'll be improving the game with each new chapter. For starters, this game really needs some design and direction (the focus of Chapter 5). By the time you're finished, the game will feature a scrolling background, a tile-based battlefield, sound effects…the whole works!

Chapter Quiz

You can find the answers to this chapter quiz in Appendix A, "Chapter Quiz Answers."

1. What is the primary graphics drawing function used to draw the tanks in *Tank War*?
   A. rectfill
   B. fillrect
   C. drawrect
   D. rectangle

2. What function in *Tank War* sets up a bullet to fire it in the direction of the tank?
   A. pulltrigger
   B. launchprojectile
   C. fireweapon
   D. firecannon

3. What function in *Tank War* updates the position and draws each projectile?
   A. updatecannon
   B. movebullet
   C. moveprojectile
   D. updatebullet

4. What is the name of the organization that produced GCC?
   A. Free Software Foundation
   B. GNU
   C. Freeware
   D. Open Source

5. How many players are supported in *Tank War* at the same time?
   A. 1
   B. 2
   C. 3
   D. 4

6. What is the technical terminology for handling two objects that crash in the game?
   A. Crash override
   B. Sprite insurance
   C. Collision detection
   D. Handling the crash

7. What function in *Tank War* keeps the tanks from colliding with other objects?

   A.   makepath

   B.   clearpath

   C.   buildpath

   D.   dontcollide

8. Which function in *Tank War* helps to find out whether a point on the screen is black?

   A.   getpixel

   B.   findcolor

   C.   getcolor

   D.   checkpixel

9. What is the standard constant used to run Allegro in windowed mode?

   A.   GFX_RUNINA_WINDOW

   B.   GFX_DETECT_WINDOWED

   C.   GFX_AUTODETECT_WINDOWS

   D.   GFX_AUTODETECT_WINDOWED

10. What function in Allegro is used to slow the game down?

   A.   pause

   B.   slow

   C.   rest

   D.   stop

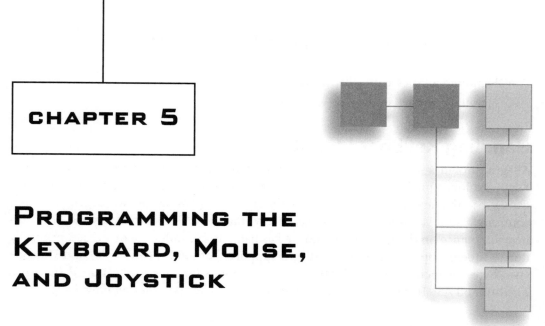

CHAPTER 5

PROGRAMMING THE KEYBOARD, MOUSE, AND JOYSTICK

Welcome to the input chapter, focusing on programming the keyboard, mouse, and joystick! This chapter is a lot of fun, and I know you will enjoy learning about these three input devices because there are some great example programs here to demonstrate how to get a handle on this subject. By the time you have finished this chapter, you will be able to scan for individual keys, read their scan codes, and detect multiple button presses. You will learn about Allegro's buffered keyboard input routines and discover ASCII. (See Appendix B, "Useful Tables," for a table of ASCII values.) You will learn how to read the mouse position, create a custom graphical mouse pointer, check up on the mouse wheel, and discover something called mickeys. You will also learn how to read the joystick, find out what features the currently installed joystick provides (such as analog/digital sticks, buttons, hats, sliders, and so on), and read the joystick values to provide input for a game. As you go through this chapter, you will discover several sample programs that make the subjects easy to understand, including a stargate program, a missile defense system, a hyperspace teleportation program, and a joystick program that involves bouncing balls. Are you ready to dig into the fun subject of device input? I thought so! Let's do it.

Here is a breakdown of the major topics in this chapter:

- Handling keyboard input
- Detecting key presses
- Dealing with buffered keyboard input
- Handling mouse input
- Reading the mouse position
- Working with relative mouse motion
- Handling joystick input

- Handling joystick controller movement
- Handling joystick button presses

Handling Keyboard Input

Allegro provides functions for handling buffered input and individual key states. Keyboard input might seem strange to gamers who have dedicated their lives to console games, but the keyboard has been the mainstay of PC gaming for two dozen years and counting, and it is not likely to be replaced anytime soon. The joystick has had only limited acceptance on the PC, but the mouse has had a larger influence on games, primarily due to modern operating systems. Allegro supports both ANSI (one-byte) and Unicode (two-byte) character systems. (By the way, ANSI stands for *American National Standards Institute* and ASCII stands for *American Standard Code for Information Interchange*.)

The Keyboard Handler

Allegro abstracts the keyboard from the operating system so the generic keyboard routines will work on any computer system you have targeted for your game (Windows, Linux, Mac, and so on). However, that abstraction does not take anything away from the inherent capabilities of any system because the library is custom-written for each platform. The Windows version of Allegro utilizes DirectInput for the keyboard handler. Since there really is no magic to the subject, let's just jump right in and work with the keyboard.

Before you can start using the keyboard routines in Allegro, you must initialize the keyboard handler with the install_keyboard function.

```
int install_keyboard();
```

If you try to use the keyboard routines before initializing, the program will likely crash (or at best, it won't respond to the keyboard). Once you have initialized the keyboard handler, there is no need to uninitialize it—that is handled by Allegro via the allegro_exit function (which is called automatically before Allegro stops running). But if you do find a need to remove the keyboard handler, you can use remove_keyboard.

```
void remove_keyboard();
```

Some operating systems, such as those with preemptive multitasking, do not support the keyboard interrupt handler that Allegro uses. You can use the poll_keyboard function to poll the keyboard if your program will need to be run on systems that don't support the keyboard interrupt service routine. Why would this be the case? Allegro is a multi-threaded library. When you call allegro_init and functions such as install_keyboard, Allegro creates several threads to handle events, scroll the screen, draw sprites, and so on.

```
int poll_keyboard();
```

When you first call `poll_keyboard`, Allegro switches to polled mode, after which the keyboard *must* be polled even if an interrupt or a thread is available. To determine when polling mode is active, use the `keyboard_needs_poll` function.

```
int keyboard_needs_poll();
```

Detecting Key Presses

Allegro makes it very easy to detect key presses. To check for an individual key, you can use the `key` array that is populated with values when the keyboard is polled (or during regular intervals, when run as a thread).

```
extern volatile char key[KEY_MAX];
```

Most of the keys on computer systems are supported by name using constant key values defined in the Allegro library header files. If you want to see all of the key definitions yourself, look in the Allegro library folder for a header file called keyboard.h, in which all the keys are defined. Note also that Allegro defines individual keys, not ASCII codes, so the main numeric keys are not the same as the numeric keypad keys, and the Ctrl, Alt, and Shift keys are treated individually. Pressing Shift+A results in two key presses, not just the "A" key. The buffered keyboard routines (covered next) will differentiate lowercase "a" from uppercase "A." Table 5.1 lists a few of the most common key codes.

Table 5.1 Common Key Codes

Key	Description
KEY_A...KEY_Z	Standard alphabetic keys
KEY_0...KEY_9	Standard numeric keys
KEY_0_PAD...KEY_9_PAD	Numeric keypad keys
KEY_F1...KEY_F12	Function keys
KEY_ESC	Esc key
KEY_BACKSPACE	Backspace key
KEY_TAB	Tab key
KEY_ENTER	Enter key
KEY_SPACE	Space key
KEY_INSERT	Insert key
KEY_DEL	Delete key
KEY_HOME	Home key
KEY_END	End key
KEY_PGUP	Page Up key
KEY_PGDN	Page Down key
KEY_LEFT	Left arrow key
KEY_RIGHT	Right arrow key
KEY_UP	Up arrow key
KEY_DOWN	Down arrow key
KEY_LSHIFT	Left Shift key
KEY_RSHIFT	Right Shift key

The sample programs in the chapters thus far have used the keyboard handler without fully explaining it because it's difficult to demonstrate anything without some form of keyboard input. The typical game loop looks like this:

```
while (!key[KEY_ESC])
{
    //do some stuff
}
```

This loop continues to run until the Esc key is pressed, at which point the loop is exited. Direct access to the key codes means the program does not use the keyboard buffer; rather, it checks each key individually, bypassing the keyboard buffer entirely. You can still check the key codes while also processing key presses in the keyboard buffer using the buffered input functions, such as readkey.

The Stargate Program

The *Stargate* program demonstrates how to use the keyboard scan codes to detect when specific keys have been pressed. You will use this technology to decipher the ancient hiero-glyphs on the gate and attempt to open a wormhole to Abydos. If all scholarly attempts fail, you can resort to trying random dialing sequences using the keys on the keyboard. Our scientists have thus far failed in their attempt to decipher the gate symbols, as you can see in Figure 5.1. What this program really needs are some sound effects, but that will have to wait for Chapter 15, "Mastering the Audible Realm: Allegro's Sound Support."

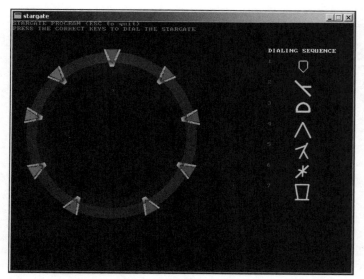

Should you successfully crack the gate codes, the result will look like Figure 5.2.

Figure 5.1 The gate symbols have yet to be deciphered. Are you up to the challenge?

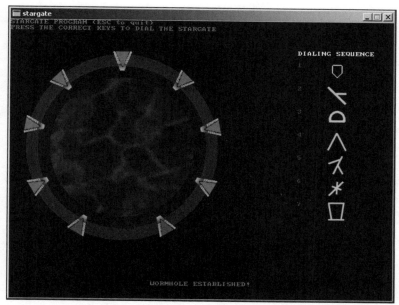

Figure 5.2 Opening a gateway to another world—speculative fantasy or a real possibility?

```
#include "allegro.h"

#define WHITE makecol(255,255,255)
#define BLUE makecol(64,64,255)
#define RED makecol(255,64,64)

typedef struct POINT
{
    int x, y;
} POINT;

POINT coords[] = {{25,235},
                  {15,130},
                  {60,50},
                  {165,10},
                  {270,50},
                  {325,135},
                  {315,235}};

BITMAP *stargate;
BITMAP *water;
```

```
BITMAP *symbols[7];
int count = 0;

//helper function to highlight each shevron
void shevron(int num)
{
    floodfill(screen, 20+coords[num].x, 50+coords[num].y, RED);

    if (++count > 6)
    {
        masked_blit(water,screen,0,0,67,98,water->w,water->h);
        textout_centre(screen,font,"WORMHOLE ESTABLISHED!",
            SCREEN_W/2, SCREEN_H-30, RED);
    }
}

//main function
void main(void)
{
    int n;

    //initialize program
    allegro_init();
    set_color_depth(16);
    set_gfx_mode(GFX_AUTODETECT_FULLSCREEN, 640, 480, 0, 0);
    install_keyboard();

    //load the stargate image
    stargate = load_bitmap("stargate.bmp", NULL);
    blit(stargate,screen,0,0,20,50,stargate->w,stargate->h);

    //load the water image
    water = load_bitmap("water.bmp", NULL);

    //load the symbol images
    symbols[0] = load_bitmap("symbol1.bmp", NULL);
    symbols[1] = load_bitmap("symbol2.bmp", NULL);
    symbols[2] = load_bitmap("symbol3.bmp", NULL);
    symbols[3] = load_bitmap("symbol4.bmp", NULL);
    symbols[4] = load_bitmap("symbol5.bmp", NULL);
    symbols[5] = load_bitmap("symbol6.bmp", NULL);
    symbols[6] = load_bitmap("symbol7.bmp", NULL);
```

```
//display the symbols
textout(screen,font,"DIALING SEQUENCE", 480, 50, WHITE);
for (n=0; n<7; n++)
{
    textprintf(screen,font,480,70+n*40,BLUE,"%d", n+1);
    blit(symbols[n],screen,0,0,530,70+n*40,32,32);
}


//display title
textout(screen,font,"STARGATE PROGRAM (ESC to quit)", 0, 0, RED);
textout(screen,font,"PRESS THE CORRECT KEYS (A-Z) "\
    "TO DIAL THE STARGATE", 0, 10, RED);

//main loop
while (!key[KEY_ESC])
{
    //check for proper sequence
    switch (count)
    {
        case 0:
            if (key[KEY_A]) shevron(0);
            break;
        case 1:
            if (key[KEY_Y]) shevron(1);
            break;
        case 2:
            if (key[KEY_B]) shevron(2);
            break;
        case 3:
            if (key[KEY_A]) shevron(3);
            break;
        case 4:
            if (key[KEY_B]) shevron(4);
            break;
        case 5:
            if (key[KEY_T]) shevron(5);
            break;
        case 6:
            if (key[KEY_U]) shevron(6);
            break;
    }
}
```

```
//clean up
destroy_bitmap(stargate);
destroy_bitmap(water);
for (n=0; n<7; n++)
    destroy_bitmap(symbols[n]);

allegro_exit();
}
END_OF_MAIN();
```

Buffered Keyboard Input

Buffered keyboard input is a less direct way of reading keyboard input in which individual key codes are not scanned; instead, the ASCII code is returned by one of the buffered keyboard input functions, such as readkey.

```
int readkey();
```

The readkey function returns the ASCII code of the next character in the keyboard buffer. If no key has been pressed, then readkey waits for the next key press. There is a similar function for handling Unicode keys called ureadkey, which returns the Unicode value (a two-byte value similar to ASCII) while returning the scan code as a pointer. (I have often wondered why Allegro doesn't simply return these values as a four-byte long.)

```
int ureadkey(int *scancode);
```

The readkey function actually returns two values using a two-byte integer value. The low byte of the return value contains the ASCII code (which changes based on Ctrl, Alt, and Shift keys), while the high byte contains the scan code (which is always the same regardless of the control keys). Because the scan code is included in the upper byte, you can use the predefined key array to detect buffered key presses by shifting the bits. Shifting the value returned by readkey by eight results in the scan code. For instance:

```
if ((readkey() >> 8) == KEY_TAB)
    printf("You pressed Tab\n");
```

Of course, it is easier to use just the key array unless you need to read both the scan code and the ASCII code at the same time, which is where readkey comes in handy.

As an alternative, you can also check the ASCII code and detect control key sequences at the same time using the key_shifts value.

```
extern volatile int key_shifts;
```

This integer contains a bitmask with the following possible values:

```
KB_SHIFT_FLAGKB_CTRL_FLAGKB_ALT_FLAG
KB_LWIN_FLAG
KB_RWIN_FLAG
KB_MENU_FLAG
KB_SCROLOCK_FLAG
KB_NUMLOCK_FLAG
KB_CAPSLOCK_FLAG
KB_INALTSEQ_FLAG
KB_ACCENT1_FLAG
KB_ACCENT2_FLAG
KB_ACCENT3_FLAG
KB_ACCENT4_FLAG
```

For instance:

```
if ((key_shifts & KB_CTRL_FLAG) && (readkey() == 13))
    printf("You pressed CTRL+Enter\n");
```

Of course, I personally find it easier to simply write the code this way:

```
if ((key[KEY_CTRL] && key[KEY_ENTER])
    printf("You pressed CTRL+Enter\n");
```

You can also use a support function provided by Allegro to convert the scan code to an ASCII value with the `scancode_to_ascii` function.

```
int scancode_to_ascii(int scancode);
```

One more support function that you might want to use is `set_keyboard_rate`, which changes the key repeat rate of the keyboard (in milliseconds). You can disable the key repeat by passing zeros to this function.

```
void set_keyboard_rate(int delay, int repeat);
```

Simulating Key Presses

Suppose you have written a game and you want to create a game demo, but you don't want to write a complicated program just to demonstrate a "proof of concept." There is an elegant solution to the problem—simulating key presses. Allegro provides two functions you can use to insert keys into the keyboard buffer so it will appear as if those keys were actually pressed.

The function is called `simulate_keypress`, and it has a similar support function for Unicode called `simulate_ukeypress`. Here are the definitions:

```
void simulate_keypress(int key);
void simulate_ukeypress(int key, int scancode);
```

In addition to inserting keys into the keyboard buffer, you can also clear the keyboard buffer entirely using the clear_keybuf function.

```
void clear_keybuf();
```

The KeyTest Program

I would be remiss if I didn't provide a sample program to demonstrate buffered keyboard input, although this small sample program is not as interesting as the last one. Nevertheless, it always helps to see the theory of a particular subject in action. Figure 5.3 shows the *KeyTest* program. This is a convenient program to keep handy because you'll frequently need keyboard scan codes, and this program makes it easy to look them up (knowing that you are free to use Allegro's predefined keys or the scan codes directly).

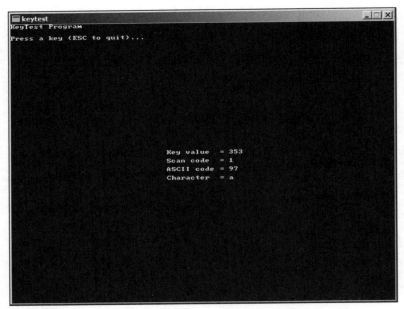

Figure 5.3 The *KeyTest* program shows the key value, scan code, ASCII code, and character.

```
#include <conio.h>
#include <stdlib.h>
#include "allegro.h"

#define WHITE makecol(255,255,255)

void main(void)
{
```

```
    int k, x, y;
    int scancode, ascii;

    //initialize program
    allegro_init();
    set_color_depth(16);
    set_gfx_mode(GFX_AUTODETECT_WINDOWED, 640, 480, 0, 0);
    install_keyboard();

    //display title
    textout(screen,font,"KeyTest Program", 0, 0, WHITE);
    textout(screen,font,"Press a key (ESC to quit)...", 0, 20, WHITE);

    //set starting position for text
    x = SCREEN_W/2 - 60;
    y = SCREEN_H/2 - 20;

    while (!key[KEY_ESC])
    {
        //get and convert scan code
        k = readkey();
        scancode = (k >> 8);
        ascii = scancode_to_ascii(scancode);

        //display key values
        textprintf(screen, font, x, y, WHITE,
            "Key value  = %-6d", k);
        textprintf(screen, font, x, y+15, WHITE,
            "Scan code  = %-6d", scancode);
        textprintf(screen, font, x, y+30, WHITE,
            "ASCII code = %-6d", ascii);
        textprintf(screen, font, x, y+45, WHITE,
            "Character  = %-6c", (char)ascii);
    }
    allegro_exit();
}
END_OF_MAIN();
```

Handling Mouse Input

Mouse input is probably even more vital to a modern game than keyboard input, so support for the mouse is not just an option, it is an assumption, a requirement (unless you are planning to develop a text game).

The Mouse Handler

Allegro is consistent with the input routines, so it is fairly easy to explain how to enable the mouse handler. The one thing you must remember is that the mouse routines (which I'll go over shortly) must only be used after the mouse handler has been installed with the install_mouse function.

```
int install_mouse();
```

Although it is not required because allegro_exit handles this aspect for you, you can use the remove_mouse function to remove the mouse handler.

```
void remove_mouse();
```

Another similarity between the mouse and keyboard handlers is the ability to poll the mouse rather than using the asynchronous interrupt handler to feed values to the mouse variables and functions at your disposal.

```
int poll_mouse();
```

When you have forced mouse polling by calling this function, or when your program is running under an operating system that doesn't support asynchronous interrupt handlers, you can check the polled state using mouse_needs_poll. If you suspect that polling might be necessary (based on the operating system you are targeting for the game), it's a good idea to call this function to determine whether polling is indeed needed.

```
int mouse_needs_poll();
```

Reading the Mouse Position

After you install the mouse handler, you automatically have access to the mouse values and functions without much ado (or any more effort). The mouse_x and mouse_y variables are defined and populated with the mouse position by Allegro.

```
extern volatile int mouse_x;
extern volatile int mouse_y;
```

The mouse_z variable contains the current value of the mouse wheel (if supported by the mouse driver and the operating system). I think it's a great idea to support the mouse wheel in a game whenever possible because it's a frequent and popular option, and most new mice have mouse wheels.

```
extern volatile int mouse_z;
```

Detecting Mouse Buttons

Obviously you can't do much with just the mouse position, so wouldn't it be helpful to also have the ability to detect mouse button clicks? You can do just that by using the mouse_b variable.

```
extern volatile int mouse_b;
```

This single integer variable contains the button values in packed bit format, where the first bit is button one, the second bit is button two, and the third bit is button three. If you want to check for a specific button, you can just use the & (logical and) operator to compare a bit inside mouse_b.

```
if (mouse_b & 1)
    printf("Left button was pressed");
if (mouse_b & 2)
    printf("Right button was pressed");
if (mouse_b & 4)
    printf("Center button was pressed");
```

Showing and Hiding the Mouse Pointer

Since an Allegro game will usually run in full-screen mode (or at least take over the entire window in windowed mode), you need a way to display a graphical mouse pointer. Anything other than the default operating system pointer is needed to really personalize a game. To facilitate this, Allegro provides the set_mouse_sprite function.

```
void set_mouse_sprite(BITMAP *sprite);
```

As you can see from the function definition, show_mouse needs a bitmap to display as the mouse pointer. Although I won't cover bitmaps and sprites until later (see Chapter 7, "Basic Bitmap Handling and Blitting," and Chapter 8, "Basic Sprite Programming"), you'll have to make some assumptions at this point and just go with the code. I will show you how to load a bitmap image and display it as the mouse pointer shortly, in the *Strategic Defense* game.

You can use a helper function after you call set_mouse_sprite to draw a graphical mouse pointer. The set_mouse_sprite_focus function adjusts the center point of the mouse cursor, with a default at the upper-left corner. If you are using a mouse pointer with another focal point, you can use this function to set that point within the mouse pointer.

```
void set_mouse_sprite_focus(int x, int y);
```

Of course, you are free to continue using the system mouse in windowed mode. Even in full-screen mode the mouse position is polled, but no mouse pointer is displayed.

When you are using a graphical mouse, you must tell the mouse handler where the mouse should be displayed. Remember that the pointer is just an image treated as a transparent sprite, so you have the option to draw the mouse directly to the screen or to any other bitmap (such as a secondary image used for double-buffering the screen). Use the show_mouse function to tell the mouse handler where you want the mouse pointer drawn.

```
void show_mouse(BITMAP *bmp);
```

Now what about hiding a graphical mouse once it's been drawn? This is actually a very important consideration because the mouse is basically treated as a transparent sprite, so it will interfere with the objects being drawn on the screen. Therefore, the mouse pointer needs to be hidden during screen updates, and then enabled again after drawing is completed. It's a bit of a pun that the function to hide the mouse pointer is called scare_mouse, and the function to show the mouse again is called unscare_mouse.

```
void scare_mouse();
void unscare_mouse();
```

There is also a version of this function that hides the mouse only if the mouse is within a certain part of the screen. If you know what part of the screen is being updated, you can use scare_mouse_area instead of scare_mouse, in which case the mouse simply will be frozen until you call unscare_mouse to re-enable it.

```
void scare_mouse_area(int x, int y, int w, int h);
```

The Strategic Defense Game

I have written a short game to demonstrate how to use the basic mouse handler functions covered so far. This game is a derivation of the classic *Missile Command* and it is called *Strategic Defense*. The game uses the mouse position and the left mouse button to control a defense weapon to destroy incoming enemy missiles. Figure 5.4 shows a missile being destroyed.

The game features a graphical mouse pointer that is used as a targeting reticule, as shown in Figure 5.5.

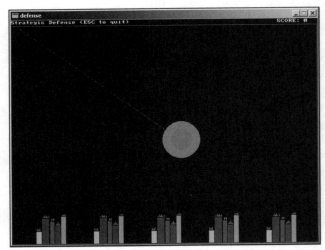

Figure 5.4 *Strategic Defense* demonstrates the mouse handler.

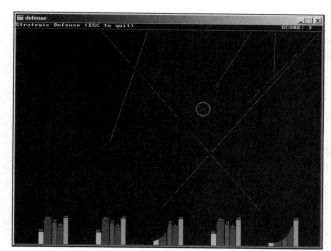

Figure 5.5 A graphical mouse pointer is used for targeting enemy missiles.

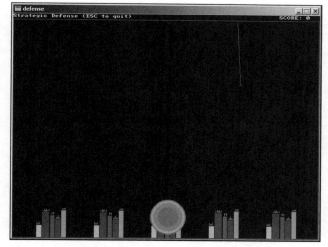

Figure 5.6 Firing on one's cities is generally frowned upon, but it is not destructive in this game.

When enemy missiles reach the ground (represented by the bottom of the screen) they will explode, taking out any nearby enemy cities.

One interesting thing about the game is how it uses a secondary screen buffer. Rather than writing extensive code to erase explosions and restore the mouse cursor, the game simply draws explosions directly on the screen rather than to the buffer (which contains the background image, including the game title and the cities). Thus, when the player fires directly on a city (as shown in Figure 5.6), that city remains intact because the explosion was drawn to the screen, while the buffer image remained intact. Perhaps it's not as realistic, but we don't want to destroy our own cities!

You might also notice in the figures that the game keeps track of the score in the upper-right corner of the screen. You gain a point for every enemy missile you destroy. Unfortunately, there is no ending to this game; it will keep running with an endless barrage of enemy missiles until you hit Esc to quit.

Type in the game's source code, and then have some fun! If you'd like to load the project off the CD-ROM, it is in the chapter08 folder and the file is called defense. This game might be overkill just to demonstrate the mouse, but it has some features that are helpful for the learning process, such as a real-time game loop, the use of bitmaps and sprites, and basic game logic. This game is far more complex than *Tank War*, but it is not without flaws. For one thing, the original *Missile Command* had multiple incoming enemy missiles and allowed the player to target them, after which a missile would fire from turrets on the ground to take out the enemy missiles. These features would really make the game a lot more fun, so I encourage you to add them if you are so inclined.

Want a hint? You can add a dimension to the points array to support many "lines" for incoming missiles. How would you fire anti-ballistic missiles from the ground up to the mouse-click spot? Reverse-engineer the enemy missile code, add another array (perhaps something like mypoints), add another line callback function that doesn't interfere with the existing one, and reverse the direction (with the starting position at the bottom, moving upward toward the mouse click). When the friendly missile reaches the end of its line, it will explode. It's like adding an intermediate step between the time you press the mouse button and when the explosion occurs.

```c
#include <conio.h>
#include <stdlib.h>
#include "allegro.h"

//create some colors
#define WHITE makecol(255,255,255)
#define BLACK makecol(0,0,0)
#define RED makecol(255,0,0)
#define GREEN makecol(0,255,0)
#define BLUE makecol(0,0,255)
#define SMOKE makecol(140,130,120)

//point structure used to draw lines
typedef struct POINT
{
    int x,y;
}POINT;

//points array holds do_line points for drawing a line
POINT points[2000];
int curpoint,totalpoints;

//bitmap images
BITMAP *buffer;
BITMAP *crosshair;
BITMAP *city;

//misc variables
int x1,y1,x2,y2;
int done=0;
```

```
int destroyed=1;
int n;
int mx,my,mb;
int score = -1;

void updatescore()
{
    //update and display the score
    score++;
    textprintf_right(buffer,font,SCREEN_W-5,1,WHITE,
        "SCORE: %d  ", score);
}

void explosion(BITMAP *bmp, int x,int y,int finalcolor)
{
    int color,size;

    for (n=0; n<20; n++)
    {
        //generate a random color
        color = makecol(rand()%255,rand()%255,rand()%255);
        //random explosion size
        size = 20+rand()%20;
        //draw the random filled circle
        circlefill(bmp, x, y, size, color);
        //short pause
        rest(2);
    }
    //missile tracker looks for this explosion color
    circlefill(bmp, x, y, 40, finalcolor);
}


void doline(BITMAP *bmp, int x, int y, int d)
{
    //line callback function...fills the points array
    points[totalpoints].x = x;
    points[totalpoints].y = y;
    totalpoints++;
}

void firenewmissile()
{
```

```
    //activate the new missile
    destroyed=0;
    totalpoints = 0;
    curpoint = 0;

    //random starting location
    x1 = rand() % (SCREEN_W-1);
    y1 = 20;

    //random ending location
    x2 = rand() % (SCREEN_W-1);
    y2 = SCREEN_H-50;

    //construct the line point-by-point
    do_line(buffer,x1,y1,x2,y2,0,&doline);
}

void movemissile()
{
    //grab a local copy of the current point
    int x = points[curpoint].x;
    int y = points[curpoint].y;

    //hide mouse pointer
    scare_mouse();

    //erase missile
    rectfill(buffer,x-6,y-3,x+6,y+1,BLACK);

    //see if missile was hit by defense weapon
    if (getpixel(screen,x,y) == GREEN)
    {
        //missile destroyed! score a point
        destroyed++;
        updatescore();
    }
    else
    //no hit, just draw the missile and smoke trail
    {
        //draw the smoke trail
        putpixel(buffer,x,y-3,SMOKE);
        //draw the missile
        circlefill(buffer,x,y,2,BLUE);
```

```
    }

    //show mouse pointer
    unscare_mouse();

    //did the missile hit a city?
    curpoint++;
    if (curpoint >= totalpoints)
    {
        //destroy the missile
        destroyed++;
        //animate explosion directly on screen
        explosion(screen, x, y, BLACK);
        //show the damage on the backbuffer
        circlefill(buffer, x, y, 40, BLACK);
    }
}

void main(void)
{
    //initialize program
    allegro_init();
    set_color_depth(16);
    set_gfx_mode(GFX_AUTODETECT_WINDOWED, 640, 480, 0, 0);
    install_keyboard();
    install_mouse();
    install_timer();
    srand(time(NULL));

    //create a secondary screen buffer
    buffer = create_bitmap(640,480);

    //display title
    textout(buffer,font,"Strategic Defense (ESC to quit)",0,1,WHITE);

    //display score
    updatescore();

    //draw border around screen
    rect(buffer, 0, 12, SCREEN_W-2, SCREEN_H-2, RED);

    //load and draw the city images
    city = load_bitmap("city.bmp", NULL);
```

```
        for (n = 0; n < 5; n++)
            masked_blit(city, buffer, 0, 0, 50+n*120,
                SCREEN_H-city->h-2, city->w, city->h);

    //load the mouse cursor
    crosshair = load_bitmap("crosshair.bmp", NULL);
    set_mouse_sprite(crosshair);
    set_mouse_sprite_focus(15,15);
    show_mouse(buffer);

    //main loop
    while (!key[KEY_ESC])
    {
        //grab the current mouse values
        mx = mouse_x;
        my = mouse_y;
        mb = (mouse_b & 1);

        //fire another missile if needed
        if (destroyed)
            firenewmissile();

        //left mouse button, fire the defense weapon
        if (mb)
            explosion(screen,mx,my,GREEN);

        //update enemy missile position
        movemissile();

        //update screen
        blit(buffer,screen,0,0,0,0,640,480);

        //pause
        rest(10);
    }

    set_mouse_sprite(NULL);
    destroy_bitmap(city);
    destroy_bitmap(crosshair);
    allegro_exit();

}
END_OF_MAIN();
```

Setting the Mouse Position

You can set the mouse position to any point on the screen explicitly using the position_mouse function.

```
void position_mouse(int x, int y);
```

This could be useful if you have a dialog on the screen and you want to move the mouse there automatically. You could also use position_mouse to create a tutorial for your game. (Show the player what to click by sliding the mouse around the screen using an array of coordinates, which could be captured by repeatedly grabbing the mouse position and storing the values.)

The *PositionMouse* program demonstrates how to use this function for an interesting effect. Moving the mouse over one location on the screen transports the mouse to another location. Figure 5.7 shows the program running. There are two wormholes, with a spaceship representing the mouse cursor. The only potentially confusing part of the program is the mouseinside function, so I'll give you a quick overview. This function checks to see whether the mouse is within the boundary of a rectangle passed to the function (x1, y1,x2,y2); it returns 1 (true) if the mouse is inside the rectangular area.

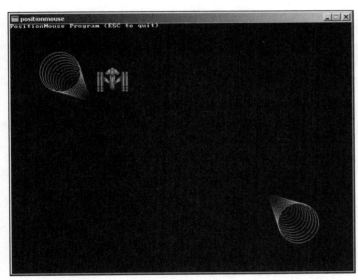

Figure 5.7 The *PositionMouse* program demonstrates the pros and cons of hyperspace travel. Ship image courtesy of Ari Feldman.

```
#include <conio.h>
#include <stdlib.h>
#include "allegro.h"

#define WHITE makecol(255,255,255)

int mouseinside(int x1,int y1,int x2,int y2)
{
    if (mouse_x > x1 && mouse_x < x2 && mouse_y > y1 && mouse_y < y2)
```

```
            return 1;
        else
            return 0;
}

void main(void)
{
    int n, x, y;

    //initialize program
    allegro_init();
    set_color_depth(16);
    set_gfx_mode(GFX_AUTODETECT_WINDOWED, 640, 480, 0, 0);
    install_keyboard();
    install_mouse();
    textout(screen,font,"PositionMouse Program (ESC to quit)",0,0,WHITE);

    //load the custom mouse pointer
    BITMAP *ship = load_bitmap("spaceship.bmp", NULL);
    set_mouse_sprite(ship);
    set_mouse_sprite_focus(ship->w/2,ship->h/2);
    show_mouse(screen);

    //draw the wormholes
    for (n=0;n<20;n++)
    {
        circle(screen,150-3*n,150-3*n,n*2,makecol(10*n,10*n,10*n));
        circle(screen,480+3*n,330+3*n,n*2,makecol(10*n,10*n,10*n));
    }

    while (!key[KEY_ESC])
    {
        if (mouseinside(90,90,150,150))
            position_mouse(550,400);

        if (mouseinside(480,330,540,390))
            position_mouse(80,80);
    }
    set_mouse_sprite(NULL);
    destroy_bitmap(ship);
    allegro_exit();
}
END_OF_MAIN();
```

Limiting Mouse Movement and Speed

There are two helper functions that you will likely never use, but which are available nonetheless. The set_mouse_range function limits the mouse pointer to a specified rectangular region on the screen. Obviously, the default range is the entire screen, but you can limit the range if you want.

```
void set_mouse_range(int x1, int y1, int x2, int y2);
```

The second helper function is set_mouse_speed, which overrides the default mouse pointer speed set by the operating system. (Note that the mouse speed is not affected outside your program.) Greater values for the xspeed and yspeed parameters result in slower mouse movement. The default is 2 for each.

```
void set_mouse_speed(int xspeed, int yspeed);
```

Relative Mouse Motion

When it comes to game programming, relative mouse motion can be a very important feature at your disposal. Often, games will need to track the mouse movement without regard to the position of a pointer on the screen. Indeed, many games (especially first-person shooters) don't even have a mouse pointer; rather, they use the mouse to adjust the viewpoint of the player in the game world. This is called *relative mouse motion* because you can continue to move the mouse to the left (lifting the mouse and dragging it to the left again) over and over again, resulting in the game world spinning around the player continuously. Keep this in mind as you design your own games. The mouse need not be limited to the boundaries of the screen; it can return an infinite range of mouse movement.

```
void get_mouse_mickeys(int *mickeyx, int *mickeyy);
```

To use the mickeys returned by this function, you will want to create two integer variables to keep track of the last values, and then compare them to the new values returned by get_mouse_mickeys. You can then determine whether the mouse has moved up, down, left, or right, with the result having some effect in the game.

Using a Mouse Wheel

The mouse wheel is another great feature to support in your games. Although I would not assign any critical gameplay controls to the mouse wheel (because it might not be present), it is definitely a nice accessory of which you should take advantage when available. The mouse wheel is abstracted by Allegro into a simple variable that you can check at your leisure.

```
extern volatile int mouse_z;
```

Allegro provides a mouse wheel support function that seems rather odd at first glance, but it allows you to set the mouse wheel variable to a specific starting value, after which successive "reads" will result in values to and from that central value. In effect, position_mouse_z sets the current mouse wheel position as the starting position. Technically, the mouse wheel doesn't have starting and ending points because it is freewheeling.

```
void position_mouse_z(int z);
```

I have written a short program that demonstrates how to use the mouse wheel. The *MouseWheel* program doesn't really do anything; it displays a fictional throttle ramp (or any other lever, for that matter) and displays a small image that moves up or down based on the mouse wheel value. The program is shown in Figure 5.8. What was I thinking about when I wrote this program? I have no idea, and it makes no sense at all, does it? I think the idea is that this represents a reactor core temperature gauge, and if it goes critical, the reactor will explode. But you have your mouse wheel handy to prevent that. Your mouse *does* have a wheel, right? Perhaps you can turn this into a real game. I find it convenient to have one of those Microsoft Office keyboards with the big spinning wheel—yeah, you can spin that sucker like a top! Hey, why don't you turn this into an interesting game?

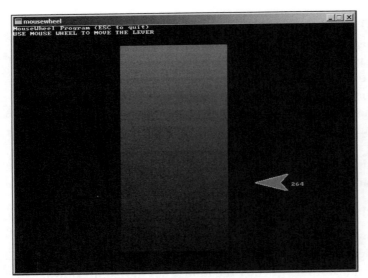

Figure 5.8 The *MouseWheel* program demonstrates how to use the mouse wheel. (Duh!)

```
#include <conio.h>
#include <stdlib.h>
#include "allegro.h"

#define WHITE makecol(255,255,255)
#define BLACK makecol(0,0,0)
#define AQUA makecol(0,200,255)

void main(void)
```

```
{
    int n, color, value;

    //initialize program
    allegro_init();
    set_color_depth(16);
    set_gfx_mode(GFX_AUTODETECT_WINDOWED, 640, 480, 0, 0);
    install_keyboard();
    install_mouse();
    textout(screen,font,"MouseWheel Program (ESC to quit)",0,0,WHITE);
    textout(screen,font,"USE MOUSE WHEEL TO MOVE THE LEVER",0,10,WHITE);

    //load the control lever image
    BITMAP *lever = load_bitmap("lever.bmp", NULL);

    //draw the throttle control
    for (n=0; n<200; n++)
    {
        color = makecol(255-n,10,10);
        rectfill(screen, 200, 40 + n * 2, 400, 42 + n * 2, color);
    }

    value=200;
    position_mouse_z(value);

    while (!key[KEY_ESC])
    {
        //erase the lever
        rectfill(screen, 450, 29 + value, 550, value + 65, BLACK);

        //update lever position
        value = mouse_z;
        if (value < 0)
            value = 0;
        if (value > 390)
            value = 390;

        //draw the lever
        blit(lever, screen, 0, 0, 450, 30 + value, lever->w, lever->h);

        //display value
        textprintf(screen, font, 520, 30 + value + lever->h / 2,
            AQUA,"%d", value);
```

```
        rest(30);
    }

    allegro_exit();
}
END_OF_MAIN();
```

Handling Joystick Input

Joysticks are not as common on the PC as they used to be, and the accessory controller market has fallen significantly since the late 1990s—to such a degree that Microsoft has dropped its Sidewinder line of gamepads and flight sticks (although at least one stick is still available from Microsoft to support its legendary *Flight Simulator* and *Combat Flight Simulator* products). I have personally been a Logitech fan for many years, and I appreciate the high quality of their mouse and joystick peripherals. The Logitech WingMan RumblePad is still my favorite gamepad because it has two analog sticks that make it useful for flight and space sims. In this section, I'll show you how to add joystick support to your bevy of new game development skills made possible with the Allegro library.

The Joystick Handler

At this point, it's becoming redundant, but we still have to initialize the joystick handler like we did for the keyboard and mouse. At least Allegro is consistent, which is not something that can be said about all libraries. The first function you need to learn is install_joystick.

```
int install_joystick(int type);
```

What is the type parameter, you might wonder? Actually, I have no idea, so I just plug random values into it to see what happens—so far with no result.

Just kidding! The type parameter specifies the type of joystick being used, while JOY_TYPE_AUTODETECT is currently the only supported value. Because Allegro abstracts the DirectInput library to provide a generic joystick controller interface, it provides functionality for supporting digital and analog buttons and sticks. If you ever need to remove the joystick handler, you can call remove_joystick.

```
void remove_joystick();
```

Allegro's joystick handler can handle at most four joysticks, which is more than I have ever seen in a single game. If you have written a game that needs more than four joysticks, let me know because I'd like to help you redesign the game! Seriously, what this really means is that you can use a driving wheel with foot pedals, which are usually treated as two joystick devices. To find out how many joysticks have been detected by Allegro, you can use num_joysticks.

```
extern int num_joysticks;
```

As was the case with the two previous hardware handlers, some systems do not support asynchronous interrupt handlers. However, this point is moot when it comes to joysticks, which must be polled. Here is the function:

```
int poll_joystick();
```

Remember, most (if not all) systems require you to poll the joystick because there is no automatic joystick interrupt handler running like there is for the keyboard and mouse handlers. Keep this in mind! If your joystick routine is not responding, it could be that you forgot to poll the joystick during the game loop!

tip

> The joystick handler has no interrupt routine, so you must poll the joystick inside your game loop or the joystick values will not be updated. The keyboard and mouse usually do not need to be polled, but the joystick does need it!

This function fills the JOYSTICK_INFO struct, which has this definition:

```
typedef struct JOYSTICK_INFO
{
    int flags;
    int num_sticks;
    int num_buttons;
    JOYSTICK_STICK_INFO stick[n];
    JOYSTICK_BUTTON_INFO button[n];
} JOYSTICK_INFO;
```

Allegro defines an array to handle any joysticks plugged into the system based on this struct.

```
extern JOYSTICK_INFO joy[n];
```

The default joystick should therefore be joy[0], which is what you will use most of the time if you are writing a game with joystick support.

Detecting Controller Stick Movement

The JOYSTICK_INFO struct contains two sub-structs, as you can see, and these sub-structs contain all of the actual joystick status information (analog/digital values). The JOYSTICK_STICK_INFO struct contains information about the sticks, which may be digital (such as an eight-way directional pad) or analog (with a range of values for position). Here is what that struct looks like:

```
typedef struct JOYSTICK_STICK_INFO
{
```

```
    int flags;
    int num_axis;
    JOYSTICK_AXIS_INFO axis[n];
    char *name;
} JOYSTICK_STICK_INFO;
```

I'll explain the flags element in a moment. For now, you need to know about num_axis and the axis[n] elements. char *name contains the name of the stick (if supported by your operating system's joystick driver). num_axis will tell you how many axes are provided by that stick. (Remember, there could be more than one stick on a joystick.) A normal stick will have two axes: X and Y. Therefore, most of the time num_axis will equal 2, and you will be able to read those axis values by looking at axis[0] and axis[1]. Some sticks are special types (such as a throttle control) that may only have one axis. If you are writing a large and complex game and you want to support as many joystick options as possible, you will want to look at all of these structs and their values to come up with a list of features available. For instance, if there are two sticks, and the first has two axes, while the second has one axis, it's a sure bet that this represents a flight-style joystick with a single stick and a throttle control. Obviously, for a large game it will be worth the time investment to create a joystick configuration option screen.

A single joystick might provide several different stick inputs (such as the two analog sticks on the Logitech WingMan RumblePad), but it is safe to assume that the first element in the stick array will always be the main directional stick. (Most joysticks have a single stick; the duals are the exception most of the time.)

Allegro really doesn't provide many support functions for decoding these structs—something that I found disappointing. However, the structs contain everything you need to read the joystick in real time, so there's no room for complaint as long as all the data is available. Besides, it's a far cry from programming a joystick using assembly language, as I did way back when—during the development of *Starship Battles*, which I talked about in Chapter 1.

Reading the Axes

To read the stick positions, you must take a look at the JOYSTICK_AXIS_INFO struct.

```
typedef struct JOYSTICK_AXIS_INFO
{
    int pos;
    int d1, d2;
    char *name;
} JOYSTICK_AXIS_INFO;
```

This struct provides one analog input (pos) and two digital inputs (d1, d2) that describe the same axis. While pos may contain a value of −128 to 128 (or 0 to 255, depending on the type of axis), the d1 and d2 values will be 0 or 1, based on whether the axis was moved left or right. A digital stick will provide just a single yes or no type result using d1 and d2, but the analog values are more common.

Reading the Joystick Flags

I want to digress for a moment to talk about the joystick flags defined as flags in the JOYSTICK_STICK_INFO struct. Table 5.2 shows the possible values stored in flags as a bit mask.

Table 5.2 Joystick Bit Mask Values

Flag	Description
JOYFLAG_DIGITAL	This control is currently providing digital input.
JOYFLAG_ANALOG	This control is currently providing analog input.
JOYFLAG_CALIB_DIGITAL	This control will be capable of providing digital input once it has been calibrated, but it is not doing this at the moment.
JOYFLAG_CALIB_ANALOG	This control will be capable of providing analog input once it has been calibrated, but it is not doing this at the moment.
JOYFLAG_CALIBRATE	This control needs to be calibrated. Many devices require multiple calibration steps, so you should call the calibrate_joystick() function from a loop until this flag is cleared.
JOYFLAG_SIGNED	The analog axis position is in signed format, ranging from −128 to 128. This is the case for all 2D directional controls.
JOYFLAG_UNSIGNED	The analog axis position is in unsigned format, ranging from 0 to 255. This is the case for all 1D throttle controls.

Thus, if you want to know whether the specified stick is analog or digital, you can check the flags member variable.

```
if (flags & JOYFLAG_DIGITAL)
    printf("This is a digital stick");
```

Allegro provides a series of functions for calibrating a joystick; these are useful for older operating systems (such as MS-DOS) where calibration was necessary. Most modern joysticks are calibrated at the driver level. In Windows, go to Start, Settings, Control Panel and look for Gaming Options or Game Controllers to find the joystick dialog. Windows 2000 uses the Gaming Options dialog box, as shown in Figure 5.9.

Clicking on the Properties button opens the calibration and test dialog box, as shown in Figure 5.10.

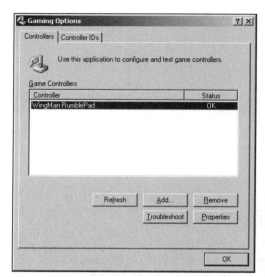

Figure 5.9 The Gaming Options dialog box in Windows 2000

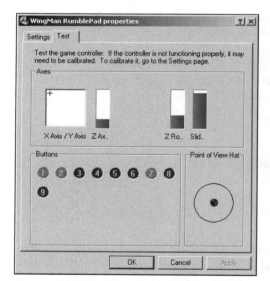

Figure 5.10 The Gaming Options properties dialog box for my WingMan RumblePad joystick

Using the Properties dialog box, you can verify that the joystick is operating (first and foremost) and that all the buttons and sticks are functioning.

Under Windows XP, the control panel applet for configuring your joystick seems to be about 12 levels deep inside the operating system, like an epithermal vein in the earth. For this reason, I recommend switching the Control Panel to Classic View so you can see exactly what you want without wading through Microsoft's patronizing interface. As a follower of the philosophies of Alan Cooper, my personal opinion is that too much interface is condescending. ("Hello sir. I believe you are too stupid to figure this out, so let me bury it for you.") However, I do appreciate and enjoy most of Microsoft's latest products—this company does get it right after eight or nine versions. It's all a matter of personal preference, though. Wouldn't you agree?

I digress again. Windows XP provides a similar applet called Game Controllers, with a similar joystick properties dialog box you can use to test your joystick. (In most cases, calibration is not needed with modern USB joysticks.)

Detecting Controller Buttons

Referring back to the primary joystick struct, JOYSTICK_INFO, you'll recall that the second sub-struct is called JOYSTICK_BUTTON_INFO.

```
JOYSTICK_BUTTON_INFO button[n];
```

This struct can be read with the help of num_buttons to determine the size of the button array.

```
int num_buttons;
```

The final struct you need to see to deal with joystick buttons has this definition:

```
typedef struct JOYSTICK_BUTTON_INFO
{
    int b;
    char *name;
} JOYSTICK_BUTTON_INFO;
```

The b element will simply be 0 or 1, based on whether the button is being pushed or not, while char *name describes that button.

Testing the Joystick Routines

I could call it a wrap at this point, but what I'd like to do now is provide two sample programs that demonstrate how to use the joystick routines. The first sample program, *ScanJoystick*, iterates through these structs to print out information about the joystick. The second program, *TestJoystick*, is a simple example of how to use the joystick in a real-time program.

The ScanJoystick Program

The *ScanJoystick* program goes through the joystick structs and prints out logistical information, including number of sticks, stick names, number of buttons, and button names. The output from the program is shown in Figure 5.11.

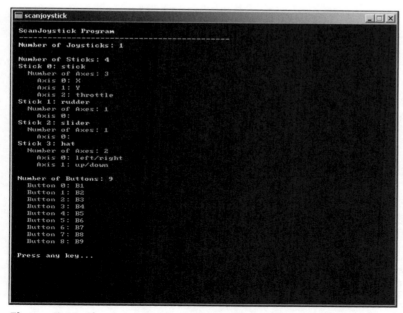

Figure 5.11 The *ScanJoystick* program prints out the vital information about the first joystick device.

```c
#include <conio.h>
#include <stdlib.h>
#include <stdio.h>
#include "allegro.h"

#define WHITE makecol(255,255,255)
#define LTGREEN makecol(192,255,192)
#define LTRED makecol(255,192,192)
#define LTBLUE makecol(192,192,255)
int curline = 1;

void print(char *s, int color)
{
    //print text with automatic linefeed
    textout(screen, font, s, 10, (curline++) * 12, color);
}

void printjoyinfo()
{
    char *s;
    int n, ax;

    //display joystick information
    sprintf(s, "Number of Joysticks: %d", num_joysticks);
    print(s, WHITE);
    print("",0);

    //display stick information
    sprintf(s, "Number of Sticks: %d", joy[0].num_sticks);
    print(s, LTGREEN);
    for (n=0; n<joy[0].num_sticks; n++)
    {
        sprintf(s, "Stick %d: %s", n, joy[0].stick[n].name);
        print(s, LTGREEN);
        sprintf(s, "  Number of Axes: %d", joy[0].stick[n].num_axis);
        print(s, LTBLUE);
        for (ax=0; ax<joy[0].stick[n].num_axis; ax++)
        {
            sprintf(s,"    Axis %d: %s", ax,
                joy[0].stick[n].axis[ax].name);
            print(s, LTRED);
        }
    }
}
```

```
        //display button information
        print("",0);
        sprintf(s, "Number of Buttons: %d", joy[0].num_buttons);
        print(s, LTGREEN);
        for (n=0; n<joy[0].num_buttons; n++)
        {
            sprintf(s," Button %d: %s", n, joy[0].button[n].name);
            print(s, LTBLUE);
        }
}

void main(void)
{
    int n, color, value;

    //initialize program
    allegro_init();
    set_color_depth(16);
    set_gfx_mode(GFX_AUTODETECT_WINDOWED, 640, 480, 0, 0);
    install_keyboard();

    //install the joystick handler
    install_joystick(JOY_TYPE_AUTODETECT);
    poll_joystick();

    //display title
    print("ScanJoystick Program", WHITE);
    print("---------------------", WHITE);

    //look for a joystick
    if (num_joysticks > 0)
        printjoyinfo();
    else
        print("No joystick could be found", WHITE);

    //pause and exit
    print("",0);
    print("Press any key...", WHITE);
    while (!keypressed()) { }
    allegro_exit();
}

END_OF_MAIN();
```

The TestJoystick Program

To really see what Allegro's joystick routines can do would require a full-blown game using the sticks for movement and the buttons for perhaps firing weapons. Hey, it sounds like *Tank War* would be a great candidate for just that! But for the time being, it is prudent to focus on a simple joystick demonstration that simply makes clear what you must do to get basic joystick support into your games. Thus, I have written a quick-and-dirty game with a functional name; it's just a ball bouncing around on the screen, with a paddle that is controlled by the joystick. Stop the ball from hitting the floor and gain a point; fail to stop the ball and lose a point. It's a very simple game in that respect. However, this game does use several bitmaps and blitting routines (including masked_blit to draw transparently). Unfortunately, these routines have not been explained yet, and I'm loath to do so now, when an entire chapter is dedicated to this subject! (See Chapter 7 for a complete explanation of how to use the bitmap loading and blitting functions.) For now, I would like to leave that discussion for Chapter 7 and just use this functionality to make the game more interesting.

Figure 5.12 shows this very simple and limited *Arkanoid/Breakout* style game in action. Again, I am indebted to Ari Feldman for the artwork (http://www.arifeldman.com), which comes from his free SpriteLib collection. The source code is only a few pages long, so I'll leave it to you to read my code comments and see how it works. I hope the game is simple enough that you will find it very easy to read the code and learn some new tricks from it.

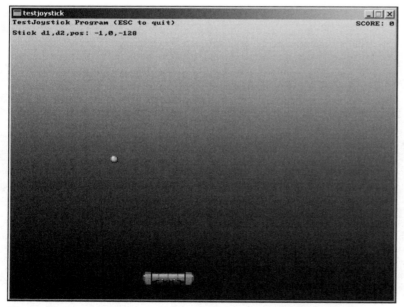

Figure 5.12 The *TestJoystick* program demonstrates how to use the joystick in a simple game.

```c
#include <conio.h>
#include <stdlib.h>
#include "allegro.h"

#define WHITE makecol(255,255,255)
#define BLACK makecol(0,0,0)

BITMAP *back;
BITMAP *paddle;
BITMAP *ball;

int score = 0, paddlex, paddley = 430;
int ballx = 100, bally = 100;
int dirx = 1, diry = 2;

void updateball()
{
    //update ball x
    ballx += dirx;

    //hit left?
    if (ballx < 0)
    {
        ballx = 1;
        dirx = rand() % 2 + 4;
    }

    //hit right?
    if (ballx > SCREEN_W - ball->w - 1)
    {
        ballx = SCREEN_W - ball->w - 1;
        dirx = rand() % 2 - 6;
    }

    //update ball y
    bally += diry;

    //hit top?
    if (bally < 0)
    {
        bally = 1;
        diry = rand() % 2 + 4;
    }
```

```
    //hit bottom?
    if (bally > SCREEN_H - ball->h - 1)
    {
        score--;
        bally = SCREEN_H - ball->h - 1;
        diry = rand() % 2 - 6;
    }


    //hit the paddle?
    if (ballx > paddlex && ballx < paddlex+paddle->w &&
        bally > paddley && bally < paddley+paddle->h)
    {
        score++;
        bally = paddley - ball->h - 1;
        diry = rand() % 2 - 6;
    }


    //draw ball
    masked_blit(ball, screen, 0, 0, ballx, bally, ball->w, ball->h);
}

void main(void)
{
    int d1, d2, pos, startpos;

    //initialize program
    allegro_init();
    set_color_depth(16);
    set_gfx_mode(GFX_AUTODETECT_WINDOWED, 640, 480, 0, 0);
    srand(time(NULL));
    install_keyboard();

    //install the joystick handler
    install_joystick(JOY_TYPE_AUTODETECT);
    poll_joystick();

    //look for a joystick
    if (num_joysticks == 0)
    {
        textout(screen,font,"No joystick could be found",0,20,WHITE);
        while(!keypressed());
        return;
    }
```

```
//store starting stick position
startpos = joy[0].stick[0].axis[0].pos;

//load the background image
back = load_bitmap("background.bmp", NULL);

//load the paddle image and position it
paddle = load_bitmap("paddle.bmp", NULL);
paddlex = SCREEN_W/2 - paddle->w/2;

//load the ball image
ball = load_bitmap("ball.bmp", NULL);

//set text output to transparent
text_mode(-1);

//main loop
while (!key[KEY_ESC])
{
    //clear screen the slow way (redraw background)
    blit(back, screen, 0, 0, 0, 0, back->w, back->h);

    //update ball position
    updateball();

    //read the joystick
    poll_joystick();
    d1 = joy[0].stick[0].axis[0].d1;
    d2 = joy[0].stick[0].axis[0].d2;
    pos = joy[0].stick[0].axis[0].pos;

    //see if stick moved left
    if (d1 || pos < startpos+10) paddlex -= 4;
    if (paddlex < 2) paddlex = 2;

    //see if stick moved right
    if (d2 || pos > startpos-10) paddlex += 4;
    if (paddlex > SCREEN_W - paddle->w - 2)
        paddlex = SCREEN_W - paddle->w - 2;

    //display text messages
    textout(screen, font, "TestJoystick Program (ESC to quit)",
        2, 2, BLACK);
```

```
            textprintf(screen, font, 2, 20, BLACK,
                "Stick d1,d2,pos: %d,%d,%d", d1, d2, pos);
            textprintf_right(screen, font, SCREEN_W - 2, 2, BLACK,
                "SCORE: %d", score);

            //draw the paddle
            blit(paddle,screen,0,0,paddlex,paddley,paddle->w,paddle->h);

            rest(20);
        }

    destroy_bitmap(back);
    destroy_bitmap(paddle);
    destroy_bitmap(ball);
    return;
}

END_OF_MAIN();
```

Summary

I don't know about you, but I got more from this chapter than I had intended! There were many new functions presented in this chapter, with absolutely no explanation for some of them! I'm talking about load_bitmap, blit, masked_blit, and so on. That is breaking a rule I had intended to follow about only using what I have covered thus far; however, I think it's a helpful learning experience to see some of what is to come.

This chapter presented Allegro's input routines and explained how to read the keyboard, mouse, and joystick—which, it turns out, is not difficult at all thanks to the way in which Allegro abstracted these hardware input devices.

The big question you might have is, why didn't we update *Tank War* to support a joystick? That's a good question. As a matter of fact, I wanted to plug in the joystick support at this point, but I felt that it would make the game too complicated this early along in the book, when the goal is really to demonstrate each chapter's new graphics features in the game. In a nutshell, the game is just too primitive and underdeveloped at this point to warrant joystick support. Therefore, I make this vow: We will add joystick support to *Tank War* in a future chapter. I guarantee it!

Chapter Quiz

You can find the answers to this chapter quiz in Appendix A, "Chapter Quiz Answers."

1. Which function is used to initialize the keyboard handler?
   - A.   `initialize_keyboard`
   - B.   `install_keyboard`
   - C.   `init_keyboard`
   - D.   `install_keyboard_handler`

2. What does ANSI stand for?
   - A.   American Negligible Situation Imperative
   - B.   American Nutritional Studies Institute
   - C.   American National Standards Institute
   - D.   American National Scuba Institute

3. What is the name of the array containing keyboard scan codes?
   - A.   `key`
   - B.   `keyboard`
   - C.   `scancodes`
   - D.   `keys`

4. Where is the real stargate located?
   - A.   Salt Lake City, Utah
   - B.   San Antonio, Texas
   - C.   Colorado Springs, Colorado
   - D.   Cairo, Egypt

5. Which function provides buffered keyboard input?
   - A.   `scankey`
   - B.   `getkey`
   - C.   `readkey`
   - D.   `buffered_input`

6. Which function is used to initialize the mouse handler?
   - A.   `install_mouse`
   - B.   `instantiate_mouse`
   - C.   `initialize_mouse`
   - D.   `ingratiate_mouse`

7. Which values or functions are used to read the mouse position?
   A. mouse_x and mouse_y
   B. get_mouse_x and get_mouse_y
   C. mousex and mousey
   D. mouse_position_x and mouse_position_y

8. Which function is used to read the mouse x and y mickeys for relative motion?
   A. mickey_mouse
   B. read_mouse_mickeys
   C. mouse_mickeys
   D. get_mouse_mickeys

9. What is the name of the main JOYSTICK_INFO array?
   A. joysticks
   B. joy
   C. sticks
   D. joystick

10. Which struct contains joystick button data?
   A. JOYSTICK_BUTTONS
   B. JOYSTICK_BUTTON
   C. JOYSTICK_BUTTON_INFO
   D. JOYSTICK_BUTTON_DATA

PART II

2D GAME THEORY, DESIGN, AND PROGRAMMING

CHAPTER 6
Introduction to Game Design 187

CHAPTER 7
Basic Bitmap Handling and Blitting 215

CHAPTER 8
Basic Sprite Programming 237

CHAPTER 9
Advanced Sprite Programming 279

CHAPTER 10
Programming Tile-Based Backgrounds with Scrolling .339

CHAPTER 11
Timers, Interrupt Handlers, and Multi-Threading 381

CHAPTER 12
Creating a Game World 429

CHAPTER 13
Vertical Scrolling Arcade Games 455

CHAPTER 14
Horizontal Scrolling Platform Games 489

Welcome to Part II of *Game Programming All in One, 2nd Edition*. Part II includes nine chapters that form the bulk of the crucial game programming subjects of the book. In this section, you will learn about game design, bitmaps, blitting, basic sprite handling, advanced sprite programming, tile-based backgrounds, background scrolling, timers, interrupt handling, multi-threading, and map editors. This section also includes chapters on vertical and horizontal scrolling games!

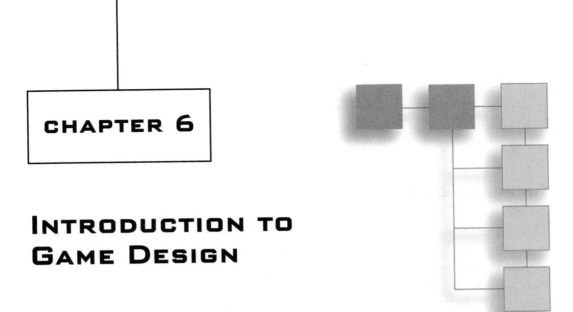

CHAPTER 6

INTRODUCTION TO GAME DESIGN

Many years have passed since the days when games were designed in a couple of hours at the family barbeque. Today, games are required to be fun and addictive, but at the same time meaningful and intuitive. The latest games released by the big companies take months to design—and that is with the help of various designers. Contrary to popular belief, a game designer's sole purpose isn't to think of an idea, and then give it to the programmers so they can make a game. A designer must think of the game idea, elaborate it, illustrate it, define it, and describe just about everything from the time the CD is inserted into the CD-ROM drive to the time when the player quits the game. This chapter will help you understand a little more about game design, as well as give you some tips about it, and in the end show you a small game design document for a very popular game.

This chapter goes over the software development process for game development, describing the main steps involved in taking a game from inspiration to completion. This is not about creating a hundred-page document with all the screens, menus, characters, settings, and storyline of the game. Rather, this chapter is geared toward the programmer, with tips for following a design process that keeps a game in development until it is completed. Without a simple plan, most game programmers will become bored with a game that only weeks before had them up all night with earnest fervor.

Here is a breakdown of the major topics in this chapter:

- Understanding game design basics
- Understanding game development phases
- Recognizing post-production woes
- Future-proofing your design
- Understanding the dreaded design document

- Recognizing the importance of good game design
- Recognizing the two types of designs
- Looking at a sample design document
- Looking at a sample game design: *Space Invaders*

Game Design Basics

Creating a computer game without at least a minimal design document or a collection of notes is like building a plastic model of a car or airplane from a kit without the instructions. More than likely, a game that is created without the instructions will end up with missing pieces and loose ends. The tendency is always to jump right in and get some code working, and there is room for that step in the development of a new game! However, the initial coding session should be used to build enthusiasm for yourself and any others in the project, and should be nothing more than a proof of concept or an incomplete prototype.

Like most creative individuals, game programmers must have the discipline to stick to something before moving on, or they will fall into the trap of half-completing a dozen or so games without much to show for the effort. The real difference between a hobbyist and a professional is simply that a professional game programmer will see the game through to completion no matter how long it takes.

Inspiration

Take a look at classic console games for inspiration, and you will have no trouble coming up with an idea for a cool new game. Any time I am bug-eyed and brain-dead from a long coding session, I take a walk outside and then return for a gaming session (preferably with a friend). Consoles are great because they are usually fast paced and they are often based on arcade machines.

PC games, on the other hand, can be quite slow and even boring in comparison because they have so much more depth. If you are in a hurry and just want to have a little fun, go with a console. Video games are full of creativity and interesting technology that PC gamers usually fail to notice.

Game Feasibility

The feasibility of a game is difficult to judge because so much is possible once you get started, and it is easy to underestimate your own capabilities (especially if you have a few people helping you). One thing that you must be careful about when designing a new game is scope. How big will the game be? You also don't want to bite off more than you can chew, to use the familiar expression.

Feasibility is the process of deciding how far you will go with the game and at what point you will stop adding new features. But at the very least, feasibility is a study of whether the game can be created in the first place. Once you are certain that you have the capability to create a certain type of game and you have narrowed the scope of the game to a manageable level, work can begin.

Feature Glut

As a general rule, you should get the game up and running before you work on new features (the bells and whistles). Never spend more than a day working on code without testing it! This is critical. Any time you change a major part of the game, you must completely recompile the game and run it to make sure you haven't broken any part of it in the process.

I can't tell you how many times I have thought up a new way to do something and gone through all the source code for a game, making changes here and there, with the result being that the game won't compile or won't run. Every change you make during the development of the game should be small and easy to undo if it doesn't work.

My personal preference is to keep the game running throughout the day. Every time I make even a minor change, I test the game to make sure it works before I move on to a new section of code. This is really where object-oriented coding pays off. By moving tried-and-tested code into a class, it is relatively safe to assume the code works as expected because you are not modifying it as often.

It really helps to eliminate bugs when you have put the startup and shutdown code inside a class (or within the Allegro library, where the library handles these routines automatically). There is also another tremendous benefit to wrapping code inside a library—information overload.

There is a point at which we humans simply can't handle any more information, and our memory starts to fail. If you try to keep track of too many loose ends in a game, you are bound to make a mistake! By putting common code in classes (or in a separate library file altogether), you reduce the amount of information that you must remember. It is such a relief when you need to do something quickly and you realize that all the code is ready to do your bidding at a moment's notice. The alternative (and old-school) method of copying sections of code and pasting them into your project is error-prone and will introduce bugs into your game.

Back Up Your Work

Follow this simple advice or learn the hard way: Back up your work several times a day! If you don't, you are going to make a significant change to the game code that completely breaks it and you will not be able to figure out how to get the game back up and running.

This is the point at which you return to a backup and start again. Even if the backup is a few hours old, it is better than spending half a day figuring out the problem with the changes you made.

I have an informal method of backing up my work. I use an archive program to zip the entire project directory for a game—including all the graphics, sounds, and source code—into a file with the date and time stamped into the filename, such as Game_070204_1030.zip.

The backup file might be huge, but what is disk space today? You don't always need to back up the entire project directory if you haven't made any changes to the graphics or sound files for the game (which can be quite large). If you are working on source code for days at a time without making any changes to media files, you might just make a complete backup once a day, and then make smaller backups during the day for code changes. As a general rule, I don't use the incremental backup feature available with many compression programs because I prefer to create an entirely new backup file each time.

If you get into the habit of backing up your files every hour or two, you will not be faced with the nightmare of losing a whole day's work if you mess up the source code or if something happens to your hard drive. For this reason, I recommend that you copy all backup files directly to CD (using packet-writing technology, which provides drag-and-drop capability from Windows Explorer). CD-RW drives are very affordable and indispensable when it comes to saving your work, giving you the ability to quickly erase and save your work repeatedly. DVD burners are also very affordable now, and they offer enough storage space to easily back up everything in an entire game project.

In the end, how much is your time worth? Making regular backups is the smart thing to do.

Game Genres

The gaming press seems to differentiate between console and PC games, but the line that separates the two is diminishing as games are ported back and forth. I tend to group console and PC games together in shared genres, although some genres do not work well on both platforms. The following sections detail a number of game genres; they contain a description of each genre and a list of sample games within that genre. It is important to consider the target genre for your game because this affects your target audience. Some gamers are absolutely fanatical about first-person shooters, while others prefer real-time strategy, and so on. It is a good idea to at least identify the type of game you are working on, even if it is a unique game.

Fighting Games

2D and 3D fighting games are almost entirely bound to the console market due to the way these games are played. A PC equipped with a gamepad is a fine platform, but fighting games really shine on console systems with multiple controllers.

One of my favorite Dreamcast fighting games is called *Power Stone 2*. This game is hilarious! Four players can participate on varied levels in hand-to-hand combat, with numerous obstacles and miscellaneous items strewn about on each level, and the action is fast paced.

Here is a list of my favorite fighting game series:

- *Dead or Alive*
- *Mortal Kombat*
- *Power Stone*
- *Ready 2 Rumble*
- *Soul Calibur*
- *Street Fighter*
- *Tekken*
- *Virtua Fighter*

Action/Arcade Games

Action/arcade games turned the fledgling video game industry into a worldwide phenomenon in the 1980s and 1990s, but started to drop off in popularity in arcades in the 2000s. The action/arcade genre encompasses a huge list of games, and here are some of my favorites:

- *Akari Warriors*
- *Blasteroids*
- *Elevator Action*
- *Rolling Thunder*
- *Spy Hunter*
- *Star Control*
- *Super R-Type*
- *Teenage Mutant Ninja Turtles*

Adventure Games

The adventure game genre was once comprised of the largest collection of games in the computer game industry, with blockbuster hits like *King's Quest* and *Space Quest*. Adventure games have fallen out of style in recent years, but there is still an occasional new adventure game that inspires the genre to new heights. For instance, *Starflight III: Mysteries of the Universe* is an official sequel to the original *Starflight* games, with a fantastic galaxy-spanning adventure story with the engaging mystery of space exploration. I am a member of the development team for this game, so I am naturally biased to appreciate the game. For more information, visit http://www.starflight3.net. My definition of adventure game might differ from someone else's, but most of the following games may be categorized as adventure games:

- *King's Quest*
- *Mean Streets*
- *Myst*
- *Space Quest*
- *Starflight*

First-Person Shooters

The first-person shooter genre is the dominant factor in the gaming industry today, with so many new titles coming out every year that it is easy to overlook some extremely cool games while playing some others. This list is by no means complete, but it includes the most common first-person shooters:

- *Doom*
- *Half-Life*
- *Jedi Knight*
- *Max Payne*
- *Quake*
- *Unreal*
- *Wolfenstein 3-D*

Flight Simulators

Flight simulators (flight sims) are probably the most important type of game in the industry, although they are not always recognized as such. When you think about it, the technology required to render the world is quite a challenge. The best of the best in flight sims usually push the envelope of realism (pun intended) and graphical wizardry. Here is my list of favorites, old and new:

- *Aces of the Pacific*
- *B-17*
- *Battlehawks 1942*
- *Falcon 4.0*
- *Jane's WWII Fighters*
- *Red Baron*

Galactic Conquest Games

Galactic conquest games have seen mixed success at various times, with a popular title about once a year. One early success was a game called *Stellar Crusade*, which focused heavily on the economics of running a galactic empire. This may be debatable, but I believe that *Master of Orion* popularized the genre, while *Master of Orion II* perfected it. Even today, *MOO2* (as it is fondly referred to) still holds its own against modern wonders, such as *Imperium Galactica II*.

- *Imperium Galactica*
- *Master of Orion*
- *Stellar Crusade*

Real-Time Strategy Games

Real-time strategy (RTS) games are second only to first-person shooters in popularity and success, with blockbuster titles selling in the millions. Westwood is generally given kudos for inventing the genre with *Dune II*, although the *Command & Conquer* series gave the genre a lot of mileage. *Warcraft* and *Starcraft* (both by Blizzard) were huge in their time and are still popular today. My personal favorites are *Age of Empires* and the follow-up games in the series. Here are the best RTS games on the market today:

- *Age of Empires*
- *Command & Conquer*
- *Dark Reign*
- *MechCommander*
- *Real War*
- *Starcraft*
- *Total Annihilation*
- *Warcraft*

Role-Playing Games

What would the computer industry be without role-playing games? RPGs go back as far as most gamers can remember, with early games such as *Ultima* and *Might and Magic* appearing on some of the earliest PCs. *Ultima Online* followed in the tradition of *Meridian 59* as a massively multiplayer online role-playing game (MMORPG), along with *EverQuest* and *Asheron's Call*. Here are some classic favorites:

- *Baldur's Gate: Dark Alliance*
- *Darkstone*
- *Diablo*

- *Fallout*
- *Forgotten Realms*
- *Might and Magic*
- *The Bard's Tale*
- *Ultima*

Sports Simulation Games

Sports sims have long held a strong position in the computer game industry as a mainstay group of products covering all the major sports themes—baseball, football, soccer, basketball, and hockey. Here are some of my favorites:

- *Earl Weaver Baseball*
- *Madden 2004*
- *Wayne Gretzky and the NHLPA All-Stars*
- *World Series Baseball 2K3*

Third-Person Shooters

The third-person shooter genre was spawned by first-person shooters, but it sports an "over the shoulder" viewpoint. *Tomb Raider* is largely responsible for the popularity of this genre. Here are some favorite third-person shooters:

- *Delta Force*
- *Tom Clancy's Rainbow Six*
- *Resident Evil*
- *Tomb Raider*

Turn-Based Strategy Games

Turn-based strategy (TBS) games have a huge fan following because this genre allows for highly detailed games based on classic board games, such as *Axis & Allies*. Because TBS games do not run in real time, each player is allowed time to think about his next move, providing for some highly competitive and long-running games. Here is a list of the most popular games in the genre:

- *Axis & Allies*
- *Panzer General*
- *Shogun: Total War*
- *Steel Panthers*
- *The Operational Art of War*

Space Simulation Games

Space sims are usually grand in scope and provide a compelling story to follow. Based loosely on movies such as *Star Wars*, space sims usually feature a first-person perspective inside the cockpit of a spaceship. Gameplay is similar to that of a flight sim, but with science fiction themes. Here is a list of popular space sims:

- *Tachyon: The Fringe*
- *Wing Commander*

Real-Life Games

Real-life sims are affectionately referred to as *God games*, although the analogy is not perfect. How do you categorize a game like *Dungeon Keeper*? Peter Molyneux seems to routinely create his own genres. These games usually involve some sort of realistic theme, although it may be based on fictional characters or incidents. Here are some of the most popular real-life games:

- *Black & White*
- *Dungeon Keeper*
- *Populous*
- *SimCity*
- *The Sims*
- *Tropico*

Massively Multiplayer Online Games

I consider this a genre of its own, although the games herein may be categorized elsewhere. The most popular online games are called MMORPGs—massively multiplayer online role-playing games. This convoluted phrase describes an RPG that you can play online with hundreds or thousands of players—at least in theory.

- *Anarchy Online*
- *Asheron's Call*
- *Conquest: Frontier Wars*
- *EverQuest*
- *Ultima Online*
- *Final Fantasy Online*

Game Development Phases

Although there are entire volumes dedicated to software development life cycles and software design, I am going to cover only the basics that you will need to design a game. You might want to go into finer detail with your game designs, or you might want to skip a few steps. It is all a matter of preference. But the important thing is that you at least attempt to document your ideas before you get started on a new game.

Initial Design

The initial design for a game is usually a hand-drawn figure showing what the game screen will look like, with the game's user interface or game elements shown in roughly the right places on the sketched screen. You can also use a program such as Visio to create your initial design screens.

The initial design should also include a few pages with an overview of the components needed by the game, such as the DirectX components or any third-party software libraries. You should include a description of how the game will be played and what forms of user input will be supported, and you should describe how the graphics will be rendered (in 2D or 3D).

Game Engine

Once you have an initial design for the game down on paper, you can get started on the game engine. This will usually be the most complicated core component of the game, such as the graphics renderer.

In the case of a 2D sprite-based game, the game engine will be a simple game loop with a double-buffer, a static or rendered background, and a few sprites moving around for good measure. If the game runs in real time, you will want to develop the collision detection routine and start working on the physics for the game.

By the end of this phase in development—before you get started on a real prototype—you should try to anticipate (based on the initial design) some of the possible graphics and miscellaneous routines you will need later. Obviously, you will not know in advance all of the functionality the game will need, but you should at least code the core routines up front.

Alpha Prototype

After you have developed the engine that will power your game, the next natural step in development is to create a prototype of the game. This phase is really a natural result of testing the game engine, so the two phases are often seamless. But if you treat the prototype as a single complete program without the need for modification, then you will have recognized this phase of the game.

Once you have finished the prototype, I recommend you compile and save it as an individual program or demo. At this point, you might want to send it to a few friends to get some feedback on general gameplay. This version of the game will not even remotely look as if it is complete. Bitmaps will be incomplete, and there might not even be any sound or music in the prototype.

However, one thing that the multiplayer prototype must have from the start is network capabilities. If you are developing a multiplayer game, you must code the networking along with the graphics and the game engine early in development. It is a mistake to start adding multiplayer code to the game after it is half finished, because most likely you will have written routines that are not suited for multiple players and you will have to rewrite a lot of code.

Game Development

The game development phase is clearly the longest phase of work done on a game. It consists of taking the prototype code base—along with feedback received by those who ran the demo—and building the game. Since this phase is the most important one, there are many different ways that you can accomplish it. First, you will most likely be building on the prototype that you developed in the previous phase because it usually does not make sense to start over from scratch unless there are some serious design flaws in the prototype.

You might want to stub out all of the functionality needed to complete the game so there is at least some sort of minimal response from the game when certain things happen or when a chain of events occurs. For instance, if you plan to support a high-score server on the Internet, you might code the high-score server with a simple response message so you can send a request to the server and then display the reply. This way, there is at least some sort of response from this part of the game, even if you do not intend to complete it until later.

Another positive note for stubbing out functionality is that you get to see the entire game as it will eventually appear when completed. This allows you to go back to the initial design phase and make some changes before you are half finished with the game. Stubbing out nonessential functionality lets you see an overview of the entire game. You can then freeze the design and complete each piece of the game individually until the game is finished.

Quality Control

Individuals like you who are working on a game alone might be tempted to skip some of the phases of development, since the formality of it might seem humorous. But even if you are working on a game by yourself, it is a good practice to get into the habit of going through the motions of the formal game development life cycle as if you have a team of people working with you on the game. Someday, you might find yourself working on a professional game with others, and the professionalism that you learned early on will pay off later.

Quality control is the formal testing process that is required to correct bugs in a game. Because the lead developers of a game have been staring at the code and the game screens for months or years, a fresh set of eyes is needed to properly test a game. If you are working solo, you need to recruit one or more friends to help you test the game. I guarantee that they will be able to find problems that you have overlooked or missed completely.

Because this is your pet project, you are very likely to develop habits when playing the game, while anyone else might find your machinations rather strange. Goofy keyboard shortcuts or strange user interface decisions might seem like the greatest thing since ketchup to you, but to someone else the game might not even be fun to play.

Consider quality control as an audit of your game. You need an objective person to point out flaws and gameplay issues that might not have been present in the prototype. It is a critical step when you think about it. After all the work you have put into a game, you certainly don't want a simple and easily correctable bug to tarnish the impression you want your game to have on others.

Beta Testing

Beta testing is a phase that follows the completion of the game's development phase, and it should be recognized as significantly separate from the previous quality control phase. The beta version of a game absolutely should not be released if the game has known bugs. Any time you send out a game for beta testing and you know there are bugs, you should recognize that you are really still in the quality control phase. Only when you have expunged every conceivable bug in the game should you release it to a wider audience for beta testing.

At this point in the game's life cycle, the game is complete and 100 percent functional, and you are only looking for a larger group of users to identify bugs that might have slipped past quality control. Before you release a game to beta testers, make absolutely certain that all of the graphics, sound effects, and music are completely ready to go, as if the game is ready to be sent out to stores. If you do not feel confident that the game is ready to sit on a retail shelf, then that is a sure sign that it is not yet out of the quality control phase. When you identify bugs during the beta test phase, you should collect them at regular time intervals and send out new releases—whether your schedule is daily or weekly.

When users stop thinking of the game as a beta version and they actually start to play it to have fun (with general trust in the game's stability), and when no new bugs have been identified for a length of time (such as a couple weeks or a month), then you can consider the game complete.

Post-Production

Post-production work on a game includes creating the install program that installs the game onto a computer system and writing the game manual. If you will be distributing the game via the Internet, you will definitely want to create a Web site for your game, with a bunch of screenshots and a list of the key features of the game.

Official Release

Once you have a complete package ready to go, burn the complete game installer with everything you need to play the game to a CD and give it to a few people who were not involved in the beta testing process. If you feel that the game is ready for prime time, you might send out copies of it to online- and printed-magazine editors for review.

Out the Door or Out the Window?

One thing is for certain: When you work on a game project for an employer who knows nothing about software development, you can count on having marketing run the show, which is not always good. Some of the best studios in the world are run by a small group of individuals who actually work on games but know very little about how to run a business or advertise a game to the general public. Far too often, those award-winning game designers and developers will turn over the reins of their small company to a fulltime manager (or president) because the pressure of running the business becomes too much for developers (who would rather write code than balance the accounts).

Managing the Game

The manager of a game studio might have learned the strategies to make a retail or wholesale company succeed. These strategies include concepts such as just-in-time inventory, employee management, cost control, and customer relationship management—all very good things to know when running a grocery store or sales department. The problem is, many managers fail to realize that software development is not a business, and programmers should not be treated like factory workers; rather, they should be treated like members of a research and development team.

Consider the infamous Bell Laboratories (or Bell Labs), an R&D center that has come up with hundreds of patents and innovations that have directly affected the computer industry (not the least of which was the transistor). A couple of intelligent guys might have invented the microprocessor, but the transistor was a revolutionary step that made the microprocessor possible. Now imagine if someone had treated Bell Labs like a factory, demanding results on a regular basis. Is that how human creativity works, through schedules and deadlines?

The case might be made that true genius is both creative and timely. Along that same train of thought, it might be said that genius is nothing but an extraordinary amount of hard work with a dash of inspiration here and there.

There are some really terrific game publishers that give development teams the leeway to add every last bell and whistle to a game, and those publishers should be applauded!

But—you knew that was coming, didn't you?—far too often, publishers simply want results without regard for the quality of a game. When shareholders become more important than developers in a game company, it's time to find a new job.

A Note about Quality

What is the best way to work with game developers or the best way to work with management? The goal, after all, is to produce a successful game. Learn the meaning behind the buzzwords. If you are a developer, try to explain the technology behind your game throughout the development life cycle and provide options to managers. By offering several technical solutions to any given problem, and then allowing the decision makers to decide which path to follow, you will succeed in completing the game on time and within budget.

The accusations and jibes actually go both ways! Management is often faced with developers who are competing with other developers in the industry. The goal might be a sound one; high-end game engines are often so difficult to develop that many companies would rather license an existing engine than build their own. Quite often a game is nothing more than a technology demo for the engine, because licensing might provide even more income than actual game sales (especially if royalties are involved). When a game is nearing completion and a competitor's game comes out with some fancy new feature, such as a software renderer with full anisotropic filtering (okay, that is impossible, but you get the point), the tendency is to cram a similar new feature into the game at the last minute for bragging rights. However, the new feature will have absolutely no bearing on the playability or fun factor of the game, and it might even reduce game stability.

This tendency is something that managers must deal with on a daily basis in a struggle to keep developers from modifying the game's design (resulting in a game that is never finished). Rather than constantly modify the design, developers should be promised work on a sequel or a new game so they can use all the new things they learned while working on the current game.

Empowering the Engine

Consider the game *Unreal*, by Epic Games. (As an aside, Epic Games was once called Epic Megagames, and they produced some very cool shareware games.) The *Unreal* engine was touted as a *Quake II* killer, with unbelievable graphics all rendered in software. Of course, 3D acceleration made *Unreal* even more impressive. But the problem with *Unreal* was not the technology behind the mesmerizing graphics in the game, but rather the gameplay. Gamers were playing tournament-style games, a trend that was somewhat missed by the developers, publishers, and gaming media at the time. In contrast, *Quake II* had a large and engaging single-player game in addition to multiplayer support that spawned a cult following and put the game at the top of the charts.

Unreal was developed from the start as a multiplayer game, since the game was in development for several years. Epic Games released *Unreal Tournament* about two years later, and it was simply awesome—a perfect example of putting additional efforts into a second game, rather than delaying the first. The only single-player component of *Unreal Tournament* is a game mode in which you can play against computer-controlled bots; it is undeniably a multiplayer game throughout.

Quality versus Trends

Blizzard was once a company that set the industry standard for creating extremely high-quality games, such as *Warcraft II, Starcraft,* and *Diablo.* These games alone have outsold the entire lineup from some publishers, with multiple millions of copies sold worldwide. Why was Blizzard so successful with these early games? In a word: quality. From the installer to the end of the game, Blizzard exuded quality in every respect. Then something happened. The company announced a new game, and then cancelled it. A new installment of *Warcraft* was announced (*Warcraft Adventures: Lord of the Clans,* a cartoon-style game that had the potential to supercede the coming "cell shading" trend pioneered by *Jet Set Radio* for the Dreamcast—not to mention that Blizzard missed out on the resurgence of the adventure game genre), and then forgotten for several years. *Diablo II* came out in 2001, and many scratched their heads, wondering why it took three years to develop a sequel that looked so much like the original.

Consider Future Trends

The problem is often not related to the quality of a game as much as it is related to trends. When it takes several years to develop an extremely complicated game, design decisions must be made in advance, and the designers have to do a little guesswork to try to determine where gaming trends are headed, and then take advantage of those trends in a game. A blockbuster game does not necessarily need to follow every new trend; on the contrary, the trends are set *by* the blockbuster games. An otherwise fantastic game that was revolutionary and ambitious at one point might find itself outdated by the time it is released.

Take Out the Guesswork

Age of Empires was released for the holiday season in 1997, at the dawn of the real-time strategy revolution in the gaming industry. This game was in development for perhaps two years before its release. That means work started on *Age of Empires* as early as 1995! Now, imagine the trends of the time and the average hardware on a PC, and it is obvious that the designer of the game had a good grasp of future trends in gaming.

Those RTS games that were developed with complete 3D environments still haven't seemed to catch on. In many ways, *Dark Reign II* is far superior to *Age of Empires II,* with gorgeous graphics and stunning 3D particle effects. Yet *Age of Empires II* has become more of a LAN party favorite, along with *Quake III Arena*, *Unreal Tournament*, and *Counter-Strike*. Perhaps RTS fans are not interested in complete 3D environments. My personal suspicion is that the 3D element is distracting to a gamer who would prefer to focus on his strategy rather than navigating the 3D terrain.

Innovation versus Inspiration

As an aspiring game designer, what is the solution to the technology/trend problem? My advice is to play every game you can get your hands on (if you are not already an avid gamer). Play games that don't interest you to get a feel for a variety of games. Download and play every demo that comes out, regardless of the type of game. Demos are a great way for marketing departments to promote a game before it is finished, but they are also a great way for competitors to see what you have planned. As with most things in business or leisure, there is a tradeoff. It is great to have some fun while you play games, but try to determine how the game works and what is under the hood. If the game is based on a licensed engine rather than custom code, you might try to identify which engine powers the game.

Half-Life is probably one of the oldest games in the industry that is still being improved upon and packaged for sale on retail shelves. One of the most significant reasons for the success of *Half-Life* (along with the compelling story and gameplay) is the *Half-Life* SDK. This software development kit for the *Half-Life* engine is available for free download. While hundreds of third-party modifications (MODs) have been created for *Half-Life*, by far the most popular is *Counter-Strike* (which was finally packaged for retail sale after more than a year in beta, and then ported to Xbox).

The Infamous Game Patch

Regardless of the good intentions of developers, many games are rushed and sent out to stores before they are 100-percent complete. This is a result of a game that went over budget, a publisher that decided to drop the game but was convinced to complete it, or a publisher that is interested only in a first run of sales, without regard to quality.

A common trap that publishers have fallen into is the belief that they can rush a game, and then release a downloadable patch for it. The reasoning is that customers are already used to downloading new versions and updates to software, so there is nothing wrong with getting a game out the door a week before Christmas to make it for the holiday season. The flaw behind this reasoning is that games are largely advertised by word of mouth, not by marketing schemes. Due to the huge number of newsgroups and discussion lists (such as Yahoo! Groups) that allow millions of members to share information, ideas, and stories, it is impossible for a killer new game to be released without a few hundred thousand gamers knowing about it.

But now you see the trap. The same gamers who swap war stories online about their favorite games will rip apart a shoddy game that was released prematurely. This is a sign of sure death for a game. Only rarely will a downloadable patch be acceptable for a game that is released before it is complete.

Expanding the Game

Most successful games are followed by an expansion pack of some sort, whether it is a map pack or a complete conversion to a new theme. One of my favorite games of all time is *Homeworld*, which was created by Relic and published by Sierra. *Homeworld* is an extraordinary game of epic proportions, and it is possibly the most engaging and realistic game I have ever played. (The same applies to *Homeworld 2*, the excellent sequel.)

When the expansion game *Homeworld: Cataclysm* was released, I found that not only was there a new theme to the game (in fact, it takes place a number of years after the events in the original game), but the developers had actually added some significant new features to the game engine. The new technologies and ships in *Cataclysm* were enough to warrant buying the game, but *Cataclysm* is also a standalone expansion game that does not require the original to run.

Expansion packs and enhanced sequels allow developers to complete a game on schedule while still exercising their creative and technical skill on an additional product based on the same game. This is a great idea from a marketing perspective because the original game has already been completed, so the amount of work required to create an expansion game is significantly less and allows for some fine-tuning of the game.

Future-Proof Design

Developing a game with code reuse is one thing, but what about designing a game to make it future-proof? That is quite a challenge given that computer technology improves at such a rapid pace. The ironic thing about computer games is that developers usually target high-end systems when building the game, even though they can't fully estimate where mainstream computer hardware will be a year in the future. Yet, when a new high-end game is released, many gamers will go out and purchase upgrades for their computers to play the new game. You can see the circular cause-and-effect that results.

Overall, designing a game for the highest end of the hardware spectrum is not a wise decision because there are thousands of gamers in the world who do not have access to the latest hardware innovations—such as striped hard drives attached to RAID (*Redundant Array of Independent Disks*) controllers or a 64-MB DDR (*Double-Data Rate memory*) GeForce 3 video card. While hardware improvements are increasing as rapidly as prices seem to be dropping, the average gaming rig is still light-years beyond the average consumer PC, and that should be taken into account when you are targeting system hardware.

Game Libraries

A solid understanding of game development usually precedes work on a game library for a particular platform, and this usually takes place during the initial design and prototype phases of game development. It is becoming more common for publishers to contract with developers for multiple platforms. Whether the developers build an entirely new game library for each platform or develop a multi-platform game library is usually irrelevant to the publisher, who is only interested in a finished product. You can see now why Allegro is such a powerful ally and why I selected it for this book!

A development studio is likely to reap incredible rewards by developing a multi-platform game library that can be easily recompiled for any of the supported computer platforms. It is not unheard of to develop a library that supports PC, PlayStation 2, GameCube, and Xbox, all with the same code base. In the case of this book, you are able to write games directly for Windows or Linux without much effort, and for Mac and a few other systems with a little work. Allegro takes care of the details within the library.

Game Engines and SDKs

Game engines are far overrated in the media and online discussion groups as complete solutions to a developer's needs. Not true! Game engines are based on game libraries for one or more platforms, and the game engine is likely optimized to an incredible degree for a particular game. Common engines today include the *Half-Life* SDK, the *Unreal* engine, and the *Quake III* engine. These game engines can be used to create a completely new game, but that game is really just a total conversion for the existing engine. Some studios are up to the challenge of modifying the existing engine for their own needs, but far more often, developers will use the existing engine as is and simply customize it for their own game projects.

Examples of games based on an existing engine include *Star Trek Voyager: Elite Force II*, *Counter-Strike*, and even *Quake IV* (which is based on the *Doom III* engine). *Half-Life 2* is promising to be a strong contender in the *engine* business, pushing the envelope of realism to an even higher level than has been seen to date.

What Is Game Design?

Now that you have some background on the theory of game design and a good overview of the various game genres your game might fit into, I'll go over some real-world examples and cover information you might need when you want to take your game into the retail market.

So what exactly is game design? It is the ancient art of creating and defining games. Well, that's at least the short definition. *Game design* is the entire process of creating a game idea, from research, to the graphical interface, to the unit's capabilities. Having an idea for a game is easy; making a game from that idea is the hard part—and that is just the design part! When creating a game, some of the jobs of a designer are to:

- Define the game idea
- Define all the screens and how they relate to each other and to the menus
- Explain how and why the interaction with the game is done
- Create a story that makes sense
- Define the game goals
- Write dialogues and other specific game texts
- Analyze the balance of the game and modify it accordingly
- And much, much more…

The Dreaded Design Document

Now that you finally have decided what kind of game you are making and you have almost everything planned out, it's time to prepare a design document. For a better understanding of what a design document should be, think of the movie industry.

When a movie is shot, the story isn't in anyone's head; it is completely described in the movie script. Actually, the movie script is usually written long before shooting starts. The author writes the script and then needs to take it to a big Hollywood company to get the necessary means to produce the movie, but this is a long process. After a company picks the movie, each team (actors, camera people, director, and so on) will get the copies of the script to do their job. When the wardrobe is done, the actors know the lines and emotion, and the director is ready, they start shooting the movie.

When dealing with game design, the process is sort of the same, in that the designers do the design document, and then they pitch to the company they work for to see whether the company has any interest in the idea. (No, trying to sell game designs to companies isn't a very nice future.) When the company gives the go for a game—probably after revising the design and for sure messing it up—each team (artists, programmers, musicians, and so on) gets the design document and starts doing its job. When some progress is made by all the teams, the actual production starts (such as testing the code with the art and including the music).

One more thing before I proceed: Just because some feature or menu is written in the design document, it doesn't mean it has to be that way no matter what. This is also similar to the movies, in that the actors follow the script, but sometimes they improvise, which makes the movie even more captivating.

The Importance of Good Game Design

Many young and beginning game programmers defend the idea that the game is in their head, and thus they refuse to do any kind of formal design. This is a bad approach for several reasons. The first one is probably the most important if you are working with a team. If you are working with other people on the game and you have the idea in your head, there are two possibilities: Your team members are psychic or you spend 90 percent of the time you should be developing your game explaining why the heck the player can't use the item picked in the first level to defeat the second boss. The second option is in no way fun.

Another valid reason to keep a formal design document is to keep focus. When you have the idea in your head, you will be working on it and modifying it even when you are finishing the programming part. This is bad because it will eventually force you to change code and lose time. I'm not saying that when you write something down, it is written in stone. All the aspects of the design document can and should change during development. The difference is that when you have a formal design, it's easy to keep focus and progress, whereas if you keep it in your head, it will be hard to progress because you won't settle with something and you will always be thinking of other stuff.

The last reason why you shouldn't keep the designs in your head is because you are human. We tend to forget stuff. Suppose you have the design in your head and you are about 50 percent done programming the game, but for some reason you have to stop developing the game for three weeks (due to vacation, exams month, aliens invading, or whatever the reason). When you get back to developing the game, most of the stuff that was previously so clear will not be as obvious, thus causing you lose to time rethinking it.

The Two Types of Designs

Even if there isn't an official distinction between design types, separating the design process into two types makes it easier to understand which techniques are more advantageous to the games you are developing.

Mini Design

You can do the mini design in about a week or so. It features a complete but general description of the game. A mini design document should be enough that any team member can pick it up, read it, and get the same idea of the game as the designer—but be allowed to include a little bit of his own ideas for the game (such as the artist designing the main character or the programmer adding a couple of features, such as cloud movement or parallax scrolling). Mini designs are useful when you are creating a small game or one that is heavily based on another game or a very well-known genre. Some distinctive aspects of a mini design document are

- General overview of the game
- Game goals

- Interaction of player and game
- Basic menu layout and game options
- Story
- Overview of enemies
- Image theme

Complete Design

The complete design document looks like the script from *Titanic*. It features every possible aspect of the game, from the menu button color to the number of hit points the barbarian can have. It is usually designed by various people, with help from external people, such as lead programmers or lead artists.

The complete design document takes too much time to make to be ignored or misinterpreted. Anyone reading it should see exactly the same game, colors, and backgrounds as the designer(s). This kind of design is reserved for big companies that have much money to spare. Small teams or lone developers should stay away from this type of design because most of the time they don't have the resources to do it. Some of the aspects a complete design should have are

- General overview of the game
- Game goals
- Game story
- Characters' stories and attributes
- NPC (*Non-Player Character*) attributes
- Player/NPC/other rule charts
- All the rules defined
- Interaction of the player and the game
- Menu layout and style and all game options
- Music description
- Sound description
- Description of the levels and their themes and goals

A Sample Design Document Template

The following sections describe a sample design document you can use for your own designs, but remember—these are just guidelines that you don't have to follow exactly. If you don't think a section applies to your game or if you think it is missing something, don't think twice about changing it.

General Overview

This is usually a paragraph or two describing the game very generally. It should briefly describe the game genre and basic theme, as well as the objectives of the player. It is a summary of the game.

Target System and Requirements

This should include the target system—Windows, Macintosh, or any other system, such as consoles—and a list of requirements for the game.

Story

Come on, this isn't any mind breaker—it is the game story. This covers what happened in the past (before the game started), what is happening when the player starts the game, and possibly what will happen while the game progresses.

Theme: Graphics and Sound

This section describes the overall theme of the game, whether it is set in ancient times in a land of fantasy or two thousand years in the future on planet Neptune. It should also contain descriptions or at least hints of the scenery and sound to be used.

Menus

This section should contain a short description and the objectives of the main menus, such as Start Game or the Options menu.

Playing a Game

This is probably the trickiest section. It should describe what happens from the time the user starts the game to when he starts to play—what usually happens, and how it ends. This should be set up as if you were describing what you would see on the screen if you were playing the game yourself.

Characters and NPCs Description

This section should describe the characters and the NPCs as well as possible. This description should include their names, backgrounds, attributes, special attacks, and so on.

Artificial Intelligence Overview

There are two options for this section. You can give an all-around general description of the game AI (*Artificial Intelligence*) and let the programmers pick that and develop their own set of rules, or you can describe almost every possible reaction and action an NPC can have.

Conclusion

The conclusion is usually a short paragraph covering—obviously—a conclusion to the game. It might feature your motivation in creating the game or some explanation of why the game is the way it is. They basically say the same thing, so just pick the one you prefer.

A Sample Game Design: Space Invaders

This section presents a sample mini design document for a *Space Invaders* type of game. *Space Invaders* is a relatively old game that you are probably familiar with. After reading this design document, you should be able to develop it on your own using the Mirus framework you developed earlier. Figure 16.1 shows a sample sketch of the game screen.

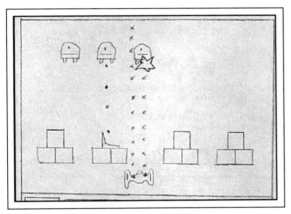

General Overview

Space Invaders is a typical arcade shooter game. The objective of the game is to destroy all the enemy ships in each level. The player controls a ship that can move horizontally at the bottom of the screen while it tries to avoid the bullets from the alien ships.

Figure 6.1 *Space Invaders* prototype

Target System and Requirements

Space Invaders is targeted for Windows 32-bit machines with DirectX 8.0 installed. Being such a low-end game, the basic requirements are minimal:

- Pentium 200 MHz
- 32 MB of memory
- 10 MB of free disk space
- SVGA DirectX-compatible video card

Story

Around 2049 A.D., aliens arrived on our planet, and they were not peaceful. They have destroyed two of the major cities in the world and are now threatening to destroy more.

The United Defense Force has decided to send their special agent, Gui Piskounov (don't ask), to destroy the alien force with the new experimental ship: ZS 3020 Airborne. You play the role of Piskounov. Your mission: To destroy all the alien scum.

Theme: Graphics and Sound

The whole game has a futuristic feeling to it. The main menus are heavily based on metallic walls and wire. The game itself is played in space, and as such, most of the backgrounds are stars or small planets. The ships have a very futuristic look to them. The game is full of heavy trance techno music with a very fast beat. Sounds are generally based on metal beating, explosions, and firing-bullet effects.

Menus

When the game starts, the user is presented with the main menu, in which he has five options.

Start New Game

This option starts a new game. The player is sent to the new game menu, where he can enter his name and chose the game difficulty.

Continue Previously Saved Game

This option starts a game that was previously saved. The player is sent to the load game menu, where he can choose a game from a list of previous saved games.

See Table of High Scores

This option shows the high scores table.

Options

This option shows the options menu. The player is sent to the options menu, where he can change the graphics, sound, and control settings.

Exit

This option exits the game.

Playing a Game

When the game starts, a company splash screen is shown for three seconds. After the three seconds, the screen fades to black and a splash screen starts to fade in. After four seconds, the screen fades to black again, and the player is sent to the main menu. When the player starts a new game, he is presented with a new menu screen, where he can enter his name and choose the game difficulty. After this is done, the user is sent to the game itself.

When each level starts, there is a three-second countdown for the game to start. The player can move his ship to the left or right and shoot using the controls defined in the options menu. When all the enemies are destroyed, the player advances a level. When the player is shot by an alien, he loses a life. If the player loses all the lives, the game ends. If the aliens reach the bottom of the screen, the game is also over.

If the player presses the Esc key while playing, the game is paused and a dialog box appears, asking what the user wants to do. He can choose from the following options:

- **Save game.** This option saves the game.
- **Options.** This option shows the options menu.
- **Quit game.** This option returns the player to the main menu.

Character and NPC Description

In this version of *Space Invaders*, there are two versions of alien ships. The first version consists of the normal ships that are constantly on the screen trying to destroy the player; the second version consists of ships that randomly appear and, if shot, give bonus points to the player.

Normal Ships

Normal ships are the typical enemies of the player. They can have various images, but their functionality is the same. They move left and right and randomly shoot bullets at the player vertically. When the ships reach a vertical margin, they move down a bit. These ships are destroyed with a single shot, and each ship destroyed gives 100 points to the player. As the levels progress, the ships move faster.

Bonus Ships

Bonus ships appear randomly at the top of the screen. They move horizontally and very quickly. These ships exist only to give bonus points to the player; they don't affect the gameplay because they don't shoot at the player and they don't have to be destroyed. When a bonus ship is destroyed, the game awards 500 points to the player.

Artificial Intelligence Overview

This game is very simple and requires almost no artificial intelligence. The ships move horizontally only until they reach one of the vertical margins, where they move down. They also randomly shoot bullets in a vertical-only direction.

Conclusion

The decision to keep this game simple but addictive was made to appeal to younger players, but also to almost any age genre, especially hardcore arcade gamers.

Game Design Mini-FAQ

Q: Why should I care about designing if I want to be a programmer?

A: Tough question. The first reason is because you will probably start developing your small games before you move to a big company and have to follow 200-page design documents in which you don't have any say. Next, being able to at least understand the concept of designing games will make your life a lot easier. If and when you are called for a meeting with the lead designer, you will at least understand what is happening.

Q: What is the best way to get a position as a fulltime game designer in some big game company?

A: First, chances of doing that are very slim, really. But the best way to try would be to start low and eventually climb the ladder. Start by working on the beta testing team, then maybe try to move to quality assurance or programming, and eventually try to give a game design to your boss. Please be aware that there are many steps from beta testing to even being a guest designer for a section of a game; time, patience, and perseverance are very important.

Summary

This chapter covered the subject of game design and discussed the phases of the game development life cycle. You learned how to classify your games by genre, how to manage development and testing, how to release and market your game, how to improve quality while meeting deadlines, and how to recognize some of the pitfalls of releasing an incomplete product. You then learned how to follow trends, how to expand and enhance a game with expansion packs, and how game libraries and game engines work together.

This was a rather short chapter for such an important topic, but this is a book mostly about programming, not design. If you have been paying attention, by now you should have a vague idea why designs are important and you should be able to pick up some of the topics covered here and design your own games. If you are having trouble, just use the fill-in template design document provided in this chapter and start designing.

Chapter Quiz

You can find the answers to this chapter quiz in Appendix A, "Chapter Quiz Answers."

1. What is the best way to get started creating a new game?
    A.   Write the source code for a prototype.
    B.   Create a game design document.
    C.   Hire the cast and crew.
    D.   Play other games to engender some inspiration.

2. What types of games are full of creativity and interesting technology that PC gamers often fail to notice?

   A.   Console games

   B.   Arcade games

   C.   PC games

   D.   Board games

3. What phrase best describes the additional features and extras in a game?

   A.   Bonus levels

   B.   Easter eggs

   C.   Bells and whistles

   D.   Updates and patches

4. What is usually the most complicated core component of a game, also called the graphics renderer?

   A.   The DirectX library

   B.   The Allegro library

   C.   The double-buffer

   D.   The game engine

5. What is the name of an initial demonstration of a game that presents the basic gameplay elements before the actual game has been completed?

   A.   Beta

   B.   Prototype

   C.   Demo

   D.   Release

6. What is the name of the document that contains the blueprints for a game?

   A.   Game document

   B.   Blueprint document

   C.   Design document

   D.   Construction document

7. What are the two types of game designs presented in this chapter?

   A.   Mini and complete

   B.   Partial and full

   C.   Prototype and final

   D.   Typical and sarcastic

8. What does NPC stand for?

   A.   Non-Pertinent Character

   B.   Non-Practical Condition

   C.   Non-Perfect Caricature

   D.   Non-Player Character

9. What are the chances of a newcomer finding a job as a fulltime game programmer or designer?

   A.   Guaranteed

   B.   Pretty good

   C.   Questionable

   D.   Negligible

10. What is the most important aspect of game development?

   A.   Design

   B.   Artwork

   C.   Programming

   D.   Implementation

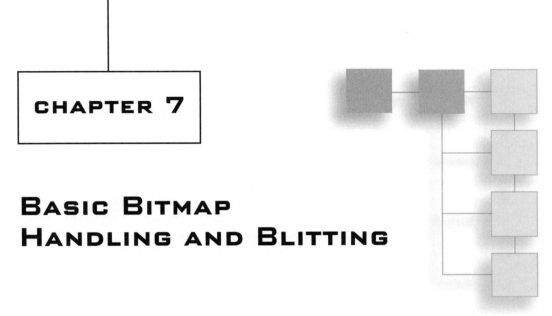

CHAPTER 7

BASIC BITMAP
HANDLING AND BLITTING

The time has come to move into the core of the subject of this book on 2D game programming. Bitmaps are that core, and they are also at the very core of the Allegro game library. This chapter is not only an overview of bitmaps, but also of the core subject of blitting—two subjects that are closely related. In fact, because blitting is the process of displaying a bitmap, it might just be considered the workhorse for working with bitmaps. By the end of this chapter, you will have a solid understanding of how to create, load, draw, erase, and delete bitmaps, and you will use this new information to enhance the *Tank War* game that you started back in Chapter 4 by converting it to a bitmap-based game.

Here is a breakdown of the major topics in this chapter:

- Creating and deleting bitmaps
- Drawing and clipping bitmaps
- Reading a bitmap from disk
- Saving a screenshot to disk
- Enhancing *Tank War*

Introduction

The infamous *sprite* is at the very core of 2D game programming, representing an object that moves around on the screen. That object might be a solid object or it might be transparent, meaning that you can see through some parts of the object, revealing the background. These are called *transparent sprites*. Another special effect called *translucency*, also known as *alpha blending*, causes an object on the screen to blend into the background by a variable degree, from opaque to totally transparent (and various values in between).

215

Sprite programming is one of the most enjoyable aspects of 2D game programming, and it is essential if you want to master the subject.

Before you can actually draw a sprite on the screen, you must find a way to create that sprite. Sprites can be created in memory at run time, although that is not usually a good way to do it. The usual method is to draw a small graphic figure using a graphic editing tool, such as Paint Shop Pro, and then save the image in a graphic file (such as .bmp, .lbm, .pcx, or .tga). Your program can then load that image and use it as a sprite. Of course, you can create precisely the sort of image your sprite needs and load one file per sprite, but that is a time-consuming task that can get really confusing and difficult when the sprites start to add up! Imagine instead that you have many sprites stored in a single bitmap file, gathered in an arrangement so you can "grab" a sprite out of the image when you need it. This way you have to load only one bitmap image into memory, and that image serves as the "home" for all of your sprites. This is a much faster method, and it works better, too!

But how do you grab the sprites out of the bitmap image? That will be the focus of the next chapter. For now, I'll focus on how to create a bitmap in memory and then draw it to the screen. You can actually use this method to create an entire game (maybe one like *Tank War* from Chapter 4?) by drawing graphics right onto a small bitmap when the program starts, and then displaying that bitmap as often as needed. It makes sense that this would be a lot faster than doing all the drawing at every step along the way. This is how *Tank War* handled the graphics—by drawing every time the tanks needed to be displayed. As you might imagine, it is much faster to render the tanks beforehand and then quickly display that bitmap on the screen. Take a look at this code:

```
BITMAP *tank = create_bitmap(32, 32);
clear_bitmap(tank);
putpixel(tank, 16, 16, 15);
blit(tank, screen, 0, 0, 0, 0, 32, 32);
```

note

Render is a graphical term that can apply to any act of drawing.

There are some new functions here that you haven't seen before, so I'll explain what they do. The first function, called create_bitmap, does exactly what it appears to do—it creates a new bitmap of the specified size. The clear_bitmap function zeroes out the new bitmap, which is necessary because memory allocation does not imply a clean slate, just the space—sort of like buying a piece of property that contains trees, bushes, and shrubbery that must be cleared before you build a house. Now take notice of the third line, with a call to putpixel. Look at the first parameter, tank. If you'll recall the putpixel function from Chapter 3, you might remember that the first parameter was always screen, which caused drawing to go directly to the screen. In this instance, you want the pixel to be drawn on the new bitmap!

The blit function is something entirely new and a little bit strange, won't you agree? If you have heard of sprites, you have probably also heard of blitting—but just in case you haven't, I'll go over it. *Blit* is shorthand for the process called "bit-block transfer." This is a fancy way of describing the process of quickly copying memory (a bit block) from one location to another. I have never quite agreed with the phrase because it's not possible to copy individual bits haphazardly; only entire bytes can be copied. To access bits, you can peer into a byte, but there's no way to copy individual bits using the blit function. Semantics aside, this is a powerful function that you will use often when you are writing games with Allegro.

Isn't it surprising that you're able to draw a pixel onto the tank bitmap rather than to the screen? Allegro takes care of all the complicated details and provides a nice clean interface to the graphics system. On the Windows platform, this means that Allegro is doing all the DirectX record-keeping behind the scenes, and other platforms are similar with their respective graphics libraries. Now it starts to make sense why all of those graphics functions you learned back in Chapter 3 required the use of screen as the first parameter. I don't know about you, but I think it's kind of amazing how just a few short lines of code (such as those shown previously) can have such a huge impact. To validate the point, you'll open the *Tank War* game project at the end of this chapter and tweak it a little, giving it a technological upgrade using bitmaps. In the context of role playing, the game will go up a level.

There is so much information to cover regarding bitmaps and blitting that I'll get into the specifics of sprites and animation in the next chapter.

Dealing with Bitmaps

Now what I'd like to do is introduce you to all of the bitmap-related functions in Allegro so you'll have a complete toolbox before you get into sprites—because sprites depend entirely on bitmaps to work. There are many aspects of Allegro that I don't get into in this book because the library has support for functionality (such as audio recording) that is not directly applicable to a game—unless you want to add voice recognition, perhaps?

You are already familiar with the screen bitmap. Essentially, this is a very advanced and complicated mapping of the video display into a linear buffer—in other words, it's easy to draw pixels on the screen without worrying about the video mode or the type of computer on which it's running. The screen buffer is also called the *frame buffer*, which is a term borrowed from reel-to-reel projectors in theaters. In computing, you don't already have a reel of film waiting to be displayed; instead, you have conditional logic that actually constructs each frame of the reel as it is being displayed. The computer is fast enough to usually do this at a very high frame rate. Although films are only displayed at 24 frames per second (fps) and television is displayed at 30 fps, it is generally agreed that 60 fps is the minimum for computer games. Why do you suppose movies and TV run at such low frame rates? Actually, the human eye is only capable of discerning about 30 fps. But it's a little different on the computer screen, where refresh rates and contrast ratios play a part, since quality is not always a constant thing as it is on a theater screen. Although a video card is capable of displaying more than 60 fps, if the monitor is only set to 60 Hertz (Hz), then a discernable flicker will be apparent, which is annoying at best and painful at worst. Very low vertical refresh rates can easily give you a headache after only a few minutes.

Although we deal with the screen in two dimensions (X and Y), it is actually just a single-dimensional array. You can figure out how big that array is by using the screen width and height.

```
Array_Size = Screen_Width * Screen_Height
```

A resolution of 800×600 therefore results in:

```
Array_Size = 800 * 600
Array_Size = 480,000
```

That's a pretty large number of pixels, wouldn't you agree? Just imagine that a game running 60 fps is blasting 480,000 pixels onto the screen 60 times per second! That comes to (480,000 * 60 =) 28,800,000 pixels per second. I'm not even talking about bytes here, just pixels. Most video modes use 3 bytes per pixel (bpp) in 24-bit color mode, or 2 bpp in 16-bit color mode. Therefore, what I'm really talking about is on the order of 90 million bytes per second in a typical game. And when was the last time you played a game at the lowly resolution of 800×600? I usually set my games to run at 1280×960. If you were to use 1600×1200, your poor video card would be tasked with pushing 180 million bytes per second. Now you can start to see what all the fuss is about regarding high-speed memory, with all the acronyms such as RDRAM, SDRAM, DDR, and so on. Your PC doesn't need 180 MB of video memory in this case—just very, very fast memory to keep the display going at 60 fps. The latest video cards with 256-MB DDR really use most of that awesome video memory for storing textures used in 3D games. The actual video buffer only requires 32 MB of memory at most.

That's quite a lot of new information (or maybe it's not so new if you are a videophile), and I've only talked about the screen itself. For reference, here is how the screen buffer is declared:

```
extern BITMAP *screen;
```

The real subject here is how to work with bitmaps, so take a look inside that bitmap structure:

```
typedef struct BITMAP          // a bitmap structure
{
    int w, h;                  // width and height in pixels
    int clip;                  // flag if clipping is turned on
    int cl, cr, ct, cb;        // clip left, right, top and bottom values
```

```
    GFX_VTABLE *vtable;            // drawing functions
    void *write_bank;             // C func on some machines, asm on i386
    void *read_bank;              // C func on some machines, asm on i386
    void *dat;                    // the memory we allocated for the bitmap
    unsigned long id              // for identifying sub-bitmaps
    void *extra;                  // points to a structure with more info
    int x_ofs;                    // horizontal offset (for sub-bitmaps)
    int y_ofs;                    // vertical offset (for sub-bitmaps)
    int seg;                      // bitmap segment
    ZERO_SIZE_ARRAY(unsigned char *, line);
} BITMAP;
```

The information in the BITMAP structure is not really useful to you as a programmer because it is almost entirely used by Allegro internally. Some of the values are useful, such as w and h (width and height) and perhaps the clipping variables.

Creating Bitmaps

The first thing you should know when learning about bitmaps is that they are not stored in video memory; they are stored in main system memory. Video memory is primarily reserved for the screen buffer, but it can also store textures. However, video memory is not available for storing run-of-the-mill bitmaps. Allegro supports a special type of bitmap called a *video bitmap*, but it is reserved for page flipping and double-buffering—something I'll get into in the next chapter.

As you have already seen, you use the create_bitmap function to create a memory bitmap.

```
BITMAP *create_bitmap(int width, int height);
```

By default, this function creates a bitmap using the current color depth. If you want your game to run at a specific color depth because all of your artwork is at that color depth, it's a good idea to call set_color_depth after set_gfx_mode when your program starts. The bitmap created with create_bitmap has clipping enabled by default, so if you draw outside the boundary of the bitmap, no memory will be corrupted. There is actually a related version of this function you can use if you want to use a specific color depth.

```
BITMAP *create_bitmap_ex(int color_depth, int width, int height);
```

If you do use create_bitmap_ex in lieu of create_bitmap with the assumed default color depth, you can always retrieve the color depth of a bitmap using this function:

```
int bitmap_color_depth(BITMAP *bmp);
```

After you create a new bitmap, if you plan to draw on it and blit it to the screen or to another bitmap, you must clear it first. The reason is because a new bitmap has random pixels on it based on the contents of memory at the space where the bitmap is now located.

To clear out a bitmap quickly, call this function:

```
void clear_bitmap(BITMAP *bitmap);
```

There is also an alternative version called clear_to_color that fills the bitmap with a specified color (while clear_bitmap fills in with 0, which equates to black).

```
void clear_to_color(BITMAP *bitmap, int color);
```

Possibly my absolute favorite function in Allegro is create_sub_bitmap because there is so much opportunity for mischief with this awesome function! Take a look:

```
BITMAP *create_sub_bitmap(BITMAP *parent, int x, y, width, height);
```

This function creates a sub-bitmap of an existing bitmap that actually shares the memory of the parent bitmap. Any changes you make to the sub-bitmap will be instantly visible on the parent and vice versa (if the sub-bitmap is within the portion of the parent that was drawn to). The sub-bitmap is clipped, so drawing beyond the edges will not cause changes to take place on the parent beyond that border. Now, about that little mention of mischief? You can create a sub-bitmap of the *screen*!

I'll wait a minute for that to sink in.

Do you have an evil grin yet? That's right, you can use sub-bitmaps to update or display portions of the screen, which you can use to create a windowing effect. This is absolutely awesome for building a scrolling background—something I'll spend a lot of time talking about in future chapters. Another point is, you can create a sub-bitmap of a sub-bitmap of a bitmap, but I wouldn't recommend creating a feedback loop by creating a bitmap of a sub-bitmap of a bitmap because that could cause your video card or monitor to explode. (Well, maybe not, but you get the picture.)

Okay, not really, but to be honest, that's the first thing I worry about when the idea of a feedback loop comes to mind. Feedback is generally good when you're talking about movies, books, video games, and so on, but feedback is very, very, very bad in electronics, as well as in software. Have you ever hooked up a video camera to a television and then pointed the camera at the screen? What you end up with is a view into eternity. Well, it *would* be infinite if the camera were centered perfectly, so the lens and TV screen are perfectly parallel, but you get the idea. If you try this, I recommend turning the volume down. Then again, leaving the volume on might help to drive the point home—feedback is dangerous, so naturally, let's try it.

```
BITMAP *hole = create_sub_bitmap(screen, 0, 0, 400, 300);
blit(hole, screen, 0, 0, 0, 0, 400, 300);
```

This snippet of code creates a sub-bitmap of the screen, and then blits that region onto itself. You can get some really weird effects by blitting only a portion of the sub-bitmap and by moving the sub-bitmap while drawing onto the screen. The point is, this is just the sort of reason you're involved in computer science in the first place—to try new things, to test new hypotheses, and to boldly go where no…let's leave it at that.

Cleaning House

It's important to throw away your hamburger wrapper after you're finished eating, just as it is important to destroy your bitmaps after you're finished using them. To leave a bitmap in memory after you're finished is akin to tossing a wrapper on the ground. You might get away with it without complaint if no one else is around, but you might feel a tinge of guilt later (unless you're completely dissociated from your conscience and society in general). This is a great analogy, which is why I've used it to nail the point home. Leaving a bitmap in memory after your program has ended might not affect anything or anyone right now. After all, it's just one bitmap, and your PC has tons of memory, right? But eventually the trash is going to pile up, and pretty soon the roads, sidewalks, and parks in your once-happy little town will be filled with trash and you'll have to reboot the town…er, the computer. destroy_bitmap is your friend.

```
void destroy_bitmap(BITMAP *bitmap);
```

By the way, stop littering. You can't really reboot your town, but that would be convenient, wouldn't it? If Microsoft Windows was the mayor, we wouldn't have to worry about litter.

Bitmap Information

You probably won't need to use the bitmap information functions often, but they can be very useful in some cases. For starters, the most useful function is bitmap_mask_color, which returns the transparency color of a bitmap.

```
int bitmap_mask_color(BITMAP *bmp);
```

Allegro defines the transparency for you so there is really no confusion (or choice in the matter). For an 8-bit (256-color) bitmap, the mask/transparent color is 0, the first entry in the palette. All other color depths use pink as the transparent color (255, 0, 255). That's fine by me because I use these colors for transparency anyway, and I'm sure you would too if given the choice. I have occasionally used black (0, 0, 0) for transparency in the past, but I've found pink to be far easier to use. For one thing, the source images are much easier to edit with a pink background because dark-shaded pixels stand out clearly when they are superimposed over pink. Actually, Allegro assumes that transparency is always on. This surprised me at first because I always made use of a transparency flag with my own sprite engines in the past. But this assumption really does make sense when the transparent color is assumed to be the mask color, which implies hardware support. On the Windows platform, Allegro tells DirectDraw that pink (255, 0, 255) is the mask color, and DirectDraw handles the rest. What if you don't want transparency? Don't use pink! For example, in later chapters I'll get into backgrounds and scrolling using tiles, and you certainly won't need transparency. Although you will use the same blit function to draw background tiles and foreground sprites, there is no speed penalty for doing so because drawing background tiles is handled at a lower level (within DirectX, SVGAlib, or whatever library Allegro uses on your platform of choice).

An American president brought the simple word "is" into the forefront of attention a few years back, and that's what you're going to do now—focus on several definitions using the word "is." The first is called is_same_bitmap.

```
int is_same_bitmap(BITMAP *bmp1, BITMAP *bmp2);
```

This function returns true if the two bitmaps share the same region of memory, with one being a sub-bitmap of another or both being sub-bitmaps of the same parent.

The is_linear_bitmap function returns true if the layout of video memory is natively linear, in which case you would have an opportunity to write optimized graphics code. This is not often the case, but it is available nonetheless.

```
int is_linear_bitmap(BITMAP *bmp);
```

A related function, is_planar_bitmap, returns true if the parameter is an extended-mode or mode-x bitmap. Given the cross-platform nature of Allegro, this *might* be true in some cases because the source code for your game *might* run if compiled for MS-DOS or console Linux.

```
int is_planar_bitmap(BITMAP *bmp);
```

The is_memory_bitmap function returns true if the parameter points to a bitmap that was created with create_bitmap, loaded from a data file or an image file. Memory bitmaps differ from screen and video bitmaps in that they can be manipulated as an array (such as bitmap[y][x] = color).

```
int is_memory_bitmap(BITMAP *bmp);
```

The related functions is_screen_bitmap and is_video_bitmap return true if their respective parameters point to screen or video bitmaps or sub-bitmaps of either.

```
int is_screen_bitmap(BITMAP *bmp);
int is_video_bitmap(BITMAP *bmp);
```

So if you create a sub-bitmap of the screen, such as:

```
BITMAP *scrn = screen;
```

then calling the function like this:

```
if (is_screen_bitmap(scrn))
```

will return true. Along that same line of thinking, is_sub_bitmap returns true if the parameter points to a sub-bitmap.

```
int is_sub_bitmap(BITMAP *bmp);
```

Acquiring and Releasing Bitmaps

Most modern operating systems use bitmaps as the basis for their entire GUI (*Graphical User Interface*), and Windows is at the forefront. There is an advanced technique for speeding up your program's drawing and blitting functions called "locking the bitmap." This means that a bitmap (including the screen buffer) can be locked so that only your code is able to modify it at a given moment. Allegro automatically locks and unlocks the screen whenever you draw onto it.

That is the bottleneck! Do you recall how many drawing functions were needed in *Tank War* to draw the tanks on the screen? Well, converting those drawing functions into bitmaps not only sped up the game thanks to blitting, but it also sped it up because each call to rectfill caused a lock and unlock of the screen, which was very, very time consuming (as far as clock cycles are concerned). But even a well-designed game with a scrolling background, transparent sprites, and so on will suffer if the screen or destination bitmap is not locked first. This process involves locking the bitmap, performing all drawing, and then unlocking it.

To lock a bitmap, you call the acquire_bitmap function.

```
void acquire_bitmap(BITMAP *bmp);
```

A shortcut function called acquire_screen is also available and simply calls acquire_bitmap(screen) for you.

```
void acquire_screen();
```

There is a danger to this situation, however, if you fail to release a bitmap after you have acquired (or locked) it. So always be sure to release any bitmaps that you have locked! More than likely you'll notice the mistake because your program will likely crash from repeated acquires and no releases (in which case the screen might never get updated). This situation is akin to falling into a black hole—the closer you get, the faster you fall! Note also that there is another function called lock_bitmap that is similar but only used by Allegro programs running under MS-DOS (which likely will never be the case—even the lowliest PC is capable of running at least Windows 95 or Linux, so I see no reason to support DOS).

After you update a locked bitmap, you want to release the bitmap with this function:

```
void release_bitmap(BITMAP *bmp);
```

and the related shortcut for the screen:

```
void release_screen();
```

Bitmap Clipping

Clipping is the process of ensuring that drawing to a bitmap or the screen does not occur beyond the boundary of that object. In most cases this is handled by the underlying architecture (DirectDraw, SVGAlib, and so on), but it is also possible to set a portion of the screen or a bitmap with clipping in order to limit drawing to a smaller region using the set_clip function.

```
void set_clip(BITMAP *bitmap, int x1, int y1, int x2, int y2);
```

The screen object in Allegro and all bitmaps that are created or loaded will automatically have clipping turned on by default and set to the boundary of the bitmap. However, you might want to change the default clip region using this function. If you want to turn clipping off, then you can pass zeros to the x1, y1, x2, and y2 parameters, like this:

```
set_clip(bmp, 0, 0, 0, 0);
```

Why would you ever want to turn off clipping? It is a very real possibility. For one thing, if you are very careful how you update the screen in your own code, you might want to turn off automatic clipping of the screen to gain a slight improvement in the drawing speed. If you are very careful with your own created bitmaps, you can also turn off clipping of those objects if you are certain that clipping is not necessary. If you only read from a bitmap and you do not draw onto it, then clipping is irrelevant and not a performance factor at all. Clipping is only an issue with drawing to a bitmap. I highly recommend that you leave clipping alone at the default setting. More than likely, you will not need the slight increase in speed that comes from a lack of clipping, and you are more than likely to crash your program without it.

Loading Bitmaps from Disk

Not too long ago, video memory was scarce and a video palette was needed to allow low-end video cards to support more than a measly 256 colors. Even an 8-bit display is capable of supporting more colors, but they must be palettized, meaning that a custom selection of 256 colors may be active out of a palette of many thousands of available colors. I once had an 8-bit video card, and at one time I used to work with an 8-bit video mode. (If you must know, VGA mode 13h was extremely popular in the DOS days.) Today you can assume that anyone who will play your games will have at least a 16-bit display. Even that is up for discussion, and it can be argued that 24- and 32-bit color will always be available on any computer system likely to run your games.

I think 24-bit color (also called *true color*) is the best mode to settle on, as far as a standard for my own games, and I feel pretty confident about it. If anyone is still stuck with a 16-bit video card, then perhaps it's time for an upgrade. After all, even an old GeForce 2 or Radeon 7500 card can be had for about 30 dollars. Of course, as often happens, someone with a 15-year-old laptop will want to run your game and will complain that it doesn't support 16-bit color. In the world we live in today, it's not always safe to walk the streets, but it is safe to assume that 24-bit color is available. For one thing, 16-bit modes are slower than 24-bit modes, even if they are supported in the GPU. Video drivers get around the problem of packing 24 bits into 16 bits by prepacking them when a game first starts (in other words, when the bitmaps are first loaded), after which time all blitting (or 3D texture drawing) is as fast as any other color depth. If you want to target the widest possible audience for your game, 16-bit is a better choice. The decision is up to you because Allegro doesn't care which mode you choose; it will work no matter what.

You were given a glimpse at how to load a bitmap file way back in Chapter 3, but now I'm going to go over all the intricate details of Allegro's graphics file support. Allegro supports several formats, which is really convenient. If I were discussing only DirectX in this book, I would be limited to just .bmp files (or I could write the code to load other types of files). Windows .bmp files are fine in most cases, but some programmers prefer other formats—not for any real technical reason, but sometimes artwork is delivered in another format.

Allegro natively supports the graphics file formats in Table 7.1.

Table 7.1 Natively Supported Graphics File Formats

Graphics Format	Extension	Color Depths
Windows / OS/2 Bitmap	BMP	8, 24
Truevision Targa	TGA	8, 16, 24, 32
Z-Soft's PC Paintbrush	PCX	8, 24
Deluxe Paint / Amiga	LBM	8

Reading a Bitmap File

The easiest way to load a bitmap file from disk is to call the load_bitmap function.

```
BITMAP *load_bitmap(const char *filename, RGB *pal);
```

This function will load the specified file by looking at the file extension (.bmp, .tga, .pcx, or .lbm) and returning a pointer to the bitmap data loaded into memory. If there is an error, such as if the file is not found, then the function returns NULL. The first parameter is the filename, and the second parameter is a pointer to a palette that you have already defined. In most cases this will simply be NULL because there is no need for a palette unless you are using an 8-bit video mode. Just for the sake of discussion, if you are using an 8-bit video mode and you load a true color image, passing a pointer to the palette parameter will cause an optimized palette to be generated when the image is loaded. If you want to use the current palette in an 8-bit display, simply pass NULL, and the current palette will be used.

As I mentioned, load_bitmap will read any of the four supported graphics formats based on the extension. If you want to specifically load only one particular format from a file, there are functions for doing so. First, you have load_bmp.

```
BITMAP *load_bmp(const char *filename, RGB *pal);
```

As was the case with load_bitmap, you can simply pass NULL to the second parameter unless you are in need of a palette. Note that in addition to these loading functions, Allegro also provides functions for saving to any of the supported formats. This means you can write your own graphics file converter using Allegro if you have any special need (such as doing batch conversions).

To load a Deluxe Paint/Amiga LBM file, you can call load_lbm:

```
BITMAP *load_lbm(const char *filename, RGB *pal);
```

which does pretty much the same thing as load_bmp, only with a different format. The really nice thing about these loaders is that they provide a common bitmap format in memory that can be used by any Allegro drawing or blitting function. Here are the other two loaders:

```
BITMAP *load_pcx(const char *filename, RGB *pal);
BITMAP *load_tga(const char *filename, RGB *pal);
```

Saving Images to Disk

What if you want to add a feature to your game so that when a certain button is pressed, a screenshot of the game is written to disk? This is a very useful feature you might want to add to any game you work on. Allegro provides the functionality to save to BMP, PCX, and TGA files, but not LBM files. Here's the save_bitmap function:

```
int save_bitmap(const char *filename, BITMAP *bmp, const RGB *pal);
```

This couldn't be any easier to use. You just pass the filename, source bitmap, and optional palette to save_bitmap, and it creates the image file. Here are the individual versions of the function:

```
int save_bmp(const char *filename, BITMAP *bmp, const RGB *pal);
int save_pcx(const char *filename, BITMAP *bmp, const RGB *pal);
int save_tga (const char *filename, BITMAP *bmp, const RGB *pal);
```

Saving a Screenshot to Disk

Now how about that screen-save feature? Here's a short example of how you might do that (assuming you have already initialized graphics mode and the game is running):

```
BITMAP *bmp;
bmp = create_sub_bitmap(screen, 0, 0, SCREEN_W, SCREEN_H);
save_bitmap("screenshot.pcx", bmp, NULL);
destroy_bitmap(bmp);
```

Whew, that's a lot of functions to remember! But don't worry, I don't expect you to memorize them. Just use this chapter as a flip-to reference whenever you need to use these functions. It's also helpful to see them and get a little experience with the various bitmap functions that you will be using frequently in later chapters.

Blitting Functions

Blitting is the process of copying one bit block to another location in memory, with the goal of doing this as quickly as possible. Most blitters are implemented in assembly language on each specific platform for optimum performance. The inherent low-level libraries (such as DirectDraw) will handle the details, with Allegro passing it on to the blitter in DirectDraw.

Standard Blitting

You have already seen the blit function several times, so here's the definition:

```
void blit(BITMAP *source, BITMAP *dest, int source_x, int source_y,
    int dest_x, int dest_y, int width, int height);
```

Table 7.2 provides a rundown of the parameters for the blit function.

Table 7.2 Parameters for the blit Function

Parameter	Description
BITMAP *source	The source bitmap (copy from)
BITMAP *dest	The destination bitmap (copy to)
int source_x	The x location on the source bitmap to copy from
int source_y	The y location on the source bitmap to copy from
int dest_x	The x location on the destination bitmap to copy to
int dest_y	The y location on the destination bitmap to copy to
int width	The width of the source rectangle to be copied
int height	The height of the source rectangle to be copied

Don't be intimidated by this function; blit is always this messy on any platform and with every game library I have ever used. But trust me, this is the bare minimum information you need to blit a bitmap (in fact, one of the simplest I have seen), and once you've used it a few times, it'll be old nature to you. The important thing to remember is how the source rectangle is copied into the destination bitmap. The rectangle's upper-left corner starts at (source_x, source_y) and extends right by width pixels and down by height pixels. In addition to raw blitting, you can use the blit function to convert images from one pixel format to another if the source and destination bitmaps have different color depths.

Scaled Blitting

There are several more blitters provided by Allegro, including the very useful stretch_blit function.

```
void stretch_blit(BITMAP *source, BITMAP *dest, int source_x, source_y,
    source_width, source_height, int dest_x, dest_y, dest_width, dest_height);
```

The stretch_blit function performs a scaling process to squeeze the source rectangle into the destination bitmap. Table 7.3 presents a rundown of the parameters.

Table 7.3 Parameters for the stretch_blit Function

Parameter	Description
BITMAP *source	The source bitmap
BITMAP *dest	The destination bitmap
int source_x	The x location on the source bitmap to copy from
int source_y	The y location on the source bitmap to copy from
int source_width	The width of the source rectangle
int source_height	The height of the source rectangle
int dest_x	The x location on the destination bitmap to copy to
int dest_y	The y location on the destination bitmap to copy to
int dest_width	The width of the destination rectangle (scaled into)
int dest_height	The height of the destination rectangle (scaled into)

The stretch_blit function is really useful and can be extremely handy at times for doing special effects, such as scaling the sprites in a game to simulate zooming in and out. However, take care when you use stretch_blit because it's not as hardy as blit. For one thing, the source and destination bitmaps must have the same color depth, and the source must be a memory bitmap. (In other words, the source can't be the screen.) You should also take care that you don't try to specify a rectangle outside the boundary of either the source or the destination. This means if you are copying the entire screen into a smaller bitmap, be sure to specify (0,0) for the upper-left corner, (SCREEN_W - 1) for the width, and (SCREEN_H - 1) for the height. The screen width and height values are counts of pixels, not screen positions. If you specify a source rectangle of (0, 0, 1024, 768), it could crash the program. What you want instead is (0, 0, 1023, 767) and likewise for other resolutions. The same rule applies to memory bitmaps—stay within the boundary or it could cause the program to crash.

Masked Blitting

A masked blit involves copying only the solid pixels and ignoring the transparent pixels, which are defined by the color pink (255, 0, 255) on high color and true color displays or by the color at palette index 0 in 8-bit video modes (which I will not discuss anymore beyond this point). Here is the definition for the masked_blit function:

```
void masked_blit(BITMAP *source, BITMAP *dest, int source_x, int source_y,
    int dest_x, int dest_y, int width, int height);
```

This function has the exact same list of parameters as blit, so to learn one is to understand both, but masked_blit ignores transparent pixels while blit draws everything! This function is the basis for sprite-based games, as you will see later in this chapter. Although there are custom sprite-drawing functions provided by Allegro, they essentially call upon masked_blit to do the real work of drawing sprites. However, unlike blit, the source and destination bitmaps must have the same color depth.

Masked Scaled Blitting

One of the rather odd but potentially very useful alternative blitters in Allegro is masked_stretch_blit, which does both masking of transparent pixels and scaling.

```
void masked_stretch_blit(BITMAP *source, BITMAP *dest, int source_x,
    source_y, source_w, source_h, int dest_x, dest_y, dest_w, dest_h);
```

The parameters for this function are identical to those for stretch_blit, so I won't go over them again. Just know that this combines the functionality of masking and scaling. However, you should be aware that scaling often mangles the transparent pixels in an image, so this function can't guarantee perfect results, especially you are when dealing with non-aligned rectangles. In other words, for best results, make sure the destination rectangle is a multiple of the source so that scaling is more effective.

Enhancing Tank War—From Graphics Primitives to Bitmaps

Well, are you ready to start making enhancements to *Tank War*, as promised back in Chapter 4? The last two chapters have not been very forthcoming with this sort of information, so now that you have more knowledge, let's put it to good use.

Tank War was developed in Chapter 4 to demonstrate all of the vector graphics support in Allegro, and also to provide a short break from all the theory. If I had my way, each new subject would be followed by a short game to demonstrate how a new feature works, but that would take too much time (and paper). Instead of going the creative route and creating a fun new game in every chapter, I think it's helpful to enhance an existing game with the new technology you learn as you go along. It has a parallel in real life, and it demonstrates the life cycle of game development from early concept through the prototype stage and on to completion. One benefit to enhancing the game with new tricks and techniques you learn as you go along is that changes only affect a few lines of code here and there, while entirely new games take up pages of code. Besides, this is not a "101 games" type of book, like those that were popular years ago; instead, you are learning both high- and low-level game programming techniques that will work across different operating systems.

I have huge plans for *Tank War*, and you will snicker at these early versions later because you will be making all kinds of improvements to the game in the coming chapters—a scrolling background, animated sprites, joystick control, sound effects, and other great things. Who knows, maybe the game will eventually be playable over the Internet!

Now, returning to the new code you just learned (which I will explain completely in the next section), what you need to do is create a bitmap surface for both of the tanks so that blitting will work. Create two tank bitmaps.

```
BITMAP *tank_bmp1 = create_bitmap(32, 32);
BITMAP *tank_bmp2 = create_bitmap(32, 32);
```

That will do nicely in theory, but the tank variables will be put in tankwar.h so the declaration will have to be separated from the initialization. (You can't use create_bitmap on the same line—more on that in a moment.) There's also the problem that each tank requires four directions, so each one will actually need four bitmaps. Now you need to clear out the bitmap memory so it's a nice clean slate.

```
clear_bitmap(tank_bmp1);
clear_bitmap(tank_bmp2);
```

Great! Now what? Now all you have to do is modify *Tank War* so it draws the tanks using blit instead of calling drawtank every time. Here is that blitting code:

```
blit(tank1, screen, 0, 0, X, Y, 32, 32);
blit(tank2, screen, 0, 0, X, Y, 32, 32);
```

Of course, this pseudo-code doesn't take into account the need for a separate bitmap for each direction the tank can travel (north, south, east, and west). But in theory, this is how it will work. On the CD-ROM, there is a project in the chapter07 folder for *Tank War* with the completed changes. But I encourage you to load up the initial Chapter 4 version of *Tank War* and make these minor changes yourself so you can get the full effect of this lesson.

When you open the tankwar project, you'll see the two files that comprise the source code: main.c and tankwar.h. Open the tankwar.h header file and add the following line after the gameover variable line:

```
//declare some variables
int gameover = 0;
BITMAP *tank_bmp[2][4];
```

This will take care of four bitmaps for each tank, and it's all wrapped nicely into a single array so it will be easy to use. Based on how the game uses tanks[0] and tanks[1] structures to keep track of the tanks, it will be easier if the bitmaps are stored in this array. Now open the main.c source code file. The goal here is to make as few changes as possible, keeping to the core of the original game at this point and just making those changes necessary to convert the game from vector-based graphics to bitmap-based graphics.

You can't really create the bitmaps in the header file, so this line just created the bitmap variables; you'll actually create the bitmaps in main.c. Do you remember how the tanks were set up back in Chapter 4? It was actually done by a function called setuptanks. All that needs to be done here is to create the two bitmaps, so put that code inside setuptanks. Look in main.c for the function and modify it as shown. (The changes are in bold.)

```
void setuptanks()
{
    int n;

    //player 1
    tanks[0].x = 30;
    tanks[0].y = 40;
    tanks[0].speed = 0;
    tanks[0].color = 9;
    tanks[0].score = 0;
    for (n=0; n<4; n++)
    {
        tank_bmp[0][n] = create_bitmap(32, 32);
        clear_bitmap(tank_bmp[0][n]);
        tanks[0].dir = n;
        drawtank(0);
    }
    tanks[0].dir = 1;

    //player 2
    tanks[1].x = SCREEN_W-30;
    tanks[1].y = SCREEN_H-30;
    tanks[1].dir = 3;
```

```
    tanks[1].speed = 0;
    tanks[1].color = 12;
    tanks[1].score = 0;
    for (n=0; n<4; n++)
    {
        tank_bmp[1][n] = create_bitmap(32, 32);
        clear_bitmap(tank_bmp[1][n]);
        tanks[1].dir = n;
        drawtank(1);
    }
}
```

It has required a lot of jumping around in the code, but so far you've only added a few lines of code. Not bad for starters! But now you're going to make some major changes to the drawtank function. This is where all those rectfill function calls will be pointed to the new tank bitmaps instead of directly to the screen. The actual logic hasn't changed, just the destination bitmap. I realize there are better and easier ways to rewrite this game to use bitmaps, but again, the goal is not to rewrite half the game, it is to make the fewest changes to get the job done. Note the changes in bold and make these changes in the drawtank function so it looks like this:

```
void drawtank(int num)
{
    int x = 15; //tanks[num].x;
    int y = 15; //tanks[num].y;
    int dir = tanks[num].dir;

    //draw tank body and turret
    rectfill(tank_bmp[num][dir], x-11, y-11, x+11, y+11, tanks[num].color);
    rectfill(tank_bmp[num][dir], x-6, y-6, x+6, y+6, 7);

    //draw the treads based on orientation
    if (dir == 0 || dir == 2)
    {
        rectfill(tank_bmp[num][dir], x-16, y-16, x-11, y+16, 8);
        rectfill(tank_bmp[num][dir], x+11, y-16, x+16, y+16, 8);
    }
    else
    if (dir == 1 || dir == 3)
    {
        rectfill(tank_bmp[num][dir], x-16, y-16, x+16, y-11, 8);
        rectfill(tank_bmp[num][dir], x-16, y+16, x+16, y+11, 8);
    }
```

```
//draw the turret based on direction
switch (dir)
{
    case 0:
        rectfill(tank_bmp[num][dir], x-1, y, x+1, y-16, 8);
        break;
    case 1:
        rectfill(tank_bmp[num][dir], x, y-1, x+16, y+1, 8);
        break;
    case 2:
        rectfill(tank_bmp[num][dir], x-1, y, x+1, y+16, 8);
        break;
    case 3:
        rectfill(tank_bmp[num][dir], x, y-1, x-16, y+1, 8);
        break;
}
}
```

Now that wasn't difficult at all, was it? Just a single parameter on all the rectfill function calls to point the drawing onto the tank bitmaps instead of onto the screen, and a minor change to the x and y variables. The original *Tank War* would draw the tanks directly on the screen using the x and y values for each tank, so I just modified it here to base the x and y on the center of the tank bitmap instead. So let's summarize what has been done so far.

1. Define the tank bitmap variables.
2. Create the tank bitmaps in memory.
3. Draw the tank images onto the tank bitmaps.

What is left to do? Just one more thing! Instead of calling drawtank in the main game loop, this has to be changed to blit! Let's do it. Scroll down to the end of the main.c file, look for the two drawtank lines of code, and replace them with the blit functions as the following listing shows:

```
//game loop
while(!gameover)
{
    //erase the tanks
    erasetank(0);
    erasetank(1);

    //check for collisions
    clearpath(0);
    clearpath(1);
```

```
//move the tanks
movetank(0);
movetank(1);

//draw the tanks
blit(tank_bmp[0][tanks[0].dir], screen, 0, 0,
    tanks[0].x-16, tanks[0].y-16, 32, 32);
blit(tank_bmp[1][tanks[1].dir], screen, 0, 0,
    tanks[1].x-16, tanks[1].y-16, 32, 32);

//update the bullets
updatebullet(0);
updatebullet(1);

//check for keypresses
if (keypressed())
    getinput();

//slow the game down (adjust as necessary)
rest(30);
}
```

The blit function really is only complicated by the multi-dimensional tank_bmp array, but this array results in far fewer lines of code than would otherwise be necessary using a switch or an if statement to draw the appropriate bitmap.

Summary

This chapter was an essential step in the path to writing great 2D games. Bitmaps are the core of 2D games and of Allegro, and in this chapter you learned to create, draw, erase, load, and delete bitmaps using a variety of Allegro functions. You also learned quite a bit about blitting, the process of drawing a bitmap to the screen really quickly.

Chapter Quiz

1. What does "blit" stand for?

    A.   Blitzkrieg

    B.   Bit-block transfer

    C.   Bit-wise transparency

    D.   Basic logarithmic infrared transmitter

2. What is a DHD?

   A.   Dynamic hard drive

   B.   Destructive hyperactivity disorder

   C.   Dial home device

   D.   That wasn't in the chapter!

3. How many pixels are there in an 800×600 screen?

   A.   480,000

   B.   28,800,000

   C.   65,538

   D.   47

4. What is the name of the object used to hold a bitmap in memory?

   A.   `hold_bitmap`

   B.   `create_bitmap`

   C.   `OBJECT`

   D.   `BITMAP`

5. Allegorically speaking, why is it important to destroy bitmaps after you're done using them?

   A.   Because bitmaps are evil and must be destroyed.

   B.   Because Microsoft Windows is the mayor.

   C.   Because the trash will pile up over time.

   D.   Because you can't reboot your hometown.

6. Which Allegro function has the potential to create a black hole if used improperly?

   A.   `acquire_bitmap`

   B.   `create_supernova`

   C.   `do_feedback`

   D.   `release_bitmap`

7. What types of graphics files are supported by Allegro?

   A.   PCX, LBM, BMP, and GIF

   B.   BMP, PCX, LBM, and TGA

   C.   GIF, JPG, PNG, and BMP

   D.   TGA, TIF, JPG, and BMP

8. What function is used to draw a scaled bitmap?
    A.   `draw_scaled_bitmap`
    B.   `stretch_blit`
    C.   `scaled_blit`
    D.   `masked_scaled_blit`

9. Why would you want to lock the screen while drawing on it?
    A.   If it's not locked, Allegro will lock and unlock the screen for every draw.
    B.   To prevent anyone else from drawing on your screen.
    C.   To keep the screen from getting away while you're using it.
    D.   To prevent a feedback loop that could destroy your monitor.

10. What is the name of the game you've been developing in this book?
    A.   *Super Allegro Bros.*
    B.   *Barbie's Motorhome Adventure*
    C.   *Teenage Neutered Midget Poodles*
    D.   *Tank War*

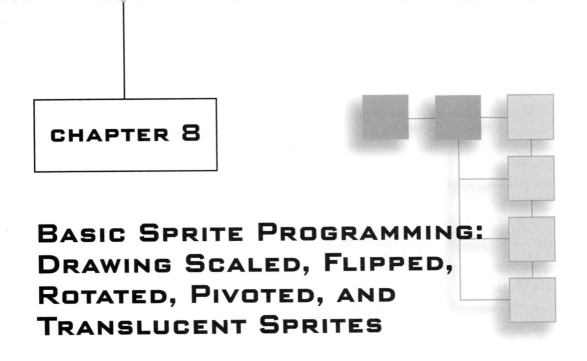

CHAPTER 8

BASIC SPRITE PROGRAMMING: DRAWING SCALED, FLIPPED, ROTATED, PIVOTED, AND TRANSLUCENT SPRITES

It is amazing to me that in the year 2004, we are still talking about, writing about, and developing games with sprites. There are just some ideas that are so great that no amount of new technology truly replaces them entirely. A *sprite* is a small image that is moved around on the screen. Many programmers misuse the term to describe any small graphic image in a game. Static, unmoving objects on the screen are not sprites because by very definition a *sprite* is something that moves around and does something on the screen, usually in direct relation to something the player is doing within the game. The analogy is to a mythical sprite—a tiny, mischievous, flying creature that quickly flits about, looking something like a classical fairy, but smaller. Of course the definition of a sprite has grown to include any onscreen game object, regardless of size or speed.

While the previous chapter provided all the prerequisites for working with sprites, this chapter delves right into the subject at full speed. Technically, a sprite is no different than a bitmap as far as Allegro is concerned. In fact, the sprite-handling functions in this chapter define sprites using the BITMAP * pointer. You can also draw a sprite directly using any of the bitmap drawing functions. However, Allegro provided a number of custom sprite functions that help to make your life as a 2D game programmer a little easier, in addition to some special effects that will knock your socks off! What I'm talking about is the ability to add dynamic lighting effects to one or more sprites on the screen! That's right—in this chapter you will learn to not only load, create, and draw sprites, but also how to apply lighting effects to those sprites. Combine this with alpha blending and transparency, and you'll learn to do some really amazing things in this chapter.

This chapter uses the word "basic" in the title because, although this is a complete overview of Allegro's sprite support, the upcoming chapters will feature a lot of the more advanced coverage. At this point, I believe it's more important to provide you with some exposure to all of the sprite routines available so you can see how they'll be used as you go along. If you don't see the big picture yet, that's understandable, but it's very helpful to grasp the key topics in this chapter because they're vital to the rest of the book. To help solidify the new information in your mind, you'll dig into *Tank War* a little more at the end of the chapter and enhance it with some sprites!

Here is a breakdown of the major topics in this chapter:

- Drawing regular and scaled sprites
- Drawing flipped sprites
- Drawing rotated and pivoted sprites
- Enhancing *Tank War*

Basic Sprite Handling

Now that you've had a thorough introduction to bitmaps in the last chapter—how to create them, load them from disk, make copies, and blit them—you have the prerequisite information for working with sprites. A sprite image is simply a bitmap image. What you do with a sprite image (and the sprite functionality built into Allegro) differentiates sprites from mere bitmaps.

Drawing Regular Sprites

The first and most important function to learn is draw_sprite.

```
void draw_sprite(BITMAP *bmp, BITMAP *sprite, int x, int y);
```

This function is similar to masked_blit in that it draws the sprite image using transparency. As you'll recall from the previous chapter, the transparent color in Allegro is defined as pink (255, 0, 255). Therefore, if your source bitmap uses pink to outline the image, then that image will be drawn transparently by draw_sprite. Did you notice that there are no source_x, source_y, width, or height parameters in this function call? That is one convenience provided by this function. It is assumed that you intend to draw the whole sprite, so those values are provided automatically by draw_sprite and you don't need to worry about them. This assumes that the entire bitmap is comprised of a single sprite. Of course, you can use this technique if you want, but a far better method is to store multiple sprites in a single bitmap and then draw the sprites by "grabbing" them out of the bitmap (something I'll cover later in this chapter).

The most important factor to consider up front when you are dealing with sprites is the color depth of your game. Until now, you have used the default color depth and simply called set_gfx_mode before drawing to the screen. Allegro does not automatically use a high-color or true-color color depth even if your desktop is running in those modes. By default, Allegro runs in 8-bit color mode (the mode that has been used automatically in all the sample programs thus far). Figure 8.1 shows a sprite drawn to the screen with the default color depth.

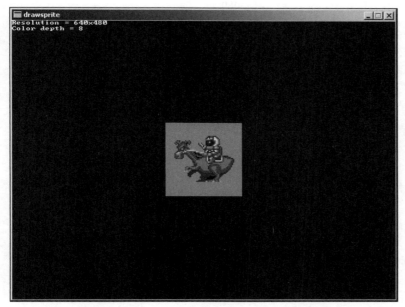

Figure 8.1 A high-color sprite drawn to the screen with a default 8-bit color depth. Sprite image courtesy of Ari Feldman.

Drawing that same sprite using a 16-bit high-color mode results in the screen shown in Figure 8.2. Notice how the sprite is now drawn with the correct transparency, whereas the pink transparent color was incorrectly drawn on the 8-bit display shown in Figure 8.1.

The program to produce these sprites is provided in the following listing and included on the CD-ROM under the name drawsprite.

```
#include <conio.h>
#include <stdlib.h>
#include "allegro.h"

#define WHITE makecol(255,255,255)

int main()
```

```
{
    BITMAP *dragon;
    int x, y;

    //initialize the program
    allegro_init();
    install_keyboard();
    set_color_depth(16);
    set_gfx_mode(GFX_AUTODETECT_FULLSCREEN, 640, 480, 0, 0);

    //print some status information
    textprintf(screen,font,0,0,WHITE,"Resolution = %ix%i",
        SCREEN_W, SCREEN_H);
    textprintf(screen, font, 0, 10, WHITE, "Color depth = %i",
        bitmap_color_depth(screen));

    //load the bitmap
    dragon = load_bitmap("spacedragon1.bmp", NULL);
    x = SCREEN_W/2 - dragon->w/2;
    y = SCREEN_H/2 - dragon->h/2;

    //main loop
    while (!key[KEY_ESC])
    {
        //erase the sprite
        rectfill(screen, x, y, x+dragon->w, y+dragon->h, 0);

        //move the sprite
        if (x-- < 2)
            x = SCREEN_W - dragon->w;

        //draw the sprite
        draw_sprite(screen, dragon, x, y);

        textprintf(screen,font,0,20,WHITE, "Location = %ix%i", x, y);
        rest(1);
    }

    //delete the bitmap
    destroy_bitmap(dragon);

    return 0;
}
END_OF_MAIN();
```

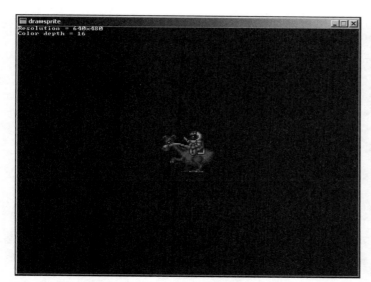

Figure 8.2 The high-color sprite is drawn to the screen with 16-bit color. Sprite image courtesy of Ari Feldman.

Transparency is an important subject when you are working with sprites, so it is helpful to gain an understanding of it right from the start. Figure 8.3 shows an example of a sprite drawn with and without transparency, as you saw in the sample drawsprite program when an 8-bit color depth was used.

When a sprite is drawn transparently, all but the transparent pixels are copied to the destination bitmap (or screen). This is necessary because the sprite has to be stored in a bitmap image of one type or another (.bmp, .pcx, and so on), and the computer can only deal with rectangular bitmaps in memory. In reality, the computer only deals with chunks of memory anyway, so it cannot draw images in any other shape but rectangular (see Figure 8.4).

In the next chapter, I'll show you a technique you can use to draw only the actual pixels of a sprite and completely ignore the transparent pixels during the drawing process. This is a special feature built into Allegro called *compiled sprites*. Compiled sprites, as well as run-length encoded (compressed) sprites, can be drawn much faster than regular sprites drawn with draw_sprite, so the next chapter will be very interesting indeed!

Figure 8.3 The difference between a sprite drawn with and without transparency. Sprite image courtesy of Ari Feldman.

Figure 8.4 The actual sprite is contained inside a rectangular image with transparent pixels. Sprite image courtesy of Ari Feldman.

Drawing Scaled Sprites

Scaling is the process of zooming in or out of an image, or in another context, shrinking or enlarging an image. Allegro provides a function for drawing a sprite within a specified rectangle on the destination bitmap; it is similar to `stretched_blit`. The function is called `stretch_sprite` and it looks like this:

```
void stretch_sprite(BITMAP *bmp, BITMAP *sprite,
    int x, int y, int w, int h);
```

The first parameter is the destination, and the second is the sprite image. The next two parameters specify the location of the sprite on the destination bitmap, while the last two parameters specify the width and height of the resulting sprite. You can only truly appreciate this function by seeing it in action. Figure 8.5 shows the *ScaledSprite* program, which displays a sprite at various resolutions.

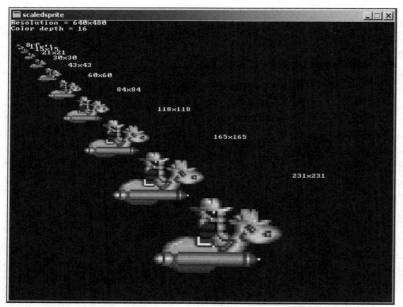

Figure 8.5 A high-resolution sprite image scales quite well. Sprite image courtesy of Ari Feldman.

```c
#include <conio.h>
#include <stdlib.h>
#include "allegro.h"

#define WHITE makecol(255,255,255)

int main()
{
    BITMAP *cowboy;
      int x, y, n;
    float size = 8;

    //initialize the program
    allegro_init();
      install_keyboard();
      set_color_depth(16);
    set_gfx_mode(GFX_AUTODETECT_FULLSCREEN, 640, 480, 0, 0);

    //print some status information
    textprintf(screen,font,0,0,WHITE,"Resolution = %ix%i",
        SCREEN_W, SCREEN_H);
    textprintf(screen, font, 0, 10, WHITE, "Color depth = %i",
        bitmap_color_depth(screen));

    //load the bitmap
      cowboy = load_bitmap("spacecowboy1.bmp", NULL);

    //draw the sprite
    for (n = 0; n < 11; n++)
    {
        y = 30 + size;
        stretch_sprite(screen, cowboy, size, y, size, size);
        textprintf(screen,font,size+size+10,y,WHITE,"%ix%i",
            (int)size,(int)size);
        size *= 1.4;
    }

    //delete the bitmap
    destroy_bitmap(cowboy);

    while(!key[KEY_ESC]);
    return 0;
}
END_OF_MAIN();
```

Drawing Flipped Sprites

Suppose you are writing a game called *Tank War* that features tanks able to move in four directions (north, south, east, and west), much like the game we have been building in the last few chapters. As you might recall, the last enhancement to the game in the last chapter added the ability to blit each tank image as a bitmap, which sped up the game significantly. Now imagine eliminating the east-, west-, and south-facing bitmaps from the game by simply drawing the north-facing bitmap in one of the four directions using a special version of draw_sprite for each one. In addition to the standard draw_sprite, you now have the use of three more functions to flip the sprite three ways:

```
void draw_sprite_v_flip(BITMAP *bmp, BITMAP *sprite, int x, int y);
void draw_sprite_h_flip(BITMAP *bmp, BITMAP *sprite, int x, int y);
void draw_sprite_vh_flip(BITMAP *bmp, BITMAP *sprite, int x, int y);
```

Take a look at Figure 8.6, a shot from the *FlipSprite* program.

```
#include <conio.h>
#include <stdlib.h>
#include "allegro.h"

int main()
{
    int x, y;

    //initialize the program
    allegro_init();
    install_keyboard();
    set_color_depth(16);
    set_gfx_mode(GFX_AUTODETECT_WINDOWED, 640, 480, 0, 0);

    //load the bitmap
    BITMAP *panel = load_bitmap("panel.bmp", NULL);

    //draw the sprite
    draw_sprite(screen, panel, 200, 100);
    draw_sprite_h_flip(screen, panel, 200+128, 100);
    draw_sprite_v_flip(screen, panel, 200, 100+128);
    draw_sprite_vh_flip(screen, panel, 200+128, 100+128);

    //delete the bitmap
    destroy_bitmap(panel);

    while(!key[KEY_ESC]);
    return 0;
}
END_OF_MAIN();
```

Figure 8.6 A single sprite is flipped both vertically and horizontally.

Drawing Rotated Sprites

Allegro has some very cool sprite manipulation functions that I'm sure you will have fun exploring. I have had to curtail my goofing off with all these functions in order to finish writing this chapter; otherwise, there might have been 90 sample programs to go over here! It really is incredibly fun to see all of the possibilities of these functions, which some might describe as "simple" or "2D."

Perhaps the most impressive (and incredibly useful) sprite manipulation function is `rotate_sprite`.

```
void rotate_sprite(BITMAP *bmp, BITMAP *sprite, int x, int y,
    fixed angle);
```

This function rotates a sprite using an advanced algorithm that retains a high level of quality in the resulting sprite image. Most sprite rotation is done in a graphic editor by an artist because this is a time-consuming procedure in the middle of a high-speed game. The last thing you want slowing your game down is a sprite rotation occurring while you are rendering your sprites.

However, what about rotating and rendering your sprites at game startup, and then using the resulting bitmaps as a sprite array? That way, sprite rotation is provided at run time, and you only need to draw the first image of a sprite (such as a tank) facing north, and then rotate all of the angles you need for the game. For some programmers, this is a wonderful and welcome feature because many of us are terrible artists. Chances are, if you are a good artist, you aren't a game programmer, and vice versa. Why would an artistically creative person be interested in writing code? Likewise, why would a programmer be interested in fooling with pixels? Naturally, there are exceptions (maybe you?), but in general, this is the way of things.

Who cares? Oh, right. Okay, let's try it out then. But first, here are the details. The `rotate_sprite` function draws the sprite image onto the destination bitmap with the top-left corner at the specified x and y position, rotated by the specified angle around its center. The tricky part is understanding that the angle does not represent a usual 360-degree circle; rather, it represents a set of floating-point angles from 0 to 256. If you would like to rotate a sprite at each of the usual 360 degrees of a circle, you can rotate it by (256 / 360 =) 0.711 for each angle.

Eight-Way Rotations

In reality, you will probably want a rotation scheme that generates eight, 16, or 32 rotation frames for each sprite. I've never seen a game that needed more than 32 frames for a full rotation. A highly spatial 2D shooter such as Atari's classic *Blasteroids* probably used 16 frames at most. Take a look at Figure 8.7 for an example of a tank sprite comprised of eight rotation frames.

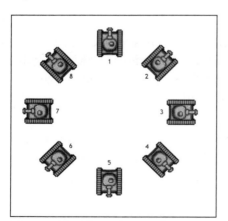

Figure 8.7 The tank sprite (courtesy of Ari Feldman) rotated in eight directions

When you want to generate eight frames, rotate each frame by 45 degrees more than the last one. This presumes that you are talking about a graphic editor, such as Paint Shop Pro, that is able to rotate images by any angle. Table 8.1 provides a rundown of the eight-frame rotation angles and the equivalent Allegro angles (based on 256). In the Allegro system, each frame is incremented by 32 degrees, which is actually easier to use from a programming perspective.

note

Even an eight-way sprite is a lot better than what we have done so far in *Tank War*, with only four pathetic sprite frames! What a travesty! Now that you've seen what is possible, I'm sure you have lost any ounce of respect you had for the game. Just hold on for a little while because you'll give the *Tank War* game a facelift at the end of this chapter with some proper sprites. It's almost time to do away with those ugly vector-based graphics once and for all!

Table 8.1 Eight-Frame Rotation Angles

Frame	Standard Angle (360)	Allegro Angle (256)
1	0	0
2	45	32
3	90	64
4	135	96
5	180	128
6	225	160
7	270	192
8	315	224

Sixteen-Way Rotations

A 16-way sprite is comprised of frames that are each incremented 22.5 degrees from the previous frame. Using this value, you can calculate the angles for an entire 16-way sprite, as shown in Figure 8.8.

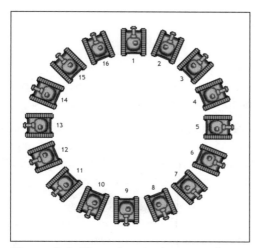

Figure 8.8 The tank sprite (courtesy of Ari Feldman) rotated in 16 directions

One glance at the column of Allegro angles in Table 8.2, and you can see why Allegro uses the 256-degree circle system instead of the 360-degree system; it is far easier to calculate the common angles used in games! Again, to determine what each angle should be, just divide the maximum angle (360 or 256, in either case) by the maximum number of frames to come up with a value for each frame.

Thirty-Two-Way Rotations

Although it's certainly a great goal to try for 24 or 32 frames of rotation in a 2D game, such as *Tank War*, each new set of frames added to the previous dimension of rotation adds a whole new complexity to the game. Remember, you need to calculate how the gun will fire in all of these directions! If your tank (or other sprite) needs to shoot in 32 directions, then you will have to calculate how that projectile will travel for each of those directions, too! To put it mildly, this is not easy to do. Combine that with the fact that the whole point of using higher rotations is simply to improve the quality of the game, and you might want to scale back to 16 if it becomes too difficult. I would suggest working from

Table 8.2 Sixteen-Frame Rotation Angles

Frame	Standard Angle (360)	Allegro Angle (256)
1	0.0	0
2	22.5	16
3	45.0	32
4	67.5	48
5	90.0	64
6	112.5	80
7	135.0	96
8	157.5	112
9	180.0	128
10	202.5	144
11	225.0	160
12	247.5	176
13	270.0	192
14	292.5	208
15	315.0	224
16	337.5	240

that common rotation count and adding more later if you have time, but don't delay the game just to get in all those frames so the game will be even better. My first rule is always to make the game work first, and then add cool factors (the bells and whistles).

Take a look at Figure 8.9 for an example of what a pre-rendered 32-frame sprite looks like. Each rotation frame is 11.25 degrees. In Allegro's 256-degree math, that's just a simple eight degrees per frame. You could write a simple loop to pre-rotate all of the images for *Tank War* using eight degrees, assuming you wanted to use a 32-frame tank.

That's a lot of sprites. In addition, they must all be perfectly situated in the bitmap image so that when it is drawn, the tank doesn't behave erratically with small jumps due to incorrect pixel alignment on each frame. What's a good solution? It probably would be a good idea to simply use a single tank image and rotate it through all 32 frames when the game starts up, and then store the rotation frames in a sprite array. Allegro makes it easy to do this. This is also a terrific solution when you are working on smaller platforms that have limited memory. Don't be surprised by the possibility that if you are serious about game programming, you might end up writing games for cell phones, Nokia N-Gage, and other small platforms where memory is a premium. Of course, Allegro isn't available for those platforms, but speaking in general terms, rotating a sprite based on a single image is very

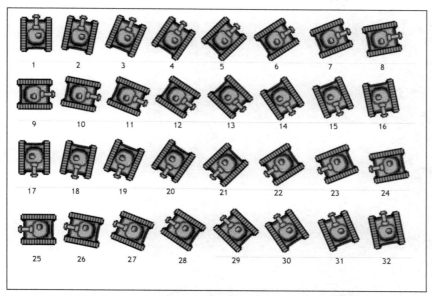

Figure 8.9 The tank sprite (courtesy of Ari Feldman) rotated in 32 directions

efficient and a smart way to develop under limited resources. You can get away with a lot of sloppy code under a large operating system, when it is assumed that the player must have a minimum amount of memory. (512 MB and 1 GB are common on Windows machines nowadays.)

The RotateSprite Program

Now it's time to put some of this newfound knowledge to use in an example program. This program is called *RotateSprite*, and it simply demonstrates the rotate_sprite function. You can use the left and right arrow keys to rotate the sprite in either direction. There is no fixed angle used in this sample program, but the angle is adjusted by 0.1 degree in either direction, giving it a nice steady rotation rate that shouldn't be too fast. If you are using a slower PC, you can increase the angle. Note that a whole number angle will go so fast that you'll have to slow down the program the hard way, using the rest function. Take a look at Figure 8.10, which shows the *RotateSprite* program running.

The only aspect of the code listing for the *RotateSprite* program that I want you to keep an eye out for is the actual call to rotate_sprite. I have set the two lines that use rotate_sprite in bold so you will be able to identify them easily. Note the last parameter, itofix(angle). This extremely important function converts the angle to Allegro's fixed 16.16 numeric format used by rotate_sprite. You will want to pass your floating-point value (float, double) to itofix to convert it to a fixed-point value.

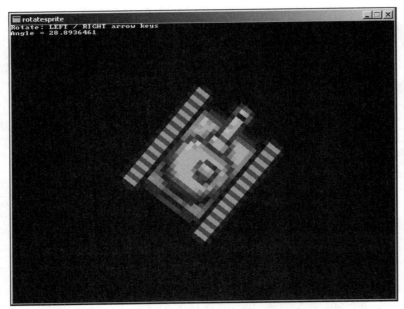

Figure 8.10 The tank sprite (courtesy of Ari Feldman) is rotated with the arrow keys.

tip

Fixed-point is much faster than floating-point—or so says the theory, which I do not subscribe to due to the modern floating-point power of processors. Remember that you must use `itofix` with all of the rotation functions.

```
#include <conio.h>
#include <stdlib.h>
#include "allegro.h"

#define WHITE makecol(255,255,255)

void main(void)
{
    int x, y;
    float angle = 0;

    //initialize program
    allegro_init();
    install_keyboard();
    set_color_depth(32);
```

```
    set_gfx_mode(GFX_AUTODETECT_WINDOWED, 640, 480, 0, 0);
    textout(screen, font, "Rotate: LEFT / RIGHT arrow keys",
        0, 0, WHITE);

    //load tank sprite
    BITMAP *tank = load_bitmap("tank.bmp", NULL);

    //calculate center of screen
    x = SCREEN_W/2 - tank->w/2;
    y = SCREEN_H/2 - tank->h/2;

    //draw tank at starting location
    rotate_sprite(screen, tank, x, y, 0);

    //main loop
    while(!key[KEY_ESC])
    {
        //wait for keypress
        if (keypressed())
        {
            //left arrow rotates left
            if (key[KEY_LEFT])
            {
                angle -= 0.1;
                if (angle < 0) angle = 256;
                rotate_sprite(screen, tank, x, y, itofix(angle));
            }

            //right arrow rotates right
            if (key[KEY_RIGHT])
            {
                angle += 0.1;
                if (angle > 256) angle = 0;
                rotate_sprite(screen, tank, x, y, itofix(angle));
            }

            //display angle
            textprintf(screen, font, 0, 10, WHITE, "Angle = %f", angle);
        }
    }
}
END_OF_MAIN()
```

Additional Rotation Functions

Allegro is generous with so many great functions, and that includes alternative forms of the rotate_sprite function. Here you have a rotation function that includes vertical flip, another rotation function that includes scaling, and a third function that does both scaling and vertical flip while rotating. Whew! You can see from these functions that the creators of Allegro were not artists, so they incorporated all of these wonderful functions to make it easier to conjure artwork for a game! These functions are similar to rotate_sprite so I won't bother with a sample program. You already understand how it works, right?

```
void rotate_sprite_v_flip(BITMAP *bmp, BITMAP *sprite,
    int x, int y, fixed angle)
```

The preceding function rotates and also flips the image vertically. To flip horizontally, add itofix(128) to the angle. To flip in both directions, use rotate_sprite() and add itofix(128) to its angle.

```
void rotate_scaled_sprite(BITMAP *bmp, BITMAP *sprite,
    int x, int y, fixed angle, fixed scale)
```

The preceding function rotates an image and scales (stretches to fit) the image at the same time.

```
void rotate_scaled_sprite_v_flip(BITMAP *bmp, BITMAP *sprite,
    int x, int y, fixed angle, fixed scale)
```

The preceding function rotates the image while also scaling and flipping it vertically, simply combining the functionality of the previous two functions.

Drawing Pivoted Sprites

Allegro provides the functionality to pivot sprites and images. What does pivot mean? The *pivot point* is the location on the image where rotation occurs. If a sprite is 64×64 pixels, then the default pivot point is at 31×31 (accounting for zero); a sprite sized at 32×32 would have a default pivot point at 15×15. The pivot functions allow you to change the position of the pivot where rotation takes place.

```
void pivot_sprite(BITMAP *bmp, BITMAP *sprite, int x, int y,
    int cx, int cy, fixed angle)
```

The x and y values specify where the sprite is drawn, while cx and cy specify the pivot *within* the sprite (not globally to the screen). Therefore, if you have a 32×32 sprite, you can draw it anywhere on the screen, but the pivot points cx and cy should be values of 0 to 31.

The PivotSprite Program

The *PivotSprite* program demonstrates how to use the pivot_sprite function by drawing two blue lines on the screen, showing the pivot point on the sprite. You can use the arrow keys to adjust the pivot point and see how the sprite reacts while it is rotating in real time (see Figure 8.11).

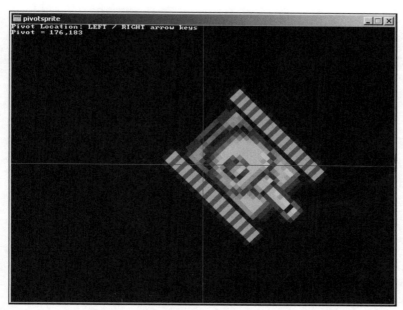

Figure 8.11 The *PivotSprite* program demonstrates how to adjust the pivot point. Image courtesy of Ari Feldman.

```c
#include <conio.h>
#include <stdlib.h>
#include "allegro.h"

#define WHITE makecol(255,255,255)
#define BLUE makecol(64,64,255)

void main(void)
{
    int x, y;
    int pivotx, pivoty;
    float angle = 0;

    //initialize program
    allegro_init();
    install_keyboard();
    set_color_depth(32);
    set_gfx_mode(GFX_AUTODETECT_WINDOWED, 640, 480, 0, 0);
```

```
//load tank sprite
BITMAP *tank = load_bitmap("tank.bmp", NULL);

//calculate center of screen
x = SCREEN_W/2;
y = SCREEN_H/2;
pivotx = tank->w/2;
pivoty = tank->h/2;

//main loop
while(!key[KEY_ESC])
{
    //wait for keypress
    if (keypressed())
    {
        //left arrow moves pivot left
        if (key[KEY_LEFT])
        {
            pivotx -= 2;
            if (pivotx < 0)
                pivotx = 0;
        }

        //right arrow moves pivot right
        if (key[KEY_RIGHT])
        {
            pivotx += 2;
            if (pivotx > tank->w-1)
                pivotx = tank->w-1;
        }

        //up arrow moves pivot up
        if (key[KEY_UP])
        {
            pivoty -= 2;
            if (pivoty < 0)
                pivoty = 0;
        }

        //down arrow moves pivot down
        if (key[KEY_DOWN])
        {
            pivoty += 2;
```

```
                    if (pivoty > tank->h-1)
                        pivoty = tank->h-1;
                }
            }

            //pivot/rotate the sprite
            angle += 0.5;
            if (angle > 256) angle = 0;
            pivot_sprite(screen, tank, x, y, pivotx, pivoty, itofix(angle));

            //draw the pivot lines
            hline(screen, 0, y, SCREEN_W-1, BLUE);
            vline(screen, x, 0, SCREEN_H-1, BLUE);

            //display information
            textout(screen, font, "Pivot Location: LEFT / RIGHT arrow keys",
                0, 0, WHITE);
            textprintf(screen, font, 0, 10, WHITE, "Pivot = %3d,%3d ",
                pivotx, pivoty);
            rest(1);
        }
    }
END_OF_MAIN()
```

Additional Pivot Functions

As usual, Allegro provides everything including the clichéd kitchen sink. Here are the additional pivot functions that you might have already expected to see, given the consistency of Allegro in this matter. Here you have three functions—pivot with vertical flip, pivot with scaling, and pivot with scaling and vertical flip. It's nice to know that Allegro is so consistent, so any time you are in need of a special sprite manipulation within your game, you are certain to be able to accomplish it using a combination of rotation, pivot, scaling, and flipping functions that have been provided.

```
void pivot_sprite_v_flip(BITMAP *bmp, BITMAP *sprite, int x, int y,
        int cx, int cy, fixed angle);


void pivot_scaled_sprite(BITMAP *bmp, BITMAP *sprite, int x, int y,
        int cx, int cy, fixed angle, fixed scale));


void pivot_scaled_sprite_v_flip(BITMAP *bmp, BITMAP *sprite,
    int x, int y, fixed angle, fixed scale)
```

Drawing Translucent Sprites

Allegro provides many special effects that you can apply to sprites, as you saw in the previous sections. The next technique is unusual enough to warrant a separate discussion. This section explains how to draw sprites with translucent alpha blending. Two more special effects (sprite lighting and Gouraud shading) are covered in the next chapter.

Translucency is a degree of "see-through" that differs from *transparency*, which is entirely see-through. Think of the glass in a window as being translucent, while an open window is transparent. There is quite a bit of work involved in making a sprite translucent, and I'm not entirely sure it's necessary for a game to use this feature, which is most definitely a drain on the graphics hardware. Although a late-model video card can handle translucency, or *alpha blending*, with ease, there is still the issue of supporting older computers or those with non-standard video cards. As such, many 2D games have steered clear of using this feature. One of the problems with translucency in a software implementation is that you must prepare both bitmaps before they will render with translucency. Some hardware solutions are likely available, but they are not provided for in Allegro.

Translucency is provided by the draw_trans_sprite function.

```
void draw_trans_sprite(BITMAP *bmp, BITMAP *sprite, int x, int y);
```

Unfortunately, it's not quite as cut-and-dried as this simple function makes it appear. To use translucency, you have to use an alpha channel blender, and even the Allegro documentation is elusive in describing how this works. Suffice it to say, translucency is not something you would probably want to use in a game because it was really designed to work between just two bitmaps. You could use the same background image with multiple foreground sprites that are blended with the background using the alpha channel, but each sprite must be adjusted pixel by pixel when the program starts. This is a special effect that you might find a use for, but I would advise against using it in the main loop of a game.

Here is the source code for the *TransSprite* program, shown in Figure 8.12. I will explain how it works after the listing.

```
#include <conio.h>
#include <stdlib.h>
#include "allegro.h"

int main()
{
    int x, y, c, a;

    //initialize
    allegro_init();
    install_keyboard();
```

Figure 8.12 The *TransSprite* program demonstrates how to draw a translucent sprite.

```
install_mouse();
set_color_depth(32);
set_gfx_mode(GFX_AUTODETECT_WINDOWED, 640, 480, 0, 0);

//load the background bitmap
BITMAP *background = load_bitmap("mustang.bmp", NULL);

//load the translucent foreground image
BITMAP *alpha = load_bitmap("alpha.bmp", NULL);
BITMAP *sprite = create_bitmap(alpha->w, alpha->h);

//set the alpha channel blend values
drawing_mode(DRAW_MODE_TRANS, NULL, 0, 0);
set_write_alpha_blender();
//blend the two bitmap alpha channels
for (y=0; y<alpha->h; y++) {
    for (x=0; x<alpha->w; x++) {
        //grab the pixel color
        c = getpixel(alpha, x, y);
        a = getr(c) + getg(c) + getb(c);
        //find the middle alpha value
        a = MID(0, a/2-128, 255);
        //copy the alpha-enabled pixel to the sprite
        putpixel(sprite, x, y, a);
    }
```

```
    }

    //create a double buffer bitmap
    BITMAP *buffer = create_bitmap(SCREEN_W, SCREEN_H);

    //draw the background image
    blit(background, buffer, 0, 0, 0, 0, SCREEN_W, SCREEN_H);

    while (!key[KEY_ESC])
    {
        //get the mouse coordinates
        x = mouse_x - sprite->w/2;
        y = mouse_y - sprite->h/2;

        //draw the translucent image
        set_alpha_blender();
        draw_trans_sprite(buffer, sprite, x, y);

        //draw memory buffer to the screen
        blit(buffer, screen, 0, 0, 0, 0, SCREEN_W, SCREEN_H);

        //restore the background
        blit(background, buffer, x, y, x, y, sprite->w, sprite->h);
    }

    destroy_bitmap(background);
    destroy_bitmap(sprite);
    destroy_bitmap(buffer);
    destroy_bitmap(alpha);

    return 0;
}
END_OF_MAIN();
```

Now for some explanation. First, the program loads the background image (called "background"), followed by the foreground sprite (called "alpha"). A new image called "sprite" is created with the same resolution as the background; it receives the alpha-channel information. The drawing mode is set to DRAW_MODE_TRANS to enable translucent drawing with the graphics functions (putpixel, line, and so on). The pixels are then copied from the alpha image into the sprite image.

After that, another new image called "buffer" is created and the background is blitted to it. At this point, the main loop starts. Within the loop, the mouse is polled to move the sprite around on the screen, demonstrating the alpha blending. The actual translucency is accomplished by two functions.

```
set_alpha_blender();
draw_trans_sprite(buffer, sprite, x, y);
```

The alpha blender is enabled before `draw_trans_sprite` is called, copying the "sprite" image onto the buffer. The memory buffer is blitted to the screen, and then the background is restored for the next iteration through the loop.

```
blit(buffer, screen, 0, 0, 0, 0, SCREEN_W, SCREEN_H);
```

Enhancing Tank War

Now it's time to use the new knowledge you have gained in this chapter to enhance *Tank War*. First, how about a quick recap on the state of the game? Take a look at Figure 8.13, showing *Tank War* as it appeared in the last chapter.

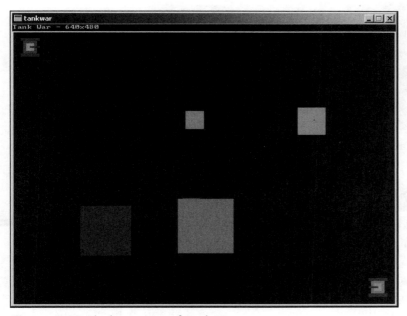

Figure 8.13 The last version of *Tank War*

Not very attractive, is it? It looks like something that would run on an Atari 2600. I have been skirting the issue of using true bitmaps and sprites in *Tank War* since it was first conceived several chapters ago. Now it's time to give this pathetic game a serious upgrade!

What's New?

First, to upgrade the game, I made a design decision to strip out the pixel collision code and leave the battlefield blank for this enhancement. The game will look better overall with the eight-way tank sprites, but the obstacles will no longer be present. Take a look at Figure 8.14, showing a tank engulfed in an explosion.

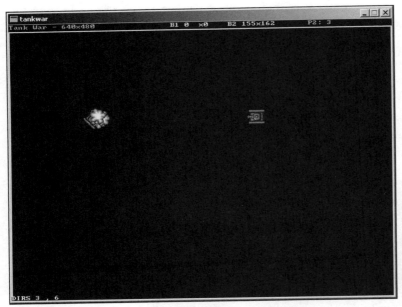

Figure 8.14 *Tank War* now features bitmap-based sprites.

It's really time to move out of the vector theme entirely. Because I haven't covered sprite-based collision detection yet to determine when a tank or bullet hits an actual sprite (rather than just checking the color of the pixel at the bullet's location), I'll leave that for the next chapter, in which I'll get into sprite collision as well as animation and other essential sprite behaviors. What that means right now is that *Tank War* is getting smaller and less complicated, at least for the time being! By stripping the pixel collision code, the source code is shortened considerably. You will lose checkpath, clearpath, and setupdebris, three key functions from the first version of the game. (Although they are useful as designed, they are not very practical.) In fact, that first version had a lot of promise and could have been improved with just the vector graphics upon which it was based. If you are still intrigued by the old-school game technology that used vector graphics, I encourage you to enhance the game and see what can be done with vectors alone. I am forging ahead because the topics of each chapter demand it, but we have not fully explored all the possibilities by any means.

New Tanks

Now what about the new changes for *Tank War*? This will be the third enhancement to the game, but it is somewhat of a backward step in gameplay because there are no longer any obstacles on the battlefield. However, the tanks are no longer rendered with vector graphics functions; rather, they are loaded from a bitmap file. This enhancement also includes a new bitmap for the bullets and explosions. The source code for the game is much shorter than it was before, but due to all the changes, I will provide the entire listing here, rather than just highlighting the changes (as was the case with the previous two enhancements). Much of the original source code is the same, but many seemingly untouched functions have had minor changes to parameters and lines of code that are too numerous to point out. Figure 8.15 shows both tanks firing their newly upgraded weapons.

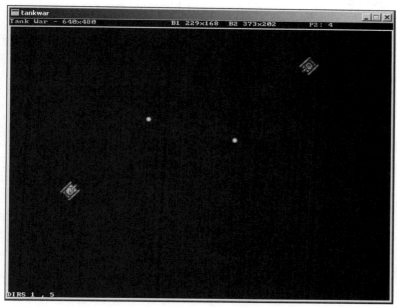

Figure 8.15 The tanks now fire bitmap-based projectiles.

If you'll take a closer look at Figure 8.15, you might notice that the same information is displayed at the top of the screen (name, resolution, bullet locations, and score). I have added a small debug message to the bottom-left corner of the game screen, showing the direction each tank is facing. Since the game now features eight-way directional movement rather than just four-way, I found it useful to display the direction each tank is facing because the new directions required modifications to the `movetank` and `updatebullet` functions.

New Sprites

Figure 8.16 shows the new projectile sprite, and Figure 8.17 shows the new explosion sprite. These might not look like much zoomed in close like this, but they look great in the game.

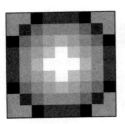

Figure 8.16
The new projectile (bullet) sprite

Figure 8.17
The new explosion sprite

Modifying the Source Code

Here is the new version of tankwar.h, the header file used by the game. You should be able to simply modify your last version to make it look like this. You might notice the new bullet and explosion bitmaps in addition to the changes to tank_bmp, which now supports eight bitmaps, one for each direction. Now that color no longer plays a part in drawing the tanks, the color variable has been removed from the tank structure, tagTank. The three function prototypes for collision detection are included: clearpath, checkpath, and setupdebris. Since the game loop has been sped up, I have also modified BULLETSPEED so that it is now six instead of 10 (which was too jumpy).

The Tank War Header File

```
/////////////////////////////////////////////////////////////////////
// Game Programming All In One, Second Edition
// Source Code Copyright (C)2004 by Jonathan S. Harbour
// Chapter 8 - Tank War Header (Enhancement 3)
/////////////////////////////////////////////////////////////////////

#ifndef _TANKWAR_H
#define _TANKWAR_H

#include <conio.h>
#include <stdlib.h>
#include "allegro.h"

//define some game constants
#define MODE GFX_AUTODETECT_WINDOWED
#define WIDTH 640
#define HEIGHT 480
#define MAXSPEED 2
#define BULLETSPEED 6
```

```
//define some colors
#define TAN makecol(255,242,169)
#define BURST makecol(255,189,73)
#define BLACK makecol(0,0,0)
#define WHITE makecol(255,255,255)

//define tank structure
struct tagTank
{
    int x,y;
    int dir,speed;
    int score;

} tanks[2];

//define bullet structure
struct tagBullet
{
    int x,y;
    int alive;
    int xspd,yspd;

} bullets[2];

//declare some variables
int gameover = 0;

//sprite bitmaps
BITMAP *tank_bmp[2][8];
BITMAP *bullet_bmp;
BITMAP *explode_bmp;

//function prototypes
void drawtank(int num);
void erasetank(int num);
void movetank(int num);
void explode(int num, int x, int y);
void updatebullet(int num);
void fireweapon(int num);
void forward(int num);
void backward(int num);
void turnleft(int num);
```

```
void turnright(int num);
void getinput();
void setuptanks();
void score(int);
void setupscreen();

#endif
```

The Tank War Source Code File

Now I want to focus on the new source code for *Tank War*. As I mentioned previously, nearly every function has been modified for this new version, so if you have any problems running it after you modify your last copy of the game, you have likely missed some change in the following listing. As a last resort, you can load the project off the CD-ROM, located in \chapter08\tankwar for your favorite compiler (devcpp, kdevelop, or msvc).

I'll walk you through each major change in the game, starting with the first part. Here you have a new drawtank, erasetank, and movetank that support sprites and eight directions.

```
//////////////////////////////////////////////////////////////////
// Game Programming All In One, Second Edition
// Source Code Copyright (C)2004 by Jonathan S. Harbour
// Chapter 8 - Tank War Game (Enhancement 3)
//////////////////////////////////////////////////////////////////

#include "tankwar.h"

//////////////////////////////////////////////////////////////////
// drawtank function
// display the tank bitmap in the current direction
//////////////////////////////////////////////////////////////////
void drawtank(int num)
{
    int dir = tanks[num].dir;
    int x = tanks[num].x-15;
    int y = tanks[num].y-15;
    draw_sprite(screen, tank_bmp[num][dir], x, y);
}

//////////////////////////////////////////////////////////////////
// erasetank function
// erase the tank using rectfill
//////////////////////////////////////////////////////////////////
void erasetank(int num)
```

```
{
    int x = tanks[num].x-17;
    int y = tanks[num].y-17;
    rectfill(screen, x, y, x+33, y+33, BLACK);
}


/////////////////////////////////////////////////////////////////////
// movetank function
// move the tank in the current direction
/////////////////////////////////////////////////////////////////////
void movetank(int num){
    int dir = tanks[num].dir;
    int speed = tanks[num].speed;

    //update tank position based on direction
    switch(dir)
    {
        case 0:
            tanks[num].y -= speed;
            break;
        case 1:
            tanks[num].x += speed;
            tanks[num].y -= speed;
            break;
        case 2:
            tanks[num].x += speed;
            break;
        case 3:
            tanks[num].x += speed;
            tanks[num].y += speed;
            break;
        case 4:
            tanks[num].y += speed;
            break;
        case 5:
            tanks[num].x -= speed;
            tanks[num].y += speed;
            break;
        case 6:
            tanks[num].x -= speed;
            break;
        case 7:
            tanks[num].x -= speed;
```

```
                    tanks[num].y -= speed;
                    break;
        }

        //keep tank inside the screen
        if (tanks[num].x > SCREEN_W-22)
        {
            tanks[num].x = SCREEN_W-22;
            tanks[num].speed = 0;
        }
        if (tanks[num].x < 22)
        {
            tanks[num].x = 22;
            tanks[num].speed = 0;
        }
        if (tanks[num].y > SCREEN_H-22)
        {
            tanks[num].y = SCREEN_H-22;
            tanks[num].speed = 0;
        }
        if (tanks[num].y < 22)
        {
            tanks[num].y = 22;
            tanks[num].speed = 0;
        }
    }
```

The next section of code includes highly modified versions of explode, updatebullet, and fireweapon, which, again, must support all eight directions. One significant change is that explode no longer includes the code that checks for a tank hit—that code has been moved to updatebullet. You might also notice in explode that the explosion is now a bitmap rather than a random-colored rectangle. This small effect alone dramatically improves the game.

```
/////////////////////////////////////////////////////////////////
// explode function
// display an explosion image
/////////////////////////////////////////////////////////////////
void explode(int num, int x, int y)
{
    int n;

    //load explode image
    if (explode_bmp == NULL)
    {
```

```
        explode_bmp = load_bitmap("explode.bmp", NULL);
    }

    //draw the explosion bitmap several times
    for (n = 0; n < 5; n++)
    {
        rotate_sprite(screen, explode_bmp,
            x + rand()%10 - 20, y + rand()%10 - 20,
            itofix(rand()%255));

        rest(30);
    }

    //clear the explosion
    circlefill(screen, x, y, 50, BLACK);

}


////////////////////////////////////////////////////////////////////
// updatebullet function
// update the position of a bullet
////////////////////////////////////////////////////////////////////
void updatebullet(int num)
{
    int x = bullets[num].x;
    int y = bullets[num].y;

    //is the bullet active?
    if (!bullets[num].alive) return;

    //erase bullet
    rectfill(screen, x, y, x+10, y+10, BLACK);

    //move bullet
    bullets[num].x += bullets[num].xspd;
    bullets[num].y += bullets[num].yspd;
    x = bullets[num].x;
    y = bullets[num].y;

    //stay within the screen
    if (x < 6 || x > SCREEN_W-6 || y < 20 || y > SCREEN_H-6)
    {
        bullets[num].alive = 0;
```

```
        return;
    }

    //look for a direct hit using basic collision
    //tank is either 0 or 1, so negative num = other tank
    int tx = tanks[!num].x;
    int ty = tanks[!num].y;
    if (x > tx-16 && x < tx+16 && y > ty-16 && y < ty+16)
    {
        //kill the bullet
        bullets[num].alive = 0;

        //blow up the tank
        explode(num, x, y);
        score(num);
    }
    else
    //if no hit then draw the bullet
    {
        //draw bullet sprite
        draw_sprite(screen, bullet_bmp, x, y);

        //update the bullet positions (for debugging)
        textprintf(screen, font, SCREEN_W/2-50, 1, TAN,
            "B1 %-3dx%-3d  B2 %-3dx%-3d",
            bullets[0].x, bullets[0].y,
            bullets[1].x, bullets[1].y);
    }
}


/////////////////////////////////////////////////////////////////
// fireweapon function
// set bullet direction and speed and activate it
/////////////////////////////////////////////////////////////////
void fireweapon(int num)
{
    int x = tanks[num].x;
    int y = tanks[num].y;

    //load bullet image if necessary
    if (bullet_bmp == NULL)
    {
```

```
        bullet_bmp = load_bitmap("bullet.bmp", NULL);
}


//ready to fire again?
if (!bullets[num].alive)
{
    bullets[num].alive = 1;

    //fire bullet in direction tank is facing
    switch (tanks[num].dir)
    {
        //north
        case 0:
            bullets[num].x = x-2;
            bullets[num].y = y-22;
            bullets[num].xspd = 0;
            bullets[num].yspd = -BULLETSPEED;
            break;
        //NE
        case 1:
            bullets[num].x = x+18;
            bullets[num].y = y-18;
            bullets[num].xspd = BULLETSPEED;
            bullets[num].yspd = -BULLETSPEED;
            break;
        //east
        case 2:
            bullets[num].x = x+22;
            bullets[num].y = y-2;
            bullets[num].xspd = BULLETSPEED;
            bullets[num].yspd = 0;
            break;
        //SE
        case 3:
            bullets[num].x = x+18;
            bullets[num].y = y+18;
            bullets[num].xspd = BULLETSPEED;
            bullets[num].yspd = BULLETSPEED;
            break;
        //south
        case 4:
            bullets[num].x = x-2;
            bullets[num].y = y+22;
```

```
                bullets[num].xspd = 0;
                bullets[num].yspd = BULLETSPEED;
                break;
        //SW
        case 5:
                bullets[num].x = x-18;
                bullets[num].y = y+18;
                bullets[num].xspd = -BULLETSPEED;
                bullets[num].yspd = BULLETSPEED;
                break;
        //west
        case 6:
                bullets[num].x = x-22;
                bullets[num].y = y-2;
                bullets[num].xspd = -BULLETSPEED;
                bullets[num].yspd = 0;
                break;
        //NW
        case 7:
                bullets[num].x = x-18;
                bullets[num].y = y-18;
                bullets[num].xspd = -BULLETSPEED;
                bullets[num].yspd = -BULLETSPEED;
                break;
        }
    }
}
```

The next section of code covers the keyboard input code, including forward, backward, turnleft, turnright, and getinput. These functions are largely the same as before, but they now must support eight directions (evident in the if statement within turnleft and turnright).

```
/////////////////////////////////////////////////////////////////
// forward function
// increase the tank's speed
/////////////////////////////////////////////////////////////////
void forward(int num)
{
    tanks[num].speed++;
    if (tanks[num].speed > MAXSPEED)
        tanks[num].speed = MAXSPEED;
}
```

```
///////////////////////////////////////////////////////////////////
// backward function
// decrease the tank's speed
///////////////////////////////////////////////////////////////////
void backward(int num)
{
    tanks[num].speed--;
    if (tanks[num].speed < -MAXSPEED)
        tanks[num].speed = -MAXSPEED;
}


///////////////////////////////////////////////////////////////////
// turnleft function
// rotate the tank counter-clockwise
///////////////////////////////////////////////////////////////////
void turnleft(int num)
{
//***
    tanks[num].dir--;
    if (tanks[num].dir < 0)
        tanks[num].dir = 7;
}


///////////////////////////////////////////////////////////////////
// turnright function
// rotate the tank clockwise
///////////////////////////////////////////////////////////////////
void turnright(int num)
{
    tanks[num].dir++;
    if (tanks[num].dir > 7)
        tanks[num].dir = 0;
}


///////////////////////////////////////////////////////////////////
// getinput function
// check for player input keys (2 player support)
///////////////////////////////////////////////////////////////////
void getinput()
{
    //hit ESC to quit
    if (key[KEY_ESC])    gameover = 1;
```

```
//WASD - SPACE keys control tank 1
if (key[KEY_W])     forward(0);
if (key[KEY_D])     turnright(0);
if (key[KEY_A])     turnleft(0);
if (key[KEY_S])     backward(0);
if (key[KEY_SPACE]) fireweapon(0);

//arrow - ENTER keys control tank 2
if (key[KEY_UP])    forward(1);
if (key[KEY_RIGHT]) turnright(1);
if (key[KEY_DOWN])  backward(1);
if (key[KEY_LEFT])  turnleft(1);
if (key[KEY_ENTER]) fireweapon(1);

//short delay after keypress
rest(20);
}
```

The next short code section includes the score function that is used to update the score for each player.

```
/////////////////////////////////////////////////////////////////
// score function
// add a point to a player's score
/////////////////////////////////////////////////////////////////
void score(int player)
{
    //update score
    int points = ++tanks[player].score;

    //display score
    textprintf(screen, font, SCREEN_W-70*(player+1), 1,
        BURST, "P%d: %d", player+1, points);
}
```

The setuptanks function has changed dramatically from the last version because that is where the new tank bitmaps are loaded. Since this game uses the rotate_sprite function to generate the sprite images for all eight directions, this function takes care of that by first creating each image and then blitting the source tank image into each new image with a specified rotation angle. The end result is two tanks fully rotated in eight directions.

```
/////////////////////////////////////////////////////////////////
// setuptanks function
// load tank bitmaps and position the tank
/////////////////////////////////////////////////////////////////
```

```
void setuptanks()
{
    int n;

    //configure player 1's tank
    tanks[0].x = 30;
    tanks[0].y = 40;
    tanks[0].speed = 0;
    tanks[0].score = 0;
    tanks[0].dir = 3;

    //load first tank bitmap
    tank_bmp[0][0] = load_bitmap("tank1.bmp", NULL);

    //rotate image to generate all 8 directions
    for (n=1; n<8; n++)
    {
        tank_bmp[0][n] = create_bitmap(32, 32);
        clear_bitmap(tank_bmp[0][n]);
        rotate_sprite(tank_bmp[0][n], tank_bmp[0][0],
            0, 0, itofix(n*32));
    }

    //configure player 2's tank
    tanks[1].x = SCREEN_W-30;
    tanks[1].y = SCREEN_H-30;
    tanks[1].speed = 0;
    tanks[1].score = 0;
    tanks[1].dir = 7;

    //load second tank bitmap
    tank_bmp[1][0] = load_bitmap("tank2.bmp", NULL);

    //rotate image to generate all 8 directions
    for (n=1; n<8; n++)
    {
        tank_bmp[1][n] = create_bitmap(32, 32);
        clear_bitmap(tank_bmp[1][n]);
        rotate_sprite(tank_bmp[1][n], tank_bmp[1][0],
            0, 0, itofix(n*32));
    }
}
```

The next section of the code includes the setupscreen function. The most important change to this function is the inclusion of a single line calling set_color_depth(32), which causes the game to run in 32-bit color mode. Note that if you don't have a 32-bit video card, you might want to change this to 16 (which will still work).

```
/////////////////////////////////////////////////////////////////////
// setupscreen function
// set up the graphics mode and draw the game screen
/////////////////////////////////////////////////////////////////////
void setupscreen()
{
    //set video mode
    set_color_depth(32);
    int ret = set_gfx_mode(MODE, WIDTH, HEIGHT, 0, 0);
    if (ret != 0) {
        allegro_message(allegro_error);
        return;
    }

    //print title
    textprintf(screen, font, 1, 1, BURST,
        "Tank War - %dx%d", SCREEN_W, SCREEN_H);

    //draw screen border
    rect(screen, 0, 12, SCREEN_W-1, SCREEN_H-1, TAN);
    rect(screen, 1, 13, SCREEN_W-2, SCREEN_H-2, TAN);
}
```

Finally, the last section of code in the third enhancement to *Tank War* includes the all-important main function. Several changes have been made in main, notably the removal of the calls to clearpath (which checked for bullet hits by looking directly at pixel color). The call to rest now has a value of 10 to speed up the game a bit in order to have smoother bullet trajectories. There is also a line of code that displays the direction of each tank, as I explained previously.

```
/////////////////////////////////////////////////////////////////////
// main function
// start point of the program
/////////////////////////////////////////////////////////////////////
void main(void)
{
    //initialize the game
```

```
        allegro_init();
        install_keyboard();
        install_timer();
        srand(time(NULL));
        setupscreen();
        setuptanks();

        //game loop
        while(!gameover)
        {
            textprintf(screen, font, 0, SCREEN_H-10, WHITE,
                "DIRS %d , %d", tanks[0].dir, tanks[1].dir);
            //erase the tanks
            erasetank(0);
            erasetank(1);

            //move the tanks
            movetank(0);
            movetank(1);

            //draw the tanks
            drawtank(0);
            drawtank(1);

            //update the bullets
            updatebullet(0);
            updatebullet(1);

            //check for keypresses
            if (keypressed())
                getinput();

            //slow the game down
            rest(10);
        }

        //end program
        allegro_exit();
}
END_OF_MAIN();
```

Summary

This marks the end of perhaps the most interesting chapter so far, at least in my opinion. The introduction to sprites that you have received in this chapter provided the basics without delving too deeply into sprite programming theory. The next chapter covers some advanced sprite programming topics, including the sorely needed collision detection. I will also get into sprite animation in the next chapter. There are many more changes on the way for *Tank War* as well. The next several chapters will provide a huge amount of new functionality that you can use to greatly enhance *Tank War*, making it into a truly top-notch game with a scrolling background, animated tanks, a radar screen, and many more new features!

Chapter Quiz

You can find the answers to this chapter quiz in Appendix A, "Chapter Quiz Answers."

1. What is the term given to a small image that is moved around on the screen?
   A. Bitmap
   B. Sprite
   C. Fairy
   D. Mouse cursor

2. Which function draws a sprite?
   A. `draw_sprite`
   B. `show_sprite`
   C. `display_sprite`
   D. `blit_sprite`

3. What is the term for drawing all but a certain color of pixel from one bitmap to another?
   A. Alpha blending
   B. Translucency
   C. Transparency
   D. Telekinesis

4. Which function draws a scaled sprite?
   A. `stretch_sprite`
   B. `draw_scaled_sprite`
   C. `draw_stretched_sprite`
   D. `scale_sprite`

5. Which function draws a vertically-flipped sprite?

   A. `draw_vertical_flip`

   B. `draw_sprite_v_flip`

   C. `flip_v_sprite`

   D. `draw_flipped_sprite`

6. Which function draws a rotated sprite?

   A. `rotate_angle`

   B. `draw_rotated_sprite`

   C. `draw_rotation`

   D. `rotate_sprite`

7. Which function draws a sprite with both rotation and scaling?

   A. `draw_sprite_rotation_scaled`

   B. `rotate_scaled_sprite`

   C. `draw_rotated_scaled_sprite`

   D. `scale_rotate_sprite`

8. What function draws a pivoted sprite?

   A. `draw_pivoted_sprite`

   B. `draw_pivot_sprite`

   C. `pivot_sprite`

   D. `draw_sprite_pivot`

9. Which function draws a pivoted sprite with scaling and vertical flip?

   A. `pivot_scaled_sprite_v_flip`

   B. `pivot_stretch_v_flip_sprite`

   C. `draw_scaled_pivoted_flipped_sprite`

   D. `scale_pivot_v_flip_sprite`

10. Which function draws a sprite with translucency (alpha blending)?

   A. `alpha_blend_sprite`

   B. `draw_trans_sprite`

   C. `draw_alpha`

   D. `trans_sprite`

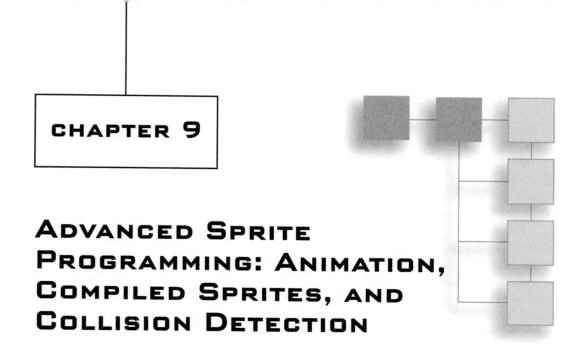

CHAPTER 9

ADVANCED SPRITE PROGRAMMING: ANIMATION, COMPILED SPRITES, AND COLLISION DETECTION

I f Chapter 7 provided the foundation for developing bitmap-based games, then Chapter 8 provided the frame, walls, plumbing, and wiring. (House analogies are frequently used to describe software development, so they may be used to describe game programming as well.) Therefore, what you need from this chapter are the sheetrock, finishing, painting, stucco, roof tiles, appliances, and all the cosmetic accessories that complete a new house—yes, including the kitchen sink.

The other sections of this chapter (on RLE sprites, compiled sprites, and collision detection) are helpful, but might be considered the Italian tile of floors, whereas linoleum will work fine for most people. But the segment on animated sprites is absolutely crucial in your quest to master the subject of 2D game programming. So what is an animated sprite? You already learned a great deal about sprites in the last chapter, and you have at your disposal a good tool set for loading and blitting sprites (which are just based on common bitmaps). An *animated sprite*, then, is an array of sprites drawn using new properties, such as timing, direction, and velocity.

Here is a breakdown of the major topics in this chapter:

- Working with animated sprites
- Using run-length encoded sprites
- Working with compiled sprites
- Understanding collision detection

Animated Sprites

The sprites you have seen thus far were handled somewhat haphazardly, in that no real structure was available for keeping track of these sprites. They have simply been loaded using load_bitmap and then drawn using draw_sprite, with little else in the way of control or handling. To really be able to work with animated sprites in a highly complex game (such as a high-speed scrolling shooter like *R-Type* or *Mars Matrix*), you need a framework for drawing, erasing, and moving these sprites, and for detecting collisions. For all of its abstraction, Allegro leaves this entirely up to you—and for good reason. No single person can foresee the needs of another game programmer because every game has a unique set of requirements (more or less). Limiting another programmer (who may be far more talented than you) to using your concept of a sprite handler only encourages that person to ignore your handler and write his own. That is exactly why Allegro has no sprite handler; rather, it simply has a great set of low-level sprite routines, the likes of which you have already seen.

What should you do next, then? The real challenge is not designing a handler for working with animated sprites; rather, it is designing a game that will need these animated sprites, and then writing the code to fulfill the needs of the game. In this case, the game I am targeting for the sprite handler is *Tank War*, which you have improved in each new chapter—and this one will be no exception. In Chapter 8, you modified *Tank War* extensively to convert it from a vector- and bitmap-based game into a sprite-based game, losing some gameplay along the way. (The battlefield obstacles were removed.) At the end of this chapter, you'll add the sprite handler and collision detection—finally!

Drawing an Animated Sprite

To get started, you need a simple example followed by an explanation of how it works. I have written a quick little program that loads six images (of an animated cat) and draws them on the screen. The cat runs across the screen from left to right, using the sprite frames shown in Figure 9.1.

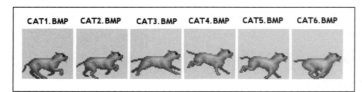

Figure 9.1 The animated cat sprite, courtesy of Ari Feldman

The *AnimSprite* program loads these six image files, each containing a single frame of the animated cat, and draws them in sequence, one frame after another, as the sprite is moved across the screen (see Figure 9.2).

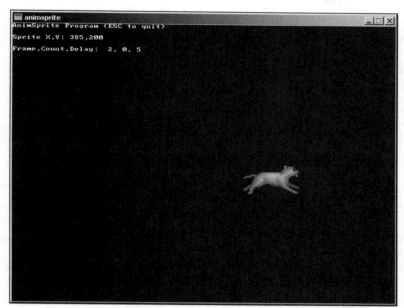

Figure 9.2 The *AnimSprite* program shows how you can do basic sprite animation.

```
#include <conio.h>
#include <stdlib.h>
#include <stdio.h>
#include "allegro.h"

#define WHITE makecol(255,255,255)
#define BLACK makecol(0,0,0)

BITMAP *kitty[7];
char s[20];
int curframe=0, framedelay=5, framecount=0;
int x=100, y=200, n;

int main(void)
{
    //initialize the program
    allegro_init();
    install_keyboard();
    install_timer();
    set_color_depth(16);
    set_gfx_mode(GFX_AUTODETECT_WINDOWED, 640, 480, 0, 0);
```

```
textout(screen, font, "AnimSprite Program (ESC to quit)",
    0, 0, WHITE);

//load the animated sprite
for (n=0; n<6; n++)
{
    sprintf(s,"cat%d.bmp",n+1);
    kitty[n] = load_bitmap(s, NULL);
}

//main loop
while(!key[KEY_ESC])
{
    //erase the sprite
    rectfill(screen, x, y, x+kitty[0]->w, y+kitty[0]->h, BLACK);

    //update the position
    x += 5;
    if (x > SCREEN_W - kitty[0]->w)
        x = 0;

    //update the frame
    if (framecount++ > framedelay)
    {
        framecount = 0;
        curframe++;
        if (curframe > 5)
            curframe = 0;
    }

    acquire_screen();

    //draw the sprite
    draw_sprite(screen, kitty[curframe], x, y);

    //display logistics
    textprintf(screen, font, 0, 20, WHITE,
        "Sprite X,Y: %3d,%3d", x, y);
    textprintf(screen, font, 0, 40, WHITE,
        "Frame,Count,Delay: %2d,%2d,%2d",
        curframe, framecount, framedelay);

    release_screen();
```

```
        rest(10);
    }

    return 0;
}
END_OF_MAIN();
```

Now for that explanation, as promised. The difference between *AnimSprite* and *DrawSprite* (from the previous chapter) is multifaceted. The key variables, curframe, framecount, and framedelay, make realistic animation possible. You don't want to simply change the frame every time through the loop, or the animation will be too fast. The frame delay is a static value that really needs to be adjusted depending on the speed of your computer (at least until I cover timers in Chapter 11, "Timers, Interrupt Handlers, and Multi-Threading"). The frame counter, then, works with the frame delay to increment the current frame of the sprite. The actual movement of the sprite is a simple horizontal motion using the x variable.

```
//update the frame
if (framecount++ > framedelay)
{
    framecount = 0;
    curframe++;
    if (curframe > 5)
        curframe = 0;
}
```

A really well thought-out sprite handler will have variables for both the velocity (x, y) and velocity (x speed, y speed), along with a velocity delay to allow some sprites to move quite slowly compared to others. If there is no velocity delay, each sprite will move at least one pixel during each iteration of the game loop (unless velocity is zero, which means that sprite is motionless).

```
//update the position
x += 5;
if (x > SCREEN_W - kitty[0]->w)
    x = 0;
```

This concept is something I'll explain shortly.

Creating a Sprite Handler

Now that you have a basic—if a bit rushed—concept of sprite animation, I'd like to walk you through the creation of a sprite handler and a sample program with which to test it. Now you'll take the animation code from the last few pages and encapsulate it into a struct. If you were using the object-oriented C++ language instead of C, you'd no doubt "class it." That's all well and good, but I don't care what C++ programmers claim—it's more difficult to understand, which is the key reason why this book focuses on C. That Allegro itself is written in C only supports this decision. The actual bitmap images for the sprite are stored separately from the sprite struct because it is more flexible that way.

In addition to those few animation variables seen in *AnimSprite*, a full-blown animated sprite handler needs to track several more variables. Here is the struct:

```
typedef struct SPRITE
{
      int x,y;
      int width,height;
      int xspeed,yspeed;
      int xdelay,ydelay;
      int xcount,ycount;
      int curframe,maxframe,animdir;
      int framecount,framedelay;
}SPRITE;
```

The variables inside a struct are called *struct elements*, so I will refer to them as such (see Figure 9.3).

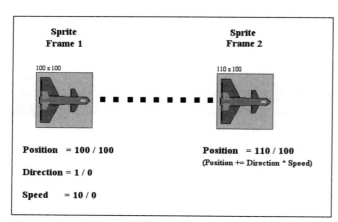

Figure 9.3 The SPRITE struct and its elements help abstract sprite movement into reusable code.

The first two elements (x, y) track the sprite's position. The next two (width, height) are set to the size of the sprite image (stored outside the struct). The velocity elements (xspeed, yspeed) determine how many pixels the sprite will move in conjunction with the velocity delay (xdelay, xcount and ydelay, ycount). The velocity delay allows some sprites to move much slower than other sprites on the screen—even more slowly than one pixel per frame. This gives you a far greater degree of control over how a sprite behaves. The animation elements (curframe, maxframe, animdir) help the sprite animation, and the animation delay elements (framecount, framedelay) help slow down the animation rate. The animdir element is of particular interest because it allows you to reverse the direction that the sprite frames are drawn (from 0 to maxframe or from maxframe to 0, with looping in either direction). The main reason why the BITMAP array containing the sprite images is not stored inside the struct is because that is wasteful—there might be many sprites sharing the same animation images.

Now that we have a sprite struct, the actual handler is contained in a function that I will call updatesprite:

```
void updatesprite(SPRITE *spr)
{
    //update x position
    if (++spr->xcount > spr->xdelay)
    {
        spr->xcount = 0;
        spr->x += spr->xspeed;
    }

    //update y position
    if (++spr->ycount > spr->ydelay)
    {
        spr->ycount = 0;
        spr->y += spr->yspeed;
    }

    //update frame based on animdir
    if (++spr->framecount > spr->framedelay)
    {
        spr->framecount = 0;
        if (spr->animdir == -1)
        {
            if (--spr->curframe < 0)
                spr->curframe = spr->maxframe;
        }
        else if (spr->animdir == 1)
        {
            if (++spr->curframe > spr->maxframe)
                spr->curframe = 0;
        }
    }
}
```

As you can see, updatesprite accepts a pointer to a SPRITE variable. A pointer is necessary because elements of the struct are updated inside this function. This function would be called at every iteration through the game loop because the sprite elements should be closely tied to the game loop and timing of the game. The delay elements in particular should rely upon regular updates using a timed game loop. The animation section checks animdir to increment or decrement the framecount element.

However, updatesprite was not designed to affect sprite behavior, only to manage the logistics of sprite movement. After updatesprite has been called, you want to deal with that sprite's behavior within the game. For instance, if you are writing a space-based shooter featuring a spaceship and objects (such as asteroids) that the ship must shoot, then you might assign a simple warping behavior to the asteroids so that when they exit one side of the screen, they will appear at the opposite side. Or, in a more realistic game featuring a larger scrolling background, the asteroids might warp or bounce at the edges of the universe rather than just the screen. In that case, you would call updatesprite followed by another function that affects the behavior of all asteroids in the game and rely on custom or random values for each asteroid's struct elements to cause it to behave slightly differently than the other asteroids, but basically follow the same behavioral rules. Too many programmers ignore the concept of behavior and simply hard-code behaviors into a game.

I love the idea of constructing many behavior functions, and then using them in a game at random times to keep the player guessing what will happen next. For instance, a simple behavior that I often use in example programs is to have a sprite bounce off the edges of the screen. This could be abstracted into a bounce behavior if you go that one extra step in thinking and design it as a reusable function.

One thing that must be obvious when you are working with a real sprite handler is that it seems to have a lot of overhead, in that the struct elements must all be set at startup. There's no getting around that unless you want total chaos instead of a working game! You have to give all your sprites their starting values to make the game function as planned. Stuffing those variables into a struct helps to keep the game manageable when the source code starts to grow out of control (which frequently happens when you have a truly great game idea and you follow through with building it).

The SpriteHandler Program

I have written a program called *SpriteHandler* that demonstrates how to put all this together into a workable program that you can study. This program uses a ball sprite with 16 frames of animation, each stored in a file (ball1.bmp, ball2.bmp, and so on to ball16.bmp). One thing that you must do is learn how to store an animation sequence inside a single bitmap image and grab the frames out of it at run time. I'll show you how to do that shortly. Figure 9.4 shows the *SpriteHandler* program running. Each time the ball hits the edge, it changes direction and speed.

```
#include <conio.h>
#include <stdlib.h>
#include <stdio.h>
#include "allegro.h"

#define BLACK makecol(0,0,0)
#define WHITE makecol(255,255,255)
```

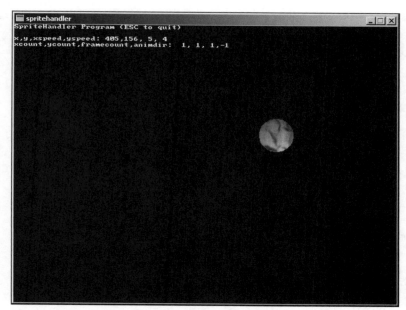

Figure 9.4 The *SpriteHandler* program demonstrates a full-featured animated sprite handler.

```
//define the sprite structure
typedef struct SPRITE
{
      int x,y;
      int width,height;
      int xspeed,yspeed;
      int xdelay,ydelay;
      int xcount,ycount;
      int curframe,maxframe,animdir;
      int framecount,framedelay;

}SPRITE;

//sprite variables
BITMAP *ballimg[16];
SPRITE theball;
SPRITE *ball = &theball;

//support variables
char s[20];
int n;
```

```
void erasesprite(BITMAP *dest, SPRITE *spr)
{
    //erase the sprite using BLACK color fill
    rectfill(dest, spr->x, spr->y, spr->x + spr->width,
        spr->y + spr->height, BLACK);
}


void updatesprite(SPRITE *spr)
{
    //update x position
    if (++spr->xcount > spr->xdelay)
    {
        spr->xcount = 0;
        spr->x += spr->xspeed;
    }

    //update y position
    if (++spr->ycount > spr->ydelay)
    {
        spr->ycount = 0;
        spr->y += spr->yspeed;
    }

    //update frame based on animdir
    if (++spr->framecount > spr->framedelay)
    {
        spr->framecount = 0;
        if (spr->animdir == -1)
        {
            if (--spr->curframe < 0)
                spr->curframe = spr->maxframe;
        }
        else if (spr->animdir == 1)
        {
            if (++spr->curframe > spr->maxframe)
                spr->curframe = 0;
        }
    }
}


void bouncesprite(SPRITE *spr)
{
```

```
    //simple screen bouncing behavior
    if (spr->x < 0)
    {
        spr->x = 0;
        spr->xspeed = rand() % 2 + 4;
        spr->animdir *= -1;
    }

    else if (spr->x > SCREEN_W - spr->width)
    {
        spr->x = SCREEN_W - spr->width;
        spr->xspeed = rand() % 2 - 6;
        spr->animdir *= -1;
    }

    if (spr->y < 40)
    {
        spr->y = 40;
        spr->yspeed = rand() % 2 + 4;
        spr->animdir *= -1;
    }

    else if (spr->y > SCREEN_H - spr->height)
    {
        spr->y = SCREEN_H - spr->height;
        spr->yspeed = rand() % 2 - 6;
        spr->animdir *= -1;
    }
}


void main(void)
{
    //initialize
    allegro_init();
    set_color_depth(16);
    set_gfx_mode(GFX_AUTODETECT_WINDOWED, 640, 480, 0, 0);
    install_keyboard();
    install_timer();
    srand(time(NULL));
    textout(screen, font, "SpriteHandler Program (ESC to quit)",
        0, 0, WHITE);
```

```
//load sprite images
for (n=0; n<16; n++)
{
    sprintf(s,"ball%d.bmp",n+1);
    ballimg[n] = load_bitmap(s, NULL);
}

//initialize the sprite with lots of randomness
ball->x = rand() % (SCREEN_W - ballimg[0]->w);
ball->y = rand() % (SCREEN_H - ballimg[0]->h);
ball->width = ballimg[0]->w;
ball->height = ballimg[0]->h;
ball->xdelay = rand() % 2 + 1;
ball->ydelay = rand() % 2 + 1;
ball->xcount = 0;
ball->ycount = 0;
ball->xspeed = rand() % 2 + 4;
ball->yspeed = rand() % 2 + 4;
ball->curframe = 0;
ball->maxframe = 15;
ball->framecount = 0;
ball->framedelay = rand() % 3 + 1;
ball->animdir = 1;

//game loop
while (!key[KEY_ESC])
{
    erasesprite(screen, ball);

    //perform standard position/frame update
    updatesprite(ball);

    //now do something with the sprite--a basic screen bouncer
    bouncesprite(ball);

    //lock the screen
    acquire_screen();

    //draw the ball sprite
    draw_sprite(screen, ballimg[ball->curframe], ball->x, ball->y);

    //display some logistics
    textprintf(screen, font, 0, 20, WHITE,
        "x,y,xspeed,yspeed: %2d,%2d,%2d,%2d",
```

```
            ball->x, ball->y, ball->xspeed, ball->yspeed);
        textprintf(screen, font, 0, 30, WHITE,
            "xcount,ycount,framecount,animdir: %2d,%2d,%2d,%2d",
            ball->xcount, ball->ycount, ball->framecount,
            ball->animdir);

        //unlock the screen
        release_screen();
        rest(10);
    }
    for (n=0; n<15; n++)
        destroy_bitmap(ballimg[n]);
    return;
}
END_OF_MAIN();
```

Grabbing Sprite Frames from an Image

In case you haven't yet noticed, the idea behind the sprite handler that you're building in this chapter is not to encapsulate Allegro's already excellent sprite functions (which were covered in the previous chapter). The temptation of nearly every C++ programmer would be to drool in anticipation over encapsulating Allegro into a series of classes. What a shame and what a waste of time! I can understand classing up an operating system service, which is vague and obscure, to make it easier to use. In my opinion, a class should be used to simplify very complex code, not to make simple code more complex just to satisfy an obsessive-compulsive need to do so.

On the contrary, you want to use the existing functionality of Allegro, not replace it with something else. By "something else" I mean not necessarily better, just different. The wrapping of one thing and turning it into another thing should arise out of use, not compulsion. Add new functions (or in the case of C++, new classes, properties, and methods) as you need them, not from some grandiose scheme of designing a library before using it.

Thus, you have a basic sprite handler and now you need a function to grab an animation sequence out of a tiled image. So you can get an idea of what I'm talking about, Figure 9.5 shows a 32-frame tiled animation sequence in a file called sphere.bmp.

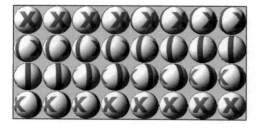

Figure 9.5 This bitmap image contains 32 frames of an animated sphere used as a sprite. Courtesy of Edgar Ibarra.

The frames would be easy to capture if they were lined up in a single row, so how would you grab them out of this file with eight columns and four rows? It's easy if you have the sprite tile algorithm. I'm sure someone described this in some mathematics or computer graphics book at one time or another in the past; I derived it on my own years ago. I suggest you print this simple algorithm in a giant font and paste it on the wall above your computer—or better yet, have a T-shirt made with it pasted across the front.

```
int x = startx + (frame % columns) * width;
int y = starty + (frame / columns) * height;
```

Using this algorithm, you can grab an animation sequence that is stored in a bitmap file, even if it contains more than one animation. (For instance, some simpler games might store all the images in a single bitmap file and grab each sprite at run time.) Now that you have the basic algorithm, here's a full function for grabbing a single frame out of an image by passing the width, height, column, and frame number:

```
BITMAP *grabframe(BITMAP *source,
                  int width, int height,
                  int startx, int starty,
                  int columns, int frame)
{
    BITMAP *temp = create_bitmap(width,height);

    int x = startx + (frame % columns) * width;
    int y = starty + (frame / columns) * height;

    blit(source,temp,x,y,0,0,width,height);

    return temp;
}
```

Note that grabframe doesn't destroy the temp bitmap after blitting the frame image to it. That is because the smaller temp bitmap is the return value for the function. It is up to the caller (usually main) to destroy the bitmap after it is no longer needed—or just before the game ends.

note

The grabframe function really should have some error detection code built in, such as a check for whether the bitmap is NULL after blitting it. As a matter of fact, all the code in this book is intentionally simplistic—with no error detection code—to make it easier to study. In an actual game, you would absolutely want to add checks in your code.

The SpriteGrabber Program

The *SpriteGrabber* program demonstrates how to use grabframe by modifying the *SpriteHandler* program and using a more impressive animated sprite that was rendered (courtesy of Edgar Ibarra). See Figure 9.6 for a glimpse of the program.

Figure 9.6 The *SpriteGrabber* program demonstrates how to grab sprite images (or animation frames) from a tiled source image.

I'm going to list the entire source code for *SpriteGrabber* and set in boldface the lines that have changed (or been added) so you can note the differences. I believe it would be too confusing to list only the changes to the program. There is a significant learning experience to be had by observing the changes or improvements to a program from one revision to the next.

```
#include <conio.h>
#include <stdlib.h>
#include <stdio.h>
#include "allegro.h"

#define BLACK makecol(0,0,0)
#define WHITE makecol(255,255,255)
```

```
//define the sprite structure
typedef struct SPRITE
{
      int x,y;
      int width,height;
      int xspeed,yspeed;
      int xdelay,ydelay;
      int xcount,ycount;
      int curframe,maxframe,animdir;
      int framecount,framedelay;

}SPRITE;

//sprite variables
BITMAP *ballimg[32];
SPRITE theball;
SPRITE *ball = &theball;

int n;

void erasesprite(BITMAP *dest, SPRITE *spr)
{
    //erase the sprite using BLACK color fill
    rectfill(dest, spr->x, spr->y, spr->x + spr->width,
        spr->y + spr->height, BLACK);
}

void updatesprite(SPRITE *spr)
{
    //update x position
    if (++spr->xcount > spr->xdelay)
    {
        spr->xcount = 0;
        spr->x += spr->xspeed;
    }

    //update y position
    if (++spr->ycount > spr->ydelay)
    {
        spr->ycount = 0;
        spr->y += spr->yspeed;
    }
```

```
    //update frame based on animdir
    if (++spr->framecount > spr->framedelay)
    {
        spr->framecount = 0;
        if (spr->animdir == -1)
        {
            if (--spr->curframe < 0)
                spr->curframe = spr->maxframe;
        }
        else if (spr->animdir == 1)
        {
            if (++spr->curframe > spr->maxframe)
                spr->curframe = 0;
        }
    }
}

void bouncesprite(SPRITE *spr)
{
    //simple screen bouncing behavior
    if (spr->x < 0)
    {
        spr->x = 0;
        spr->xspeed = rand() % 2 + 4;
        spr->animdir *= -1;
    }

    else if (spr->x > SCREEN_W - spr->width)
    {
        spr->x = SCREEN_W - spr->width;
        spr->xspeed = rand() % 2 - 6;
        spr->animdir *= -1;
    }

    if (spr->y < 40)
    {
        spr->y = 40;
        spr->yspeed = rand() % 2 + 4;
        spr->animdir *= -1;
    }

    else if (spr->y > SCREEN_H - spr->height)
    {
```

```
            spr->y = SCREEN_H - spr->height;
            spr->yspeed = rand() % 2 - 6;
            spr->animdir *= -1;
        }

}


BITMAP *grabframe(BITMAP *source,
                  int width, int height,
                  int startx, int starty,
                  int columns, int frame)
{
    BITMAP *temp = create_bitmap(width,height);

    int x = startx + (frame % columns) * width;
    int y = starty + (frame / columns) * height;

    blit(source,temp,x,y,0,0,width,height);

    return temp;
}

void main(void)
{
    BITMAP *temp;

    //initialize
    allegro_init();
    set_color_depth(16);
    set_gfx_mode(GFX_AUTODETECT_WINDOWED, 640, 480, 0, 0);
    install_keyboard();
    install_timer();
    srand(time(NULL));
    textout(screen, font, "SpriteGrabber Program (ESC to quit)",
        0, 0, WHITE);

    //load 32-frame tiled sprite image
    temp = load_bitmap("sphere.bmp", NULL);
    for (n=0; n<32; n++)
    {
        ballimg[n] = grabframe(temp,64,64,0,0,8,n);
    }
    destroy_bitmap(temp);
```

```
//initialize the sprite with lots of randomness
ball->x = rand() % (SCREEN_W - ballimg[0]->w);
ball->y = rand() % (SCREEN_H - ballimg[0]->h);
ball->width = ballimg[0]->w;
ball->height = ballimg[0]->h;
ball->xdelay = rand() % 2 + 1;
ball->ydelay = rand() % 2 + 1;
ball->xcount = 0;
ball->ycount = 0;
ball->xspeed = rand() % 2 + 4;
ball->yspeed = rand() % 2 + 4;
ball->curframe = 0;
ball->maxframe = 31;
ball->framecount = 0;
ball->framedelay = 1;
ball->animdir = 1;

//game loop
while (!key[KEY_ESC])
{
    erasesprite(screen, ball);

    //perform standard position/frame update
    updatesprite(ball);

    //now do something with the sprite--a basic screen bouncer
    bouncesprite(ball);

    //lock the screen
    acquire_screen();

    //draw the ball sprite
    draw_sprite(screen, ballimg[ball->curframe], ball->x, ball->y);

    //display some logistics
    textprintf(screen, font, 0, 20, WHITE,
        "x,y,xspeed,yspeed: %2d,%2d,%2d,%2d",
        ball->x, ball->y, ball->xspeed, ball->yspeed);
    textprintf(screen, font, 0, 30, WHITE,
        "xcount,ycount,framecount,animdir: %2d,%2d,%2d,%2d",
        ball->xcount, ball->ycount, ball->framecount, ball->animdir);

    //unlock the screen
```

```
            release_screen();

            rest(10);
        }

    for (n=0; n<31; n++)
        destroy_bitmap(ballimg[n]);

    return;
    }
END_OF_MAIN();
```

The Next Step: Multiple Animated Sprites

You might think of a single sprite as a single-dimensional point in space (thinking in terms of geometry). An animated sprite containing multiple images for a single sprite is a two-dimensional entity. The next step, creating multiple copies of the sprite, might be compared to the third dimension. So far you have only dealt with and explored the concepts around a single sprite being drawn on the screen either with a static image or with an animation sequence. But how many games feature only a single sprite? It is really a test of the sprite handler to see how well it performs when it must contend with many sprites at the same time.

Because performance will be a huge issue with multiple sprites, I will use a double-buffer in the upcoming program for a nice, clean screen without flicker. I will add another level of complexity to make this even more interesting—dealing with a bitmapped background image instead of a blank background. rectfill will no longer suffice to erase the sprites during each refresh; instead, the background will have to be restored under the sprites as they move around.

Instead of a single sprite struct there is an array of sprite structs, and the code throughout the program has been modified to use the array. To initialize all of these sprites, you need to use a loop and make sure each pointer is pointing to each of the sprite structs.

```
//initialize the sprite
for (n=0; n<MAX; n++)
{
    sprites[n] = &thesprites[n];
    sprites[n]->x = rand() % (SCREEN_W - spriteimg[0]->w);
    sprites[n]->y = rand() % (SCREEN_H - spriteimg[0]->h);
    sprites[n]->width = spriteimg[0]->w;
    sprites[n]->height = spriteimg[0]->h;
    sprites[n]->xdelay = rand() % 3 + 1;
```

```
    sprites[n]->ydelay = rand() % 3 + 1;
    sprites[n]->xcount = 0;
    sprites[n]->ycount = 0;
    sprites[n]->xspeed = rand() % 8 - 5;
    sprites[n]->yspeed = rand() % 8 - 5;
    sprites[n]->curframe = rand() % 64;
    sprites[n]->maxframe = 63;
    sprites[n]->framecount = 0;
    sprites[n]->framedelay = rand() % 5 + 1;
    sprites[n]->animdir = rand() % 3 - 1;
}
```

This time I'm using a much larger animation sequence containing 64 frames, as shown in Figure 9.7. The source frames are laid out in an 8×8 grid of tiles.

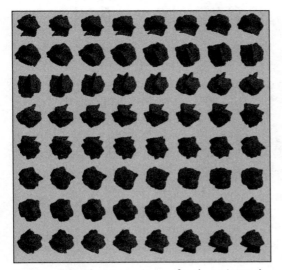

Figure 9.7 The source image for the animated asteroid contains 64 frames.

To load these frames into the sprite handler, a loop is used to grab each frame individually.

```
//load 64-frame tiled sprite image
temp = load_bitmap("asteroid.bmp", NULL);
for (n=0; n<64; n++)
{
    spriteimg[n] = grabframe(temp,64,64,0,0,8,n);
}
destroy_bitmap(temp);
```

The MultipleSprites Program

The *MultipleSprites* program animates 100 sprites on the screen, each of which has 64 frames of animation! Had this program tried to store the actual images with every single sprite instead of sharing the sprite images, it would have taken a huge amount of system memory to run—so now you see the wisdom in storing the images separately from the structs. Figure 9.8 shows the *MultipleSprites* program running at 1024×768. This program differs from *SpriteGrabber* because it uses a screen warp rather than a screen bounce behavior.

This program uses a second buffer to improve performance. Could you imagine the speed hit after erasing and drawing 100 sprites directly on the screen? Even locking and unlocking the screen wouldn't help much with so many writes taking place on the screen. That is why this program uses double-buffering—so all blitting is done on the second buffer, which is then quickly blitted to the screen with a single function call.

Figure 9.8 The *MultipleSprites* program animates 100 sprites on the screen.

```
//update the screen
acquire_screen();
blit(buffer,screen,0,0,0,0,buffer->w,buffer->h);
release_screen();
```

The game loop in *MultipleSprites* might look inefficient at first glance because there are four identical for loops for each operation—erasing, updating, warping, and drawing each of the sprites.

```
//erase the sprites
for (n=0; n<MAX; n++)
    erasesprite(buffer, sprites[n]);

//perform standard position/frame update
for (n=0; n<MAX; n++)
```

```
        updatesprite(sprites[n]);

//apply screen warping behavior
for (n=0; n<MAX; n++)
    warpsprite(sprites[n]);

//draw the sprites
for (n=0; n<MAX; n++)
    draw_sprite(buffer, spriteimg[sprites[n]->curframe],
        sprites[n]->x, sprites[n]->y);
```

It might seem more logical to use a single for loop with these functions inside that loop instead, right? Unfortunately, that is not the best way to handle sprites. First, all of the sprites must be erased before anything else happens. Second, all of the sprites must be moved before any are drawn or erased. Finally, all of the sprites must be drawn at the same time, or else artifacts will be left on the screen. Had I simply blasted the entire background onto the buffer to erase the sprites, this would have been a moot point. The program might even run faster than erasing 100 sprites individually. However, this is a learning experience. It's not always practical to clear the entire background, and this is just a demonstration—you won't likely have 100 sprites on the screen at once unless you are building a very complex scrolling arcade shooter or strategy game.

Following is the complete listing for the *MultipleSprites* program. If you are typing in the code directly from the book, you will want to grab the asteroids.bmp and ngc604.bmp files from the CD-ROM. (They are located in \chapter09\multiplesprites.)

```c
#include <conio.h>
#include <stdlib.h>
#include <stdio.h>
#include "allegro.h"

#define BLACK makecol(0,0,0)
#define WHITE makecol(255,255,255)

#define MAX 100
#define WIDTH 640
#define HEIGHT 480
#define MODE GFX_AUTODETECT_WINDOWED

//define the sprite structure
typedef struct SPRITE
{
    int x,y;
    int width,height;
```

```
            int xspeed,yspeed;
            int xdelay,ydelay;
            int xcount,ycount;
            int curframe,maxframe,animdir;
            int framecount,framedelay;

}SPRITE;

//variables
BITMAP *spriteimg[64];
SPRITE thesprites[MAX];
SPRITE *sprites[MAX];
BITMAP *back;

void erasesprite(BITMAP *dest, SPRITE *spr)
{
    //erase the sprite
    blit(back, dest, spr->x, spr->y, spr->x, spr->y,
        spr->width, spr->height);
}

void updatesprite(SPRITE *spr)
{
    //update x position
    if (++spr->xcount > spr->xdelay)
    {
        spr->xcount = 0;
        spr->x += spr->xspeed;
    }

    //update y position
    if (++spr->ycount > spr->ydelay)
    {
        spr->ycount = 0;
        spr->y += spr->yspeed;
    }

    //update frame based on animdir
    if (++spr->framecount > spr->framedelay)
    {
        spr->framecount = 0;
        if (spr->animdir == -1)
        {
```

```
                    if (--spr->curframe < 0)
                        spr->curframe = spr->maxframe;
            }
            else if (spr->animdir == 1)
            {
                    if (++spr->curframe > spr->maxframe)
                        spr->curframe = 0;
            }
        }
    }
}


void warpsprite(SPRITE *spr)
{
    //simple screen warping behavior
    if (spr->x < 0)
    {
        spr->x = SCREEN_W - spr->width;
    }

    else if (spr->x > SCREEN_W - spr->width)
    {
        spr->x = 0;
    }

    if (spr->y < 40)
    {
        spr->y = SCREEN_H - spr->height;
    }

    else if (spr->y > SCREEN_H - spr->height)
    {
        spr->y = 40;
    }

}


BITMAP *grabframe(BITMAP *source,
                    int width, int height,
                    int startx, int starty,
                    int columns, int frame)
{
    BITMAP *temp = create_bitmap(width,height);
```

```
        int x = startx + (frame % columns) * width;
        int y = starty + (frame / columns) * height;

        blit(source,temp,x,y,0,0,width,height);

        return temp;
}

void main(void)
{
    BITMAP *temp, *buffer;
    int n;

    //initialize
    allegro_init();
    set_color_depth(16);
    set_gfx_mode(MODE, WIDTH, HEIGHT, 0, 0);
    install_keyboard();
    install_timer();
    srand(time(NULL));

    //create second buffer
    buffer = create_bitmap(SCREEN_W, SCREEN_H);

    //load & draw the background
    back = load_bitmap("ngc604.bmp", NULL);
    stretch_blit(back, buffer, 0, 0, back->w, back->h, 0, 0,
        SCREEN_W, SCREEN_H);

    //resize background to fit the variable-size screen
    destroy_bitmap(back);
    back = create_bitmap(SCREEN_W,SCREEN_H);
    blit(buffer,back,0,0,0,0,buffer->w,buffer->h);

    text_mode(-1);
    textout(buffer, font, "MultipleSprites Program (ESC to quit)",
        0, 0, WHITE);

    //load 64-frame tiled sprite image
    temp = load_bitmap("asteroid.bmp", NULL);
    for (n=0; n<64; n++)
    {
        spriteimg[n] = grabframe(temp,64,64,0,0,8,n);
```

```
    }
    destroy_bitmap(temp);


    //initialize the sprite
    for (n=0; n<MAX; n++)
    {
        sprites[n] = &thesprites[n];
        sprites[n]->x = rand() % (SCREEN_W - spriteimg[0]->w);
        sprites[n]->y = rand() % (SCREEN_H - spriteimg[0]->h);
        sprites[n]->width = spriteimg[0]->w;
        sprites[n]->height = spriteimg[0]->h;
        sprites[n]->xdelay = rand() % 3 + 1;
        sprites[n]->ydelay = rand() % 3 + 1;
        sprites[n]->xcount = 0;
        sprites[n]->ycount = 0;
        sprites[n]->xspeed = rand() % 8 - 5;
        sprites[n]->yspeed = rand() % 8 - 5;
        sprites[n]->curframe = rand() % 64;
        sprites[n]->maxframe = 63;
        sprites[n]->framecount = 0;
        sprites[n]->framedelay = rand() % 5 + 1;
        sprites[n]->animdir = rand() % 3 - 1;
    }

    //game loop
    while (!key[KEY_ESC])
    {
        //erase the sprites
        for (n=0; n<MAX; n++)
            erasesprite(buffer, sprites[n]);

        //perform standard position/frame update
        for (n=0; n<MAX; n++)
            updatesprite(sprites[n]);

        //apply screen warping behavior
        for (n=0; n<MAX; n++)
            warpsprite(sprites[n]);

        //draw the sprites
        for (n=0; n<MAX; n++)
            draw_sprite(buffer, spriteimg[sprites[n]->curframe],
```

```
                    sprites[n]->x, sprites[n]->y);

        //update the screen
        acquire_screen();
        blit(buffer,screen,0,0,0,0,buffer->w,buffer->h);
        release_screen();

        rest(10);
    }

    for (n=0; n<63; n++)
        destroy_bitmap(spriteimg[n]);

    return;
}
END_OF_MAIN();
```

I think that wraps up the material for animated sprites. You have more than enough information to completely enhance *Tank War* at this point. But hang on for a few more pages so I can go over some more important topics related to sprites.

Run-Length Encoded Sprites

Allegro provides a custom type of sprite that is compressed to save memory. Run-length encoded (RLE) sprite images can have significantly smaller memory footprints than standard bitmaps. In addition, there is some overhead in the header for each bitmap that also consumes memory. If you have an image that is not modified but only copied *from*, then it is a good candidate for RLE compression. (In this case they should be called RLE bitmaps instead of sprites because the image doesn't necessarily need to be small to be RLE compressed.)

There are several drawbacks to using RLE sprites, so some flexibility is sacrificed to save memory (and perhaps increase speed at the same time). RLE sprites can't be flipped, rotated, stretched, or copied *into*. All you can do is copy an RLE sprite to a destination bitmap using one of the custom RLE sprite-drawing functions.

RLE sprite images are stored in a simple run-length encoded format, where repeated zero pixels are replaced by a single length value and strings of normal pixels start with a counter that gives the length of the solid run. RLE sprites are usually much smaller than normal bitmaps because of the compression and because they avoid most of the overhead of the standard bitmap structure (which must support flipping, scaling, and so on). RLE sprites are often faster than normal bitmaps because rather than having to compare every single pixel with zero to determine whether it should be drawn, you can skip over a whole series of transparent pixels with a single instruction.

Creating and Destroying RLE Sprites

You can convert a normal memory bitmap (loaded with load_bitmap or created at run time) into an RLE sprite using the get_rle_sprite function.

```
RLE_SPRITE *get_rle_sprite(BITMAP *bitmap);
```

When you are using RLE sprites, you must be sure to destroy the sprites just as you destroy regular bitmaps. To destroy an RLE sprite, you will use a custom function created just for this purpose, called destroy_rle_sprite.

```
void destroy_rle_sprite(RLE_SPRITE *sprite);
```

Drawing RLE Sprites

Drawing an RLE sprite is very similar to drawing a normal sprite, and the parameters are similar in draw_rle_sprite.

```
void draw_rle_sprite(BITMAP *bmp, const RLE_SPRITE *sprite, int x, int y);
```

Note that the only difference between draw_rle_sprite and draw_sprite is the second parameter, which refers directly to an RLE_SPRITE instead of a BITMAP. Otherwise, it is quite easy to convert an existing game to support RLE sprites.

Allegro provides two additional blitting functions for RLE sprites. The first one, draw_trans_rle_sprite, draws a sprite using translucent alpha-channel information and is comparable to draw_trans_sprite (only for RLE sprites, of course). This involves the use of blenders, as described in the previous chapter.

```
void draw_trans_rle_sprite(BITMAP *bmp, const RLE_SPRITE *sprite,
    int x, int y);
```

Another variation of the RLE sprite blitter is draw_lit_rle_sprite, which uses lighting information to adjust a sprite's brightness when it is blitted to a destination bitmap. These functions are next to useless for any real game, so I am not planning to cover them here in any more detail. However, you can adapt the *TransSprite* program from the previous chapter with a little effort to use draw_trans_rle_sprite.

```
void draw_lit_rle_sprite(BITMAP *bmp, const RLE_SPRITE *sprite,
    int x, y, color);
```

The RLESprites Program

To assist with loading an image file into an RLE sprite, I have modified the grabframe function to return an RLE_SPRITE directly so conversion from a normal BITMAP is not necessary. As you can see from the short listing for this function, it creates a temporary BITMAP as a scratch buffer for the sprite frame, which is then converted to an RLE sprite, after which the scratch bitmap is destroyed and the RLE_SPRITE is returned by the function.

```
RLE_SPRITE *rle_grabframe(BITMAP *source,
                   int width, int height,
                   int startx, int starty,
                   int columns, int frame)
{
    RLE_SPRITE *sprite;
    BITMAP *temp = create_bitmap(width,height);

    int x = startx + (frame % columns) * width;
    int y = starty + (frame / columns) * height;

    blit(source,temp,x,y,0,0,width,height);
    sprite = get_rle_sprite(temp);
    destroy_bitmap(temp);

    return sprite;
}
```

The *RLESprites* program is unique in that it is the first program to really start using background tiling—something that is covered in the next chapter. As you can see in Figure 9.9, a grass and stone tile is used to fill the bottom portion of the screen, while the dragon sprite flies over the ground. This is a little more realistic and interesting than the sprite being drawn to an otherwise barren, black background (although background scenery and a sky would help a lot).

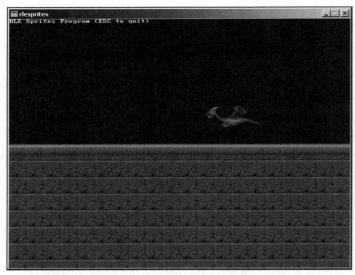

Figure 9.9 The *RLESprites* program demonstrates how to use run-length encoded sprites to save memory and speed up sprite blitting.

The actual dragon sprite is comprised of six frames of animation, as shown in Figure 9.10. This sprite was created by Ari Feldman, as were the ground tiles.

Using the previous *SpriteGrabber* program as a basis, you should be able to adapt the code for the RLE sprite demo. I will highlight the differences in bold.

Figure 9.10 The animated dragon sprite used by the *RLESprites* program. Images courtesy of Ari Feldman.

```
#include <conio.h>
#include <stdlib.h>
#include <stdio.h>
#include "allegro.h"

#define BLACK makecol(0,0,0)
#define WHITE makecol(255,255,255)

//define the sprite structure
typedef struct SPRITE
{
    int x,y;
    int width,height;
    int xspeed,yspeed;
    int xdelay,ydelay;
    int xcount,ycount;
    int curframe,maxframe,animdir;
    int framecount,framedelay;
}SPRITE;

//sprite variables
RLE_SPRITE *dragonimg[6];
SPRITE thedragon;
SPRITE *dragon = &thedragon;

void erasesprite(BITMAP *dest, SPRITE *spr)
{
```

```
    //erase the sprite using BLACK color fill
    rectfill(dest, spr->x, spr->y, spr->x + spr->width,
        spr->y + spr->height, BLACK);
}

void updatesprite(SPRITE *spr)
{
    //update x position
    if (++spr->xcount > spr->xdelay)
    {
        spr->xcount = 0;
        spr->x += spr->xspeed;
    }

    //update y position
    if (++spr->ycount > spr->ydelay)
    {
        spr->ycount = 0;
        spr->y += spr->yspeed;
    }

    //update frame based on animdir
    if (++spr->framecount > spr->framedelay)
    {
        spr->framecount = 0;
        if (spr->animdir == -1)
        {
            if (--spr->curframe < 0)
                spr->curframe = spr->maxframe;
        }
        else if (spr->animdir == 1)
        {
            if (++spr->curframe > spr->maxframe)
                spr->curframe = 0;
        }
    }
}

void warpsprite(SPRITE *spr)
{
    //simple screen warping behavior
    if (spr->x < 0)
    {
```

```
            spr->x = SCREEN_W - spr->width;
    }

    else if (spr->x > SCREEN_W - spr->width)
    {
        spr->x = 0;
    }

    if (spr->y < 40)
    {
        spr->y = SCREEN_H - spr->height;
    }

    else if (spr->y > SCREEN_H - spr->height)
    {
        spr->y = 40;
    }

}

RLE_SPRITE *rle_grabframe(BITMAP *source,
                  int width, int height,
                  int startx, int starty,
                  int columns, int frame)
{
    RLE_SPRITE *sprite;
    BITMAP *temp = create_bitmap(width,height);

    int x = startx + (frame % columns) * width;
    int y = starty + (frame / columns) * height;

    blit(source,temp,x,y,0,0,width,height);
    sprite = get_rle_sprite(temp);
    destroy_bitmap(temp);

    return sprite;
}

void main(void)
{
    BITMAP *temp;
    int n, x, y;
```

```
//initialize
allegro_init();
set_color_depth(16);
set_gfx_mode(GFX_AUTODETECT_WINDOWED, 640, 480, 0, 0);
install_keyboard();
install_timer();
srand(time(NULL));
textout(screen, font, "RLE Sprites Program (ESC to quit)",
    0, 0, WHITE);

//load and draw the blocks
temp = load_bitmap("block1.bmp", NULL);
for (y=0; y < SCREEN_H/2/temp->h+temp->h; y++)
    for (x=0; x < SCREEN_W/temp->w; x++)
        draw_sprite(screen, temp, x*temp->w, SCREEN_H/2+y*temp->h);
destroy_bitmap(temp);

temp = load_bitmap("block2.bmp", NULL);
for (x=0; x < SCREEN_W/temp->w; x++)
    draw_sprite(screen, temp, x*temp->w, SCREEN_H/2);
destroy_bitmap(temp);

//load rle sprite
temp = load_bitmap("dragon.bmp", NULL);
for (n=0; n<6; n++)
    dragonimg[n] = rle_grabframe(temp,128,64,0,0,3,n);
destroy_bitmap(temp);

//initialize the sprite
dragon->x = 500;
dragon->y = 150;
dragon->width = dragonimg[0]->w;
dragon->height = dragonimg[0]->h;
dragon->xdelay = 1;
dragon->ydelay = 0;
dragon->xcount = 0;
dragon->ycount = 0;
dragon->xspeed = -4;
dragon->yspeed = 0;
dragon->curframe = 0;
dragon->maxframe = 5;
dragon->framecount = 0;
dragon->framedelay = 10;
```

```
    dragon->animdir = 1;

    //game loop
    while (!key[KEY_ESC])
    {
        //erase the dragon
        erasesprite(screen, dragon);

        //move/animate the dragon
        updatesprite(dragon);
        warpsprite(dragon);

        //draw the dragon
        acquire_screen();
        draw_rle_sprite(screen, dragonimg[dragon->curframe],
            dragon->x, dragon->y);
        release_screen();

        rest(10);
    }

    for (n=0; n<6; n++)
        destroy_rle_sprite(dragonimg[n]);

    return;
}
END_OF_MAIN();
```

Compiled Sprites

RLE sprites are interesting because they are rendered with a custom function called draw_rle_sprite that actually decompresses the bitmap as it is being drawn to the destination bitmap (or screen). To truly speed up the blitting of these sprites, they would need to contain many repeated pixels. Therefore, a complex sprite with many colors and different pixels will not benefit at all from run-length encoding—don't always assume that just because an RLE sprite sounds cool, it is necessarily better than a regular sprite. Sometimes the good old-fashioned brute-force method works best.

However, if you are using sprites with many pixel runs of the same color in a row, then RLE sprites will draw faster. But isn't there yet another method that would draw them even faster? Given that you will choose the method to use for certain sprites while writing the code, it is up to you to decide whether a sprite contains long runs of pixels (good for packed blitting) or a diversity of pixels (good for brute-force blitting). Why not take RLE sprites to the next step and actually pre-compile the sprite itself? After all, a blitter is nothing more than a function that copies a source bitmap to a destination bitmap one line at a time (often using fast assembly language copy instructions). How about coding those assembly language instructions directly into the sprites instead of storing pixels?

Intriguing idea? Personally, I love it, for no other reason than that it sounds cool! But what about performance? I'll leave that up to you to decide. Each game is different and each sprite is different, so it's largely up to you. Will standard, RLE, or compiled sprites work best with certain images but not with others? Suppose you are developing a role-playing game. These games typically have beautiful game worlds filled with plants, animals, houses, rivers, forests, and so on. An RLE or compiled sprite would just slow down this type of game compared to a standard sprite. But take a game like *Breakout* or *Tetris* that uses solid blocks for game pieces...now these blocks are absolutely perfect candidates for compressed or compiled sprites!

Using Compiled Sprites

What's the scoop with compiled sprites? They store the actual machine code instructions that draw a specific image onto a bitmap, using assembly language copy instructions with the colors of each pixel directly plugged into these instructions. Depending on the source image, a compiled sprite can render up to five times faster than a regular sprite using draw_sprite!

However, one of the drawbacks is that compiled sprites take up much more memory than either standard or RLE sprites, so you might not be able to use them for all the sprites in a game without causing the game to use up a lot of memory. By their very nature, compiled sprites are also quite constricted. Obviously, if you're talking about assembly instructions, a compiled sprite isn't really a bitmap any longer, but a miniature program that knows how to draw the image. Knowing this, one point is fairly evident, but I will enunciate it anyway: If you draw a compiled sprite outside the boundary of a bitmap (or the screen), bad things will happen because parts of program memory will be overwritten! The memory could contain anything—instructions, images, even the Allegro library itself. You must be very careful to keep track of compiled sprites so they are never drawn outside the edge of a bitmap or the screen, or the program will probably crash.

Now, how about another positive point? You can convert regular bitmaps into compiled sprites at run time, just like you could with RLE sprites. There is no need to convert your game artwork to any special format before use—you can do that when the program starts.

From this point, compiled sprites are functionally similar to RLE sprites. The first function you might recognize from the previous section—get_compiled_sprite. That's right, this function is almost exactly the same as get_rle_sprite, but it returns a pointer to a COMPILED_SPRITE.

```
COMPILED_SPRITE *get_compiled_sprite(BITMAP *bitmap, int planar);
```

The bitmap in the first parameter must be a memory bitmap (not a video bitmap or the screen). The second parameter is obsolete and should always be set to FALSE, specifying that the bitmap is a memory bitmap and not a multi-plane video mode (a holdover from a time when mode-x was popular with MS-DOS games).

In similar fashion, Allegro provides a custom function for destroying a compiled sprite in the destroy_compiled_sprite function.

```
void destroy_compiled_sprite(COMPILED_SPRITE *sprite);
```

What remains to be seen? Ah yes, the blitter. There is a single function for drawing a compiled sprite, and that concludes the discussion. (See, I told you compiled sprites were limited, if powerful.)

```
void draw_compiled_sprite(BITMAP *bmp, const COMPILED_SPRITE *sprite,
    int x, int y);
```

The first parameter is the destination bitmap, then comes the actual COMPILED_SPRITE to be blitted, followed by the x and y location for the sprite. Remember that draw_compiled_sprite does not do any clipping at the edges of the screen, so you could hose your program (and perhaps the entire operating system) if you aren't careful!

What if you are used to allowing sprites to go just beyond the boundaries of the screen so that they will warp to the other side more realistically? It certainly looks better than simply popping them to the other side when they near the edge (something that the *SpriteHandler* program did). There is a trick you can try if this will be a problem in your games. Create a memory bitmap (such as the second buffer) that is slightly larger than the actual screen, taking care to adjust the blitter when you are drawing it to the screen. Then you have some room with which to work when you are drawing sprites, so you won't have to be afraid that they will blow up your program.

Testing Compiled Sprites

To save some paper I've simply modified the *RLESprites* program for this section on compiled sprites; I will point out the differences between the programs. You can open the *RLESprites* program and make the few changes needed to test compiled sprites. Also, on the CD-ROM there is a complete *CompiledSprites* program that is already finished; you can load it up if you want. I liked the dragon so much that I've used it again in this program (giving credit again where it is due—thanks to Ari Feldman for the sprites).

Up near the top of the program where the variables are declared, there is a single line that changed from RLE_SPRITE to COMPILED_SPRITE.

```
//sprite variables
COMPILED_SPRITE *dragonimg[6];
```

Then skip down past erasesprite, updatesprite, and warpsprite, and you'll see the rle_grabframe function. I have converted it to compiled_grabframe, and it looks like the following. (The changes are in bold.)

```
COMPILED_SPRITE *compiled_grabframe(BITMAP *source,
                    int width, int height,
                    int startx, int starty,
                    int columns, int frame)
{
    COMPILED_SPRITE *sprite;
    BITMAP *temp = create_bitmap(width,height);

    int x = startx + (frame % columns) * width;
    int y = starty + (frame / columns) * height;

    blit(source,temp,x,y,0,0,width,height);

    //remember FALSE is always used in second parameter
    sprite = get_compiled_sprite(temp, FALSE);

    destroy_bitmap(temp);
    return sprite;
}
```

Moving along to the main function, you change the title.

```
textout(screen, font, "CompiledSprites Program (ESC to quit)",
    0, 0, WHITE);
```

Cruising further into the main function, make a change to the code that loads the dragon sprite images.

```
//load compiled sprite of dragon
temp = load_bitmap("dragon.bmp", NULL);
for (n=0; n<6; n++)
    dragonimg[n] = compiled_grabframe(temp,128,64,0,0,3,n);
destroy_bitmap(temp);
```

Down in the game loop where the dragon sprite is drawn to the screen, you need to change the code to use draw_compiled_sprite.

```
//draw the dragon
acquire_screen();
draw_compiled_sprite(screen, dragonimg[dragon->curframe],
    dragon->x, dragon->y);
release_screen();
```

There is one last change where the compiled sprite images are destroyed.

```
for (n=0; n<6; n++)
    destroy_compiled_sprite(dragonimg[n]);
```

That's it! Now try out the program and gain some experience with compiled sprites. You might not notice any speed improvement; then again, you might notice a huge improvement. It really depends on the source image, so experiment a little and make use of this new type of sprite whenever the need arises.

Collision Detection

Collision detection is the process of detecting when one sprite intersects (or collides with) another sprite. Although this is treated as a one-to-one interaction, the truth is that any one sprite can collide with many other sprites on the screen while a game is running. Collision detection is much easier once you have a basic sprite handler (which I have already gone over) because it is necessary to abstract the animation and movement so that any sprite can be accommodated (whether it's a space ship or an asteroid or an enemy ship—in other words, controlled versus behavioral sprites).

The easiest (and most efficient) way to detect when two sprites have collided is to compare their bounding rectangles. Figure 9.11 shows the bounding rectangles for two sprites, a jet airplane and a missile. As you can see in the figure, the missile will strike the plane when it contacts the wings, but it has not collided with the plane yet. However, a simple bounding-rectangle collision detection routine would mark this as a true collision because the bounding rectangle of the missile intersects with the bounding rectangle of the plane.

One way to increase the accuracy of bounding-rectangle collision detection is to make the source rectangle closely follow the boundaries of the actual sprite so there is less empty space around the sprite. For instance, suppose you were using a 64×64 image containing a bullet sprite that only uses 8×8 pixels in the center of the image—that's 56 pixels of empty space in each direction around the sprite that will foul up collision detection. There's no reason why you can't use different sizes for each sprite—make each one as small as possible to contain the image. The load_bitmap function certainly doesn't care how big the sprite is, and the blitting and collision routines don't care either. But you will speed up the game and make collision detection far more accurate by eliminating any unneeded empty space around a sprite. Keep them lean!

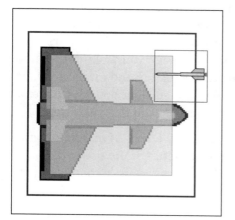

Figure 9.11 Sprite collision using bounding rectangles

Another way to increase collision detection accuracy is by reducing the virtual bounding rectangle used to determine collisions; that is, not by reducing the size of the image, but just the rectangular area used for collision detection. By reducing the bounding rectangle by some value, you can make the collisions behave in a manner that is more believable for the player. In the case of Figure 9.11 again, do you see the shaded rectangle inside the plane image? That represents a virtual bounding rectangle that is slightly smaller than the actual image. It might fail in some cases (look at the rear wings, which are outside the virtual rectangle), but in general this will improve the game. When sprites are quickly moving around the screen, small errors are not noticeable anyway.

Take a look at Figure 9.12, which shows three missiles (A, B, and C) intersecting with the jet airplane sprite. Right away you might notice a problem—the missiles have a lot of empty space. It would improve matters if the missile images were reduced to a smaller image containing only the missile's pixels, without all the blank space above and below the missile. Why? Missile A is clearly missing the plane sprite, but a "dumb" collision routine would see this is a collision using simple intersection. A smarter collision routine using a virtual rectangle would improve the situation, but the bounding rectangles for these missiles are so large that clear misses are likely to be treated as collisions more often than not.

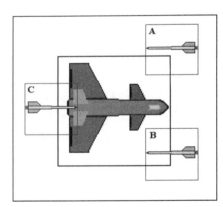

Figure 9.12 Sprite collision is more accurate using a virtual bounding rectangle with very little blank space.

Now take a look at Missile B in Figure 9.12. In this situation, the missile is intersecting the plane sprite's bounding rectangle, resulting in a true collision in most cases, but you can clearly see that it is not a collision. However, a virtual bounding rectangle would have compensated for the position of Missile B and recognized this as a miss. Missile C is clearly intersecting the plane's bounding rectangle, and the actual pixels in each image are intersecting so this is a definite collision. Any collision routine would have no problem with C, but it might have a problem with B and it would definitely have a problem with A. So you should design your collision routine to accommodate each situation and make sure your game's art resources are efficient and use the least amount of blank space necessary.

Following is a generic collision routine. This function accepts two SPRITE pointers as parameters, comparing their bounding rectangles for an intersection. A more useful collision routine might have included parameters for the virtual bounding rectangle compensators, but this function uses a hard-coded value of five pixels (bx and by), which you can modify as needed.

I have included the first glob of code only to simplify the collision code because so many variables are in use. This function works by comparing the four corners of the first sprite with the bounding rectangle of the second sprite, using a virtual rectangle that is five pixels smaller than the actual size of each sprite (which really should be passed as a parameter or calculated as a percentage of the size for the best results).

```
int collided(SPRITE *a, SPRITE *b)
{
    int wa = a->x + a->width;
    int ha =a->y + a->height;
    int wb = b->x + b->width;
    int hb = b->y + b->height;
    int bx = 5;
    int by = 5;

    if (inside(a->x, a->y, b->x+bx, b->y+by, wb-bx, hb-by) ||
        inside(a->x, ha, b->x+bx, b->y+by, wb-bx, hb-by) ||
        inside(wa, a->y, b->x+bx, b->y+by, wb-bx, hb-by) ||
        inside(wa, ha, b->x+bx, b->y+by, wb-bx, hb-by))
        return 1;
    else
        return 0;
}
```

The second part of the function uses the shortcut variables to perform the collision detection based on the four corners of the first sprite. If any one of the points at each corner is inside the virtual bounding rectangle of the second sprite, then a collision has occurred and the result is returned to the calling routine.

The CollisionTest Program

I've made some changes to the *SpriteGrabber* program to demonstrate collision detection (rather than writing an entirely new program from scratch). Figure 9.13 shows the *CollisionTest* program in action. By changing a few lines and adding the collision routines, you can adapt *SpriteGrabber* and turn it into the *CollisionTest* program.

The first thing you need to add are some defines for the graphics mode and a define to specify the number of sprites used in the program. Note the additions in bold.

```
#include <conio.h>
#include <stdlib.h>
#include <stdio.h>
#include "allegro.h"
```

```
#define BLACK makecol(0,0,0)
#define WHITE makecol(255,255,255)


#define NUM 10
#define WIDTH 640
#define HEIGHT 480
#define MODE GFX_AUTODETECT_FULLSCREEN
```

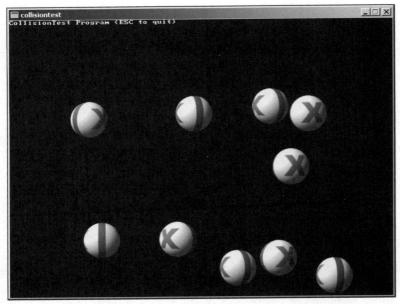

Figure 9.13 The *CollisionTest* program demonstrates how sprites can interact. Sprite image courtesy of Edgar Ibarra.

The next section of code declares the sprite variables below the SPRITE struct. All you need to do here is make these variables plural because this program uses many sprites instead of just the one sprite in the original *SpriteGrabber* program. The array of pointers will point to the struct array inside main because it is not possible to set the pointers in the declaration. (Each element of the array must be set individually.)

```
//sprite variables
BITMAP *ballimg[32];
SPRITE theballs[NUM];
SPRITE *balls[NUM];
```

After these minor changes, skip down a couple pages in the source code listing (ignoring the functions erasesprite, updatesprite, bouncesprite, and grabframe) and add the following functions after grabframe:

```
int inside(int x,int y,int left,int top,int right,int bottom)
{
    if (x > left && x < right && y > top && y < bottom)
        return 1;
    else
        return 0;
}


int collided(SPRITE *a, SPRITE *b)
{
    int wa = a->x + a->width;
    int ha =a->y + a->height;
    int wb = b->x + b->width;
    int hb = b->y + b->height;
    int bx = 5;
    int by = 5;

    if (inside(a->x, a->y, b->x+bx, b->y+by, wb-bx, hb-by) ||
        inside(a->x, ha, b->x+bx, b->y+by, wb-bx, hb-by) ||
        inside(wa, a->y, b->x+bx, b->y+by, wb-bx, hb-by) ||
        inside(wa, ha, b->x+bx, b->y+by, wb-bx, hb-by))
        return 1;
    else
        return 0;
}


void checkcollisions(int num)
{
    int n,cx1,cy1,cx2,cy2;

    for (n=0; n<NUM; n++)
    {
        if (n != num && collided(balls[n], balls[num]))
        {
            //calculate center of primary sprite
            cx1 = balls[n]->x + balls[n]->width / 2;
            cy1 = balls[n]->y + balls[n]->height / 2;

            //calculate center of secondary sprite
            cx2 = balls[num]->x + balls[num]->width / 2;
            cy2 = balls[num]->y + balls[num]->height / 2;
```

```
//figure out which way the sprites collided
if (cx1 <= cx2)
{
    balls[n]->xspeed = -1 * rand() % 6 + 1;
    balls[num]->xspeed = rand() % 6 + 1;
    if (cy1 <= cy2)
    {
        balls[n]->yspeed = -1 * rand() % 6 + 1;
        balls[num]->yspeed = rand() % 6 + 1;
    }
    else
    {
        balls[n]->yspeed = rand() % 6 + 1;
        balls[num]->yspeed = -1 * rand() % 6 + 1;
    }
}
else
{
    //cx1 is > cx2
    balls[n]->xspeed = rand() % 6 + 1;
    balls[num]->xspeed = -1 * rand() % 6 + 1;
    if (cy1 <= cy2)
    {
        balls[n]->yspeed = rand() % 6 + 1;
        balls[num]->yspeed = -1 * rand() % 6 + 1;
    }
    else
    {
        balls[n]->yspeed = -1 * rand() % 6 + 1;
        balls[num]->yspeed = rand() % 6 + 1;
    }
}
            }
        }
    }
}
```

The `main` function has been modified extensively from the original version in *SpriteGrabber* to accommodate multiple sprites and calls to the collision functions, so I'll provide the complete `main` function here. This is similar to the previous version but now includes `for` loops to handle the multiple sprites on the screen, in addition to calling the collision routine.

```c
void main(void)
{
    BITMAP *temp;
    BITMAP *buffer;
    int n;

    //initialize
    allegro_init();
    set_color_depth(16);
    set_gfx_mode(MODE, WIDTH, HEIGHT, 0, 0);
    install_keyboard();
    install_timer();
    srand(time(NULL));

    //create second buffer
    buffer = create_bitmap(SCREEN_W, SCREEN_H);

    text_mode(-1);
    textout(buffer, font, "CollisionTest Program (ESC to quit)",
        0, 0, WHITE);

    //load sprite images
    temp = load_bitmap("sphere.bmp", NULL);
    for (n=0; n<32; n++)
        ballimg[n] = grabframe(temp,64,64,0,0,8,n);
    destroy_bitmap(temp);

    //initialize the sprite
    for (n=0; n<NUM; n++)
    {
        balls[n] = &theballs[n];
        balls[n]->x = rand() % (SCREEN_W - ballimg[0]->w);
        balls[n]->y = rand() % (SCREEN_H - ballimg[0]->h);
        balls[n]->width = ballimg[0]->w;
        balls[n]->height = ballimg[0]->h;
        balls[n]->xdelay = 0;
        balls[n]->ydelay = 0;
        balls[n]->xcount = 0;
        balls[n]->ycount = 0;
        balls[n]->xspeed = rand() % 5 + 1;
        balls[n]->yspeed = rand() % 5 + 1;
        balls[n]->curframe = rand() % 32;
        balls[n]->maxframe = 31;
        balls[n]->framecount = 0;
        balls[n]->framedelay = 0;
```

```
            balls[n]->animdir = 1;
    }


    //game loop
    while (!key[KEY_ESC])
    {
        //erase the sprites
        for (n=0; n<NUM; n++)
            erasesprite(buffer, balls[n]);

        for (n=0; n<NUM; n++)
        {
            updatesprite(balls[n]);
            bouncesprite(balls[n]);
            checkcollisions(n);
        }

        //draw the sprites
        for (n=0; n<NUM; n++)
            draw_sprite(buffer, ballimg[balls[n]->curframe],
                balls[n]->x, balls[n]->y);

        //update the screen
        acquire_screen();
        blit(buffer,screen,0,0,0,0,buffer->w,buffer->h);
        release_screen();

        rest(10);
    }

    for (n=0; n<32; n++)
        destroy_bitmap(ballimg[n]);

    return;
}
END_OF_MAIN();
```

Enhancing Tank War

The next enhancement to *Tank War* will incorporate the new features you learned in this chapter, such as the use of a sprite handler and collision detection. For this modification, you'll follow the same strategy used in previous chapters and only modify the latest version of the game, adding new features.

You need to add the SPRITE struct to the tankwar.h header file. But the struct needs two more variables before it will accommodate *Tank War* because the tanks and bullets included variables that are not yet part of the sprite handler. The SPRITE struct must also contain an int called dir and another called alive. Open the tankwar.h file and add the struct to this file just below the color definitions. After declaring the struct, you should also add the sprite arrays. At the same time, you no longer need the tagTank or tagBullet structs, so delete them! Also, you need to fill in a replacement for the "score" variables for each tank, so declare this as a new standalone int array.

```
//define the sprite structure
typedef struct SPRITE
{
    //new elements
    int dir, alive;

    //current elements
    int x,y;
    int width,height;
    int xspeed,yspeed;
    int xdelay,ydelay;
    int xcount,ycount;
    int curframe,maxframe,animdir;
    int framecount,framedelay;
}SPRITE;

SPRITE mytanks[2];
SPRITE *tanks[2];
SPRITE mybullets[2];
SPRITE *bullets[2];

//replacement for the "score" variable in tank struct
int scores[2];
```

Replacing the two structs with the new SPRITE struct will have repercussions throughout the entire game source code because the new code uses pointers rather than struct variables directly. Therefore, you will need to modify most of the functions to use the -> symbol in place of the period (.) to access elements of the struct when it is referenced with a pointer. The impact of converting the game to use sprite pointers won't be truly apparent until the next chapter, when you add a background to the game (finally!).

Now I want to go over the changes to the main source code file for *Tank War* with the changes in place.

```
///////////////////////////////////////////////////////////////////
// Game Programming All In One, Second Edition
// Source Code Copyright (C)2004 by Jonathan S. Harbour
// Chapter 9 - Tank War Game (Enhancement 4)
///////////////////////////////////////////////////////////////////

#include "tankwar.h"

int inside(int x,int y,int left,int top,int right,int bottom)
{
    if (x > left && x < right && y > top && y < bottom)
        return 1;
    else
        return 0;
}

int collided(SPRITE *a, SPRITE *b)
{
    int wa = a->x + a->width;
    int ha =a->y + a->height;
    int wb = b->x + b->width;
    int hb = b->y + b->height;
    int bx = 5;
    int by = 5;

    if (inside(a->x, a->y, b->x+bx, b->y+by, wb-bx, hb-by) ||
        inside(a->x, ha, b->x+bx, b->y+by, wb-bx, hb-by) ||
        inside(wa, a->y, b->x+bx, b->y+by, wb-bx, hb-by) ||
        inside(wa, ha, b->x+bx, b->y+by, wb-bx, hb-by))
        return 1;
    else
        return 0;
}

void drawtank(int num)
{
    int dir = tanks[num]->dir;
    int x = tanks[num]->x-15;
    int y = tanks[num]->y-15;
    draw_sprite(screen, tank_bmp[num][dir], x, y);
```

```
    }

void erasetank(int num)
{
    int x = tanks[num]->x-17;
    int y = tanks[num]->y-17;
    rectfill(screen, x, y, x+33, y+33, BLACK);
}

void movetank(int num){
    int dir = tanks[num]->dir;
    int speed = tanks[num]->xspeed;

    //update tank position based on direction
    switch(dir)
    {
        case 0:
            tanks[num]->y -= speed;
            break;
        case 1:
            tanks[num]->x += speed;
            tanks[num]->y -= speed;
            break;
        case 2:
            tanks[num]->x += speed;
            break;
        case 3:
            tanks[num]->x += speed;
            tanks[num]->y += speed;
            break;
        case 4:
            tanks[num]->y += speed;
            break;
        case 5:
            tanks[num]->x -= speed;
            tanks[num]->y += speed;
            break;
        case 6:
            tanks[num]->x -= speed;
            break;
        case 7:
            tanks[num]->x -= speed;
            tanks[num]->y -= speed;
```

```
                break;
    }

    //keep tank inside the screen
    //use xspeed as a generic "speed" variable
    if (tanks[num]->x > SCREEN_W-22)
    {
        tanks[num]->x = SCREEN_W-22;
        tanks[num]->xspeed = 0;
    }
    if (tanks[num]->x < 22)
    {
        tanks[num]->x = 22;
        tanks[num]->xspeed = 0;
    }
    if (tanks[num]->y > SCREEN_H-22)
    {
        tanks[num]->y = SCREEN_H-22;
        tanks[num]->xspeed = 0;
    }
    if (tanks[num]->y < 22)
    {
        tanks[num]->y = 22;
        tanks[num]->xspeed = 0;
    }

    //see if tanks collided
/*    if (collided(tanks[0], tanks[1]))
    {
        textout(screen,font,"HIT",tanks[0]->x, tanks[0]->y,WHITE);
        tanks[0]->xspeed = 0;
        tanks[1]->xspeed = 0;
    }
    */
}

void explode(int num, int x, int y)
{
    int n;

    //load explode image
    if (explode_bmp == NULL)
    {
```

```
        explode_bmp = load_bitmap("explode.bmp", NULL);
    }

    //draw the explosion bitmap several times
    for (n = 0; n < 5; n++)
    {
        rotate_sprite(screen, explode_bmp,
            x + rand()%10 - 20, y + rand()%10 - 20,
            itofix(rand()%255));

        rest(30);
    }

    //clear the explosion
    circlefill(screen, x, y, 50, BLACK);

}

void updatebullet(int num)
{
    int x, y, tx, ty;
    int othertank;

    x = bullets[num]->x;
    y = bullets[num]->y;

    if (num == 1)
        othertank = 0;
    else
        othertank = 1;

    //is the bullet active?
    if (!bullets[num]->alive) return;

    //erase bullet
    rectfill(screen, x, y, x+10, y+10, BLACK);

    //move bullet
    bullets[num]->x += bullets[num]->xspeed;
    bullets[num]->y += bullets[num]->yspeed;
    x = bullets[num]->x;
    y = bullets[num]->y;
```

```
    //stay within the screen
    if (x < 6 || x > SCREEN_W-6 || y < 20 || y > SCREEN_H-6)
    {
        bullets[num]->alive = 0;
        return;
    }

    //look for a direct hit using basic collision
    tx = tanks[!num]->x;
    ty = tanks[!num]->y;
    //if (collided(bullets[num], tanks[!num]))
    if (inside(x,y,tx,ty,tx+16,ty+16))
    {
        //kill the bullet
        bullets[num]->alive = 0;

        //blow up the tank
        explode(num, x, y);
        score(num);
    }
    else
    //if no hit then draw the bullet
    {
        //draw bullet sprite
        draw_sprite(screen, bullet_bmp, x, y);

        //update the bullet positions (for debugging)
        textprintf(screen, font, SCREEN_W/2-50, 1, TAN,
            "B1 %-3dx%-3d  B2 %-3dx%-3d",
            bullets[0]->x, bullets[0]->y,
            bullets[1]->x, bullets[1]->y);
    }
}

void fireweapon(int num)
{
    int x = tanks[num]->x;
    int y = tanks[num]->y;

    //ready to fire again?
    if (!bullets[num]->alive)
    {
        bullets[num]->alive = 1;
```

```
//fire bullet in direction tank is facing
switch (tanks[num]->dir)
{
    //north
    case 0:
        bullets[num]->x = x-2;
        bullets[num]->y = y-22;
        bullets[num]->xspeed = 0;
        bullets[num]->yspeed = -BULLETSPEED;
        break;
    //NE
    case 1:
        bullets[num]->x = x+18;
        bullets[num]->y = y-18;
        bullets[num]->xspeed = BULLETSPEED;
        bullets[num]->yspeed = -BULLETSPEED;
        break;
    //east
    case 2:
        bullets[num]->x = x+22;
        bullets[num]->y = y-2;
        bullets[num]->xspeed = BULLETSPEED;
        bullets[num]->yspeed = 0;
        break;
    //SE
    case 3:
        bullets[num]->x = x+18;
        bullets[num]->y = y+18;
        bullets[num]->xspeed = BULLETSPEED;
        bullets[num]->yspeed = BULLETSPEED;
        break;
    //south
    case 4:
        bullets[num]->x = x-2;
        bullets[num]->y = y+22;
        bullets[num]->xspeed = 0;
        bullets[num]->yspeed = BULLETSPEED;
        break;
    //SW
    case 5:
        bullets[num]->x = x-18;
        bullets[num]->y = y+18;
        bullets[num]->xspeed = -BULLETSPEED;
```

```
                bullets[num]->yspeed = BULLETSPEED;
                break;
        //west
        case 6:
                bullets[num]->x = x-22;
                bullets[num]->y = y-2;
                bullets[num]->xspeed = -BULLETSPEED;
                bullets[num]->yspeed = 0;
                break;
        //NW
        case 7:
                bullets[num]->x = x-18;
                bullets[num]->y = y-18;
                bullets[num]->xspeed = -BULLETSPEED;
                bullets[num]->yspeed = -BULLETSPEED;
                break;
        }
    }
}


void forward(int num)
{
    //use xspeed as a generic "speed" variable
    tanks[num]->xspeed++;
    if (tanks[num]->xspeed > MAXSPEED)
        tanks[num]->xspeed = MAXSPEED;
}


void backward(int num)
{
    tanks[num]->xspeed--;
    if (tanks[num]->xspeed < -MAXSPEED)
        tanks[num]->xspeed = -MAXSPEED;
}


void turnleft(int num)
{
    tanks[num]->dir--;
    if (tanks[num]->dir < 0)
        tanks[num]->dir = 7;
}
```

```c
void turnright(int num)
{
    tanks[num]->dir++;
    if (tanks[num]->dir > 7)
        tanks[num]->dir = 0;
}

void getinput()
{
    //hit ESC to quit
    if (key[KEY_ESC])   gameover = 1;

    //WASD - SPACE keys control tank 1
    if (key[KEY_W])     forward(0);
    if (key[KEY_D])     turnright(0);
    if (key[KEY_A])     turnleft(0);
    if (key[KEY_S])     backward(0);
    if (key[KEY_SPACE]) fireweapon(0);

    //arrow - ENTER keys control tank 2
    if (key[KEY_UP])    forward(1);
    if (key[KEY_RIGHT]) turnright(1);
    if (key[KEY_DOWN])  backward(1);
    if (key[KEY_LEFT])  turnleft(1);
    if (key[KEY_ENTER]) fireweapon(1);

    //short delay after keypress
    rest(20);
}

void score(int player)
{
    //update score
    int points = ++scores[player];

    //display score
    textprintf(screen, font, SCREEN_W-70*(player+1), 1,
        BURST, "P%d: %d", player+1, points);
}

void setuptanks()
{
```

```
    int n;

    //configure player 1's tank
    tanks[0] = &mytanks[0];
    tanks[0]->x = 30;
    tanks[0]->y = 40;
    tanks[0]->xspeed = 0;
    scores[0] = 0;
    tanks[0]->dir = 3;

    //load first tank bitmap
    tank_bmp[0][0] = load_bitmap("tank1.bmp", NULL);

    //rotate image to generate all 8 directions
    for (n=1; n<8; n++)
    {
        tank_bmp[0][n] = create_bitmap(32, 32);
        clear_bitmap(tank_bmp[0][n]);
        rotate_sprite(tank_bmp[0][n], tank_bmp[0][0],
            0, 0, itofix(n*32));
    }

    //configure player 2's tank
    tanks[1] = &mytanks[1];
    tanks[1]->x = SCREEN_W-30;
    tanks[1]->y = SCREEN_H-30;
    tanks[1]->xspeed = 0;
    scores[1] = 0;
    tanks[1]->dir = 7;

    //load second tank bitmap
    tank_bmp[1][0] = load_bitmap("tank2.bmp", NULL);

    //rotate image to generate all 8 directions
    for (n=1; n<8; n++)
    {
        tank_bmp[1][n] = create_bitmap(32, 32);
        clear_bitmap(tank_bmp[1][n]);
        rotate_sprite(tank_bmp[1][n], tank_bmp[1][0],
            0, 0, itofix(n*32));
    }
```

```
    //load bullet image
    if (bullet_bmp == NULL)
        bullet_bmp = load_bitmap("bullet.bmp", NULL);

    //initialize bullets
    for (n=0; n<2; n++)
    {
        bullets[n] = &mybullets[n];
        bullets[n]->x = 0;
        bullets[n]->y = 0;
        bullets[n]->width = bullet_bmp->w;
        bullets[n]->height = bullet_bmp->h;
    }
}

void setupscreen()
{
    int ret;

    //set video mode
    set_color_depth(32);
    ret = set_gfx_mode(MODE, WIDTH, HEIGHT, 0, 0);
    if (ret != 0) {
        allegro_message(allegro_error);
        return;
    }

    //print title
    textprintf(screen, font, 1, 1, BURST,
        "Tank War - %dx%d", SCREEN_W, SCREEN_H);

    //draw screen border
    rect(screen, 0, 12, SCREEN_W-1, SCREEN_H-1, TAN);
    rect(screen, 1, 13, SCREEN_W-2, SCREEN_H-2, TAN);
}

void main(void)
{
    //initialize the game
    allegro_init();
    install_keyboard();
    install_timer();
```

```
    srand(time(NULL));
    setupscreen();
    setuptanks();

    //game loop
    while(!gameover)
    {
        //erase the tanks
        erasetank(0);
        erasetank(1);

        //move the tanks
        movetank(0);
        movetank(1);

        //draw the tanks
        drawtank(0);
        drawtank(1);

        //update the bullets
        updatebullet(0);
        updatebullet(1);

        //check for keypresses
        if (keypressed())
            getinput();

        //slow the game down
        rest(20);
    }

    //end program
    allegro_exit();
}
END_OF_MAIN();
```

Summary

This chapter was absolutely packed with advanced sprite code! You learned about animation, a subject that could take up an entire book of its own. (For instance, see Ari Feldman's book *Designing Arcade Computer Game Graphics*—http://www.arifeldman.com/reference.) Indeed, there is much to animation that I didn't get into in this chapter, but the most important points were covered here and as a result, you have some great code that will be used in the rest of the book (especially that grabframe function) and perhaps many of your own Allegro game projects. You also learned about a couple subjects that are seldom discussed in game programming books—compiled and compressed sprite images. Using run-length encoded sprites, your game will use less memory, and by using compiled sprites, your game will run much faster. But possibly the most important subject in this chapter is the discussion of collision detection and how to implement it.

What comes next? We aren't done with sprites yet, not by a long shot! The next chapter delves into scrolling backgrounds. Get ready for some huge changes to *Tank War* because I've got some huge plans for the battlefield!

Chapter Quiz

You can find the answers to this chapter quiz in Appendix A, "Chapter Quiz Answers."

1. Which function draws a standard sprite?
    A. `draw_standard_sprite`
    B. `standard_sprite`
    C. `draw_sprite`
    D. `blit_sprite`

2. What is a frame in the context of sprite animation?
    A. A single image in the animation sequence
    B. The bounding rectangle of a sprite
    C. The source image for the animation sequence
    D. A buffer image used to store temporary copies of the sprite

3. What is the purpose of a sprite handler?
    A. To provide a consistent way to animate and manipulate many sprites on the screen
    B. To prevent sprites from moving beyond the edges of the screen
    C. To provide a reusable sprite drawing function
    D. To keep track of the sprite position

4. What is a struct element?
    A. A property of a struct
    B. A sprite behavior
    C. The underlying Allegro sprite handler
    D. A variable in a structure

5. Which term describes a single frame of an animation sequence stored in an image file?

   A. Snapshot

   B. Tile

   C. Piece

   D. Take

6. Which Allegro function is used frequently to erase a sprite?

   A. `rectfill`

   B. `erase_sprite`

   C. `destroy_sprite`

   D. `blit`

7. Which term describes a reusable activity for a sprite that is important in a game?

   A. Collision

   B. Animation

   C. Bounding

   D. Behavior

8. Which function converts a normal sprite into a run-length encoded sprite?

   A. `convert_sprite`

   B. `get_rle_sprite`

   C. `convert_to_rle`

   D. `load_rle_sprite`

9. Which function draws a compiled sprite to a destination bitmap?

   A. `draw_compiled`

   B. `draw_comp_sprite`

   C. `draw_compiled_sprite`

   D. `compiled_sprite`

10. What is the easiest (and most efficient) way to detect sprite collisions?

   A. Bounding rectangle intersection

   B. Pixel comparison

   C. Bilinear quadratic evaluation

   D. Union of two spheres

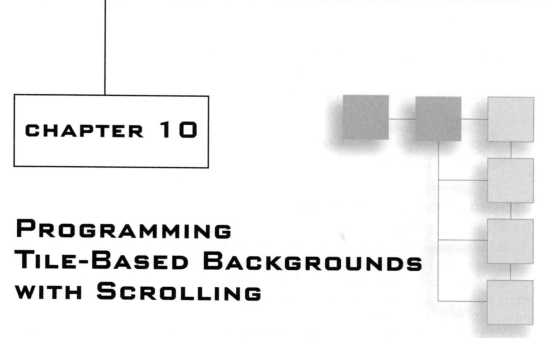

CHAPTER 10

PROGRAMMING TILE-BASED BACKGROUNDS WITH SCROLLING

llegro has a history that goes way back to the 1980s, when it was originally developed for the Atari ST computer, which was a game programmer's dream machine (as were the Atari 800 that preceded it and the Commodore Amiga that was in a similar performance class). While IBM PC users were stuck playing text adventures and ASCII role-playing games (in which your player was represented by @ or P), Atari and Amiga programmers were playing with tile-based scrolling, hardware-accelerated sprites, and digital sound. If you revel in nostalgia as I do, I recommend you pick up *High Score! The Illustrated History of Electronic Games* by DeMaria and Wilson (McGraw-Hill Osborne Media, 2003). Given such roots, it is no surprise that Allegro has such terrific support for scrolling and sprites.

However, there is a drawback to the scrolling functionality—it is very platform dependent. Modern games simply don't use video memory for scrolling any longer. Back in the old days, it was a necessity because system memory was so limited. We take for granted a gigabyte of memory today, but that figure was as unbelievable in the 1980s as a manned trip to Mars is today. Allegro's scrolling functionality works with console-based operating systems such as MS-DOS and console Linux, where video memory is not a graphical handle provided by the operating system as it is today. Even so, the virtual screen buffers were very limited because they were designed for video cards with 256 to 1024 KB of video memory. You were lucky to have two 320×240 screens, let alone enough for a large scrolling world. Therefore, this chapter will focus on creating tile-based backgrounds with scrolling using secondary buffers. As you will discover, this is far easier than trying to wrangle memory out of a video card as programmers were forced to do years ago. A memory buffer will work well with either full-screen or windowed mode.

Here is a breakdown of the major topics in this chapter:

- Scrolling
- Working with tile-based backgrounds
- Enhancing *Tank War*

Introduction to Scrolling

What is scrolling? In today's gaming world, where 3D is the focus of everyone's attention, it's not surprising to find gamers and programmers who have never heard of scrolling. What a shame! The heritage of modern games is a long and fascinating one that is still relevant today, even if it is not understood or appreciated. The console industry puts great effort and value into scrolling, particularly on handheld systems, such as the Game Boy Advance. Given the extraordinary sales market for the GBA, would you be surprised to learn that more 2D games may be sold in a given day than 3D games? Oh, you're already sold on 2D games? Right; I digress. Figure 10.1 illustrates the concept of scrolling.

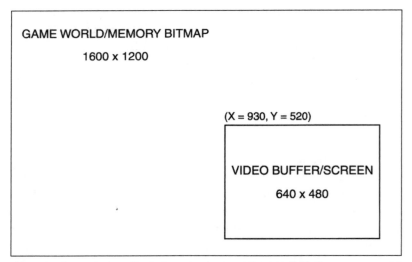

Figure 10.1 The scroll window shows a small part of a larger game world.

note

Scrolling is the process of displaying a small window of a larger virtual game world.

The key to scrolling is actually having something in the virtual game world to display in the scroll window. Also, I should point out that the entire screen need not be used as the scroll window. It is common to use the entire screen in scrolling-shooter games, but role-playing games often use a smaller window on the screen for scrolling, using the rest of the screen for gameplay (combat, inventory, and so on) and player/party information (see Figure 10.2).

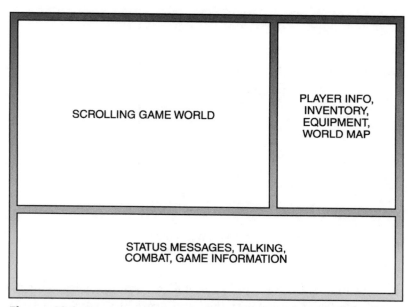

Figure 10.2 Some games use a smaller scroll window on the game screen.

You could display one huge bitmap image in the virtual game world representing the current level of the game, and then copy (blit) a portion of that virtual world onto the screen. This is the simplest form of scrolling. Another method uses tiles to create the game world, which I'll cover shortly. First, you'll write a short program to demonstrate how to use bitmap scrolling.

A Limited View of the World

I have written a program called *ScrollScreen* that I will show you. The \chapter10\ScrollScreen folder on the CD-ROM contains the bigbg.bmp file used in this program. Although I encourage you to write the program yourself, feel free to load the project in either KDevelop, Dev-C++, or Visual C++. Figure 10.3 shows the bigbg.bmp file.

When you run the program, the program will load the bigbg.bmp image into the virtual buffer and display the upper-left corner in the 640×480 screen. (You can change the resolution if you want, and I also encourage you to try running the program in full-screen mode using GFX_AUTODETECT_FULLSCREEN for the best effect.) The program detects when the

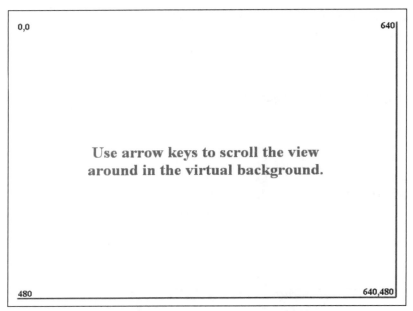

Figure 10.3 The bigbg.bmp file is loaded into the virtual memory buffer for scrolling.

arrow keys have been pressed and adjusts the x and y variables accordingly. Displaying the correct view is then a simple matter of blitting with the x and y variables (see Figure 10.4).

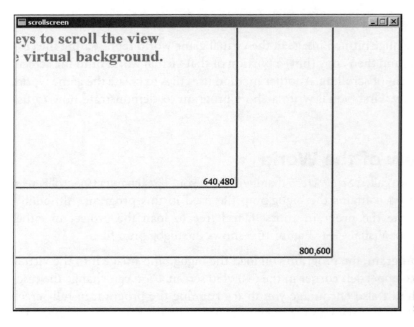

Figure 10.4 The *ScrollScreen* program demonstrates how to perform virtual buffer scrolling.

note

You could just as easily create a large virtual memory bitmap at run time and draw on that bitmap using the Allegro drawing functions you have learned thus far. I have chosen to create the bitmap image beforehand and load it into the program to keep the code listing shorter. Either method works the same way.

```c
#include <conio.h>
#include <stdlib.h>
#include "allegro.h"

//define some convenient constants
#define MODE GFX_AUTODETECT_FULLSCREEN
#define WIDTH 640
#define HEIGHT 480
#define STEP 8

//virtual buffer variable
BITMAP *scroll;

//position variables
int x=0, y=0;

//main function
void main(void)
{
    //initialize allegro
    allegro_init();
    install_keyboard();
    install_timer();
    set_color_depth(16);
    if (set_gfx_mode(MODE, WIDTH, HEIGHT, 0, 0) != 0)
    {
        set_gfx_mode(GFX_TEXT, 0, 0, 0, 0);
        allegro_message(allegro_error);
        return;
    }

    //load the large bitmap image from disk
    scroll = load_bitmap("bigbg.bmp", NULL);
    if (scroll == NULL)
    {
        set_gfx_mode(GFX_TEXT, 0, 0, 0, 0);
```

```
        allegro_message("Error loading bigbg.bmp file");
        return;
    }

    //main loop
    while (!key[KEY_ESC])
    {
        //check right arrow
        if (key[KEY_RIGHT])
        {
            x += STEP;
            if (x > scroll->w - WIDTH)
                x = scroll->w - WIDTH;
        }

        //check left arrow
        if (key[KEY_LEFT])
        {
            x -= STEP;
            if (x < 0)
                x = 0;
        }

        //check down arrow
        if (key[KEY_DOWN])
        {
            y += STEP;
            if (y > scroll->h - HEIGHT)
                y = scroll->h - HEIGHT;
        }

        //check up arrow
        if (key[KEY_UP])
        {
            y -= STEP;
            if (y < 0)
                y = 0;
        }

        //draw the scroll window portion of the virtual buffer
        blit(scroll, screen, x, y, 0, 0, WIDTH-1, HEIGHT-1);
```

```
        //slow it down
        rest(20);
    }
    destroy_bitmap(scroll);
    return;
}
END_OF_MAIN();
```

The first thing I would do to enhance this program is create two variables, lastx and lasty, and set them to equal x and y, respectively, at the end of the main loop. Then, before blitting the window, check to see whether x or y has changed since the last frame and skip the blit function. There is no need to keep blitting the same portion of the virtual background if it hasn't moved.

If you have gotten the *ScrollScreen* program to work, then you have taken the first step to creating a scrolling arcade-style game (or one of the hundred-thousand or so games released in the past 20 years). In the old days, getting the scroller working was usually the first step to creating a sports game. In fact, that was my first assignment at Semi-Logic Entertainments back in 1994, during the prototype phase of *Wayne Gretzky and the NHLPA All-Stars*—to get a hockey rink to scroll as fast as possible.

Back then, I was using Borland C++ 4.5, and it just wasn't fast enough. First of all, this was a 16-bit compiler, while the 80×86- and Pentium-class PCs of the day were capable of 32-bit memory copies (mov instruction) that could effectively draw four pixels at a time in 8-bit color mode or two pixels at a time in 16-bit mode. Fortunately, Allegro already uses high-speed assembly instructions for blitting, as the low-level functions are optimized for each operating system using assembly language.

Introduction to Tile-Based Backgrounds

You have seen what a simple scroller looks like, even though it relied on keyboard input to scroll. A high-speed scrolling arcade game would automatically scroll horizontally or vertically, displaying a ground-, air-, or space-based terrain below the player (usually represented by an airplane or a spaceship). The point of these games is to keep the action moving so fast that the player doesn't have a chance to rest from one wave of enemies to the next. Two upcoming chapters have been dedicated to these very subjects! For the time being, I want to keep things simple to cover the basics of scrolling before you delve into these advanced chapters.

tip

For an in-depth look at vertical scrolling, see Chapter 13, "Vertical Scrolling Arcade Games." If you prefer to go horizontal, you can look forward to Chapter 14, "Horizontal Scrolling Platform Games."

Backgrounds and Scenery

A background is comprised of imagery or terrain in one form or another, upon which the sprites are drawn. The background might be nothing more than a pretty picture behind the action in a game, or it might take an active part, as in a scroller. When you are talking about scrollers, they need not be relegated only to the high-speed arcade games. Role-playing games are usually scrollers too, as are most sports games.

You should design the background around the goals of your game, not the other way around. You should not come up with some cool background and then try to build the game around it. (However, I admit that this is often how games are started.) You never want to rely on a single cool technology as the basis for an entire game, or the game will be forever remembered as a trendy game that tried to cash in on the latest fad. Instead of following and imitating, set your own precedents and make your own standards!

What am I talking about, you might ask? You might have the impression that anything and everything that could possibly have been done with a scrolling game has already been done ten times over. Not true. Not true! Remember when *Doom* first came out? Everyone had been imitating *Wolfenstein 3-D* when Carmack and Romero bumped up the notch a few hundred points and raised everyone's expectations so high that shockwaves reverberated throughout the entire game industry—console and PC alike.

Do you really think it has all been done before and there is no more room for innovation, that the game industry is saturated and it's impossible to make a successful "indie" game? That didn't stop Bungie from going for broke on their first game project. *Halo* has made its mark in gaming history by upping everyone's expectations for superior physics and intelligent opponents. Now, a few years hence, what kinds of games are coming out? What is the biggest industry buzzword? *Physics.* Design a game today without it, and suddenly your game is *so 1990s* in the gaming press. It's all about physics and AI now, and that started with *Halo.* Rather, it was perfected with *Halo*—I can't personally recall a game with that level of interaction before *Halo* came along. There is absolutely no reason why you can't invent the next innovation or revolution in gaming, even in a 2D game.

tip

Eh…all this philosophizing is giving me a headache. Time for some Strong Bad. Check out http://www.homestarrunner.com/sbemail94.html for one of my favorites. Okay, back to business.

Creating Backgrounds from Tiles

The real power of a scrolling background comes from a technique called tiling. *Tiling* is a process in which there really is no background, just an array of tiles that make up the background as it is displayed. In other words, it is a virtual virtual background and it takes up very little memory compared to a full bitmapped background (such as the one in *ScrollScreen*). Take a look at Figure 10.5 for an example.

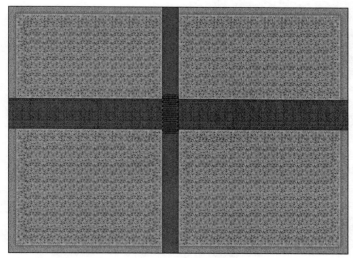

Figure 10.5 A bitmap image constructed of tiles

Can you count the number of tiles used to construct the background in Figure 10.5? Eighteen tiles make up this image, actually. Imagine that—an entire game screen built using a handful of tiles, and the result is pretty good! Obviously a real game would have more than just grass, roads, rivers, and bridges; a real game would have sprites moving on top of the background. How about an example? I thought you'd like that idea.

Tile-Based Scrolling

The *TileScroll* program uses tiles to fill the large background bitmap when the program starts. Other than that initial change, the program functions exactly like the *ScrollScreen* program. Take a look at Figure 10.6.

You might wonder why the screen looks like such a mess. That was intentional, not a mistake. The tiles are drawn to the background randomly, so they're all jumbled incoherently— which is, after all, the nature of randomness. After this, I'll show you how to place the tiles in an actual order that makes sense. Also, you can look forward to an entire chapter dedicated to this subject in Chapter 12, "Creating a Game World: Editing Tiles and Levels."

Figure 10.6 The *TileScroll* program demonstrates how to perform tile-based background scrolling.

Why an entire chapter just for this subject? Because it's huge! You're just getting into the basics here, but Chapter 12 will explore map editors, creating game worlds, and other higher-level concepts. The actual bitmap containing the tiles is shown in Figure 10.7.

Figure 10.7 The source file containing the tiles used in the *TileScroll* program

Here's the source code for the *TileScroll* program:

```
#include <conio.h>
#include <stdlib.h>
#include "allegro.h"

//define some convenient constants
#define MODE GFX_AUTODETECT_FULLSCREEN
#define WIDTH 640
#define HEIGHT 480
```

```
#define STEP 8
#define TILEW 32
#define TILEH 32
#define TILES 39
#define COLS 10

//temp bitmap
BITMAP *tiles;

//virtual background buffer
BITMAP *scroll;

//position variables
int x=0, y=0, n;
```

```
int tilex, tiley;

//reuse our friendly tile grabber from chapter 9
BITMAP *grabframe(BITMAP *source,
                  int width, int height,
                  int startx, int starty,
                  int columns, int frame)
{
    BITMAP *temp = create_bitmap(width,height);

    int x = startx + (frame % columns) * width;
    int y = starty + (frame / columns) * height;

    blit(source,temp,x,y,0,0,width,height);

    return temp;
}

//main function
void main(void)
{
    //initialize allegro
    allegro_init();
    install_keyboard();
    install_timer();
    srand(time(NULL));
    set_color_depth(16);

    //set video mode
    if (set_gfx_mode(MODE, WIDTH, HEIGHT, 0, 0) != 0)
    {
        set_gfx_mode(GFX_TEXT, 0, 0, 0, 0);
        allegro_message(allegro_error);
        return;
    }

    //create the virtual background
    scroll = create_bitmap(1600, 1200);
    if (scroll == NULL)
    {
        set_gfx_mode(GFX_TEXT, 0, 0, 0, 0);
        allegro_message("Error creating virtual background");
        return;
```

```
    }

    //load the tile bitmap
    tiles = load_bitmap("tiles.bmp", NULL);
    if (tiles == NULL)
    {
        set_gfx_mode(GFX_TEXT, 0, 0, 0, 0);
        allegro_message("Error loading tiles.bmp file");
        return;
    }

    //now draw tiles randomly on virtual background
    for (tiley=0; tiley < scroll->h; tiley+=TILEH)
    {
        for (tilex=0; tilex < scroll->w; tilex+=TILEW)
        {
            //pick a random tile
            n = rand() % TILES;
            //use the result of grabframe directly in blitter
            blit(grabframe(tiles, TILEW+1, TILEH+1, 0, 0, COLS, n),
                scroll, 0, 0, tilex, tiley, TILEW, TILEH);
        }
    }

    //main loop
    while (!key[KEY_ESC])
    {
        //check right arrow
        if (key[KEY_RIGHT])
        {
            x += STEP;
            if (x > scroll->w - WIDTH)
                x = scroll->w - WIDTH;
        }

        //check left arrow
        if (key[KEY_LEFT])
        {
            x -= STEP;
            if (x < 0)
                x = 0;
        }
```

```
        //check down arrow
        if (key[KEY_DOWN])
        {
            y += STEP;
            if (y > scroll->h - HEIGHT)
                y = scroll->h - HEIGHT;
        }

        //check up arrow
        if (key[KEY_UP])
        {
            y -= STEP;
            if (y < 0)
                y = 0;
        }

        //draw the scroll window portion of the virtual buffer
        blit(scroll, screen, x, y, 0, 0, WIDTH-1, HEIGHT-1);

        //slow it down
        rest(20);
    }

    destroy_bitmap(scroll);
    destroy_bitmap(tiles);
    return;
}
END_OF_MAIN();
```

Creating a Tile Map

Displaying random tiles just to make a proof-of-concept is one thing, but it is not very useful. True, you have some code to create a virtual background, load tiles onto it, and then scroll the game world. What you really need won't be covered until Chapter 12, so as a compromise, you can create game levels using an array to represent the game world. In the past, I have generated a realistic-looking game map with source code, using an algorithm that matched terrain curves and straights (such as the road, bridge, and river) so that I created an awesome map from scratch, all by myself. The result, I'm sure you'll agree, is one of the best maps ever made. Some errors in the tile matching occurred, though, and a random map doesn't have much point in general. I mean, building a random landscape is one thing, but constructing it at run time is not a great solution—even if your map-generating routine is very good. For instance, many games, such as *Warcraft III*,

Age of Mythology, and *Civilization III*, can generate the game world on the fly. Obviously, the programmers spent a lot of time perfecting the world-generating routines. If your game would benefit by featuring a randomly generated game world, then your work is cut out for you but the results will be worth it. This is simply one of those design considerations that you must make, given that you have time to develop it.

Assuming you don't have the means to generate a random map at this time, you can simply create one within an array. Then you can modify the *TileScroll* program so it uses the array. Where do you start? First of all, you should realize that the tiles are numbered and should be referenced this way in the map array.

Here is what the array looks like, as defined in the *GameWorld* program:

```
int map[MAPW*MAPH] = {
    0,0,0,0,0,0,0,0,0,0,0,0,0,0,0,0,0,0,0,0,0,0,0,0,0,
    0,2,2,2,2,2,2,2,2,2,2,2,2,2,2,2,2,2,2,2,2,2,2,2,0,
    0,2,2,2,2,2,2,2,2,2,2,2,2,2,2,2,2,2,2,2,2,2,2,2,0,
    0,2,2,2,2,2,2,2,2,2,2,2,2,2,2,2,2,2,2,2,2,2,2,2,0,
    0,2,2,2,2,2,2,2,2,2,2,2,2,2,2,2,2,2,2,2,2,2,2,2,0,
    0,2,2,2,2,2,2,2,2,2,2,2,2,2,2,2,2,2,2,2,2,2,2,2,0,
    0,2,2,2,2,2,2,2,2,2,2,2,2,2,2,2,2,2,2,2,2,2,2,2,0,
    0,2,2,2,2,2,2,2,2,2,2,2,2,2,2,2,2,2,2,2,2,2,2,2,0,
    0,2,2,2,2,2,2,2,2,2,2,2,2,2,2,2,2,2,2,2,2,2,2,2,0,
    0,2,2,2,2,2,2,2,2,2,2,2,2,2,2,2,2,2,2,2,2,2,2,2,0,
    0,2,2,2,2,2,2,2,2,2,2,2,2,2,2,2,2,2,2,2,2,2,2,2,0,
    0,2,2,2,2,2,2,2,2,2,2,2,2,2,2,2,2,2,2,2,2,2,2,2,0,
    0,2,2,2,2,2,2,2,2,2,2,2,2,2,2,2,2,2,2,2,2,2,2,2,0,
    0,2,2,2,2,2,2,2,2,2,2,2,2,2,2,2,2,2,2,2,2,2,2,2,0,
    0,2,2,2,2,2,2,2,2,2,2,2,2,2,2,2,2,2,2,2,2,2,2,2,0,
    0,2,2,2,2,2,2,2,2,2,2,2,2,2,2,2,2,2,2,2,2,2,2,2,0,
    0,2,2,2,2,2,2,2,2,2,2,2,2,2,2,2,2,2,2,2,2,2,2,2,0,
    0,2,2,2,2,2,2,2,2,2,2,2,2,2,2,2,2,2,2,2,2,2,2,2,0,
    0,2,2,2,2,2,2,2,2,2,2,2,2,2,2,2,2,2,2,2,2,2,2,2,0,
    0,2,2,2,2,2,2,2,2,2,2,2,2,2,2,2,2,2,2,2,2,2,2,2,0,
    0,2,2,2,2,2,2,2,2,2,2,2,2,2,2,2,2,2,2,2,2,2,2,2,0,
    0,2,2,2,2,2,2,2,2,2,2,2,2,2,2,2,2,2,2,2,2,2,2,2,0,
    0,2,2,2,2,2,2,2,2,2,2,2,2,2,2,2,2,2,2,2,2,2,2,2,0,
    0,2,2,2,2,2,2,2,2,2,2,2,2,2,2,2,2,2,2,2,2,2,2,2,0,
    0,0,0,0,0,0,0,0,0,0,0,0,0,0,0,0,0,0,0,0,0,0,0,0,0,
};
```

It's not complicated—simply a bunch of twos (grass) bordered by zeroes (stone). The trick here is that this is really only a single-dimensional array, but the listing makes it obvious how the map will look because there are 25 numbers in each row—the same number of tiles in each row. I did this intentionally so you can use this as a template for creating your own maps. And you can create more than one map if you want. Simply change the name of each map and reference the map you want in the blit function so that your new map will show up. You are not limited in adding more tiles to each row. One interesting thing you can try is making map a two-dimensional array containing many maps, and then changing the map at run time! How about looking for the keys 1–9 (KEY_1, KEY_2,...KEY_9), and then changing the map number to correspond to the key that was pressed? It would be interesting to see the map change right before your eyes without re-running the program (sort of like warping). Now are you starting to see the potential? You could use this simple scrolling code as the basis for any of a hundred different games if you have the creative gumption to do so.

I have prepared a legend of the tiles and the value for each in Figure 10.8. You can use the legend while building your own maps.

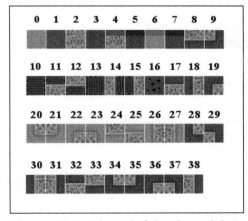

Figure 10.8 A legend of the tiles and their reference numbers used to create a map in the *GameWorld* program

note

All of the tiles used in this chapter were created by Ari Feldman, and I also owe him a debt of gratitude for creating most of the artwork used in this book. If you would like to contact Ari to ask him about custom artwork for your own game, you can reach him at http://www.arifeldman.com.

Call the new program *GameWorld*. This new demo will be similar to *TileScroll*, but it will use a map array instead of placing the tiles randomly. This program will also use a smaller virtual background to cut down on the size of the map array. Why? Not to save memory, but to make the program more manageable. Because the virtual background was 1600×1200 in the previous program, it would require 50 columns of tiles across and 37 rows of tiles down to fill it! That is no problem at all for a map editor program, but it's too much data to type in manually. To make it more manageable, the new virtual background will be 800 pixels across. I know, I know—that's not much bigger than the 640×480 screen. The point is to demonstrate how it will work, not to build a game engine, so don't worry about it. If you want to type in the values to create a bigger map, by all means, go for it! That would be a great learning experience, as a matter of fact. For your purposes here (and with my primary goal of being able to print an entire row of numbers in a single source code line in the book), I'll stick to 25 tiles across and 25 tiles down. You can work with a map that is deeper than it is wide, which will allow you to test scrolling up and down fairly well. Figure 10.9 shows the output from the *GameWorld* program.

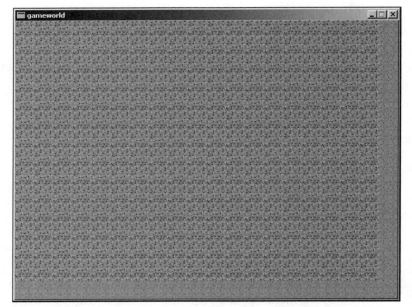

Figure 10.9 The *GameWorld* program scrolls a map that was defined in the map array.

How about that source code? Let's just add a few lines to the *TileScroll* program to come up with this new version. I recommend creating a new project called *GameWorld*, setting up the linker options for Allegro's library file, and then pasting the source code from *TileScroll* into the new main.c file in the *GameWorld* program. If you don't feel like doing all that, fine; go ahead and mess up the *TileScroll* program!

First, up near the top with the other defines, add these lines:

```
#define MAP_ACROSS 25
#define MAP_DOWN 25
#define MAPW MAP_ACROSS * TILEW
#define MAPH MAP_DOWN * TILEH
```

Then, of course, add the map array definition below the defines. (Refer back a few pages for the listing.) Only one more change and you're finished. You need to make a slight change to the section of code that draws the tiles onto the virtual background bitmap. You can remove the line that sets n to a random number; simply change the blit line, noting the change in bold. Note the last parameter of grabframe, which was changed from n to map[n++]. That's the only change you need to make. Now go ahead and build this puppy, and take it for a spin.

```
//now draw tiles randomly on virtual background
for (tiley=0; tiley < scroll->h; tiley+=TILEH)
```

```
{
    for (tilex=0; tilex < scroll->w; tilex+=TILEW)
    {
        //use the result of grabframe directly in blitter
        blit(grabframe(tiles, TILEW+1, TILEH+1, 0, 0, COLS, map[n++]),
            scroll, 0, 0, tilex, tiley, TILEW, TILEH);
    }
}
```

It's a lot more interesting with a real map to scroll instead of jumbled tiles randomly thrown about. I encourage you to modify and experiment with the *GameWorld* program to see what it can do. Before you start making a lot of modifications, you'll likely need the help of some status information printed on the screen. If you want, here is an addition you can make to the main loop, just following the blit. Again, this is optional.

```
//display status info
text_mode(-1);
textprintf(screen,font,0,0,makecol(0,0,0),
    "Position = (%d,%d)", x, y);
```

Enlarge the map to see how big you can make it. Try having the program scroll the map (with wrapping) without requiring user input. This is actually a fairly advanced topic that will be covered in future chapters on scrolling. You should definitely play around with the map array to come up with your own map, and you can even try a different set of tiles. If you have found any free game tiles on the Web (or if you have hired an artist to draw some custom tiles for your game), note the layout and size of each tile, and then you can modify the constants in the *GameWorld* program to accommodate the new tile set. See what you can come up with; experimentation is what puts the "science" in computer science.

Enhancing Tank War

I have been looking forward to this edition of *Tank War* since the first chapter in which the program was introduced (Chapter 4). If you thought the previous chapter introduced many changes to *Tank War*, you will be pleasantly surprised by all that will be put into the game in this chapter! The only drawback is that at least half of the game has been revised, but the result is well worth the effort. The game now features two (that's right, *two*!) scrolling game windows on the screen—one for each player. Shall I count the improvements? There's a new bitmap to replace the border and title; the game now uses scrolling backgrounds that you can edit to create your own custom battlefields (one for each player); the game is now double-buffered; debug messages have been removed; and the interface has been spruced up. Take a look at Figure 10.10 for a glimpse of the new game.

Terrific, isn't it? This game could seriously use some new levels with more creativity. Remember, this is a tech demo at best, something to be used as a learning experience, so

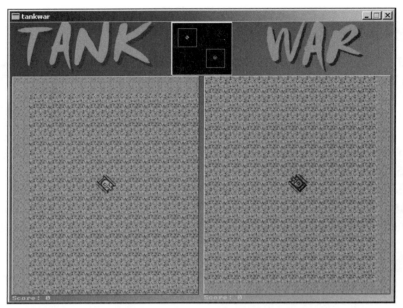

Figure 10.10 *Tank War* now features two scrolling windows, one for each player.

it has to be easy to understand, not necessarily as awesome as it could be. I leave that to you! After I've done the hard work and walked you through each step of the game, it's your job to create awesome new levels for the game. Of course, the game would also greatly benefit from some sound effects, but that will have to wait for Chapter 15, "Mastering the Audible Realm: Allegro's Sound Support."

Exploring the All-New Tank War

Since you'll be spending so much time playing this great game with your friends (unless you suffer from multiple personality disorder and are able to control both tanks at the same time), let me give you a quick tour of the game, and then we'll get started on the source code. Figure 10.11 shows what the game looks like when player 2 hits player 1. The explosion should occur on both windows at the same time, but herein lies a problem: We haven't covered timers yet! Soon enough; the next chapter covers this very important (and sorely needed) subject.

Figure 10.12 shows both tanks engulfed in explosions. D'oh! Talk about mutually assured destruction. You might be wondering where these ultra-cool explosions came from. Again, thanks to Ari Feldman's wonderful talent, we have an explosion sprite that can be rotated, tweaked, and blitted to make those gnarly boom-booms. Imagine what this game will be like with sound effects. I'm tempted to jump to that chapter right now so I can find out!

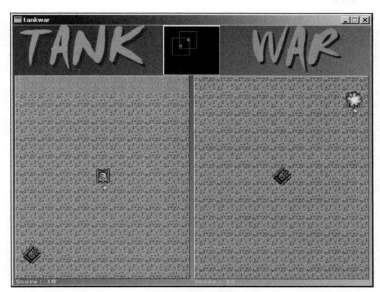

Figure 10.11 Both of the scrolling windows in *Tank War* display the bullets and explosions.

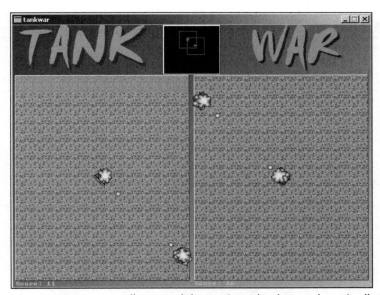

Figure 10.12 Mutually assured destruction: It's what total war is all about.

The next two figures show a sequence that is sad but true: Someone is going to die. Figure 10.13 shows player 1 having fired a bullet.

Referring to Figure 10.14—ooooh, direct hit; he's toast.

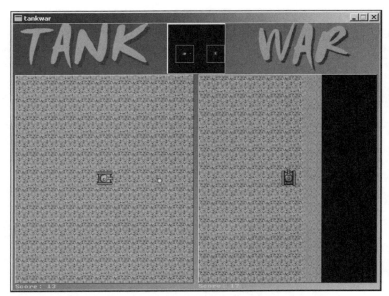

Figure 10.13 Player 1 has fired. Bullet trajectory looks good....

Figure 10.14 Player 1 would like to thank his parents, his commander, and all his new fans.

The last image shows something interesting that I want to bring to your attention when you are designing levels. Take a look at Figure 10.15.

Figure 10.15 The border around the game world is filled with a blank tile.

See how the border of the game world is black? That's not just empty space; it's a blank tile from the tiles.bmp image. It is necessary to insert blanks around the edges of the map so the tanks will seem to actually move up to the edge of the map. If you omit a border like this, the tanks will not be able to reach the true border of the map. Just a little trick for you at no cost, although I'm fairly certain someone has written a book about this.

The New Tank War Source Code

It's time to get down and dirty with the new source code for *Tank War*. Let me paint the picture this way and explain things straight up. Almost everything about the source has been changed. I'm afraid a line-by-line change list isn't possible this time because more than half the game has been modified. I mean, come on—it's got dual scrolling. What do you expect, a couple of line changes? Er, sorry about that—been watching too much Strong Bad. Let's get started.

The first significant change to the game is that it is now spread across several source code files. I decided this was easier to maintain and would be easier for you to understand, so you don't have to wade through the 10-page source code listing in a single main.c file. I'll go over this with you, but you feel free to load the project from \chapter10\tankwar on the CD-ROM if you are in a hurry. I heartily recommend you follow along because there's a lot of real-world experience to be gained by watching how this game is built. Don't be a copy-paster!

Header Definitions

First up is the tankwar.h file containing all the definitions for the game.

```
/////////////////////////////////////////////////////////////////////
// Game Programming All In One, Second Edition
// Source Code Copyright (C)2004 by Jonathan S. Harbour
// Tank War Enhancement 5 - tankwar.h
/////////////////////////////////////////////////////////////////////

#ifndef _TANKWAR_H
#define _TANKWAR_H

#include <conio.h>
#include <stdlib.h>
#include "allegro.h"

//define some game constants
#define MODE GFX_AUTODETECT_WINDOWED
#define WIDTH 640
#define HEIGHT 480
#define MAXSPEED 4
#define BULLETSPEED 10
#define TILEW 32
#define TILEH 32
#define TILES 39
#define COLS 10
#define MAP_ACROSS 31
#define MAP_DOWN 33
#define MAPW MAP_ACROSS * TILEW
#define MAPH MAP_DOWN * TILEH
#define SCROLLW 310
#define SCROLLH 375

//define some colors
#define TAN makecol(255,242,169)
#define BURST makecol(255,189,73)
#define BLACK makecol(0,0,0)
#define WHITE makecol(255,255,255)
#define GRAY makecol(128,128,128)
#define GREEN makecol(0,255,0)

//define the sprite structure
typedef struct SPRITE
```

```
{
//new elements
    int dir, alive;

    int x,y;
    int width,height;
    int xspeed,yspeed;
    int xdelay,ydelay;
    int xcount,ycount;
    int curframe,maxframe,animdir;
    int framecount,framedelay;
}SPRITE;

SPRITE mytanks[2];
SPRITE *tanks[2];
SPRITE mybullets[2];
SPRITE *bullets[2];

//declare some variables
int gameover;
int scores[2];
int scrollx[2], scrolly[2];
int startx[2], starty[2];
int tilex, tiley, n;
int radarx, radary;

//sprite bitmaps
BITMAP *tank_bmp[2][8];
BITMAP *bullet_bmp;
BITMAP *explode_bmp;

//the game map
extern int map[];

//double buffer
BITMAP *buffer;

//bitmap containing source tiles
BITMAP *tiles;

//virtual background buffer
BITMAP *scroll;
```

```
//screen background
BITMAP *back;

//function prototypes
void drawtank(int num);
void erasetank(int num);
void movetank(int num);
void explode(int num, int x, int y);
void movebullet(int num);
void drawbullet(int num);
void fireweapon(int num);
void forward(int num);
void backward(int num);
void turnleft(int num);
void turnright(int num);
void getinput();
void setuptanks();
void setupscreen();
int inside(int,int,int,int,int,int);
BITMAP *grabframe(BITMAP *, int, int, int, int, int, int);

#endif
```

Bullet Functions

I have transplanted all of the routines related to handling bullets and firing the weapons into a file called bullet.c. Isolating the bullet code in this file makes it easy to locate these functions without wading through a huge single listing. If you haven't already, add a new file to your *Tank War* project named bullet.c and type the code into this new file.

```
///////////////////////////////////////////////////////////////////////
// Game Programming All In One, Second Edition
// Source Code Copyright (C)2004 by Jonathan S. Harbour
// Tank War Enhancement 5 - bullet.c
///////////////////////////////////////////////////////////////////////

#include "tankwar.h"

void explode(int num, int x, int y)
{
    int n;

    //load explode image
    if (explode_bmp == NULL)
```

```
    {
        explode_bmp = load_bitmap("explode.bmp", NULL);
    }

    //draw the explosion bitmap several times
    for (n = 0; n < 5; n++)
    {
        rotate_sprite(screen, explode_bmp,
            x + rand()%10 - 20, y + rand()%10 - 20,
            itofix(rand()%255));
        rest(30);
    }
}

void drawbullet(int num)
{
    int n;
    int x, y;

    x = bullets[num]->x;
    y = bullets[num]->y;

    //is the bullet active?
    if (!bullets[num]->alive) return;

    //draw bullet sprite
    for (n=0; n<2; n++)
    {
        if (inside(x, y, scrollx[n], scrolly[n],
            scrollx[n] + SCROLLW - bullet_bmp->w,
            scrolly[n] + SCROLLH - bullet_bmp->h))

            //draw bullet, adjust for scroll
            draw_sprite(buffer, bullet_bmp, startx[n] + x-scrollx[n],
                starty[n] + y-scrolly[n]);
    }

    //draw bullet on radar
    putpixel(buffer, radarx + x/10, radary + y/12, WHITE);

}

void movebullet(int num)
```

```
{
    int x, y, tx, ty;

    x = bullets[num]->x;
    y = bullets[num]->y;

    //is the bullet active?
    if (!bullets[num]->alive) return;

    //move bullet
    bullets[num]->x += bullets[num]->xspeed;
    bullets[num]->y += bullets[num]->yspeed;
    x = bullets[num]->x;
    y = bullets[num]->y;

    //stay within the virtual screen
    if (x < 0 || x > MAPW-6 || y < 0 || y > MAPH-6)
    {
        bullets[num]->alive = 0;
        return;
    }

    //look for a direct hit using basic collision
    tx = scrollx[!num] + SCROLLW/2;
    ty = scrolly[!num] + SCROLLH/2;
    if (inside(x,y,tx-15,ty-15,tx+15,ty+15))
    {
        //kill the bullet
        bullets[num]->alive = 0;

        //blow up the tank
            x = scrollx[!num] + SCROLLW/2;
            y = scrolly[!num] + SCROLLH/2;

            if (inside(x, y,
                scrollx[num], scrolly[num],
                scrollx[num] + SCROLLW, scrolly[num] + SCROLLH))
            {
                //draw explosion in my window
                explode(num, startx[num]+x-scrollx[num],
                    starty[num]+y-scrolly[num]);
            }
```

```
        //draw explosion in enemy window
        explode(num, tanks[!num]->x, tanks[!num]->y);
        scores[num]++;
    }
}

void fireweapon(int num)
{
    int x = scrollx[num] + SCROLLW/2;
    int y = scrolly[num] + SCROLLH/2;

    //ready to fire again?
    if (!bullets[num]->alive)
    {
        bullets[num]->alive = 1;

        //fire bullet in direction tank is facing
        switch (tanks[num]->dir)
        {
            //north
            case 0:
                bullets[num]->x = x-2;
                bullets[num]->y = y-22;
                bullets[num]->xspeed = 0;
                bullets[num]->yspeed = -BULLETSPEED;
                break;
            //NE
            case 1:
                bullets[num]->x = x+18;
                bullets[num]->y = y-18;
                bullets[num]->xspeed = BULLETSPEED;
                bullets[num]->yspeed = -BULLETSPEED;
                break;
            //east
            case 2:
                bullets[num]->x = x+22;
                bullets[num]->y = y-2;
                bullets[num]->xspeed = BULLETSPEED;
                bullets[num]->yspeed = 0;
                break;
            //SE
            case 3:
                bullets[num]->x = x+18;
```

```
                    bullets[num]->y = y+18;
                    bullets[num]->xspeed = BULLETSPEED;
                    bullets[num]->yspeed = BULLETSPEED;
                    break;
                //south
                case 4:
                    bullets[num]->x = x-2;
                    bullets[num]->y = y+22;
                    bullets[num]->xspeed = 0;
                    bullets[num]->yspeed = BULLETSPEED;
                    break;
                //SW
                case 5:
                    bullets[num]->x = x-18;
                    bullets[num]->y = y+18;
                    bullets[num]->xspeed = -BULLETSPEED;
                    bullets[num]->yspeed = BULLETSPEED;
                    break;
                //west
                case 6:
                    bullets[num]->x = x-22;
                    bullets[num]->y = y-2;
                    bullets[num]->xspeed = -BULLETSPEED;
                    bullets[num]->yspeed = 0;
                    break;
                //NW
                case 7:
                    bullets[num]->x = x-18;
                    bullets[num]->y = y-18;
                    bullets[num]->xspeed = -BULLETSPEED;
                    bullets[num]->yspeed = -BULLETSPEED;
                    break;
            }
        }
}
```

Tank Functions

Next up is a listing containing the code for managing the tanks in the game. This includes the drawtank and movetank functions. Note that erasetank has been erased from this version of the game. As a matter of fact, you might have noticed that there is no more erase code in the game. The scrolling windows erase everything, so there's no need to erase sprites. Add a new file to your *Tank War* project named tank.c and type this code into the new file.

```
///////////////////////////////////////////////////////////////////////
// Game Programming All In One, Second Edition
// Source Code Copyright (C)2004 by Jonathan S. Harbour
// Tank War Enhancement 5 - tank.c
///////////////////////////////////////////////////////////////////////

#include "tankwar.h"

void drawtank(int num)
{
    int dir = tanks[num]->dir;
    int x = tanks[num]->x-15;
    int y = tanks[num]->y-15;
    draw_sprite(buffer, tank_bmp[num][dir], x, y);

    //what about the enemy tank?
    x = scrollx[!num] + SCROLLW/2;
    y = scrolly[!num] + SCROLLH/2;
    if (inside(x, y,
        scrollx[num], scrolly[num],
        scrollx[num] + SCROLLW, scrolly[num] + SCROLLH))
    {
        //draw enemy tank, adjust for scroll
        draw_sprite(buffer, tank_bmp[!num][tanks[!num]->dir],
            startx[num]+x-scrollx[num]-15, starty[num]+y-scrolly[num]-15);
    }
}

void movetank(int num){
    int dir = tanks[num]->dir;
    int speed = tanks[num]->xspeed;

    //update tank position
    switch(dir)
    {
        case 0:
            scrolly[num] -= speed;
            break;
        case 1:
            scrolly[num] -= speed;
            scrollx[num] += speed;
            break;
        case 2:
            scrollx[num] += speed;
            break;
```

```
        case 3:
            scrollx[num] += speed;
            scrolly[num] += speed;
            break;
        case 4:
            scrolly[num] += speed;
            break;
        case 5:
            scrolly[num] += speed;
            scrollx[num] -= speed;
            break;
        case 6:
            scrollx[num] -= speed;
            break;
        case 7:
            scrollx[num] -= speed;
            scrolly[num] -= speed;
            break;
    }

    //keep tank inside bounds
    if (scrollx[num] < 0)
        scrollx[num] = 0;
    if (scrollx[num] > scroll->w - SCROLLW)
        scrollx[num] = scroll->w - SCROLLW;
    if (scrolly[num] < 0)
        scrolly[num] = 0;
    if (scrolly[num] > scroll->h - SCROLLH)
        scrolly[num] = scroll->h - SCROLLH;
}
```

Keyboard Input Functions

The next listing encapsulates (I just love that word!) the keyboard input functionality of
the game in a single file named input.c. Herein you will find the forward, backward, turnleft,
turnright, and getinput functions. Add a new file to your *Tank War* project named input.c
and type the code into this new file.

```
///////////////////////////////////////////////////////////////////////
// Game Programming All In One, Second Edition
// Source Code Copyright (C)2004 by Jonathan S. Harbour
// Tank War Enhancement 5 - input.c
///////////////////////////////////////////////////////////////////////
```

```c
#include "tankwar.h"

void forward(int num)
{
    //use xspeed as a generic "speed" variable
    tanks[num]->xspeed++;
    if (tanks[num]->xspeed > MAXSPEED)
        tanks[num]->xspeed = MAXSPEED;
}

void backward(int num)
{
    tanks[num]->xspeed--;
    if (tanks[num]->xspeed < -MAXSPEED)
        tanks[num]->xspeed = -MAXSPEED;
}

void turnleft(int num)
{
    tanks[num]->dir--;
    if (tanks[num]->dir < 0)
        tanks[num]->dir = 7;
}

void turnright(int num)
{
    tanks[num]->dir++;
    if (tanks[num]->dir > 7)
        tanks[num]->dir = 0;
}

void getinput()
{
    //hit ESC to quit
    if (key[KEY_ESC])    gameover = 1;

    //WASD - SPACE keys control tank 1
    if (key[KEY_W])     forward(0);
    if (key[KEY_D])     turnright(0);
    if (key[KEY_A])     turnleft(0);
    if (key[KEY_S])     backward(0);
    if (key[KEY_SPACE]) fireweapon(0);
```

```
    //arrow - ENTER keys control tank 2
    if (key[KEY_UP])    forward(1);
    if (key[KEY_RIGHT]) turnright(1);
    if (key[KEY_DOWN])  backward(1);
    if (key[KEY_LEFT])  turnleft(1);
    if (key[KEY_ENTER]) fireweapon(1);

    //short delay after keypress
    rest(20);

}
```

Game Setup Functions

The game setup functions are easily the most complicated functions of the entire game, so it is a good thing that they are run only once when the game starts. Here you will find the setupscreen and setuptanks functions. Add a new file to your *Tank War* project named setup.c and type the following code into this new file.

```
///////////////////////////////////////////////////////////////////////
// Game Programming All In One, Second Edition
// Source Code Copyright (C)2004 by Jonathan S. Harbour
// Tank War Enhancement 5 - setup.c
///////////////////////////////////////////////////////////////////////

#include "tankwar.h"

void setuptanks()
{
    int n;

    //configure player 1's tank
    tanks[0] = &mytanks[0];
    tanks[0]->x = 30;
    tanks[0]->y = 40;
    tanks[0]->xspeed = 0;
    scores[0] = 0;
    tanks[0]->dir = 3;

    //load first tank bitmap
    tank_bmp[0][0] = load_bitmap("tank1.bmp", NULL);

    //rotate image to generate all 8 directions
    for (n=1; n<8; n++)
```

```
{
    tank_bmp[0][n] = create_bitmap(32, 32);
    clear_to_color(tank_bmp[0][n], makecol(255,0,255));
    rotate_sprite(tank_bmp[0][n], tank_bmp[0][0],
        0, 0, itofix(n*32));
}

//configure player 2's tank
tanks[1] = &mytanks[1];
tanks[1]->x = SCREEN_W-30;
tanks[1]->y = SCREEN_H-30;
tanks[1]->xspeed = 0;
scores[1] = 0;
tanks[1]->dir = 7;

//load second tank bitmap
tank_bmp[1][0] = load_bitmap("tank2.bmp", NULL);

//rotate image to generate all 8 directions
for (n=1; n<8; n++)
{
    tank_bmp[1][n] = create_bitmap(32, 32);
    clear_to_color(tank_bmp[1][n], makecol(255,0,255));
    rotate_sprite(tank_bmp[1][n], tank_bmp[1][0],
        0, 0, itofix(n*32));
}

//load bullet image
if (bullet_bmp == NULL)
    bullet_bmp = load_bitmap("bullet.bmp", NULL);

//initialize bullets
for (n=0; n<2; n++)
{
    bullets[n] = &mybullets[n];
    bullets[n]->x = 0;
    bullets[n]->y = 0;
    bullets[n]->width = bullet_bmp->w;
    bullets[n]->height = bullet_bmp->h;
}

//center tanks inside scroll windows
tanks[0]->x = 5 + SCROLLW/2;
```

```
        tanks[0]->y = 90 + SCROLLH/2;
        tanks[1]->x = 325 + SCROLLW/2;
        tanks[1]->y = 90 + SCROLLH/2;
}


void setupscreen()
{
        int ret;

        //set video mode
        set_color_depth(16);
        ret = set_gfx_mode(MODE, WIDTH, HEIGHT, 0, 0);
        if (ret != 0) {
            allegro_message(allegro_error);
            return;
        }

        text_mode(-1);

        //create the virtual background
        scroll = create_bitmap(MAPW, MAPH);
        if (scroll == NULL)
        {
            set_gfx_mode(GFX_TEXT, 0, 0, 0, 0);
            allegro_message("Error creating virtual background");
            return;
        }

        //load the tile bitmap
        tiles = load_bitmap("tiles.bmp", NULL);
        if (tiles == NULL)
        {
            set_gfx_mode(GFX_TEXT, 0, 0, 0, 0);
            allegro_message("Error loading tiles.bmp file");
            return;
        }

        //now draw tiles on virtual background
        for (tiley=0; tiley < scroll->h; tiley+=TILEH)
        {
            for (tilex=0; tilex < scroll->w; tilex+=TILEW)
            {
                //use the result of grabframe directly in blitter
```

```
            blit(grabframe(tiles, TILEW+1, TILEH+1, 0, 0, COLS,
                map[n++]), scroll, 0, 0, tilex, tiley, TILEW, TILEH);
        }
    }

    //done with tiles
    destroy_bitmap(tiles);

    //load screen background
    back = load_bitmap("background.bmp", NULL);
    if (back == NULL)
    {
        set_gfx_mode(GFX_TEXT, 0, 0, 0, 0);
        allegro_message("Error loading background.bmp file");
        return;
    }

    //create the double buffer
    buffer = create_bitmap(WIDTH, HEIGHT);
    if (buffer == NULL)
    {
        set_gfx_mode(GFX_TEXT, 0, 0, 0, 0);
        allegro_message("Error creating double buffer");
        return;
    }

    //position the radar
    radarx = 270;
    radary = 1;

    //position each player
    scrollx[0] = 100;
    scrolly[0] = 100;
    scrollx[1] = MAPW - 400;
    scrolly[1] = MAPH - 500;

    //position the scroll windows
    startx[0] = 5;
    starty[0] = 93;
    startx[1] = 325;
    starty[1] = 93;

}
```

Main Function

You have greatly simplified the main.c source code file for *Tank War* by moving so much code into separate source files. Now in main.c, you have a declaration for the map array. Why? Because it was not possible to include the declaration inside the tankwar.h header file, only an extern reference to the array definition inside a source file. As with the previous code listings, this one is heavily commented so you can examine it line by line. Take particular note of the map array definition. To simplify and beautify the listing, I have defined B equal to 39; as you can see, this refers to the blank space tile around the edges of the map.

The game also features a new background image to improve the appearance of the game. Figure 10.16 shows the image, which acts as a template for displaying game graphics.

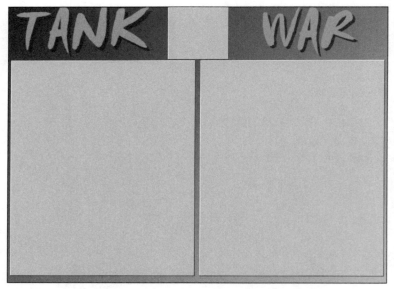

Figure 10.16 The background image of the new *Tank War*

```
/////////////////////////////////////////////////////////////////////
// Game Programming All In One, Second Edition
// Source Code Copyright (C)2004 by Jonathan S. Harbour
// Tank War Enhancement 5 - main.c
/////////////////////////////////////////////////////////////////////

#include "tankwar.h"

#define B 39
```

```
int map[MAPW*MAPH] = {
    B,B,B,B,B,B,B,B,B,B,B,B,B,B,B,B,B,B,B,B,B,B,B,B,B,B,B,B,B,B,B,B,
    B,B,B,B,B,B,B,B,B,B,B,B,B,B,B,B,B,B,B,B,B,B,B,B,B,B,B,B,B,B,B,B,
    B,B,B,B,B,B,B,B,B,B,B,B,B,B,B,B,B,B,B,B,B,B,B,B,B,B,B,B,B,B,B,B,
    B,B,B,B,B,B,B,B,B,B,B,B,B,B,B,B,B,B,B,B,B,B,B,B,B,B,B,B,B,B,B,B,
    B,B,B,0,0,0,0,0,0,0,0,0,0,0,0,0,0,0,0,0,0,0,0,0,0,0,0,0,0,B,B,B,
    B,B,B,0,2,2,2,2,2,2,2,2,2,2,2,2,2,2,2,2,2,2,2,2,2,2,2,0,B,B,B,
    B,B,B,0,2,2,2,2,2,2,2,2,2,2,2,2,2,2,2,2,2,2,2,2,2,2,2,0,B,B,B,
    B,B,B,0,2,2,2,2,2,2,2,2,2,2,2,2,2,2,2,2,2,2,2,2,2,2,2,0,B,B,B,
    B,B,B,0,2,2,2,2,2,2,2,2,2,2,2,2,2,2,2,2,2,2,2,2,2,2,2,0,B,B,B,
    B,B,B,0,2,2,2,2,2,2,2,2,2,2,2,2,2,2,2,2,2,2,2,2,2,2,2,0,B,B,B,
    B,B,B,0,2,2,2,2,2,2,2,2,2,2,2,2,2,2,2,2,2,2,2,2,2,2,2,0,B,B,B,
    B,B,B,0,2,2,2,2,2,2,2,2,2,2,2,2,2,2,2,2,2,2,2,2,2,2,2,0,B,B,B,
    B,B,B,0,2,2,2,2,2,2,2,2,2,2,2,2,2,2,2,2,2,2,2,2,2,2,2,0,B,B,B,
    B,B,B,0,2,2,2,2,2,2,2,2,2,2,2,2,2,2,2,2,2,2,2,2,2,2,2,0,B,B,B,
    B,B,B,0,2,2,2,2,2,2,2,2,2,2,2,2,2,2,2,2,2,2,2,2,2,2,2,0,B,B,B,
    B,B,B,0,2,2,2,2,2,2,2,2,2,2,2,2,2,2,2,2,2,2,2,2,2,2,2,0,B,B,B,
    B,B,B,0,2,2,2,2,2,2,2,2,2,2,2,2,2,2,2,2,2,2,2,2,2,2,2,0,B,B,B,
    B,B,B,0,2,2,2,2,2,2,2,2,2,2,2,2,2,2,2,2,2,2,2,2,2,2,2,0,B,B,B,
    B,B,B,0,2,2,2,2,2,2,2,2,2,2,2,2,2,2,2,2,2,2,2,2,2,2,2,0,B,B,B,
    B,B,B,0,2,2,2,2,2,2,2,2,2,2,2,2,2,2,2,2,2,2,2,2,2,2,2,0,B,B,B,
    B,B,B,0,2,2,2,2,2,2,2,2,2,2,2,2,2,2,2,2,2,2,2,2,2,2,2,0,B,B,B,
    B,B,B,0,2,2,2,2,2,2,2,2,2,2,2,2,2,2,2,2,2,2,2,2,2,2,2,0,B,B,B,
    B,B,B,0,2,2,2,2,2,2,2,2,2,2,2,2,2,2,2,2,2,2,2,2,2,2,2,0,B,B,B,
    B,B,B,0,2,2,2,2,2,2,2,2,2,2,2,2,2,2,2,2,2,2,2,2,2,2,2,0,B,B,B,
    B,B,B,0,2,2,2,2,2,2,2,2,2,2,2,2,2,2,2,2,2,2,2,2,2,2,2,0,B,B,B,
    B,B,B,0,2,2,2,2,2,2,2,2,2,2,2,2,2,2,2,2,2,2,2,2,2,2,2,0,B,B,B,
    B,B,B,0,2,2,2,2,2,2,2,2,2,2,2,2,2,2,2,2,2,2,2,2,2,2,2,0,B,B,B,
    B,B,B,0,0,0,0,0,0,0,0,0,0,0,0,0,0,0,0,0,0,0,0,0,0,0,0,0,0,B,B,B,
    B,B,B,B,B,B,B,B,B,B,B,B,B,B,B,B,B,B,B,B,B,B,B,B,B,B,B,B,B,B,B,B,
    B,B,B,B,B,B,B,B,B,B,B,B,B,B,B,B,B,B,B,B,B,B,B,B,B,B,B,B,B,B,B,B,
    B,B,B,B,B,B,B,B,B,B,B,B,B,B,B,B,B,B,B,B,B,B,B,B,B,B,B,B,B,B,B,B,
    B,B,B,B,B,B,B,B,B,B,B,B,B,B,B,B,B,B,B,B,B,B,B,B,B,B,B,B,B,B,B,B
};

//perform basic collision detection
int inside(int x,int y,int left,int top,int right,int bottom)
{
    if (x > left && x < right && y > top && y < bottom)
        return 1;
    else
        return 0;
```

```
    }

    //reuse our friendly tile grabber from chapter 9
    BITMAP *grabframe(BITMAP *source,
                      int width, int height,
                      int startx, int starty,
                      int columns, int frame)
    {
        BITMAP *temp = create_bitmap(width,height);

        int x = startx + (frame % columns) * width;
        int y = starty + (frame / columns) * height;

        blit(source,temp,x,y,0,0,width,height);

        return temp;
    }

    //main function
    void main(void)
    {
        //initialize the game
        allegro_init();
        install_keyboard();
        install_timer();
        srand(time(NULL));
        setupscreen();
        setuptanks();

        //game loop
        while(!gameover)
        {
            //move the tanks and bullets
            for (n=0; n<2; n++)
            {
                movetank(n);
                movebullet(n);
            }

            //draw background bitmap
            blit(back, buffer, 0, 0, 0, 0, back->w, back->h);
```

```
//draw scrolling windows
for (n=0; n<2; n++)
    blit(scroll, buffer, scrollx[n], scrolly[n],
        startx[n], starty[n], SCROLLW, SCROLLH);

//update the radar
rectfill(buffer,radarx+1,radary+1,radarx+99,radary+88,BLACK);
rect(buffer,radarx,radary,radarx+100,radary+89,WHITE);

//draw mini tanks on radar
for (n=0; n<2; n++)
    stretch_sprite(buffer, tank_bmp[n][tanks[n]->dir],
        radarx + scrollx[n]/10 + (SCROLLW/10)/2-4,
        radary + scrolly[n]/12 + (SCROLLH/12)/2-4,
        8, 8);

//draw player viewport on radar
for (n=0; n<2; n++)
    rect(buffer,radarx+scrollx[n]/10, radary+scrolly[n]/12,
        radarx+scrollx[n]/10+SCROLLW/10,
        radary+scrolly[n]/12+SCROLLH/12, GRAY);

//display score
for (n=0; n<2; n++)
    textprintf(buffer, font, startx[n], HEIGHT-10,
        BURST, "Score: %d", scores[n]);

//draw the tanks and bullets
for (n=0; n<2; n++)
{
    drawtank(n);
    drawbullet(n);
}

//refresh the screen
acquire_screen();
blit(buffer, screen, 0, 0, 0, 0, WIDTH, HEIGHT);
release_screen();

//check for keypresses
if (keypressed())
    getinput();
```

```
        //slow the game down
        rest(20);
    }

    //destroy bitmaps
    destroy_bitmap(explode_bmp);
    destroy_bitmap(back);
    destroy_bitmap(scroll);
    destroy_bitmap(buffer);
    for (n=0; n<8; n++)
    {
        destroy_bitmap(tank_bmp[0][n]);
        destroy_bitmap(tank_bmp[1][n]);
    }
    return;
}
END_OF_MAIN();
```

Summary

This marks the end of yet another graphically intense chapter. In it, I talked about scrolling backgrounds and spent most of the time discussing tile-based backgrounds—how they are created and how to use them in a game. Working with tiles to create a scrolling game world is by no means an easy subject! If you skimmed over any part of this chapter, be sure to read through it again before you move on because the next three chapters dig even deeper into scrolling. You also opened up the *Tank War* project and made some huge changes to the game, not the least of which was creating dual scrolling windows—one for each player! This is the last major change to the game. From this point forward, you will make only minor additions (such as sound effects, music, and timing) in upcoming chapters. So, be happy in the knowledge that you have completed the vast majority of the work on *Tank War*.

Chapter Quiz

You can find the answers to this chapter quiz in Appendix A, "Chapter Quiz Answers."

1. Does Allegro provide support for background scrolling?

   A. Yes, but the functionality is obsolete.

   B. Yes, and it works great!

   C. Yes, but it needs some work.

   D. Not even.

2. What does a scroll window show?

    A.   A small part of a larger game world.

    B.   A window filled with sprites.

    C.   A scroll that explains the rules of the game.

    D.   A portion of the double-buffer.

3. Which of the programs in this chapter demonstrated bitmap scrolling for the first time?

    A.   *Tank War*

    B.   *TileScroll*

    C.   *ScrollScreen*

    D.   *GameWorld*

4. Why should a scrolling background be designed?

    A.   To sell it as a marketable game engine.

    B.   To devise a new programming technique.

    C.   To mesmerize the gaming public.

    D.   To achieve the goals of the game.

5. Which process uses an array of images to construct the background as it is displayed?

    A.   Iterating

    B.   Blitting

    C.   Tiling

    D.   Constructing

6. What is the best way to create a tile map of the game world?

    A.   By using a map editor.

    B.   By randomly generating the map at run time.

    C.   By using an array.

    D.   By stealing maps off the Internet.

7. What type of object comprises a typical tile map?

    A.   Variables

    B.   Arrays

    C.   Numbers

    D.   Breakpoints

8. What was the size of the virtual background in the *GameWorld* program?

    A.   800×800

    B.   16384×65536

    C.   640×480

    D.   1600×1200

9. How many virtual backgrounds are used in the new version of *Tank War?*

    A.   0

    B.   1

    C.   2

    D.   3

10. How many scrolling windows are used in the new *Tank War?*

    A.   0

    B.   1

    C.   2

    D.   3

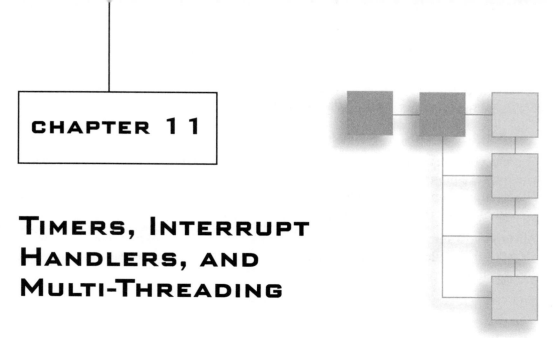

CHAPTER 11

TIMERS, INTERRUPT HANDLERS, AND MULTI-THREADING

This chapter covers the extremely critical subject of timing as it relates to game programming. Until now, you have used the primitive rest function to slow down your example programs in the past 10 chapters, and it has been hit or miss as far as how well it worked. In this chapter, I'll go over Allegro's support for timers and interrupt handlers to calculate the frame rate and slow down a program to a fixed rate. This chapter also delves into the compelling subject of multi-threading with an explanation of how to use threads to enhance a game. It also contains a demonstration program.

Here is a breakdown of the major topics in this chapter:

- Understanding timers
- Working with interrupt handlers
- Using timed game loops
- Understanding multi-threading

Timers

Timing is critical in a game. Without an accurate means to slow down a game to a fixed rate, the game will be influenced by the speed of the computer running it, adversely affecting gameplay. (This usually renders the game unplayable.) Allegro has support for timing a game using rest, but a far more powerful feature is the interrupt handler, which you can use to great effect.

Installing and Removing the Timer

You have already used Allegro's timer functions without much explanation in prior chapters because it's almost impossible to write even a simple demonstration program without some kind of timing involved. To install the primary timer in Allegro that makes it possible to use the timer functions and interrupt handlers, you use the `install_timer` function.

```
int install_timer();
```

You must be sure to call `install_timer` before you create any timer routines and also before you display a mouse pointer or play FLI animations or MIDI music because these features all rely on the timer. So it's up to you! This function returns zero on success, although it is so unlikely to error out that I never check it.

Allegro will automatically remove the timer when the program ends (or when `allegro_exit` is called), but you can call the `remove_timer` function if you want to remove the timer before the program ends.

```
void remove_timer();
```

Slowing Down the Program

You have seen the `rest` function used frequently in the sample programs in prior chapters, so it should be familiar to you. For reference, here is the declaration:

```
void rest(long time);
```

You can pass any number of milliseconds to `rest` and the program will pause for that duration, after which control will pass to the next line in the program. This is very effective for slowing down a game, of course, but it can also be used to pause for a short time when you are waiting for threads to terminate (as you'll learn about later in this chapter). Once Allegro has taken over the timer, the standard `delay` function will no longer work, although you haven't been using `delay` so that should not come as a surprise.

One feature that I haven't gone over yet is the `rest_callback` function. Have you noticed that Allegro provides a callback for almost everything it does? This is a fine degree of control seldom found in game development libraries; obviously, Allegro was developed by individuals with a great deal of experience, who had the foresight to include some very useful callback functions. Here is the declaration:

```
void rest_callback(long time, void (*callback)())
```

This function works like `rest`, but instead of doing nothing, a callback function is called during the delay period so your program can continue working even while timing is in effect to slow the game down.

Here's an example of how you would call the function:

```
//slow the game down
rest_callback(8, rest1);
```

The rest1 callback function is very simple; it contains no parameters.

```
void rest1(void)
{
    //time to rest, or do some work?
}
```

This is a good time to update some values, such as the frame rate, but I would not recommend doing any time-intensive processing during the rest callback because it must return quickly to avoid messing up the game's timing. The *TimedLoop* program later in this chapter will demonstrate how to use the rest_callback function.

The TimerTest Program

Because none of the sample programs in the book up to this point have used effective timing techniques, I've written a program to calculate the frame rate and display this value along with a count of seconds passing. The *TimerTest* program will be used in the next two segments of the chapter, so its listing is somewhat extensive at this point. However, the next two segments will provide simple code changes to this program to save time and space.

Figure 11.1 shows the *TimerTest* program running. As you can see, it is very graphical, with a background and many sprites moving across the screen. I owe a debt of thanks to Ari Feldman (http://www.arifeldman.com) again for allowing me to use his excellent SpriteLib to populate this chapter with such interesting, high-quality sprites.

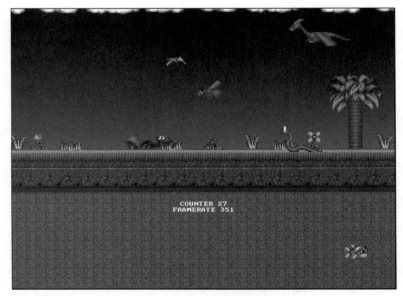

Figure 11.1 The *TimerTest* program animates many sprites over a background scene. Sprites courtesy of Ari Feldman.

The first section of code includes the defines, structs, and variables.

```
#include <stdio.h>
#include <time.h>
#include <stdlib.h>
#include "allegro.h"

#define MODE GFX_AUTODETECT_FULLSCREEN
#define WIDTH 640
#define HEIGHT 480
#define MAX 6
#define BLACK makecol(0,0,0)
#define WHITE makecol(255,255,255)

//define the sprite structure
typedef struct SPRITE
{
    int dir, alive;
    int x,y;
    int width,height;
    int xspeed,yspeed;
    int xdelay,ydelay;
    int xcount,ycount;
    int curframe,maxframe,animdir;
    int framecount,framedelay;
}SPRITE;

//variables
BITMAP *back;
BITMAP *temp;
BITMAP *sprite_images[10][10];
SPRITE *sprites[10];
BITMAP *buffer;
int n, f;

//timer variables
int start;
int counter;
int ticks;
int framerate;
```

The next section of code for the *TimerTest* program includes the sprite-handling functions updatesprite, warpsprite, grabframe, and loadsprites. These functions should be familiar from previous chapters.

```c
void updatesprite(SPRITE *spr)
{
    //update x position
    if (++spr->xcount > spr->xdelay)
    {
        spr->xcount = 0;
        spr->x += spr->xspeed;
    }

    //update y position
    if (++spr->ycount > spr->ydelay)
    {
        spr->ycount = 0;
        spr->y += spr->yspeed;
    }

    //update frame based on animdir
    if (++spr->framecount > spr->framedelay)
    {
        spr->framecount = 0;
        if (spr->animdir == -1)
        {
            if (--spr->curframe < 0)
                spr->curframe = spr->maxframe;
        }
        else if (spr->animdir == 1)
        {
            if (++spr->curframe > spr->maxframe)
                spr->curframe = 0;
        }
    }
}


void warpsprite(SPRITE *spr)
{
    //simple screen warping behavior
    //Allegro takes care of clipping
    if (spr->x < 0 - spr->width)
    {
        spr->x = SCREEN_W;
    }
```

```
    else if (spr->x > SCREEN_W)
    {
        spr->x = 0 - spr->width;
    }

    if (spr->y < 0)
    {
        spr->y = SCREEN_H - spr->height-1;
    }

    else if (spr->y > SCREEN_H - spr->height)
    {
        spr->y = 0;
    }


}

//reuse our friendly tile grabber from chapter 9
BITMAP *grabframe(BITMAP *source,
                  int width, int height,
                  int startx, int starty,
                  int columns, int frame)
{
    BITMAP *temp = create_bitmap(width,height);

    int x = startx + (frame % columns) * width;
    int y = starty + (frame / columns) * height;

    blit(source,temp,x,y,0,0,width,height);

    return temp;
}

void loadsprites(void)
{
    //load dragon sprite
    temp = load_bitmap("dragon.bmp", NULL);
    for (n=0; n<6; n++)
        sprite_images[0][n] = grabframe(temp,128,64,0,0,3,n);
    destroy_bitmap(temp);

    //initialize the dragon (sprite 0)
    sprites[0] = malloc(sizeof(SPRITE));
```

```
sprites[0]->x = 500;
sprites[0]->y = 0;
sprites[0]->width = sprite_images[0][0]->w;
sprites[0]->height = sprite_images[0][0]->h;
sprites[0]->xdelay = 1;
sprites[0]->ydelay = 0;
sprites[0]->xcount = 0;
sprites[0]->ycount = 0;
sprites[0]->xspeed = -5;
sprites[0]->yspeed = 0;
sprites[0]->curframe = 0;
sprites[0]->maxframe = 5;
sprites[0]->framecount = 0;
sprites[0]->framedelay = 5;
sprites[0]->animdir = 1;

//load fish sprite
temp = load_bitmap("fish.bmp", NULL);
for (n=0; n<3; n++)
    sprite_images[1][n] = grabframe(temp,64,32,0,0,3,n);
destroy_bitmap(temp);

//initialize the fish (sprite 1)
sprites[1] = malloc(sizeof(SPRITE));
sprites[1]->x = 300;
sprites[1]->y = 400;
sprites[1]->width = sprite_images[1][0]->w;
sprites[1]->height = sprite_images[1][0]->h;
sprites[1]->xdelay = 1;
sprites[1]->ydelay = 0;
sprites[1]->xcount = 0;
sprites[1]->ycount = 0;
sprites[1]->xspeed = 3;
sprites[1]->yspeed = 0;
sprites[1]->curframe = 0;
sprites[1]->maxframe = 2;
sprites[1]->framecount = 0;
sprites[1]->framedelay = 8;
sprites[1]->animdir = 1;

//load crab sprite
temp = load_bitmap("crab.bmp", NULL);
for (n=0; n<4; n++)
```

```
            sprite_images[2][n] = grabframe(temp,64,32,0,0,4,n);
destroy_bitmap(temp);

//initialize the crab (sprite 2)
sprites[2] = malloc(sizeof(SPRITE));
sprites[2]->x = 300;
sprites[2]->y = 212;
sprites[2]->width = sprite_images[2][0]->w;
sprites[2]->height = sprite_images[2][0]->h;
sprites[2]->xdelay = 6;
sprites[2]->ydelay = 0;
sprites[2]->xcount = 0;
sprites[2]->ycount = 0;
sprites[2]->xspeed = 2;
sprites[2]->yspeed = 0;
sprites[2]->curframe = 0;
sprites[2]->maxframe = 3;
sprites[2]->framecount = 0;
sprites[2]->framedelay = 20;
sprites[2]->animdir = 1;

//load bee sprite
temp = load_bitmap("bee.bmp", NULL);
for (n=0; n<6; n++)
    sprite_images[3][n] = grabframe(temp,50,40,0,0,6,n);
destroy_bitmap(temp);

//initialize the bee (sprite 3)
sprites[3] = malloc(sizeof(SPRITE));
sprites[3]->x = 100;
sprites[3]->y = 120;
sprites[3]->width = sprite_images[3][0]->w;
sprites[3]->height = sprite_images[3][0]->h;
sprites[3]->xdelay = 1;
sprites[3]->ydelay = 0;
sprites[3]->xcount = 0;
sprites[3]->ycount = 0;
sprites[3]->xspeed = -3;
sprites[3]->yspeed = 0;
sprites[3]->curframe = 0;
sprites[3]->maxframe = 5;
sprites[3]->framecount = 0;
sprites[3]->framedelay = 8;
```

```
    sprites[3]->animdir = 1;

//load skeeter sprite
    temp = load_bitmap("skeeter.bmp", NULL);
    for (n=0; n<6; n++)
        sprite_images[4][n] = grabframe(temp,50,40,0,0,6,n);
    destroy_bitmap(temp);

    //initialize the skeeter (sprite 4)
    sprites[4] = malloc(sizeof(SPRITE));
    sprites[4]->x = 500;
    sprites[4]->y = 70;
    sprites[4]->width = sprite_images[4][0]->w;
    sprites[4]->height = sprite_images[4][0]->h;
    sprites[4]->xdelay = 1;
    sprites[4]->ydelay = 0;
    sprites[4]->xcount = 0;
    sprites[4]->ycount = 0;
    sprites[4]->xspeed = 4;
    sprites[4]->yspeed = 0;
    sprites[4]->curframe = 0;
    sprites[4]->maxframe = 4;
    sprites[4]->framecount = 0;
    sprites[4]->framedelay = 2;
    sprites[4]->animdir = 1;

//load snake sprite
    temp = load_bitmap("snake.bmp", NULL);
    for (n=0; n<8; n++)
        sprite_images[5][n] = grabframe(temp,100,50,0,0,4,n);
    destroy_bitmap(temp);

    //initialize the snake (sprite 5)
    sprites[5] = malloc(sizeof(SPRITE));
    sprites[5]->x = 350;
    sprites[5]->y = 200;
    sprites[5]->width = sprite_images[5][0]->w;
    sprites[5]->height = sprite_images[5][0]->h;
    sprites[5]->xdelay = 1;
    sprites[5]->ydelay = 0;
    sprites[5]->xcount = 0;
    sprites[5]->ycount = 0;
    sprites[5]->xspeed = -2;
```

```
    sprites[5]->yspeed = 0;
    sprites[5]->curframe = 0;
    sprites[5]->maxframe = 4;
    sprites[5]->framecount = 0;
    sprites[5]->framedelay = 6;
    sprites[5]->animdir = 1;
}
```

The last section of code for the *TimerTest* program includes the main function, which initializes the program and includes the main loop. This program is lengthy in setup but efficient in operation because all the sprites are contained within arrays that can be updated as a group within a for loop. I have highlighted timer-related code in bold.

```
void main(void)
{
    //initialize
    allegro_init();
    set_color_depth(16);
    set_gfx_mode(MODE, WIDTH, HEIGHT, 0, 0);
    srand(time(NULL));
    text_mode(-1);
    install_keyboard();
    install_timer();

    //create double buffer
    buffer = create_bitmap(SCREEN_W,SCREEN_H);

    //load and draw the blocks
    back = load_bitmap("background.bmp", NULL);
    blit(back,buffer,0,0,0,0,back->w,back->h);

    //load and set up sprites
    loadsprites();

    //game loop
    while (!key[KEY_ESC])
    {
        //restore the background
        for (n=0; n<MAX; n++)
            blit(back, buffer, sprites[n]->x, sprites[n]->y,
                sprites[n]->x, sprites[n]->y,
                sprites[n]->width, sprites[n]->height);
```

```
    //update the sprites
    for (n=0; n<MAX; n++)
    {
        updatesprite(sprites[n]);
        warpsprite(sprites[n]);
        draw_sprite(buffer, sprite_images[n][sprites[n]->curframe],
            sprites[n]->x, sprites[n]->y);
    }

    //update ticks
    ticks++;

    //calculate framerate once per second
    if (clock() > start + 1000)
    {
        counter++;
        start = clock();
        framerate = ticks;
        ticks = 0;
    }

    //display framerate
    blit(back, buffer, 320-70, 330, 320-70, 330, 140, 20);
    textprintf_centre(buffer,font,320,330,WHITE,"COUNTER %d",
        counter);
    textprintf_centre(buffer,font,320,340,WHITE,"FRAMERATE %d",
        framerate);

    //update the screen
    acquire_screen();
    blit(buffer,screen,0,0,0,0,SCREEN_W-1,SCREEN_H-1);
    release_screen();
}

//remove objects from memory
destroy_bitmap(back);
destroy_bitmap(buffer);

for (n=0; n<MAX; n++)
{
    for (f=0; f<sprites[n]->maxframe+1; f++)
        destroy_bitmap(sprite_images[n][f]);
```

```
        free(sprites[n]);
    }

    return;
}

END_OF_MAIN();
```

Interrupt Handlers

The rest and rest_callback functions are useful for slowing down a game, but Allegro's support for interrupt handlers is the real power of the timer functionality. Allegro allows you to easily create an interrupt handler routine that will execute at a specified interval. This is a limited form of multi-threading in concept, although interrupt handlers do not run in parallel, but sequentially and based on the interval. Because no two interrupt handlers will ever be running at the same time, you don't need to worry about corrupted data as you do with threading.

Creating an Interrupt Handler

After you have installed the timer using install_timer, you can create one or more interrupt handlers using the install_int function.

```
int install_int(void (*proc)(), int speed);
```

This function accepts the name of an interrupt handler callback function and the duration by which that function should be called. After you install the interrupt handler, you don't need to call it because the handler function is called automatically at the interval specified (in milliseconds).

tip

If you forget to call install_timer before you create an interrupt handler, don't worry; Allegro is smart enough to call install_timer automatically if it is not already running.

There are a limited number of interrupt handlers available for your program's use, so if the function fails to create a new handler it will return a non-zero, with a zero on success. The interrupt callback function is called by Allegro, not the operating system, so it doesn't need any special wrapper code (as with traditional interrupt handlers); it can be a regular C function. Because timing is crucial, I recommend that you don't use an interrupt callback function for any real processing; use it to set flags, increment a frame rate counter, and that sort of thing, and then do any real work in the main function using these flags or counters. Try not to take too much time in an interrupt callback, in other words.

Not all operating systems require it, but Allegro provides a means to secure variables and functions that are used by an interrupt. You can use LOCK_VARIABLE and LOCK_FUNCTION to identify them to Allegro. You will also want to declare any global variables used by the interrupt as volatile.

Removing an Interrupt Handler

It is not absolutely necessary to remove an interrupt handler from your program because allegro_exit will remove the handler for you, but it is nevertheless a good idea to have your programs clean up after themselves to eliminate even the possibility of a difficult-to-find bug. You can use the remove_int function to remove an interrupt handler.

```
void remove_int(void (*proc)());
```

Simply pass the name of the interrupt callback function to remove_int and that will stop the interrupt from calling the function.

The InterruptTest Program

The real power of an interrupt handler is obvious in practice, when you do something essential (such as calculate the frame rate) inside the interrupt callback function. I have made some changes to the *TimerTest* program you saw in the last section. Instead of using a ticks variable and the clock function to determine when to mark each second, this new program uses an interrupt handler that is set to 1,000 milliseconds to automatically tick off a second. To make things easier, I have modified the *TimerTest* program (which was quite lengthy) to use an interrupt instead of a simple timer; only a few lines of code need to be changed. Figure 11.2 shows the output of the new version of the program, which is now called *InterruptTest*.

Figure 11.2 The *InterruptTest* program demonstrates how you can use an interrupt callback function to calculate the frame rate.

If you look back a few pages to Figure 11.1, you might notice that it had a slightly higher frame rate than this new *InterruptTest* program (from 351 fps to 346 fps). The difference is negligible and would not be noticed in a timed game loop in which the frame rate is fixed. However, this does demonstrate that the interrupt handler adds some overhead to the program; it is further proof that the callback function should run as quickly as possible to avoid adding to that overhead.

Let's get started on the changes, few that they are. The first change is up near the top of the program, where the counter, ticks, and framerate variables are declared. Add volatile to their definitions.

```
//timer variables
volatile int counter;
volatile int ticks;
volatile int framerate;
```

Next, you need to add the interrupt handler callback function, timer1, to the program. You can add this function right above main or up at the top of the program, as long as it's visible to main. Note how simple this function is; it increments counter (for seconds), sets the framerate variable, and resets the ticks variable.

```
//calculate framerate once per second
void timer1(void)
{
    counter++;
    framerate = ticks;
    ticks=0;
}
END_OF_FUNCTION(timer1)
```

The next change takes place in main, where the variables and callback function are identified to Allegro as interrupt-aware and the interrupt handler is created. You can add this code right above the while loop inside main.

```
//lock interrupt variables
LOCK_VARIABLE(counter);
LOCK_VARIABLE(framerate);
LOCK_VARIABLE(ticks);
LOCK_FUNCTION(timer1);
//create the interrupt handler
install_int(timer1, 1000);
```

Okay, now for the last change, which is really only a deletion. Because the timer code was moved into the interrupt callback function, you need to delete it from main. Look for the code highlighted in bold in the following listing (and commented out), and remove those lines from the program.

```
//update ticks
ticks++;

//calculate framerate once per second
//if (clock() > start + 1000)
//{
//      counter++;
//      start = clock();
//      framerate = ticks;
//      ticks = 0;
//}

//display framerate
blit(back, buffer, 320-70, 330, 320-70, 330, 140, 20);
textprintf_centre(buffer,font,320,330,WHITE,"COUNTER %d", counter);
textprintf_centre(buffer,font,320,340,WHITE,"FRAMERATE %d", framerate);
```

Using Timed Game Loops

You have now learned how to use a timer to calculate the frame rate of the program with a simple timer and also an interrupt handler. But so what if you know the frame rate; how does that keep the game running at a stable rate regardless of the computer hardware running it? You need to use this new functionality to actually limit the speed of the game so it will look the same on any computer.

Slowing Down the Gameplay...Not the Game

The key point here is not to slow down the gameplay, but the graphics rendering on the screen. Any blitting going on will (and should) be as fast as possible, but the pace of the game must be maintained or it will be unplayable. You have already seen what a high-speed game loop looks like by running the *TimerTest* and *InterruptTest* programs. What you need now is a way to slow down the program to a predictable rate.

Now you return to the rest_callback function introduced at the start of this chapter to help create a timed game loop. There is no new functionality in this section, just an example of how to use what you've learned so far to improve gameplay. You are free to use any target frame rate you want for your game, but as a general rule a value between 30 and 60 fps is a good target to shoot for. Why? Any slower than 30 fps and the game will seem sluggish; any faster than 60 and the game will feel too frenetic. You do want to blit all the graphics as quickly as possible, and then if there are cycles left over after that is done, you need to slow down the game so one frame of the game is displayed at a fixed interval.

The TimedLoop Program

Now you can modify the program again to give it a timed loop that will keep the program running fluidly and predictably whether it's running on a Pentium II 450 or an Athlon XP 3700+ CPU. First, open up the *InterruptTest* program as a basis, so the program will still include the interrupt handler to calculate the frame rate. The new program, which will be called *TimedLoop*, is simply a modification of that previous program, so only a few line changes are needed. Figure 11.3 shows the program running. Take note of the new status message that displays the resting value.

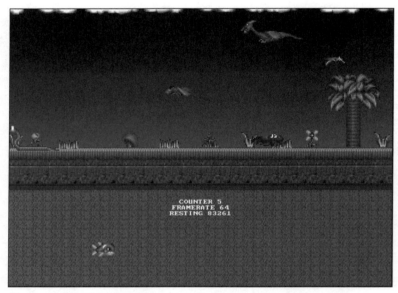

Figure 11.3 The *TimedLoop* program demonstrates how to slow a program down to a consistent frame rate.

First, up near the top of the program, add another `volatile` variable.

```
//timer variables
volatile int counter;
volatile int ticks;
volatile int framerate;
volatile int resting, rested;
```

Scroll down to the `timer1` interrupt callback function and add a line to it.

```
//calculate framerate every second
void timer1(void)
{
    counter++;
```

```
        framerate = ticks;
        ticks=0;
        rested=resting;
}
END_OF_FUNCTION(timer1)
```

Now you create the function that is called by rest_callback. You can add this function below timer1.

```
//do something while resting (?)
void rest1(void)
{
        resting++;
}
```

The next change takes place in main, adding the code to call the rest_callback function, which is a call to rest1, just added. Note also the changes to the section of code that displays the counter and frame rate. I have changed the last parameter of blit from 20 to 30 to erase the new line, which is also listed below, highlighted in bold. This displays the number of ticks that transpired while the program was waiting inside the rest1 callback function.

```
//update ticks
ticks++;

//slow the game down
resting=0;
rest_callback(8, rest1);

//display framerate
blit(back, buffer, 320-70, 330, 320-70, 330, 140, 30);
textprintf_centre(buffer,font,320,330,WHITE,"COUNTER %d", counter);
textprintf_centre(buffer,font,320,340,WHITE,"FRAMERATE %d", framerate);
textprintf_centre(buffer,font,320,350,WHITE,"RESTING %d", rested);
```

Multi-Threading

Every modern operating system uses threads for essential and basic operation and would not be nearly as versatile without threads. A *thread* is a process that runs within the memory space of a single program but is executed separately from that program. This section will provide a short overview of multi-threading and how it can be used (fairly easily) to enhance a game. I will not go into the vast details of threaded programming because the topic is too huge and unwieldy to fully explain in only a few pages. Instead, I will provide you with enough information and example code that you will be able to start using threads.

To be multi-threaded, a program will create at least one thread that will run in addition to that program's main loop. Any time a program uses more than one thread, you must take extreme caution when working with data that is potentially shared between threads. It is generally safe for a program to share data with a single thread (although it is not recommended), but when more than one thread is in use, you must use a protection scheme to protect the data from being manipulated by two threads at the same time.

To protect data, you can make use of mutexes that will lock data inside a single thread until it is safe to unlock the data for use in the main program or in another thread. The locking and unlocking must be done inside a loop that runs continuously inside the thread callback function. Note that if you do not have a loop inside your thread function, it will run once and terminate. The idea is to keep the thread running—doing something— while the main program is doing the delegating work. You should think of a thread as a new employee who has been hired to alleviate the amount of work done by the program (or rather, by the main thread). To demonstrate, at the end of this section I'll walk you through a multi-threaded example in which two distinct threads control two identical sprites on the screen, with one thread running faster than the other, while the program's main loop does nothing more than blit the double-buffer to the screen.

Abstracting the Parallel Processing Problem

We disseminate the subject as if it's just another C function, but threads were at one time an extraordinary achievement that was every bit as exciting as the first connection of ARPAnet in 1969 or the first working version of UNIX. In the 1980s, parallel programming was as hip as virtual reality, but like the latter term, it was not to be a true reality until the early 1990s. *Multi-threaded programming* is the engineer's term for parallel processing and is a solution that has been proven to work. The key to parallel processing came when software engineers realized that the processor is not the focus; rather, software design is. In the words of Agent Smith from *The Matrix*, "We lacked a programming language with which to construct your world."

A single-processor system should be able to run multiple threads. Once that goal was realized, adding two or more processors to a system provided the ability to delegate those threads, and this was a job for the operating system. No longer tasked with designing a parallel-processing architecture, engineers in both the electronics and software fields abstracted the problem so the two were not reliant upon each other. A single program can run on a motherboard with four CPUs and push all of those processors to the limit, if that single program invokes multiple threads. As such, the programs themselves were treated as single threads. And yet, there can be many non-threaded programs running on our fictional quad-processor system, and it might not be taxed at all. It depends on what each program is doing.

Math-intensive processes, such as 3D rendering, can eat a CPU for breakfast. But with the advent of threading in modern operating systems, programs such as 3D Studio Max, Maya, Lightwave, and Photoshop can invoke threads to handle intense processes, such as scene rendering and image manipulation. Suddenly, that dual-G5 Mac is able to process a Photoshop image in four seconds, whereas it took 45 seconds on your G3 Mac! Why? Threads.

However, just because a single program is able to share four CPUs, that doesn't mean each thread is an independent entity. Any global variables in the program (main thread) can be used by the invoked threads as long as care is taken that data is not damaged. Imagine 10 children grasping for an ice cream cone at the same time and you get the picture. What your threaded program must do is isolate the ice cream cone for each child, and only make the ice cream cone available to the others after that child has released it. Get the picture?

How does this concept of threading relate to processes? As you know, modern operating systems treat each program as a separate process, allocating a certain number of milliseconds to each process. This is where you get the term *multi-tasking;* many processes can be run at the same time using a time-slicing mechanism. A process has its own separate heap and stack and can contain many threads. A thread, on the other hand, has its own stack but shares the heap with other threads within the process. This is called a *thread group.*

The Pthreads-Win32 Library

The vast majority of Linux and UNIX operating system flavors will already have the pthread library installed because it is a core feature of the kernel. Other systems might not be so lucky. Windows uses its own multi-threading library. Of course, a primary goal of this book is to keep this code 100-percent portable. So what you need is a pthread library that is compatible with the POSIX systems. After all, that is what the "p" in pthreads stands for—POSIX threads.

An important thing you should know about the Windows implementation of pthread is that it abstracts the Windows threading functionality, molding it to conform to pthread standards.

There is one excellent open-source pthreads library for Windows systems, distributed by Red Hat, that I have chosen for this chapter because it includes makefiles for Visual C++ and Dev-C++. I have included the compiled version of pthread for Visual C++ and Dev-C++ on the CD-ROM in the \pthread folder, as Table 11.1 shows. These files are also provided in the MultiThread project folder on the CD-ROM. I recommend copying the lib file to your compiler's lib folder (for Visual C++ 6, this will usually be C:\Program Files\Microsoft Visual Studio\VC98\Lib) and the header files (pthread.h and sched.h) to your compiler's include folder (for Visual C++ 6, this will usually be C:\Program Files\Microsoft Visual Studio\VC98\Include). The dll can reside with the executable.

Table 11.1 pthread Library Files

Compiler	Lib	DLL
Visual C++	pthreadVC.lib	pthreadVC.dll
Dev-C++	libpthreadGC.a	pthreadGC.dll

Although Red Hat's pthread library is open source, I have chosen not to distribute it with the book and have only included the libs, dlls, and key headers. You can download the pthread library and find extensive documentation at http://sources.redhat.com/pthreads-win32. I encourage you to browse the site and get the latest version of Pthreads-Win32 from Red Hat. Makefiles are provided so it is easy to make the pthread library using whatever recent version of the sources you have downloaded. If you are intimidated by the prospect of having to compile sources, I encourage you to try. I, too, was once intimidated by down-loading open source projects; I wasn't sure what to do with all the files. These packages were designed to be easy to make using GCC or Visual C++. All you really need to do is open a command prompt, change to the folder where the source code files are located, and set the path to your compiler. If you are using Dev-C++, for instance, you can type the following command to bring the GCC compiler online.

```
path=C:\Dev-Cpp\bin;%path%
```

What next? Simply type `make GC` and presto, the sources will be compiled. You'll have the libpthreadGC.a and pthreadGC.dll files after it's finished. The GC option is a parameter used by the makefile. If you want to see the available options, simply type `make` and the options will be displayed.

If you are really interested in this subject and you want more in-depth information, look for Butenhof's *Programming with POSIX Threads* (Addison-Wesley, 1997). Because the Pthreads-Win32 library is functionally compatible with Posix threads, the information in this book can be applied to pthread programming under Windows.

Programming with Posix Threads

I am going to cover the key functions in this section and let you pursue the full extent of multi-threaded programming on your own using the references I have suggested. For the purposes of this chapter, I want you to be able to control sprites using threads outside the main loop. Incidentally, the `main` function in any Allegro program is a thread too, although it is only a single thread. If you create an additional thread, then your program will be using two threads.

Creating a New Thread

First of all, how do you create a new thread? New threads are created with the pthread_create function.

```
int pthread_create (
    pthread_t *tid,
    const pthread_attr_t *attr,
    void *(*start) (void *),
    void *arg);
```

Yeah! That's what I thought at first, but it's not a problem. Here, let me explain. The first parameter is a pthread_t struct variable. This struct is large and complex, and you really don't need to know about the internals to use it. If you want more details, I encourage you to pick up Butenhof's book as a reference.

The second parameter is a pthread_attr_t struct variable that usually contains attributes for the new thread. This is usually not used, so you can pass NULL to it.

The third parameter is a pointer to the thread function used by this thread for processing. This function should contain its own loop, but should have exit logic for the loop when it's time to kill the thread. (I used a done variable.)

The fourth parameter is a pointer to a numeric value for this thread to uniquely identify it. You can just create an int variable and set it to a value before passing it to pthread_create.

Here's an example of how to create a new thread:

```
int id;
pthread_t pthread0;
int threadid0 = 0;
id = pthread_create(&pthread0, NULL, thread0, (void*)&threadid0);
```

So you've created this thread, but what about the callback function? Oh, right. Here's a minimal example:

```
void* thread0(void* data)
{
    int my_thread_id = *((int*)data);
    while(!done)
    {
        //do something!
    }
    pthread_exit(NULL);
    return NULL;
}
```

Killing a Thread

This brings us to the `pthread_exit` function, which terminates the thread. Normally you'll want to call this function at the end of the function after the loop has exited. Here's the definition for the function:

```
void pthread_exit (void *value_ptr);
```

You can get away with just passing NULL to this function because `value_ptr` is an advanced topic for gaining more control over the thread.

Mutexes: Protecting Data from Threads

At this point you can write a multi-threaded program with only the `pthread_create` and `pthread_exit` functions, knowing how to create the callback function and use it. That is enough if you only want to create a single thread to run inside the process with your program's main thread. But more often than not, you will want to use two or more threads in a game to delegate some of the workload. Therefore, it's a good idea to use a mutex for all your threads. Recall the ice cream cone analogy. Are you sure that new thread won't interfere with any globals? Have you considered timing? When you call `rest` to slow down the main loop, it has absolutely no effect on other threads. Each thread can call `rest` for timing independently of the others. What if you are using a thread to blit the double-buffer to the screen while another thread is writing to the buffer? Most memory chips cannot read and write data at the same time. It is very likely is that you'll update a small portion of the buffer (by drawing a sprite, for instance) while the buffer is being blitted to the screen. The result is some unwanted flicker—yes, even when using a double-buffer. What you have here is a situation that is similar to a vertical refresh conflict, only it is occurring in memory rather than directly on the screen. Do you need a `dbsync` type of function that is similar to `vsync`? I wouldn't go that far. What I am trying to point out is that threads can step on each other's toes, so to speak, if you aren't careful to use a mutex.

A *mutex* is a block used in a thread function to prevent other threads from running until that block is released. Assuming, of course, that all threads use the same mutex, it is possible to use more than one mutex in your program. The easiest way is to create a single mutex, and then block the mutex at the start of each thread's loop, unblocking at the end of the loop.

Creating a mutex doesn't require a function; rather, it requires a struct variable.

```
//create a new thread mutex to protect variables
pthread_mutex_t threadsafe = PTHREAD_MUTEX_INITIALIZER;
```

This line of code will create a new mutex called `threadsafe` that, when used by all the thread functions, will prevent data read/write conflicts.

You must destroy the mutex before your program ends; you can do so using the `pthread_ mutex_destroy` function.

```
int pthread_mutex_destroy (pthread_mutex_t *mutex);
```

Here is an example of how it would be used:

```
pthread_mutex_destroy(&threadsafe);
```

Next, you need to know how to lock and unlock a mutex inside a thread function. The `pthread_mutex_lock` function is used to lock a mutex.

```
int pthread_mutex_lock (pthread_mutex_t * mutex);
```

This has the effect of preventing any other threads from locking the same mutex, so any variables or functions you use or call (respectively) while the mutex is locked will be safe from manipulation by any other threads. Basically, when a thread encounters a locked mutex, it waits until the mutex is available before proceeding. (It uses no processor time; it simply waits.)

Here is the unlock function:

```
int pthread_mutex_unlock (pthread_mutex_t * mutex);
```

The two functions just shown will normally return zero if the lock or unlock succeeded immediately; otherwise, a non-zero value will be returned to indicate that the thread is waiting for the mutex. This should not happen for unlocking, only for locking. If you have a problem with `pthread_mutex_unlock` returning non-zero, it means the mutex was locked while that thread was supposedly in control over the mutex—a bad situation that should never happen. But when it comes to game programming, bad things do often happen while you are developing a new game, so it's helpful to print an error message for any non-zero return.

The MultiThread Program

At this point, you have all the information you need to use multi-threading in your own games and other programs. To test this program in a true parallel environment, I used my dual Athlon MP 1.2-GHz system under Windows 2000 and also under Windows XP. I like how XP is more thread-friendly (the Task Manager shows the number of threads used by each program), but any single-processor system will run this program just fine. Most dual systems should blow away even high-end single systems with this simple sprite demo because each sprite has its own thread. I have seen rates on my dual Athlon MP system that far exceed a much faster Pentium 4 system, but all that has changed with Intel's Hyper-Threading technology built into their high-end CPUs. This essentially means that Intel CPUs are thread-friendly and able to handle multiple threads in a single CPU.

Processors have boasted multiple pipelines for a decade, but now those pipelines are optimized to handle multiple threads.

The *MultiThread* program (shown in Figure 11.4) creates two threads (thread0 and thread1) with similar functionality. Each thread moves a sprite on the screen with a bounce behavior, with full control over erasing, moving, and drawing the sprite on the double-buffer. This leaves the program's main loop with just a single task of blitting the buffer to the screen.

Figure 11.4 The *MultiThread* program uses threads to control sprite animation on the screen.

If you are using Visual C++, you'll want to create a new Win32 Application project, add a new source code file called main.c to the project, and then open the Project Settings dialog box, as shown in Figure 11.5.

On the Link tab, you'll want to type in **alleg.lib** and **pthreadVC.lib** separated by a space in the Object/Library Modules field, like this:

```
alleg.lib pthreadVC.lib
```

If you are using Dev-C++, you'll want to create a new Windows Application C-language project. Open the Project Options dialog box, go to the Parameters tab, and add the following two options:

```
-lalleg -lpthreadGC
```

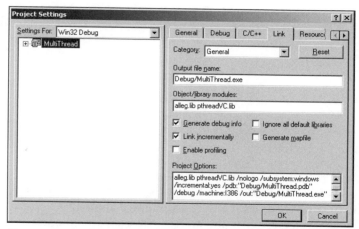

Figure 11.5 Adding pthreadVC.lib as a library file required by
MultiThread program

Now you are ready to type in the source code for the *MultiThread* program. This project
uses the sphere.bmp image containing the 32-frame animated ball from the *CollisionTest*
project in Chapter 9. The project is located in completed form in the \chapter11\multi-
thread directory on the CD-ROM. Here is the first section of code for the program:

```
#include <pthread.h>
#include "allegro.h"

#define MODE GFX_AUTODETECT_FULLSCREEN
#define WIDTH 640
#define HEIGHT 480
#define BLACK makecol(0,0,0)
#define WHITE makecol(255,255,255)

//define the sprite structure
typedef struct SPRITE
{
    int dir, alive;
    int x,y;
    int width,height;
    int xspeed,yspeed;
    int xdelay,ydelay;
    int xcount,ycount;
    int curframe,maxframe,animdir;
    int framecount,framedelay;
}SPRITE;
```

```
//variables
BITMAP *buffer;
BITMAP *ballimg[32];
SPRITE theballs[2];
SPRITE *balls[2];
int done;
int n;

//create a new thread mutex to protect variables
pthread_mutex_t threadsafe = PTHREAD_MUTEX_INITIALIZER;
```

As you can see, you just created the new mutex as a struct variable. Really, there is no processing done on a mutex at the time of creation; it is just a value that threads recognize when you pass &threadsafe to the pthread_mutex_lock and pthread_mutex_unlock functions.

The next section of code in the *MultiThread* program includes the usual sprite-handling functions that you should recognize.

```
void erasesprite(BITMAP *dest, SPRITE *spr)
{
    //erase the sprite
    rectfill(dest, spr->x, spr->y, spr->x + spr->width,
        spr->y + spr->height, BLACK);
}

void updatesprite(SPRITE *spr)
{
    //update x position
    if (++spr->xcount > spr->xdelay)
    {
        spr->xcount = 0;
        spr->x += spr->xspeed;
    }

    //update y position
    if (++spr->ycount > spr->ydelay)
    {
        spr->ycount = 0;
        spr->y += spr->yspeed;
    }

    //update frame based on animdir
    if (++spr->framecount > spr->framedelay)
    {
```

```
        spr->framecount = 0;
        if (spr->animdir == -1)
        {
            if (--spr->curframe < 0)
                spr->curframe = spr->maxframe;
        }
        else if (spr->animdir == 1)
        {
            if (++spr->curframe > spr->maxframe)
                spr->curframe = 0;
        }
    }
}


//this version doesn't change speed, just direction
void bouncesprite(SPRITE *spr)
{
    //simple screen bouncing behavior
    if (spr->x < 0)
    {
        spr->x = 0;
        spr->xspeed = -spr->xspeed;
        spr->animdir *= -1;
    }

    else if (spr->x > SCREEN_W - spr->width)
    {
        spr->x = SCREEN_W - spr->width;
        spr->xspeed = -spr->xspeed;
        spr->animdir *= -1;
    }

    if (spr->y < 0)
    {
        spr->y = 0;
        spr->yspeed = -spr->yspeed;
        spr->animdir *= -1;
    }

    else if (spr->y > SCREEN_H - spr->height)
    {
        spr->y = SCREEN_H - spr->height;
        spr->yspeed = -spr->yspeed;
```

```
            spr->animdir *= -1;
        }
}


BITMAP *grabframe(BITMAP *source,
                  int width, int height,
                  int startx, int starty,
                  int columns, int frame)
{
    BITMAP *temp = create_bitmap(width,height);
    int x = startx + (frame % columns) * width;
    int y = starty + (frame / columns) * height;
    blit(source,temp,x,y,0,0,width,height);
    return temp;
}


void loadsprites()
{
    BITMAP *temp;

    //load sprite images
    temp = load_bitmap("sphere.bmp", NULL);
    for (n=0; n<32; n++)
        ballimg[n] = grabframe(temp,64,64,0,0,8,n);
    destroy_bitmap(temp);

    //initialize the sprite
    for (n=0; n<2; n++)
    {
        balls[n] = &theballs[n];
        balls[n]->x = rand() % (SCREEN_W - ballimg[0]->w);
        balls[n]->y = rand() % (SCREEN_H - ballimg[0]->h);
        balls[n]->width = ballimg[0]->w;
        balls[n]->height = ballimg[0]->h;
        balls[n]->xdelay = 0;
        balls[n]->ydelay = 0;
        balls[n]->xcount = 0;
        balls[n]->ycount = 0;
        balls[n]->xspeed = 5;
        balls[n]->yspeed = 5;
        balls[n]->curframe = rand() % 32;
        balls[n]->maxframe = 31;
```

```
        balls[n]->framecount = 0;
        balls[n]->framedelay = 0;
        balls[n]->animdir = 1;
    }
}
```

Now you come to the first thread callback function, thread0. I should point out that you can use a single callback function for all of your threads if you want. You can identify the thread by the parameter passed to it, which is retrieved into my_thread_id in the function listing that follows. You will want to pay particular attention to the calls to pthread_mutex_lock and pthread_mutex_unlock to see how they work. Note that these functions are called in pairs above and below the main piece of code inside the loop. Note also that pthread_exit is called after the loop. You should always provide a way to exit the loop, so this function can be called before the program ends. More than likely, all threads will terminate with the main process, but it is good programming practice to free memory before exiting.

```
//this thread updates sprite 0
void* thread0(void* data)
{
    //get this thread id
    int my_thread_id = *((int*)data);

    //thread's main loop
    while(!done)
    {
        //lock the mutex to protect variables
        if (pthread_mutex_lock(&threadsafe))
            textout(buffer,font,"ERROR: thread mutex was locked",
                0,0,WHITE);

        //erase sprite 0
        erasesprite(buffer, balls[0]);

        //update sprite 0
        updatesprite(balls[0]);

        //bounce sprite 0
        bouncesprite(balls[0]);

        //draw sprite 0
        draw_sprite(buffer, ballimg[balls[0]->curframe],
            balls[0]->x, balls[0]->y);
```

```
        //print sprite number
        textout(buffer, font, "0", balls[0]->x, balls[0]->y,WHITE);

        //display sprite position
        textprintf(buffer,font,0,10,WHITE,
            "THREAD ID %d, SPRITE (%3d,%3d)",
            my_thread_id, balls[0]->x, balls[0]->y);

        //unlock the mutex
        if (pthread_mutex_unlock(&threadsafe))
            textout(buffer,font,"ERROR: thread mutex unlock error",
                0,0,WHITE);

        //slow down (this thread only!)
     rest(10);
    }

    // terminate the thread
    pthread_exit(NULL);

    return NULL;
}
```

The second thread callback function, thread1, is functionally equivalent to the previous thread function. In fact, these two functions could have been combined and could have used my_thread_id to determine which sprite to update. This is something you should keep in mind if you want to add more sprites to the program to see what it can do. I separated the functions in this way to better illustrate what is happening. Just remember that many threads can share a single callback function, and that function is executed inside each thread separately.

```
//this thread updates sprite 1
void* thread1(void* data)
{
    //get this thread id
    int my_thread_id = *((int*)data);

    //thread's main loop
    while(!done)
    {
        //lock the mutex to protect variables
        if (pthread_mutex_lock(&threadsafe))
            textout(buffer,font,"ERROR: thread mutex was locked",
                0,0,WHITE);
```

```
            //erase sprite 1
            erasesprite(buffer, balls[1]);

            //update sprite 1
            updatesprite(balls[1]);

            //bounce sprite 1
            bouncesprite(balls[1]);

            //draw sprite 1
            draw_sprite(buffer, ballimg[balls[1]->curframe],
                balls[1]->x, balls[1]->y);

            //print sprite number
            textout(buffer, font, "1", balls[1]->x, balls[1]->y,WHITE);

            //display sprite position
            textprintf(buffer,font,0,20,WHITE,
                "THREAD ID %d, SPRITE (%3d,%3d)",
                my_thread_id, balls[1]->x, balls[1]->y);

            //unlock the mutex
            if (pthread_mutex_unlock(&threadsafe))
                textout(buffer,font,"ERROR: thread mutex unlock error",
                    0,0,WHITE);

            //slow down (this thread only!)
        rest(20);
        }


    // terminate the thread
    pthread_exit(NULL);

    return NULL;
}
```

The final section of code for the *MultiThread* program contains the main function of the program, which creates the threads and processes the main loop to update the screen. Note that I have used the mutex in the main loop as well, just to be safe. You wouldn't want the double-buffer to get hit by multiple threads at the same time, which is what would happen without the mutex being called. Of course, that doesn't stop the main loop from impacting the buffer while a thread is using it. That is a situation you would want to take into account in a real game.

```c
//program's primary thread
void main(void)
{
    int id;
    pthread_t pthread0;
    pthread_t pthread1;
    int threadid0 = 0;
    int threadid1 = 1;

    //initialize
    allegro_init();
    set_color_depth(16);
    set_gfx_mode(MODE, WIDTH, HEIGHT, 0, 0);
    srand(time(NULL));
    install_keyboard();
    install_timer();

    //create double buffer
    buffer = create_bitmap(SCREEN_W,SCREEN_H);

    //load ball sprite
    loadsprites();

    //create the thread for sprite 0
    id = pthread_create(&pthread0, NULL, thread0, (void*)&threadid0);

    //create the thread for sprite 1
    id = pthread_create(&pthread1, NULL, thread1, (void*)&threadid1);

    //main loop
    while (!key[KEY_ESC])
    {
        //lock the mutex to protect double buffer
        pthread_mutex_lock(&threadsafe);

        //display title
        textout(buffer, font, "MultiThread Program (ESC to quit)",
            0, 0, WHITE);

        //update the screen
        acquire_screen();
        blit(buffer,screen,0,0,0,0,SCREEN_W-1,SCREEN_H-1);
        release_screen();
```

```
        //unlock the mutex
        pthread_mutex_unlock(&threadsafe);

        //note there is no delay
    }

    //tell threads it's time to quit
    done++;
    rest(100);

    //kill the mutex (thread protection)
    pthread_mutex_destroy(&threadsafe);

    //remove objects from memory
    destroy_bitmap(buffer);

    //delete sprites
    for (n=0; n<32; n++)
        destroy_bitmap(ballimg[n]);

    return;
}


END_OF_MAIN();
```

Enhancing Tank War

The current version of *Tank War* (from Chapter 10) includes two scrolling windows (one for each player), a radar screen, tank sprites, bullet sprites, and scorekeeping. The game needs a few more things to make it complete. First of all, it needs better timing, particularly for explosions (which momentarily pause the game), and it could use a little more animation. In Chapter 15, "Mastering the Audible Realm: Allegro's Sound Support," you'll add sound support to the game.

For the time being, you can work on adding some better animation, as well as on that terrible explosion code that pauses the game. I'd like the explosions to be drawn on the screen without affecting the timing of the game. As for the new animation, I'd like the tank treads to move with respect to the speed that the tank is moving. So let's work on the sixth enhancement to the game now!

Description of New Improvements

To draw animated treads, I have modified the tank1.bmp and tank2.bmp files, adding seven additional frames to each tank from Ari Feldman's SpriteLib (from which the tanks were originally derived). Figure 11.6 shows the updated tank bitmaps.

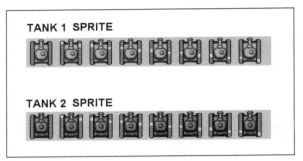

To plug these new animated tanks into the game, you'll need to make some modifications to the routines that load, move, and draw the tanks, and you'll need to add a new function to animate the tanks. Figure 11.7 shows the game running with the animated tanks.

Figure 11.6 *Tank War* now features animated tanks.

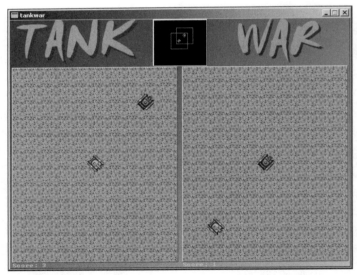

Figure 11.7 The tanks are now equipped with new military technology—animated treads.

The next enhancement to *Tank War* that I'll show you is an update to the explode function and addition of some new explosion sprites to handle the explosions so the game won't pause to render them. Figure 11.8 shows an explosion drawn over one of the tanks without pausing gameplay. Now both explosions can occur at the same time (instead of one after the other).

Figure 11.8 *Tank War* now draws animated explosions in the game loop without pausing the game.

Modifying the Tank War Project

The complete new version of *Tank War* is available in \chapter11\tankwar on the CD-ROM; you can load up the project or simply run the game from that location if you want. I recommend you follow along and make the changes yourself because it is a valuable learning experience. To do so, you'll want to open the *Tank War* project from Chapter 10 to make the following changes. Be sure to copy the tank1.bmp and tank2.bmp files off the CD-ROM so the new version of the game will work, because these bitmap files contain the new animated tanks.

Updating tankwar.h

First, you need to make a few minor changes to the tankwar.h header file. Look for the section of code that defines the sprites and add the new line of code shown in bold.

```
SPRITE mytanks[2];
SPRITE *tanks[2];
SPRITE mybullets[2];
SPRITE *bullets[2];
SPRITE *explosions[2];
```

Next, modify the tank_bmp array, which contains the bitmap images for the tanks. Scroll down in tankwar.h a little further to find the sprite bitmap definitions and make the change noted in bold. (It's a small change to the tank_bmp array—just add another dimension to the array as shown.)

```
//sprite bitmaps
BITMAP *tank_bmp[2][8][8];
BITMAP *bullet_bmp;
BITMAP *explode_bmp;
```

Now scroll down a little further in tankwar.h to the function prototypes and add the following three function definitions noted in bold:

```
//function prototypes
void animatetank(int num);
void updateexplosion(int num);
void loadsprites();
void drawtank(int num);
void erasetank(int num);
void movetank(int num);
```

Updating tank.c

Now you can make some changes to the tank.c source code file, which contains all the code for loading, moving, and drawing the tanks. Add a new function to the top of tank.c to accommodate the new animated tanks.

```
//new function added in chapter 11
void animatetank(int num)
{
    if (++tanks[num]->framecount > tanks[num]->framedelay)
    {
        tanks[num]->framecount = 0;
        tanks[num]->curframe += tanks[num]->animdir;
        if (tanks[num]->curframe > tanks[num]->maxframe)
            tanks[num]->curframe = 0;
        else if (tanks[num]->curframe < 0)
            tanks[num]->curframe = tanks[num]->maxframe;
    }
}
```

Now you have to make some changes to drawtank, the most important function in tank.c, because it is responsible for actually drawing the tanks. You need to add support for the new animated frames in the tank_bmp array. Make the changes noted in bold. (You'll notice that the only changes are made to draw_sprite function calls.)

```
void drawtank(int num)
{
    int dir = tanks[num]->dir;
    int x = tanks[num]->x-15;
    int y = tanks[num]->y-15;
```

```
draw_sprite(buffer, tank_bmp[num][tanks[num]->curframe][dir], x, y);

//what about the enemy tank?
x = scrollx[!num] + SCROLLW/2;
y = scrolly[!num] + SCROLLH/2;
if (inside(x, y,
    scrollx[num], scrolly[num],
    scrollx[num] + SCROLLW, scrolly[num] + SCROLLH))
{
    //draw enemy tank, adjust for scroll
    draw_sprite(buffer, tank_bmp[!num][tanks[!num]->curframe][tanks[!num]->dir],
        startx[num]+x-scrollx[num]-15, starty[num]+y-scrolly[num]-15);

}
}
```

Next, you need to make some changes to the movetank function to accommodate the new animated tanks. The way this works now is that the tank is animated only when it is moving. You need to determine when the tank is moving by looking at the speed of the tank, and then update the sprite frame accordingly. You also need to make some changes to the code that keeps the tanks inside the bounds of the map so that when a tank reaches the edge, it will stop animating. Make the changes noted in bold.

```
void movetank(int num)
{
    int dir = tanks[num]->dir;
    int speed = tanks[num]->xspeed;

    //animate tank when moving
    if (speed > 0)
    {
        tanks[num]->animdir = 1;
        tanks[num]->framedelay = MAXSPEED - speed;
    }
    else if (speed < 0)
    {
        tanks[num]->animdir = -1;
        tanks[num]->framedelay = MAXSPEED - abs(speed);
    }
    else
        tanks[num]->animdir = 0;

    //update tank position
    switch(dir)
```

```
    {
        case 0:
            scrolly[num] -= speed;
            break;
        case 1:
            scrolly[num] -= speed;
            scrollx[num] += speed;
            break;
        case 2:
            scrollx[num] += speed;
            break;
        case 3:
            scrollx[num] += speed;
            scrolly[num] += speed;
            break;
        case 4:
            scrolly[num] += speed;
            break;
        case 5:
            scrolly[num] += speed;
            scrollx[num] -= speed;
            break;
        case 6:
            scrollx[num] -= speed;
            break;
        case 7:
            scrollx[num] -= speed;
            scrolly[num] -= speed;
            break;
    }

    //keep tank inside bounds
    if (scrollx[num] < 0)
    {
        scrollx[num] = 0;
        tanks[num]->xspeed = 0;
    }
    else if (scrollx[num] > scroll->w - SCROLLW)
    {
        scrollx[num] = scroll->w - SCROLLW;
        tanks[num]->xspeed = 0;
    }
    if (scrolly[num] < 0)
```

```
    {
        scrolly[num] = 0;
        tanks[num]->xspeed = 0;
    }
    else if (scrolly[num] > scroll->h - SCROLLH)
    {
        scrolly[num] = scroll->h - SCROLLH;
        tanks[num]->xspeed = 0;
    }
}
```

That is the last change to tank.c. Now you can move on to the setup.c file.

Updating setup.c

You must make extensive changes to setup.c to load the new animation frames for the tanks and initialize the new explosion sprites. You'll end up with a new loadsprites function and a lot of changes to setuptanks. First, add the new loadsprites function to the top of the setup.c file. I won't use bold because you need to add the whole function to the program.

```
void loadsprites()
{
    //load explosion image
    if (explode_bmp == NULL)
    {
        explode_bmp = load_bitmap("explode.bmp", NULL);
    }

    //initialize explosion sprites
    explosions[0] = malloc(sizeof(SPRITE));
    explosions[1] = malloc(sizeof(SPRITE));
}
```

Next up, the changes to setuptanks. There are a lot of changes to be made in this function to load the new tank1.bmp and tank2.bmp files, and then extract the individual animation frames. Make all changes noted in bold.

```
void setuptanks()
{
    BITMAP *temp;
    int anim;
    int n;

    //configure player 1's tank
    tanks[0] = &mytanks[0];
```

```
    tanks[0]->x = 30;
    tanks[0]->y = 40;
    tanks[0]->xspeed = 0;
    tanks[0]->dir = 3;
    tanks[0]->curframe = 0;
    tanks[0]->maxframe = 7;
    tanks[0]->framecount = 0;
    tanks[0]->framedelay = 10;
    tanks[0]->animdir = 0;
    scores[0] = 0;

    //load first tank
    temp = load_bitmap("tank1.bmp", NULL);
    for (anim=0; anim<8; anim++)
    {
        //grab animation frame
        tank_bmp[0][anim][0] = grabframe(temp, 32, 32, 0, 0, 8, anim);

        //rotate image to generate all 8 directions
        for (n=1; n<8; n++)
        {
            tank_bmp[0][anim][n] = create_bitmap(32, 32);
            clear_to_color(tank_bmp[0][anim][n], makecol(255,0,255));
            rotate_sprite(tank_bmp[0][anim][n], tank_bmp[0][anim][0],
                0, 0, itofix(n*32));
        }
    }
    destroy_bitmap(temp);

    //configure player 2's tank
    tanks[1] = &mytanks[1];
    tanks[1]->x = SCREEN_W-30;
    tanks[1]->y = SCREEN_H-30;
    tanks[1]->xspeed = 0;
    tanks[1]->dir = 7;
    tanks[1]->curframe = 0;
    tanks[1]->maxframe = 7;
    tanks[1]->framecount = 0;
    tanks[1]->framedelay = 10;
    tanks[1]->animdir = 0;
    scores[1] = 0;
```

```
//load second tank
temp = load_bitmap("tank2.bmp", NULL);
for (anim=0; anim<8; anim++)
{
    //grab animation frame
    tank_bmp[1][anim][0] = grabframe(temp, 32, 32, 0, 0, 8, anim);

    //rotate image to generate all 8 directions
    for (n=1; n<8; n++)
    {
        tank_bmp[1][anim][n] = create_bitmap(32, 32);
        clear_to_color(tank_bmp[1][anim][n], makecol(255,0,255));
        rotate_sprite(tank_bmp[1][anim][n], tank_bmp[1][anim][0],
            0, 0, itofix(n*32));
    }
}
destroy_bitmap(temp);

//load bullet image
if (bullet_bmp == NULL)
    bullet_bmp = load_bitmap("bullet.bmp", NULL);

//initialize bullets
for (n=0; n<2; n++)
{
    bullets[n] = &mybullets[n];
    bullets[n]->x = 0;
    bullets[n]->y = 0;
    bullets[n]->width = bullet_bmp->w;
    bullets[n]->height = bullet_bmp->h;
}

//center tanks inside scroll windows
tanks[0]->x = 5 + SCROLLW/2;
tanks[0]->y = 90 + SCROLLH/2;
tanks[1]->x = 325 + SCROLLW/2;
tanks[1]->y = 90 + SCROLLH/2;
}
```

That wasn't so bad because the game was designed well and the new code added in Chapter 10 was highly modifiable. It always pays to write clean, tight code right from the start.

Updating bullet.c

Now you can make the necessary changes to the bullet.c source file to accommodate the new friendly explosions. (How's that for a contradiction of terms?) What I mean by *friendly* is that the explosions will no longer use the rest function to draw. This is really bad because it causes the whole game to hiccup every time there is an explosion to be drawn. There weren't many bullets flying around in this game, or I never would have gotten away with this quick solution. Now let's correct the problem.

Open the bullet.c file. You'll be adding a new function called updateexplosion and modifying the existing explode function. Here is the new updateexplosion you should add to the top of the bullet.c file.

```c
//new function added in chapter 11
void updateexplosion(int num)
{
    int x, y;

    if (!explosions[num]->alive) return;

    //draw explosion (maxframe) times
    if (explosions[num]->curframe++ < explosions[num]->maxframe)
    {
        x = explosions[num]->x;
        y = explosions[num]->y;

        //draw explosion in enemy window
        rotate_sprite(buffer, explode_bmp,
            x + rand()%10 - 20, y + rand()%10 - 20,
            itofix(rand()%255));

        //draw explosion in "my" window if enemy is visible
        x = scrollx[!num] + SCROLLW/2;
        y = scrolly[!num] + SCROLLH/2;
        if (inside(x, y,
            scrollx[num], scrolly[num],
            scrollx[num] + SCROLLW, scrolly[num] + SCROLLH))
        {
            //but only draw if explosion is active
            if (explosions[num]->alive)
                rotate_sprite(buffer, explode_bmp,
                    startx[num]+x-scrollx[num] + rand()%10 - 20,
                    starty[num]+y-scrolly[num] + rand()%10 - 20,
                    itofix(rand()%255));
```

```
        }
    }
    else
    {
        explosions[num]->alive = 0;
        explosions[num]->curframe = 0;
    }
}
```

Now modify `explode` so it will properly set up the explosion, which is actually drawn by `updateexplosion` later on in the animation process of the game loop. Make the changes noted in bold. The entire function has been rewritten, so simply delete existing code and add the new lines to `explode`.

```
void explode(int num, int x, int y)
{
    //initialize the explosion sprite
    explosions[num]->alive = 1;
    explosions[num]->x = x;
    explosions[num]->y = y;
    explosions[num]->curframe = 0;
    explosions[num]->maxframe = 20;
}
```

That's the end of the changes to bullet.c. Now you can make the last few changes needed to update the game. Next you'll turn to the main.c file.

Updating main.c

The last changes will be made to main.c to call the new functions (such as `animatetank` and `updateexplosion`). The only changes to be made will be to the `main` function. You need to add a line that creates a new variable and calls `loadsprites` and `animatetank`, and finally, you need a call to `updateexplosion`. Be careful to catch the changes to `tank_bmp` and note the cleanup code at the end. Make the changes noted in bold.

```
//main function
void main(void)
{
    int anim;

    //initialize the game
    allegro_init();
    install_keyboard();
    install_timer();
    srand(time(NULL));
```

```
setupscreen();
setuptanks();
loadsprites();

//game loop
while(!gameover)
{
    //move the tanks and bullets
    for (n=0; n<2; n++)
    {
        movetank(n);
        animatetank(n);
        movebullet(n);
    }

    //draw background bitmap
    blit(back, buffer, 0, 0, 0, 0, back->w, back->h);

    //draw scrolling windows
    for (n=0; n<2; n++)
        blit(scroll, buffer, scrollx[n], scrolly[n],
            startx[n], starty[n], SCROLLW, SCROLLH);

    //update the radar
    rectfill(buffer,radarx+1,radary+1,radarx+99,radary+88,BLACK);
    rect(buffer,radarx,radary,radarx+100,radary+89,WHITE);

    //draw mini tanks on radar
    for (n=0; n<2; n++)
        stretch_sprite(buffer, tank_bmp[n][tanks[n]->curframe][tanks[n]->dir],
            radarx + scrollx[n]/10 + (SCROLLW/10)/2-4,
            radary + scrolly[n]/12 + (SCROLLH/12)/2-4,
            8, 8);

    //draw player viewport on radar
    for (n=0; n<2; n++)
        rect(buffer,radarx+scrollx[n]/10, radary+scrolly[n]/12,
            radarx+scrollx[n]/10+SCROLLW/10,
            radary+scrolly[n]/12+SCROLLH/12, GRAY);

    //display score
    for (n=0; n<2; n++)
```

```
            textprintf(buffer, font, startx[n], HEIGHT-10,
                BURST, "Score: %d", scores[n]);

        //draw the tanks and bullets
        for (n=0; n<2; n++)
        {
            drawtank(n);
            drawbullet(n);
        }

        //explosions come last (so they draw over tanks)
        for (n=0; n<2; n++)
            updateexplosion(n);

        //refresh the screen
        acquire_screen();
        blit(buffer, screen, 0, 0, 0, 0, WIDTH-1, HEIGHT-1);
        release_screen();

        //check for keypresses
        if (keypressed())
            getinput();

        //slow the game down
        rest(20);
    }

    //destroy bitmaps
    destroy_bitmap(explode_bmp);
    destroy_bitmap(back);
    destroy_bitmap(scroll);
    destroy_bitmap(buffer);

    //free tank bitmaps
    for (anim=0; anim<8; anim++)
        for (n=0; n<8; n++)
        {
            destroy_bitmap(tank_bmp[0][anim][n]);
            destroy_bitmap(tank_bmp[1][anim][n]);
        }
```

```
    //free explosion sprites
    for (n=0; n<2; n++)
        free(explosions[n]);

    return;
}
END_OF_MAIN();
```

Future Changes to Tank War

I must admit that this game is really starting to become fun, not only as a very playable game, but also as an Allegro game project. It is true that if you design and program a game that *you* find interesting and fun, others will be attracted to the game as well. I did just that, and I have enjoyed sharing the vision of this game with you. What do you think of the result so far? It needs a little bit more work (such as sound effects), but otherwise it is very playable. If you have any great ideas to make the game even better, by all means, go ahead and try them!

You can use this example game as a basis for your own games. Are you interested in RPGs? Go ahead and convert it to a single scrolling window and replace the tank with your own character sprite, and you almost have an RPG framework right there. As for future changes, the next chapter adds customizable levels to the game with a level-editing program called Mappy.

Summary

This was an advanced chapter that dealt with the intriguing subjects of timers, interrupts, and threads. I started with a *TimerTest* program that animated several sprites on the screen to demonstrate how to calculate and display the frame rate. You then modified the program to use an interrupt handler to keep track of the frame rate outside of the main loop (*InterruptTest*). This was followed by another revision that demonstrated how to set a specific frame rate for the program (*TimedLoop*). The last section of the chapter was devoted to multi-threading, with a tutorial on the Posix Threads library and Red Hat's Pthreads-Win32 project. The result was an interesting program called *MultiThread* that demonstrated how to use threads for sprite control. The potential for increased frame-rate performance in a game is greatly encouraged with the use of threads to delegate functionality from a single loop because this provides support for multiple-processor systems.

Chapter Quiz

You can find the answers to this chapter quiz in Appendix A, "Chapter Quiz Answers."

1. Why is it important to use a timer in a game?

   A.   To maintain a consistent frame rate

   B.   To include support for interrupts

   C.   To make the program thread-safe

   D.   To delegate code to multiple threads

2. Which Allegro timer function slows down the program using a callback function?

   A.   `callback_rest`

   B.   `sleep_callback`

   C.   `rest`

   D.   `rest_callback`

3. What is the name of the function used to initialize the Allegro timer?

   A.   `init_timer`

   B.   `install_timer`

   C.   `timer_reset`

   D.   `start_timer`

4. What is the name of the function that creates a new interrupt handler?

   A.   `create_handler`

   B.   `create_interrupt`

   C.   `int_callback`

   D.   `install_int`

5. What variable declaration keyword should be used with interrupt variables?

   A.   `danger`

   B.   `cautious`

   C.   `volatile`

   D.   `corruptible`

6. What is a process that runs within the memory space of a single program but is executed separately from that program?

   A.   Mutex

   B.   Process

   C.   Thread

   D.   Interrupt

7. What helps protect data by locking it inside a single thread, preventing that data from being used by another thread until it is unlocked?

   A. Mutex

   B. Process

   C. Thread

   D. Interrupt

8. What does pthread stand for?

   A. Protected Thread

   B. Public Thread

   C. Posix Thread

   D. Purple Thread

9. What is the name of the function used to create a new thread?

   A. `create_posix_thread`

   B. `pthread_create`

   C. `install_thread`

   D. `thread_callback`

10. What is the name of the function that locks a mutex?

    A. `lock_pthread_mutex`

    B. `lock_mutex`

    C. `pthread_lock_mutex`

    D. `pthread_mutex_lock`

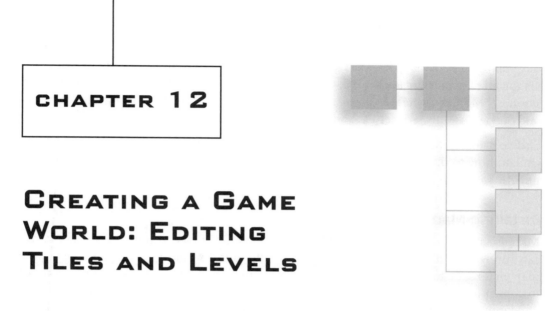

CHAPTER 12

CREATING A GAME WORLD: EDITING TILES AND LEVELS

The game world defines the rules of the game and presents the player with all of the obstacles he must overcome to complete the game. Although the game world is the most important aspect of a game, it is not always given proper attention when a game is being designed. This chapter provides an introduction to world building—or more specifically, map editing. Using the skills you learn in this chapter, you will be able to enhance *Tank War* and learn to create levels for your own games. This chapter provides the prerequisite information you'll need in the next two chapters, which discuss horizontal and vertical scrolling games.

Here is a breakdown of the major topics in this chapter:

- Creating the game world
- Loading and drawing Mappy level files

Creating the Game World

Mappy is an awesome map editing program, and it's freeware so you can download and use it to create maps for your games at no cost. If you find Mappy to be as useful as I have, I encourage you to send the author a small donation to express your appreciation for his hard work. The home page for Mappy is http://www.tilemap.co.uk.

Why is Mappy so great, you might ask? First of all, it's easy to use. In fact, it couldn't be any easier to use without sacrificing features. Mappy allows you to edit maps made up of the standard rectangular tiles, as well as isometric and hexagonal tiles! Have you ever played hexagonal games, such as *Panzer General*, or isometric games, such as *Age of Empires*? Mappy lets you create levels that are similar to the ones used in these games. Mappy has been used to create many retail (commercial) games, some of which you might have played. I personally know of several developers who have used Mappy to create levels for retail games for Pocket PC, Game Boy Advance, Nokia N-Gage, and wireless (cell phones). MonkeyStone's *Hyperspace Delivery Boy* (created by Tom Hall, John Romero, and Stevie Case) for Pocket PC and Game Boy Advance is one example.

Suffice it to say, Mappy is an unusually great map editor released as freeware, and I will explain how to use it in this chapter. You'll also have an opportunity to add Mappy support to *Tank War* at the end of the chapter.

Installing Mappy

Mappy is included in the \mappy folder on the CD-ROM that accompanies this book. You can run Mappy directly without installing it, although I would recommend copying the mapwin.exe file to your hard drive. Mappy is so small (514 KB) that it's not unreasonable to copy it to any folder where you might need it. If you want to check for a newer version of Mappy, the home page is located at http://www.tilemap.co.uk. In addition to Mappy, there are sample games available for download and the Allegro support sources for Mappy. (See the "Loading and Drawing Mappy Level Files" section later in this chapter for more information.) If you do copy the executable without the subfolders, INI file, and so on, you'll miss out on the Lua scripts and settings, so you might want to copy the whole folder containing the executable file.

Creating a New Map

Now it's time to fire up Mappy and create a new map. Locate mapwin.exe and run it. The first time it is run, Mappy displays two blank child windows (see Figure 12.1).

Now open the File menu and select New Map to bring up the New Map dialog box, shown in Figure 12.2.

As the New Map dialog box shows, you must enter the size of each tile in your tile image file. The tiles used in *Tank War* (and in most of the chapters of this book) are 32×32 pixels, so I have typed 32 in the width box and 32 in the height box. Next you must enter the size of the map. The default 100×100 map probably is too large to be useful as a good example at this point. If you recall from Chapter 10, the *GameWorld* program used a map that had an area of 31×33 tiles. You should use that program as a basis for testing Mappy. Of course, you can use any values you want, but be sure to modify the source code (in the next section) to accommodate the dimensions of the map you have created.

tip

Mappy allows you to change the size of the map after it has been created, so if you need more tiles in your map later, it's easy to enlarge the map. Likewise, you can shrink the map; Mappy has an option that lets you choose the part of the map you want to resize.

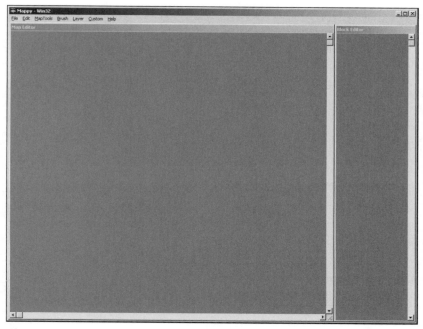

Figure 12.1 Mappy is a simple and unassuming map editor.

Figure 12.3 shows the dimensions that I have chosen for this new map. Note also the option for color depth. This refers to the source image containing the tiles; in most cases you will want to choose the Truecolour option because most source artwork will be 16-bit, 24-bit, or 32-bit. (Any of these will work with Mappy if you select this option.)

If you click on the Advanced button in the New Map dialog box, you'll see the additional options shown in Figure 12.4. These additional options allow you to select the exact color depth of the source tiles (8-bit through 32-bit), the map file version to use, and dimensions for non-rectangular map tiles (such as hexagonal and isometric).

Mappy: New map (easy)

Make a new standard rectangular tilemap (FMP0.5)

See the helpfile for details (cancel this, then press F1)

Each tile is [32] pixels wide and [32] pixels high

I want my map to be [100] tiles wide and [100] tiles high

Colours (if unsure use truecolour)   ⊙ Truecolour   ○ Paletted (8bit)

[Advanced]   [OK]   [Cancel]

Figure 12.2 You can use the New Map dialog box to configure a new game level.

Mappy: New map (easy)

Make a new standard rectangular tilemap (FMP0.5)

See the helpfile for details (cancel this, then press F1)

Each tile is [32] pixels wide and [32] pixels high

I want my map to be [31] tiles wide and [33] tiles high

Colours (if unsure use truecolour)   ⊙ Truecolour   ○ Paletted (8bit)

[Advanced]   [OK]   [Cancel]

Figure 12.3 Changing the size of the new map

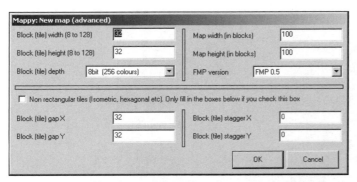

Figure 12.4 The advanced options in the New Map dialog box

When you click on the OK button, a new map will be created and filled with the default black tile (tile #0). At this point, you must import the tile images to be used to create this map. This is where things really get interesting because you can use multiple image files containing source artwork, and Mappy will combine all the source tiles into a new image source with correctly positioned tiles. (Saving the tile bitmap file is an option in the Save As dialog box.)

Importing the Source Tiles

Now open the File menu and select Import. The Open File dialog box will appear, allowing you to browse for an image file, which can be of type BMP, PCX, PNG, or MAR/P (map array file—something that can be exported by Mappy). I have created a larger tile image file containing numerous tiles from Ari Feldman's SpriteLib (http://www.arifeldman.com). The maptiles.bmp file is located in the \chapter12\ArrayMapTest folder on the CD-ROM. After you choose this file, Mappy will import the tiles into the tile palette, as shown in Figure 12.5. Recall that you specified the tile size when you created the map file; Mappy used the dimensions provided to automatically read in all of the tiles. You must make the image resolution reasonably close to the edges of the tiles, but it doesn't need to be perfect —Mappy is smart enough to account for a few pixels off the right or bottom edges and move to the next row.

Now I'd like to show you a convenient feature that I use often. I like to see most of the level on the screen at once to get an overview of the game level. Mappy lets you change the zoom level of the map editor display. Open the MapTools menu and select one of the zoom levels to change the zoom. Then, select a tile from the tile palette and use the mouse to draw that tile on the map edit window to see how the chosen zoom level appears. I frequently use 0.5 (1/2 zoom). Until you have added some tiles to the map window, you won't see anything happen after you change the zoom.

Now let me show you a quick shortcut for filling the entire map with a certain tile. Select a neutral tile that is good as a backdrop, such as the grass, dirt, or stone tile. Open the Custom menu. This menu contains scripts that you can run to manipulate a map. (You can write your own scripts if you learn the Lua language—visit http://www.lua.org for more information.) Select the script called Solid Rectangle, which brings up the dialog box shown in Figure 12.6.

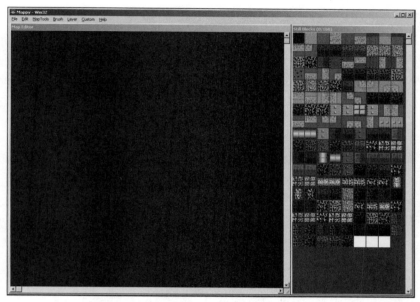

Figure 12.5 The SpriteLib tiles have been imported into Mappy's tile palette for use in creating game levels.

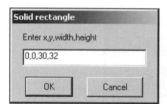

Figure 12.6 Mappy includes scripts that can manipulate a map, and you can create new scripts.

Modify the width and height parameters for the rectangle, using one less than the value you entered for the map when it was created (31–1 = 30 and 33–1 = 32). Click on OK, and the map will be filled with the currently selected tile, as shown in Figure 12.7.

Play around with Mappy to gain familiarity with it. You can erase tiles using the right mouse button and select tiles in the palette using the left button. You can use the keyboard arrow keys to scroll the map in any direction, which is very handy when you want to keep your other hand on the mouse for quick editing. Try to create an interesting map, and then I'll show you how to save the map in two different formats you'll use in the sample programs that follow.

Saving the Map File as FMP

Have you created an interesting map that can be saved? If not, go ahead and create a map, even if it's just a hodgepodge of tiles, because I want to show you how to save and use the map file in an Allegro program. Are you ready yet? Good! As a reference for the figures that follow in this chapter, the map I created is shown in Figure 12.8.

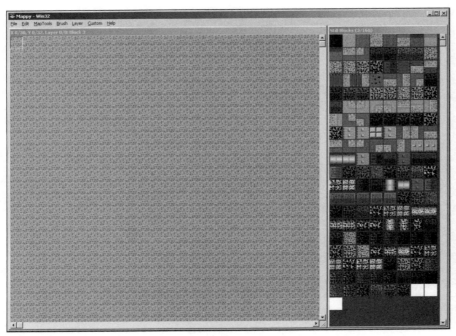

Figure 12.7 The Solid Rectangle script fills a region of the map with a tile.

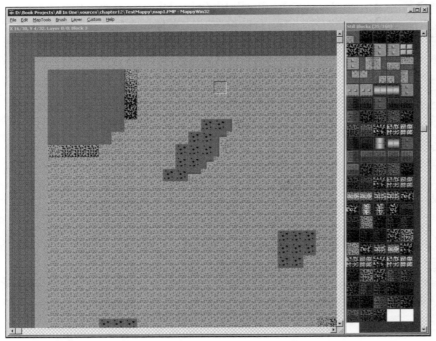

Figure 12.8 The sample map file used in this chapter

I'll show you how to save the map file first, and then you'll export the map to a text file and try to use it in sample programs later. For now, open the File menu and select Save As to bring up the Save As dialog box shown in Figure 12.9.

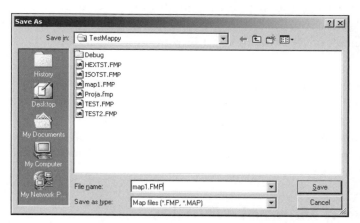

Figure 12.9 The Save As dialog box in Mappy is used to save a map file.

Type a map filename, such as map1.fmp, and click on Save. The interesting thing about the FMP file format is that the tile images are stored along with the map data, so you don't need to load the tiles *and* the map file to create your game world. You might not like losing control over the tile images, but in a way it's a blessing—one less thing to worry about when you'd rather focus your time on gameplay.

Saving the Map File as Text

Now that you have saved the new level in the standard Mappy file format, I'd like to show you how to export the map to a simple text file that you can paste into a program. The result will be similar to the *GameWorld* program from Chapter 10, in which the map tile data was stored in an array in the program's source code.

Open the File menu and select Export. Do *not* select Export As Text. That is an entirely different option used to export a map to a binary array used for the Game Boy Advance and other systems. Just select Export to bring up the Export dialog box shown in Figure 12.10.

You can explore the uses for the various formats in the Export dialog box when you have an opportunity; I will only explain the one option you need to export the map data as text. You want to select the third check box from the top, labeled Map Array as Comma Values Only (?.CSV).

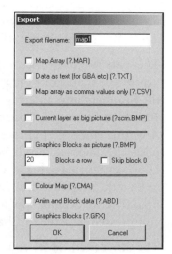

Figure 12.10 The Export dialog in Mappy lets you choose options for exporting the map.

If you want to build an image containing the tiles in the proper order, as they were in Mappy, you can also select the check box labeled Graphics Blocks as Picture (?.BMP). I strongly recommend exporting the image. For one thing, Mappy adds the blank tile that you might have used in some parts of the map; it also numbers the tiles consecutively starting with this blank tile unless you check the option Skip Block 0. Normally, you should be able to leave the default of 20 in the Blocks a Row input field. Click on OK to export the map.

Mappy outputs the map with the name provided in the Export dialog box as two files—map1.BMP and map1.CSV. (Your map name might differ.) The CSV format is recognized by Microsoft Excel, but there is no point loading it into Excel (even if you have Microsoft Office installed). Instead, rename the file map1.txt and open it in Notepad or another text editor. You can now copy the map data text and paste it into a source code file, and you have the bitmap image handy as well.

Loading and Drawing Mappy Level Files

Mappy is far more powerful than you need for *Tank War* (or the rest of this book, for that matter). Mappy supports eight-layer maps with animated tiles and has many helpful features for creating game worlds. You can create a map, for instance, with a background layer, a parallax scrolling layer with transparent tiles, and a surface layer that is drawn over sprites (such as bridges and tunnels). I'm sure you will become proficient with Mappy in a very short time after you use it to create a few games, and you will find some of these features useful in your own games. For the purposes of this chapter and the needs of your *Tank War* game, Mappy will be used to create a single-layer map.

There are two basic methods of using map files in your own games. The first method is to export the map from Mappy as a text file. You can then paste the comma-separated map tile numbers into an array in your game. (Recall the *GameWorld* program from Chapter 10, which used a hard-coded map array.) There are drawbacks to this method, of course. Any time you need to make changes to a map file, you'll need to export the map again and paste the lines of numbers into the map array definition in your game's source code. However, storing game levels (once completed) inside an array means that you don't need to load the map files into your game—and further, this prevents players from editing your map files. I'll explain how to store game resources (such as map files) inside an encrypted/compressed data file in Chapter 16, "Using Datafiles to Store Game Resources."

The other method, of course, is to load a Mappy level file into your game. This is a more versatile solution, which makes sense if your game has a lot of levels and/or is expandable. (Will players be able to add their own levels to the game and make them available for download, and will you release expansion packs for your game?)

The choice is obvious for large, complex games, such as *StarCraft*, but for smaller games like *Arkanoid*, my personal preference is to store game levels inside the source code. Given the advanced features in Mappy, it is really only practical to export map files if your game is using a single layer with no animation. When your game needs multiple layers and animated tiles, it is better to load the Mappy level file. Why? Because source code is available to load and draw complex Mappy files. (See the "Using a Mappy Level File" section later in this chapter.). Another consideration you should keep in mind is that Mappy files include both the map data *and* the artwork! That's right; the Mappy file includes the tiles as well as the data, so you don't need to load the tiles separately when you're using a Mappy file directly. This is a great feature, particularly when you are dealing with huge, complex game world maps.

Next, I'll demonstrate how to load a map that has been exported to a text file, and then I'll follow that explanation with another sample program that demonstrates how to load a Mappy file directly.

Using a Text Array Map

I want to write a short program to demonstrate how to load a Mappy level that has been exported to a text file. You'll recall from the previous section that you exported a map to a text file with a bitmap file filled with the source tiles that correspond to the values in the text data. I'm going to open the *GameWorld* program from Chapter 10 and modify it to demonstrate the text map data that was exported. Create a new project and add a reference to the Allegro library as usual. Then, type the following code into the main.c file. Figure 12.11 shows the program running.

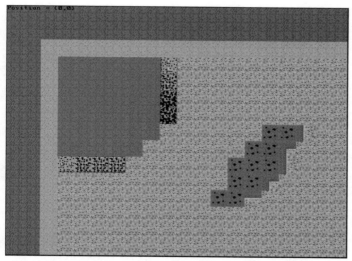

Figure 12.11 The *ArrayMapTest* program demonstrates how to use an exported Mappy level.

If you are using *GameWorld* as a basis, just take note of the differences. On the CD-ROM, this project is called ArrayMapTest, and it is located in the \chapter12\ArrayMapTest folder.

```
#include "allegro.h"

//define some convenient constants
#define MODE GFX_AUTODETECT_FULLSCREEN
#define WIDTH 640
#define HEIGHT 480
#define STEP 8

//very important! double check these values!
#define TILEW 32
#define TILEH 32

//20 columns across is the default for a bitmap
//file exported by Mappy
#define COLS 20

//make sure this exactly describes your map data
#define MAP_ACROSS 31
#define MAP_DOWN 33

#define MAPW MAP_ACROSS * TILEW
#define MAPH MAP_DOWN * TILEH

int map[] = {
    //
    //PASTE MAPPY EXPORTED TEXT DATA HERE!!!
    //
};

//temp bitmap
BITMAP *tiles;

//virtual background buffer
BITMAP *scroll;

//position variables
int x=0, y=0, n;
int tilex, tiley;
```

```
//reuse our friendly tile grabber from chapter 9
BITMAP *grabframe(BITMAP *source,
                  int width, int height,
                  int startx, int starty,
                  int columns, int frame)
{
    BITMAP *temp = create_bitmap(width,height);
    int x = startx + (frame % columns) * width;
    int y = starty + (frame / columns) * height;
    blit(source,temp,x,y,0,0,width,height);
    return temp;
}

//main function
void main(void)
{
    //initialize allegro
    allegro_init();
    install_keyboard();
    install_timer();
    srand(time(NULL));
    set_color_depth(16);

    //set video mode
    if (set_gfx_mode(MODE, WIDTH, HEIGHT, 0, 0) != 0)
    {
        set_gfx_mode(GFX_TEXT, 0, 0, 0, 0);
        allegro_message(allegro_error);
        return;
    }

    //create the virtual background
    scroll = create_bitmap(MAPW, MAPH);
    if (scroll == NULL)
    {
        set_gfx_mode(GFX_TEXT, 0, 0, 0, 0);
        allegro_message("Error creating virtual background");
        return;
    }

    //load the tile bitmap
    //note that it was renamed from chapter 10
```

```
tiles = load_bitmap("maptiles.bmp", NULL);
if (tiles == NULL)
{
    set_gfx_mode(GFX_TEXT, 0, 0, 0, 0);
    allegro_message("Error loading maptiles.bmp file");
    return;
}

//now draw tiles on virtual background
for (tiley=0; tiley < scroll->h; tiley+=TILEH)
{
    for (tilex=0; tilex < scroll->w; tilex+=TILEW)
    {
        //use the result of grabframe directly in blitter
        //change: TILEW-1, TILEH-1 are just TILEW,TILEH now
        blit(grabframe(tiles, TILEW, TILEH, 0, 0, COLS, map[n++]),
            scroll, 0, 0, tilex, tiley, TILEW, TILEH);
    }
}

//main loop
while (!key[KEY_ESC])
{
    //check right arrow
    if (key[KEY_RIGHT])
    {
        x += STEP;
        if (x > scroll->w - WIDTH)
            x = scroll->w - WIDTH;
    }

    //check left arrow
    if (key[KEY_LEFT])
    {
        x -= STEP;
        if (x < 0)
            x = 0;
    }

    //check down arrow
    if (key[KEY_DOWN])
    {
```

```
            y += STEP;
            if (y > scroll->h - HEIGHT)
                y = scroll->h - HEIGHT;
        }


        //check up arrow
        if (key[KEY_UP])
        {
            y -= STEP;
            if (y < 0)
                y = 0;
        }


        //draw the scroll window portion of the virtual buffer
        blit(scroll, screen, x, y, 0, 0, WIDTH-1, HEIGHT-1);

        //display status info
        text_mode(-1);
        textprintf(screen,font,0,0,makecol(0,0,0),
            "Position = (%d,%d)", x, y);

        //slow it down
        rest(20);
    }

    destroy_bitmap(scroll);
    destroy_bitmap(tiles);
    return;
}


END_OF_MAIN();
```

In case you didn't catch the warning (with sirens, red alerts, and beseechings), you must paste your own map data into the source code in the location specified. The map data was exported to a map1.CSV file in the previous section of the chapter, and you should have renamed the file map1.txt to open it in Notepad. Simply copy that data and paste it into the map array.

This is the easiest way to use the maps created by Mappy for your game levels, and I encourage you to gain a working knowledge of this method because it is probably the best option for most games. When you have progressed to the point where you'd like to add some advanced features (such as blocking walls and obstacles on the level), you can move on to loading and drawing Mappy files directly.

Using a Mappy Level File

The Mappy file structure is binary and includes not only the data, but also the tiles. A library has been created to support Mappy within Allegro programs and is available for download on the Mappy Web site at http://www.tilemap.co.uk. The library is called MappyAL, and the current release at the time of this writing is 11D. For distribution and licensing reasons, I have chosen not to include this library on the book's CD-ROM (although the author offers it for free on the Web site). When you download MappyAL (which is currently called mapalr11.zip, but that is likely to change), extract the zip file to find some source code files therein.

All you need are the mappyal.c and mappyal.h files from the zip archive to use Mappy map files in your own programs. Because I will not be going into the advanced features of Mappy or the MappyAL library, I encourage you to browse the Mappy home page, view the tutorials, and download the many source code examples (including many complete games) to learn about the more advanced features of Allegro.

The MappyAL library is very easy to use. Basically, you call MapLoad to open a Mappy file. MapDrawBG is used to draw a background of tiles, and MapDrawFG draws foreground tiles (specified by layer number). There is one drawback to the MappyAL library—it was written quite a long time ago, back in the days when VGA mode 13h (320×200) was popular. Unfortunately, the MappyAL library only renders 8-bit (256 color) maps correctly.

You can convert a true color map to 8-bit color. Simply open the MapTools menu and select Useful Functions, Change Block Size/Depth. This will change the color depth of the map file; you can then import 8-bit tiles and the map will be restored. Paint Shop Pro can easily convert the tiles used in this chapter to 8-bit without too much loss of quality. Ideally, I recommend using the simple text map data due to this drawback.

Now it's time to write a short test program to see how to load a native Mappy file containing map data and tiles, and then display the map on the screen with the ability to scroll the map. Create a new project, add a reference to the Allegro library, and add the mappyal.c and mappyal.h files to the project. (These source code files provide support for Mappy in your Allegro programs.) Then, type the following code into the main.c file. You can use the map1.FMP file you saved earlier in this chapter—or you can use any Mappy file you want to test, because this program can render any Mappy file regardless of dimensions (which are stored inside the map file rather than in the source code). Figure 12.12 shows the *TestMappy* program running.

```
#include <conio.h>
#include <stdlib.h>
#include "allegro.h"
#include "mappyal.h"
```

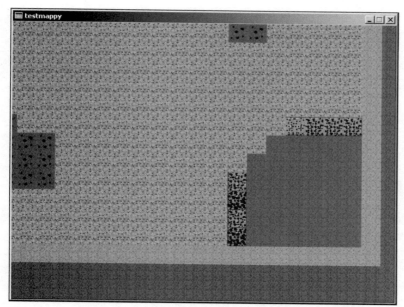

Figure 12.12 The *TestMappy* program demonstrates how to load a native Mappy file.

```
#define MODE GFX_AUTODETECT_FULLSCREEN
#define WIDTH 640
#define HEIGHT 480
#define WHITE makecol(255,255,255)

//x, y offset in pixels
int xoffset = 0;
int yoffset = 0;

//double buffer
BITMAP *buffer;

void main (void)
{
    //initialize program
    allegro_init();
    install_timer();
    install_keyboard();
    set_gfx_mode(MODE, WIDTH, HEIGHT, 0, 0);
    text_mode(-1);
```

```
//create the double buffer and clear it
buffer = create_bitmap(SCREEN_W, SCREEN_H);
if (buffer==NULL)
{
    allegro_message("Error creating double buffer");
    return;
}
clear(buffer);

//load the Mappy file
if (MapLoad("map1.fmp"))
{
    allegro_message ("Can't find map1.fmp");
    return;
}

//set palette
MapSetPal8();

//main loop
while (!key[KEY_ESC])
{
    //draw map with single layer
    MapDrawBG(buffer, xoffset, yoffset, 0, 0, SCREEN_W-1, SCREEN_H-1);

    //blit the double buffer
    blit (buffer, screen, 0, 0, 0, 0, SCREEN_W-1, SCREEN_H-1);

    //check for keyboard input
    if (key[KEY_RIGHT])
    {
        xoffset+=4;
        //make sure it doesn't scroll beyond map edge
        if (xoffset > 31*32) xoffset = 31*32;
    }
    if (key[KEY_LEFT])
    {
        xoffset-=4;
        if (xoffset < 0) xoffset = 0;
    }
    if (key[KEY_UP])
    {
```

```
            yoffset-=4;
            if (yoffset < 0) yoffset = 0;
        }
        if (key[KEY_DOWN])
        {
            yoffset+=4;
            //make sure it doesn't scroll beyond map edge
            if (yoffset > 33*32) yoffset = 33*32;
        }

    }

    //delete double buffer
    destroy_bitmap(buffer);

    //delete the Mappy level
    MapFreeMem();

    allegro_exit();
    return;
}

END_OF_MAIN()
```

Enhancing Tank War

Now it's time for an update to *Tank War*—the seventh revision to the game. Chapter 11 provided some great fixes and new additions to the game, including animated tanks and non-interrupting explosions. As you might have guessed, this chapter brings Mappy support to *Tank War*. It should be a lot of fun, so let's get started! This is going to be an easy modification (only a few lines of code) because *Tank War* was designed from the start to be flexible. However, a lot of code that will be *removed* from *Tank War* because MappyAL takes care of all the scrolling for you.

Do you remember the dimensions of the map1.fmp file that was used in this chapter? They were 100 tiles across by 100 tiles down. However, the actual map only uses 30 tiles across and 32 tiles down. This is a bit of a problem for *Tank War* because MappyAL will render the entire map, not just the visible portion. The reason the map was set to 100×100 was to make the Mappy tutorial easier to explain, and at the time it did not matter. Now you're dealing with a map that is 3,200×3,200 pixels, which won't work in *Tank War*. (Actually, it will run just fine, but the tanks won't be bounded by the edge of the map.)

To remedy this situation, I have created a new version of the map file used in this chapter.

It is called map3.fmp, and it is located in \chapter12\tankwar along with the project files for this new revision of *Tank War*.

What's great about this situation? You can create a gigantic battlefield map for *Tank War*! There's no reason why you should limit the game to a mere 30×32 tiles. Go ahead and create a huge map with lots of different terrain so that it isn't so easy to find the other player. Of course, if you create a truly magnificent level, you'll need to modify the bullet code. It wasn't designed for large maps, so you can't fire again until the bullet reaches the edge of the map. Just put in a timer so the bullet will expire if it doesn't hit anything after a few seconds.

Proposed Changes to Tank War

The first thing to do is add mappyal.c and mappyal.h to the project to give *Tank War* support for the MappyAL library. I could show you how to render the tiles directly in *Tank War*, which is how the game works now, but it's far easier to use the functions in MappyAL to draw the two scrolling game windows. You can open the completed project from \chapter12\tankwar, or open the Chapter 11 version of the game and make the following changes.

How about a quick overview? Figure 12.13 shows *Tank War* using the map file from the *TestMappy* program! In Figure 12.14, player two is invading the base of player one!

Figure 12.13 *Tank War* now supports the use of Mappy files instead of a hard-coded map.

Figure 12.14 Support for Mappy levels gives *Tank War* a lot of new potential because anyone can create a custom battlefield for the game.

Modifying Tank War

Now you can make the necessary changes to *Tank War* to replace the hard-coded background with support for Mappy levels.

Modifying tankwar.h

First up is the tankwar.h header file. Add a new #define line to include the mappyal.h file in the project. Note the change in bold.

```
//////////////////////////////////////////////////////////////////////
// Game Programming All In One, Second Edition
// Source Code Copyright (C)2004 by Jonathan S. Harbour
// Tank War Enhancement 7 - tankwar.h
//////////////////////////////////////////////////////////////////////

#ifndef _TANKWAR_H
#define _TANKWAR_H

#include <conio.h>
#include <stdlib.h>
#include "allegro.h"
#include "mappyal.h"
```

Next, remove the reference to the hard-coded map array. (I have commented out the line so you will see what to remove.) This line follows the bitmap definitions.

```
//the game map
//extern int map[];
```

Next, delete the definition for the `tiles` bitmap pointer. Because Mappy levels contain the tiles, your program doesn't need to load them; it only needs to load the map file. (Isn't that great?)

```
//bitmap containing source tiles
//BITMAP *tiles;
```

Finally, delete the reference to the `scroll` bitmap, which is also no longer needed.

```
//virtual background buffer
//BITMAP *scroll;
```

You've ripped out quite a bit of the game with only this first file! That is one fringe bene-fit to using MappyAL—a lot of source code formerly required to do scrolling is now built into MappyAL.

Modifying setup.c

Next up is the setup.c source code file. Scroll down to the `setupscreen` function and slash the code that loads the tiles and draws them on the virtual background image. You can also delete the section of code that created the virtual background. I'll list the entire func-tion here with the code commented out that you should delete. Note the changes in bold.

```
void setupscreen()
{
    int ret;

    //set video mode
    set_color_depth(16);
    ret = set_gfx_mode(MODE, WIDTH, HEIGHT, 0, 0);
    if (ret != 0) {
        allegro_message(allegro_error);
        return;
    }

    text_mode(-1);

/*  REMOVE THIS ENTIRE SECTION OF COMMENTED CODE
    //create the virtual background
    scroll = create_bitmap(MAPW, MAPH);
```

```
if (scroll == NULL)
{
    set_gfx_mode(GFX_TEXT, 0, 0, 0, 0);
    allegro_message("Error creating virtual background");
    return;
}

//load the tile bitmap
tiles = load_bitmap("tiles.bmp", NULL);
if (tiles == NULL)
{
    set_gfx_mode(GFX_TEXT, 0, 0, 0, 0);
    allegro_message("Error loading tiles.bmp file");
    return;
}

//now draw tiles on virtual background
for (tiley=0; tiley < scroll->h; tiley+=TILEH)
{
    for (tilex=0; tilex < scroll->w; tilex+=TILEW)
    {
        //use the result of grabframe directly in blitter
        blit(grabframe(tiles, TILEW+1, TILEH+1, 0, 0, COLS, map[n++]),
            scroll, 0, 0, tilex, tiley, TILEW, TILEH);
    }
}

//done with tiles
destroy_bitmap(tiles);

END OF THE CHOPPING BLOCK
*/

//load screen background
back = load_bitmap("background.bmp", NULL);
if (back == NULL)
{
    set_gfx_mode(GFX_TEXT, 0, 0, 0, 0);
    allegro_message("Error loading background.bmp file");
    return;
}
```

```
//create the double buffer
buffer = create_bitmap(WIDTH, HEIGHT);
if (buffer == NULL)
{
    set_gfx_mode(GFX_TEXT, 0, 0, 0, 0);
    allegro_message("Error creating double buffer");
    return;
}

//position the radar
radarx = 270;
radary = 1;

//position each player
scrollx[0] = 100;
scrolly[0] = 100;
scrollx[1] = MAPW - 400;
scrolly[1] = MAPH - 500;

//position the scroll windows
startx[0] = 5;
starty[0] = 93;
startx[1] = 325;
starty[1] = 93;
}
```

Modifying tank.c

Now open up the tank.c file and scroll down to the movetank function. Down at the bottom of the function, you'll see the section of code that keeps the tank inside the boundary of the map. This was based on the virtual background bitmap's width and height, but now it needs to be based on the Mappy level size instead. The mapwidth, mapblockwidth, mapheight, and mapblockheight variables are global and found inside mappyal.h. Make the changes noted in bold.

```
//keep tank inside bounds
if (scrollx[num] < 0)
{
    scrollx[num] = 0;
    tanks[num]->xspeed = 0;
}

else if (scrollx[num] > mapwidth*mapblockwidth - SCROLLW)
```

```
    {
        scrollx[num] = mapwidth*mapblockwidth - SCROLLW;
        tanks[num]->xspeed = 0;
    }

    if (scrolly[num] < 0)
    {
        scrolly[num] = 0;
        tanks[num]->xspeed = 0;
    }
    else if (scrolly[num] > mapheight*mapblockheight - SCROLLH)
    {
        scrolly[num] = mapheight*mapblockheight - SCROLLH;
        tanks[num]->xspeed = 0;
    }
}
```

Modifying main.c

Now open up the main.c file. The first thing you need to do in main.c is remove the huge map[] array definition (with included map tile values). Just delete the whole array, including the #define B 39 line. I won't list the commented-out code here because the map definition was quite large, but here are the first three lines (for the speed readers out there who tend to miss entire pages at a time):

```
//#define B 39
//int map[MAPW*MAPH] = {
//     B,B,B,B,B,B,B,B,B,B,B,B,B,B,B,B,B,B,B,B,B,B,B,B,B,B,B,B,B,
```

Don't forget to delete the rest of the map array definition that follows these lines.

Next, scroll down to the main function and add the code that loads the Mappy file, as shown in the bold lines that follow.

```
//main function
void main(void)
{
    int anim;

    //initialize the game
    allegro_init();
    install_keyboard();
    install_timer();
    srand(time(NULL));
    setupscreen();
```

```
setuptanks();
loadsprites();

//load the Mappy file
if (MapLoad("map3.fmp"))
{
    allegro_message ("Can't find map3.fmp");
    return;
}

//set palette
MapSetPal8();
```

Next, you need to modify the lines that used to draw the scrolling background and replace them with a call to MapDrawBG, which is all you need to draw the background. You can use the same variables as before.

```
//game loop
while(!gameover)
{
    //move the tanks and bullets
    for (n=0; n<2; n++)
    {
        movetank(n);
        animatetank(n);
        movebullet(n);
    }

    //draw background bitmap
    blit(back, buffer, 0, 0, 0, 0, back->w, back->h);

    //draw scrolling windows (now using Mappy)
    for (n=0; n<2; n++)
        MapDrawBG(buffer, scrollx[n], scrolly[n],
            startx[n], starty[n], SCROLLW, SCROLLH);
```

Remove the line of code near the end of main that destroys the scroll bitmap, which is no longer used.

```
//destroy bitmaps
destroy_bitmap(explode_bmp);
destroy_bitmap(back);
//destroy_bitmap(scroll);
destroy_bitmap(buffer);
```

Only one more change to main, and you'll be finished. Add the following line of code at the bottom of main to free the MappyAL tile map:

```
//free the MappyAL memory
MapFreeMem();

return;
}
END_OF_MAIN();
```

Summary

This chapter provided the information you need to create maps, levels, and worlds for your games. This very important subject is often glossed over until one finds that a game simply doesn't work without some way to store data to represent the game world. Mappy is an excellent tool for creating game levels. You also gained some experience using Mappy to create some sample maps, along with the source code to load and display those maps. You then added Mappy support to *Tank War*, giving the game a huge boost in playability. Now anyone can create battlefield maps for *Tank War* and fight it out with friends.

Chapter Quiz

1. What is the home site for Mappy?

    A. http://www.mappy.com

    B. http://www.maptiles.com

    C. http://www.tilemap.co.uk

    D. http://www.mappy.co.uk

2. What kind of information is stored in a map file?

    A. Data that represent the tiles comprising a game world

    B. Data that specify the game environment

    C. Data that describe the characters in a game

    D. Data that identify the background images of a game

3. What name is given to the graphic images that make up a Mappy level?

    A. Sprites

    B. Levels

    C. Maps

    D. Tiles

4. What is the default extension of a Mappy file?
   A. SMF
   B. MAP
   C. FMP
   D. BMP

5. Where does Mappy store the saved tile images?
   A. Inside a new bitmap file
   B. Inside the map file
   C. In individual bitmap files
   D. At a location specified by the user

6. What is one example of a retail game that uses Mappy levels?
   A. *Hot Wheels: Stunt Track Driver 2*
   B. *Hyperspace Delivery Boy*
   C. *Real War: Rogue States*
   D. *Wayne Gretzky and the NHLPA All-Stars*

7. What is the recommended format for an exported Mappy level?
   A. Binary
   B. Hexadecimal
   C. C binary array
   D. Text map data

8. Which macro in Mappy fills a map with a specified tile?
   A. Solid Rectangle
   B. Filled Rectangle
   C. Flood Fill Tile
   D. Paste Tiles

9. How much does a licensed copy of Mappy cost?
   A. $10
   B. $20
   C. $50
   D. It's free!

10. Which MappyAL library function loads a Mappy file?
   A. `MapLoad`
   B. `LoadMap`
   C. `MappyLoad`
   D. `OpenMap`

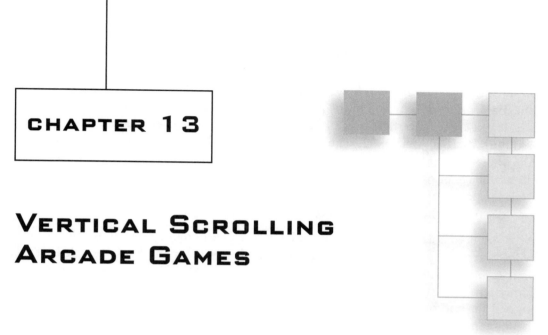

CHAPTER 13

VERTICAL SCROLLING ARCADE GAMES

Most arcade games created and distributed to video arcades in the 1980s and 1990s were scrolling shoot-em-up games (also called simply *shooters*). About an equal number of vertical and horizontal shooters were released. This chapter focuses on vertical shooters (such as *Mars Matrix*) and the next chapter deals with the horizontal variety (although it focuses on platform "jumping" games, not shooters). Why focus two whole chapters on the subject of scrolling games? Because this subject is too often ignored. Most aspiring game programmers know what a shooter is but have no real idea how to develop one. That's where this chapter comes in! This chapter discusses the features and difficulties associated with vertical shooters and explains how to develop a vertical scroller engine, which is used to create a sample game called *Warbirds Pacifica*, a *1942*-style arcade game with huge levels and professionally-drawn artwork.

Here is a breakdown of the major topics in this chapter:

- Building a vertical scroller engine
- Writing a vertical scrolling shooter

Building a Vertical Scroller Engine

Scrolling shooters are interesting programming problems for anyone who has never created one before (and who has benefited from an experienced mentor). In the past, you have created a large memory bitmap and blitted the tiles into their appropriate places on that bitmap, which could then be used as a large game world (for instance, in an earlier revision of *Tank War*). A scrolling shooter, on the other hand, has a game world that is far too large for a single bitmap. For that matter, most games have a world that is too large for a single bitmap, and using such a bitmap goes against good design practices. The world is comprised of tiles, after all, so it would make sense to draw only the tiles needed by the current view.

But for the sake of argument, how big of a world bitmap would you have to use? Mappy (the map editor tool covered in the previous chapter) supports a map of around 30,000 tiles. If you are using a standard 640-pixels-wide screen for a game, that is 20 tiles across, assuming each tile is 32×32. Thirty-thousand tiles divided by 20 tiles across gives you…how many? Fifteen-hundred tiles spread vertically. At 32 pixels each, that is a bitmap image of 640×48,000. That is ridiculously large—so large that I do not need to argue the point any further. Of course, the game world can be much smaller than this, but a good scrolling shooter will have nice, large levels to conquer.

What you need is a vertical scrolling game engine capable of blitting only those tiles needed by the current display. I once wrote a game called *Warbirds* for another book titled *Visual Basic Game Programming with DirectX* (Premier Press, 2002). The game featured a randomly generated vertical scrolling level with warping. This meant that when the scrolling reached the end of the level, it wrapped around to the start of the level and continued scrolling the level without interruption (see Figure 13.1).

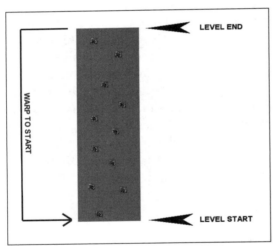

Figure 13.1 Level warping occurs when the end of the level is reached in a scrolling game.

Given that the levels were generated randomly, the game could go on forever without the need for new levels. Unfortunately, as you might have guessed, the levels were quite boring and repetitive. Even with a fairly good warping technique and random map generator, the levels were not very attractive. See Figure 13.2 for a screenshot of *Warbirds*.

If you don't want to use wraparound, or warping, then what happens when the scroller reaches the end? Of course, that's the end of the level. At this point, you want to display the score, congratulate the player, add bonus points, and then proceed to load the next level of the game.

The vertical scroller engine that you'll put together shortly will just sort of stop when it reaches the end of the level; this is a design decision, because I want you to take it from there (load the next level). Then, you can add the custom artwork for a new scrolling shooter, and I'll provide a template by having you build a sample game at the end of this chapter: *Warbirds Pacifica*.

Figure 13.2 *Warbirds* featured a randomly-generated scrolling map.

Creating Levels Using Mappy

The *Warbirds Pacifica* game developed later in this chapter will use high-quality custom levels created with Mappy (which was covered in the previous chapter). Although I suggested using a data array for the maps in simple games, that is not suitable for a game like a scrolling shooter—this game needs variety! To maximize the potential for this game, I'm going to create a huge map file that is 20 tiles wide and 1,500 tiles high! That's equivalent to an image that is 640×48,000 pixels in size. This game *will* be fun; oh yes, it will be!

If you read the previous chapter, then you should have Mappy handy. If not, I recommend you go back and read Chapter 12 because familiarity with Mappy is crucial for getting the most out of this chapter and the one that follows.

Assuming you have Mappy fired up, open the File menu and select New Map. First, be sure to select the Paletted (8bit) option. You want to use simple 8-bit tiles when possible to lighten the memory load with MappyAL, although you may use hi-color or true color tiles if you want. (I wouldn't recommend it generally.) You might recall from the last chapter that MappyAL is a public domain source code library for reading and displaying a Mappy level, and that is what you'll use in this chapter to avoid having to create a tile engine from scratch. Next, for the width and height of each tile, enter 32 and 32, respectively. Next, for the map size, enter 20 for the width and 1500 for the height, as shown in Figure 13.3.

tip

Be sure to select Paletted (8bit) for the color depth of a new map in Mappy if you intend to use the MappyAL library in your Allegro games.

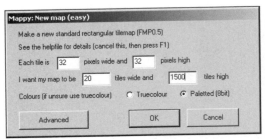

Mappy will create a new map based on your specifications, and then will wait for you to import some tiles (see Figure 13.4).

Figure 13.3 Creating a new map in Mappy for the vertical scroller demo

Figure 13.4 Mappy has created the new map and is now waiting for tiles.

Now open the File menu and select Import to bring up the File Open dialog box. This is the part where you have some options. You can use the large collection of tiles I have put together for this chapter or you can create your own tiles and use them. Your results will certainly look different, but if you have your own tiles, by all means use them. Otherwise, I recommend that you copy the maptiles8.bmp file from the CD-ROM to a folder on your hard drive. The tile image is located in \chapter13\VerticalScroller on the CD-ROM under the sources folder for the environment you are using (Visual C++, KDevelop, or Dev-C++). Select this file using the File Open dialog box, and the 32×32 tiles will be added to the tile palette in Mappy (see Figure 13.5).

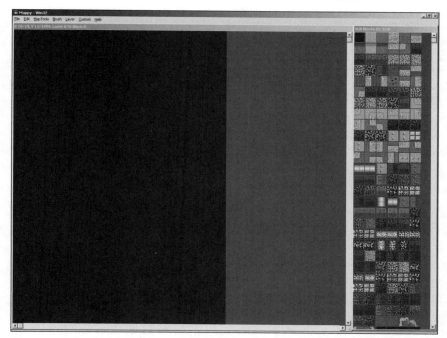

Figure 13.5 The tile palette has been filled with tiles imported from a bitmap file.

If the tiles look familiar, it's because most of them were used in the last chapter. I added new tiles to the maptiles.bmp file while working on the *Warbirds Europa* game. Note that when you add new tiles, you must add them to the bottom row of tiles, not to a column on the right. Mappy reads the tiles from left to right, top to bottom. You can add new tiles to the bottom of the maptiles.bmp file (which I have called maptiles8.bmp to reflect that it is an 8-bit image with 256 colors), and then import the file again into your Mappy map to start using new tiles. Simply select the first tile in the tile palette before you import again, and the existing tiles will be replaced with the new tiles.

Filling in the Tiles

Now that you have a big blank slate for the level, I want to show you how to create a template map file. Because the sample game in this chapter is a World War II shooter based on the arcade game *1942*, you can fill the entire level with a neutral water tile and then save it as a template. At that point, it will be relatively easy to use this template to create a number of levels for the actual game.

tip

All of the graphics in this game are available in the free SpriteLib GPL at http://www.arifeldman. com. Thanks to Ari Feldman for allowing me to use his tiles and sprites in this chapter.

Locate a water tile that is appealing to you. I have added two new water tiles just for this chapter, again from SpriteLib. Again, this was created by Ari Feldman and released into the public domain with his blessing. However, I encourage you to visit Ari's Web site at http://www.arifeldman.com to contact him about commissioning custom artwork for your own games. These are high-quality sprite tiles, and I am grateful to Ari for allowing me to use them.

Because this map is so big, it would take a very long time to fill in all the tiles manually. Thankfully, Mappy suports the Lua scripting language. Although it's beyond the scope of this chapter, you can edit Lua scripts and use them in Mappy. One such script is called Solid Rectangle, and it fills a region of the map with the selected tile. Unfortunately, there's a bug in this Lua script so it leaves out the last row and column of tiles. On a map this big, it takes a long time just to fill in a single column or row. I fixed the bug and have included the script on the CD-ROM. If you have just copied Mappy off the CD-ROM, then you should have the fix. If you have downloaded a new version of Mappy, then you'll have to fill in the unfilled tiles manually.

Having selected an appropriate water tile, open the Custom menu and select Solid Rectangle. A dialog box will appear, asking you to enter four numbers separated by commas. Type in these values:

0,0,20,1500

If you have the buggy version of this script, then type in:

0,0,19,1499

Now save the map as template.fmp so it can be reused to create each level of the game. By the way, while you have one large ocean level available, why not have some fun playing with Mappy? See what kind of interesting ocean level you can create using the available tiles. The map should look interesting, but it won't be critical to the game because all the action will take place in the skies.

Let's Scroll It

Now that you have a map ready to use, you can write a short program to demonstrate the feasibility of a very large scrolling level. Figure 13.6 shows the output from the *VerticalScroller* program. As was the case in the last chapter, you will need the MappyAL files to run this program. The mappyal.c and mappyal.h files are located on the CD-ROM under \chapter13\VerticalScroller.

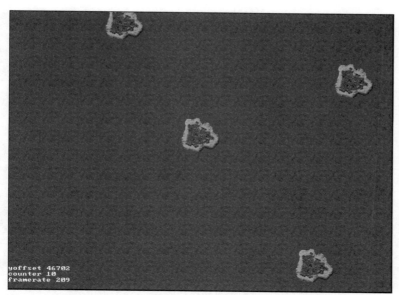

Figure 13.6 The *VerticalScroller* program contains the code for a basic vertical scroller engine.

```
#include "allegro.h"
#include "mappyal.h"

//this must run at 640x480
#define MODE GFX_AUTODETECT_FULLSCREEN
//#define MODE GFX_AUTODETECT_WINDOWED
#define WIDTH 640
#define HEIGHT 480
#define WHITE makecol(255,255,255)

#define BOTTOM 48000 - HEIGHT
//y offset in pixels
int yoffset = BOTTOM;

//timer variables
volatile int counter;
volatile int ticks;
volatile int framerate;

//double buffer
BITMAP *buffer;
```

```c
//calculate framerate every second
void timer1(void)
{
    counter++;
    framerate = ticks;
    ticks=0;
}
END_OF_FUNCTION(timer1)


void main (void)
{
    //initialize program
        allegro_init();
        install_timer();
        install_keyboard();
        set_gfx_mode(MODE, WIDTH, HEIGHT, 0, 0);
        text_mode(-1);

    //create the double buffer and clear it
        buffer = create_bitmap(SCREEN_W, SCREEN_H);
        if (buffer==NULL)
    {
         set_gfx_mode(GFX_TEXT, 0, 0, 0, 0);
         allegro_message("Error creating double buffer");
         return;
    }
        clear(buffer);

    //load the Mappy file
        if (MapLoad("level1.fmp"))
    {
         set_gfx_mode(GFX_TEXT, 0, 0, 0, 0);
            allegro_message ("Can't find level1.fmp");
            return;
        }

    //set palette
    MapSetPal8();

    //identify variables used by interrupt function
    LOCK_VARIABLE(counter);
    LOCK_VARIABLE(framerate);
```

```
LOCK_VARIABLE(framerate);
LOCK_VARIABLE(ticks);
LOCK_FUNCTION(timer1);

//create new interrupt handler
install_int(timer1, 1000);

//main loop
while (!key[KEY_ESC])
    {
    //check for keyboard input
        if (key[KEY_PGUP]) yoffset-=4;
        if (key[KEY_PGDN]) yoffset+=4;
    if (key[KEY_UP])    yoffset-=1;
    if (key[KEY_DOWN]) yoffset+=1;

    //make sure it doesn't scroll beyond map edge
    if (yoffset < 0) yoffset = 0;
    if (yoffset > BOTTOM) yoffset = BOTTOM;

    //draw map with single layer
    MapDrawBG(buffer, 0, yoffset, 0, 0, SCREEN_W-1, SCREEN_H-1);

    //update ticks
    ticks++;

    //display some status information
    textprintf(buffer,font,0,440,WHITE,"yoffset %d",yoffset);
    textprintf(buffer,font,0,450,WHITE,"counter %d", counter);
    textprintf(buffer,font,0,460,WHITE,"framerate %d", framerate);

    //blit the double buffer
    acquire_screen();
        blit (buffer, screen, 0, 0, 0, 0, SCREEN_W-1, SCREEN_H-1);
    release_screen();

    }

//delete double buffer
   destroy_bitmap(buffer);

//delete the Mappy level
   MapFreeMem();
```

```
        allegro_exit();
        return;
}

END_OF_MAIN()
```

Writing a Vertical Scrolling Shooter

To best demonstrate a vertical scroller, I have created a simple scrolling shooter as a sample game that you can use as a template for your own games of this genre. Simply replace the map file with one of your own design and replace the basic sprites used in the game, and you can adapt this game for any theme—water, land, undersea, or outer space.

Whereas the player's airplane uses local coordinates reflecting the display screen, the enemy planes use world coordinates that range from 0–639 in the horizontal and 0–47,999 in the vertical. Hey, I told you these maps were huge! The key to making this game work is that a test is performed after each sprite is drawn to determine whether it is within the visible range of the screen. Keep in mind that while the enemy fighters are moving toward the player, the map itself is scrolling downward to simulate forward movement.

Describing the Game

I have called this game *Warbirds Pacifica* because it was based on my earlier *Warbirds* game but set in the Pacific campaign of World War II. The game is set over ocean tiles with frequent islands to help improve the sense of motion (see Figure 13.7).

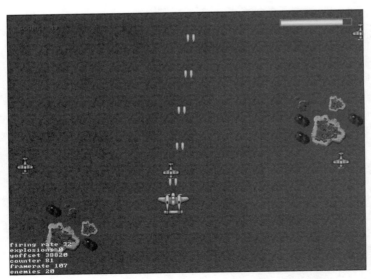

Figure 13.7 *Warbirds Pacifica* is a vertical scrolling shooter.

This is a fast-paced game and even with numerous sprites on the screen, the scrolling engine (provided by MappyAL) doesn't hiccup at all. Take a look at Figure 13.8. The player has a variable firing rate that is improved by picking up power-ups.

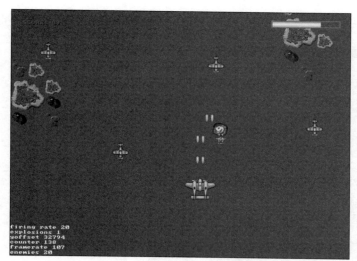

Figure 13.8 The firing rate of the player's P-38 fighter plane is improved with power-ups.

Another cool aspect of the game, thanks to Allegro's awesome sprite handling, is that explosions can overlap power-ups and other bullet sprites due to internal transparency within the sprites (see Figure 13.9). Note also the numerous debug-style messages in the bottom-left corner of the screen. While developing a game, it is extremely helpful to see status values that describe what is going on in order to tweak gameplay. I have modified many aspects of the game thanks to these messages.

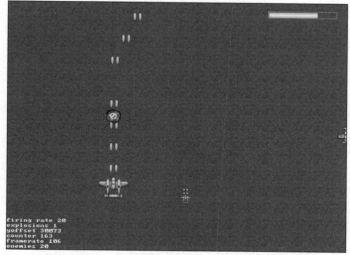

Figure 13.9 Destroying enemy planes releases power-ups that will improve the player's P-38 fighter.

Of course, what would the game be like without any challenge? Although this very early alpha version of *Warbirds Pacifica* does not have the code to allow enemy planes to fire at the player, it does detect collisions with enemy planes, which cause the player's P-38 to explode. (Although gameplay continues, the life meter at the top drops.) One of the first things you will want to do to enhance the game is add enemy firepower (see Figure 13.10).

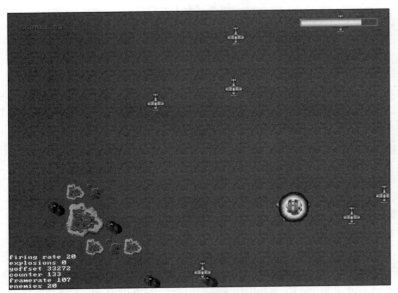

Figure 13.10 The enemy planes might not have much firepower, but they are still capable of Kamikaze attacks!

The Game's Artwork

This game is absolutely loaded with potential! There is so much that could be done with it that I really had to hold myself back when putting the game together as a technology demo for this chapter. It was so much fun adding just a single power-up that I came very close to adding all the rest of the power-ups to the game, including multi-shots! Why such enthusiasm? Because the artwork is already available for building an entire game, thanks to the generosity of Ari Feldman. The artwork featured in this game is a significant part of Ari's SpriteLib.

Let me show you some examples of the additional sprites available that you could use to quickly enhance this game. Figure 13.11 shows a set of enemy bomber sprites. The next image, Figure 13.12, shows a collection of enemy fighter planes that could be used in the game. Notice the different angles. Most shooters will launch squadrons of enemies at the player in formation, which is how these sprites might be used.

Figure 13.11 A set of enemy bomber sprites. Courtesy of Ari Feldman.

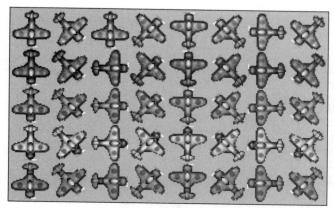

Figure 13.12 A collection of enemy fighter planes. Courtesy of Ari Feldman.

The next image, Figure 13.13, is an animated enemy submarine that comes up out of the water to shoot at the player. This would be a great addition to the game!

Yet another source of sprites for this game is shown in Figure 13.14—an enemy battleship with rotating gun turrets! The next image, Figure 13.15, shows a number of high-quality power-up sprites and bullet sprites. I used the shot power-up in the game as an example so that you can add more power-ups to the game.

Of course, a high-quality arcade game needs a high-quality font that looks really great on the screen. The default font with Allegro looks terrible and should not be used in a game like *Warbirds Pacifica*. Take a look at Figure 13.16 for a sample of the font available for the game with SpriteLib. You can use the existing menus and messages or construct your own using the provided alphabet.

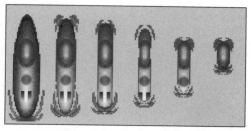

Figure 13.13 An enemy submarine sprite. Courtesy of Ari Feldman.

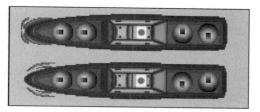

Figure 13.14 An enemy battleship with rotating gun turrets. Courtesy of Ari Feldman.

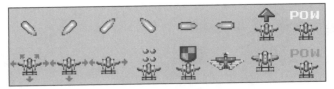

Figure 13.15 A collection of high-quality power-ups and bullets. Courtesy of Ari Feldman.

Figure 13.16 A high-quality font suitable for a scrolling shooter, such as *Warbirds Pacifica.* Courtesy of Ari Feldman.

Writing the Source Code

The source code for *Warbirds Pacifica* is designed to be easy to enhance because my intent was to provide you with a template, something to which you can apply your imagination to complete. The game has all the basic functionality and just needs to be well-rounded and, well, finished.

I recommend you use the *VerticalScroller* program as a basis because it already includes the two support files from the MappyAL library (mappyal.c and mappyal.h). If you are creating a new project from scratch, simply copy these two files to your new project folder and add them to the project by right-clicking on the project name and selecting Add Files to Project.

All the artwork for this game is located on the CD-ROM under \chapter13\Warbirds. You can open the project directly if you are not inclined to type in the source code; however, the more code you type in, the better programmer you will become. In my experience, just the act of typing in a game from a source code listing is a great learning experience. I see aspects of the game—and how it was coded—that are not apparent from simply paging through the code listing. It helps you to become more intimate and familiar with the source code. This is an absolute must if you intend to learn how the game works in order to enhance or finish it.

warbirds.h

All of the struct and variable definitions are located in the warbirds.h file. You should add a new file to the project (File, New, C/C++ Header File) and give it this name.

```
#ifndef _WARBIRDS_H
#define _WARBIRDS_H

#include "allegro.h"
#include "mappyal.h"

//this must run at 640x480
//#define MODE GFX_AUTODETECT_FULLSCREEN
#define MODE GFX_AUTODETECT_WINDOWED
#define WIDTH 640
#define HEIGHT 480

#define WHITE makecol(255,255,255)
#define GRAY makecol(60,60,60)
#define RED makecol(200,0,0)

#define MAX_ENEMIES 20
#define MAX_BULLETS 20
#define MAX_EXPLOSIONS 10
#define BOTTOM 48000 - HEIGHT

//define the sprite structure
typedef struct SPRITE
{
    int dir, alive;
    int x,y;
    int width,height;
    int xspeed,yspeed;
    int xdelay,ydelay;
    int xcount,ycount;
    int curframe,maxframe,animdir;
    int framecount,framedelay;
}SPRITE;

//y offset in pixels
```

```
int yoffset = BOTTOM;

//player variables
int firecount = 0;
int firedelay = 60;
int health = 25;
int score = 0;

//timer variables
volatile int counter;
volatile int ticks;
volatile int framerate;

//bitmaps and sprites
BITMAP *buffer;
BITMAP *temp;
BITMAP *explosion_images[6];
SPRITE *explosions[MAX_EXPLOSIONS];
BITMAP *bigexp_images[7];
SPRITE *bigexp;
BITMAP *player_images[3];
SPRITE *player;
BITMAP *bullet_images[2];
SPRITE *bullets[MAX_BULLETS];
BITMAP *enemy_plane_images[3];
SPRITE *enemy_planes[MAX_ENEMIES];
BITMAP *progress, *bar;
BITMAP *bonus_shot_image;
SPRITE *bonus_shot;

#endif
```

main.c

Now for the main source code file. The main.c file will contain all of the source code for
the *Warbirds Pacifica* template game. Remember, this game is not 100-percent functional
for a reason—it was not designed to be a polished, complete game; rather, it was designed
to be a template. To make this a complete game, you will want to create additional levels
with Mappy; add some code to handle the loading of a new level when the player reaches
the end of the first level; and add the additional enemy planes, ships, and so on, as
described earlier. Then this game will rock! Furthermore, you will learn how to add sound
effects to the game in Chapter 15, "Mastering the Audible Realm: Allegro's Sound
Support," which will truly round out this game!

```c
#include "warbirds.h"

//reuse our friendly tile grabber from chapter 9
BITMAP *grabframe(BITMAP *source,
                  int width, int height,
                  int startx, int starty,
                  int columns, int frame)
{
    BITMAP *temp = create_bitmap(width,height);

    int x = startx + (frame % columns) * width;
    int y = starty + (frame / columns) * height;

    blit(source,temp,x,y,0,0,width,height);

    return temp;
}


void loadsprites(void)
{
    int n;

    //load progress bar
    temp = load_bitmap("progress.bmp", NULL);
    progress = grabframe(temp,130,14,0,0,1,0);
    bar = grabframe(temp,6,10,130,2,1,0);
    destroy_bitmap(temp);

    //load bonus shot
    bonus_shot_image = load_bitmap("bonusshot.bmp", NULL);
    bonus_shot = malloc(sizeof(SPRITE));
    bonus_shot->alive=0;
    bonus_shot->x = 0;
    bonus_shot->y = 0;
    bonus_shot->width = bonus_shot_image->w;
    bonus_shot->height = bonus_shot_image->h;
    bonus_shot->xdelay = 0;
    bonus_shot->ydelay = 2;
    bonus_shot->xcount = 0;
    bonus_shot->ycount = 0;
    bonus_shot->xspeed = 0;
    bonus_shot->yspeed = 1;
    bonus_shot->curframe = 0;
```

```
bonus_shot->maxframe = 0;
bonus_shot->framecount = 0;
bonus_shot->framedelay = 0;


//load player airplane sprite
temp = load_bitmap("p38.bmp", NULL);
for (n=0; n<3; n++)
    player_images[n] = grabframe(temp,64,64,0,0,3,n);
destroy_bitmap(temp);

//initialize the player's sprite
player = malloc(sizeof(SPRITE));
player->x = 320-32;
player->y = 400;
player->width = player_images[0]->w;
player->height = player_images[0]->h;
player->xdelay = 1;
player->ydelay = 0;
player->xcount = 0;
player->ycount = 0;
player->xspeed = 0;
player->yspeed = 0;
player->curframe = 0;
player->maxframe = 2;
player->framecount = 0;
player->framedelay = 10;
player->animdir = 1;

//load bullet images
bullet_images[0] = load_bitmap("bullets.bmp", NULL);

//initialize the bullet sprites
for (n=0; n<MAX_BULLETS; n++)
{
    bullets[n] = malloc(sizeof(SPRITE));
    bullets[n]->alive = 0;
    bullets[n]->x = 0;
    bullets[n]->y = 0;
    bullets[n]->width = bullet_images[0]->w;
    bullets[n]->height = bullet_images[0]->h;
    bullets[n]->xdelay = 0;
    bullets[n]->ydelay = 0;
```

```
        bullets[n]->xcount = 0;
        bullets[n]->ycount = 0;
        bullets[n]->xspeed = 0;
        bullets[n]->yspeed = -2;
        bullets[n]->curframe = 0;
        bullets[n]->maxframe = 0;
        bullets[n]->framecount = 0;
        bullets[n]->framedelay = 0;
        bullets[n]->animdir = 0;
    }

    //load enemy plane sprites
    temp = load_bitmap("enemyplane1.bmp", NULL);
    for (n=0; n<3; n++)
        enemy_plane_images[n] = grabframe(temp,32,32,0,0,3,n);
    destroy_bitmap(temp);

    //initialize the enemy planes
    for (n=0; n<MAX_ENEMIES; n++)
    {
        enemy_planes[n] = malloc(sizeof(SPRITE));
        enemy_planes[n]->alive = 0;
        enemy_planes[n]->x = rand() % 100 + 50;
        enemy_planes[n]->y = 0;
        enemy_planes[n]->width = enemy_plane_images[0]->w;
        enemy_planes[n]->height = enemy_plane_images[0]->h;
        enemy_planes[n]->xdelay = 4;
        enemy_planes[n]->ydelay = 4;
        enemy_planes[n]->xcount = 0;
        enemy_planes[n]->ycount = 0;
        enemy_planes[n]->xspeed = (rand() % 2 - 3);
        enemy_planes[n]->yspeed = 1;
        enemy_planes[n]->curframe = 0;
        enemy_planes[n]->maxframe = 2;
        enemy_planes[n]->framecount = 0;
        enemy_planes[n]->framedelay = 10;
        enemy_planes[n]->animdir = 1;
    }

    //load explosion sprites
    temp = load_bitmap("explosion.bmp", NULL);
    for (n=0; n<6; n++)
        explosion_images[n] = grabframe(temp,32,32,0,0,6,n);
```

```
    destroy_bitmap(temp);

    //initialize the sprites
    for (n=0; n<MAX_EXPLOSIONS; n++)
    {
        explosions[n] = malloc(sizeof(SPRITE));
        explosions[n]->alive = 0;
        explosions[n]->x = 0;
        explosions[n]->y = 0;
        explosions[n]->width = explosion_images[0]->w;
        explosions[n]->height = explosion_images[0]->h;
        explosions[n]->xdelay = 0;
        explosions[n]->ydelay = 8;
        explosions[n]->xcount = 0;
        explosions[n]->ycount = 0;
        explosions[n]->xspeed = 0;
        explosions[n]->yspeed = -1;
        explosions[n]->curframe = 0;
        explosions[n]->maxframe = 5;
        explosions[n]->framecount = 0;
        explosions[n]->framedelay = 15;
        explosions[n]->animdir = 1;
    }

    //load explosion sprites
    temp = load_bitmap("bigexplosion.bmp", NULL);
    for (n=0; n<8; n++)
        bigexp_images[n] = grabframe(temp,64,64,0,0,7,n);
    destroy_bitmap(temp);

    //initialize the sprites
    bigexp = malloc(sizeof(SPRITE));
    bigexp->alive = 0;
    bigexp->x = 0;
    bigexp->y = 0;
    bigexp->width = bigexp_images[0]->w;
    bigexp->height = bigexp_images[0]->h;
    bigexp->xdelay = 0;
    bigexp->ydelay = 8;
    bigexp->xcount = 0;
    bigexp->ycount = 0;
    bigexp->xspeed = 0;
    bigexp->yspeed = -1;
```

```
    bigexp->curframe = 0;
    bigexp->maxframe = 6;
    bigexp->framecount = 0;
    bigexp->framedelay = 10;
    bigexp->animdir = 1;

}

int inside(int x,int y,int left,int top,int right,int bottom)
{
    if (x > left && x < right && y > top && y < bottom)
        return 1;
    else
        return 0;
}

void updatesprite(SPRITE *spr)
{
    //update x position
    if (++spr->xcount > spr->xdelay)
    {
        spr->xcount = 0;
        spr->x += spr->xspeed;
    }

    //update y position
    if (++spr->ycount > spr->ydelay)
    {
        spr->ycount = 0;
        spr->y += spr->yspeed;
    }

    //update frame based on animdir
    if (++spr->framecount > spr->framedelay)
    {
        spr->framecount = 0;
        if (spr->animdir == -1)
        {
            if (--spr->curframe < 0)
                spr->curframe = spr->maxframe;
        }
        else if (spr->animdir == 1)
        {
```

```
                if (++spr->curframe > spr->maxframe)
                    spr->curframe = 0;
        }
    }
}

void startexplosion(int x, int y)
{
    int n;
    for (n=0; n<MAX_EXPLOSIONS; n++)
    {
        if (!explosions[n]->alive)
        {
            explosions[n]->alive++;
            explosions[n]->x = x;
            explosions[n]->y = y;
            break;
        }
    }

    //launch bonus shot if ready
    if (!bonus_shot->alive)
    {
        bonus_shot->alive++;
        bonus_shot->x = x;
        bonus_shot->y = y;
    }
}

void updateexplosions()
{
    int n, c=0;

    for (n=0; n<MAX_EXPLOSIONS; n++)
    {
        if (explosions[n]->alive)
        {
            c++;
            updatesprite(explosions[n]);
            draw_sprite(buffer, explosion_images[explosions[n]->curframe],
                explosions[n]->x, explosions[n]->y);
```

```
            if (explosions[n]->curframe >= explosions[n]->maxframe)
            {
                explosions[n]->curframe=0;
                explosions[n]->alive=0;
            }
        }
    }
    textprintf(buffer,font,0,430,WHITE,"explosions %d", c);

    //update the big "player" explosion if needed
    if (bigexp->alive)
    {
        updatesprite(bigexp);
        draw_sprite(buffer, bigexp_images[bigexp->curframe],
            bigexp->x, bigexp->y);
        if (bigexp->curframe >= bigexp->maxframe)
        {
            bigexp->curframe=0;
            bigexp->alive=0;
        }
    }
}


void updatebonuses()
{
    int x,y,x1,y1,x2,y2;

    //add more bonuses here

    //update bonus shot if alive
    if (bonus_shot->alive)
    {
        updatesprite(bonus_shot);
        draw_sprite(buffer, bonus_shot_image, bonus_shot->x, bonus_shot->y);
        if (bonus_shot->y > HEIGHT)
            bonus_shot->alive=0;

        //see if player got the bonus
        x = bonus_shot->x + bonus_shot->width/2;
        y = bonus_shot->y + bonus_shot->height/2;
        x1 = player->x;
        y1 = player->y;
```

```
        x2 = x1 + player->width;
        y2 = y1 + player->height;

        if (inside(x,y,x1,y1,x2,y2))
        {
            //increase firing rate
            if (firedelay>20) firedelay-=2;

            bonus_shot->alive=0;
        }
    }

}

void updatebullet(SPRITE *spr)
{
    int n,x,y;
    int x1,y1,x2,y2;

    //move the bullet
    updatesprite(spr);

    //check bounds
    if (spr->y < 0)
    {
        spr->alive = 0;
        return;
    }

    for (n=0; n<MAX_ENEMIES; n++)
    {
        if (enemy_planes[n]->alive)
        {
            //find center of bullet
            x = spr->x + spr->width/2;
            y = spr->y + spr->height/2;

            //get enemy plane bounding rectangle
            x1 = enemy_planes[n]->x;
            y1 = enemy_planes[n]->y - yoffset;
            x2 = x1 + enemy_planes[n]->width;
            y2 = y1 + enemy_planes[n]->height;
```

```
                //check for collisions
                if (inside(x, y, x1, y1, x2, y2))
                {
                    enemy_planes[n]->alive=0;
                    spr->alive=0;
                    startexplosion(spr->x+16, spr->y);
                    score+=2;
                    break;
                }
            }
        }
    }
}

void updatebullets()
{
    int n;
    //update/draw bullets
    for (n=0; n<MAX_BULLETS; n++)
        if (bullets[n]->alive)
        {
            updatebullet(bullets[n]);
            draw_sprite(buffer,bullet_images[0], bullets[n]->x, bullets[n]->y);
        }
}

void bouncex_warpy(SPRITE *spr)
{
    //bounces x off bounds
    if (spr->x < 0 - spr->width)
    {
        spr->x = 0 - spr->width + 1;
        spr->xspeed *= -1;
    }

    else if (spr->x > SCREEN_W)
    {
        spr->x = SCREEN_W - spr->xspeed;
        spr->xspeed *= -1;
    }

    //warps y if plane has passed the player
    if (spr->y > yoffset + 2000)
```

```
    {
        //respawn enemy plane
        spr->y = yoffset - 1000 - rand() % 1000;
        spr->alive++;
        spr->x = rand() % WIDTH;
    }

    //warps y from bottom to top of level
    if (spr->y < 0)
    {
        spr->y = 0;
    }

    else if (spr->y > 48000)
    {
        spr->y = 0;
    }
}


void fireatenemy()
{
    int n;
    for (n=0; n<MAX_BULLETS; n++)
    {
        if (!bullets[n]->alive)
        {
            bullets[n]->alive++;
            bullets[n]->x = player->x;
            bullets[n]->y = player->y;
            return;
        }
    }
}

void displayprogress(int life)
{
    int n;
    draw_sprite(buffer,progress,490,15);

    for (n=0; n<life; n++)
        draw_sprite(buffer,bar,492+n*5,17);
}
```

```
void updateenemyplanes()
{
    int n, c=0;

    //update/draw enemy planes
    for (n=0; n<MAX_ENEMIES; n++)
    {
        if (enemy_planes[n]->alive)
        {
            c++;
            updatesprite(enemy_planes[n]);
            bouncex_warpy(enemy_planes[n]);

            //is plane visible on screen?
            if (enemy_planes[n]->y > yoffset-32 && enemy_planes[n]->y <
                yoffset + HEIGHT+32)
            {
                //draw enemy plane
                draw_sprite(buffer, enemy_plane_images[enemy_planes[n]->curframe],
                    enemy_planes[n]->x, enemy_planes[n]->y - yoffset);
            }
        }
        //reset plane
        else
        {
            enemy_planes[n]->alive++;
            enemy_planes[n]->x = rand() % 100 + 50;
            enemy_planes[n]->y = yoffset - 2000 + rand() % 2000;
        }
    }
    textprintf(buffer,font,0,470,WHITE,"enemies %d", c);
}

void updatescroller()
{
    //make sure it doesn't scroll beyond map edge
    if (yoffset < 5)
    {
        //level is over
        yoffset = 5;
        textout_centre(buffer, font, "END OF LEVEL", SCREEN_W/2,
            SCREEN_H/2, WHITE);
    }
```

```
        if (yoffset > BOTTOM) yoffset = BOTTOM;


    //scroll map up 1 pixel
    yoffset-=1;

    //draw map with single layer
    MapDrawBG(buffer, 0, yoffset, 0, 0, SCREEN_W-1, SCREEN_H-1);
}

void updateplayer()
{
    int n,x,y,x1,y1,x2,y2;

    //update/draw player sprite
    updatesprite(player);
    draw_sprite(buffer, player_images[player->curframe],
        player->x, player->y);

    //check for collision with enemy planes
    x = player->x + player->width/2;
    y = player->y + player->height/2;
    for (n=0; n<MAX_ENEMIES; n++)
    {
        if (enemy_planes[n]->alive)
        {
            x1 = enemy_planes[n]->x;
            y1 = enemy_planes[n]->y - yoffset;
            x2 = x1 + enemy_planes[n]->width;
            y2 = y1 + enemy_planes[n]->height;
            if (inside(x,y,x1,y1,x2,y2))
            {
                enemy_planes[n]->alive=0;
                if (health > 0) health--;
                bigexp->alive++;
                bigexp->x = player->x;
                bigexp->y = player->y;
                score++;
            }
        }
    }
}
```

```
void displaystats()
{
    //display some status information
    textprintf(buffer,font,0,420,WHITE,"firing rate %d", firedelay);
    textprintf(buffer,font,0,440,WHITE,"yoffset %d",yoffset);
    textprintf(buffer,font,0,450,WHITE,"counter %d", counter);
    textprintf(buffer,font,0,460,WHITE,"framerate %d", framerate);

    //display score
    textprintf(buffer,font,22,22,GRAY,"SCORE: %d", score);
    textprintf(buffer,font,20,20,RED,"SCORE: %d", score);
}

void checkinput()
{
    //check for keyboard input
    if (key[KEY_UP])
    {
        player->y -= 1;
        if (player->y < 100)
            player->y = 100;
    }
    if (key[KEY_DOWN])
    {
        player->y += 1;
        if (player->y > HEIGHT-65)
            player->y = HEIGHT-65;
    }
    if (key[KEY_LEFT])
    {
        player->x -= 1;
        if (player->x < 0)
            player->x = 0;
    }
    if (key[KEY_RIGHT])
    {
        player->x += 1;
        if (player->x > WIDTH-65)
            player->x = WIDTH-65;
    }

    if (key[KEY_SPACE])
    {
```

```
            if (firecount > firedelay)
            {
                firecount = 0;
                fireatenemy();
            }
        }
    }
}

//calculate framerate every second
void timer1(void)
{
    counter++;
    framerate = ticks;
    ticks=0;
    rest(2);
}
END_OF_FUNCTION(timer1)

void initialize()
{
    //initialize program
        allegro_init();
        install_timer();
        install_keyboard();
    set_color_depth(16);
        set_gfx_mode(MODE, WIDTH, HEIGHT, 0, 0);
    text_mode(-1);
    srand(time(NULL));

    //create the double buffer and clear it
        buffer = create_bitmap(SCREEN_W, SCREEN_H);
        if (buffer==NULL)
    {
        set_gfx_mode(GFX_TEXT, 0, 0, 0, 0);
        allegro_message("Error creating double buffer");
        return;
    }
        clear(buffer);

    //load the Mappy file
        if (MapLoad("level1.fmp"))
        {
```

```
        set_gfx_mode(GFX_TEXT, 0, 0, 0, 0);
      allegro_message ("Can't find level1.fmp");
      return;
    }

    //set palette
    MapSetPal8();

    //identify variables used by interrupt function
    LOCK_VARIABLE(counter);
    LOCK_VARIABLE(framerate);
    LOCK_VARIABLE(ticks);
    LOCK_FUNCTION(timer1);

    //create new interrupt handler
    install_int(timer1, 1000);
}

void main (void)
{
    int n;

    //init game
    initialize();
    loadsprites();

    //main loop
    while (!key[KEY_ESC])
       {
        checkinput();

        updatescroller();

        updateplayer();
        updateenemyplanes();

        updatebullets();
        updateexplosions();
        updatebonuses();

        displayprogress(health);
        displaystats();
```

```
        //blit the double buffer
        acquire_screen();
                blit (buffer, screen, 0, 0, 0, 0, SCREEN_W-1, SCREEN_H-1);
        release_screen();

        ticks++;
        firecount++;
    }

//delete the Mappy level
    MapFreeMem();

//delete bitmaps
destroy_bitmap(buffer);
destroy_bitmap(progress);
destroy_bitmap(bar);

for (n=0; n<6; n++)
    destroy_bitmap(explosion_images[n]);

for (n=0; n<3; n++)
{
    destroy_bitmap(player_images[n]);
    destroy_bitmap(bullet_images[n]);
    destroy_bitmap(enemy_plane_images[n]);
}

//delete sprites
free(player);
for (n=0; n<MAX_EXPLOSIONS; n++)
    free(explosions[n]);
for (n=0; n<MAX_BULLETS; n++)
    free(bullets[n]);
for (n=0; n<MAX_ENEMIES; n++)
    free(enemy_planes[n]);

    allegro_exit();
    return;
}

END_OF_MAIN()
```

Summary

Vertical scrolling shooters were once the mainstay of the 1980s and 1990s video arcade, but have not been as prevalent in recent years due to the invasion of 3D, so to speak. Still, the scrolling shooter as a genre has a large and loyal fan following, so it will continue to be popular for years to come. This chapter explored the techniques involved in creating vertical scrollers and produced a sample template game called *Warbirds Pacifica* using the vertical scroller engine (which is really powered by the MappyAL library). I hope you enjoyed this chapter because this is not the end of the scroller! The next chapter takes a turn—a 90-degree turn, as a matter of fact—and covers the horizontal scroller.

Chapter Quiz

You can find the answers to this chapter quiz in Appendix A, "Chapter Quiz Answers."

1. In which game genre does the vertical shooter belong?
    A. Shoot-em-up
    B. Platform
    C. Fighting
    D. Real-time strategy

2. What is the name of the support library used as the vertical scroller engine?
    A. ScrollerEngine
    B. VerticalScroller
    C. MappyAL
    D. AllegroScroller

3. What are the virtual pixel dimensions of the levels in *Warbirds Pacifica*?
    A. 640×480
    B. 48,000×640
    C. 20×1500
    D. 640×48,000

4. What is the name of the level-editing program used to create the first level of *Warbirds Pacifica*?
    A. Happy
    B. Mappy
    C. Snappy
    D. Frappy

5. How many tiles comprise a level in *Warbirds Pacifica*?

    A. 30,000

    B. 1,500

    C. 48,000

    D. 32,768

6. Which of the following games is a vertical scrolling shooter?

    A. *R-Type*

    B. *Mars Matrix*

    C. *Contra*

    D. *Castlevania*

7. Who created the artwork featured in this chapter?

    A. Ray Kurzweil

    B. Clifford Stoll

    C. Ari Feldman

    D. Nicholas Negroponte

8. Which MappyAL function loads a map file?

    A. LoadMap

    B. MapLoad

    C. LoadMappy

    D. ReadLevel

9. Which MappyAL function removes a map from memory?

    A. destroy_map

    B. free_mappy

    C. DeleteMap

    D. MapFreeMem

10. Which classic arcade game inspired *Warbirds Pacifica*?

    A. *Pac-Man*

    B. *Mars Matrix*

    C. *1942*

    D. *Street Fighter II*

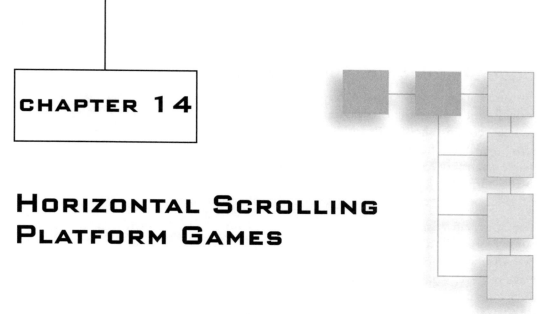

CHAPTER 14

HORIZONTAL SCROLLING PLATFORM GAMES

Everyone has his own opinion of the greatest games ever made. Many games are found on bestseller lists or gamer polls, but there are only a few games that stand the test of time, capable of drawing you in again from a mere glance. One such game is *Super Mario World*, originally released as the launch title for the SNES and now available for the Game Boy Advance. This game is considered by many to be the greatest platformer ever made—if not the best game of all time in any genre. What is it about *Super Mario World* that is so appealing? Aside from the beautiful 2D graphics, charming soundtrack, and likable characters, this game features perhaps the best gameplay ever devised, with levels that are strikingly creative and challenging. The blend of difficulty and reward along with boss characters that go from tough to tougher only scratch the surface of this game's appeal.

Super Mario World is a horizontal scrolling platform game that takes place entirely from the side view (with the exception of the world view). That is the focus of this chapter; it is an introduction to platform games with an emphasis on how to handle tile collisions. Strictly speaking, platform games do not make up the entirety of the horizontal scroller genre; there are perhaps more shoot-em-ups (such as *R-Type* and *Gradius*) in this orientation than there are platformers. I am as big a fan of shooters as I am of platformers; however, because the last chapter focused on a shooter, this chapter will take on the subject of platform game programming.

Using a special feature of Mappy, I'll show you how to design a platform game level that requires very little source code to implement. By the time you have finished this chapter, you will know what it takes to create a platform game and you will have written a sample game that you can tweak and modify to suit your own platform game creations. Here is a list of the major topics in this chapter:

- Understanding horizontal scrolling games
- Developing a scrolling platform game

Understanding Horizontal Scrolling Games

I'm sure you have played many shoot-em-up and platform games in your life, but I will provide you with a brief overview anyway. Although it's tough to beat the gameplay of a vertical scrolling shooter, there is an equal amount of fun to be had with a horizontal scrolling game. The traditional shooters in this genre (*R-Type*, *Gradius*, and so on) have had long and successful runs, with new versions of these classic games released regularly. *R-Type* for Game Boy Color was followed a few years later by *R-Type Advance*, and this is a regular occurrence for a popular game series such as this one.

The other sub-genre of the horizontal scrolling game is the platformer—games such as *Super Mario World* and a vast number of other games of this type. *Kien* is a recent Game Boy Advance platform game with RPG elements. Another old favorite is *Ghosts 'n Goblins*. Have you ever wondered how these games are developed? Such games differ greatly from their horizontal shoot-em-up cousins because platformers by their very nature have the simulated effect of gravity that draws the player down. The goal of the game is to navigate a series of levels comprised of block tiles of various shapes and sizes, such as the game shown in Figure 14.1.

Developing a Platform Scroller

Although it would seem logical to modify the vertical scroller engine from the last chapter to adapt it to the horizontal direction, that only solves the simple problem of how to get tiles on the screen, which is relatively easy to do. The majority of the source code for *Warbirds Pacifica* in the last chapter handled animating the airplanes, bullets, and explosions. Likewise, the real challenge to a platform game is not getting the level to scroll horizontally, but designing the level so that solid tiles can be used as obstacles by the player without requiring a lot of custom code (or worse, a separate data file describing the tiles stored in the map file). In other words, you really want to do most of the work in Mappy, and then perform a few simple function calls in the game to determine when a collision has occurred.

Figure 14.1 Platform games feature a character who walks and jumps.

Some code is required to cause a sprite to interact with tiles in a level, such as when you are blocking the player's movement, allowing the player to jump up on a solid tile, and so on. As you will soon see, the logic for accomplishing this key ingredient of platform gameplay is relatively easy to understand because it uses a simple collision detection routine that is based on the properties of the tiles stored in the Mappy-generated level file.

Creating Horizontal Platform Levels with Mappy

There are many ways to write a platform game. You might store map values in an array in your source code, containing the tile numbers for the map as well as solid block information used for collision detection. This is definitely an option, especially if you are writing a simple platform game. However, why do something the hard way when there is a better way to do it? As you saw in the last two chapters, Mappy is a powerful level-editing program used to create map files (with the .fmp extension). These map files can contain multiple layers for each map and can include animated tiles as well.

In Chapter 10, I explained how to develop a simple scrolling engine using a single large bitmap. (This engine was put to use to enhance the *Tank War* game.) Later, in Chapter 12, I introduced you to Mappy and explained how to walk the level (or preview it with source code). Now that you are using the MappyAL library, introduced in the previous chapter on vertical scrolling, there is no longer any need to work with the map directly. You have seen and experienced a logical progression from simple to advanced, while the difficulty has been reduced in each new chapter. This chapter is even simpler than the last one, and I will demonstrate with a sample program shortly.

Before you can delve into the source code for a platform game, I need to show you some new tricks in Mappy because you need to create a level with two types of blocks—

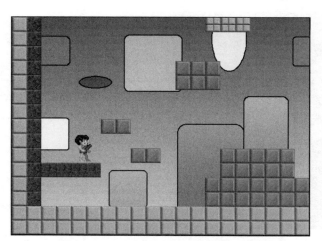

background and foreground. Try not to confuse block type with layering. Mappy supports multiple layers, but I am not using layers to accomplish platform-style gameplay. Instead, the background tiles are static and repeated across the entire level, whereas the foreground tiles are used basically to support the player. Take a look at Figure 14.2 for an example. You can see the player standing on a ledge, which is how this template game looks at startup.

Figure 14.2 The solid tile blocks keep the player from falling through the bottom of the screen.

In the background you see a colorful image containing various shapes, while the foreground contains solid tiles. However, as far as Mappy is concerned, this map is made up of a single layer of tiles.

Allow me to explain. There are basically two ways to add a background to a Mappy level. You can simply insert generic neutral tiles in the empty spaces or you can insert a bitmap image. You might be wondering how to do that. Mappy includes a feature that can divide a solid bitmap into tiles and then construct a map out of it. The key is making sure your starting level size has the same dimensions as the source bitmap.

Run Mappy, open the File menu, and select New Map. Set each tile to 32×32 and set the map size to 20×15 tiles. The result of these dimensions is a 640×480-pixel map. Also, you will be working with true color (16-bit or higher color depth) in this chapter (see Figure 14.3).

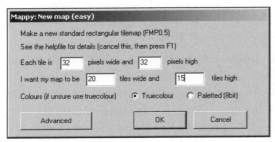

Figure 14.3 The New Map dialog box in Mappy

Now, use your favorite graphic editor to create a 640×480 bitmap image or use one of your favorite bitmaps resized to these dimensions. Normally at this point, you would use Import to load a tile map into Mappy, but the process for converting a solid image into tiles is a little different. Open the MapTools menu. Select the Useful Functions menu item and select Create Map from Big Picture, as shown in Figure 14.4.

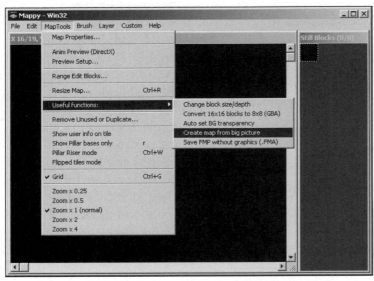

Figure 14.4 Creating a map from a large bitmap image

To demonstrate, I created a colorful bitmap image and used it as the basis for a new map in Mappy using this special feature. But before you create a new map, let me give you a little pointer. The background tiles must be stored with the foreground tiles. You'll want to create a new source bitmap that has room for your background image and the tiles used in the game. Paste your background image into the new bitmap at the top, with the game tiles located underneath. Also be sure to leave some extra space at the bottom so it is easier to add new tiles as you are developing the game (see Figure 14.5).

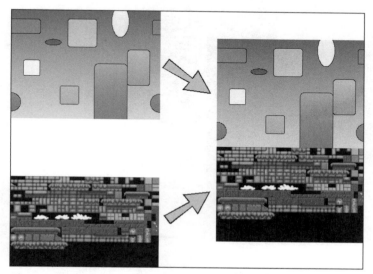

Figure 14.5 The background image and game tiles are stored in the same bitmap image and imported into Mappy.

Using this combined source bitmap, go into Mappy and, after having created the 640×480 map (20 tiles across, 15 tiles down, 32×32 pixels per tile), select Useful Functions, Create Map from Big Picture. The resulting map should look similar to the one shown in Figure 14.6. If you scroll down in the tile palette, you should see the foreground tiles below the background image tiles. See how Mappy has divided the image into a set of tiles? Naturally, you could do this sort of thing with source code by blitting a transparent tile map over a background image, but doing this in Mappy is more interesting (and saves you time writing source code).

You might be wondering, "What next? Am I creating a scrolling game out of a 640×480 tile map?" Not at all; this is only the first step. You must use a tile map that is exactly the same size as the background image in your source bitmap, or the background tiles will be tweaked. Once the background has been generated, you can resize the map.

Open the MapTools menu and select Resize Map to bring up the Resize Map Array dialog box shown in Figure 14.7.

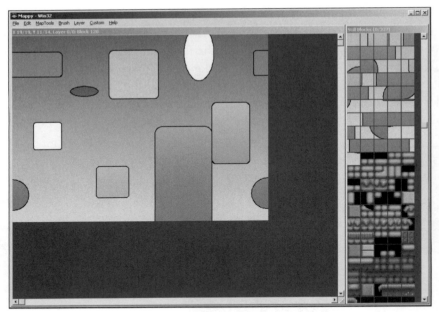

Figure 14.6 A new tile map has been generated based on the source bitmap image.

Press the button labeled 4 to instruct the resize routine to preserve the existing tiles during the resize. The new map can be any size you want, but I normally choose the largest map size possible until I've designed the level, to provide a lot of work space. Besides, it's more fun to include large levels in your games than smaller ones. Just keep in mind that Mappy supports a maximum of 30,000 tiles. If you want your game to scroll upward (as the player is jumping on tiles), keep that in mind. Fifteen tiles deep equates to 480 pixels. You can enter 20 for the height if you want. That is probably a better idea after all, to allow some room for jumping.

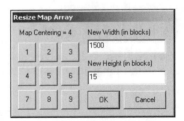

Figure 14.7 The Resize Map Array dialog box

Next, you can experiment with the Brush menu to duplicate the background tiles across the entire level, unless you intend to vary the background. I created a background that meshes well from either side to provide a seamless image when scrolling left or right. Basically, you can choose Grab New Brush, then use the mouse to select a rectangular set of tiles with which to create the brush, and then give the new brush a name. From then on, anywhere you click will duplicate that section of tiles. I used this method to fill the entire level with the same small background tiles. The beautiful thing about this is you end up with a very small memory footprint for such an apparently huge background image.

After resizing and filling the map with the background tiles, the result might look something like Figure 14.8.

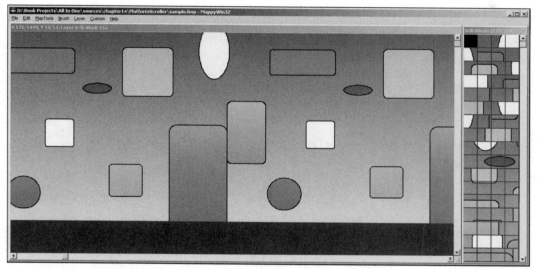

Figure 14.8 A very large horizontally oriented level in Mappy with a bitmap background image

Separating the Foreground Tiles

After you have filled the level with the background tiles, it's time to get started designing the level. But first, you need to make a change to the underlying structure of the foreground tiles, setting them to the FG1 property to differentiate them from the background tiles. This will allow you to identify these tiles in the game to facilitate collision detection on the edges of the tiles.

If you decided to skip over the step earlier in which I suggested adding tiles below the bitmap image, you will need to complete it at this time because the background tiles are not suitable for creating a game level.

The tiles provided on the CD-ROM in the \chapter14\PlatformScroller project folder will suffice if you want to simply copy the file off the CD-ROM. I have called the original tile image blocks1.bmp and the combined image blocks2.bmp. (This second one will be used in the *PlatformScroller* demo shortly.)

Throughout this discussion, I want to encourage you to use your own artwork in the game. Create your own funky background image as I have done for the *PlatformScroller* program that is coming up. As for the tiles, that is a more difficult matter because there is no easy way to draw attractive tiles. As expected, I am using a tileset from Ari Feldman's SpriteLib in this chapter as well. (See http://www.arifeldman.com for more information.)

SpriteLib is a good place to start when you need sprites and tiles with which to develop your game, although it is not a replacement for your own commissioned artwork. Contact Ari to find out how to order a custom sprite set.

Assuming you are using the blocks2.bmp file I created and stored in the project folder for this chapter, you'll want to scroll down in the tile palette to tile 156, the first foreground tile in the tile set (see Figure 14.9).

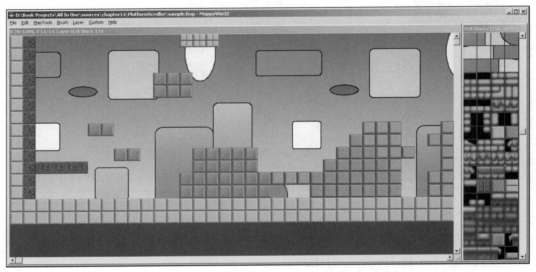

Figure 14.9 Highlighting the first foreground tile in Mappy (right side of the screen)

After you have identified the first foreground tile, you can use this number in the next step. What you are going to do is change the property of the tiles. Double-click on tile #156 to bring up the tile editor. By default, tiles that have been added to the map are assigned to the background, which is the standard level used in simple games (see Figure 14.10).

Do you see the four small boxes on the bottom-left of the Block Properties dialog box? These represent the tile image used for each level (BG, FG1, FG2, FG3). Click on the BG box to bring up the Pick Block Graphic dialog box. Scroll up to the very first tile, which is blank, and select it, and then close the dialog box (see Figure 14.11).

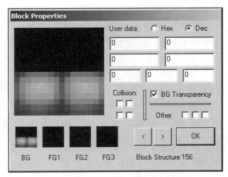

Figure 14.10 The Block Properties dialog box provides an interface for changing the properties of the tiles.

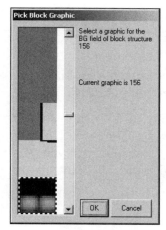

Figure 14.11 The Pick Block Graphic dialog box is used to select a tile for each of the four scroll layers.

Next, click on the FG1 map layer box and locate the tile image you just removed from BG. If you have a hard time locating tiles, I recommend first selecting FG1 before you remove the BG tile. After you have selected the correct tile, you have essentially moved the tile from BG to FG1. In a moment, I will show you a method to quickly make this change on a range of tiles.

The next property to change on the foreground tiles is the collision. If you look for the Collision boxes near the middle of the Block Properties dialog box, you'll see four check boxes. Check all of them so the tile properties look like Figure 14.12.

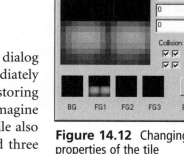

Figure 14.12 Changing the collision properties of the tile

Have you noticed that the Block Properties dialog box has many options that don't immediately seem useful? Mappy is actually capable of storing quite a bit of information for each tile. Imagine being able to set the collision property while also having access to seven numeric values and three Booleans. This is more than enough information for even a highly complex RPG, which typically has more complicated maps than other games. You can set these values in Mappy for use in the game, and you can also read or set the values in your program using the various properties and arrays in MappyAL. For reference, open the mappyal.h file, which contains all the definitions. You can also examine some of the sample programs that come with MappyAL (included on the CD-ROM under \mappy\mappyal).

For the purpose of creating a simple platform game, you only need to set the four collision boxes. (Note that you can fine-tune the collision results in your game by setting only certain collision boxes here.)

Performing a Range Block Edit

Open the MapEdit menu and select Range Edit Blocks to bring up the Range Alter Block Properties dialog box shown in Figure 14.13.

In the From field, enter the number of the first foreground tile. If you are using the blocks2.bmp file for this chapter project, the tile number is 156.

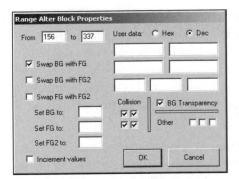

Figure 14.13 The Range Alter Block Properties dialog box

In the To field, enter the number of the last tile in the foreground tile set, which is 337 in this case.

You now have an opportunity to set any of the property values for the range of blocks. Make sure all four collision boxes are fully checked.

The most important thing to do with this range edit is swap the BG for the FG1 layer. This will have the same effect as the manual edit you performed earlier, and it will affect all of the tiles in one fell swoop.

After clicking on OK to perform the action, you can save the map file and move on to the next section. You might want to double-click on one of the tiles to ensure that the change from BG to FG1 has been made.

If you have not added any tiles to your map, you must do that before you continue. As a general rule, the edges of the map should be walled, and a floor should be across the bottom, or at least insert a platform for the start position if your level design does not include a floor. You might want to let the player "fall" as part of the challenge for a level, in which case you'll need to check the Y position of the player's sprite to determine when the player has dropped below the floor. Just be careful to design your level so that there is room for the player to fall. The *PlatformScroller* program to follow does not account for sprites going out of range, but normally when the player falls below the bottom edge of the screen, he has lost a life and must restart the level.

Developing a Scrolling Platform Game

The *PlatformScroller* program included on the CD-ROM is all ready to run, but I will go over the construction of this program and the artwork used by it. You already created the map in the last section, but you can also use the provided map file (sample.fmp) if you want.

Describing the Game

The *PlatformScroller* demo features an animated player character who can run left or right (controlled by the arrow keys) and jump (controlled by the spacebar). The map is quite large, 1,500 tiles across (48,000 pixels) by 15 tiles down (480 pixels). The *PlatformScroller* engine is capable of handling up and down scroll directions, so you can design maps that go up, for instance, by allowing the player to jump from ledge to ledge, by flying, or by some other means. Figure 14.14 shows the player jumping. It is up to the level designer to ensure that the player has a path on which to walk, and it is up to the programmer to handle cases in which the player falls off the screen (and usually dies).

The background image is an example; you should design your own background imagery, as described earlier in this chapter. Although I have not gotten into the subject in this book, you can also feature parallax scrolling using MappyAL by creating additional layers in the map file. MappyAL has the code to draw parallax layers. Of course, you can draw multiple layers yourself using the standard Allegro `blit` function.

Figure 14.14 The *PlatformScroller* program demonstrates how the player's sprite can interact with tiles using the collision properties set within Mappy.

The Game Artwork

The artwork for the *PlatformScroller* demo is primarily comprised of the background image and foreground tiles you have already seen. For reference, the tiles are shown in Figure 14.15.

Figure 14.15 The source tiles used in *PlatformScroller* (which you may use to modify the level)

The only animated artwork in the game is the player character that moves around the level, running and jumping (see Figure 14.16). This character is represented by a sprite with eight frames of animation. Four additional animation frames are provided in the guy.bmp file that you can use for a jumping animation. I have not used these frames to keep the source code listing relatively short (in contrast to the long listing for *Warbirds Pacifica* in the previous chapter).

Figure 14.16 The source image containing the animated player character in the *PlatformScroller* demo

Using the Platform Scroller

Most of the source code for the *PlatformScroller* demo is familiar from previous chapters, including the SPRITE struct and so on. The new information that might need clarification has to do with tile collision.

You might recall from the Block Properties dialog box in Mappy that you set four collision boxes. These values are stored in a struct called BLKSTR.

```
//structure for data blocks
typedef struct {
long int bgoff, fgoff;      //offsets from start of graphic blocks
long int fgoff2, fgoff3;    //more overlay blocks
unsigned long int user1, user2;     //user long data
unsigned short int user3, user4;    //user short data
unsigned char user5, user6, user7;  //user byte data
unsigned char tl : 1;        //bits for collision detection
unsigned char tr : 1;
unsigned char bl : 1;
unsigned char br : 1;
unsigned char trigger : 1;  //bits to trigger an event
unsigned char unused1 : 1;
unsigned char unused2 : 1;
unsigned char unused3 : 1;
} BLKSTR;
```

You might be able to identify the members of the struct after seeing them represented in the Block Properties dialog box. You might notice the seven integer values (user1 to user7) and the three values (unused1, unused2, unused3).

The values you need for collision detection with tiles are called tl and tr (for top-left and top-right) and bl and br (you guessed it, for bottom-left and bottom-right). What is needed to determine when a collision takes place? It's remarkably easy thanks to MappyAL. You can retrieve the block number from an (x,y) position (presumably, the player's sprite location), and then simply return a value specifying whether that tile has one or more of the collision values (tl, tr, bl, br) set to 1 or 0. Simply returning the result is enough to pass a true or false response from a collision function. So here you have it:

```
int collided(int x, int y)
{
    BLKSTR *blockdata;
    blockdata = MapGetBlock(x/mapblockwidth, y/mapblockheight);
    return blockdata->tl;
}
```

The MapGetBlock function accepts a (row,column) value pair and simply returns a pointer to the block located in that position of the map. This is extremely handy, isn't it?

Writing the Source Code

Because the collision and ability to retrieve a specific tile from the map are so easy to handle, the source code for the *PlatformScroller* program is equally manageable. There is some code to manage the player's position, but a small amount of study reveals the simplicity of this code. The player's position is tracked as player->x and player->y and is compared to the collision values to determine when the sprite should stop moving (left, right, or down). There is currently no facility for handling the bottom edge of tiles; the sprite can jump through a tile from below, but not from above (see Figure 14.17). This might be a feature you will need, depending on the requirements of your own games.

The source code for the *Platform Scroller* demo follows. As was the case with the projects in the last chapter, you will need to include the mappyal.h and mappyal.c files (which make up the MappyAL library) and include a linker reference to alleg.lib as usual (or -lalleg, depending on your compiler). I have highlighted in bold significant sections of new code that contribute to the logic of the game or require special attention.

Figure 14.17 The player can jump through tiles from below, but will stop when landing on top of a tile.

```
#include <stdio.h>
#include <allegro.h>
#include "mappyal.h"

#define MODE GFX_AUTODETECT_FULLSCREEN
#define WIDTH 640
#define HEIGHT 480
#define JUMPIT 1600

//define the sprite structure
typedef struct SPRITE
{
    int dir, alive;
    int x,y;
    int width,height;
    int xspeed,yspeed;
    int xdelay,ydelay;
    int xcount,ycount;
    int curframe,maxframe,animdir;
    int framecount,framedelay;
}SPRITE;

//declare the bitmaps and sprites
BITMAP *player_image[8];
SPRITE *player;
BITMAP *buffer;
BITMAP *temp;

//tile grabber
BITMAP *grabframe(BITMAP *source,
                    int width, int height,
                    int startx, int starty,
                    int columns, int frame)
{
    BITMAP *temp = create_bitmap(width,height);
    int x = startx + (frame % columns) * width;
    int y = starty + (frame / columns) * height;
    blit(source,temp,x,y,0,0,width,height);
    return temp;
}

int collided(int x, int y)
{
```

```
        BLKSTR *blockdata;
        blockdata = MapGetBlock(x/mapblockwidth, y/mapblockheight);
        return blockdata->tl;
}

int main (void)
{
        int mapxoff, mapyoff;
        int oldpy, oldpx;
        int facing = 0;
        int jump = JUMPIT;
        int n;

        allegro_init();
        install_timer();
        install_keyboard();
        set_color_depth(16);
        set_gfx_mode(MODE, WIDTH, HEIGHT, 0, 0);

        //load the player sprite
        temp = load_bitmap("guy.bmp", NULL);
        for (n=0; n<8; n++)
            player_image[n] = grabframe(temp,50,64,0,0,8,n);
        destroy_bitmap(temp);

        //initialize the sprite
        player = malloc(sizeof(SPRITE));
        player->x = 80;
        player->y = 100;
        player->curframe=0;
        player->framecount=0;
        player->framedelay=6;
        player->maxframe=7;
        player->width=player_image[0]->w;
        player->height=player_image[0]->h;

        //load the map
        if (MapLoad("sample.fmp")) exit(0);

        //create the double buffer
        buffer = create_bitmap (WIDTH, HEIGHT);
        clear(buffer);
```

```
//main loop
while (!key[KEY_ESC])
{
    oldpy = player->y;
    oldpx = player->x;

    if (key[KEY_RIGHT])
    {
        facing = 1;
        player->x+=2;
        if (++player->framecount > player->framedelay)
        {
            player->framecount=0;
            if (++player->curframe > player->maxframe)
                player->curframe=1;
        }
    }
    else if (key[KEY_LEFT])
    {
        facing = 0;
        player->x-=2;
        if (++player->framecount > player->framedelay)
        {
            player->framecount=0;
            if (++player->curframe > player->maxframe)
                player->curframe=1;
        }
    }
    else player->curframe=0;

    //handle jumping
    if (jump==JUMPIT)
    {
        if (!collided(player->x + player->width/2,
            player->y + player->height + 5))
            jump = 0;

        if (key[KEY_SPACE])
            jump = 30;
    }
    else
    {
```

```
        player->y -= jump/3;
        jump--;
    }


    if (jump<0)
    {
        if (collided(player->x + player->width/2,
            player->y + player->height))
        {
            jump = JUMPIT;
            while (collided(player->x + player->width/2,
                player->y + player->height))
                player->y -= 2;
        }
    }

    //check for collision with foreground tiles
    if (!facing)
    {
        if (collided(player->x, player->y + player->height))
            player->x = oldpx;
    }
    else
    {
        if (collided(player->x + player->width,
            player->y + player->height))
            player->x = oldpx;
    }


    //update the map scroll position
    mapxoff = player->x + player->width/2 - WIDTH/2 + 10;
    mapyoff = player->y + player->height/2 - HEIGHT/2 + 10;

    //avoid moving beyond the map edge
    if (mapxoff < 0) mapxoff = 0;
    if (mapxoff > (mapwidth * mapblockwidth - WIDTH))
        mapxoff = mapwidth * mapblockwidth - WIDTH;
    if (mapyoff < 0)
        mapyoff = 0;
    if (mapyoff > (mapheight * mapblockheight - HEIGHT))
        mapyoff = mapheight * mapblockheight - HEIGHT;
```

```
    //draw the background tiles
    MapDrawBG(buffer, mapxoff, mapyoff, 0, 0, WIDTH-1, HEIGHT-1);

    //draw foreground tiles
    MapDrawFG(buffer, mapxoff, mapyoff, 0, 0, WIDTH-1, HEIGHT-1, 0);

    //draw the player's sprite
    if (facing)
        draw_sprite(buffer, player_image[player->curframe],
            (player->x-mapxoff), (player->y-mapyoff));
    else
        draw_sprite_h_flip(buffer, player_image[player->curframe],
            (player->x-mapxoff), (player->y-mapyoff));

    //blit the double buffer
    vsync();
    acquire_screen();
    blit(buffer, screen, 0, 0, 0, 0, WIDTH-1, HEIGHT-1);
    release_screen();
    } //while

//clean up
for (n=0; n<9; n++)
    destroy_bitmap(player_image[n]);
free(player);
destroy_bitmap(buffer);
MapFreeMem();
allegro_exit();
}
END_OF_MAIN();
```

Summary

This chapter provided an introduction to horizontal scrolling platform games, explained how to create platform levels with Mappy, and demonstrated how to put platforming into practice with a sample demonstration program that you could use as a template for any number of platform games. This subject might seem dated to some, but when does great gameplay ever get old? If you take a look at the many Game Boy Advance titles being released this year, you'll notice that most of them are scrolling arcade-style games or plat-formers! The market for such games has not waned in the two decades since the inception of this genre and it does not look like it will let up any time soon. So have fun and create the next *Super Mario World*, and I guarantee you, someone will publish your game.

Chapter Quiz

You can find the answers to this chapter quiz in Appendix A, "Chapter Quiz Answers."

1. Which term is often used to describe a horizontal-scrolling game with a walking character?
   A. Shooter
   B. Platform
   C. RPG
   D. Walker

2. What is the name of the map-editing tool you have used in the last several chapters?
   A. Mappy
   B. Map Editor
   C. Mapper
   D. Tile Editor

3. What is the identifier for the Mappy block property representing the background?
   A. BG1
   B. BACK
   C. BG
   D. BGND

4. What is the identifier for the Mappy block property representing the first foreground layer?
   A. FG1
   B. FORE1
   C. FG
   D. LV1

5. Which dialog box allows the editing of tile properties in Mappy?
   A. Tile Properties
   B. Map Tile Editor
   C. Map Block Editor
   D. Block Properties

6. Which menu item brings up the Range Alter Block Properties dialog?

    A. Range Alter Block Properties

    B. Range Edit Blocks

    C. Range Edit Tile Properties

    D. Range Block Edit

7. What is the name of the MappyAL struct that contains information about tile blocks?

    A. BLOCKS

    B. TILEBLOCK

    C. BLKSTR

    D. BLKINFO

8. What MappyAL function returns a pointer to a block specified by the (x,y) parameters?

    A. MapGetBlock

    B. GetDataBlock

    C. GetTileAt

    D. MapGetTile

9. What is the name of the function that draws the map's background?

    A. MapDrawBG

    B. DrawBackground

    C. DrawMapBack

    D. DrawMapBG

10. Which MappyAL block struct member was used to detect collisions in the sample program?

    A. bl

    B. br

    C. tl

    D. tr

PART III

TAKING IT TO THE NEXT LEVEL

CHAPTER 15

Mastering the Audible Realm: Allegro's Sound Support 511

CHAPTER 16

Using Datafiles to Store Game Resources 539

CHAPTER 17

Playing FLIC Movies 551

CHAPTER 18

Introduction to Artificial Intelligence 563

CHAPTER 19

The Mathematical Side of Games 585

CHAPTER 20

Publishing Your Game 611

Welcome to Part III of *Game Programming All in One, 2nd Edition*. Part III includes six chapters that push the boundaries of your game development skills to the limit. You will find coverage of sound mixing and sample playback, storing game resources in datafiles, and playing FLIC movies before you delve into the complex subjects of artificial intelligence and mathematics. The book ends with a chapter about how to get your games published.

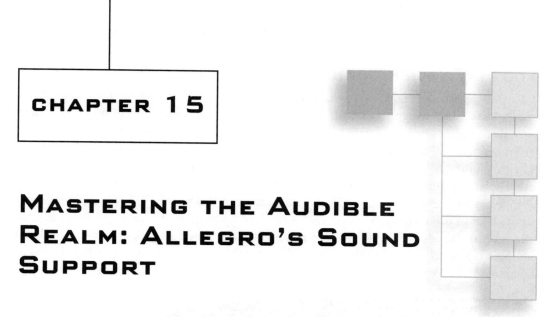

CHAPTER 15

Mastering the Audible Realm: Allegro's Sound Support

Most game programmers are interested in pushing graphics to the limit, first and foremost, and few of us really get enthusiastic about the sound effects and music in a game. That is natural, since the graphics system is the most critical aspect of the game. Sound can be an equal partner with the graphics to provide a memorable, challenging, and satisfying game experience far beyond pretty graphics alone. Indeed, the sound effects and music are often what gamers love most about a game.

This chapter provides an introduction to the sound support that comes with Allegro, and Allegro is significantly loaded with features! Allegro provides an interface to the underlying sound system available on any particular computer system first, and if some features are not available, Allegro will emulate them if necessary. For instance, a basic digital sound mixer is often the first request of a game designer considering the sound support for a game because this is the core of a sound engine. Allegro will interface with DirectSound on Windows systems to provide the mixer and many more features and will take advantage of any similar standardized library support in other operating systems to provide a consistent level of performance and function in a game on any system.

Here is a breakdown of the major topics in this chapter:

- Understanding sound initialization routines
- Working with standard sample playback routines
- Using low-level sample playback routines

The PlayWave Program

I want to get started right away with a sample program to demonstrate how to load and play a WAV file through the sound system because this is the usual beginning of a more complex sound system in a game. Figure 15.1 shows the output from the *PlayWave* program. As with all the other support functions in Allegro, you only need to link to the Allegro library file (alleg.lib or liballeg.a) and include allegro.h in your program—no other special requirements are needed. Essentially, you have a built-in sound system along with everything else in Allegro. Go ahead and try out this program; I will explain how it works later in this chapter. All you need to run it is a sample WAV file, which you can usually find in abundance on the Web in public domain sound libraries. I have included a sample clapping.wav file in the project folder for this program on the CD-ROM; it is in \chapter15\PlayWave.

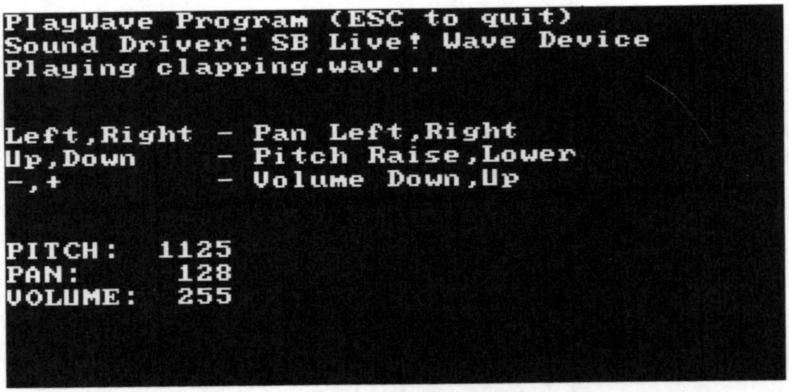

Figure 15.1 The *PlayWave* program demonstrates how to initialize the sound system and play a WAV file.

```
#include <allegro.h>

#define MODE GFX_AUTODETECT_WINDOWED
#define WIDTH 640
#define HEIGHT 480
#define WHITE makecol(255,255,255)

void main(void)
{
    SAMPLE *sample;
    int panning = 128;
    int pitch = 1000;
    int volume = 128;
```

```
//initialize the program
allegro_init();
install_keyboard();
install_timer();
set_color_depth(16);
set_gfx_mode(MODE, WIDTH, HEIGHT, 0, 0);
text_mode(0);

//install a digital sound driver
if (install_sound(DIGI_AUTODETECT, MIDI_NONE, "") != 0)
{
    allegro_message("Error initializing sound system");
    return;
}

//display program information
textout(screen,font,"PlayWave Program (ESC to quit)",0,0,WHITE);
textprintf(screen,font,0,10,WHITE,"Sound Driver: %s",digi_driver->name);
textout(screen,font,"Playing clapping.wav...",0,20,WHITE);
textout(screen,font,"Left,Right - Pan Left,Right",0,50,WHITE);
textout(screen,font,"Up,Down    - Pitch Raise,Lower",0,60,WHITE);
textout(screen,font,"-,+        - Volume Down,Up",0,70,WHITE);

//load the wave file
sample = load_sample("clapping.wav");
if (!sample)
{
    allegro_message("Error reading wave file");
    return;
}

//play the sample with looping
play_sample(sample, volume, pan, pitch, TRUE);

//main loop
while (!key[KEY_ESC])
{
    //change the panning
    if ((key[KEY_LEFT]) && (panning > 0))
        panning--;
    else if ((key[KEY_RIGHT]) && (panning < 255))
        panning++;
```

```
//change the pitch (rounding at 512)
if ((key[KEY_UP]) && (pitch < 16384))
    pitch = ((pitch * 513) / 512) + 1;
else if ((key[KEY_DOWN]) && (pitch > 64))
    pitch = ((pitch * 511) / 512) - 1;

//change the volume
if (key[KEY_EQUALS] && volume < 255)
    volume++;
else if (key[KEY_MINUS] && volume > 0)
    volume--;

//adjust the sample
adjust_sample(sample, volume, pan, pitch, TRUE);

//pause
rest(5);

//display status
textprintf(screen,font,0,100,WHITE,"PITCH: %5d", pitch);
textprintf(screen,font,0,110,WHITE,"PAN:   %5d", panning);
textprintf(screen,font,0,120,WHITE,"VOLUME:%5d", volume);
}

//destroy the sample
destroy_sample(sample);

//remove the sound driver
remove_sound();

return;
}

END_OF_MAIN();
```

Now I want go over some of the functions in the *PlayWave* program and more Allegro sound routines that you'll need. This gives you a preview of what is possible with Allegro, but don't limit your imagination to this meager example because much more is possible.

Sound Initialization Routines

As with the graphics system, you must initialize the sound system before you use the sound routines. Why is that? Allegro runs as lean as possible and only allocates memory when it is needed. It would be a shame if every Allegro feature were allocated and initialized automatically with even the smallest of programs (such as a command-line utility).

Now I'll go over some of the sound initialization routines you'll be using most often. If you require more advanced features, you can refer to the Allegro documentation, header files, and online sources for information on topics such as sound recording, MIDI, and streaming. I will not cover those features here because they are not normally needed in a game.

Detecting the Digital Sound Driver

The detect_digi_driver function determines whether the specified digital sound device is available. It returns the maximum number of voices that the driver can provide or zero if the device is not available. This function must be called before install_sound.

```
int detect_digi_driver(int driver_id);
```

Reserving Voices

The reserve_voices function is used to specify the number of voices that are to be used by the digital and MIDI sound drivers, respectively. This must be called before install_sound. If you reserve too many voices, subsequent calls to install_sound will fail. The actual number of voices available depends on the driver, and in some cases you will actually get more than you reserve. To restore the voice setting to the default, you can pass −1 to the function. Be aware that sound quality might drop if too many voices are in use.

```
void reserve_voices(int digi_voices, int midi_voices);
```

Setting an Individual Voice Volume

The set_volume_per_voice function is used to adjust the volume of each voice to compensate for mixer output being too loud or too quiet, depending on the number of samples being mixed (because Allegro lowers the volume each time a voice is added to help reduce distortion). This must be called before calling install_sound. To play a sample at the maximum volume without distortion, use 0; otherwise, you should call this function with 1 when panning will be used. It is important to understand that each time you increase the parameter by one, the volume of each voice will be halved. So if you pass 2, you can play up to eight samples at maximum volume without distortion (as long as panning is not used). If all else fails, you can pass −1 to restore the volumes to the default levels. Table 15.1 provides a guide.

Here is the definition of the function:

```
void set_volume_per_voice(int scale);
```

Table 15.1 Channel Volume Parameters

Number of Voices	Recommended Parameters
1–8 voices	set_volume_per_voice(2)
16 voices	set_volume_per_voice(3)
32 voices	set_volume_per_voice(4)
64 voices	set_volume_per_voice(5)

Initializing the Sound Driver

After you have configured the sound system to meet your needs with the functions just covered, you can call install_sound to initialize the sound driver. The default parameters are DIGI_AUTODETECT and MIDI_AUTODETECT, which instruct Allegro to read hardware settings from a configuration file (which was a significant issue under MS-DOS and is no longer needed with the sound drivers of modern operating systems).

```
int install_sound(int digi, int midi, const char *cfg_path);
```

tip

The third parameter of install_sound generally is not needed any longer with modern operating systems that use a sound card device driver model.

Removing the Sound Driver

The remove_sound function removes the sound driver and can be called when you no longer need to use the sound routines.

```
void remove_sound();
```

Changing the Volume

The set_volume function is used to change the overall volume of the sound system (both digital and MIDI), with a range of 0 to 255. To leave one parameter unchanged while updating the other, pass –1. Most systems with sound cards will have hardware mixers, but Allegro will create a software sound mixer if necessary.

```
void set_volume(int digi_volume, int midi_volume);
```

Standard Sample Playback Routines

The digital sample playback routines can be rather daunting because there are so many of them, but many of these routines are holdovers from when Allegro was developed for MS-DOS. I will cover the most important and useful sample playback routines. Because sound mixers are common in the sound card now, many of the support functions are no longer needed; it is usually enough for any game that a sound mixer is working and sound effects can be played simultaneously.

If some of this listing seems like a header file dump, it is because there are so many sound routines provided by Allegro to manipulate samples and voice channels that a code example for each one would be too difficult (and time consuming). Suffice it to say, many of the seldom-used functions are included here for your reference.

Loading a Sample File

The `load_sample` function will load a .wav or .voc file. The .voc file format was created by Creative Labs for the first Sound Blaster sound card, and this format was very popular with MS-DOS games. It is nice to have the ability to load either file format with this routine because .voc might still be a better format for some older systems.

```
SAMPLE *load_sample(const char *filename);
```

Loading a WAV File

The `load_wav` function will load a standard Windows or OS/2 RIFF WAV file. This function is called by `load_sample` based on the file extension.

```
SAMPLE *load_wav(const char *filename);
```

Loading a VOC File

The `load_voc` function will load a Creative Labs VOC file. This function is called by `load_sample` based on the file extension.

```
SAMPLE *load_voc(const char *filename);
```

Playing a Sample

The `play_sample` function starts playback of a sample using the provided parameters to set the properties of the sample prior to playback. The available parameters are volume, panning, frequency (pitch), and a Boolean value for looping the sample.

The volume and pan range from 0 to 255. Frequency is relative rather than absolute—1000 represents the frequency at which the sample was recorded, 2000 is twice this, and so on. If the loop flag is set, the sample will repeat until you call stop_sample and can be manipulated during playback with adjust_sample. This function returns the voice number that was allocated for the sample (or –1 if it failed).

```
int play_sample(const SAMPLE *spl, int vol, int pan, int freq, int loop);
```

Altering a Sample's Properties

The adjust_sample function alters the properties of a sample during playback. (This is usually only useful for looping samples.) The parameters are volume, panning, frequency, and looping. If there is more than one copy of the same sample playing (as in a repeatable sound, such as an explosion), this will adjust the first one. If the sample is not playing it has no effect.

```
void adjust_sample(const SAMPLE *spl, int vol, int pan, int freq, int loop);
```

Stopping a Sample

The stop_sample function stops playback and is often needed for samples that are looping in playback. If more than one copy of the sample is playing (such as an explosion sound), this function will stop all of them.

```
void stop_sample(const SAMPLE *spl);
```

Creating a New Sample

The create_sample function creates a new sample with the specified bits (sampling rate), stereo flag, frequency, and length. The returned SAMPLE pointer is then treated like any other sample.

```
SAMPLE *create_sample(int bits, int stereo, int freq, int len);
```

Destroying a Sample

The destroy_sample function is used to remove a sample from memory. You can call this function even when the sample is playing because Allegro will first stop playback.

```
void destroy_sample(SAMPLE *spl);
```

Low-Level Sample Playback Routines

If you need more detailed control over how samples are played, you can use the lower-level voice functions as an option rather than using the sample routines. The voice routines require more work because you must allocate and free voice data in memory rather than letting Allegro handle such details, but you do gain more control over the mixer and playback functionality.

Allocating a Voice

The `allocate_voice` function allocates memory for a sample in the mixer with default parameters for volume, centered pan, standard frequency, and no looping. After voice playback has finished, it must be removed using `deallocate_voice`. This function returns the voice number or −1 on error.

```
int allocate_voice(const SAMPLE *spl);
```

Removing a Voice

The `deallocate_voice` function removes a voice from the mixer after stopping playback and releases any resources it was using.

```
void deallocate_voice(int voice);
```

Reallocating a Voice

The `reallocate_voice` function changes the sample for an existing voice, which is equivalent to deallocating the voice and then reallocating it again using the new sample.

```
void reallocate_voice(int voice, const SAMPLE *spl);
```

Releasing a Voice

The `release_voice` function releases a voice and allows it to play through to completion without any further manipulation. After playback has finished, the voice is automatically removed. This is equivalent to deallocating the voice at the end of playback.

```
void release_voice(int voice);
```

Activating a Voice

The `voice_start` function activates a voice using the properties configured for the voice.

```
void voice_start(int voice);
```

Stopping a Voice

The `voice_stop` function stops (or rather, pauses) a voice at the current playback position, after which playback can be resumed with a call to `voice_start`.

```
void voice_stop(int voice);
```

Setting Voice Priority

The voice_set_priority function sets the priority of the sample in the mixer with a priority range of 0 to 255. Lower-priority voices are cropped when the mixer becomes filled.

```
void voice_set_priority(int voice, int priority);
```

Checking the Status of a Voice

The voice_check function determines whether a voice has been allocated, returning a copy of the sample if it is allocated or NULL if the sample is not present.

```
SAMPLE *voice_check(int voice);
```

Returning the Position of a Voice

The voice_get_position function returns the current position of playback for that voice or −1 if playback has finished.

```
int voice_get_position(int voice);
```

Setting the Position of a Voice

The voice_set_position function sets the playback position of a voice in sample units.

```
void voice_set_position(int voice, int position);
```

Altering the Playback Mode of a Voice

The voice_set_playmode function adjusts the loop status of a voice and can be called even while a voice is engaged in playback.

```
void voice_set_playmode(int voice, int playmode);
```

The playmode parameters listed in Table 15.2 can be passed to this function.

Table 15.2 Play Mode Parameters

Play Mode Parameter	Description
PLAYMODE_PLAY	Plays the sample once; this is the default without looping.
PLAYMODE_LOOP	Loops repeatedly through the sample.
PLAYMODE_FORWARD	Plays the sample from start to end; supports looping.
PLAYMODE_BACKWARD	Plays the sample in reverse from end to start; supports looping.
PLAYMODE_BIDIR	Plays the sample forward and backward, reversing direction each time the start or end position is reached during playback.

Returning the Volume of a Voice

The `voice_get_volume` function returns the current volume of a voice in the range of 0 to 255.

```
int voice_get_volume(int voice);
```

Setting the Volume of a Voice

The `voice_set_volume` function sets the volume of a voice in the range of 0 to 255.

```
void voice_set_volume(int voice, int volume);
```

Ramping the Volume of a Voice

The `voice_ramp_volume` functions starts a volume ramp up (crescendo) or down (diminuendo) from the current volume to the specified volume for a specified number of milliseconds.

```
void voice_ramp_volume(int voice, int time, int endvol);
```

Stopping a Volume Ramp

The `voice_stop_volumeramp` function interrupts a volume ramp that was previously started with `voice_ramp_volume`.

```
void voice_stop_volumeramp(int voice);
```

Returning the Pitch of a Voice

The `voice_get_frequency` function returns the current pitch of the voice in Hertz (Hz).

```
int voice_get_frequency(int voice);
```

Setting the Pitch of a Voice

The `voice_set_frequency` function sets the pitch of a voice in Hertz (Hz).

```
void voice_set_frequency(int voice, int frequency);
```

Performing a Frequency Sweep of a Voice

The `voice_sweep_frequency` function performs a frequency sweep (glissando) from the current frequency (or pitch) to the specified ending frequency, lasting for the specified number of milliseconds.

```
void voice_sweep_frequency(int voice, int time, int endfreq);
```

Stopping a Frequency Sweep

The voice_stop_frequency_sweep function interrupts a frequency sweep that was previously started with voice_sweep_frequency.

```
void voice_stop_frequency_sweep(int voice);
```

Returning the Pan Value of a Voice

The voice_get_pan function returns the current panning value from 0 (left speaker) to 255 (right speaker).

```
int voice_get_pan(int voice);
```

Setting the Pan Value of a Voice

The voice_set_pan function sets the panning position of a voice with a range of 0 (left speaker) to 255 (right speaker).

```
void voice_set_pan(int voice, int pan);
```

Performing a Sweeping Pan on a Voice

The voice_sweep_pan function performs a sweeping pan from left to right (or vice versa) from the current panning value to the specified ending value with a duration in milliseconds.

```
void voice_sweep_pan(int voice, int time, int endpan);
```

Stopping a Sweeping Pan

The voice_stop_pan_sweep function interrupts a panning sweep operation that was previously started with the voice_sweep_pan function.

```
void voice_stop_pan_sweep(int voice);
```

The SampleMixer Program

I think you will be pleasantly surprised by the simplicity of the next demonstration program in this chapter. *SampleMixer* is a short program that shows you how easy it is to feature multi-channel digital sample playback in your own games (and any other programs) using Allegro's digital sound mixer. Figure 15.2 shows the output from the program. As you can see, there is only a simple interface with no bells or whistles.

The WAV files used in this sample program are included on the CD-ROM in the \chapter15\ SampleMixer folder.

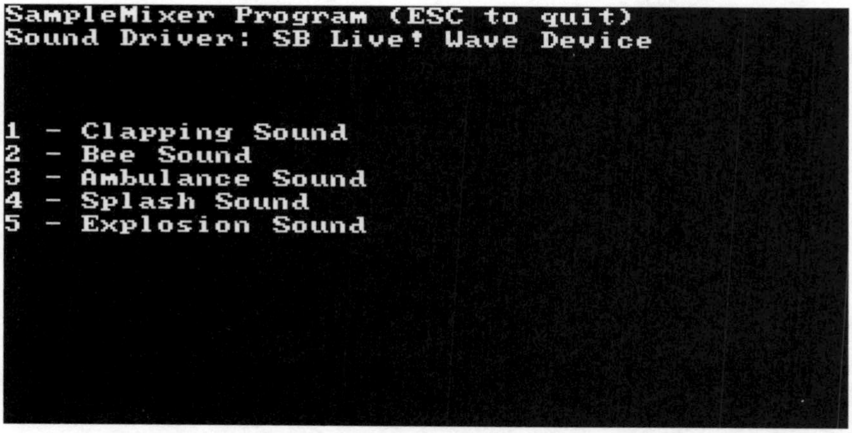

Figure 15.2 The *SampleMixer* program demonstrates the sound mixer provided by Allegro.

```c
#include <allegro.h>

#define MODE GFX_AUTODETECT_WINDOWED
#define WIDTH 640
#define HEIGHT 480
#define WHITE makecol(255,255,255)

void main(void)
{
    SAMPLE *samples[5];
    int volume = 128;
    int pan = 128;
    int pitch = 1000;
    int n;

    //initialize the program
    allegro_init();
    install_keyboard();
    install_timer();
    set_color_depth(16);
    set_gfx_mode(MODE, WIDTH, HEIGHT, 0, 0);
    text_mode(0);

    //install a digital sound driver
    if (install_sound(DIGI_AUTODETECT, MIDI_NONE, "") != 0)
    {
```

```
        allegro_message("Error initializing the sound system");
        return;
    }

    //display program information
    textout(screen,font,"SampleMixer Program (ESC to quit)",0,0,WHITE);
    textprintf(screen,font,0,10,WHITE,"Sound Driver: %s", digi_driver->name);

    //display simple menu
    textout(screen,font,"1 - Clapping Sound",0,50,WHITE);
    textout(screen,font,"2 - Bee Sound",0,60,WHITE);
    textout(screen,font,"3 - Ambulance Sound",0,70,WHITE);
    textout(screen,font,"4 - Splash Sound",0,80,WHITE);
    textout(screen,font,"5 - Explosion Sound",0,90,WHITE);

    //load the wave file
    //normally you would want to include error checking here
    samples[0] = load_sample("clapping.wav");
    samples[1] = load_sample("bee.wav");
    samples[2] = load_sample("ambulance.wav");
    samples[3] = load_sample("splash.wav");
    samples[4] = load_sample("explode.wav");

    //main loop
    while (!key[KEY_ESC])
    {
        if (key[KEY_1])
            play_sample(samples[0], volume, pan, pitch, FALSE);
        if (key[KEY_2])
            play_sample(samples[1], volume, pan, pitch, FALSE);
        if (key[KEY_3])
            play_sample(samples[2], volume, pan, pitch, FALSE);
        if (key[KEY_4])
            play_sample(samples[3], volume, pan, pitch, FALSE);
        if (key[KEY_5])
            play_sample(samples[4], volume, pan, pitch, FALSE);

        //block fast key repeats
        rest(50);
    }

    //destroy the samples
    for (n=0; n<5; n++)
```

```
    destroy_sample(samples[n]);

    //remove the sound driver
    remove_sound();

    return;
}
END_OF_MAIN();
```

Enhancing Tank War

This chapter will see the final enhancement to *Tank War*! It's been a long journey for this game, from a meager vector-based demo, through the various stages to bitmaps, sprites, scrolling backgrounds, and animation. The final revision to the game (the ninth) will add sound effects. In addition, since this is the last update that will be made to *Tank War*, I have decided to throw in a few extras for good measure. Back in Chapter 5, it was premature to add joystick support to *Tank War*. But much time has passed, and you have learned a great deal in the intervening 10 chapters, so now you'll finally have the opportunity to add joystick support to the game. Along the way, I'll show you how to limit the input routines a little to make the tanks move more realistically.

By the time you have finished this section, *Tank War* will have sound effects, joystick support, and improved gameplay. All that will remain is for you to create some new map files using Mappy to see how far you can take the game! I also suggest you play with the techniques from Chapter 14 for testing collisions with Mappy tiles to add solid blocks to *Tank War*. Because that is beyond the scope of this chapter, I leave the challenge to you. Now let's get started on the changes to the game.

Modifying the Game

The last revision to the game was back in Chapter 12, when you added Mappy support to it. Now you can work on adding sound effects and joystick support, and tweaking the gameplay a little. If you haven't already, open the *Tank War* project from Chapter 12 to make the proposed changes. You can also open the completed project in \chapter15 \tankwar if you want. At the very least, you need to copy the wave files out of the folder and into the project folder on your hard drive. Here is a list of the files you need for this enhancement:

- ammo.wav
- fire.wav
- goopy.wav
- harp.wav

- hit1.wav
- hit2.wav
- ohhh.wav
- scream.wav

Modifying tankwar.h

The first change occurs in tankwar.h because there are some variables needed for this enhancement, as well as a new function prototype. Scroll down in tankwar.h to the variables section and add the lines noted in bold.

```
//variables used for sound effects
#define PAN 128
#define PITCH 1000
#define VOLUME 128
#define NUM_SOUNDS 8
#define AMMO 0
#define HIT1 1
#define HIT2 2
#define FIRE 3
#define GOOPY 4
#define HARP 5
#define SCREAM 6
#define OHHH 7
SAMPLE *sounds[NUM_SOUNDS];

//some variables used to slow down keyboard input
int key_count[2];
int key_delay[2];

//function prototypes
void loadsounds();
void readjoysticks();
void animatetank(int num);
void updateexplosion(int num);
```

Modifying setup.c

Now open the setup.c source code file. Add the new loadsounds function to the top of the file. This function loads all the new sound effects that will be used in *Tank War*.

```
void loadsounds()
{
    //install a digital sound driver
```

```c
if (install_sound(DIGI_AUTODETECT, MIDI_NONE, "") != 0)
{
    allegro_message("Error initializing sound system");
    return;
}

//load the ammo sound
sounds[AMMO] = load_sample("ammo.wav");
if (!sounds[AMMO])
{
    allegro_message("Error reading ammo.wav");
    return;
}

//load the hit1 sound
sounds[HIT1] = load_sample("hit1.wav");
if (!sounds[HIT1])
{
    allegro_message("Error reading hit1.wav");
    return;
}
//load the hit2 sound
sounds[HIT2] = load_sample("hit2.wav");
if (!sounds[HIT2])
{
    allegro_message("Error reading hit2.wav");
    return;
}
//load the fire sound
sounds[FIRE] = load_sample("fire.wav");
if (!sounds[FIRE])
{
    allegro_message("Error reading fire.wav");
    return;
}
//load the goopy sound
sounds[GOOPY] = load_sample("goopy.wav");
if (!sounds[GOOPY])
{
    allegro_message("Error reading goopy.wav");
    return;
}
```

```
//load the harp sound
sounds[HARP] = load_sample("harp.wav");
if (!sounds[HARP])
{
    allegro_message("Error reading harp.wav");
    return;
}
//load the scream sound
sounds[SCREAM] = load_sample("scream.wav");
if (!sounds[SCREAM])
{
    allegro_message("Error reading scream.wav");
    return;
}
//load the ohhh sound
sounds[OHHH] = load_sample("ohhh.wav");
if (!sounds[OHHH])
{
    allegro_message("Error reading ohhh.wav");
    return;
}

//cannons are reloading
play_sample(sounds[0], VOLUME, PAN, PITCH, FALSE);
}
```

Modifying bullet.c

Now open the bullet.c file to add some function calls to play sounds at various points in the game (for instance, during an explosion). The first function in this file is updateexplosion. Down at the bottom of this function is an else statement. Add the play_sample line as shown.

```
    }
    else
    {
        //play "end of explosion" sound
        play_sample(sounds[HARP], VOLUME, PAN, PITCH, FALSE);

        explosions[num]->alive = 0;
        explosions[num]->curframe = 0;
    }
}
```

Now scroll down a little to the explosion function. Add the new lines of code as shown. You might be wondering why there are three sounds being played at the start of an explosion. It's for variety! The three sounds together add a distinctive explosion sound, along with a light comical twist. Remember that Allegro mixes sounds, so these are all played at basically the same time.

```
void explode(int num, int x, int y)
{
    //initialize the explosion sprite
    explosions[num]->alive = 1;
    explosions[num]->x = x;
    explosions[num]->y = y;
    explosions[num]->curframe = 0;
    explosions[num]->maxframe = 20;

    //play explosion sounds
    play_sample(sounds[GOOPY], VOLUME, PAN, PITCH, FALSE);
    play_sample(sounds[HIT1], VOLUME, PAN, PITCH, FALSE);
    play_sample(sounds[HIT2], VOLUME, PAN, PITCH, FALSE);
}
```

Now scroll down to the movebullet function. You'll make a ton of changes to this function, basically to add more humorous elements to the game. Whenever a bullet hits the edge of the map, a reload sound is played (ammo.wav), which tells the player that he can fire again. Remember that bullets will keep going until they strike the enemy tank or the edge of the map. The next change to this function is quite funny, in my opinion. Whenever there is a near miss of a bullet close to your tank, one of two samples is played. If it's player 1, the scream.wav sample is played, while ohhh.wav is played for a near miss with player 2. This really adds a nice touch to the game, as you'll see when you play it. Now, just make all the changes noted in bold.

```
void movebullet(int num)
{
    int x, y, tx, ty;

    x = bullets[num]->x;
    y = bullets[num]->y;

    //is the bullet active?
    if (!bullets[num]->alive) return;

    //move bullet
    bullets[num]->x += bullets[num]->xspeed;
    bullets[num]->y += bullets[num]->yspeed;
```

```
x = bullets[num]->x;
y = bullets[num]->y;

//stay within the virtual screen
if (x < 0 || x > MAPW-6 || y < 0 || y > MAPH-6)
{
    //play the ammo sound
    play_sample(sounds[AMMO], VOLUME, PAN, PITCH, FALSE);

    bullets[num]->alive = 0;
    return;
}

//look for a direct hit using basic collision
tx = scrollx[!num] + SCROLLW/2;
ty = scrolly[!num] + SCROLLH/2;
if (inside(x,y,tx-15,ty-15,tx+15,ty+15))
{
    //kill the bullet
    bullets[num]->alive = 0;

    //blow up the tank
    x = scrollx[!num] + SCROLLW/2;
    y = scrolly[!num] + SCROLLH/2;

    //draw explosion in enemy window
    explode(num, tanks[!num]->x, tanks[!num]->y);
    scores[num]++;

    //kill any "near miss" sounds
    if (num)
        stop_sample(sounds[SCREAM]);
    else
        stop_sample(sounds[OHHH]);
}

else if (inside(x,y,tx-30,ty-30,tx+30,ty+30))
{
    //it's a near miss!
    if (num)
        //player 1 screams
        play_sample(sounds[SCREAM], VOLUME, PAN, PITCH, FALSE);
    else
```

```
    //player 2 ohhhs
    play_sample(sounds[OHHH], VOLUME, PAN, PITCH, FALSE);
  }
}
```

Now, scroll down a little more to the fireweapon function. I have added a single play_sample function call that plays a sound whenever a player fires a bullet. This is the basic fire sound. Add the line shown in bold.

```
void fireweapon(int num)
{
    int x = scrollx[num] + SCROLLW/2;
    int y = scrolly[num] + SCROLLH/2;

    //ready to fire again?
    if (!bullets[num]->alive)
    {
        //play fire sound
        play_sample(sounds[FIRE], VOLUME, PAN, PITCH, FALSE);

        bullets[num]->alive = 1;
```

Modifying input.c

Next, open the input.c file. The first thing you must do is add a new function called readjoysticks. This function first verifies that a joystick is connected, and then tries to scan the input of one or two joysticks, if present. If you have two joysticks or gamepads, try plugging them into your PC to see how much fun *Tank War* can be when played like a console game! Add the new readjoysticks function to the top of input.c.

```
void readjoysticks()
{
    int b, n;

    if (num_joysticks)
    {
        //read the joystick
        poll_joystick();

        for (n=0; n<2; n++)
        {
            //left stick
            if (joy[n].stick[0].axis[0].d1)
                turnleft(n);
```

```
        //right stick
        if (joy[n].stick[0].axis[0].d2)
            turnright(n);

        //forward stick
        if (joy[n].stick[0].axis[1].d1)
            forward(n);

        //backward stick
        if (joy[n].stick[0].axis[1].d2)
            backward(n);

        //any button will do
        for (b=0; b<joy[n].num_buttons; b++)
            if (joy[n].button[b].b)
            {
                fireweapon(n);
                break;
            }
      }
    }
}
```

Next, you need to make some modifications to the forward, backward, turnleft, and turnright functions. These changes help slow down the device input so it's easier to control the tanks. (Previously, you might recall, the tanks would turn far too fast.) This also makes the tank movement feel more realistic because you must speed up gradually, rather than going from 0 to 60 in 0.5 seconds, as the game was played before. Note the changes in bold.

```
void forward(int num)
{
    if (key_count[num]++ > key_delay[num])
    {
        key_count[num] = 0;

        tanks[num]->xspeed++;
        if (tanks[num]->xspeed > MAXSPEED)
            tanks[num]->xspeed = MAXSPEED;
    }
}


void backward(int num)
{
    if (key_count[num]++ > key_delay[num])
```

```
    {
        key_count[num] = 0;

        tanks[num]->xspeed--;
        if (tanks[num]->xspeed < -MAXSPEED)
            tanks[num]->xspeed = -MAXSPEED;
    }
}

void turnleft(int num)
{
    if (key_count[num]++ > key_delay[num])
    {
        key_count[num] = 0;

        tanks[num]->dir--;
        if (tanks[num]->dir < 0)
            tanks[num]->dir = 7;
    }
}

void turnright(int num)
{
    if (key_count[num]++ > key_delay[num])
    {
        key_count[num] = 0;

        tanks[num]->dir++;
        if (tanks[num]->dir > 7)
            tanks[num]->dir = 0;
    }
}
```

The last change you'll make is to the getinput function. There has been a rest function call in here since the first version of the game, while the timing of the game belongs in the main loop. Simply delete the line indicated in bold (and commented out).

```
void getinput()
{
    //hit ESC to quit
    if (key[KEY_ESC])    gameover = 1;

    //WASD - SPACE keys control tank 1
    if (key[KEY_W])      forward(0);
```

```
    if (key[KEY_D])     turnright(0);
    if (key[KEY_A])     turnleft(0);
    if (key[KEY_S])     backward(0);
    if (key[KEY_SPACE]) fireweapon(0);

    //arrow - ENTER keys control tank 2
    if (key[KEY_UP])    forward(1);
    if (key[KEY_RIGHT]) turnright(1);
    if (key[KEY_DOWN])  backward(1);
    if (key[KEY_LEFT])  turnleft(1);
    if (key[KEY_ENTER]) fireweapon(1);

    //short delay after keypress
    //rest(20);
}
```

Modifying main.c

Next up is the main.c file, the primary source code file for *Tank War*, which contains (among other things) that game loop. Scroll down to main and add the call to loadsounds, as indicated in bold.

```
//main function
void main(void)
{
    int anim;

    //initialize the game
    allegro_init();
    install_keyboard();
    install_timer();
    srand(time(NULL));
    setupscreen();
    setuptanks();
    loadsprites();
    loadsounds();
```

Next, scroll down a little bit past the section of code that loads the Mappy file and add the new code shown in bold. This code initializes the joystick(s) and sets the input delay variables.

```
    //load the Mappy file
    if (MapLoad("map3.fmp"))
    {
        allegro_message ("Can't find map3.fmp");
```

```
    return;
}

//set palette
MapSetPal8();

//install the joystick handler
install_joystick(JOY_TYPE_AUTODETECT);
poll_joystick();

//setup input delays
key_count[0] = 0;
key_delay[0] = 2;
key_count[1] = 0;
key_delay[1] = 2;
```

Now, scroll down to the end of the game loop and insert or change the following lines of code after the call to getinput, as shown in bold. You'll insert a call to readjoysticks and modify the rest function call to increase the delay a bit (because the delay in getinput was removed).

```
        //check for keypresses
        if (keypressed())
            getinput();

        readjoysticks();

        //slow the game down
        rest(30);
}
```

Now let's clean up the memory that was used by these new changes. Scroll down a little bit more and insert the following code after the call to MapFreeMem, as shown in bold.

```
//free the MappyAL memory
MapFreeMem();

//free the samples
for (n=0; n<NUM_SOUNDS; n++)
    destroy_sample(sounds[n]);

//remove the sound driver
remove_sound();

//remove the joystick driver
```

```
    remove_joystick();

    return;
}
END_OF_MAIN();
```

Final Comments about Tank War

Figure 15.3 shows the final version of *Tank War*. It's been a long haul, and you've seen the game grow from a meager vector game to the current incarnation with animated sprites and scrolling backgrounds. Here's a list of the features of the final version of the game:

- Two-player split-screen gameplay
- A scrolling battlefield
- Support for new maps created with Mappy
- Advanced update code to show all the action in both windows
- Keyboard and dual joystick support
- Sixty-four animated frames for each tank
- Support for stereo sound cards
- Numerous sound effects to enhance gameplay
- Support for maps with up to 30,000 tiles
- A battlefield that can be up to 5,500×5,500 pixels in size
- Ability to run on Windows, Linux, Mac OS X, and many other systems

Well, what are you waiting for? Go ahead and get started on the tenth revision to *Tank War*!

Figure 15.3 The final version of *Tank War*

Summary

This chapter provided an introduction to the sound support routines provided by Allegro for including sound effects in a game. Allegro provides an interface to the underlying operating system (with support for DirectSound) that, along with a software sound mixer, provides a consistent level of functionality and performance from one computer system to another. In this chapter, you learned how to initialize the sound system, load a WAV file, and play back the WAV file with or without looping. You were also provided with an example that demonstrated Allegro's automatic mixing of samples that are played. In a nutshell, it requires very little effort to play a sound effect, and mixing is handled automatically, allowing you to focus on gameplay rather than the mechanics of an advanced sound system.

Chapter Quiz

You can find the answers to this chapter quiz in Appendix A, "Chapter Quiz Answers."

1. What is the name of the function that initializes the Allegro sound system?
   A. `install_sound`
   B. `init_sound`
   C. `initialize_sound_system`
   D. `init_snd`

2. Which function can you use to play a sound effect in your own games?
   A. `start_playback`
   B. `play_sound`
   C. `play_sample`
   D. `digi_snd_play`

3. What is the name of the function that specifically loads a RIFF WAV file?
   A. `load_riff`
   B. `load_wav`
   C. `load_wave`
   D. `load_riff_wav`

4. Which function can be used to change the frequency, volume, panning, and looping properties of a sample?
   A. `modify_sample`
   B. `change_sample`
   C. `alter_sample`
   D. `adjust_sample`

5. What function would you use to shut down the Allegro sound system?

    A.   `uninstall_sound`

    B.   `remove_sound`

    C.   `close_sound`

    D.   `close_sound_system`

6. Which function provides the ability to change the overall volume of sound output?

    A.   `set_volume`

    B.   `change_volume`

    C.   `fix_volume`

    D.   `set_vol`

7. What is the name of the function used to stop playback of a sample?

    A.   `stop_playback`

    B.   `stop_playing`

    C.   `halt_playback`

    D.   `stop_sample`

8. Within what range must a panning value remain?

    A.   −32,768 to 32,767

    B.   0 to 65,536

    C.   1 to 100

    D.   0 to 255

9. What parameter should you pass to `install_sound` to initialize the standard digital sound driver?

    A.   `SND_AUTODETECT`

    B.   `SND_AUTODETECT_DIGITAL`

    C.   `DIGI_AUTODETECT`

    D.   `DIGI_AUTODETECT_SOUND`

10. What is the name of the function that plays a sample through the sound mixer?

    A.   `start_playback`

    B.   `play_sample`

    C.   `play_sample_mix`

    D.   `start_mix_playback`

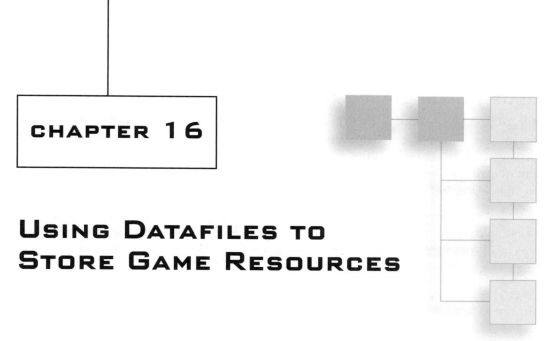

CHAPTER 16

Using Datafiles to Store Game Resources

Suppose you have written one of the greatest new games to come out of the indie market in years, and you are chomping at the bit to get the game out into the world. You poured your blood, sweat, and tears into the game and it has cost you every moment of your free time for three years. Your friends and relatives have abandoned you, and you haven't emerged from your room in months, focused on and dedicated to one goal—making this the most unbelievable game ever. You have come up with a new gaming technology that you think will create a whole new genre. It's the next *Doom* or *Warcraft*.

There's just one problem. You have spent so much time getting the game running and polished that you have paid no attention to the game's resources. Now, faced with distribution, you are struggling to come up with a plan for protecting your game's resources—all the amazing artwork (that you had commissioned from a professional artist), sound effects and music (commissioned from a sound studio), and professional voice acting at various parts throughout the game. You have valuable assets to protect. You have thought about finding a ZIP decompression library, but are not looking forward to the problems associated with temp files.

Luckily for you, you planned ahead and developed your new cutting-edge game with Allegro. And it just so happens that Allegro has support for data files to store all of your game resources with encryption and compression. Best of all, it's extremely easy to use, and you don't need to deal with temp files. Ready to learn how to do this?

Here is a breakdown of the major topics in this chapter:

- Understanding Allegro datafiles
- Creating Allegro datafiles
- Using Allegro datafiles
- Testing Allegro datafiles

Understanding Allegro Datafiles

Allegro data files (*datafiles*) are similar to ZIP archive files in that they can contain multiple files of different types and sizes, with support for encryption and compression. However, Allegro datafiles differ from the files of general-purpose archival programs in that Allegro is geared entirely to store game resources. Allegro datafiles use the LZSS compression algorithm when compression is used.

Datafiles are created by the Allegro Datafile archiving utility and have a .dat extension. They can contain bitmaps, sounds, FLI animations, Mappy levels, text files, and any other type of file or binary data that your game will need. You can distribute your game with a single executable and a single datafile.

One of the best things about datafiles is that, because they are so easy to create and use, you can use a datafile for any program you write, not just games. This really adds a strong degree of appeal to Allegro even for general-purpose programming, developing command-line utilities and support programs in addition to full-blown game editors and similar programs. Instead of distributing a background image, sprite image, and sound file in a small game, simply bundle it all together in a datafile and send it off to your friends with the program file. In other words, you don't have to reserve datafile use only for big projects; you can feel free to use datafiles frequently even on non-game projects.

Datafiles use a struct to keep track of their resources. The struct looks like this:

```
typedef struct DATAFILE
{
   void *dat;     //pointer to the actual data
   int type;      //type of the data
   long size;     //size of the data in bytes
   void *prop;    //list of object properties
} DATAFILE;
```

When you refer to an object in a datafile, you must use a DATAFILE struct to get at the resource. Usually you will not need to be concerned with anything other than the dat member variable, which is a void pointer to the object in the file (or in memory after the datafile has been loaded).

Would you like a quick example? Although I haven't covered the load_datafile function yet, here is an example of how you might load a datafile into memory and then grab a sprite directly out of the datafile:

```
DATAFILE *data = load_datafile("game.dat");
draw_sprite(screen, data[PLAYER_SPRITE].dat, x, y);
```

If you want to identify a resource by type (for instance, to verify that the resource is a valid type), you can use the type member variable of the DATAFILE struct. Table 16.1 provides a list of the various types of objects that can be stored in a datafile.

Table 16.1 Datafile Object Types and Formats

Data Type	Format	Description
DAT_FILE	"FILE"	Nested data file
DAT_DATA	"DATA"	Block of binary data (miscellaneous)
DAT_FONT	"FONT"	Font object
DAT_SAMPLE	"SAMP"	Sound sample structure
DAT_MIDI	"MIDI"	MIDI file
DAT_PATCH	"PAT"	GUS patch file
DAT_FLI	"FLIC"	FLI animation
DAT_BITMAP	"BMP"	BITMAP structure
DAT_RLE_SPRITE	"RLE"	RLE_SPRITE structure
DAT_C_SPRITE	"CMP"	Linear compiled sprite
DAT_XC_SPRITE	"XCMP"	Mode-X compiled sprite
DAT_PALETTE	"PAL"	Array of 256 RGB structures
DAT_END	N/A	Special flag to mark the end of the data list

Creating Allegro Datafiles

Before you can practice using datafiles, you need to learn how to create and manage them. This will also give you a heads-up on extracting the game resources from other people's games that use Allegro datafiles! Not that I would condone the theft of artwork...but it is interesting to see how some people develop their artwork.

Allegro comes with a command-line utility program called dat.exe that you will use to create and manage your datafiles. The Allegro utilities are located in the tools folder inside the root Allegro folder, wherever you installed it (based on the sources). If you have extracted Allegro to your root drive folder, then the dat.exe program is likely to be found in \allegro\tools. You will need to open a command prompt or shell and change to that folder to run the program. Alternatively, you might want to just add \allegro\tools to your system path. In Windows, you would do that by typing

```
path=C:\allegro\tools;%path%
```

After you do this, you will be able to maintain your datafiles from any folder on the hard drive because dat.exe will be included in the path. Here is the output from dat.exe if you run it with no parameters:

```
Datafile archiving utility for Allegro 4.0.3, MSVC.s
By Shawn Hargreaves, 2003

Usage: dat [options] filename.dat [names]

Options:
        '-a' adds the named files to the datafile
        '-bpp colordepth' grabs bitmaps in the specified format
        '-c0' no compression
        '-c1' compress objects individually
        '-c2' global compression on the entire datafile
        '-d' deletes the named objects from the datafile
        '-dither' dithers when reducing color depths
        '-e' extracts the named objects from the datafile
        '-g x y w h' grabs bitmap data from a specific grid location
        '-h outputfile.h' sets the output header file
        '-k' keeps the original file names when grabbing objects
        '-l' lists the contents of the datafile
        '-m dependencyfile' outputs makefile dependencies
        '-o output' sets the output file or directory when extracting data
        '-p prefixstring' sets the prefix for the output header file
        '-pal objectname' specifies which palette to use
        '-s0' no strip: save everything
        '-s1' strip grabber specific information from the file
        '-s2' strip all object properties and names from the file
        '-t type' sets the object type when adding files
        '-transparency' preserves transparency through color conversion
        '-u' updates the contents of the datafile
        '-v' selects verbose mode
        '-w' always updates the entire contents of the datafile
        '-007 password' sets the file encryption key
        'PROP=value' sets object properties
```

I'm not going over all these options; consider it your homework for the day. The really important thing to know about the dat.exe syntax is the usage.

```
Usage: dat [options] filename.dat [names]
```

When you run dat.exe, first you must include any options, then the name of the datafile, followed by the files you want to add to (or extract from) the datafile. Looking through the options, I see that -a is the parameter that adds files to a datafile. But you must also use the -t option to tell dat what kind of file you are adding. Go ahead and try it. Locate a bitmap file, change to that directory from the command prompt (or shell), and adapt the following command to suit the bitmap file you intend to add to the datafile.

```
dat -a -t BMP -bpp 16 test.dat back.bmp
```

Do you see the -bpp 16 parameter? You must specify the color depth of the bitmaps you are adding to the datafile or it will treat them as 8-bit images (one byte per pixel). I have used the -bpp 16 parameter to instruct the dat program to store the file as a 16-bit bitmap. The output from dat should look something like this:

```
test.dat not found: creating new datafile
Inserting back.bmp -> BACK_BMP
Writing test.dat
```

Now you can find out whether the bitmap image is actually stored inside the test.dat file.

```
dat -l test.dat
```

You should see a result that looks something like this:

```
Reading test.dat
- BMP  - BACK_BMP                - bitmap (640x480, 16 bit)
```

Great, it worked! Now there's just one problem. I see from the options list that I can add compression to the datafile using the -c2 option, so I'd like to reduce the size of the file. Here is the command to do that:

```
dat -c2 test.dat
```

The output looks like this:

```
Reading test.dat
Writing test.dat
```

I see that the file has been reduced from 900 KB to about 100 KB. Perfect!

Now I want to another file (a sprite), and then I'll demonstrate how to get to these objects from an Allegro program.

```
dat -a -t BMP -bpp 16 test.dat ship.bmp
```

results in this output, so I know it's good:

```
Reading test.dat
Inserting ship.bmp -> SHIP_BMP
Writing test.dat
```

Now that you have added two files to the datafile, take a peek inside:

```
dat -l test.dat
```

produces this output:

```
Reading test.dat
```

```
- BMP   - BACK_BMP                - bitmap (640x480, 16 bit)
- BMP   - SHIP_BMP                - bitmap (111x96, 16 bit)
```

If you take a look at the file size, you'll see that it is still compressed. Trying to compress it again results in the same file size, so it's apparent that once -c2 has been applied to a datafile, compression is then applied to any new files added to it.

I should also point out that you should reference the objects in the file in the order they are displayed using dat -l test.dat. You can reference the back.bmp file using array index 0, explode.wav using array index 1, and so on.

The dat tool is able to generate a header file containing the datafile definition of values using the -h option.

```
dat test.dat -h defines.h
```

produces a file that looks like this:

```
/* Allegro datafile object indexes, produced by dat v4.0.3, MSVC.s */
/* Datafile: test.dat */
/* Date: Thu Apr 15 20:49:59 2004 */
/* Do not hand edit! */

#define BACK_BMP                 0        /* BMP  */
#define SHIP_BMP                 1        /* BMP  */
```

It is best to include this header file directly in your project and not edit it manually (although for the simple demonstration program later in the chapter, I have simply pasted the defines into the program).

Using Allegro Datafiles

You have learned some details about what datafiles are made of and how to create and update them. Now it's time to put them to the test in a real Allegro program that will load the datafile and retrieve game objects directly out of the datafile. First you need to go over the datafile functions to learn how to manipulate a datafile with source code.

Loading a Datafile

The load_datafile function loads a datafile into memory and returns a pointer to it or NULL. If the datafile has been encrypted, you must first use the packfile_password function to set the appropriate key. See grabber.txt for more information. If the datafile contains true color graphics, you must set the video mode or call set_color_conversion() before loading the datafile.

```
DATAFILE *load_datafile(const char *filename);
```

note

If you are programming in C++, you will get an error unless you include a cast for the type of object being referenced in the datafile. Here is an example:

```
draw_sprite(screen, (BITMAP *)data[SPRITE].dat, x, y);
```

Unloading a Datafile

The `unload_datafile` function frees all the objects in a datafile and removes the datafile from memory.

```
void unload_datafile(DATAFILE *dat);
```

Loading a Datafile Object

The `load_datafile_object` will load a specific object from a datafile, returning the object as a single `DATAFILE *` pointer (instead of the usual array).

```
DATAFILE *load_datafile_object(const char *filename, const char *objectname);
```

Here is an example:

```
sprite = load_datafile_object("datafile.dat", "SPRITE_BMP");
```

Unloading a Datafile Object

The `unload_datafile_object` function will free an object that was loaded with the `load_datafile_object` function.

```
void unload_datafile_object(DATAFILE *dat);
```

Finding a Datafile Object

The `find_datafile_object` function searches an opened datafile for an object with the specified name, returning a pointer to the object or NULL.

```
DATAFILE *find_datafile_object(const DATAFILE *dat, const char *objectname);
```

Testing Allegro Datafiles

Now that you have a basic understanding of how datafiles are created and what the data inside a datafile looks like, it's time to learn how to read a datafile in an Allegro program. I have written a short program that loads the test.dat file you created earlier in this chapter and displays the back.bmp and ship.bmp files stored in the datafile. You should be able to use this basic example (along with the list of data file object types) to use any other type of file in your programs (such as samples or Mappy files). Figure 16.1 shows the output of the *TestDat* program.

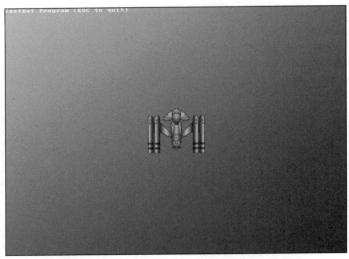

Figure 16.1 The *TestDat* program demonstrates how to read bitmaps from an Allegro datafile.

```
#include <allegro.h>

#define MODE GFX_AUTODETECT_WINDOWED
#define WIDTH 640
#define HEIGHT 480
#define WHITE makecol(255,255,255)

//define objects in datafile
#define BACK_BMP 0
#define SHIP_BMP 1


void main(void)
{
    DATAFILE *data;
    BITMAP *sprite;
```

```
    //initialize the program
    allegro_init();
    install_keyboard();
    install_timer();
    set_color_depth(16);
    set_gfx_mode(MODE, WIDTH, HEIGHT, 0, 0);
    text_mode(-1);

    //load the datafile
    data = load_datafile("test.dat");

    //blit the background image using datafile directly
    blit(data[BACK_BMP].dat, screen, 0, 0, 0, 0, WIDTH-1, HEIGHT-1);

    //grab sprite and store in separate BITMAP
    sprite = (BITMAP *)data[SHIP_BMP].dat;
    draw_sprite(screen, sprite, WIDTH/2-sprite->w/2,
        HEIGHT/2-sprite->h/2);

    //display title
    textout(screen,font,"TestDat Program (ESC to quit)",0,0,WHITE);

    //pause
    while(!key[KEY_ESC]) { }

    //remove datafile from memory
    unload_datafile(data);

    allegro_exit();
}
END_OF_MAIN();
```

Summary

This chapter provided an introduction to Allegro datafiles and showed you how to create them, modify them, and read them into an Allegro program or game. Datafiles make it much easier to distribute your games to others because you need only include the datafile and executable program file. Datafiles can contain any type of file, but some items are predefined so they are recognized and handled properly by Allegro.

Chapter Quiz

You can find the answers to this chapter quiz in Appendix A, "Chapter Quiz Answers."

1. What is the shorthand term for an Allegro data file?

   A.   datafile

   B.   datfile

   C.   data file

   D.   ADF

2. What compression algorithm does Allegro use for compressed datafiles?

   A.   LZSS

   B.   LZH

   C.   ZIP

   D.   RAR

3. What is the command-line program that is used to manage Allegro datafiles?

   A.   data.exe

   B.   datafile.exe

   C.   datafile.exe

   D.   dat.exe

4. What is the Allegro datafile object struct called?

   A.   DATA_FILE

   B.   DATAFILE

   C.   DAT_FILE

   D.   AL_DATFILE

5. What function is used to load a datafile into memory?

   A.   open_data_file

   B.   load_dat

   C.   load_datfile

   D.   load_datafile

6. What is the data type format shortcut string for bitmap files?

   A.   BITMAP_IMAGE

   B.   BITMAP

   C.   BMP

   D.   DATA_BITMAP

7. What is the data type constant for wave files, defined by Allegro for use in reading datafiles?

    A.   `DAT_RIFF_WAV`

    B.   `DAT_WAVE`

    C.   `DAT_SAMPLE`

    D.   `DAT_SOUND`

8. What is the `dat` option to specify the type of file being added to the datafile?

    A.   `-t <type>`

    B.   `-a <type>`

    C.   `-d <type>`

    D.   `-s <type>`

9. What is the `dat` option to specify the color depth of a bitmap file being added to the datafile?

    A.   `-c <depth>`

    B.   `-d <depth>`

    C.   `-bpp <depth>`

    D.   `-color <depth>`

10. Which function loads an individual object from a datafile?

    A.   `load_data_object`

    B.   `load_object_file`

    C.   `load_datafile`

    D.   `load_datafile_object`

CHAPTER 17

PLAYING FLIC MOVIES

FLI is an animation format developed by Autodesk for creating and playing computer-generated animations at high resolutions using Autodesk Animator, while the FLC format was the standard format used in Autodesk Animator Pro. These two formats (FLI and FLC) are both referred to as the FLIC format. The original FLI format was limited to a resolution of 320×200, while FLC provided higher resolutions and file compression. This chapter focuses on the functions built into Allegro for reading and playing FLIC movies, which are especially useful as cut-scenes within a game or as the opening video often presented as a game begins.

Here is a breakdown of the major topics in this chapter:

- Playing FLI animation files
- Loading FLIs into memory

Playing FLI Animation Files

Animated or rendered movies are often used in games to fill in a cut-scene at a specified point in the game or to tell a story as the game starts. Of course, you can use an animation for any purpose within a game using Allegro's built-in support for FLI loading and playback (both from memory and from disk file). The only limitation is that you can only play one FLI at a time. If you need multiple animations to run at the same time, I recommend converting the FLI file to one or more bitmap images and treating the movie as an animated sprite—although I'll leave implementation of that concept up to you. (First you would need to convert the FLI to individual bitmap images.)

The easiest way to play an FLI animation file with Allegro is by using the play_fli function, which simply plays an FLI or FLC file directly to the screen or to another destination bitmap.

```
int play_fli(const char *filename, BITMAP *bmp, int loop,
        int (*callback)());
```

The first parameter is the FLI/FLC file to play; the second parameter is the destination bitmap where you would like the animation to play; and the third parameter, loop, determines whether the animation is looped at the end (1 is looped, 0 is not). In practice, however, you will want to intercept playback in the callback function and pass a return value of 1 from the callback to stop playback.

As you can see from the function definition, play_fli supports a callback function. The purpose for this is so that your game can continue running while the FLI is played; otherwise, playback would run without interruption. The callback function is very simple—it returns an int but accepts no parameters.

When you are playing back an animation file, keep in mind that play_fli draws each frame at the upper-left corner of the destination bitmap (which is usually the screen). If you want more control over the playback of an FLI, you have two options. First, you can tell play_fli to draw the frames on a memory bitmap and then draw that bitmap to the screen yourself. (See the following section on using the callback function.)

The FLI Callback Function

The callback function makes it possible to do other things inside your program after each frame of the animation is displayed. Note that you should return from the callback function as quickly as possible or the playback timing will be off. When you want to use a callback function, simply declare a function like this:

```
int fli_callback(void)
{
}
```

You can then use play_fli to start playback of an FLI file, including the fli_callback function.

```
play_fli("particles.fli", screen, 1, fli_callback);
```

The PlayFlick Program

The play_fli function is not really very useful if you don't also use the callback function. I have written a test program called *PlayFlick* that demonstrates how to use play_fli along with the callback to play an animation with logistical information printed after each frame of the FLI is displayed on the screen. Figure 17.1 shows the output from the *PlayFlick* program.

Figure 17.1 The *PlayFlick* program demonstrates how to play an Autodesk Animator FLI/FLC file.

If you are writing this program from scratch (as follows), you will of course need an FLI file to use for testing. You can copy one of the FLI files off the CD-ROM from the folder for this chapter and project, \chapter17\playflick. The sample file is called particles.fli, and there are several other sample FLI files in other project folders for this chapter.

```
#include <stdio.h>
#include "allegro.h"

#define WHITE makecol(255,255,255)

int ret;

int fli_callback(void)
{
    //display some info after each frame
    textprintf(screen, font, 0, 0, WHITE,
        "FLI resolution: %d x %d", fli_bitmap->w, fli_bitmap->h);
    textprintf(screen, font, 0, 10, WHITE,
        "Current frame: %2d", fli_frame);
```

```
    //ESC key stops animation
    if (key[KEY_ESC])
        return 1;
    else
        return 0;
}

void main(void)
{
    //initialize Allegro
    allegro_init();
    set_color_depth(16);
    set_gfx_mode(GFX_AUTODETECT_WINDOWED, 640, 480, 0, 0);
    install_timer();
    install_keyboard();

    //play fli with callback
    play_fli("particles.fli", screen, 1, fli_callback);

    //time to leave
    allegro_exit();
}
END_OF_MAIN();
```

Playing an FLI from a Memory Block

Allegro provides you with a way to play a raw FLI file that has been mass copied from disk into memory with header and all. The play_memory_fli function will play a memory FLI as if it were a disk file. The FLI routines must still work with only one file at a time, even if that file was loaded into a memory block (which you must create with malloc and read into memory using your own file input code). You would also use this function when you have stored an FLI inside a datafile. (For more information about datafiles, refer to Chapter 16.)

```
int play_memory_fli(const void *fli_data, BITMAP *bmp,
        int loop, int (*callback)());
```

Loading FLIs into Memory

The two functions covered thus far were designed for simple FLI playback with little to no control over the frames inside the animation. Fortunately, Allegro provides a low-level interface for FLI playback, allowing you to read an FLI file and manipulate it frame by frame, adjusting the palette and blitting the frame to the screen manually.

Opening and Closing FLI Files

To open an FLI file for low-level playback, you'll use the open_fli function.

```
int open_fli(const char *filename);
```

If you are using a datafile (or you have loaded an entire FLI file into memory byte for byte), you'll use the open_memory_fli function to open it for low-level access.

```
int open_memory_fli(const void *fli_data);
```

If the file was opened successfully, a value of FLI_OK will be returned; otherwise, FLI_ERROR will be returned by these functions. Information about the current FLI is held in global variables, so you can only have one animation open at a time.

n o t e

> The FLI routines make use of interrupts, so you must install the timer by calling install_timer at the start of the program.

After you have finished playing an FLI animation, you can close the file by calling close_fli.

```
void close_fli();
```

Processing Each Frame of the Animation

After you have opened the FLI file, you are ready to begin handling the low-level processing of the animation playback. Allegro provides a number of functions and global variables for dealing with each animation frame; you'll see that they are easy to use in practice.

For starters, take a look at the next_fli_frame function.

```
int next_fli_frame(int loop);
```

This function reads the next frame of the current animation file. If loop is set, the player will cycle when playback reaches the end of the file; otherwise, the function will return FLI_EOF. If no error occurs, this function will return FLI_OK, but if an error has occurred, it will return FLI_ERROR or FLI_NOT_OPEN. One useful return value is FLI_EOF, which tells you that the playback has reached the last frame of the file.

What about drawing each frame image? The frame is read into the global variables fli_bitmap (which contains the current frame image) and fli_palette (which contains the current frame's palette).

```
extern BITMAP *fli_bitmap;
extern PALETTE fli_palette;
```

Even if you are running a program in a high-color or true-color video mode, you will need to set the current palette to render the animation frames properly. (This at least applies to 8-bit FLI files; FLC files might not need a palette.)

After each call to next_fli_frame, Allegro sets a global variable indicating the current frame in the animation sequence of the FLI file, called fli_frame.

```
extern int fli_frame;
```

The current frame is helpful to know, but it doesn't help with timing, which will differ from one FLI file to another. Allegro takes care of the problem by automatically incrementing a global variable called fli_timer whenever a new frame should be displayed. This works regardless of the computer's speed because it is handled by an interrupt. It is important to pay attention to timing unless you are only concerned with the image of each frame and not playback speed.

```
extern volatile int fli_timer;
```

Each time you call next_fli_frame, the fli_timer variable is decremented, so if playback is in sync with timing, this variable will always be 0 unless a new frame is ready to be displayed. This makes it easy to determine when each frame should be drawn.

The LoadFlick Program

To demonstrate the low-level FLI animation routines, I've written a short program called *LoadFlick*. The output from this program is shown in Figure 17.2. *LoadFlick* pretty much demonstrates everything you need to know about the low-level FLI routines, including how to load an FLI file, keep track of each frame, manage timing, and blit the image to the screen.

```
#include <stdio.h>
#include "allegro.h"

#define WHITE makecol(255,255,255)

int ret;

void main(void)
{
    //initialize Allegro
    allegro_init();
    set_color_depth(16);
    set_gfx_mode(GFX_AUTODETECT_WINDOWED, 640, 480, 0, 0);
    install_timer();
    install_keyboard();
```

Figure 17.2 The *LoadFlick* program handles each frame of the FLI animation individually.

```
//load the fli movie file
ret = open_fli("octahedron.fli");
if (ret != FLI_OK)
{
    textout(screen, font, "Error loading octahedron.fli",
        0, 30, WHITE);
    readkey();
    return;
}

//display movie resolution
textprintf(screen, font, 0, 0, WHITE,
    "FLI resolution: %d x %d", fli_bitmap->w, fli_bitmap->h);

//main loop
while (!key[KEY_ESC])
{
    //is it time for the next frame?
    if (fli_timer)
    {
```

```
            //open the next frame
            next_fli_frame(1);

            //adjust the palette
            set_palette(fli_palette);

            //copy the FLI frame to the screen
            blit(fli_bitmap, screen, 0, 0, 0, 30,
                fli_bitmap->w, fli_bitmap->h);

            //display current frame
            textprintf(screen, font, 0, 10, WHITE,
                "Current frame: %4d", fli_frame);
        }
    }

    //remove fli from memory
    close_fli();

    //time to leave
    allegro_exit();
}
END_OF_MAIN();
```

The ResizeFlick Program

Let's do something fun just to see how useful the low-level FLI routines can be when you want full control over each frame in the animation. The *ResizeFlick* program is similar to *LoadFlick* in that it opens an FLI into memory before playback. The difference in this new program is that the resulting FLI frames are resized to fill the screen (using a proper ratio for the height). Note that the FLI file must be in landscape orientation—wider than it is tall—or the bottom of each frame image might be cropped. It's best to use FLI files with a resolution that is similar to one of the common screen resolutions, such as 320×240, 640×480, and so on.

Figure 17.3 shows the *ResizeFlick* program running with a short animation of a jet aircraft (the U.S. Air Force SR-71 Blackbird). Note the black area at the bottom of the screen— this is due to the fact that the original FLI animation was 320×200, so when it was scaled there were pixels left blank on the bottom. If you want to truly fill the entire screen, you can do away with the width and height variables and simply pass SCREEN_W-1 and SCREEN_H-1 as the last two parameters of stretch_blit, which will cause the FLI to be played back in true full-screen mode (although with image artifacts if the scaling is not a multiple of the original resolution).

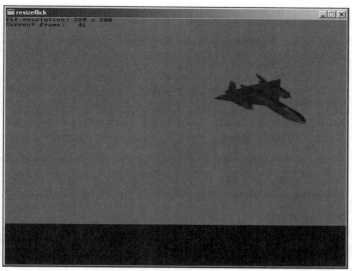

Figure 17.3 The *ResizeFlick* program shows how to play an FLI at any scaled resolution.

```c
#include "allegro.h"

#define WHITE makecol(255,255,255)
#define BLACK makecol(0,0,0)

int ret,width,height;

void main(void)
{
    //initialize Allegro
    allegro_init();
    install_timer();
    install_keyboard();
    text_mode(-1);

    //set video mode--color depth defaults to 8-bit
    set_gfx_mode(GFX_AUTODETECT_WINDOWED, 640, 480, 0, 0);

    //load the fli movie file
    ret = open_fli("sr-71.fli");
    if (ret != FLI_OK)
    {
        textout(screen, font, "Error loading sr-71.fli",
```

```
                  0, 30, WHITE);
        readkey();
        return;
    }


    //main loop
    while (!key[KEY_ESC])
    {
        //is it time for the next frame?
        if (fli_timer)
        {
            //open the next frame
            next_fli_frame(1);

            //adjust the palette
            set_palette(fli_palette);

            //calculate scale
            width = SCREEN_W;
            height = fli_bitmap->h * (SCREEN_W / fli_bitmap->w);

            //draw scaled FLI (note: screen must be in 8-bit mode)
            stretch_blit(fli_bitmap, screen, 0, 0, fli_bitmap->w,
                fli_bitmap->h, 0, 0, width, height);

            //display movie resolution
            textprintf(screen, font, 0, 0, BLACK,
                "FLI resolution: %d x %d", fli_bitmap->w, fli_bitmap->h);

            //display current frame
            textprintf(screen, font, 0, 10, BLACK,
                "Current frame: %4d", fli_frame);

        }
    }

    //remove fli from memory
    close_fli();

    //time to leave
    allegro_exit();
}
END_OF_MAIN();
```

Summary

This chapter provided an overview of the FLIC animation routines available with Allegro. You learned how to play an FLI/FLC file directly from disk as well as how to load an FLI/FLC file into memory and manipulate the animation frame by frame. There were three sample programs in this chapter to demonstrate the routines available for playback of an FLIC file, including a program at the end of the chapter that displayed a movie scaled to the entire screen.

Chapter Quiz

You can find the answers to this chapter quiz in Appendix A, "Chapter Quiz Answers."

1. Which company developed the FLI/FLC file format?
   A. Autodesk
   B. Borland
   C. Microsoft
   D. Bungie

2. Which product first used the FLI format?
   A. 3D Studio Max
   B. WordPerfect
   C. Animator
   D. PC Paintbrush

3. Which product premiered the more advanced FLC format?
   A. Animator Pro
   B. PC Animation
   C. Dr. Halo
   D. CorelDRAW

4. What is the common acronym used to describe both FLI and FLC files?
   A. FLICK
   B. FLICKS
   C. FLI/C
   D. FLIC

5. Which function plays an FLIC file directly?

   A. play_fli

   B. direct_play

   C. play_animation

   D. play_flic

6. How many FLIC files can be played back at a time by Allegro?

   A. 1

   B. 2

   C. 3

   D. 4

7. Which function loads an FLIC file for low-level playback?

   A. load_fli

   B. read_fli

   C. open_fli

   D. shoo_fli

8. Which function moves the animation to the next frame in an FLIC file?

   A. next_fli_frame

   B. get_next_frame

   C. move_frame

   D. next_fli

9. What is the name of the variables used to set the timing of FLIC playback?

   A. flic_frames

   B. playback_timer

   C. fli_playback

   D. fli_timer

10. What is the name of the variable that contains the bitmap of the current FLIC frame?

   A. fli_frame

   B. fli_bitmap

   C. fli_image

   D. current_fli

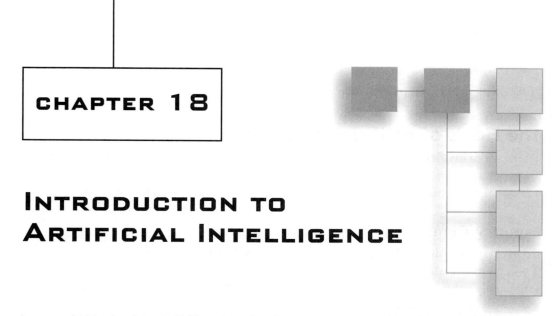

CHAPTER 18

INTRODUCTION TO ARTIFICIAL INTELLIGENCE

Probably the thing I dislike most about some games is how the computer cheats. I'm playing my strategy game and I have to spend 10 minutes finding their units while they automatically know where mine are, which type they are, their energies, and so on. It's not the fact that they cheat to make the game harder, it's the fact that they cheat because the artificial intelligence is very weak. The computer adversary should know just about the same information as the player. If you look at a unit, you don't see their health, their weapons, and their bullets. You just see a unit and, depending on your units, you respond to it. That's what the computer should do; that's what artificial intelligence is all about.

In this chapter I will first give you a quick overview of several types of artificial intelligence, and then you will see how you can apply one or two to games. In this chapter, I'm going to go against the norm for this book and explain the concepts with little snippets of code instead of complete programs. The reason I'm doing this is because the implementation of each field of artificial intelligence is very specific, and where is the fun in watching a graph give you the percentage of the decisions if you can't actually see the bad guy hiding and cornering you? Complete examples would basically require a complete game! For this reason, I will go over several concrete artificial intelligence examples, giving only the theory and some basic code for the implementation, and it will be up to you to choose the best implementation for what you want to do.

Here is a breakdown of the major topics in this chapter:

- Understanding the various fields of artificial intelligence
- Using deterministic algorithms
- Recognizing finite state machines
- Identifying fuzzy logic

563

- Understanding a simple method for memory
- Using artificial intelligence in games

The Fields of Artificial Intelligence

There are many fields of artificial intelligence; some are more game-oriented and others are more academic. Although it is possible to use almost any of them in games, there are a few that stand out, and they will be introduced and explained in this section.

Expert Systems

Expert systems solve problems that are usually solved by specialized humans. For example, if you go to a doctor, he will analyze you (either by asking you a set of questions or doing some analysis himself), and according to his knowledge, he will give you a diagnosis.

An expert system could be the doctor if it had a broad enough knowledge base. It would ask you a set of questions, and depending on your answers, it would consult its knowledge base and give you a diagnosis. The system checks each of your answers with the possible answers in its knowledge base, and depending on your answer, it asks you other questions until it can easily give you a diagnosis.

For a sample knowledge tree, take a look at Figure 18.1. As you can see, a few questions would be asked, and according to the answers, the system would follow the appropriate tree branch until it reached a leaf.

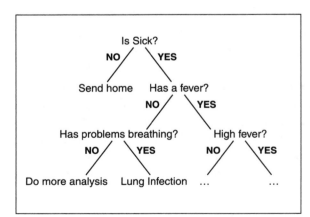

Figure 18.1 An expert system's knowledge tree

A very simple expert system for a doctor could be something like the following code. Note that this is all just pseudo-code, based on a fictional scripting language, and it *will not compile* in a compiler, such as Dev-C++ or Visual C++. This is not intended to be a functional example, just a glimpse at what an expert system's scripting language might look like.

```
Answer = AskQuestion ("Do you have a fever?");
if (Answer == YES)
  Answer = AskQuestion ("Is it a high fever (more than 105.8 F)?");
```

```
  if (Answer == YES)
      Solution = "Go to a hospital now!";
  end if
  Is Sick?
  NO YES
  Has a fever?
  NO YES
  Has problems breathing?
  NO YES
  High fever?
  NO YES
  Send home
  . . . Lung Infection Do more analysis . . .
else
  Answer = AskQuestion ("Do you feel tired?");
  if (Answer == YES)
    Solution = "You probably have a virus, rest a few days!";
  else
    Solution = "Knowledge base insufficient. Further diagnosis needed.";
  end if
else
  Answer = AskQuestion ("Do you have problems breathing?");
  if (Answer == YES)
    Solution = "Probably a lung infection, need to do exams."
  else
    Solution = "Knowledge base insufficient. Further diagnosis needed.";
  end if
end if
```

As you can see, the system follows a set of questions, and depending on the answers, either asks more questions or gives a solution.

note

For the rest of this chapter, you can assume that the strings work exactly like other variables, and you can use operators such as = and == to the same effect as in normal types of variables.

Fuzzy Logic

Fuzzy logic expands on the concept of an expert system. While an expert system can give values of either true (1) or false (0) for the solution, a fuzzy logic system can give values in between. For example, to know whether a person is tall, an expert system would do the following (again, this is fictional script):

```
Answer = AskQuestion ("Is the person's height more than 5' 7"?");
if (Answer == YES)
  Solution = "The person is tall.";
else
  Solution = "The person is not tall.";
end if
```

A fuzzy set would appear like so:

```
Answer = AskQuestion ("What is the person's height?");
if (Answer >= 5' 7")
  Solution = "The person is tall.";
end if
if ((Answer < 5' 7") && (Answer < 5' 3"))
  Solution = "The person is almost tall.";
end if
if ((Answer < 5' 3") && (Answer < 4' 11"))
  Solution = "The person isn't very tall.";
else
  Solution = "The person isn't tall.";
end if
```

The result would be fuzzy. Usually a fuzzy set returns values from 0 (false) to 1 (true), representing the membership of the problem. In the last example, a more realistic fuzzy system would use the graph shown in Figure 18.2 to return a result.

As you can see from the graph, for heights greater than 5' 7", the function returns 1; for heights less than 4' 11", the function returns 0; and for values in between, it returns the corresponding value between 5' 7" and 4' 11". You could get this value by subtracting the height from 5' 7" (the true statement) and dividing by 20 (5' 7"–4' 11", which is the variance in the graph). In code, this would be something like the following:

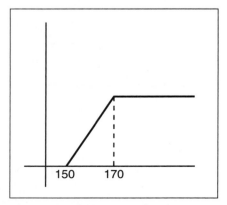

Figure 18.2 Fuzzy membership

```
Answer = AskQuestion ("What is the person's height?");
if (Answer >= 5' 7")
  Solution = 1
end if
if (Answer <= 4' 11")
  Solution = 0
else
  Solution = (Answer - 5' 7") / (5' 7" - 4' 11")
end if
```

You might be wondering why you don't simply use the equation only and discard the if clauses. The problem with doing so is that if the answer is more than 5' 7" or less than 4' 11", it will give values outside the 0 to 1 range, thus making the result invalid.

Fuzzy logic is extremely useful when you need reasoning in your game.

Genetic Algorithms

Using genetic algorithms is a method of computing solutions that relies on the concepts of real genetic concepts (such as evolution and hereditary logic). You might have had a biology class in high school that explained heredity, but in case you didn't, the field of biology studies the evolution of subjects when they reproduce. (Okay, maybe there is a little more to it than that, but you are only interested in this much.)

As you know, everyone has a blood type, with the possible types being A, B, AB, and O, and each of these types can be either positive or negative. When two people have a child, their types of blood will influence the type of blood the child has. All that you are is written in your DNA. Although the DNA is nothing more than a collection of bridges between four elements, it holds all the information about you, such as blood type, eye color, skin type, and so on. The little "creatures" that hold this information are called *genes.*

What you might not know is that although you have only one type of blood, you have two genes specifying which blood type you have. How can that be? If you have two genes describing two types of blood, how can you have only one type of blood?

Predominance! Certain genes' information is stronger (or more influential) than that of others, thus dictating the type of blood you have. What if the two genes' information is equally strong? You get a hybrid of the two. For the blood type example, both type A and type B are equally strong, which makes the subject have a blood type AB. Figure 18.3 shows all the possible combinations of the blood types. From this table, you can see that both the A and B types are predominant, and the O type isn't. You can also see that positive is the predominant type.

So, how does this apply to the computer? There are various implementations that range from solving mathematical equations to fully generating artificial creatures for scientific research. Implementing a simple genetics algorithm in the computer isn't difficult. The necessary steps are described here:

1. Pick up a population and set up initial information values.
2. Order each of the information values to a flat bit vector.
3. Calculate the fitness of each member of the population.
4. Keep only the two with the highest fitness.
5. Mate the two to form a child.

Parent 1	Parent 2	Offspring
A	A	A
A	O	A
A	B	AB
B	B	B
B	O	B
B	A	AB
O	O	O

Figure 18.3 Gene blood type table

And thus you will have a child that is the product of the two best subjects in the population. Of course, to make a nice simulator you wouldn't use only two of the subjects—you would group various subjects in groups of two and mate them to form various children, or *offspring*. Now I'll explain each of the steps.

You first need to use the initial population (all the subjects, including creatures, structures, or mathematical variables) and set them up with their initial values. (These initial values can be universally known information, previous experiences of the subject, or completely random values.) Then you need to order the information to a bit vector, as shown in Figure 18.4.

Figure 18.4 Bit vectors (or binary encoding) of information—the virtual DNA

Although some researchers say that an implementation of a genetic algorithm must be done with bit vectors, others say that the bit vectors can be replaced by a function or equation that will analyze each gene of the progenitors and generate the best one out of the two. To be consistent with the DNA discussion earlier, I will use bit vectors (see Figure 18.4).

You now have to calculate the fitness of each subject. The fitness value indicates whether you have a good subject (for a creature, this could be whether the creature was strong, smart, or fast, for example) or a bad subject. Calculating the fitness is completely dependent on the application, so you need to find some equation that will work for what you want to do.

After you calculate the fitness, get the two subjects with the highest fitness and mate them. You can do this by randomly selecting which gene comes from which progenitor or by intelligently selecting the best genes of each to form an even more perfect child. If you want to bring mutation to the game, you can switch a bit here and there after you get the final offspring. That's it—you have your artificial offspring ready to use. This entire process is shown in Figure 18.5.

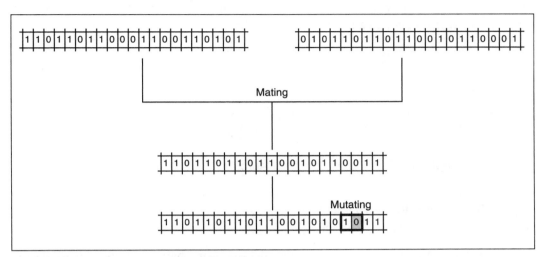

Figure 18.5 Mating and mutation of an offspring

A good use of this technology in games is to simulate artificial environments. Instead of keeping the same elements of the environment over and over, you could make elements (such as small programs) evolve to stronger, smarter, and faster elements (or objects) that can interact with the environment and you.

Neural Networks

Neural networks attempt to solve problems by imitating the workings of a brain. Researchers started trying to mimic animal learning by using a collection of idealized neurons and applying stimuli to them to change their behavior. Neural networks have evolved much in the past few years, mostly due to the discovery of various new learning algorithms, which made it possible to implement the idea of neural networks with success. Unfortunately, there still aren't major discoveries in this field that make it possible to simulate the human brain efficiently.

The human brain is made of around 50 billion neurons (give or take a few billion). Each neuron can compute or process information and send this information to other neurons. Trying to simulate 50 billion neurons in a computer would be disastrous. Each neuron takes various calculations to be simulated, which would lead to around 200 billion calculations. You can forget about modeling the brain fully, but you can use a limited set of neurons (the human brain only uses around 5 to 10 percent of its capacity) to mimic basic actions of humans.

In 1962, Rosenblatt created something called a *perceptron*, one of the earliest neural network models. A perceptron is an attempt to simulate a neuron by using a series of inputs, weighted by some factor, which will output a value of 1 if the sum of all the weighted inputs is greater than a threshold, or 0 if it isn't. Figure 18.6 shows the idea of a perceptron and its resemblance to a neuron.

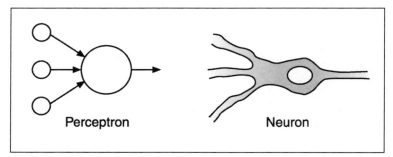

Figure 18.6 A perceptron and a neuron

While a perceptron is just a simple way to model a neuron, many other ideas evolved from this, such as using the same values for various inputs, adding a bias or memory term, and mixing various perceptrons using the output of one as input for others. All of this together formed the current neural networks used in research today.

There are several ways to apply neural networks to games, but probably the most predominant is by using neural networks to simulate memory and learning. This field of artificial intelligence is probably one of its most interesting parts, but unfortunately, the topic is too vast to give a proper explanation of it here. Fortunately, neural networks are becoming more and more popular these days, and numerous publications are available about the subject.

Deterministic Algorithms

Deterministic algorithms are more of a game technique than an artificial intelligence concept. *Deterministic algorithms* are predetermined behaviors of objects in relation to the universe problem. You will consider three deterministic algorithms in this section—random motion, tracking, and patterns. While some say that patterns aren't a deterministic algorithm, I've included them in this section because they are predefined behaviors.

note

The universe (or universe problem) is the current state of the game that influences the subject, and it can range from the subject's health to the terrain slope, number of bullets, number of adversaries, and so on.

Random Motion

The first, and probably simplest, deterministic algorithm is random motion. Although random motion can't really be considered intelligence (because it's random), there are a few things you can make to simulate some simple intelligence.

As an example, suppose you are driving on a road, you reach a fork, and you really don't know your way home. You would usually take a random direction (unless you are superstitious and always take the right road). This isn't very intelligent, but you can simulate it in your games like so:

```
NewDirection = rand() % 2;
```

This will give a random value that is either 0 or 1, which would be exactly the same thing as if you were driving. You can use this kind of algorithm in your games, but it isn't very much fun. However, there are things to improve here. Another example? Okay. Suppose you are watching some guard patrolling an area. Two things might happen: The guard could move in a logical way, perhaps a circle or straight line, but most of the time he will move randomly. He will move from point A to B, then to C, then go to B, then C again, then D, then back to A, and repeat this in a totally different form. Take a look at Figure 18.7 to see this idea in action.

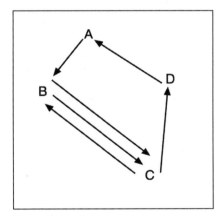

Figure 18.7 A very bad guard

His movement can be described in code something like this:

```
Vector2D kGuardVelocity;
Vector2D kGuardPosition;
int kGuardCycles;
/* Initialize random velocity and cycles */
kGuardVelocity[0] = rand () % 10 - 5;
```

```
kGuardVelocity[1] = rand () % 10 - 5;
kGuardCycles = rand () % 20;
while (GameIsRunning)
{
  // If we still have some cycles with the current movement
  while (kGuardCycles- > 0)
  {
    A
    D
    C
    B
    kGuardPosition += kGuardVelocity;
  }
  // Change velocity and cycles
  kGuardVelocity [0] = rand () % 10 - 5;
  kGuardVelocity [1] = rand () % 10 - 5;
  kGuardCycles = rand () % 20;
}
```

And you have your guard. You might think this isn't very intelligent, but if you were only playing the game, you would simply see that the guard was patrolling the place, and you would think that he was being intelligent.

note

Some of the psuedo-code in this chapter is based on the code developed to represent vectors in Chapter 19, "The Mathematical Side of Games."

Tracking

When you are trying to catch someone, there are a few things you must do. First, move faster than him, or else you will never catch him, and move in the direction he is from you. There is no logic in running south if he is north of you.

To solve this problem and add a little more intelligence to your games, you can use a tracking algorithm. Suppose the guard spots an intruder. He would probably start running toward him. If you wanted to do this in your game, you would use the following code:

```
Vector2D kGuardVelocity;
Vector2D kGuardPosition;
Vector2D kIntruderPosition;
int iGuardSpeed;
// Intruder was spotted, run to him
Vector2D kDistance;
```

```
kDistance = kIntruderPosition - kGuardPosition;
kGuardVelocity = kDistance.Normalize();
kGuardVelocity *= iGuardSpeed;
kGuardPosition += kGuardVelocity;
```

This code gets the direction from the intruder to the guard (the normalized distance) and moves the guard to that direction by a speed factor. Of course, there are several improvements you could make to this algorithm, such as taking into account the intruder's velocity and maybe doing some reasoning about the best route to take.

The last thing to learn with regard to tracking algorithms is about anti-tracking algorithms. An *anti-tracking algorithm* uses the same concepts as the tracking algorithm, but instead of moving toward the target, it runs away from the target. In the previous guard example, if you wanted the intruder to run away from the guard, you could do something like this:

```
mrVector2D kGuardVelocity;
mrVector2D kGuardPosition;
mrVector2D kIntruderPosition;
mrUInt32 iGuardSpeed;
// Guard has spotted the intruder, intruder run away from him
mrVector2D kDistance;
kDistance = kGuardPosition - kIntruderPosition;
kGuardVelocity = -kDistance.Normalize();
kGuardVelocity *= iGuardSpeed;
kGuardPosition += kGuardVelocity;
```

As you can see, the only thing you need to do is negate the distance to the target (the distance from the guard to the intruder). You could also use the distance from the intruder to the guard and not negate it, because it would produce the same final direction.

Patterns

A *pattern*, as the name indicates, is a collection of actions. When those actions are performed in a determined sequence, a pattern (repetition) can be found. Take a look at my rice-cooking pattern, for example. There are several steps I take when I'm cooking rice:

1. Take the ingredients out of the cabinet.
2. Get the cooking pan from under the counter.
3. Add about two quarts of water to the pan.
4. Boil the water.
5. Add 250 grams of rice, a pinch of salt, and a little lemon juice.
6. Let the rice cook for 15 minutes.

And presto, I have rice ready to be eaten. (You don't mind if I eat while I write, do you?) Whenever I want to cook rice, I follow these steps or this pattern. In games, a pattern can be as simple as making an object move in a circle or as complicated as executing orders, such as attacking, defending, harvesting food, and so on. How is it possible to implement a pattern in a game? First you need to decide how a pattern is defined. For your small implementation, you can use a simple combination of two values—the action description and the action operator. The *action description* defines what the action does, and the *action operator* defines how it does it. The action operator can express the time to execute the action, how to execute it, or the target for the action, depending on what the action is.

Of course, your game might need a few more arguments to an action than only these two; you can simply add the necessary parameters. Take another look at the guard example. Remember that there were two things the guard might be doing if he was patrolling the area—moving randomly (as you saw before) or in a logical way. For this example, assume the guard is moving in a logical way—that he is performing a square-styled movement, as shown in Figure 18.8.

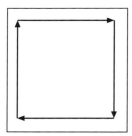

Figure 18.8 A good guard patrolling the area

As you can see, the guard moves around the area in a square-like pattern, which is more realistic than moving randomly. Now, doing this in code isn't difficult, but you first need to define how an action is represented. For simple systems like yours, you can define an action with a description and an operator. The description field describes the action (well, duh!), but the operator can have various meanings. It can be the time the action should be performed, the number of shots that should be fired, or anything else that relates to the action. For the guard example, the operator would be the number of feet to move. Although this system works for many actions, you might want to introduce more data to the pattern. Doing so is easy; you simply need to include more operators in the action definition. A simple example could be:

```
class Action
{
public:
string Description;
string Operator;
};
```

To make your guard pattern, you could do something like this:

```
Action GuardPattern [4];
GuardPattern[0].Description = "MoveUp";
GuardPattern[0].Operator = "10";
GuardPattern[1].Description = "MoveRight";
```

```
GuardPattern[1].Operator = "10";
GuardPattern[2].Description = "MoveDown";
GuardPattern[2].Operator = "10";
GuardPattern[3].Description = "MoveLeft";
GuardPattern[3].Operator = "10";
```

And your guard pattern would be defined. The last thing you need to do is the pattern processor. This isn't hard; you simply need to check the actual pattern description and, depending on the pattern description, perform the action like so:

```
mrUInt32 iNumberOfActions = 4;
mrUInt32 iCurrentAction;
for (iCurrentAction = 0; iCurrentAction < iNumberOfActions;
iCurrentAction++)
{
  if (GuardPattern [iCurrentAction].Description == "MoveUp";
  {
    kGuardPosition [1] += GuardPattern [iCurrentAction].Operator;
  }
  if (GuardPattern [iCurrentAction].Description == "MoveRight';
  {
    kGuardPosition [0] += GuardPattern [iCurrentAction].Operator;
  }
  if (GuardPattern [iCurrentAction].Description == "MoveDown";
  {
    kGuardPosition [1] -= GuardPattern [iCurrentAction].Operator;
  }
  if (GuardPattern [iCurrentAction].Description == "MoveUp";
  {
    kGuardPosition [0] -= GuardPattern [iCurrentAction].Operator;
  }
}
```

This would execute the pattern to make the guard move in a square. Of course, you might want to change this to only execute one action per frame or execute only part of the action per frame, but that's another story.

Finite State Machines

Random logic, tracking, and patterns should be enough to enable you to create some intelligent characters for your game, but they don't depend on the actual state of the problem to decide what to do. If for some reason a pattern tells the subject to fire the weapon, and there isn't any enemy near, then the pattern doesn't seem very intelligent, does it? That's where finite state machines (or software) enter.

A *finite state machine* has a finite number of states that can be as simple as a light switch (either on or off) or as complicated as a VCR (idle, playing, pausing, recording, and more, depending on how much you spend on it).

A *finite state software application* has a finite number of states. These states can be represented as the state of the playing world. Of course, you won't create a state for each difference in an object's health. (If the object had a health ranging from 0 to 1,000, and you had 10 objects, that would mean 100,010 different states, and I don't even want to think about that case!) However, you can use ranges, such as whether an object's health is below a number, and only use the object's health for objects that are near the problem you are considering. This would reduce the states from 100,010 to about four or five.

Let's resume the guard example. If an intruder were approaching the area, until now you would only make your guard run to him. But what if the intruder is too far? Or too near? And what if the guard had no bullets in his gun? You might want to make the guard act differently. For example, consider the following cases:

1. Intruder is in a range of 1000 feet: Just pay attention to the intruder.
2. Intruder is in a range of 500 feet: Run to him.
3. Intruder is in a range of 250 feet: Tell him to stop.
4. Intruder is in a range of 100 feet and has bullets: Shoot first, ask questions later.
5. Intruder is in a range of 100 feet and doesn't have bullets: Sound the alarm.

You have five scenarios, or more accurately, states. You could include more factors in the decision, such as whether there are any other guards in the vicinity, or you could get more complicated and use the guard's personality to decide. If the guard is too much of a coward, you probably never shoot, but just run away. The previous steps can be described in code like this:

```
// State 1
if ((DistanceToIntruder () > 500) && (DistanceToIntruder () < 1000))
{
    Guard.TakeAttention ();
}
// State 2
if ((DistanceToIntruder () > 250) && (DistanceToIntruder () < 500))
{
  Guard.RunToIntruder ();
}
// State 3
if ( (DistanceToIntruder () > 100) && (DistanceToIntruder () < 250))
{
  Guard.WarnIntruder ();
```

```
}
// State 4
if (DistanceToIntruder () < 100)
{
  if (Guard.HasBullets ())
  {
    Guard.ShootIntruder();
  }

  // State 5
  else
  {
    Guard.SoundAlarm();
  }
}
```

Not hard, was it? If you combine this with the deterministic algorithms you saw previously, you can make a very robust artificial intelligence system for your games.

Fuzzy Logic

I have already covered the basics of fuzzy logic, but this time I will go into several of the fuzzy logic techniques more deeply, and explain how to apply them to games.

Fuzzy Logic Basics

Fuzzy logic uses some mathematical sets theory, called *fuzzy set theory*, to work. If you're rusty with sets, check the mathematics chapter (Chapter 19, "The Mathematical Side of Games") before you continue. Fuzzy logic is based on the membership property of things. For example, while all drinks are included in the liquids group, they aren't the only things in the group; some detergents are liquids too, and you don't want to drink them, do you? The same way that drinks are a subgroup—or more accurately, a subset—of the liquids group, some drinks can also be subsets of other groups, such as wine and soft drinks. In the wine group, there are red and white varieties. In the soft drink group, there are carbonated and non-carbonated varieties.

All this talk about alcoholic and non-alcoholic drinks was for demonstration purposes only, so don't go out and drink alcohol just to see whether I'm right. Alcohol damages your brain and your capacity to code, so stay away from it (and drugs, too).

Okay, I'll stop being so paternal and get back to fuzzy logic. Grab a glass and fill it with some water (as much as you want). The glass can have various states—it can be empty, half full, or full (or anywhere in between). How do you know which state the glass is in? Take a look at Figure 18.9.

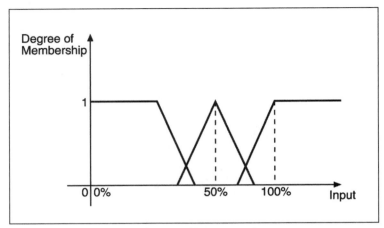

Figure 18.9 Group membership for a glass of water

As you can see, when the glass has 0 percent water, it is totally empty; when it has 50 percent water, it is half full (or half empty, if you prefer). When it has 100 percent of its size in water, then it is full. What if you only poured 30 percent of the water? Or 10 percent? Or 99 percent? As you can see from the graph, the glass will have a membership value for each group. If you want to know the membership values of whatever percentage of water you have, you will have to see where the input (the percentage) meets the membership's graphs to get the degree of membership of each, as shown in Figure 18.10.

Memberships graphs can be as simple as the ones in Figure 18.10, or they can be trapezoids, exponentials, or other equation-derived functions. For the rest of this section, you will only use normal triangle shapes to define memberships. As in Figure 18.10, you can see that the same percentage of water can be part of two or more groups, where the greater membership value will determine the value's final membership.

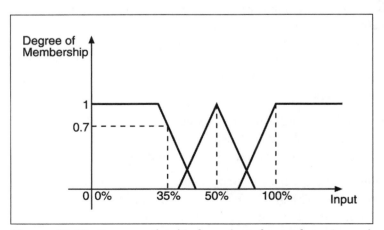

Figure 18.10 Group membership for a glass of water for various values

You can also see that the final group memberships will range from zero to one. This is one of the requirements for a consistent system. To calculate the membership value on a triangle membership function, assuming that the value is inside the membership value (if it isn't, the membership is just zero), you can use the following code:

```
float fCenterOfTriangle = (fMaximumRange - fMinimumRange) / 2;
/* Value is in the center of the range */
if (fValue == fCenterTriangle)
{
  fDegreeOfMembership = 1.0;
}
/* Value is in the first half of the range */
if (fValue < fCenterTriangle)
{
  fDegreeOfMembership = (fValue - fMinimumRange) /
    (fCenterTriangle - fMinimumRange);
}
/* Value is in the second half of the range */
if (fValue > fCenterTriangle)
{
  fDegreeOfMembership = ((fMaximumRange - fCenterTriangle) - (fValue -
    fCenterTriangle)) / (fMaximumRange - fCenterTriangle);
}
```

And you have the degree of membership. If you played close attention, what you did was use the appropriate line slope to check for the vertical intersection of fValue with the triangle.

Fuzzy Matrices

The last topic about fuzzy logic I want to cover is fuzzy matrices. This is what really makes you add intelligence to your games. First, I need to pick a game example to demonstrate this concept. Anyone like soccer?

You will be defining three states of the game.

1. The player has the ball.
2. The player's team has the ball.
3. The opposite team has the ball.

Although there are many other states, you will only be focusing on these three. For each of these states, there is a problem state for the player. You will be considering the following:

1. The player is clear.
2. The player is near an adversary.
3. The player is open for a goal.

Using these three states, as well as the previous three, you can define a matrix that will let you know which action the player should take when the two states overlap. Figure 18.11 shows the action matrix.

	Player has ball	Player team has ball	Adversaries have ball
Player is clear	Run for goal	Try to get a good position	Run to nearest adversary
Player is near adversary	Pass the ball	Try to get clear	Try to tackle the adversary
Player is open for goal	Shoot	Get a good position to shoot	Run to nearest adversary

Figure 18.11 The action matrix for a soccer player

Using this matrix would make the player react like a normal player would. If he is clear and doesn't have the ball, he will try to get in a favorable position for a goal. If he has the ball at a shooting position, he will try to score. You get the idea.

But how do you calculate which state is active? It's easy—you use the group membership of each state for both inputs, and multiply the input row by the column row to get the final result for each cell. (It's not matrix multiplication; you simply multiply each row position by the column position to get the row column value.) This will give you the best values from which to choose. For example, if one cell has a value of 0.34 and the other cell has a value of 0.50, then the best choice is probably to do what the cell with 0.50 says. Although this isn't an exact action, it is the best you can take. There are several ways to improve this matrix, such as using randomness, evaluating the matrix with another matrix (such as the personality of the player), and many more.

A Simple Method for Memory

Although programming a realistic model for memory and learning is hard, there is a method that I personally think is pretty simple to implement—you can store game states as memory patterns. This method will save the game state for each decision it makes (or for each few, depending on the complexity of the game) and the outcome of that decision; it will store the decision result in a value from zero to one (with zero being a very bad result and one being a very good result).

For example, consider a fighting game. After every move the subject makes, the game logs the result (for example, whether the subject hit the target, missed the target, caused much damage, or was hurt after the attack). Calculate the result and adjust the memory result for that attack. This will make the computer learn what is good (or not) against a certain player, especially if the player likes to follow the same techniques over and over again.

You can use this method for almost any game, from Tic-Tac-Toe, for which you would store the player's moves and decide which would be the best counter-play using the current state of the game and the memory, to racing games, for which you would store the movement of the cars from point to point and, depending on the result, choose a new way to get to the path. The possibilities are infinite, of course. This only simulates memory, and using only memory isn't the best thing to do—but it is usually best to act based on memory instead of only pure logic.

Artificial Intelligence and Games

There are various fields of artificial intelligence, and some are getting more advanced each day. The use of neural networks and genetic algorithms for learning is pretty normal in today's games. Even if all these techniques are being applied to games nowadays and all the hype is out, it doesn't mean you need to use it in your own games. If you need to model a fly, just make it move randomly. There is no need to apply the latest techniques in genetic algorithms to make the fly sound like a fly; random movement will do just as well (or better) than any other algorithm. There are a few rules I like to follow when I'm developing the artificial intelligence for a game.

1. If it looks intelligent, then your job is done.
2. Put yourself in the subject's place and code what you think you would do.
3. Sometimes the simpler technique is the needed one.
4. Always pre-design the artificial intelligence.
5. When nothing else works, use random logic.

Summary

This chapter has provided a small introduction to artificial intelligence. Such a broad topic could easily take a few sets of books to explain—and even then, many details would have to be left out. The use of artificial intelligence depends much on the type of game you are developing, so it is usually also very application-specific. While 3D engines can be used repeatedly, it is less likely that artificial intelligence code can. Although this chapter covered some of the basics of artificial intelligence, it was just a small subset of what you might use, so don't be afraid to experiment!

Chapter Quiz

You can find the answers to this chapter quiz in Appendix A, "Chapter Quiz Answers."

1. Which of the following is *not* one of the three deterministic algorithms covered in this chapter?

    A. Random logic

    B. Tracking

    C. Conditions

    D. Patterns

2. Can fuzzy matrices be used without multiplying the input memberships? Why or why not?

    A. No, it is absolutely necessary to multiply the input memberships.

    B. Yes, but only after negating the matrix.

    C. Yes, it is possible using AND and OR operators, and then randomly selecting action for the active cell.

    D. Yes, it is possible using XOR and NOT operators after multiplying the matrix.

3. Which type of system solves problems that are usually solved by specialized humans?

    A. Expert system

    B. Deterministic algorithm

    C. Conditional algorithm

    D. If-then-else

4. Which type of intelligence system is based on an expert system, but is capable of determining fractions of complete answers?

    A. Genetic algorithm

    B. Fuzzy logic

    C. Deterministic algorithm

    D. Expert system

5. Which type of intelligence system uses a method of computing solutions for a hereditary logic problem?

    A. Expert system

    B. Fuzzy logic

    C. Genetic algorithm

    D. Conditional logic

6. Which type of intelligence system solves problems by imitating the workings of a brain?

 A. State machine

 B. Genetic algorithm

 C. Fuzzy logic

 D. Neural network

7. Which of the following uses predetermined behaviors of objects in relation to the universe problem?

 A. Genetic algorithm

 B. Deterministic algorithm

 C. Fuzzy logic

 D. Neural network

8. Which type of deterministic algorithm "fakes" intelligence?

 A. Patterns

 B. Tracking

 C. Random motion

 D. Logic

9. Which type of deterministic algorithm will cause one object to follow another?

 A. Tracking

 B. Conditional

 C. Patterns

 D. Random motion

10. Which type of deterministic algorithm follows preset templates?

 A. Tracking

 B. Random motion

 C. Genetic

 D. Patterns

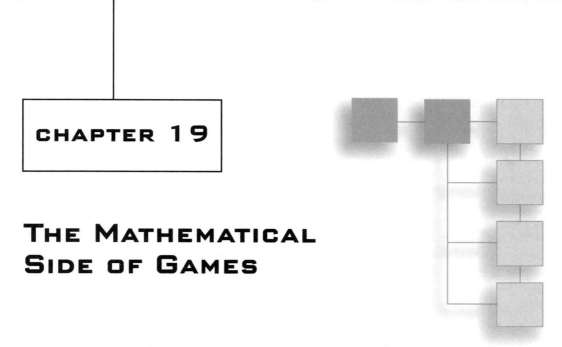

CHAPTER 19

THE MATHEMATICAL SIDE OF GAMES

As you might already know, math is an extremely important subject in high-level computer programming, especially in game programming. Behind the scenes, in the graphics pipeline, and in the physics engine, heavy math is being processed by your computer, often with direct implementation in the silicon (as is the case with most graphics chips). While a huge amount of heavy math is needed to get a polygon on the screen with a software renderer, that is all handled by highly optimized (and fantastically complex) mathematics built into the latest graphics processors. Vectors, matrices, functions, and other math-related topics comprise an indispensable section in any game-programming curriculum. In this chapter, I will go over basic linear algebra, such as vector operations, matrices, and probability, with a bit of calculus when I get into the basics of functions. Please note that this is an extremely simple primer on basic algebra and calculus and should accomplish little more than whetting your appetite. For a really solid treatment of game mathematics, please refer to *Mathematics for Game Developers* (Course Technology PTR, 2004) by Christopher Tremblay, who has tackled the subject with a tenacity that is sure to enhance your math skills.

Here is a breakdown of the major topics in this chapter:

- Using trigonometry
- Understanding vectors
- Working with matrices
- Using probability
- Working with functions

Trigonometry

Trigonometry is the study of angles and their relationships to shapes and various other geometries. You will use some of the material covered here as support for some advanced operations you will build later.

Visual Representation and Laws

Before I go into the details of trigonometry, let me introduce a new concept—radians. A *radian* is a measurement of an angle, just like a degree. One radian is the angle formed in any circle where the length of the arc defined by the angle and the circle radius are of same length, as shown in Figure 19.1. You will use radians as your measurement because they are the units C++ math functions use for angles. Because you are probably accustomed to using degrees as your unit of measurement, you need to be able to convert from radians to degrees and vice versa. As you might know, π radians is the angle that contains half a circle, as you can see in Figure 19.2. And you probably know that 180 degrees is also the angle that contains half a circle. Knowing this, you can convert any radian unit to degrees, as shown in Equation 19.1, and vice versa using Equation 19.2.

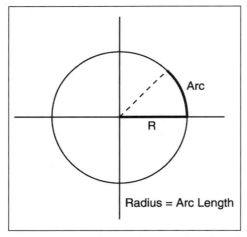

Figure 19.1 Relation of the arc length and radius of the circle

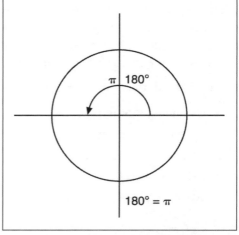

Figure 19.2 Half a circle denoted by radians and degrees

$$Radians = \frac{Degrees * \pi}{180}$$

Equation 19.1

$$Degrees = \frac{Radians * 180}{\pi}$$

Equation 19.2

```
double DegreeToRadian(double degree)
{
    return (degree * PI / 180);
}
double RadianToDegree(double radian)
{
    return (radian * 180 / PI);
}
```

Now that you know what a radian is, I'll explain how to use them. Take a look at Figure 19.3. From the angle and the circle radius, you can get the triangle's sides and angles. If you examine that circle a little bit closer, you will see that in any triangle that contains the center of the circle and the end of the arc as vertices, the hypotenuse of that triangle is the line formed

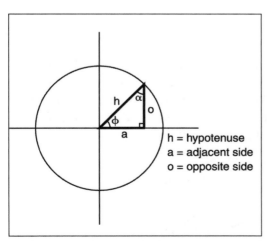

from the circle's center to the end of the arc. Now you need to find the two other lines' lengths that form the triangle. You will find these using the cosine and sine functions. The three equations that are important in geometry are cosine, sine, and tangent, and they are directly related to the triangle. See the cosine Equation 19.3, the sine Equation 19.4, and the tangent Equation 19.5.

h = hypotenuse
a = adjacent side
o = opposite side

Figure 19.3 A triangle formed by a circle radius and an angle; π radians = 180 degrees

$$\text{cosine}(\phi) = \frac{\text{Adjacent Side}}{\text{Hypotenuse}}$$

Equation 19.3

$$\text{sine}(\phi) = \frac{\text{Opposite Side}}{\text{Hypotenuse}}$$

Equation 19.4

$$\text{tangent}(\phi) = \frac{\sin(\phi)}{\cos(\phi)} = \frac{\text{Opposite Side}}{\text{Adjacent Side}}$$

Equation 19.5

You can calculate these trigonometric operations using the MacLaurin series, but that is beyond the scope of this book. Now you can determine the length of the adjacent side of the triangle on the circle by using the cosine, as shown in Equation 19.6.

$$\text{cosine}(\phi) = \frac{\text{Adjacent Side}}{\text{Hypotenuse}} \Longleftrightarrow$$

$$\text{Adjacent Side} = \text{Circle Radius} * \text{cosine}(\phi)$$

Equation 19.6

What if you want to know the angles at each side of the triangle? You use exactly the same equations as you used before to get the sine or the cosine. When you have them, you use the inverse of those operations to get the angles. Taking the triangle in Figure 19.3, you find two of the angles. You don't need to find one of the angles because you already know that the triangle is a right angle triangle, and as such, the angle formed is 90 degrees, or one-half π.

$$\text{cosine}(\phi) = \frac{\text{Adjacent Side}}{\text{Hypotenuse}} \Longleftrightarrow$$

$$\phi = \text{cosine}^{-1}\left(\frac{\text{Adjacent Side}}{\text{Circle Radius}}\right)$$

Equation 19.7

$$\text{cosine}(\alpha) = \frac{\text{Opposite Side}}{\text{Hypotenuse}} \Longleftrightarrow$$

$$\alpha = \text{cosine}^{-1}\left(\frac{\text{Opposite Side}}{\text{Circle Radius}}\right)$$

Equation 19.8

What is the difference between the two equations? If you look carefully, you are trying to get the angle ⟨ using the cosine and the opposite side. You do this because the opposite side of the angle ⟨ is actually the adjacent side in relation to that angle. So what does this mean? It means that the terms *adjacent* and *opposite* are relative to the angle to which they are referred. In the second calculation, the opposite side should actually be the adjacent side of that angle. Table 19.1 shows you the list of trigonometric functions. This might seem complicated, but it will become clearer when you start using all of this later.

Table 19.1 C Trigonometric Functions

Trigonometric	C Function	C Function Inversed
cosine	cos	acos
sine	sin	asin
tangent	tan	atan/atan2

* These functions are all defined in math.h.

Angle Relations

A couple of relations can prove useful when you are dealing with angles and trigonometric functions. One of the most important relations is the trigonometric identity shown in Equation 19.9.

$$sine^2(\phi) + cosine^2(\phi) = 1$$

Equation 19.9

This equation is the base of all the other relations. To be honest, these relations are used only for problem solving or optimizations. For that reason, I will not go over them in detail; I will simply show them to you so you can use them at your discretion. The following equations are derived from Equation 19.9 and should be used to optimize your code.

$$sine(2\phi) = 2sine(\phi) * cosine(\phi)$$

Equation 19.10

$$\text{cosine}(2\phi) = \text{cosine}^2(\phi) - \text{sine}^2(\phi)$$

Equation 19.11

$$\text{tangent}(2\phi) = \frac{2\text{tangent}(\phi)}{1 - \text{tangent}^2(\phi)}$$

Equation 19.12

Now you are done with trigonometry. Trigonometry isn't very useful per se, but it will prove an indispensable tool later when you use it with other concepts, such as vectors or matrices.

Vectors

A vector is an n-tuple of ordered real values that can represent anything with more than one dimension—for example, a 2D or 3D Euclidean space. Basically, vectors are nothing more than a set of components.

$$\vec{\text{Vector}} = \begin{pmatrix} V_1 \\ V_2 \\ V_3 \\ V_n \end{pmatrix} \in R^n$$

Equation 19.13

Vectors describe both magnitude and direction. In the two-dimensional case, the X and Y components represent the distance from the relative origin to the end of the vector, as you can see in Figure 19.4. Because you are using a 2D world, you define vectors using two components for convenience, with a commonly known notation (x, y). You can also represent just one component of the vector by using a subscript either with the order of the element or with the component identification, as shown in Equation 19.14.

```
#include <math.h>

typedef struct vector2d
```

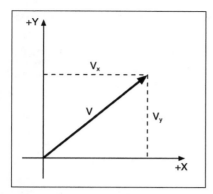

Figure 19.4 A 2D vector composed of two scalars defining the orientation

$$\vec{\text{Vector}} = (V_1;V_2) = (V_x;V_y)$$
$$\vec{\text{Vector}} = (12;9)$$

Equation 19.14

```
{
    double components[2];
}
vector2d;
```

As you can see, the vector is constituted by an array of two components: X (`components[0]`) and Y (`components[1]`).

Addition and Subtraction

Vectors can be added or subtracted to form new vectors. You can see in Equation 19.15 that the addition of two vectors is completed component by component, which is true for subtraction as well.

$$\vec{\text{Added Vector}} = \vec{A} + \vec{B} \Longleftrightarrow$$
$$\vec{\text{Added Vector}} = (A_x + B_x; A_y + B_y)$$

Equation 19.15

Equation 19.15 also shows that vector addition can be done in any order, but this isn't true for vector subtraction. If you take a look at Figure 19.5, you can see how the same vectors subtracted in different order produce a vector that is the same in length but different in orientation. Before I move on, I want to create your addition method.

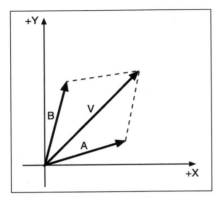

Figure 19.5 Addition of two vectors

```
vector2d vector2d_add(vector2d first, vector2d second)
{
    vector2d newvector;
    newvector.components[0] = first.components[0] + second.components[0];
    newvector.components[1] = first.components[1] + second.components[1];
    return newvector;
}
```

As you can see in Figure 19.6, the subtraction of two vectors gives you the distance between them, but it isn't commutative. If you subtract A – B you get the distance from A to B, whereas in B – A you get the distance from B to A. This is shown in Equation 19.16.

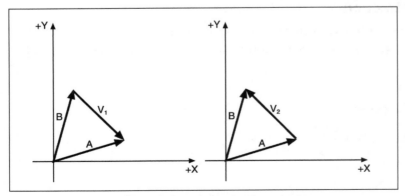

Figure 19.6 Subtraction of two vectors in different order

$$\vec{\text{S}}\text{ubtracted Vector} = \vec{A} + \vec{B} \Longleftrightarrow$$

$$\vec{\text{S}}\text{ubtracted Vector} = (A_x + B_x; A_y + B_y)$$

Equation 19.16

note

In Figure 19.6, you can see that the product of the subtraction has its origin on the end of the first vector. This is incorrect. The vector origin should be the origin of the world.

To finalize this section, let's build the subtraction function.

```
vector2d vector2d_subtract(vector2d first, vector2d second)
{
    vector2d newvector;
    newvector.components[0] = first.components[0] - second.components[0];
    newvector.components[1] = first.components[1] - second.components[1];
    return newvector;
}
```

Scalar Multiplication and Division

You can scale vectors by multiplying or dividing them by scalars, just like normal scalar-to-scalar operations. To do this, you multiply or divide each vector component by the scalar. You can see this in Equation 19.17, which shows multiplication of each of the vector components by a scalar to produce a new vector.

$$\vec{\text{M}}\text{ultiplied Vector} = (V_x * \text{Scalar}; V_y * \text{Scalar})$$

Equation 19.17

In code you have:

```
vector2d vector2d_multiply(vector2d vect, double multiplier)
{
    vector2d newvector;
    newvector.components[0] = vect.components[0] * multiplier;
    newvector.components[1] = vect.components[1] * multiplier;
    return newvector;
}
```

You do the same thing for division, as you can see in Equation 19.18.

$$\vec{\text{Divided Vector}} = \left(\frac{V_x;V_y}{\text{Scalar}} \right)$$

Equation 19.18

To end the normal operations, let's build a division function.

```
vector2d vector2d_divide(vector2d vect, double divisor)
{
    vector2d newvector;
    newvector.components[0] = vect.components[0] / divisor;
    newvector.components[1] = vect.components[1] / divisor;
    return newvector;
}
```

Length

The length is the *size* of the vector. The length is used in several other vector operations, so it should be the first one you learn. If you remember the Pythagorean Theorem, you know that the square of the hypotenuse is equal to the sum of the square of each side. You use the same theorem to get the length of the vector, as you can see in Equation 19.19.

$$\| \vec{\text{Vector}} \| = \sqrt{V_x^2 + V_y^2}$$

Equation 19.19

As usual, I'll write a function to calculate the length of a vector.

```
double vector2d_length(vector2d vect)
{
    return (double) sqrt (vect.components[0] * vect.components[0] +
        vect.components[1] * vect.components[1]);
}
```

Normalization

As you saw earlier, vectors have both an orientation and a length, also referred to as the *norm*. Some calculations you use will need a vector of length 1.0. To force a vector to have a length of 1.0, you must normalize the vector—in other words, divide the components of the vector by its total length, as shown in Equation 19.20.

$$\vec{\text{Normalized Vector}} = \left(\frac{V_x; V_y}{\|\vec{V}\|}\right)$$

Equation 19.20

```
vector2d vector2d_normalize(vector2d vect)
{
    vector2d newvector = vect;
    double length = vector2d_length(vect);
    if (length > 0)
    {
        newvector.components[0] /= length;
        newvector.components[1] /= length;
    }
    return newvector;
}
```

Perpendicular Operation

Finding the perpendicular of a vector is one of those operations you'll use once a year, but let's briefly talk about it anyway. A vector perpendicular to another is a vector that forms a 90-degree angle, or a half-π radians angle with the other. In Figure 19.7, you can see that vector B forms a 90-degree, counterclockwise angle with vector A.

Finding the perpendicular vector of a 2D vector is easy; you simply need to negate the Y component and swap it with the X component of the vector, as shown in Equation 19.21.

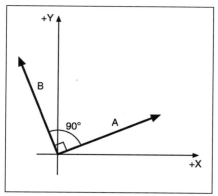

Figure 19.7 A perpendicular vector forming a 90-degree, counterclockwise angle with another vector

$$\vec{\text{Perpendicular Vector}}_{\perp} = (-V_y; V_x)$$

Equation 19.21

Just one little thing.... You see that reversed T in Equation 19.21? That is the perpendicular symbol.

```
vector2d vector2d_perpendicular(vector2d vect)
{
    vector2d newvector = vect;
    newvector.components[0] = vect.components[1] * -1;
    newvector.components[1] = vect.components[0];
    return newvector;
}
```

Dot Product

The dot product is probably the most used operation with vectors. You can use it to multiply two vectors, as shown in Equation 19.22.

$$\vec{A} \cdot \vec{B} = A_x * B_x + A_y * B_y$$

Equation 19.22

```
double vector2d_dotproduct(vector2d first, vector2d second)
{
    return (double) first.components[0] * second.components[0] +
        first.components[1] * second.components[1];
}
```

Using the dot product isn't very informative per se, but the dot product can also be defined by Equation 19.23.

This equation gives a little more information, don't you agree? In case you didn't know, ø is the smallest angle formed by the two vectors. With a little thought and by combining Equations 19.22 and 19.23, you can get the equation to find the smallest angle of two vectors (see Equation 19.24).

$$\vec{A} \cdot \vec{B} = ||\vec{A}|| * ||\vec{B}|| * cosine(\phi)$$

Equation 19.23

$$cosine(\phi) = \frac{\vec{A} \cdot \vec{B}}{||\vec{A}|| * ||\vec{B}||} \Longleftrightarrow$$

$$\phi = cosine^{-1}\left(\frac{\vec{A} \cdot \vec{B}}{||\vec{A}|| * ||\vec{B}||}\right)$$

Equation 19.24

You finally have some use for the dot product. If you calculate the arc cosine of the dot product of the two vectors divided by the product of their lengths, you have the smallest angle between them. Now you can build the angle function.

```
double vector2d_angle(vector2d first, vector2d second)
{
    return (double) acos (
        vector2d_dotproduct(first, second) /
        (vector2d_length(first) * vector2d_length(second)));
}
```

Perp-Dot Product

The perp-dot product is nothing new. It is the dot product of a calculated perpendicular vector. This operation is mostly used in physics, as you will see later. How do you find the perp-dot product? Easy—you find the perpendicular of a vector and calculate the dot product of that vector with another, as shown in Equation 19.25.

$$\vec{Perp\ Dot} = \vec{A}_\perp \cdot \vec{B}$$

Equation 19.25

```
double vector2d_perpdotproduct(vector2d first, vector2d second)
{
    return vector2d_dotproduct(vector2d_perpendicular(first), second);
}
```

Matrices

A simple way of defining a *matrix* is to say that it is a table of values. You can see in Equation 19.26 that a matrix is defined by a set of rows and columns. The number of columns is given by p and the number of rows by q. You can also access any element of the matrix using the letter i for the row and the letter j for the column. This is shown in Equation 19.27.

$$\text{Matrix}_{pq} = \begin{bmatrix} m_{11} & m_{12} & \cdots & m_{1q} \\ m_{21} & m_{22} & \cdots & m_{2q} \\ \cdots & \cdots & \cdots & \cdots \\ m_{p1} & m_{p2} & \cdots & m_{pq} \end{bmatrix} \in R$$

Equation 19.26

$$m_{ij} = \begin{bmatrix} \cdots & \cdots & \cdots \\ \cdots & \cdots & m_{23} \\ \cdots & \cdots & \cdots \end{bmatrix}$$
$$i = 2; j = 3$$

Equation 19.27

Addition and Subtraction

Matrix addition and subtraction is done exactly the same way as the vector addition and subtraction. You add (or subtract) each element of one matrix to (or from) the other to produce a third matrix, as shown in Equation 19.28 (for the addition operation).

Matrix addition is commutative (that is, independent of the order), but this isn't the case for subtraction, as you can see in Equation 19.29.

Scalars with Multiplication and Division

Again, to multiply or divide a matrix by a scalar, you multiply or divide each matrix element by the scalar, as shown in Equation 19.30 for multiplication.

$$\text{Matrix Added}_{ij} = A_{ij} + B_{ij}$$

$$\text{Matrix Added} = \begin{bmatrix} a & b \\ c & d \end{bmatrix} + \begin{bmatrix} 1 & 2 \\ 3 & 4 \end{bmatrix} \Longleftrightarrow$$

$$\text{Matrix Added} = \begin{bmatrix} a+1 & b+2 \\ c+3 & d+4 \end{bmatrix}$$

Equation 19.28

$$\text{Matrix Subtracted}_{ij} = A_{ij} - B_{ij}$$

$$\text{Matrix Subtracted} = \begin{bmatrix} a & b \\ c & d \end{bmatrix} - \begin{bmatrix} 1 & 2 \\ 3 & 4 \end{bmatrix} \Longleftrightarrow$$

$$\text{Matrix Subtracted} = \begin{bmatrix} a-1 & b-2 \\ c-3 & d-4 \end{bmatrix}$$

Equation 19.29

$$\text{Matrix Multiplied}_{ij} = A_{ij} * \text{Scalar}$$

$$\text{Matrix Multiplied} = \begin{bmatrix} a & b \\ c & d \end{bmatrix} * \text{Scalar} \Longleftrightarrow$$

$$\text{Matrix Multiplied} = \begin{bmatrix} a * \text{Scalar} & b * \text{Scalar} \\ c * \text{Scalar} & d * \text{Scalar} \end{bmatrix}$$

Equation 19.30

This is exactly the same for the division process, shown in Equation 19.31.

Scalar operations in matrices are pretty easy and usually unnecessary. Next I will go over the most useful matrix operations.

Special Matrices

There are two special matrices I want to go over—the zero matrix and the identity matrix. First, the *zero matrix* is a matrix that, when added to any other matrix, produces the matrix shown in Equation 19.32.

$$\text{Matrix Divided}_{ij} = \frac{A_{ij}}{\text{Scalar}}$$

$$\text{Matrix Divided} = \frac{\begin{bmatrix} a & b \\ c & d \end{bmatrix}}{\text{Scalar}} \iff$$

$$\text{Matrix Divided} = \begin{bmatrix} \dfrac{a}{\text{Scalar}} & \dfrac{b}{\text{Scalar}} \\ \dfrac{c}{\text{Scalar}} & \dfrac{d}{\text{Scalar}} \end{bmatrix}$$

Equation 19.31

$$\text{Matrix} = \text{Zero Matrix} + \text{Matrix}$$

$$\text{Zero Matrix} = \begin{bmatrix} 0 & 0 \\ 0 & 0 \end{bmatrix}$$

Equation 19.32

As long as it is a 2×2 matrix, the result of the operation is M—no matter what M is. The *identity matrix* is a matrix that, when multiplied by any other matrix, produces the same matrix as shown in Equation 19.33.

$$\text{Matrix} = \text{Identity Matrix} * \text{Matrix}$$

$$\text{Identity Matrix} = \begin{bmatrix} 1 & 0 \\ 0 & 1 \end{bmatrix}$$

Equation 19.33

Again, as long as it is a 2×2 matrix, the result of this operation is M—no matter what M is.

Transposed Matrices

A *transposed matrix* is a matrix in which the matrix values are swapped with the other diagonal element, proving Equation 19.34 true. This operation is usually used to change coordinate systems in 3D.

$$\text{Matrix Transposed}_{ij} = M_{ji}$$

$$\begin{bmatrix} 1 & 2 \\ 3 & 4 \end{bmatrix} = \begin{bmatrix} 1 & 3 \\ 2 & 4 \end{bmatrix}$$

Equation 19.34

Matrix Concatenation

You have reached one of the most needed (and one of the most complicated) matrix operations—matrix multiplication, or more correctly, concatenation. *Concatenation* is the real name for matrix multiplication. This operation enables you to concatenate matrices to produce various effects, such as rotating or shearing. Equation 19.35 presents an example of matrix multiplication.

$$\text{Matrix Concatenated}_{ij} = \sum_{u-1}^{3} A_{iu} * B_{uj}$$

Equation 19.35

Well, you have a new symbol in your game. The Σ symbol, in English, represents the sum. Look at the math in Equation 19.36.

$$\sum_{i=0}^{n} \text{mass}_i$$

Equation 19.36

There are three things to explain—the symbol, the number above it, and the number below it. What you do with this bit of math is sum all the masses you have in the equation above n. Suppose that mass is an array, such as int mass [n], and you want to add every element of mass from i = 0 to n.

It's easy if you think of it like a programmer would, isn't it? So basically, the sum symbol means that you will add each element of an array from i to n. In Equation 19.37, what you actually do is add all the products of the row of matrix A with the column of matrix B to get each element of the result matrix. It's easier to check this with the example in Equation 19.37.

$$\text{Matrix Concatenated} = \begin{bmatrix} a & b \\ c & d \end{bmatrix} * \begin{bmatrix} 1 & 2 \\ 3 & 4 \end{bmatrix} \Leftrightarrow$$

$$\text{Matrix Concatenated} = \begin{bmatrix} a*1+b*3 & a*2+b*4 \\ c*1+d*3 & c*2+d*4 \end{bmatrix}$$

Equation 19.37

I want to go over how you actually come to these results. First, you will find Matrix Concatenated$_{ij}$. If you look at Equation 19.38, you can see that:

MatrixConcatenated$_{ij}$ = A$_{iu}$* B$_{uj}$ + A$_{i(u+i)}$ * B$_{(u+i)j}$

$$\text{Matrix Concatenated}_{ij} = \sum_{u=1}^{2} A_{iu} * B_{uj}$$

Equation 19.38

Since u starts at 1 and ends at 2, you can say that:

MatrixConcatenated$_{11}$ = A$_{11}$* B$_{11}$ + A$_{12}$ * B$_{21}$, or MatrixConcatenated$_{11}$ = a*1+b*3

You do the same for each element, as follows:

MatrixConcatenated$_{12}$ = A$_{11}$* B$_{12}$ + A$_{12}$ * B$_{22}$ = a*2+b*4

MatrixConcatenated$_{21}$ = A$_{21}$* B$_{11}$ + A$_{22}$ * B$_{21}$ = c*1+d*3

MatrixConcatenated$_{22}$ = A$_{21}$* B$_{12}$ + A$_{22}$ * B$_{22}$ = c*2+d*4

Vector Transformation

Being able to transform vectors by matrices is one of the fundamental tasks for 2D manipulation, but the concept behind it is very simple. If you treat a 2D vector as a matrix of size 1×2, you can multiply the *matrix vector* by another matrix the same way you would with two matrices, as shown in Equation 19.39.

You just treat the vector as a matrix, and there you have it.

$$\vec{\text{Vector Transformed}} = A * \vec{V}$$

$$\vec{\text{Vector Transformed}} = \begin{bmatrix} a & b \\ c & d \end{bmatrix} * \begin{bmatrix} 1 \\ 2 \end{bmatrix} \Leftrightarrow$$

$$\vec{\text{Vector Transformed}} = \begin{bmatrix} a*1+b*2 \\ c*1+d*2 \end{bmatrix}$$

Equation 19.39

Probability

Probability is a study of math that analyzes events and then tries to evaluate the odds of those events happening. I want to go over a simple example.

From yesterday's weather forecast, there is a good probability of heavy wind and a 50-percent chance of rain.

This forecast actually tells you the probability of heavy wind or rain happening. The text says there is a good probability of heavy wind, so you can say heavy wind has about a 75–90-percent chance of happening—and as for rain, only a 50-percent chance. What does this tell you? Well, if you had 100 days with the exact same forecast, you would probably end up with about 75–90 days with heavy wind, and 50 days with rain. In case you didn't know, 50 percent is actually 0.5.

Sets

A *set* is an unordered collection of objects. You evaluate the objects when you are dealing with probability. They can be numbers, letters, real objects, or just about anything. A set is denoted by a capital letter, and the objects in it are listed between curly braces, such as `SetA = {2, 5, 12, 22}`. Sets are usually defined as a circle with the letter caption and the objects contained, as shown in Figure 19.8.

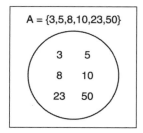

Figure 19.8 Graphical representation of sets

Union

The union operation creates a new set that combines both of the existing sets. You can see this in Equation 19.40.

Figure 19.9 shows a visual representation of the union of two sets.

$$A = \{1,3,6,9\}$$
$$B = \{2,7,10\}$$
$$A \cup B = \{1,3,6,9\} + \{2,7,10\} \Longleftrightarrow$$
$$A \cup B = \{1,2,3,6,7,9,10\}$$

Equation 19.40

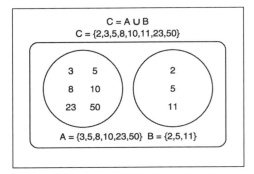

Figure 19.9 Union of two sets

Here is an example in pseudo-code:

```
List unionset;
List setA;
List setB;
unionset = setA;
For each element of setB
Begin
   If element exists in setA, do nothing
   Otherwise, add it to unionset
End
```

Intersection

The intersection operation is straightforward. You compare each element of a set to another set. The elements that are contained in both sets are elements that appear in the *intersected* set, as shown in Equation 19.41 and Figure 19.10.

$$A = \{1,2,5,9\}$$
$$B = \{2,5,7,10\}$$
$$A \cap B = \{1,2,5,9\} - \{2,5,7,10\} \Longleftrightarrow$$
$$A \cap B = \{2,5\}$$

Equation 19.41

Here is some pseudo-code that describes the process:

```
List IntersectionSet;
List ListA;
```

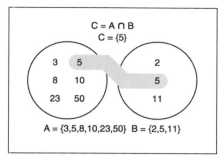

Figure 19.10 Intersection of two sets

```
List ListB;
For each element of SetB
Begin
  If element exists in SetA, add it to IntersectionSet
  Otherwise, do nothing
End
```

As you can see from the code, you go over each element of the set and see whether it exists in the other set. If it does, it is added to the final set; if it doesn't exist, it is ignored.

Functions

A function is really an equation, but because you used equation names for all the formulas before, you need to distinguish these functions from equations. I think an example will help. If I gain 0.22 pounds ever day, how much weight will I have gained after 15 days? You can multiply 0.22 pounds by 15 to get 3.31 pounds. This is correct, but what if you want to know how much I will weigh after 23 days? And what about after 93 days? You can mathematically represent this as a function, as shown in Equation 19.42.

Weight Gained (Days) = 100 * Days

Equation 19.42

You can see this graphically in Figure 19.11. Functions can be used to express various series, ideas, and so on. They are very helpful as a programming tool.

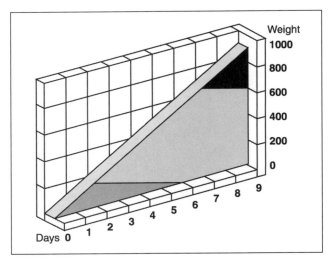

Figure 19.11 Graphical representation of a function

Integration

Differentiation and integration are advanced calculus math topics. I will go over some basic theories related to physics, since you will need it later. If you are driving a car and you press the gas pedal, producing an acceleration of 11.16 miles per hour, how do you get to the velocity and position functions? First you need to define your acceleration function, as shown in Equation 19.43.

$$\text{Acceleration (time)} = 5\text{m/s}^2$$

Equation 19.43

Looking at Equation 19.43, how do you get the velocity function? You need to integrate this function. How? This is a rather simple function, so you can easily do it, as shown in Equation 19.44.

$$\text{Velocity (time)} = \int \text{Acceleration (time)} * \Delta\text{time} \iff$$
$$\text{Velocity (time)} = \text{Initial Velocity} + \text{Acceleration} * \text{time} \iff$$
$$\text{Velocity (time)} = 5 * \text{time}$$

Equation 19.44

How do you know the integration is like this? You cheat. In Appendix B, "Useful Tables," you will find a table of useful integration constants. Now that you have the velocity function, how about getting the position function? Take a look at Equation 19.45.

$$\text{Position (time)} = \int \text{Velocity (time)} * \Delta\text{time} \Longleftrightarrow$$

$$\text{Position (time)} = \text{Initial Position} + \text{Initial Velocity} * \text{time} + \tfrac{1}{2} \text{Acceleration} * \text{time}^2 \Longleftrightarrow$$

$$\text{Position (time)} = 0 + 0 * \text{time} + \tfrac{1}{2} \, 5 * \text{time}^2 \Longleftrightarrow$$

$$\text{Position (time)} = \tfrac{1}{2} \, 5 * \text{time}^2$$

Equation 19.45

You also can cheat and use Appendix B to get to the final equation.

Differentiation

A function differentiation gives you the slope of the function at any given position. Differentiating a function is the exact opposite of integrating. Using the example given in the integration section, you can get acceleration from velocity, and velocity from position, as shown in Equations 19.46 and 19.47.

$$\text{Velocity (time)} = \text{Position (time)}' \Longleftrightarrow$$

$$\text{Velocity (time)} = (\tfrac{1}{2} \, 5 * \text{time}^2)' \Longleftrightarrow$$

$$\text{Velocity (time)} = (5 * \text{time})$$

Equation 19.46

$$\text{Acceleration (time)} = \text{Velocity (time)}' \Longleftrightarrow$$

$$\text{Acceleration (time)} = (5 * \text{time})' \Longleftrightarrow$$

$$\text{Acceleration (time)} = 5$$

Equation 19.47

As in the integration process, you also can cheat and use the Appendix B tables to get the derivatives. Why am I not going through all of the integration and derivation processes? Honestly, because they would require an entire chapter by themselves.

Summary

I have covered a lot of ground here. Math is one of the fundamental aspects of game programming, but it has been mostly tucked away by game libraries such as DirectX and Allegro. This chapter introduced you to the basics and provided you with enough theory to get you through the basics so you will be prepared (at least marginally) for the mathematical calculations you are likely to find in many game engines today. There are many other mathematical concepts you will need to know during your game programming career, so don't hesitate to check the references in Appendix D for further reading.

Chapter Quiz

You can find the answers to this chapter quiz in Appendix A, "Chapter Quiz Answers."

1. What is the study of angles and their relationships to shapes and various other geometries?

   A. Calculus

   B. Algebra

   C. Arithmetic

   D. Trigonometry

2. What is the name of the C function that calculates cosine?

   A. `cosine`

   B. `cos`

   C. `sine`

   D. `cosineof`

3. What is the name of the C function that calculates sine?

   A. `sin`

   B. `calc_sine`

   C. `sine`

   D. `sineof`

4. What is the name of the C function that calculates tangent?

   A. `tan`

   B. `tangent`

   C. `calc_tan`

   D. `tangentof`

5. Which C function calculates the inverse sine?

   A.   `asine`

   B.   `acos`

   C.   `atan`

   D.   `asin`

6. Which C function calculates the inverse tangent?

   A.   `arctangent`

   B.   `arctan`

   C.   `atan`

   D.   `calc_arctan`

7. What does a set intersection contain?

   A.   The elements not contained in either set

   B.   The elements inversely shared by both sets

   C.   The elements that are contained in both sets

   D.   The union of elements not shared by either set

8. What does a function differentiation return?

   A.   The slope of the function at any given position

   B.   The multiplication matrix for two parallel lines

   C.   The vector points at both ends of a line

   D.   The difference between two matrices

9. What is the opposite of function differentiation?

   A.   Interpolation

   B.   Conflagration

   C.   Integration

   D.   Congestion

10. What Greek letter is most often used in calculations of degrees or radians of a circle?

    A.   Alpha

    B.   Omega

    C.   Pi

    D.   Theta

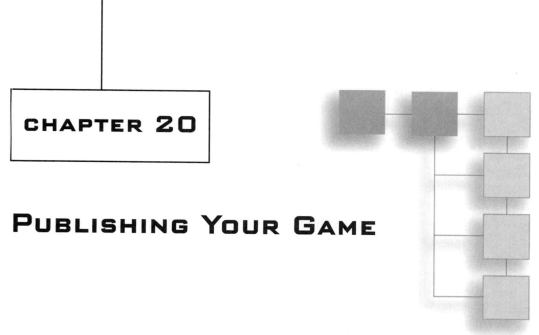

CHAPTER 20

PUBLISHING YOUR GAME

You have finally made it. You have finished your game and you want to publish it. Now you can read the following pages for some advice on how you can do it.

Here is a breakdown of the major topics in this chapter:

- Is your game worth publishing?
- Whose door should you knock on?
- Understanding contracts
- Meeting milestones
- Interviews

Is Your Game Worth Publishing?

Before you seek a publisher, you must evaluate your game. Be truthful to yourself, and also ask friends, family, and even strangers to play your games and give you some feedback. Put yourself in the position of the buyer—would you buy your own game if you saw it in the stores? And if so, how much would you pay for it? These are very important questions to ask yourself when you are thinking about approaching a publisher. In this section, I'll go over a few steps you can follow to see whether your game is worth publishing. Please note that these aren't strict rules.

Probably the most important thing to evaluate in your game is whether it is graphically attractive. Don't get me wrong; I play my old Spectrum games (the good old days) more often than the new 3D perspective mumbo jumbo out there. But unfortunately, only a small group of people do so. Users want their $250 video cards to be stretched to the last polygon. They want to see an infinite number of lights, models, and huge maps, and unfortunately, games of that size require much time from many people.

Don't despair! There is still room for 2D games out there, but they must be very good to beat the new 3D ones. A nice user interface, friendly graphics, and some tricks can do the job, but understand that this is difficult to do. So, your game is fascinating? It has nice graphics and animations and even plays smoothly? Great, move on to the next topic.

The sound is not as important, but it's still a consideration. Does the sound match the actions? Is it immersive? One good way to test this would be to play the game and have a friend sit with his back to the computer and try to describe what the sounds depict to him. If he says that it sounds like a machine gun when you have exploded a mine, it isn't a good sign. You should also pay extra attention to the music. Music should immerse the player in the game, not make him deaf. Make sure the music is pleasing to the ears but still contains the mood of the game. An example of a bad soundtrack would be if you were doing a horror game and your soundtrack consisted of the Bee Gees and the Spice Girls. The music shouldn't force the user to turn it off; rather, it should make him feel he is in the game itself.

One thing to be critical about when evaluating your game is, does it have a beginning, a middle, and an end? Does the player progress through various parts of the game feeling as if he has achieved something? Nowadays, you can't just throw a game to the player and expect him to play if you don't reward him for accomplishing something or you don't explain why he should do things. Don't overlook this part of the game, because it's ten times more important than having cool alpha blend effects. The era of games that consisted of putting a player in a dungeon with a pistol and just letting him play are long gone, my friend.

You should also be concerned with whether the game pulls the player back to play. Is it attractive? Will it make the player be late to his job because he had the desire to kill the boss in level seven? If he does, then you have probably done your job well.

To see whether your game is worth publishing, you can finally determine whether it fits into any hardcore genre. For example, if your game isn't very pretty or doesn't have nice sound but it has a million and one options to run an army, it will probably be interesting to a small hardcore group. The people in these groups tend to buy the game that fits their genre (even if it isn't very impressive graphically) if it excels at simulating a subject in that genre or hobby. There are many types of games that fall into the sub-genres and niche product categories, such as war games, strategy games, and puzzle games.

Whose Door to Knock On

Whose door you should knock on depends much on the type of game and its quality. You can't expect Codemasters to pick your *Pac-Man* clone. Nor should you expect a company that is strictly into the strategy genres to pick your shooter. Knowing what type of game genres publishers are more interested in could help you immensely.

If you have no previous game published, it might be hard to find a publisher even if you have a very good game. You should start at the bottom and build up. Do some small games and sell them online or through budget publishers. Then, start to do more complex games and try to get some small publisher to take them. As you build a name for yourself or for your company, make a lot of contacts along the way, and it will be easier to get to publishers and work out some deals.

Another suggestion is to attend conferences, such as E3 (*Electronic Entertainment Expo*) and GDC (*Game Developers Conference*), and try to get the latest scoop about what publishers are looking for. You can even make some contacts and exchange business cards with some of them.

Learn to Knock Correctly

One of the worst errors new developers make is to get too excited about their games and bombard almost every publisher 20 times about their game. Learning to go through the correct channels to submit a game can help you greatly.

First, check the publisher's Web site and try to find information on how to submit games to them. If you can't find any information, such as a phone number or e-mail address, then e-mail the Webmaster and politely ask whom you should contact to talk about publishing opportunities. This usually works. If you know a publisher's phone number, you can call to get this information and take a chance to do some scouting.

When you have your contact, it's time to let him know you have a game. Send an e-mail to the person and say you have a game of a certain genre, give a two- to three-line description of the game, and explain that you would be interested in working some deal with them. If you have a Web site for the game, send the person a URL for the game's demo and/or screenshots. If the publisher is interested in your game, he will probably send an NDA (*non-disclosure agreement*) and give you the guidelines to submit the game.

Now it's up to you to convince the publisher that your game is worth publishing and that they should be the ones publishing it. Don't ever disrespect or attack the publisher even if they refuse your game. They might not want this game, but they might be interested in another one, and if you do anything to make them angry, you can forget about trying to go to that publisher again.

No Publisher, So Now What?

You couldn't get any publisher to take your game? Don't despair, because it isn't over yet. You can still sell the game yourself. Start a Web site, find a host that can handle credit card purchases (or pay for a payment service), and do a lot of advertising. You might still have a chance to profit from your game.

Contracts

The most important advice I can give you when you start dealing with a contract is, get a lawyer. Get a good lawyer. If possible, try to find a lawyer who has experience negotiating publishing contracts. The ideal one, of course, has experience in the game industry.

Getting a lawyer to analyze the contract for you, check for any loopholes, and see whether it is profitable for you is a must if you plan to publish your games. Don't count on only common sense when you are reading a contract. There are many paragraphs we law-impaired people might think we understand, but we don't. Again, get a good lawyer.

Also, make sure you put everything in writing. Don't count on oral agreements. If they promise you something, make sure it is documented in writing. Now that I gave you my advice, here's an overview of the types of papers you will need to sign.

Non-Disclosure Agreement

The NDA is probably the first thing the publisher will ask you to sign, even before any negotiation is made. This legally-bound paper works as a protection for both you and the publisher. Some people think the NDA is sort of a joke; beware, it isn't. A breach of any paragraph in the NDA can, and probably will, get you into trouble. NDAs are usually safe to sign without much hassle, but you should still check with a lawyer or someone with expertise in the field just to be safe.

The main objective of the NDA is to protect the confidentiality of all talks, papers, files, or other information shared between the publisher and the developer. Some NDAs also include some legal protection (mostly for the publisher) about future disputes that might arise from working together. Some topics the typical NDA covers are

- Confidentiality
- Protection of material submitted by either party
- The fact that all materials submitted by either party will not breach any existing law
- Damage liability
- Time of execution

The Actual Publishing Contract

The actual publishing contract is what you are looking for. The NDA doesn't give you any assurance on the part of the publisher that they will even take your game for review, but the actual contract ensures that you and the publisher have to execute all the paragraphs implied. There isn't much general information I can give you on this one because these contracts change depending on publisher, game type, and game budget. My main advice is to run the contract by a lawyer because he will be able to help you more than I will. Just be sure to analyze dates and numbers yourself because your lawyer doesn't know how much time you need and how much money you want. Some of the typical topics a normal agreement covers are

- Distribution rights
- Modifications to the original game
- Schedule for milestones
- Royalties
- Confidentiality
- Dates for publishing

Milestones

So, you finally got the contract signed; it's time to lay back and expect the money to pour into your pocket, right? Wrong! You are now at the publisher's mercy. You have to make all the changes in your game that you agreed to in the contract, fix bugs that for some reason don't occur on your computer but happen on others, include the publisher's messages and splash images (including their logos), build demos, and do just about everything stated in the contract. It's a time-consuming task for sure. There are generally three main milestones in the development of a game—the alpha prototype (in which most artwork and programming is complete), the beta version (in which all artwork is final, but programming bugs are still being worked out), and finally the gold release (in which all artwork and programming is finished and a master CD-ROM is sent to the publisher).

Bug Report

You thought you were finished with debugging and bug fixing until the publisher sent you a list with 50-plus bugs? Don't worry; it's natural! When you get a bug report from the publisher, there are usually three types of bugs—critical, normal, and minimal (by order of importance). Some publishers require that you fix all the bugs; others only force you to fix the first two types. My advice is to fix them all! If it becomes public that your game has bugs, it will be a disaster!

Release Day

You made it to release day! Congratulations—not many do. It's time to start thinking of your next game. Start designing, program, and create art so you can have your second game on the shelves as soon as possible!

Interviews

Nothing better than a little insider input from the ones in the business, is there ? Paul Urbanis of Urbonix, Inc; Niels Bauer from Niels Bauer Software Design; and André LaMothe of Xtreme Games LLC were kind enough to answer the following questions.

Paul Urbanus: Urbonix, Inc.

Paul Urbanis is a longtime video game programmer whose experience goes back to the golden age of the video game industry (the 1970s and 1980s), when he was involved in designing both the hardware and software of early game machines.

Q: Thank you for agreeing to be interviewed for this book. Care to give our readers a little background about yourself and your experience?

A: I'm pretty blown away by the tools that are available today. I'm a former video game programmer myself, but I certainly didn't plan it. When I was in school for my electrical engineering degree, I took a cooperative education [co-op] job in the Home Computer Division of Texas Instruments in Lubbock, Texas. At that time, Texas Instruments was manufacturing and selling the TI 99/4. The 99/4 was enhanced in 1981 by adding another graphics mode and a more typewriter-like keyboard, and was called the TI 99/4A, which replaced the 99/4.

I had two co-op phases with TI, and when I returned to school after my first co-op phase, I had a single board TMS9900 [the TI 16-bit micro used in the 99/4A] computer with an instant assembler, a dumb terminal, a 99/4A system, and a complete listing of the monitor ROM. I spent way too much time understanding that machine and too little time on school. I didn't flunk out, but that system for me was like a light bulb for a moth—I was mesmerized and on a quest for knowledge. My ultimate use for this knowledge was to write a video game, since I also spent time playing video games that would have been better spent in homework.

When I returned to TI for my second co-op stint after a year in school, I was much more knowledgeable about the TI-99 architecture. TI was about to introduce their improved machine, the 99/4A. My first assignment was to generate a pass/fail matrix of video chip supply voltage versus temperature. So, I would put the 99/4A into a temperature chamber, set the voltage, wait for the temperature to stabilize, and then log the pass/fail result for all of the voltages. As you can imagine, this was B-O-R-I-N-G, but exactly the kind of work that was pushed off to a co-op student. And I couldn't complain, because I was making good money [$7 per hour in 1982].

Q: What was it like having an electronics degree, working for a computer hardware company, and then finding yourself working on games?

A: Well, when I returned to TI, I discovered that they were working on an editor/assembler package. I was very excited because up to that point, all of my 9900 assembly language programming had been on the single-board computer, and there was no source code storage except for the thermal printer on my dumb terminal. The editor/ assembler was in the internal testing phase. This is where the video chip testing re-enters the picture.

While waiting for the temperature chamber to stabilize, I would be playing around/testing the new editor/assembler package. How cool was this—you could type in code for an hour, and it *wasn't lost* when the computer was turned off? Soon, I was reading about the new graphics mode and had some assembly-language eye candy (screensaver-like stuff) on the screen. This bit of eye candy dramatically changed my co-op job in the Home Computer Division. Because a few days later the head of the HC division, Don Bynum, was walking around, just visiting with everyone—as was his practice—and he saw my graphics experimentation and asked questions such as, "Who are you and what do you have running here?" I explained that I was testing the new graphics chip and the editor/assembler package, and wanted to play with the new graphics mode because no one in the software development group was doing anything with it. He nodded in acknowledgement and continued his visit with the troops.

Later that day, I was called into Don's office, and he told me that I was being reassigned from the Hardware Development group to the Advanced Development group. Now, the real fun started. The first thing I did was get the source code to the assembler on the TI single-board computer I had used to learn TMS9900 assembly language, and port this code to a new cartridge we were working on. I also included my "Lines" eye-candy demo in source and object format so buyers of this cartridge would have an example of using the new graphics mode. After I finished this project, Don Bynum called me and Jim Dramis into his office and told us he wanted us to work on a game together. He suggested a space game, but told us that wasn't written in stone. And we had carte blanche to do whatever we wanted. There was no storyboard, script, or anything else. Just collaborate and write a game. Wow! Life couldn't get any better unless I could get the royal treatment at the Playboy Mansion. By the way, Jim Dramis was responsible for developing TI's best-selling games, *Car Wars* and *Munchman* (a *Pac-Man* clone). Eventually, we wrote a space game and it was named (not by us) *Parsec*.

Q: Believe it or not, I actually owned a TI-44/Plus computer and jury-rigged my dad's tape recorder to save/load programs! What else can you tell me about this space game?

A: *Parsec* was a horizontal scroller, somewhat similar to *Defender*. Unfortunately, due to the architecture of the 99/4A, the graphics memory was not directly in the memory map of the CPU, but instead was accessible only through some video chip control registers. Mainly, there was a 14-bit address register (two consecutive writes to the same 8-bit address) and an 8-bit data register. So the sequence to read/write one or more bytes of graphics memory was

1. Write first byte of address N.
2. Write second byte of address N.
3. Read/write byte of data at N.
4. Read/write byte of data at N+1.
5. Continue until non-contiguous address is needed, then go back to Step 1.

As you can see, random access of graphics memory to do bit-blitting was painfully slow and a real competitive disadvantage when using the 99/4A for gaming. And, in the early 1980s, video games were hot! Of course, that whole market crashed big in 1983/1984 and Nintendo stepped in to fill the void, but that's another story entirely.

Back to *Parsec*. In writing *Parsec*, Jim did most of the game flow and incorporated my suggestions. I contributed two technical breakthroughs to allow *Parsec* to do things that hadn't been possible before—and both of these contributions were directly attributable to my background as a hardware guy and reading the chip specs in detail. I was able to use a small amount of SRAM that only required two clock cycles to cache both the code and scroll buffer for the horizontal scrolling routine. This increased the speed about two times (my best recollection) and made scrolling feasible. The other thing I did was figure out how to use a new user hook [added in the /4A version] into the 60-Hz vertical interrupt to allow speech synthesis [when the speech module was connected] data to be transferred during the vertical interrupt. Prior to this, when any speech was needed the application stopped completely while the speech synthesizer was spoon-fed in a polled loop. I also did the graphics for the asteroid belt. These were actually done using TI LOGO, a LISP-like language enhanced with direct support of the 99/4A graphics. The LOGO files were converted to assembler DATA statements using a utility I wrote.

Q: LOGO! Now that brings back some fond memories, doesn't it? I actually did a lot of "Turtle Graphics" programming when I was just starting to learn how to program.

A: I've been told that TI actually produced around one million *Parsec* games. Of course, after they exited the home computer business at the end of 1983, many of these may have been buried in a landfill somewhere. Also, *Parsec* was the first TI game where the programmers' names were allowed to be included in the manual—at the beginning, no less.

Q: What did you do after that game was completed?

A: After *Parsec*, it was time for me to go back to school, which was New Mexico State University in Las Cruces. I was in school for the fall semester of 1982, and at that time I began to have conversations with two ex-TIers who had opened a computer store in Lubbock, where the Home Computer Division was located. We talked about forming a video gaming company patterned after Activision. The company would initially consist of the two business/marketing guys and the three top TI game programmers—myself, Jim Dramis, and Garth Dollahite. Garth had written *TI-Invaders*, an improved *Space Invaders* knockoff, while he was a co-op student and was hired by TI after he completed his degree. At that time, the home computer video game market was extremely hot. So, in January of 1983, I moved to Lubbock. But Jim and Garth hadn't quit TI yet, even though they had agreed they would do so. And I was sharing an apartment with Garth, as we were both single. In February, they both resigned and Sofmachine was born.

Q: How was the company organized?

A: The stock in Sofmachine was evenly divided between the five principals. The plan was for the business types to raise money by selling shares in a limited partnership, and we programmers would each write a game. As it turned out, I ended up doing lots of work making development tools, since I was the hardware guy. I designed and built emulator cartridges [not much different in principle than GBA flash carts], as well as an eprom programmer for the 99/4A. I also modified the TI debugger so all I/O was through the serial port because our games were too hooked into the video system to share it with the debugger. I also added a disassembler to the TI debugger.

Q: So your new company focused mainly on the TI-99?

A: Our games were progressing fine, although mine was behind because of all of the support development I needed to do. However, the business guys weren't having much success. In fact, by mid-summer they had raised exactly *zero* dollars. Keep in mind, they had income from a computer store they were running, while we had quit our jobs. Their only additional expense was to install a phone line in their store that they answered as "Sofmachine." Of course, there was expense for preparing and printing up the limited partnership prospectus. Needless to say, we were getting nervous. Jim was married with two kids, so he was burning through his savings at a high rate. And I had taken out a personal loan, co-signed with my dad, and it wasn't going to float me too much longer.

In the middle of the summer, Sofmachine was contacted by Atarisoft. Atarisoft had been buying the rights to port the popular full-size arcade games to game consoles and home computers of the day. And Atarisoft wanted us to convert three games: *Jungle Hunt*, *Pole Position*, and *Vangard*. We agreed to do so, at $35,000 for each game—except for *Pole Position*, which we managed to get $50,000 to do. So we started coding in earnest. Meanwhile, absolutely *no* funding of Sofmachine was happening. So Jim Dramis and I decided that the business guys needed to be out of the corporation because it would be unfair for them to get 40 percent of the Atarisoft revenue for doing *nothing*. We had delivered 99/4A games to be manufactured and marketed, but they hadn't delivered the means to manufacture and market them. This was complicated even more because Garth was a former high school student of one of the business people, whose name was Bill Games. In fact, Bill had recruited Garth to TI as a co-op student. Garth didn't think we should kick out the business types, but eventually he relented. We had a meeting and we agreed to pay all expenses incurred in the limited partnership offering, as well as other tangible expenses—phone and copy costs—plus five percent of the Atarisoft contract. Everyone agreed, and they signed their shares over to us programmers.

Q: I played those games quite a bit as a kid. It must have been fun working on arcade ports. How did that go?

A: We finished both *Jungle Hunt* and *Pole Position* at the end of 1983. About midway through the *Vangard* project, which I was doing, Atarisoft cancelled the project and agreed to pay half of the $35,000. When Jim finished *Jungle Hunt*, he accepted a job with IBM in Florida. Meanwhile, Garth and I were waiting on Atarisoft to decide whether they wanted us to port *Pole Position* to the ColecoVision game console. We really wanted that because we knew the game and already had the graphics. And, while the ColecoVision used a Z80 CPU, it had a TMS9918A video chip—the same as the TI 99/4A. I had already reverse-engineered the ColecoVision and generated a schematic. In fact, I designed a TMS9900-based single-board computer [SBC] that attached to the ColecoVision expansion bus, and used DMA to access the ColecoVision memory space. That way, we were able to use a slightly modified version of our 99/4A debugger that was ported to the SBC. In fact, Garth even modified the 9900 disassembler so it would disassemble the Z80 code in a ColecoVision cartridge. We were all set to make some easy money on the *Pole Position* conversion. But the video game industry was in the midst of imploding, so Atarisoft decided they didn't want to do this project. Garth moved back to

California and took a job with a defense contractor, and I used my Home Computer connections to get a job back at TI in their Central Research Laboratories [CRL].

Q: So you went full circle. What was the CRL all about?

A: At TI's CRL, I joined the Optical Processing branch, which was researching and developing the DMD. This is a light modulator technology along the lines of an LCD. It uses an array of small mirrors—17 microns on a side originally, now 14 microns—to display an image. This image is magnified by projection optics. TI now refers to this technology as DLP [*Digital Light Processing*], and it is used in over 50 percent of the conference room portable projectors and almost all of the digital cinema installations. In 1990, this technology was moved out of CRL and spun into its own operating group. While in CRL, I was the systems engineer for DMD, even though I didn't actually have a degree. In 1989, thirteen years after graduating high school, I received my BSEE from the University of Texas at Dallas. Of course, TI paid for my books and tuition while I worked on my degree.

I worked at TI as an employee until 1995. When I left, I had a project lined up with Cyrix, which was making X86 clone products at the time. This project lasted about a year, and just after it was completed, I got a call from the DLP guys, and they needed some help for about six months. I ended up doing contract engineering for them for five years. Then, they decided I either needed to become an employee or leave. So I left.

Q: Now tell me a little something about the company you founded and are still involved with at this time.

A: I formed Urbonix, Inc. (http://www.urbonix.com), which in reality had existed as a DBA [*Doing Business As*] since 1995. Before I cut the cord with TI, I was contacted by a company on the East coast, Dimensional Media Associates, who was getting ready to produce a 3D display using TI's DLP. This company, now LightSpace Technologies (http://www.lightspacetech.com), is still developing and marketing this product. Urbonix designed and built the first prototypes for the DMD display boards, as well as the image processor/formatter board that is used in the ZI1024 product that you see on the LightSpace Technologies Web site. My company, Urbonix, currently has a contract with Texas Instruments, where I am developing and supporting FPGA-based boards and peripherals for ASIC emulation.

Q: Thank you very much for your time.

A: Through all of this, I'm still interested in game design. It's been a pleasure; thank you.

Niels Bauer: Niels Bauer Software Design

Niels Bauer has been programming since he was 10 years old. He owns Niels Bauer Software Design and is studying law at the University of Freiburg in Germany. Niels Bauer Software Design (http://www.nbsd.de), located in Germany, has concentrated on complex (but still easy to learn) games. One of their best games, *Smugglers 2*, is an elite-like game from a strategic point of view. It features a lot of new ideas, such as crew management, boarding enemy ships, attacking planets, treasure hunting, and smuggling. If you want to make a game in the *Smugglers* universe under the loose guidance of this company, get in touch with them. You can reach them via the Web sites just mentioned or by e-mail, at contact@nbsd.de. Niels Bauer is now working on *Smugglers 3*.

Q: You founded Niels Bauer Software Design in 1999. Was it hard for a single person to develop the games alone?

A: In two years, I finished three games. Unfortunately, they weren't very successful. In spring of 2001, I wanted to leave the game business and do something else. Finally, I decided to make only one more game, *Smugglers*, and just for myself and nobody else. I decided to use Delphi because I wanted to concentrate 100 percent on the gameplay. I wanted a game that I would really like to play myself, even after weeks of development. When the game was finished, after about one month I showed it to some friends, and they immediately became addicted. Suddenly I became aware of the potential of the game and decided to release it. As you can see from this little story, the most difficult part of working alone is keeping yourself motivated until you have the first hit. *Smugglers 2* is the last game where I wrote most of the code myself. In the future, I will concentrate more on the business and design part.

Q: I've noticed that *Smugglers* has been a cover mount on some computer magazines. How easy or difficult was it to achieve this?

A: I would say it was very difficult and pure luck that I got the necessary contacts. I sent e-mails to many magazines, but from most I didn't even get a reply. The main [reason] for this could have been that *Smugglers 1* didn't have cool graphics and you needed to play the game to become addicted. Those editors became addicted and so they made a very good offer that I couldn't turn down, but unfortunately, from the feedback I got this is very uncommon.

Q: What do you think made *Smugglers* so popular?

A: Well, this is a difficult question. There are a lot of elite-like games out there. Unfortunately, most are too complex to be understood by the casual player. Even [I], as an experienced player, have problems with most. *Smugglers*, on the other hand, is very easy to learn and play. With the short interactive tutorial, you can really start off immediately. On the other hand, it could have been so successful because it provided the player with a lot of freedom while still keeping the complexity low. For example, he can be a trader, a smuggler, a pirate, or even fight for the military. Or, for example, you can fly capital ships and attack planets. These are a lot of options. What I especially liked was the opportunity to receive ranks and medals depending on your own success. The last time I saw something like this was in *Wing Commander 1*, and this was a while back.

Q: You released *Smuggler 2* recently. Any projects for the future?

A: Yes, definitely. The team [has] already begun work on an online version. This time we say goodbye to the menu system used in previous *Smugglers* titles and use a very nice top-down view of the universe. I am very excited about the possibility of such a game.

Q: From a developer's perspective, what do you think of the game industry at this moment?

A: I feel very sorry for it. Where [have] all the cool games like *Pirates*, *Wing Commander*, *Civilization*, *Ultima 7*, and *Elite* gone to? I can tell you. They all landed in the trashcan because they don't have high-tech graphics. Only those games with the best graphics get bought these days in huge masses, and unfortunately, these games are the least fun and have the most bugs. I can't imagine a single game—except *Counter-Strike* and that was a mod—that I really liked to play for longer than a couple of hours. I don't believe I can change this with *Smugglers*, but maybe I can provide a safe haven for some people who feel like I do. Considering the attention I got for *Smugglers*, it might not be a few.

Q: Any final advice to the starting game developer?

A: Concentrate on the gameplay. I needed two years to understand that it's not C++ and DirectX that make a game cool. There are thousands of those games out there. What makes a game really good are two important factors:

1. It's extremely easy to learn. (Your mother needs to be able to play it right off.)
2. You need to like it to play it yourself all day long.

Someone said in a book, which I unfortunately don't remember [the name of] now, that you most likely need to make 10 crappy games before you will finally make a good game. This is definitely true.

André LaMothe: Xtreme Games LLC

André LaMothe has been in the computing industry for more than 24 years. He has worked in just about every field of computing and he even worked for NASA. He currently owns Xtreme Games LLC, a computer games publishing company. Xtreme Games LLC was founded five years ago and develops and publishes games for the PC, Palm, and Pocket PC platforms.

Q: At this time, with gamers wanting 3D environments with cube mapping and realistic particle systems, what game type do you think a small developer would have more luck with?

A: That's really hard to say. Even if a small developer makes a game better than *Quake III*, it really doesn't matter since it's nearly impossible to get distribution these days, and publishers screw developers with percentage rates of 5 to 10 percent being common. So my advice is, simply make what you want to play.

Q: Being Xtreme Games LLC, a publisher, what are the minimum requirements for publishing a game with you?

A: That the game be of professional quality, bug-free, and competitive with other value games on the market.

Q: With the new growth of Xtreme Games LLC, what kind of games would you be more interested in seeing?

A: Value sports games, 3D games leveraging the Genesis engine, etc., and quality Palm and Pocket PC games.

Q: What steps are involved? And what is the process from the point that a developer gives you a complete game to retail distribution?

A:

1. The game is tested until all bugs are removed.
2. The packaging of the product is created.
3. Buyers at chains make purchase orders for the product.
4. The product is manufactured and units are shipped to distribution points and warehouses.
5. The product is shelved.
6. The money for the product is paid. (It takes three to six months.)
7. Royalties are dispersed.

Q: From a developer's perspective, what do you think of the current state of the industry at this time?

A: Very bad. I'm sorry to say, corporate America has got into it really deep now, and completely taken the fun out of game development. Programmers work 100+ hours a week trying to meet impossible schedules dictated by marketing, distribution, and manufacturing that aren't even "real," and in the end 99 percent of all games don't even break even. On top of that, game programmers are not paid well; their average pay is less than programmers that are nowhere near as technically skilled but work in more mainstream software endeavors like Internet, database, etc. The problem with the entire game development industry is that the people running it still to this day don't understand it. If the developers ran it, we would all be a lot happier. Just because we are nerds doesn't mean we aren't smarter than MBAs when it comes to business. They better not ever let us in charge. Instead of a business that is replete with failure, huge losses, and dismal earnings to gross revenues, we would actually make money!

Q: Do you have any final advice to the small developer who wants to try to get into this challenging industry?

A: Don't think about how to make "them" happy; just do what makes you happy, stay focused, and finish what you start. Keep this up and sooner or later something good has to happen.

Xtreme Games is always looking for good products to license. If you're interested, contact us at:

Xtreme Games LLC
http://www.xgames3d.com
info@xgames3d.com

Summary

You have been through a crash course in software publishing, and this was just the tip of the iceberg. There are many options, many contracts, and many publishers you need to check, and that's just the beginning. As you get more experience, you will start to easily recognize the good and bad contracts, as well as the good and bad publishers. So what are you waiting for? Finish the game and start looking!

References

Below are some URLs of publishing companies. Please note that neither I nor Premier Press recommend any one publisher over another; the list is alphabetical.

Codemasters: http://www.codemasters.com
E3: http://www.e3expo.com
ECTS: http://www.ects.com
eGames: http://www.egames.com
Game Developers Conference: http://www.gdconf.com
GarageGames: http://www.garagegames.com
MonkeyByte Games: http://www.mbyte.com
On Deck Interactive: http://www.odigames.com
RealArcade Games: http://realguide.real.com/games
Xtreme Games Conference: http://www.xgdx.com
Xtreme Games LLC: http://www.xgames3d.com

Chapter Quiz

You can find the answers to this chapter quiz in Appendix A, "Chapter Quiz Answers."

1. What is the first step you must take before attempting to get your game published?
   A. Evaluate the game.
   B. Sell the game.
   C. Test the game.
   D. Release the game.

2. What is the most important question to consider in a game before seeking a publisher?
   A. Is it challenging?
   B. Is it fun to play?
   C. Is it graphically attractive?
   D. Is it marketable?

3. What is the second most important aspect of a game?
   A. Graphics
   B. Sound
   C. Music
   D. Input

4. What is an important factor of gameplay, in the sense of a beginning, middle, and ending, that must be considered?

   A. Progression

   B. Goals

   C. Difficulty

   D. Continuity

5. What adjective best describes a best-selling game?

   A. Large

   B. Complex

   C. Cute

   D. Addictive

6. What is an NDA?

   A. Never Diverge Anonymity

   B. No Disco Allowed

   C. Non-Disclosure Agreement

   D. Non-Discussion Agreement

7. What is a software bug?

   A. An error in the source code

   B. A mistake in the design

   C. A digital life form

   D. A tracking device

8. What term describes a significant date in the development process?

   A. Deadline

   B. Milestone

   C. Achievement

   D. Release

9. Who created the game *Smugglers 2*?

   A. Niels Bauer

   B. André LaMothe

   C. John Carmack

   D. Ellie Arroway

10. For whom should you create a game for the purpose of entertainment?

   A. Yourself

   B. Gamers

   C. Publishers

   D. Marketers

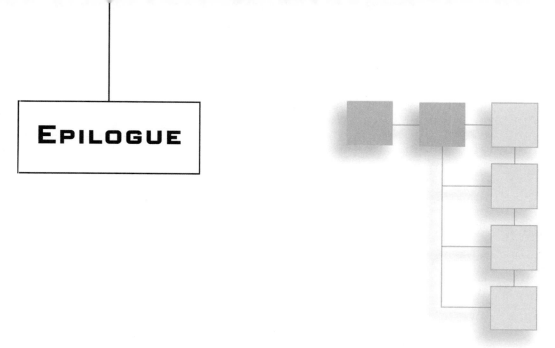

EPILOGUE

I tend to say this each time I reach this point, but I can honestly say that this book has been the most enjoyable book I have written so far. Exploring the vast feature set of the Allegro library has been an absolute blast, and I am grateful to have had the opportunity to write this book on such a fascinating subject. I hope you have enjoyed it, too!

Although I do not know you personally, I have gotten to know many readers through online forums, so there is a certain feeling of coming full circle at this point. I hope you have found this book not just helpful, but invaluable as a reference and enjoyable to read. I have strived to cover all the bases of 2D game programming, and I hope you have enjoyed it.

Although every effort was made to ensure that the content and source code presented in this book is error-free, it is possible that errors in print or bugs in the sample programs might have missed scrutiny (especially when multiple compilers are involved, as was the case here). If you have any problems with the source code, sample programs, or general theory in this book, please let me know! You can contact me at support@jharbour.com. I'll do my best to help you work though any problems (and I'll try to respond within a day or so). I also welcome constructive criticism and comments that you might have regarding the content of this book. Reader feedback was the reason for this dramatic revision to a book that was once based on Windows and DirectX, but is now cross-platform and based on open-source tools!

Finally, whether you are an absolute beginner or a seasoned professional, I welcome you to visit my online forum at http://www.jharbour.com to share your games, ideas, and questions with other Allegro fans! Membership is free and open to the public.

As always, I look forward to hearing from you!

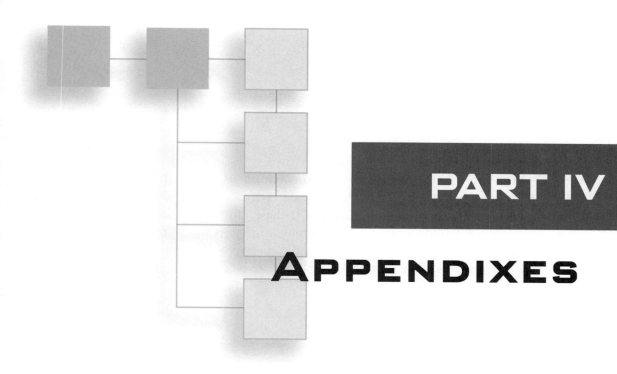

PART IV

APPENDIXES

APPENDIX A
Chapter Quiz Answers 633

APPENDIX B
Useful Tables 651

APPENDIX C
Numbering Systems: Binary and Hexadecimal .657

APPENDIX D
Recommended Books and Web Sites 663

APPENDIX E
Configuring Allegro for Microsoft Visual C++ and Other Compilers . . .671

APPENDIX F
Compiling the Allegro Source Code 685

APPENDIX G
Using the CD-ROM 691

Welcome to Part IV of *Game Programming All in One, 2nd Edition.* Part IV includes seven appendixes that provide reference information for your use, including some useful tables, an ASCII chart, a list of helpful books and Web sites, an overview of hexadecimal and binary numbering systems, a tutorial on configuring Allegro and compiling the Allegro library, and an overview of the included CD-ROM.

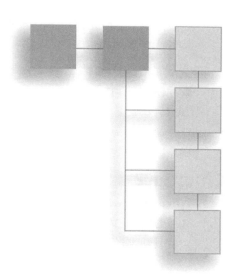

Appendix A

Chapter Quiz Answers

Chapter 1

1. What programming language is used in this book?

   A. C

2. What is the name of the free multi-platform game library used in this book?

   C. Allegro

3. What compiler can you use to compile the programs in this book?

   D. All of the above

4. Which operating system does Allegro support?

   D. All of the above

5. Which of the following is a popular strategy game for the PC?

   C. *Real War*

6. What is the most important factor to consider when working on a game?

   C. Gameplay

7. What is the name of the free open-source IDE/compiler included on the CD-ROM?

   B. Dev-C++

8. What is the name of the most popular game development library in the world?

   C. DirectX

9. Which of the following books discusses the gaming culture of the late 1980s and early 1990s with strong emphasis on the exploits of id Software?

   A. *Masters of Doom*

10. According to the author, which of the following is one of the best games made in the 1980s?

   D. *Starflight*

Chapter 2

1. What game features an Avatar and takes place in the land of Brittania?

   B. *Ultima VII: The Black Gate*

2. GNU is an acronym for which of the following phrases?

   A. GNU is Not Unix

3. What is the primary Web site for Dev-C++?

   B. http://www.bloodshed.net

4. What is the name of the compiler used by Dev-Pascal?

   A. GNU Pascal

5. What is the name of the powerful automated update utility for Dev-C++?

   D. WebUpdate

6. What are the Dev-C++ update packages called?

   B. DevPaks

7. What distinctive feature of Dev-C++ sets it apart from commercial development tools?

   D. All of the above

8. What is the name of the game programming library featured in this chapter?

   D. Allegro

9. What function must be called before you use the Allegro library?

   C. `allegro_init()`

10. What statement must be included at the end of `main()` in an Allegro program?

   B. `END_OF_MAIN()`

Chapter 3

1. What is the term used to describe line-based graphics?

    A. Vector

2. What does CRT stand for?

    C. Cathode Ray Tube

3. What describes a function that draws a simple geometric shape, such as a point, line, rectangle, or circle?

    B. `Graphics Primitive`

4. How many polygons does the typical 3D accelerator chip process at a time?

    C. 1

5. What is comprised of three small streams of electrons of varying shades of red, green, and blue?

    D. Pixel

6. What function is used to create a custom 24- or 32-bit color?

    A. `makecol`

7. What function is used to draw filled rectangles?

    D. `rectfill`

8. Which of the following is the correct definition of the circle function?

    A. `void circle(BITMAP *bmp, int x, int y, int radius, int color);`

9. What function draws a set of curves based on a set of four input points stored in an array?

    C. `spline`

10. Which text output function draws a formatted string with justification?

    D. `textprintf_justify`

Chapter 4

1. What is the primary graphics drawing function used to draw the tanks in *Tank War*?

    A. `rectfill`

2. What function in *Tank War* sets up a bullet to fire it in the direction of the tank?

    C. `fireweapon`

3. What function in *Tank War* updates the position and draws each projectile?

D.   `updatebullet`

4. What is the name of the organization that produced GCC?

A.   Free Software Foundation

5. How many players are supported in *Tank War* at the same time?

B.   2

6. What is the technical terminology for handling two objects that crash in the game?

C.   Collision detection

7. What function in *Tank War* keeps the tanks from colliding with other objects?

B.   `clearpath`

8. Which function in *Tank War* helps to find out whether a point on the screen is black?

A.   `getpixel`

9. What is the standard constant used to run Allegro in windowed mode?

D.   `GFX_AUTODETECT_WINDOWED`

10. What function in Allegro is used to slow the game down?

C.   `rest`

Chapter 5

1. Which function is used to initialize the keyboard handler?

B.   `install_keyboard`

2. What does ANSI stand for?

C.   American National Standards Institute

3. What is the name of the array containing keyboard scan codes?

A.   `key`

4. Where is the real stargate located?

C.   Colorado Springs, Colorado

5. Which function provides buffered keyboard input?

C.   `readkey`

6. Which function is used to initialize the mouse handler?

 A. `install_mouse`

7. Which values or functions are used to read the mouse position?

 A. `mouse_x` and `mouse_y`

8. Which function is used to read the mouse x and y mickeys for relative motion?

 D. `get_mouse_mickeys`

9. What is the name of the main `JOYSTICK_INFO` array?

 B. `joy`

10. Which struct contains joystick button data?

 C. `JOYSTICK_BUTTON_INFO`

Chapter 6

1. What is the best way to get started creating a new game?

 D. Play other games to engender some inspiration.

2. What types of games are full of creativity and interesting technology that PC gamers often fail to notice?

 A. Console games

3. What phrase best describes the additional features and extras in a game?

 C. Bells and whistles

4. What is usually the most complicated core component of a game, also called the graphics renderer?

 D. The game engine

5. What is the name of an initial demonstration of a game that presents the basic gameplay elements before the actual game has been completed?

 B. Prototype

6. What is the name of the document that contains the blueprints for a game?

 C. Design document

7. What are the two types of game designs presented in this chapter?

 A. Mini and complete

8. What does NPC stand for?

   D.   Non-Player Character

9. What are the chances of a newcomer finding a job as a full-time game programmer or designer?

   D.   Negligible

10. What is the most important aspect of game development?

   A.   Design

Chapter 7

1. What does "blit" stand for?

   B.   Bit-block transfer

2. What is a DHD?

   C.   Dial home device

3. How many pixels are there in an 800×600 screen?

   A.   480,000

4. What is the name of the object used to hold a bitmap in memory?

   D.   `BITMAP`

5. Allegorically speaking, why is it important to destroy bitmaps after you're done using them?

   C.   Because the trash will pile up over time.

6. Which Allegro function has the potential to create a black hole if used improperly?

   A.   `acquire_bitmap`

7. What types of graphics files are supported by Allegro?

   B.   BMP, PCX, LBM, and TGA

8. What function is used to draw a scaled bitmap?

   B.   `stretch_blit`

9. Why would you want to lock the screen while drawing on it?

   A.   If it's not locked, Allegro will lock and unlock the screen for every draw.

10. What is the name of the game you've been developing in this book?

   D.   *Tank War*

Chapter 8

1. What is the term given to a small image that is moved around on the screen?

    B.   Sprite

2. Which function draws a sprite?

    A.   draw_sprite

3. What is the term for drawing all but a certain color of pixel from one bitmap to another?

    C.   Transparency

4. Which function draws a scaled sprite?

    A.   stretch_sprite

5. Which function draws a vertically-flipped sprite?

    B.   draw_sprite_v_flip

6. Which function draws a rotated sprite?

    D.   rotate_sprite

7. Which function draws a sprite with both rotation and scaling?

    B.   rotate_scaled_sprite

8. What function draws a pivoted sprite?

    C.   pivot_sprite

9. Which function draws a pivoted sprite with scaling and vertical flip?

    A.   pivot_scaled_sprite_v_flip

10. Which function draws a sprite with translucency (alpha blending)?

    B.   draw_trans_sprite

Chapter 9

1. Which function draws a standard sprite?

    C.   draw_sprite

2. What is a frame in the context of sprite animation?

    A.   A single image in the animation sequence

3. What is the purpose of a sprite handler?

A. To provide a consistent way to animate and manipulate many sprites on the screen

4. What is a struct element?

D. A variable in a structure

5. Which term describes a single frame of an animation sequence stored in an image file?

B. Tile

6. Which Allegro function is used frequently to erase a sprite?

A. `rectfill`

7. Which term describes a reusable activity for a sprite that is important in a game?

D. Behavior

8. Which function converts a normal sprite into a run-length encoded sprite?

B. `get_rle_sprite`

9. Which function draws a compiled sprite to a destination bitmap?

C. `draw_compiled_sprite`

10. What is the easiest (and most efficient) way to detect sprite collisions?

A. Bounding rectangle intersection

Chapter 10

1. Does Allegro provide support for background scrolling?

A. Yes, but the functionality is obsolete.

2. What does a scroll window show?

A. A small part of a larger game world

3. Which of the programs in this chapter demonstrated bitmap scrolling for the first time?

C. *ScrollScreen*

4. Why should a scrolling background be designed?

D. To achieve the goals of the game

5. Which process uses an array of images to construct the background as it is displayed?

   C. Tiling

6. What is the best way to create a tile map of the game world?

   A. By using a map editor

7. What type of object comprises a typical tile map?

   C. Numbers

8. What was the size of the virtual background in the *GameWorld* program?

   A. 800×800

9. How many virtual backgrounds are used in the new version of *Tank War*?

   B. 1

10. How many scrolling windows are used in the new *Tank War*?

   C. 2

Chapter 11

1. Why is it important to use a timer in a game?

   A. To maintain a consistent frame rate

2. Which Allegro timer function slows down the program using a callback function?

   D. `rest_callback`

3. What is the name of the function used to initialize the Allegro timer?

   B. `install_timer`

4. What is the name of the function that creates a new interrupt handler?

   D. `install_int`

5. What variable declaration keyword should be used with interrupt variables?

   C. `volatile`

6. What is a process that runs within the memory space of a single program but is executed separately from that program?

   C. Thread

7. What helps protect data by locking it inside a single thread, preventing that data from being used by another thread until it is unlocked?

   A. Mutex

8. What does pthread stand for?

C.   Posix Thread

9. What is the name of the function used to create a new thread?

B.   `pthread_create`

10. What is the name of the function that locks a mutex?

D.   `pthread_mutex_lock`

Chapter 12

1. What is the home site for Mappy?

C.   http://www.tilemap.co.uk

2. What kind of information is stored in a map file?

A.   Data that represent the tiles comprising a game world

3. What name is given to the graphic images that make up a Mappy level?

D.   Tiles

4. What is the default extension of a Mappy file?

C.   FMP

5. Where does Mappy store the saved tile images?

B.   Inside the map file

6. What is one example of a retail game that uses Mappy levels?

B.   *Hyperspace Delivery Boy*

7. What is the recommended format for an exported Mappy level?

D.   Text map data

8. Which macro in Mappy fills a map with a specified tile?

A.   Solid Rectangle

9. How much does a licensed copy of Mappy cost?

D.   It's free!

10. Which MappyAL library function loads a Mappy file?

A.   `MapLoad`

Chapter 13

1. In which game genre does the vertical shooter belong?

   A.   Shoot-em-up

2. What is the name of the support library used as the vertical scroller engine?

   C.   MappyAL

3. What are the virtual pixel dimensions of the levels in *Warbirds Pacifica*?

   D.   640×48,000

4. What is the name of the level-editing program used to create the first level of *Warbirds Pacifica*?

   B.   Mappy

5. How many tiles comprise a level in *Warbirds Pacifica*?

   A.   30,000

6. Which of the following games is a vertical scrolling shooter?

   B.   *Mars Matrix*

7. Who created the artwork featured in this chapter?

   C.   Ari Feldman

8. Which MappyAL function loads a map file?

   B.   `MapLoad`

9. Which MappyAL function removes a map from memory?

   D.   `MapFreeMem`

10. Which classic arcade game inspired *Warbirds Pacifica*?

   C.   *1942*

Chapter 14

1. Which term is often used to describe a horizontal-scrolling game with a walking character?

   B.   Platform

2. What is the name of the map-editing tool you have used in the last several chapters?

   A.   Mappy

3. What is the identifier for the Mappy block property representing the background?

A.   BG1

4. What is the identifier for the Mappy block property representing the first foreground layer?

A.   FG1

5. Which dialog box allows the editing of tile properties in Mappy?

D.   Block Properties

6. Which menu item brings up the Range Alter Block Properties dialog box?

B.   Range Edit Blocks

7. What is the name of the MappyAL struct that contains information about tile blocks?

C.   BLKSTR

8. What MappyAL function returns a pointer to a block specified by the (x,y) parameters?

A.   MapGetBlock

9. What is the name of the function that draws the map's background?

A.   MapDrawBG

10. Which MappyAL block struct member was used to detect collisions in the sample program?

C.   tl

Chapter 15

1. What is the name of the function that initializes the Allegro sound system?

A.   install_sound

2. Which function can you use to play a sound effect in your own games?

C.   play_sample

3. What is the name of the function that specifically loads a RIFF WAV file?

B.   load_wav

4. Which function can be used to change the frequency, volume, panning, and looping properties of a sample?

D.   adjust_sample

5. What function would you use to shut down the Allegro sound system?

    B.   `remove_sound`

6. Which function provides the ability to change the overall volume of sound output?

    A.   `set_volume`

7. What is the name of the function used to stop playback of a sample?

    D.   `stop_sample`

8. Within what range must a panning value remain?

    D.   0 to 255

9. What parameter should you pass to `install_sound` to initialize the standard digital sound driver?

    C.   `DIGI_AUTODETECT`

10. What is the name of the function that plays a sample through the sound mixer?

    B.   `play_sample`

Chapter 16

1. What is the shorthand term for an Allegro data file?

    B.   datafile

2. What compression algorithm does Allegro use for compressed datafiles?

    A.   LZSS

3. What is the command-line program that is used to manage Allegro datafiles?

    D.   dat.exe

4. What is the Allegro datafile object struct called?

    B.   `DATAFILE`

5. What function is used to load a datafile into memory?

    D.   `load_datafile`

6. What is the data type format shortcut string for bitmap files?

    C.   `BMP`

7. What is the data type constant for wave files, defined by Allegro for use in reading datafiles?

    C.   `DAT_SAMPLE`

8. What is the `dat` option to specify the type of file being added to the datafile?

   A.   `-t <type>`

9. What is the `dat` option to specify the color depth of a bitmap file being added to the datafile?

   C.   `-bpp <depth>`

10. What function loads an individual object from a datafile?

   D.   `load_datafile_object`

Chapter 17

1. Which company developed the FLI/FLC file format?

   A.   Autodesk

2. Which product first used the FLI format?

   C.   Animator

3. Which product premiered the more advanced FLC format?

   A.   Animator Pro

4. What is the common acronym used to describe both FLI and FLC files?

   D.   FLIC

5. Which function plays an FLIC file directly?

   A.   `play_fli`

6. How many FLIC files can be played back at a time by Allegro?

   A.   1

7. Which function loads an FLIC file for low-level playback?

   C.   `open_fli`

8. Which function moves the animation to the next frame in an FLIC file?

   A.   `next_fli_frame`

9. What is the name of the variable used to set the timing of FLIC playback?

   D.   `fli_timer`

10. What is the name of the variable that contains the bitmap of the current FLIC frame?

   B.   `fli_bitmap`

Chapter 18

1. Which of the following is *not* one of the three deterministic algorithms covered in this chapter?

    C.   Conditions

2. Can fuzzy matrices be used without multiplying the input memberships? Why or why not?

    A.   No, it is absolutely necessary to multiply the input memberships.

3. Which type of system solves problems that are usually solved by specialized humans?

    A.   Expert system

4. Which type of intelligence system is based on an expert system, but is capable of determining fractions of complete answers?

    B.   Fuzzy logic

5. Which type of intelligence system uses a method of computing solutions for a hereditary logic problem?

    C.   Genetic algorithm

6. Which type of intelligence system solves problems by imitating the workings of a brain?

    D.   Neural network

7. Which of the following uses predetermined behaviors of objects in relation to the universe problem?

    B.   Deterministic algorithm

8. Which type of deterministic algorithm "fakes" intelligence?

    C.   Random motion

9. Which type of deterministic algorithm will cause one object to follow another?

    A.   Tracking

10. Which type of deterministic algorithm follows preset templates?

    D.   Patterns

Chapter 19

1. What is the study of angles and their relationships to shapes and various other geometries?

   D. Trigonometry

2. What is the name of the C function that calculates cosine?

   B. cos

3. What is the name of the C function that calculates sine?

   A. sin

4. What is the name of the C function that calculates tangent?

   A. tan

5. Which C function calculates the inverse sine?

   D. asin

6. Which C function calculates the inverse tangent?

   C. atan

7. What does a set intersection contain?

   C. The elements that are contained in both sets

8. What does a function differentiation return?

   A. The slope of the function at any given position

9. What is the opposite of function differentiation?

   C. Integration

10. What Greek letter is most often used in calculations of degrees or radians of a circle?

    C. Pi

Chapter 20

1. What is the first step you must take before attempting to get your game published?

   A. Evaluate the game.

2. What is the most important question to consider in a game before seeking a publisher?

   C. Is it graphically attractive?

3. What is the second most important aspect of a game?

   B.   Sound

4. What is an important factor of gameplay, in the sense of a beginning, middle, and ending, that must be considered?

   D.   Continuity

5. What adjective best describes a best-selling game?

   D.   Addictive

6. What is an NDA?

   C.   Non-Disclosure Agreement

7. What is a software bug?

   A.   An error in the source code

8. What term describes a significant date in the development process?

   B.   Milestone

9. Who created the game *Smugglers 2*?

   A.   Niels Bauer

10. For whom should you create a game for the purpose of entertainment?

   A.   Yourself

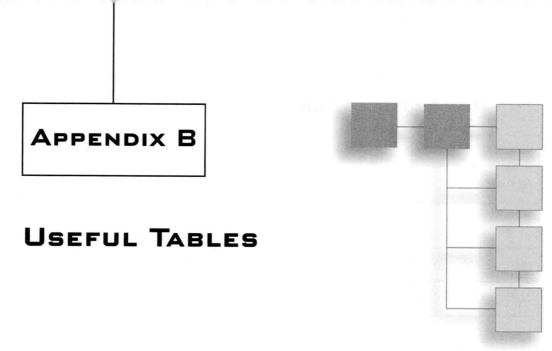

APPENDIX B

USEFUL TABLES

This appendix includes an ASCII table and three mathematical tables containing integral equations, derivative equations, and inertia equations.

Integral Equations Table

$\int x^x dx = \frac{x^{(y+1)}}{n+1} + C$
$\int \frac{1}{x} dx = 1n\ |x| + C$
$\int e^x dx = e^x + C$
$\int b^x dx = \frac{b^{(r+1)}}{1n(b)} + C$
$\int 1n(x)dx = x\ 1n(x) - x + C$
$\int \sin(x)dx = -\cos(x) + C$
$\int \cos(x)dx = s1n(x) + C$
$\int \tan(x)dx = -1n|\cos(x)| + C$
$\int \arcsin(x)dx = x\ \arcsin(x)x + \sqrt{1 - x^2} + C$
$\int \arccos(x)dx = x\ \arccos(x)x - \sqrt{1 - x^2} + C$
$\int \arctan(x)dx = x\ \arctan(x)x - \frac{1}{2}1n(1 + x^2) + C$

Derivative Equations Table

$(u^x)' = xu^{n-1}$
$(e^x)' = x'e^x$
$1n(u)' = \dfrac{u'}{u}$
$sin(u)' = u'cos(u)$
$cos(u)' = -u'sen(u)$
$tan(u)' = \dfrac{u'}{cos^2(u)}$

Inertia Equations Table

Object	Inertia Equations
Solid cylinder (horizontal axis)	$I = \dfrac{1}{2} mr^2$
Solid cylinder (vertical axis)	$I = \dfrac{1}{4} mr^2 + \dfrac{1}{12} ml^2$
Ring (horizontal axis)	$I = mr^2$
Ring (vertical axis)	$I = \dfrac{1}{2} mr^2 + \dfrac{1}{12} ml^2$
Empty sphere	$I = \dfrac{2}{3} mr^2$
Solid sphere	$I = \dfrac{2}{5} mr^2$
Cone	$I = \dfrac{3}{10} mr^2$

ASCII Table

This is a standard ASCII chart of character codes 0 to 255. To use an ASCII code, simply hold down the ALT key and type the value next to the character in the table to insert the character. This method works in most text editors; however, some editors are not capable of displaying the special ASCII characters (codes 0 to 31).

Char	Value	Char	Value	Char	Value
null	000	∟	028	8	056
☺	001	↔	029	9	057
●	002	▲	030	:	058
♥	003	▼	031	;	059
♦	004	space	032	<	060
♣	005	!	033	=	061
♠	006	"	034	>	062
•	007	#	035	?	063
◘	008	$	036	@	064
○	009	%	037	A	065
◙	010	&	038	B	066
♂	011	'	039	C	067
♀	012	(	040	D	068
♪	013	)	041	E	069
♫	014	*	042	F	070
☼	015	+	043	G	071
►	016	,	044	H	072
◄	017	-	045	I	073
↕	018	.	046	J	074
‼	019	/	047	K	075
¶	020	0	048	L	076
§	021	1	049	M	077
▬	022	2	050	N	078
↨	023	3	051	O	079
↑	024	4	052	P	080
↓	025	5	053	Q	081
→	026	6	054	R	082
←	027	7	055	S	083

Char	Value	Char	Value	Char	Value
T	084	u	117	û	150
U	085	v	118	ù	151
V	086	w	119	ÿ	152
W	087	x	120	Ö	153
X	088	y	121	Ü	154
Y	089	z	122	¢	155
Z	090	{	123	£	156
[	091	|	124	¥	157
\	092	}	125	Pts	158
]	093	~	126	ƒ	159
^	094	⌂	127	á	160
_	095	Ç	128	í	161
`	096	ü	129	ó	162
a	097	é	130	ú	163
b	098	â	131	ñ	164
c	099	ä	132	Ñ	165
d	100	à	133	ª	166
e	101	å	134	º	167
f	102	ç	135	¿	168
g	103	ê	136	⌐	169
h	104	ë	137	¬	170
i	105	è	138	½	171
j	106	ï	139	¼	172
k	107	î	140	¡	173
l	108	ì	141	«	174
m	109	Ä	142	»	175
n	110	Å	143	░	176
o	111	É	144	▒	177
p	112	æ	145	▓	178
q	113	Æ	146	│	179
r	114	ô	147	┤	180
s	115	ö	148	╡	181
t	116	ò	149	╢	182

Char	Value	Char	Value	Char	Value
╖	183	╪	216	·	249
╕	184	╛	217	·	250
╣	185	╚	218	√	251
║	186	█	219	ⁿ	252
╗	187	▄	220	²	253
╝	188	▌	221	■	254
╜	189	▐	222		255
╞	190	▀	223		
┐	191	α	224		
└	192	ß	225		
┴	193	Γ	226		
┬	194	π	227		
├	195	Σ	228		
─	196	σ	229		
┼	197	µ	230		
╟	198	τ	231		
╠	199	Φ	232		
╚	200	Θ	233		
╔	201	Ω	234		
╩	202	δ	235		
╦	203	∞	236		
╠	204	φ	237		
═	205	ε	238		
╬	206	∩	239		
╧	207	≡	240		
╨	208	±	241		
╤	209	≥	242		
╥	210	≤	243		
╙	211	⌠	244		
╘	212	⌡	245		
╒	213	÷	246		
╓	214	≈	247		
╫	215	°	248		

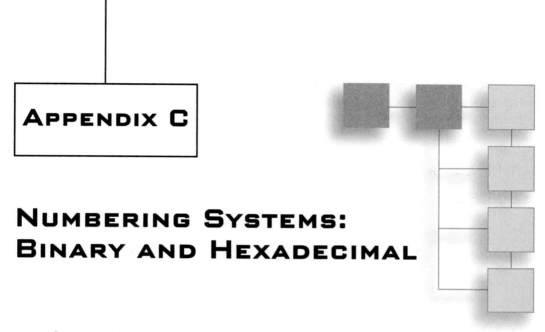

APPENDIX C

NUMBERING SYSTEMS: BINARY AND HEXADECIMAL

There are three numbering systems commonly used in computer programming—binary, decimal, and hexadecimal. The binary numbering system is called Base-2 because it has only two digits: 0 and 1. The decimal system is called Base-10; it is the one with which you are most familiar because it is used in everyday life. The hexadecimal system is called Base-16 and is comprised of the numerals 0–9 and the letters A–F to represent values from 0–15. Computers use the binary system exclusively in the hardware, but to make programming easier, compilers support decimal and hexadecimal (and the little-used Octal numbering system—Base-8).

Binary

Binary numbers use the Base-2 system, in which the numbers are represented by digits of either 0 or 1. This is the system the computer uses to store all the data in memory. Each digit in the number represents a power of two. Table C.1 shows the values in the binary system.

Table C.1 Binary System

Position	Digit
1	0
2	1

The best way to read a binary number is right to left; the first digit is to the far right and the last digit is to the far left. The number 1101, read from right to left, has the order 1, 0,

1, 1. The position of each digit determines the value of that digit, and each position is twice as large as the previous (with the first digit representing 0 or 1). Table C.2 provides a breakdown.

Table C.2 Binary Values Table

Position	Value
1	1
2	2
3	4
4	8
5	16
6	32
7	64
8	128
9	256
10	512
11	1,024
12	2,048
13	4,096
14	8,192
15	16,384
16	32,768
17	65,536
18	131,072
19	262,144
20	524,288
21	1,048,576
22	2,097,152
23	4,194,304
24	8,388,608
25	16,777,216
26	33,554,432
27	67,108,864
28	134,217,728
29	268,435,456
30	536,870,912
31	1,073,741,824
32	2,147,483,648

Using this table you can decode any binary number as long as you remember to read the number from right to left and add up each value. How about an example?

The number 10101110 can be decoded as:

```
0 * 1 = 0
1 * 2 = 2
1 * 4 = 4
1 * 8 = 8
0 * 16 = 0
1 * 32 = 32
0 * 64 = 0
1 * 128 = 128
```

Adding up the values 2 + 4 + 8 + 32 + 128 = 174. Anyone can read a binary number in this way, as long as it is read from right to left. With a little practice you will be converting binary numbers in your head in only a few seconds.

Decimal

You have probably been using the decimal system since childhood and you don't even think about counting numbers in specific digits because you have been practicing for so long. The Base-10 numbering system is a very natural way for humans to count because we have 10 fingers. But from a scientific point of view, it's possible to decode a decimal number by adding up its digits, as you do for binary.

For example, try to decode the number 247. What makes this number "two hundred forty seven?" The decimal system has 10 digits (thus the name *decimal*) that go from 0–9. Just as with the binary system, you decode the number from right to left (although it is read from left to right in normal use). Because each digit in 247 represents a value to the power of 10, you can decode it as:

```
7 * 1 = 7
4 * 10 = 40
2 * 100 = 200
```

Adding up the values 7 + 40 + 200 = 247. Now this is asinine for the average person, but for a programmer, this is a good example for understanding the other numbering systems and it is a good lesson.

Hexadecimal

The hexadecimal system is a Base-16 numbering system that uses the numbers 0–9 and the letters A–F (to represent the numbers 10–15, since each position must be represented by a single digit). Decoding a hexadecimal number works exactly the same as it does for binary and decimal—from right to left, by adding up the values of each digit. For reference, Table C.3 provides a breakdown of the values in the hexadecimal system.

Table C.3 Hexadecimal Table

Value	Digit
0	0
1	1
2	2
3	3
4	4
5	5
6	6
7	7
8	8
9	9
10	A
11	B
12	C
13	D
14	E
15	F

To read a hexadecimal number (in other words, to convert it to decimal so a human can understand it), just decode the hexadecimal digits from right to left using the table of values and multiply each digit by a successive power of 16. It was easy to calculate Base-2 multipliers, but it is a little more difficult with hexadecimal. Since hex numbers increase quickly in value, there are usually very few digits in a hex number—just look at the huge number after only 10 digits! Table C.4 shows multipliers for Base-16.

Using this newfound information, you should be able to decode any hex number. For instance, the hex number 9C56D is decoded like this:

D: 1 * 13 = 13
6: 16 * 6 = 96
5: 256 * 5 = 1,280
C: 4,096 * 12 = 49,152
9: 65,536 * 9 = 589,824

Table C.4 Hexadecimal Table

Position	Multiplier
0	1
1	16 (16^1)
2	16 (16^2)
3	256 (16^3)
4	4096 (16^4)
5	65,536 (16^5)
6	1,048,576 (16^6)
7	16,777,216 (16^7)
8	268,435,456 (16^8)
9	4,294,967,296 (16^9)
10	68,719,476,736 (16^10)

Adding these values results in $13 + 96 + 1,280 + 49,152 + 589,824 = 640,365$. Because these numbers grow so quickly in Base-16, they are usually grouped in twos and fours when humans need to read them. Any hex number beyond four digits is usually too much for the average programmer to calculate in his head. However, the small size of a hex number usually means it cuts out several digits from a decimal number, which makes for more efficient storage in a file system. For this reason, hex numbers are used in compression and cryptography.

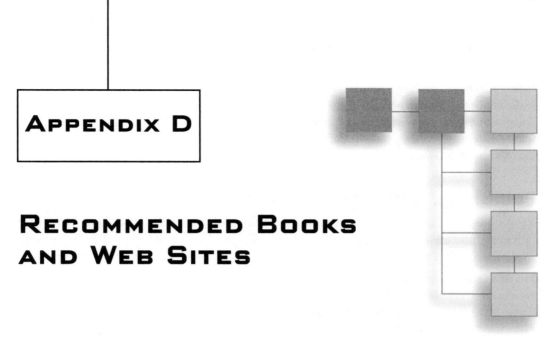

Appendix D

Recommended Books and Web Sites

Here is a collection of sites related to game development that I highly recommend.

All in One Support on the Web

I have set up a Web site to provide online support for this book. This site features an overview, sample programs and screenshots, related links, and downloads: http://www. jharbour.com/ allinone.

In addition, I have set up an online forum dedicated to game development, focused on providing additional support for this book from other readers and fans of Allegro. The online forums are at http://www.jharbour.com/forums.

Game Development Web Sites

Here are some excellent game development sites on the Web that I visit frequently:

Allegro Home Site: http://www.talula.demon.co.uk/allegro
GameDev LCC: http://www.gamedev.net
FlipCode: http://www.flipcode.com
MSDN DirectX: http://msdn.microsoft.com/directx
MSDN Visual C++: http://msdn.microsoft.com/visualc
Game Development Search Engine: http://www.gdse.com
CodeGuru: http://www.codeguru.com
Programmers Heaven: http://www.programmersheaven.com
AngelCode.com: http://www.angelcode.com
OpenGL: http://www.opengl.org

NeHe Productions: http://nehe.gamedev.net
NeXe: http://nexe.gamedev.net
Game Institute: http://www.gameinstitute.com
Game Developer: http://www.gamedeveloper.net
Wotsit's Format: http://www.wotsit.org

Publishing, Game Reviews, and Download Sites

Keeping up with all that is happening is a daunting task, to say the least. New things happen every minute all over the world, and hopefully, the next set of links will help you keep up to date with it all.

Thomson/Course Technology: http://www.course.com
Premier Press: http://www.premierpressbooks.com
Games Domain: http://www.gamesdomain.com
Blue's News: http://www.bluesnews.com
Happy Puppy: http://www.happypuppy.com
Download.com: http://www.download.com
Tucows: http://www.tucows.com
Slashdot: http://slashdot.org
Imagine Games Network (IGN): http://www.ign.com

Engines

Sometimes it is not worth reinventing the wheel. There are several good engines, both 2D and 3D, out there. Following are some of the engines I have had the pleasure (or pain) of working with that I want to recommend to you. Some are expensive, but then again, some are free. See which is best for you and start developing.

Touchdown Entertainment (LithTech Engine): http://www.lithtech.com
Jet3D: http://www.jet3d.com
Genesis3D: http://www.genesis3d.com
RenderWare: http://www.renderware.com
Crystal Space: http://crystal.sourceforge.net

Independent Game Developers

You know, almost everyone started as you are starting, by reading books and magazines or getting code listings from friends or relatives. Some of the developers in the following list have worked hard to complete some great games.

Longbow Digital Arts: http://www.longbowdigitalarts.com
Spin Studios: http://www.spin-studios.com
Positech Games: http://www.positech.co.uk

Samu Games: http://www.samugames.com
QUANTA Entertainment: http://www.quanta-entertainment.com
Satellite Moon: http://www.satellitemoon.com
Myopic Rhino Games: http://www.myopicrhino.com

Industry

If you want to be in the business, you need to know the business. Reading magazines and visiting association meetings will help you for sure.

Game Developers Magazine: http://www.gdmag.com
GamaSutra: http://www.gamasutra.com
International Game Developers Association: http://www.igda.com
Game Developers Conference: http://www.gdconf.com
Xtreme Game Developers eXpo: http://www.xgdx.com
Association of Shareware Professionals: http://www.asp-shareware.org
RealGames: http://www.real.com/games

Computer Humor

Here are some great sites to visit when you are looking for a good laugh.

Homestar Runner (Strong Bad!): http://www.homestarrunner.com
User Friendly: http://www.userfriendly.org
Geeks!: http://www.happychaos.com/geeks
Off the Mark: http://www.offthemark.com/computers.htm
Player Versus Player: http://www.pvponline.com

Recommended Books

I've provided a short description for each of the books in this list because they are either books I have written (plug!) or that I highly recommend and have found useful, relaxing, funny, or essential on many an occasion. You will find this list of recommended books useful as references to the C language and as complementary titles and references to subjects covered in this book, such as Linux and Mac game programming (with a few unrelated but otherwise interesting titles thrown in for good measure).

3D Game Engine Programming

Oliver Duvel, et al; Premier Press; ISBN 1-59200-351-6

"Are you interested in learning how to write your own game engines? With [this book] you can do just that. You'll learn everything you need to know to build your own game engine as a tool that is kept strictly separate from any specific game project, making it a tool that you can use again and again for future projects. You won't have to give a second thought to your engine. Instead, you'll be able to concentrate on your game and the gameplay experience."

3D Game Programming All in One
Kenneth Finney; Premier Press; ISBN 1-59200-136-X

An introduction to programming 3D games using the Torque engine by GarageGames.

AI Techniques for Game Programming
Mat Buckland; Premier Press; ISBN 1-931841-08-X

"[This book] takes the difficult topics of genetic algorithms and neural networks and explains them in plain English. Gone are the torturous mathematic equations and abstract examples to be found in other books. Each chapter takes you through the theory a step at a time, explaining clearly how you can incorporate each technique into your own games."

Beginner's Guide to DarkBASIC Game Programming
Jonathan S. Harbour and Joshua R. Smith; Premier Press; ISBN 1-59200-009-6

This book provides a good introduction to programming Direct3D, the 3D graphics component of DirectX, using the C language.

Beginning C++ Game Programming
Michael Dawson; Premier Press; ISBN 1-59200-205-6

"If you're ready to jump into the world of programming for games, [this book] will get you started on your journey, providing you with a solid foundation in the game programming language of the professionals. As you cover each programming concept, you'll create small games that demonstrate your new skills. Wrap things up by combining each major concept to create an ambitious multiplayer game. Get ready to master the basics of game programming with C++!"

Beginning DirectX 9
Wendy Jones; Premier Press; ISBN 1-59200-349-4

An excellent introduction to the new features in DirectX 9.

C Programming for the Absolute Beginner
Michael Vine; Premier Press; ISBN 1-931841-52-7

This book teaches C programming using the free GCC compiler as its development platform, which is the same compiler used to write Game Boy programs! As such, I highly recommend this starter book if you are just learning the C language. It sticks to the basics. You will learn the fundamentals of the C language without any distracting material or commentary—just the fundamentals of what you need to be a successful C programmer.

C++ Programming for the Absolute Beginner

Dirk Henkemans and Mark Lee; Premier Press; ISBN 1-931841-43-8

If you are new to programming with C++ and you are looking for a solid introduction, this is the book for you. This book will teach you the skills you need for practical C++ programming applications and how you can put these skills to use in real-world scenarios.

Character Development and Storytelling for Games

Lee Sheldon; Premier Press; ISBN 1-59200-353-2

"[This book] begins with a history of dramatic writing and entertainment in other media. It then segues to writing for games, revealing that while proven techniques in linear media can be translated to games, games offer many new challenges on their own, such as interactivity, non-linearity, player input, and more. It then moves beyond linear techniques to introduce the elements of the craft of writing that are particularly unique to interactive media. It takes us from the relatively secure confines of single-player games to the vast open spaces of virtual worlds and examines player-created stories, and shows how even here writers on the development team are necessary to the process, and what they can do to aid it."

Game Design: The Art and Business of Creating Games

Bob Bates; Premier Press; ISBN 0-7615-3165-3

This very readable and informative book is a great resource for learning how to design games—the high-level process of planning the game prior to starting work on the source code or artwork.

Game Programming for Teens

Maneesh Sethi; Premier Press; ISBN 1-59200-068-1

An excellent introduction to Windows game programming with DirectX.

High Score! The Illustrated History of Electronic Games

Rusel DeMaria and Johnny L. Wilson; McGraw-Hill/Osborne; ISBN 0-07-222428-2

This is a gem of a book that covers the entire video game industry, including arcade machines, consoles, and computer games. It is jam-packed with wonderful interviews with famous game developers and is chock full of color photographs.

Mac Game Programming

Mark Szymczyk; Premier Press; ISBN 1-931841-18-7

"Covering the components that make up a game and teaching you to program these components for use on your Macintosh, you will work your way through the development of a complete game. With detailed information on everything from graphics and sound to physics and artificial intelligence, [this book] covers everything that you need to know as you create your first game on your Mac."

Mathematics for Game Developers

Christopher Tremblay; Premier Press; ISBN 1-59200-038-X

"[This book] explores the branches of mathematics from the game developer's perspective, rejecting the abstract, theoretical approach in favor of demonstrating real, usable applications for each concept covered. Use of this book is not confined to users of a certain operating system or enthusiasts of particular game genres; the topics covered are universally applicable."

Microsoft C# Programming for the Absolute Beginner

Andy Harris; Premier Press; ISBN 1-931841-16-0

Using game creation as a teaching tool, this book teaches not only C#, but also the fundamental programming concepts you need to learn any computer language. You will be able to take the skills you learn from this book and apply them to your own situations. *Microsoft C# Programming for the Absolute Beginner* is a unique book aimed at the novice programmer. Developed by computer science instructors, the *Absolute Beginner* series is the ideal tool for anyone with little to no programming experience.

Microsoft Visual Basic .NET Programming for the Absolute Beginner

Jonathan S. Harbour; Premier Press; ISBN 1-59200-002-9

Whether you are new to programming with Visual Basic .NET or you are upgrading from Visual Basic 6.0 and looking for a solid introduction, this is the book for you. It teaches the basics of Visual Basic .NET by working through simple games that you will learn to create. You will acquire the skills you need for more practical Visual Basic .NET programming applications and learn how you can put these skills to use in real-world scenarios.

Linux Game Programming

Mark Collins, et al; Premier Press; ISBN 0-7615-3255-2

"This book offers Linux users the information they need to create a game using their OS of choice. Featuring an overview of the game development cycle, using tools and libraries, developing graphics applications, and adding extras such as sound, this book provides clear, concise information on developing games for and with the Linux OS."

Pocket PC Game Programming: Using the Windows CE Game API

Jonathan S. Harbour; Premier Press; ISBN 0-7615-3057-6

This book will teach you how to program a Pocket PC handheld computer using Visual Basic and Visual C++. It includes coverage of graphics, sound, stylus and button input, and even multiplayer capability. Numerous sample programs and games demonstrate the key topics you need to know to write complete Pocket PC games.

Programming Role Playing Games with DirectX, Second Edition
Jim Adams; Premier Press; ISBN 1-59200-315-X

"In the second edition of this popular book, you'll learn how to use DirectX 9 to create a complete role-playing game. Everything you need to know is included! You'll begin by learning how to use the various components of DirectX 9.... Once you have a basic understanding of DirectX 9, you can move on to building the basic functions needed to create a game—from drawing 2D and 3D graphics to creating a scripting system. Wrap things up as you see how to create an entire game—from start to finish!"

Swords & Circuitry: A Designer's Guide to Computer Role-Playing Games
Neal and Jana Hallford; Premier Press; ISBN 0-7615-3299-4

This book is a fascinating overview of what it takes to develop a commercial-quality role-playing game, from design to programming to marketing. This is a helpful book if you would like to write a game like *Zelda*.

Visual Basic Game Programming with DirectX
Jonathan S. Harbour; Premier Press; ISBN 1-931841-25-X

This book is a comprehensive programmer's tutorial and a reference for everything related to programming games with Visual Basic. After a complete explanation of the Windows API graphics device interface meant to supercharge 2D sprite programming for normal applications, the book delves into DirectX 7.0 and 8.1 and covers every component of DirectX in detail, including Direct3D. Four complete games are included, demonstrating the code developed in the book.

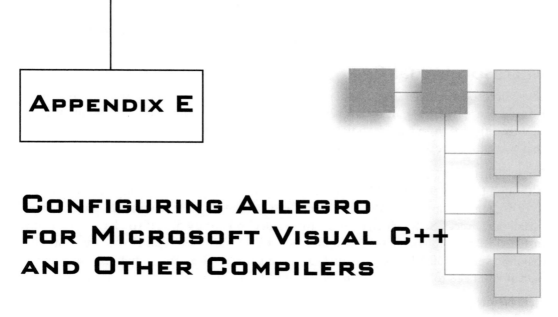

APPENDIX E

CONFIGURING ALLEGRO FOR MICROSOFT VISUAL C++ AND OTHER COMPILERS

This appendix provides instructions for configuring Allegro with the most popular compilers, including Microsoft Visual C++, KDevelop 3.0 (Linux), and Dev-C++ 5. It is amazing how there are so many compilers that support Allegro, and several of them are free! In the past, high-caliber development tools like these were very expensive and hard to find. These tutorials assume that you have already compiled the Allegro source code (per Appendix F, "Compiling the Allegro Source Code") or you have copied the headers and library files provided on the CD-ROM that accompanies this book.

I have pre-compiled the Allegro library and made it available. The easiest way to examine the configuration is to open one of the pre-configured source code projects from the CD-ROM. The second option is to read further and find out how to set up the compiler yourself. Linking is a complicated subject. If you run into any problems, be sure to refer to Appendixes E and F whenever necessary.

To make things as easy as possible (especially for those who are not as experienced with configuring compilers), I have included on the CD-ROM the completed project files for every program in the book for all three primary compilers that are supported: Dev-C++, Visual C++, and KDevelop. It is more common to use the dynamic library with Visual C++, so those projects all reference the dynamic library and require the DLL (alleg40.dll). Dev-C++ and KDevelop projects are configured for the statically linked library. If you examine the CD-ROM that accompanies this book, you'll find a folder called \sources, in which the source code projects for the book are separated into three subfolders: msvc, devcpp, and kdevelop. Within each of these folders you will find all of the projects for each chapter. You can simply open the projects directly if you do not want to configure the compilers yourself. The project files for Visual C++ have an extension of .dsw; project files for Dev-C++ have an extension of .dev; and project files for KDevelop have an extension of .kdevprj.

Microsoft Visual C++

The Microsoft compilers are all very similar in options and configuration, so this short tutorial is applicable to all recent versions of Visual C++. The dialog boxes might look slightly different from what is shown here in VC5 or VC7, but the process is simple enough that you should be able to adapt the basic concept to your needs.

These instructions take for granted that the DirectX SDK is installed on your system. Although DirectX 9 is available at the time of this writing, you really only need DirectX 8 to compile programs with Allegro. I'm not just talking about the run time—you need to install the DirectX SDK, which includes the header and library files. If you have not already installed it, refer to the CD-ROM folder called \libraries. Note that if you are using the dynamic version of Allegro, you don't need the DirectX SDK. You only need the DirectX SDK if you need to compile Allegro or if you plan to statically link it to your programs.

Here is how you can configure Visual C++ 6 to use the Allegro library. Create a new Win32 Application type project (see Figure E.1).

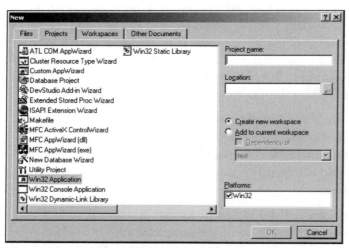

Figure E.1 The New Project dialog box in Visual C++ 6

Next, open the Project menu and select Settings to bring up the Project Settings dialog box (see Figure E.2). Click on the Link tab and look for the Object/Library Modules text field. Clear the entire field and type in **alleg.lib** in place of the other library files.

Now you need to make sure the linker can find Allegro. Add a new source file to the project and type in the following code. This program does very little, but it verifies that Allegro has been linked to your program.

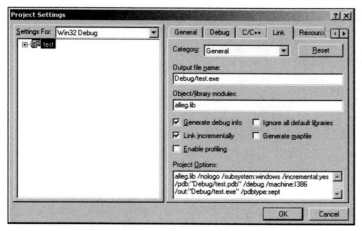

Figure E.2 The Project Settings dialog box in Visual C++ 6

```
#include "allegro.h"
int main(void)
{
    allegro_init();
    allegro_message("Welcome To Allegro!");
    return 0;
}
END_OF_MAIN();
```

If all goes as expected, the compilation output window should show "0 error(s), 0 warning(s)" (see Figure E.3), and upon running the program, you should see a message box with the phrase "Welcome To Allegro!" If there are any errors, be sure to check for typos, and then refer to Appendix F to verify that you have compiled and installed Allegro correctly.

If you want to use the static library of Allegro in Visual C++ (which is not usually the case), then you'll want to replace the single alleg.lib entry in the Object/Library Modules text box with the following entries. (Be sure to separate each with a space.)

```
alleg_s.lib
gdi32.lib
winmm.lib
ole32.lib
dxguid.lib
dinput.lib
ddraw.lib
dsound.lib
```

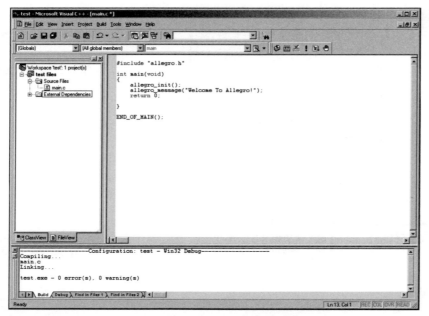

Figure E.3 Compiling an Allegro program with Visual C++ 6

You also need to tell Allegro to use the static library by including the following line at the top of any program that will be compiled static:

```
#define ALLEGRO_STATICLINK
```

Dev-C++

Dev-C++ was covered briefly in Chapter 2, but this is a more thorough explanation of configuring Allegro, assuming that you have already compiled the sources or copied the Allegro library files and headers as described in Appendix F. Dev-C++ comes with a WebUpdate tool that will automatically download and install the Allegro headers and library files into Dev-C++ so it's ready to use (covered in Chapter 2). But in this tutorial, I'm going to explain how to set up Dev-C++ without the benefit of WebUpdate.

Dev-C++ is a fully capable Windows compiler with support for all the usual Windows libraries (kernel32, user32, gdi32, and so on), including DirectX. If you have ever installed Microsoft's DirectX SDK, you'll recall how big it is—hundreds of files, hundreds of megabytes. There is a much smaller public domain implementation of DirectX 8 for the MinGW32 system (the version of GCC used by Dev-C++) included on the CD-ROM that accompanies this book. You will find it in the folder \directx, in the file dx80_mgw.zip. Extract the \include and \lib folders from dx80_mgw.zip inside the main Dev-C++ folder on your hard drive. (This will usually be C:\Dev-Cpp.) The easiest way to do this is to copy dx80_mgw.zip to C:\Dev-Cpp and unzip it there, where the header and library files will be extracted into the existing include and lib folders. That's all there is to installing DirectX for Dev-C++ (or more specifically, for GCC). You might note that the header files are copyrighted by Microsoft, while the lib files actually have the usual GCC library extension of .a. This way, you can differentiate between the official Microsoft DirectX SDK and the public domain implementation.

You should note that MinGW32 (bundled with Dev-C++) also includes public domain implementations of the entire Windows 32-bit API. This means that someone actually wrote compatible versions of the entire Windows API for use with tools such as MinGW32 to make GCC compatible with Windows. This provides you with all the power of Visual C++ in a very tight, small package. Because I do not write Windows GUI apps with C/C++ (involving dialogs, windows, and controls, for which I use Visual Basic), I find Dev-C++ with DirectX, OpenGL, and other libraries (such as Allegro) to be an awesome alternative to Visual C++ for game programming. The real benefit to Visual C++ is the comprehensive documentation in the form of MSDN, the dialog editor/form designer, and other value-added features. Because Dev-C++ includes the MinGW32 implementation of the Win32 API, I find it useful to keep Internet Explorer open to the Microsoft Developer Network Web site at http://msdn.microsoft.com/visualc, where the latest edition of MSDN is available online (and is equivalent to the distributed version of the MSDN subscription).

I won't debate the fact that Microsoft produces an exemplary and untouchable C/C++ compiler and IDE for Windows in the form of Visual C++. What I find most convenient about Dev-C++ is the very small footprint in memory (only about 12 MB), the small install file, and the simple installer. Combined with the MinGW32 implementation of the Windows API and the third-party implementation of DirectX, you have a great little game development package for Windows.

Now that I have presented the pros and cons of using Dev-C++, allow me to explain how to set up Allegro for this compiler for either dynamic or static link. You must first install Allegro. Even if you install the Allegro DevPak, I still recommend copying the Allegro 4.0.3 library and header files over to C:\Dev-Cpp. The header files should be copied to C:\Dev-Cpp\include and the library files should be copied to C:\Dev-Cpp\lib. (Your path might be different depending on where you chose to install Dev-C++.) While I have included the library and dll files in \libraries on the CD-ROM, you'll want to copy the contents of \include from the CD-ROM to C:\Dev-Cpp\include as well. This is especially important if you are upgrading to a new version of Allegro. For instance, the DevPak included on the CD-ROM only supports Allegro 4.0.0, but you need 4.0.3 for the programs in this book. So even if you install the DevPak, you still need to copy the 4.0.3 includes and libraries over to C:\Dev-Cpp into their respective folders. If this whole process is confusing, just follow these simple guidelines:

- Copy CD-ROM\include*.* into C:\Dev-Cpp\include.
- Copy CD-ROM\libraries\devcpp*.* into C:\Dev-Cpp\lib.

If you still have trouble getting the sample programs to compile, refer to Appendix F to actually compile the Allegro sources. You will benefit from an install script included with Allegro that installs everything where it's supposed to go. I have provided the include and lib files on the CD-ROM so you can just copy them over and get up and running quickly. Compiling the sources is pretty easy, so you should give it a try even if your compiler is configured and working correctly.

Now I want to cover how to set up Dev-C++ for the static library. Run Dev-C++ and open the File menu, and then select New, Project to bring up the New Project dialog box (Figure E.4).

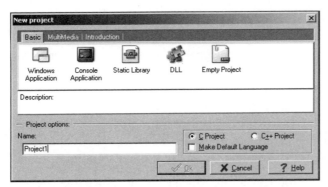

Figure E.4 The New Project dialog box in Dev-C++

If you have installed the Allegro DevPak as explained in Chapter 2, then you have the option of using one of the Allegro project templates (see Figure E.5).

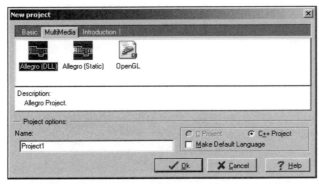

Figure E.5 Allegro project template choices for a new project in Dev-C++

If you choose to create an Allegro (Static) project, I need to inform you of a little bug in the template. The ALLEGRO_STATICLINK option is in the wrong box for the C compiler when the template is designed for the C++ compiler. Move -DALLEGRO_STATICLINK from the first options box to the second box, labeled C++ compiler, and then it will compile correctly (see Figure E.6). This bug might be fixed in a new release of the Allegro.DevPak, and it is not an issue at all if you configure the project yourself. (More on that in a minute.)

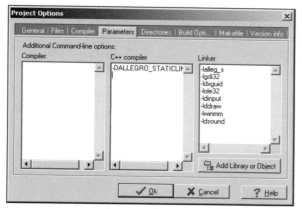

Figure E.6 The Project Options dialog box in Dev-C++

The other option is to configure a Dev-C++ project yourself, without using the templates. You would need to do this, for instance, if you have not installed the Allegro.DevPak. The DevPaks are really useful because they install the appropriate files in the correct folders for compiling a program with the requisite library. But if you want to just create a standard project, here's how to do it.

First, fire up Dev-C++, and then click on File, New, Project to bring up the New Project dialog box (see Figure E.7). Choose Windows Application for the project type, and be sure to select C Project instead of the C++ option because you will be setting up the project for the standard C compiler. This will be very similar to the settings that were applied with the project template.

Once the project is created, open the Project Options dialog box and click on the Parameters tab. All you have to do to create a dynamically linked Allegro program is add -lalleg to the Linker box. Note that the -l is a linker switch that tells the linker to include the library file named liballeg.a. (Remember that the lib at the front and .a at the end are assumed.) You could also simply insert the actual filename with the full path if you want; for instance, -lc:\allegro\lib\liballeg.a is a valid option. It is generally a good idea to copy library files into the lib folder for the compiler you're using. In the case of Dev-C++, that folder is usually C:\Dev-Cpp\lib.

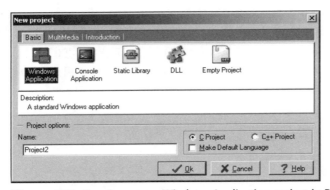

Figure E.7 Creating a new Windows Application project in Dev-C++

If you want to configure the project to use the static library, it requires two extra steps. In the first box, labeled Compiler, type in the static library option **-DALLEGRO_STATICLINK**. In the Linker box, enter the following options:

```
-lalleg_s
-lgdi32
-lwinmm
-lole32
-ldxguid
-ldinput
-lddraw
-ldsound
```

Figure E.8 shows the Project Options dialog box with the settings needed for a statically linked Allegro program.

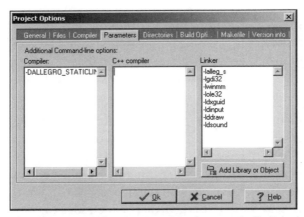

Figure E.8 Configuring Dev-C++ for a statically linked Allegro program

That's all there is to configuring the static library the manual way. Now you can write a short program to test the configuration and make sure Allegro is properly installed and the compiler is properly configured. Type the following program into the code window. (Delete any existing code first.)

```
#include "allegro.h"
int main(void)
{
    char version[80];
    allegro_init();
    sprintf(version, "Allegro library version = %s", allegro_id);
    allegro_message(version);
    return 0;
}
END_OF_MAIN();
```

Compile and run the program, and you should see a message pop up on the screen with the following text, which will indicate that Allegro is configured:

```
Allegro library version = Allegro 4.0.3, MinGW32.s
```

If you have any problems compiling the program at this point, it is most likely due to missing DirectX files, missing Allegro include files, or missing Allegro library files. You do not need alleg40.dll to run the static version. If you have double-checked these issues and you still have problems compiling, refer to Appendix F to do a full install of Allegro for Dev-C++.

KDevelop for Linux

The Linux operating system is a good choice for writing games with Allegro because the GCC compiler is always installed with the operating system, and you can type in programs with a simple text editor and get them to run with very little effort. However, Linux is not for the faint at heart, so if you are a beginner trying to get up to speed with Linux, you might have to pick up a book on using Linux. It's beyond the scope of this meager appendix to explain how to install KDevelop, the development tool used in this book for compiling Allegro programs for Linux. Assuming you have KDevelop already installed (as part of the KDE window system/user interface), then you can forge ahead. Even if you are using another window manager, such as GNOME, you can still run KDevelop by simply installing the KDE libraries. More than likely your distribution of choice provided KDevelop as an install option, or might have simply installed it with KDE automatically. If you want to download the latest version of KDevelop for your Linux box, browse to http://www.kdevelop.org. By the way, KDevelop is merely a front-end GUI for GCC (and a fine IDE at that).

Now you need to configure KDevelop for the Allegro library. If you haven't installed Allegro yet, jump to Appendix F and follow the instructions for compiling and installing Allegro under Linux. Because Allegro's installer script copies files into so many locations, it is really foolhardy to attempt a manual install by copying the includes and libraries yourself. Besides, that's the hard way. Compiling the sources is the single best way to install Allegro! Once you have done that, then return here and proceed to configure KDevelop as the following instructions explain.

First, fire up KDevelop, and then create a new project by opening the Project menu and selecting New. Choose a C terminal program (as shown in Figure E.9).

Figure E.9 Creating a new C terminal program in KDevelop

In the ApplicationWizard dialog box that appears, I recommend disabling the following three unneeded options:

- GNU-Standard-Files (INSTALL,README,COPYING...)
- User-Documentation
- Ism-File - Linux Software Map

However, you should keep the Generate Sources and Headers option selected, as shown in Figure E.10.

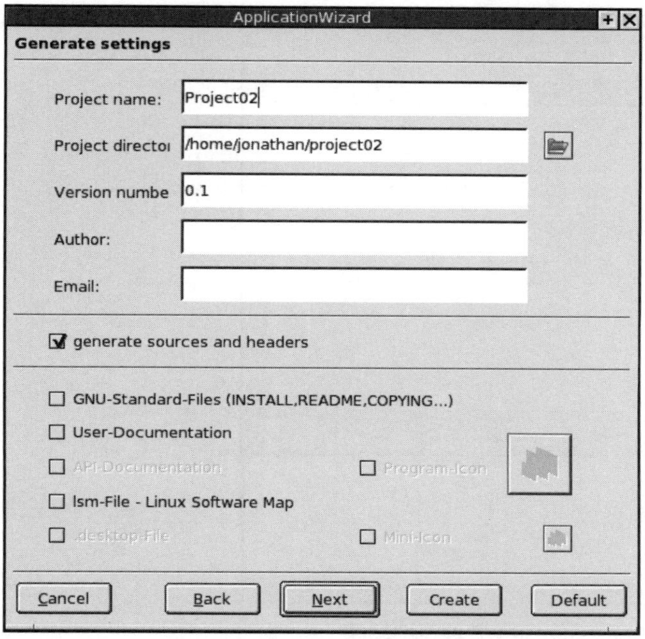

Figure E.10 Setting parameters in KDevelop's ApplicationWizard

You can skip the Version Control System Support dialog box. In the next two dialog boxes, turn off Headertemplate for .h-files and Headertemplate for .c-files, which clog up the source code. Finally, you will come to a Processes dialog box in the ApplicationWizard. Click on Create to build the new project, and ignore any obscure errors that appear regarding missing files. When you are finished, click on the Exit button. KDevelop will create a new project for you, as shown in Figure E.11.

Now you can set up the project for Allegro. Open the Project menu and select Options to bring up the Project Options dialog box. Click on the Linker Options icon on the left. Select the X11 and kdeui library check boxes, and type the following in the Additional Libraries text box:

```
-L/usr/local/lib
-L/usr/X11R6/lib
-lalleg
-lpthread
-lXxf86dga
-lXxf86vm
-ldl
```

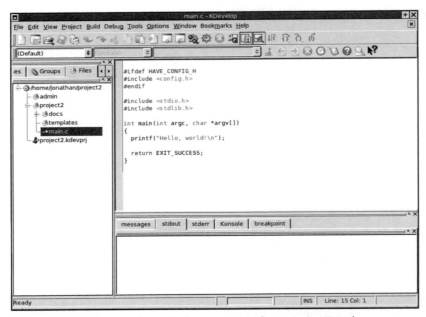

Figure E.11 The new C terminal program, ready to run in KDevelop

Note the uppercase L in the first two linker options; these tell the linker to include every library file found in the supplied folder name, if required by the smart linker (see Figure E.12).

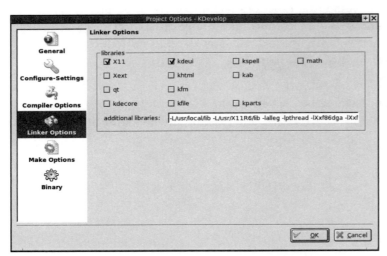

Figure E.12 The Project Options dialog box for compiling an Allegro program with KDevelop

Returning to the editor window, you can type in a program that actually demonstrates that the Allegro library is indeed working as expected. Here is a short program that will do just that.

```c
#include "allegro.h"
int main(void)
{
    char version[80];
    allegro_init();
    sprintf(version, "Allegro library version = %s", allegro_id);
    allegro_message(version);
    return 0;
}
END_OF_MAIN();
```

If the project has been configured correctly and if Allegro was installed correctly, the program should compile and run with an output like the one shown in Figure E.13.

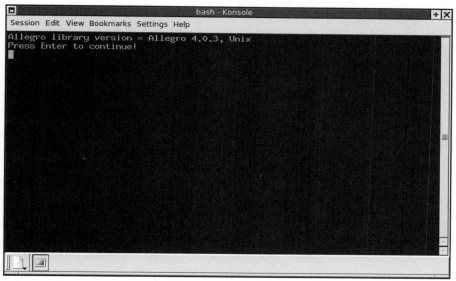

Figure E.13 Testing the Allegro program compiled with KDevelop

Final Comments

One final note on the Allegro game library: There are online discussions currently raging about the future of Allegro. It is very possible that future versions of Allegro will not be backward compatible with the 4.0.3 version used in this book. If that is the case, then I suggest using 4.0.3 and not getting tied up trying to get a newer version to work. It's very possible that 5.0 and later will support 4.0.3 programs, but based on my experience with as recent a version as 4.1.12, which is not compatible with 4.0.3, it seems that the developers of Allegro are facing the dilemma of providing new functionality without breaking existing code. If you download a new version of Allegro, it will be up to you to get it to work. I am only officially supporting 4.0.3 (the most stable version, in my opinion) in this book.

APPENDIX F

COMPILING THE ALLEGRO SOURCE CODE

This appendix will walk you through the process of compiling the Allegro source code. Allegro is an open-source game programming library that is distributed in source code form. You must compile Allegro in order to use it. There are some friendly people on the Web who have compiled Allegro for various operating systems, but it is best to compile Allegro yourself, if for no better reason than to verify that your compiler is compatible with the version of Allegro you intend to use. (I strongly recommend sticking with 4.0.3.) This is a fairly simple process that I'll walk you through for Microsoft Visual C++ 6.0, Borland C++ 5.5 (including C++Builder 3.0 or later), Bloodshed Dev-C++ 4.9 (or later), and KDevelop 2.1 (or later).

Note that Visual C++ 7.0 or later should be similar to 6.0; if you have problems, refer to the tutorials at http://www.allegro.cc or visit http://www.jharbour.com for assistance. A good collection of pre-compiled Allegro library files (and DLLs) is also located at http://www.allegro.cc/files, including makefiles for MSVC6, MSVC7, and Borland C++ Builder. If you have trouble compiling Allegro yourself, you can use these pre-built versions.

Microsoft Visual C++

There is good news and bad news about working with Visual C++. The good news is that Allegro compiles just fine under Visual C++. The bad news is that Microsoft's make utility was created just for Microsoft projects and does not support any type of standard makefile format.

So, you have to use the make.exe program that comes with Dev-C++ (or any version of GCC, for that matter). This shouldn't be a problem because Dev-C++ is rather small, and you can install a simple version of GCC by downloading it off the Web if you want, just to acquire the make.exe program. (Browse to http://gcc.gnu.org.) The Allegro makefiles were designed specifically for the GCC make, not the make program that comes with the various compilers. If you haven't installed Dev-C++ but you want to use Visual C++ anyway, install Dev-C++ to the default folder, which should be C:\Dev-Cpp. After you have done so, add it to your path so the make program will work.

```
set path=C:\Dev-Cpp\bin;%path%
```

You also will need to add the path to Visual C++ in a moment.

Before you can compile the Allegro library, you must extract it from the ZIP file. If you look on the CD-ROM under \allegro, you will find a file called all403.zip. This file contains the complete Allegro 4.0.3 source code distribution for all platforms.

Extract the all403.zip file to the root of your hard drive (which is usually C:\) using WinZip, WinRar, or another archiving utility. Be sure to extract with the directory structure intact (which is usually the default with WinZip and similar programs). This will create a new folder on your root called C:\allegro. The Allegro sources (including tools and examples) will use up about 15.5 MB of disk space after they are extracted.

Open a command prompt window. (Select Start, Run, and type cmd.exe on most Windows systems.) Change to the C:\allegro folder.

```
CD \allegro
```

Now type in the following line at the command prompt:

```
fix msvc
```

This invokes the fix.bat batch file to configure the Allegro sources for Microsoft Visual C++. By default, the Allegro makefiles are set up to compile the standard optimized version of Allegro (which you would want to use for the release build of a game).

You are almost ready to compile Allegro. But first, have you set a path to your installation of Visual C++? The standard installation of Visual C++ includes a batch file that will configure the environment variables and paths for Visual C++. If you have installed Visual C++ to the default folder, you can use this command to set the path:

```
set path=C:\Program Files\Microsoft Visual Studio\VC98\Bin;%path%
```

Now you're ready to compile Allegro. There are three versions that you can compile (standard optimized version, debug version, and profiler version) for the three standard project types in a C/C++ compiler. If you want to compile the debug version, you must first set an environment variable.

```
set DEBUGMODE=1
```

That is followed by this command:

```
make lib
```

If you want to compile the profile version of Allegro, type the following lines:

```
set PROFILEMODE=1
make lib
```

For your purposes, you want to compile all three versions of Allegro, along with all the example programs. So type the following line:

```
make all
```

It will usually take several minutes for the entire Allegro library to compile, along with all of the support programs (such as dat.exe and grabber.exe) and example programs that demonstrate Allegro's features.

Finally, as I discussed in Appendix E, you can compile the static version of Allegro in order to link Allegro inside the executable file of your game. The static library can be compiled like so:

```
set STATICLINK=1
make lib
```

In general, just remember the `fix msvc` and `make all` commands, and you'll have no problems. After you have compiled the Allegro source code, you'll want to look inside \allegro \lib\msvc for the compiled library files and DLL, and then copy these files to your Visual C++ lib folder (usually located in \Program Files\Microsoft Visual Studio\VC98\Lib). You will also want to look in \allegro\include and copy all files and subfolders to the include folder for Visual C++ (usually located in \Program Files\Microsoft Visual Studio\VC98 \Include).

Borland C++/C++Builder

I did not formally support Borland C++ in the book because it was quite a feat just to keep my sanity with three different compilers! However, Allegro should compile for Borland C++ 5.5 (but not 5.0), as well as C++Builder 3.0 or later. The cool thing about this is that if you have been a Borland fan for many years, or you just prefer to use a compiler other than GCC, you can download the command-line compiler from Borland's Web site for free; it is perfectly suitable for compiling Allegro, as well as the source code from this book. (Browse to http://www.borland.com/products/downloads/download_cbuilder.html.) However, Borland C++ does not enjoy as much support from Allegro as MSVC and Dev-Cpp.

The process of compiling the Allegro library sources is the same as for Microsoft Visual C++, with one exception. First, you must configure the Allegro makefiles for Borland using this command:

```
fix bcc32
```

Aside from this change, you can follow the instructions in the previous section for compiling Allegro for Visual C++, because the remaining instructions are the same. After you have compiled the Allegro source code, you'll want to look inside \allegro\lib\bcc32 for the compiled library files and DLL, and copy these files to your Borland C++ lib folder. You will also want to look in \allegro\include and copy all files and subfolders to the include folder for Borland C++.

Dev-C++

Dev-C++ is the free integrated development environment provided by Bloodshed Software. It used throughout the book interchangeably with Visual C++ and KDevelop. The instructions for Dev-C++ are similar to Borland C++/C++Builder. You can follow the instructions laid out for Visual C++ with a single exception: You must configure the Allegro makefiles for Dev-C++ (which *really* means you need to configure the makefiles for MinGW32/GCC).

```
fix mingw32
```

From here, you can set the environment variables for compiling the standard, debug, and profile versions of Allegro (along with the optional STATICLINK option to create a statically-linked library file, if you want).

But first, have you set a path to your installation of Dev-C++? If you have a question about this, refer to Chapter 2 and Appendix E for instructions on how to install and configure Dev-C++. The default install folder is C:\Dev-Cpp, so you might need to set a path as follows:

```
set path=C:\Dev-Cpp\bin;%path%
```

From this point, follow the directions for Visual C++ to set the options and compile Allegro using the makefiles. After you have compiled the Allegro source code, you'll want to look inside \allegro\lib\mingw32 for the compiled library files and DLL, and copy these files to your Dev-C++ lib folder (usually located in \Dev-Cpp\lib). You will also want to look in \allegro\include and copy all files and subfolders to the include folder for Dev-C++ (usually located in \Dev-Cpp\include).

KDevelop for Linux

I'm going to have to assume you are somewhat familiar with Linux already because it is a little more difficult to compile Allegro under Linux than it is under Windows. But once you have Allegro extracted and you are in the Allegro folder, it's very easy and automated for the most part.

Open a command-shell window. Locate the Allegro sources on the CD-ROM in a file called allegro-4.0.3.tar.gz. You can extract the Allegro library sources using gzip and tar from the command line, or just use Nautilus or another GUI program that can read archive files.

Type this command first to extract the tar file out of the gz file:

```
gzip -d allegro-4.0.3.tar.gz
```

Next, type this to extract the files out of the tar archive:

```
tar -xf allegro-4.0.3.tar
```

If you look in the current folder, you should now see a subfolder called allegro-4.0.3. Move into this folder using cd allegro-4.0.3.

Now for the steps involved in configuring the project files for compilation. First, assuming you are in shell and currently in allegro-4.0.3, type this command:

```
./configure
```

This will configure the Allegro sources and makefiles and prepare them for the GCC compiler. After the configuration script runs, you should convert the files to UNIX format and set the makefile. This is not absolutely necessary, especially if you just extracted Allegro from a tar file, but it's worth knowing how to configure the sources for UNIX.

```
./fix.sh unix
```

Now you're ready to compile the Allegro library source code. It's best to just build all the versions (standard, debug, and profile) at the same time.

```
make all
```

The compilation might take several minutes because all of the utility programs (such as dat.exe and grabber.exe) are compiled, along with all of the example programs that demonstrate the features of Allegro.

If all goes well (compilation errors are rare due to the configuration script), you should soon be ready to compile Allegro programs using KDevelop. You can refer to Appendix E for instructions on how to set up an Allegro project in KDevelop. After the Allegro sources have been compiled, you will need to install Allegro into the proper directories for it to work properly with KDevelop and other development environments. (Make sure you have root access.) Type the following line:

```
su -c "make install"
```

This command will copy the Allegro library and header files into the shared locations. Next, you can install the manuals (man pages) and info docs using these commands:

```
su -c "make install-man"
su -c "make install-info"
```

APPENDIX G

USING THE CD-ROM

The CD that comes with this book contains some important files you will want to use when you are working through the sample programs in the book. The CD comes preloaded with a very nice Autorun program that includes a menu for installing the various programs and files to your hard drive.

The most important files on the CD are the source code files for the sample programs in the book. The programs are stored in folders on the CD that are organized by chapter from the root \sources folder. Inside \sources, you will find the platform subfolders \sources\msvc, \sources\devcpp, and \sources\kdevelop, which contain the chapter folders \sources\msvc\chapter01, \sources\msvc\chapter02, and so on. I recommend that you copy the entire \sources folder for your particular platform/compiler to your hard drive and turn off the read-only property for all of the files so you will be able to peruse the sample projects for the book more easily. Zip files have also been provided for each compiler: sources_msvc.zip, sources_devcpp.zip, and sources_kdevelop.tar.gz.

Because this book focuses mainly on using Dev-C++ with the GCC compiler, Dev-C++ has also been provided on the CD-ROM in the \dev-cpp folder. You can run the installer from the Premier Press CD-ROM menu or directly off the CD by running the devcpp4980.exe installer. To save you time downloading DevPaks for Dev-C++, I have also included a folder called \devpaks, which contains the most useful updates for the content in this book.

The Allegro Game Library has been provided on the CD-ROM in the \allegro folder for both Windows (all403.zip) and Linux (allegro-4.0.3.tar.gz). I have also included the Allegro header files in \allegro\include. Most importantly, I have compiled the Allegro library for Visual C++, Dev-C++, and KDevelop. You can avoid the difficulty of compiling Allegro yourself by simply copying the appropriate library files into \lib, where your compiler is located. The dynamic, static, and debug builds of Allegro have been provided in \allegro\ libraries.

Windows programmers will need to install the DirectX SDK. (Version 8 or later will work.) If you are using Visual C++, you will want to install Microsoft's official DirectX SDK. However, if you are using Dev-C++ and GCC, you will need a special version of DirectX that has been compiled into .a files (the library format used by GCC). The GCC version of DirectX 8 is located in \directx in a file called dx80_mgw.zip.

INDEX

Numbers

1942, 455
2D games market, 14-15
3D cards, 73-74

A

acquiring bitmaps, 223-224
action/arcade game design genre, 191
adventure game design genre, 191-192
AI (artificial intelligence), 563
    deterministic algorithms, 570-575
        patterns, 573-575
        random motion, 571-572
        tracking motion, 572-573
    expert systems, 564-565
    fields, 564-570
    finite state machines, 575-577
    fuzzy logic, 565-567, 577-580
        group membership, 577-579
        matrices, 579-580
    game states, 580-581
    genetic algorithms, 567-569
    knowledge trees, 564-565
    memory, 580-581
    neural networks, 569-570
    overview, 563-564
    perceptrons, 570
    tips, 581
algorithms
    deterministic algorithms, 570-575
        patterns, 573-575
        random motion, 571-572
        tracking motion, 572-573
    genetic algorithms, 567-569

Allegro
    backward compatibility, 683-684
    CD-ROM, 691-692
    compiling source code
        Borland C++, 687-688
        C++ Builder, 687-688
        Dev-C++, 688
        KDevelop, 689-690
        Linux, 689-690
        overview, 685
        Visual C++, 685-687
    configuring
        Dev-C++, 674-679
        KDevelop, 679-683
        Linux, 679-683
        overview, 671
        Visual C++, 672-674
        Windows, 672-679
    cross-platform capabilities, 43
    DevPaks, 42-43
    DLLs, 42-43
    features, 27-28
    game development, 26-28
    installing, 41-43
    operating systems, 27
    source code, 42-43
    support, 26-28
    templates, 63
    testing, 53-63
    troubleshooting functions, 65-66
    versions, 683-684
    Web site, 26
allegro_exit function, 79
allegro_id function, 53-54
allegro_init function, 53

allegro_message function, 78
alpha blending, 215
animated sprites
    collision detection, 317-324
    compiled sprites, 313-317
    compression, 306
    creating, 280-283
    creating speed, 313
    flickering, 298
    grabbing frames, 291-298
    handlers, 283-291, 324-336
    multiple, 298-306
    overview, 279-280
    performance, 298
    PlatformScroller game, 499-500
    RLE, 306-313
    Tank War
        handlers, 324-336
        treads, 413-426
    tiling, 292
    troubleshooting, 298
    updating, 285-286
animation. *See* FLIC animation
AnimSprite program, 280-283
answers, chapter quizzes, 633-650
Arkanoid game, 178
ArrayMapTest program, 437-441
arrays, tile-based backgrounds, 351-355
artificial intelligence. *See* AI
artwork, 353
ASCII values, 653-655
associations, Web sites, 664
audio. *See* sound
author Web site, 663
Axis & Allies, 22-24

B
backgrounds
    scrolling bitmaps, 220
    tile-based. *See also* tiles
        arrays, 351-355
        buffers, 339
        graphics, 346
        horizontal scrolling platform maps, 491-498
        overview, 345-347
        scrolling, 347-351
        Tank War, 355-378
        tile maps, 351-355

backups, game design, 189-190
backward compatibility (Allegro), 683-684
Base-2 numbers, 657-659
Base-8 numbers, 657
Base-10 numbers, 657-659
Base-16 numbers, 657-661
Bauer, Niels, 622-623
beta testing, 198
binary numbers, 657-659
bit-block transfer. *See* blitting
bitmaps
    acquiring, 223-224
    blitting, 79-82, 217
        masked, 229
        scaled, 228-229
        standard, 227-228
        stretching, 228-229
    buffers, 217-219
    clearing, 220
    clipping, 224
    color, 219-222
    creating, 216-221
    datafiles, 542-543
    destroying, 221
    feedback loops, 220-221
    formats, 225-226
    linear, 222
    loading, 79-82, 224-227
    locking, 223-224
    memory, 222
    planar, 222
    refresh rates, 218
    releasing, 223-224
    saving, 226-227
    screens, 222
    scrolling backgrounds, 220
    sprites relationship, 216
    Tank War, 229-334
    transparency, 221-222
blitting
    bitmaps, 79-82, 217
        masked, 229
        scaled, 228-229
        standard, 227-228
        stretching, 228-229
    graphics, 73
blocks, 491-498

book, this
    artwork, 353
    goals, 6
books, 665-669
Borland C++, compiling code, 687-688
Breakout game, 178
buffering/buffers
    bitmaps, 217-219
    double-buffering, 75, 159
    frames, 74
    keyboard, 152-153
    scrolling, 339
    tile-based backgrounds, 339
bug reports, 615
bullets
    creating, 122-125
    moving, 122-125
    troubleshooting, 422-426
business. *See* industry
buttons
    joysticks, 174-175
    mouse, 157

C

C/C++
    Borland C++, 687-688
    C++ Builder, 687-688
    cross-platform compatibility, 29, 45
    defined, 12
    Dev-C++
        CD-ROM, 691
        compiling source code, 688
        configuring compiler, 674-679
        DevPaks, 39
        GCC (GNU Compiler Collection), 29, 36,
        45, 691-692
        overview, 29-30
        Package Manager, 41-42
        testing, 44-53
        updating, 37-40
    support, 29-30
    Visual C++
        compiling source code, 685-687
        configuring compiler, 672-674
C++ Builder, 687-688
callbacks
    circles, 101-102
    FLIC animation, 552-554

lines, 92-95
    timers, 382-383
capturing animated sprites, 291-298
CD-ROM, 691-692
chapter quiz answers, 633-650
characters (ASCII values), 653-655
chips, graphics, 72-74
circle function, 95-97
circlefill function, 97-98
CircleFill program, 97-98
circles
    callbacks, 101-102
    drawing, 95-98
Circles program, 95-97
classes, game design, 189
clearing bitmaps, 220
clipping bitmaps, 224
closing FLIC animation, 555
code. *See* source code
collision detection
    animated sprites, 317-324
    Tank War, 122-126, 324-336
    Warbirds Pacifica, 466
CollisionTest program, 319-324
color
    bitmaps, 219-222
    maps, 431
    sprites, 239
companies, publishing games, 626
compatibility
    backward (Allegro), 683-684
    cross-platform compatibility
        Allegro, 43
        C/C++, 29, 45
        CD-ROM, 691
        market, 13-14
        scrolling, 339
compiled animated sprites, 313-317
CompiledSprites program, 315-317
compilers
    configuring
        Dev-C++, 674-679
        KDevelop, 679-683
        Linux, 679-683
        overview, 671
        Visual C++, 672-674
        Windows, 672-679

compilers *(continued)*
   Dev-C++
      CD-ROM, 691
      compiling source code, 688
      configuring compiler, 674-679
      DevPaks, 39
      GCC (GNU Compiler Collection), 29, 36, 45, 691-692
      overview, 29-30
      Package Manager, 41-42
      testing, 44-53
      updating, 37-40
compiling
   programs, 51-53
   source code
      Borland C++, 687-688
      C++ Builder, 687-688
      Dev-C++, 688
      KDevelop, 689-690
      Linux, 689-690
      overview, 685
      Visual C++, 685-687
   sprites, 241
compression
   animated sprites, 306
   datafiles, 540, 543
conferences, Web sites, 664
configuring Allegro, compilers
   Dev-C++, 674-679
   KDevelop, 679-683
   Linux, 679-683
   overview, 671
   Visual C++, 672-674
   Windows, 672-679
contracts, publishing games, 614-615
conventions, Web sites, 664
creating. *See also* installing
   bitmaps, 216-221
   bullets, 122-125
   circles, 95-98
   datafiles, 541-544
   demos, 153-154
   ellipses, 98-101
   filling, 109-112
   interrupt handlers (timers), 392-393
   lines
      any, 88-89
      callback, 92-95

      horizontal, 85-87
      vertical, 87-88
   maps, 430-432
      FMP, 442-445
      overview, 436-437
      text, 437-441
      vertical scrollers, 456-460
   pixels, 82-84
   polygons, 107-109
   POSIX threads, 401
   programs (Greetings), 46-51
   rectangles, 89-92
   scrolling, 341-345
   sound, 518
   splines, 103-105
   sprites, 238-242
      animated sprites, 280-283, 313
      flipped, 244-245
      pivoted, 252-255
      rotated, 245-252
      scaled, 242-243, 252
      stretching, 242-243, 252
      translucent, 256-259
   tanks, 120-122
criticism, 24-25
cross-platform compatibility
   Allegro, 43
   C/C++, 29, 45
   CD-ROM, 691
   market, 13-14
   scrolling, 339

D

datafiles
   bitmaps, 542-543
   compression, 540, 543
   creating, 541-544
   encryption, 540
   finding, 545
   formats, 541
   loading, 544-545
   overview, 539-541
   referencing, 544
   searching, 545
   sprites, 543
   storing resources, 539-541
   testing, 545-547
   unloading, 545

DDR graphics, 73-74
debugging games
    creating, 465
    publishing, 615
decimal numbers, 657-659
delaying timers, 382-383
demos
    creating, 153-154
    game development, 202
derivative equations, 652
design. *See* game design
design document, 205-209
destroying
    bitmaps, 221
    POSIX threads, 402
    sound, 518
detecting sound, 515
deterministic algorithms (AI), 570-575
    patterns, 573-575
    random motion, 571-572
    tracking motion, 572-573
Dev-C++
    CD-ROM, 691
    compiling source code, 688
    configuring compiler, 674-679
    DevPaks, 39
    GCC (GNU Compiler Collection), 29
        CD-ROM, 691-692
        overview, 44-45
        support, 45
        Web site, 45
        installing, 36
    overview, 29-30
    Package Manager, 41-42
    testing, 44-53
    updating, 37-40
development, games. *See* game development
DevPaks
    Allegro, 42-43
    Dev-C++, 39
DirectX, 4
    game development, 25-26
    SDK, 692
DLLs, 42-43
do_circle function, 101-102
DoCircles program, 101-102
doline_callback function, 92-95
DoLines program, 92-95

double-buffering, 75, 159
downloads, Web sites, 663
DrawBitmap program, 79-82
drawing. *See* creating
DrawSprite program, 239-240

E

editing
    maps, 429
    sound, 518
education, game industry, 10-12
ellipse function, 98-100
ellipsefill function, 100-101
EllipseFill program, 100-101
ellipses, 98-101
Ellipses program, 98-100
encryption (datafiles), 540
engines
    game development, 196, 200-201
    vertical scrollers, 455-456
    Web sites, 663
equations. *See* math
erasing tiles, 433
evaluating games, 611-612
expansion packs, 203
expectations, 24-25
expert systems (AI), 564-565
explosions. *See* bullets
exporting. *See* saving
expo Web sites, 664

F

feasability, 188-190
features
    Allegro, 27-28
    game design, 189
    Tank War final version, 536
feedback loops (bitmaps), 220-221
Feldman, Ari, Web site, 353
fields (AI), 564-570
fighting game design genre, 190-191
files, CD-ROM, 691
filling
    graphics, 109-112
    horizontal scrolling platform maps, 494-495
    tiles, maps, 432-433
finding datafiles, 545

finite state machines (AI), 575-577
firing. *See* bullets
first-person shooters, 192
FLIC animation
    callback function, 552-554
    closing, 555
    frames, 555-558
    loading, 554-558
    memory, 554
    opening, 555
    overview, 551
    playing, 551-554
    scaling, 558-560
    stretching, 558-560
flickering animated sprites, 298
flight simulators, 192
flipped sprites, 244-245
FlipSprite program, 244-245
floodfill function, 109-112
FloodFill program, 109-112
FMP maps, 433-435, 442-445
foreground (horizontal scrolling platform maps),
    495-497
formats
    bitmaps, 225-226
    datafiles, 541
forums, Web sites, 663
frames
    animated sprites, 291-298
    buffers, 74
    FLIC animation, 555-558
functions
    allegro_exit, 79
    allegro_id, 53-54
    allegro_init, 53
    allegro_message, 78
    circle, 95-97
    circlefill, 97-98
    do_circle, 101-102
    doline_callback, 92-95
    ellipse, 98-100
    ellipsefill, 100-101
    floodfill, 109-112
    get_mouse_mickeys, 167
    hline, 85-87
    install_joystick, 170
    install_keyboard, 146-147
    install_mouse, 156
    keyboard_needs_poll, 148

    line, 88-89
    makecol, 78
    math, 605-607
    mouse_needs_poll, 156
    mouseinside, 165-166
    num_joysticks, 170-171
    poll_joystick, 171
    poll_keyboard, 146-148
    poll_mouse, 156
    polygon, 107-109
    position_mouse, 165-166
    position_mouse_z, 168-170
    putpixel, 82-84
    readkey, 152
    rect, 89-91
    rectfill, 91-92
    remove_joystick, 170
    remove_keyboard, 146-147
    remove_mouse, 156
    scancode_to_ascii, 153
    scare_mouse, 158
    scare_mouse_area, 158
    set_gfx_mode, 75-78
    set_keyboard_rate, 153
    set_mouse_range, 167
    set_mouse_speed, 167
    set_mouse_sprite, 157-158
    set_mouse_sprite_focus, 157
    show_mouse, 158
    simulate_keypress, 153-154
    spline, 103-105
    srand, 84
    text_mode, 112
    textout, 112-113
    textprintf, 78, 113-114
    triangle, 105-107
    troubleshooting, 65-66
    unscare_mouse, 158
    ureadkey, 152
    vline, 87-88
    voices (sound), 518-522
fuzzy logic (AI), 565-567, 577-580
    group membership, 577-579
    matrices, 579-580

G

galactic conquest game design genre, 193

game design
  backups, 189-190
  classes, 189
  design document, 205-209
  feasability, 188-190
  features, 189
  game development, 196
  genres
    action/arcade, 191
    adventure, 191-192
    fighting, 190-191
    first-person shooters, 192
    flight simulators, 192
    galactic conquest, 193
    MMORPGs, 195
    overview, 190
    real-life simulators, 195
    RPGs, 193-194
    RTS, 193
    space simulators, 195
    sports simulators, 194
    TBS, 194
    third-person shooters, 194
  inspiration, 188, 346
  job market, 212
  libraries, 204
  OOP, 189
  overview, 187-188, 204-205
  planning, 203-204
  SDKs, 204
  Space Invaders, 209-211
game developer Web sites, 663-664
game development
  Allegro, 26-28
  Axis & Allies, 22-24
  beta testing, 198
  criticism, 24-25
  demos, 202
  DirectX, 25-26
  engines, 196, 200-201
  expansion packs, 203
  expectations, 24-25
  game design, 196
  horizontal scrolling platforms, 490-491, 498-506
  innovation, 202
  input controls, 13
  inspiration, 202
  keyboards, 13

  management, 199-200
  marketing, 199, 202
  motivation, 9-10
  niches, 15-17
  operating systems, 26
  overview, 6-9, 195-196
  patches, 202-203
  Perfect Match, 17
  planning, 201-202
  Pocket Trivia, 16
  post-production, 198-199
  profit, 16-17
  prototypes, 196-197
  quality, 200-202
  quality control, 197-198
  releases, 199
  RenderWare Studio, 25-26
  schedules, 199-200
  Star Trek, 18
  Starship Battles, 18-22
  storyboards, 8-9
  Tactical Starship Combat, 18
  trends, 201-202
  war games, 22-24
  Web sites, 663
  wrapper code, 13
game engines. *See* engines
Game Programming All in One Web site, 663
games
  1942, 455
  Arkanoid, 178
  artwork, 353
  Breakout, 178
  CD-ROM, 691
  debugging, 465
  demos, 153-154
  design. *See* game design
  developer Web sites
  development. *See* game development
  double-buffering, 159
  industry
    2D games, 14-15
    cross-platform market, 13-14
    education, 10-12
    history, 9
    specialization, 12-13
  Mappy, 430
  Missile Command, 158

games *(continued)*
  programming overview, 4-6
  publishing
    bug reports, 615
    companies, 626
    contracts, 614-615
    debugging, 615
    evaluating, 611-612
    milestones, 615
    NDAs, 614
    releases, 615
    selling, 612-613
  real-time loops, 159
  RPGs, 34-35
  Space Invaders, 209-211
  speed, 395-397
  states (AI), 580-581
  Strategic Defense
    overview, 158-160
    source code, 160-164
  strategy games, 35
  Super Mario World, 489
  Tank War. *See* Tank War
  timed game loops, 395-397
  Warbirds Pacifica
    collision detection, 466
    overview, 464-468
    power-ups, 465
    source code, 468-486
    sprite handling, 465
    sprites, 466-468
    text, 467-468
GameWorld program, 352-355
GCC (GNU Compiler Collection), 29
  CD-ROM, 691-692
  overview, 44-45
  support, 45
  Web site, 45
General Public License (GNU), 36
genetic algorithms (AI), 567-569
genres (game design)
  action/arcade, 191
  adventure, 191-192
  fighting, 190-191
  first-person shooters, 192
  flight simulators, 192
  galactic conquest, 193
  MMORPGs, 195
  overview, 190

real-life simulators, 195
  RPGs, 193-194
  RTS, 193
  space simulators, 195
  sports simulators, 194
  TBS, 194
  third-person shooters, 194
get_mouse_mickeys function, 167
GetInfo program
  operating systems, 57-61
  overview, 53-56
  running, 56-57, 62-63
  source code, 61-62
GNU
  GCC, 29
    CD-ROM, 691-692
    overview, 44-45
    support, 45
    Web site, 45
  General Public License, 36
GNU Compiler Collection. *See* GCC
goals, this book, 6
grabbing frames, 291-298
graphics
  3D cards, 73-74
  bitmaps
    acquiring, 223-224
    blitting, 79-82, 217, 227-229
    buffers, 217-219
    clearing, 220
    clipping, 224
    color, 219-222
    creating, 216-221
    datafiles, 542-543
    destroying, 221
    feedback loops, 220-221
    formats, 225-226
    linear, 222
    loading, 79-82, 224-227
    locking, 223-224
    memory, 222
    planar, 222
    refresh rates, 218
    releasing, 223-224
    saving, 226-227
    screens, 222
    scrolling backgrounds, 220
    sprites relationship, 216

Tank War, 229-334
transparency, 221-222
blitting, 73
chips, 72-74
circles, 95-98, 101-102
DDR, 73-74
double-buffering, 75
ellipses, 98-101
Feldman, Ari, 353
filling, 109-112
frame buffers, 74
games. *See* games
initializing, 75-79
lines
any, 88-89
callback, 92-95
horizontal, 85-87
vertical, 87-88
overview, 71-74
pixels
drawing, 82-84
overview, 74-75
polygons, 107-109
rectangles, 89-92
splines, 103-105
sprites. *See* sprites
tile-based backgrounds, 346
triangles, 105-107
vertices, 73
video cards, 72-74
Greetings program
compiling, 51-53
creating, 46-51
naming, 48
overview, 44-45
running, 51-53
saving, 48
source code, 48-52
group membership (fuzzy logic), 577-579
guns. *See* bullets

H

handlers
animated sprites, 283-291
Tank War, 324-336
Warbirds Pacifica, 465
joysticks, 170-171
keyboard, 146-148
mouse, 156

HelloWorld program, 63-65
hexadecimal numbers, 657-661
hexagonal maps, 431
history, games industry, 9
hline function, 85-87
HLines program, 85-87
horizontal lines, 85-87
horizontal scrolling platforms
developing, 490-491, 498-506
maps, 491-498
blocks, 491-498
filling, 494, 495
foreground, 495-497
layers, 491-498
size, 493, 494
tile-based backgrounds, 491-498
overview, 489-490
humorous Web sites, 664
hyperspace program, 165-166

I

IDEs (Integrated Development Environments).
See Dev-C++
images. *See* graphics
importing tiles, 432-434
industry
games
2D games, 14-15
cross-platform market, 13-14
education, 10-12
specialization, 12-13
history, 9
interviews
Bauer, Niels, 622-623
LaMothe, André, 624-625
Urbanus, Paul, 616-621
job market, 212
management, game development, 199-200
market, 13-15
marketing game development, 199, 202
publishing games
bug reports, 615
companies, 626
contracts, 614-615
debugging, 615
evaluating, 611-612
milestones, 615
NDAs, 614

industry *(continued)*
    releases, 615
    selling, 612-613
  Web sites, 663-664
inertia equations, 652
InitGraphics program, 75-79
initializing
  graphics, 75-79
  sound, 514-516
innovation, 202
input
  games, 13
  joysticks
    buttons, 174-175
    handlers, 170-171
    moving, 171-174
    multiple, 531-534
    testing, 175-182
  keyboard
    buffering, 152-153
    games, 13
    handlers, 146-148
    input, 146-155
    key presses, 148-149, 153-154
    key repeat, 153
    Stargate program, 149-152
    Tank War source code, 368-371
  mouse
    buttons, 157
    handlers, 156
    input, 155-170
    MouseWheel program, 168-170
    moving, 167
    pointer, 157-158
    position, 156, 165-166
    PositionMouse program, 165-166
    speed, 167
    Strategic Defense game, 158-164
    tracking, 167
    wheels, 167-170
  overview, 145-146
inspiration
  game design, 188, 346
  game development, 202
install_joystick function, 170
install_keyboard function, 146-147
install_mouse function, 156

installing. *See also* creating
  Allegro, 41-43
  Dev-C++, 36
  Mappy, 430
  sound, 515-516
  timers, 381-382
integral equations, 651
Integrated Development Environments.
  See Dev-C++
interrupt handlers
  Tank War, 413-426
  timers
    creating, 392-393
    multi-threading, 392
    removing, 393-395
InterruptTest program, 393-395
interviews
  Bauer, Niels, 622-623
  LaMothe, André, 624-625
  Urbanus, Paul, 616-621
isometric maps, 431

J

job market, 212
joysticks, 170-182
  buttons, 174-175
  handlers, 170-171
  moving, 171-174
  multiple, 531-534
  testing, 175-182
Jupiter Research Web site, 13

K

KDevelop
  compiling source code, 689-690
  configuring compiler, 679-683
key presses, 148-149, 153-154
key repeat, 153
keyboard
  buffering, 152-153
  games, 13
  handlers, 146-148
  input, 146-155
  key presses, 148-149, 153-154
  key repeat, 153
  Stargate program, 149-152
  Tank War source code, 368-371

keyboard_needs_poll function, 148
KeyTest program, 154-155
knowledge trees (AI), 564, 565

L

LaMothe, André, 624-625
layers (horizontal scrolling platform maps), 491-498
levels. *See* maps
libraries
    Allegro. *See* Allegro
    DirectX, 4
        game development, 25-26
        SDK, 692
    DLLs, 42-43
    game design, 204
line function, 88-89
linear bitmaps, 222
lines
    any, 88-89
    callback, 92-95
    horizontal, 85-87
    vertical, 87-88
Lines program, 88-89
Linux
    CD-ROM, 691
    compiling source code, 689-690
    configuring compiler, 679-683
listings. *See* source code
LoadFlick program, 556-558
loading
    bitmaps, 79-82, 224-227
    datafiles, 544-545
    FLIC animation, 554-558
    maps
        FMP, 442-445
        overview, 436-437
        text, 437-441
    sound, 517
locking bitmaps, 223-224
loops
    bitmaps, 220-221
    real-time games, 159
    timed game loops, 395-397

M

magazines, 664
makecol function, 78

management, game development, 199-200
Mappy
    installing, 430
    overview, 429-430
    sample games, 430
    Web site, 429
maps
    color, 431
    creating, 430-432
        FMP, 442-445
        overview, 436-437
        text, 437-441
        vertical scrollers, 456-460
    editing, 429
    hexagonal, 431
    horizontal scrolling platforms, 491-498
        developing, 490-491, 498-506
        blocks, 491-498
        filling, 494, 495
        foreground, 495-497
        layers, 491-498
        overview, 489-490
        size, 493, 494
        tile-based backgrounds, 491-498
    isometric, 431
    loading
        FMP, 442-445
        overview, 436-437
        text, 437-441
    Mappy
        installing, 430
        overview, 429-430
        sample games, 430
        Web site, 429
    PlatformScroller game, 499-500
    saving
        FMP, 433-435
        text, 435-436
    scrolling (FMP), 442-445
    size, 430
    tiles
        erasing, 433
        filling, 432-433
        importing, 432-434
        number, 430
        palettes, 432-433
        scrolling, 433
        Tank War, 445-453

maps *(continued)*
   tile-based backgrounds, 351-355
   vertical scrollers, 459-460
  vertical scrollers
   creating, 456-460
   engines, 455-456
   overview, 455-456
   tiles, 459-460
  Warbirds Pacifica
   collision detection, 466
   overview, 464-468
   power-ups, 465
   source code, 468-486
   sprite handling, 465
   sprites, 466-468
   text, 467-468
  zooming, 432
market, 13-15
marketing game development, 199, 202
masked blitting (bitmaps), 229
math
  AI. *See* AI
  derivative equations, 652
  functions, 605-607
  inertia equations, 652
  integral equations, 651
  matrices, 598-602
  overview, 585-586
  probability, 603-605
  radians, 586-587
  trigonometry, 586-590
  vectors, 590-598
matrices, 579-580, 598-602
membership (fuzzy logic), 577-579
memory
  AI, 580-581
  bitmaps, 222
  FLIC animation, 554
Microsoft Visual C++
  compiling source code, 685-687
  configuring compiler, 672-674
milestones, 615
Missile Command, 158
MMORPGs game design genre, 195
motivation, 9-10
mouse
  buttons, 157
  handlers, 156
  input, 155-170

MouseWheel program, 168-170
  moving, 167
  pointer, 157-158
  position, 156, 165-166
  PositionMouse program, 165-166
  speed, 167
  Strategic Defense game
   overview, 158-160
   source code, 160-164
  tracking, 167
  wheels, 167-170
mouse_needs_poll function, 156
mouseinside function, 165-166
MouseWheel program, 168-170
movies. *See* FLIC animation
moving
  bullets, 122-125
  joysticks, 171-174
  mouse, 167
  random motion (AI), 571-572
  tanks, 125-126
  tracking motion (AI), 572-573
multichannel sound, 522
multiple animated sprites, 298-306
multiple joysticks, 531-534
MultipleSprites program, 300-306
MultiThread program, 403-413
multi-threading
  interrupt handlers (timers), 392
  mutexes, 398
  overview, 397-398
  parallel processing, 398-399
  POSIX threads
   creating, 401
   destroying, 402
   mutexes, 402-403
   overview, 399-400
  Tank War, 413-426
  threads, 397-398
mutexes
  multi-threading, 398
  POSIX threads, 402-403

N

naming programs, 48
NDAs (non-disclosure agreements), 614
neural networks (AI), 569-570
niches, 15-17

non-disclosure agreements (NDAs), 614
num_joysticks function, 170-171
numbers
    Base-2, 657-659
    Base-8, 657
    Base-10, 657-659
    Base-16, 657-661
    binary, 657-659
    decimal, 657-659
    hexadecimal, 657-661
    octal, 657
    systems, 657
    tiles, maps, 430
    voices, sound, 515

O

octal numbers, 657
OOP game design, 189
opening FLIC animation, 555
operating systems
    Allegro, 27
    game development, 26
    GetInfo program, 57-61

P

Package Manager, 41-42
packages
    Allegro, 42-43
    Dev-C++, 39
palettes, tiles, 432-433
parallel processing, multi-threading, 398-399
patches, game development, 202-203
patterns (AI deterministic algorithm), 573-575
perceptrons (AI), 570
Perfect Match, 17
performance, animated sprites, 298
pivoted sprites, 252-255
PivotSprite program, 252-255
pixels, 82-84
Pixels program, 82-84
planar bitmaps, 222
planning
    game design, 203-204
    game development, 201-202
platforms
    CD-ROM, 691
    horizontal scrolling platforms
        developing, 490-491, 498-506

    blocks, 491-498
    filling, 494, 495
    foreground, 495-497
    layers, 491-498
    maps, 491-498
    overview, 489-490
    size, 493, 494
    tile-based backgrounds, 491-498
PlatformScroller program
    animated sprites, 499-500
    map, 499-500
    overview, 498-501
    source code, 501-506
playback, sound, 517-522
PlayFlick program, 552-554
playing
    FLIC animation, 551-554
    sound, 517-518
PlayWave program, 512-514
Pocket Trivia, 16
pointer (mouse), 157-158
poll_joystick function, 171
poll_keyboard function, 146-148
poll_mouse function, 156
polygon function, 107-109
polygons, 107-109
Polygons program, 107-109
position (mouse), 156-166
position_mouse function, 165-166
position_mouse_z function, 168-170
PositionMouse program, 165-166
POSIX threads
    creating, 401
    destroying, 402
    mutexes, 402-403
    overview, 399-400
post-production, 198-199
power-ups, 465
primitives. *See* graphics
printing text, 112-114
probability, 603-605
profit, 16-17
programming games overview, 4-6
programs
    AnimSprite, 280-283
    ArrayMapTest, 437-441
    CD-ROM, 691
    CircleFill, 97-98
    Circles, 95-97

programs *(continued)*

  CollisionTest, 319-324

  CompiledSprites, 315-317

  DoCircles, 101-102

  DoLines, 92-95

  DrawBitmap, 79-82

  DrawSprite, 239-240

  EllipseFill, 100-101

  Ellipses, 98-100

  FlipSprite, 244-245

  FloodFill, 109-112

  games. *See* games

  GameWorld, 352-355

  GetInfo

    operating systems, 57-61

    overview, 53-56

    running, 56-63

    source code, 61-62

  Greetings

    compiling, 51-53

    creating, 46-51

    naming, 48

    overview, 44-45

    running, 51-53

    saving, 48

    source code, 48-52

  HelloWorld, 63-65

  HLines, 85-87

  hyperspace, 165-166

  InitGraphics, 75-79

  InterruptTest, 393-395

  KeyTest, 154-155

  Lines, 88-89

  LoadFlick, 556-558

  MouseWheel, 168-170

  MultipleSprites, 300-306

  MultiThread, 403-413

  PivotSprite, 252-255

  Pixels, 82-84

  PlatformScroller

    animated sprites, 499-500

    map, 499-500

    overview, 498-501

    source code, 501-506

  PlayFlick, 552-554

  PlayWave, 512-514

  Polygons, 107-109

  PositionMouse, 165-166

  Rect, 89-91

  RectFill, 91-92

  ResizeFlick, 558-560

  RLESprites, 307-313

  RotateSprite, 249-251

  sample, 65-67

  SampleMixer, 522-525

  ScaledSprite, 242-243

  ScanJoystick, 175-177

  ScrollScreen, 341-345

  Splines, 103-105

  SpriteGrabber, 293-298

  SpriteHandler, 286-291

  Stargate, 149-152

  TestDat, 546-547

  TestJoystick, 178-182

  TestMappy, 442-445

  TextOutput, 114-115

  TileScroll, 347-351

  TimedLoop, 396-397

  TimerTest, 383-392

  TransSprite, 256-259

  Triangles, 105-107

  VerticalScroller, 460-464

  VLines, 87-88

  wormhole, 165-166

prototypes, 196-197

pthreads. *See* POSIX

publishing

  games

    bug reports, 615

    companies, 626

    contracts, 614-615

    debugging, 615

    evaluating, 611-612

    milestones, 615

    NDAs, 614

    releases, 615

    selling, 612-613

  Web sites, 663

putpixel function, 82-84

Q-R

quality, 200-202

quality control, 197-198

quiz answers, 633-650

radians, 586-587

random motion deterministic algorithm (AI), 571-572

readkey function, 152

real-life simulators, 195

real-time loops, 159

real-time strategy (RTS) genre, 193

rect function, 89-91

Rect program, 89-91

rectangles, 89-92

rectfill function, 91-92

RectFill program, 91-92

referencing datafiles, 544

refresh rates (bitmaps), 218

releases
 game development, 199
 publishing games, 615

releasing bitmaps, 223-224

remove_joystick function, 170

remove_keyboard function, 146-147

remove_mouse function, 156

removing
 interrupt handlers, 393-395
 sound, 516
 timers, 381-382, 393-395

rendering. *See* creating

RenderWare Studio, 25-26

ResizeFlick program, 558-560

resources
 books, 665-669
 game publishers, 626
 storing, 539-541
 Web sites
  Allegro, 26
  associations, 664
  author, 663
  conferences, 664
  conventions, 664
  downloads, 663
  expos, 664
  Feldman, Ari, 353
  forums, 663
  game developers, 663-664
  game development, 663
  game engines, 663
  Game Programming All in One, 663
  GCC, 45
  humor, 664
  industry, 664
  Jupiter Research, 13

  magazines, 664
  Mappy, 429
  publishing, 663
  reviews, 663
  studios, 663-664

resting timers, 382-383

reviews, Web sites, 663

RLE animated sprites, 306-313

RLESprites program, 307-313

role-playing games. *See* RPGs

rotated sprites, 245-252

RotateSprite program, 249-251

RPGs (role-playing games), 34-35, 193-194

RTS game design genre, 193

run-length encoding, 306-313

running
 GetInfo program, 56-63
 Greetings program, 51-53

S

sample programs, 65-67

SampleMixer program, 522-525

saving
 bitmaps, 226-227
 maps
  FMP, 433-435
  text, 435-436
 programs (Greetings), 48
 screenshots, 227

ScaledSprite program, 242-243

scaling
 horizontal scrolling platform maps, 493-494
 FLIC animation, 558-560
 maps, 430
 scaled blitting, 228-229
 scaled sprites, 242-243, 252

scancode_to_ascii function, 153

ScanJoystick program, 175-177

scare_mouse function, 158

scare_mouse_area function, 158

schedules (game development), 199-200

screens
 bitmaps, 222
 text, 112-114

screenshots, saving, 227

scrolling
 backgrounds (bitmaps), 220
 buffers, 339

scrolling *(continued)*
  creating, 341-345
  cross-platform compatibility, 339
  horizontal scrolling platforms
    developing, 490-491, 498-506
    blocks, 491-498
    filling, 494, 495
    foreground, 495-497
    layers, 491-498
    maps, 491-498
    overview, 489-490
    size, 493, 494
    tile-based backgrounds, 491-498
  maps
    FMP, 442-445
    tiles, 433
  overview, 340-341
  Tank War
    overview, 355-359
    source code, 359-378
  tile-based backgrounds, 347-351
  vertical scrollers
    creating, 456-460
    engines, 455-456
    overview, 455-456
    tiles, 459-460
ScrollScreen program, 341-345
SDKs
  DirectX, 692
  game design, 204
searching datafiles, 545
selling games, 612-613
set_gfx_mode function, 75-78
set_keyboard_rate function, 153
set_mouse_range function, 167
set_mouse_speed function, 167
set_mouse_sprite function, 157-158
set_mouse_sprite_focus function, 157
setting sound, 516
shapes. *See* graphics
shooting. *See* bullets
show_mouse function, 158
simulate_keypress function, 153-154
size. *See* scaling
sound
  creating, 518
  destroying, 518
  detecting, 515
  editing, 518

initializing, 514-516
installing, 515-516
loading, 517
multichannel, 522
overview, 511-512
playback, 517-522
playing, 517-518
removing, 516
SampleMixer program, 522-525
setting volume, 516
stopping, 518
Tank War, 525-536
voices
  functions, 518-522
  number, 515
  volume, 515-516
WAV, 512-514
source code
  Allegro, 42-43
  AnimSprite program, 280-283
  Arkanoid game, 178
  ArrayMapTest program, 437-441
  Breakout game, 178
  C/C++ cross-compatibility, 29
  CD-ROM, 691
  CircleFill program, 97-98
  Circles program, 95-97
  CollisionTest program, 319-324
  CompiledSprites program, 315-317
  compiling
    Borland C++, 687-688
    C++ Builder, 687-688
    Dev-C++, 688
    KDevelop, 689-690
    Linux, 689-690
    overview, 685
    Visual C++, 685-687
  DoCircles program, 101-102
  DoLines program, 92-95
  DrawBitmap program, 79-82
  DrawSprite program, 239-240
  EllipseFill program, 100-101
  Ellipses program, 98-100
  FlipSprite program, 244-245
  FloodFill program, 109-112
  GameWorld program, 352-355
  GetInfo program, 61-62
  Greetings, 48-52
  HLines program, 85-87

hyperspace program, 165-166
InterruptTest program, 393-395
KeyTest, 154-155
Lines program, 88-89
LoadFlick program, 556-558
MouseWheel program, 168-170
MultipleSprites program, 300-306
MultiThread program, 403-413
PivotSprite program, 252-255
Pixels program, 82-84
PlatformScroller, 501-506
PlayFlick program, 552-554
PlayWave program, 512-514
Polygons program, 107-109
PositionMouse program, 165-166
Rect program, 89-91
RectFill program, 91-92
RLESprites program, 307-313
RotateSprite program, 249-251
SampleMixer program, 522-525
ScaledSprite program, 242-243
ScanJoystick program, 175-177
ScrollScreen program, 341-345
Splines program, 103-105
SpriteGrabber program, 293-298
SpriteHandler program, 286-291
Strategic Defense game, 160-164
Tank War, 126-141
    animated sprite handlers, 324-336
    bitmaps, 229-334
    bullets, 422-426
    collision detection, 324-336
    interrupt handlers, 413-426
    keyboards, 368-371
    multiple joysticks, 531-534
    multi-threading, 413-426
    scrolling, 359-378
    sound, 525-536
    sprites, 262-275
    tile maps, 445-453
    tile-based backgrounds, 359-378
    treads, 413-426
TestDat program, 546-547
TestJoystick program, 178-182
TestMappy program, 442-445
TextOutput program, 114-115
TileScroll program, 347-351
TimedLoop program, 396-397

TimerTest program, 383-392
TransSprite program, 256-259
Triangles program, 105-107
VerticalScroller program, 460-464
VLines program, 87-88
Warbirds Pacifica, 468-486
wormhole program, 165-166
wrapper code, 13
Space Invaders game design, 209-211
space simulators, 195
specialization, 12-13
speed
    creating animated sprites, 313
    games, 395-397
    mouse, 167
    timers, 382-383
spline function, 103-105
splines, 103-105
Splines program, 103-105
sports simulators, 194
SpriteGrabber program, 293-298
SpriteHandler program, 286-291
sprites
    alpha blending, 215
    animated sprites
        collision detection, 317-324
        compiled sprites, 313-317
        compression, 306
        creating, 280-283
        creating speed, 313
        flickering, 298
        grabbing frames, 291-298
        handlers, 283-291, 324-336
        multiple, 298-306
        overview, 279-280
        performance, 298
        PlatformScroller game, 499-500
        RLE, 306-313
        Tank War, 324-336, 413-426
        tiling, 292
        treads, 413-426
        troubleshooting, 298
        updating, 285-286
    bitmaps relationship, 216
    color, 239
    compiling, 241
    creating, 238-242
        flipped, 244-245

sprites *(continued)*
  pivoted, 252-255
  rotated, 245-252
  scaled, 242-243, 252
  stretching, 242-243, 252
  translucent, 256-259
datafiles, 543
handling, Warbirds Pacifica, 465
overview, 215-217, 237-238
Tank War
  animated sprites, 324-336, 413-426
  overview, 259-262
  source code, 262-275
translucency, 215
transparency, 215, 238-242
Warbirds Pacifica, 466-468
srand function, 84
standard blitting, 227-228
Star Trek, 18
Stargate program, 149-152
Starship Battles, 18-22
states (AI), 580-581
stopping sound, 518
storing resources, 539-541
storyboards, 8-9
Strategic Defense game
  overview, 158-160
  source code, 160-164
strategy games, 35
stretching
  blitting bitmaps, 228-229
  FLIC animation, 558-560
  sprites, 242-243, 252
studios, 663-664
Super Mario World, 489
support
  Allegro, 26-28
  books, 665-669
  C/C++, 29-30
  GCC, 45
  Web sites
    Allegro, 26
    associations, 664
    author, 663
    conferences, 664
    conventions, 664
    downloads, 663
    expos, 664

Feldman, Ari, 353
forums, 663
game developers, 663-664
game development, 663
game engines, 663
Game Programming All in One, 663
GCC, 45
humor, 664
industry, 664
Jupiter Research, 13
magazines, 664
Mappy, 429
publishing, 663
reviews, 663
studios, 663-664
systems, numbers, 657

T

Tactical Starship Combat, 18
Tank War
  bitmaps, 229-334
  bullets
    creating, 122-125
    moving, 122-125
    troubleshooting, 422-426
  collision detection, 122-126, 324-336
  final version features, 536
  interrupt handlers, 413-426
  joysticks, multiple, 531-534
  keyboards, 368-371
  maps, tiles, 445-453
  multi-threading, 413-426
  overview, 119-120
  scrolling
    overview, 355-359
    source code, 359-378
  sound, 525-536
  source code, 126-141
    bitmaps, 229-334
    keyboard, 368-371
    scrolling, 359-378
    sprites, 262-275
    tile-based backgrounds, 359-378
  sprites
    animated sprite handlers, 324-336
    animated sprite treads, 413-426
    overview, 259-262
    source code, 262-275

tanks
    creating, 120-122
    moving, 125-126
    tile-based backgrounds
        overview, 355-359
        source code, 359-378
tanks
    creating, 120-122
    moving, 125-126
TBS, 194
templates, Allegro, 63
terrain. *See* maps
TestDat program, 546-547
testing
    Allegro, 53-63
    datafiles, 545-547
    Dev-C++, 44-53
    joysticks, 175-182
    timers, 383-392
TestJoystick program, 178-182
TestMappy program, 442-445
text, 112-114
    ASCII values, 653-655
    maps, 435-441
    Warbirds Pacifica, 467-468
text_mode function, 112
textout function, 112-113
TextOutput program, 114-115
textprintf function, 78, 113-114
third-person shooters, 194
threads
    multi-threading, 397-398
    POSIX
        creating, 401
        destroying, 402
        mutexes, 402-403
        overview, 399-400
tile-based backgrounds. *See also* tiles
    arrays, 351-355
    buffers, 339
    graphics, 346
    horizontal scrolling platform maps, 491-498
    overview, 345-347
    scrolling, 347-351
    Tank War
        overview, 355-359
        source code, 359-378
    tile maps, 351-355

tiles. *See also* tile-based backgrounds
    animated sprites, 292
    maps
        erasing, 433
        filling, 432-433
        importing, 432-434
        number, 430
        palettes, 432-433
        scrolling, 433
        Tank War, 445-453
        tile-based backgrounds, 351-355
        vertical scrollers, 459-460
TileScroll program, 347-351
timed game loops, 395-397
TimedLoop program, 396-397
timers
    callbacks, 382-383
    delaying, 382-383
    installing, 381-382
    interrupt handlers
        creating, 392-393
        multi-threading, 392
        removing, 393-395
        Tank War, 413-426
    multi-threading. *See* multi-threading
    overview, 381
    removing, 381-382
    resting, 382-383
    speed, 382-383
    testing, 383-392
    timed game loops, 395-397
TimerTest program, 383-392
tips (AI), 581
tracking, mouse, 167
tracking motion deterministic algorithm (AI), 572-573
translucent sprites, 215, 256-259
transparency
    bitmaps, 221-222
    sprites, 215, 238-242
TransSprite program, 256-259
treads (Tank War), 413-426
trends (game development), 201-202
triangle function, 105-107
triangles, 105-107
Triangles program, 105-107
trigonometry, 586-590

troubleshooting
    animated sprites, 298
    bullets, 422-426
    functions, 65-66
turn-based strategy (TBS), 194
twitch generation, 6

U

unloading datafiles, 545
unscare_mouse function, 158
updating
    animated sprites, 285-286
    Dev-C++, 37-40
Urbanus, Paul, 616-621
ureadkey function, 152

V

values (ASCII), 653-655
vectors, 590-598
versions (Allegro), 683-684
vertical lines, 87-88
vertical scrollers
    engines, 455-456
    maps
        creating, 456-460
        tiles, 459-460
    overview, 455-456
    Warbirds Pacifica
        collision detection, 466
        overview, 464-468
        power-ups, 465
        source code, 468-486
        sprite handling, 465
        sprites, 466-468
        text, 467-468
VerticalScroller program, 460-464
vertices (graphics), 73
video cards (graphics), 72-74
Visual C++
    compiling source code, 685-687
    configuring compiler, 672-674
vline function, 87-88
VLines program, 87-88
voices (sound)
    functions, 518-522
    number, 515
    volume, 515-516

volume (sound), 515-516

W-Z

war games, 22-24
Warbirds Pacifica
    collision detection, 466
    overview, 464-468
    power-ups, 465
    source code, 468-486
    sprite handling, 465
    sprites, 466-468
    text, 467-468
WAV sound, 512-514
Web sites
    Allegro, 26
    associations, 664
    author, 663
    conferences, 664
    conventions, 664
    downloads, 663
    expos, 664
    Feldman, Ari, 353
    forums, 663
    game developers, 663-664
    game development, 663
    game engines, 663
    Game Programming All in One, 663
    GCC, 45
    humor, 664
    industry, 664
    Jupiter Research, 13
    magazines, 664
    Mappy, 429
    publishing, 663
    reviews, 663
    studios, 663-664
wheels, mouse, 167-170
Windows
    CD-ROM, 691-692
    configuring compiler, 672-679
wormhole program, 165-166
wrapper code, 13
zooming, maps, 432

GNU GENERAL PUBLIC LICENSE

Version 2, June 1991

Copyright (C) 1989, 1991 Free Software Foundation, Inc.

59 Temple Place - Suite 330, Boston, MA 02111-1307, USA

Preamble

The licenses for most software are designed to take away your freedom to share and change it. By contrast, the GNU General Public License is intended to guarantee your freedom to share and change free software—to make sure the software is free for all its users. This General Public License applies to most of the Free Software Foundation's software and to any other program whose authors commit to using it. (Some other Free Software Foundation software is covered by the GNU Library General Public License instead.) You can apply it to your programs, too.

When we speak of free software, we are referring to freedom, not price. Our General Public Licenses are designed to make sure that you have the freedom to distribute copies of free software (and charge for this service if you wish), that you receive source code or can get it if you want it, that you can change the software or use pieces of it in new free programs; and that you know you can do these things.

To protect your rights, we need to make restrictions that forbid anyone to deny you these rights or to ask you to surrender the rights. These restrictions translate to certain responsibilities for you if you distribute copies of the software, or if you modify it.

For example, if you distribute copies of such a program, whether gratis or for a fee, you must give the recipients all the rights that you have. You must make sure that they, too, receive or can get the source code. And you must show them these terms so they know their rights.

We protect your rights with two steps: (1) copyright the software, and (2) offer you this license which gives you legal permission to copy, distribute and/or modify the software.

Also, for each author's protection and ours, we want to make certain that everyone understands that there is no warranty for this free software. If the software is modified by someone else and passed on, we want its recipients to know that what they have is not the original, so that any problems introduced by others will not reflect on the original authors' reputations.

Finally, any free program is threatened constantly by software patents. We wish to avoid the danger that redistributors of a free program will individually obtain patent licenses, in effect making the program proprietary. To prevent this, we have made it clear that any patent must be licensed for everyone's free use or not licensed at all.

The precise terms and conditions for copying, distribution and modification follow.

TERMS AND CONDITIONS FOR COPYING, DISTRIBUTION AND MODIFICATION

0. This License applies to any program or other work which contains a notice placed by the copyright holder saying it may be distributed under the terms of this General Public License. The "Program", below, refers to any such program or work, and a "work based on the Program" means either the Program or any derivative work under copyright law: that is to say, a work containing the Program or a portion of it, either verbatim or with modifications and/or translated into another language. (Hereinafter, translation is included without limitation in the term "modification".) Each licensee is addressed as "you".

   Activities other than copying, distribution and modification are not covered by this License; they are outside its scope. The act of running the Program is not restricted, and the output from the Program is covered only if its contents constitute a work based on the Program (independent of having been made by running the Program). Whether that is true depends on what the Program does.

1. You may copy and distribute verbatim copies of the Program's source code as you receive it, in any medium, provided that you conspicuously and appropriately publish on each copy an appropriate copyright notice and disclaimer of warranty; keep intact all the notices that refer to this License and to the absence of any warranty; and give any other recipients of the Program a copy of this License along with the Program.

   You may charge a fee for the physical act of transferring a copy, and you may at your option offer warranty protection in exchange for a fee.

2. You may modify your copy or copies of the Program or any portion of it, thus forming a work based on the Program, and copy and distribute such modifications or work under the terms of Section 1 above, provided that you also meet all of these conditions:

   a) You must cause the modified files to carry prominent notices stating that you changed the files and the date of any change.

   b) You must cause any work that you distribute or publish, that in whole or in part contains or is derived from the Program or any part thereof, to be licensed as a whole at no charge to all third parties under the terms of this License.

   c) If the modified program normally reads commands interactively when run, you must cause it, when started running for such interactive use in the most ordinary way, to print or display an announcement including an appropriate copyright notice and a notice that there is no warranty (or else, saying that you provide a warranty) and that users may redistribute the program under these conditions, and telling the user how to view a copy of this License. (Exception: if the Program itself is interactive but does not normally print such an announcement, your work based on the Program is not required to print an announcement.)

These requirements apply to the modified work as a whole. If identifiable sections of that work are not derived from the Program, and can be reasonably considered independent and separate works in themselves, then this License, and its terms, do not apply to those sections when you distribute them as separate works. But when you distribute the same sections as part of a whole which is a work based on the Program, the distribution of the whole must be on the terms of this License, whose permissions for other licensees extend to the entire whole, and thus to each and every part regardless of who wrote it.

Thus, it is not the intent of this section to claim rights or contest your rights to work written entirely by you; rather, the intent is to exercise the right to control the distribution of derivative or collective works based on the Program.

In addition, mere aggregation of another work not based on the Program with the Program (or with a work based on the Program) on a volume of a storage or distribution medium does not bring the other work under the scope of this License.

3. You may copy and distribute the Program (or a work based on it, under Section 2) in object code or executable form under the terms of Sections 1 and 2 above provided that you also do one of the following:

a) Accompany it with the complete corresponding machine-readable source code, which must be distributed under the terms of Sections 1 and 2 above on a medium customarily used for software interchange; or,

b) Accompany it with a written offer, valid for at least three years, to give any third party, for a charge no more than your cost of physically performing source distribution, a complete machine-readable copy of the corresponding source code, to be distributed under the terms of Sections 1 and 2 above on a medium customarily used for software interchange; or,

c) Accompany it with the information you received as to the offer to distribute corresponding source code. (This alternative is allowed only for noncommercial distribution and only if you received the program in object code or executable form with such an offer, in accord with Subsection b above.)

The source code for a work means the preferred form of the work for making modifications to it. For an executable work, complete source code means all the source code for all modules it contains, plus any associated interface definition files, plus the scripts used to control compilation and installation of the executable. However, as a special exception, the source code distributed need not include anything that is normally distributed (in either source or binary form) with the major components (compiler, kernel, and so on) of the operating system on which the executable runs, unless that component itself accompanies the executable.

If distribution of executable or object code is made by offering access to copy from a designated place, then offering equivalent access to copy the source code from the same place counts as distribution of the source code, even though third parties are not compelled to copy the source along with the object code.

4. You may not copy, modify, sublicense, or distribute the Program except as expressly provided under this License. Any attempt otherwise to copy, modify, sublicense or distribute the Program is void, and will automatically terminate your rights under this License. However, parties who have received copies, or rights, from you under this License will not have their licenses terminated so long as such parties remain in full compliance.

5. You are not required to accept this License, since you have not signed it. However, nothing else grants you permission to modify or distribute the Program or its derivative works. These actions are prohibited by law if you do not accept this License. Therefore, by modifying or distributing the Program (or any work based on the Program), you indicate your acceptance of this License to do so, and all its terms and conditions for copying, distributing or modifying the Program or works based on it.

6. Each time you redistribute the Program (or any work based on the Program), the recipient automatically receives a license from the original licensor to copy, distribute or modify the Program subject to these terms and conditions. You may not impose any further restrictions on the recipients' exercise of the rights granted herein. You are not responsible for enforcing compliance by third parties to this License.

7. If, as a consequence of a court judgment or allegation of patent infringement or for any other reason (not limited to patent issues), conditions are imposed on you (whether by court order, agreement or otherwise) that contradict the conditions of this License, they do not excuse you from the conditions of this License. If you cannot distribute so as to satisfy simultaneously your obligations under this License and any other pertinent obligations, then as a consequence you may not distribute the Program at all. For example, if a patent license would not permit royalty-free redistribution of the Program by all those who receive copies directly or indirectly through you, then the only way you could satisfy both it and this License would be to refrain entirely from distribution of the Program.

If any portion of this section is held invalid or unenforceable under any particular circumstance, the balance of the section is intended to apply and the section as a whole is intended to apply in other circumstances.

It is not the purpose of this section to induce you to infringe any patents or other property right claims or to contest validity of any such claims; this section has the sole purpose of protecting the integrity of the free software distribution system, which is implemented by public license practices. Many people have made generous contributions to the wide range of software distributed through that system in reliance on consistent application of that system; it is up to the author/donor to decide if he or she is willing to distribute software through any other system and a licensee cannot impose that choice.

This section is intended to make thoroughly clear what is believed to be a consequence of the rest of this License.

8. If the distribution and/or use of the Program is restricted in certain countries either by patents or by copyrighted interfaces, the original copyright holder who places the Program under this License may add an explicit geographical distribution limitation excluding those countries, so that distribution is permitted only in or among countries not thus excluded. In such case, this License incorporates the limitation as if written in the body of this License.

9. The Free Software Foundation may publish revised and/or new versions of the General Public License from time to time. Such new versions will be similar in spirit to the present version, but may differ in detail to address new problems or concerns.

   Each version is given a distinguishing version number. If the Program specifies a version number of this License which applies to it and "any later version", you have the option of following the terms and conditions either of that version or of any later version published by the Free Software Foundation. If the Program does not specify a version number of this License, you may choose any version ever published by the Free Software Foundation.

10. If you wish to incorporate parts of the Program into other free programs whose distribution conditions are different, write to the author to ask for permission. For software which is copyrighted by the Free Software Foundation, write to the Free Software Foundation; we sometimes make exceptions for this. Our decision will be guided by the two goals of preserving the free status of all derivatives of our free software and of promoting the sharing and reuse of software generally.

NO WARRANTY

11. BECAUSE THE PROGRAM IS LICENSED FREE OF CHARGE, THERE IS NO WARRANTY FOR THE PROGRAM, TO THE EXTENT PERMITTED BY APPLICABLE LAW. EXCEPT WHEN OTHERWISE STATED IN WRITING THE COPYRIGHT HOLDERS AND/OR OTHER PARTIES PROVIDE THE PROGRAM "AS IS" WITHOUT WARRANTY OF ANY KIND, EITHER EXPRESSED OR IMPLIED, INCLUDING, BUT NOT LIMITED TO, THE IMPLIED WARRANTIES OF MERCHANTABILITY AND FITNESS FOR A PARTICULAR PURPOSE. THE ENTIRE RISK AS TO THE QUALITY AND PERFORMANCE OF THE PROGRAM IS WITH YOU. SHOULD THE PROGRAM PROVE DEFECTIVE, YOU ASSUME THE COST OF ALL NECESSARY SERVICING, REPAIR OR CORRECTION.

12. IN NO EVENT UNLESS REQUIRED BY APPLICABLE LAW OR AGREED TO IN WRITING WILL ANY COPYRIGHT HOLDER, OR ANY OTHER PARTY WHO MAY MODIFY AND/OR REDISTRIBUTE THE PROGRAM AS PERMITTED ABOVE, BE LIABLE TO YOU FOR DAMAGES, INCLUDING ANY GENERAL, SPECIAL, INCIDENTAL OR CONSEQUENTIAL DAMAGES ARISING OUT OF THE USE OR INABILITY TO USE THE PROGRAM (INCLUDING BUT NOT LIMITED TO LOSS OF DATA OR DATA BEING RENDERED INACCURATE OR LOSSES SUSTAINED BY YOU OR THIRD PARTIES OR A FAILURE OF THE PROGRAM TO OPERATE WITH ANY OTHER PROGRAMS), EVEN IF SUCH HOLDER OR OTHER PARTY HAS BEEN ADVISED OF THE POSSIBILITY OF SUCH DAMAGES.

END OF TERMS AND CONDITIONS

How to Apply These Terms to Your New Programs

If you develop a new program, and you want it to be of the greatest possible use to the public, the best way to achieve this is to make it free software which everyone can redistribute and change under these terms.

To do so, attach the following notices to the program. It is safest to attach them to the start of each source file to most effectively convey the exclusion of warranty; and each file should have at least the "copyright" line and a pointer to where the full notice is found.

one line to give the program's name and an idea of what it does.

Copyright (C) yyyy name of author

This program is free software; you can redistribute it and/or modify it under the terms of the GNU General Public License as published by the Free Software Foundation; either version 2 of the License, or (at your option) any later version.

This program is distributed in the hope that it will be useful, but WITHOUT ANY WARRANTY; without even the implied warranty of MERCHANTABILITY or FITNESS FOR A PARTICULAR PURPOSE. See the GNU General Public License for more details.

You should have received a copy of the GNU General Public License along with this program; if not, write to the Free Software Foundation, Inc., 59 Temple Place - Suite 330, Boston, MA 02111-1307, USA. Also add information on how to contact you by electronic and paper mail.

If the program is interactive, make it output a short notice like this when it starts in an interactive mode:

Gnomovision version 69, Copyright (C) year name of author

Gnomovision comes with ABSOLUTELY NO WARRANTY; for details type `show w'. This is free software, and you are welcome to redistribute it under certain conditions; type `show c' for details.

The hypothetical commands `show w' and `show c' should show the appropriate parts of the General Public License. Of course, the commands you use may be called something other than `show w' and `show c'; they could even be mouse-clicks or menu items—whatever suits your program.

You should also get your employer (if you work as a programmer) or your school, if any, to sign a "copyright disclaimer" for the program, if necessary. Here is a sample; alter the names:

Yoyodyne, Inc., hereby disclaims all copyright interest in the program `Gnomovision' (which makes passes at compilers) written by James Hacker. signature of Ty Coon, 1 April 1989 Ty Coon, President of Vice

This General Public License does not permit incorporating your program into proprietary programs. If your program is a subroutine library, you may consider it more useful to permit linking proprietary applications with the library. If this is what you want to do, use the GNU Lesser General Public License instead of this License.